D0106099

FLORIDA BEACHES

PARKE PUTERBAUGH & ALAN BISBORT

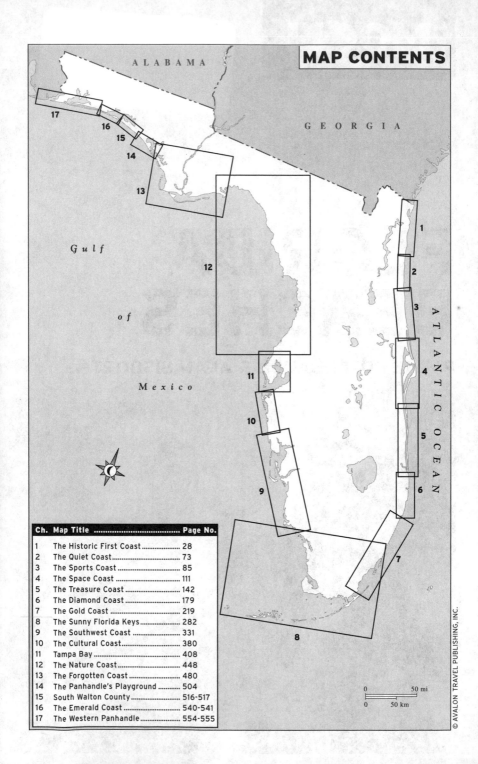

MAP CONTENTS

ALABAMA

GEORGIA

17
16
15
14
13

Gulf

of

Mexico

12

11

10

9

1
2
3
4
5
6
7

8

ATLANTIC OCEAN

Ch.	Map Title	Page No.
1	The Historic First Coast	28
2	The Quiet Coast	73
3	The Sports Coast	85
4	The Space Coast	111
5	The Treasure Coast	142
6	The Diamond Coast	179
7	The Gold Coast	219
8	The Sunny Florida Keys	282
9	The Southwest Coast	331
10	The Cultural Coast	380
11	Tampa Bay	408
12	The Nature Coast	448
13	The Forgotten Coast	480
14	The Panhandle's Playground	504
15	South Walton County	516-517
16	The Emerald Coast	540-541
17	The Western Panhandle	554-555

0   50 mi

0   50 km

© AVALON TRAVEL PUBLISHING, INC.

Contents

How to Use This Book 14

Introduction 17
Preface to the Third Edition 17
Best Beaches 22

Jacksonville, St. Augustine, and the Historic First Coast 27
Fort Clinch State Park 28
Fernandina Beach 30
Summer Beach 36
American Beach 36
Amelia Island Plantation 39
Amelia Island (south end) 41
Big Talbot Island State Park and Little Talbot Island State Park 42
Fort George Island 44
Jacksonville 45
Mayport 46
Atlantic Beach 47
Neptune Beach 49
Jacksonville Beach 50
Ponte Vedra Beach 56
Guana River 58
South Ponte Vedra Beach 59
Vilano Beach 60
St. Augustine 62
Anastasia State Park 68
St. Augustine Beach 69

Special Topics
Best Beaches 29; Where's the Beach? 32; Geology of Amelia Island 35; The Amazing Story of MaVynee Betsch 37; Nuts for Golf 54; The Comic Rituals of the Guard Gate 57; Henry Morrison Flagler 63; An Opinionated Guide to St. Augustine Attractions 64

Flagler Beach and the Quiet Coast 72

Crescent Beach. 72

Fort Matanzas National Monument 74

Summer Haven 75

Marineland 75

Washington Oaks Gardens State Park 77

Palm Coast and Hammock 77

Painters Hill. 79

Beverly Beach. 79

Flagler Beach 80

Gamble Rogers Memorial State Recreation Area 82

Special Topics
Best Beaches 74; Marineland: A Buried Treasure 76

Daytona Beach and the Sports Coast. 84

Ormond-by-the-Sea 84

Ormond Beach 86

Daytona Beach and Daytona Beach Shores. 89

Wilbur-by-the-Sea. 102

Ponce Inlet 102

New Smyrna Beach. 105

Special Topics
Best Beaches 87; Daytona USA: A 250 MPH Tourist Trap 90; How a Minor Leaguer Made Major History in Daytona Beach 93; Wheels on the Beach 100

Cocoa Beach and the Space Coast. 110

Canaveral National Seashore 111

Merritt Island National Wildlife Refuge. 115

Cape Canaveral. 116

Cocoa Beach 119

Patrick Air Force Base and South Patrick Shores 129

Satellite Beach 130

Indian Harbour Beach. 132

Canova Beach 133

Indialantic 134
Melbourne Beach and Melbourne Shores. 136
Floridana Beach and Sunnyland Beach 140

Special Topics
Best Beaches 112; Playalinda Beach: Nude and Proud 114; Space Is the Place: A Tour of Kennedy Space Center 116; Mousin' Around Orlando: The Lowdown on Disney World 120; Ron Jon Surf Shop 123; "The Sea Turtle Preservation Society" 137

Vero Beach, Hutchinson Island, and the Treasure Coast. 141
Sebastian Inlet State Park 141
North Indian River County 144
Indian River Shores. 148
Vero Beach 148
Round Island Park. 154
North Hutchinson Island. 155
Fort Pierce Inlet State Park 156
Fort Pierce 157
Hutchinson Island (mid-island) 159
Jensen Beach 164
Stuart 168
Port Salerno 173
St. Lucie Inlet Preserve State Park 174
Hobe Sound National Wildlife Refuge. 175
Hobe Sound. 176
Blowing Rocks Preserve 177

Special Topics
Best Beaches 143; Indian River Fruit 147; Dodgertown 149; We Don't Love Lucie 160; Hurricane Frances 169; Hurricane Jeanne 171; Jonathan Dickinson State Park 174

Palm Beach, Boca Raton, and the Diamond Coast. 178
Tequesta 179
Jupiter. 180

Juno Beach 185
John D. MacArthur Beach State Park 187
Singer Island: Riviera Beach and Palm Beach Shores 189
Palm Beach 194
Lake Worth 203
South Palm Beach, Lantana, and Manalapan 205
Boynton Beach, Ocean Ridge, Briny Breezes, and Gulfstream 206
Delray Beach 208
Highland Beach 212
Boca Raton 212

Special Topics
Best Beaches 180; The Burt Reynolds Story 182; The Golf Coast 193; The Big House Problem 195; Worth Avenue: Shops Without End, Amen 196; Flea Circus 198; The Ballad of the Butterfly Ballot 202; Gumbo Limbo Nature Center 213

Fort Lauderdale, Miami Beach, and the Gold Coast
. . . . 218
Deerfield Beach 219
Hillsboro Beach 223
Pompano Beach 223
Lauderdale-by-the-Sea 226
Fort Lauderdale 228
John U. Lloyd Beach State Park 240
Dania Beach 241
Hollywood 242
Hallandale Beach 251
Golden Beach 252
Sunny Isles Beach 253
Bal Harbour and Surfside 256
Miami Beach 258
Fisher Island 274
Key Biscayne and Virginia Key 275
Matheson Hammock County Park 278
Homestead 279
Biscayne National Park 279

Special Topics
*Best Beaches **220**; Naked Came the Strangers **224**; Hurricane Wilma **229**;*
*The Death of Fun on Fort Lauderdale's Strip **230**; So You Want to Be a Gator*
*Wrestler? **233**; Sandy Soap Opera on Hollywood Beach **244**; Seminole Paradise:*
*Reservations About the Reservation **248**; Renourishing South Florida's Eroded*
*Beaches **250**; Little Havana: The Cuban Community in Miami **258**; Doing the Art*
*Deco Dance in Miami Beach **261**; The Wolfsonian **262**; Eat at Joe's **268**; Get Thee*
*Behind Me, Miami **271**; Who Will Unlock Virginia Key's Potential? **274**; Hurricane*
*Katrina **277***

Key West and the Sunny Florida Keys 281
Key Largo 283
John Pennekamp Coral Reef State Park 289
Islamorada 290
Lignumvitae Key Botanical State Park 294
Indian Key Historic State Park 294
Anne's Beach 295
Long Key 296
Duck Key 296
Grassy Key 297
Curry Hammock State Park 298
Marathon and Key Colony Beach 298
Boot Key 304
Pigeon Key 304
Little Duck Key and Ohio Key 305
Bahia Honda State Park 305
West Summerland Key 307
Big Pine Key 307
Looe Key 308
Little Torch Key 309
Ramrod Key 309
Summerland Key and Cudjoe Key 309
Sugarloaf Key 309
Big Coppitt Key and Boca Chica Key 310
Key West 311

Dry Tortugas National Park   322

Everglades National Park   323

Special Topics

Best Beaches 283; Highway to the Keys 285; Port Bougainville: Entering the Twilight Zone 286; Fishing the Florida Keys 292; Key Lime Pie 299; Hurricane Rita 310; The Conch Republic 312; Florida Keys to Hurricanes: No Mas, Por Favor 321; Waist Deep in the Big Muddy Everglades 326

Naples, Sanibel-Captiva, and the Southwest Coast   330

Cape Romano and Kice Island.   331

Marco Island   332

Naples   337

Vanderbilt Beach.   342

Delnor-Wiggins Pass State Park.   343

Barefoot Beach County Park and Barefoot Beach Access.   343

Bonita Beach.   344

Lovers Key State Park   347

Fort Myers Beach   349

Bunch Beach.   354

Sanibel Island and J. N. "Ding" Darling National Wildlife Refuge.   355

Captiva Island   363

North Captiva Island.   367

Cayo Costa Island State Park   368

Boca Grande   369

Little Gasparilla Island, Don Pedro Island,
   Knight Island, and Palm Island   373

Manasota Key   375

Special Topics

Best Beaches 332; Cape Marco: Big City Skyline on a Small Florida Island 334; Corkscrew Swamp Sanctuary 339; Stranger Than Fiction: The Bizarre Tale of the Koreshans 346; Singing the Toll Bridge Blues on Sanibel Island 354; Seashellology 101 356; Sanibel-Captiva Conservation Foundation 362; Hurricane Charley 366; Cowards of the County 374

Sarasota, Bradenton, and the Cultural Coast 379

Venice 380

Nokomis and Casey Key 384

Siesta Key 386

Sarasota 392

Lido Key and St. Armands Key 394

Longboat Key 397

Anna Maria Island: Bradenton Beach,
    Holmes Beach, and Anna Maria 402

Special Topics
*Best Beaches 381; Open Midnight Pass! 387; Step Right Up: The Ringling Museums 393;
Mote Marine Aquarium and Laboratory 395; The Wrong People Have All the
Money 398*

St. Petersburg, Clearwater, and the Beaches of Tampa Bay 407

Egmont Key 409

Apollo Beach 410

Fort De Soto Park 411

Pass-a-Grille 413

St. Pete Beach 414

Treasure Island and Sunset Beach 418

Madeira Beach 422

Redington Beach, North Redington Beach, and Redington Shores 425

Indian Shores and Indian Rocks Beach 426

Belleair Shore and Belleair Beach 429

Sand Key County Park 431

Clearwater Beach 431

Dunedin 437

Caladesi Island State Park and Honeymoon Island State Park 439

Ozona, Palm Harbor, and Crystal Beach 441

Tarpon Springs 442

Anclote Key Preserve State Park 445

Special Topics

Best Beaches 409; Bridge to the Sky: St. Petersburg's Sunshine Skyway 411; Ted Peters Is Smokin'! 418; Sand Key: A Sliver of Old Florida 422; Suncoast Seabird Sanctuary 427; Clearwater vs. the Church of Scientology 430; Pinellas County Recreation Trail 432; A Day in the Life of Clearwater Beach 434

The Nature Coast

The Nature Coast 447

Holiday, New Port Richey, and Port Richey 447

Hudson and Aripeka 452

Hernando Beach 453

Bayport and Pine Island 454

Chassahowitzka National Wildlife Refuge
  and Crystal River National Wildlife Refuge 456

Homosassa Springs and Homosassa 457

Ozello 458

Crystal River 459

Yankeetown 461

Cedar Key 462

Waccasassa Bay Preserve State Park and
  Cedar Key Scrub State Reserve 467

Cedar Keys National Wildlife Refuge and
  Lower Suwannee National Wildlife Refuge 467

Suwannee 469

Shired Island County Park 469

Horseshoe Beach 470

Steinhatchee 470

Big Bend Wildlife Management Area 472

Keaton Beach 472

Dekle Beach 474

Adams Beach 474

Econfina River State Park and Aucilla River State Canoe Trail 474

Newport 475

St. Marks National Wildlife Refuge 476

Edward Ball Wakulla Springs State Park 476

Shell Point. 477
Panacea. 478

Special Topics
Best Beaches 449; The Eight Counties of the Nature Coast 450; Manatee Springs State Park 468

Apalachicola, St. George Island, and the Forgotten Coast 479

Alligator Point. 479
Lanark Village. 481
Carrabelle and Carrabelle Beach 481
Dog Island 483
St. George Island. 484
Little St. George Island (Cape St. George State Reserve) 489
Apalachicola 489
St. Vincent Island National Wildlife Refuge 492
Indian Pass 493
Cape San Blas 495
St. Joseph Peninsula State Park 496
Port St. Joe. 496
St. Joe Beach and Beacon Hill 497
Mexico Beach 498
Tyndall Air Force Base 499

Special Topics
Best Beaches 481; We Dream of Jeanni 485; Refrigerator Magnate: The John Gorrie Story 490

Panama City Beach: The Panhandle's Playground. 502

St. Andrews State Park. 502
Panama City Beach. 504

Special Topics
Best Beaches 503; Enter Sandman: Dr. Beach and the Ratings Game 506; Look Out Joe, Here Comes Arvida 508

Seaside and the Stylish Communities of South Walton County 515

Inlet Beach and Carillon Beach. 516

Rosemary Beach. 517

Seacrest Beach. 520

Seagrove Beach 520

Seaside 523

WaterColor 527

Grayton Beach State Park 528

Grayton Beach 530

Blue Mountain Beach, Santa Rosa Beach, and Dune-Allen Beach 531

Topsail Hill Preserve State Park 534

Sandestin 535

Miramar Beach 536

Special Topics
*Best Beaches **518**; South Walton County **519**; Eden Gardens State Park **522**; Bed Taxes for Better Beaches **532***

Destin, Fort Walton Beach, and the Emerald Coast 539

Destin 539

Eglin Air Force Base 547

Fort Walton Beach and Okaloosa Island 548

Special Topics
*Best Beaches **542**; The World's Luckiest Fishing Village **544**; Fish Out of Water: A Californian Cleans Up Destin Harbor **546***

Pensacola Beach, Perdido Key, and the Western Panhandle 553

Navarre Beach 554

Gulf Breeze 556

Santa Rosa Area (Gulf Islands National Seashore). 558

Pensacola Beach. 559

Fort Pickens Area (Gulf Islands National Seashore). 566
Big Lagoon State Park 567
Perdido Key Area (Gulf Islands National Seashore). 568
Perdido Key. 569

Special Topics
*Best Beaches 556; Navarre Beach Blues 557; Hurricane Dennis 558; Hurricane
Ivan 570; The Fall and Rise of the Flora-Bama Lounge 572*

Resources 574

Travel Resources. 574
Beach Activities 579
Health and Safety 582
Flora and Fauna. 584
Environmental Concerns. 587

Special Topics
*Florida's Pro Sports Teams 575; Top 10 Reasons Hurricane Season Is Like
Christmas 588; Summary of Hurricanes and Tropical Storms Impacting
Florida, 2004 590; Summary of Hurricanes and Tropical Storms Impacting
Florida, 2005 591*

Index 595

How to Use This Book

Florida Beaches is organized so that the narrative proceeds in a clockwise direction. We begin north of Jacksonville (on the Georgia border), move south to the Keys, head up the West Coast along the Gulf of Mexico, curve around the Big Bend, and finally head west along the Panhandle to the Alabama line. Thirty-five Florida counties touch the coast, and we've organized them into 17 regional chapters.

Each chapter begins with an introduction to the region and a list of its best beaches. The chapter will also include one or more maps of the area it covers. Beaches are identified with numbers, which correspond to the numbers on the maps. Following the introduction, write-ups of each community or locale open with a general essay outlining what readers can expect to see and do there. We delve into a locale's physical look and layout, as well as its appeal and attractions, history and sociology, and anything else that might provide a useful overview. We've also provided contact information—including street addresses, phone numbers, and URLs—for local chambers of commerce, convention and visitors bureaus, and tourist development councils.

Additional information follows under the following headings: Beaches, Recreation and Attractions, Accommodations, Coastal Cuisine, and Nightlife.

BEACHES

We offer the lowdown on what you can expect to see and do at every publicly accessible beach. This includes a description of a beach's natural features and any other relevant observations. Each beach also has its own "beach profile": a list of practical information, including directions, activities, parking and day-use fees, hours, facilities, and contact number. A **BEST(** symbol also appears in the profiles of a region's best beaches or coastal locales.

Each beach profile also includes symbols for certain activities beyond the beach basics of swimming and sunbathing. Since one can surf cast on any beach, we haven't included a special fishing symbol. However, our jetty and pier symbols indicate when those particular angling opportunities are available. The 8 activity symbols are as follows:

Beach driving (driving on beach permitted)

Pier (wooden or concrete structure from which people fish or stroll)

Camping (developed campground or campgrounds)

Surfing (sufficiently sizable and well-formed waves that draw more than the occasional surfer)

Diving/snorkeling (popular spot for diving and/or snorkeling)

Volleyball (volleyball nets and standards on the beach or park grounds)

Hiking (trail or trails for nature observation and/or exercise)

Jetty (rock structure extending seaward from the mouth of an inlet or harbor, making for good fishing, snorkeling and surfing)

We've also included information on facilities available at each beach:

- Concession (food and drink available at or near beach)
- Lifeguards (year-round, unless identified as "seasonal")
- Picnic area
- Restrooms (anything from Portolets to modern facilities)
- Showers
- Visitors center (staffed facility with information and exhibits)

RECREATION AND ATTRACTIONS

This selective listing of up to 12 attractions and recreational services is a kind of quick-and-dirty Yellow Pages that we've compiled for selected communities.

- Bike/Skate Rentals (bicycles, in-line skates, and other fun stuff)
- Boat Cruise (sightseeing trips on the water)
- Dive Shop (diving equipment and/or dive trips)
- Ecotourism (canoe/kayak outfitter or site for ecotourist outing)
- Fishing Charters (guided fishing trips)
- Lighthouse
- Marina (boat dockage)
- Pier
- Rainy-Day Attraction (something to do indoors when the weather is inclement)
- Shopping/Browsing (shopping district, center, or mall of note)
- Surf Shop (surfboards and surf gear)
- Vacation Rentals (beach houses and/or condos for short-term rental)

ACCOMMODATIONS

We offer a general overview of lodging options in a given community, as well as brief descriptions of selected hotels, motels, and resorts we'd recommend when planning a beach vacation. Our write-ups are based on actual stays and site visits made by us. Because room rates fluctuate, we provide general guidelines of price range. Our $–$$$$ symbols are offered as indicators of the nightly cost of a standard room with two beds in season (i.e., in the summer months along the Panhandle and during winter in South Florida).

 $ = inexpensive (under $80 per night)
 $$ = moderate ($80–129)
 $$$ = moderately expensive ($130–179)
 $$$$ = expensive ($180 and up)

COASTAL CUISINE

We offer a general overview of the dining scene in each locale, as well as descriptive write-ups of restaurants specializing in seafood and/or regional cuisine that are located on or near the beach. We cast a favorable eye upon places that have been around awhile and have maintained a reputation for consistency and quality. Our $–$$$$ symbols are general indicators that reflect the median cost of an à la carte dinner entree at a given restaurant.

 $ = inexpensive (under $10)
 $$ = moderate ($10–16)
 $$$ = moderately expensive ($17–23)
 $$$$ = expensive ($24 and up)

NIGHTLIFE

Our concept of nightlife is people gathering to relax or blow off steam after the sun sets. Our listings run the gamut from tiki bars and coffeehouses to clubs with live music or deejays—in other words, anywhere you can kick back and have fun during and after sunset. Quite honestly, our interest in certain aspects of modern nightlife has waned as live rock bands have given way to deejayed dance music. Nonetheless, we still make the rounds looking for the liveliest good times to be had. And we let you know when you're better off not wasting your time.

Map Symbols

Expressway	Interstate Freeway	Airfield
Primary Road	US Highway	Airport
Secondary Road	State Highway	City/Town
Unpaved Road	County Highway	Mountain
Ferry	Lake	Park
National Border	Dry Lake	Pass
State Border	Seasonal Lake	State Capital

INTRODUCTION
Preface to the Third Edition

The book you are holding is the completely reworked, rewritten, and re-researched third edition of *Florida Beaches*. Frankly, we were shocked by how extensively the state had changed since the publication of the second edition in 2001. Perhaps we shouldn't have been, as change has become a dependable constant in Florida. The state's population, for instance, grew by 23 percent in the 1990s and grew by another 10 percent in the first half of the current decade. The natural and manmade environments are in perpetual flux as well, with the latter growing by leaps and bounds at the expense of the former.

Florida is a 447-mile-long peninsula that possesses the longest tidal coastline in the lower 48 states. Incredibly, Florida has more miles of sandy beaches than California. As the crow flies, Florida claims 1,800 miles of coastline, and 1,100 miles of that are sand beaches. When all the undulations around bays and inlets are figured in, Florida's shoreline totals 8,462 miles.

Because the state is bounded by water, Florida can be said to have several coastlines: the East Coast (facing the Atlantic Ocean); the Keys (extending into the Straits of Florida); and the Gulf Coast (on the Gulf of Mexico), which includes Florida's West Coast and Panhandle—not to mention the interior elbow known as the "Big Bend."

Florida is largely fringed by long, narrow barrier islands. It is a coastline more influenced by waves than tides, making it conducive to the formation of sandy-beached barrier islands and spits. On the Panhandle and the northern peninsula, the quartz sand is fine-grained and white. Further down the peninsula, the sand is brown and composed of shells. Out on the Keys, crushed

© PARKE PUTERBAUGH

coral enters into the equation. Unfortunately, many Florida beaches are no longer natural, since they have been "renourished" with sand dredged from offshore—a procedure necessitated by beach erosion due to human interference with sand-deposition processes. In the wake of Florida's recent run of hurricanes, the entire state has become one big beach-renourishment project.

However, we're still enthusiastic champions of Florida's sandy beaches. How can you not love Florida, with its subtropical climate and generally relaxed lifestyle? Florida is sunshine and beaches, palm trees and coral reefs, Panama hats and flip-flops, orange groves and limestone springs, alligators and manatees. The very word "Florida" seems to warm up a room. (In the era of global climate change, it often gets *too* darned hot.)

In this book, we've written about every publicly accessible beach in the state of Florida, which we've broken down into chapters organized around well-known beach locales, such as "Daytona Beach and the Sports Coast" and "Sarasota, Bradenton, and the Cultural Coast."

Public beach access is a key concept in this book. According to state law, descended from principles of common law dating back to Roman times, the beach is public property seaward of the mean high-tide line. In other words, the wet-sand portion of the beach—much of which is not inundated most of the time—is held in public trust, and therefore everyone has a right to be on it.

Ah, but there's a catch. Getting onto the public part of the beach means crossing private property, and without access in the form of easements or public ownership of a beachfront parcel (by a local, county, state, or federal government), the beach is technically inaccessible.

This book therefore focuses on public beaches and beach accesses. If you are staying at an oceanfront hotel, motel, cottage, or condo, beach access will be of no concern. For everyone else, however, the issue of access is critical. The initial edition of *Florida Beaches* represented the first comprehensive inventory of Florida's public beaches and beach accesses in 15 years, and this third edition has allowed us to fine-tune and update the inventory. There is no other book like it on the market.

But *Florida Beaches* is way more than an access guide. We offer an insider's look at the communities along the coast. We talk about history and sociology, flora and fauna, roads and bridges, food and drink, sun and sand, locals and tourists, rock and roll, and all the other elements that make beach life what it is.

Florida Beaches is a book for vacationers, natives, and people who simply enjoy reading about other places. We've packed it with facts, stats, and hard information, including the lowdown on where to play, stay, eat, and go out at night. At the same time, we've provided subjective commentary, humorous asides, and plainspoken opinions. We've also stocked *Florida Beaches* with dozens of stand-alone essays on various Florida-related subjects.

We want *Florida Beaches* to be a book that people consult as a guidebook and travel planner. We also want it to be read and enjoyed as a work of travel literature. Our goal is to be both informative and entertaining, utilitarian and readable, soberingly critical and laugh-out-loud funny.

So pull up an armchair and circumnavigate Florida's bountiful coastline with us. Traveling in a clockwise direction, we begin on the Georgia border at Amelia Island, which has flown under eight flags in its stormy history. We inch our way south along the East Coast, passing through Daytona Beach (NASCAR country) and Cocoa Beach (NASA headquarters) while lingering at wilderness beaches like Canaveral National Seashore and John D. MacArthur Beach State Park.

Then it's on to South Florida, with all the glamour and glitz of Palm Beach, Fort Lauderdale, and Miami Beach. Next we visit the Keys, a grouping of narrow, coral-spined islands that barely poke above sea level. From here we move up the West Coast, home to appealing and enlightened cities like Naples and Sarasota, as well as gorgeous sunsets over the Gulf of Mexico. The population thins out on the Nature Coast, along Florida's Big Bend. Sand beaches are scarce but natural beauty is abundant. Finally, we traipse the snow-white beaches of the Panhandle, from St. George Island to Perdido Key, finishing on the Alabama state line.

With a population of 17.4 million, Florida is the nation's fourth most populous state. Despite the crush of humanity, parts of Florida still teem with wildlife and natural wonder. No other state can match its bounty of parks and preserves, which includes two national seashores, three national parks, 28 national wildlife refuges (24 of which are on or near the coast), and 162 state parks and historic sites. Florida's coastal counties and communities have also seeded the shoreline with beach parks and accesses. It is easy to understand why Florida rates so highly with beachcombers—not to mention anglers, golfers, boaters, divers, surfers, and others—and why tourism is the state's leading industry.

We've profiled a total of 400 beaches in 35 coastal counties. We've done everything but hand you suntan lotion and swimsuits. Now, storm the beaches!

A SPECIAL WORD ABOUT HURRICANES

We've been writing about Florida since the early 1980s and first began visiting Florida as kids in the early 1960s, so we can truthfully claim to have watched the state grow and develop in the modern era. However, nothing can match the cataclysmic changes that have rocked the Sunshine State since the publication of the last edition of *Florida Beaches* in 2001.

The changes have been meteorological, demographic, developmental, and environmental. You name it, and Florida has been impacted—and mostly not for the better. What's happened to Florida has been no day at the beach.

The most visible culprits have been hurricanes—especially the unprecedented glut of them in 2004 and 2005, when hurricanes hit Florida hard and repeatedly. They eroded the state's coastline, collectively caused an estimated $65 billion in property damage and agricultural losses, took a number of lives (162 in all), and exacted a psychological toll upon those who live here. Tourism has suffered as well, since beaches and buildings washed away in the storms. (For a breakdown of the most damaging hurricanes—Charley, Frances, Ivan, and Jeanne in 2004, and Dennis, Katrina, Rita, and Wilma in 2005—see the annotated table in the *Resources* chapter at the end of the book.)

We've branded this latest version of *Florida Beaches* the "Hurricane Edition." During our latest round of beach-by-beach research, we were saddened to see many favorite places battered and beaten by hurricanes. We must stress that hurricanes didn't just "hit" Florida. They took extreme umbrage with the state. They'd damage multiple areas, entering one side and exiting the other, stalking the coast in destructive and almost vindictive ways.

Hurricane Charley was the first monumental storm in this two-year period. Forecast to hit near Tampa, it abruptly changed course and made landfall further south at Cayo Costa Island, on August 13, 2004. Given little chance to prepare or evacuate, the communities of Fort Myers and Punta Gorda were devastated. Charley was the most powerful hurricane to hit Florida since Andrew in 1992. And that was just the beginning.

Hurricane Frances made landfall on Hutchinson Island, along Florida's central East Coast, on September 5, 2004. This mammoth system slowly crossed the state, exiting on the West Coast at New Port Richey, where it caused record flood stages in the Tampa–St. Pete area. Even then, it wasn't done with Florida. Tropical Storm Frances entered the open gulf, turned north and made a second landfall on the eastern Panhandle. Frances ultimately spun off 106 tornadoes, the second-greatest number in hurricane history.

Incredibly enough, Hurricane Jeanne made landfall on Hutchinson Island three weeks later (on September 25). Never before had two hurricanes come ashore at the same place in a single hurricane season. That is the kind of destructive anomaly Mother Nature has been throwing at Florida.

Perhaps it's unfair to blame Mother Nature, since human activities have played a role in generating the kinds of super-hurricanes we've seen in recent times. The 800-pound gorilla no one wants to mention is global warming, which—according to a preponderance of scientific evidence—has been driving the recent spate of larger and more powerful hurricanes (as well as those projected for the coming years). And it's also been killing the coral reefs.

Some would argue that we are reaping the consequences of our reckless automotive lifestyle, due to accelerating fossil fuel emissions in an age of gas-guzzling vehicles. We've actually been hit with a double whammy: the impact of global warming combined with the cyclical upturn of hurricanes in the North Atlantic basin. (Hurricanes operate on roughly 30-year cycles of greater and lesser intensity.)

The repeated scenario in which a massive hurricane strengthens while crossing the Gulf of Mexico, feeding on the unusually warm waters as if sucking up rocket fuel, is proof enough to us that natural systems have been thrown out of balance. Which brings us to the mother of all hurricanes, the cataclysm named Katrina…

Before Hurricane Katrina leveled New Orleans, it entered Florida near Miami on August 25, 2005. People tend to forget the property damage ($2 billion) and loss of life (14 fatalities) Katrina caused in South Florida. Instead of weakening as it crossed the Florida peninsula, Katrina passed over the watery Everglades and then built up Frankenstein strength in the open gulf. As we write this more than half a year later, they're still pulling bodies out of condemned homes in New Orleans. We're told that Katrina was the worst natural disaster in U.S. history, but much of its damage was *un*natural. That is to say, the post-hurricane levee failures that destroyed a major American city can be blamed on the actions and inactions of FEMA and the feds. We mention this because Florida's own response after two years' worth of hurricanes—including further devastation from Rita and Wilma, which followed Katrina—has set the table for another Katrina-like tragedy—or a whole string of them.

Along many parts of Florida, the reaction to hurricanes has been not one of wise, cautious planning but the looniest sort of new beachfront construction. An unholy alliance of powerful developers, profit-driven financial institutions, and pliable county commissions has ignited a coastal building boom in the aftermath of eight catastrophic hurricanes. In many places, the response to beach erosion and property destruction has been even *taller* buildings constructed even *closer* to the ocean.

Panama City Beach, Daytona Beach Shores, Fort Lauderdale, Hallandale Beach: We're talking to you. These are all places we've enjoyed, to varying degrees, as vacation spots and homes away from home. However, we harbor extreme reservations about the overbuilding that has dramatically reshaped their beachfronts, and we cannot turn our heads and act like nothing's wrong.

It's no secret that Florida is spinning out of control, with beaches and natural environments gobbled up by reckless development. Some parts of Florida's coast have become nothing more than sun-baked asphalt parking lots adjacent to soulless gray condo towers named for landscape features they've displaced, with endless Publix and Eckerds lining frantic four-lane thoroughfares with gas stations on every corner and sickly palms listing in the wind.

Until the feds get out of the business of underwriting flood insurance along the coast, cranes will keep erecting ugly condo towers on Florida's beaches. The beneficiaries are usually absentee owners looking not for a place to live but for investment income and/or second-home tax write-offs. In other words, these constructions serve no useful purpose beyond profit. And eventually hurricanes will knock them down like bowling pins, if erosion doesn't get to them first.

Unlike a lot of travel books, you will find the unvarnished and up-to-date truth about every corner of Florida's coastline in this book. We are not writing to please business interests, chambers of commerce, tourist development councils, or the state's tourism agency. We are reporting the truth as we have researched and witnessed it. That's the least we can do for our readers and the state of Florida, which is in dire need of a reality check. Call it tough love.

You should also know there's much we still love about Florida. Many communities and counties have acted smartly and with conscience, and there are still scenic, swimmable beaches and abundant natural beauty along the coast. Just recognize that by avoiding the bad places and patronizing the good, using this book as your guide, you will be acting in the most effective way—i.e., by making choices as an informed consumer and traveler—to effect positive change.

Let us tell one more hurricane tale before moving on. The most anomalous storm track of all belonged to Hurricane Ivan. It hit Florida's western Panhandle as a Category 3 hurricane on September 16, 2004, decimating Pensacola Beach, Perdido Key, and Navarre Beach. Ivan killed 19 people in Florida and heavily damaged the bridge that crosses Escambia Bay in Pensacola. It then tracked inland, flooding the Southeast before exiting into the Atlantic Ocean along North Carolina's Outer Banks.

Here's where the storm track truly got weird. Over open water off the Carolina coast, Ivan split into several subsystems, one of which tracked south and struck Florida *again*. Yes, Hurricane Ivan made a gigantic loop and returned to punish Florida a second time, crossing the state from east to west and entering the Gulf of Mexico, where it regained tropical storm strength. For its encore, Ivan menaced the Panhandle, Louisiana, and Texas coasts with up to 10 inches of rain. By this point, the storm was three weeks old.

We regard the hurricane rampage not as the hand of God but partly as nature's response to human-altered natural systems. More highways, shopping malls, SUVs, condo towers, and subdivisions are not the answer. In fact, they're the problem. Florida must emerge from its state of denial and change the way it allows people to do business. If they don't, Florida could lose it all.

Ominously, the 2006 hurricane season kicked off early when Tropical Storm Alberto made landfall at Horseshoe Beach, Florida, on June 13th. Given that forecasters are predicting 15–20 more years of hurricane activity like those recently endured, it's safe to say that nothing will ever be the same in the Sunshine State.

—Parke Puterbaugh and Alan Bisbort, July 2006

Best Beaches

From among 400 beaches in the Sunshine State, we've picked our Top 25 overall favorites, plus our Top 5 for selected beach activities. Hurricanes and overdevelopment have forced us to revamp our Top 25 list from previous editions. Ten former favorites have been purged and 10 deserving beaches added. For the first time, we've also rank-ordered our lists in order to make them more meaningful.

◖ FLORIDA'S TOP 25 BEACHES

1. **Siesta Key Public Beach,** the Cultural Coast, page 389. Fine-grained, hard-packed white quartz sand on a wide, breezy beach. As perfect a mix of nature and people as you could conjure.
2. **Lummus Park/South Beach,** the Gold Coast, page 265. The most sociable beach in America, with near-naked beautiful people enjoying the scenery (and each other).
3. **Little Talbot Island State Park,** the Historic First Coast, page 44. Five miles of sandy bliss in Florida's northeast corner. This is a classic Southeastern barrier island, narrow and long, with a wide beach.
4. **Caladesi Island State Park,** Tampa Bay, page 440. Accessible by boat only, this uninhabited jewel in the Gulf of Mexico has fluffy, floury sand.
5. **North Beach,** Tampa Bay, page 412. An entire island set in Tampa Bay, south of St. Petersburg, offers beaches on several sides and abundant facilities. We consider it the best county park in Florida—no, in America.
6. **Grayton Beach State Park,** South Walton County, page 529. The Panhandle's symphony of white sand, salt marshes, coastal lakes, pine flatlands, and scrub-hickory hammock reaches a crescendo here.
7. **St. Joseph Peninsula State Park,** the Forgotten Coast, page 496. Nine deserted miles of gulf beaches backed by sandy dunes so white they look like snowdrifts.
8. **Bowman's Beach,** the Southwest Coast, page 360. The westernmost beach on Sanibel Island, the shelling capital of America, has an absolutely splendid setting.
9. **Playalinda Beach,** the Space Coast, page 113. This long, gorgeous wilderness beach at the south end of Canaveral National Seashore is within sight of NASA's launching pads.
10. **Bahia Honda State Park,** the Sunny Florida Keys, page 306. You can walk way out in the shallow waters offshore of this beach, one of the Keys' few sandy enclaves.
11. **Sebastian Inlet State Park (north side),** the Treasure Coast, page 143. Great fishing, radical surfing, scenic camping, and more along a relaxed stretch of A1A between Cocoa Beach and Vero Beach.
12. **Delray Beach Public Beach,** the Diamond Coast, page 210. One of the most likeable communities in South Florida also has one of the best lifeguard staffs in the country.
13. **Lori Wilson Park,** the Space Coast, page 124. Cocoa Beach is conveniently near Kennedy Space Center and the theme parks of Orlando, yet sparkling beach parks like Lori Wilson will tempt you to stay put.
14. **Main Street Pier and Beach,** the Sports Coast, page 95. Yes, it's big, built-up, noisy, and a bit red in the neck, but it's also a hell of a lot of fun. Let your hair down.
15. **Lovers Key State Park,** the Southwest Coast, page 348. This expansive parkland offers mangrove swamps, inner-island habitats, and—best of all—wide, shell-covered beaches. Bring your canoe and fishing pole.
16. **St. George Island State Park,** the Forgotten Coast, page 486. Occupying the east end

of a family-friendly barrier island way off the mainland, this park is great for biking, camping, nature exploration, and getting away from it all.

17. **Topsail Hill Preserve State Park,** South Walton County, page 535. This isolated park, one of the last true nature preserves on the Panhandle, has towering dunes and coastal dune lakes.

18. **South Beach Park,** the Treasure Coast, page 151. We're always pleasantly surprised by the size and attractiveness of this sandy gem on the south side of well-mannered Vero Beach.

19. **Juno Beach Park,** the Diamond Coast, page 186. Some towns "get it," and Juno Beach is one of them. Numerous stairs provide access to Juno's lengthy beach, and there's virtually no building on the beach side of A1A—as it should be.

20. **Kathryn Abby Hanna Beach Park,** the Historic First Coast, page 46. Towering, vegetated dunes overlook a beach that runs for 1.5 generally deserted miles. Hard to believe you're so close to Jacksonville.

21. **Anastasia State Park,** the Historic First Coast, page 68. Windsurfing in and camping on the inlet are two good reasons to come here. A four-mile, table-flat beach you can drive on is another.

22. **Deerfield Public Beach,** the Gold Coast, page 221. One of the nicest urban beaches in South Florida offers walkways, benches, palm trees, and a pier. Come here to de-stress.

23. **Casperson Park,** the Cultural Coast, page 383. This park preserves not only a two-mile stretch of pristine gulfside beach but also what lies behind it—a coastal hammock, tidal flats, and mangrove forests.

24. **Hobe Sound National Wildlife Refuge,** the Treasure Coast, page 176. Beloved by sea turtles and humans who appreciate quiet, unspoiled beaches, some of the best beach hiking in Florida can be done here.

25. **Coquina Beach,** the Cultural Coast, page 403. Behind the broad beach are picnic tables set in pine groves. Blessed relief from the snob appeal of neighboring Longboat Key.

◖ BEST BEACHES FOR FAMILIES

1. **Lori Wilson Park,** the Space Coast, page 124.
2. **Daytona Beach,** the Sports Coast, page 95.
3. **Treasure Island Beach Access,** Tampa Bay, page 420.
4. **Manatee Beach,** the Cultural Coast, page 404.
5. **Jacksonville Beach,** the Historic First Coast, page 52.

◖ BEST BEACHES FOR PEOPLE-WATCHING

1. **Lummus Park/South Beach,** the Gold Coast, page 265.
2. **Fort Lauderdale City Beach (Central Beach),** the Gold Coast, page 235.
3. **Midtown Beach,** the Diamond Coast, page 199.
4. **Hollywood Beach (Central Beach),** the Gold Coast, page 246.
5. **Siesta Key Public Beach,** the Cultural Coast, page 389.

◖ BEST BEACHES FOR SURFING

1. **Sebastian Inlet State Park (north side),** the Treasure Coast, page 143.
2. **Cocoa Beach (north end),** the Space Coast, page 124.
3. **Main Street Pier and Beach,** the Sports Coast, page 95.
4. **Smyrna Dunes Park,** the Sports Coast, page 107.
5. **North Jetty Park,** the Cultural Coast, page 385.

◖ BEST COASTAL LOCALES FOR FISHING

1. **Destin,** the Emerald Coast, page 539.
2. **Islamorada,** the Sunny Florida Keys, page 290.
3. **Marathon,** the Sunny Florida Keys, page 298.
4. **Treasure Island,** Tampa Bay, page 418.
5. **St. George Island,** the Forgotten Coast, page 484.

◖ BEST BEACHES FOR CAMPING

1. **St. Joseph Peninsula State Park,** the Forgotten Coast, page 496.
2. **St. Andrews State Park,** the Panhandle's Playground, page 504.
3. **Bahia Honda State Park,** the Sunny Florida Keys, page 306.
4. **Gamble Rogers Memorial State Recreation Area,** the Quiet Coast, page 83.
5. **Fort De Soto Park,** Tampa Bay, page 411.

◖ BEST COASTAL LOCALES FOR DIVING AND SNORKELING

1. **Looe Key,** the Sunny Florida Keys, page 308.
2. **John Pennekamp Coral Reef State Park,** the Sunny Florida Keys, page 289.
3. **Biscayne National Park,** the Gold Coast, page 280.
4. **Kings Bay,** the Nature Coast, page 456.
5. **St. Andrews State Park,** the Panhandle's Playground, page 504.

◖ BEST COASTAL LOCALES FOR CANOEING AND KAYAKING

1. **J. N. "Ding" Darling National Wildlife Refuge,** the Southwest Coast, page 355.
2. **Cedar Keys National Wildlife Refuge,** the Nature Coast, page 468.
3. **Chassahowitzka National Wildlife Refuge,** the Nature Coast, page 456.
4. **Gulf Coast Keys,** the Sunny Florida Keys, page 329.
5. **Big Talbot Island State Park,** the Historic First Coast, page 44.

◖ BEST COASTAL LOCALES FOR BIRDWATCHING AND WILDLIFE-VIEWING

1. **Merritt Island National Wildlife Refuge,** the Space Coast, page 115.
2. **J. N. "Ding" Darling National Wildlife Refuge,** the Southwest Coast, page 355.
3. **Gulf Coast Keys,** the Sunny Florida Keys, page 329.
4. **Homosassa Springs State Wildlife Park,** the Nature Coast, page 457.
5. **St. Marks National Wildlife Refuge,** the Southwest Coast, page 476.

◖ BEST BEACHES FOR COLLECTING SHELLS

1. **Bowman's Beach,** the Southwest Coast, page 360.
2. **Cayo Costa Island State Park,** the Southwest Coast, page 368.
3. **Captiva Beach,** the Southwest Coast, page 365.
4. **Lovers Key State Park,** the Southwest Coast, page 348.
5. **Fort Clinch State Park,** the Historic First Coast, page 29.

◖ BEST NUDE BEACHES

1. **Playalinda Beach,** the Space Coast, page 113.
2. **Haulover Beach,** the Gold Coast, page 255.
3. **Lummus Park/South Beach,** the Gold Coast, page 265.
4. **Apollo Beach,** the Space Coast, page 113.
5. **Navarre Beach,** the Western Panhandle, page 556.

JACKSONVILLE, ST. AUGUSTINE, AND THE HISTORIC FIRST COAST

They call northeast Florida the "First Coast," because it was the first place that Europeans landed in the New World. Looking for the Fountain of Youth, Ponce de Leon and his posse came ashore near Guana River in 1513. He was followed by Pedro Menendez de Aviles, who founded the city of St. Augustine in 1565. The area's subsequent history has been tumultuous and bloody, and local boosters make hay out of the fact that Amelia Island has flown under eight flags and St. Augustine under five since the conquistadors first rolled ashore.

Today, the First Coast is notable for its beaches, pressed between the historic towns of Fernandina Beach (in Nassau County, up by the Georgia state line) and St. Augustine (in St. Johns County). You'll find unique coastal geography on Amelia Island and Little Talbot Island, where the dunes are steeper than elsewhere on Florida's East Coast. You'll even find an important chapter of African-American history residing in American Beach.

The Big Kahuna in these parts is the bulging metropolis of Jacksonville—a city that occupies 841 square miles, taking up almost all of Duval County. If you like golfing, boating, beer-drinking, and Lynyrd Skynyrd (as we do), you'll love the Jacksonville area. East of the city, three beach towns—Jacksonville Beach, Atlantic Beach, and Neptune Beach, collectively known as the "Jax Beaches"—are slowly transforming into viable vacation destinations. Duval County's beaches run for 16 miles, from the Talbot Islands to Jacksonville Beach, and they're as wide and fine as they come. As word gets out, people are putting on the brakes instead of speeding down I-95 to points south.

St. Johns County is bordered by water—the Atlantic Ocean on the east, the St. Johns River on the west, and the Nassau and Matanzas

© PARKE PUTERBAUGH

Inlets to the north and south—and blessed with 24 miles of beaches. Its coastline varies from upscale (Ponte Vedra Beach) to unpretentious (Vilano Beach), from raw and wide (Guana River) to narrowed to nothing (St. Augustine Beach). The historic centerpiece of the county is St. Augustine, which bills itself as "America's Oldest City," celebrating that fact with attractions trading on its colonial past. Still, St. Johns County is very much attuned to the present, cultivating an upscale image as a county of golf resorts and shopping malls.

Fort Clinch State Park

The first beach in Florida instantly establishes Sunshine State's unrivaled reputation for sandy shores. Fort Clinch's 2.3 miles of beach—nearly a mile along the Atlantic Ocean, plus another 1.5 miles along the Cumberland Sound—can be found inside **Fort Clinch State Park,** just north of Fernandina Beach. One of Florida's oldest state parks, Fort Clinch comprises 1,121 acres of salt marsh, tidal estuaries, a coastal hardwood hammock (with oaks whose limbs are draped with Spanish moss), and huge sand dunes.

All of this bounty is centered around a restored 19th-century fortification. Park personnel, dressed in period uniforms, offer programs to showcase the daily life of a Union garrison in 1864. Built in 1847, the fort was named for General Duncan Lamont Clinch, a hero of the Seminole War of the 1830s. In 1861, the fort was occupied by Confederate troops who abandoned it in 1862, when it was claimed by Union forces. Fort Clinch even played a minor role in World War II, as beach patrollers kept a lookout for invading Germans and a navigational beacon helped guide seaplanes home from training missions.

The park itself has an interesting history. The state of Florida purchased the abandoned fort, along with 256 acres, in 1935 and then began

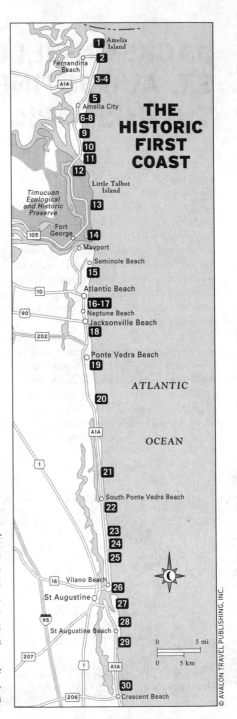

THE HISTORIC FIRST COAST

© AVALON TRAVEL PUBLISHING, INC.

BEST BEACHES

(Fort Clinch State Park: Best for Collecting Seashells (page 29).

(Big Talbot Island State Park: Best for Canoeing and Kayaking (page 44)

(Little Talbot Island State Park: Top 25 (page 44)

(Kathryn Abby Hannah Beach Park: Top 25 (page 46)

(Jacksonville Beach: Best for Families (page 52)

(Anastasia State Park: Top 25 (page 68)

buying adjacent land as funds became available. They were the fortuitous beneficiaries of FDR's New Deal legislation in 1937, as the Civilian Conservation Corps built the initial hiking trails, roads, and facilities for what would become the state's showcase park the following year. They also restored the old fort.

Today, the park has two campgrounds, a six-mile loop hiking trail that penetrates dense forest and tall dunes, and a shorter trail that circles two freshwater ponds. The park's most striking feature is its fishing pier, which juts into the mouth of Cumberland Sound. It is 0.5-mile long; we have never seen a longer pier anywhere (former bridges turned piers excepted).

In addition to a breathtaking view of the south end of Georgia's Cumberland Island, the pier rewards eagle-eyed visitors with an occasional manatee spotting. We saw two of the sweet old sea cows during our long march out on the fishing pier one dazzling summer day. (Note: If you want to see more of Cumberland Island—which is both a sparsely inhabited island and a campable National Seashore—it can be visited via passenger ferry out of the Georgia port town of St. Mary's, Georgia.)

If you're going to camp, especially in warmer months, we'd recommend the more shaded Amelia River location. The Atlantic Beach campground, built around a circle at the end of a spur road, is exposed to the full force of the sun with no relief.

Fort Clinch is a textbook case of a healthy barrier-island beach, with wide, hard-packed sand backed by fields of vegetation-covered dunes. No lifeguards are on duty, and swimming is prohibited north of the pier due to unpredictable currents. Beside the pier is a sliver of beach protected by a small breakwater of rocks. The shelling is surprisingly good along this strip. We found intact whelk shells and more. Shark's teeth are also said to be plentiful, but we saw none of those. You'll notice that part of the beach and all of the dunes south of the pier have been roped off for the benefit of nesting shorebirds. Don't be a piggy human and cross the rope, or you'll set the poor endangered things all atwitter.

With Fort Clinch State Park, the Florida coast sets a high standard right off the bat. Happily, most of the beaches along the so-called First Coast—from Fort Clinch to St. Augustine—maintain this level of excellence.

For more information, contact Fort Clinch State Park, 2601 Atlantic Avenue, Fernandina Beach, FL 32034, 904/277-7274, www.floridastateparks.org.

BEACHES

1 FORT CLINCH STATE PARK

BEST (

Location: From Fernandina Beach's historic district, drive east for two miles along Atlantic

Avenue (A1A) and then turn north at park entrance. It is three miles from here to Fort Clinch, with beach accesses marked along the way.

Parking/Fees: $5 entrance fee per vehicle. An additional $2 per person (free for children under six) is charged for touring the fort. Camping fee is $22 per night.

Hours: 8 A.M.-sunset

Facilities: restrooms, picnic tables, showers, and visitors center. There are 62 developed sites in two campgrounds (Atlantic Beach and Amelia River).

Contact: Fort Clinch State Park, 904/277-7274

Fernandina Beach

Fernandina Beach is a charming, well-preserved town at the north end of Amelia Island, Florida's northernmost barrier island. That officially makes it Florida's first beach town. It also marks the beginning of the First Coast, a chunk of Florida's northeast that is too often sped past by vacationers who are headed down I-95 toward Orlando and the beaches of central and south Florida. If you're looking for some storied history and an intact piece of the quickly vanishing "Old Florida," do not hesitate to detour off the traffic-choked interstate to check out Fernandina Beach for a few hours, days, or longer.

Fernandina Beach—and indeed, all of Amelia Island—is the only place in the United States to have flown under eight different flags. In addition to the flags of France, Spain, England, and the United States, a few off-brands have flown over this strategically situated island. The most short-lived was the "Patriots of Amelia Island," an anti-Spanish splinter group whose blue-and-white standard fluttered in the breeze for all of one day in 1812. As disarrayed as its early history was, Fernandina has—with the exception of 1861-1862, when the Confederate flag flew over Fort Clinch—flown the Stars and Stripes since 1821.

The federal occupation of the bustling port town brought an initial burst of prosperity after the Civil War. This segued into the Gilded Age (1875-1900), a real boom time for Fernandina Beach. Much of the town's wealth came from Florida's first cross-state railroad, completed in 1861, which ran from Fernandina to Cedar Key. That wealth was evident in the town's Victorian architecture. Two luxury hotels were built by the railroad, drawing wealthy guests from the north. Along Centre Street, near the natural harbor provided by the Amelia River, shipping magnates constructed huge Victorian mansions.

When Henry Flagler's East Coast Railway began siphoning wealthy tourists off to South Florida, Fernandina Beach relied on its fishing industry to bail it out of economic hard times. Specifically, the modern shrimping industry was founded in Fernandina Beach, with the first offshore shrimp trawlers pushing off in 1913. Shrimpers still dock at City Marina, which has the signal honor of harboring Florida's only marine welcome station. Shrimping was augmented by oyster harvesting and crabbing, which led to the construction of several canneries. The sweet Fernandina shrimp is still the unofficial town mascot, and you should definitely order them off any menu when in the area.

By contrast, the unofficial town nuisance has been the malodorous nearby Rayonier paper mills. Though they helped pull Fernandina out of the Great Depression, the belching mills were determined in the 1990s to be a primary cause of declining plankton species vital to the food chain in the Amelia River. However, a million-dollar cleanup in 2001 has made Rayonier an altogether better corporate neighbor.

There's nothing shrimpy about the town's ambitious and ongoing restoration. The 50-square-block "Olde Town" area has been designated a historic district in the National Register of Historic Places. A number of popular walking tours of the district, including a "Cemetery Crawl," are offered at the **Amelia Island Museum of History** (233 South 3rd Street, 904/261-7378). You can conduct your

THE HISTORIC FIRST COAST

© PARKE PUTERBAUGH

Fernandina Beach harbor

own guided walking tour with a brochure obtained at the Chamber of Commerce (102 Centre Street, 904/261-3248), located inside the restored 1899 train depot.

The theme of preservation and renewal extends to the shopping district, where storefronts re-create the style of the previous century. Things might, in fact, be going a little too well, as recent arrivals on Centre Street include Aveda and Seattle's Best Coffee. The good news is that Fernandina Beach largely remains a real community. Much of it is low-key and residential, and the residents seem committed to keeping it that way. In 2005, the county commissioners voted down a fancy new hotel on South Fletcher Avenue, preferring that the area retain its unaffected, residential character. They also implemented a four-story height restriction on new construction in Fernandina Beach.

And so Fernandina Beach remains a pleasant surprise for those who venture by, offering great beaches in town and at Fort Clinch State Park, plus loads of Victoriana and charm in the Centre Street historic district. The area is so unpretentiously inviting that you might consider renting one of the almost ridiculously af-

fordable beach homes that line South Fletcher for a family vacation. Hey, the thought has crossed our minds.

For more information, contact the Amelia Island Tourist Development Council, 102 Centre Street, Fernandina Beach, FL 32034, 800/2-AMELIA (800/226-3542), www.ameliaisland.org.

BEACHES

From I-95, A1A zigs and zags through town before finally turning south to begin its shore-hugging way south along Fletcher Avenue. To get to the beach from the historic "Olde Town" district, head east on Centre Street, which becomes Atlantic Avenue (A1A) at 8th Street and ends at **Main Beach.** Because of its abundant parking and facilities, including lifeguard stands and a grassy playground, the vast majority of Fernandina Beach visitors—especially those with children—gravitate to Main Beach. Ample free parking is provided at two large paved lots. Beside them are picnic areas, gazebos, restrooms, showers, and a boardwalk. Right by the water is Sandy Bottoms, an unfancy place for a beer and a bite to eat.

WHERE'S THE BEACH?

Tales of beach renourishment, which begin right on the Florida border at Fernandina Beach and Amelia Island Plantation, are a recurring theme in this book, since beach erosion has occurred all over Florida. A good measure of the credit for Florida's sand-starved beaches has to go to the U.S. Army Corps of Engineers, whose jetties, groins, seawalls, and other hardened structures have often created and then worsened the problem. The Corps is responsible in another sense, as well. By damming rivers throughout the Southeast, they've cut off the primary source of sediment to the beaches. If you're pondering the whereabouts of all the sand that should be keeping your favorite beach wide and healthy, look upstream: it's likely trapped behind a dam.

Real-estate builders and developers must bear some of the blame, too, since they've often destroyed or severely altered the dune structure in seaside communities in order to make it possible to live directly on the beach. Sand dunes are like bank accounts. The more money you have in the bank, the better you'll be able to survive a financial emergency. Likewise, the more sand that's banked into dunes, the better able the beach will be to absorb the force of wind and waves from hurricanes and storms. Flattening dunes eliminates the protective buffer between land and ocean. Think of it this way: If you have a clear and unobstructed view of the ocean, then it has a clear and unobstructed path to you, too. Now think of the billions in damage caused by hurricanes in Florida, including four big blows in 2004 alone. Finally, ponder what lies ahead as we move deeper into a natural cycle of heightened hurricane activity – not to mention hurricanes made unusually powerful due to global warming.

Now, do you still want to live on the beach?

In season Main Beach is lifeguarded noon–7 P.M. daily (and from 11 A.M. on weekends). While it's all the same long strand, running south from Fort Clinch State Park, the beach has thinned at Main Beach, augmented by riprap and a squat seawall. The shore face is steeper and shellier here than at Fort Clinch, but the beach widens again as you move farther down Amelia Island. Check out the water color, which is a more deep, opaque green than the emerald and azure hues seen elsewhere in Florida.

The "beach" part of the town name does not lie. From Main Beach down to the southern city limits sign, we measured 4.5 miles of beach and counted 50 public accesses. Each is clearly marked with rectangular wooden signs. All are brought to you courtesy of the city of Fernandina Beach. Most of the northern accesses are for pedestrians only. Further south a limited number of free parking spaces (10–20) are provided. Surfing is not allowed at Main Beach, so board bums head down

to popular **Seaside Park,** at Sadler Road and South Fletcher Avenue (A1A), where the waves break better anyway. Seaside Park has gazebos, picnic tables, boardwalks, and more, and this gleaming addition to the beachfront (located next to Slider's Seaside Restaurant) opened in 2003.

Fernandina Beach has generally displayed foresight in its residential zoning, with homes built well behind the 40-foot-tall sand dunes. Most of the beach houses are modest in size, and some are appealingly eccentric. Two are shaped like miniature lighthouses.

Peter's Point Beach Front Park is the most desirable of the beach parks south of Main Beach. In addition to a wide, walkable strand, it offers decent facilities and adequate parking. It's a healthy, one-eighth-mile beach with three distinct beach ridges between the parking and beach. On the west side of the park is a decent swatch of maritime forest, which provides a glimpse

THE HISTORIC FIRST COAST

of what once covered the area. This is also a drive-on beach, though the sand is soft and recommended only for four-wheel-drive vehicles. The only bummer is that it's bordered by the Carlton Dunes, one of those unseemly architectural colossuses devoted to "luxury oceanfront living."

Driving on the beach is permitted at Peter's Point, Scott Road, and Burney Beach. You can buy a one-day ($5) or one-year ($20) permit at the Nassau County Courthouse (76347 Veterans Way, 904/548-4700) in Yulee or at Hall's Beach Store (2021 South Fletcher Avenue, 904/261-7007) in Fernandina Beach.

🄴 MAIN BEACH

Location: A1A (Fletcher Avenue) at Trout Street in Fernandina Beach
Parking/Fees: free parking lots
Hours: 8 A.M.–9 P.M.
Facilities: lifeguards (seasonal), restrooms, picnic tables, a playground, and showers
Contact: Fernandina Beach Parks and Recreation Department, 904/277-7350

🄴 SEASIDE PARK

Location: Sadler Road at South Fletcher Avenue (A1A) in Fernandina Beach
Parking/Fees: free parking lot
Hours: 8 A.M.–9 P.M.
Facilities: lifeguards (seasonal), restrooms, picnic tables, and showers
Contact: Fernandina Beach Parks and Recreation Department, 904/277-7350

🄴 FERNANDINA BEACH ACCESSES

Location: There are 50 beach accesses at

street ends off South Fletcher Avenue (A1A) between Main Beach and Peter's Point.
Parking/Fees: limited free street parking
Hours: 8 A.M.–9 P.M.
Facilities: none
Contact: Fernandina Beach Parks and Recreation Department, 904/277-7350

🄴 PETER'S POINT BEACH FRONT PARK

Location: south end of Fletcher Avenue (A1A), just outside city limits
Parking/Fees: free parking lots
Hours: sunrise–sunset
Facilities: lifeguards (seasonal), restrooms, picnic tables, and showers
Contact: Nassau County Recreation Department, 904/321-5790

🄴 SCOTT ROAD BEACH ACCESS

Location: Scott Road at Amelia Island Parkway, south of Fernandina Beach
Parking/Fees: free parking lot
Hours: sunrise–sunset
Facilities: none
Contact: Nassau County Recreation Department, 904/321-5790

RECREATION AND ATTRACTIONS

- **Ecotourism:** Kayak Amelia, 904/321-0697 or 888/30-KAYAK (888/305-2925)

- **Fishing Charters:** Amelia Island Charter Boat Association, 1 Front Street, 904/261-2870

- **Lighthouse:** Amelia Island Lighthouse, ½ Lighthouse Circle, 904/261-3248

- **Marina:** Fernandina Harbour Marina, 1 Front Street, 904/261-0355

- **Pier:** Fort Clinch State Park, 2601 Atlantic Avenue, Fernandina Beach, 904/277-7274
- **Rainy-Day Attraction:** Amelia Island Museum of History, 233 South 3rd Street, Fernandina Beach 904/261-7378
- **Shopping/Browsing:** Centre Street ("Historic Downtown Fernandina Beach")
- **Surf Shop:** Pipeline Surf Shop, 2022 1st Avenue, Fernandina Beach, 904/277-3717
- **Vacation Rentals:** Fernandina Beach Reality, 2057 South Fletcher Avenue, Fernandina Beach, 904/261-4011 or 800/741-4011

ACCOMMODATIONS

You can make history a part of your stay in Fernandina Beach by choosing from among nearly a dozen bed-and-breakfast inns, some of which legitimately date from the Victorian era. Yesteryear is very much alive at the venerable **Amelia Island Williams House** (103 South 9th Street, 904/277-2328, $$$). The Williams House, which has four rooms to rent, has won numerous awards and been selected a "Top Inn of the Year" by *Country Inns* magazine. Built in 1856, it was bought three years later by Marcellus Williams, a railroad surveyor. He added a gingerbread-style porch in the 1880s, and not much has changed beyond that in more than a century.

Pure Victoriana, inside and out, is available nearby at the five-room **Bailey House** (28 South 7th Street, 904/261-5390, $$). Built in 1895 by an agent for a steamship company, the Bailey House was one of the most elaborately constructed homes of its day, with many turrets, gables, and bay windows, plus period antiques, brass beds, and carved furniture.

While the above two inns are located in the historic district (a mile from the beach), **Elizabeth Pointe Lodge** (98 South Fletcher Avenue, 904/277-4851, $$$) is situated right behind the sand dunes. This airy, gray-shingled 25-unit lodge offers a full breakfast, and some rooms have kitchenettes. The smaller, six-room **1735 House** (584 South Fletcher Avenue, 904/261-5878, $$$) also boasts an excellent location and architectural distinction.

COASTAL CUISINE

On the culinary front, Fernandina Beach is famous for the shrimp its local fleet continues to haul from local waters, despite the struggles that dog small, independent shrimpers these days. The price of shrimp fluctuates according to catch size, but they are available all over town and usually served steamed in the shell with cocktail sauce and lemon. Nothing fancy, but when shrimp are this fresh, they don't need dressing up. If you don't mind peeling and eating, it's the way to go here.

Brett's Waterway Cafe (1 South Front Street, 904/261-2660, $$$) has the best location in town: at the foot of Centre Street in downtown Fernandina Beach, overlooking the harbor. Try coming as the sun is going down for a great view. It's a bustling, noisy place that attracts a happy mix of families, locals, tourists, and folks from Jacksonville who know a meal worth driving for. They feature the best in local seafood, such as crab-crusted grouper and cornmeal-dusted flounder. For those who like to keep it simple, there's "Good Ole' [sic] Fried Shrimp," served with fries and slaw. From appetizers to desserts, Brett's delivers the goods in a grand setting.

The **Marina Seafood Restaurant** (101 Centre Street, 904/261-5310, $$) is the hands-down favorite in town for seafood. It's not so much that it's fancy as that it's fresh. They serve fish all day long, from fish and eggs (with cheese grits!) in the morning to a killer grouper sandwich for lunch, and fisherman's platters ($20.95 fried and $21.95 broiled) at the dinner hour. You can't miss going for the shrimp dishes. We like the fact they serve limes to squeeze on the seafood and in the iced tea. Tables full of locals make a happy racket. Family owned and operated, they've built on a history of good dining at this address that dates back to the early 1900s. Incidentally, you haven't really seen a jumbo shrimp until you've studied the preserved monster on display at the Marina.

Asking around for further recommendations, we were tipped off by a local to the **Crab Trap** (31 North 2nd Street, 904/261-4749,

GEOLOGY OF AMELIA ISLAND

Amelia Island is the name of the northeasternmost barrier island in Florida. It's separated from the state of Georgia by St. Mary's River. Geographically, Amelia Island and the neighboring Big Talbot and Little Talbot Islands (see separate entry), are the southernmost in a chain of barrier islands that start with the Outer Banks way up in North Carolina. Amelia and Talbot Islands have more in common with Georgia's "sea islands" – a special type of barrier island – than the rest of Florida's East Coast. They are all part of the "Golden Isle chain," which also includes several islands in South Carolina.

Sea islands are found along the Georgia embayment, a wide arc extending from North Carolina to Florida, with its center near Jekyll Island, Georgia. The head is subject to greater tidal exchange and lesser wave energy than the ends. At Amelia Island, for instance, the mean tidal range – the average difference between high and low tide – is more than two meters (about six feet). By comparison, the rest of Florida's East Coast has a mean tidal range tide of one meter (three feet) or less.

Sea islands form along coastlines where the tidal range is 2.5 meters (which classifies them as "mesotidal"). The 2.1-meter tidal range found at the Georgia-Florida border allows inlets to form and remain open, creating barrier islands. Sand and sediment are transported by currents running parallel to the coast – a process known as "longshore drift" – and their deflection by ebbing tides results in the buildup of deltas that emerge to form beach ridges at the tips. Sea islands such as Amelia are typically short and stubby in form. They are called "drumstick barriers," because they're shaped like chicken drumsticks. These sea islands' most prominent feature is an extensive, well-developed salt marsh on the inlet side. Between the dunes and marshes lie dense forests of palms, Southern magnolias, and magnificently gnarly live oaks draped with Spanish moss.

What all this technical talk means to the average vacationer is that Amelia Island and the Talbot Islands are unique in Florida – and that you might want to put this often overlooked corner of the state on your vacation itinerary.

$$). The ambience is casual, it's a few blocks away from the Centre Street bustle, and the fried, blackened, or broiled seafood is among Amelia Island's best.

For something a bit dressier, the **Beech Street Grill** (8th and Beech Streets, 904/277-3662, $$$) is a gourmet New American eatery in an old Victorian setting. They specialize in Cajun blackened and light Italian seafood preparations utilizing fresh herbs and sauces.

The **Down Under Restaurant** (A1A, 904/261-1001, $$), family owned and operated since 1982, is a good place to go to partake of fresh, locally caught seafood. The name refers to its scenic location "down under" the Thomas J. Shave Bridge, which crosses the Amelia River.

The **Florida House Inn** (22 South 3rd Street, 904/261-3300, $$) serves home-style Southern cooking: fried chicken, BBQ pork, catfish, collards, biscuits, cornbread. The heaping platters and bowls back up their claim to give you "always all you care to eat." You might pay a bit more at the Florida House, but you get a more evocative setting: it's Florida's oldest hotel, dating back to 1857, and still operates as an 11-room bed-and-breakfast.

NIGHTLIFE

By virtue of being Florida's oldest continuously operating bar, the **Palace Saloon** (117 Centre Street, 904/261-6320) is an interesting spot to duck into while shuffling around the historic district. Built in 1878, it thrived in the Gay '90s and continued to lure curious folks with its period appointments (hand-carved oak bar, brass rails, tin ceiling, murals) a century later. In fact, a lot of visitors began and ended their nightlife right here. Sadly, an electrical fire gutted the Palace Saloon in February 1999, claiming the priceless 1907 wall murals and damaging the black mahogany bar. Still, you can't keep a good bar down, and the Palace reopened three months later and slowly but surely has been restored to its former glory. Even the murals depicting ships and pirates have been meticulously re-created.

In the historic district, we also like **O'Kane's** (318 Centre Street, 904/261-1000), a friendly Irish pub and eatery. Your best bet for finding rock and roll down by the beach is the ramshackle, dark, and beer-stained **Sliders** (1998 South Fletcher Avenue, 904/261-0954).

A decent place to spend your beachside evening is on the patio of **The Surf** (3199 South Fletcher Avenue, 904/261-5711), where breezes will serenade you between sets by (more than likely) a one-man band or a local DJ. The music starts nightly at 6 P.M.; simple, serviceable food (smoked fish dip, seafood plates) can be ordered; and on a balmy, moonlit evening, The Surf's wooden deck makes a fine place to knock back a brew or two. There's also a motel, cut from the plainest possible cloth, on the premises.

Summer Beach

Summer Beach is an upscale resort development of homes, condos and villas. It's just south of the Fernandina Beach city limits, so the mailing address is Amelia Island. The layout is not dissimilar to its much larger neighbor, Amelia Island Plantation, which preceded it by a few decades. You can arrange a vacation rental or stay at the five-star Ritz-Carlton Amelia Island. It's all very posh, upscale, and (of course) ridiculously expensive.

For more information, contact Summer Beach Resort Central, 5000 Amelia Island Parkway, Amelia Island, FL 32034, 904/277-0905, www.summerbeach.com.

ACCOMMODATIONS

We needn't go on about how bedazzled you'll be by the 445-unit **Ritz-Carlton Amelia Island** (4750 Amelia Island Parkway, 904/277-1100, $$$$) or how much you'll pay to stay here. Rates range from $289 for an oceanfront room in season to $2,200 for the massive "Presidential Suite." Suffice it to say that the Ritz has earned AAA's five-star rating, that it has 1.5 miles of pristine Amelia Island beachfront, and that the property is an almost obscenely genteel paradise. It boasts of being the only mainland Ritz-Carlton tethered to a championship golf course. In addition to the 18-hole Golf Club of Amelia Island, other resort amenities include indoor/outdoor pools, tennis courts, a croquet lawn, pathways that meander over plush landscaped grounds, four on-premises restaurants. ... In short, the works.

COASTAL CUISINE

The **Grill at the Ritz-Carlton** (4750 Amelia Island Parkway, 904/277-1100, $$$$) is the five-star culinary centerpiece at the Ritz, excelling in grilled steak and seafood. Do be aware that you won't get out of here for less than $60 a head, however.

American Beach

Though bigots and greedy developers might argue otherwise, American Beach is aptly named. It is emblematic of a major aspect of American life and history: the African-American experience. It is proudly and defiantly a black beach pressed between two sentinels of upscale white hegemony: the Ritz-Carlton Amelia Island and Amelia Island Plantation. Its appearance is shockingly poor compared to the marble-walled Ritz-Carlton and the villas of the neighboring "plantation." American Beach is, to all outward appearances, a down-on-its-heels place that developers have been angling to acquire, lot by lot, and turn into yet another soulless, gated resort for America's golfing gentry.

THE AMAZING STORY OF MAVYNEE BETSCH

More than a decade ago, when we first made the turn off A1A into American Beach, the only living figure we saw was a black woman. Her long hair was gathered into a single elephant trunk–sized dreadlock. Eight-inch fingernails sprouted from her hands. This striking figure wandered between a squat house near the ocean and a dumpster that was covered with political bumper stickers. We circled around to have a closer look at the only ambulatory soul in American Beach but spun out of town when she began barking what we thought to be some sort of reprimand at us.

Would that we had stuck around. It turns out that we had encountered MaVynee Betsch. She was the great-granddaughter of A. L. Lewis, founder of the Afro-American Insurance Company, an enormously successful Jacksonville-based firm launched in 1901 (and since absorbed by a larger firm). Afro-American purchased and founded American Beach back in the 1930s, which is why it's remained "in the family," so to speak, all these years.

Betsch, who died in 2005, was for many decades known as the "Beach Lady," because of her tireless support for American Beach's preservation and recognition of its historic past. She didn't much care for or about money. At points in her life she literally lived on the beach. A former opera singer and a graduate of Oberlin College, she patrolled the town as its de facto guardian and conscience. And every word she said made a hell of a lot of sense to us.

In 1995, there was another of the periodic flare-ups between the defiant citizens of American Beach and the resort developers on either side of them. That year, the issue was the proposed development of 83 acres that had been acquired by Amelia Island Plantation. When the specter of yet another golf course surrounded by 60 or 70 "luxury single-family homes" appeared to be in the cards – this one right in American Beach's backyard – Betsch had this to say in the *Miami Herald*:

"I found [the attitude] insulting that we should be honored they were building a golf course next to us. I said to them: 'You should be honored to be living next to one of the most historic black communities in the South.'"

Well, the development (known as Osprey Village) came to pass, and it does indeed butt up against what's left of American Beach. However, the contrasting worlds of the upscale and new and that of the poor and historic has seemingly arrived at some sort of mutual accommodation in the new millennium. In 2003, Amelia Island Plantation donated nearly 10 acres of dunes that separate American Beach and Osprey Village to the National Park Service's Timucuan Ecological and Historic Preserve. Moreover, it was announced that the county intended to build an American Beach museum at the local community center. A member of the board of the A. L. Lewis Historical Society, established to preserve the legacy of American Beach, said: "We're hopeful that this will be the beginning of community coming together and good things happening."

Betsch passed away on September 5, 2005, ending a long bout with cancer. Two months later, she received a special acknowledgement and blessing from (of all people) the Dalai Lama. This pair of appreciative beach bums would also like to add their posthumous kudos to Ms. Betsch for a job well done. We wish there were more like her looking after Florida's beaches, both from the standpoint of environmental health and human history.

Should you happen to be driving down A1A between Fernandina Beach and Amelia Island Plantation, you may spy a nondescript road sign that points east toward "Historic American Beach." If you are a tourist or passer-through, it is not a turn you'll want to make. If you are white, your presence in this tumble-down town of concrete-block bungalows might elicit raised eyebrows—that is, if anyone is around to check you out.

American Beach used to come alive on weekends, when black youths from the Jacksonville area headed up to party on the beach. Sometimes these parties got out of hand, leading to confrontations with the authorities. As the result of a beefed-up police presence, however, the crowds dwindled and disappeared. These days, American Beach is as devoid of life as if a neutron bomb had hit it.

Lewis Street runs down to the beach and Gregg Street runs along it. At present, although American Beach preservationists have won some victories (see *The Amazing Story of MaVynee Betsch* sidebar), it still looks like a ghost town in dire need of an overhaul. It is an odd collage of crumbling cinderblock homes, modest new construction, and vacant lots. To what it is transitioning is unclear. Despite the push to recognize its historicity, it is currently a listless place. What survives of American Beach is, ironically, almost an affront. Out on A1A sit the decaying remains of a liquor store and a tavern called the Honey Dripper—mute testament to the days when people partied hearty hereabouts.

In our view, the best thing that could happen to American Beach would be for some visionary African-American entrepreneurs to build a resort community of oceanfront hotels and villas that would attract black-owned businesses and vacationers. Doing so would allow American Beach to again function as a viable community and allow it to compete on a proud and equal footing with the resorts around it.

If you want to learn more about this fascinating place, read *American Beach: A Saga of Race, Wealth and Memory,* by Russ Rymer (HarperCollins, 1998).

For more information, contact the American Beach Property Owners Association, P.O. Box 6123, Fernandina Beach, FL 32035, 904/261-4396.

BEACHES

At the south end of American Beach is **Burney Beach Front Park,** a Nassau County facility with picnic tables and a large parking lot. Every time we've come here—including several beautiful summer days—it's been virtually empty. Leaving the tortured matter of race relations and the war between the haves and the have-nots aside, we were impressed by Burney Park, with its big, bountiful dune bluffs and unspoiled beach. There was not a golf cart in sight, although we did once have to dodge a kid on a go-cart who seemed to want to mow us down. We also saw a turtle racing across the parking lot here. Yes, racing: you might think turtles are slow, but this one was really making time.

7 AMERICAN BEACH

Location: From Amelia Island Parkway (A1A), turn east onto Lewis Street and follow to beach. American Beach is seven miles south of Fernandina Beach.
Parking/Fees: free street parking
Hours: none posted
Facilities: none
Contact: Nassau County Recreation Department, 904/321-5790

8 BURNEY BEACH FRONT PARK

Location: From Amelia Island Parkway (A1A) turn east onto Burney Street and follow to beach. The park is 7.5 miles south of Fernandina Beach.
Parking/Fees: free parking lots
Hours: sunrise-sunset
Facilities: restrooms, picnic tables, and showers
Contact: Nassau County Recreation Department, 904/321-5790

Amelia Island Plantation

We appreciate the efforts at environmental preservation and a respectful coexistence with nature made by planners of Amelia Island Plantation. In many respects we regard it as a model of how to develop without destroying the natural surroundings. The key concept is a harmonious blending with nature, and while the principle has become incrementally compromised over time—there are now 54 holes of golf and only seven miles of biking and nature trails—Amelia Island Plantation's claims of "environmental integrity" have merit. We'd put it right up there with Kiawah Island, South Carolina—another planned resort community where environmental disruption has been held to a relative minimum.

Amelia Island very nearly might have turned out looking like hell's half-acre had an enlightened developer named Charles Fraser not come along. The Union Carbide Corporation originally held title to the land upon which Amelia Island Plantation now sits. (That is, of course, after the Timucuan Indians, the flags of eight nations, and a now-vanished black community named Franklintown.) The chemical firm intended to strip-mine the land for potassium. Fortunately, the enlightened Fraser—whose Sea Pines Company had developed Hilton Head Island—purchased 900 acres and began looking for ways to design a resort community that would preserve and highlight the fragile barrier island ecology.

The plantation's overseers drafted a plan to protect salt marshes and oceanfront dunes while buffering waterways with strips of natural vegetation to minimize runoff from golf courses and habitations. Foot traffic was restricted to boardwalks. Covenants defining the restrictions and obligations of property owners were devised. Codified guidelines ensured that buildings were "aesthetically pleasing, functionally convenient, and part of the landscape design."

It's no coincidence that Amelia Island Plantation was plotted at the dawn of the 1970s, near the environmental awakening that found its most universal expression with the first Earth Day observance in April 1970. This broadly shared perspective began influencing

© PARKE PUTERBAUGH

Amelia Island Plantation

the kinds of things people wanted to do and see on vacation. Fraser anticipated that people of means were beginning to desire more natural settings—not silo-like monstrosities rising out of tree-strafed sandlots but tasteful condominiums burrowed in the cooling shade of oak trees and sabal palms. At the same time, they also wanted the very best golf courses and tennis courts, as well as top-quality instructors.

In the more than three decades that have passed since the master plan was drafted, Amelia Island Plantation has stuck to the script pretty faithfully. The resort has increased its holdings so that, at 1,330 acres, it is now nearly half again as large. To be sure, there is a lot more on the grounds than there was back when we first visited in the mid-1980s. But a general air of preservation continues to allow Amelia Island Plantation to rate way above the competition along Florida's grossly overbuilt East Coast. Here, you can at least see the forest *and* the trees—not to mention the beach. This was driven home to us one recent summer morning when we stepped outside our room at the Amelia Island Inn, looked out over the forest and marsh and really could not see a building for all the trees. Kudos to Amelia Island Plantation for a job well done.

For more information, contact Amelia Island Plantation, 3000 First Coast Highway, Amelia Island, FL 32034, 888/261-6161, www.aipfl.com.

BEACHES

Amelia Island Plantation claims 3.5 miles of beach, which is quite an expanse. They have occasionally been forced to renourish the eroding beach, but it was satisfyingly wide upon our last visit in late 2005. There is a good length of it at Amelia Island Plantation to walk, lie, or play on—that is, if you can tear yourself away from the tennis and golf (three 18-hole courses), which are the resort's main recreational calling cards. If you're a beach person, one positive effect of all these other distractions is that you can easily find

a spot where you'll literally have the beach to yourself.

This is a high-energy beach, judging from all the coarse "shell hash" in the surf zone. It reminded us a bit of the Outer Banks of North Carolina. One of us brought our daughter down for a stay, and she had endless hours of fun riding her inflatable plastic crocodile up and down the beach face as waves broke and receded. We've seen surfers get surprisingly decent rides here. The Beach Club, located adjacent to the Amelia Island Inn, has a pair of free-form pools (accessible to guests) that offer a calmer alternative to the ocean.

9 AMELIA ISLAND PLANTATION

Location: 10 miles south of Fernandina Beach and 15 miles north of Jacksonville, on First Coast Highway (A1A)
Parking/Fees: Beaches and facilities are for the use of residents, registered guests, and their visitors only.
Hours: none posted
Facilities: concessions, restrooms, showers, and a visitors center
Contact: Amelia Island Plantation, 904/261-6161 or 800/874-6878

ACCOMMODATIONS

With the addition of the 249-unit **Amelia Inn** (Amelia Island Plantation, 3000 First Coast Highway, 904/261-6161, $$$$) in 1998, there are now nearly 700 guest accommodations available at Amelia Island Plantation. These range from rooms at the inn (all of them oceanfront) to villas with up to three bedrooms. Villas range in age, decor, location (seaside, woods, marsh, golf course), and on and on. We've sampled a few of Amelia's villas over the years, most recently staying at a development called (appropriately for us) Beachwalker. The bedrooms were commodious, the appointments quite comfortable.

We could get used to living like this with no trouble at all.

If you're thinking of buying at Amelia Island Plantation, there are more than 900 villa units among 17 developments bearing names like Piper Dunes, Fairway Oaks, and Sandcastles, all of them self-evidently describing their location. If you want to book a vacation, a two-bedroom ocean-view villa goes for $409–774 per night or $2023–3318 per week. Peak season is mid-March–May. During Amelia Island's low season, which spans the winter months—a contrast to the resorts of South Florida, where winter is peak season—you will get the best deals. Rooms at the inn go for $236–296 per night. Finally, they offer package deals—centered around golf, tennis, and "romantic getaways"—that are worth asking about.

COASTAL CUISINE

As you'd expect of a gargantuan golf, beach, and tennis resort, there are all manner of places to wet your whistle at Amelia Island Plantation. The **Ocean Grill** inside the Amelia Inn (904/321-5050, $$$$) specializes in upscale atmosphere and hearty food, simply but elegantly prepared. On any given night, you will find chophouse fare like beef tenderloin, veal chop, and free-range chicken counterpointed by seafood offerings.

The **Verandah** (Amelia Island Plantation, 904/321-5050, $$$)—our favorite on-premises eatery, refurbished after a fire in 1999—does terrific things with seafood. Entrees we've tried include blackened red snapper with crabmeat in ginger-herb sauce, grouper with lobster meat in herb-garlic sauce, and herb-crusted ahi with mango chili sauce. On our most recent visit, Baked Red House Grouper (with a blue-crab crust and sauvignon blanc sauce) and pecan-dusted fried flounder with a spicy remoulade were the star entrees. If you can't decide, the Verandah Seafood Platter (shrimp, fish, scallops, and crab cake) is your best bet (and their top-seller). But we'd suggest letting the kitchen strut its stuff and choose one of the more elaborate sauced entrees.

NIGHTLIFE

While wandering the grounds of the Amelia Island Plantation some years back, we heard a siren go off, accompanied by a message delivered and repeated in an amplified robotic voice: "Island is being tampered with! Island is being tampered with!" We never figured out exactly who was "tampering" with the island, but this is the most excitement we've ever scared up after dark here. There's little in the way of nightlife to be found beyond a civilized drink at the **Amelia Inn.** Your best bet is the **Beach Club Sports Bar,** where you'll find pool tables and TV screens. But it is only open seasonally. If it's nightlife you want, head up the road to Fernandina Beach.

Amelia Island (south end)

After all the buildup at Fernandina Beach, Summer Beach, and Amelia Island Plantation, it's good to find a few public accesses and some wilderness acreage on the island. First of all, the county has wrangled an access path between private construction south of Amelia Island Plantation. **South Beach Access** is one of 110 numbered beach walkovers in the county (outside of Fernandina Beach, which has 50 of its own), so we salute Nassau County for its attentiveness to the matter of public beach access. South Beach Access is unique among them at this end of the county in that it has a parking lot. The path to the beach is long and narrow, bordered by private residences and, on one side, a chain-link fence.

If you're a wild-beach type, **Amelia Island State Park,** along A1A at the south end of Nassau County, offers 200 acres on which to roam. Visitors can swim, fish, and ride horses on the beach. Lines can be cast from the shore or the mile-long George Crady Bridge—an abandoned vehicular bridge that was replaced by a new one—which extends into Nassau Sound. The state record flounder was hauled in here and redfish and speckled trout are common catches.

Kelly Seahorse Ranch (7500 First Coast Highway, Amelia Island, 904/491-5166) serves the park with guided beach horseback rides that cost $45 and go out four times daily. You must be 13 or over; call for times and reservations. This is the only state-endorsed horse ranch. The horses saunter from their stables through some woods and out to the beach. It's a nice ride, though not quite the wilderness experience one might imagine, thanks to all the private-home construction on the beach.

For more information, contact Amelia Island State Park, c/o Little Talbot Island State Park, 12157 Heckscher Drive, Jacksonville, FL 32226, 904/251-2320, www.floridastateparks.org.

BEACHES

10 SOUTH BEACH ACCESS

Location: off First Coast Highway (A1A), a mile north of Amelia Island State Park in southern Nassau County
Parking/Fees: free parking lot
Hours: sunrise-sunset
Facilities: none
Contact: Nassau County Recreation Department, 904/321-5790

11 AMELIA ISLAND STATE PARK

Location: 10 miles south of Fernandina Beach along First Coast Highway (A1A)
Parking/Fees: $1 per person
Hours: 8 A.M.-sunset
Facilities: restrooms
Contact: Kelly Seahorse Ranch, 904/491-5166, or Little Talbot Island State Park, 904/251-2320

Big Talbot Island State Park and Little Talbot Island State Park

In the northeast corner of Duval County, between Nassau Sound and Fort George Inlet, three islands lie side by side like lazy gators

Big Talbot Island

© PARKE PUTERBAUGH

basking in the sun. They are, from north to south, Big Talbot, Long, and Little Talbot Islands, and you'll cross all of them if you're driving south on A1A between Amelia Island and Jacksonville. In this instance, the old saying "less is more" holds true, because Little Talbot Island is the gem in the chain, at least from the perspective of beach access.

Bounded by Simpson Creek and Nassau Sound, **Big Talbot Island** is characterized by steep bluffs instead of dunes, and one descends to the beach by way of stairs. High tide comes right up to the bluffs' base, and natural erosion causes the gnarly live oaks to topple seaward from time to time. The beach is narrow and dark in color, and the look of the island is wild, with the silvery skeletons of dead trees reposing in the surf zone. Big Talbot's proximity to Nassau Sound makes it great for fishing, so bring a pole and/or boat to explore the teeming sound and tidal creeks. Kayak Amelia (904/251-0016, www.kayakamelia.com) leads paddling expeditions, some of which depart from Big Talbot Island. Also, hikers will want to keep an eye out for trailheads along A1A as it crosses Big Talbot Island. Facilities at Big Talbot Island are minimal—a dirt parking lot with a shoreline-access trail—so if it's beach recreation you're seeking, head down to Little Talbot Island.

Long Island lies between Big and Little Talbot Islands. Only its northern tip is exposed to Nassau Sound, so there is no beach out here. Mostly covered with maritime forest, this narrow island has lately become part of the state's expanding inventory of parkland.

Little Talbot Island, whose entrance lies four mile south of Big Talbot's bluffs, is entirely preserved as a state park. Narrow and elongated, it is the southernmost barrier island in the extensive Golden Isles chain, which begins way up on North Carolina's Outer Banks. Boardwalks at both ends of Little Talbot Island lead to five miles of beaches backed by a well-developed dune system. And what a beach this is: wide and flat, usually uncrowded, and simply perfect. The only caveat is that swimming has been banned since 2003 at the south end of the island because of dangerous currents in and around Fort George Inlet.

Surfers swarm to Little Talbot. On a gorgeous weekday, board bums were coming and going along the boardwalk as if it were an assembly line, trading impromptu surf reports and accounts of rides. It was a great day for wave riders, with 3–4' barrels rolling ashore and little competition for the waves. It must be worth the trouble it takes to get here, because we saw several surfers who'd ridden their bikes, driving with one hand while holding a board under the other. This trying form of locomotion seemed to be a form of extreme sports in itself. If it's any help, it appeared to us as if surfers favored the north end while anglers flocked to the south.

Little Talbot's beaches, having never been developed, are broader and healthier than those of Amelia Island. The island's midsection is a great place to get away from the crowds, if you're up for a hike from either the north or south parking lot. The whole island is worth exploring and appreciating. Seaward dunes are covered with sea oats and beach morning glory. Older, inland dune ridges support slash pines, red cedars, and cabbage palms. Grasses and sedges thrive in the interdune swales. A coastal hammock thick with live oaks, Southern magnolia, and American holly occupies the northeast corner of the island. An unnamed nature trail, whose head is located just west of the ranger station, proceeds 2.4 miles through the hammock before ending on the beach. To complete a scenic loop, walk 1.7 miles south along the beach to the north boardwalk and then return via the boardwalk and park road.

The island's west side is a classic Southern sea island salt marsh of grass-covered flats interlaced with tidal creeks. The park's 40-site campground is located on the west side of the island, a short walk from the marsh's edge.

You might even stumble onto some interesting wildlife out here. A ranger told us that bobcat sightings have become more common; only days

THE HISTORIC FIRST COAST

before, he'd seen a mother leading four kittens across the road. Another happy piece of news has to do with sea turtles. There were only 15 turtle nests laid on Little Talbot Island in 2004, but that number jumped to 40 nests in 2005.

For more information, contact Talbot Islands State Park, 12157 Heckscher Drive, Jacksonville, FL 32226, 904/251-2320, www.floridastateparks.org.

BEACHES

12 BIG TALBOT ISLAND STATE PARK

Location: Big Talbot Island is between Amelia and Little Talbot Islands on A1A, just south of the bridge over Nassau Sound.
Parking/Fees: $1 entrance fee per vehicle (honor system); $2 to access bluff-top picnic area
Hours: 8 A.M. to one hour before sunset
Facilities: restrooms, boat launch ($3)
Contact: Talbot Islands State Park, 904/251-2320

13 LITTLE TALBOT ISLAND STATE PARK

 BEST (

Location: 13 miles north of Jacksonville and 7 miles south of Amelia Island, along A1A.
Parking/Fees: $4 entrance fee per vehicle. Camping fees are $19 per night.
Hours: 8 A.M.-sunset
Facilities: lifeguards (seasonal), restrooms, picnic tables, showers, and visitors center
Contact: Talbot Islands State Park, 904/251-2320

Fort George Island

When Jacksonville city dwellers want to spend a day on the beach in a more natural setting than Jacksonville Beach, they head up to Fort George Island. This triangular island lies over the St. Johns River from the naval town of Mayport. It is bounded on the east by the Fort George River, which separates it from Little Talbot Island, while the Intracoastal Waterway divides it from the swampy mainland. The drawing card is the city-owned **Huguenot Memorial Park,** named for French Protestants who sought refuge from persecution in the New World during the 16th and 17th centuries.

Fort George Island is far less urbanized than the Jax Beaches. You are likely to spy sand dollars and starfish on the beach at Huguenot Memorial Park, while it is unlikely you'd turn up either on Jacksonville Beach. By contrast to their dune-flattened city cousins, the dune fields at Huguenot are extensive, tall, and heavily vegetated. Huguenot's two miles of beach magically expand in length and width at low tide.

Not surprisingly, Huguenot is popular with families, who bring the kids to fish, camp, or swim. One cause for concern is the area where the Fort George River meets the ocean, creating turbulent currents that led to drownings in the past. Lifeguards were introduced to the park in 1999, and they've had their hands full, making more than 40 water rescues in each season since their arrival. Families with young children should head to the calmer inlet side of the island. In addition to swimmers and sunbathers, windsurfers carve their way around the inlet. Birdwatchers train field glasses on the abundant avian life, including painted bunting. An observation area has been set aside strictly for birders. Anglers toss lines from beach, jetty, and riverbank. Many come early in the morning, stake out a prime location, and fish all day—a pleasant way to while away the hours. Three camping areas—by the inlet, on the river, and in the woodsy "middle ground"—offer a total of 88 sites in the park, which are rented cheaply at $5 (tents) and $7 (RVs) per night.

Because Huguenot's beach frontage is abun-

THE HISTORIC FIRST COAST

dant and unspoiled, crowds of 5,000 or more show up on sunny weekends. The park is readily accessible from Jacksonville by taking the Mayport–Fort George Ferry ($2.50 per car, reachable via A1A north of Mayport) or the Heckscher Drive exit off I-95. Beach access near an urban area doesn't get much cheaper than Huguenot's admission fee of $0.50 per person.

For more information, contact Huguenot Park, 10980 Heckscher Drive, Jacksonville, FL 32226, 904/251-3335.

BEACHES

14 HUGUENOT MEMORIAL PARK

Location: On Fort George Island, northeast of Jacksonville. Take the Heckscher Drive (S.R. 105) exit off I-95 (Exit 358) and head east. Turn north on A1A and follow it to the park.
Parking/Fees: $0.50 per person entrance fee. Camping fees are $5 per night for tents and $7 for RVs; there are no hookups.
Hours: 8 A.M.–6 P.M. (till 8 P.M. April–October)
Facilities: concessions, lifeguards (seasonal), restrooms, picnic tables, and showers
Contact: Huguenot Memorial Park, 904/251-3335

Jacksonville

Every time we roll through this resurgent Southern city, we're bowled over by the changes. For starters, Jacksonville (pop. 780,000) has the largest incorporated land area of any city in the United States, a whopping 841 square miles (almost twice the size of Los Angeles). With its population having increased by 50 percent over the past decade, Jacksonville is worthy of a nickname like the Amazing Inflatable City. Currently it is the 13th largest and the 18th fastest-growing city in the U.S. It is a headquarters for Fortune 500 firms and

insurance companies. Here's another telling statistic: Jacksonville has the youngest average age of any large city in Florida. It also boasts the largest urban park system of any U.S. city, encompassing 80,000 acres.

The county of Duval and the city of Jacksonville are essentially one and the same, as the city expanded to the county borders in the late 1960s. Its vastness renders Jacksonville a kind of an endless blank slate that keeps filling with more people, businesses, bridges, developments, home teams, and, of course, traffic. As large towns go, it's vibrant and likeable, if beset with traffic and other assorted other urban ills that accompany rapid growth.

Jacksonville's boomtown ways are reflected in the city boosters' trumpeting of its many amenities. Among these are a wealth of museums, including the Museum of Science and History (MOSH) and the Cummer Museum of Art & Gardens; a striking Edward Rouse–designed waterfront on the St. Johns River, anchored by a linear park and festival marketplace known as Jacksonville Landing; and the Jacksonville Jaguars. This hugely successful NFL franchise has marshaled a rabid fan base that amounts to a citywide pep rally. They play at Alltel Stadium, near downtown Jacksonville, and tickets are nearly impossible to come by. The city further raised its football profile by hosting the 39th Super Bowl in 2005.

Jacksonville is, first and foremost, an aquatic city. The St. Johns River defines the city and its recreational prerogatives. If you live here, you almost have to have a boat. Enjoying a bottle of wine on the water at sunset, "tailboating" (the marine equivalent of a tailgate party) to a Jags game, trolling tidal creeks for redfish, kayaking around an estuary or out to an ocean sandbar—these are some of the recreational options that inspire Jacksonville natives to balance work with play in a way that's reminiscent of Southern California.

One other aspect of life in the Jacksonville area that residents justifiably boast about is their beaches. Located 15 miles east of downtown (via Atlantic, Beach, or Butler boulevards) is a trifecta of beach towns: Atlantic Beach, Neptune Beach, and Jacksonville Beach. They are collectively known as the "Jax Beaches." If downtown Jacksonville is all business, then the Jax Beaches are completely casual, as in flip-flops, cutoffs, jukeboxes, and cold beer. In a sense, they are two different worlds. Beach residents refer to Jacksonville as being "across the ditch" (the St. Johns River).

In contrast to much of Florida's overbuilt east coast, the Jax Beaches are in no hurry to have their neighborhoods razed and replaced with condos and luxury hotels. In recent years they have begun a gradual, and mostly positive, transformation into more of a vacation destination to the outside world. Unpretentious and affordable, they are much like the whole of Jacksonville: informal and neighborly, optimistic and engaging. As a result, increasing carloads of travelers are discovering that all they could ever want in a beach adventure is right here.

For more information, contact Jacksonville and the Beaches Convention and Visitors Bureau, 550 Water Street, Suite 1000, Jacksonville, FL 32202, 904/798-9111, www.jaxcvb.com.

Mayport

Mayport is no Mayberry. It's a Navy town, and Naval Station Mayport (commissioned in 1942) is the third-largest naval facility in the U.S., employing more than 14,000 active-duty personnel. Much to the relief of the broader community, it did not turn up on the list of recommended base closings by the Pentagon's Base Realignment and Closure (BRAC) commission. In fact, it will be absorbing another naval station (in Pascagoula, Mississippi) that is being shut down.

Really, the only reasons a visitor who doesn't have Navy kin would detour to Mayport are to board the Mayport-Fort George Ferry, which crosses the St. Johns River, or to go to Kathryn Abby Hanna Beach Park. The ferry makes the

half-mile passage across the St. Johns River in a matter of minutes, saving considerable miles and time for those headed from Jacksonville to the parks of northern Duval County and Amelia Island. It costs $2.50 per car; call 904/241-9969 for schedules and information. For a rundown on the unsurpassable Hanna Park, read on.

For more information, contact Kathryn Abby Hanna Beach Park, 500 Wonderwood Drive, Jacksonville, FL 32233, 904/249-4700.

BEACHES

The stellar 450-acre **Kathryn Abby Hanna Beach Park,** run by the city of Jacksonville, is located just south of the Mayport Naval Station. Hanna Park offers access to a gorgeous, lifeguarded 1.5-mile-long beach. The main draw, however, is the park's 20-mile network of hiking and biking trails.

The mountain-bike trails are maintained by local bike shops to be challenging, championship-level courses. The biking trails—about a half dozen of them, each two miles or so in length and bearing names like "Misery" and "Logjam"—ramble over the extensive park grounds, which include a 65-acre man-made lake and 293 campsites with full hookups. With an entrance fee of $2 a head, Hanna Park is one of the best recreational bargains on the First Coast. The beach is blessed by some of the tallest and most solidly vegetated dunes we've seen on the state's east coast. There are frontal, secondary, and tertiary dunes, a rare trifecta in the Sunshine State. It is a rejuvenating spritz of nature amid Jacksonville's urban sprawl.

15 KATHRYN ABBY HANNA BEACH PARK

Location: 3.5 miles north of Jacksonville Beach, off Mayport Road, in Mayport
Parking/Fees: $2 per person entrance fee and free for those under six. Camping fees are $13.50 per night for tents and $18 for RVs.

THE HISTORIC FIRST COAST

© PARKE PUTERBAUGH

Hanna Park in Mayport

Hours: 8 A.M.–6 P.M. (till 8 P.M. April–October)
Facilities: concessions, lifeguards (seasonal), restrooms, picnic tables, showers, and visitors center
Contact: Kathryn Abby Hanna Beach Park, 904/249-4700

COASTAL CUISINE

Worth a detour, or right on your way if you're crossing the St. Johns River via the Mayport Ferry, is the unpretentious but excellent **Singleton's Seafood Shack** (4728 Ocean Street, 904/246-4442, $$). Specialties of the shack are steamed shrimp and rock shrimp, but you'll also find grouper, dolphin, snapper, flounder, and other catches on the ample menu. We feasted on fish dip, steamed shrimp, and blackened grouper one balmy afternoon after working up an appetite kayaking around the Timucuan Preserve. We can scarcely imagine a better way to spend a weekend in the Jacksonville area than paddling the marsh and scarfing shrimp afterward. The floors at Singleton's are wooden, diners sit at unfancy picnic tables, the waitresses are busy but friendly, and the whole casual enterprise

is a modest monument to seafood that bustles at lunch and dinner seven days a week. It's on the south bank of the river, just a block from the Mayport Ferry.

Atlantic Beach

The most immediately appealing of the three separate but contiguous communities that run along Jacksonville's oceanfront, Atlantic Beach (pop. 13,400) tries hard to be all things to all beachgoers. Most importantly, it's a solid year-round community with a clearly delineated "Town Center" of shops, restaurants, and nicely landscaped sidewalks, which it shares with neighboring Neptune Beach. Atlantic Boulevard is the line of demarcation between the two communities (to confuse you, Ragtime Tavern in Atlantic Beach and Sun Dog Diner in Neptune Beach each claim 207 Atlantic Boulevard as their address, though they sit across the street from each other). They also welcome outside visitors while keeping the resultant commercial zone on Atlantic Boulevard free of low-end blight and upscale snobbery.

In short, little Atlantic Beach (three square miles) has the right mix for a beach town, in our estimation.

Perhaps this relaxed posture derives from the town's resort history. Atlantic Beach was created in 1900, growing up around a depot of Henry Flagler's East Coast Railway. In 1901, Flagler built the Continental Hotel here. It was so staggeringly huge that its three-block verandah could hold 3,000 rocking chairs! In 1910, Atlantic Boulevard was laid down to connect this saltwater playground with Jacksonville. Today, it's still the town's main east-west thoroughfare, as well as its southern boundary. Unlike standoffish Neptune, however, Atlantic has retained an open-arms policy to visitors.

For more information, contact Jacksonville and the Beaches Convention & Visitors Bureau, Beaches Visitor Center, 403 Beach Boulevard, Jacksonville Beach, FL 32250, 904/242-0024, www.jaxcvb.com.

BEACHES

The town's newsletter, compiled by a well-meaning local booster, claims two miles of beachfront for **Atlantic Beach,** but our rented car's odometer gauged it at no more than one mile, and that's being charitable. Running north from the main beach access at Atlantic Boulevard, there are additional public access points at each of the 15 street endings. As this is the most popular of the three "Jax Beaches," Atlantic Beach presents day-trippers with a major parking problem, as does neighboring Neptune Beach. Jacksonville Beach, with its considerably longer stretch of oceanfront, doesn't have that problem. Some parking spots near the beach can be found on the streets, but they are snapped up quickly and relinquished rarely. A large pay lot is located between 18th and 19th Streets.

Lifeguards are on duty at Atlantic Beach daily, 8 A.M.–6 P.M. The beach itself is as wide, flat, and healthy as we've seen it in the more than 20 years we've been visiting. For one thing, the Jacksonville area is rarely visited by hurricanes. Unlike the rest of hurricane-besieged Florida, Jacksonville is in a kind of hurricane shadow, protected by virtue of its location relative to the islands of the Carib-

Neptune Beach

© PARKE PUTERBAUGH

bean. Jacksonville has not received a direct hit from a hurricane since 1964, when Hurricane Dora tore up the North Florida coast.

16 ATLANTIC BEACH

Location: Beach access points are located at street ends north of Atlantic Boulevard.
Parking/Fees: free street parking
Hours: none posted
Facilities: lifeguards (seasonal)
Contact: Atlantic Beach Recreation Department, 904/247-9828

ACCOMMODATIONS

The **Sea Turtle Inn** (1 Ocean Boulevard, 904/249-7402, $$$) has the beach blanketed in Atlantic Beach, as it's the oldest oceanfront "inn" in town (actually, it's a high-rise hotel). The Sea Turtle is also the largest hotel on the Jax Beaches, taking up a full city block and boasting 194 rooms. Other amenities: a swimming pool, a lounge, and an oceanfront restaurant/lounge (Plantains). Last but not least, staying at the Sea Turtle means you've got a coveted parking space in Atlantic Beach. Since it's located within walking distance of the best bars and restaurants, you have no reason to move the car, either. We've heard that it's a favorite of writer John Grisham, if that counts as a recommendation.

COASTAL CUISINE

It's rare to find a hot nightspot that also serves fine food, but such is the case at **Ragtime Tavern** (207 Atlantic Boulevard, 904/241-7877, $$$). A hint of New Orleans infuses a menu that's gloriously top-heavy with fresh Florida seafood, such as charcoal-grilled grouper and seafood skewers. Ragtime is extremely popular, so be prepared to wait a while at one of its three bars. If the pangs get too loud, calm them with an order of Cajun-style popcorn shrimp.

NIGHTLIFE

Not only is Ragtime Tavern a top-notch restaurant, but once the plates are cleared this is a popular nightspot for yuppie party animals from the Jacksonville area. We've run its gauntlet of preppies in starched shirts, each with an imported beer in hand, fixed smile on face, perfect facial hair and tan, and a ready line of bar patter. Outside, lined up alongside a theater rope with an usher letting in the horde a few at a time, an army of gorgeous, jewelry-bedecked, and salon-coifed women wait their turn. Despite or maybe in addition to its meat-market rep, Ragtime does have an undeniable appeal. There are three full-service bars, each with its own seating and gathering area, plus decent live rock and roll on weekends. Ragtime has survived all the trendy comings and goings that have claimed lesser hotspots and seems like it's here to stay.

Neptune Beach

More residential than recreational, Neptune Beach (pop. 7,300) is caught between the rock of Atlantic Beach to the north and the hard place of Jacksonville Beach to the south. Clearly trying to hold both ends at bay, Neptune Beach has made obvious attempts to curb crowds, with speed bumps on side streets and virtually no public beach parking. The idea is to let the mostly year-round population enjoy its well-earned place in the sun. It seems to have worked. Established in 1931, originally as part of Jacksonville Beach, Neptune Beach is a nice enough small town that occupies only 2.5 square miles. You can move here, but don't plan a beach vacation around it.

For more information, contact Jacksonville and the Beaches Convention & Visitors Bureau, Beaches Visitor Center, 403 Beach Boulevard, Jacksonville Beach, FL 32250, 904/242-0024, www.jaxcvb.com.

BEACHES

In **Neptune Beach,** the town's half-mile beachfront runs along North 1st Street, two blocks east of 3rd Street (A1A), which is the main north-south artery through all three of the Jax Beaches. Each of Neptune Beach's 23 streets ends with a public beach access onto the sand. Only two of these access points (Lemon and Hopkins Streets) have parking spaces, and those are limited. A few other parking spots can be had along the sandy shoulder of Strand Street, a short one-way street along the ocean.

Lifeguards are on duty 9 A.M.–5 P.M. on weekdays, and 9 A.M.–7 P.M. on weekends in season.

17 NEPTUNE BEACH

Location: Beach access points are located at street ends from Atlantic Boulevard south to Seagate Avenue.
Parking/Fees: free limited street parking
Hours: none posted
Facilities: lifeguards (seasonal) and a shower
Contact: Neptune Beach Public Works Department, 904/270-2423

ACCOMMODATIONS

There's little in the way of accommodations in Neptune Beach, with the exception of the **Sea Horse Oceanfront Inn** (120 Atlantic Boulevard, 904/246-2175), which is technically on Neptune's border with Atlantic Beach. If the Sea Turtle's full up, as happens on busy weekends, try the Sea Horse, a more than adequate alternative two blocks down the beach. This appealing 37-unit motel has been given a facelift in recent years. You just roll out of bed, into your flip-flops and onto the amber sands.

COASTAL CUISINE

Art deco American diner is the visual motif at the chrome-shiny **Sun Dog Diner** (207 Atlantic Boulevard, 904/241-8221, $$), while the food takes its cues from the tropics. Don't miss the brick-oven pizza or Italian specialties at

Mezza Luna Vagabondo Ristorante (110 1st Street, 904/246-5100), either. And **Sliders** (218 1st Street, 904/246-0681) is the ultimate casual beach hangout in these parts. The food is affordable (a bulging seafood burrito goes for $7) and save room for the signature dessert: "Florida Snowballs," ice cream rolled in coconut and covered with raspberry sauce.

NIGHTLIFE

Despite Neptune's penchant for privacy, some of the best watering holes in the Jax Beaches area are located here. **Sun Dog Diner** (207 Atlantic Boulevard, 904/241-8221) is a long-time favorite of the locals, who often stick around after dinner for the nightly live music. **Papa Joe's** (100 1st Street, 904/246-6406) is a less preppy version of Ragtime Tavern in Atlantic Beach. Another beloved local hangout is **Pete's Bar** (117 1st Street, 904/249-9158), "where the crowd is the entertainment" and cheap beer and pool tables run a close second. This venerable institution was the inspiration for the bar scenes in *The Brethren* by John Grisham, purportedly a regular at Pete's when he's in town. This is an unselfconscious den of imbibers. We saw a woman who was 60 if she was a day hoisting a bottle of Bud as she danced around the room like an MTV coquette.

Jacksonville Beach

By far the largest of the "Jax Beaches," Jacksonville Beach (pop. 21,000) has a lot going for it in terms of its sandy endowment. While the town had been stumbling along like a dragster stuck in beach sand for the past quarter century, it has lately been putting the pedal to the metal. The urban decay and boarded-up storefronts that once lined 1st Street have been filled by new businesses and destination clubs and restaurants, as well as a middling number of high-rise condominiums. Fortunately, the town mandated that public beach access could not be restricted by new development, and renovation of existing older properties

© PARKE PUTERBAUGH

Jacksonville Beach

has been encouraged. Lots of neat little shops line 3rd Street.

The changes have been for the better, giving Jacksonville Beach a thriving quality without destroying its age-old appeal as a relaxed and unpretentious beach town. This isn't to suggest that Jax Beach—as it's known to everyone but cartographers—was exactly dangerous (although even the local newspaper often referred to its "rowdy and lawless" reputation in the past). Let's just say it always seemed ripe for the renaissance it is currently undergoing. We only hope it doesn't go too far in the other direction. At least the local population is trying to see to it that it doesn't.

"We are very proud of being Jax Beach locals," one booster told us over breakfast platters at the Beach Hut Cafe. "We don't want to become another Miami. We don't want to have the traffic issues of Fort Lauderdale. We want to manage growth."

The first boom heard down this way was provided by Henry Flagler's East Coast Railway. The next stop down the line from Atlantic Beach was Pablo Beach (named for the San Pablo River, to the west), which was renamed

Jacksonville Beach in 1925. **Pablo Historical Park** (425 Beach Boulevard, 904/246-0093) goes into great detail about the area's past, and members of the Beaches Historical Society offer guided tours of the remnants of the town's railroad origins. A thriving boardwalk developed in 1916, with dance halls, shooting galleries, boxing and wrestling matches, auto racing on the sand, and "other forms of entertainment" (use your imagination). This scene flourished until the late 1950s, when gambling and other forms of vice were chased out of town. Driving was allowed on the beach until the late 1970s, when it was sensibly banned within city limits.

Trust us when we say that Jacksonville Beach will grow on you, as it has steadily grown on us over the years. Certainly, it's an alternative to the severely upscale affectations of Ponte Vedra Beach to the south and the parking headaches of Atlantic and Neptune Beaches. On a late Saturday afternoon when a rock band is playing on the deck at a beach bar or on a Sunday morning over a plate of grits and eggs at Jacksonville Beach Fishing Pier, the place seems like paradise to us. There's a real warts-and-all beach-life feel about Jacksonville Beach that we find preferable to the soulless upscaling that has claimed so may other beach communities. This is, after all, Lynyrd Skynyrd country. The Southern-rock legends came together in these parts, and their career is celebrated at the hard-rocking Freebird Cafe, which is emblematic of the let-it-all-hang-out aesthetic that rules here.

For more information, contact Jacksonville and the Beaches Convention & Visitors Bureau, Beaches Visitor Center, 403 Beach Boulevard, Jacksonville Beach, FL 32250, 904/242-0024, www.jaxcvb.com.

BEACHES

"We try to keep the beach as open and accessible as possible," we were told by a beach booster. Indeed, the beachfront along the trio of "Jax Beaches" extends for more than 100 blocks along 1st Street. It would be the envy of any in America, were it not for the area's longtime economic problems. Because roughly 60 of those city blocks belong to **Jacksonville Beach,** the southernmost and most welcoming of the bunch, it has traditionally been the destination of choice. Though Atlantic and Neptune Beaches are part of the same lengthy strand, Jacksonville Beach boasts the widest beach of all. The hard-packed, blindingly white sand is backed by the remnants of sugary soft dunes. The most popular stretch of beach runs from around 4th Avenue North down to 6th Avenue South, with Beach Boulevard the approximate midpoint. Twenty-five lifeguards are on duty from 10 A.M.–5 P.M. in summer. In 2001, a half million cubic yards of sand were spread along 7.5 miles of thinning beach from Mayport down to Jacksonville Beach ("a minor tune-up" is how it was described to us). The sand looks to have stayed in place, making this one of the more cost-effective beach renourishment projects we've seen.

The town has provided beach-access points at the end of 64 avenues. Many of these accesses have a few free parking spaces, and if you don't luck into one of those, plenty of parking can be found a block or so west. The 983-foot Jacksonville Beach Fishing Pier, at the end of 6th Avenue South, charges $3.50 per adult to fish ($5 more to rent a pole) and $0.75 to stroll. The rickety restaurant on the pier is a favorite breakfast spot. The damage the pier sustained in 1999 from Hurricane Floyd has been fully repaired, and it miraculously escaped harm during the 2004 hurricane season. Both sides of the pier are popular with surfers.

18 JACKSONVILLE BEACH

 BEST (

Location: Jax Beach's half-mile shorefront is accessible from the ends of 64 east-west avenues. The heart of the beach area is at Beach Boulevard (U.S. 90/S.R. 212) and 1st Street.
Parking/Fees: free street parking
Hours: sunrise–sunset
Facilities: lifeguards (seasonal), restrooms, and showers
Contact: Jacksonville Beach Recreation Department, 904/247-6236

RECREATION AND ATTRACTIONS

- **Dive Shop:** Divers Supply, 9701 Beach Boulevard, 904/646-3828
- **Ecotourism:** Outdoor Adventures, 1625 Emerson Street, Jacksonville, 904/393-9030
- **Fishing Charters:** Salty Feather Guide Service, 2683 St. Johns Bluff Road, Jacksonville, 904/645-8998
- **Lighthouse:** American Lighthouse and Maritime Museum, 1011 North 3rd Street, 904/241-8845
- **Marina:** Beach Marina, 2315 Beach Boulevard, Intracoastal Waterway Marker 34, 904/249-8200
- **Pier:** Jacksonville Beach Fishing Pier, 3 6th Avenue South, 904/246-6001

- **Rainy-Day Attraction:** Museum of Science and History, 1025 Museum Circle, 904/396-7062
- **Shopping/Browsing:** Jacksonville Landing, 2 Independent Drive, Jacksonville, 904/353-1188
- **Surf Report:** 904/249-4452, 904/828-4848, or 904/241-0933
- **Surf Shops:** Aqua East Surf Shop, 696 Atlantic Boulevard, Neptune Beach, 904/246-2550; Austin's, 615 South 3rd Street, 904/249-9848, Jacksonville Beach; and Sunrise Surf Shop, 834 Beach Boulevard, Jacksonville Beach, 904/241-0822
- **Vacation Rentals:** Seaside Realty, 1639 Beach Boulevard, 904/247-7000

ACCOMMODATIONS

Jax Beach tries hard to be accommodating. At least, it offers a lot of accommodations. The **Ramada Resort** (1201 North 1st Street, 904/241-5333, $$) used to be the oceanfront venue of choice. Though you can't argue with its location, the Ramada is beginning to show its age. **Days Inn Oceanfront** (1031 South 1st Street, 904/249-7231, $) and **Comfort Inn Oceanfront** (1515 North 1st Street, 904/241-2311, $$) have stolen some of Ramada's thunder. They are nicer, newer, cheaper, and have beach access and pools. Both places offer just enough in the way of cleanliness and comfort so that you'll sleep well, but not so much that you'll be tempted to waste your day hanging around the room. And that is exactly how it should be at the beach.

Are you getting the idea that Jacksonville Beach is a Days Inn/Comfort Inn kind of beach town? Well, that's because it is. Jacksonville Beach's top-of-the-line is the **Holiday Inn Sunspree Resort** (1617 North 1st Street, 904/249-9071, $$$). In addition to brand-name quality, the Sunspree designation means modernized facilities and activity programs for kids. The key word here is "family"; they're pushing it all over Jacksonville Beach these days.

Nearly touching Ponte Vedra Beach from the south end of Jacksonville Beach, the **Hampton Inn** (1220 Marsh Landing Parkway, 904/280-9101, $$) combines Ponte Vedra comfort with Jax Beach address and price. It's off the beach by half a mile, next door to a high-end shopping mall, and has the leafy views and peace and quiet of the surrounding neighborhood going for it.

COASTAL CUISINE

For breakfast or lunch, hit the **Beach Hut Cafe** (1281 South 3rd Street, 904/249-3516, $), which is good 'n' cheap and perennially line-out-the-door popular. You'll catch a lot of local wisdom and interesting conversations from the wait staff and nearby patrons. For dinner, a longtime favorite is **First Street Grille** (807 North 1st Street, 904/246-6555, $$$), which serves grilled steaks and seafood with fresh seasonings and an ocean view. Specialties of the eclectic menu include Cajun-spiced sauteed red snapper and Pablo Beach shrimp. (Jacksonville Beach used to be known as Pablo Beach, and some old-timers still call it that.)

Another reliable venue is **Island Grille** (981 North 1st Street, 904/241-1881, $$$), which features tropical seafood, fruits, and vegetables of Florida and the West Indies, as well as an ocean-facing deck. A pair of more upscale restaurants have become favorites of ours on recent visits: **Dolphin Depot** (704 North 1st Street, 904/270-1424, $$$) and **Magellan's** (333 North 1st Street, 904/247-2644, $$$). The latter features seared sea scallops and Florida lobster tail.

Back toward town, on the west bank of the Intracoastal Waterway, **Marker 32** (14549 Beach Boulevard, 904/223-1534, $$$) offers casual ambience, sumptuous food, and a splendid setting. Fresh-fish specials might include cilantro-grilled tuna and pan-fried red snapper atop okra and tomatoes. Another temptation is smoked salmon carpaccio with potato pancakes. Great service and a good wine list round out an exemplary dining experience.

NIGHTLIFE

The beach has become a hub of nightlife for the entire Jacksonville area. Red-faced locals, who have been shaken and baked all day on the beach, are likely to hang out afterward at unpretentious bar/restaurants like **Bukkets Baha Beach Club** (222 North Ocean Street, 904/246-7701). A good time is had by all, especially when local rock bands provide a soundtrack for the revelry in the upstairs nightclub. Another beachside bar-restaurant combo that packs 'em in is **Manatee Ray's** (314 1st Avenue North, 904/241-3138), which serves food and drink with a Caribbean flair.

Nearby, a pair of friendly bars serve as the epicenter for late-night frivolity: the **Atlantic** (333 North 1st Street, 904/249-3338) and **Lynch's Irish Pub** (514 North 1st Street, 904/249-5181). The beach's best sports bar is **R.P. McMurphy's Sports Bar & Grill** (798 South 3rd Street, 904/247-0196), named after the protagonist in Ken Kesey's *One Flew Over the Cuckoo's Nest*. A willing staff of Nurse Ratcheds dispense liquid medication from behind the bar. A close second is **Moon Grille & Oyster Bar** (1396 Beach Boulevard, 904/241-1894), where you can shuck your own bivalves and play pool.

Every time we come to Jacksonville Beach, we make a pilgrimage to the **Freebird Cafe**

NUTS FOR GOLF

People have gone nuts over golf on the First Coast. Literally. As a result, what was once a wondrously intriguing piece of Old Florida – an enchanting mix of primordial swampland, palmetto-laden coastal habitat, and Floridian culture – has become a place of second homes to rich snowbirds in loudly colored slacks scooting about carpets of manicured grass in motorized carts while waving obscenely expensive implements to swat around golf balls. Knocking a ball around a public golf course is one thing, but turning an entire stretch of coast into a private country club is quite another.

Do you think we exaggerate? Ponder this statistic: There are 64 private, public, and resort golf courses along the First Coast. The local press – whose responsibility it is to question dramatic transformations to the landscape – has been one of the leading cheerleaders for this prodigious conversion. Here are some quotes taken from a puff piece found in the business section of the *Florida Times-Union*, Jacksonville's daily newspaper:

- A local golf-club maker: "We have the perfect climate, great courses, the PGA Tour and now the World Golf Village. ... It's a hotbed."

- A golf pro, with absolutely no irony: "It's like traffic on Butler Boulevard – the golf industry just keeps coming and coming."

- A real-estate developer: "The economic impact will be incredibly significant. Already it's enhancing the value of real estate along the I-95 corridor. Now we have to figure out how we're going to tie that into our marketing and piggyback off what they're doing. There's a lot of potential there."

- A local politico: "I think we're very lucky. We're in the middle of an industry that's going nuts. ... We're sitting on a rocket that's slowly exploding, and it will only get better."

Well maybe not. Golf-mania in northeast Florida culminated and arguably peaked with a boondoggle called World Golf Village, which opened in 1998 near St. Augustine. This 6,300-acre "village" has a hall of fame, two golf courses (King & Bear, Slammer & Squire), four lodging options (from Comfort Suites to "The Residences"), convention center, homesites, retail shopping, golf academy, and the World Golf Hall of Fame.

(200 North 1st Street, 904/246-BIRD), which is to devotees of Southern rock the equivalent of The Vatican. It's owned by the widow of Ronnie Van Zant, the Lynyrd Skynyrd vocalist who died in the 1978 plane crash that also killed two other band members and injured all of them. Hoping to have lunch at the Freebird on a 2005 visit, we pulled up to the curb with the latest album by the surviving Van Zant brothers, Johnny and Donnie (of 38 Special fame), blaring loudly from our car. We were being both ironic and tributary, but our gesture was wasted, as the Freebird was closed. Turns out that this one-time restaurant is now operating solely as a nighttime music venue—one of

the finest in north Florida, without question. Little Feat was playing at the Freebird that very night. Feats don't fail us now!

Back in Jacksonville proper, **River City Brewing Company** (835 Museum Circle, 904/398-2299) produces a smashing lineup of home brews (try the Pale Ale or English Porter) to go with its menu of seafood and bar food. The stunning view of downtown Jacksonville's skyline is all the more reason to "cross the ditch" for lunch or to watch a sunset.

A musical aside: the group Yellowcard, one of the most popular of the youthful "emo" bands, hails from Jacksonville. Locals used to refer to them as the "baby band," because they

---

Yet the public response has been underwhelming. Several years after it opened, a *Florida Times-Union* columnist wrote that the attraction was "awesome but often idle." He went on to note:

"When it opened, there were expectations that visitors would flock to the place. One St. Johns County official told the *Times-Union* that when she looked at the World Golf Village, what she saw was Epcot. [Talk about blind optimism!]

"That hasn't. While the complex keeps adding new features, most recently a golf academy, many of the shops in the complex have closed due to lack of foot traffic and, in August, the staff selling time shares for the 102-unit Sheraton Vistana Resort was laid off."

Developers got cold feet and canceled plans for a spa and industrial park in 1999. That same year, the resort fell behind in payments to St. Johns County for a loan to build its convention center, and the county has had to pick up shortfalls in the years since. The unkindest cut came when Liberty Mutual Legends of Golf tournament – which had moved to the World Golf Village's" Slammer & Squire" course in 1999 – pulled out in 2002 due to poor attendance.

You know that something's not working when a flak for the World Golf Hall of Fame admits in euphemistic P.R.-speak that it's "reorganizing some existing exhibit content to provide a more compelling and emotional guest experience." In other words, they're desperately trying to make a yawn-inducing assortment of putters, trophies, scorecards, and knickknacks suck less badly. Attendance rose to 210,000 in 2004 – their best year yet, but far less than the 500,000 annual visitors predicted by project boosters. "The direct impact has been slower than what we were looking for," admitted the executive director of the St. Johns County Tourism Development Council.

How did this private enterprise get funded? With loans of public money! The state of Florida issued $40 million in bonds, which covered 80 percent of the construction and exhibit costs for the World Golf Hall of Fame. St. Johns County anted up $16 million in bond money to build the convention center.

If you wish to point your golf cart in the direction of the World Golf Hall of Fame (1 World Golf Place, St. Augustine, 904/940-4000, www.wgv.com), be advised that the entrance fee is steep: $15 for adults and $10 for kids 12 and under. IMAX films cost additional.

were barely high-school age when they began working the local club scene. Now they're big stars, and many around here brag that they knew them when.

Ponte Vedra Beach

Ponte Vedra Beach (pop. 23,000) is a world-class golf and tennis resort destination and an exclusive bedroom community for the executive class of Jacksonville, which lies 20 miles northwest. Ponte Vedra often gets lumped in with the "Jax Beaches," but it's a decidedly different creature. Located in a separate county (St. Johns) from Jacksonville (which is in Duval County), Ponte Vedra is a world apart. Here, you will find the same emphasis on "golf course living" that's made Orange County, CA, such a bastion of rock-ribbed Republicanism, although in this neck of what used to be woods they call it "country club values." Either way, it translates into an aggressive attempt to keep at arm's length anyone without a briefcase or golf club in his hand. As if to emphasize this point, Ponte Vedrans equip their beachfront mansions with security fences and serpentine shrubbery.

While the name "Ponte Vedra Beach" may suggest ocean breezes and verdant stands of sea oats swaying atop sand dunes, most of the community lies west of A1A and a few miles from the beach. Every available piece of real estate out that way is unnaturally and obsessively landscaped and contoured. Many of the beautiful residential neighborhoods were constructed on filled-in wetlands, and they derive their names from the very natural features they've replaced (Marsh Landing, Old Palm Valley, etc.).

The biggest controversy in town during one of our visits was over the size of some beachfront houses that were awaiting permit approval. This proposed development—with the ridiculously self-inflated name "The Enclave"—had some of the old-timer beachfront homeowners steamed. Their beef? These new homes wouldn't be big enough! There goes the neighborhood.

"This isn't like Daytona Beach," one owner huffed from behind his security fence. "There is a real residential feel here."

"This can't be permitted," they all vowed. Hear, hear!

Part of the community does run beside the beach, and it includes both private homes and country-club villas. An inspection of the beachfront after a wicked nor'easter revealed waves lapping at the base of seawalls and splashing up on lawns, making homesteads at Ponte Vedra Beach seem not so terribly secure after all, guard gates or not.

For more information, contact the Ponte Vedra Chamber of Commerce, Four Sawgrass Village, Suite 104F, Ponte Vedra Beach, FL 32082, 904/285-2004, www.pontevedrachamber.org; or the St. Augustine, Ponte Vedra & The Beaches Visitors & Convention Bureau, 88 Riberia Street, Suite 400, St. Augustine, FL 32084, 800/653-2489, www.visitoldcity.com.

BEACHES

From the Duval County line to the south end of Ponte Vedra Beach is a distance of 6.5 miles, all of it fronted by an inviting beach. However, as if sensing that it's not welcome by the uptight bluebloods, A1A swerves inland. The oceanfront is instead approached via a loop road, Ponte Vedra Boulevard (S.R. 203). The rabble are discouraged from entering, as there are no public places to park to gain access to the beach. The exceptions are a trio of exclusive resorts (see *Accommodations,* below) and a single public access (Mickler's Landing) at the south end of S.R. 203, just before it reconnects with A1A.

Mickler's Landing is the accommodating exception to Ponte Vedra's leave-us-alone attitude. You'll find a paved 300-space lot along with modern showers and restrooms. A narrow beach crossover has been pinned between ostentatious private homes. On one of our visits, the automatic sprinkler system for a mansion abutting the Mickler's Landing access was

THE COMIC RITUALS OF THE GUARD GATE

In places like Ponte Vedra Beach, residential subdevelopments are guarded via gated checkpoints. While this song and dance no doubt affords a measure of comfort and security to those who live here, it can be off-putting to those who come calling – even for a couple of veteran beach bums dropping in on an old friend who's sunk roots into these waterlogged soils. Dealing with these "security" minders and their flimsy, flapping gate can also seem as pointless as removing one's shoes for an airport screener. If nothing else, the paranoid rituals of the gated community limit one's options for being sociable and all but prohibit a drive-through out of curiosity.

While trying to locate the home of our friend several years back, we became unwilling participants in a slapstick routine at a development called Marsh Landing, in Ponte Vedra Beach. The boob in charge – a dead ringer for Floyd the barber from *The Andy Griffith Show* – opened the gate for us, but when we made to drive through, he quickly lowered it, nearly karate-chopping the hood of our rented car. Then he shouted at us, as though we were looters who'd come up from New Orleans: "Come back here!"

We dutifully backed up and said, "But you opened the gate. ... "

"I hit the wrong button!" he angrily retorted, as if this were somehow our fault.

He insisted on calling to obtain authorization for us, two obviously dangerous criminals, to enter the neighborhood. We gave him our friend's name, and he promptly dialed two wrong numbers, holding us up for five minutes as he went through the painfully protracted process of explaining himself and then apologizing to each recipient of his wayward calls. Even after we wrote out the correct phone number for him, he misdialed it, necessitating another lengthy apology. On his fourth attempt, he managed to connect with our friend. Not just content to be incompetent, he had to prove he was unobservant, too, as he announced us as "Mr. and Mrs. Parke, here to see you." Though confused, our friend okayed our passage, and we were on our way.

Whoops, not so fast! Our man still had to fill out a guest pass, a Magna Carta-sized document that had to be "displayed on the dashboard at all times." When the gate was finally raised, we burned rubber lest he shatter the windshield by lowering it again for no apparent reason.

---

flicking its spray into the wind, dousing beachgoers. The wooden walkway crosses thickly vegetated dunes to a sloping beach with shelly, coarse brown sand. The park is popular with families and surfers who are otherwise denied Ponte Vedra's beach bounty.

MICKLER'S LANDING

Location: Ponte Vedra Beach Boulevard (S.R. 203) at A1A

Parking/Fees: free parking lot

Hours: October 1-April 30, 24 hours; May 1-September 30, 5 A.M.-10 P.M.

Facilities: lifeguards (seasonal), showers, and restrooms

Contact: St. Johns County Recreation Department, 904/471-6616

ACCOMMODATIONS

The centerpiece of Ponte Vedra Beach is Sawgrass, "an uncrowded resort community with a commitment to excellence." Its 4,800 acres offer three golf courses—including Pete Dye's "masterpiece," the Tournament Players Club—13 tennis courts, a wilderness preserve, the **Sawgrass Marriott Resort Inn** (1000 TPC Boulevard, 904/285-7777, $$$$), and the luxury Beach Club (which boasts of having three pools). Oddly, the beach itself is downplayed.

In other words, Sawgrass has roped off one of the nicest beaches in northern Florida while its guests are encouraged to sit around swimming pools, nursing drinks and jawing about the good life. This all goes to prove an adage of ours: Much as youth can be said to be wasted on the young, some of the best beaches in America are wasted on the rich.

The **Lodge and Beach Club at Ponte Vedra Beach** (607 Ponte Vedra Boulevard, 904/273-9500, $$$$) is similar in amenities to Sawgrass but not so intimidating. Its 66 rooms and villas overlook the beach from gracefully behind the dunes. The Mediterranean architecture and tasteful furnishings give it an air of relaxed elegance.

More venerable elegance is available at the **Ponte Vedra Inn and Club** (200 Ponte Vedra Boulevard, 904/285-1111, $$$$), the first beach resort built here (in 1927). Again, golf, tennis, and swimming pools are touted at both resorts, but the beach is right out back. The bounty of beach rentals (chairs, umbrellas, cabanas, boogie boards, and kayaks) encourages visitors to immerse themselves in the ocean rather than ignore it.

COASTAL CUISINE

For all its world-class affectations, Ponte Vedra Beach is oddly devoid of interesting or unique dining spots. The places touted by locals are dining areas found inside the **Marriott at Sawgrass Resort** (1000 TPC Boulevard, 904/285-7777): **Cafe on the Green** ($$) and the **Augustine Room** ($$$). The latter requires semiformal attire, which seems a little over the top at the beach. More interesting meals and settings can be had seven miles north at the Jax Beaches or 20 miles south in St. Augustine.

Guana River

One of Florida's most farsighted acquisitions, Guana River is a coastal reserve that covers 2,600 acres of barrier island between Ponte

Vedra Beach and Vilano. It offers public access to five miles of the finest barrier-island beach in northern Florida. Formerly a state park, Guana River has been absorbed into the larger Guana Tolomato Matanzas National Estuarine Research Reserve (GTMNERR, for short).

In addition to towering, thickly vegetated dunes and a long, primeval beach, the park's varied habitat attracts a diversity of wildlife, including more than 240 species of birds. Where there are birds, there must also be fish, and the Guana and Tolomato Rivers' tidal waters are teeming with them: redfish, bluefish, black drum, and flounder, as well as shrimp and blue crab. Judging from the number of lines we've seen in the water, fishing is excellent at Guana Dam, too. In addition, anglers can fish freshwater Guana Lake for trout and striped bass. (Note that boats are restricted to 10 horsepower.)

Nine miles of trails and old service roads allow bikers and hikers to see the various plant communities: hardwood hammock, salt marsh, inland marsh, pine flatwoods, and scrub coastal strand. The GTMNERR–Guana River Environmental Educational Center will help visitors interpret it all.

For more information, contact GTM-NERR–Guana River, 505 Guana River Road, Ponte Vedra Beach, FL 32082, 904/823-4500, www.dep.state.fl.us/coastal/sites/gtm/guana_river.htm.

BEACHES

Guana River has three beach-use areas, known as North, Middle, and South Beach. Entrances and parking lots for all three areas are on the inlet (west) side of A1A. The fee at the beach parking lots is a modest $3 per car, self-paid on the honor system. All beach-access areas have paved lots with a few portable toilets and not much else.

We offer one word of warning: Be careful crossing A1A, lest you become road kill. To reach the beach, you must dash across the highway, at which point you'll take a wooden dune crossover the rest of the way. It's worth the sprint, though you should be mindful of traffic, especially if dragging kiddies. We know that elevated highway crossovers are probably outside of the reserve's budget, but they wouldn't be a bad investment.

Guana River is a case study of a healthy beach, a veritable mountain range of dunes held in place by glistening sea oats, sea grapes, a jumble of vines and grasses, and a few squat palm trees. The beach itself is composed of coarse, brownish sand with shell fragments. There are no lifeguards at Guana River, yet plenty of swimmers on warm, sunny days. You can always hike your way to isolation by heading in either direction. An observation tower beside the boardwalk at the South Beach area affords stunning views of the wetlands to the west and miles of unbroken, undeveloped beach to the north and south.

If all that isn't enough for you, Guana River marks the approximate location of Ponce de Leon's first landing and explorations in the area he proclaimed "La Florida." The name came from the Spanish *Pascua florida* ("flowery Passover"), as his arrival came near Easter.

20 GUANA RIVER

Location: three marked lots and walkovers along A1A between Ponte Vedra Beach and St. Augustine
Parking/Fees: $3 per vehicle entrance fee
Hours: 8 A.M.-sundown
Facilities: restrooms
Contact: Guana River, 904/825-5071

South Ponte Vedra Beach

The 10-mile drive on A1A from Ponte Vedra Beach through the Guana River reserve on down to Vilano Beach rates among the nicer automotive excursions in northeast Florida. It is a veritable tunnel of green created by grass- and scrub-covered dunes the size of small mountains (on the ocean side) and by mangrove- and tree-filled wetlands (on the inland side). About five miles of this stretch passes through the unincorporated community of South Ponte Vedra Beach. What development there is out here is more scaled-down than Ponte Vedra Beach, but filled with similarly exclusive private residences.

For more information, contact St. Augustine, Ponte Vedra & The Beaches Visitors & Convention Bureau, 88 Riberia Street, Suite 400, St. Augustine, FL 32084, 800/653-2489, www.visitoldcity.com.

BEACHES

A few county-maintained beach accesses exist along this stretch, including a small lot and dune crossover at a Gate service station just past the southern boundary of Guana River (which is why it is known as **Gate Station Beach**). **South Ponte Vedra Beach Recreation Area** is another access point (with a dirt lot and minimal facilities) to the same unspoiled stretch of orange coquina sand beach.

Usina Beach is accessed in two places: at a ramp across from a private campground (North Beach Campground, popular with RVs) about three miles south of the state park and at a parking lot about a quarter mile south of the ramp in the 2900 block of A1A. At the former, the ramp is open 5 A.M.–10 P.M., but driving is impossible at high tide and unreasonable any other time. McMulvie's Reef Restaurant (4100 Coastal Highway, 904/824-8008, $$) sits next door, for those who'd rather sit it out altogether. At the latter, you'll find shaded picnic areas, fire rings, wooden stairwell accesses, and portable restrooms. Signs read "No Loud Music Over 55 dB" and "Caution: Soft Sand and Strong Currents." The surf did look a little choppy, but the sand was wide and hard-packed and the water filled with swimmers.

21 GATE STATION BEACH

Location: below the southern boundary of Guana River at Gate Trading Post (2700 South A1A)
Parking/Fees: free parking lot
Hours: October 1-April 30, 24 hours; May 1-September 30, 5 A.M.-10 P.M.
Facilities: none
Contact: St. Johns County Recreation Department, 904/471-6616

22 SOUTH PONTE VEDRA BEACH RECREATION AREA

Location: 2.25 miles south of Guana River beaches on A1A
Parking/Fees: free parking lot
Hours: October 1-April 30, 24 hours; May 1-September 30, 5 A.M.-10 P.M.
Facilities: restrooms and picnic tables
Contact: St. Johns County Recreation Department, 904/471-6616

23 USINA BEACH

Location: four miles north of Vilano Beach, at North Beach Avenue and A1A
Parking/Fees: free parking lot or on-beach parking and driving ($5 per day or $20-35 annually)
Hours: October 1-April 30, 24 hours; May 1-September 30, 5 A.M.-10 P.M.
Facilities: restrooms
Contact: St. Johns County Recreation Department, 904/471-6616

Vilano Beach

Vilano Beach is a small beach community just north of St. Augustine. Over the years, that small city has been converted to a giant historical theme park, and some long-time residents have escaped the tourist mayhem to Vilano Beach. Unfortunately, gentrification has also begun creeping in this direction, judging from a massive new development called Ocean Grande, which occupies both sides of A1A in Vilano. Yet Vilano Beach still retains a bit of its "old Florida" ambience. You'll find a smattering of motels and RV parks, unpretentious restaurants along the ocean and marshes, and a modest surfing and fishing scene at the south end of Vilano Beach, by St. Augustine Inlet.

For more information, contact St. Johns County Visitors and Convention Bureau, 88 Riberia Street, Suite 400, St. Augustine, FL 32084, 800/653-2489, www.visitoldcity.com.

BEACHES

The first thing we saw in **Vilano Beach** was a pickup truck stuck in the sand, wheels furiously pumping their stiff green gallop in mute nostril agony (to borrow from the Doors' "Horse Latitudes"). The ancient vehicle was occupied by a family who had burned out their transmission trying to get unstuck—but only dug themselves deeper. A good Samaritan in a Ford Bronco tried towing them out to no avail. The occupants looked about helplessly, their fishing expedition having suddenly turned into an AAA emergency.

We tell this story only to discourage driving along the beach in Vilano Beach. It is allowed, for reasons that are unfathomable to us. The sand is coarser and softer than that found on other places where beach driving is permitted, like Anastasia State Park (in St. Augustine Beach) and Daytona Beach. Besides, this is a turtle-nesting beach, and the notion of jeeps digging ruts around turtle nests is unconscionable—as if the hazards of getting stuck weren't reason enough to forbid the practice.

Vilano Beach, located at St. Augustine Inlet, is a high-energy beach with a sloping face and big waves crashing and churning the shelly sand. A1A hugs the very lip of the beach, and

© PARKE PUTERBAUGH

North Beach Park in Vilano Beach

(on the inland side of A1A), plus a walkway to the beach that crosses above A1A. Another access point is **Surfside,** a half-mile north of St. Augustine Inlet. Otherwise, all the dune crossovers you'll see leading onto the beach are on private property, and signs attest to that fact in no uncertain terms.

24 NORTH BEACH PARK

Location: off A1A between Gardner and Meadow Avenues in Vilano Beach
Parking/Fees: free parking lot or on-beach parking and driving ($5 per day or $20-35 annually)
Hours: October 1-April 30, 24 hours; May 1-September 30, 5 A.M.-10 P.M.
Facilities: lifeguards (seasonal), restrooms, and showers
Contact: St. Johns County Recreation Department, 904/471-6616

erosion would seem to be a constant worry. Most of the action is down at the inlet, where public parking and access are provided. It's a colorful scene down here. The waves are particularly good for skimboarding—kind of like surfing in reverse. A small board is tossed onto the wet sand of a receding wave, and the skimboarder hops on for a ride down the beach and up a wave face, where it briefly looks like he or she's surfing.

If you like fishing, Vilano Beach affords a gold mine of opportunity on both sides of the highway. Anglers pilot their four-wheel drives out on the beach, where they then drive out to Porpoise Point (under the bridge and up along the inlet) or head north on the beach. The beach sand is too soft for driving by anything other than 4WD's, so don't get any fancy ideas with that rented Hyundai.

A recent arrival, up where South Ponte Vedra Beach meets Vilano Beach, is **North Beach Park.** This county facility offers a playground and restrooms by its parking lot

25 SURFSIDE

Location: 0.5 mile north of the Vilano Beach entrance ramp on A1A
Parking/Fees: free parking lot or on-beach parking and driving ($5 per day or $20-35 annually)
Hours: October 1-April 30, 24 hours; May 1-September 30, 5 A.M.-10 P.M.
Facilities: lifeguards (seasonal), restrooms, and showers
Contact: St. Johns County Recreation Department, 904/471-6616

26 VILANO BEACH

Location: two miles north of downtown St. Augustine, on A1A just over the New Vilano Bridge at the end of Vilano Road

Parking/Fees: off-beach parking lot (free) or on-beach parking and driving ($5 per day or $20-35 annually)

Hours: October 1-April 30, 24 hours; May 1-September 30, 5 A.M.-10 P.M.

Facilities: lifeguards (seasonal) and restrooms

Contact: St. Johns County Recreation Department, 904/471-6616

ACCOMMODATIONS

If nothing else, you have to see the **Magic Beach Motel** (50 Vilano Road, 904/829-2651, $). Formerly known as the Vilano Beach Motel, it's done up in 1950s art-deco style with a rooftop flamingo; not bad for this far north of Miami Beach. It has a pool and easy beach access, and is friendly to surfers and families. Just don't come expecting a concierge and turndown service, and you'll be fine.

Up the road a mile or so is the **Ocean Sands Beach Inn** (3465 North A1A, 904/824-1112, $$), which has clean, comfortable rooms and free coffee and doughnuts in the morning. Guests get to use the Beachcomber Club's dune crossover to the beach, as well as a 1,000-foot pier that extends into the marshes bordering the Intracoastal Waterway.

Vilano Beach's newest arrival is **Casa del Mar** (95 Vilano Road, 904/824/1599, $$$), a Clarion hotel and the first whiff of "class" accommodations to arrive out this way. It's kind of telling that they located here instead of St. Augustine Beach, and it may be a harbinger of what's to come. In any case, you have the best of both worlds out here: access to a viable beach and downtown St. Augustine's myriad attractions.

COASTAL CUISINE

Fiddler's Green (2750 Anahma Drive, 904/824-8897, $$$) is a clubby beach establishment on a site formerly occupied by the historic Vilano Beach Casino (which burned in the 1930s). It's got a distinctive atmosphere and tasty fish, shellfish, and pasta dishes (e.g., shrimp Vilano with mushrooms, spinach, and three cheeses), brought to you by the same folks who

own Salt Water Cowboy's—one of our favorite Florida eateries—in St. Augustine Beach.

Another local favorite is **The Reef** (4100 A1A, 904/824-8008, $$), a casual-dining spot with a far-ranging menu (go for the fresh catch, fried shrimp, or jambalaya) and one of the most popular weekend brunches in the area.

Located at the end of a side road off A1A, **Oscar's Old Florida Grill** (614 Euclid Avenue, 904/829-3794, $$) lists lazily in a picturesque setting beside a marsh. The atmosphere of Old Florida has been preserved in a classic cracker-style pavilion (built in 1909) with green-checked tablecloths and unfinished wood floors. You can dine inside or out on a deck overlooking the waterway; the latter is preferable if it's not too hot and buggy. The menu consists of fresh local food from the surf and marsh. Those with adventurous palates will want to take on the "Swamp Thing," a platter consisting of frog legs, gator tail, and whole catfish. One of us had butternut grouper: a butter-marinated grouper fillet baked with pecan stuffing that's a house specialty. (Note: They're closed on Monday and Tuesday.)

NIGHTLIFE

If you do nothing else, quaff a drink or two in the Irish ambience of Fiddler's Green. The Reef offers live music and dancing on weekends, while Oscar's Old Florida Grill has country and bluegrass bands at midweek. See *Coastal Cuisine* for more information on all three of these.

St. Augustine

If you've come to Florida for beaches, you will not find them in St. Augustine proper. The town is surrounded by two rivers (the San Sebastian and the Matanzas) and the St. Augustine Inlet, but you're only a bridge away from sandy swaths in Vilano Beach, just north of town, and St. Augustine Beach, right over the Bridge of Lions. If you're en route to points

HENRY MORRISON FLAGLER

Henry Morrison Flagler (1830-1913) opened up Florida to travel and tourism. His handiwork is evident all over the state, from the luxury hotels and private mansions he constructed to his crowning achievement, the Florida East Coast Railway, which ran down the coast and out to Key West. The foundations for his railroad bridges survived several hurricanes and served as supports for the construction of the Overseas Highway.

Flagler made his millions as a cofounder of Standard Oil (now Exxon). John D. Rockefeller, Sr., was his partner in this and other enterprises. Flagler remained director of Standard Oil's board until two years before his death. A trip to Florida in 1878 filled his head with visions of possibilities for the state, which was then a swampy backwater. He recognized the need for a transportation network and hotel facilities. In the 1880s, he bought and combined several rail lines into the Florida East Coast Railway, offering service from Jacksonville to Daytona. But he didn't stop there.

In 1892, he began laying track south to Palm Beach and, ultimately, Miami. Towns along the route began to develop as Flagler's railroad opened them up to trade and tourism. Flagler also constructed luxury hotels in places like Palm Beach (The Breakers) and St. Augustine (Ponce de Leon Hotel). By 1896, Flagler's Florida East Coast Railway reached down to Biscayne Bay. Flagler was a prime mover in the development of Miami, dredging channels, paving streets, laying power and water lines, and bankrolling the town's first newspaper. So central a figure was he that when Miami incorporated in 1896, the residents wanted to name the town "Flagler." He declined the honor.

In 1905, Flagler extended his railway to Key West. Many thought the project a doomed folly, and indeed its completion required engineering innovations, a workforce of 4,000 and seven years of hard labor, and triumph over numerous setbacks wrought by five hurricanes. The monetary incentive for linking the Keys with the mainland was to open trade with Cuba and Latin America – particularly since construction of the Panama Canal had been announced in 1905. Flagler lived to see the project to completion, riding the first train into Key West in 1912. He died a year later at his palatial home, Whitehall, in Palm Beach.

Flagler's legacy is still keenly felt in St. Augustine, most acutely in the splendid architecture of the former Ponce de Leon Hotel (now Flagler College) and the Memorial Presbyterian Church, built in memory of his daughter and grandchild. The spectacular church – with a 150-foot dome copied from St. Mark's Cathedral in Venice – is an Italian Renaissance-style masterpiece.

We recommend a visit to Flagler College's tranquil courtyard to cool your heels. As you sit by its circular fountain, watching terra-cotta frogs gurgle water, try imagining the scene a century ago, when the wealthy took their ease at the Ponce de Leon Hotel during its brief but lively winter season. Those were different times, but some of the flavor of a less harried age still seeps through the nooks and crannies in and around St. Augustine.

in southern or central Florida, St. Augustine makes an ideal place to spend the night. Boasting an abundance of motels and restaurants, it beats the heck out of your average highway interchange. Even the sightseeing, though a mixed bag, is leagues more interesting than you'll find elsewhere in Florida.

St. Augustine (pop. 14,000) is one of the more interesting, mold-breaking communities in Florida. There's a little bit of everything here, the sum total of which is a mosaic of contradictory impressions. On the one hand, it is among the nation's most historic communities, and there are endless informative and

AN OPINIONATED GUIDE TO ST. AUGUSTINE ATTRACTIONS

Over the years we've spent quite a few days visiting St. Augustine's tourist attractions. To separate the wheat from the chaff, we've drawn up a list of preferred sites (as well as ones we didn't like so well). We don't pretend to speak for all tourists and travelers. Some folks love saltwater taffy, tacky T-shirts, and tourist traps, and more power to them. We enjoy such things ourselves, albeit ironically and in small doses.

We've compiled this list with our idealized traveler in mind. This person is (like us) reasonably well-educated and curious, appreciative of history and art, and casts a fairly jaundiced eye at the trivialization of culture and insistent consumer arm-twisting that goes on in tourist towns. With that in mind, here we go:

Top Five Attractions in St. Augustine

1. **Castillo de San Marcos National Monument** (1 S. Castillo Drive, 904/829-6506, $6 adult admission): The oldest masonry fort in the United States, constructed in 1695 from coquina, still looms impressively over old St. Augustine. The castle grounds make for great strolling, the aura of history is authentic, the exhibits are interesting and informative, and you can even have your picture taken with soldiers in Spanish military garb.

2. **Lightner Museum** (75 King Street, 904/824-2874, $8 adult admission): Relics of the 19th century, including furnishings, costumes, housewares, and musical instruments, are on display. Not to be missed: the stained-glass room, featuring the work of Louis Comfort Tiffany. Civility, good taste, and refined manners survive at the Lightner.

3. **Mission of Nombre de Dios** (27 Ocean Avenue, 904/824-2809, no admission fee): St. Augustine, the first permanent Christian settlement in the New World, was founded on this site on September 8, 1565. On the grounds are a mission chapel and shrine, the 208-foot Great Cross, and some blessed peace and quiet from the downtown bustle. Daily masses at Prince of Peace Church (on the mission grounds) are open to the public. We bought St. Christopher's medals at the Mission Gift Shop, and they haven't failed us yet.

legitimate ways to explore its storied past. On the other, it is a tourist trap that assaults the traveler with cheesy attractions, trinket shops, and stop-and-go traffic.

There is yet another side to this small city. St. Augustine is something of a bohemian community, mixing a bit of New Orleans' festive, back-alley spirit with a shot of enlightened, Greenwich Village-style dropout culture. This side of St. Augustine was perhaps best expressed by a pair of bumper stickers we saw affixed to a pair old vans: "Plants and Animals Disappear to Make Room for Your Fat Ass" and "Strike a Blow for Justice—Punch an At-

torney." Coffeehouses and bookstores abound, which is impressive for a town of modest dimensions that's otherwise preoccupied with herding tourists into wax museums. You'll find expressions of entrepreneurial personality ranging from Jasmine's Coffee House (big and lavender) to the Surf Station, which has a car crashing out of its storefront.

Nearly two million people a year visit St. Augustine, which offers something for everybody. As you survey the lengthy list of attractions, ask yourself one question: Would you rather tour the genteel Lightner Museum or see what came out of a cow's stomach at

4. St. Augustine Lighthouse and Museum (81 Lighthouse Avenue, 904/829-0745, $7.50 adult admission): Nautical exhibits, lighthouse lenses, and period artifacts are on display. A calf-burning, 219-stair climb leads up the lighthouse. You won't want to miss the view from the top.

5. St. Augustine Alligator Farm (999 Anastasia Boulevard, 904/824-3337, $17.95 adult admission): Not the typical gator and pony show, this is an educational display of reptiles, tropical birds, and more, all on well-landscaped grounds that preserve the look of Old Florida. Best of all, there's not an alligator wrestler in sight – just naturalists who can give you the real lowdown on the world of reptiles.

Bottom Five Attractions in St. Augustine

1. Fountain of Youth (11 Magnolia Avenue, 904/829-3168, $6 adult admission): This tourist traps claims to be a "national archaeological park" and "North America's first historical site," but it is nothing quite that grand. It costs six bucks to enter and sip from Ponce de Leon's "Fountain of Youth." What you get is a miserly plastic cup of sulfur water poured from a pitcher. Other on-site attractions: a pile of sticks identified as an Indian "roasting spit" and a tacky gift shop where the same vile-tasting sulfur water is retailed by the fifth.

2. Ripley's Believe It or Not! (19 San Marco Avenue, 904/824-1606, $12.95 adult admission): Here's a spot for those with an appetite for the bizarre (come see the six-legged cow!) and little sense of, or interest in, the real history of St. Augustine.

3. Oldest Wooden Schoolhouse (14 St. George Street, 904/824-0192, $2.75 adult admission): You will feel like donning the dunce cap on display after paying to tour this tiny museum.

4. Museum of Weapons and Early American History (81C King Street, 904/829-3727, $4 adult admission): Guns, swords, rifles, pistols, muskets, and more fill this violence-themed museum.

5. Zorayda Castle (83 King Street, 904/824-3097, $6.50 adult admission): The burning question about this 1:10 scale re-creation of a Moorish palace is, why? Highlights: a "sacred cat rug," a mummy's foot, and John Tyler's piano.

Ripley's Believe It or Not? St. Augustine is equipped to satisfy any visitor's appetite, with the only serious bugaboo being that traffic can knot up into an unholy mess along the main thoroughfares.

We're told that the average length of stay in St. Augustine is three days, which seems about a day too long to us. Most of the worthwhile sites can be toured in a day or two, if you start early and follow a reasonable itinerary with time-outs for hot dogs, fudge, and T-shirt browsing.

The town is a veritable museum of American history, having seen considerable bloodshed and flag-hoisting over the centuries. St. Augustine claims to be "America's Oldest City." Indeed, it is the oldest continuously settled city in America, dating back to the Spanish explorer Ponce de Leon's landing in 1513 and the town's founding by the Spanish admiral Pedro Menendez de Aviles in 1565. Menendez named the town for St. Augustine, upon whose feast day he sighted the coast. For the next two and a half centuries—with the exception of the years 1763–1783, when it was occupied by the British—St. Augustine belonged to the Spanish. It has been part of the United States since 1821.

The unremitting cycles of fire, famine, disaster, and warfare in St. Augustine's past are appalling and make one grateful for its relatively peaceful state these days. While traveling the pockmarked highway of history, St. Augustine has claimed a lot of firsts. It was, as previously noted, the first European settlement in what is now America, having been founded a full 55 years before the Pilgrims' landing at Plymouth, Massachusetts. The first Catholic mass in America was conducted here on September 8, 1565. The citrus industry was born here. St. Augustine was the first planned city in North America. What would St. Augustine's original planners make of it now, with its Pizza Huts and 7-Elevens, not to mention a Ramada Inn that sits squarely on the site of the continent's first orange grove? Ah, progress!

St. Augustine is also the site of the oldest stone fort in the country, the Castillo de San Marcos. It is constructed of coquina, a rocklike substance built from the calcified remains of butterfly clams into a coral-type reef. The coquina was quarried by a chain gang of convicts and Native American slaves, and the edifice, which took 15 years to complete, proved an impregnable fortress that withstood every attack upon it. This grand old fortress and other buildings made of coquina are among the architectural highlights of St. Augustine.

After centuries of hardship and an almost inconceivable record of violence and cruelty, oil magnate Henry Flagler helped turn St. Augustine into a peaceful subtropical getaway. An era of gracious living came to St. Augustine in the late 1800s and early 1900s, as wealthy northerners trekked down to stay at Flagler's Ponce de Leon Hotel. With its balmy winters and appealing setting amid palm trees and orange groves, how could they resist? Neither as war-torn nor as rarefied these days, St. Augustine is a bustling tourist town in which you can study the relics and remnants of the past without having to worry about whizzing cannonballs, smoking muskets, or flaming tomahawks.

When you get to St. Augustine, head straight for the **Visitor Information Center** (10 Castillo Drive, 904/825-1000), where maps, brochures, and information can be had. Traffic and parking in St. Augustine are a problem, and the large, inexpensive ($3 per day) lot at the information center is by far the best deal in town. It's within walking distance of downtown attractions, as well as train and trolley tours. If you've got time, stick around to watch the 52-minute film *Dream of Empire,* about the city's rich history. If you're in a hurry, at least watch the 12-minute capsule video on local attractions. If you're too pooped to hoof it around town, you have options. **Red Sightseeing Trains** (170 San Marco Avenue, 904/829-6545) offers package deals that include a narrated train tour and various attractions. **St. Augustine Trolley Tours** (167 San Marco Avenue, 904/829-3800) sells passes good for all-day rides around town and vends discounted attraction tickets as well.

For more information, contact St. Johns County Visitors and Convention Bureau, 88 Riberia Street, Suite 400, St. Augustine, FL 32084, 800/653-2489, www.visitoldcity.com.

RECREATION AND ATTRACTIONS

- **Bike/Skate Rentals:** Sunshine Shop, 546 A1A Beach Boulevard, St. Augustine Beach, 904/471-6899

- **Dive Shop:** Sea Hunt Scuba, 309 S.R. 16, St. Augustine 904/824-0831

- **Ecotourism:** GTMNERR–Guana River Environmental Education Center, 505 Guana River Road, Ponte Vedra Beach, 904/823-4500

- **Fishing Charters:** St. Augustine Fishing Charters, Conch House Marina, 57 Comares Avenue, St. Augustine, 904/797-6499

- **Lighthouse:** St. Augustine Lighthouse, 81 Lighthouse Avenue, St. Augustine, 904/829-0745

- **Marina:** Municipal Marina, 111 Avenida Menendez, St. Augustine, 904/825-1026
- **Pier:** St. Johns County Pier, 350 A1A Beach Boulevard, St. Augustine Beach, 904/461-0119
- **Rainy-Day Attraction:** Lightner Museum, 75 King Street, St. Augustine, 904/824-2874
- **Shopping/Browsing:** St. George Street, between Cathedral Place and Hypolita Street, St. Augustine
- **Surf Shop:** Surf Station, 1020 Anastasia Boulevard, St. Augustine Beach, 904/471-4694 (store) and 904/471-1122 (surf report)
- **Vacation Rentals:** Ocean Village Realty, 1009 A1A Beach Boulevard, St. Augustine Beach, 904/471-9329

ACCOMMODATIONS

St. Augustine is ruled by chain motels and hotels, which are clustered on or near San Marco Avenue, close to the downtown historic district, and along Anastasia Boulevard, over the Bridge of Lions in the direction of St. Augustine Beach. If you want to see the sights and soak up history, stay downtown. There's a brand-new **Hilton** (32 Avenida Menendez, 904/829-2277, $$$$), a Spanish Colonial fortress that blends in well with the surrounding area. You might need to plunder a treasure ship to afford the tariff, though.

Other dependable name-brand chains with good downtown locations and more affordable rates are **Hampton Inn** (2050 North Ponce de Leon Boulevard, 904/829-1996, $$), **Holiday Inn Downtown** (1300 Ponce de Leon Boulevard, 904/824-3383, $$), the **Best Western Spanish Quarters Inn** (6 Castillo Drive, 904/824-4457, $$), and the **Ramada Inn** (116 San Marco Avenue, 904/824-4352, $$). Prices vary by time of year, and you're best advised to make advance reservations instead of showing up and hoping for the best.

On a more upscale note, there are 26 historic bed-and-breakfast inns in St. Augustine. For more information, visit the St. Augustine

Historic Inns website at www.staugustineinns.com. Two of the better ones are the **Cedar House Inn** (79 Cedar Street, 904/829-0079, $$$), near the Lightner Museum, and **Casa de la Paz** (22 Avenida Menendez, 904/829-2915, $$$), located on Matanzas Bay.

Finally, St. Augustine can be a cheap date, if you're willing to stay at a Scottish Inn or Sunrise Inn, both of which were advertising $32 single rooms last time we passed through. As we said earlier, there's something for everybody in St. Augustine.

COASTAL CUISINE

Several of the better restaurants in St. Augustine are located over the Bridge of Lions, which deposits traffic on the north end of Anastasia Island. This side of Anastasia, which is still in St. Augustine proper, wasn't originally part of the island. A man named Davis created it in the 1920s by extending the island with landfill. (He did a similar thing in Tampa.) So while you may be on dry land, it's a man-made extension. Motels, restaurants, and the odd surf shop line Anastasia Boulevard (A1A) before you round a curve and begin hugging the shore in St. Augustine Beach.

The **Gypsy Cab Company** (828 Anastasia Boulevard, 904/824-8244, $$$) is a healthy, cosmopolitan bistro that does creative things with fish, chicken, and beef. A favorite of discriminating diners, it's been around for many years. On the changing menu you might find pepper-seared grouper in spicy Dijon sauce, flounder with white wine mustard, or something similarly intriguing.

Osteen's (205 Anastasia Boulevard, 904/829-6974, $$) is the place to go for fried shrimp; no one does it better, anywhere. The plump, perfectly breaded shrimp—listed as "Our Famous St. Augustine Fried Shrimp" on the menu—are served at lunch and dinner and are worth every penny ($9.95 for nine, $10.95 for 12). Squirt a few drops of Osteen's own sweet 'n' hot datil sauce (datil is a kind of pepper grown locally), and you'll be in shrimp heaven. Osteen's also does oysters, scallops, fish, catfish, crab, and clam strips, and they sell their bottled "Datil Squeezings" at the cash register. (Note: They're closed on Sunday and Monday.)

Conch House Marina Resort (57 Comares Avenue, 904/829-8646, $$) is a full-service resort that includes a 23-unit motel, restaurant, lounge, 100-slip marina, sportfishing charter, outfitter (Raging Watersports), sports bar, and gift shop. Dining on the Conch House's outdoor deck, with its thatched-roof huts and direct views onto the inlet, is the way to enjoy the Caribbean-themed menu. Try anything conchy, like cracked conch or conch fritters. The complex remains in the Ponce family of Minorcan bluebloods who founded St. Augustine.

There are dozens more dining options downtown, too. A personal favorite is the **Raintree** (120 San Marco Avenue, 904/824-7211, $$$). Located in an exquisitely furnished two-story home, the Raintree will make you forget you're mere feet from busy San Marco Avenue. The menu is continental, with such dishes as veal Oscar (topped with asparagus, blue crab, and hollandaise) and brandy pepper steak (among the best filet mignons we've ever tasted), plus seafood specialties like grouper Raintree (sauteed in white wine, mushrooms, and cream).

NIGHTLIFE

In the vicinity of St. George Street, you can wet your whistle at several English-style pubs. Two of the more frequented among them are the **Mill Top Tavern** (19½ St. George Street, 904/829-2329) and the **White Lion Tavern** (20 Cuna Street, 904/829-2388). A popular gathering spot of longstanding is **Scarlett O'Hara's** (70 Hypolita Street, 904/824-6535), a longtime jazz-blues club and restaurant located in a two-story house. There are rocking chairs on Scarlett O'Hara's front porch, which sums up the low-key tenor of nightlife in downtown St. Augustine. For a noisier and younger scene, head out to St. Augustine Beach to fritter the night away.

Anastasia State Park

Anastasia State Park, located on the northeast corner of Anastasia Island, is blessed with one of the finest beaches on Florida's east coast. The healthy condition of this beach stands in stark contrast to the degraded beaches below the pier and behind the hotels of St. Augustine Beach (just below the park's southern border). The comparison is instructional, as it dramatically demonstrates the negative impact that seawalls and development can have on shoreline width. There is no beach at the north end of St. Augustine Beach, where waves slap against walls and rock revetments, whereas the undeveloped shoreline of Anastasia State Park is an awesome beach. Take a close look: you'll never see a stronger argument against beach development in your life than that on display here.

At Anastasia's fine-grained, hard-packed, table-flat, four-mile beach, cars travel in both directions and park several rows deep. There is no charge, beyond the $5 park entrance fee, to drive on Anastasia Beach. And there's more to do at Anastasia in the way of outdoor recreation. A wooded, 139-site campground borders the inlet. There's also a windsurfing area, complete with parking lot and launch site, on the inlet. Surfboards, windsurfers, kayaks, and canoes can be rented at a park concession operated by the Surf Station (904/471-4694), which also operates a complete surf shop just outside the park's gates. In addition to equipment rentals, the Surf Station offers instruction on board surfing and windsurfing.

For more information, contact Anastasia State Park, 1340A A1A South, St. Augustine, FL 32084, 904/461-2033, www.floridastateparks.org.

BEACHES

27 ANASTASIA STATE PARK

Location: one mile east of downtown St. Augustine on A1A, at the mouth of St. Augustine inlet

Parking/Fees: $5 entrance fee per vehicle.
Camping fee is $23 per night.
Hours: 8 A.M.-sundown
Facilities: concessions, lifeguards (seasonal),
restrooms, picnic tables, and showers
Contact: Anastasia State Park, 904/461-2033

St. Augustine Beach

They really ought to think of shortening the name of St. Augustine Beach (pop. 5,000) to St. Augustine, because the distinction between the two adjacent communities is minimal. That is to say, at least in 2005, there was no beach to speak of in the main part of St. Augustine Beach. We've always known this area, especially by St. Johns County Pier, to be a particularly sand-starved stretch of coast, but for a brief while earlier in this decade it did have a nice, wide (albeit artificial) beach. St. Augustine Beach spent millions on a renourishment project that extended its beach all the way out to the end of the pier. The new beach lasted all of one season before the hurricanes of 2004 washed it away. "Easy come, easy go" is how a disgusted native put it to us. Now the waves once again break against the riprap piled up at the base of a seawall.

There is a silver lining to this calamitous waste of taxpayers' money: Anglers can once again drop a line from the pier. (It costs $2 to fish and $0.50 to walk on the pier.) Meanwhile, the narrowing of the beach behind the oceanfront hotels has again left them fighting a rearguard action—with boulders, riprap, and seawalls—to keep from washing away. And the debate over using federal funds to renourish Florida's beaches continues, though the money spigot has been dripping less wastefully for this dubious investment.

This is worth bearing in mind, because if you come to St. Augustine Beach expecting a typical Florida beach vacation, you may be sorely disappointed. Chain-link fences be-

St. Augustine Beach

© PARKE PUTERBAUGH

hind some hotels, in fact, keep people from attempting to climb over the seawall onto the wave-battered rocks. The rock revetment runs from St. Johns County Pier down to A Street. The situation improves at the south end of St. Augustine Beach.

For more information, contact the South Beaches Information Center, St. Johns County Pier, 350 A1A South, St. Augustine, FL 32084, 904/471-1596, www.visitoldcity.com.

BEACHES

The saving grace of St. Augustine's beach scene is Anastasia State Park. Contrarily, the question at **St. Augustine Beach** proper is, "What beach?" Beach erosion has been noted out here as far back as the 1880s. In our opinion, they ought to forbid driving on the beach in St. Johns County, as it creates weak spots that worsen the erosion that occurs during storms and overwash. It would at least be a start. As it is, about the best you can do is cast a line from St. Johns County Pier, which also is the site of a visitors center for the "South Beaches" area, where you can load up on maps, brochures, and local info, or wander up to Anastasia State Park.

The street-end accesses in the "south beach" area of St. Augustine Beach are in marginally better shape than the seawalled area around the pier. At **Frank Butler Park, East** you can park, picnic, and cross a dune walkover to the beach. The larger "west" unit of Frank Butler Park lies along the Intracoastal Waterway.

28 ST. AUGUSTINE BEACH (COUNTY PIER)

Location: east of St. Augustine on A1A at St. Johns County Pier.
Parking/Fees: free street and lot parking
Hours: October 1-April 30, 24 hours; May 1-September 30, 5 A.M.-10 P.M.
Facilities: lifeguards (seasonal), restrooms, picnic tables, showers, and a visitors center
Contact: St. Johns County Recreation Department, 904/471-6616

29 ST. AUGUSTINE BEACH (SOUTH BEACH)

Location: numerous access points at street ends for four miles south of St. Johns County Pier along A1A
Parking/Fees: free street and lot parking
Hours: sunrise-sunset
Facilities: none
Contact: St. Johns County Recreation Department, 904/471-6616

30 FRANK BUTLER PARK, EAST

Location: A1A near Dune Street, between St. Augustine Beach and Crescent Beach
Parking/Fees: free parking lot

Hours: sunrise-sunset
Facilities: picnic tables and showers
Contact: St. Johns County Recreation Department, 904/471-6616

ACCOMMODATIONS

The lodging situation out on St. Augustine Beach is certainly not hopeless, but without a beach, it may seem pointless. The oceanfront hotels back up to a seawall bordered by chain-link fencing and beaches that vanish at high tide. The safest bet may be the **Best Western Ocean Inn** (3955 A1A South, 904/471-8010, $$), which is, ironically, on the side of the road opposite the ocean.

Still, some remain undaunted in their desire to build upon the ocean on this dicey stretch of coast. The newest entry in this high-stakes game is the spiffy mid-rise **Hampton Inn** (430 A1A Beach Boulevard, 904/471-4000, $$). Its on-site amenities (pool, Jacuzzi, fitness center, volleyball) are the best hereabouts. Also on the ocean is a longstanding **Holiday Inn** (860 A1A Beach Blvd., 904/471-2555, $$), which has a protected gazebo overlooking the waves. An on-site sports bar can get mildly raucous, depending on what team, rock band, or convention is staying at the motel.

COASTAL CUISINE

If we could compose a menu that expressed what we like most about food, it would resemble the menu at **Salt Water Cowboy's** (299 Dondanville Road, 904/471-2332, $$), two miles south of St. Augustine Beach. Everything about the place speaks to our sensibilities. The restaurant, started by a rugged Floridian whose nickname was "Cowboy," has been in business since 1964. This tin-roofed marshside institution is a cracker paradise. It looks like an 1890s fish camp, with personal artifacts and weird photographs of gator carcasses on the walls. The wood flooring came from the old Jacksonville train station. Rustic willow furniture occupies the plant-filled rooms. Twisted, serpentine trees, including some enormous live oaks, grow both inside and outside the restaurant.

Salt Water Cowboy's has a no-reservation policy. Your Lexus and net worth mean nothing here; it's strictly first-come, first-served. Come expecting to wait for a spell on the rambling wooden porch, and knock back a drink while the sun sets over the marsh. Once seated, you will dine in either the Snake, Gator, or Hibiscus room.

Salt Water Cowboy's iced tea is served in mason jars. Delicious, cold, and not too sickly sweet, it is the perfect accompaniment to the spread of broiled or fried seafood laid out before you. While it's all good, we'd steer you to the locally harvested oysters and shrimp. If you have an adventurous palate, they'll oblige with a bodacious Florida Cracker Combo appetizer: frog legs, cooter (soft-shell turtle), and alligator tail. Some entrees—chicken, catfish, steak, catch of the day, and "shrimp on a stick"—can be ordered blackened. You can also get chicken, shrimp, and ribs barbecued to a turn over an open pit. It's all too darn good, and if you have any room left they serve a key lime pie as tart and tasty as any you'll find this side of Miami.

One of our favorite beachside haunts in Florida, the **Beachcomber** (2 A Street, 904/471-3744, $), will fill your belly without emptying your wallet. It's front and center on the beach, where A Street meets the ocean and everyone in town meets each other. Here, "proper attire" means only "shoes and shirt required after 5:30 A.M." They serve three meals a day, and the menu is surprisingly varied, from steamed shrimp and burgers to seafood specialties, dinner platters, and salads. The prices are reasonable and the helpings plentiful. Downside: There's precious little parking here, so the best way to visit the Beachcomber is when you are, uh, combing the beach.

Just up the street, the morning port of call and unofficial community bulletin board is **Stir It Up** (18 A Street, 904/461-4552). Even the roughest morning-after can be jumpstarted here with fruit smoothies and fresh-roasted coffee blends. Diagonally across the street and fronting A1A is **Sharky's Shrimp Shack** (700 A1A, 904/461-9992), which offers "beachy casual ocean breeze dining" and 23 preparations of fresh local shrimp.

Sunset Grille (421 Beach Boulevard, 904/471-5555, $$$) has an airy wood-and-glass interior with big picture windows that look out onto A1A and the beach beyond. For lunch, try the spinach salad with blackened grouper and wild mushroom and bacon dressing. (Both of us got it.) At dinner, you'll likely have a hard time deciding between cedar-planked roasted grouper and Mediterranean mahimahi—and the coconut shrimp is plenty appealing, too.

NIGHTLIFE

St. Augustine Beach has always had the nightlife, as if St. Augustine, bowing under the awful weight of history, couldn't be bothered with such trifles as deejays and flashing lights. But over the years, the nightlife has eroded away much like the beach. Gone are the days when we would indulge in footloose escapism at hangouts on A1A, trying to keep pace with the collegiate Gen X-ers and their wacky techno music. Even if we wanted to now, there are few places left to get yer freak on. Only the "world-famous" **Oasis Deck and Restaurant** (4000 A1A Beach Boulevard, 904/471-3424) with its 24-ounce drafts and nightly live music (e.g., Vince and the Viceroys, Bush Doctors) carries the torch for rock and roll revelry at the beach.

FLAGLER BEACH AND THE QUIET COAST

South of St. Augustine Beach, the population thins out and the coastline turns quiet. This break in the buildup along Florida's East Coast is as welcome as it is unexpected. There's a small beach community (Crescent Beach) and a trio of beaches—Butler, Crescent, and Matanzas—between St. Augustine Beach and the southern border of St. Johns County.

The quietude continues in Flagler County. Nineteen miles of Atlantic Ocean beach are its calling card, and the one-horse town of Flagler Beach its modest centerpiece. The pace is picking up, however. Thanks to luxury golf communities like Palm Coast, Flagler County is officially the fastest-growing county in the U.S., its population having shot up by 10.1 percent between 2003 and 2004. Since 2000, the county population has increased by 40 percent. (They must be so proud!) That's still small potatoes, as with its current population of 70,000, Flagler County still accounts for only 0.4 percent of the state's population. But it is a sign that things are changing quickly. Our favorite place: Marineland, a roadside attraction from the past that's struggled and somehow survived into the new millennium. It's reassuring that places like this are still able to exist in Florida. But for how long?

Crescent Beach

Crescent Beach, a small beach community at the south end of Anastasia Island, offers a glimpse at the magical lure of Old Florida. Looking for a cool, off-the-beaten-track spot to vacation? Crescent Beach is it. The central artery into Crescent Beach is SR 206, which meets the ocean at a vehicular ramp leading onto the beach. Sun-baked cottages flare out north and south of the ramp.

© PARKE PUTERBAUGH

For more information, contact South Beaches Information Center, St. Johns County Pier, 350 A1A South, St. Augustine, FL 32084, 904/471-1596, www.visitoldcity.com.

BEACHES

There are 24 beach-access points from St. Augustine Beach through Crescent Beach (an eight-mile-long stretch generally referred to as the "South Beaches"). The beaches down this way are wide, white, and sufficiently hard-packed to allow for beach driving (though we're not wild about the practice).

Crescent Beach Park is a four-acre park along where A1A meets Cubbedge Road in Crescent Beach. You'll find a decent-sized parking lot and a ramp onto the beach. The dunes are still intact and the beach has retained a decent width. This is a sharp contrast to the thinning strand up in St. Augustine Beach. The county maintains five street-end access points along Crescent Beach's five miles of shorefront, along with a full complement of facilities, including seasonal lifeguards.

Further down A1A, between Crescent Beach and Fort Matanzas, is another county maintained beach adjoining a condominium. **Spyglass Beach** (beside Spyglass Condominium) has a 23-space parking lot and beach access at one of the wider points on Anastasia Island

1 CRESCENT BEACH PARK

Location: three miles south of St. Augustine Beach at A1A and Cubbedge Road in Crescent Beach
Parking/Fees: off-beach parking lot (free) or on-beach parking and driving ($5 per day or $35 annually)
Hours: October 1–April 30, 24 hours; May 1–September 30, 5 A.M.–10 P.M.
Facilities: restrooms
Contact: St. Johns County Recreation Department, 904/209-0333

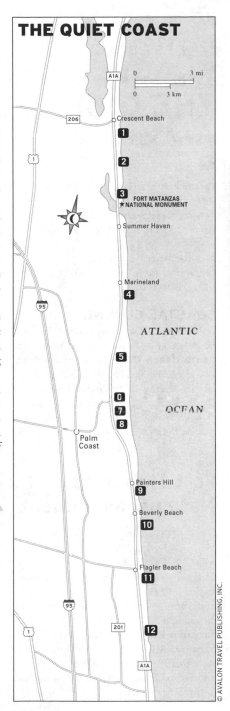

THE QUIET COAST

© AVALON TRAVEL PUBLISHING, INC.

THE QUIET COAST

BEST BEACHES

 Gamble Rogers Memorial State Recreation Area: Best for Camping (page 83)

2 SPYGLASS BEACH

Location: between Crescent Beach and Fort Matanzas at 8200 A1A
Parking/Fees: free parking lot
Hours: October 1–April 30, 24 hours; May 1–September 30, 5 A.M.–10 P.M.
Facilities: none
Contact: St. Johns County Recreation Department, 904/209-0333

COASTAL CUISINE

Located beside the beach ramp in Crescent Beach is a funky community landmark called **South Beach Grill** (45 Cubbedge Road, 904/471-8700, $). This two-story bar-restaurant serves great shrimp and seafood baskets and sandwiches (the blackened fish wrap is a personal favorite), and you're made to feel right at home in this great yellow wonder.

Fort Matanzas National Monument

Down at the south end of the island, Fort Matanzas National Monument (8635 A1A South, 904/471-0116) stands sentry in the Matanzas Inlet. A free ferry from the mainland to Matanzas Island and its namesake 18th-century stone fort leaves every hour on the half hour 9:30 A.M.–4:30 P.M. The fort sits on Rattlesnake Island, located in the Matanzas River/Intracoastal Waterway. It came by its name honestly (read: beware of rattlers) and is one of the oldest historic sites in North America.

Matanzas, in fact, means "slaughter," which is what occurred here in 1565 when a force of French Huguenots attacked the Spanish settlers (and lost). The fort itself was constructed 1740–1742 and marked Spain's futile last stand at staving off British encroachment.

Though it sits on federal property, the three-mile **Matanzas Beach** is maintained by St. Johns County. The beach is wonderfully natural and secluded—a real find. A separate access a quarter-mile south takes you via a wooden walk through a "living dune." One of the chief attractions at this end of Anastasia Island is fishing, judging from all the anglers casting lines into the inlet from the Matanzas Bridge.

For more information, contact the South Beaches Information Center, St. Johns County Pier, 350 A1A South, St. Augustine, FL 32084, 904/471-1596, www.visitoldcity.com.

BEACHES

3 MATANZAS BEACH

Location: 7.5 miles south of St. Augustine Beach on A1A
Parking/Fees: off-beach parking lot (free) or on-beach parking and driving ($5 per day or $35 annually)
Hours: October 1–April 30, 24 hours; May 1–September 30, 5 A.M.–10 P.M.
Facilities: lifeguards (seasonal), restrooms, picnic tables, showers, and a visitors center
Contact: St. Johns County Recreation Department, 904/209-0333

ACCOMMODATIONS

At **Beacher's Lodge** (6970 A1A South, 904/471-8849, $$), the rates are good (especially from Labor Day till the end of January, which is the off-season in northeast Florida), and the dunes out back are high and healthy. King- and queen-bed suites (with a sleeper sofa in the living room) face the ocean. You'll save a little more by staying on the ground floor, because the dunes are tall enough to partially obstruct the ocean view.

Summer Haven

On the south side of bridge over Matanzas Inlet, you'll notice that "Old A1A" lurches toward the ocean while the real A1A continues south. If you want to see the Florida beach equivalent of Atlantis, pay heed and take the turn onto Old A1A. Along an old, washed-out road barely protected by riprap sits the sleepy cottage colony of Summer Haven. Founded by one Albert Graves in the 1870s, it used to be a literal summer haven for moneyed folk. Nowadays, it looks like the end of the world. At the point where the road spills jaggedly onto the beach, we saw a hand-painted sign warning "YOUR GONNA GET STUK" [sic].

Back out on the "real" A1A, head south for a mile and you'll come to the other end of "Old A1A"—another entry point into this lost colony. The road here is, if possible, even less inviting than the northern end. Covered in sand drifts and barely accessible to the local residents, it is so narrow that cars cannot travel two abreast. Out of deference to an approaching resident, we drove in reverse for a quarter mile to let him pass. One circular house attracted our notice. Raised high on stilts above the rising sand and water of the marsh, it looks like "The Mothership" from the old funk group Parliament's stage show. It just adds to the eerie look of Summer Haven.

Surfers are particularly drawn to Summer Haven, parking along Old A1A and hopping over the riprap with their boards. Meanwhile, the ever-eroding beach continues to threaten houses, chew at Old A1A, elicit calls for responsible beach management, and do its darnedest to become again what it was in historical times: an inlet.

For more information, contact the South Beaches Information Center, St. Johns County Pier, 350 A1A South, St. Augustine, FL 32084, 904/471-1596, www.visitoldcity.com.

Marineland

Just inside Flagler County sits Marineland, the world's first "oceanarium" (see the *Marineland: A Buried Treasure* sidebar). On its property is the seaward component of the River to Sea Preserve. This preserve was established ten years ago by local residents along the Marineland/Palm Coast boundary, partly in hopes of reviving the dwindling scrub jay population, which activists have called a "condominium casualty." The town of Marineland and the county of Flagler jointly purchased the 90-acre preserve in 1999, with a grant from a state land preservation program. It's a modest area, to be sure, given how much nearby acreage has been swallowed by gated high-rise condos and "luxury golf communities" in the last two decades. The town of Palm Coast alone has grown by 15,000 Homo sapiens in the last five years!

Listen to this local official dissembling over his failure to comply with the goal of the 1999 purchase, which was to set aside a 30-acre habitat for the threatened scrub jay population: "Any criticism is just totally unfounded," he prevaricated. "The partners decided that the focus should be on revegetation, bathrooms, parking lot, and other amenities. We decided they should be the primary focus so we can get that preserve opened to the public."

Bird droppings! Preserves are, by definition, for the benefit of native flora and fauna. If biologists say the land base is too small to

MARINELAND: A BURIED TREASURE

Marineland opened in 1938 as the world's first "oceanarium," and it quickly became the world's most popular marine-oriented tourist attraction. For a spell, it was the most popular tourist attraction in the whole of Florida. But Marineland did not keep up with the changing times, steadily losing ground later in the century to more contemporary attractions like Sea World, Disney World, and the Kennedy Space Center. Even though Marineland faltered, it remained the top tourist destination in Flagler County – which speaks volumes about Flagler County. After falling into near decrepitude in the 1990s, Marineland got a reprieve as a study center for the University of Florida, which maintained its Graduate School of Marine Biology here.

When several structures were damaged by hurricanes in 2004, Marineland used the downtime for repairs and an extensive, overdue remodeling. Marineland has reopened with a new Dolphin Conservation Center, including revamped lagoons for its dolphin performers.

A park spokesman said, "Our desire is to create more than just a dolphin swim program. We want our guests to walk away with an appreciation for the fragility of the ocean's ecosystems by being immersed in interactive dolphin research. It's not your standard encounter, that's for sure."

The new, improved Marineland reopened in March 2006. General admission is $5 for adults and $2.50 for kids, and the facility is open daily 8:30 A.M.-4:30 P.M. Five interactive dolphin programs are offered, ranging from relatively inexpensive ($60 for Dolphin Designs, $65 for Flippers & Fins) to fairly pricy ($120 for Discover Dolphins, $150 for "The Immersion") to gold card–busting expensive ($275 for "The Quest," an in-depth, afternoon-long opportunity to spend quality time with your fellow mammals).

For more information, contact Marineland, 9600 Oceanshore Boulevard, Marineland, FL 32086, 904/471-1111 or 888/279-9194, www.marineland.net.

---

sustain a population of scrub jays, there's a simple solution for the county and state: Buy up more land out here before developers make a mockery of the county's slogan, "The Quiet Side of Florida."

For more information, contact Marineland, 9600 Oceanshore Boulevard, Marineland, FL 32086, 904/460-1275 or 888/279-9194, www. marineland.net.

BEACHES

Insofar as beach at the **River to Sea Preserve** is concerned, you can clamber down to a strip of orange coquina sand with hard outcroppings in the nearshore water. It's hardly a prime swimming beach, though, so you're best advised to stick to Marineland's dolphin shows or launching a canoe or kayak into the Intracoastal Waterway or Matanzas River.

4 RIVER TO SEA PRESERVE

Location: beside Marineland, at 9600 North Oceanshore Boulevard (A1A)
Parking/Fees: free parking lot
Hours: sunrise-11 P.M.
Facilities: concession, restrooms, picnic tables, shower, and a visitors center
Contact: Flagler County Parks and Recreation Department, 386/437-7589

Washington Oaks Gardens State Park

The 390 sublime acres of this lovely park were deeded to the state by its former owners. Located three miles south of Marineland, Washington Oaks Gardens State Park looks like much of coastal Florida did prior to European colonization. Great ecological diversity is displayed within a brief distance. At the ocean's edge, a "coquina beach" of fine orange coquina sand and rocks hosts a variety of shorebirds and marine life, including crabs and starfish in the tidal pools and mussels and anemones glued to the rocks. Known as "the Rocks," about 0.4 mile of beach falls within park boundaries. The "rocks" are hardened outcrops of coquina sand sculpted by wind and sea into lovely formations. An informative display explains "Life on Beach Rocks." People come out here to study and/or sun themselves on the unusual (and usually deserted) beach.

Moving inland, you proceed from coastal scrub (stunted vegetation that serves as habitat for the rare Florida scrub jay) to coastal hammock (live oak, hickory, magnolia) and, finally, to a tidal marsh bordering the Matanzas River. A short nature trail winds through the hammock and along the river. The park's gardens—whose cultivation dates from the mid-1800s—occupy a coastal swale awash in colorful flowers and exotic plants like the giant elephant's ear. Dirt pathways wander through the oaks, their limbs overhung with Spanish moss, past a spring-fed pond and beautiful patches of roses, camellias, and azaleas. All in all, Washington Oaks Gardens is one of the most peaceful spots on Florida's East Coast. It makes an ideal place for a picnic in a setting that's as picturesque as they come.

For more information, contact Washington Oaks Gardens State Park, 6400 North Ocean Boulevard, Palm Coast, FL 32137, 386/446-6780, www.floridastateparks.org.

BEACHES

5 WASHINGTON OAKS GARDENS STATE PARK

Location: three miles south of Marineland, along A1A
Parking/Fees: $4 entrance fee per vehicle ($2 for beach side only)
Hours: 8 A.M. to sundown
Facilities: restrooms, picnic tables, and visitors center
Contact: Washington Oaks Gardens State Park, 386/446-6780

Palm Coast and Hammock

Flagler County is a less-traveled stretch of A1A between the tourist meccas of St. Augustine and Daytona Beach. With a population of only 70,000, the county—particularly the stretch from Painters Hill to Flagler Beach—can honestly market itself as "the Quiet Side of Florida," but we wonder for how much longer. The mid-county communities of Palm Coast and Hammock have fallen to architects of gated luxury resorts and "private golf communities." That is to say, "golf course living" (a phrase we first heard used in California) has staked its claim here, creating an entirely different climate than that found in the funky beach towns at the southern end of the county.

Palm Coast bears the prefab look of a community that didn't even exist a quarter century ago. Rich and tony golf resorts, gated residential communities, and a fortress mentality are what you'll find at inland Palm Coast (pop. 60,000) and coastal Hammock (pop. 750). Yes, you read correctly. Palm Coast, which was incorporated in 1999—and which takes up 65 square miles—accounts for 85 percent of Flagler County's population. It was founded by the ITT

Corporation and is one of those soulless instant cities that send so many rootless Americans into existential tailspins. Needless to say, we won't steer you anywhere near Palm Coast.

The premier development on the coast in these parts is Hammock Dunes ("A Private Oceanfront Golf Community"). You practically expect to hear "Also Sprach Zarathustra" rising to a crescendo as you approach its hallowed guard gates. These are the sorts of places where golf courses are referred to in glossy brochures as "masterpieces." If so, then Tom Fazio, Jack Nicklaus, Gary Player, and Arnold Palmer are the Bach, Beethoven, Mozart, and Brahms of the golfing set in Palm Coast. All we needed to know about the tenor of development here was expressed on a billboard along A1A: "Hammock Beach Is Expanding… by 18 Holes." Putting as polite a spin on it as we can, we travel in different circles than these folks.

The Hammock Dunes Toll Bridge ($0.75) connects A1A with I-95 and Hammock with Palm Coast. Though the privatization of the shoreline goes against the grain, we will give them this much: the oceanfront development out here is low-density, leaving lots of room for nature's manic tangle of trees, shrubs, and dune grasses. A paved biking/jogging path runs for miles on the east side of A1A and you can still catch glimpses of how A1A used to be in these parts as you whiz by abandoned roadside stands from bygone eras.

One curious sociological phenomenon in Hammock is the palpable tension between the exclusive new "communities" being built here and the old spreads of trailer parks, RV campgrounds, flyblown motels, and biker bars along A1A. You can witness this collision most dramatically on 16th Street, where an earth-rattling upscale golf-and-condo development has been wedged alongside a long-time community of mobile homes and saltbox-style houses. One can't help but imagine that the resentment among the long-time residents who haven't sold out must be extreme. Either way, nature looks to be the big loser in Hammock, however this thing plays out culturally.

It's really a shame—and a black mark—that Flagler County has not done better by its long-time residents than to sell them out like this. They should have bought some of this prime oceanfront land for their own park system before it was completely gone. As it is, there is one decent-sized county-run beach park (Malacompra) and two small accesses (Jungle Hut, Old Salt Road). A local land conservancy took matters into their own hands to create the River to Sea Preserve at the north end of Palm Coast, where it abuts Marineland.

For more information, contact the Flagler County Palm Coast Chamber of Commerce, 20 Airport Road, Bunnell, FL 32110, 386/437-0106, www.flaglercounty.com.

BEACHES

There are three county beaches in the Palm Coast/Hammock area. All have free parking lots, wooden dune walkovers, and restrooms. From north to south, they are **Malacompra Beach Park, Old Salt Road Park,** and **Jungle Hut Road Park;** all are found at the ends of roads bearing those names. Old Salt is not as rocky as the others, Jungle Hut is the only one with a shower, and at 36 acres, Malacompra is by far the largest.

At Malacompra, a sign warns of "strong undercurrent. Swim at own risk." As if to reinforce the warning, uprooted coastal scrub lines the beach like battle corpses. On one visit we spied a sun-beaten, old salty dog perched atop the handrail of the crossover, having a smoke and watching the waves. As wealthy, golf-club-toting retirees find their way to Flagler County, his like is becoming an endangered species, like the scrub jay.

⑥ MALACOMPRA BEACH PARK

Location: at the end of Malacompra Road in Hammock

Parking/Fees: free parking lot
Hours: sunrise–11 P.M.
Facilities: restrooms
Contact: Flagler County Parks and Recreation Department, 386/437-7589

⑦ OLD SALT ROAD PARK

Location: at the end of Old Salt Road in Palm Coast
Parking/Fees: free parking lot
Hours: sunrise–11 P.M.
Facilities: restrooms
Contact: Flagler County Parks and Recreation Department, 386/437-7589

⑧ JUNGLE HUT ROAD PARK

Location: at the end of Jungle Hut Road in Palm Coast
Parking/Fees: free parking lot
Hours: sunrise–11 P.M.
Facilities: restrooms and shower
Contact: Flagler County Parks and Recreation Department, 386/437-7589

ACCOMMODATIONS

If you're coming to Palm Coast for golf, tennis, boating, and beaching—which is why most people head down this way—the **The Lodge at Ocean Hammock** (105 16th Road, 386/445-3000, $$$) will fit the bill. (Note: They closed down their "older" property, the Harborside Inn at Palm Coast.) You can also rent condos at all sorts of exclusive gated resort communities hereabouts, but since we're not really fond of gates or exclusivity, we'll let you do the legwork.

COASTAL CUISINE

J.T.'s Seafood Shack (5225 North Oceanshore Boulevard, 386/446-4337, $$) and **Norriss Crazy Crab** (5949 North Oceanshore Boulevard, 386/447-5731, $$) are two roadside eateries that offer a bit of the vanishing "Old Florida."

Painters Hill

Painters Hill (pop. 400) serves as a buffer between the upper-crust golf communities of Hammock and Palm Coast and the RV and trailer parks of Beverly Beach. Its chief feature, insofar as this book is concerned, is **Varn Beach Park,** a county-run park with a free lot and dune walkovers that lead across healthy dunes to an orange-sand beach. Varn is a little larger than the trio of accesses in neighboring Hammock. There's not much out here but relative peace and quiet—and who could ask for anything more?

Somewhat anomalously, there's a biker bar in Painters Hill: the **Iron Boot Pub** (2982 North Oceanshore Boulevard, 386/439-0912). Please make no disparaging remarks about Dixie, if you wish to leave without an iron boot in your backside.

For more information, contact the Flagler County/Palm Coast Chamber of Commerce, 20 Airport Road, Bunnell, FL 32110, 386/437-0106, www.flaglercounty.com.

BEACHES

⑨ VARN BEACH PARK

Location: 3665 North Oceanshore Boulevard (A1A) in Painters Hill
Parking/Fees: free parking lot
Hours: sunrise–11 P.M. daily
Facilities: restrooms
Contact: Flagler County Parks and Recreation Department, 386/437-7589

Beverly Beach

Beverly Beach (pop. 450) hangs by its fingernails to Flagler County's coastline. An RV campground sits directly across the road from a mobile home park—not exactly the most scenic sight on A1A. But it is bound to be even less scenic when it is, inevitably, bought up and transformed into condos. "For Sale" signs dot the landscape where new homes will be built during the next market upturn.

For now, the community's most redeeming feature is **Beverly Beach,** a public park with a smattering of concrete picnic tables on the south side of town. From here access can be gained to the town's two-mile beach. But you can do better than that without going much farther by continuing south on A1A, just below Flagler Beach, to Gamble Rogers Memorial State Park (see separate write-up).

Beverly Beach's other prominent feature is the **Shark House** (2929 North Oceanshore Boulevard, 386/439-1000), which is "Home of Sharky's Lounge." This bar-restaurant perches precariously atop beachside bluffs, drawing crowds from miles in either direction.

For more information, contact Flagler County Palm Coast Chamber of Commerce, 20 Airport Road, Bunnell, FL 32110, 386/437-0106, www.flaglercounty.com.

BEACHES

BEVERLY BEACH

Location: at the south end of Beverly Beach, on A1A
Parking/Fees: free parking lot
Hours: 8 A.M.-10 P.M.
Facilities: restrooms and picnic tables
Contact: Beverly Beach Town Hall, 386/439-6888

Flagler Beach

Flagler Beach possesses a peculiar charm that comes from being an old-school type of fish. The pier is action central in "downtown" Flagler Beach. The old white wooden letters that spell out the town name on both sides of the pier shack's roof look so out-of-date, one wonders if they've been changed since Dwight Eisenhower was president. We found

Flagler Beach's step-back-in-time quality to be refreshing. Posted at the pier entrance are a multitude of snapshots of happy anglers holding their quarry. Some of the fish look bigger than the little boys holding them, while many of the older gents pictured here will no doubt die contented with a rod in their hands on this pier.

Flagler Beach stands out from the rest of Florida's East Coast for another reason. Its unusual-looking beach is stained a ruddy orange by coquina shells unique to the area. Finally, we must note that the beach is encroaching on the highway and it wouldn't surprise us to learn that sections of A1A will have to be relocated inland in the not-too-distant future. Already, the edges of the short cliffs at the back of the beach are inching precariously close to the highway's shoulder.

Flagler Beach (pop. 5,411) is, in many ways, the land that time forgot. They call it "the Peaceful Beach," but its peace is engendered not by conscious design but by a lack of interest from the outside world. The town's squat cinder-block cottages, modest homes, and low-rent motor courts appear unchanged since the 1950s. Modernity has passed by this little town, which celebrated its 85th birthday in 2005. Flagler Beach has an off-the-beaten-path charm, and we always enjoy passing through just to remember "how it was" in Florida not so many decades past.

How slow is it here? Practically every town in America has a website, and each of these websites usually has a section of Frequently Asked Questions (FAQs). Here is the FAQ for Flagler Beach, in its entirety:

- Q: Does the schedule for trash pickup change if there is a holiday?

- A: No. The City's Sanitation Department continues to provide trash pickup on holidays (including Christmas). There is no change in schedule.

Its beach runs for six miles. A1A hugs the shoreline closely here, its shoulder flirting with the edge of the eroding short bluffs that drop down to the beach. The bluffs are held in place with sea grass and prickly pear cactus. Numerous private dune crossovers lead to the beach, which is relatively narrow and steep in profile. The sand is a ruddy orange, colored by coquina from an offshore formation.

The town of Flagler Beach has been struggling almost from the beginning. Formerly named Ocean City and later renamed for railroad and tourism magnate Henry Flagler in 1923, the town was the site of the apparently magnificent four-story Flagler Beach Hotel, which thrived during the 1920s and died during the Depression.

If truth be told, Flagler Beach hasn't made great strides since the Depression. It's holding on but hasn't kept pace with the rest of Florida's East Coast beach towns. To our thinking that is a good thing. There is something comforting about a coastal community that continues to resist change. No doubt this is what attracts the same families here year after year. We wonder how long it will be able to manage the feat of walking in place. But we've been wondering that for a long time now.

In town, there's the 844 foot Flagler Beach Pier ($4 to fish, $1 to walk out) and a lot of angle-in free parking in its vicinity. The outer 30 feet of the pier collapsed from the force of waves kicked up by Hurricane Jeanne, but repairs have been made. Lining the west side of A1A are nondescript motels, restaurants whose specialties tend toward pizza, and a pretty cool-looking surf shop. The town doesn't project much character, but for those families who want nothing more from a vacation than a rented house or motel room with a beach across the road, it's perfectly fine. And here's a neat piece of trivia: Exit 284 (Flagler Beach) is closest to the beach of any exit along I-95 between Maine and Florida.

For more information, contact the Flagler Beach Palm Coast Chamber of Commerce, 20 Airport Road, Bunnell, FL 32110, 386/437-0106, www.flaglercounty.com/fbcc.

BEACHES

Flagler Beach offers nothing more (or less) than a modest good time on a beach that has to rank as one of the state's most undiscovered coastal locales. Metered parking is available near the Flagler Beach Pier. A gray wooden boardwalk runs along the beach for a short distance. Families and surfers hoot and holler in the water. The break by the pier makes for the best surfing, especially after a storm. Running for several miles along the length of the town are pull-offs for roadside parking and secluded access to the beach (no facilities).

Interestingly, a public pool in nearby Palm Coast, the **Frieda Zamba Aquatic Complex** (4520 Belle Terre Parkway, 386/986-4741), bears the name of a famous local female surfer who still makes her home in Flagler Beach and can sometimes be seen riding waves by the pier.

11 FLAGLER BEACH

Location: Flagler Beach's six-mile municipal beach has its center at Moody Boulevard (S.R. 100) and Oceanshore Boulevard (A1A), at Flagler Beach Pier.

Parking/Fees: free street parking

Hours: none posted

Facilities: lifeguards (seasonal), restrooms, and showers

Contact: Flagler Beach City Hall, 386/517-2000

RECREATION AND ATTRACTIONS

- **Ecotourism:** Tropical Kayaks and Boat Rentals, Palm Coast Marina, Palm Coast, 386/445-0506

- **Marina:** Flagler Bridge Marina, 131 Lehigh Avenue, Flagler Beach, 386/439-0081

- **Pier:** Flagler Beach Pier, 215 South Oceanshore Boulevard, Flagler Beach, 386/439-3891

THE QUIET COAST

- **Rainy-Day Attraction:** Marineland, 9600 North Oceanshore Boulevard (A1A), Marineland, 904/460-1275 or 888/279-9194

- **Shopping/Browsing:** Oceanshore Boulevard (A1A) between Moody Boulevard (S.R. 100) and South 7th Street, Flagler Beach

- **Surf Shop:** Z Wave Surf Shop, 400 South Oceanshore Boulevard, 386/439-9283, Flagler Beach

- **Vacation Rentals:** Palm Coast Flagler Beach Realty, 500 North Oceanshore Boulevard, Flagler Beach, 386/439-2699

ACCOMMODATIONS

A1A is lined with small, old motels. They're the kind of places that only a surfer—which is to say, someone oblivious to his or her surroundings—could love. There's one notable exception: **Topaz** (1224 South Oceanshore Boulevard, 386/439-3301, $$), a unique and well-maintained "motel, hotel, cafe, and porch." Its antique-filled parlor, including an authentic player piano, is worth checking out. The pipe-roofed, red-doored, white stucco buildings are a striking sight on an otherwise bland stretch of highway. You can stay in the motel or the more quaintly done-up hotel section. Nightly rates range from an unbelievable $46 (for a motel room) up to $140 (for an antique-filled hotel room with Jacuzzi). You can even book a room for an entire month for $1,300—a bargain at any beach, on any coastline.

Of the less stylish lodgings, two of the more appealing ones are **Whale Watch Motel** (2448 South Oceanshore Boulevard, 386/439-2545, $) and **Beach Front Motel** (1544 South Oceanshore Boulevard, 386/439-0089, $). Their names tell their tales.

COASTAL CUISINE

The pickings are pretty plain in Flagler Beach. **Kings' Oceanside Restaurant & Patio Cafe** (208 South Oceanshore Boulevard, 386/439-0380, $$) sits across from the pier. We noticed that the list of early-bird specials didn't include any seafood entrees, although we were tempted to return for their Friday-night Buffalo-style fish fry.

Two miles south of town lies **High Tides at Snack Jack** (2805 South A1A, 386/439-3344, $$), a modest-looking seafood restaurant perched directly above the ocean. In the small, sandy parking lot is a sign that ludicrously offers "Valet Parking." (Out here in the middle of nowhere?!)

NIGHTLIFE

The Golden Lion Cafe (500 North A1A, 386/439-3004, $$) is not as regal as the name might lead you to believe—this is, after all, Flagler Beach—but it's kind of the hub of activity in this little town. They book live music—folk, C&W, lite-rock duos, that kind of thing.

To our eyes and ears, the best place to hang ten in Flagler Beach is **Finnegan's Beachside Pub** (101 North A1A, 386/439-7755). You can't miss it: the mural outside depicts leprechauns on surfboards.

Gamble Rogers Memorial State Recreation Area

Gamble Rogers State Recreation Area is about 2.5 miles south of A1A's junction with S.R. 100 in Flagler Beach. Purchased by the state back in 1954, and originally known as Flagler Beach State Park, it was renamed for beloved Florida folksinger/storyteller James Gamble Rogers, who died in 1991 while trying to save a drowning victim.

This 145-acre park makes the most of its relatively compact size. On the east side of A1A are 34 oceanfront campsites and beach access. On the west side are picnic areas, a boat basin on the Intracoastal, and a nature trail. The beach is typical of those in Flagler County: orange-hued and narrow, with a somewhat steep profile. The fishing is great on both the ocean side (pompano, bluefish, drum) and in the Intracoastal (speckled trout, redfish, flounder). Bring a tent and some fishing gear, and you'll have it made in the shade.

For more information, contact Gamble Rogers Memorial State Park, 3100 South A1A, Flagler Beach, FL 32136, 386/517-2086, www.floridastateparks.org.

BEACHES

12 GAMBLE ROGERS MEMORIAL STATE RECREATION AREA

   BEST (

Location: 2.5 miles south of Flagler Beach, along A1A

Parking/Fees: $4 entrance fee per vehicle. Camping fees are $23.

Hours: 8 A.M.-sundown

Facilities: restrooms, picnic tables, and showers

Contact: Gamble Rogers Memorial State Recreation Area, 386/517-2086, www.floridastateparks.org

THE QUIET COAST

DAYTONA BEACH AND THE SPORTS COAST

The Daytona area is known as the "Birthplace of Speed." It was on the hard-packed sands of Ormond Beach that the sport of automobile racing got its start 1903. It has evolved into the billion-dollar phenomenon known as the National Association for Stock Car Auto Racing (NASCAR, for short), which these days is claimed to be America's second-most popular sport. The city of Daytona has been NASCAR's headquarters since its founding here in 1948, and car racing generates $800 million in economic activity for Volusia County. Daytona International Speedway is the site of the Daytona 500 and a full calendar of other races.

The Daytona area also caters to America's other national pastimes: golf and baseball. There are 30 golf courses in Volusia County, and the minor-league Daytona Cubs play a 34-game home schedule at Jackie Robinson Stadium. Jackie Robinson—one of the game's greatest players, and a bonafide national hero who broke the color line in baseball's Major Leagues—played here before being called up to the Brooklyn Dodgers.

Beyond all that, many millions of yearly visitors surf, swim, boat, and drive along the beach. In Volusia County, 16 out of 47 miles of beach are open to vehicular traffic (speed limit: 10 mph). For all these reasons, we regard Daytona Beach and surrounding communities as Florida's "Sports Coast."

Ormond-by-the-Sea

Ormond-by-the-Sea (pop. 14,328) is "an unincorporated residential community" on the barrier island east of the Halifax River. Its isolation is accentuated by its seemingly precarious geography. Up here at Volusia County's north end, the island narrows to a thin point.

© PARKE PUTERBAUGH

This neck of the county is the site of North Peninsula State Park, another jewel in Florida's peerless park system.

For more information, contact the Ormond Beach Chamber of Commerce, 165 West Granada Boulevard, Ormond Beach, FL 32174, 386/677-3454, www.ormond-chamber.com.

BEACHES

The relative lack of development in Ormond-by-the-Sea has had positive consequences on its beachfront. With the possible exception of Lighthouse Point (down by Ponce Inlet), Ormond-by-the-Sea and neighboring North Peninsula State Park are home to the healthiest dune fields in all of Volusia County's 43 miles of beaches.

North Peninsula State Park is a 900-acre work-in-progress created as part of a massive, multi-state effort to save the endangered loggerhead sea turtle. It is primarily a nature preserve and refuge. No parking is allowed along the road (there is a free lot), and no dune crossovers are provided. However, you can hike north from Ormond-by-the-Sea (no beach driving!) and have a beautiful, secluded two-mile beach all to yourself.

An avuncular park ranger reported that couples stroll up and, under cover of dark, "do what young couples will do." For the less amorous, surfcasting along this stretch of coast—for redfish, whitefish, and bluefish—is enough to make an angler's eyes well up with salt water. Fish get trapped inside the offshore bars, and fishermen have a field day casting for them.

Ormond-by-the-Sea has 2.5 miles of beachfront, with dune walkovers provided from Essex Street down to Ocean Breeze Court. There are two county-run beach parks here: **Bicentennial Park,** which stretches from the Halifax River to the ocean, and **Tom Renick Park,** a few blocks south. Ormond-by-the-Sea is off limits to beach driving. At this erosion-prone end of Volusia County, the beaches require occasional renourishment after hard winter storms.

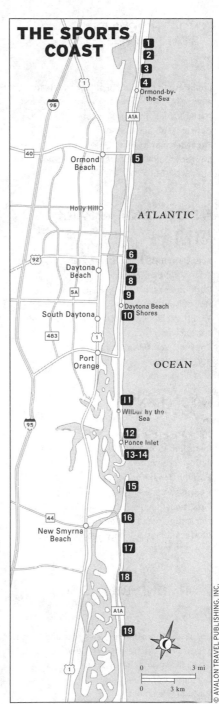

THE SPORTS COAST

© AVALON TRAVEL PUBLISHING, INC.

1 NORTH PENINSULA STATE PARK

Location: 10 miles north of Ormond Beach along A1A
Parking/fees: free parking lot
Hours: 8 A.M.-sunset
Facilities: none
Contact: Gamble Rogers Memorial State Park, 386/517-2086

2 BICENTENNIAL PARK

Location: 1800 North Oceanshore Boulevard in Ormond-by-the-Sea
Parking/fees: free parking lot
Hours: sunrise-sunset
Facilities: lifeguards, restrooms, picnic tables, and showers
Contact: Volusia County Beach Services, 386/239-7873

3 TOM RENICK PARK

Location: 1565 North Oceanshore Boulevard in Ormond-by-the-Sea
Parking/fees: free parking lot
Hours: sunrise-sunset
Facilities: lifeguards (seasonal), restrooms, picnic tables, and showers
Contact: Volusia County Beach Services, 386/239-7873

4 ORMOND-BY-THE-SEA

Location: approximately 25 street-end beach accesses with dune walkovers between Essex Street and Ocean Breeze Court in Ormond-by-the-Sea
Parking/fees: none

Hours: sunrise-sunset
Facilities: none
Contact: Volusia County Beach Services, 386/239-7873

COASTAL CUISINE

Alfie's Restaurant (1666 Oceanshore Boulevard, 386/441-7024, $) has won several "best breakfast in Volusia County" awards. You can eat your omelette while staring out to sea. They also serve lunch and dinner, including early-bird specials noon–6 P.M., with emphases on seafood, steak, and Italian dishes.

Ormond Beach

Ormond Beach (pop. 36,000) lays claim to the title "Birthplace of Speed" because automobile racing debuted here in 1903. That was when Ransom E. Olds and Alexander Winston raced each other at Ormond Beach, reaching the then-amazing speed of 68 mph. Races would continue to be held on the hard-packed sands until 1935, during which year a record speed of nearly 300 mph (you read right) was reached.

On first glance, Ormond Beach and Daytona Beach might appear to be more or less the same: more of the same beach, more hotels and motels lining A1A. Yet Ormond Beach is a sizable and unique town in its own right, stretching west onto the mainland via S.R. 40 (Granada Boulevard) and U.S. 1 (Dixie Highway). Look closer and there are obvious aesthetic differences between them. Stated simply, Ormond Beach is a more calm, composed residential community that has resisted the urge to turn its beachfront into a vertical Lego project.

There are beachside hotels on Ormond Beach, to be sure, and restaurants and shopping centers occupy the inland side of A1A. But Ormond Beach is a cut above its neighbor's towering sprawl. Let us make this argument by describing what happens where the two towns meet. Even if there weren't a town-limits sign,

THE SPORTS COAST

BEST BEACHES

(Daytona Beach: Best for Families (page 95)

(Main Street Pier and Beach: Top 25, Best for Surfing (page 95)

(Smyrna Dunes Park: Best for Surfing (page 107)

the line between Ormond Beach and Daytona Beach is plain as day, as the latter commences with the twin eyesores of a McDonald's and a 25-story condo construction site.

Ormond Beach wears its size well, investing its considerable wealth in home improvements and public services. Its sterling pedigree dates back to the days of John D. Rockefeller, who built a winter home ("The Casements") here. The Casements (25 Riverside Drive, 386/676-3216) has been beautifully restored and is open to the public as a free museum and cultural center. It's noted for its Hungarian folk art and Boy Scout memorabilia.

Other local residents have carried forward Rockefeller's moneyed legacy, most notably Ron Rice, president of Hawaiian Tropic tanning products, whose corporate headquarters and palatial home are found in Ormond Beach. You can't miss the latter, with its "RR" monogram on the iron fence along Oceanshore Boulevard. Rice has been a generous citizen, too, underwriting a lot of the cost to equip Volusia County's award-winning beach patrol.

One of the legends of the surfing world, Lisa Andersen, makes her home in Ormond Beach, too. Winner of three consecutive world titles, Andersen has been described by *Surfing* magazine as "the mother of all champions, perhaps the most radical woman surfer of all time."

Ormond Beach is naturally blessed in other ways. It's home to two state parks, and both offer unique natural settings. **Bulow Creek State Park** (3351 Old Dixie Highway, 386/677-4645) is centered around the 800-year-old Fairchild live oak tree, which serves

as a monument to local preservationists. It has, according to the park brochure, "withstood Seminole Indian wars, developers, fires, and countless owners, each with his own vision of the land's purpose." A short hiking trail leads through an oak hammock. Not far away are the ruins of the old Bulow Plantation, a former cotton, rice, sugar, and indigo plantation that is now a state historic site.

The other notable parkland is **Tomoka State Park** (2099 North Beach Street, 386/676-4050), near the confluence of the Tomoka and Halifax Rivers. It was the site of a "Nocoroco," a Timucuan Indian village that was cleared (along with much of the forest) to make way for a plantation in the 1770s. Tomoka is presently returning to its natural state as an oak hammock. A tents-only campground on the river affords access to the inland tidal waterways. Canoes are rented, and a guided canoe tour explores the plantation ruins. There's also a short nature trail and even a sandy riverside beach at the north picnic area.

For more information, contact the Ormond Beach Chamber of Commerce, 165 West Granada Boulevard, Ormond Beach, FL 32174, 386/677-3454, www.ormondchamber.com.

BEACHES

Ormond Beach has a three-mile beach, running from Neptune Avenue to Harvard Drive, with a handful of publicly accessible dune crossovers. Most of the Ormond Beach crossovers are private, which explains their gates, locks, and makeshift appearances. Ormond

THE SPORTS COAST

Beach has proven to be a tough nut to crack, in terms of public beach access. It's easier to drive on the beach here than it is to park off the beach and walk onto it.

The sand has a different texture and color up this way than it does in Daytona Beach. Its reddish-brown hue comes from an offshore coquina reef and is most pronounced in the spring and summer. The particles are coarser and therefore don't pack so well. It's a blessing in disguise, because the softer sand makes for difficult beach driving. Even under the best conditions, only a small portion of Ormond Beach—near the intersection of Oceanshore Boulevard and S.R. 40—can be driven.

5 ORMOND BEACH

Location: three miles of beach, from Neptune Avenue to Harvard Drive in Ormond Beach
Parking/fees: $5 per day to park on the beach (free in December and January)
Hours: sunrise-sunset
Facilities: none
Contact: Volusia County Beach Services, 386/239-7873

ACCOMMODATIONS

Ormond Beach handles the spillover from Daytona Beach during special events like Bike Week, Race Weekends, and what's left of Spring Break. The city has a loyal following among vacationing families, too. The huge flagship hotels are located at its southern end, near Daytona Beach, along Atlantic Avenue (A1A). The top choice is the **Casa Del Mar Beach Resort** (621 South Atlantic Avenue, 386/672-4550, $$$). A huge beachside pool deck and kitchen facilities in every room are pluses. Another beachside tower with similar amenities is the **Granada Inn** (51 South Atlantic Avenue, 386/672-7550, $$$). If you're thinking of staying at either during summer weekends or special events, make reservations well in advance. You can also get a per-

fectly fine oceanfront room at the **Quality Inn Oceanside** (251 South Atlantic Avenue, 386/672-8510, $$). All three are in a beach-driving zone, so watch out for vehicles on your way to the water's edge.

The **Coral Sands Inn** (1009 Oceanshore Boulevard, 386/441-1831, $$$) offers a quieter alternative at the north end of Ormond Beach There are 86 rooms in the main building and several seaside cottages on the spacious property, which also includes a pool and volleyball and badminton courts. All rooms have refrigerators, and many have fully equipped kitchens.

COASTAL CUISINE

Stonewood Grill and Tavern (100 S. Atlantic Ave., 386/671-1200 $$$) originated in Ormond Beach and has grown to half a dozen franchises. Simply prepared but sensationally tasty oak-grilled seafood items are served here. The blackened salmon and grilled mahi, weighing in at a hefty nine ounces, are among the best we've had in Florida. Accompaniments included rice pilaf and creamed spinach, both quite good. Unlike a lot of restaurants that pad the bill with à la carte charges, fresh-fish entrees at Stonewood include a salad and two sides, and they're priced fairly at $18–20. Smaller, six-ounce cuts of fish with more elaborate preparations—such as Creole grouper, Caribbean mahimahi, and a dynamite citrus-flavored salmon—are other tempting options. The atmosphere is Early Steakhouse—dark wood and low lighting—and the entire operation, from servers to servings, is first-rate.

Other than Stonewood Grill, Ormond Beach shares with Daytona Beach the same mix of franchises and unexceptional non-franchised restaurants.

NIGHTLIFE

The "World Famous" **Iron Horse Saloon** (1068 North U.S. 1, 386/677-1550) is a biker bar whose main attraction is the Wall of Death, upon whose banked track Harley riders strut their stuff. This biker palace is located out on Dixie Highway (U.S. 1), a good five miles from the beach. You can call us a couple of Dixie chickens, but we steered clear of the Iron Horse, pointing our wheels instead to **Billy's Tap Room** (58 East Granada Boulevard, 386/672-1910). Billy's has the decided advantages of beach proximity, a local crowd, and a storied history. Billy's was founded in 1922 as a *tea*room, affiliated with the old Ormond Hotel. Billy MacDonald, who'd managed the lounges at the Astor and Plaza hotels in New York City, was brought down to run the place, which eventually began selling homemade beer. With those roots, it's no wonder that Billy's closely resembles the Plaza Hotel's famed Oak Room.

Daytona Beach and Daytona Beach Shores

Before we get started, let us state up front that in many ways we like Daytona Beach. It has a long history as an affordable family beach,

and we are all in favor of communities with a come-one, come-all attitude. After all, everyone deserves a day at the beach. But Daytona Beach and its neighboring shoreline communities are in a period of transition, and this has created some instability and confusion, in our opinion. There's still much to like about Daytona Beach, though it appears to be moving away from its core constituency (or at least trying to do so). Maybe there's nothing town planners can do about it, since money flows into a community and does what it will. But if the following few paragraphs seem unduly harsh, it's only because we're calling it exactly as we've seen and experienced it.

Daytona Beach is a tale of two sides of the street. On the ocean side of Atlantic Avenue, new and recently arrived hotel towers—such as the Hilton Oceanfront and Ocean Walk Resort—set an upscale agenda. By contrast, the landward side of the street is replete with single-story businesses geared toward those with shallower pockets: cheap motels, convenience marts, pizza stands, and shops advertising henna tattoos, body piercing, biker gear, cat-house lingerie, and liquor.

© PARKE PUTERBAUGH

Daytona Beach

THE SPORTS COAST

DAYTONA USA: A 250 MPH TOURIST TRAP

Daytona USA is billed as "the Ultimate Motorsports Attraction." It is part museum, part shopping mall, and as complete a tourist trap as has ever been devised.

Many visitors to the Daytona area come to immerse themselves in the sport. If car racing can be said to be a religion, then Daytona USA — located next to Daytona International Speedway — is its temple. Even though this NASCAR theme park makes a ton of money, it's all a little crass. For instance, Daytona USA is, like racing itself, as rife with product placement as Washington, D.C. is with special interests. Let's not beat around the Busch. Everywhere you look, there's a corporate logo. They're affixed to every square foot of every racecar on display and stitched onto every square inch of clothing worn by the drivers. At Daytona USA, logos are plastered onto every conceivable surface upon which your eyes might fall, your feet might tread, and your ass might rest. They are draped from the rafters. They hang from the walls. They are attached to every TV monitor, loudspeaker, banner, stanchion, pole, beam, pipe, window, curtain, writing implement, brochure, turnstile, door handle, button, knob and slot. They are even emblazoned on your admission ticket.

Despite massive corporate underwriting, you must pay through the nose to enter Daytona USA. It costs $21.50 per person to get in ($18.50 for seniors, $15.50 for children 6-12, free for kids five and under). This fee gains visitors admittance to the main building, half of whose space is devoted to a gift shop and video game arcade where nothing is free and little is reasonably priced. Admission also includes access to a 45-minute IMAX movie, entitled *NASCAR 3D: The IMAX Experience,* which is basically a glorified NASCAR advertorial that runs six times daily.

Here's what you get for your money. For starters, you learn about the early days of competitive motoring. It originated in 1902 atop the hard-packed sands of Daytona Beach and Ormond Beach, which are refereed to as "Birthplace of Speed." Through vintage artifacts and display copy, you see how the sport developed into the big-time enterprise it is today.

Visitors also have access to interactive programs. You can pretend to be on a pit crew or interview a driver via computer. These hands-on attractions are far and away the most popular part of the exhibit space. Thus they're typically 10-deep with

On our first night in town during a recent visit, we got a taste of Daytona Beach's less savory side. We were walking along the sidewalk from our hotel to the Oyster Bar, one of our favorite hangouts in Florida. It had recently rained, and some dirty water had puddled beside the curb. A carload of yahoos swerved into the gutter as they passed, intentionally splashing us with oily liquid. After cursing, gesticulating and then slowly drying out, we came to see some humor in the situation. We decided we'd been paid a visit by the Daytona Beach Welcome Wagon. We later learned that a few days earlier, a house painter who'd had several too many fell to his death from a parking garage onto the very slab of sidewalk where

we'd been soaked. So it goes in Daytona Beach. Just check the local paper on any given day, and you are likely to read the most unbelievable—to the point of black comedy—tales of death and criminal mayhem.

"Big Beach. Big Fun." is the upbeat motto of Daytona Beach (pop. 65,000). It's a town in transition, trying to upgrade its image without driving away its steadiest customers. Ordinary folks—families, collegians, Harley riders, and party animals from all over the country—have been streaming here for decades. The drawing card has been the promise of a "big beach" and "big fun" at relatively small prices. Not every coastal community can be South Beach or Palm Beach. The reality is that some places

kids waiting their turn to twirl the bolts, so you can forget about taking a crack at the tire jack if there's a crowd. A bit of trivia: Did you know that a good pit crew can change four tires, fill two tanks of gas, and tend to the biological needs of a driver in 20 seconds?

A tram tour of **Daytona International Speedway** costs an additional $7.50. On the tour, you are driven slowly around one lap of the 2.5-mile track and given a viewing of the 31° banked curves (which must be driven at speeds of at least 95 mph to maintain control), the grandstands (seating capacity 100,000), and the infield (which can accommodate another 40,000). The Daytona 500 is run on this very track each February, and various other races are staged here from October to March.

Our tram tour guide was given to well-practiced witticisms and histrionic patter. "Forty-two gallons of 110-octane fuel would barely supply these voracious beasts for the first 100 miles!" he exclaimed. (In a time of gas shortages, how is this a good thing?) Were we to recommend anything at Daytona USA, it would be the tram tour (which is offered on the half-hour 9:30 A.M.–5:30 P.M.) But please don't misinterpret that as an endorsement.

Annual racing events at Daytona International Speedway include the Rolex 24, the Budweiser Shootout, the Gatorade Dual, and the absolutely darling Hershey's Kissables 300. Then there's racing's premier event, the Daytona 500, which is held in mid-February (in 2006 it fell on February 19) and is, for now, free of corporate attachment. Tickets to the "Great American Race," as it's known, currently go for $99 and are looking to break that $100 threshold any year now.

"Fan Zone" has become a popular race-day attraction. Purchase of this pre-race pass lets fans to stroll across the track and grassy oval over to Pit Road, where there's entertainment and the opportunity to hang out where the action is. Fan Zone passes run $20–35 for most races (and $90 for the Daytona 500).

For race information, contact Daytona International Speedway, 1801 West International Speedway Boulevard, Daytona Beach, FL 32114, 386/254-2700 (general information) or 386/253-7223 (ticket office), www.daytonaintlspeedway.com. For attraction information, contact Daytona USA, 1801 West International Speedway Boulevard, Daytona Beach, FL 32114, 386/947 6800, www.daytonausa.com. Daytona USA is open 9 A.M.–7 P.M. every day except Christmas.

THE SPORTS COAST

exist to serve those who don't run in the same circles as Paris Hilton and Donald Trump. Such a place is Daytona Beach. It is indeed a big beach, and we don't begrudge them their fair share of convention hotels and luxury condominiums. However, we'd urge them to remain mindful of their blue-collar roots.

We might be a few years too late with our counsel, however. There are 30+ new condo projects in various states of construction in Daytona Beach and neighboring Daytona Beach Shores (to the south), joining those already existing. The talk is that "big money" has finally found Daytona Beach, taking advantage of the fact that the area has been overlooked, undervalued, and ripe for plun-

der. The spate of hurricanes in 2004 created a fire-sale scenario that, ironically, further ignited the building boom. Damaged properties—often mom-and-pop motels well past their prime—sold out to developers who are erecting condos and "condo hotels" in their place. This epidemic of verticality is particularly evident at the south end of Daytona Beach and throughout Daytona Beach Shores. Wilbur by the Sea has retained its residential character, but disappointingly, the building boom resumes in parts of Ponce Inlet, which ought to have known better.

It struck us how architecturally undistinguished these constructions are. With their institutional facades, drab colors and numberless beehive-like cells, they resemble hospitals and dormitories, not living quarters (at least from the outside). Some of them reach 20 stories in Daytona Beach Shores, which has become as unrecognizably overbuilt as Panama City Beach on the Florida Panhandle. Constructed too close to the surf zone, as usual, they all look like an easy mark for the next big hurricane.

It's no wonder developers have targeted Daytona Beach. The Daytona Beach area has sandy assets in abundance: 23 miles of hard-packed beaches, 11 miles of which are open to vehicular traffic. Beach driving has given the area its unique identity. The practice dates back to the days when car races were held on the sands of Volusia County—Ormond, Daytona, and New Smyrna beaches—between 1903 and 1935. These days, pro-racing rituals are conducted at the days-of-thunder cathedral known as the Daytona International Speedway, five miles inland. But beach driving (not racing) is still permitted on Daytona Beach. You ought to try it sometime: pay your five bucks, drive onto the beach, and pull right up to wherever you want to drop your beach towel for the day.

Much talk has been made about reshaping Daytona as an ecotourist destination, a family destination, and a place where historical attractions and the arts can flourish. Traces of all of those elements are already in place. Still, despite its lately more rarefied self-image, Daytona has a somewhat oversimplified reputation as a party town to live down. To be blunt about it, any makeover can only be so radical, since auto racing, beach driving, and the periodic influx of bikers will have to remain a viable part of whatever new identity the community hopes to assume. It's a matter of recognizing economic realities and striking the proper balance.

One tradition it's largely managed to tame is Spring Break. In the 1980s Daytona Beach become known as a mecca for misbehavior, and Spring Breakers faithfully trekked here on various colleges' staggered mid-semester breaks. The collegiate crush peaked in 1989,

when 400,000 kids showed up. A few too many balcony-diving mishaps put the city on alert that it "had to take the edge off Spring Break," as one local official euphemistically put it. In the words of one lifelong resident, "People thought we were a rundown party town."

In fact, Daytona Beach toned down their Spring Break dependency by appealing to other elements, courting convention business, motorcycle enthusiasts, and those ever-reliable NASCAR fans. Spring Break now draws less than half the former inundation, spaced out over a longer period. Also, it no longer attracts the rowdiest Spring Breakers. They moved on to Panama City Beach and then to more un-bridled resort towns in Mexico and the Caribbean, where one can legally imbibe at 18.

In their place, Daytona Beach welcomes bikers with open arms. The biggest week on Daytona's calendar year is Bike Week (the first week of March), when as many as 400,000 two-wheelers arrive. Equally popular is Bike-toberfest, a Halloween bacchanal that caters to the Harley crowd. The image painted by local merchants is a far cry from the bikers depicted in old Roger Corman flicks, where town fathers hid their women, boarded up the windows, and oiled the shotgun as leather-jacketed heathens roared down Main Street. As one motel owner put it, "I wish all our guests were as courteous and generous as the bikers. They're the biggest spenders and the best tippers. And the nicest people you'll ever want to deal with."

The world's largest, sleekest, and most successful Harley-Davidson dealership is located in downtown Daytona. It's as stylish and neon-laden as any Mercedes-Benz franchise in Bremen, Frankfurt, or Palm Beach. Think about it: Anyone who can afford to drop $30,000 on a Harley isn't exactly an indigent outlaw. It may seem ironic, but room rates get jacked up for Bike Week and then fall again for Spring Break. "The hotels charge what the market will bear, and the kids don't have that kind of money," we were told.

All of this biker boosterism notwithstand-

HOW A MINOR LEAGUER MADE MAJOR HISTORY IN DAYTONA BEACH

Daytona Beach is home to a rich legacy of African-American history. Among the noteworthy figures were educators Howard Thurman and Mary McLeod Bethune, the latter having opened the Daytona Literary and Industrial School for Training Negro Girls in 1904. Bethune's school is now, as Bethune-Cookman, one of the premier black universities in the nation. Its 60-acre campus contains 33 buildings, many listed as National Historic Landmarks.

Another great, if overlooked, event in black history occurred here on March 17, 1946. On that date, a scuffling young second baseman for the minor league Montreal Royals played in a preseason game against his team's parent club, the Brooklyn Dodgers. Many fans are under the mistaken impression that the so-called "color line" – that segregationist code that barred black players from Major League Baseball – was not broken until the following April, when Robinson played his first game at Brooklyn's Ebbets Field. Not true. Robinson got a taste of the pressure-cooker that awaited him over the next two decades in Daytona Beach in 1946.

The ballgame was to have taken place in a neighboring town, but the Florida Crackers there raised a holy stink. A black man playing against white men! Well, we never! Due largely to the intercession of Mary Bethune, Daytona Beach opened its arms to the future Hall of Famer. The game was played, the color line was broken, and America was incalculably richer for the gesture.

Daytona Beach continues to open her arms to the late baseball legend. The city has renamed the field where this historic game took place Jackie Robinson Ballpark. In 2005, the town oversaw a $1.4 million renovation that will establish a museum onsite to honor the great player. The ballpark is located in the downtown waterfront area and is now home to the Daytona Beach Cubs (www.daytonacubs.com), a farm team for the Chicago Cubs that plays in the Florida State League. We dropped by the ballpark during the 2005 season and, even though torrential rain was forecast, a crowd had lined up early to catch the action – including busloads of schoolkids. Ah, baseball.

ing, half a million bikers is still half a million bikers, and the bars and storefronts on Main Street cater to that lifestyle with darkened windows, rebel flags, and skull-and-crossbones imagery. There is little here that suggests the "family vacationer" the city aims to court. But to give the bikers their due, with half a million hogs on the streets during Bike Week 2005, there were only five misdemeanor arrests, two minor accidents, and no fatalities. You couldn't get that many church folk together and have so little trouble.

To be fair, there are some genuine oases of culture hereabouts. Daytona is home to the **Southeast Museum of Photography** (Daytona Beach Community College, 1200 International Speedway Boulevard, 386/254-

4475), Bethune-Cookman College (which has one of the world's richest collections of African-American culture and history), and the **Museum of Arts and Sciences** (1040 Museum Boulevard, 386/255-0285). During one of our trips, the art museum had both a room full of Picasso's handmade pottery and a remarkable exhibit on Florida's cracker culture. Now that is what we mean by "striking the proper balance"!

Make no mistake, though. Daytona Beach will always have a lived-in look, sound, and smell. Try as they might, there are pockets of seediness and blight that won't go away anytime soon. They are the occupational hazards of being an affordable, egalitarian beach destination. Daytona continues to attract a mixed bag: Canadians and Cajuns, car nuts and tree huggers, hard-bodies and lard-asses, body piercers and business people. The town is a funhouse mirror of society. You can peer into it and find elements both appealing and ugly. Nothing will change or hide that fact. You can't make a silk purse out of a sea cow's ear. But we love sea cows, and we generally like Daytona Beach just fine.

There's one more thing, besides cars and beachgoers, that moves across the sand: sea turtles. In their slow-going way, they've helped to modify the character of Volusia County's beaches. The establishment of "natural conservation zones" has provided sea turtles with stretches of sand where they can nest in peace. As a consequence, life in Volusia County, while still motoring at a pleasurable velocity, has slowed to a more relaxed pace.

For more information, contact the Daytona Beach Area Convention and Visitors Bureau, 126 East Orange Avenue, Daytona Beach, FL 32114, 386/255-0415 or 800/544-0415, www.daytonabeach.com; or the Daytona Beach Shores Chamber of Commerce, 3048 South Atlantic Avenue, Daytona Beach Shores, FL 32118, 386/761-7163, www.db-schamber.com.

BEACHES

The beach in **Daytona Beach** has narrowed somewhat over the years. We can remember when it was a few football fields wide at low tide. These days, high tide brings it creeping ever closer to the seawalls. Hurricanes have not been kind to Daytona Beach in recent years, and you see signs of damage along the oceanfront. The main casualties have been mom-and-pop hotels that didn't survive the big blows.

The heart of Daytona Beach (what they call the "Core Area") is the **Main Street Pier and Beach** and the concrete boardwalk that stretches north from it for about half a mile, up to Ocean Front Resort. It's nothing fancy. There's some boardwalk food stalls and a few thrill rides, and it's a good place to stroll as

the sun starts retiring for the day. The pier is open 6 A.M.–10 P.M. ($3.50 to fish, $1 to walk out on it). You might recall that a 200-foot section of the pier collapsed into the ocean during Hurricane Floyd in 1999, but it withstood the onslaught of hurricanes in 2004 without problem.

The only developed beachfront park per se in Daytona Beach is **Sun Splash Park,** which is six blocks south of the pier. An interactive water fountain is the most striking feature. It also has a playground, volleyball nets, picnic areas, two ramps onto the beach, and a decent-sized parking lot. It's a nice surprise, all the way around, and Daytona Beach could stand to have more places like it.

From Ormond Beach to Ponce Inlet, the shoreline runs for 23 unbroken miles. The most noticeable thing about this strand, besides its remarkable length, is that vehicles—including RVs and trucks under 33 feet long—are allowed on 11 of those 23 miles. The sand is composed of fine quartz grains, with few rock or shell fragments, which results in a smooth, hard-packed surface. On sunny days over busy weekends, as many as 10,000 vehicles crowd the beach. During spring tides—the highest high tides, occurring during full moons—the beach might be closed to wheeled traffic, especially if there's a rough winter storm, too.

Daytona Beach (5 miles) and Daytona Beach Shores (5.5 miles) are neighboring communities. Daytona Beach is the wild and crazy beach town, dense with people, cars, and bars, while **Daytona Beach Shores** is, as they used to put it, "the quiet end of the world's most famous beach." The differences have been eroding (like the beach) as condominium construction imposes architectural uniformity, but in a general sense it still applies that Daytona Beach is lively and Daytona Beach Shores less so. Knowing that, you can aim your car and beach blanket accordingly.

Daytona Beach Shores (like Daytona Beach and Ormond Beach) is pretty darn stingy with public beach access. (To us, pedestrian accessways between condos don't count for much of anything.) **Frank Rendon Park** is a respite from the cranes and jackhammers. Named for a community activist who would probably be horrified at what's become of his community, this recently expanded park is a family-friendly spot with picnic shelters, a playground, and a decent-sized parking lot.

Besides driving, the beach here is great for walking, jogging, bicycling, volleyball, surfing, and swimming. Water temperatures climb well into the eighties in summer, making for easy immersion. There are occasional problems with rip currents on outgoing tides. We mention this only as a precaution and will quickly console you with the fact that the Volusia County Beach Patrol maintains a staff of 65 full-time Beach Patrol officers and 300 part-time lifeguards in its stands and towers. This eagle-eyed, cross-trained, award-winning crew surveys 47 miles of shoreline in Volusia County, including Ormond Beach and New Smyrna Beach. In addition to the beach towers, they maintain five large substations, each equipped with an observation tower that allows for a long view of the beaches. Annually, they average 3,000 rescues. Given that as many as 200,000 people may be on the beach at one time, some of them having imbibed a bit of "liquid courage"—in the words of a beach-patrol officer—this is indeed an impressive and heroic feat.

Surfers try their luck on either side of the Main Street Pier (especially the north side). They must stay a 100 yards minimum from the pier's pilings. It isn't Southern California, but when the surf's hitting right, a steady string of two-foot waves can provide decent rides. If you want to learn how, check out the **Daytona Beach Surfing School** (91 Ormwood Drive, 386/441-1110), which is actually in Ormond Beach.

In summer, free weekly concerts are held at the open-air band shell near the pier. It's worth checking out for its architectural history, too. Built entirely of coquina rock in 1937, it's a stellar example of the good works done by the Civilian Conservation Corps.

6 DAYTONA BEACH

Location: five miles of beach along South Atlantic Avenue in Daytona Beach
Parking/fees: $5 per day to park on the beach (free in December and January); free off-beach parking lots
Hours: sunrise-sunset
Facilities: lifeguards
Contact: Volusia County Beach Services, 386/239-7873

7 MAIN STREET PIER AND BEACH

Location: Main Street at South Atlantic Avenue in Daytona Beach
Parking/fees: metered street parking and free off-beach parking lots
Hours: sunrise-sunset
Facilities: concessions, lifeguards, restrooms, and showers
Contact: Volusia County Beach Services, 386/239-7873

8 SUN SPLASH PARK

Location: 611 South Atlantic Avenue, at Revilo Boulevard, in Daytona Beach
Parking/fees: free parking lot
Hours: sunrise-sunset
Facilities: lifeguards, picnic tables, restrooms, and showers
Contact: Volusia County Beach Services, 386/239-7873

9 DAYTONA BEACH SHORES

Location: 5.5 miles of beach between Daytona Beach, but few public accesses onto it

THE SPORTS COAST

Parking/fees: $5 per day to park on the beach (free in December and January)
Hours: sunrise–sunset (autos only), 24 hours (pedestrians)
Facilities: lifeguards
Contact: Volusia County Beach Services, 386/239-7873

10 FRANK RENDON PARK

Location: 2705 South Atlantic Avenue in Daytona Beach Shores
Parking/fees: free parking lot
Hours: sunrise–sunset
Facilities: lifeguards, picnic tables, restrooms, and showers
Contact: Volusia County Beach Services, 386/239-7873

RECREATION AND ATTRACTIONS

- **Bike/Skate Rentals:** Ducer Cruzer Bicycle, 137 Sunrise Boulevard, Daytona Beach, 386/383-7433

- **Dive Shop:** Discover Diving Dive Center, 92 Dunlawton Avenue, Port Orange, 386/760-3483

- **Ecotourism:** Doris Leeper Spruce Creek Preserve (between Port Orange and New Smyrna Beach), Volusia County Land Acquisition and Management, 386/740-5261

- **Fishing Charters:** Critter Fleet, Lighthouse Landing, 4940 South Peninsula Drive, Ponce Inlet, 386/761-9271

- **Lighthouse:** Ponce de Leon Inlet Lighthouse, 4931 South Peninsula Drive, Ponce Inlet, 386/761-1821

- **Marina:** Halifax Harbor Marina and Park, 450 Basin Street, Daytona Beach, 386/253-0575; Inlet Harbor Marina, 133 Inlet Harbor Road, Ponce Inlet, 386/767-8755

- **Pier:** Main Street Pier, Main Street at Ocean Avenue, Daytona Beach, 386/253-1212; Sunglow Pier, 3701 South Atlantic Avenue, Daytona Beach Shores, 386/756-4219

- **Rainy-Day Attraction:** Museum of Arts and Sciences, 1040 Museum Boulevard, Daytona Beach, 386/255-0285

- **Shopping/Browsing:** Volusia Mall, 1700 West International Speedway Boulevard (U.S. 92), Daytona, 386/253-6783; Fountain Square Shopping Village, 142 East Granada Boulevard, Ormond Beach, 386/677-3845

- **Surf Shop:** Mad Dog Surf Shop, 3634 South Atlantic Avenue, Daytona Beach, 386/761-5999 (surf shop) or 386/761-1853 (surf report)

- **Vacation Rentals:** Ponce Inlet Realty, 4000 South Atlantic Avenue, Port Orange, 386/761-3004 or 888/882-8870

ACCOMMODATIONS

The hotel of first choice in Daytona Beach is the **Daytona Beach Hilton Oceanfront Resort** (100 North Atlantic Avenue, 386/254-8200, $$$). Formerly the Adam's Mark, this property anchored the "Core Area" when the first attempts at urban renewal were made back in the previous decade. The Hilton would look to be the spot convention planners would want to patronize, if they could be lured to Daytona Beach. It offers all the amenities one could want (pool, Jacuzzi, fitness center, comfortable common spaces) plus the kind of cleanliness and comfort you won't find in Daytona's one- and two-star motels. However, its rack rates may be a bit pricey for working families, who tend to gravitate to the modest motor courts. If you do stay here, try to wrangle an upper-floor oceanfront room. It's worth the extra tariff, as you can sit out on the balcony and savor a late-afternoon breeze or an early-morning sunrise. Leave the sliding door open and listen to the waves serenade you all night long.

Next to the Hilton is **Ocean Walk Resort** (300 North Atlantic Avenue, 386/323-4800, $$$$). It's a time-share place with some nightly rentals. A cluster of shops and restaurants is at ground level, including a Starbucks. Based on that fact alone, Daytona Beach has come a long way.

Also located on the north end of the Core Area, the **Plaza Resort & Spa** (600 North Atlantic Avenue, 386/255-4471, $$$) is a 323-room behemoth that boasts the area's largest pool deck, as well as a playground, fitness center, restaurant, and lounge.

While towering hotels and condos have staked their inevitable claim to much of the shoreline in Daytona Beach, a good number of accommodations are still modest and affordable. If you thought a Florida beach vacation was an unaffordable luxury, Daytona Beach says otherwise. With 13,000 rentable rooms, there are often plenty of vacancies. The exceptions are summer weekends and special events like Daytona International Speedway's eight Race Weekends, Spring Break, Bike Week, and Biketoberfest. At other times, rooms along Atlantic Avenue (A1A) might go for $35. Prices are often printed on the motel sign, and they tend to be identical. It's a buyer's market, if you aren't too particular about where you lay your head. After Labor Day is a good time to visit because the crowds are gone and prices drop, but water temperature is still as warm and air temperature is not so blisteringly hot.

The hurricane season of 2004 affected the lodging scene in Daytona Beach and Daytona Beach Shores. They got attacked from the west by Hurricane Charley, from the south by Hurricane Francis, and from the east by Hurricane Jeanne, which did the greatest damage to this stretch of coast. And it didn't end with the 'canes. A series of winter nor'easters brought even more wind, rain and erosion to the area. Many months after the storms, you could still see indications of damage: blown-out signs, vacated storefronts, palm trees with tops missing. We were told that "condominium restoration" became a hot new business in Florida in the wake of the 2004 hurricane season.

Roughly 10 percent of Daytona Beach's accommodations were put out of commission. Small hotels like the Beachcomber shut their doors forever. Others, like the Southern Shores (in Daytona Beach Shores) used insurance settlements as an opportunity to repair and upgrade. As a result, the Southern Shores is now **The Shores Resort & Spa** (2637 South Atlantic Avenue, 386/767-7350), a Noble House Resort and Daytona's first four-star hotel ("Daytona refined," they take pains to note). The opulence carries through to its restaurant (Baleen) and spa (Spa Terra at The Shores).

Given a 23-mile stretch of motels from which to choose, it's a difficult task. You might narrow the pack by checking out a listing of "Superior Small Lodgings." These are "guaranteed high-quality places with no more than 50 rooms or units." (For a brochure describing the full roster of Superior Small Lodgings, call 800/854-1234.) Among them, we are partial to the **Key West Village** (1901 South Atlantic Avenue, 386/255-5394, $$), with 22 oceanside rooms surrounding a courtyard with tropical garden and pool; and the **Ocean Court Motel** (2315 South Atlantic Avenue, 386/253-8185, $$), a quiet, family-run place with a pool and cookout area facing the beach. Most rooms have kitchens.

Reliable hotel towers in the Daytona Beach Shores area include **Holiday Inn** (3209 South Atlantic Avenue, 386/761-2030, $$) and **Daytona Surfside Inn & Suites** (3125 South Atlantic Avenue, 386/788-1000, $$). The 10-story **Treasure Island Inn** (2025 South Atlantic Avenue, 386/257-1950, $$$) used to be the flagship of several fine area hotels owned by a local family and managed as Oceans Eleven Resorts. Four of them, including Treasure Island Inn, were sold in 1999 and are now operated as Ocean Resorts.

Moving up A1A toward Ormond Beach are a number of decent quality mom-and-pops. Those we like include the **Ocean Villa Motel** (828 North Atlantic Avenue, 386/252-4644, $). It has 38 units, many with kitchens, two pools, a water slide, back-door beach access, and a loyal clientele. It's more homey than fancy, which suits the folks who come back year after year just fine.

Finally, Daytona is home to a handful of

bed-and-breakfasts with historical legacies. Built in 1884, the six-room **Lillian Place** (111 Silver Beach Avenue, 386/323-9913, $$) is where Stephen Crane recuperated from injuries sustained in a shipwreck in Ponce Inlet and wrote the short story "The Open Boat." The seven-room **Miss Pat's Inn** (1209 South Peninsula Drive, 386/248-8420, $$) has been around since 1898. Both are big yellow Victorian houses with wraparound porches, and both are set a few blocks back from the beach in quieter neighborhoods.

COASTAL CUISINE

Even a tony corporate tower like the Hilton trades on the fact that it's located at the "Birthplace of Speed" and that NASCAR rules here. Their **North Turn Restaurant** (100 North Atlantic Avenue, 386/254-8200, $) has NASCAR-themed food items: Fried Piston Rings (onion rings), Darlington Dawgs (hot dogs), Talladega Tenders (chicken strips), Pit Row Popcorn Shrimp, and other strained attempts to milk the motorsports metaphor. The fact that an upscale hotel would serve such mediocre grub illustrates how difficult it is to get a decent meal in Daytona Beach.

Because 10 million visitors a year come through here—the great majority of them bikers, college kids, racing fans, and vacationing families—the restaurants tend to be more serviceable than memorable. Fast food, fried seafood platters, pancakes, barbecue—this is the lay of the land along Atlantic Avenue. Daytona Beach is a monument to culinary mediocrity: "All U Can Eat" buffet troughs, burger stands, and convenience marts with microwavable burritos for the truly desperate. Those who come to Daytona Beach harbor simple notions about what constitutes good food: large portions, fried golden brown, preferably with free seconds. Food is just a means to an end here: a way to fuel the body for more fun on the beach or at the racetrack. Pick your pit stop and start scarfing.

Incidentally, we learned a new way to say grace ("The Cracker Prayer") at Daytona's Museum of Arts and Sciences, courtesy of an exhibit entitled "Cracker Culture in Florida History." The blessing goes like this: "God, we thank you for all the food we got, especially the grits."

We uttered those words over our plates at **Aunt Catfish's on the River** (4009 Halifax Drive, 386/762-4768, $$), where we got our grits and a mess of other rib-tickling victuals done up in "Down South River Cooking" style. The "river" is the Halifax (which serves as the Intracoastal Waterway through here), and the restaurant is located on its west bank. It's in Port Orange, beside Dunlawton Bridge—the southernmost of six bridges that link Daytona's barrier island to the mainland.

Nailed to the wall by the restaurant entrance is a plaque with a metal catfish. You are urged to "Rub the Wish Fish" and make a wish. Here are ours:

- Parke: "I wish upon a metal catfish that Florida gets restored to environmental sanity before it's too late."

- Alan: "To quote Beat poet Lawrence Ferlinghetti, I wish for a rebirth of wonder in America."

Soon after you're seated a waitress comes over and introduces herself as kin—"Hello, I'm Cousin Chrissie"—and takes your order. The food is as fine as a covered-dish church supper down yonder in the Bible Belt, with all the trimmings and extra helpings. The star menu item is, unsurprisingly, catfish. It is farm raised and served Cajun-grilled or lightly breaded and fried. If you're hungry and indecisive try the Gone Fishin' Lunch Seafood Platter (catfish, clam strips, scallops, shrimp), all for $9.99. That comes with gratis visits to the Fish Camp Hot Bar, where you can help yourself to baked beans, cheese grits, cole slaw, and cornbread squares. (Overheard: "I'm gonna git me another helping of them beans," said Hungry Male #1. "You're gonna hafta git another plate t'hold all that cornbread, buddy," replied Hungry Male #2.)

They serve iced tea in mason jars, and sugar

is spooned from a gray porcelain boot. A fresh-baked cinnamon roll accompanies every order. For dessert, try the Boatsinker's Pie: fudge pie with two scoops of chocolate ice cream served in a chocolate shell and topped with whipped cream and a cherry. Have your doctor's card on your person in case you stroke out.

The servers at Aunt Catfish are so disarmingly pleasant we think they must take nice pills. Our young waitress's mood darkened only once—when we asked her what she thought of all the high-rise construction occurring on the beachfront. "I don't like it," she said with a frown, staring across the bridge at Daytona Beach Shore's new skyline. "I don't like it at all."

Another good riverside haven is **Park's Seafood** (951 North Beach Street, 386/258-7272, $$), a large family-oriented restaurant. The nautical motif is prevalent, but the tableside aquarium briefly took us aback when, just as we were cutting into a fillet of broiled grouper, a large fish stared forlornly at us through the glass. A full catfish or catch-of the-day (gray sole when we visited) dinner runs about $10, and the menu tops out with red snapper and broiled pompano for under $17. Meals are served with mullet dip and crackers, tomato-based seafood chowder, salad, and two side dishes. Indeed, a solid meal at bargain prices.

Back at the beach, the **Ocean Deck** (127 South Ocean Avenue, 386/253-5224, $$) is the quintessential Daytona Beach bar and grill. A two-decked local institution for as long as anyone can remember (not to mention being ranked #1 on NASCAR's Top 10 list of "places to hang out"), Ocean Deck takes casual dining to an appealing extreme. You can wander in from the beach downstairs or enjoy slightly classier digs upstairs.

Right in the heart of Daytona Beach along the Seabreeze Boulevard bazaar, the **Oyster Pub** (555 Seabreeze Boulevard, 386/255-6348, $) is our perennial favorite for raw bivalves and cold brew. They have a decent lunch menu (seafood salads, sandwiches), but the drawing card is the oysters and lots of beer to wash it down.

For a healthy meal, dance on down to the **Dancing Avocado** (110 South Beach Street, 386/947-2022, $), where you can get smoothies, sandwiches, and vegetarian dishes. We've enjoyed their avocado, cheese, and tomato-filled omelette. For lunch, try the "Susan Burger": a vegetarian patty with all the fixings that's named for a regular who takes her vegan lifestyle seriously. There's a lot of colorful bric-a-brac on the walls, and the place is a downtown hub for the alternative community.

NIGHTLIFE

Despite being marketed as a "family" beach, Daytona also draws its fair share of singles—college kids, bikers, party animals. That said, the nightlife of Daytona Beach is a well-oiled machine built for partying and centered around three distinct tracks: along Main Street and the Main Street Pier; along Seabreeze Boulevard; and in downtown Daytona (on the mainland), near the historic district. Each has its own appeal.

After an unsuccessful attempt at urban upscaling, downtown Daytona spent some years wearing the appearance of an expensive failure, with "For Sale" and "For Rent" signs hanging in storefront windows. That was, no doubt, the price they paid for aiming above the heads of their core clientele of car freaks, bikers, teens, and blue-collar families from western Volusia County and beyond.

Downtown Daytona is starting to stabilize, however, around a waterfront park, a minor-league ballpark named for Jackie Robinson, and small shops along Beach Avenue. The area has a good, relaxed feeling, like it's finally beginning to find its rhythm. One place that piqued our curiosity is **The Love Bar** (116 North Beach Street, 386/252-7600), which uses the unusual lettering of the 1960s' band Love on its sign. It's a dark, hip kind of place with a young, goth clientele. At the other extreme is the **Stock Exchange** (125 Basin Street, 386/255-6477), which appeals to the

THE SPORTS COAST

WHEELS ON THE BEACH

As virtually everyone in the Western world is aware, you can drive on parts of Daytona, Ormond, and New Smyrna Beaches. Elsewhere in Florida, you can drive on selected beaches near St. Augustine and on Amelia Island. The only other beaches in America we've seen where people are legally and physically able to drive their cars are Pismo Beach, California; Ocean Shores, Washington; and Long Beach Peninsula, Washington. But Daytona Beach is the best known of the bunch.

This unusual privilege is a curious holdover from the area's days as the Birthplace of Speed. Over the years, it has accrued the status of an inalienable right, up there with gun ownership, flag protection, and lawn watering. It was upon these beaches that the first racing cars were tested and, so the logic goes, anyone on wheels should be allowed to drive on them now. At present, 16 miles of beach from Ormond Beach to Ponce Inlet are open to wheeled vehicles.

But, before you floor your car, motorcycle, or dune buggy in a due easterly direction, you might want to ponder "The Rules." They've changed a bit over the years, beginning with the establishment of conservation zones created to protect endangered sea turtles. A 1995 lawsuit filed against Volusia County listed various species of sea turtles as plaintiffs in an attempt to have beach driving banned. As a result, the Habitat Conservation Plan was implemented in 1996. The county's shoreline was divided into Natural (conservation), Transitional, and Urban zones.

The new rules restricted beach driving to Urban zones and banned night driving entirely. The situation changed further in 2000, when driving was eliminated for one mile, from Seabreeze Boulevard down to Main Street, in Daytona Beach's Core Area. This opened up more of the busiest stretch of beach to pedestrians only. Those parts of the beach that have been declared off-limits to vehicles – be it by the Main Street Pier in Daytona Beach or on some of the quieter sections of beach in the county – have since become pleasurable havens for sunbathers, surfers, swimmers, sand dunes, and sea turtles.

If you wish to drive on the beach, here are "The Rules":

* The beach is open to motorized traffic sunrise-sunset November–April and 8 A.M.–7 P.M. the rest of the year. The beach will be closed to driving if sand conditions are wrong or the beach has narrowed, usually because of a high tide, big storm, or both. For instance, after the hurricane season of 2004, the number of miles of drivable beaches temporarily shrank from 16 to 6 – and, even then, only as tides permitted.

older set and is located on the west bank of the Halifax River at the Halifax Marina. Phones on the tables at this "playground for big kids" let you ring up other patrons. We haven't seen that gimmick since the disco era. Dinner, dancing, and deejays keep the martini-and-sirloin crowd bopping.

The other two night districts, though always fun, are not for the faint of heart. Let's start with Main Street. No matter how hard they try to market "Historic Main Street" as a family entertainment mecca, it's impossible to over-look its bad-ass image. Frankly, we have never seen so hardcore a biker image as that flaunted on and around Main Street in Daytona Beach. Just check out the names of the establishments: John's Rock 'n' Ride, Dirty Harry's, Choppers World, Harley Davidson, Tombstone Cycles, Badlands Bodyworks, Bulldog Leathers, Shotguns, Hot Leathers, and a strip club or two. This is family fare? One bumper sticker we spied summed up the mind set: "American by Birth. Harley Rider by Choice."

The flavor of Main Street is best sampled at

- There are between 25 and 30 – the number varies according to season – marked entrance gates from north Volusia County (Ormond Beach) to south Volusia County (New Smyrna Beach).

- Vehicles for which entrance fees are required are cars, trucks (under 33 feet long only), motorcycles, vans, and RVs. Bicycles are allowed on the beach free of charge.

- The fee to enter the beach at designated gates is $5 per vehicle. This fee allows you unlimited entry all day long. Seasonal passes are available to residents for $20 and nonresidents for $40.

- Transitional zones are located on either side of the urban zones, plus the north end of New Smyrna Beach. Sea turtle nesting here is moderate, and you must not drive within 30 feet of the dunes or seawalls.

- Natural zones are where dune habitats are largely intact and sea-turtle nesting is highly concentrated. These areas are found north of Granada Boulevard on Ormond Beach, between Emilia Avenue in Daytona Beach and Beach Street in Ponce Inlet, and from 27th Avenue south in New Smyrna Beach. The no-driving rule is strictly enforced in conservation zones (which are clearly marked), with a $500 fine for parking or operating any vehicle there.

- The speed limit is 10 miles per hour at all times. Park either facing the ocean or the dunes, but not parallel to the water.

A word to the wise: If you do park on the beach, keep an eye on the tide. If the water starts lapping at the hubcaps, you may need the Beach Patrol to pull you out. On busy days in peak season, we've been told they extract as many as 200 stuck vehicles. Beyond having to be towed, you can do appalling damage to a car by bringing it to the beach. Salt water, salt spray, and windblown sand will induce "dramatic rot," as one local put it, to a vehicle's underside. A three-year life span is normal for beach-driven vehicles.

While driving on the beach will always be a hot issue in Volusia County, the compromises that have already been made were unthinkable in previous decades. As one veteran of the Volusia County Beach Patrol put it, "A lot of different agendas are in play here. I used to think a driving ban would never happen, but now I'd say the chances are about 50-50."

For up-to-date information on driving and beach conditions, call the Volusia County Beach Hotline at 386/239-7873 (Daytona Beach) or 386/423-3330 (New Smyrna Beach).

THE SPORTS COAST

Boot Hill Saloon (310 Main Street, 386/258-9506), a biker bar of the most benign kind. Their slogan says it all: "You're better off here than across the street." Boot Hill sits opposite an old cemetery. During Bike Week, of course, you can't get near the door, but any other time it's worth checking out for the ambience and live music. A Boot Hill Saloon T-shirt is one of Daytona's most popular and cherished souvenirs. Just down the street is the **Bank & Blues Club** (701 Main Street, 386/257-9272), a nationally known blues venue.

Our favorite after-dark hangout in Daytona Beach is the Seabreeze corridor. That's because it's the home of one of our favorite bars in all of Christendom, the **Oyster Pub** (555 Seabreeze Boulevard, 386/255-6348). You breathe a sigh of relief just entering its doors (at least we do). They have a great jukebox, relaxed atmosphere, enormous horseshoe-shaped bar, and multiple TV sets soundlessly broadcasting sporting events. If you can hold out till midnight, the price of oysters drops to $0.25 apiece. Many's the night we've allowed our hunger pangs to extend to the witching hour just to take advantage of this deal. Good golly, you can actually have friendly conversations with strangers here!

Directly across the street from the Oyster Pub is **Molly Brown's** (542 Seabreeze Boulevard, 255-5966), a strip club, if you're looking for entertainment of a more "adult" sort. Two other clubs that have made the biggest splash along Seabreeze are the **Fuel** (640 North Grandview Avenue, 386/248-3151) and **Razzles** (611 Seabreeze Boulevard, 386/257-6236). Fuel occupies the former site of Baja Beach Club, and bills itself as "Daytona's #1 Party Complex" (five bars! three dance floors!). Razzles has been Razzles for a long time, and is likewise a high-energy dance club. And that is the yin and yang of nightlife in Daytona Beach: biker bars and dance clubs.

Finally, one of the most enduring acts on the Daytona Beach scene is the Atlantic Ocean. There is no cover charge, and now that cars can no longer drive on the beach past 7 P.M., it's safe to sit back and dig the sound of the waves and the look of the moon rising overhead. (As many as 25 people used to get run over on the beach each year, most of them at night.) An equally relaxing experience is a moonlight drive along the west bank of the Halifax River. Riverside Drive is a palm-lined thoroughfare buffeted by breezes coming off the water.

Wilbur-by-the-Sea

Wilbur-by-the-Sea is a small, mostly residential colony between Daytona Beach and Ponce Inlet. Its low-key profile remains intact, despite all the skyscraping new real estate that's brought jolting (and unwelcome) changes to the surrounding communities of Daytona Beach Shores and Ponce Inlet. The quiet beach in Wilbur-by-the-Sea can be vehicularly accessed via Toronita Avenue, while pedestrians can get onto the beach at seven publicly accessible dune walkovers.

For more information, contact the Daytona Beach Area Convention and Visitors Bureau, 126 East Orange Avenue, Daytona Beach, FL 32114, 386/255-0415 or 800/544-0415, www. daytonabeach.com.

BEACHES

 WILBUR-BY-THE-SEA

Location: seven miles south of Daytona Beach
Parking/fees: $5 per day to enter and park on the beach via the Toronita Avenue approach (free in December and January) and off-beach parking lots
Hours: sunrise–sunset
Facilities: lifeguards and showers
Contact: Volusia County Beach Services, 386/239-7873

Ponce Inlet

Though officially part of the Daytona Beach strand, occupying the southernmost chunk of the barrier island, Ponce Inlet (pop. 3,200) has little in common with the heavily trafficked commercial build-up above it. A local we know even refers to it as the "Un-Daytona." Consisting of mostly residential homes, Ponce Inlet is well endowed with a natural conservation zone, conferring a bit of tropical seclusion upon parts of the area. As recently as the late 1960s, Ponce Inlet was too far off the beaten path (and evacuation routes) to be worth the trouble and expense of development. However, the property here is among the most coveted along the central Florida coast, and it pains us to report that developers have been planting condos along South Atlantic Avenue as quickly as permits can be wrangled. You'll still find one- and two-story homes up at the north end, providing a bit of visual respite from Daytona Beach Shores' overgrowth, but further down Ponce Inlet is chockablock with bland, sand-brown, eight-story condos that bear a drab institutional look.

Since some of its low-density development and natural character have gone by the wayside, we feel compelled to cheer less loudly about Ponce Inlet in this edition. But we will still cheer, albeit with reservations, as it remains a special place in many ways. For instance, they have done a good job of preserving some of the Old Florida constructions out here. The most noteworthy example is the Ponce de Leon Inlet Lighthouse, which is open daily 10 A.M.–5 P.M. ($4 for adults, $1 for children under 11). Built in 1887, this 175-foot monolith of red brick and granite is the second-tallest lighthouse in America. The light was disabled in 1970 and rekindled in 1982. The lighthouse is the centerpiece of a park that has eight additional buildings on the grounds. They form a larger "museum" that includes such things as the lighthouse worker's dwellings, an old tugboat, and a Museum of the Sea. You can also walk a short nature trail that follows the park's perimeter, preserving a patch of woodlands. It was here

© PARKE PUTERBAUGH

Ponce de Leon Inlet Lighthouse

we literally saw "leaping lizards": little black reptiles that hopped from the ground onto tree trunks.

As for the lighthouse, it takes 203 steps to reach the top. You can purchase a T-shirt attesting to the feat in the gift shop. (Heck, you don't even have to hike to the top to buy the T-shirt—who'll know?) It's Florida's tallest lighthouse and the second tallest in the country. (The tallest is Cape Hatteras Lighthouse, on North Carolina's Outer Banks, which takes 269 steps to ascend). Built of bricks shipped down from New York State, Ponce Inlet Lighthouse still shines a beacon warning boats away from the coast. Several years ago the modern electric light was replaced with a new Fresnal lens, so the look is closer to the beacon that shone many years ago. (A word of warning: Don't climb the lighthouse if there's lightning in the area. We were told that a bolt recently struck the electrical transformer at its base, hurtling it 100 feet away.)

The Marine Science Center (100 Lighthouse Drive, 386/304-5545) is a welcome addition to Ponce Inlet. Open 10 A.M.–4 P.M. daily, it specializes in environmental education and sea critter rehabilitation. Enthusiastic volunteers lead informative tours. From "Turtle Terrace," a wooden deck, you can peer into the Sea Turtle Intensive Care Unit, where injured turtles recover in circular pools while being fed and attended to by marine specialists. The smallish museum doesn't yet have a lot to display—you can easily tour it in 15 minutes—but the $3 admission fee goes to a great cause.

There is an enlightening display on litter at the beach. We were not thrilled to learn that Americans annually discard 4.5 trillion cigarette butts, which become wildlife-threatening litter. The display also poses questions like, "Can a sea turtle tell the difference between a plastic bag and a jellyfish?" (Answer: no.) The gift shop sells some unusually attractive T-shirts. Between us, we stocked up on tie-dyed shirts that read "Peace Love & Turtles."

A number of deep-sea sportfishing charters

leave out of Ponce Inlet's harbor. A ban on netfishing within three miles of shore, enacted in the mid-1990s, has paid dividends, allowing populations of shrimp and scallops—and the fish that feed on them—to bounce back.

For more information, contact the Daytona Beach Area Convention and Visitors Bureau, 126 East Orange Avenue, Daytona Beach, FL 32114, 386/255-0415 or 800/544-0415, www.daytonabeach.com.

BEACHES

Ponce Inlet's beach is entered at Beach Street, but one can only drive south (because of the conservation zone) to the jetty at Lighthouse Point Park. In this exceedingly private community, it is hard to enjoy the beach without wheels. A small beachfront park, **Winterhaven Park,** has been wedged in here, and this little board-walked sanctuary is indeed very welcome. However, the Big Kahuna in Ponce Inlet, in terms of beach access and activity, is **Lighthouse Point Park and Recreation Area.**

Located at the end of Peninsula Drive, it is a state-owned, county-run facility that includes a jetty, oceanfront pavilion, and nature trails. At one point some of the highest concentrations of sea turtle nesting sites were found here and it was arguably among the nicest beaches in the county. The surf was popular with surfers (though not quite as good as the south side of Ponce Inlet) and dog owners, being that it's the only county beach park that allows dogs.

Then, from 1999–2002, the U.S. Army Corps of Engineers undertook a gargantuan and costly project to extend Ponce Inlet's North Jetty (by 800 feet). They also built a ghastly 1,540-foot rock revetment along the beach. The purpose of this was to hold Ponce Inlet open for navigation. Even the Army Corps seemed to recognize that the loss of the beach at Lighthouse Point Park would be an inevitable consequence: "Over time, it is anticipated that the interior inlet shoreline at Lighthouse Point Park will erode to a point where its contour follows the new jetty extension and revetment." By way of reasoning,

they argued, "The project is *essential* to correct severe erosion and navigation problems at Ponce de Leon Inlet." In other words, they had to destroy the beach in order to save the inlet. The project was subject to delays and overruns, concluding in 2002 at a cost of $10 million.

Fixing us with a disgusted expression, a gatekeeper at the park explained, "Any time the Corps of Engineers gets involved, you know what happens. ... "

PONCE INLET

Location: Ponce Inlet's 2.5 miles of beach lie nine miles south of Daytona Beach along South Atlantic Avenue
Parking/fees: $5 per day to park on the beach at the Beach Street entrance (free in December and January)
Hours: sunrise-sunset
Facilities: concessions, lifeguards, restrooms, picnic tables, and showers
Contact: Volusia County Beach Services, 386/239-7873

WINTERHAVEN PARK

Location: 4590 South Atlantic Avenue, in Ponce Inlet
Parking/fees: free parking lot
Hours: sunrise-sunset
Facilities: restrooms, picnic tables, and showers
Contact: Volusia County Beach Services, 386/239-7873

LIGHTHOUSE POINT PARK AND RECREATION AREA

Location: 5000 Robert Merrill Parkway, off A1A in Ponce Inlet

THE SPORTS COAST

Parking/fees: $3.50 entrance fee per vehicle
Hours: 6 A.M.–9 P.M.
Facilities: lifeguards, restrooms, picnic tables, showers, and a visitors center
Contact: Lighthouse Point Park and Recreation Area, 386/756-7488

COASTAL CUISINE

One of the most venerable meal tickets in the area is **Lighthouse Landing Restaurant & Raw Bar** (4940 South Peninsula Drive, 386/761-9271, $$), which bills itself as "the oldest restaurant on the East Coast." We asked when it opened. "That I couldn't tell you," said the hostess. "But the family who owns it now has had it for 40 years." Well, alright, then. This eatery does look like it's seen its share of history. Lighthouse Landing sits by the marina where the Critter Fleet (a deep-sea fishing fleet) docks. The casual setting enhances the dark, Old Florida ambience of the restaurant. Lighthouse Landing caters to an older crowd who've been coming here since Lawrence Welk was a young man.

The newer star of the Ponce dining scene is **Inlet Harbor Restaurant and Marina** (133 Inlet Harbor Road, 386/767-8/55, $$). Opened in 1997, it immediately began packing them in, with two-hour waits on weekends not uncommon. The wait is worth it and painlessly enough done at Riverdance, the restaurant's breezy patio bar. Riverdance has its own excellent appetizer menu featuring fresh shrimp, oysters, stone crab claws, conch fritters, and a blackened seafood burrito. The patio overlooks the blue-green inlet waters and surrounding protected wetlands. If you get really impatient, stroll over to the marina and watch the fishing fleet unload their daily catch. The Inlet Harbor dinner menu offers an assortment of fresh and simply prepared seafood, cooked to your choosing (grilled, fried, broiled, blackened) at prices that won't bust a move on your wallet. We dug the Calypso crab cakes with spicy remoulade sauce and the Florida jumbo shrimp, which is Inlet Harbor's claim to fame.

New Smyrna Beach

New Smyrna Beach is Daytona Beach's hipper southern neighbor. It shares Daytona's obsession for driving cars on the sand, but that's about where it ends. Separated from its better-known neighbor by an inlet, New Smyrna Beach has a different atmosphere and mindset.

"I've lived my entire life on New Smyrna Beach, but I have never been on Daytona Beach," a native told us. "My feet have never actually touched the sand. I prefer the quiet stability here. I tried to move away once, but I came home after six days." She, like all locals, pronounces Smyrna not as it looks but with an extra syllable: "Sa-myrna."

There is more to this town than initially meets the eye. In years past, what the eye met as it approached New Smyrna Beach on U.S. 1 was a string of rickety motels and biker bars. But that's only the outer layer. Downtown New Smyrna and its beach are a 10-minute drive east from U.S. 1 via the A1A causeway.

It is only fair to warn you that New Smyrna Beach, while still a far cry from Daytona Beach, is no longer the quaint, quiet beach town it used to be. Not only has a second causeway bridge been built to the barrier Island—the North Causeway, an extension of Flagler Avenue—but the bulk of New Smyrna's eight-mile beach has become a wall of high-rise condos and second homes for the part-time use of folks from Orlando. As a member of the Volusia County Beach Patrol told us, "On weekends and during special events, New Smyrna is just as packed as Daytona." We are impressed with the town's retail makeover—particularly Flagler Avenue, which is lined with boutiques, bakeries, and surf shops. Just how good the surfing is here can be gleaned from the abundance of surf shops and surf bars. Even a local bakeshop is called Beach Bums Bakery and Cafe.

The town's name originated with its founder, Dr. Andrew Turnbull. He christened it New Smyrna Beach in honor of his wife, who came from Smyrna, in Asia Minor. Prior to

European colonization, the area had been home to Timucuan Indians. Juan Ponce de Leon landed somewhere in the vicinity in 1513 (thus the name Ponce Inlet). New Smyrna Beach was briefly the most lucrative of the British colonies in the New World.

Little of this local history has been preserved. For instance, the only Timucuan shell mound that wasn't used to pave local roads can be found inside Canaveral National Seashore. The roads have lately reached the saturation point, in terms of development. If they would only leave well enough alone, we'd certainly look forward to future visits to New Smyrna Beach.

For more information, contact the Southeast Volusia Chamber of Commerce, 115 Canal Street, P.O. Box 129, New Smyrna Beach, FL 32069, 386/428-2449, www.sevchamber.com.

BEACHES

From Ponce Inlet to the entrance into Canaveral National Seashore, **New Smyrna Beach** and neighboring Bethune Beach account for 13.2 miles of beach. Seven miles of that strand, from Ponce Inlet to 27th Avenue, has been designated a "transitional zone," which means beach driving and parking are allowed 30 feet seaward of the dunes or seawalls. South of 27th Avenue the beach is a "natural conservation zone," meaning no motorized vehicles are permitted. Even at peak season, the crush on Smyrna's beaches never quite achieves Daytona's intensity, but it's a popular and busy beach all the same.

Surfers claim that New Smyrna Beach has "the most consistent surf break in Florida." The best spot is on the south side of Ponce Inlet. The waves are said to peak two feet higher here than anywhere in the county. This surfer's Shangri-La is accessed via **Smyrna Dunes Park,** at the end of Peninsula Avenue. The county has leased this pristine, dune-covered acreage from the Coast Guard and created an intriguing park. Behind the shaded picnic area and shower facilities, a 1.5-mile boardwalk runs in a loop out to and around

Ponce Inlet, with two beach accesses provided en route. It can be a blisteringly hot and dry hike on a summer day, and there isn't one square inch of shade, so bring water and plan to stay on the beach for long enough to make the trip worthwhile.

That said, it's worth every drop of sweat to get here for the view from the wetlands observation deck and access to the inlet and a gorgeous, secluded beach. The only sour note to the view is Inlet Marina Villages, an eyesore condo on the boundary of this unspoiled park. Seldom have we seen dune fields so broad and dense with vegetation, including prickly pear cactus, sea oats, and railroad vine creeping along the white sand. It's also worth hiking out here to surf or watch the surfers. This tireless, dauntless, and usually penniless contingent will hike barefoot over the splintering boardwalk and sizzling asphalt with boards in tow. Smyrna Dunes reminds us of Trestles, a famous surf spot in San Clemente, California, necessitating a similar hike-in. Smyrna Dunes, with its cross-jurisdictional partnership, should serve as a template for beach communities who want to broaden their public access.

South of Smyrna Dunes, Atlantic Avenue winds its way to that stretch of beach most favored by locals. Found at the end of Esther Street, just north of a 7-Eleven, this area is called "The Wall." There's a seawall over which you must hop to gain beach access. Upon the seawall is a faded but colorful mural painted by local schoolchildren. It depicts sea life and contains this polite, plaintive plea: "Save Our Oceans, Please." On hot summer days, the beach just below the wall and for several hundred yards in either direction is packed with nubile bodies and cruised by cars enjoying the flesh parade. You can park for free on the sandy shoulder, if you can find a spot.

Flagler Park lies at the end of Flagler Avenue, where a concrete entrance ramp allows vehicular access onto the sand and a huge dirt parking lot lets you enjoy the beach sans wheels. Unfortunately, New Smyrna Beach took a major hit from the hurricanes of 2004, and Flagler Park was closed for repair for much of 2005. The park's covered walkways and stairs to the beach got hammered, and a chain-link fence had been built around them to keep people away. Seawalls that were destroyed couldn't immediately be rebuilt because construction would interfere with the sea turtles' egg-laying.

From Flagler Park down to 30th Avenue, beach accesses are generously provided every three or four blocks and are marked by blue signs along Atlantic Avenue (A1A). **27th Avenue Park** has been nicely developed by the county with beach cabanas, picnic tables, boardwalk, playground, and a large parking lot.

South of 27th Avenue, New Smyrna Beach erupts in an endless, mind-numbing chain of condos. A merciful break in that chain occurs at **Mary McLeod Bethune Beach Park,** in Bethune Beach, which derives its name from the great African-American educator who helped create Bethune-Cookman College in Daytona Beach. This county-run beachside park sits on a sandy bluff and offers a pier, picnic area, boardwalk, beach access, and tennis, volleyball and basketball.

15 SMYRNA DUNES PARK

BEST (

Location: 2995 North Peninsula Drive in New Smyrna Beach
Parking/fees: $3.50 entrance fee per vehicle
Hours: 6 A.M.-7 P.M. (8 P.M. in summer)
Facilities: restrooms, picnic tables, showers, and a visitors center
Contact: Smyrna Dunes Parks, 386/424-2935

16 NEW SMYRNA BEACH

Location: beach accesses are located at street ends from Ocean Drive down to 30th Avenue in New Smyrna Beach

Parking/fees: limited free parking
Hours: sunrise-sunset
Facilities: none
Contact: Contact: Volusia County Beach Services, 386/239-7873

17 FLAGLER PARK

Location: Flagler Avenue at Atlantic Avenue in New Smyrna Beach
Parking/fees: $5 per day to park on the beach (free in December and January) and a free parking lot
Hours: sunrise-sunset
Facilities: lifeguards, restrooms, picnic tables, and showers
Contact: Volusia County Beach Services, 386/239-7873

18 27TH AVENUE PARK

Location: 27th Avenue at Atlantic Avenue in New Smyrna Beach
Parking/fees: free parking lot
Hours: sunrise-sunset
Facilities: lifeguards, restrooms, picnic tables, and showers
Contact: Volusia County Beach Services, 386/239-7873

19 MARY MCLEOD BETHUNE BEACH PARK

Location: 6656 South Atlantic Avenue in Bethune Beach
Parking/fees: free parking lot
Hours: sunrise-sunset
Facilities: concessions, lifeguards, restrooms, picnic tables, and showers
Contact: Volusia County Beach Services, 386/239-7873

RECREATION AND ATTRACTIONS

- **Ecotourism:** Apollo Beach and Mosquito Lagoon, Canaveral National Seashore, 386/428-3384
- **Fishing Charters:** Captain J.B.'s Fish Camp, 859 Pompano Street, New Smyrna Beach, 386/427-5747
- **Marina:** Fishin' Cove Marina, 111 North Riverside Drive, New Smyrna Beach, 386/428-7827
- **Rainy-Day Attraction:** Atlantic Center for the Arts, 1414 Art Center Avenue, New Smyrna Beach, 386/427-6975
- **Surf Shop:** Inlet Charley's, 510 Flagler Avenue, New Smyrna Beach, 386/427-5674; Nicols Surf Shop, 411 Flagler Avenue, New Smyrna Beach, 386/427-5050
- **Vacation Rentals:** Ocean Properties, 3506 South Atlantic Avenue, New Smyrna Beach, 386/428-0513

ACCOMMODATIONS

Condo-mania has gripped New Smyrna Beach. Unfortunately, a Great Wall of condos has screened out almost any other viable option for staying on the beach. The most obvious exception is the **Holiday Inn** (1401 South Atlantic Avenue, 386/426-0020, $$$), which directly overlooks one of the busiest sections of beach. Prices can be a touch on the high side since the town is a seller's market. But all units have kitchens and ocean-view balconies, the pool is large, and the property is well maintained. The only other viable option is the **Oceania Beach Resort,** which has both a hotel (425 Atlantic Avenue, 386/427-4636, $$$) and a beach club (421 South Atlantic Avenue, 386/423-8400). The latter is operated as a time-share resort, as so many beachside properties in Florida are these days.

COASTAL CUISINE

Norwood's Seafood Restaurant (400 Second Avenue, 386/428-4621, $$$) opened 60 years ago in what had formerly been a gas station, general store, mosquito control center, and piggy-bank factory. Tastefully and unobtrusively set among a grove of palms and fruit trees, Norwood's specializes in fresh seafood. In fact, they go through 2,000 pounds of fresh fish a week. Owners Don and Helen Simmons have won numerous awards, including several from Wine Spectator for their 40-page wine list. Despite these sophisticated touches, Norwood's remains firmly grounded in tradition.

After sampling appetizers of wood-smoked trout and sun-dried tomato brochette, we had entrees of char-broiled grouper and golden tilefish. The latter was topped with capers and salsa. Both were sensational. Non-fish eaters take note: Norwood's is also among the top servers of Angus beef in the nation.

Though nothing can touch Norwood's for dinner, you shouldn't miss **Captain J.B.'s Fish Camp** (859 Pompano Street, 386/427-5747, $$) for lunch. It's in the community of Bethune Beach, seven miles south of New Smyrna Beach and near the north entrance to Canaveral National Seashore. A ramshackle complex set along the Intracoastal Waterway, J.B.'s is indeed a working fish camp, with guides for hire, a bait and tackle shop, and a dock near which a "resident manatee" hangs his snout. Best of all, this lovably sloppy eatery serves "Southern Seafood at Its Finest" inside a large porch cooled by ceiling fans.

At the entrance, a smiling stuffed alligator sits on its tail (the Gator d'?). A notice warns that "Unattended Children Will Be Used As Crab Bait." Once inside, you take a seat at a picnic table covered in butcher paper, flag down a hard-working waitress, and rattle off your order. Start with conch fritters and proceed to any of a number of blackened specialties, including gator. We can also vouch for the steamed spiced shrimp and lightly fried oysters. While waiting for your order, wander around and admire the odd collection of artifacts. They could never franchise a place like J.B.'s—"Where Fun Is Legal"—because it's one of a kind. They sell great souvenir T-shirts, too.

NIGHTLIFE

Some of the old saloons on the edge of town are still in business, boasting names like **Bottom's Up Club** (2520 North Dixie Highway, 386/427-0364) and **Last Resort Bar** (5812 South Ridgewood Avenue, 386/761-5147) and catering to Harley crowd. A more appealing alternative, **Gilly's Pub 44** (1889 S.R. 44, 386/428-6523), is popular with rhinestone cowboys, sun-baked tourists, and motorcyclists alike. Located in a strip mall west of the causeway bridge, Gilly's is named for owner Gilly Aguiar, who was running for county commissioner the last time we looked. "Keep the charm and quality of life of New Smyrna Beach" was his motto. Hear, hear.

In the downtown area, there are a few friendly pubs along Flagler Avenue. There's not as many as used to exist when one was able to do the "Flagler crawl" from one to another, but you can still quaff a drink or two in friendly surroundings at **Traders** (317 Flagler Avenue, 386/428-9141) and **Flagler Tavern** (414 Flagler Avenue, 386/426-2080). Both get our nod of approval.

THE SPORTS COAST

COCOA BEACH AND THE SPACE COAST

America's space program went into orbit when the first manned flight was launched from Cape Canaveral in 1961. Even though our jaded modern world doesn't quite snap to attention like it did back in the heady days of the Apollo missions, the Kennedy Space Center—in north Brevard County, near Titusville and above Cocoa Beach—remains one of the top draws in Florida. To our thinking, it is the worthiest tourist attraction in the entire Sunshine State, celebrating the best ambitions and capabilities of the American spirit.

NASA's grand initiatives have given the Space Coast (which essentially means Brevard County and a nip of southern Volusia County) its publicity handle. Brevard County claims 72 miles of shoreline—more than any other county in Florida. The abundant beaches range from the isolation of Canaveral National Seashore to the surfable and sociable sands of Cocoa Beach. South Brevard County is a lengthy stretch of contiguous communities—including Satellite Beach, Indialantic, and Melbourne Beach—that run down to Sebastian Inlet.

The 33 miles of coast from Patrick Air Force Base to Sebastian Inlet are known as South Brevard County. The area used to have an understated appeal, until it turned up on developers' radar in recent yeas. Through most of this corridor, "Land For Sale" signs are jabbed into nearly every vacant lot along A1A. Condominiums are noticeable beyond the borders of the many county beach parks and accesses that are the area's saving grace. The community names change every few miles, and some (Satellite Beach, Canova Beach) are noticeably worse than others when it comes to yielding to developmental pressure.

Another decade down the road, it's anybody's guess what kind of zany high-rise crap will be plopped down out here. For now, the

© PARKE PUTERBAUGH

Old Florida beach ambience—mom-and-pop motels, local seafood joints, and watering holes—can still be turned up here and there, though the new-money imperatives of towering condos and gated communities encroach on them month by month and acre by acre. In late 2004, Hurricanes Jeanne and Frances both made landfall in the area, seriously chewing up South Brevard County's beaches. Oddly, we were told, rather than scare people away from the county, the hurricanes "put Melbourne on the map," triggering an even more active land rush. Many mom-and-pops took the developers' lucre and headed for higher ground.

Some of the names encountered in south Brevard County don't yet appear on maps, and even the locals can't always tell you where one town ends and another begins. To add to the confusion, most of the businesses out this way are listed under the city of Melbourne. But the beaches are nice, and some of them are exceptional.

Canaveral National Seashore

One of the longest and most gorgeous stretches of beach in the United States is Canaveral National Seashore—a pristine, undefiled ribbon of sand that runs for 33 miles. Canaveral, meaning "place of canes," is one of the oldest geographical names in America, originating with Ponce de Leon's claiming of the area for Spain in 1513. Canaveral and Merritt Island were originally set aside as buffers for NASA's activities back in the 1950s. Today, the former is administered by the National Park Service as Canaveral National Seashore, while the U.S. Fish and Wildlife Service oversees the latter as Merritt Island National Wildlife Refuge. Their mission goes far beyond the space program. These preserves serve as vital habitat for numerous types of flora and fauna—1,045 plant and 310 bird species—including 15 that are endangered or threatened. In particular, the

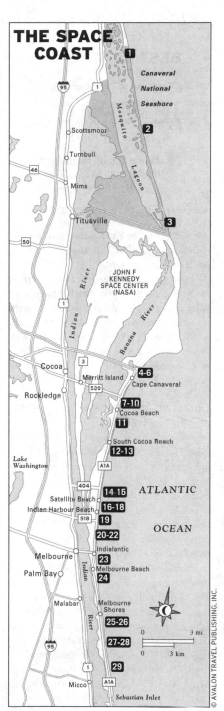

THE SPACE COAST

THE SPACE COAST

© AVALON TRAVEL PUBLISHING, INC.

BEST BEACHES

◖ **Apollo Beach:** Best Nude Beach (page 113)

◖ **Playalinda Beach:** Top 25, Best Nude Beach (page 113)

◖ **Merritt Island National Wildlife Refuge:** Best for Birdwatching and Wildlife-Viewing (page 115)

◖ **Cocoa Beach (north end):** Best for Surfing (page 124)

◖ **Lori Wilson Park:** Top 25, Best for Families (page 124)

marshes and diked impoundments of Merritt Island National Wildlife Refuge provide vital sanctuary for waterfowl.

Canaveral National Seashore is entered from the north end at Apollo Beach (roughly 10 miles south of New Smyrna Beach). A park road runs for seven miles along the beach, with five paved parking areas strewn along its length. Camping is permitted at four primitive sites November 1–April 30 and costs nothing beyond the $5 daily entrance fee.

The shallow body of water behind the beach at Canaveral is called Mosquito Lagoon. Running the length of Cape Canaveral National Seashore, it is the northernmost body of water in the 156-mile Indian River Lagoon. Mosquito Lagoon supports an ecosystem of extremely high biological diversity, but it has become a system out of balance. Various human-generated problems include wastewater pumped into it from Edgewater and New Smyrna Beach, sediment-laden storm runoff from developments, seagrass scarring by boat props, and bacterial contamination from leaking septic tanks. Researchers have been studying biodiversity and "biological fouling" in Mosquito Lagoon.

Mosquito Lagoon also used to be a haven for saltwater mosquitoes. (Here's a scary statistic: The area's salt marshes are capable of producing a million mosquitoes per square yard per day!) The conversion of 69,000 acres of salt marsh into diked freshwater impoundments has allowed for pest control on a grand scale.

However, efforts are underway to restore the salt marsh and reconnect the lagoon with the impoundments. If you want to learn more about the lagoon and its restoration, contact the Environmental Learning Center, 255 Live Oak Drive, Vero Beach, FL 32963, 561/589-5050, www.indian-river.fl.us/elc.

A short trail at the south end of **Apollo Beach**—accessed on the west side of the park road—leads to Eldora Hammock and the Eldora fishing piers, where you can cast into a tidal creek. Catches include redfish and spotted trout. Clam and oyster beds also thrive in the shallows. There's also a boat dock on Mosquito Lagoon at Shipyard Island, just before the Canaveral National Seashore Visitor Information Center. Boat ramps into the lagoon are located at parking area #5 and at Eddy Creek. Primitive camping is allowed at 11 designated island sites throughout the lagoon.

Canaveral National Seashore is entered from the south—via S.R. 406 and S.R. 402, which cut across Merritt Island National Wildlife Refuge—at **Playalinda Beach.** The launching pads of Kennedy Space Center are visible from the beach. (However, no one is allowed on the beach on launch days.) A four-mile road runs along Playalinda Beach, with parking lots every one-third mile or so. Nudity prevails on Playalinda Beach north of parking area #13. Not everyone likes the fact that this is a nude beach (one of a relatively small number in Florida), and it's been a controversial political hot potato over the years (see the *Playalinda Beach: Nude and Proud* sidebar). Incidentally, nudity is practiced, though in lesser numbers, at Apollo Beach, too. Walk south from the #5 dune crossover and take it all off, if you're so inclined.

What lies along the roadless stretch between Apollo and Playalinda beaches is perhaps most intriguing: 24 miles of isolated shoreline known as **Klondike Beach.** Yes, on a particularly built-up stretch of Florida's East Coast—between the speedway at Daytona and the space center at Titusville—exists a wilderness beach of great magnitude. Getting onto this desolate, striking beach means walking south from Apollo or north from Playalinda. Saw palmettos and Spanish bayonet rustle at the edge of short, sandy bluffs that drop to the beach. There's rarely another soul in sight.

Admission to Canaveral National Seashore is $5 per day, per vehicle; an annual pass is available for $35 per vehicle. Facilities are few: restrooms and drinking fountains at the Apollo and Playalinda Visitor Centers (which also feature informative exhibits) and portable restrooms at parking lots along the beach. A word of advice. Bring a cooler filled with beverages. In the blazing heat of summer, you will dehydrate quickly without frequent replenishment.

For more information, contact Canaveral National Seashore, 308 Julia Street, Titusville, FL 32796, 321/267-1110, www.nps.gov/cana.

BEACHES

1 APOLLO BEACH

BEST (

Location: Canaveral National Seashore
Parking/fees: $5 daily charge per vehicle to enter Cape Canaveral National Seashore. There is no additional fee for camping.
Hours: 6 A.M.-6 P.M.
Facilities: lifeguards (seasonal), restrooms, and a visitors center

Contact: Canaveral National Seashore, 386/428-3384

2 KLONDIKE BEACH

Location: 24 miles of wilderness beach, accessible only by foot, are located between Apollo Beach (south end of Volusia County) and Playalinda Beach (north end of Brevard County).
Parking/Fees: $5 daily charge per vehicle to enter Cape Canaveral National Seashore. There is no additional fee for camping.
Hours: 6 A.M.-6 P.M.
Facilities: none
Contact: Canaveral National Seashore, 321/267-1110

3 PLAYALINDA BEACH

BEST (

Location: From I-95, take Exit 80 (S.R. 406) at Titusville. After crossing the Indian River, take a right fork onto S.R. 402 and continue east to the beach. From Cocoa Beach, take A1A north to S.R. 528 and proceed west to S.R. 3. Follow S.R. 3 north to S.R. 402, then turn right (east) and proceed to the beach.
Parking/Fees: $5 daily charge per vehicle to enter Cape Canaveral National Seashore. There is no additional fee for camping.
Hours: 6 A.M.-6 P.M.
Facilities: restrooms and a visitors center
Contact: Canaveral National Seashore, 321/267-1110. For information on surf conditions and launch closures at Playalinda Beach, call 321/867-2805.

COASTAL CUISINE

Canaveral National Seashore headquarters are in Titusville, which lies on the west bank of the Indian River. I-95 passes through it, so if you're headed north or south to other points in Florida or east to the national seashore, you'll pass through it, too. Titusville is home to

THE SPACE COAST

PLAYALINDA BEACH: NUDE AND PROUD

Unlike liberated California, the state of Florida is not exactly overrun with clothing-optional beaches. There are really very few of note: Haulover and South Beach in Miami Beach, which attract more of an international clientele, are the obvious exceptions. Then there's Playalinda Beach, part of Canaveral National Seashore in Brevard County. Unlike the decadence that is accepted as a fact of life in Miami Beach, nudity still raises eyebrows on the Space Coast. This despite the fact that there is no dearth of strip clubs and X-rated video stores. Consequently, Playalinda Beach – whose north end is frequented by nude swimmers and sunbathers – has been a political hot potato. Brevard County has instituted an anti-nudity ordinance but it's ignored as legal challenges continue. Also, the National Park Service staff doesn't enforce county ordinances on federal property.

The babble of voices, pro and con, has made the issue a cause celebre from time to time. Here's the lay of the land: As often occurs on federally owned beaches, an area (usually remote) becomes known by word of mouth and force of habit as a nude beach. Up at Playalinda Beach the bathing suits melt away at the north end of Lot 13, where the road that follows the beach for four miles gives out. North of dune crossover 13B is where the fun really begins. The line of demarcation is pretty sharp. On one side, you have fishermen clad in jeans and T-shirts, happily casting away. On the other, you have people who aren't wearing a stitch, happily baring their privates to wind, sun, and water.

The situation grew heated in the early 1990s, when park superintendent Wendell Simpson cracked down on what he saw as "lewd and lascivious behavior." In 1993, he oversaw the arrest of more than 100 nudists on sex charges. When no federal and state laws held up in court, he worked in concert with the conservative, Arizona-based National Family Legal Foundation to implement a law at the local level banning nudity. Brevard County ordinance 95-21 makes it illegal to be nude or wear a thong bathing suit in public. Adding fuel to the fire was a congressman who checked out the scene after receiving complaints from constituents. Of course, he promptly pronounced himself offended.

The nudists have continued disrobing, testing both the legality and enforce-

one of our favorite Florida restaurants: **Dixie Crossroads** (1475 Garden Street, 321/268-5000, $$). It's located near the "crossroads" of Park Avenue and Garden Street, two miles east of I-95. Shrimp is the specialty here, especially rock shrimp. Caught hereabouts, they have hard, purplish shells and taste a bit like lobster. They serve two other kinds of shrimp—"boat run" and "large"—along with scallops and various fresh catches. We're partial to the "Cape Canaveral"—a platter that includes two dozen rock shrimp, a dozen boat-run shrimp, and a quarter pound of scallops, all for $20.99 (and $12 more if you add a whole Maine lobster). Our second favorite is the "Indian River" platter: fish (especially if it's

triggerfish), rock shrimp, scallops, and stuffed crab for $14.99.

Folks, it just doesn't get any better than this, especially when your platter is proceeded by a basket of hot corn fritters dusted in confectioner's sugar. If you're traveling with the family, they have cheap ($2.99) kids' plates, too. You might have to wait if you come at the height of the lunch or dinner rushes but that's okay because there are lots of benches and you can feed the fish in the outdoor pond. Another plus: The owners are good stewards of the land, being involved with habitat preservation and environmental education at Merritt Island National Wildlife Refuge. Good folks, good food.

ability of the prohibition. An exasperated park ranger to whom we spoke had this to say: "How can we enforce an ordinance like that when there's 40 miles of beach and maybe one ranger on duty, and he's got to worry about collecting entrance fees and any *real* crimes that might get committed? We've got more important things to do."

To which we can only add, folks, it's really no big deal. We saw no orgies nor heard any talk of a sexual nature on the beach. Just a bunch of naked people in the sand, tanning areas of the flesh that normally don't see the light of day. On a warm summer Saturday, we witnessed approximately 100 nude sunbathers along about a mile's worth of beach. They were mainly clumped a short distance north of the No. 13B crossover and thereafter thinned out quickly. Statistically, the crowd looked to be 80 percent male and 20 percent female. Most of the nude sunbathers appeared to be gay males. Maybe a third of the remainder were true naturists and the rest heterosexual couples. You'd really have to go out of your way to be offended by the docile scene at Playalinda Beach, and it's really not worth the trouble. There's too much beach out here to let a sliver of naturism ruin your day.

Although the standoff continues, it's simmered down somewhat since park superintendent Simpson took a new assignment in 1997. The Brevard County ordinance banning beach nudity is still on the books, but goes unenforced. Only four citations were issued in 1999, and in the ensuing years, the furor has died down as cooler heads have prevailed. One of us felt compelled to break the law as a kind of statement of personal freedom. For those who have never tried it, swimming nude in the great, balmy Atlantic in summertime is indeed a liberating feeling – unless visions of stinging jellyfish and Portuguese man-of-wars begin playing havoc with your mind, at which point a swimsuit does seem practical. And what of sunburn in tender places?

By and large, we side with the nudists of Playalinda Beach, as long as they remain discreet. (As discreet as one can be in public without clothing, that is.) As for those naysayers who are ashamed of their bodies and everyone else's, we have one bit of advice: Mind your own business.

For the record, nudity is tolerated at Apollo Beach, up at the north end of Canaveral National Seashore, too. The "traditional naturist area" at Apollo Beach is south of the last dune crossover (#5).

BEST❶ Merritt Island National Wildlife Refuge

Originally set aside as a buffer zone for NASA's operations at Cape Canaveral, Merritt Island has, quite frankly, gone to the birds—310 species of them, as a matter of fact. More endangered and threatened species of all kinds visit or make their home on Merritt Island than any other continental wildlife refuge. They include bald eagles, wood storks, Florida scrub jays, peregrine falcons, and brown pelicans, as well as manatees and sea turtles on the non-avian side. Then there's

the inundation of non-endangered species. In winter, as many as 70,000 migratory waterfowl are on the refuge. There's a lot of room for them, as Merritt Island National Wildlife Refuge (140,000 acres) and Canaveral National Seashore (which adjoins it to the east) collectively preserve 239,000 acres of prime central Florida coast real estate.

The centerpiece of the refuge for visitors is Black Point Wildlife Drive. This unpaved, one-way road makes a seven-mile circuit through piney flatwoods and along the edges of diked impoundments that serve as habitat for waterfowl. You'll want to move slowly, stopping to sight bald-eagle nests or skinny ospreys spearing a meal from the water. Better

THE SPACE COAST

SPACE IS THE PLACE: A TOUR OF KENNEDY SPACE CENTER

The closest place to the moon in this world is the Kennedy Space Center (KSC), east of Titusville and just above Port Canaveral on Florida's Space Coast. We've toured the complex repeated times and are impressed by the tours and exhibits. In fact, we've left the grounds dreaming the dream of every kid who grew up in the 1960s of wanting to become an astronaut. It's a little late for us, but you can still entertain that fantasy by visiting KSC. We consider it the premier man-made attraction in Florida, because it speaks so eloquently to the most high-minded strivings of the human species.

The Kennedy Space Center is surrounded by the isolated acreage of Canaveral National Seashore and Merritt Island National Wildlife Refuge. Roughly 1.5 million people visit the space center yearly. The continued obsession with the space program was driven home on July 13, 2005, when we got caught in a 50-mile traffic jam to watch what was supposed to be the first Space Shuttle launch in two and a half years. We were headed from Orlando to a viewing site, duly obtained KSC passes in hand, but traffic quickly ground to a halt on the so-called Beeline (S.R. 528). So we turned around. Wise move, because the launch was delayed anyway, finally going up on July 26.

If you were to relocate the United Nations inside Grand Central Station, you'd have an idea of the Kennedy Space Center Visitor Complex, which teems with chatter made in many languages. This is where you pay up and begin your tour. When we say "pay up," we are not kidding, as admission is not cheap: a flat fee of $30 per adult and $20 per child (aged 3-11) for the basic Kennedy Space Center Tour. That ticket is good for all Visitor Complex movies, exhibits, and shows – except for the nearby Astronaut Hall of Fame and its space-flight simulators. A "Maximum Access" costing $37 ($27 for kids) includes these, too.

Beyond these basics, there are other, pricier tours you can take: "NASA Up Close," a small-group guided tour that visits the launch pads and Vehicle Assembly building ($52 for adults, $36 for kids) and "Cape Canaveral: Then and Now," a more historical look at the facilities that costs the same price.

Since a basic ticket will cost $100 for a family of four, we would urge you to come early and plan on spending most of the day to make it worth your while. There is plenty to do here. The tour is taken by bus, which begins at the visitor center complex and drops you off at two sites – the LC-39 Observation Gantry and the Apollo/Saturn V Center – before returning you to the visitor center. There are things to do at all three places.

yet, bring bikes and meander along the drive at ground level. Early morning and late afternoon are the best times for wildlife viewing, and the winter months are optimum in terms of bird numbers. Linger a while and soak up some of nature's slower rhythms; you won't be sorry.

To get to Merritt Island National Wildlife Refuge from I-95, take Exit 80 (S.R. 406) and then follow S.R. 402 east (to the visitors center) or continue on S.R. 406 to Black Point Wildlife Drive.

For more information, contact Merritt Is-land National Wildlife Refuge, P.O. Box 6504, Titusville, FL 32782, 321/861-0667, www.fws.gov/merrittisland.

Cape Canaveral

Cape Canaveral (pop. 9,200) lies east of Kennedy Space Center and above Cocoa Beach. It is so close to the latter that residential Cape Canaveral is practically indistinguishable from north Cocoa Beach. In fact, the two

Plan to spend the most time at the Apollo/Saturn V Center, which is a jaw-dropper. The *Saturn V* rocket that launched *Apollo VIII* has been arrayed end-to-end inside the exhibit building, and it is longer than a football field. The very idea that this 363-foot and 6.2 million-pound behemoth overcame gravity and propelled a capsule into space seems impossible. This it did with more horsepower (160,000,000 hp) than 8,000 starting fields in the Daytona 500. It is claimed that Saturn V/Apollo 8 tandem is the most complex machine ever built by humans. En route to the LC-39 Observation Gantry, you'll pass the Vehicle Assembly Building, a 525-foot-high building where these marvels are put together.

Back at the Visitor Complex, two IMAX films – *The Dream Is Alive,* a space shuttle documentary, and *L5: First City in Space,* a fictional view of a future space settlement – play all day. The first of these documents a shining moment in the domestic space program and contains outstanding footage of our little blue marble from the depths of space.

At the height of the Apollo program, the space center employed 3,000 workers. The average *Apollo* astronaut was 32 years old, 5 feet 10 inches tall, and weighed 164 pounds. Wanna meet an astronaut? Every day of the year a real live space sojourner takes questions from tour groups and reminisces about his or her adventures. It's a guaranteed thrill for children of all ages – including baby boomers like us who grew up watching the space race. One of our kids, Hayley Puterbaugh, got to meet and pose with astronaut Charlie Walker, who flew on a few shuttle missions.

If we recited all the facts thrown at us on the various tours we've taken here, we'd be well on our way toward writing another book. Suffice it to say that you'll have a wonderful time at the Kennedy Space Center. A visit here is will provide an instant cure for wavering patriotism. It recalls a more inspired time when unity of mission, civility of discourse and soaring ambition allowed this country to send a man to the moon and more. In the words of astronaut Neil Armstrong, the first man to walk on the moon, "With courage, imagination and the will to explore, no dream is impossible."

To get here from I-95 or U.S. 1, take S.R. 405 east to NASA Parkway and follow signs to the Kennedy Space Center Visitor Complex. From Cocoa Beach, take S.R. 520 north to S.R. 528 west, then proceed north on S.R. 3 to NASA Parkway and the visitor complex. Kennedy Space Center Visitor Complex is open daily, except Christmas and certain launch days, 9 A.M.–5:30 P.M.

For more information, contact the Kennedy Space Center Visitor Complex, Kennedy Space Center, FL 32899, 321/449-4444, www.kennedyspacecenter.com.

communities merge seamlessly, at least on the ocean. There is nothing particularly appealing about Cape Canaveral or north Cocoa Beach, unless you really like donut shops, gas stations, and mile after mile of unspectacular franchised commerce or have some reason to be here on business.

To a visitor, the most interesting part of Cape Canaveral is Port Canaveral, off A1A up at the north end. The port is an enormous complex of container and cruise ships, charter boats, storage facilities, docks, restaurants, and parks. Whether you're heading to the Bahamas aboard Canaveral Cruise Lines or merely want a seafood dinner on the waterfront, Port Canaveral is the busy, bustling heart of Cape Canaveral.

For more information, contact the Cocoa Beach Area Chamber of Commerce, 400 Fortenberry Road, Merritt Island, FL 32952, 321/459-2200, www.cocoabeachchamber.com; or the Space Coast Office of Tourism, 2725 Judge Fran Jamieson Way, B-105, Viera, FL 32940, 321/637-5483, www.space-coast.com.

BEACHES

Jetty Park is one of three parks run by the Canaveral Port Authority. Its 150-site campground is close to the park's half-mile beach, which offers views of ships coming and going from the port. On the grounds are a bait-and-tackle shop, concession stand, and a 1,200-foot fishing pier. Beach rentals and year-round lifeguards, too! All for a $5 per car entrance fee. Many improvements were made in 2000, all aimed at making Jetty Park "one of the best recreational park's on Florida's East Coast," in the Port Authority's own words.

Cape Canaveral also lays claim to peachy-keen **Cherie Down Park,** a charming seven-acre beachside park with a boardwalk and dune walkovers at either end. It's a bit off the beaten track for tourists but well worth seeking out. Also within Cape Canaveral, public beach access is offered via dune walkovers along more than two miles of beach.

4 JETTY PARK

Location: 400 East Jetty Road, at the east end of S.R. 528 in Cape Canaveral. From the entrance to Port Canaveral, bear right and follow signs to Jetty Park.

Parking/Fees: $5 per car entrance fee ($7 for RVs). Depending on time of year, camping fees are $25-31 for "improved" RV sites, $18-24 for rustic tent sites, and $22-28 for "semi-improved" (water and sewer) sites.

Hours: 24 hours

Facilities: concession, lifeguards, restrooms, picnic tables, and showers

Contact: Jetty Park Campground, 321/783-7111

5 CHERIE DOWN PARK

Location: 8492 Ridgewood Avenue in Cape Canaveral. From North Atlantic Avenue, turn east on Harrison Avenue and then north on Ridgewood Avenue. Park is a half-mile north.

Parking/Fees: free parking lot

Hours: 7 A.M.-sunset

Facilities: lifeguards (seasonal), restrooms, picnic tables, and showers

Contact: Brevard County Parks and Recreation Department (central area), 321/455-1380

6 CAPE CANAVERAL

Location: There are 2.3 miles of beaches, from Washington Avenue south to Wilson Avenue, off Ridgewood Avenue in Cape Canaveral.

Parking/Fees: free street parking and parking lots at the ends of Grant, Hayes, Garfield, Arthur, and Wilson Avenues

Hours: sunrise-sunset

Facilities: none

Contact: Cape Canaveral Public Works Department, 321/868-1240

ACCOMMODATIONS

If you want to stay directly on the beach, the options are limited in Cape Canaveral. The newly arrived exception is **Ron Jon Cape Caribe Resort** (1100 Shorewood Drive, 321/784-4922, $$$$). Of course, nothing's quite as easy as it seems in the modern world. A hotel is not a hotel but a vacation-ownership resort through which one may rent a villa for a night or longer. If you do stay here, you'll hear all about opportunities to become an owner. Hey, the hard sell starts down at Ron Jon Surf Shop, where a table is set up by the entrance and hirelings thrust brochures and pitches at shoppers before they can even enter the store to browse for Ron Jon–branded merchandise.

Ron Jon Cape Caribe Resort is a Caribbean-themed resort with an on-premises grill and recreation galore (basketball and tennis courts, miniature golf course, huge pool with waterslide). Whether you want to pay sky-high rates to stay "nestled" (their word) between Cocoa Beach and Cape Canaveral is up to you. But we frankly prefer the ease of transaction of checking into a motel or hotel and using the savings for dining and attractions. And we're worried that these high-priced spreads might be setting a bad precedent here on the largely affordable Space Coast.

There are alternatives to Ron Jon. If you want to be near Port Canaveral, book at the **Radisson Cape Canaveral Resort** (8701 Astronaut Boulevard, 321/784-0000, $$$). **Cape Winds Resort** (7400 Ridgewood Drive, 321/783-6226, $$$$) is a 67-unit condo hotel that preceded Ron Jon; it too has tennis and basketball courts.

COASTAL CUISINE

Locals and visitors alike head up to "The Cove at Port Canaveral," an area of restaurants, bars, and boats where ample servings of dinner and nightlife can be had. We're fondest of **Grills Seafood Deck & Tiki Bar** (505 Glen Creek Drive, 321/868-2226, $$), an indoor-outdoor restaurant and bar whose menu is refreshingly blunt on one point: "If you want fried fish, go to Long John Silver's." True to their name, they serve grilled fish here. The offerings change nightly, depending on whatever's fresh (tuna, mahi, grouper, cobia), but the price remains the same. a reasonable $15.99. The surroundings are unfancy (beer lights, unvarnished wood, hanging plants), the servers are unpretentious (tattoos, bared midriffs), and there's a special parking area for choppers. Sunbeaten bikers and Midwestern families of five alike come here for some serious grilled fish. Appetizers include a killer Bahamian chowder (brown, thick, and spicy), steamed shrimp, conch fritters, "voodoo wings," and a few sushi offerings. Wash it all down with a tropical drink. Forget about desserts, which aren't made in-house.

Rusty's Seafood & Oyster Bar (628 Glen Cheek Drive, 321/783-2033, $$)—which has a sister operation in Cocoa Beach—is casual and inexpensive. It serves $0.25 oysters at happy hour (3 p.m.–6 p.m. daily) and a raft of dinner choices: sandwiches, fried seafood baskets, early-bird specials, and nightly deals on entrees like blackened grouper and mahimahi.

Wander around Port Canaveral and you'll find more spots that serve grouper, oysters, beer, and live music in casual surroundings.

NIGHTLIFE

The bar at Rusty's (see *Coastal Cuisine*) makes a cool spot to down beer and oysters. There's often live music, usually reggae, blaring from various places on the water at Port Canaveral. Just keep your antennae up as you stroll along, and duck inside when you hear something agreeable. Or keep walking and enjoy the bobbing vessels, if you don't.

Cocoa Beach

Cocoa Beach (pop. 13,000) is indelibly linked to two things: the Kennedy Space Center and its world-class beach. Its accessibility to these attractions is a sufficient draw for the middle-brow tourism that pumps up everything out here. Everything about Cocoa Beach—sand, meals, motels, nightlife—seems aimed at striking the Golden Mean.

It's a family-friendly beach town whose selling point is affordability. Several years back, the local tourist board boasted that the average price of a Cocoa Beach motel room is $47 per night. It's gone up a bit; we'd guess that $60 sounds right, averaged out over the course of a year. Still, given its world-class beach, Cocoa Beach remains a real bargain. In fact, we'd argue that with Orlando only an hour away and the Kennedy Space Center close by, Cocoa Beach makes the most sensible home base for a central Florida vacation. The town occupies a long, narrow barrier island between the Banana River and the Atlantic Ocean. It has swaying palms, tree-lined neighborhoods, good traffic flow, and an appealingly low-key demeanor. Cocoa Beach still bears scars from the catastrophic 2004 hurricane season, though storm damage is far more evident in southern Brevard County.

Cocoa Beach first asserted its modest claim

MOUSIN' AROUND ORLANDO: THE LOWDOWN ON DISNEY WORLD

In 20 years of researching and writing about Florida's beaches, we've rarely ventured more than a few miles inland. We've taken great pains *not* to write about Orlando or Disney World in *Florida Beaches*. In fact, we've touted past editions as being a "Disney-free zone."

And then we had kids. When they got old enough, we took them to Disney World. They had a great time (no surprise). Lo and behold, we had a good time, too (big surprise). Return visits to Orlando have been made. In other words, pigs have flown and hell has frozen over.

The truth is, most Americans who have children will become willing prisoners of the Mouse at some point. How does that relate to this book? It may surprise you to learn that Orlando is only 60 miles from Cocoa Beach, a straight shot west on S.R. 528 (a.k.a. the Bee Line). The trip can be made in either direction in an hour. If you're vacationing in Cocoa Beach, you can easily check out Disney World (and vice versa). Their proximity makes for a good dual-destination vacation – hitting one or more of Orlando's theme parks (Disney World, Universal Studios, and Sea World being the Holy Trinity) and then chilling out by the ocean in Cocoa Beach.

Having softened toward Disney in our middle-aged senility, we offer the following suggestions – based on our own experiences – on how to approach this mother of all theme parks.

Tip #1: You don't need a separate guidebook to plan a trip to Disney. Folding maps that detail each of the four theme parks – Magic Kingdom, Epcot, MGM-Disney, and Animal Kingdom – are available for free from Disney (407/934-7639). You can also pick up these guide maps at any hotel or resort on Disney property and at the gates of the four theme parks and their guest-relations kiosks. They offer brief descriptions of rides and attractions, plus places to eat or snack on property. You can quickly plot out your day(s) by poring over them.

Tip #2: Don't pay through the nose to stay in a room at a hotel or resort where you'll spend little time. You can ante up $300-500 (or more) a night for "deluxe" Disney lodgings like the Grand Floridian and the Yacht & Beach Club. They're top-of-the-line alright, but why pay an exorbitant tariff if you'll be using your room mainly as a place to sleep, shower, and store luggage? We recommend the "moderate" lodges – especially Caribbean Beach and Port Orleans – which cost half or even a third as much ($134-165 per night). Port Orleans has "French Quarter" (1,000 rooms) and "Riverside" (2,000 rooms) sections that faithfully re-create the look and ambience of New Orleans (without the crime). In fact, you'll find more of New Orleans at Disney World than in Louisiana in the wake of Hurricane Katrina. The "value" lodgings ($77-111 per night) are best for families on a budget. All-Star Movies, with its animated-film motifs, is a kid-pleasing choice. If you do want to go deluxe, Animal Kingdom Lodge is the most reasonably priced and appealing. It's worth paying extra for a savanna-side room to watch African wildlife graze outside your window. And the lodge has our favorite restaurant – Boma, an African-food buffet – in all of Disney.

Tip #3: Ask about specials and package deals when calling for reservations. Disney has begun offering all-inclusive vacations that include lodgings, theme-park tickets and meals. For $1,243.04 (including tax) one of us purchased a five-day, four-night package that included a riverside room at Port Orleans French Quarter. The family wore out its feet in the theme parks and ate like kings and queens at Cinderella's Royal Castle and other restaurants. More than a deal, it felt like a steal and may indicate the tourism pinch that even Disney is feeling in these down times.

Tip #4: When it comes to purchasing tickets to Disney World, be aware that there's really very little difference in cost between five- and 10-day passes. A five-day ticket, good for visiting one park per day, costs $193 ($155 for kids 3-9). A 10-day ticket costs just $15 more (and only $12 more for kids). Prices jump from 12 percent to 15 percent if you choose the "Park Hopper" option, which lets you visit multiple parks each day. Annual passes cost $395 ($336 for kids 3-9) and are worth considering if you'll be down more than once in a 12-month period.

Tip #5: Favorite restaurants: Wolfgang Puck's, in Downtown Disney (try the sushi platter or pasta dishes). Le Cellier at the Canadian area in Epcot's World Showcase (great steak and filet mignon). Boma, at Animal Kingdom Lodge (incredible African food). Coral Reef, at Epcot's Living Seas pavilion (good seafood dishes, like the tilapia/crabcake combo, and a six million gallon aquarium). Cinderella's Royal Table, in Magic Kingdom (little girls will love it, and the food is first-rate). Crystal Palace, in Magic Kingdom (Disney characters circulate while diners graze from a buffet whose offerings range from rotisserie chicken to green Thai curry). A word of warning: you can't help but eat a lot at Disney, but you tend to walk it off.

Tip #6: Favorite rides: Rock 'n' Roller Coaster (your "limo" to an Aerosmith show accelerates from zero to 60 in 2.8 seconds and spins you through two loops and a corkscrew). Tower of Terror (Twilight Zone-theme elevator lifts and drops you 13 stories; it's less jarring than it sounds.) Space Mountain (indoor coaster simulates space travel and darkness adds to thrills). Soarin' (hang-glide above the Napa Valley using IMAX technology). Fast Track (simulated automotive test track subjects you to white-knuckle extremes, including speed and curves; cars actually reach 65 mph on straightaway). Splash Mountain (our favorite ride lasts longer than most others and has great scenery and songs – plus a thrilling final plunge). A must to avoid: Mission: SPACE (unless you relish the thought of throwing up your last meal).

Tip #7: Favorite shows: Lights! Motors! Action! Extreme Stunt Show and Indiana Jones Epic Stunt Spectacular (fast-paced, informative, and entertaining, with plenty of thrills, chills, explosions, and stunts). Mickey's Philharmagic (best 3D movie at Disney World and a guaranteed child-pleaser). Honey, I Shrunk the Audience (3D comedy short starring Eric Idle and Rick Moranis; a snake's flicking tongue is the best special effect). Maelstrom (located in Norway, this is our favorite boat cruise in Epcot's World Showcase). Kilimanjaro Safari (jeep tour of the Serengeti that culminates with the "arrest" of poachers; good message for kiddies about protecting wildlife)

Tip #8: Don't come to Disney with infants or very small children. They don't know what's going on and will spend a lot of time crying unhappily due to crowds, noise, intense Florida sun, and all the scary, jostling rides their witless parents drag them on. Why spend thousands of dollars on a vacation that will mean little or nothing to them? They can't (or shouldn't) be allowed on many of these rides at that age anyway. Wait until they're old enough to "feel the magic" – at around age four, in our opinion. If you do come with infants or young kids, bring a stroller or rent one when you get here. (You'll thank us for this last bit of advice.) And don't stick them on inappropriate rides. Even if your little tyke meets the height requirement, he or she may well wind up traumatized and squalling on the Tower of Terror.

Tip #9: Stay away from Disney World in the summertime. It's the busiest, hottest and most uncomfortable time to be here. Avoid the week after Christmas and Easter season, as they're also crowded. At these times, wait times for rides can grow uncomfortably long. Worse, the hot, humid Central Florida summer will leave you wilted and cranky, while the predictable afternoon thunderstorms will soak you from head to toe. At other times of year, prices and temperatures go down considerably. Try coming anytime from Labor Day through Thanksgiving. If you do show up in hot weather, plan to arrive in the park early each day, head back to your hotel for a break in the afternoon, and then return around sundown for more fun.

Tip #10: Use Fast Passes. The most popular rides and attractions offer Fast Pass distribution, which minimizes time spent in line by giving you a sort of reservation that's good for quick entry during a specified hour-long block of time. You can get a Fast Pass, go elsewhere, and then return to take the ride without a frustrating wait.

One final tip: Leave your Disney preconceptions and prejudices at the gates and have fun.

THE SPACE COAST

to fame when John F. Kennedy ignited the space race back in the early 1960s. His exact words: "Surely the opening vistas of space promise high costs and hardships, as well as high rewards. But man in his quest for knowledge and progress is determined and cannot be deterred. For the eyes of the world now look into space, to the moon, and to the planets beyond." The luster and pizzazz of the space program helped bring to life an area that was otherwise known largely for citrus groves.

With NASA's burgeoning budget came an influx of professionals: engineers, designers, technicians, and assistants. Before the astronauts, Tom Wolfe wrote in *The Right Stuff,* "Cocoa Beach was the resort town for all the low-rent folks who couldn't afford the resort towns further south." After they arrived, "Cocoa Beach [began] to take on the raw excitement of a boom town and the manic and motley cast of characters that goes with it." In other words, it evolved from a low-rent resort town to one with a quicker pulse and more money.

What held true of Cocoa Beach in the 1960s remains true today, to a great degree. Hemmed in by the Kennedy Space Center to the north and Patrick Air Force Base to the south, Cocoa Beach combines the nondescript look of a military town with the unpretentious air of a populist beach destination. Steady growth has brought malls, restaurants, gas stations, and convenience marts, particularly along a 10-mile stretch on S.R. 520 between Cocoa Beach and the western edge of Cocoa (a mainland town with a population of 16,500). Along the ocean, particularly north of the modest town center, Cocoa Beach offers its share of hotels, motels, and condos. Yet the town somehow manages to be way more pleasant and low-key than, say, Daytona Beach. Beachside parks break up the monotony of buildings and retail commerce, and south Cocoa Beach is highly residential.

One nice thing about Cocoa Beach is that the beachside thoroughfare—Ocean Beach Boulevard—is discontinuous. This makes for a less car-choked beachfront with discrete pockets of activity, such as Cocoa Beach Pier. It's not exactly bursting with personality, but there is something appealingly sunny and unchanging about Cocoa Beach. How can you not like a community that named one of its side streets after Major Anthony Nelson, the fictional astronaut of *I Dream of Jeannie* fame?

For more information, contact the Cocoa Beach Area Chamber of Commerce, 400 Fortenberry Road, Merritt Island, FL 32952, 321/459-2200, www.cocoabeachchamber.com; or the Space Coast Office of Tourism, 8810 Astronaut Boulevard, Suite 102, Cape Canaveral, FL 32920, 321/868-1126 or 800/93-OCEAN, www.space-coast.com.

BEACHES

Cocoa Beach is the most crowded stretch of Brevard County's long, unbroken strand, which runs from Port Canaveral to Sebastian Inlet. This is a quintessential American beach: green water and a wide, medium-grained brown-sand beach peopled with visitors of every race, creed, color, and swimsuit size. They tend to congregate most densely around Cocoa Beach Pier, located on Atlantic and Meade Avenues up toward the north end of town. Surfers catch waves on both sides of the pier. Kids splash and frolic. Parents repose on chaise lounges and surf chairs. The only thing missing from this picture is lifeguards. The lack of lifeguards around the populated pier and city beaches seems an obvious demerit against Cocoa Beach, and one that should be addressed and remedied, because the beach itself is a treasure. The pier is pretty remarkable, with 270 pilings pounded 15 feet into the sand to keep this 800-foot-long beast structurally sound. It proved itself seaworthy once again during the hurricanes of 2004, when it closed for only two days after Frances and five days after Jeanne.

In addition to a vast beach strand accessible from 40 street ends (useful if you're not staying on the ocean), a quartet of beachside parks

RON JON SURF SHOP

One thing you can do at Cocoa Beach that can be done nowhere else, aside from watching space shuttle launches at close range, is shop for surfwear in the middle of the night. If Cocoa Beach nightlife is pedestrian and disappointing, there's always **Ron Jon Surf Shop** (3850 South Banana River Boulevard, 321/799-8888 or 888/RJ-SURFS), which is open 24 hours a day, seven days a week, all year round. We've certainly availed ourselves of the opportunity to buy T-shirts at 3 A.M. One time we even browsed the racks at Ron Jon's during a hurricane (no lie!). It was Hurricane Irene, which blew through on October 16, 1999. The store remained open, even as hotels and restaurants in the area lost electricity and roads flooded. While rain and wind pelted the windows, we calmly tried on logoed T-shirts.

Located where Minuteman Causeway (S.R. 520) meets Atlantic Avenue (A1A), Ron Jon is the Taj Mahal of surf shops. A complex of buildings bathed in hot neon pink and turquoise, it dominates the landscape like nothing else in Cocoa Beach, including its tallest hotels. First, there's Ron Jon's "sports park," a combination sculpture garden and parking lot with towering life-size depictions of surfers frozen in the act of catching a monster wave. The main building is the cathedral, devoted to retailing a holy kingdom's worth of T-shirts, walking shorts, swimsuits, ball caps, and other apparel. Two other buildings rent and sell recreation equipment, from surfboards to Jet Skis. At midnight on a Friday, Ron Jon's is likely to be doing more business than most nightclubs in Cocoa Beach.

Indeed, one cannot leave town without a Ron Jon T-shirt. If you're a modest suburbanite, a three-button henley with a discreet Ron Jon logo will suffice. If you're a hip, urban-dwelling Gen X-er, a T-shirt with a huge glow-in-the-dark Ron Jon logo on the back is a must.

The irony is that if you're a real surfer, you'll probably be found nowhere near Ron Jon. It's simply too big, too touristy. Surfers prefer more dedicated, less commercial shops run by members of the tribe: fellow board bums and board shapers. To them, a place like Ron Jon – 52,000 square feet of clothing, souvenirs, and surfboards – is a blasphemy better suited to tourists. We're not quite so elitist about it, so we've had a fine time browsing the racks at Ron Jon over the years. It's especially fun in the wee hours.

A visit to Ron Jon can be entertaining, but it also must be noted that it's a little like historian Daniel Boorstin's definition of "celebrity" in his book *The Image*: i.e., someone who's famous for being famous. Endless Ron Jon billboards line I-95 in a visual assault second only to South of the Border's infamous roadside procession in the Carolinas. Ron Jon's billboards are as well known as the store itself.

Incidentally, Ron Jon now has its own resorts: one in Ormond Beach and a recent arrival in Cape Canaveral. This drives home the point that Ron Jon is not only a surf shop, but a burgeoning commercial empire. After awhile, even we've found ourselves asking, What does this have to do with surfing?

offer free picnic shelters and basic facilities. They are, from north to south, Sheppard Park, Sidney Fischer Park, Lori Wilson Park, and Robert P. Murkshe Memorial Park. Among them, all but Murkshe Park post lifeguards (albeit only from Easter through Labor Day and on weekends through late October).

Sheppard Park is named for astronaut Alan Sheppard, and it's located where Minuteman Causeway (S.R. 520) meets Ridgewood Avenue at the beach. It's a great place to bring a picnic and/or watch anything that's launching from Cape Canaveral. A half-mile south is **Sidney Fischer Park,** named for a former Cocoa Beach mayor, which offers more of the same. Both charge a $5 parking fee.

We are especially fond of the county-run **Lori Wilson Park,** at which a boardwalk nature trail winds through a patch of maritime forest. The park claims 1,000 feet of beachfront right in the heart of Cocoa Beach, bounded by north and south parking areas. There's also a sand volleyball court, picnic area and playground, and a nature center with some hands-on exhibits.

Below this area, the east-west streets are numbered, the island thins a bit, and A1A hugs the shore more closely. In South Cocoa Beach, the beach can be accessed via street ends from 4th Street north to 15th Street south. Down at this end you'll find a modest residential neighborhood where it's not unusual to find homes with pink flamingos staked into the front yards. The beaches themselves are narrower but pleasantly uncrowded. The last of the city beaches, located at 16th Street South, is **Robert P. Murkshe Memorial Park.** Named for yet another mayor, Murkshe Park is a small oceanfront park with a few picnic shelters and a free parking lot.

The island reaches its narrowest point around **South Cocoa/North Patrick Beach,** roughly from Olive Street south to 35th Street. The most popular spot along this strip is located at the end of Crescent Beach Drive. All of the town's beaches suffered erosion, from minor to severe, during both Hurricanes Frances and Jeanne in 2004. But Cocoa Beach was spared the worst effects of these storms due to an ongoing beach restoration project that buffered some of the flood and storm-surge damage.

Incidentally, if you'd like to hear a prerecorded surf report, you've got your choice of three, each provided by a Cocoa Beach surf shop: **Ron Jon** (800/717-BEACH), **Quiet Flight** (321/783-6640), and **Natural Art** (321/784-2400). The concentration of surf shops in Cocoa Beach reflects the fact that the area offers some of the best surfing in Florida—especially at Cocoa Beach Pier, Patrick Air Force Base, and Sebastian Inlet.

7 COCOA BEACH (NORTH END)

 BEST

Location: 1.5 miles of beach, from Harding Avenue south to Flagler Lane in Cocoa Beach

Parking/Fees: metered parking lots at the ends of Harding, Barlow, Meade, Pulsipher, and Winslow Avenues, and at the ends of Leon, Osceola, Gadsden, Marion, Palm, and Flagler Lanes. The Cocoa Beach Pier is at the end of Meade Avenue.

Hours: sunrise-sunset

Facilities: concession and restrooms (at Cocoa Beach Pier)

Contact: Cocoa Beach Parks Department, 321/868-3274

8 SHEPPARD PARK

Location: east end of S.R. 520 at Ridgewood Avenue in Cocoa Beach

Parking/Fees: $5 per vehicle entrance fee

Hours: sunrise-sunset

Facilities: restrooms, picnic tables, and showers

Contact: Cocoa Beach Parks Department, 321/868-3274

9 SIDNEY FISCHER PARK

Location: 0.5 mile south of S.R. 520 on A1A in Cocoa Beach

Parking/Fees: $5 per vehicle entrance fee

Hours: sunrise-sunset

Facilities: restrooms, picnic tables, and showers

Contact: Cocoa Beach Parks Department, 321/868-3274

10 LORI WILSON PARK

 BEST

Location: 1.4 miles south of Minuteman Cause-

way (S.R. 520) at North Atlantic Avenue (A1A)
in Cocoa Beach
Parking/Fees: $1 per vehicle parking fee
Hours: 7 A.M.-sunset
Facilities: lifeguards (seasonal), restrooms,
picnic tables, showers, and a visitors center
(Johnnie Johnson Nature Center)
Contact: Brevard County Parks and Recre-
ation Department (central area), 321/455-1380

11 COCOA BEACH (SOUTH END)

Location: between North 4th Street and South
15th Street in Cocoa Beach
Parking/Fees: metered street parking
Hours: sunrise-sunset
Facilities: none
Contact: Cocoa Beach Parks Department,
321/868-3274

12 ROBERT P. MURKSHE MEMORIAL PARK

Location: South Atlantic Avenue (A1A) at
South 16th Street in Cocoa Beach
Parking/Fees: free parking lot
Hours: 7 A.M.-sunset
Facilities: restrooms, picnic tables, and
showers
Contact: Brevard County Parks and Recre-
ation Department (central area), 321/455-1380

13 SOUTH COCOA/NORTH PATRICK BEACH

Location: between Olive Street (in south
Cocoa Beach) and Patrick Drive (in North Patrick), on A1A
Parking/Fees: free parking lots at Fern Street,
and free street parking at the end of Summer

Street, Sunny Lane, between 26th and 35th
Streets, and South Patrick and East Patrick
Drives
Hours: sunrise-sunset
Facilities: none
Contact: Cocoa Beach Parks Department,
321/868-3274

RECREATION AND ATTRACTIONS

- **Bike/Skate Rentals:** Ten Speed Drive
  Bicycle Center, 166 North Atlantic Avenue,
  321/783-1196

- **Ecotourism:** Cocoa Beach Kayaking, 170
  South 26th Street, Cocoa Beach, 321/784-
  4545; Funday Eco Tours, 1905 Atlantic
  Street, Melbourne, 321/725-0796; Adven-
  ture Kayak of Cocoa Beach, Ramp Road
  Park (west end of Ramp Road), Cocoa
  Beach, 321/480-8632

- **Fishing Charters:** Canaveral Charter
  Captains' Association, www.fishingspace-
  coast.org

- **Marina:** Sunrise Marina, 505 Glen Cove
  Drive, Port Canaveral, 321/783-9535; In-
  dian Cove Marina, 14 Myrtice Avenue,
  Merritt Island, 321/452-8540

- **Pier:** Cocoa Beach Pier, 401 Meade Avenue,
  Cocoa Beach, 321/783-7549

- **Rainy-Day Attractions:** Kennedy Space
  Center Visitor Complex, S.R. 405, Titusville, 321/449-4444; Cocoa Beach Surf Museum (at Watersports), 4151 North Atlantic
  Avenue, Cocoa Beach, 321/783-0764

- **Shopping/Browsing:** Cocoa Village, U.S.
  1 at S.R. 520, Cocoa, 321/631-9075

- **Surf Shops:** Ron Jon Surf Shop, 4151
  North Atlantic Avenue, Cocoa Beach,
  321/799-8820; Natural Art Surf Shop,
  2370 South Atlantic Avenue, Cocoa Beach,
  321/783-0764

- **Vacation Rentals:** Cocoa Beach Realty, 120 Canaveral Plaza, Cocoa Beach,
  321/783-4200

ACCOMMODATIONS

Cocoa Beach is ideally situated for a beach vacation, Kennedy Space Center tours and Orlando theme-park side trips. For this reason, accommodations are bountiful. In keeping with its no-frills image, however, the upscaling of Cocoa Beach's oceanfront has thankfully been held to a relative minimum. What you have on the oceanfront are a lot of perfectly attractive and comfortable chain accommodations. Motels of the Days Inn, Comfort Inn, and Econo Lodge class are plentiful, and they are absolutely adequate for a stay at the beach.

In our less-prosperous early days as beach writers, we actually bunked down at **Motel 6** (3701 North Atlantic Avenue, 321/783-3103, $) for three nights and found it perfectly acceptable and ridiculously inexpensive. Moreover, it's a mere street-width shy of the beach and only a few blocks south of the Taj Mahal of beach stores, Ron Jon Surf Shop. You probably passed 100 or so billboards along I-95 alerting you to its presence in Cocoa Beach.

Another lodging surprise: The **Cocoa Beach Days Inn** (5500 North Atlantic Avenue, 321/784-2550, $$$) is an exemplar of that generally downscale chain and one of the nicer accommodations on Cocoa's oceanfront. It's certainly the best situated, being a few steps north of the pier and extending back from the beach for a block and a half. The well-maintained grounds are attractively landscaped with palm trees and tropical vegetation.

Our first choice on the Space Coast is the 500-unit **Holiday Inn Cocoa Beach** (1300 North Atlantic Avenue, 321/783-2271, $$), a full-service resort offering all you will ever need, including a restaurant, three bars, pools for kids and adults, workout room, hot tub, shuffleboard and tennis courts, and beach access. Try to get one of the ocean-facing suites, which have a bedroom, kitchenette, and living room. Any time a hotel's bath towels are colored sage and goldenrod, you know it's a cut above. The furniture is classy, the beds are extremely comfortable, and the layout allows those who want to read or rest get away from the TV-watchers and night owls. The hotel extends from Atlantic Avenue to the Atlantic Ocean and is bordered on its north side by Lori Wilson Park. You won't need to leave the grounds—unless, of course, you're headed up to Kennedy Space Center or an off-premises meal.

Hilton Oceanfront Cocoa Beach (1550 North Atlantic Avenue, 321/799-0003, $$$) is top-of-the-line in Cocoa Beach, with seven stories of creature comforts, a pool deck, and a wide, quiet sliver of beach. While vacationing with the family, one of us actually broke down and rented a cabana setup here, enjoying a peaceful, restorative day on the beach. Hurricane damage necessitated some noisy repairs in 2005—in lieu of wake-up calls, we had the sound of hammers jolting us out of bed—but the hotel is back and better than ever. There is one downside: late check-in (4 P.M.) and early check-out (11 A.M.).

Regardless of your choice of beachfront lodging, they're all set back well behind the dunes in Cocoa Beach, partly explaining why the beaches here are so consistently wide. In terms of cost, summer is the high season here and elsewhere on Florida's central coast. Prices fluctuate according to demand, day of week, time of year and general state of the economy. One hot July morning, we conducted an informal survey of room rates at oceanfront hotels and motels in Cocoa Beach while jogging. This exercise in data collection gave us an excuse to duck into hotel lobbies for water breaks. We asked the price for a standard room (two persons, two beds) on a busy weekend and came up with a range from $99–225. Out of season, rates will drop by half or more (except over holidays and during shuttle launches). Rounding out your beachside choices are the following:

- **Best Western Oceanfront Resort** (5600 North Atlantic Avenue, 321/783-7621, $$) is a half-block back from the beach and quite affordable.

- **Comfort Inn and Suites Resort** (3901

North Atlantic Avenue, 321/783-2221, $$)
is right next to Ron Jon Surf Shop.

- **Discovery Beach Resort and Tennis Club** (300 Barlow Avenue, 321/868-7777, $$$) is an older property with tennis courts atop its parking garage.
- **Doubletree** (2080 North Atlantic Avenue, 321/783-9222, $$) has rooms in a courtyard and plaza tower, plus a grand ocean observation deck.
- **Hampton Inn** (3425 North Atlantic Avenue, 321/799-4099, $$$) is a relatively new arrival in Cocoa Beach.
- **Inn at Cocoa Beach** (4300 Ocean Beach Boulevard, 321/799-3460, $$$) is a pink oceanfront beauty that's a cross between a hotel and a bed-and-breakfast.
- **Ocean Suites Hotel** (5500 Ocean Beach Boulevard, 321/784-4343, $$) is a bargain—and it's pierside, to boot.

COASTAL CUISINE

We've got a couple favorite Cocoa Beach restaurants at the high end of the dining scene. They are near one another in "downtown" Cocoa Beach, where North and South Atlantic Avenues meet.

First up is **Bernard's Surf** (2 South Atlantic Avenue, 321/783-2401, $$$$). This old reliable has been in business since 1948. Nearly six decades of success in a fickle beach town is saying something. Bernard's has kept pace with changing times and tastes while sticking to the basics done well. Gone are the exotic menu items that made the restaurant a gourmet novelty in bygone decades—things like zebra and antelope steak and various appetizer preparations of ants, grasshoppers, caterpillars, and baby bees. When the Customs Service tightened up on importation of such comestibles, they were dropped from the menu.

The atmosphere at Bernard's Surf has 1950s-ish overtones and is casual yet classy. It's clubby and informal in the manner of an old, established New York restaurant that knows it's good and doesn't have to put on airs. On our most recent visit, our French waiter steered us

to one of the best pieces of fish we've ever had: snapper française. It was a generous portion of snapper, as tender as could be, dipped in egg wash, gently sauteed, and served with a lemon butter dipping sauce. It was heaven on a plate, pure and simple.

They serve about half a dozen fresh catches. Other popular menu items include blackened tuna with Grand Marnier and raspberries, and almond-crusted grouper. They make a great, tangy Caesar salad at your table, and the house salad had deep-red, ripe tomatoes, not those salmon-colored, hothouse-raised abominations so many restaurants serve. For starters, be sure to try the Cajun gator tail (tasty little nuggets of tenderized gator) or mushroom caps stuffed with crabmeat. There are a number of dessert choices, but Bernard's flambeaus—peppered strawberries and bananas Foster—are irresistible. They're prepared tableside, and it's quite a show. They'll even set a cup of alcohol-fortified coffee on fire for you at meal's end.

Bernard's Surf is actually part of a restaurant triplex, all occupying the same address. Each one appeals to different clienteles. We've tried and liked them all. **Fischer's Seafood Bar and Grill** (2 South Atlantic Avenue, 321/783-2401, $$$) is for heartier, more robust appetites. **Rusty's Seafood & Oyster Bar** (2 South Atlantic Avenue, 321/783-2401, $$) is more casual and inexpensive.

Then there's the **Mango Tree Inn** (118 North Atlantic Avenue, 321/799-0513, $$$$), a superlative restaurant set in an old home on Atlantic Avenue. The building has been expanded over the years to accommodate demand. Inside, the house is packed with artwork, aquariums, and greenery. Outside is a lavish jungle of gardens. The owners cultivate orchids as a pastime, and they've turned the Mango Tree's gardens into a world unto itself. The only thing missing is an actual mango tree; they grow well on nearby Merritt Island but, for some reason, don't take to Cocoa Beach.

The cuisine is sophisticated and cosmopolitan. An extensive wine list complements a delectable menu. Here's a meal savored by

THE SPACE COAST

one of us, from start to finish: An appetizer of seared ahi with wasabi and teriyaki. Seafood bisque. Cornmeal-crusted grouper with Dijon-hollandaise sauce. Coffee with a shot of Godiva dark chocolate liqueur. Homemade key lime pie. On the other side of the table: Maryland-style lump crabcakes for an appetizer. Salad with homemade vinaigrette dressing. Seared filet mignon of tuna... Ah, this is beginning to sound too much like bragging. Come find out for yourself.

For a simpler seafood dinner (hold the atmosphere), there's **Florida's Seafood Bar & Grill** (480 West Cocoa Beach Causeway, 321/784-0892, $$), located on the S.R. 520 causeway between Cocoa and Cocoa Beach. We'd recommend the rock shrimp or one of the sampler platters that has rock shrimp as an option. Rock shrimp are spiny-shelled shrimp that taste like lobster. Dip these tasty little suckers in butter and/or cocktail sauce. The motto here is "Where Shrimp Happens," but don't overlook the stone crab cakes and calico scallops, either. The atmosphere is pure Florida kitsch, with burbling aquariums, nautical-themed wall murals, carved fish and birds, and a youthful wait staff.

You can't help but have a fine and filling meal at **Jack Baker's Lobster Shanty** (2200 South Orlando Avenue, 321/783-1350, $$), a large and long-lived institution on the Banana River in south Cocoa Beach. The food starts arriving from the second you sit down, when they place powdered sugar-dusted corn fritters and cole slaw on the table. Meals here are a good deal. Entrees run in the $16–22 range, and they include a bowl of chowder or trip to their well-stocked, tasty and healthy salad bar, plus two side items. Fish are served herb-grilled, broiled, blackened, or with several sauces. If you're indecisive, try the "Triple Treat": a sampling of grouper, mahi, and salmon prepared grilled or blackened. Try to get a table overlooking the river; if the weather's nice, there's outdoor seating on the deck.

Additionally, there are four restaurants on the Cocoa Beach Pier, the most notable among them (for seafood lovers) being **Atlantic Ocean Grille** (401 Meade Avenue, 321/783-7549, $$).

And finally, a stoic nod to the **Cape Codder New England Seafood Restaurant** (2960 South Atlantic Avenue, 321/868-2500, $), which makes an ideal stop for homesick Yankees or for Southerners who need a break from grouper sandwiches. Haddock, cod, and scallops are shipped down from the north and served fried or broiled (and in baskets at lunchtime). Specialties of the house include full-belly Ipswich clams and lobster rolls—two New England classics. (Believe us, we know from clams, having dined at Ipswich's famed Clam Box and other spots on Cape Ann.) Homemade chowder, too! The Cape Codder is a little bit of Beantown in Cocoa Beach and will satisfy your craving for such fare till you get to the similarly themed Boston's on the Beach in Delray Beach.

NIGHTLIFE

In years past, we've been surprised by how tame the "surfing capital of the East Coast" gets after the sun goes down. We had visions of Animal House by the sea, with hooting, hollering crowds knocking back Coronas while the mother of all wet T-shirt contests rages on into the wee hours. A local surfer, however, schooled us on what really goes on in "sleepy old Cocoa Beach"—i.e., not much at all. We were skeptical and had to go out and find the sorry truth for ourselves. More often than not our nighttime prowls turned up such things as a Caucasian trio plodding through the Bob Marley catalog or flush-faced, potbellied middle-agers attempting to rekindle lost adolescence to the familiar strains of beach music.

But there are some oases of activity after dark. A great place to start your evening is **Oh Shucks Seafood Bar** (401 Meade Avenue, 321/783-4050), one of four venues on capacious Cocoa Beach Pier. A late-afternoon crowd of locals gathers for raw oysters, raucous chatter, and live music until 10 P.M. There's also a tiki bar at the end of the pier. In late May, the pier is home to a four-day "Beachfest," underwritten by every major purveyor of alcohol (Absolut,

Jose Cuervo, Bud, Michelob, etc.) and featuring a multitude of musical performers, not to mention this yin/yang combo: a bikini contest and military beach Olympics.

The party revs hottest at **Coconuts on the Beach** (2 Minutemen Causeway, 321/784-1422), a mile or so south of the pier. Overlooking the beach, Coconuts is party central, starting with generous happy hour specials that segue into a full dinner menu, live entertainment, and packed houses nightly until 2 A.M. The food here is surprisingly decent for a beach bar, with fresh local seafood among the specialties. Bikini contests on weekends attempt to show how little material a woman can wear while avoiding indecent exposure charges. On weekend mornings, Coconuts also serves as a party recovery zone, offering bracing breakfast 6:30 A.M.–10:30 A.M. In other words, this joint is closed for all of four hours a day! As you can tell, we're cuckoo for Coconuts.

Cocoa Beach has, of course, always had another side. As is customary near military installations—and Patrick Air Force Base, Cape Canaveral Air Force Station, and Kennedy Space Center are all close by—strip clubs and porn emporiums in the area serve as steam-release valves for the pent-up male libido. Some are seedy places servicing seedy people, but others make an effort to erect a "classy" front. Rather than call themselves strip clubs or topless bars, these businesses refer to themselves as "cabarets" and "gentlemen's clubs." By any name, we have no problem with them, though we patronize them strictly for (ahem) research purposes. If you are the sort who enjoys such cheap thrills, you won't have any trouble finding an outlet hereabouts.

Patrick Air Force Base and South Patrick Shores

The first five miles of south Brevard County's beaches fall under the stealthy wing of an air force base. From all outward appearances (read: staring enviously through iron fencing along the west side of A1A), Patrick AFB (pop. 1,400) is the place to be stationed if you want to become a Top Gun. The grounds are as lush and well maintained as a country club, the housing neat and tidy, and the beach access is second to none for military bases in the United States. Patrick AFB survived Donald Rumsfeld's base-closing mania in 2005, and you can bet they're glad of that down here.

South Patrick Shores is a nondescript community that serves partly as a commercial zone for residents of the air base. Some low-rise condominiums are going up, a small taste of sights to come farther south, but otherwise there are no accommodations, restaurants, or nightlife.

For more information, contact Patrick Air Force Base, FL 32925, 407/494-1110, www.patrick.af.mil.

BEACHES

Locals refer to south Brevard County as the "small wave capital of the East Coast," and the beach along Patrick Air Force Base is considered one of the three best areas for surfing these small waves. (The other two are 5th Avenue Boardwalk at James H. Nance Park, in Indialantic, and the north jetty at Sebastian Inlet.) Happily, civilians can enjoy a healthy measure of beach access at Patrick Air Force Base. Accesses are provided along the east side of A1A in designated parking areas. Driving through, you will find two large lots with dune walkovers north of the main gate, a smaller lot directly across from it, and two more large lots with dune walkovers south of it. One of the latter is near the "central gate," while the other is near the intersection of A1A and S.R. 404 (Pineda Causeway), the first of three causeways that connect South Brevard's beaches with the mainland.

These beaches are free of charge and open to all—even those who protested the Vietnam and Iraq wars. We saw happy folks of all stripes, from seniors to surfers, hopping over the walkovers.

The beaches are clean and relatively safe, which is a good thing as there are no lifeguards or facilities. They are considerably thinner after the hurricanes of 2004, sustaining major beach and dune erosion that will take years to restore.

Beach access in South Patrick Shores consists of two small county parks: **Seagull Park** (1.6 acres) and **South Patrick Residents Association Park** (0.8 acres). Seagull Park has a couple picnic shelters, is attractively landscaped and can accommodate 15 cars. South Patrick Residents Association (S.P.R.A.) Park is smaller still but is notable for its memorial to the space shuttle *Challenger*.

14 SEAGULL PARK

Location: 0.5 mile south of Pineda Causeway (S.R. 404) on A1A in South Patrick Shores
Parking/Fees: free parking lot
Hours: 7 A.M.-sunset
Facilities: picnic tables and shower
Contact: Brevard County Parks and Recreation Department (south area), 321/952-4580

15 SOUTH PATRICK RESIDENTS ASSOCIATION PARK (A.K.A. S.P.R.A. PARK)

Location: 0.7 miles south of Pineda Causeway (S.R. 404) on A1A in South Patrick Shores
Parking/Fees: free parking lot
Hours: sunrise-sunset
Facilities: shower
Contact: Brevard County Parks and Recreation Department (south area), 321/952-4580

Satellite Beach

Appropriately named, Satellite Beach (pop. 10,275) has fired its retro rockets for develop-

ment. It is the largest of South Brevard's beach towns and is the commercial hub. The town has soared so far into the stratosphere of high finance that the oxygen supply appears to have been cut off to its brain.

In Satellite Beach, *Saturn* rocket-sized cranes hoist slabs of steel into place at oceanfront construction sites. Prefab walls and balconies follow, then a parking lot, pool and perhaps a ridiculous guard gate. Units in these vertical monstrosities are unloaded by sleazy developers to dupes with more money than sense who don't understand the first thing about shoreline dynamics and the destructive meteorological peril that their little cell in this artificial paradise will eventually and inevitably face.

Strip malls, unimaginatively planned and mindlessly sprawling, run the length of this grossly unappealing town, creating a depressing tableau that makes you want to high-tail out of here. The same cartoonish real-estate mistakes made in South Florida during the era of Reaganomics are being repeated here. The credo seems to be "Build it and they will come." By contrast, ours is "Leave it alone and they will thank you profusely a century from now."

For more information, contact the Melbourne/Palm Bay and the Beaches Convention and Visitors Bureau, 1005 East Strawbridge Avenue, Melbourne, FL 32901, 321/724-5400 or 800/771-9922, www.melpb-chamber.org.

BEACHES

Satellite Beach runs for two miles, with dune crossovers at street ends providing access to the town's generally narrow (especially at high tide) beach. The brown sand and inviting water are good for the beach basics of sunbathing and swimming, but watch out for rocks in the water. The best beach-related reason to come to this overbuilt community is **Pelican Beach Park.** Located a few hundred yards north of the intersection of DeSoto Parkway and A1A, it's a county-owned, city-run park with ample free parking, two dune crossovers, picnic shelters, and an observation tower. The beach has been looking a little

© PARKE PUTERBAUGH

Satellite Beach

narrow and steep the last few times we passed through; in a previous edition, we noted that it was, by contrast, wide and hard packed, with "some of the only intact dune structure left in the area." The ocean giveth and the ocean taketh away. The ocean took away a huge chunk of Satellite Beach in 2004, due mainly to, according to the state government storm report, "the lack of a beach restoration project along the critically eroded beaches of Satellite Beach, Indian Harbour Beach, and the City of Melbourne."

The next best beach in the area is **Hightower Beach Park,** a two-acre county beach at the town's north end. There's a small lot, outdoor shower, and dune walkover onto a narrow, sloping and often deserted beach.

16 HIGHTOWER BEACH PARK

Location: 4.5 miles south of Pineda Causeway (S.R. 404) on A1A in Satellite Beach
Parking/Fees: free parking lot
Hours: sunrise-sunset

Facilities: shower
Contact: Brevard County Parks and Recreation Department (south area), 321/952-4580

17 SATELLITE BEACH

Location: between Grant Street and Palmetto Avenue, off A1A in Satellite Beach
Parking/Fees: free street parking at the ends of (from north to south) Grant Street, Park Lane, Ellwood Street, Cassia Boulevard, DeSoto Parkway, and Magellan, Sunrise, and Palmetto Avenues
Hours: sunrise-sunset
Facilities: none
Contact: Satellite Beach Parks and Recreation Department, 321/773-6458

18 PELICAN BEACH PARK

Location: 2.5 miles north of S.R. 518 (Royal Palm Boulevard) on A1A in Satellite Beach

Parking/Fees: free parking lot
Hours: sunrise-sunset
Facilities: restrooms, picnic tables, and showers
Contact: Satellite Beach Parks and Recreation Department, 321/773-6458

ACCOMMODATIONS

About the only hotel or motel we would have conceivably thought to recommend in this ill-conceived town was an oceanfront Ramada Plaza Hotel, but that got sandblasted into oblivion by the one-two punch of Hurricanes Jeanne and Frances in September 2004. If you must stay in Satellite Beach, the **Days Inn** (180 A1A, 321/777-3552, $) held fast through the hurricanes, no doubt owing to the fact that it's on the landward side of A1A and is only two stories.

COASTAL CUISINE

Aside from its beach parks, the only reason we would ever come to Satellite Beach is **Bunky's Seafood Grill and Raw Bar** (1390 A1A, 321/777-CLAM, $). This authentically funky and unpretentious eatery has been here for 20 years. It is exactly the sort of enterprise that all beach towns should be grateful to claim as their own. Bunky's is a sports bar, a locals' haven, and a great place for cheap, fresh, and simply prepared seafood. We'd always come in to pull the trigger on their "38 Special": 38 plump, juicy, iced, raw Indian River oysters for $12.95. Sadly, this is no longer offered; too much labor-intensive shucking, we were informed. But you can get 'em by the half-dozen or dozen.

At Bunky's you can take aim at fish sandwiches (the blackened grouper is killer!), seafood salads, crab cakes, grouper fingers, Cajun-style mahimahi, salmon, and other satisfying and inexpensive fare. The staff is super friendly. While you're here, look around: collegiate sports banners, race-car memorabilia, and beer logos take up seemingly every available square inch of wall and ceiling space. Bunky's is also a popular late-night hangout, with weekly microbrew specials and sporting events playing on numerous television screens. Happiest ending of all: though Bunky's lost its sign in the 2004 hurricane season, it remained structurally sound. In fact, unlike a lot of bruised and battered buildings in the area—including a few hotels that were still closed a year after the hurricanes hit—Bunky's shut down briefly only because its staff evacuated the beachfront. You can't keep a good bar down.

Indian Harbour Beach

Indian Harbour Beach (pop. 8,024) has one mile of oceanfront that is fast becoming a facsimile of its northern neighbor, Satellite Beach. On the plus side, it is also home to a nice but small city-run facility, Richard G. Edgeton Bicentennial Park. One-fifth of all homes in town were damaged by Hurricanes Frances and Jeanne. More than a year later, the scars still show. Indeed, that is true all over south Brevard County: listing and pockmarked signs, blue plastic tarps protecting leaky roofs, damaged homes, and small businesses that remain unfixed and abandoned.

For more information, contact the Melbourne/Palm Bay and the Beaches Convention and Visitors Bureau, 1005 East Strawbridge Avenue, Melbourne, FL 32901, 321/724-5400 or 800/771-9922, www.melpb-chamber.org.

BEACHES

Located where Pine Tree Road meets A1A, **Richard G. Edgeton Bicentennial Park** has a free parking lot (36 spaces), picnic tables, and an outdoor shower. This sylvan park—an oasis of green amid a glut of development—has picnic tables, palm trees, volleyball nets, showers, and a broad wooden deck. Look north from the deck and you'll see all the visual evidence you'll ever need to argue against coastal development: a gross orange condo complex that hogs way too much of A1A in Indian Harbour Beach.

19 RICHARD G. EDGETON BICENTENNIAL PARK

Location: end of Ocean Dunes Drive, off A1A in Indian Harbour Beach
Parking/Fees: free parking lot
Hours: sunrise-10 P.M.
Facilities: picnic tables and shower
Contact: Indian Harbour Beach Parks and Recreation Department, 321/773-0552

Canova Beach

Canova Beach (pop. 1,500) occupies only a half-mile-square parcel of oceanfront real estate, but they've gotten around that limitation by building up. We wonder why they bother to give separate names to the towns out there since they're all starting to look alike: overbuilt and unsightly.

For more information, contact the Melbourne/Palm Bay and the Beaches Convention and Visitors Bureau, 1005 East Strawbridge Avenue, Melbourne, FL 32901, 321/724-5400 or 800/771-9922, www.melpb-chamber.org.

BEACHES

Canova Beach has two small, county-run beach parks in extremely close proximity near the foot of the Eau Galle Causeway (S.R. 518). They are **Irene H. Canova Park** and **Canova Beach Park.** (Obviously, someone is indebted to the Canova family around here.) There's nothing much (yet) at Irene H. Canova beyond a parking lot and dune crossover, but we expect it will eventually look much like neighboring Canova Beach Park, which has a beach pavilion, picnic shelters, and three dune crossovers. Parking costs $1. One caveat: Just beyond where the waves break is a rocky reef that would seem to present a potential hazard to the unwary. No signs are posted and no lifeguards are on duty, so swim at your own risk. Erosion has narrowed the beach so much that waves wash at the foot of the stairs. Up on the

bluff, this green, clean park is large and nicely landscaped. A tantalizing tangle of sea grape provides a glimpse of what Florida's East Coast once looked like. Look in either direction from here to see what's replaced it.

20 IRENE H. CANOVA PARK

Location: 0.1 mile north of Eau Galle Causeway (S.R. 518) on A1A in Canova Beach
Parking/Fees: $1 per vehicle entrance fee
Hours: 7 A.M.-sunset
Facilities: none
Contact: Brevard County Parks and Recreation Department (south area), 321/952-4580

21 CANOVA BEACH PARK

Location: east of Melbourne at the foot of Eau Galle Causeway (S.R. 518) in Canova Beach
Parking/Fees: $1 per vehicle entrance fee
Hours: 7 A.M.-sunset
Facilities: restrooms, picnic tables, and showers
Contact: Brevard County Parks and Recreation Department (south area), 321/952-4580

ACCOMMODATIONS

One place in south Brevard County that sticks out like a sore thumb is the **Radisson Suite Hotel Oceanfront** (3101 North A1A, 321/773-0260, $$$). It is an absurdly huge building that dominates the landscape like the Vehicle Assembly Building at the Kennedy Space Center. Although it looks impregnable, it had to shut down for about a month in the wake of 2004's hurricanes. It looks indistinguishable from the high-rise condos in the area. All 168 rooms are oceanfront suites.

The Holiday Inn Beach Resort in Canova Beach was so badly damaged by the hurricanes of 2004 that it was torn down and rebuilt almost from scratch to become the **Crowne**

THE SPACE COAST

Canova Beach Park

Plaza Melbourne Oceanfront (2605 North A1A, 321/777-4100, $$$$). After being closed for more than a year, it reopened with its new name and look on January 1, 2006.

COASTAL CUISINE

Each night, **Flamingo Crab Co.** (A1A and Eau Galle Causeway, 321/777-8069, $), located across the street from Canova Beach Park, features an awesome special, such as all-you-can-eat grouper and shrimp on Tuesday. For an inexpensive happy-hour treat, hit the Flamingo 4–6 P.M. daily, when raw oysters are just two bits apiece.

Indialantic

Indialantic (pop. 3,000) is the most pleasant, established, and clearly defined of the south Brevard County beach communities, occupying one compact and tidy square mile. Its backbone is 5th Avenue (S.R. 500), which, unlike the one in New York, is an unassuming commercial zone that is anything but highfalutin or overpriced. It's all of five blocks long—the width of the barrier island. To give an idea of the quiet civility that awaits you in Indialantic, the town center boasts two decently stocked used bookshops. As for its oceanfront, Indialantic embraces 1.5 miles of beach whose understated appeal centers around two excellent parks. And there you have the town in a nutshell: grab a used paperback and head for the sand.

If you follow 5th Avenue westward, you'll hit Melbourne Causeway (S.R. 500/U.S. 192), an east-west thoroughfare that brings beachgoers across the Indian River from "the Harbour City" of Melbourne, a small city on a fast track with a population of 75,000. Named after the first postmaster's home city in Australia back in the 1880s, Melbourne rode a wave of growth in the 1980s and 1990s generated by computer and electronics firms that relocated here. While the area has gained a host of big-city amenities, it's also gathered some of the concomitant problems. That includes an ungodly strip-mall sprawl that clings to U.S. 192 all the way out to I-95.

For more information, contact the Melbourne/Palm Bay and the Beaches Convention

THE SPACE COAST

© PARKE PUTERBAUGH

and Visitors Bureau, 1005 East Strawbridge Avenue, Melbourne, FL 32901, 321/724-5400 or 800/771-9922, www.melpb-chamber.org.

BEACHES

Howard E. Futch Memorial Park at Paradise Beach (formerly Paradise Beach Park) lies south of the Eau Galle Causeway in Indialantic. Yes, that mouthful of a name is its official title. It's yet another nicely landscaped county park—the largest one of all, by the look of it—that charges a nominal self-pay fee of $1. Endless parking lots stretch along A1A in the vicinity of Paradise Boulevard. It's also loaded with facilities: picnic shelters, volleyball nets, a concession stand, seasonal lifeguards, and a bathhouse. It's worth mentioning that directly across the island from Futch Park, at the foot of the Eau Galle Causeway (S.R. 518), is a popular boat ramp and windsurfing site.

Conveniently located in the heart of Indialantic, where 5th Avenue dead-ends into A1A, is **James H. Nance Park.** It's another huge park with zigzagging maze-like walkways. Ample metered parking (400 spaces) is available, and a concrete boardwalk runs along Wavecrest Avenue for Nance's half-mile length. At the

James H. Nance Park, Indialantic

© PARKE PUTERBAUGH

north end of Nance Park is Bizarro's Famous NY Pizza (4 Wavecrest Avenue, 321/724-4799, $), the perfect stop if you're a famished surfer.

HOWARD E. FUTCH MEMORIAL PARK AT PARADISE BEACH

Location: between Eau Galle Causeway (S.R. 518) and Melbourne Causeway (S.R. 516) at the north end of Indialantic
Parking/Fees: $1 per vehicle entrance fee
Hours: 7 A.M.-sunset
Facilities: concessions, lifeguards (seasonal), restrooms, picnic tables, and showers
Contact: Brevard County Parks and Recreation Department (south area), 321/952-4580

JAMES H. NANCE PARK

Location: end of 5th Avenue, off A1A in Indialantic
Parking/Fees: metered parking lot
Hours: sunrise-9 P.M.
Facilities: lifeguards (seasonal), restrooms, picnic tables, and showers
Contact: Indialantic Town Hall, 321/723-2242

ACCOMMODATIONS

Since first staying here back in the early 1980s, we've been partial to the Sharrock Shores Resort, which changed owners and names in 1999 to **Tuckaway Shores Resort** (1441 South Miramar Avenue, 321/723-3355, $$). It's a reasonably priced complex with picture-window views of the churning ocean. Rooms have kitchenettes, refrigerators, sofas, and balconies, and are as comfortable as a beach house. Nice outdoor pool deck, too. Some folks rent rooms here by the week or month. It's located not quite a mile south of 5th Avenue and A1A, and only a miracle spared it from Hurricanes Frances and Jeanne.

THE SPACE COAST

Another sentimental favorite is the **Oceanside** (745 North A1A, 321/727-2723, $), the sort of well-tended mom-and-pop motel Florida's central coast used to have in abundance. There's a pool on the premises, and some of the efficiency units have full kitchens. Since bed-and-breakfasts are as rare in central Florida as ski slopes, the stately **Windemere Inn By the Sea** (815 South Miramar Avenue, 321/728-9334, $$), a sunny, antique-filled guest home, is worth considering. At the other extreme, **Quality Suites** (1665 North A1A, 321/723-4222, $$$) is a modern 10-story, twin-tower complex with 208 oceanfront suites, a pool, hot tub, sauna, exercise room, and complimentary breakfast.

NIGHTLIFE

Lou's Blues (3191 North A1A, 321/779-2299) has picked up some of the live music business at this end of the county since the Sebastian Beach Inn (written up elsewhere) scaled back. Housed in a soulless rectangular box next door to the ghastly Radisson, Lou's nonetheless has an impressive stage and plenty of room for biker mamas to get their groove on. Lou's tries to be many things to many people, with jams being its stock-in-trade: bluegrass jams, '60s–'80s jams, and obligatory "blues jams" are on the weekly schedule. Weekend nights feature regional and national bands. Blues jams rank toward the low end of our personal taste in music, right down there with New Age and death metal, but if this sort of thing gets you off, head for Lou's.

Melbourne Beach and Melbourne Shores

Melbourne Beach (pop. 3,300) and Melbourne Shores offer a bit of suburbia at the beach. Fascinating fact: Founded in 1883, Melbourne Beach is the oldest beach community in Brevard County. That may explain why it has a better grasp of reality than some of its fast-growth

neighbors. The development here is predominantly residential, with a decided emphasis on middle-class values: S-shaped backstreets, sloped curbs, men with Weed Eaters and hedge trimmers prowling their lawns like big-game hunters, enormous SUVs parked in the driveways. These communities are not the least bit downtrodden, but neither are they exclusive. They're right down the middle of the road.

That is exactly where we found ourselves late one afternoon during a torrential summer rainstorm, the likes of which we'd never before seen. We were driving right down the middle of A1A, afraid to veer too close to either shoulder lest we be washed out to sea, afraid to stop because of the traffic on our tail. Adding to our fear of catastrophe was a glance at the map, which revealed how amazingly thin is the barrier island upon which these seemingly safe, tidy, and quiet communities sit. The strangest sight of all was a golf course being heavily watered by an automated sprinkler system while this mother of all monsoons flooded the fairways.

Once the clouds passed—often within minutes on summer afternoons in Florida—we realized what a homey and appealing place Melbourne Beach is. No wonder so many have chosen to live here and tried to rein in attempts to convert it to a resort town.

For more information, contact the Melbourne/Palm Bay and the Beaches Convention and Visitors Bureau, 1005 East Strawbridge Avenue, Melbourne, FL 32901, 321/724-5400 or 800/771-9922, www.melpb-chamber.org.

BEACHES

At one time the beaches hereabouts were almost as wide as Daytona's, but Brevard County's beaches have thinned considerably over the last few decades. The erosion is due to the construction of Port Canaveral, in Volusia County, back in the 1950s, whose jetties have kept sand from "bypassing" the inlet and moving south to Brevard County's beaches, as had been the natural order of things. As a result, occasional beach renourishment, at times on an emergency basis, has been necessary, especially in

"THE SEA TURTLE PRESERVATION SOCIETY"

(sung to the tune of "The Village Green Preservation Society," by the Kinks)
We are the sea turtle preservation society
God bless loggerheads, leatherbacks, and Kemp's ridley
We are the condominium condemnation affiliate
Down with developers, realtors, and their advocates

(chorus)
Preserving the beaches for me and for you
Protecting sea turtles, water quality, too
What more can we do?
We use the beach bum surfing addict vernacular
God bless Surfrider and ocean waves spectacular
We are the Jet-Ski elimination authority
Personal watercraft is offensive to the majority

(chorus)
Preserving the beaches for me and for you
Protecting sea turtles, water quality, too
What more can we do?
We are the raw oyster consumer consortium
Pass the cocktail sauce, horseradish, and lemon
We are the thong bikini appreciation society
God bless Ron Jon, Candy, Lexus, and Foxy

(chorus)
Preserving the beaches for me and for you
Protecting sea turtles, water quality, too
What more can we do?

Note: If you want to contact the real Sea Turtle Preservation Society — yes, there is such an organization — it is located at 111 South Miramar Avenue, Indialantic Beach, 321/676-1701, www.seaturtlespacecoast.org. They are open II A.M.-5 P.M.

the Melbourne Beach and Indialantic area. A major beach renourishment project to pump sand onto 13 thinning miles of beaches began in late 2000. The cost to Volusia County alone was $39 million. It's amazing to us that after all this time they still haven't figured out a way to bypass sand around ports and jetties.

There's plenty of public beach access out here to supply the needs of residents, tourists, and the weekend swarm that head over from Melbourne. Pedestrian access, used mostly by town residents, is available at street ends from B Street down to 6th Avenue. **Ocean Park,** a small beach park with picnic tables and volleyball nets, is located at the east end of Ocean Avenue (A1A). This provides some visual relief from the Breakers, a quarter mile of cheesy stucco condos that obscure a driver's view of the beach along A1A south of the little park. At the west end of Ocean Avenue is Ryckman Park, a larger public park on the river that has a gazebo, picnic tables, playground, and the Melbourne Beach Pier.

More access is gained at **Spesser Holland**

North Beach Park and **Spesser Holland South Beach Park.** Located two miles south of Melbourne Causeway (U.S. 192), this linear beach park has north and south entrances, divided by a Patrick Air Force Base tracking station. Ample parking lots run for a quarter mile at each end, and pavilions and facilities are available at both. The south entrance got nailed by hurricanes and was undergoing a massive renovation when we passed through late in 2005. Incidentally, the namesake for these parks was a beloved Florida politician who served as governor 1941–1945 and U.S. Senator from 1946 until his death in 1971.

The main appeal of **Coconut Point Park,** a short distance south in Melbourne Shores, is botanical, as it is set amid a pleasing 37-acre tangle of sea grapes, saw palmettos, and short coconut palm trees. Less than a mile south of Coconut Point is a new county-run beach park, **Juan Ponce de Leon Landing.** It commemorates the landing of Spanish explorer Juan Ponce de Leon at this very spot on April 2, 1513. This park is another feather in the cap of the county. Any effort to counter the condo invasion is as welcome to us as a mermaid holding a key lime pie.

Various parcels of beachfront in the Melbourne vicinity make up the Archie Carr National Wildlife Refuge, a protected habitat for sea turtles and other endangered species. The 20 miles of coastline between Melbourne Beach and Wabasso Beach (in Indian River County) is the most important nesting site for loggerhead turtles in the western hemisphere and second most important in the world. Astonishingly, 25 percent of all loggerheads and 35 percent of all green sea turtles in the United States nest on this brief stretch of shoreline. It was Dr. Archie Carr, a renowned ecologist and sea turtle expert at the University of Florida, whose research and advocacy led to the designation of a National Wildlife Refuge that now bears his name.

Attempting to save vital nesting habitat on what was still a relatively undisturbed coastline, Congress established the refuge in 1991. It consists of discontinuous sections along the Melbourne-area coastline, with fill-in parcels

acquired as money becomes available. When completed, it will total 900 acres and 9.4 miles of coastline. The refuge encompasses only the beach and dune system. These sandy shores are important nesting sites for sea turtles but also provide habitat for the endangered Florida beach mouse. A couple of access points along its length are indicated by signs. If you want to do something on the turtles' behalf, urge your senators and representatives to support increased funding for the Archie Carr National Wildlife Refuge.

24 OCEAN PARK

Location: east end of Ocean Avenue at Riverside Drive in Melbourne Beach
Parking/Fees: free parking lot at Ocean Avenue and free street parking at the ends of A and B Streets and from 1st to 6th Avenues
Hours: 7:30 A.M.-sunset
Facilities: lifeguards (seasonal) and picnic tables
Contact: Melbourne Beach Town Hall, 321/724-5860

25 SPESSER HOLLAND NORTH BEACH PARK

Location: two miles south of Melbourne Causeway (U.S. 192) on A1A in Melbourne Beach
Parking/Fees: $1 per vehicle entrance fee
Hours: 7 A.M.-sunset
Facilities: lifeguards (seasonal), restrooms, picnic tables, and showers
Contact: Brevard County Parks and Recreation Department (south area), 321/952-4580

26 SPESSER HOLLAND SOUTH BEACH PARK

Location: 2.2 miles south of Melbourne Causeway (U.S. 192) on A1A in Melbourne Beach

THE SPACE COAST

Parking/Fees: $1 per vehicle entrance fee
Hours: 7 A.M.-sunset
Facilities: lifeguards (seasonal), restrooms, picnic tables, and showers
Contact: Brevard County Parks and Recreation Department (south area), 321/952-4580

27 COCONUT POINT PARK

Location: 5.5 miles south of Melbourne Causeway (S.R. 192) in Melbourne Beach along A1A
Parking/Fees: free parking lot
Hours: 7 A.M.-sunset
Facilities: restrooms, picnic tables, and showers
Contact: Brevard County Parks and Recreation Department (south area), 321/952-4580

28 JUAN PONCE DE LEON LANDING

Location: 0.7 miles south of Coconut Point Park along A1A
Parking/Fees: free parking lot
Hours: 7 A.M.-sunset
Facilities: restrooms, picnic table, and showers
Contact: Brevard County Parks and Recreation Department (south area), 321/952-4580

ACCOMMODATIONS

As in neighboring Indialantic, mom-and-pop motels rule the waves in Melbourne Beach. **Samperton's on the Atlantic** (3135 A1A, 321/951-8200, $) provides clean, comfortable, and unostentatious oceanfront rooms and efficiencies. Also on the grounds is the best seafood restaurant in the area. Just down the road, **Sandy Shores Motel** (3455 A1A, 321/723-5586, $) offers much the same, though it's a bit more attractively decorated. The **Sea Dunes Resort** (5485 South A1A, $) offers rooms and efficiencies and has Loggerhead's Restaurant

and Lounge on the premises. Howard Hughes was alleged to be a frequent visitor. **Tiara by the Sea** (5815 A1A, 321/725-0525, $) may not be as diamond-studded as its name suggests, but it is on the ocean.

A number of other motels and rental properties are available for the next eight miles as you approach Sebastian Inlet. None will ever be mistaken for a Ritz-Carlton, but they'll do. In fact, their abundance makes this part of the coast something of a charming throwback to yesteryear.

COASTAL CUISINE

Samperton's on the Atlantic (3135 A1A, 321/951-8200, $$) offers the seafood basics most folks expect but also goes out on a limb with creative preparations such as seared tuna in ginger. Local catches like blackened grouper are simply and expertly prepared. The signature dish is a seafood saute of shrimp, scallops, crab, scallions, and mushrooms in white wine sauce served over rice or pasta. The restaurant doesn't lie about being on the Atlantic, either. The view from the upstairs dining room is so close to the ocean that it's like being inside an aquarium. From this vantage point, we witnessed an awe-inspiring lightning storm that had every table oohing and aahing.

A bit off the beaten track, overlooking the Indian River in Melbourne, is **Conchy Joe's Seafood Restaurant** (1477 Pineapple Avenue, 321/253-3131, $$). One of the area's old reliables, it's made to look like an Old Florida fish house, and it specializes in tried-and-true native Florida cuisine (gator tail, conch fritters, raw oysters), as well as Bahamian seafood dishes. Reggae and calypso bands play during the dinner hour.

NIGHTLIFE

One of Florida's most venerable beachside hangouts and live-music venues has been the **Sebastian Beach Inn** (7035 South A1A, 321/728-4311). Known as "SBI," for short, this sprawling oceanfront restaurant, lounge, and live-music room is housed inside one of

Florida's last coastal watch stations (ca. 1900). SBI, however, got nailed by the hurricanes of 2004, with chunks of its former glory turning the grounds into a junkyard worthy of *Sanford and Son*. In the past, the proprietor produced a free bimonthly publication called *The Real Paper*, which was among our favorite local reads. The quirky rag reflected the personality of the place, abounding in misspellings and consisting mainly of rambling, often hilarious commentary on everything from nude sunbathing controversies to Allen Ginsberg's lasting significance.

SBI's "House of Bluez" [*sic*] is a spacious room where national acts (including Steve Miller, Albert King, Foghat, and Burning Spear) have played on weekends. Live music of some kind—be it a national or local act, or an open-mike blues jam—used to go on every night of the week. Not any more. Like the restaurant, which once did a brisk business in prime rib and seafood, the House of Bluez is now only open on weekends. The SBI still hosts Saturday and Sunday beach parties (11 A.M.–9 P.M.) on the sands below its patio, replete with a "Jamaican Limbo contest" and "progressive reggae." The party goes on, but some of SBI's magic has undeniably been sundered by the hurricanes. We've even heard talk that they're looking to sell the place.

And now for a significant piece of local rock and roll trivia. Did you know that the late Jim Morrison, the charismatic vocalist and frontman for the Doors, was born in Melbourne? The son of Rear Admiral Steve Morrison (who was stationed here) and his wife Clara entered the world on September 8, 1943.

Floridana Beach and Sunnyland Beach

A land rush is on in these two unincorporated hamlets between Melbourne Beach and Sebastian Inlet. A development called Aquarina Country Club—which bills itself as "ocean-to-river golf and tennis"—takes up virtually all of Sunnyland Beach. For now, Floridana Beach is an unincorporated stretch of thickly vegetated hammock and coastal dunes, though "For Sale" signs are staked every few hundred yards. The devastation of 2004 has not stopped development, which blithely carries on along the west side of A1A.

For more information, contact the Melbourne/Palm Bay and the Beaches Convention and Visitors Bureau, 1005 East Strawbridge Avenue, Melbourne, FL 32901, 321/724-5400 or 800/771-9922, www.melpb-chamber.org.

BEACHES

The only beach access around here is **Bonsteel Park.** It's county run, with free parking in a small dirt lot. One dune crossover, no lifeguards. Like the beaches north of here, the sand slopes dramatically to the water's edge and the waves crash hard and loud. It's easy to see why this part of Florida's coast is popular with surfers and less so with families. This would be even more the case after 2004, when Hurricane Frances inflicted major beach and dune damage to 15 miles of beaches in southern Brevard County. Further, according to a state report, "With no opportunity to recover [from Frances], Hurricane Jeanne inflicted the most severe erosion seen in the area in recorded history."

A short distance south of Bonsteel Park lies Sebastian Inlet, which is where the Treasure Coast can properly be said to begin.

29 BONSTEEL PARK

Location: 2.4 miles north of Sebastian Inlet on A1A in south Brevard County
Parking/Fees: free parking lot
Hours: 7:30 A.M.-sunset
Facilities: restrooms
Contact: Brevard County Parks and Recreation Department (south area), 321/952-4580

VERO BEACH, HUTCHINSON ISLAND, AND THE TREASURE COAST

When they call this area the Treasure Coast, they're not just talking about sunken Spanish galleons. The Gold Coast of Fort Lauderdale and Miami Beach beckons travelers to keep heading south, but the beaches of the three Treasure Coast counties—Indian River, St. Lucie, and Martin—are the overlooked treasures of Florida's East Coast. If you've not made their acquaintance, you might wish to put on the brakes and explore their sandy treasures.

At the north, Indian River County is blessed with 29 miles of golden sand beaches. By Florida standards, it's quiet and untamed, with Vero Beach the only community of any size along A1A. The beaches are safe, too, with an offshore coquina reef taming the waves before they roll ashore.

St. Lucie County has 22 miles of beautiful beaches, many of them in an unspoiled state. The only rhinestones along the Treasure Coast can be found on the overbuilt St. Lucie

County mainland. The prized jewel of the Treasure Coast is Martin County, one of the most enlightened and far-sighted counties in the state. Martin has been a reliable steward of its 20 miles of oceanfront real estate long before beach preservation became a concern elsewhere in the state. The icing on its cake are a state preserve and national wildlife refuge in Hobe Sound, at the county's southern end, which account for seven miles of wilderness beach.

Sebastian Inlet State Park

Sebastian Inlet is a man-made cut that splits a long, narrow barrier island. Private attempts to dig a cut here date back to the late 1800s, and in 1924 the Sebastian Inlet Tax District did the job with bond money, digging an inlet 100

© PARKE PUTERBAUGH

THE TREASURE COAST

feet wide and six feet deep. Without it, Cocoa Beach and Vero Beach would occupy the same landform. Straddling both sides of the inlet is Sebastian Inlet State Park. Great surfing and fishing are the main draws, though many come simply to relax, dragging coolers and folding chairs into the ankle-deep water of the lagoon on the park's north side.

The state park is split into units on either side of the inlet, which is also the dividing line between Brevard County and Indian River County. On the more popular north side is a fishing jetty, calm-water lagoon (with kid-safe swimming), and surfing at what has been called "the best break in Florida." The beach near the north jetty also gets packed with boogie boarders. To us, this high-energy area looks to pose hazards for kids (though that doesn't stop families from parking their beach blankets here). Big waves rise close to shore, crash dramatically, and run and back down up a steeply sloping beach face.

Surfing is best by the north jetty but can be dangerous on the south side—an area called "Monster Hole" whose hazards include sharks that enter the inlet on incoming tides in search of food. Also on the south side is a 51-unit campground and boat launch. A sandy parking lot is located a half mile south of the Sebastian Inlet bridge, allowing access to the 1.8 miles of state-park beach that fall inside Indian River County. No fee is charged to park here. A $5 day-use fee is, however, charged to access the campground, marina, and south jetty via the park road on the west side of A1A, just south of the inlet bridge. Access to the north unit and its facilities also costs $5. Incidentally, your entrance fee gains access to both sides of Sebastian Inlet State Park.

Inlets are high-energy areas, particularly in the vicinity of man-made jetties that keep the channel fixed for boat traffic. The tidal exchange through Sebastian Inlet is extreme. On a rising tide, the water rushes in with such speed and fury that stiff winds are stirred in its vicinity. These cooling breezes can best be enjoyed from catwalks that run under the

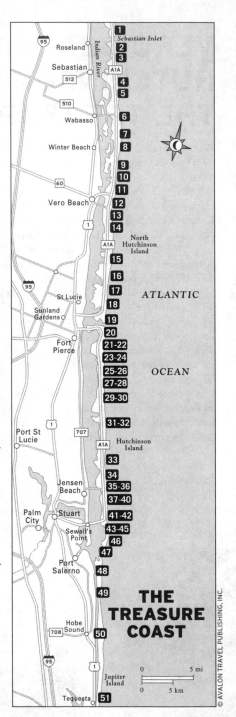

© AVALON TRAVEL PUBLISHING, INC.

BEST BEACHES

(Sebastian Inlet State Park (north side): Top 25, Best for Surfing (page 143)

(South Beach Park: Top 25 (page 151)

(Hobe Sound National Wildlife Refuge: Top 25 (page 176)

inlet bridge. To experience the raw power of the ocean, walk to the end of the jetty. The collisions that result when incoming waves meet outgoing tides fling water and spray onto the jetty. Pelicans hang out at both spots; they know where the fishing is best.

Sebastian Inlet State Park claims three miles of ocean beach. One of the more highly developed and popular state parks in Florida, it offers concessions (food and drink, camping and fishing supplies, and rental of boogie boards, surfboards, and beach umbrellas), a full-service marina, canoe and kayak rentals, and guided ecotours (call 321/724-5424). On a wall inside the snack bar, we found "Greg Noll's East Coast Surf Legends Hall of Fame," listing those Atlantic board bums who get the thumbs up from this West Coast legend. In terms of wave size and quality, Sebastian Inlet is as close to Southern California you'll get in the Sunshine State.

Also within the boundaries of the park are two museums: **McLarty Treasure Museum** (772/589-2147) and **Sebastian Fishing Museum.** Named for Robert McLarty, who donated land to the park, the treasure museum tells the story, via exhibits and recovered treasures, of a Spanish fleet that wrecked offshore in 1715. Laden with gold and silver from Mexico and Peru, the ship and its scattered treasure have remained on the ocean floor for nearly three centuries. Salvage operations began in the mid-1950s, and major finds have been made as recently as 1990. Hence, the nickname "Treasure Coast," bestowed upon a stretch of coast that extends from Sebastian Inlet down to Hobe

Sound. The museum, which is open 10 A.M.– 4:30 P.M. daily, charges a small admission of $1 per person on top of the park's entrance fee. The small Sebastian Fishing Museum occupies a house just down the road and tells the story of the local fishing industry.

Outside the park, in the town of Sebastian, is **Mel Fisher's Treasure Museum** (1322 U.S. 1, 772/589-9875). It also houses a collection of Spanish artifacts salvaged from the same 1715 fleet's wreckage. Open daily, it charges an admission fee of $6.50 for adults and $2 for children. Incidentally, Sebastian is also the site of Pelican Island National Wildlife Refuge. Founded in 1903 by President Theodore Roosevelt, it was the first in a chain that now numbers 545 refuges totaling nearly 100 million acres.

For more information, contact Sebastian Inlet State Park, 9700 South A1A, Melbourne Beach, FL 32951, 321/984-4852. For camping reservations, call 772/589-9659 or check out www.floridastateparks.org.

BEACHES

1 SEBASTIAN INLET STATE PARK (NORTH SIDE)

Location: north side of Sebastian Inlet, between Melbourne Beach and Vero Beach on A1A
Parking/Fees: $5 per vehicle entrance fee. $1 per person admission fee to McLarty Treasure Museum.

© PARKE PUTERBAUGH

Sebastian Inlet

Hours: 24 hours
Facilities: concessions, lifeguards (seasonal), restrooms, picnic tables, showers, and two museums (McLarty Treasure Museum and Sebastian Fishing Museum)
Contact: Sebastian Inlet State Park, 321/984-4852

⊒ SEBASTIAN INLET STATE PARK (SOUTH SIDE)

Location: South side of Sebastian Inlet, between Melbourne Beach and Vero Beach on A1A. The entrance road to the campground, marina, and south jetty are at the foot of Sebastian Inlet bridge. A free beach parking lot is located a half-mile south of the bridge on A1A.
Parking/Fees: $5 per vehicle entrance fee for developed areas of the park (campground, marina, jetty). Camping fee is $23 per night. There is no charge to use the beach parking lot.
Hours: 24 hours

Facilities: concessions, restrooms, picnic tables, and showers
Contact: Sebastian Inlet State Park, 772/589-9659

North Indian River County

A magnificent string of public beaches runs the length of Orchid Island from Sebastian Inlet to Vero Beach. This well-preserved, less-populous north end of Indian River County is one of the less-heralded wonders along Florida's East Coast. We are impressed by their number, the facilities provided, and the beaches themselves. Hats off to Indian River County for ensuring that residents and visitors have ample beach access. The county uses its natural assets and opportunities for ecotourism as a selling point. We wish that more counties followed its example!

For more information, contact the Indian River County Chamber of Commerce, 1216

THE TREASURE COAST

21st Street, Vero Beach, FL 32960, 772/567-3491 or 800/338-2678, ext. 17802, www.indianriverchamber.com.

BEACHES

Up near the top of Orchid Island, just below the southern boundary of Sebastian Inlet State Park, is the first in a strand of county beaches. Unfortunately, **Amber Sands Beach** is the weak link in this otherwise illustrious chain, having already suffered from steady erosion (thanks to the nearby Sebastian Inlet jetties) that was compounded by flattening punches administered when Hurricanes Frances and Jeanne blew through in 2004. On a 2005 visit, we saw a chain-link fence and "Do Not Enter" sign staked at what had been an entrance, and although dune-stabilizing seedlings were beginning to sprout, Amber Sands did not look ripe for reopening anytime soon.

The beach profile improves further south along A1A. Located about a mile apart, **Treasure Shores Beach Park** and **Golden Sands Beach Park** are splendid examples of how a county can both provide beach access and make it aesthetically pleasing. The grounds for both parks are meticulously maintained. Teeming with colorful vegetation, they're virtual botanical gardens of subtropical species. A coarse-sand beach with a steep profile is backed by heavily vegetated dunes. If you look north, in the direction of Sebastian Inlet, the beach seems to stretch into an infinity of unbuilt-upon coastal wilderness. These county-run parks do post lots of "no's," however—no scuba diving (at Treasure Shores), no surfing, no fishing, etc. And these parks did lose some vegetation and beach width as a result of the big blows of 2004.

Wabasso Beach Park lies six miles north of Vero Beach, east of the mainland town of Wabasso and south of the tiny community of Orchid (pop. 150). Wabasso took a debilitating hit from the hurricanes. It used to be an idyllic stretch of sandy paradise—so much so that Disney sited its first beach resort right next to it after searching for years for the perfect spot

in Florida. The serial hurricanes of 2004 put a serious hurting on both Wabasso Beach and Disney's Vero Beach Resort. We previously gave Wabasso a five-star thumbs-up, but it's an eroded shell of its former self that was, in fact, closed to the public when we passed through in 2005.

Moving south, two accesses situated in close proximity are **Sea Grape Beach Access** and **Turtle Trail Beach Access.** Long, paved parking lots extend from A1A to the dune crossover at each access. Both are fine examples of nature held in public trust for the enjoyment of all, preserving bits and pieces of the fast disappearing Old Florida.

3 AMBER SANDS BEACH

Location: 4.4 miles north of the Wabasso Bridge (C.R. 510), on A1A
Parking/Fees: free parking lots
Hours: 8 A.M.-sunset
Facilities: none
Contact: Indian River County Recreation Department, 772/567-2144

4 TREASURE SHORES BEACH PARK

Location: 2.4 miles north of the Wabasso Bridge (C.R. 510), on A1A
Parking/Fees: free parking lots
Hours: 8 A.M.-sunset
Facilities: lifeguards, restrooms, picnic tables, and showers
Contact: Treasure Shores Beach Park, 772/589-6411

5 GOLDEN SANDS BEACH PARK

Location: 1.4 miles north of the Wabasso Bridge (C.R. 510), on A1A
Parking/Fees: free parking lots
Hours: 8 A.M.-sunset

THE TREASURE COAST

© PARKE PUTERBAUGH

Treasure Shores Beach Park

Facilities: lifeguards, restrooms, picnic tables, and showers
Contact: Golden Sands Beach Park, 772/589-6411

6 WABASSO BEACH PARK

Location: east of the Wabasso Bridge (C.R. 510), beside Disney's Vero Beach Resort on A1A
Parking/Fees: free parking lots
Hours: 8 A.M.–sunset
Facilities: lifeguards, restrooms, picnic tables, and showers
Contact: Wabasso Beach Park, 772/589-8291

7 SEA GRAPE BEACH ACCESS

Location: 1.5 miles south of the Wabasso Bridge (C.R. 510), on A1A
Parking/Fees: free parking lot
Hours: 8 A.M.–sunset
Facilities: none

Contact: Indian River County Recreation Department, 772/567-2144

8 TURTLE TRAIL BEACH ACCESS

Location: 2.3 miles south of the Wabasso Bridge (C.R. 510), near Old Winter Beach Road on A1A
Parking/Fees: free parking lot
Hours: 8 A.M.–sunset
Facilities: none
Contact: Indian River County Recreation Department, 772/567-2144

ACCOMMODATIONS

Disney's Vero Beach Resort (9250 Island Grove Terrace, 772/234-2000, $$$$) was the first foray into time-share vacation resorts for the House of Mouse. (They now operate beach resorts in Key West and Hilton Head Island, too.) But the location turns out to have been jinxed, as the Vero Beach area has been pummeled by hurricanes and plagued with beach erosion. In fact a trio of hurricanes in 2004 inflicted so much damage on Disney's Vero Beach Resort that it had to close down nearly three months for repairs. We're certain that was not part of the original business plan.

During our post hurricane stay, numerous signs on the property read: "Please Pardon Our Appearance: We Are Refurbishing This Area for Your Future Enjoyment." Landscaping crews seemed to outnumber guests as they scurried to re-create the air of an unruffled paradise that is the hallmark of everything Disney touches. This property is a vacation ownership resort where rooms are also rented out to non-owners by the night or week. Disney's Vero Beach Resort is painted a cheerful yellow, and you will find Goofy, Mickey, and pals wandering the spacious, wood-floored lobby at specified times. The rooms are nicely appointed and the entire resort functions flawlessly as a vacation sanctuary. However, we do

feel compelled to lodge one complaint: Somewhat disappointingly, soundproofing doesn't seem to have been a high priority. One of us stayed in a studio room, and the noisy children in an adjacent room could be heard plain as day. They loudly played hide-and-seek till 10 P.M. and were up and howling again with the dawn. We don't expect anything different from kids on vacation, and we've been known to make a racket ourselves. We just don't feel that at these rates guests should be able to hear each other quite so clearly.

You'll pay $165–305 a night for an ocean-view room and $60–70 more per night for a one-bedroom villa. They call Disney's Vero Beach Resort a "turn-of-the-century seaside inn," but at those prices, they must mean the 22nd Century. On the positive side, it is a great place to get away with the family. There are programs to occupy the kids, a huge heated pool with a two-story water slide, and easy

INDIAN RIVER FRUIT

The term "Indian River fruit" denotes the best that Florida has to offer in the way of oranges and grapefruits. This is true for three main reasons:

1. The oak-hammock soil and underlying limestone are a rich storehouse of nutrients.

2. High annual rainfall (52 inches) makes for juicy, thin-skinned fruit.

3. Winters are sufficiently cool to trigger sugar production but not too cold – most years, at least – to kill off the citrus crop.

The Indian River Citrus District extends from Daytona Beach south to West Palm Beach. Indian River County alone accounts for nearly one-third of the 220,000 acres under commercial cultivation. How good is Indian River fruit? Testing of citrus by the U.S. Department of Agriculture ranked Indian River citrus first in several categories, including juice content and peel thinness. Your own taste buds can confirm its supremacy by stopping at any of the grower/packers that sell to the public at stands on or near U.S. 1 in Indian River County, including **Hale Groves** (U.S. 1 at 4th Street, Vero Beach, 561/562-3653). Naval oranges are the most celebrated variety grown along the Indian River, but there are also wonderfully sweet red and white grapefruit, plus pineapple, Temple and Valencia oranges, tangerines, and tangelos.

If you would like to learn more about the citrus industry, a charming small museum in Vero Beach is devoted to the subject. The **Indian River Heritage and Citrus Museum** (Heritage Center, 2140 14th Avenue, 772/770-2263) offers exhibits, tools, images, and artifacts that explore four centuries of citrus history in Florida. The gift shop sells such things as original orange crate labels.

THE TREASURE COAST

beach access. They've made an effort to be nature-friendly, the architecture blends in nicely, and it's two hours from Orlando—worth keeping in mind if you want to combine a beach stay with a theme-park visit.

As for the beach, Disney must have to truck in a lot of sand to maintain their sliver of beach at a people-pleasing width. On either side of the resort—Wabasso County Beach to the north and some private estates to the south—the beach was noticeably narrower. Since sand is reworked and evens out along a stretch of beach by wind, wave, and currents, Disney will be fighting a costly, long-term battle to hold its parcel of beach in place. And one day it will lose that battle, because it sits too close to the ocean.

Indian River Shores

Browsing through the annual edition of *Treasure Coast*—a glossy magazine for those looking to relocate or build second homes—we found everything that is developmentally problematic about Florida in general—and Indian River Shores in particular—neatly summed up in one un-ironic sentence: "In Vero Beach, Indian River Shores and the tiny town of Orchid, gated communities are winter residential retreats for the affluent." Now that we've told you all you need to know about Indian River Shores (pop. 3,500), an exclusive appendage of Vero Beach, we'll get straight to the only real thing worth writing about: its beachside park.

For more information, contact the Indian River County Chamber of Commerce, 1216 21st Street, Vero Beach, FL 32960, 772/567-3491 or 800/338-2678, ext. 17802, www.indianriverchamber.com.

BEACHES

Tracking Station Beach, was named for the radar-tracking station that adjoins the property. (Fascinating fact: The station was used by NASA from the early days of the space program through the Saturn moon launches.) This park preserves the dense vegetation that is the most striking feature of Florida's East Coast in its natural state. A series of parking lots are surrounded by a tropical forest of sea grape and palm trees. A boardwalk crossover leads to a coarse, brown-sand beach backed by high, humpbacked dunes held in place by a healthy vegetative cover. It is the sort of semi-isolated spot where an inveterate beach lover could happily spend an entire day.

9 TRACKING STATION BEACH

Location: one mile north of Beachland Boulevard, on A1A in Indian River Shores
Parking/Fees: free parking lots
Hours: 8 A.M.-sunset
Facilities: lifeguards, restrooms, picnic tables, and showers
Contact: Tracking Station Beach, 772/231-2485

Vero Beach

Vero Beach (pop. 18,000) suffers from an identity crisis, insofar as tourism is concerned. Every other major town along Florida's East Coast is associated with something, be it recreation or history, that instantly fixes it in people's minds. Cocoa Beach's calling card is Kennedy Space Center, while Daytona Beach has NASCAR racing, St. Augustine preserves pre- and early-colonial history, and Jacksonville claims pro football's Jaguars. Further down the coast, Palm Beach, Fort Lauderdale, and Miami Beach define the South Florida resort experience and are known to one and all.

Vero Beach is the rather invisible center of Florida's citrus industry and the spring-training site for pro baseball's Los Angeles Dodgers. Now there's nothing wrong with Dodgertown or Indian River fruit (read the *Dodgertown* and *Indian River Fruit* sidebars),

DODGERTOWN

In 2007, the Los Angeles Dodgers will celebrate the 60th season of spring training at their "Dodgertown" complex in Vero Beach. In a game that's not exactly known for loyalty or constancy, this ongoing relationship between the Dodgers and Vero Beach is worth celebrating.

Of the 18 major-league baseball teams that train in Florida, the Dodgers' spring-training program is the one most grounded in tradition. The association with Vero dates back to 1948, when the team set up camp on the site of an old naval training station. Their loyalty to Vero Beach survived the franchise's relocation from Brooklyn to Los Angeles a decade later, and both team and town have been enamored of one another — though in the age of big money, those bonds have been tested. Still, the Dodgers remain the only West Coast team that trains in Florida.

The term "mystique" is often invoked by fans and players alike, and the ready accessibility of players to spectators in the casual environment at Dodgertown is cited as a big reason. The team has helped put Vero Beach on the map, such as it is. In the words of longtime Dodgers broadcaster Vin Scully, "I don't believe Vero Beach would be known anywhere outside of Vero Beach except for the presence of the Dodgers."

The Dodgers practice at Holman Stadium, which is part of the larger Dodgertown complex. Dodgertown also serves as home to a class-A minor-league team, the Vero Beach Dodgers. Football team practices and fantasy baseball camps are held here. There are six practice fields, a conference center, housing, swimming pools, tennis courts, two golf courses, and a commercial citrus grove. But the springtime version of the summer game by the Los Angeles Dodgers is the biggest attraction at the 468-acre camp, whose centerpiece is Holman Stadium, where the lack of dugouts means that players sit on benches, always visible and audible to those in the stands.

Players begin arriving at camp in mid-February and leave around April 1. They play roughly 30 exhibition games with other major-league teams throughout the month of March, half of them away and half at Holman Stadium (named for Bud Holman, a local entrepreneur). Most games begin around 1 P.M.; a few start at 6 P.M. or 7 P.M. Once the major leaguers have vacated, the Vero Beach Dodgers launch a 140-game minor-league schedule that begins in early April and ends in early September. Tickets to major-league exhibition games cost $16-18. Minor-league games cost $5 for adults and $4 for kids ages 6-12 and seniors over 50. Entertainment doesn't come much cheaper than that.

In the late 1990s, the Dodgers began scouting elsewhere for spring training, with Las Vegas the top contender. However, after much wrangling Florida governor Jeb Bush allocated funds in June 2000 to help the county of Indian River and the city of Vero Beach keep the Dodgers in Dodgertown. This was done by buying Dodgertown from the Dodgers, making millions of dollars in improvements to the facility, and then leasing it back to the ball club. A deal signed in 2002 will keep the Los Angeles Dodgers in Vero Beach through 2022. So for now and hopefully forever, the Dodgers will continue to call Holman Stadium home when spring comes calling.

To find out more about spring training and game schedules for both the Los Angeles Dodgers and the Vero Beach Dodgers, contact Dodgertown, 4101 26th Street, Vero Beach, FL 32966, www.dodgertown.com. Call 772/569-4900 for Dodgertown information, and call Ticketmaster (866-DODGERS) for tickets to major- and minor-league games. Tickets for the L.A. Dodgers' spring-training season generally go on sale around February 3.

By the way, in 2005 the Vero Beach Dodgers finished second in the Florida State League's East Division but got upset in the playoffs by the Palm Beach Cardinals.

but they're hardly comparable to space-shuttle launches, the Daytona 500, and South Beach's jet-setting nightlife. However, Vero Beach and Indian River County have lately been repositioning themselves as an ecotourism destination. That's just fine with us, as it requires vigilant preservation of open space and natural resources to pull it off.

On previous visits, Vero Beach struck us as a pretty dull place geared toward a graying population of retirees. Maybe because we're a little older now ourselves, Vero Beach looks a lot more appealing these days. It is a charming, habitable small city boasting well-tended beachside parks, lovely older residential neighborhoods, and a modest tourist trade. An obvious demerit is severe beach erosion at the center of town, where Beachland Boulevard meets Ocean Drive. To combat the ocean's incursions, they've built seawalls. The beach regains a modest amount of width as you head away from Beachland Boulevard in either direction, and the town itself is a thoroughly pleasant place that moves at a sea turtle's unhurried crawl.

What can you do here? Well, they've got good restaurants; great recreational opportunities in the Indian River Lagoon, Atlantic Ocean, and Sebastian and Fort Pierce Inlets; a healthy accent on ecotourism; the first-rate **Vero Beach Museum of Art** (3001 Riverside Drive, 772/231-0707); two treasure museums; two National Wildlife Refuges (Archie Carr and Pelican); and one of the most popular state parks in Florida (Sebastian Inlet). Need we say more?

For more information, contact the Indian River County Chamber of Commerce, 1216 21st Street, Vero Beach, FL 32960, 772/567-3491 or 800/338-2678, ext. 17802, www.indianriverchamber.com.

BEACHES

The beach at the heart of town is so eroded they should consider changing the town name from Vero Beach to just Vero. Besides saving five letters, it would be closer to the truth.

The situation looked bad when we researched our first beach book in 1984 and is no better now. It's been this way for decades, and Hurricanes Frances and Jeanne, which made landfall within three weeks of each other in September 2004, inflicted even more damage on Vero Beach. At **Sexton Plaza,** where Beachland Boulevard meets the ocean, waves lap at the seawall. North and south of the center the beach gradually regains width. An offshore reef installed by the U.S. Army Corps of Engineers is supposed to help protect the shoreline. As with all Corps projects, *caveat emptor* is the rule.

Starting up north, **Jaycee Beach Park** has a large, grassy area for playing and picnicking (volleyball, playground equipment, covered picnic tables) and plenty of parking. A bench-lined wooden boardwalk runs along the beach to some on-street parking in the vicinity of **Conn Beach,** which it adjoins. This is the place to come with the family with a picnic basket or to grill your dinner. It's very Mayberry-like here. There's even a sandwich and ice-cream shop!

It's worth noting that all of the lifeguarded beaches in Vero Beach and Indian River County have a full complement of facilities—including playgrounds, picnic pavilions, and grills—and are exquisitely landscaped. There is no public fishing pier in Vero Beach but people cast lines from walkways over Barber Bridge, which crosses the Indian River.

Humiston Park, which is a few blocks south of Sexton Plaza, is another green, clean park that includes not just a beach but a grassy quadrangle. Burdened by development on all sides, this beach too is backed by a seawall. It is narrow at low tide and practically vanishes at high tide. A little retail area consisting of a deli, bakery, and convenience store gives the area a modest neighborhood feel and the greenspace is a delight.

Riomar Beach, located east of the intersection of Riomar and Ocean Drives, is a popular spot with surfers. It's a private residential neighborhood, but there's a public beach access and limited street parking.

The pearl in Vero Beach's sandy chain is **South Beach Park.** Vero Beach chills out at its south end, giving way to a modest complex of beach homes and small motels. It is a likable area and the beach earns an A+. A mixed bag of young families, elderly retirees, and comely singles in bikinis—more than we expected to see in Vero Beach—crowds a markedly wide beach with clean, gleaming light-brown sand and emerald green waters. Walk along the beach for a quarter-mile north and you'll have a virtual wilderness beach all to yourself. Parking is free at South Beach and all other city and county beach parks. Yahoo!

As a final note, Vero Beach has some fine parks along the Indian River, including Mac-William Park and Riverside Park (north and south of the east end of Merrill Barber Bridge, respectively). On the west bank of the river, Royal Palm Point Park has picnic tables, fishing and boat docks, and a fountain in which kids can cool off.

10 JAYCEE BEACH PARK/ CONN BEACH

Location: A1A at Mango Avenue in Vero Beach
Parking/Fees: free parking lot
Hours: sunrise-sunset
Facilities: concessions, lifeguards, restrooms, picnic tables, and showers
Contact: Jaycee Beach Park, 772/231-0578

11 SEXTON PLAZA

Location: Ocean Drive at Beachland Boulevard in Vero Beach
Parking/Fees: free street parking
Hours: 8 A.M.-sunset
Facilities: none
Contact:: Vero Beach Recreation Department, 772/231-4700

12 HUMISTON PARK

Location: Ocean Drive at Easter Lily Lane, just south of Beachland Boulevard in Vero Beach
Parking/Fees: free street and lot parking
Hours: sunrise-sunset
Facilities: concessions, lifeguards, restrooms, picnic tables, and showers
Contact: Humiston Park, 772/231-5790

13 RIOMAR BEACH

Location: Ocean Drive at Riomar Drive, south of the Riomar Country Club, in Vero Beach
Parking/Fees: free street parking
Hours: 8 A.M.-sunset
Facilities: none
Contact: Vero Beach Recreation Department, 772/231-4700

14 SOUTH BEACH PARK

Location: South Ocean Drive and East Causeway Boulevard (17th Street Bridge), in Vero Beach. South Beach Park can also be entered from the ends of Coquina, Flamevine, Jasmine, Pirate Cove, Sandpiper, and Turtle Cove lanes, though no parking is available at these accesses.
Parking/Fees: free parking lots at park entrance
Hours: 8 A.M.-sunset
Facilities: lifeguards, restrooms, picnic tables, and showers
Contact: South Beach Park, 772/231-4700

RECREATION AND ATTRACTIONS
- **Bike/Skate Rentals:** Bicycle Sport, Vero Beach, 772/569-5990
- **Dive Shop:** Deep Six Dive & Watersports, 416 21st Street, Vero Beach, 772/562-2883

South Beach Park

- **Ecotourism:** Indian River Kayak and Canoe, 3435 Aviation Boulevard, Vero Beach, 772/569-5757
- **Fishing Charters:** Vero's Tackle and Marina, 3321 Bridge Plaza Drive, Vero Beach, 772/234-9585
- **Marina:** Grand Harbor Marina, 5510 North Harbor Village Drive, Vero Beach, 772/770-4470
- **Rainy-Day Attraction:** Indian River Heritage and Citrus Museum, 2140 14th Avenue, Vero Beach, 772/770-2263
- **Shopping/Browsing:** Indian River Mall, 6200 20th Street, Vero Beach, 772/770-9404
- **Surf Shop:** Inner Rhythm Surf and Sport, 2053 Indian River Boulevard, Vero Beach, 772/778-9038
- **Vacation Rentals:** Seaside Realty of Vero Beach, 3247 Ocean Drive, Vero Beach, 772/231-7741

ACCOMMODATIONS

America loves an eccentric, and Vero Beach had a dandy. His name was Waldo Sexton, and he was an art collector, builder, entrepreneur, and borderline nut case. He constructed three restaurants and one hotel here in the early 1900s. Their outlandish nature is remarkable in a town this foursquare. His piece de resistance was the **Driftwood Inn** (3150 Ocean Drive, 772/231-0550, $$$). Sexton was not a trained architect, but he designed the Driftwood with verbal instructions, improvising as he went. As its name suggests, the inn was constructed entirely from wood that had washed ashore, and the rooms were decorated with whatever nautical bric-a-brac—ship bells, lanterns, cannons, boat parts—the sea coughed up. After it opened, Sexton continued to festoon the interior with artifacts obtained at estate auctions, flea markets, and his own world travels. Paintings, treasure chests, mastodon bones, ever more bells. The Driftwood is a museum of the eclectic, unified by its general nautical theme. The original Driftwood Inn is intact, though it is now flanked by more modern lodgings and the whole complex has been renamed the Driftwood Resort.

Also at Sexton Plaza is **Holiday Inn Oceanside** (3384 Ocean Drive, 772/231-2300, $$). One of the town's more attractive properties, **Vero Beach Hotel and Club**

(3500 Ocean Drive, 772/231-5666, $$$)—formerly the Doubletree Inn & Suites—got clobbered by hurricanes and, we're told, might possibly reopen as a combined hotel/condo project. The eroded condition of the beach, combined with damage that Vero Beach hotels and buildings have repeatedly suffered at the hands of hurricanes, makes us hesitant to recommend the town per se as a place to come and enjoy the shore.

If you want to stay on a wide, healthy beach in Vero Beach proper, head south to the modestly appealing **Aquarius Oceanfront Resort** (1526 South Ocean Drive, 772/231-5218, $), a clean, well-kept, and inexpensive motel located by South Beach Park. Or you could head north to Disney's Vero Beach Resort—which isn't in Vero Beach but six miles north of it (see write-up under *Accommodations* in the *North Indian River County* section).

COASTAL CUISINE

There's money in Vero Beach, which means good restaurants. On the high end is **Black Pearl Brasserie** (2855 Ocean Drive, 772/234-7426, $$$$). It's elegant, so forget about wearing a Mickey Mouse T-shirt and cutoffs to dinner. Done up in dark and mauve tones, the dining room is a feast for the eyes, while the entree creations are a feast, pure and simple. Black Pearl concedes nothing in the way of gourmet excellence to the upscale brasseries of South Florida. Try the yellowtail snapper with lobster beurre blanc or blackened tuna with crab Creole. They do a great jerk-spiced dolphin and a Rockefeller-style fresh catch (pan roasted with spinach, bacon, and Pernod *veloute*). This easily places among our favorite restaurants between Jacksonville and Miami. The Black Pearl also has a location on the Indian River in Vero Beach (4445 North A1A, 772/234-4426, $$$$), to which a gourmet deli is appended.

Another of Florida's finest restaurants is **Tango's** (3001 Ocean Drive, 772/231-1550, $$$$). Who would've thought we'd wind up in Vero Beach, Florida, eating Maine lobster? It

was not just any lobster, mind you, but Tango's signature "Southern-fried Lobster." Imagine two lobster tails rolled in a light breading and flash-fried, then served atop garlic mashed potatoes and baby asparagus in a pool of key lime butter sauce. Yum! This is just one of the tasty menu offerings at Tangos, which has been around for a decade but for the past few years has occupied a new building across the street from the beach at Humiston Park. It's not an inexpensive place to dine—dinner for two might top $150 if you go all the way and order appetizers, dessert, and wine, as we did—but one where the tab is well worth it. Off-menu specials might include such treats as gray grouper in chive butter sauce and almond-crusted flounder with tropical fruit salsa. Fried oysters in a buttery remoulade with a seriously spicy hot sauce dotted about the plate is a favorite appetizer, as are lobster fritters and a quarter-pound crab cake. Don't miss the key lime cheesecake with strawberry marmalade for dessert. Bananas Foster soufflé is another after-dinner specialty, but must be ordered with your entree to allow for preparation time. The room and service are class personified, and a dinner here is an unforgettable event.

Appended to the Driftwood Inn (see *Accommodations*) is another of Waldo Sexton's architectural curiosities. The **Ocean Grill** (1050 Sexton Plaza, 772/231-5409, $$$) overlooks the water at the end of Beachland Boulevard, a prime oceanfront location in Vero Beach. In fact, the location might be a little too good. In 1984, the Ocean Grill was washed into the sea by a vicious winter nor'easter. With it went a priceless collection of nautical bric-a-brac. According to one account, "Old driftwood and European artifacts that decorated the popular bar were lost when the building collapsed into the sea." However, it's been rebuilt and still sways on pilings over the water, which just proves you can't keep a good restaurant down. Go for the seafood: broiled grouper, grilled swordfish, or the house specialty—Indian River crab fingers.

For another kind of dining experience

that's also on the water—the Intracoastal Waterway, in this case—point your car or boat to the **Riverside Cafe** (1 Beachland Boulevard, 772/234-5550, $$). It is located almost directly under the New Merrill Barber Bridge. (Follow signs from Beachland Avenue, near the eastern foot of the bridge.) It's a great spot to watch the sun set as cars and joggers cross the gracefully arching bridge. With its open-air deck, the Riverside is a pleasant place to nibble bar food and listen to bar bands. They make a savory bowl of conch chowder, and the fish tostada—a grilled slab of mahimahi served atop a cheesy tostada with a mound of yellow rice and black beans—makes a filling entree. Hearty appetizers like baked stuffed oysters and Buffalo wings are done decently and served in an archetypal Florida setting.

Capt. Hiram's Restaurant (1606 Indian River Drive, 772/589-4345, $$$) is neither on the ocean nor in Vero Beach, but it's close enough. This multidimensional "fun complex" is built around a Key West–style restaurant on the banks of the Indian River in the town of Sebastian at the north end of Orchid Island. Seafood, including raw-bar items, are the house specialties at Capt. Hiram's. On the premises you'll also find a motel, two bars (Ramp Lounge and Sand Bar, both with seasonal entertainment), and a full-service marina. There's even a sand beach—albeit on the banks of the Indian River.

By the way, if you're staying at Disney's Vero Beach Resort, **Shutters** is the casual restaurant on the Disney property. You can nab a healthy, fairly priced meal here. At breakfast, you might opt for "The Healthy Floridian"—an artfully arranged pile of fresh fruit, served with a muffin and small helping of yogurt and granola—or a basil, tomato, and asparagus omelette.

NIGHTLIFE

Coming to Vero Beach in search of nightlife is like driving to Orlando in search of surf. About the best you can hope for is a group

with a name like the Landsharks playing rock and reggae at an outdoor tiki bar. That was exactly what we heard on the deck of the Riverside Cafe (see *Coastal Cuisine*). Their alternative-lite covers got an entire table of elderly Swedish tourists all worked up. They bolted out of their seats and boogied as if they'd just won the lottery. America—such a wild and crazy place!

Round Island Park

Beach access isn't as bountiful south of Vero Beach as in the northern part of the county. In fact, the only beach park in southern Indian River County is Round Island Park, which is mainly centered around the Indian River, on the west side of Ocean Drive (A1A).

It's a welcome break in the wall of development, and anglers love to toss a line from the shore. Moreover, it's been upgraded quite a bit in recent years with palm trees, picket fences, and a playground. The brown-sand beach is

© PARKE PUTERBAUGH

Be alert to lifeguard notification signs for a safer visit.

wide and steep-sloped. There's also a bit of World War II history hereabouts, as a German U-boat torpedoed three right off the coast from this beach.

For more information, contact the Indian River County Recreation Department, 1725 17th Avenue, Vero Beach, FL 32960, 772/567-2144, www.indian-river.fl.us/playing/parkirc.html.

BEACHES

15 ROUND ISLAND PARK

Location: A1A at the St. Lucie County line
Parking/Fees: free parking lot
Hours: sunrise-sunset
Facilities: restrooms, picnic tables, and showers
Contact: Indian River County Recreation Department, 772/567-2144

North Hutchinson Island

First of all, let us make one thing perfectly unclear: North Hutchinson Island is also known as Orchid Island. Depending on which county you are in, the same island goes by different names. The south end belongs to St. Lucie County and is known as North Hutchinson Island, while the north end belongs to Indian River County and is known as Orchid Island. Confused? Join the club.

North Hutchinson Island is schizophrenic, being divided between wild, windswept beach parks and tall stands of condominiums. In places it is one large construction zone moonscape. Heading south on our latest visit, the first three signs we saw in St. Lucie County all advertised various amounts of "Acres for Sale." The buildup of 15-story condos, exhibiting all the architectural panache of college dormitories, runs for miles

above Fort Pierce Inlet on North Hutchinson Island, blocking views of the ocean for those driving along A1A. It seemed curious to us that at the height of summer, parking lots at these oceanfront fortresses are nearly empty. It's the absentee owner phenomenon! You know, privatizing the beach for phantom guests whose check-writing ability is nonetheless held in esteem because it pumps up the county tax base.

A marked dichotomy exists along stretches along A1A on North Hutchinson Island: towering condos on the ocean side and manufactured housing on the inland side. Neither is a pretty sight. The good news is that several beach parks and accesses exist between the fortress-like condos.

For more information, contact the St. Lucie County Tourist Development Council, 2300 Virginia Avenue, Fort Pierce, FL 34982, 772/462-1535 or 800/344-8443, www.visit-stluciefla.com.

BEACHES

Driving down North Hutchinson Island, you'll encounter Avalon Beach, Bryn Mawr Beach, and Pepper Park. **Avalon Beach** is a state property with nothing much more than two entrance points, free lots, restrooms, and dune walkovers over a broad meadow thick with beach grasses. The beach is unspoiled and often deserted. A dune restoration is in progress and the beach has been noticeably thinned by the hurricanes of 2004. St. Lucie County has provided a parking lot and dune crossover at **Bryn Mawr Access,** about a half-mile south of Avalon, and it's more of the appealing (but recovering) same.

The gem of North Hutchinson Island is **Pepper Park,** a full-tilt ocean-to-river park that's busting out with things to do and places to do them. It's got volleyball, tennis, and basketball courts. On the lagoon side are boat docks and fishing piers. Picnic tables occupy a large, grassy quadrangle. There's also the intriguing **Navy Seal Museum** (3300 North

A1A, Pepper Park, 772/595-5845, $5 adults, $2 kids), devoted to those amphibious men in uniform—a.k.a. "frogmen"—who helped guard the coast from German U-boats during World War II. Best of all, there's nearly 2,000 feet of expansive, gently sloping beach at Pepper Park, though condos loom like enemy ramparts in both directions. The Fort Pierce Inlet jetties are visible to the south. All in all, this is a very inviting place that gets our highest commendations.

16 AVALON BEACH

Location: 1.5 miles south of Indian River County line at A1A on North Hutchinson Island
Parking/Fees: free parking lots
Hours: 8 A.M.-sunset
Facilities: restrooms
Contact: Fort Pierce Inlet State Park, 772/468-3985

17 BRYN MAWR ACCESS

Location: two miles south of the Indian River County line along A1A on North Hutchinson Island
Parking/Fees: free parking lot
Hours: sunrise-sunset
Facilities: none
Contact: St. Lucie County Recreation Office, 772/462-1521

18 PEPPER PARK

Location: 2.5 miles south of the Indian River County line along A1A on North Hutchinson Island
Parking/Fees: free parking lots
Hours: sunrise-sunset
Facilities: lifeguards (seasonal), restrooms, picnic tables, showers, and a visitors center (Navy Seal Museum)
Contact: St. Lucie County Recreation Office, 772/462-1521

Fort Pierce Inlet State Park

The main attraction at the south end of the island is Fort Pierce Inlet State Park. This two-part park consists of the north shore of Fort Pierce Inlet (a.k.a. North Jetty Park) and Jack Island Preserve, a peninsula on the Indian River side of the island. Jack Island is a mile and a half north of the jetty along A1A. Good surf is occasionally kicked up at North Jetty Park when swells roll in from the north or northeast. On an ominously overcast day in October, a long line of surfers had staked out positions in the water.

The swimming is fine all of the time on this lifeguarded beach. The sand is a natural brown-orange, not at all like the mocha-colored fill south of the jetty on the beaches of Fort Pierce. At Fort Pierce Inlet and Jack Island Preserve, trails wend their way through coastal plant communities—maritime hammock and mangrove wetlands, respectively—both of which are rarer than they deserve to be. Bring a canoe and paddle around the mangrove swamp at Dynamite Point (so named for the Navy's Underwater Demolition Team, who drilled here during World War II), on the west side of the inlet. Also, be advised that the fishing is exceptional on every flank of the park, from jetty to estuary.

For more information, contact Fort Pierce Inlet State Park, 905 Shorewinds Drive, Fort Pierce, FL 34949, 772/468-3985, www.floridastateparks.org.

BEACHES

19 FORT PIERCE INLET STATE PARK

Location: southern tip of North Hutchinson Island at the end of Shorewinds Drive
Parking/Fees: $5 per vehicle entrance fee
Hours: 8 A.M.-sunset

Facilities: lifeguards (seasonal), restrooms, picnic tables, and showers
Contact: Fort Pierce Inlet State Park, 772/468-3985

Fort Pierce

As is the case with Vero Beach, Fort Pierce (pop. 37,516) is largely situated on the west side of the Indian River, but the town also spills over onto the north end of Hutchinson Island. Fort Pierce Inlet, the Intracoastal Waterway, and the Atlantic Ocean provide boundless opportunities for boaters and anglers. Marinas and docks line Fort Pierce Harbor, and a few motels and waterfront pubs exist to service the boat people.

The section of Fort Pierce on Hutchinson Island is low-key and unpretentious—a throwback to an earlier time, which is amazing given the mad growth scenarios on the mainland in St. Lucie County. A string of green, clean beach parks and accesses adds to the appeal. Few of Florida's beach communities have changed less than Fort Pierce since we began keeping tabs. Unfortunately, recent hurricanes have whipped up on Fort Pierce, and buildings and signs still bear scars from twin assaults by Frances and Jeanne like a punch-drunk boxer who can't quite stand up after being knocked to the canvas.

By the way, you really don't want to have much to do with mainland Fort Pierce, especially along the hellish U.S. 1 corridor. We spent what felt like half a lifetime in a McDonald's parking lot here.

For more information, contact the St. Lucie County Tourist Development Council, 2300 Virginia Avenue, Fort Pierce, FL 34982, 772/462-1535 or 800/344-8443, www.visit-stluciefla.com.

BEACHES

The beaches of Hutchinson Island (nicknamed "Sunrise City") are about all we like about St. Lucie County, and we haven't always liked the ones in Fort Pierce. When we first spent time here more than 20 years ago, littering and lax enforcement were taking their toll. We found vegetation-smashing tire tracks from joyriding Jeeps and mounds of trash and tackle left behind by anglers. **South Jetty Park,** located where A1A meets the island in Fort Pierce, looks a bit more spruced up these days, though it can still get trashed on bad days. On our most recent visit, for example, wads of litter choked a dune restoration project. What kind of rabble would discard trash in roped-off dunes?

This park is defined by a 1,200-foot rock and concrete jetty that is the longest in Florida. (In terms of jurisdiction, the jetties on either side of Fort Pierce Inlet belong to the federal government, while the park on the north side is Fort Pierce Inlet State Park while that on the south side is city-owned South Jetty Park.) Constructed to keep Fort Pierce Inlet open for boating, the jetty and park were also designed with fishing and other forms of recreation in mind. Picnic tables are distributed around the parking area, with a fish-cleaning station at the center of the action. You can catch it, clean it, fillet it, and cook it right there on the barbecue grills. Best of all, just around the corner is a lifeguarded, crescent-shaped beach. The beach and adjoining grounds are connected by a boardwalk and are cooled by constant breezes that blow off the churning waters of the inlet and jetty.

Between South Jetty Park and South Beach Boardwalk, a group of dune walkovers provide access to beachgoers (including those who live in the neighborhood but not on the beach). The walkovers are located at the ends of streets between Avalon and Gulfstream Avenues along South Ocean Drive (A1A).

The quarter-mile **South Beach Boardwalk,** at the 700 block of South Ocean Drive (A1A), is the centerpiece of a beach park where you'll find free parking, picnic areas, and lifeguard stands. Less than a half mile south is another boardwalked beach, this one a side-by-side duo called **Surfside Park/Kimberly Bergalis**

Memorial Park. The latter was named for a local resident who contracted HIV and then bravely spent her remaining days speaking out for victims of the disease and petitioning for funds to research its cure. Although parking is limited, there's room for any spillover along Ocean Drive (A1A). Lifeguards are on duty in summer at the conjoined parks, which together account for about another quarter mile of sandy beach. Across the street from Surfside Park, on the west side of A1A, is Jaycee Park, which extends to the Intracoastal Waterway. Between the two, just about all of the recreational bases are covered.

Rounding out Fort Pierce's accessible beach bounty, small parking lots and dune crossovers (and nothing else) are provided at **Coconut Drive Park,** and **Exchange Park,** on the south end of town. Incidentally, at all above-mentioned parks, the sand is a chocolate color and coarser than natural Florida beach sand. It looks suspiciously like fill from inlet-dredging projects.

20 SOUTH JETTY PARK

Location: east end of Seaway Drive, off North Ocean Drive (A1A) in Fort Pierce, on the south side of Fort Pierce Inlet
Parking/Fees: free parking lot
Hours: sunrise-sunset
Facilities: lifeguards, restrooms, picnic tables, and showers
Contact: St. Lucie County Recreation Office, 772/462-1521

21 SOUTH BEACH BOARDWALK

Location: 0.25 mile south of Gulfstream Avenue on South Ocean Drive (A1A) in Fort Pierce
Parking/Fees: free parking lot
Hours: sunrise-sunset
Facilities: lifeguards, restrooms, picnic tables, and showers

Contact: South Beach Boardwalk, 772/432-2355

22 SURFSIDE PARK/ KIMBERLY BERGALIS MEMORIAL PARK

Location: one mile south of Fort Pierce Inlet, between Indialantic and Melaleuca Drives on South Ocean Drive (A1A) in Fort Pierce
Parking/Fees: free parking lots
Hours: sunrise-sunset
Facilities: lifeguards (seasonal), restrooms, picnic tables, and showers
Contact: St. Lucie County Recreation Office, 772/462-1521

23 COCONUT DRIVE PARK

Location: south end of Surfside Drive on Blue Heron Avenue in Fort Pierce
Parking/Fees: free parking lot
Hours: sunrise-sunset
Facilities: none
Contact: St. Lucie County Recreation Office, 772/462-1521

24 EXCHANGE PARK

Location: 2.25 miles south of Fort Pierce Inlet on South Ocean Drive (A1A) in Fort Pierce
Parking/Fees: free parking lot
Hours: sunrise-sunset
Facilities: none
Contact: St. Lucie County Recreation Office, 772/462-1521

RECREATION AND ATTRACTIONS

- **Dive Shop:** Dive Odyssea, 621 North 2nd Street, Fort Pierce, 772/460-1771

- **Ecotourism:** Turtle Walk, Florida Power & Light, Hutchinson Island, 800/552-8440

- **Fishing Charters:** Grand Slam Fishing Center, 101 Seaway Drive, Fort Pierce, 772/466-6775

- **Marinas:** Fort Pierce City Marina, 1 Avenue A, Fort Pierce, 772/464-1245; Harbortown Marina, 1945 Harbortown Drive, Fort Pierce 772/466-7300

- **Pier:** South Jetty Park, Fort Pierce Inlet, Seaway Drive at South Ocean Drive (A1A), Fort Pierce, 772/462-1521

- **Rainy-Day Attraction:** Harbor Branch Oceanographic Institution, 5600 U.S. 1, Fort Pierce, 772/465-7156

- **Shopping/Browsing:** Orange Blossom Mall, Okeechobee Road at Virginia Avenue, Fort Pierce

- **Surf Shop:** Blue Planet Dive and Surf, 1317B NW Port St. Lucie West Boulevard, Port St. Lucie, 772/871-9122

- **Vacation Rentals:** Ocean Village, 2400 South Ocean Drive (A1A), Fort Pierce, 772/489-6100

ACCOMMODATIONS

There's plenty of beach at the north end of Hutchinson Island but precious few hotels or motels directly on it. You'll find a couple along Fort Pierce Inlet. Cut from plain cloth, they serve the undemanding fishing and boating crowd. One is called the **Dockside Inn** (1152 Seaway Drive, 772/461-4824, $). The place closest to the beach—in fact, right where A1A makes its southern turn—is the **Beachwood Motel** (110 South Ocean Drive, 772/465-3157, $), an old reliable. One block back from the beach is **Mariners Days Inn** (1920 Seaway Drive, 772/461-8737, $). It's small by this chain's standards, with only 32 units in a one-story structure that got knocked one step closer to decrepitude after the 2004 hurricane season.

The only oceanfront lodging really worth extolling in Fort Pierce is **Ocean Village** (2400 South Ocean Drive, 772/489-0300, $$$). Located two miles south of the inlet, this condo complex offers beach access and is within walking distance of Green Turtle Beach. Ocean Village covers 120 acres and might be described as a miniature Amelia Island Plantation. On the grounds: a beach club, beautiful swimming pool, nine-hole

golf course, tennis and racquetball courts, four residential towers, and rows of two-story villas lining the fairways. Like many such places, Ocean Village is only partly open to the public. Individual units are rented by the week or month when participating owners are not using them.

COASTAL CUISINE

There's nothing much to recommend on the beach in Fort Pierce. If you can't get down to Jensen Beach or up to Vero Beach for dinner, we can only recommend, however tepidly, **Harbortown Fish House** (1930 Harbortown Drive, Taylor Creek Marina, 772/461-8732, $$). It's miles from the ocean and all over the map in terms of menu, with Key West–style conch dishes cohabiting with New England clam chowder. Nearer the ocean is **Mangrove Mattie's** (1640 Seaway Drive, 772/466-1044, $$$), whose most salient feature is a lovely view of the inlet and the beach. Mattie serves fresh seafood at inflated prices. Memo to Mattie: This is Fort Pierce, home of blown-out burger stands, not South Miami Beach.

Hutchinson Island (mid-island)

One of the most pleasant surprises along Florida's coast is Hutchinson Island, a 16-mile barrier island. The island encompasses the eastward extensions of Fort Pierce and Jensen Beach (see separate write-ups for each), plus a whole lot in between. With the glaring exception of a nuclear power facility, Hutchinson Island has pretty much been left to the natural elements. Mother Nature has, in fact, found a strange bedfellow out here in that very power plant. Florida Power & Light (FPL), the electric utility that operates St. Lucie Nuclear Power Plant at mid-island, owns a five-mile swath of undeveloped and thickly vegetated acreage that serves as a safety buffer. Sadly, the flora here was thinned considerably in September 2004

WE DON'T LOVE LUCIE

Judging from the growth spurt of cities west of Hutchinson Island, it might take the construction of another fort to protect the beaches of St. Lucie County from mainland Fort Pierce and its completely landlocked neighbor, Port St. Lucie. The latter is the worst culprit. At least Fort Pierce has tried to fix up its old downtown district and added a Manatee Observation and Education Center. Still, both cities have been attracting hordes of new arrivals in recent decades, and we don't mean vacationers. They are mostly retirees who can't afford the luxury of aging down along the Gold Coast or suckers who've been taken in by apocryphal Florida real-estate come-ons.

The U.S. Census Bureau announced in 2005 that Port St. Lucie is the fastest-growing city in the nation. Between 2003 and 2004, the population jumped by 12 percent. This is not cause for celebration but alarm, in our eyes. Consider that Port St. Lucie did not even exist in 1961. Today it is the blob-like home to 130,000 people sprawled across 77 square miles – the third largest land area of any Florida city – of former swampland and pine savanna. From the perspective of U.S. 1, it's sweltering asphalt and retail blight as far as the eye can see.

Far sadder and more troubling is the abnormally high incidence of rare brain and central nervous system cancers in children in St. Lucie County. In an earlier edition we speculated that this cancer cluster might have something to do with proximity to the nuclear plant on Hutchinson Island. Of course, when we raised this point, we were accused of all sort of nefarious motives. The sitting mayor of Port St. Lucie labeled us "outside nuts," while a former mayor opined that we were "obviously suffering from cranial suffocation caused by rectal strangulation." (Huh?) A city councilman questioned our credibility as travel writers, and another said ours was a "fairy tale."

First, after the bungled vote count in the 2000 presidential election, public officials in Florida would be well advised to avoid ever using terms like "fairy tale" or "credibility." Second, a story that ran in the *New York Times* in August 2005 sadly appears to affirm that our hunch was correct. (Not that we want to be proved "right" in such a tragic matter as this.)

According to the *Times,* records show that Florida Power and Light made numerous shipments of radioactive waste from its nuclear power facility to municipal landfills all over St. Lucie County in the 1980s. The contaminants (cobalt 60, strontium, and cesium) were contained in sludge that was sent to landfills and spread on farmland and cow pastures. Furthermore, plant workers used a sink to wash mops, rags, and

by Hurricane Jeanne, which made landfall on the southern end of Hutchinson Island. Downed trees sit like spent matchsticks on the ocean side of A1A.

Of course, there are concerns about having a nuclear plant so proximate to the Indian River and mainland populations. The Indian River watershed is hugely important to central Florida's agricultural, fishing, and tourist industries, as well as being a vital habitat for threatened and endangered sea turtle species and other forms of marine life (including many species commonly found on restaurant menus). Perhaps overcompensating for the PR woes of the much-maligned nuclear industry, FPL—whose Hutchinson Island plant has had its share of problems—has been a good steward of the land and watershed. They sponsor low-impact nighttime turtle walks, run a free educational "Energy Encounter" program for the public, conduct outreach environmental programs for area schools, and have preserved a 400-acre freshwater cypress swamp (Barley Barber Swamp) in western Martin County. (For these and other programs, call FPL's Environmental Information Line at 800/334-

THE TREASURE COAST

other heavily contaminated materials, which drained into the county's sewage system. As this edition went to press, lawsuits were pending from the parents of children who had contracted cancer.

To add insult to injury, insofar as our standing with the powers-that-be in St. Lucie County is concerned, the first edition of our book was published soon after a pan of Port St. Lucie appeared in the *New York Post*. A columnist for that paper – assigned for a month to cover the nearby New York Mets spring-training camp – had described Port St. Lucie as "a pathetic waste of map space" filled with "honky-tonk bars" and "briefly clad babes." Apparently, our book's less strident, fact-based observations struck the locals as piling on, which didn't minimize our shock at having the local tourist council call our book "inaccurate" and "sad."

Then there were the rantings of one Joe Crankshaw, a writer for the *Stuart News* who devoted an entire column to our book – or, rather, impressions of our book gleaned from the defensive rantings of local officials. His main beef with our "trashing" of Port St. Lucie was that the city has no beaches and, should therefore not have been mentioned in our book. He added, "If they don't like the St. Lucie County beaches, it is just because they are too young [Hah! We wish!] and never knew the real Florida."

Sorry to burst Crankshaw's bubble, but we have been passing through the area almost yearly since the early 1960s and have often stayed on Hutchinson Island over the years. We're guessing he never even thumbed through our book. If he had, it would have registered that we say many positive things about the beaches of St. Lucie County.

We stand by everything we've previously written and suggest the leaders of St. Lucie County start paying heed to their own citizens, who have registered disparaging comments of their own about the county's unchecked growth. This was written by a lifelong native in response to the trashing of our book by local politicians:

"I grew up here. I went to high school and college here, and I wonder where [these] City Council members live? Are they blind? Do they not see all this destruction of property? The traffic is horrible. For them to say [*Florida Beaches*] is a fairy tale or misinformation – they're completely wrong. And when the authors of the book said 90 percent of the population of Port St. Lucie does not want to see all these strip malls, they're correct. No one does. Everywhere you turn, there's a new Publix, there's a new Lowe's. There's no more land left. There's nothing. I think it's deplorable, and they need to wake up and see what Port St. Lucie is really like. It's not a beautiful city and it really does not have all that much to offer."

5483.) In short, FPL has set the right example for the ecotourism market that Hutchinson Island—if not the development-hungry St. Lucie County as a whole—badly wishes to cultivate. Lot by lot, acre by acre, the remaining unprotected areas of Hutchinson Island are going to the dogs of development even as we speak. But at least this five-mile stretch at mid-island remains in its pristine state—albeit with the concrete towers of a nuclear plant doing the babysitting.

For more information, contact the St. Lucie County Tourist Development Council, 2300 Virginia Avenue, Fort Pierce, FL 34982, 772/462-1535 or 800/344-8443, www.visit-stluciefla.com.

BEACHES

By our painstaking count, you'll find 28 developed beach parks or public beach accesses with parking on Hutchinson Island: 15 in Fort Pierce and the rest of St. Lucie County, and 13 in Jensen Beach and the rest of Martin County. The island is divided between those two counties, with the lion's share going to St. Lucie. The maddening exception to the new low-impact, ecotourist spirit of Hutchinson Island is an unbroken line, four miles in length, of high-rise condominiums along the beach. This onslaught falls on the St. Lucie side of the county line, which is unsurprising giving this county's priorities of growth and development before all else.

Still, Hutchinson Island has some of the most secluded beaches in central Florida, comparing favorably with Canaveral National Seashore and north Indian River County. The only sour note is the devastation wrought by hurricanes in 2004. Saltwater intrusion from flooding has killed off a lot of the maritime forest, which was either blown over or left standing, dead and denuded of vegetation. Moreover, the eroded shoreline has moved closer to the edge of the dead forest. These things happen and nature is quick to regenerate, but any recovery will be inevitably slowed by the fact that longshore transport of sand has been cut off by the Fort Pierce jetties. Thus, the only way to hasten the recovery process will be to renourish the beaches (which is not a natural process and typically meets with limited success). We therefore wonder if these beaches will ever look the same.

Still, like sea turtles on their annual crawl ashore, we like wandering the beaches of Hutchinson Island at an unhurried pace. We recommend you do so as well. Here is what you will find, moving south from Fort Pierce:

- **Green Turtle Beach/John Brooks Park:** This side-by-side beach park duo sits just beyond the Fort Pierce city limits. There are no facilities and limited parking. What they do have is a beach—a remarkable 8,600 feet of it, in fact, which translates to 1.6 miles of undeveloped shoreline.

- **Frederick Douglass Memorial Beach:** This St. Lucie County park is a fitting monument to a man who escaped slavery and then became one of its most articulate detractors as an orator, journalist, and author. The 1,000-foot beach named for him is suitably grand, claiming the best seashell beds in the area and unblemished

natural panoramic vistas. The park is also clean and well tended, with covered picnic areas and volleyball courts. Three Sundays a month, horseback riding is allowed. An old dune-buggy trail, now off-limits to motorized vehicles, can be used by hikers and horseback riders.

- **Middle Cove Beach Access:** This county park is located 1.5 miles south of Frederick Douglass Memorial Beach. From a small paved lot, a dirt path leads to the beach. It is a short, pleasant stroll through a cover of tall grass and scrub pine. The seclusion found here is rejuvenating and the beach consists of gently tapered brownish-tan sand with driftwood lying about. The only drawback—besides the obvious devastation of 2004—is that there are no facilities or lifeguards. But that is a hidden blessing, as it renders this spot all the more enticing for those who want to feel like castaways on a fantasy Gilligan's Island.

- **Blind Creek Beach:** Two miles south of Middle Cove, Blind Creek offers access to more of the same grand strand. A rutted road leads to a small parking lot and a short hop onto to a secluded beach. Again, there are no facilities or lifeguards—and therefore few people. The acquisition of a parcel by the county has extended the length of Blind Creek Beach to 835 feet.

- **Turtle Beach Nature Trail:** This half-mile stroll through unusually thick coastal habitat falls on the property of the Florida Power & Light's nuclear facility and is marked by a sign on A1A.

- **Walton Rocks Beach:** Located a half-mile south of the FPL nuclear plant—and managed cooperatively by the county and the utility—Walton Rocks is reached via a dirt road that leads a quarter mile to a dirt parking lot. You can settle here or keep driving further to a second lot. Both have similar facilities (restrooms, showers, picnic tables), and from each you walk through a break in the dunes—which used to be covered with sea oats and scrub pine and now stand exposed to wind and waves—to find the same beach profile as lies north of here. Living up to its name, Walton does have some rocks (known as "wormrock") in the water, which makes the ocean vista more beautiful and evocative. Despite the hazards, Walton Rocks is popular with surfers. According to some regulars we spoke with, there are five bands of wormrock, each separated by about 15 feet of sand. At high tide, the water is plenty safe for their purposes, they assured us. Running for 0.6 mile, Walton Rocks is the second-longest public beach in the county.

- **Herman's Bay and Normandy Beach Accesses:** At both of these St. Lucie County sites you'll find free parking in a dirt lot and a smallish beach (100 feet) covered with seaweed and driftwood. Both are used mainly by surfers. With all the available choices on Hutchinson Island, these spots don't rank at the top of our list because of their proximity to condos with self-important names like the Admiral and Atlantis. On the inlet side of A1A, a community of mobile homes, squat houses, and boat docks occupies Nettles Island, which was created from landfill.

- **Dollman Park:** This park has a sizable beach (1,850 feet), plus lifeguards, restrooms, and showers. Moreover, it is slated to grow both in terms of acreage and facilities, so keep this one in mind if you're down this way.

- **Waveland Beach:** This municipal park is located a mile north of the Jensen Beach Causeway (S.R. 732). Hemmed in by condos, this 320-foot beach tends to draw elderly condo dwellers and their visiting relations. Surfers flock here, too, though they're required to surf outside the lifeguarded area.

Incidentally, the county has prevailed over condo owners down in south St. Lucie County, providing a public easement onto the beach at the Islands II condominium. Located between Dollman and Waveland beaches, it exists mainly for the benefit of people who live across the road and need a legal access to get onto the beach. Putting this public easement in

place required knocking down a wall. We'll be the first to champion any effort to let the walls fall in the name of public beach access.

25 GREEN TURTLE BEACH/ JOHN BROOKS PARK

Location: just south of the Fort Pierce city limits along A1A on Hutchinson Island
Parking/Fees: free parking lot
Hours: sunrise–sunset
Facilities: none
Contact: St. Lucie County Recreation Office, 772/462-1521

26 FREDERICK DOUGLASS MEMORIAL BEACH

Location: four miles south of Fort Pierce Inlet, on A1A
Parking/Fees: free parking lot
Hours: sunrise–sunset
Facilities: lifeguards (seasonal), restrooms, picnic tables, and showers
Contact: St. Lucie County Recreation Office, 772/462-1521

27 MIDDLE COVE BEACH ACCESS

Location: five miles south of Fort Pierce Inlet, on A1A
Parking/Fees: free parking lot
Hours: sunrise–sunset
Facilities: none
Contact: St. Lucie County Recreation Office, 772/462-1521

28 BLIND CREEK BEACH

Location: eight miles south of Fort Pierce Inlet, on A1A
Parking/Fees: free parking lot

Hours: sunrise-sunset
Facilities: none
Contact: St. Lucie County Recreation Office, 772/462-1521

29 TURTLE BEACH NATURE TRAIL

Location: on property belonging to Florida Power & Light's St. Lucie Nuclear Power Plant, along A1A on Hutchinson Island
Parking/Fees: free parking lot
Hours: sunrise-sunset
Facilities: none
Contact: Florida Power & Light's Environmental Information Line, 800/552-8440

30 WALTON ROCKS BEACH

Location: south of St. Lucie Nuclear Power Plant along A1A on Hutchinson Island
Parking/Fees: free parking lot
Hours: sunrise-sunset
Facilities: restrooms, picnic tables, and showers
Contact: St. Lucie County Recreation Office, 772/462-1521

31 HERMAN'S BAY ACCESS

Location: 10 miles south of Fort Pierce Inlet, along A1A on Hutchinson Island
Parking/Fees: free parking lot
Hours: sunrise-sunset
Facilities: picnic tables
Contact: St. Lucie County Recreation Office, 772/462-1521

32 NORMANDY BEACH ACCESS

Location: 11 miles south of Fort Pierce Inlet, along A1A on Hutchinson Island
Parking/Fees: free parking lot
Hours: sunrise-sunset
Facilities: none
Contact: St. Lucie County Recreation Office, 772/462-1521

33 DOLLMAN PARK

Location: two miles north of the Jensen Beach Causeway, along A1A on Hutchinson Island
Parking/Fees: free parking lot
Hours: sunrise-sunset
Facilities: lifeguards, restrooms, and showers
Contact: St. Lucie County Recreation Office, 772/462-1521

34 WAVELAND BEACH

Location: one mile north of the Martin County line along A1A on Hutchinson Island
Parking/Fees: free parking lot
Hours: sunrise-sunset
Facilities: lifeguards, restrooms, picnic tables, and showers
Contact: St. Lucie County Recreation Office, 772/462-1521

Jensen Beach

The name "Jensen Beach" is somewhat misleading, as most of this community (pop. 15,000) sits not on the beach but on the mainland. The appeal of Jensen Beach is easy to understand, especially if you've driven south on U.S. 1 through St. Lucie County and are in desperate need of civilized relief from that asphalt morass. The bulk of Jensen Beach lies between U.S. 1 and the Indian River, west of Hutchinson Island in a unique landscape that rises to a whopping 85 feet above sea level—the highest point of land on Florida's East Coast. The large historic district—one of Martin County's earliest settlements—is now the centerpiece of a riverfront area called Old Jensen Village. It's a pedestrian-friendly and antiquarian shopping district not unlike Fernandina Beach's refurbished Victorian downtown.

Jensen Beach's initial wealth was made almost entirely from pineapples, which thrived on surrounding Indian River plantations, and from Henry Flagler's railroad, which arrived in 1894 to ship those pineapples to the rest of the world. For the next decade, one million boxes of the prized fruit rolled out of Jensen each July. But a nematode infestation and increased freight fees brought trade to a halt, giving way to a more modest fishing industry.

Hutchinson Island, due east via the Jensen Beach Causeway (S.R. 732), was seemingly an afterthought in the old days—a good place to raise fruit and graze livestock, but too prone to hurricanes to be more than that. The first bridge, a mile-long wooden span, wasn't built until 1925. Thankfully, a stampede didn't follow. The portion of Jensen Beach located on the barrier island is one of the most pleasantly understated beachfronts on Florida's East Coast.

For more information, contact the Jensen Beach Chamber of Commerce, 1910 Northeast Jensen Beach Boulevard, Jensen Beach, FL 34957, 772/334-3444, www.jensenchamber.com.

BEACHES

Martin County could well serve as a case study on how to preserve beaches and make them accessible to the public—which is why it's such a shame they took a huge hit in 2004. The Stuart/Jensen Beach area was ground zero for Hurricanes Frances and Jeanne, and they cut a wide swath of damage here and inland. Yet the damage is more evident inland, because it occurred to prop-

erty. Here and in St. Lucie County, you'll see vacated residences, abandoned stores, signs blown out or lying on the ground, and plywood and roofing tarps still shielding damaged properties from the elements. It's like time stopped in September 2004 in the more vulnerable and affected parts of these counties. Yet the beaches, while precipitously narrowed in places, are still here as nature crawls back at its own unhurried pace.

The Martin County coast is largely nature in the raw. Starting up at the north end of the county you'll encounter **Glasscock Beach,** a two-part beach access that lies between the county line and Jensen Beach Causeway. The northernmost area is little more than a parking lot and dune walkovers leading out to a beautiful strip of beach wedged between residential developments. The second Glasscock exit, which lies a few hundred yards south, is larger and more accommodating. It has a paved lot, four dune crossovers, and outdoor showers and restrooms. You could almost convince yourself you're on a wilderness beach.

Jensen Beach received a massive $11 million beach renourishment in 1996, leading to a dramatic transformation of the 4.5-mile beachfront from just north of Jensen Beach Causeway down to the southern tip of Hutchinson Island. Just as dramatic, but for opposite reasons, was the damage that Hurricanes Jeanne and Frances wrought upon these beaches in 2004. This terrible twosome made landfall right here in north Martin County. Maybe those early settlers who avoided building out on Hutchinson Island because of hurricanes and shifting sands had the right idea after all.

Sea Turtle Beach and Jensen Beach were conjoined to form a sizable beach park with the name **Jensen Beach/Sea Turtle Beach.** Located 300 yards north of the Holiday Inn (set to reopen in 2006 after hurricane damage necessitated its reconstruction), it is almost one-third mile long. Parking is plentiful and free, and amenities include concessions, boardwalk, volleyball courts, and lifeguards. The beach is 1,500 feet long but lost a lot of width

THE TREASURE COAST

due to hurricane-caused erosion. (Expect another pricey renourishment, if the feds can cough up the money.) Watch out for wormrock formations in the water. Surfing is allowed at the north end of the beach. Leashed dogs are allowed on Jensen Beach and indeed at every beach in the county.

Bob Graham Beach is located a mile south of Jensen Beach/Sea Turtle Beach. It is named for a former Florida governor, U.S. Senator, and (briefly) presidential candidate who was enlightened on environmental matters. Bob Graham Beach is nearly 2,000 feet long, and the beach profile is similar to Sea Turtle's (i.e., renourished by man, then depleted by nature). There are 35 free parking spaces in a dirt lot but no facilities or lifeguards. This is Martin County *au naturel*, which is just fine by us. Just down from that is **Beachwalk/Pasley Park,** a relatively new arrival (1999) that is similarly unadorned (dirt lot, no facilities) but functional. In the works is a half-mile trail to link Bob Graham Park with Beachwalk/Pasley Park.

The next two access points, **Bryn Mawr Beach Access** and **Alex's Beach,** lie in close proximity on A1A about a mile south of town. Another closely conjoined pair, **Stokes Beach** and **Virginia Forest Access,** are a half-mile farther south. Finally, there's **Tiger Shores Access,** located in the 1900 block of A1A, another half-mile or so down the highway. They are all virtual carbon copies of one another. Each has limited free parking in a dirt lot, with no facilities or lifeguards and about 100 feet of beach. All of the beaches, from Bob Graham to Tiger Shores, are delightfully secluded and known for excellent surfing and surfcasting. Among all of them, only Sea Turtle is wheelchair-accessible.

35 GLASSCOCK BEACH

Location: County Line Road and A1A, just north of the Jensen Beach Causeway

Parking/Fees: free parking lot
Hours: sunrise–sunset
Facilities: restrooms and showers (south area)
Contact: Martin County Parks Department, 772/221-1418

36 JENSEN BEACH/SEA TURTLE BEACH

Location: A1A just north of Jensen Beach Causeway (S.R. 732) in Jensen Beach
Parking/Fees: free parking lots
Hours: sunrise–sunset
Facilities: concessions, lifeguards, picnic tables, restrooms, and showers
Contact: Martin County Parks Department, 772/221-1418

37 BOB GRAHAM BEACH

Location: on A1A, 0.7 miles south of Jensen Beach
Parking/Fees: free parking lot
Hours: sunrise–sunset
Facilities: none
Contact: Martin County Parks Department, 772/221-1418

38 BEACHWALK/ PASLEY PARK

Location: on A1A, one mile south of Jensen Beach
Parking/Fees: free parking lot
Hours: sunrise–sunset
Facilities: none
Contact: Martin County Parks Department, 772/221-1418

39 BRYN MAWR BEACH ACCESS AND ALEX'S BEACH

Location: 1.5 miles south of Jensen Beach on A1A
Parking/Fees: free parking lots
Hours: sunrise-sunset
Facilities: none
Contact: Martin County Parks Department, 772/221-1418

40 STOKES BEACH AND VIRGINIA FOREST ACCESS

Location: 1.75 miles south of Jensen Beach on A1A
Parking/Fees: free parking lots
Hours: sunrise-sunset
Facilities: none
Contact: Martin County Parks Department, 772/221-1418

41 TIGER SHORES ACCESS

Location: two miles south of Jensen Beach on A1A
Parking/Fees: free parking lot
Hours: sunrise-sunset
Facilities: none
Contact: Martin County Parks Department, 772/221-1418

RECREATION AND ATTRACTIONS
- **Bike/Skate Rentals:** The Bike Shop, 403 SE Monterey Road, Stuart, 772/283-6186
- **Dive Shop:** Stuart Dive Center, 733 North Federal Highway (U.S. 1), Stuart, 772/692-1828
- **Ecotourism:** Jonathan Dickinson State Park, 16450 Southeast Federal Highway,

Hobe Sound, 772/546-2771 (park office) and 772/746-1466 (boat tours and rentals)
- **Fishing Charters:** Hunter Sportfishing Charters, 4897 SE Capstan Avenue, Stuart, 772/223-0073
- **Marina:** Hutchinson Island Marriot Beach Resort & Marina, 555 NE Ocean Boulevard, Stuart, 772/225-3700
- **Rainy-Day Attraction:** Florida Oceanographic Society, Coastal Science Center, 890 NE Ocean Boulevard, Stuart, 772/225-0505
- **Shopping/Browsing:** Old Jensen Beach Village, Jensen Beach Boulevard, two blocks west of the Indian River
- **Surf Shop:** Sunrise Surf Shop, 11013 South Ocean Drive (A1A), Jensen Beach, 772/229-1722
- **Vacation Rentals:** Resort Vacations/Prudential Florida WCI Realty, 2363 SE Ocean Boulevard, Suite 200, Stuart, 772/283-7706

ACCOMMODATIONS
Holiday Inn Oceanside (3793 Northeast Ocean Boulevard, 772/225-3000, $$) completed a $5 million renovation in January 2001, only to be nearly destroyed in 2004 when Hurricanes Frances and Jeanne made landfall here. We've stayed here several times, and it was eerie to peer through the windows of its brick skeleton and see clear out the other side. The hotel is being rebuilt but still hadn't reopened as we went to press.

Somewhere off the asphalt nightmare of U.S. 1 in St. Lucie County is the European-style vacation oasis **Club Med Sandpiper** (4500 S.E. Pine Valley, 772/398-510, $$$$). It is one of only two Club Med resorts in the United States (the other is in Crested Butte, Colorado) and the only one in Florida. The 400-acre resort is located in Port St. Lucie. No, it's not on the beach, but the resort runs shuttles to Hutchinson Island for its guests. At Club Med, you play hard—everything from golf and waterskiing to rollerblading and trampoline-jumping—and eat well. The resort's Spanish villas are appealing places to hang out at end of the day, after chasing balls and gorging at the buffet spreads. But it's pricey. The all-inclusive cost of a mid-autumn week at Club Med Sandpiper for a family of three: $2,811.

The most unique place on the island used to be the Hutchinson Inn, a B&B-style beach motel that made a stylish stand in a land of ever-more condos. However, the inn was destroyed by the 2004 hurricanes and the owners chose not to rebuild. It has since been demolished.

COASTAL CUISINE

A number of fine restaurants and friendly pubs can be found in downtown Jensen Beach, both in the old village and along the riverfront. The best seafood restaurant in town—rivaling the best on the entire Treasure Coast—is the **New England Fish Market & Restaurant** (1419 NE Jensen Beach Boulevard, 772/334-7328, $$$). Like the name suggests, the theme is New England seafood, and lobsters and mussels are flown down from the north. On Monday and Tuesday, you can order a "Bug in a Box"—a one-pound Maine lobster dinner for eat-in or takeout for $17.95. Garlic mussels are one of their appetizer specialties. You don't often find good mussels (or mussel preparations) in Florida, but this is an exception.

Beyond the Yankee orientation, the restaurant serves plenty of Florida seafood as well. Fish are prepared half a dozen different ways—grilled, blackened, fried, crunchy-fried, sauteed, and Jamaican jerk. The house specialty cioppino (rarely seen in Florida) is a seafood stew served over linguine that can easily serve two—and you still might take some of it home. You can make a very satisfying meal here just from appetizers. Their smoked fish dip is a winner, and we'd drive 100 miles (as some people do, we're told) for New England Fish Market's Buffalo grouper cheeks. What are grouper cheeks, you ask? Literally the meat from the cheek of a grouper. They are

tasty little medallions. Order the spicy Buffalo sauce on the side and dip 'em. Betcha can't eat just one.

It's a long way from Maine to the Caribbean, but you can make the trip (at least in a culinary sense) in a matter of minutes in Jensen Beach. **Conchy Joe's** (3945 Northeast Indian River Drive, 772/334-1130, $$) serves native Florida and Bahamian preparations in a West Indian setting. Conch is served every way it can be cooked, and other house specialties include soft-shell crabs and grouper marsala. Reggae and calypso bands entertain late into the evening. It also offers a glorious view of the Indian River.

NIGHTLIFE

If the luck of the draw brings you to Jensen Beach on a Thursday, you can partake of "Jammin' Jensen." This weekly affair starts at 5:30 P.M. in Old Jensen Village, the restored area two blocks west of the Indian River. Most of the bars offer live music and drink specials, while the restaurants cut deals on food and the shops remain open. Barring that, you can always quaff a brew at the **Jensen Beach Ale House** (3611 NW Federal Highway, 772/692-3611).

Stuart

This unprepossessing and nicely restored town is located inland of Hutchinson Island, for the most part, though a bit of it spills onto the island's southern tip. Serving as the county seat, Stuart (pop. 15,750) has a legacy of enlightenment and individuality. One of the stops along Henry Flagler's East Coast Railway, it was originally called Potsdam but renamed itself after Homer T. Stuart, a prominent resident.

In 1925, the town seceded from Palm Beach County in a dispute over taxes, leading to the creation of lovely and still relatively pristine Martin County. Stuart makes an appealing southern point of entry onto Hutchinson Island. You should stop to admire Riverwalk, a park along the St. Lucie River at its inland center. It's a pleasant place for a stroll before heading over the A1A bridge to the island.

Further proof of Stuart's good sense was evident in the community's response to a proposed development called SeaWind. This environmentally disruptive leviathan would have built 7,000 houses near Stuart but met with immediate and forceful public wrath. Here's excerpt from a concerned local citizen's letter to the editor: "There is no justification to dig up, sanitize, and pave over yet another bit of Florida in order to attract thousands of new residents and thus permanently alter the character of Stuart and Martin County. The SeaWind project is monstrous, both literally and figuratively. Not all change is progress."

Already, we count 56 golf courses along the Treasure Coast (including 21 in Martin County). An astute columnist for the *Stuart News* took the words right out of our mouth: "Golf courses ought to be banned as enemies of our environment. To make a golf course you must cut down a lot of trees, reshape the terrain, alter natural drainage, and run off a lot of wildlife. To keep your course from looking bad you have to pump in millions of gallons of water—an increasingly valuable commodity in Florida—and pour on tons of pesticides and fertilizers. Also, golf courses are restricted to the use of golfers. You can't just stroll happily about on them. Even golfers don't stroll along them." How true.

Stuart's toehold on Hutchinson Island is

HURRICANE FRANCES

Hurricane Frances triggered the largest evacuation in state history. In a particularly bad case of timing, both for residents and visitors, it hit over Labor Day weekend of 2004. Two days before making landfall, 2.5 million residents of Florida's East Coast – from Florida City to Flagler Beach – were ordered to evacuate, causing an 80 mile traffic jam through Orlando. After battering the Bahamas, the eye of the huge, slow-moving storm wobbled ashore in Florida near Stuart (on Hutchinson Island) as a strong Category 2 hurricane with 105 mph winds. It hit during the night, at 1 A.M. on Sunday, September 5.

The storm system was so large that tropical-force winds were measured simultaneously in Miami and Orlando. It inched across the state at a snail's pace, exacerbating wind and flood damage. It took two days to cross Florida. This massive hurricane – as large as the state of Texas – caused power outages to three million residents. It dumped more than 12 inches of rain on Palm Beach County, where 90 percent of homes lost power. Outages were so massive that nearly half a million customers would still be in the dark a week later, their discomfort exacerbated by heat and humidity. Schools remained closed, gas couldn't be pumped (no electricity!), and the water was unfit to drink.

Hurricane Frances caused 23 deaths and $8 billion worth of damage in Florida. The storm punished both the east and west coast of Florida, causing record storm stages in the Tampa area. Frances even made a second landfall (as a tropical storm) on the Panhandle. On the East Coast, Frances caused major beach and dune erosion throughout Indian River, St. Lucie, and Martin Counties in an area roughly from Sebastian Inlet down to St. Lucie Inlet. Homes, hotels, and even condos were destroyed, as the beach retreated 30 feet along many stretches and as much as 50-75 feet in some places.

As the state struggled to rebound from the one-two punch of Hurricanes Charley and Frances, Hurricane Ivan began bearing down on the Florida Panhandle. And Ivan was followed all too quickly by Hurricane Jeanne, which made landfall at the same place as Frances – an unprecedented occurrence in a single hurricane season.

home to a stretch of unblemished oceanfront, plus a museum and science center within sight of the waves. Built in 1875, **Gilbert's Bar House of Refuge Museum** (301 Southeast MacArthur Boulevard, 772/225-1875) is the oldest standing structure in the county. The "bar" is shorthand for the sandbar upon which it sits, the result of thousands of years of sedimentary outwash from the St. Lucie River. The House of Refuge was once a recuperative refuge for shipwrecked sailor and then a museum of marine artifacts and life-saving equipment, with an impressive seaquarium housed on the lower level. It owns the distinction, too, of being the only house of refuge still standing in America. Unfortunately, it was barely standing after the double trouble wrought by Hurricanes Frances and Jeanne. After undergoing extensive repairs, the House of Refuge reopened in the summer of 2006.

Equally interesting is the **Elliott Museum** (825 Northeast Ocean Boulevard, 772/225-1961), a hot-pink adobe-style mansion that houses quirky artifacts of Americana and invention history dating back to 1750. Its former owner, Sterling Elliott, was inventor of the stamp machine, a knot-tying device, and a four-wheeled bicycle. The last of these presaged the Stanley Steamer, a prototype for the gas-powered motorcar. (Admission is $6 for adults and $2 for kids.)

The Florida Oceanographic Society opened its **Coastal Science Center** (890 Northeast Ocean Boulevard, 772/225-0505) along the inlet side of Hutchinson Island. Though primarily a research center with a library and administrative offices, the 40-acre complex is also home to a visitors center with reef exhibits, touch tanks, and interactive computers. Nature trails along the Indian River offer abundant peace, quiet, and photo ops. It closed for renovations but reopened in early November 2005.

For more information, contact the Stuart/Martin County Chamber of Commerce, 1650 South Kanner Highway, Stuart, FL 34994, 772/287-1088, www.goodnature.org.

BEACHES

Next door to the Elliott Museum, and sharing the same entrance road, is **Stuart Beach.** Like all Martin County beach accesses, Stuart Beach is clearly designated by a pale blue wooden sign with a wave logo. The park makes the most of its location. There's ample free parking (260 spaces), restrooms, showers, a full-service food concession (Moondoggies), nicely landscaped grounds, basketball and volleyball courts, a 250-foot boardwalk, and two lifeguard stands. Because of this bounty, Stuart Beach is popular with everyone from baby-toting parents to surfboard-toting babes. There is, in fact, a minor surfer cult based in the Stuart area.

Backed by a healthy dune structure held in place by sea grape, palms, and railroad vine, the 1,200-foot stretch of sand at Stuart Beach is shelly and gray (telltale signs of beach renourishment), sloping steeply toward the water. Because of partially submerged wormrock in the nearshore waters, lifeguards are ever vigilant here. The beach itself has lost a great deal of width since the last time we visited; at high tide the water comes all the way up to the pylons of the boardwalk. The word on Stuart Beach from a surfer in the know is that it's "decent on bigger swells" but otherwise no great shakes.

Hugging the shore from this point south requires following MacArthur Boulevard, which begins at the Marriott Jensen Beach Resort. As a visual cue, it is impossible to miss. Driving down MacArthur Boulevard in 2005 put us in mind of a line from Richard Harris's epic hit "MacArthur Park": "Someone left the cake out in the rain. ... " Indeed, hurricanes rained all over MacArthur Boulevard's parade of beaches, thinning the shoreline and destroying trees and vegetation. This stretch of coast received the brunt of Hurricanes Frances and Jeanne, which made landfall within weeks of one another—an unprecedented confluence of 'canes upon a single stretch of coast in the same year.

Locals have coined unofficial names for some

HURRICANE JEANNE

The monetary damage Hurricane Jeanne did in Florida was substantial, but it pales to the loss of life in the Caribbean. On the island of Haiti, the death toll due to Jeanne ultimately reached 3,000 and another 200,000 were left homeless. That was the grisly prelude to Jeanne's assault upon Florida. The storm made landfall near Stuart (on Hutchinson Island) just before midnight on Saturday, September 25, 2004 – exactly three weeks after Hurricane Frances came ashore there. Two hurricanes hadn't made landfall in the same vicinity in a single season since 1964, when Hurricanes Cleo and Isabel hit Palm Beach County.

Battle-weary Floridians facing yet another evacuation were warned that Jeanne was, if anything, a larger, stronger and more dangerous hurricane than Frances. The state's meteorologist likened it to a "brick wall." With top sustained winds of 120 mph, Jeanne became the first Category 3 hurricane in half a century to strike the Treasure Coast. And it further damaged homes, buildings, boats, and beaches that had taken serious blows from Frances. It left 1.6 million customers without electricity. Together, Frances and Jeanne caused $14 billion in prop-erty damage in Florida, leaving St. Lucie County particularly hard-hit. The county's schools suffered $40 million in damage. The cost of repairing traffic lights alone on the Treasure Coast came to $50 million. Schools on the Treasure Coast remained closed for a week or more.

In the wake of Jeanne – the fourth major hurricane to hit Florida that year – President Bush declared 26 Florida counties to be major disaster areas. And Jeanne wasn't done with the U.S. yet. The still-potent storm system moved up the East Coast, bringing tornadoes, high winds, and torrential rains from Georgia to New Jersey. Its effects were especially pronounced in the mountains of North Carolina and in the city of Richmond, Virginia. Meanwhile, in Florida, the hurricane season many would wish to forget had broken the bank, exhausting the state's Hurricane Catastrophe Fund and straining the budgets of county governments, school districts, Florida Power & Light (which incurred $650 million in restoration charges), and the Federal Emergency Management Agency (FEMA). Little did anyone suspect that 2005 would bring more of the same. And more of the same is just what Florida did not need.

---

of the county's numbered accesses, which may confuse anyone in search of real names and designations (there aren't any). For instance, the beach that lies a half-mile south of Stuart Beach is variously known as **Fletcher Beach,** Fletcher Strip, and "The Stairs." Meanwhile, a sign out front identifies it as "Martin County Beach Access #7." By any name, it has undeniable appeal. Here, you can swim, surf, snorkel, shell, and surfcast away from the crowds up at Stuart.

Adjoining Fletcher Beach is **Santa Lucea Beach.** Martin County's newest beach—it opened in 2005—is a moody place. The narrow sand strip is dark, and the look and feel of this part of the coast downright primeval. A visit here at sundown gave us the willies. We could feel Mother Nature's power as darkness descended and the pounding surf sent geysers of water exploding through blowholes.

The next beach access, another half-mile south, shares the entrance road for Gilbert's Bar Museum and House of Refuge. Dubbed **House of Refuge Beach,** this 2,100-foot strand is wild to behold and lovely to ponder, with sculptural orange outcrops jutting from the roiling waters and tidepools. However, the setting is not nearly as inviting as Stuart Beach and the beach has eroded to nothing. In fact, on our most recent visit, the waves were crashing so hard that we could feel the ground shake under our feet from the parking area.

The next beach is variously referred to as **Chastain Access,** Sailfish Point, or Martin County Beach Access #8, but those in the know call it "The Rocks." (not to be confused with Blowing Rocks Preserve, to the south). Chastain is located a few hundred yards south of House of Refuge. It offers the familiar roll call of Martin County beach amenities: a small parking lot, restrooms, showers, and dune walkover onto a beach with a nearshore reef. Walking from the jam-packed lot and over the dunes, we had to do a double take. The sight of 21 surfers lined up in the water on a rainy Wednesday in the off-season was a sight we were more accustomed to seeing in Southern California.

Chastain would have to be considered southern Florida's Steamer Lane, where the waves break directly onto rocks and surfers take death-defying rides. This swell-fed break, we later learned, is "for pros only," and one is forewarned to "watch out for the men in the brown suits" (i.e., sharks). The rocks are actually a sharp, jagged reef formation that runs right up to the shoreline and, at low tide, is only inches below the water surface. Suffice it to say that it's fun to watch these bold souls do their thing, but nothing could entice us onto boards in that water.

The complete opposite of "The Rocks" is the reef-protected haven known as **Bathtub Reef Beach Park,** less than a mile south, at the southern tip of Hutchinson Island. This gorgeous 1,000-foot-long beach sits behind an offshore coral reef created by honeycomb worms. Most reefs are made from coral polyps, but this one is built by small marine worms. The reef covers 85 underwater acres and runs for 1.4 miles. In the area between sand and reef—the stunning blue and green "bathtub"—snorkeling is excellent and the water is as safe as mother's milk for wading tots. Owing to this fact and the park's facilities—restrooms, showers, boardwalk, observation area, informative displays, two lifeguard towers, and 200 free parking spaces—Bathtub Reef is extremely popular with families.

Fishing is popular at St. Lucie Inlet, where the Indian River meets the Atlantic Ocean. The best local purveyor of snorkeling and diving equipment, with two locations, is **Dixie Divers** (10795 South Federal Highway, 772/283-5588; 6083 SE Federal Highway, 772/286-0078). If the Indian River looks like a tempting place to paddle, it most certainly is. **Tropical Visions** in downtown Stuart (600 West 1st Street, 772/223-2097) rents kayaks and conducts pontoon-boat tours of this vast watershed.

42 STUART BEACH

Location: MacArthur Boulevard at A1A in Stuart
Parking/Fees: free parking lots
Hours: sunrise-sunset
Facilities: concessions, lifeguards, restrooms, picnic tables, showers, and a visitors center (Elliott Museum)
Contact: Martin County Parks Department, 772/221-1418

43 FLETCHER BEACH

Location: approximately one-half mile south of Stuart Beach on A1A
Parking/Fees: free parking lot
Hours: sunrise-sunset
Facilities: none
Contact: Martin County Parks Department, 772/221-1418

44 SANTA LUCEA BEACH

Location: approximately three-quarters of a mile south of Stuart Beach on A1A
Parking/Fees: free parking lot
Hours: sunrise-sunset
Facilities: showers
Contact: Martin County Parks Department, 772/221-1418

45 HOUSE OF REFUGE BEACH

Location: one mile south of Stuart Beach on A1A
Parking/Fees: free parking lot; $4 per person to tour the Gilbert's Bar House of Refuge and Museum
Hours: sunrise-sunset
Facilities: restrooms
Contact: Martin County Parks Department, 772/221-1418

46 CHASTAIN ACCESS (A.K.A. STUART ROCKS)

Location: between House of Refuge Beach and Bathtub Reef (St. Lucie Inlet) along A1A on Hutchinson Island
Parking/Fees: free parking lot
Hours: sunrise-sunset
Facilities: restrooms and showers
Contact: Martin County Parks Department, 772/221-1418

47 BATHTUB REEF BEACH PARK

Location: south end of Hutchinson Island at the St. Lucie Inlet
Parking/Fees: free parking lot
Hours: sunrise-sunset
Facilities: lifeguards, restrooms, picnic tables, and showers
Contact: Martin County Parks Department, 772/221-1418

ACCOMMODATIONS

The most exclusive place on Hutchinson Island is the **Hutchinson Island Marriott Beach Resort & Marina** (555 Northeast Ocean Boulevard, 772/225-3700, $$$$). Formerly the Indian River Plantation Beach Resort, it is located near the foot of Stuart Causeway,

where A1A swings west onto the mainland. The Hutchinson Island Marriott is the largest single resort complex on the Treasure Coast. Spread out over 200 ocean-to-riverfront acres that contain an 18-hole golf course, an "aqua range" (drive balls into a man-made lake), 13 tennis courts, four pools, and rental bikes and boats. The main hotel is a four-story luxury lodge with 200 units, but 126 Key West–style villas are also available for rent. Room rates start at $199 and go up there.

COASTAL CUISINE

The best seafood restaurant in downtown Stuart is the **Prawnbroker** (3754 SE Ocean Boulevard, 772/288-1222, $$), a fish market by day and creative eatery at dinnertime. The menu is determined by whatever fresh catches arrive that day. **Fish Tales** (5042 SE Federal Highway, 772/288-5011, $$) also features fresh seafood and Florida produce.

Port Salerno

Low-key Port Salerno is on the mainland, but it has waterfront (not oceanfront) parks worth noting, especially for those towing a boat. The first is Sand Spit Park (a.k.a. Cove Road Park), off A1A at the end of Cove Road. It's a large park with free parking and boat launch into the Intracoastal Waterway. You can paddle a canoe or kayak (but no motorized boats) to the north end of Jupiter Island and enjoy the pristine wilderness beach at St. Lucie Inlet State Preserve (see next entry).

Two miles farther south on A1A is **Seabranch Preserve State Park** (4810 SE Cove Road, Stuart, 772/219-1880), a 919-acre sand pine scrub community—rare enough habitat to be designated "globally imperiled." (To our thinking, anything within fallout range of the Hutchinson Island Nuclear Power Plant is, by definition, imperiled.) Seabranch provides habitat for gopher tortoise, eastern indigo snake, Florida scrub jay, bobcat, and Florida sandhill crane, as well as protected plant species like the

JONATHAN DICKINSON STATE PARK

This 11,328-acre park is one of South Florida's greatest natural treasures. Located off U.S. 1 in Hobe Sound, Jonathan Dickinson State Park is an easily accessible side trip from Jupiter Island. It offers eloquent commentary on the ocean-hugging estuaries that are the lifeblood of marine communities. With four hiking trails, 600 plant and 150 bird species, and access to the Loxahatchee River – the first river in Florida to be designated a National Wild and Scenic River – Dickinson is well worth your time.

Your first stop should be the Hobe Mountain Trail, an easy trek on an incline so gradual that the three flights up the observation tower at its end provide the most strenuous exercise. This 200-foot elevation passes for a "mountain" in Florida. From atop the tower, a gaze eastward takes in the layers of land starting with the ocean, the barrier spit, the Intracoastal Waterway, and finally the sand pine scrub community – isolated pine islands within a sea of scrub. A placard reads: "This is Florida's oldest plant community and contains more rare and endangered plants and animals than any other area of the park. Originally, sand pine scrub extended to Miami, but due to development, this is the only large area of its kind left on the southeast coast of Florida."

On that sobering note, we drove three miles west to the main parking area and picked up the trailhead for the Kitching Creek Trail, which piggybacks on the Wilson Creek Trail. Together, they provide an hour-long stroll that crosses two creeks and follows the shore of the Loxahatchee. The abundant plant life runs the gamut from cactus, scrub pine, and saw palmetto to lush ferns, flowers, and stunted turkey oaks. We had personal encounters with many animals, including raccoons, woodpeckers, hawks, lizards, deer, and fish that leaped from the brackish waters of Kitching Creek. The restful overlook's quiet is broken only by the plopping of acrobatic fish.

A longer hike is the 9.3-mile route that moves across the flat green horizon to the west, crossing Old Dixie Highway and the Florida East Coast Railway and passing by Trapper Nelson's Interpretive Site. This spot, on a high bank beside the river, is a tribute to the "wild man of the Loxahatchee" who lived here for almost 40 years, establishing his own nature sanctuary and wildlife zoo.

We regretted not having time to take the narrated boat "adventure" aboard the *Loxahatchee Queen II*. The river is home to alligators, manatees, and herons, and the park contracts the waterway concession to reputable guides. Canoes can also be rented for hours of family fun. For information on boat tours and canoe rentals, call 772/746-1466.

Jonathan Dickinson State Park charges a $4 per-vehicle entrance fee. Camping costs $22 per night, and cabins rent for $85 (rustic) or $95 (deluxe) nightly. For more information, contact Jonathan Dickinson State Park, 16450 Southeast Federal Highway, Hobe Sound, FL 33455, 772/546-2771, www.floridastateparks.org.

hand fern, Curtiss' milkweed, yellow bachelor button, and golden polypody. There are eight miles of hiking trails and there's a picnic area on the Intracoastal Waterway. Stop at Seabranch for the view, a chance to glimpse a stealthy bobcat, or simply to stretch your legs in a natural setting. The preserve is open daily 8 A.M.–dusk, and there is, as yet, no entrance fee.

For more information, contact the Stuart/Martin County Chamber of Commerce, 1650 South Kanner Highway, Stuart, FL 34994, 772/287-1088, www.goodnature.org.

St. Lucie Inlet Preserve State Park

St. Lucie Inlet State Preserve is located due east of Port Salerno on the northern tip of Jupiter Island. It ranks among the most beautiful beaches you've never visited in your life. Unless you have a boat or are willing to paddle a surfboard across the Indian River, you can't get to the preserve, which is buffered from vehicular access by Hobe Sound

National Wildlife Refuge (see next write-up). If you do have a boat, canoe, or kayak, you're in luck, because there are 30 slips at the preserve's dock on the east side of the Indian River. From here, a 3,300-foot boardwalk leads across the island to the ocean. Nothing could be finer than its 2.7 miles of wide, untrammeled beach. Offshore is a reef tract, comprised of hard and soft corals, that occupies six square miles.

If you're looking for a place to launch your boat toward the preserve from the west bank of the Indian River, the state would like to oblige but its hands have been tied by petty politics. Originally, plans called for the construction of a dock in Sand Spit Park, at the end of Cove Road in Port Salerno. From here, shuttle ferries and private boats could make the crossing to St. Lucie Inlet Preserve State Park. However, nervous local property owners, fearing God knows what, nipped that in the bud. As it stands, canoes and kayaks can launch from the Sand Spit Park boat ramp, but motorized boats must launch from other points on the Intracoastal Waterway and a state-run shuttle service is out for now.

For more information, contact St. Lucie Inlet Preserve State Park, 4810 SE Cove Road, Hobe Sound, FL 33455, 772/219-1880, www.floridastateparks.org.

BEACHES

48 ST. LUCIE INLET PRESERVE STATE PARK

Location: On St. Lucie Inlet, at the northern tip of Jupiter Island. The preserve is accessible only by boat.

Parking/Fees: $2 per boat and $1 per canoe berthing fee

Hours: 8 A.M.–sunset

Facilities: restrooms and picnic tables

Contact: St. Lucie Inlet Preserve State Park, 772/219-1880

Hobe Sound National Wildlife Refuge

Hobe Sound National Wildlife Refuge encompasses 735 acres on Jupiter Island and 232 acres on the mainland in southern Martin County. It was created from private land donated to the Nature Conservancy, which then turned it over to the U.S. Fish and Wildlife Service. These precious acres represent one of the Treasure Coast's most priceless and dwindling treasures: acreage protected from development, including some of the last remaining sand pine-scrub-oak habitat left in Florida. Sea turtles come ashore along its 3.5-mile beach in heavy numbers from May to August in their ritual nesting activities. Human visitors enjoy the refuge as well, parking in the lot at its southern boundary and walking out to and along the beach to enjoy such low-impact activities as swimming, surfing, surfcasting, sunbathing, and shell collecting.

Not much else is allowed on the refuge. Camping and picnicking are not permitted; bikes, ATVs, and mopeds are prohibited; and no roads or hiking trails penetrate its interior. If you're game for a lengthy wilderness-beach hike, a 13-mile round-trip will take you to the tip of St. Lucie Inlet State Preserve and back. "People do it every day," a refuge manager told us. The only way to get onto the refuge other than parking at the south end is by boating to Peck Lake Access Area, about 2.5 miles north of the refuge boundary. A 0.4-mile trail leads from the Indian River to the ocean at a point where the beach sees a whole lot less visitor use. There's an observation platform in the parking lot.

There are no facilities (other than portable restrooms) on the Jupiter Island tract. On the mainland tract, south of Bridge Road (C.R. 708) off U.S. 1, is Hobe Sound National Wildlife Refuge visitors center. The building doubles as headquarters for the Hobe Sound Nature Center, run by an environmental education group that leads turtle walks in June and July and conducts trips to Merritt Island

and other natural sites across the state. To reserve space on a turtle walk or get more information about outings and activities, call the **Hobe Sound Nature Center** at 772/546-2067. This headquarters is close to Jonathan Dickinson State Park (see the *Jonathan Dickinson State Park* sidebar), which preserves a vast tract of the same sand pine-scrub ecosystem.

Finding the refuge's Jupiter Island unit requires foreknowledge of some intentionally misleading signs. It is easy to mistake the access road to the refuge for a private road because of signs that read "Dead End" and "Designated for Golf Carts." North Beach Road is, in fact, a public right-of-way that runs for 1.5 miles north to the refuge entrance. The gall of moneyed Floridians who would try to usurp a public road for their private use does not necessarily surprise us, but the failure of governing bodies not to make this clear to visitors is another matter. Let us offer a suggestion for a great big sign that should be posted where Bridge Road meets North Beach Road: "Welcome to Hobe National Wildlife Refuge."

For more information, contact Hobe Sound National Wildlife Refuge, 13640 Southeast Federal Highway, Hobe Sound, FL 33455, 772/546-6141, www.southeast.fws.gov/hobesound.

BEACHES

49 HOBE SOUND NATIONAL WILDLIFE REFUGE

 BEST (

Location: From Hobe Sound, take Bridge Road (C.R. 708) east until it ends at North Beach Road. Turn left and proceed 1.5 miles into the refuge parking lot.

Parking/Fees: $5 parking fee per vehicle

Hours: sunrise-sunset

Facilities: restrooms and a visitors center (at the mainland tract)

Contact: Hobe Sound National Wildlife Refuge, 772/546-6141

Hobe Sound

The gold-plated community of Hobe Sound (pop. 12,400) is first prize for those seeking to make their primary residence (or second or perhaps even third home) on the Treasure Coast. The majority of the population is on the mainland, but the most rarefied and desirable part of the community lies on Jupiter Island. It is an exclusive place to live—perhaps even more rarefied than Palm Beach.

Delicately placed like a condor's egg in a gilded nest among Edenic nature preserves, this island enclave is so exclusive it's practically undetectable. Driving through the area, you catch glimpses of its golf courses and regal logo, but the ritzy sub-developments are gated and its large estates sit at a distance from the roadway behind well-landscaped fortresses of greenery. Needless to add, excepting Hobe Sound Beach, not so much as a one-foot-wide beach-access easement can be found in Hobe Sound.

For more information, contact the Hobe Sound Chamber of Commerce, 8994 Southeast Bridge Road, Hobe Sound, FL 33455, 772/546-4724, www.hobesound.org.

BEACHES

The last gasp of beach access in Martin County can be found at the east end of Bridge Road in Hobe Sound. **Hobe Sound Beach** offers a sandy exception to the reclusive privacy of the Hobe Sound area, complete with lifeguards, picnic pavilions, and free parking. Surfing is popular at the north end of the beach. On the wall of the public restroom was this scrawled message: "Hobe Sound locals do not like Mother F***ing Snowbirds. Love, HSL." A sign of the tension between fenced-out long-timers and millionaire beach hoarders?

50 HOBE SOUND BEACH

Location: from Hobe Sound, take Bridge Road (C.R. 708) east until it ends at Jupiter Island

Parking/Fees: free parking lot
Hours: sunrise-sunset
Facilities: concession, lifeguards, restrooms, picnic tables, and showers
Contact: Martin County Parks Department, 772/221-1418

COASTAL CUISINE

A down-home respite from the country-club ways of Hobe Sound, **Harry and the Natives** (11910 U.S. 1, 772/546-3061, $) is an anomalous eatery at the intersection of Bridge Road and U.S. 1. It is rather like finding a Jimmy Buffett fan in full parrothead regalia downing margaritas at the opera house. The place is run by, and full of, characters. The menu has headings like "Daily Road Kill" and lists fictitious items (e.g., Marinated Beef Lips, fresh, frozen, or petrified for $14.25) and jokey asides ("New this year… indoor plumbing outside"). If you're on a budget, you can order "The Day Before Payday Peanut Butter & Jelly," but we'd urge you instead to ante up for a mahimahi sandwich. The Caribbean-style version is a sweet and spicy treat, but they also do it grilled or sauteed in basil butter.

Blowing Rocks Preserve

The last glimpse of Martin County as you move south down A1A is one to remember. It's the Nature Conservancy's **Blowing Rocks Preserve,** a mile-long stretch of coast whose 73 acres feature a shallow limestone reef just seaward of the sandy beach. This is part of the same lithified shelf of coquina (known as the Anastasia formation) that runs all the way from St. Augustine to Boca Raton. However, the "blowing rocks" phenomenon on display

here is fairly unique. The rocky, unyielding coquina sits right in the surf zone. When breaking waves hit eroded blowholes in the reef, geysers of saltwater spew skyward in explosive plumes, especially during unusually high tides or after a winter storm kicks up swell. On a big day, incoming waves can get blown upward of 50 feet.

People come not only to watch the spectacle but also to stroll the beach and snorkel around the reef. There are a scant 18 parking spaces at the preserve. The former "suggested donation" of $3 per adult is now an established fee here (though children 12 and under get in free). Directly across A1A from the beachside lot, on the Indian River side of the preserve, is the **Hawley Education Center,** a staffed facility with a small exhibit space, butterfly garden, and a boardwalk along the Indian River Lagoon. It is open daily 9 A.M.–5 P.M.; free tours of the preserve are given Sunday at 11 A.M.

For more information, contact Blowing Rocks Preserve, 575 South Beach Road, Hobe Sound, FL 33455, 772/744-6668, www.tncflorida.org.

BEACHES

51 BLOWING ROCKS PRESERVE

Location: 574 South Beach Road (A1A) in southern Martin County
Parking/Fees: $3 entrance fee per adult, free for children 12 and under
Hours: 9 A.M.-5 P.M.
Facilities: restrooms and a visitors center
Contact: Blowing Rocks Preserve, 772/744-6668

PALM BEACH, BOCA RATON, AND THE DIAMOND COAST

Palm Beach County is huge, occupying 2,386 square miles—roughly the size of the state of Delaware—and stretching from the Everglades to the Atlantic Ocean. Though it is Florida's most populous county, home to 1.25 million South Floridians, this area was somehow missed by early Spanish conquistadors and explorers. The entrepreneur Henry Flagler made up for the lost time in the late 19th century, when he became Florida's first big-time developer. Palm Beach became the terminus of his Florida East Coast Railway in 1893. (Eventually it would be extended to Miami and then Key West.) He settled down here, building a colossal mansion ("Whitehall") that is now a museum. Flagler set an upscale example that many have tried to follow—especially in Palm Beach proper, an enclave of walled estates and obscene wealth located on the 14-mile island of Palm Beach. The words "Palm Beach" are synonymous with the good life for those who

have made it (or inherited it) and are now working hard to spend it in a land of sun, sin, and easeful decadence.

We call Palm Beach County the Diamond Coast, because it is dripping both with real gems and bejeweled waters. The county is kissed by the Gulf Stream—the closest that this warm current swings toward land. Thanks to its moderating effect, Palm Beach County's 47 miles of beaches are comfortable all year long. There are swimming areas at all 13 of the county's beach parks, and they're lifeguarded year-round (7:30 A.M.–5:30 P.M.). Moreover, they're free of charge (except for parking fees at two of them).

The city of Palm Beach is, true to its reputation, an epicenter of snobbery. Better beaches are located in less pretentious towns like Delray Beach, Juno Beach, and Riviera Beach. Even snooty Boca Raton is far preferable, having had the uncommon foresight to purchase

© PARKE PUTERBAUGH

its oceanfront acreage in the 1970s, converting it into a string of lovely, contiguous municipal beach parks.

Those beaches, unfortunately, got hammered when Hurricane Wilma blew through in late October 2005. The hurricane caused severe beach erosion along parts of the Palm Beach coast, and beach parks reopened slowly in its wake. The county suffered massive, protracted power outages, and schools were closed for two weeks. Palm Beach County had largely been spared the wrath of the 2004 and 2005 hurricane seasons but couldn't dodge this unfortunate bullet, which set hurricane records both for barometric pressure and for the rapidity at which it strengthened.

Tequesta

As recently as 1955, the village of Tequesta was such a gnarly tangle of undeveloped subtropical vegetation that it was dismissed as being "just a jungle." Two years later, it was incorporated as a golf-course community around the Tequesta Country Club. Fifty years further on, Tequesta has a year-round population of 5,300 (which swells with second home–owning snowbirds in the winter), and it most definitely would not be mistaken for a jungle. Well-tended lawns have replaced the unruly splendor of the natural ecosystem. Still, Tequesta's appeal is understandable, as the setting—along the north bank of the Loxahatchee River at Jupiter Inlet—couldn't be nicer.

For more information, contact the Jupiter/Tequesta/Juno Beach Chamber of Commerce, 800 North U.S. 1, Jupiter, FL 33477, 561/746-1111 or 800/616-7402, www.jupiterfl.org.

BEACHES

Almost all of Tequesta lies west of the Intracoastal Waterway, but there's one small sliver on Jupiter Island that belongs to the village. This is **Coral Cove Park,** a county-owned ocean-to-waterway playground that has 1,500 feet of ocean frontage, having

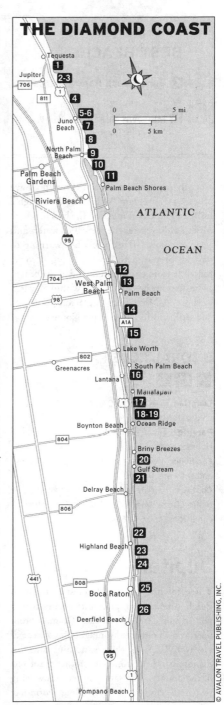

BEST BEACHES

(**Juno Beach Park:** Top 25 (page 186)

(**Midtown Beach:** Best For People-Watching (page 199)

(**Delray Beach Public Beach:** Top 25 (page 210)

recently expanded its beach through a Save Our Coasts program. Visitors walk through a lush sea grape hammock to the beach, where a lifeguard oversees the reef-filled waters and a set of colored flags offers fair warning to anyone prepared to dive in. Jagged rocks protrude from the southern end of the beach; swimmers are advised to stay within 50 yards of shore. All in all, it's as placid a setting as one will find in Palm Beach County.

1 CORAL COVE PARK

Location: 19450 S.R. 707, at A1A in Tequesta, on Jupiter Island
Parking/Fees: free parking lot
Hours: sunrise–sunset
Facilities: lifeguards, restrooms, picnic tables, and showers
Contact: Palm Beach County Parks and Recreation Department, 561/966-6631. For beach conditions, call 561/624-0065.

Jupiter

Three towns—Jupiter, Tequesta, and Juno Beach—lie in close proximity like peas in a pod in northern Palm Beach County. From the traveler's restricted vantage point of Federal Highway (U.S. 1), there is nothing much to distinguish them from one another or the rest of the county. The same clutter of low-lying strip malls clings to this main drag. Dorm-like condominiums and gated subdivisions dot the area, attesting to the fact it's one of the last coastal locales in South Florida that hasn't been completely "built out," to use developer's lingo. But it's getting there.

Jupiter (pop. 48,000) is at the heart of a watery paradise that includes the Intracoastal Waterway, the Atlantic Ocean, Jupiter Inlet, and the Loxahatchee River. There are more than 100 miles of various kinds of shoreline in the Jupiter area, making it a haven for boaters. On the north side of the Jupiter Inlet is Jupiter Beach Colony; on the south, Jupiter Beach Park, a large county-run facility. Standing sentry over it all is the fire-engine red **Jupiter Inlet Lighthouse** (805 North U.S. 1, 561/747-6639). Built in 1860, it is the oldest standing structure in Palm Beach County. A major restoration of the lighthouse was done in 2000. It can be climbed Saturday–Wednesday 10 A.M.–3:15 P.M. for $5 (which seems a bit steep for a mere 105 steps). A small museum and gift shop are on the grounds.

How did Jupiter get its name? The local Indians called themselves the Jobe, so Spanish settlers named the river after them. English settlers in the mid-18th century misheard *Jobe* River as *Jove* River. Jove, also known as Jupiter, was the Roman god of thunder and watcher of the skies. With a Jovian stroke, Jupiter stuck to the inlet and the settlement at its mouth. With another mythological thunderbolt, Jupiter has positioned itself to grow by another 50 percent with the construction of a massive development called Abacoa. This planned community has baseball at its core—specifically, a spring-training facility for major-league teams. In 1998, its first year of operation, both the Montreal Expos and the St. Louis Cardinals trained here. After the major leaguers split for the summer, the minor-league Jupiter Hammerheads take over the stadium.

Spring training is just the tip of the sand dune. According to its 20-year plan, Abacoa will cover 2,055 acres. There will be 6,000 homes, a satellite campus (the honors college of Florida Atlantic University), 400 acres of shops and offices, three public schools, and an 18-hole golf course. We'd typically decry such an undertaking, except for one extenuating factor: Abacoa is the brainchild of Andres Duany and Elizabeth Plater-Zyberk, the dynamic duo who designed Seaside on the Florida Panhandle (see *Seaside* in the *Seaside and the Stylish Communities of South Walton County* chapter). Like Seaside, Abacoa follows the blueprint for the "New Urbanism," which seeks to re-establish the sense of community that's absent in so much of America. We only hope that the results at Abacoa are compatible with higher social and environmental goals.

Incidentally, we'll never forget the time we found ourselves in Jupiter late one year. While the rest of the country had plunged into an early-December deep freeze, the midday mercury in Jupiter hit a near-perfect 78 degrees. It sure didn't seem like December (It never seems like December—or January and February, for that matter—in South Florida.) The sight of a plastic snowman on a warm, sunny day seemed particularly incongruous to us.

For more information, contact the Jupiter/Tequesta/Juno Beach Chamber of Commerce, 800 North U.S. 1, Jupiter, FL 33477, 561/746-1111 or 800/616-7402, www.jupiterfl.org.

BEACHES

Our highest commendations go to Palm Beach County for providing plentiful beach access and lovely, landscaped park environments adjoining them. Taking it from the top, **DuBois Park** is a 30-acre site along the south shore of the Jupiter Inlet. It's got a guarded beach

(a 100-foot section of its 1,200-foot ocean frontage), picnic ground, volleyball courts, great view of Jupiter Inlet Lighthouse on the opposite shore, access to a nearby fishing jetty, and **DuBois Pioneer Museum,** an 1898 pioneer home built atop an Indian shell mound. The museum can be toured Wednesday and Sunday 1 P.M.–4 P.M.; admission is $2.

DuBois Park shares space on this elongated barrier spit with **Jupiter Beach Park,** whose beach has been renourished in the recent past. Long rock jetties hold open the mouth of the inlet, south of which lies a flat, desert-like beach that runs for a third of a mile. A cluster of condos adjacent to the park provides a jarring visual note. However, Jupiter Beach is a very pleasant place. Jupiter Beach Park protects a beach hammock environment between the beach and the river. The park is a major picnicking ground. People erect protective shelters over the picnic tables to for shade. This 50-acre facility has a play area, covered picnic tables, grills, showers and more. People splash in the knee-deep water of a lagoon and stroll a path that wraps around the inlet. Incidentally the beach drops off very steeply at the ocean's edge.

Cars and portable toilets line the winding road to the inlet. The park is so popular that if you don't get here early, you're simply not going to get a space. If you ever want to see why public beach access is a good thing, come to Jupiter Beach Park. People fight for parking places, and they shouldn't have to do so in order to spend a day at the beach.

One time we struck up a conversation with a knot of friendly surfers who were about to brave the choppy surf. Two of us happened to be wearing the same T-shirt, which we'd picked up at a surfing championship at Huntington Beach, California. They bade us adieu in minimalist surfer-speak—"Later on, dude," "Cool"—and we both went our separate waves. Jupiter's surfer clique is so tightly knit that they have their own website (www.jupitersurf.com), posting photos of their moves, surf conditions, and a link to the local chapter of Surfrider. We

THE BURT REYNOLDS STORY

He is one of Florida's proudest sons, a former football hero at Florida State University who went on to become a movie star, sex symbol, and celebrity. Like Anita Bryant, Burt Reynolds is indelibly associated with the state. She had her singing voice, religious convictions, homophobia, and "Florida sunshine tree." He has his acting career and trademark mustache. Mostly associated with drive-in caliber entertainment like *Smokey and the Bandit* and *Cannonball Run,* Reynolds once jested, "My movies were the kind they show in prisons and airplanes, because nobody can leave." Yet he also worked in the critically acclaimed *Deliverance* and such fun flicks as *The Longest Yard.* He was the world's top box-office star five years in a row and has appeared in 75 films. Moving to TV, he played the lead character in *Evening Shade,* a 1990s sitcom. In 2005, he returned to film with a role in Adam Sandler's remake of *The Longest Yard.*

Reynolds' roots are buried deep in the sandy soils of north Palm Beach County. His father was chief of police in Riviera Beach. Though Reynolds found fame and fortune in Hollywood, he never lost touch with his home state, buying a ranch and starting a theater in Jupiter that bore his name. In 1988, he got hitched to platinum-maned Loni Anderson at a ceremony on the ranch.

Some years back, as we passed through Burt's hometown, national headlines were trumpeting the news that the then 60-year-old actor had declared bankruptcy. Court documents revealed that he'd accumulated $12.2 million in debts while leading a lifestyle that cost him $116,000 a month. Among other things, he'd reportedly lost nearly $20 million investing in a pair of Florida-based restaurant chains. Reynolds' financial unraveling came in the wake of a nasty separation and divorce from Anderson. The sordid details of their parting were splashed all over the supermarket tabloids and even spilled into mainstream magazines. Burt and Loni both made the rounds of tabloid talk shows while watching their misfortune serve as comic fodder for late-night TV monologists.

Bankruptcy was a particularly bitter pill for the macho Reynolds to swallow. Once Hollywood's most bankable star, he'd been reduced to taking bit parts in made-for-TV and straight-to-video action-adventure flicks. Yet he bounced back like the trooper he is, earning respectable notices for his acting in *Striptease* (a 1996 farce based on a Carl Hiaasen novel) and *Boogie Nights.* Still, the financial problems persisted and

strongly support Surfrider, a surfer's advocacy group that works to monitor and preserve water quality and keep the beaches accessible to all.

Next up is **Carlin Park,** also in Jupiter. This 118-acre county park has large lots on both sides of A1A, as well as a snack bar (Lazy Loggerhead), children's play area, baseball diamond, picnic pavilions, and amphitheater. And it's all free! "Shakespeare by the Sea" was in progress and *Macbeth* the featured play during one of our visits. There's even a Sunset at Carlin concert series. Real culture at the beach—what a concept!

Particularly appealing at Carlin Park are the sheltered picnic tables that lie behind windbreaks formed by palms, pines, shrubs, and tall dune grasses. On cooler, breezier winter days, some folks sun themselves back here rather than on the windy beach. It's a very festive, family-friendly environment. You can smell the charcoal as people grill out on the hibachis. The beach has been widened, and coarse salt-and-pepper sand runs along its 0.6-mile frontage.

Rounding out Jupiter's public beach parks is **Ocean Cay Park,** a pleasant spot on the south side of town near the Juno Beach city line. This 14-acre beauty has 700 feet of life-guarded beach with all the trimmings: volin April 1998, Reynolds' Jupiter ranch was put up for sale. Lawyers for Reynolds and his creditors haggled over his worth to determine what the latter might receive as compensation.

Our curiosity piqued, we poked around to find out what kind of mark Burt Reynolds had left on the community over the years. Here's what we found:

- **Burt Reynolds and Friends Museum** – Billed as the "largest celebrity museum in Florida," this museum opened in February 2003. It replaces the Burt Reynolds Museum that had been sited on the old Burt Reynolds Ranch. Located on the ground level of a former bank at a busy intersection (U.S. 1 at Indiantown Road, 561/743-5955), it displays movie props and memorabilia, plus sports items and miscellany. Some of what you will find: a canoe from *Deliverance;* a hat from *The Man Who Loved Cat Dancing;* a pair of boots from *The Best Little Whorehouse in Texas;* a key to the city of Buena Park, California; deputy sheriff badges from places like Leon County, Florida, and Jefferson Parish, Louisiana; and the original bill of sale for Roy Rogers' horse Trigger. Unfortunately, you can't buy a souvenir mustache at the gift shop, though $20 will get you a ballcap that reads: "Thanks, Burt."

- **Burt Reynolds Institute For Theatre Training** – Known as BRITT, for short, this was the place to come for seminars on such topics as the Stanislavski Method in Action-Adventure Filmmaking, the Semiotics of High-Speed Car Crashes, and Deconstructing *Cannonball Run.* Closed in 1997.

- **Burt Reynolds Jupiter Theatre** – Reynolds founded the theater that bore his name in 1978 in an attempt to bring culture to Jupiter, calling it "the miracle at the truck stop." We've tried to imagine what the typical stage production might have been: Shakespearean treatments of Reynolds' plebeian films, with titles such as *Romeo and the Bandit, A Midsummer Night's Drag Race,* or perhaps *Timon of Athens, Georgia.* The curtain fell on the theater in 1989, but the facility reopened with new owners and a new name – the Jupiter Theatre – before folding for good in 1996.

- **Burt Reynolds Park** – A two-part park named for Jupiter's proudest son still bears his name. The parks are located across from each other at 800 and 801 U.S. 1, south of Jupiter Inlet. The Jupiter Chamber of Commerce is headquartered in the west park and the Florida History Center and Museum in the east.

leyball courts, playground, picnic shelters, and more.

Additionally, we counted 26 beach-access dune walkovers between Carlin Park and Donald Ross Boulevard, a 3.5-mile stretch. Bike lanes run in both directions, parking beside the road is free, and a sidewalk to walk or jog on runs for a good ways.

Parking/Fees: free parking lots

Hours: sunrise–sunset

Facilities: lifeguards (seasonal), restrooms, picnic tables, showers, and a visitors center (DuBois Pioneer Home)

Contact: Palm Beach County Parks and Recreation Department, 561/966-6631. For beach conditions, call 561/624-0065.

2 DUBOIS PARK

Location: 19075 DuBois Road, on the south side of Jupiter Inlet in Jupiter

3 JUPITER BEACH PARK

Location: 1375 Jupiter Beach Road, on the south side of Jupiter Inlet

THE DIAMOND COAST

© PARKE PUTERBAUGH

Jupiter Beach Park

Parking/Fees: free parking lot
Hours: sunrise-sunset
Facilities: lifeguards, restrooms, picnic tables, and showers
Contact: Palm Beach County Parks and Recreation Department, 561/966-6631. For beach conditions, call 561/624-0065.

CARLIN PARK

Location: 400 South A1A, south of Indiantown Road in Jupiter
Parking/Fees: free parking lot
Hours: sunrise-sunset
Facilities: concessions, lifeguards, restrooms, picnic tables, and showers
Contact: Palm Beach County Parks and Recreation Department, 561/966-6631. For beach conditions, call 561/624-0065.

5 OCEAN CAY PARK

Location: 2188 Marcinski Road, at A1A in Jupiter
Parking/Fees: free parking lot

Hours: sunrise-sunset
Facilities: lifeguards, restrooms, picnic tables, and showers
Contact: Palm Beach County Parks and Recreation Department, 561/966-6631. For beach conditions, call 561/624-0065.

RECREATION AND ATTRACTIONS

- **Bike/Skate Rentals:** J-Town Bicycle, 126 Center Street, Jupiter 561/575-2453

- **Dive Shop:** Seafari Dive & Surf Shop, 75 East Indiantown Road, Jupiter, 561/747-6115

- **Ecotourism:** Canoe Outfitters of Florida, 8900 West Indiantown Road, Jupiter, 561/746-7053

- **Fishing Charters:** Waterdog Sportfishing Charters, 1095 North A1A, Jupiter, 561/744-5932

- **Lighthouse:** Jupiter Inlet Lighthouse, 500 Capt. Armour's Way (U.S. 1 and Beach Road), 561/747-8380

- **Marina:** Jupiter Hills Lighthouse Marina, 18261 U.S. 1, Tequesta, 561/744-0727

- **Rainy-Day Attraction:** Marinelife Center, 1200 U.S. 1, Juno Beach, 561/627-8280

- **Shopping/Browsing:** Loggerhead Plaza, 1225 U.S. 1, Juno Beach
- **Surf Shop:** Seafari Dive & Surf Shop, 75 East Indiantown Road, Jupiter, 561/747-6115
- **Vacation Rentals:** Oceanside Reality of Jupiter, 725 North A1A, 561/746-7476.

ACCOMMODATIONS

There are no resorts directly on the ocean and few even close to it in Jupiter. The **Jupiter Beach Resort** (5 North A1A, 561/746-2511, $$$) is the notable exception. This nine-story white wonder is easily the resort of first choice in northern Palm Beach County. You'll pay around $115 a night in the off-season and three times that during the winter to enjoy a two-bedroom oceanfront room. The resort offers a battalion of amenities: heated pool, balconies, fitness center, access to nearby golf and tennis facilities, and outstanding on-premises restaurants. Frankly, we'd rather stay here than at The Breakers in Palm Beach. For one thing, they have a beach in a natural setting with a thick buffer of vegetation between the resort and the water.

If $360–400 a night for an oceanfront room in the high season is beyond your budget, try the **Wellesley Inn** (34 Fisherman's Wharf, 561/575-7201, $), which offers clean, serviceable accommodations on the west bank of the Intracoastal Waterway at the back of a restaurant/shopping center complex. The beach is less than a mile away, and you'll save a bundle, which you can spend on crab dinners.

COASTAL CUISINE

They've got a bad case of the crabs in Jupiter. For some reason, they're really keen on Maryland-style crab houses down here, even though the Chesapeake Bay lies 1,000 miles north of here. Three crab houses—**Jupiter Crab Company** (1511 North Old Dixie Highway, 561/747-8300, $$$$), the **Crab House** (1065 North A1A, 561/744-1300, $$$), and **Charley's Crab** (1000 North U.S. 1, 561/744-4710, $$$)—sit on or near Jupiter

Inlet in close proximity. Our advice would be to order the freshest Floridian catch of the day—grouper, snapper, or whatever—and leave the Maryland crabs, the North Atlantic salmon, the Maine lobster, and the Canadian scallops to others. At the Crab House, you can arrive by boat, docking beside the restaurant, or book an after-dinner cruise aboard the Manatee Queen (561/744-2191).

The Jupiter Beach Resort has an award-winning restaurant, **Sinclair's Ocean Grill** (5 North A1A, 561/745-7120, $$$), that's both semiformal and semi-affordable, with entrees running in the $12 to 24 range. All the on-premises restaurants at the resort are serviced by the main kitchen, so quality is assured throughout.

NIGHTLIFE

You can bend an elbow in Jupiter at any number of hospitable taverns, including the **Jupiter Ale House** (126 Center Street, 561/746-6720) and **Rooney's Public House** (1153 Town Center Drive, 561/94-6610). The latter features Irish music five nights a week. The lounge at the **Jupiter Beach Resort** (5 North A1A, 561/746-2511) has live music most nights, and bands set up beside the huge heated pool on weekends.

Juno Beach

This town of 3,300 is the only one of the trio in northern Palm Beach County that has "beach" in its name. That is because most of the town does, in fact, exist between the ocean and the Intracoastal Waterway. Especially along A1A, it's a pretty low-key place, given the general bustle and boom in this populous county's beachside communities. That makes it all the harder to believe that Juno Beach was at one time the county seat of Dade County.

You read correctly. Dade County formerly encompassed 7,200 square miles, and Juno Beach was its seat during the 1890s. Then the honor was passed to Miami, and Dade County

THE DIAMOND COAST

was subsequently subdivided. Today, Juno Beach is a no-frills beach town with the usual South Florida mix of single-family homes and high-rises, with strip malls lining U.S. 1 (a.k.a. Federal Highway). Interestingly, U.S. 1 and A1A nearly converge in Juno Beach, running closely parallel at Juno Beach Park (an area referred to by surfers as "Double Roads").

Snowbirds, take note: On a typical early-December afternoon in Juno Beach, the water temperature was an inviting 76°F. Offshore, we saw windsurfers carving back and forth. Sunbathers soaked up rays on the narrow beach at the base of the stairs. We constantly had to remind ourselves it was December. Ah, Florida.

For more information, contact the Jupiter/Tequesta/Juno Beach Chamber of Commerce, 800 North U.S. 1, Jupiter, FL 33477, 561/746-1111 or 800/616-7402, www.jupiterfl.org.

BEACHES

Juno Beach has the right idea about beach access. There's lots of public beach, and it's accessible from numerous stairwells along Ocean Avenue. There aren't very many showers—they look to have been removed, and the tunnels that allow passage under A1A have been closed, too—except by the pier at **Juno Beach Park.** This concrete pier and popular beach attract the largest (and youngest) crowds. Loads of youthful, tanned teens chat and check each other out, while watching surfers by the pier and slathering the suntan lotion that keeps them bronzed and beautiful.

Opposite the Juno Beach Park Pier is a massive parking lot, which extends between Ocean Avenue (A1A) and Federal Highway (U.S. 1). Despite all the space, you still need to arrive early if you want to get a spot on weekends. Juno Beach on a nice day is a balmy sliver of Florida-style heaven.

On a cool afternoon in late spring, the ocean was slightly warmer than the air. The ocean was wild, kicking up four-foot waves that charged up the steep-sloped beach face. The water felt great, but we didn't try to fight our way beyond the shorebreak, fearing rip currents.

Juno Beach is a high-energy beach with coarse, dark sand. It extends for a few miles with no buildings (except for the Jupiter Reef Club) on the ocean side of A1A and low-key condos on the west side. In other words, Juno Beach is virtually one continuous strip of public beach access. If you want to lose the crowd, there's plenty of solitude to be found out here.

At the edge of the beach, dunes are held in place by sea grapes, which have been sculpted to a 45-degree angle by wind and salt spray. During a beach hike we picked up a lot of litter—plastic bags and bottles, Styrofoam food containers, even a half-full can of chain lubricant. Yuck! Nonetheless, this beach gets two enthusiastic thumbs-ups from us. There are lifeguards (in season) but you'll still need to keep an eye on the kids, because the strong waves can quickly pull them under. One of us, in fact, was knocked to his knees and then dragged down the shore face in the fierce backwash from a huge breaker.

Loggerhead Park boasts both a beach and an environmental education mission: informing the public about loggerhead turtles and other ocean dwellers via kid-friendly exhibits at the Marinelife Center (561/627-8280). It also houses a sea turtle hospital where the marine reptiles are nursed back to health. The park also has a bike path, nature trail, tennis courts, and play area. Not that a sensible adult would need to be warned, but in just case you have any crazy ideas, the penalties for molesting nesting loggerheads run up to $20,000. They take their loggerheads seriously here in South Florida. The center is open 10 A.M.–4 P.M. Tuesday–Saturday (noon–3 P.M. on Sunday). Admission is free, and donations are accepted.

6 JUNO BEACH PARK

BEST (

Location: 14775 A1A in Juno Beach
Parking/Fees: free parking lot
Hours: sunrise-sunset

© PARKE PUTERBAUGH

Juno Beach Park and pier

THE DIAMOND COAST

Facilities: concessions, lifeguards, restrooms, picnic tables, and showers
Contact: Palm Beach County Parks and Recreation Department, 561/966-6631. For beach conditions, call 561/624-0065.

LOGGERHEAD PARK

Location: 14200 U.S. 1 in Juno Beach
Parking/Fees: free parking lot
Hours: sunrise-sunset
Facilities: lifeguards, restrooms, picnic tables, showers, and a visitors center (Marinelife Center)
Contact: Palm Beach County Parks and Recreation Department, 561/966-6631. For beach conditions, call 561/624-0065.

ACCOMMODATIONS

A few chain motels can be found a block back from the ocean in Juno Beach, including the **Holiday Inn Express** (13950 U.S. 1, 561/626-1531, $$). It's at the intersection of Federal Highway (U.S. 1) and Donald Ross Boulevard, and that's as close as you'll get in Juno Beach. We stayed there and enjoyed the easy walk to the beach. Only steps away from the motel is **Juno Beach Fish House** (13980 U.S. 1, 561/626-2636, $$), a decent, nonfranchised island bobbing in a sea of predictable mall offerings.

COASTAL CUISINE

Look no further than the **Reef Grill** (12846 U.S. Highway 1, 561/624-9924, $$), a no-frills seafood house favored by spring-training major-leaguers (the St. Louis Cardinals train nearby) and beach bums alike. As one local pundit put it, "If you can name a fish, it'll likely be on the menu sooner or later, simply prepared and outstandingly fresh."

John D. MacArthur Beach State Park

Here is one of the real beauty spots on Florida's East Coast. John D. MacArthur Beach State Park offers a magical setting with some of the

© PARKE PUTERBAUGH

John D. MacArthur Beach State Park

last unbuilt-upon beach wilderness in South Florida. MacArthur Park is named for its benefactor, who donated nearly 800 acres of land and an undeveloped two-mile beach to the state. It is a green haven for humans and a popular nesting spot for loggerhead turtles. In addition to its lengthy beach, the park offers shaded picnic areas, playground, nature center, and kayak rentals.

The park has been intelligently planned to optimize access while minimizing impact on its four ecosystems: beach, reef, mangrove estuary, and hardwood hammock. A hiking trail roams among 225 acres of uplands, and a 1,600-foot wooden boardwalk crosses Lake Worth Lagoon en route to the beach. On a casual stroll, we saw herons, ibises, roseate spoonbills, and ospreys, as well as acres of mangrove, cabbage palms, and gumbo-limbo. On the trail through the back-dune area, we came upon spider webs so thick that walking into them would have created natural shower caps on our heads. More than 150 bird species have been sighted at MacArthur, and a helpful brochure lists them all.

The waters in and around the park are ideal

for kayaking. A kayak appears on every sign welcoming you into the park, reinforcing that very point. From the boardwalk we watched kayakers paddling on the placid waters on our latest visit and wished we could be drifting out there ourselves. Two-hour guided kayak tours are offered Monday at 9 A.M. ($20 for a single kayak, $30 for a double), and kayaks are rented daily 9 A.M.–3 P.M. ($10 for a single kayak, $15 for a double).

It's a half-mile hike out to the beach, which isn't terribly wide but nonetheless beautiful. Signs warn about the lack of lifeguards and the danger of submerged rocks. We dove right in and had no problem. We were, however, bothered by mosquitoes, so come armed with insect repellent in case they're biting. And pay heed to any warnings you might see about sea lice, too.

If you're lugging a lot of beach gear or just don't want to walk, a shuttle offers regular service from the parking area to the beach. Once we hopped aboard and had a spirited discussion with our driver about (of all things) Luddites. "Wouldn't it be great," he mused, "to have the technology of today with the values of the 1940s. It's people who kill off nature, not machines." While we've heard that unconvincing argument made with regard to handguns, it was nice to strike up an intelligent debate with a genial stranger.

One caveat: Parking can be hard to find at MacArthur at times (read: any sunny weekend or holiday), and even the park's $5 admission fee can't temper the great demand to use this special place. In this age of truck-sized SUVs, we saw too many oversized vehicles taking up more than their allotted space.

For more information, contact John D. MacArthur Beach State Park, 10900 S.R. 703 (A1A), North Palm Beach, FL 33408, 561/624-6950, www.floridastateparks.org.

BEACHES

8 JOHN D. MACARTHUR BEACH STATE PARK

Location: 2.5 miles north of Riviera Beach, on A1A
Parking/Fees: $5 per vehicle entrance fee
Hours: 8 A.M.–sunset
Facilities: restrooms and a visitors center
Contact: John D. MacArthur Beach State Park, 561/624-6950

Singer Island: Riviera Beach and Palm Beach Shores

Singer Island has always occupied a special place in our hearts for having been the winter watering hole of the late Frederick Exley, who's been one of our favorite writers since college. In *Pages from a Cold Island*—the late writer's second volume in his trilogy of memoirs—he paints an appealing picture of the island from the vantage point of a barstool. Suffering writer's block, he passed time with the island's fishermen, fry cooks, barkeeps, dropouts, and other assorted dreamers, Exley comes off as a beery Socrates warding off his "private malaise" by hanging around people he liked. So smitten was he with Singer Island that he actually experienced physical pain when he had to cross the bridge onto the mainland city of Riviera Beach (pop. 32,500) to shop for essentials.

Some of the spirit that Exley celebrated still remains, though one must look hard to find it. Without question, the toothbrush-shaped island puts on fewer airs than its neighbors. Singer Island can be reached via PGA Boulevard at the north and Blue Heron Boulevard at the south. It puts its best foot forward at the north end, where one is welcomed by the outer fringes of John D. MacArthur Beach State Park, and at Rivera Beach Municipal Beach.

From MacArthur Park south, alas, Singer Island has taken on the overbuilt look of its neighbors. A very pleasant ride along PGA Boulevard onto Singer Island on state parkland is defiled once you hit rows of indistinguishable high-rises that begin at the island's north end. We counted 30 of the abominations, each given a pompous name (Martinique II, Via del Fino, Cote d'Azur, Eastpointe), along a two-mile stretch. Even more are on the way, judging from the cranes and earth-moving machinery.

To add insult to injury, most of these condos are eerily empty in the off-season, as if a neutron bomb had struck them. John D. MacDonald, Florida's great mystery writer, may have had Singer Island in mind when he wrote his terrifying thriller *Condominium*. (Now there's the *perfect* South Florida beach read!) The beleaguered long-time residents of this formerly down-to-earth place must be seething.

Even so, parts of Singer Island remain cheerfully accommodating. At the island's central point is a pleasant, unpretentious business district anchored by Ocean Mall and a generous swath of lifeguarded beach. If one believes the local literature, the warm waters of the Gulf

THE DIAMOND COAST

Stream approach closer to land at Singer Island than at any other spot in North America. As a result, the temperature varies only slightly. Night and day, winter and summer, Tuesday and Saturday, the mercury hovers at an average of 76°F. In the hot summer months, while inland areas are baking in the humid heat, Singer is a not-unpleasant 86°F, and cooling breezes make the scorching sun bearable.

Singer Island is, by the way, noted for sportfishing, with deep-sea expeditions available at local marinas. Scenic waterway cruises also leave from **Sailfish Marina** (98 Lake Drive, 561/844-1724). **Phil Foster Park**—a pea-shaped landfill island located beneath Riviera Bridge at Blue Heron Boulevard—is the launching point for an *Island Queen Riverboat* cruise aboard a 150-seat Mississippi River paddle-wheeler. The cruise goes to and from Palm Beach, offering a scenic way of surveying the homes and lifestyles of the rich and famous. Nearby is **Peanut Island** (561/845-4445), a unique county park accessible by boat from the Intracoastal Waterway. This 87-acre islet has a fishing pier, boat dock, 18 boat slips, and 20 campsites, as well as the Kennedy Bunker. Yes, the U.S. Secret Service and the Navy Seabees constructed a secret bunker for President John F. Kennedy in the event that the Cuban Missile Crisis escalated into a nuclear war with Russia! To take a tour of Peanut Island, park at the Palm Beach Maritime Center (2400 north Flagler Drive, West Palm Beach, 561/845-4445). A tour of the island costs $7 ($5 for those age 5–17). Ferries run to the island on an irregular schedule; call for information.

With a free public beach, peerless state park, and nod of approval from Fred Exley, a beach lover would have to hail Singer Island. The inland portion of Riviera Beach is a different kettle of rotten fish. Most of this sprawling small city lies across Blue Heron Bridge on the mainland. It is even less inviting now than when Exley dreaded having to make provisioning trips there. Moving down Federal Highway (U.S. 1), fast-food stands and suburban mall sprawl give way to unbroken miles of boarded-

up storefronts, cracked sidewalks, pawnshops, and a plague of cheerless, decrepit businesses. The smell of petty crime wafts along this corridor from Riviera Beach to West Palm Beach. Yecch.

Adding insult to injury, in 2005 the city of Riviera Beach announced that it intended to displace 6,000 mostly black and poor residents in order to construct a billion-dollar waterfront yachting complex. Their rationale was a terrible Supreme Court decision—*Kelo v. City of New London* (June 25, 2005)—expanding the principle of "eminent domain." In a divided vote, they gave state and local governments the green light to seize private property for upscale commercial projects, rationalizing that private development resulting in job creation and tax revenues constitutes a public use of property. Translation: chase off the poor and court the rich. This does not sound like the American way to us.

For more information, contact the Singer Island Business Association, 1211 The Plaza, Singer Island, FL 33404, 561/842-2477, www.singerislandflorida.com.

BEACHES

At the north end of Singer Island, **Ocean Reef Park** harbors an offshore reef popular with snorkelers, as well as a 700-foot beach. Squeezed between condos, it's near the private Palm Beach Racquet Club on Ocean Drive (A1A). The main public beach on Singer Island is **Riviera Beach Municipal Beach,** which has 1,000 feet of lifeguarded beach. It is claimed to be South Florida's widest public beach. That isn't quite the boast it may first appear to be, as those beaches are often narrow and erosion-prone, and this one has been artificially widened by trucking in sand.

A sign at Riviera Beach Municipal Beach also proclaims it "Florida's best beach." This is pure hyperbole, of course, but not entirely without merit. Compared to the miles of high-rise eyesores leading onto Singer Island, Riviera Beach looks like a sandy mirage in

© PARKE PUTERBAUGH

Riviera Beach Municipal Beach

an arid desert of condo towers. And it is extremely wide. We felt like a pair of desert dwellers hoofing it across the sand to get to the water.

Riviera Beach Municipal Beach is easily found by following Ocean Drive (A1A) to the large parking area in front of Ocean Mall. (Incidentally, A1A exits the island at this point via Blue Heron Boulevard.) On these replenished and bulldozed sands, volleyball courts contribute to the look and feel of a Southern California beach during peak season. The professional volleyball circuit makes a tournament stop here. This beachside park also offers a boardwalk, children's play area, and sheltered picnic tables. It's no good for snorkeling, because of the sandy bottom, but fine for swimming.

Like many beaches in Palm Beach County, the beach is steep-faced and strewn with beards of greenish-black seaweed. As with Jupiter Beach Park, drivers compete for parking spaces along the beach or at lots a block behind it. We joined a wagon train of circling for a parking opportunity, and it took awhile to find one on a busy summer Sunday.

Much of the remaining oceanfront down to Lake Worth Inlet belongs to Palm Beach Shores. This uptight community restricts beach access to residents only. To park here, you must both live here and obtain a beach sticker for your car at Town Hall. Of course, you're within your legal rights to walk down from Riviera Beach, as long as you stay on the sand. **Palm Beach Shores Park** does have a lovely beach with a bench-lined boardwalk running alongside it and a playground for the kiddies. Surfers hike down from Riviera Beach with their boards, because the surf off the Pump House has "long rights."

⑨ OCEAN REEF PARK

Location: near Bimini Lane at Ocean Drive (A1A) on Singer Island
Parking/Fees: free parking lot
Hours: sunrise-sunset
Facilities: lifeguards, restrooms, picnic tables, and showers

Contact: Palm Beach County Parks and Recreation Department, 561/966-6631

RIVIERA BEACH MUNICIPAL BEACH

Location: Blue Heron Boulevard at Ocean Drive, beside Ocean Mall on Singer Island
Parking/Fees: metered parking lot
Hours: sunrise-sunset
Facilities: lifeguards, restrooms, picnic tables, and showers
Contact: Riviera Beach Municipal Beach, 561/845-4079

11 PALM BEACH SHORES PARK

Location: along Ocean Drive from Bamboo Road to Lake Worth Inlet in Palm Beach Shores
Parking/Fees: Parking is restricted to Palm Beach Shores residents displaying beach stickers, obtainable at Town Hall (247 Edwards Lane) for a $10 annual fee. On July 1 of every year—and only on this day—beach stickers are sold to non-residents at a cost of $100 for 10 stickers.
Hours: sunrise-sunset
Facilities: lifeguards, restrooms, picnic tables, and showers
Contact: Palm Beach Shores Town Hall, 561/844-3457

RECREATION AND ATTRACTIONS

- **Dive Shop:** Force E, 155 East Blue Heron Boulevard, Riviera Beach, 561/845-2333
- **Ecotourism:** Adventure Times Kayaking, 521 Northlake Boulevard, North Palm Beach, 561/881-7218
- **Fishing Charters:** Sailfish Marina Resort, 98 Lake Drive, Palm Beach Shores, Singer Island, 561/844-1724
- **Marina:** Riviera Beach Municipal Marina, 200 East 13th Street, Riviera Beach, 561/842-7806
- **Rainy-Day Attraction:** South Florida Science Museum, 4801 Dreher Trail North, West Palm Beach, 561/832-1988
- **Shopping/Browsing:** Ocean Mall, Ocean Drive at Blue Heron Boulevard.
- **Surf Shop:** Lazydays Surf & Skate, 12189 U.S. 1, North Palm Beach, 561/625-9283
- **Vacation Rentals:** Home Property Management, 4360 Northlake Boulevard, Palm Beach Shores, 561/624-4663

ACCOMMODATIONS

Hidden among the towering condos and luxury resort hotels are a few beach motels that have somehow survived the trend toward verticality. The **Island Beach Resort** (3100 North Ocean Drive, 561/848-6810, $$) and **Tahiti on the Ocean** (3920 North Ocean Drive, 561/848-9764, $$) are both adequate and affordable, by Palm Beach County standards. The latter offers oceanfront rooms for around $100 a night during the winter high season. The **Rutledge Inn** (3730 North Ocean Drive, 561/848-6621, $$) is holding tough between all the condos, but we'll bet it's gone before long.

For a few dollars more, a few midlevel chain motels are here, including **Days Inn Oceanfront Resort** (2700 North Ocean Drive, 561/848-8661, $$$). A bit more upscale and pricey are the **Radisson Resort Singer Island** (3200 North Ocean Drive, 561/842-6171, $$$) and the **Hilton Singer Island Oceanfront Resort** (3700 North Ocean Drive, 561/848-3888, $$$). At the latter, conveniently located near Riviera Beach Municipal Beach, in-season rates run from $350 per night for a double room.

At the top end of the scale is the **Embassy Suites Resort Hotel** (181 Ocean Drive, 561/863-4000, $$$$), which is on the Palm Beach Shores end of the island. An oceanfront room with two beds runs $325 a night in February. We could make that kind of money go a lot further than one night at the beach.

COASTAL CUISINE

Vestiges of Singer Island's relaxed beach-bum lifestyle remain in a two-block area bordering the public beach. There's just enough to allow you to grab a good meal and a helping of local color. At **Johnny Longboat's** (2401 North Ocean Drive, 561/882-1333, $$), they present an innovative menu of seafood and other items. Our favorites: the house-specialty "Grouper in a Bag"—it's been on the menu for 20 years, and they've served over 100,000 of them—and

sauteed snapper topped with crabmeat and lemon butter sauce. Another must try is Dr. Ray's fresh fillet: a piece of mahi prepared with Grand Marnier and sliced bananas.

Two sides come with each dinner plate, and choices include maple-roasted sweet potatoes and sweet plantains. Appetizers are great, too. We're partial to cherry pepper calamari (which has a nice, spicy bite), conch fritters, and escargots with mushroom caps, crabmeat, garlic and butter in puff pastry. Johnny Longboat's is both a restaurant and bar, so there's no need to leave your seat when dinner's over.

THE GOLF COAST

Golf is another of the secular religions practiced by moneyed pilgrims in Palm Beach County, which has the highest number of golf courses in the state of Florida and, for that matter, the entire nation. There are more than 160 of them. Florida, in turn, has more than 1,250 – the most of any state in the country – covering a combined ground area of over 300 square miles. Many environmental laws would have been violated had most existing courses been built today. Wetlands were drained and filled, forests razed, and chemicals dumped onto the courses (and, via storm runoff, into watersheds). Prodigious quantities of chemicals are needed to fertilize and maintain these unnatural spaces. In humid climates like Florida's, up to nine pounds per acre of herbicides, fungicides, and insecticides are sprayed and spread each year. That's three times the average rate used by the most chemically dependent agribusiness.

Water-quality analyst Richard Klein, one of the foremost authorities on the environmental impact of development, was asked by Sierra magazine to name the least desirable location for a golf course. He responded, "Near a water source in a sandy area with a shallow water table." That basically describes the state of Florida.

In recent years, vigilant citizens and tougher environmental regulations have forced golf-course developers and maintenance crews to clean up their act to some degree. Less intrusive strategies are now employed in course construction, parts of courses are allowed to remain in a natural state, and alternatives to pesticides are being developed and tried. Even so, the powerful U.S. golf industry – whose annual gross receipts run about $24 billion a year, with upward of 16,000 courses in operation and a new course opening somewhere every day – remains environmentally culpable. For one thing, golf courses cover 2.4 million acres in the U.S., and $8 billion in chemicals and equipment are spent annually to maintain them.

Scientists argue that research on runoff and sediment in golf watersheds must be conducted. Ironically, Florida's course designers and developers now employ ecological buzzwords and play up their natural settings. One new course in Palm Beach County calls attention to "the surrounding native Florida terrain, with its wetlands and abundance of wildlife." Let's be optimists here and salute what seems like a healthy trend. Maybe once they begin appreciating the wetlands and wildlife they're golfing through, the duffers will take up hiking and kayaking, too.

We also stopped in Mother Nature's Bounty, which serves smoothies and health foods—wraps and such—plus suntan lotion, T-shirts and more.

Down in Palm Beach Shores, point your sail to the local marinas if you're hungry. Both Sailfish Marina and Buccaneer Marina have popular seafood restaurants—the **Buccaneer Restaurant & Lounge** (142 Lake Drive, 561/844-3477, $$$$) and the **Sailfish Marina Restaurant** (90 Lake Drive, 561/848-1492, $$$)—which feature fresh catches hauled in daily.

NIGHTLIFE

Portofino's Barefoot Cafe (2447 North Ocean Drive, 561/844-2162, $$) has been around since 1978, which is an eternity in South Florida. Classic and hard rock blares from speakers while imbibers chat at outside tables or around the bar. The restaurant serves food with an Italian flair. It's a cool scene, but down the block, we found the music at **Johnny Longboat's** (see *Coastal Cuisine*) more to our liking. In the few hours we were there, we heard "Boogie On, Reggae Woman," "Knock On Wood," "Rock Steady," "La Bamba," and "Little Bit of Soul," all played loud enough to be enjoyable.

Johnny Longboat's is a local institution and one of the last signs of life on an island nearly tamed to extinction by condo developers. It's staffed and patronized by real beach people. Johnny Longboat's is a big place, with outdoor decks and an indoor bar/restaurant. The rectangular bar makes a great place to sip on a frosty Corona and lime or a frozen margarita. Next to us a pleasant, portly couple made a request that shocked us basketball-loving yahoos: they wanted the bartender to turn the big-screen TV from an NBA playoff game—the deciding one in a seven-game series!—to a NASCAR race. No one objected (except us, silently). Oh well. If you're seated at the bar, look up at the huge stuffed shark hanging from the rafters. In another corner, two fish hang mouth-to-mouth, as if locking lips.

Palm Beach

Palm Beach is a hedonistic place where the rich lead lives of self-indulgent ease and luxury. The prevailing attitude can best be expressed by a sight we saw one afternoon in front of The Breakers, an exclusive, world-famous beach resort. Two head-turning babes in a red Corvette cruised down the long driveway, wheeled to a stop beside the Florentine fountain and took turns photographing each other striking posing atop the car's hood. With the posh resort as a backdrop, they seemed to be saying, "Eat your heart out—all this is mine!" Of course, none of it was theirs, and even the car was likely rented or borrowed. But it's the image that counts.

Palm Beach is synonymous with money, privacy, and the opportunities for decadence afforded by both. Hunter S. Thompson captured it perfectly while covering the debauched Roxanne Pulitzer divorce trial for *Rolling Stone:* "It is the ultimate residential community, a lush sand bar lined with palm trees and mansions on the Gold Coast of Florida—millionaires

Midtown Beach, Palm Beach

© PARKE PUTERBAUGH

THE BIG HOUSE PROBLEM

The wealthy old guard of Palm Beach have really worked themselves up into a lather in recent years. Because the surrounding county is the second fastest-growing in the state, some of the nouveau riche riff-raff have begun settling in their palm-swaddled enclave. Among the sorts of people who've moved to Palm Beach are high-tech millionaires, investment bankers, architects, and celebrities. (Not many writers, though.)

The old-timers not only don't like the newer, younger people – partly on general principles (they are not "like us"). They also really don't like this new breed's propensity for showing off with gaudy, obscenely expensive McMansions. An oil billionaire who wanted to enclose his second-story porch was taken to court by an old neighbor complaining that this addition would obstruct his ocean view. Similar beefs about size of houses and extent of renovations have ended up in court of late, prompting the town to hire consultants to study the "Big House Problem." Their conclusions, detailed in a report to the town, were that zoning issues in Palm Beach have become "increasingly fractious and divisive, causing citizens to turn against one another." Moreover, "The town is faced with a paradoxical demand from citizens. 'Don't let them build any more big monster houses, and don't get in my way when I want to add rooms to my own house.'"

In *Palm Beach Houses* – a coffee-table book that's a staple of all self-respecting homeowners here – Robert A. M. Stern writes, "Without the magic of architecture, real estate is just so much land." That pretty much sums up the disconnect from reality in the castle-filled fantasy world of Palm Beach.

and old people, an elaborately protected colony for the seriously rich, a very small island and a very small world."

The term "Palm Beach" is inseparable from the word "socialite." Just for kicks, we searched the online archives of the *Miami Herald* for the phrase "Palm Beach socialite" and came up with more than 500 articles over the past 20 years. Many bore headlines like these: "Millionaire Charged in Wife's Murder, but Ex-Palm Beach Suspect Missing," "Palm Beach Socialite a Suspect in Daughters' Kidnapping," "Jewelry Missing, Police Hint Robber May Have Killed Palm Beach Socialite." And, of course, there are sad announcements of some doyenne's passing, such as this: "Nancy 'Trink' Gardiner, a philanthropist and socialite who gained notoriety by shooting her husband, has died after a brief illness."

Though Palm Beach sits beside an ocean, the resorts tend to focus on golf, tennis, and shopping. The game of golf is an obsession down here because it can be played all year long. There are 160 golf courses in Palm Beach County—more than any other county in Florida, which has more courses than any other state in the country.

Odds are you're not coming to Palm Beach for a traditional beach vacation. The town is primarily a winter playground for the wealthy, who jet down from places like New York, Newport, and Nantucket when cold weather arrives. Its reputation as an enclave of high society is a drawing card that's used to pump up Palm Beach County tourism on the theory that people like to be around money. What they don't tell you is that an outsider stands less chance of penetrating the social whirl than the domestic help. And outside of the high season (December–April), Palm Beach is honest-to-God not happening.

It is actually a rather small place, with a year-round population of 10,500 that swells to 25,000 in winter. The community's origins as a winter hideout for the wealthy dates back to Henry Flagler—yes, him again—and his

WORTH AVENUE: SHOPS WITHOUT END, AMEN

The romance of Old Palm Beach, the fresh look of couture fashion, the bloom of bougainvillea tumbling over arched doorways and tiled stone stairways. This is Worth Avenue, the heart of the Island, an international street of dreams and dramatic encounters. ... Go ahead, take a long walk on Worth Avenue. Have a tall tropical drink, fill your arms with shiny designer shopping bags, and give yourself a day or two of the really good life. After all, this is Palm Beach.

— from "Worth Avenue Adventure," an article
in a local magazine devoted to shopping

If, as has been suggested, shopping in Palm Beach is a religion, then it is most similar to the Latin High Mass. The emphasis is on *high*, as in if you gotta ask the price, you can't afford it. As it is in the cathedral, if you are uncertain about the rituals, remain seated or kneeling in your pew.

When it comes to the worship of shopping, we are defiant heretics. But because we believe in trying anything once, we offer the following list of items and observations culled from a window-shopping spree along Worth Avenue in Palm Beach, the Rodeo Drive of South Florida. We ducked into and quickly back out of a goodly number of Worth Avenue's 250 posh businesses.

Our original idea had been to paddle the Loxahatchee River in nearby Jonathan Dickinson State Park and then embark on a Worth Avenue shopping excursion, comparing and contrasting the two experiences. We got the idea to do this from Bill McKibben's *The Age of Missing Information*, wherein he compared and contrasted a week spent watching TV with an equivalent amount of time immersed in nature. Though we sadly missed the river tour due to tight scheduling and uncooperative weather, we pressed ahead with our Worth Avenue adventure. Dressed in our best wrinkled writer's clothes, we each took one side of the street, working our way down the sidewalk. Here is what we found:

- Asian straw handbag that, we were told, "the ladies love because they don't scratch their silk dresses." Don't you hate it when that happens?

- "Bandstand Bears": xylophone-playing bears as tacky as anything found on the Jersey Shore.

- "Crocodile diaries" made from the skin of this tropical reptile for $2,000.

---

construction of two resort hotels (The Breakers and the Royal Poinciana) and a splendid private mansion (Whitehall). A gift to his third wife, Mary Lily Kenan, Whitehall operates today as the **Flagler Museum** (1 Whitehall Way, 561/655-2833). It has variously been referred to as the Taj Mahal of the South, the San Simeon of the East, and the most magnificent private residence in the nation. Each room in this immense marble mansion was designed and furnished after a different period: Italian Renaissance, French Renaissance, Louis XIV,

Louis XV, Louis XVI. We fantasized a room decorated in early garage-rock: Louie, Louie. At Whitehall, Flagler fell down a flight of stairs and died of his injuries on May 20, 1913. Don't feel too sorry for him, though, as he lived to the ripe old age of 93. Admission to Whitehall is $10 for adults and $3 for children 6–12.

We can't help but think that Flagler would be pleased with the look of Palm Beach today. In a droll turn of phrase, the historic WPA *Guide to Florida* had this to say about Palm

- Facsimile of a 1925 Christofle's tea set, for $3,125, with the notation that it "includes a real coffee pot." At that price, it ought to include a house call from Juan Valdez bearing sacks of the world's finest coffee beans.
- Fur coats for men (enough said).
- Ghastly life-sized bronze sculptures of kids playing ball, playing jumprope, or swinging on a rope.
- Grace Kelly handbags that started at $4,500. Their steep price was attributed by the perky saleswoman to "craftsmanship. ... They are made partly by hand. I was lucky enough to see one of the purses being made in Paris last year."
- Hippo-tusk carving for $6,500. When asked its vintage, we were told "20th century," which suggests that endangered-species laws may have been violated.
- "King of the Road," a miniature Hummer replica that "proves to be an enjoyable way to navigate both suburbia and the wilderness."
- Needle-sharp glass-heeled snakeskin shoes.
- Puke-gold, panty-thin golf shirt for $425.
- Short note in the handwriting of Sigmund Freud — who had a thing or two to say about the libidinous underpinnings of reckless spending — for $9,500.
- Signed check from Marilyn Monroe, made out for the amount of $8.22 and noted as being "for drugs."

By local ordinance, the word "sale" cannot appear in the window of any shop on Worth Avenue. There's even a "chief code compliance officer" whose job it is to see that this and any other downscaling tendencies are discouraged. This, of course, only encourages Worth Avenue shopkeepers to further inflate their prices.

If Worth Avenue doesn't sate your shopping addiction or completely deplete your bank account, we learned in our Worth Avenue Adventure brochure that "Palm Beach-style" shopping can be done at nine other local malls, each of which has 125–200 stores. Each is variously described as "exclusive," "world-class," "world-renowned," "out of the ordinary," and "truly in a class of its own." But the most shameless advertising come-on had to be the following: "Forget the beach — south Florida's newest hot spot is Mizner Park." Of course, it is just another boutique- and gallery-filled shopping mall along Federal Highway (U.S. 1) in nearby Boca Raton.

We, of course, think just the opposite. Forget the shops! The only hot spot in any oceanfront town is the beach.

THE DIAMOND COAST

Beach in the 1930s: "Its habitués constitute a fragment of international society seeking June in January and the pleasures afforded by right of social prestige and heavy purse." In all essential aspects, the town has little changed since those words were written. The streets and "vias" of Palm Beach remain lined with private mansions hidden behind huge, boxy hedges trimmed with geometrical precision. God knows what goes on behind those hedges. Beyond the torn curtain that afforded glimpses of sordid goings-on in that world during the

Pulitzer divorce and William Kennedy Smith rape trials, we'll never know.

We will make cursory mention of West Palm Beach, a bona fide city lies on the mainland side of the Intracoastal Waterway. Its population is nearly eight times that of Palm Beach, and it is at least eight times less glamorous, too. West Palm Beach is a city of malls girdled by freeways, yet it has in recent years made remarkable strides in reclaiming its downtown and protecting its distinctive neighborhoods. It has a multicultural mix that Palm Beach decidedly does not.

There are other communities with the words "Palm Beach" in them, too: North Palm Beach, South Palm Beach, Palm Beach Gardens, Palm Beach Shores, yada yada yada. They all want a touch of that tony Palm Beach cachet, but only Palm Beach Shores even comes close.

Gradually, it sinks in that the Palm Beaches are a scaled-down, East Coast version of Southern California, specifically Los Angeles. If West Palm Beach is downtown L.A., then Palm Beach is Malibu. Various other towns (Riviera Beach, Lantana, Lake Worth, the other Palm Beaches) are arrayed around it. One travels great distances on highways and bridges to get from point to point. It all adds up to a bulging, spread-out mass of civilization that is utterly dependent on the automobile and seemingly heedless of the consequences of such dependency. On our last visit, as war raged in Iraq and oil hit $80 per barrel, a new Hummer dealership was opening on traffic-choked Okeechobee Boulevard.

In the emphasis on wealth and living well beneath the bright and sometimes blinding sun, the Palm Beaches evoke all the rewards and frustrations that also make the City of Angels tick so maniacally.

For more information, contact the Chamber of Commerce of the Palm Beaches, 45 Coconut Row, Palm Beach, FL 33840, 561/655-3282, www.palmbeaches.com; or the Palm Beach County Convention and Visitors Bureau, 1555 Palm Lakes Boulevard, Suite 204, West Palm Beach, FL 33401, 561/233-3000, www.palmbeachfl.com.

FLEA CIRCUS

The old law of science – for every action there's an equal and opposite reaction-holds true as pertains to social class in the Palm Beach area. While mini-mansions in gated communities are filled top to bottom with pricey artifacts and garages teem with His and Her Hummers, the Palm Beach area also has a fixation on bargains, as in the sort of cheap merchandise sold at flea markets. Being both scavengers and sellers at flea markets – one of us ran a book stall at a downtown Washington, D.C. flea market for five years – we can't resist their lure. So on a turn-down day at the beach, we visited two of the biggest flea markets we've ever seen. Both are in the Palm Beach area.

Dr. Flea's (1200 S. Congress Avenue, West Palm Beach, 561/965-1500) constitutes one of the more original we've encountered. Located at Exit 66 off I-95, Dr. Flea's shares a home with the county's Puppetry Arts Center. Much of the merchandise at this 55-year-old institution is discounted brand-name stuff (jeans, socks, sneakers, cowboy hats, "beauty aids"). Still, there are a few eccentric items buried in the back booths that make the pursuit as fun as the score.

Swap Shop Circus (3921 West Sunrise Boulevard, West Palm Beach, 954/791-SWAP), has a more international (read: Third World) flavor. Moreover, it claims to be "Florida's 2nd Biggest Tourist Attraction." (Ha!) It is big, with 800 vendors and 88 acres. You can purchase everything from parakeets to doo-rags, plus an astonishing array of fresh produce and "original watches."

We scored "Jesus Is My Boss" baseball caps. Sporting these, no one bothered us for the rest of our trip – not even the bouncers at Club Boca. Some of the merchandise at Swap Shop Circus is depressing: piles of what looks like soiled laundry, toe clippers, duct tape, damaged canned goods. But all of it is at least interesting from a sociological point of view and the people-watching is some of the best in Florida.

The area is pierced by loud salsa music and the smell of West Indian cooking. When you and the young'uns get burnt out, head indoors to the miniature circus, replete with trapeze artists and clowns. They perform for free 365 days a year. There are also carnival rides outside. A tip based on personal experience: If you ride the log flume, wear waterproof clothing and don't carry bags of produce.

THE DIAMOND COAST

BEACHES

Palm Beach built its reputation on the bank accounts and bloodlines of the rich and famous whose walled estates contribute to the town's air of chilly inaccessibility. You are led to believe that Palm Beach is the Hope diamond in a pure-gold setting. But if it's beaches you're looking for, the bauble is costume jewelry. South Beach in Miami is much more cosmopolitan, hip, and alive—and the wide beach down there is no mirage.

A short sand-colored wall runs along much of the oceanfront in Palm Beach, discouraging public access. That said, there is one public beach in Palm Beach proper. **Midtown Beach** is located where Worth Avenue meets South Ocean Boulevard (A1A). The public beach extends for 5,000 feet, a quarter of which is lifeguarded. There's nothing much in the way of facilities besides a public shower, not even a lousy restroom, which says everything you need to know about Palm Beach's grudging provision of public access. There's nothing much in the way of sand, either, although we were told it had been "beautifully restored." To the contrary, on a perfect spring day in 2005 we saw huge ocean-chewed ledges in the sand, signs warning of rocks in the water, a rusted and cracked seawall, and no visitors save for two weirdos wielding metal detectors in search of lost gold trinkets and spare change.

Adding to the sense of exclusion, the beach is closed 8 P.M.–8 A.M. Metered parking is available along A1A ($1 per hour). However, we got the distinct feeling that people are much more welcome on Worth Avenue, the shopping district that functions as the town's de facto beach in the sense that this is where visitors get soaked (see the *Worth Avenue: Shops Without End, Amen* sidebar).

There are two other beach parks on the south end of Palm Beach. **Phipps Ocean Park** is a lifeguarded municipal beach with a rocky, narrow shoreline that runs for a quarter-mile. Curiosity seekers will enjoy the 19th-century schoolhouse on the premises. **Richard G. Kreusler Park** is a tiny (450 feet) lifeguarded county beach that

boasts a small artificial reef for diving and snorkeling fun. While none of these spots is worth rattling your jewelry about, they are indeed all that opulent Palm Beach has to offer.

The entire stretch of coast from Palm Beach down to Boynton Beach can be viewed as the East Coast's answer to the 17-Mile Drive in Pebble Beach, California. However, it's actually worse than that, because the cement barriers along the road holding the ocean at bay undermine the area's would-be chicness. Driving Ocean Boulevard (A1A) in search of hassle-free beach access is as forbidding as entering a Worth Avenue boutique with a squadron of sales clerks on the prowl and no other customers in sight. There are no shoulders beside the road, so you can't pull over to park or get your bearings or drink in all the architectural ego gratification on view. The beachfront is gated for the private pleasure of part-time-resident millionaires or upscale sorts who maintain way stations in high-rises with names like "The Patrician." There are few utilitarian businesses to speak of, though poodle groomers and plastic surgeons hang their shingles. Everything seems designed to keep visitors moving along. We found ourselves wondering, as we did in Pebble Beach, California, why they even bother with the pretense of a public road.

12 MIDTOWN BEACH

  BEST (

Location: east end of Worth Avenue at South Ocean Boulevard (A1A) in Palm Beach
Parking/Fees: metered street parking
Hours: sunrise-sunset
Facilities: lifeguards and showers
Contact: Midtown Beach, 561/838-5483

13 PHIPPS OCEAN PARK

Location: 1.5 miles north of Lake Worth Beach, on the south end of Palm Beach at 2145 South Ocean Boulevard

Parking/Fees: metered parking lot
Hours: sunrise-sunset
Facilities: lifeguards, restrooms, picnic tables, and showers
Contact: Phipps Ocean Park, 561/585-9203

14 RICHARD G. KREUSLER PARK

Location: 2695 South Ocean Boulevard (A1A) in Palm Beach
Parking/Fees: metered parking lot
Hours: sunrise-sunset
Facilities: lifeguards, restrooms and showers
Contact: Palm Beach County Parks and Recreation Department, 561/966-6631. For beach conditions, call 561/276-3990.

RECREATION AND ATTRACTIONS

- **Bike/Skate Rentals:** Palm Beach Bicycle Trail Shop, 223 Sunrise Avenue, Palm Beach, 561/659-4583
- **Boat Cruise:** Atlantic Coastal Cruises, 900 East Heron Boulevard, West Palm Beach, 561/848-7827
- **Dive Shop:** The Scuba Club, 4708 North Flagler Drive, West Palm Beach, 561/844-2466
- **Ecotourism:** Okeeheelee Nature Center, Okeeheelee Park, West Palm Beach, 561/233-1400
- **Marina:** Palm Beach Yacht Club and Marina, 800 North Flagler Drive, West Palm Beach, 561/655-1944
- **Pier:** Lake Worth Municipal Pier, 10 South Ocean Boulevard, Lake Worth, 561/533-7367
- **Rainy-Day Attractions:** Flagler Museum (a.k.a. Whitehall), Coconut Row and Whitehall Way, Palm Beach, 561/655-2833; Society of the Four Arts, 2 Four Arts Plaza, Palm Beach, 561/655-7226
- **Shopping/Browsing:** Worth Avenue, Palm Beach, 561/659-6909; City Place, Okeechobee Boulevard, West Palm Beach
- **Surf Shop:** Cuyagua Surf Shop, 10300 West Forest Hill Boulevard, West Palm Beach, 561/790-0372
- **Vacation Rentals:** Paulette Koch, 328 Royal Poinciana Plaza, Palm Beach, 561/655-9081.

ACCOMMODATIONS

The Breakers (1 South County Road, 561/655-6611, $$$$) is the most venerable resort in Palm Beach and maybe all of Florida. Built in the Italian Renaissance style by Henry Flagler, The Breakers celebrated its centennial in 1996. A little history: Flagler's first Palm Beach hotel was not the more-celebrated Breakers but the Royal Poinciana, on Lake Worth. At first The Breakers existed to house the overflow from the Royal Poinciana. Flagler purchased and enlarged an oceanfront home, calling his new acquisition the Palm Beach Inn and opening it to the public in 1896. Five years later, he renamed it The Breakers. At the time, it was the only oceanfront hotel south of Daytona Beach, incredible as that may seem.

You will indeed hear breakers at The Breakers. They break right on the seawall that protects the 100-year-old fortress from the pounding ocean. It is almost *too* close to the ocean, whose encroachment has left the resort fighting a rear-guard action to hold the waves at bay and unable to present a proper beach behind the hotel. Since you cannot realistically swim or sun by the ocean, they've provided a beach club with a huge heated pool, vast deck area, and poolside bar and restaurant. There are two golf courses and 14 tennis courts on the premises. They also provide such activities as tennis clinics, fly-fishing, water aerobics, and a Worth Avenue shopping trip.

Unless you're attending a convention and someone else is picking up the tab, you will pay dearly to stay at this 572-room, five-star hotel (which underwent a total of $225 million in renovations since 1990). At the low end, a "partial ocean-view superior" room runs around

$315 during the low season (mid-May–October) and climbs to $510 during the high season (early January–mid-May). An oceanfront suite runs $600–1,040 a night.

Like all posh resorts that are described with such words as "venerable" and "grand," you sometimes feel like a captive going broke in high style. The nightly tariff entitles you to nothing but a room, and you'll wind up dropping big bucks on food and incidentals. The on-site restaurants are expensive (for instance, entrees run $32–59 at the Flagler Steakhouse). It costs $25 daily to use the fitness center attached to the spa. (The workout room in the hotel itself is free to guests.) It costs $20 per night to valet-park your car. Beach and pool cabanas run around $300 per day, in season. The charge for 18 holes of golf is $160. (Incidentally, the Breakers Ocean Course is the oldest golf course in Florida, dating back to 1897.) There are valets and bellhops to be tipped. (The hotel employs 1,300 people.) And on-site stores vend everything from pricey logoed merchandise to Steuben glassware.

Admittedly, part of the thrill of staying at The Breakers is getting to say you stayed at The Breakers. The rooms are quite commodious, the result of a $100 million makeover in the late 1990s. Our oceanfront room was light and airy, with coral walls and coordinated comforters and draperies done in a riotously flowered pattern. We left the sliding glass doors open so we could be serenaded to sleep by the churning sea. Public spaces include the Tapestry Bar and Florentine Dining Room, bedecked with priceless 16th- and 17th-century tapestries collected by Flagler. Guests invariably stop to gawk at the hallway photo portfolio of celebrity patrons—among them, Heather Locklear, Loni Anderson, Donald Trump, and Sally Jessy Raphael. Among all of them, only Robin Williams looked the least bit human.

The other five-star and five-diamond resort in Palm Beach is the **Four Seasons Ocean Grand** (2800 South Ocean Boulevard, 561/582-2800, $$$). Though it's five miles

south of Worth Avenue, the Ocean Grand falls within Palm Beach city limits. (The same cannot be said of the Ritz-Carlton Palm Beach, which is in Manalapan.) The Ocean Grand, which opened in 1990, was the first hotel built in Palm Beach in nearly 40 years. It's a veritable bank vault encircled by palm trees. The restaurant is so self-smitten that it calls itself "The Restaurant."

More down to earth, and therefore more to our liking, is the **Heart of Palm Beach Hotel** (160 Royal Palm Way, 561/655-5600, $$$). It's an attractive European-style hostelry conveniently located within walking distance of Midtown Beach and Worth Avenue. Rooms are spacious, the staff is helpful, the location is ideal, and there's no charge to park your car.

The **Brazilian Court Hotel** (301 Australian Avenue, 561/655-7740, $$$) is another old reliable (ca. 1928) that prizes casual elegance over ostentation. It has 134 rooms, a swimming pool, a restaurant (the Chancellor Grill Room), and a cocktail lounge. Their summer rates are a bargain, by Palm Beach standards.

If you want to stay in Palm Beach on the cheap, or relatively so, there's a **Howard Johnson's Hotel** (2870 South Ocean Boulevard, 561/586-6542, $$) along the Intracoastal Waterway on the south end of town, very near the Four Seasons Ocean Grand. Finally, as a general rule of thumb, you can get a room in Palm Beach during the summer season for about $100, but that same room will triple or quadruple in price when winter rolls around and the trunks of the well-to-do begin arriving.

COASTAL CUISINE

Testa's (221 Royal Poinciana Way, 561/832-0992, $$$$) has been in business in Palm Beach since 1921 and has been at its present location since 1946. The food and atmosphere are unpretentious and high quality. It is an indoor-outdoor restaurant that mercifully lacks the air of snootiness that hangs over Palm Beach like a suffocating fog. The lunch menu offers a good selection of salads (such as seared

THE DIAMOND COAST

THE BALLAD OF THE BUTTERFLY BALLOT

Palm Beach County is no stranger to notoriety, and in November 2000 it got a fresh dose of the stuff during the controversial presidential vote count in the state of Florida. Two species of electoral detritus – the lovely butterfly ballot and the stately hanging chad – became forever identified with Palm Beach County, thanks to one Theresa LePore. George W. Bush owes his presidency (first term, at least) to the fact that this Palm Beach County election official designed a ballot so confusing that a sizable number of voters were unable to distinguish between Democrat Al Gore and far-right firebrand Pat Buchanan. As a consequence, at least 10,000 and as many as 19,000 befuddled county residents voted for two candidates. Many others apparently voted for Buchanan by mistake. Buchanan himself agreed it was highly unlikely he could've drawn as many votes as he did in Palm Beach County, since he polled so poorly elsewhere in Florida.

A series of events in Florida resulted in a perfect storm that swept George W. Bush into office, barely tipping the electoral college in his favor. The "butterfly ballot" – so-called because it vaguely resembled a butterfly's anatomy, with candidates names staggered on both sides with punch holes running down the center – was one of the critical elements in this tempest. The *Palm Beach Post* bluntly concluded that confusion over the butterfly ballot cost Al Gore the election. A painstaking review of ballots showed that 5,330 voters clearly punched chads for both Gore and Buchanan, while another 2,908 did so for Gore and an obscure Socialist candidate. If the total of invalidated ballots (8,238) meant for Gore was reduced by the number disallowed because Bush supporters mistakenly punched chads for Bush and Buchanan (1,631), it appears that Gore suffered a net loss of 6,607 votes in Palm Beach County.

The official tally for the state of Florida gave Bush a razor-thin margin of 507 votes. In other words, if those Palm Beach County residents who were befuddled by the butterfly ballot had cast the votes they intended, Al Gore would have won the state of Florida by 6,100 votes and therefore would have been our 43rd president.

Ironically, LePore – the ballot designer and supervisor of elections – was a registered Democrat who had worked at the county election office for 30 years. Complaints about the badly designed ballet had been registered before Election Day, but a memo from LePore asking poll workers to post written instructions to avoid voter confusion didn't arrive until well after polls had opened.

LePore's flawed ballot was an honest but costly mistake. Given everything it set in motion – including world events of cataclysmic if not apocalyptic proportions – one would think she would have discreetly abandoned electoral politics. This was not the case, and it was left to the people to turn her out. Running for re-election in 2004, LePore was defeated in what was described as a "stunning victory" for local educator Arthur Anderson.

And so the saga of Theresa LePore and her butterfly ballot remains a sorry footnote to the election fiasco of 2000. No doubt it will crop up as a question in future editions of Trivial Pursuit – after the passage of time has lessened the painful memories of its consequences, that is.

tuna Caesar and poached salmon with sliced tomatoes and buffalo mozzarella), while dinner focuses on seafood and steaks, with fresh catches running in the $20–30 range. Of all the chichi eateries lining the north side of Royal Poinciana Way for several blocks, Testa's is the most inviting. And the outdoor patio makes a great place to dine while watching the passing Palm Beach parade.

The best location in town belongs to **Charley's Crab** (456 South Ocean Boulevard, 561/659-1500, $$$$). Unlike any other restaurant or retail establishment in Palm Beach, Charley's sits as close to the beach as a crab hole. We found the food to be serviceable but not good enough to merit a rave. But atmosphere and location do count for something, and Charley's is a well-placed landmark.

Here are some other dining options from Palm Beach's upscale pantry:

- **Bice Ristorante** (313½ Worth Avenue, 561/835-1600, $$$$) serves Northern Italian cuisine. Rod Stewart has been spotted here. You should come anyway.

- **Cafe L'Europe** (331 South County Road, 561/655-4020, $$$$) specializes in French fare.

- **Casablanca Cafe Americain** (101 North County Road, 561/655-1115, $$$) offers Mediterranean meals.

- **Chuck and Harold's** (207 Royal Poinciana Way, 561/659-1440, $$$$) and **Ta-Boo** (221 Worth Avenue, 561/835-3500, $$$$) are see-and-be-seen places.

- **Hamburger Haven** (314 South County Road, 561/655-5277, $) and **Green's Pharmacy** (151 North County Road, 561/832-4443, $) are good spots for an inexpensive lunch.

NIGHTLIFE

In a town where one of the hottest nightspots is called **Ta-Boo** (221 Worth Avenue, 561/835-3500)—a Worth Avenue restaurant that doubles as a bar and disco—you can be certain the nightlife is racy, bold, and fraught with decadence. A comely, young, blonde ingénue holding fast to the tailored blazer of a wealthy, older male consort is a common sight around here. The music to which these odd couples dance is from another time, ranging from big-band jazz to contemporary R&B. Vocalist/songwriter Bryan Ferry would have a field day deconstructing this scene. The social observer and critic Cleveland Amory certainly did.

They'd both ironically enjoy the tragically hip goings-on at **Au Bar** (336 Royal Poinciana Way, 561/832-4800), which is where William Kennedy Smith and uncle Ted were hanging out the night that... ah, but that's ancient history now. Au Bar attracts curious tourists and native bon vivants, so ante up the cover charge and let the champagne flow. Other necessary stops on the Palm Beach party trolley: **E.R. Bradley's Saloon** (111 Bradley Place, 561/833-3520), **Chuck and Harold's** (207 Royal Poinciana Way, 561/659-1440), and **The Breakers** (1 South County Road, 561/655-6611), which offer the only ocean-view public bars in town.

Lake Worth

The town of Lake Worth (pop. 36,000) is a thick grid of residential and commercial streets south of Palm Beach, extending westward from the Intracoastal Waterway. It seems to be a kind of clubhouse for retirees who flock here and play at one of the 15 golf courses within a tee shot of the city limits. The town was founded by immigrating Chicagoans in the 1870s. In keeping with the population explosion all over South Florida, Lake Worth has tripled since the 1950s. If you're interested in roadside history, take a spin along U.S. 1 through Lake Worth. It used to be the main route down the East Coast but tourist traffic dried up when I-95 offered a faster, multi-lane alternative. Today U.S. 1 is lined with old, sun-faded motels from yesteryear that are dying if not dead. And with that we'll now head out to Lake Worth's one window on the ocean.

For more information, contact the Greater Lake Worth Chamber of Commerce, 811 Lucerne Avenue, Lake Worth, FL 33460, 561/582-4401, www.lwchamber.com.

BEACHES

While Lake Worth is almost entirely inland, it does retain a toehold on the oceanfront via **Lake Worth Municipal Beach** and Barton Park. This enormous but unpretentious beach park is accessed via Lake Avenue (S.R. 802) at Ocean Boulevard (A1A).

Into this 1,200-foot-long public beach is squeezed a "developed beach," lifeguards, a pool (at the casino), shuffleboard courts, a picnic area, grills, and a 1,300-foot fishing pier. On the latter sits a modest, rusty, and windblown eatery. This complex was built in 1922, rebuilt in 1947, and seems to have remained unimproved since. A one-way entrance road leads to metered parking. Access to the pier costs $0.50 for walkers and $2.50 if you're fishing.

The scene always seemed to be fishing for something that had clearly eluded it, until now. Lake Worth Municipal Beach has never looked better. The sand is golden and clean, the tiki huts on the beach are as inviting as the blue-green water or friendly chatter at Benny's on the Beach, a genial outdoor bar near the pier entrance. One caveat for little ones: there's a steep drop-off in the water just a few feet from shore.

Lake Worth Municipal Beach teems with business. Shops include Beach T-Shirt Company, NYPD Pizza and Pasta, Pier Bait and Tackle, Surfside Sundries, Casino Dairy Bar, and Fox Surf and Sport. The only problem is that sometimes cars outnumber parking spaces. One busy Sunday we got caught in a monumental traffic jam trying to exit the beach parking lot via its circular drive. It was like rush-hour traffic in midtown Manhattan.

Lake Worth Municipal Beach attracts an ethnically varied makeup, obviously serving as a place for locals to get away from the sweltering mainland. South of the beach, an asphalt pathway runs alongside Lake Worth and about a mile's worth of condos.

15 LAKE WORTH MUNICIPAL BEACH

Location: 10 South Ocean Boulevard in Lake Worth, due east of Lake Worth Road
Parking/Fees: metered parking ($1 per hour) by the beach or token lot ($2 per day) on the west side of A1A
Hours: 6 A.M.-midnight
Facilities: concessions, lifeguards, restrooms, picnic tables, and showers
Contact: Lake Worth Municipal Beach, 561/533-7367

ACCOMMODATIONS

The **Beachcomber Motel** (3024 South Ocean Boulevard, South Palm Beach, FL 33480, 561/585-4646, $$) offers a rare option to those with limited budgets. At $100 or less per night, this low-key, likeable estab-

© PARKE PUTERBAUGH

Lake Worth Municipal Beach

THE DIAMOND COAST

lishment qualifies as a bargain among the Palm Beaches.

NIGHTLIFE

The classiest live music venue in Palm Beach County—**The Bamboo Room** (25 South J Street, 561/585-2583)—is located in Lake Worth. On our last visit, we caught Dave Alvin (late of the Blasters) blasting the Bamboo's rafters. Other national musicians, often tilted toward the blues, are booked here.

South Palm Beach, Lantana, and Manalapan

Palm Beach's intense privatization of beaches continues south into the adjoining towns of South Palm Beach (pop. 17,500), Lantana (pop. 9,500), and Manalapan (pop. 370). All retain discernible, though mostly private, footholds on the beach. South Palm Beach is the most community-oriented, with a quaint town hall overseeing the beach road and banners "celebrating" its 50-year history. Incidentally, tabloid newspaper addicts may be interested to learn that Lantana is home to the *National Enquirer*.

The exclusive community of Manalapan (median income: $90,000) picks up where Lantana ends and raises the stakes even higher. The spit upon which the sprawling estates of Manalapan sit is so thin that a reasonably well-struck chip shot would carry from the sand trap of the eroding beach to the water hazard of the Intracoastal Waterway. So much pricey real estate piled atop so fragile a foundation! Fish-eye mirrors at the end of every driveway allow the owners to back out their Mercedes, Lexuses, Beemers, and Hummers without getting creamed. Occasionally you can catch a glimpse of the ocean through the thick hedges and eight-foot privacy walls.

Here's a "fun fact" about Manalapan from the local historian: "Manalapan, founded in 1931 by Commodore Harold Vanderbilt—

scion of one of America's wealthiest families—prefers its low-key gentility to the noisy social scene of Palm Beach." We can just see noses raising in the air like drawbridges.

For more information, contact the Greater Lantana Chamber of Commerce, 212 Iris Avenue, Lantana, FL 33462, 561/585-8664, www.lantanachamber.com.

BEACHES

Lantana Municipal Beach is a nicely landscaped six-acre complex up where Ocean Avenue (S.R. 812) meets Ocean Boulevard (A1A). The south end of its metered parking lot is adjacent to the loading dock for the Ritz-Carlton Palm Beach. Lantana's public beach is a similar sop to the non-oceanfront-dwelling public as at Lake Worth Municipal Beach. The beach has a modest width made appealing by sea grape–gripped dunes. In addition, the park has a restaurant (Dunedeck Cafe), souvenir shop, volleyball court, playground, and offshore reef.

16 LANTANA MUNICIPAL BEACH

Location: Ocean Avenue (S.R. 812) at Ocean Boulevard (A1A) in Lantana

Parking/Fees: metered parking lot for nonresidents ($1 per hour) and free parking area for residents displaying beach stickers ($6 annually per vehicle). Beach stickers are available to nonresidents for $100 per year per vehicle.

Hours: sunrise–sunset

Facilities: concessions, lifeguards, restrooms, picnic tables, and showers

Contact: Lantana Municipal Beach, 561/540-5731. For beach conditions, call 561/540-5735.

ACCOMMODATIONS

Though South Palm Beach occupies only 0.1 square mile, it is jammed to the breaking point with high-rise condos. The lone exception to the condo-mania is the **Palm Beach**

Oceanfront Inn (3550 South Ocean Boulevard, 561/582-5631, $$$). Fronted by an appealingly kitschy tiki-roofed office, the inn is a modest two-story structure that rambles from A1A down to the water. The rooms are clean and unpretentious, and rates are affordable, by Palm Beach standards. The Tides Bar & Grille is a great spot to survey the ocean over a morning cup of coffee. This hotel, restaurant, and tiki bar is the only commercial enterprise in South Palm Beach, having been grandfathered in because it already existed when the town incorporated in 1955. We're cheered to see something hereabouts survive intact, except for a minor name change. (It used to be the Palm Beach Hawaiian Ocean Inn.)

You don't have to travel very far down A1A to go from one extreme to another. By contrast to the low-key Palm Beach Ocean Inn, the **Ritz-Carlton Palm Beach** (100 South Ocean Boulevard, 561/533-6000, $$$$) swaddles its guests in marble and marvels. A six-story, 270-room resort that boasts four on-premises restaurants and a five-star rating, it is a typically top-of-the-line Ritz-Carlton operation. The hallways are lined with original artwork, bathed in an amber glow cast by chandeliers. The palm-filled grounds feature a spacious pool deck and easy access to the beach. The rooms are simply but elegantly decorated with French Provincial furnishings. You will pay dearly for cosseting of this kind ($300–600 per night, in season), but making it and spending it is the name of the game in Palm Beach.

Boynton Beach, Ocean Ridge, Briny Breezes, and Gulfstream

The city of Boynton Beach (pop. 65,000) was named for Civil War officer Nathan South Boynton. As for the "beach" part, Boynton Beach is oddly misnamed. None of the town lies east of the Intracoastal Waterway. Out by the ocean along A1A you'll find Ocean Ridge (pop. 1,700), a small, exclusive community that once was part of Boynton Beach but spun off on its own. In order to do so, the wealthy Ocean Ridge residents made the town of Boynton Beach an offer it couldn't refuse: they paid off the debt-plagued community's sewer and water bonds during the Depression. To make matters more confusing, Boynton Beach Oceanfront Park is located in Ocean Ridge but belongs to Boynton Beach. So if you're wondering whether Boynton Beach extends out to the beach—well, it does and it doesn't.

Recreationally, the Boynton Beach area is of more interest to fishermen than to beachcombers. South Lake Worth Inlet connects Lake Worth to the ocean, providing access to a couple of the East Coast's best fishing holes, dubbed Kingfish Circle and Sailfish Alley. But Boynton Beach and the rest of south Palm Beach County may well be of most interest to golfers. As a local publication put it, intending praise and not irony, "At first glance, South County looks like a collection of golf courses, plus a little room for people." We couldn't have put it better ourselves and applaud their candor, however inadvertent. By the way, have you ever heard of so large a city that's made so negligible an impression on the general consciousness? Boynton Beach is essentially South Florida residential sprawl, albeit of a more friendly, less snooty character than in neighboring Boca Raton or any of the Palm Beaches.

Ocean Ridge, by contrast, is a luxury condo community that keeps its upper lip stiff and its building codes as flexible as the law will allow. We'll note a news item we read while passing through. A mansion-in-progress was being held up by ordinances against destroying sand dunes. The project's architectural engineer told the town commissioners that "we will not disturb the dune any more than we would have to" in constructing a pool deck and dune crossover. The easement was granted by the pliable local board, and the mansion was on its way. Among the amenities: ten bathrooms, five guest bedrooms, three "powder rooms," a game room, wine room, music room, and "grand hall." The initial buzz was that Oprah Winfrey had purchased the lot, which she vehemently denied.

Then there's Briny Breezes (pop. 400) and Gulfstream (pop. 714)—two more dots on the map with evocative names that claim a sliver of oceanfront. President George H.W. Bush once took a fishing vacation in Gulfstream, briefly putting the town on the map for the first time since its incorporation in 1926. As for Briny Breezes, what can you say about a town that occupies a mere 0.25 square mile, almost all of which is a trailer park (albeit a quiet, well-tended one)?

For more information, contact the Greater Boynton Beach Chamber of Commerce, 639 East Ocean Avenue, Suite 108, Boynton Beach, FL 33435, 561/732-9501, www.boyntonbeach.org

BEACHES

On the south side of South Lake Worth Inlet, which separates Ocean Ridge from Manalapan, is **Ocean Inlet Park,** which offers marina facilities on the Intracoastal side. While it's best for fishing (from the jetty) and surfing, families will enjoy the 600-foot lifeguarded beach, picnic tables, snack bar, and playground. The county sheriff's office is right next-door, too, in case any spin-the-bottle games get out of hand. A short distance south of here is **Ocean Ridge Hammock Park,** essentially a nature preserve that consists of a small roadside parking lot (28 spaces) and a path across the dunes to the beach.

Boynton Beach Oceanfront Park isn't very well marked (watch for a blue sign on A1A). It's free to locals with permits (which cost $30 annually) but nonresidents must pay a stiff $10 per car to park. This effectively makes Boynton Beach a locals-only park, and the locals are welcome to it. This is not said in disrespect. It's an okay spot with a healthy pla-

teau of sea oats giving way to dwarf sea grape on the dunes. It's got year-round lifeguards, plus a concession stand, barbecue grills, and picnic areas, as well as a playground and basketball court. The sand-starved beach—having been deprived, no doubt, by the groins to the north—is periodically renourished.

If you don't live in Boynton Beach, then you don't need to pay a daily ten-spot at Oceanfront Park when Delray Beach, a free and easy beach town, lies just down the road. Besides, free beach access can be had at Ocean Ridge Hammock Park and **Gulfstream County Park,** which lie due north and south, respectively. Gulfstream is an attractive 6.4-acre park with plenty of free parking, a boardwalk that leads through a hammock of scrub pine and sea grape to a picnic area, playground, and 600-foot-long beach. A popular snorkeling reef lies just of the lifeguarded area. Signs caution about underwater rocks, but the large number of families who come here would seem to indicate that Gulfstream's a pretty safe place to spread one's beach blanket.

17 OCEAN INLET PARK

Location: 6990 North Ocean Boulevard, at A1A in Ocean Ridge
Parking/Fees: free parking lot
Hours: sunrise–sunset (24 hours for fishing)
Facilities: concessions, lifeguards, restrooms, picnic tables, and showers
Contact: Palm Beach County Parks and Recreation Department, 561/966-6631. For beach conditions, call 561/276-3990.

18 OCEAN RIDGE HAMMOCK PARK

Location: 6620 North Ocean Boulevard at A1A in Ocean Ridge; look for small lot on east side of road

THE DIAMOND COAST

Parking/Fees: free parking lot
Hours: sunrise-sunset
Facilities: none
Contact: Palm Beach County Parks and Recreation Department, 561/966-6631. For beach conditions, call 561/276-3990.

19 BOYNTON BEACH OCEANFRONT PARK

Location: 6415 North Ocean Boulevard, at A1A in Ocean Ridge
Parking/Fees: Parking fee of $10 per car May 1-November 15 and $5 per car November 16-April 30. Town residents can buy a parking decal good for a year (renewable each October 1) for $30 from Boynton Beach City Hall. Non-residents can buy a decal good for slightly more than half a year (May 1-November 15) for $60.
Hours: sunrise-sunset
Facilities: concessions, lifeguards, restrooms, picnic tables, and showers
Contact: Boynton Beach Oceanfront Park, 561/742-6565. For beach conditions, call 561/742-6775.

20 GULFSTREAM COUNTY PARK

Location: 4489 North Ocean Boulevard, at A1A in Gulfstream
Parking/Fees: free parking lot
Hours: sunrise-sunset
Facilities: lifeguards, restrooms, picnic tables, and showers
Contact: Palm Beach County Parks and Recreation Department, 561/966-6631. For beach conditions, call 561/276-3990.

NIGHTLIFE

By general consensus, Boynton Beach is home to the best rock and roll club in the area:

Club Ovation (3637 South Federal Highway, 561/740-7076). It's also the biggest, having taken over a former Winn-Dixie grocery store that holds 2,000 revelers.

Delray Beach

From an enlightened traveler's perspective, Delray Beach is the light at the end of Palm Beach's tunnel of moneyed self-absorption. For beach lovers, it's the bucket of golden sand at the end of the asphalt rainbow. It is the ideal South Florida beach town, having been blessed with natural beauty and an enlightened populace. It possesses a small-town feel with big-city amenities.

Delray Beach has long been a resort community, but in recent decades it has attracted more college grads, young families, and DINKs (dual income, no kids). They're drawn by the town's relative affordability, employer base, and enviable beaches. It's a growing small city (pop. 65,000) with a dynamic outlook. *Florida Trend* magazine declared it the best-run town in the state.

On the north side, Delray Beach begins at George Bush Road and Ocean Avenue (A1A). As is the case all over Palm Beach County, you see nice beachfront homes out here, too, but the feeling is more open and accessible. For one thing, there are no buildings on the ocean side of A1A along Delray's lengthy public strand.

During peak season, Delray Beach gets wild but not crazy, perhaps because its roots are solidly Midwestern. Delray takes its name from a suburb of Detroit. The original plots were sold through advertisements in Michigan newspapers in the 1890s. A century later, we'd compare it to Capitola, California, another beach town of comparable dimensions that is well-mannered and fun, with a touch of arty gentility to balance out the sandy side of the ledger. They haven't over-commercialized the beachfront at Delray. Moreover, it is a safe, well-patrolled stretch of sand. Though Delray Beach lies only 45 miles north of Miami, its residents and visi-

THE DIAMOND COAST

THE DIAMOND COAST

© PARKE PUTERBAUGH

Delray Beach Public Beach

tors move around in comparative tranquility. You can take a moonlight walk on the beach, for instance, without fear of mugging.

The renovated downtown, with its Old School Square, gives off a homey village feel. A VFW hall, Christian Science reading room, and newly expanded public library are all within walking distance of the beach.

One of Delray's most unique attractions is the **Morikami Museum and Japanese Gardens** (4000 Morikami Park Road, 561/495-0233). Located three miles west of town, it's a living tribute to a clump of Japanese settlers who came here in the early 1900s to establish an agricultural community. Their plan was to farm tropical plants, but the commune ("Yamato Colony") didn't pan out. However, one tenacious pilgrim, George Sukeji Morikami, eventually grew rich from his pineapple plantation. He donated the 200-acre property to the town in the 1970s, along with its meticulous gardens, waterfalls, bonsai trees, nature trail, and two galleries filled with Japanese cultural artifacts. Strict adherence to customs extends to visitors, who are asked to remove their shoes before entering.

For more information, contact the Greater Delray Beach Chamber of Commerce, 64 Southeast 5th Avenue, Delray Beach, FL 33483, 561/278-0424, www.delraybeach.com.

BEACHES

What does Delray do so well to gain the unabashed praise of a couple of jaded beach bums? For starters, a local lifeguard told us that a window between the Bahamian Islands allows swell to come through unimpeded here, making for a rare stretch of decent surf along this length of coast. Moreover, the Gulf Stream swings within one and three miles of Delray Beach, depending on seasonal fluctuations. This proximity, coupled with the lack of a pier and all of the water-fouling crap it generates, makes for warm, clear, sparkling waters.

Public access to the main beach—where Atlantic Avenue meets Ocean Boulevard (A1A)—is a breeze, with more than a mile of metered parking (20 minutes for $0.25). Numerous clearly designated access points—three dozen in all, with a dune crossover and public shower at every one—lead over thickly vegetated dunes to the beach. This lengthy strand

THE DIAMOND COAST

is called **Delray Beach Public Beach.** Great spots to eat, drink, and be merry sit directly across Ocean Boulevard (A1A) from the beach, reinforcing the town's sensible philosophy of fun and good times. Sandoway Park and Anchor Park, in the 200 and 500 blocks of A1A, respectively, are part of Delray Beach's unbroken strand.

Beach activities have been segregated on the main beach so swimmers don't get whacked by surfboards and sunbathers don't get bonked by errant Frisbees. There are designated areas for swimming and sunbathing, surfing, volleyball, and boat launching. Snorkelers and divers, take note: the remnants of a 1902 shipwreck lie a few hundred yards offshore at the south end of Delray Beach.

An able contingent of EMT-trained and U.S. Lifeguard Association–certified guards patrols the main beach from several towers. Delray's lifeguards are legendary, having won national competitions, including a gold medal in "line pull rescue." With a staff of about 30 competing against teams of 500 or so from Los Angeles, Delaware, and the Jersey Shore, that is an amazing feat.

The city also maintains **Atlantic Dunes Park,** which lies 1.5 miles south of Atlantic Avenue, via a leasing arrangement with Palm Beach County. It's a small beach with one lifeguard stand and metered parking.

21 DELRAY BEACH PUBLIC BEACH

 BEST (

Location: 0.5 mile in either direction along Ocean Boulevard (A1A) from its intersection with Atlantic Avenue in Delray Beach
Parking/Fees: metered street parking
Hours: 24 hours (except no beach parking north of Atlantic Avenue 11 P.M.-5 A.M.)
Facilities: concessions, lifeguards, restrooms, and showers
Contact: Delray Beach Public Beach, 561/243-7352; recording on beach conditions, 561/272-3224

22 ATLANTIC DUNES PARK

Location: 1.5 miles south of Atlantic Boulevard, in Delray Beach
Parking/Fees: metered street parking
Hours: 24 hours
Facilities: lifeguards, restrooms, and showers
Contact: Delray Beach Parks and Recreation Department, 561/243-7250; recording on beach conditions, 561/272-3224

RECREATION AND ATTRACTIONS

- **Bike/Skate Rentals:** A1A Bike Rentals, 1155 East Atlantic Avenue, Delray Beach, 561/243-2453
- **Boat Cruise:** Intracoastal Cruises, Veterans Park, Delray Beach, 561/243-0686
- **Dive Shop:** Force E, 2181 North Federal Highway, Boca Raton, 561/368-0555
- **Ecotourism:** Gumbo Limbo Environmental Complex, 1801 North Ocean Boulevard, Boca Raton, 561/338-1473
- **Fishing Charters:** Find-a-Fish Charter, 2699 Northeast 25th Terrace, Boca Raton, 561/338-0999
- **Marina:** Ocean Inlet Marina, 9600 North Ocean Boulevard, Ocean Ridge, 561/966-6646
- **Rainy-Day Attraction:** Morikami Museum, 4000 Morikami Park Road, Delray Beach, 561/495-0233
- **Shopping/Browsing:** downtown Delray Beach, along Atlantic Avenue (S.R. 806), 0.5 mile east of Ocean Boulevard (A1A)
- **Surf Shop:** Nomad Surf & Sport, 4655 North Ocean Boulevard, Boca Raton, 561/272-2882
- **Vacation Rentals:** Artistic Assets II Rentals, 1–5 Northeast 7th Street, Delray Beach, 561/302-1033

ACCOMMODATIONS

There are a few high-styled accommodations in Delray, most notably the **Delray**

Beach Marriott (10 North Ocean Boulevard, 561/274-3211, $$$$). This arrival took over from a Holiday Inn that formerly occupied the site. A new building has been added to the refurbished old one, and the location couldn't be more prime: Atlantic Avenue at Ocean Boulevard (A1A).

The spirit of Delray Beach is best presented in the low-scaled motels and rental apartments that abound on and near the beach. The **Bermuda Inn** (64 South Ocean Boulevard, 561/276-5288, $) is typical of the pleasantly unfancy lodgings that are available. Its 20 units include motel rooms and apartments, and the ocean is well within view from the dry side of A1A. There's a small pool on the premises. As the sunbaked, gold-chained proprietor said, "You don't get lost in the shuffle here." The Bermuda is located next door to Boston's at the Beach, a beach bar and restaurant that's as fun as they come. Talk about convenience!

The **Sea Aire** (1715 South Ocean Boulevard, 561/276-7491, $) is a similar kettle of fish: villas and apartments, each with a kitchen. Book early at both because they are popular with a regular clientele. The **Colony Hotel** (525 East Atlantic Avenue, 561/276-4123, $$) is a holdover from the days of the senior influx. This lovely, three-story wooden structure (circa 1926) lies a few blocks up Atlantic Avenue from the beach. Even if you don't stay here, the Colony's rattan-dominated lobby is worth a gander. If you do—and it is only open in peak season (January–April)—breakfast and dinner come with the room tariff, and you can take a crack at a shuffleboard tournament.

At the more secluded south end of town, **Wright by the Sea** (1901 South Ocean Boulevard, 561/278-3355, $$$) is the sort of low-scale, non-franchise motel you used to see all over the East Coast of Florida.

COASTAL CUISINE

Driving down Atlantic Avenue to the beach, we spotted a popular diner called **Doc's All-American** (10 North Swinton Avenue,

561/278-3627, $). We dropped in for some remedial comfort food. To treat hunger pangs, we prescribe a visit to Doc's, followed by a half-hour rest on the beach before swimming. Doc's lunch treats included blackened mahimahi sandwiches and milkshakes.

If you want to start your day in a healthy way, head west to **Blood's Hammock Groves** (4600 Linton Boulevard, 561/498-3400, $). This family-owned institution dispenses fresh fruit and fresh juices, and jams and jellies from its kitchen. At one time, groves like these defined the look of Florida.

On the ocean, the obvious choice is **Boston's at the Beach** (40 South Ocean Boulevard, 561/278-3364, $$), which has an airy outdoor patio that catches the breezes wafting off the ocean. It is also the hottest nightspot. You can grab lunch or dinner. We've enjoyed Caesar salad and blackened swordfish at Boston's. Better yet, Boston's serves what might be the best grouper sandwich we've ever had—a big, flaky fillet spilling out of the bun.

If you're up for something more gourmet, just two blocks from the beach, along East Atlantic Avenue, are two acclaimed restaurants, **Thirty Two East** (32 East Atlantic Avenue, 561/276-7868, $$$) has a retro feel but contemporary creativity in entrees like sauteed hog snapper with brown caper butter and spaghetti squash, and cumin-encrusted tuna with avocado salsa. The other is **Dakotah 624** (270 East Atlantic Avenue, 561/274-6244, $$$), which has the same retro-martini bar look, but transcends that affectation with inventive fare and wall-to-wall beautiful people. The cuisine here, prepared by Chef Ron Radabaugh, won the 2002 DiRoNA ("Distinguished Restaurants of North America") Award.

NIGHTLIFE

Where there's interesting nightlife, we'll write about it, but we won't force the issue when there's only the blare of dance clubs or the tinkling of ivories in a piano bar to report. We'd just as soon get a good night's sleep. But

THE DIAMOND COAST

Delray Beach kept us up way past our bedtime, because it's our favorite place to hang in Palm Beach County.

Delray's best live music venue is the **Back Room** (16 East Atlantic Avenue, 561/243-9110), which books local and national acts for reasonable cover charges (under $10). During the week we were in the area, the Back Room hosted a lineup that included John Mayall and NRBQ, among others. The ambience is as ramshackle and unpretentious as, well, the music of NRBQ itself. Sofas line the walls, there's a small dance area, and only beer and wine are sold.

On the beachfront, **Boston's at the Beach** (40 South Ocean Boulevard, 561/278-3364) dresses up in all things Beantown. Its walls are covered with signed photos of Carl "Yaz" Yastrzemski, Bobby Orr's hockey sticks, and street signs for Yawkey Way and Landsdowne (the road behind "the Green Monster," the infamous left-field wall at Fenway Park). You can just imagine what it was like here when the Red Sox won the World Series (finally!) in 2004.

But Boston's is more than just another sports-themed bar. It is a place where people interface giddily at the lengthy happy hour (4 P.M.–8 P.M.) and stick around for the occasional live band upstairs at Boston's Upper Deck. Monday is "Reggae Night" at Boston's, featuring a house band. On a Sunday afternoon we walked in as an old Bruce Springsteen song ("Growin' Up") was being played. The whole place was popping with a line-out-the-door crowd of beach people. In our book, it doesn't get any better than that.

On another weekend visit (yes, we get down here a lot), we lucked into an "Island Sunday" celebration (held every Sunday 3–7 P.M.). It featured food specials (conch fritters, jerk chicken) and a band that was playing—as if they were expecting us—"Hotel California" when we walked in the door. Speaking of hotels, one of the most enticing places to stay in Delray Beach is right here at Boston's. **The Boston House** is a 13-room annex to the restaurant and bar. No need for a designated driver!

Boston's also offers the enticement and opportunity of a midnight stroll on the public beach across the street.

Highland Beach

Though there's nothing much a nonresident can do here—i.e., go to the beach or even book a room (with one exception)—we feel duty bound to mention Highland Beach. It is a town of 4,200 with as much ocean frontage as Delray Beach and Boca Raton—though neither of those communities walled off its major resource for its residents' exclusive use.

Highland Beach lies between Delray and Boca on A1A. It's a hidden community of private homes and estates, and one can only imagine the marvelous coastal hammock that was razed to make way for all the nondescript construction. Interestingly, the only commercial property in Highland Beach is a beachside **Holiday Inn** (2809 South Ocean Boulevard, at least 278-6241, $$$), which is up toward the Delray Beach side of town.

For more information, contact the Palm Beach County Convention and Visitors Bureau, 1555 Palm Lakes Boulevard, Suite 800, West Palm Beach, FL 33401, 561/233-3000, www.palmbeachfl.com.

Boca Raton

The name of the town is Boca Raton, but we have taken to calling it "Boca Right On!" The town deserves a hearty high-five for the smart things it's done with its beachfront. Before the real-estate land grab and condo-building boom began in earnest, Boca Raton (pop. 78,500) had the uncommon foresight to buy its beach. It did this with bond money raised via referendums dating back to the early 1970s. It has been money well spent. The beaches belong to the residents of Boca Raton. Not coincidentally, the paved bike trail that runs beside A1A from Boca Raton to Delray Beach

GUMBO LIMBO NATURE CENTER

It started as the dream of a high-school science teacher who wanted a place to educate and expose young minds to the biological wonders of Old Florida. It grew to become a reality through the combined efforts of the city of Boca Raton, the Palm Beach County School Board, and Florida Atlantic University. Inside the main building at the Gumbo Limbo Nature Center in Boca Raton are exhibits about the flora and fauna of the Florida coast. Can't-miss winners for the kids include huge sea turtle shells and alligator skulls. Computers allow youngsters to call up a particular class of coastal plants and animals and get a brief rundown on their physical characteristics. Fact-filled murals and cases bring this world to life in ways that are interesting to laypeople, beach bums, and schoolchildren alike.

From the main building, a left turn goes out to a boardwalk trail through the coastal hammock. Proceeding straight to the Intracoastal Waterway brings you to the underwater tanks – saltwater basins that harbor sharks, loggerhead turtles, and other live specimens. Beginning on the right side of the building, the North Trail passes a butterfly garden, a bird blind, grass flats, and mangroves. The Coastal Hammock Trail winds through a peaceful forest whose calm is interrupted only by the chirping of songbirds and lapping of water against the mangrove-lined shores of the Intracoastal Waterway. The word "hammock" derives from a Native American term meaning "shady place." It is a unique environment in that the microclimate found on the narrow strip of land between ocean and estuary allows for plant species that are otherwise found only in the tropics.

Our favorite among the many tree species native to the hammock is the strangler fig. Its roots propagate near the bases of tree trunks. Using the host tree for structure and support, the strangler fig grows upward by encircling and eventually "strangling" the host. It is nature's equivalent of the sleeper hold employed by some professional wrestlers. The site of two trees bound together in twisting, turning agony, parasite and host desperately arching skyward for light, offers mute testimony to nature's struggle for survival using ingenious adaptive techniques.

The literal high point of the Coastal Hammock Trail is the 40-foot observation tower, which protrudes above the top of the canopy. Only the green crowns of the trees are visible. As is the case in the Amazonian rain forest, all the photosynthetic action occurs in the canopy. Below is a sunless void with little understory or ground cover. Up on top lies a whole other world, as becomes clear from the observation tower. The only thing taller than the tree tops is the outline of distant condos. And to think all of Florida's coastline once looked like this.

Gumbo Limbo Nature Center is an incredible facility that should be visited by all. Best of all, it is free and open daily 9 A.M.-4 P.M. (except Sunday, when it opens at noon). It sure beats a wasted day spent haunting strip malls along Federal Highway.

For more information, contact Gumbo Limbo Nature Center, 1801 North Ocean Boulevard, Boca Raton, FL 33432, 561/338-1473, www.ns1.fau.edu/gumbo.

THE DIAMOND COAST

is as pleasant and green a passage as you'll find in South Florida.

Boca Raton is a link in the chain of bulging, burgeoning South Florida cities that are quickly growing together into a giant coastal metropolis. Boca is the last gasp of Palm Beach–style chic before you cross into Broward County, where you're greeted by the less-gilded Deerfield Beach and the altogether ghastly Pompano Beach. Boca Raton is a riches-to-rags-to-riches story. Established by Addison Mizner—the renowned architect largely responsible for the Mediterranean style with which Florida is identified—Boca Raton went from glamourville to ghost town with the collapse of the stock market in the 1930s.

A classic failed city, Boca Raton's population had declined to less than 1,000 by the early 1950s. Now it is nearly 80 times that, having benefited from the real-estate boom that has resounded all over South Florida.

Boca Raton has been swamped by a rising tide of wealthy retirees, second-home *nouveau riche,* real-estate speculators, and Europeans taking advantage of favorable exchange rates. Given its rapid growth scenario and emphasis on wealth, Boca Raton is not a very warm or interesting place, especially if you're outside the social whirl. It is a city without much history, having been virtually rebuilt and repopulated since the 1970s. The inland thoroughfares are jammed with cars and lined with fancy Italian restaurants and upscale malls.

Along A1A, however, Boca Raton shows a completely different side, having demonstrated rare good judgment in allocating revenue to the best investment a coastal community can make: beach acquisition and preservation.

For more information, contact the Greater Boca Raton Chamber of Commerce, 1800 North Dixie Highway, Boca Raton, FL 33432, 561/395-4433, www.bocaratonchamber.com.

BEACHES

Virtually the entirety of Boca Raton's beach belongs to the municipality. From Spanish River south to Palmetto Park Road, it's all city-owned. We were told by an elderly gatekeeper that Boca claims ownership of more beach (five miles of sandy splendor) than any other municipality in the United States. These are all beautiful, well-manicured parks set amid a stunning tangle of vegetation and trees.

Unless you live in Boca Raton, in which case you're entitled to use the three beach parks for a $31 annual fee, it will cost dearly to park at the beach. The charge for nonresidents is $16 per car on weekdays and $18 on weekends and holidays. That is a stiff tariff, and it means there is essentially no place where those who don't live here can use the beaches of Boca without paying. But if you use the beach all day, it's not such a bad deal for a carload of folks, being equivalent to the price of a few tickets to the latest horrific action-adventure flick playing at the local mall multiplex.

The money no doubt goes to fund not only the usual maintenance costs but also the re-nourishing of the beaches. Yes, although the beachfront parks of Boca Raton are lovely, complete with lighted boardwalks, picnic tables, and gazebos that overlook the ocean, the beach itself can get pretty skimpy. We've seen dump trucks depositing loads of coarse, dark fill-sand on the beach while bulldozers spread it around. To be honest, it looked more like Midwestern sod than beach sand. On our latest visit, Boca's beach strand looked much healthier and we enjoyed a pleasant early-fall swim at South Beach Park after a run along Boca Raton's beach-paralleling asphalt walkway.

The parks themselves, stretching a few hundred yards from the ocean to the Intracoastal Waterway, preserve the coastal hammock communities that existed before these barrier islands were descended upon by European settlers. The beachside jungle is thick with coconut palms, sea grape, and saw palmetto. The coastal hammock begins with mangroves at the edge of the Intracoastal Waterway and then becomes a rain forest–like area of tall trees—predominantly cabbage palms, mastics, pigeon plum, and paradise tree (see the *Gumbo Limbo Nature Center* sidebar).

Boca's 3.5-mile beachfront is broken into three parks. From north to south, they are **Spanish River Park, Red Reef Park,** and **South Beach Park.** Red Reef boasts a man-made offshore reef. The Boca Raton Artificial Reef consists of six reef "modules." Each reef comprises 25 limestone boulders weighing five tons apiece and arranged in two layers. In all, there are 600 tons of limestone. Some 95 fish species and 76 invertebrate species have been cataloged on the reef. Red Reef also has an executive golf course attached to it, though we're much fonder of the boardwalk.

Spanish River Park consists of 95 acres, on which there is 0.3 mile of beach, five covered shelters, picnic tables and grills, volleyball courts, a 40-foot observation tower, and a neat little nature trail.

At South Beach Pavilion, there's a no-fee overlook with a few parking spaces that lies where Palmetto Park Road dead-ends into A1A. Folks turn out early to grab a seat and contemplate the dawn's early light or bring a bagged lunch at midday to this special spot. It's something of a community gathering place, and you see a cross-section of humanity, from old men working crossword puzzles to rawboned young surfers discussing the waves kicked up by a storm out in the Caribbean. On a recent visit we overheard two sharp surfer dudes trying to pick up a pair of hot babes in scanty Abercrombie & Fitch outfits. The conversation was predictably awkward and almost beside the point. We really decided we loved the place when two outwardly tough-looking guys chided a woman for losing patience because traffic wasn't moving quickly enough around the circle for her liking. "Don't be impatient," one counseled. "This is Florida!"

The last link in Boca's beach chain is **South Inlet Park,** a county-run facility that lies just south of Camino Real Bridge. It's is a safe, lifeguarded place to spread a beach blanket, although with only 850 feet of "developed" beach, not the best Boca Raton has to offer. The real calling card at South Inlet is Buck's Cave, a great snorkeling spot with caves beneath a protruding shelf of wormrock.

SPANISH RIVER PARK

Location: 3001 North Ocean Boulevard (A1A), two miles north of Palmetto Park Road in Boca Raton
Parking/Fees: free for Boca Raton residents with beach permits ($31 per vehicle annually); $16 per car for nonresidents ($8 on weekends)
Hours: 8 A.M.-sunset
Facilities: lifeguards, restrooms, picnic tables, and showers

Contact: Boca Raton Parks and Recreation Department, 561/393-7810

RED REEF PARK

Location: 1400 North Ocean Boulevard (A1A), one mile north of Palmetto Park Road in Boca Raton
Parking/Fees: free for Boca Raton residents with beach permits ($31 per vehicle annually); $16 per car for nonresidents ($8 on weekends)
Hours: 8 A.M.-10 P.M.
Facilities: lifeguards, restrooms, picnic tables, showers, and a visitors center at Gumbo Limbo Nature Center
Contact: Boca Raton Parks and Recreation Department, 561/393-7810

SOUTH BEACH PARK

Location: Ocean Boulevard (A1A) at Northeast 4th Street in Boca Raton
Parking/Fees: free for Boca Raton residents with beach permits ($31 per vehicle annually); $16 per car for nonresidents ($18 on weekends)
Hours: 8 A.M.-sunset
Facilities: lifeguards, restrooms, picnic tables, and showers
Contact: Boca Raton Parks and Recreation Department, 561/393-7810

SOUTH INLET PARK

Location: 1298 South Ocean Boulevard, on A1A in Boca Raton
Parking/Fees: $3 per car ($5 on weekends and holidays)
Hours: sunrise-sunset
Facilities: lifeguards, restrooms, picnic tables, and showers
Contact: Palm Beach County Parks and Recreation Department, 561/966-6631

ACCOMMODATIONS

The resort of first choice in Boca is the **Boca Raton Resort & Club** (501 East Camino Real, 561/395-3000, $$$$). This Gold Coast grande dame was originally built by Addison Mizner as "The Cloisters" back in the mid-1920s. With its beveled French doors, Romanesque archways, Oriental rugs, Venetian lobby, and Spanish oil paintings, it's no wonder Mizner went bankrupt and skipped town (prompting the name change). In addition to the original Cloisters, the resort encompasses the Boca Raton Beach Club, the Boca Country Club, and the hot-pink, 27-story Tower—963 rooms in all—plus dining options that run from a rooftop restaurant in The Tower to the more atmospheric and formal Cathedral Dining Room in the Cloisters.

Entering the grounds of the Boca Raton Resort is like being transported to an earlier time when the world moved more slowly to the easy rustle of Floridian breezes. Set in a residential neighborhood, it is a huge but largely hidden (from the street) wonder. The rooms are inviting and classy without being ostentatious, and the beds are as comfortable as any we've encountered. On the premises you can savor the landscaping and architecture from a bench on a covered walkway. Inside, you can admire the furnishings or bone up on your Mizner minutiae, particularly the curious tale of Addison Mizner and his pet monkey, which is documented in words and pictures. Mizner was, apparently, the Michael Jackson of his day in that he was rarely seen without his pet spider monkey, Johnnie Brown. The two were inseparable and when death did them part, the monkey was buried at Via Mizner in Palm Beach.

What you'll find at the Boca Raton Resort, above and beyond the commodious surroundings, is something subtler that cannot be seen with the naked eye. It's the measured, unostentatious way that old money does things—and has done thing for many decades—in Florida.

The **Radisson Bridge Resort** (999 East Camino Real, 561/368-9500, $$$) is an 11-story hotel bathed in "Boca pink." It reposes beside a winding bridge at the point where Camino Real crosses the Intracoastal Waterway. The units, especially the two-room suites, are large enough to feel homey and comfortable. Many overlook the waterway and the ocean. From the Radisson, you can easily walk to the beach at South Inlet Park or take off along the bike path that runs all up the way to Delray Beach.

The **Ocean Lodge** (531 North Ocean Boulevard, 561/395-7772, $$) is cut from plainer cloth, but it's a clean, affordable, and quiet small motel directly across from the beach. In that regard, it is fairly unique in Boca Raton. Even the Boca Raton Resort & Club doesn't have such ready beach access. Each room has two double beds and a dining area. Room rates range $50–100, depending on the time of year, and weekly rates are offered as well.

COASTAL CUISINE

By and large, the dining scene in Boca Raton is elegant, formal, and pricey. There's little out on the beach, but gourmet French and Italian restaurants abound along Federal Highway (U.S. 1), Palmetto Park Road, and other inland corridors. All aim at offering an upscale (read: expensive) dining experience. For Italian, try **Ecco** (499 South Federal Highway, 561/338-8780, $$$$), **Josephine's** (5700 North Federal Highway, 561/988-0668, $$$), and—especially worth singling out, given this book's orientation toward all things oceanic—**Nick's Italian Fishery** (One Boca Place, 2255 Glades Road, 561/994-2201, $$$). At Nick's, go for the freshest catch of the day, grilled over oak. For French cuisine, the top contenders for your gold card's attention are **La Vieille Maison** (770 East Palmetto Park Road, 561/391-6701, $$$$) and **Marcel's** (1 Ocean Boulevard, 561/362-9911, $$$). We'd recommend snapper with fresh herbs at the former and shrimp with curry and saffron at the latter. And that's just a sampling; many more fine continental eateries are sprinkled around Boca Raton like Godiva chocolates.

Incidentally, if you happen to be in town on Tuesday, **Carmen's Top of the Bridge Restaurant** at the Radisson Bridge Resort (999 East Camino Real, 561/368-9500, $$$) puts out a bountiful seafood buffet for $22.95. We gorged on raw oysters, steamed shrimp, and crab legs—and that's just for starters, because you also get to order a seafood entree. We are not the sort to high-five each other, especially over food, but we were doing just that at Carmen's, which offers not only good food but also a great view.

Boca Raton abounds with fine restaurants of every ethnic description. A local steered us to **Mido's Japanese Restaurant** (508 Viaduct de Palmas, 561/361-9683, $$), where they lay out healthy and sizable servings of sushi that are especially affordable at lunch. In fact, the sushi lunch special at Mido's is one of the best bargains in Boca.

NIGHTLIFE

We are reformed party animals who have hung up our boogie shoes, more or less for good. At least part of the reason has to do with the changing environment for nightlife in the 20-odd years since we began, ahem, "researching" beaches. We simply cannot stomach a lot of contemporary dance music and the sterile, pretentious clubs where this garbage is played. Dismayed by the decibel-plagued dance clubs that proliferate in South Florida, we've got particularly grim memories of ringing ears and painful hangovers in Boca Raton.

Club Boca, a dance club we'd dutifully checked out on our visits because of its popularity, shut down a few years back. It reopened as Radius, a "hot networking spot," but the fickle herd cooled on that, too. Don't look now, but **Club Boca** (7000 West Palmetto Park Road, 561/392-3747) is back in its original space and little has changed. Beautiful but vapid night people crowd the dance floor, which deejays flood with the robotic rhythms of hip-hop, rap, dance, and trance music. If this sort of scene floats your boat, you can't sail any higher than Club Boca.

Fortunately, the entertainment options in Boca Raton aren't limited to this sort of played-out scene. We were drawn to the **Surf Cafe** (395 NE Spanish River Blvd., 561/392-1965), which has the feel of a Southern California surf bar, complete with nonstop surfing videos. They've got live rock bands on weekends and a pool tournament on Mondays. **Gatsby's** (5970 SW 18th Street, 561/393-3900) is a friendly, upscale bar that has weathered the changeable Boca Raton scene. If you're into cigars, martinis, big-screen TVs, and chatter, Gatsby's has your number. **Gigi's** (346 Plaza Real, 561/368-4488) is a thriving French bistro and tavern that houses a separate Oyster Bar and Cafe. Gigi's recently won a local award for "Best Meet Market."

Nightspots tend to come and go in Boca Raton, so check local listings in *New Times* and *City Link* (free weeklies available in boxes all over town) for the latest arrivals and hottest scenes.

FORT LAUDERDALE, MIAMI BEACH, AND THE GOLD COAST

The adjacent South Florida counties of Miami-Dade and Broward are what most Americans think of when the conversation turns to Florida. Before all the other coastal counties seriously pursued tourism as an economic boon, this area aggressively marketed itself as the "Gold Coast." While the Gold Coast has lost some of its luster since those heady days when Henry Flagler's East Coast Railway beat a path to Miami Beach, it's still the prime Florida destination for travelers from all over the world.

Fort Lauderdale and Miami Beach are the most prominent nuggets on the Gold Coast, but there is a diverse array of smaller communities lying between and around them. These range from modest Deerfield Beach to condo-filled Pompano Beach to development-crazed Hallandale to suddenly booming Sunny Isles Beach to low-slung Lauderdale-by-the-Sea. Other beach communities—Dania, Hollywood, Surfside, and North Miami Beach—still draw retirees and older visitors, harking back to the good old days of Jackie Gleason, Lawrence Welk, and Wolfie Cohen.

Fort Lauderdale has always possessed a patina of class and upward mobility, but it became so obsessed with appearances that it banished the collegiate Spring Break tradition from its beaches in the mid-1990s. Somewhat sadly, the fun seems to be setting on Fort Lauderdale, as huge, gloomy new residential towers are overtaking great stretches of its formerly accessible beachfront "Strip."

By contrast, Miami Beach—and especially that international hotbed of sun, sand, sin, and revelry known as South Beach—doesn't ever want the party to end. Sparked by South Beach's renaissance in the 1990s, the Miami area is currently experiencing another intense building boom. How high (or low) can they go? Down on the Gold Coast, as the song goes, the future's so bright you gotta wear shades.

© PARKE PUTERBAUGH

Deerfield Beach

Deerfield Beach (pop. 66,000) stretches from its pretty municipal beach onto the mainland. The city's inland area is another link—albeit one of the more appealing ones—in the South Florida megalopolis that runs from West Palm Beach to south Miami. In size, appearance and layout, Deerfield most closely resembles Delray Beach, in neighboring Palm Beach County.

On the beach, Deerfield boasts a low-key scene that serves all comers. You'll find casual restaurant-lounges with outdoor decks; a newish pier that ranks among the East Coast's finest; and a green, mile-long beach park that attracts everyone from testosterone-fueled surfers to the newspaper-reading elderly.

Deerfield's beach district hugs A1A, which makes a few 90° turns through the area, briefly running east-west along 2nd Street. This is where the center, such as it is, can be found. People-watching yields a gamut of ages and types, from old folks who gather on the boardwalk to play games and make small talk to young families with children straining at the leash to European travelers looking for sun and fun in South Florida. Unlike Fort Lauderdale and Miami Beach, you feel out of range of citified dangers and distractions in Deerfield Beach. Unlike Palm Beach and Boca Raton, you don't sense the oppressive hand of big money, either. It is, in short, a modest and likable beach town.

Deerfield Beach has maintained its essential qualities over time, which has not always been an easy task. At one point, developers and county-government allies were conspiring to convert Deerfield into another segment of what may someday be an unbroken wall of condominium and hotel towers along the South Florida coast. In 1998 former Deerfield Beach mayor Jean Robb waged a campaign opposing construction of a proposed seven-story luxury hotel called the Deerfield Ocean Grand.

"We like to say we're the most underrated and beautiful beach in South Florida, but they're trying to change all that," she told us.

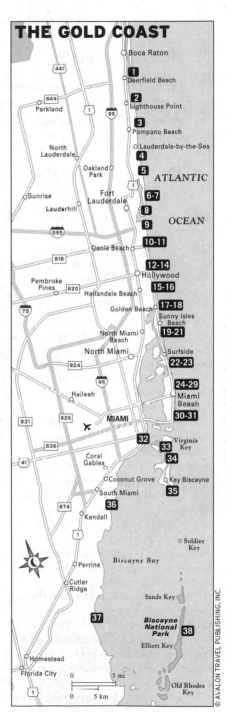

THE GOLD COAST

© AVALON TRAVEL PUBLISHING, INC.

THE GOLD COAST

BEST BEACHES

◖ Deerfield Public Beach: Top 25 (page 221)

◖ Fort Lauderdale City Beach (Central Beach): Best for People-Watching (page 235)

◖ Hollywood Beach (Central Beach): Best for People-Watching (page 246)

◖ Haulover Beach: Best Nude Beach (page 255)

◖ Lummus Park/South Beach: Top 25, Best for People-Watching, Best Nude Beach (page 265)

◖ Biscayne National Park: Best for Diving and Snorkeling (page 280)

"They want to destroy the main beach parking lot and fire station and give it to some developer to put in a 260-room hotel." Not to mention an upscale retail mall, as if there aren't already way too many of those.

The riled townsfolk formed a grassroots "Save Our Beach" committee and took their protest to the county commission. It must've worked, because there is no Deerfield Ocean Grand—just the same handful of beachfront hotels that have been here for years (Howard Johnson, Embassy Suites) and many smaller ones.

To be fair there was another side to this argument, put to us by a local lifeguard (of all unlikely pro-development boosters). He pointed out that the Deerfield Ocean Grand was a classy project that might have economically enhanced the community. While we're all for slow growth—and even no growth in certain instances—it is shortsighted to be a knee-jerk naysayer all the time, since some projects can admittedly brighten and improve a community. But Deerfield Beach isn't blighted, just low-key, and it doesn't need pretentious constructions like those that are currently going up along (and ruining) Fort Lauderdale's municipal beach. Therefore, we wish the Deerfield Beach preservationists well in this and future battles. For now, it remains a neat, unassuming little beach at a bend in the road.

For more information, contact the Greater Deerfield Beach Chamber of Commerce, 1601 East Hillsboro Boulevard, Deerfield Beach, FL 33441, 954/427-1050, www.deerfieldchamber.com.

BEACHES

Deerfield Beach owns its beach and pier, and this ownership is what gives **Deerfield Public Beach** the look and feel of a real community beach. Watched over by nine lifeguard towers, the public beach extends for one mile, with the center of the action being the 900-foot Deerfield Beach International Fishing Pier. (What makes a fishing pier "international"? Is it the fact that fish that swim up from the Caribbean?) A grassy greenbelt, wide wooden boardwalk, and rows of palm trees line the back of the beach. Benches, thatched-roof huts, and gazebos, and patterned brick walkways add to the park-like ambience. It is a pretty beach at any time of day, but especially in late afternoon, as the sun starts setting.

The beach is informally divided into three areas: north of the pier ("North Beach"); from the pier south to a beach-hogging, coral-colored monstrosity called the Cove Beach Club ("Main Beach"); and south of the Cove ("South Beach"). North Beach draws a recreation-minded crowd of youthful surfers and volleyball players. South Beach is where you head to escape the numbers. Main Beach is a happy medium between old and young, stoked and

© PARKE PUTERBAUGH

Deerfield Public Beach

laid-back. You'll see families playing Scrabble or checkers on picnic tables and elderly retirees reading newspapers from folding chairs set up in the shade of palm trees. Others gaze beatifically out to sea, as if mesmerized by the sight—and well they should be.

Deerfield Public Beach is lifeguarded 9 A.M.–5 P.M. daily. Snorkeling is permitted within 50 yards of shoreline and surfing is allowed north of the pier and south of Tower #9. Deerfield Public Beach is steep-faced and, in 2005, looked to have narrowed since our last visit. At that time, there were bulldozer tracks all over the beach, indicating a renourishment project. Well, the slow but steady drumbeat of erosion, added to what was instantly stripped away by recent hurricanes, will necessitate another expensive sand infusion before long—that is, if funds can be found to repeat this Sisyphus-like maneuver in our cash-strapped age.

There's roughly a mile of metered public parking in Deerfield Beach, which will eat up five quarters an hour (come with a roll of them). A nickel will fetch you a whopping two minutes. The meter charges are enforced 6 A.M.–11 P.M.

and parking is prohibited outside those hours. Concessionaires rent cabanas, beach chairs, and umbrellas. The fun and games end on the far side of Embassy Suites Resort, at SE 10th Street.

1 DEERFIELD PUBLIC BEACH

 BEST

Location: north and south of the Deerfield Beach International Fishing Pier, which is located at the east end of 2nd Street (A1A) in Deerfield Beach

Parking/Fees: metered street parking

Hours: 6 A.M.–11 P.M.

Facilities: concessions, lifeguards, restrooms, picnic tables, and showers

Contact: Deerfield Beach Parks and Recreation Department, 954/480-4412; beach conditions, 954/480-4413

ACCOMMODATIONS

The twin towers on Deerfield Beach are the **Howard Johnson Plaza Resort** (2096 NE 2nd Street, 954/428-2850, $$$) and the **Embassy Suites Deerfield Beach Resort**

(950 SE 20th Avenue, 954/426-0478, $$$$). The 35-year-old Howard Johnson, which opened for business in 1971, stills stands tall and proud at the center of the action, only steps away from a seafood dinner at Flanagan's and a leisurely stroll on the pier. In fact, it was completely renovated in 2003 and is looking better than ever.

Embassy Suites lies on a quieter stretch of A1A about a half-mile south of the pier. A huge heated pool sits in the middle of an attractive white-washed courtyard. The beach is just across the road, making it easy to hop from pool to ocean and back again (which we did one warm December morning). A free evening cocktail hour and a prepared breakfast come with the room charge, which is not inexpensive ($270–340 per night in winter, $150–190 in summer, and somewhere in between at other times of year).

Less vertically commanding, though equally proximate to the ocean, are a couple of so-called beach clubs—**Berkshire Beach Club** (500 North A1A, 954/428-1000, $$$) and **Rettger Resort Beach Club** (100 NE 20th Terrace, 954/427-7900, $$$)—where a room will set you back $100–200 a night, depending on time of year.

Beyond the high-rises and "beach clubs," a string of modest one- and two-story mom-and-pop motels line A1A. They are variously identified as "motel apartments," "efficiencies," and "resort motels," the idea being that you can check in for a night or two or book a longer stay. All bear idyllic names like Emerald Seas, Ocean Villa, Summerwind, and Tropic Isle, and they offer a break on price, if Embassy Suites and Howard Johnson are out of range. For instance, a one-bedroom room at the **Tropic Isle** (370 South A1A, 954/427-1000, $$) goes for $155 in season. April–November, rates drop to $55 per night. Who says the beach life is unaffordable?

COASTAL CUISINE

A couple of casual spots occupy the curve where A1A crooks its arm in the vicinity of the pier. The **Whale's Rib Raw Bar and Restaurant** (2031 NE 2nd Street, 954/421-8880, $$) offers everything from takeout sandwiches to baked mahimahi and seared garlic pepper tuna, with full dinners running around $12.

A few steps away is **Flanagan's Hi-Tide Seafood Bar** (2041 NE 2nd Street, 954/427-9304, $$), whose specialty is fresh Florida mahimahi sandwiches or fried "fingers" at lunch, and blackened, fried, sauteed, broiled, or grilled fillets at dinner.

Cagney's Crabhouse (950 SE 20th Avenue, 954/426-0478, $$$), the on-premises restaurant at Embassy Suites, specializes in seafood and regional cuisine but lacks the carefree, just-folks ambience of Flanagan's and the Whale's Rib.

NIGHTLIFE

Federal Highway (U.S. 1) slices through the contiguous cities of Boca Raton, Deerfield Beach, Pompano Beach, and Fort Lauderdale about a mile inland. It is a veritable assembly line of places to eat, drink, and shop for clothes, tires, toiletries, office supplies, liquor, and guns. It can be harrowing to navigate this congested stretch of asphalt, given all the bad drivers and outbreaks of road rage resulting in flashing blue lights at accident scenes with greater frequency than would seem statistically possible.

The fact is, basic needs for shelter, food, and nightlife can be met on the beach side of Deerfield Beach without having to cross the Hillsboro Boulevard bridge. Once you're parked and checked in, you don't need a car to get around Deerfield's compact beachside commercial district. Yes, there are places right on the beach to hang out and imbibe, and ocean breezes make them all the more inviting. **JB's on the Beach** (300 NW 21st Avenue, 954/571-5220) tends to get jammed. **Kahuna's Bar and Grill** (249 NE 21st Avenue, 954/725-0244), which is near a parking garage, is popular as well. Flanagan's and the Whale's Rib (see *Coastal Cuisine*) are the old-timers hereabouts. Saunter over to either for beer or booze and a platter of raw ones. (Hint: If you're staying at the Embassy Suites, drinks are free for two hours nightly.) **Big Daddy's**

Liquor Store adjoins Flanagan's—same address (2041 NE 2nd Street), different phone numbers (954/427-3920 and 954/427-9304, respectively).

Hillsboro Beach

Hillsboro Beach (pop. 3,000) is an exclusive residential community between Deerfield Beach and Hillsboro Inlet, where a drawbridge leads over to Pompano Beach. It's located almost entirely seaward of the Hillsboro Mile (A1A) along a narrow three-mile stretch modestly referred to as "Millionaire Mile."

In addition to municipal autonomy, Hillsboro Beach has a lot of low-to-the-ground homes and condos, a lighthouse (dating back to 1907), and a private marina. The town is similar to Highland Beach, up in adjacent Palm Beach County, in that it lacks much commercial business—with one notable exception, the Seabonay Beach Resort. As in Highland Beach, there's absolutely no beach access for anyone who doesn't own property here.

For more information, contact the Greater Fort Lauderdale Convention and Visitors Bureau, 1850 Eller Drive, Suite 303, Fort Lauderdale, FL 33316, 954/765-4466 or 800/22-SUNNY, www.sunny.com.

ACCOMMODATIONS

The **Seabonay Beach Resort** (1159 Hillsboro Mile, 954/427-2525, $$) is a six-story "apartment hotel" consisting of standard hotel rooms and one- and two-bedroom units with full cooking facilities. Outfitted with a pool deck and exercise room, it's a good hideaway for couples or families who want a relaxing vacation on the Gold Coast while avoiding its bustle and clamor.

Pompano Beach

Pompano Beach (pop. 88,000) is Fort Lauderdale's poor relation, a red-headed stepchild that lacks the brains, class, and charisma of its neighboring city. To draw a West Coast parallel, Pompano Beach is to Fort Lauderdale as Oakland is to San Francisco. Along the beach, Pompano Beach is an unappealing wall of faded resorts and drab condo towers. It's even worse along Federal Highway (U.S. 1), an endless procession of stores and signs, strip malls, and strip clubs.

Pompano Beach's 17 square miles used to be farmland, but it's been a long time since anything but condos and shopping malls have sprouted here. Incorporated in 1906 as the inland town of Pompano (after the fish), it annexed 3.5 miles of beach to become Pompano Beach in 1947. The city was one of the first to welcome and encourage condominium construction—the first oceanfront condo was built here in 1960—and it has paid a huge aesthetic price for making this deal with the devil.

On our latest pass through Pompano Beach, a sign along A1A announces that a Sonata Beach Club will soon be going up, and a project called Europa By the Sea—talk about wishful thinking—is under construction. Apparently they green-light every project presented to them, resulting in an unbroken wall of condominiums that's visually staggering (and not in a good way). Arguably such constructions have rescued Pompano from its down-at-the-heels look. But that rationalization is about the best light you can cast on it.

In addition to a plague of condos and malls, latter-day Pompano Beach exists to serve the prurient interests of Broward County, offering a glut of adult-oriented nightclubs along Federal Highway (see the *Naked Came the Strangers* sidebar). A more appealing side of the community exists at Hillsboro Inlet and Lighthouse Point, site of the scenic Hillsboro Lighthouse and boat marinas.

Fishing has traditionally been a big draw to Pompano Beach. More than 400 species have been identified in these warm South Florida waters. Popular catches include king mackerel, tarpon, snook, dolphin, sailfish, cobia, and the namesake pompano. However, these and

THE GOLD COAST

NAKED CAME THE STRANGERS

Okay, we're going to tell the truth, the whole truth, and nothing but the truth. We went to a strip club in Pompano Beach one night. Make that a "gentleman's club." It sounds more respectable. Real businessmen swarm to these places in suits and ties, so they've got to be respectable. It seemed like the thing to do, being that there are so many of them in South Florida and that the parking lots are often full.

The place we went to was called – well, the name's not important, since they all offer more or less the same experience. Let's just say it's on Federal Highway in Pompano Beach. We chose this particular establishment based on the fact that it looked "classy" from the outside. With its name outlined in purple neon, it appeared to be sufficiently upscale that the clientele wouldn't feel nervous about patronizing it.

In any case, we pushed open the enormous doors and were greeted by a gal who cheerfully chirped, "Hi, guys," as if to reassure us that being here was perfectly normal. Truth to tell, in this day and age dropping by a strip club is about as edgy as picking up a loaf of bread on the way home from work. We paid the five-buck cover and were escorted to a table. We chose not to sit ringside but less obtrusively positioned at a corner table a row back from the action.

"Ooh, the girls are going to pin you in here when they come around," giggled our hostess, who was wearing a thong.

What we found was not an obvious place of depravity but rather a secular house of worship where the female form was only the most visible object of adoration. Also celebrated herein were sports, rock and roll, television, alcohol, and money. Maintaining the veneer of faux gentility was a bouncer who circulated around the club in a black tuxedo, looking every inch the dapper fool. Everything was as controlled as a sterilized plant where computer chips are made. And the atmosphere was equally surreal.

The strip club we patronized is a warehouse-sized place with a giant, elevated dance floor in the center where girls take turns disrobing to excruciatingly loud music. We were bugged and bothered from the second we sat down. Cocktail waitresses circled the joint, forcing drinks on patrons at frequent intervals: "You guys okay?" "You doin' alright here?" "Can I get you another?" "Need anything?" "Another round?" They attempted to spirit away half-full glasses so that already self-conscious voyeurs would be further shamed into handing over another $6 (plus tip) for a bottled beer. Each woman did a four-song turn on the stage, during which she'd disrobe in increments until she was dancing to AC/DC or Metallica in her birthday suit.

They also circulated on the floor, offering table dances. This led to some awkward exchanges. A pair of dancers wandered over to our table, introducing themselves and shaking our hands as if we were peers at a corporate mixer. The blond wore a skimpy red vinyl outfit, while her raven-haired partner was squeezed into a short, diaphanous dress. They offered us a "double deal" – "Just ten bucks, apiece, guys" – which we politely declined. Like car salesmen, they wouldn't take no for an answer. We could feel their moist heat as they leaned in to close the deal.

"Later," we promised, "after we've had a few more." Since we were drinking club soda, this was simply a ruse to get them to move on.

"Okay," they giggled. "We'll be back later to take your wallets!"

others have suffered precipitous declines due to overfishing, and the state of Florida has been forced to impose increasing restrictions in order to preserve existing stocks. The deck definitely does seem stacked against our piscine friends. Sonar technology has made landing fish as easy as shooting ducks in a barrel, which doesn't make sportfishing very "sporting."

Be that as it may, fishing charters can be booked in the marinas at Hillsboro Inlet. The town calls itself the "Sportfishing Capital of the World," which beats the "Strip Club Capital of South Florida" or "The Gold Coast's Condo Capital," although all three titles are accurate.

For more information, contact the Greater Pompano Beach Chamber of Commerce, 2200 East Atlantic Boulevard, Pompano Beach, FL 33064, 954/941-2940, www.pompanobeach-chamber.com.

BEACHES

The city maintains **Pompano Public Beach,** which runs for 0.6 mile along Pompano Beach Boulevard down to its intersection with Atlantic Boulevard. There's a bit of a beach strip-mall feel on Atlantic Avenue, which has some appealing small shops and is a kind of last stand for the casual, "Old Florida" look of Pompano Beach back in the day. These golden sands include Pompano Beach Municipal Pier, which juts 0.2 mile into the ocean and never closes. Surfing is allowed north of the pier.

Up toward Hillsboro Inlet, at NE 16th Street and North Ocean Boulevard (A1A), is **North Ocean Park.** On this unguarded beach, you're allowed to launch wind-driven, non-motorized watercraft such as Hobie Cats. The noisy stuff—Jet Skis, WaveRunners, and their ilk—can be launched at Alsdorf Park, on the NE 14th Street Causeway. Offshore, they've sunk 20 freighters to create an artificial reef that's a haven for fish and anglers.

In addition, Pompano Beach provides access points at street ends from NE 10th Street down to SE 8th Street. A particularly hot surfing break can be found at SE 2nd Street.

2 NORTH OCEAN PARK

Location: NE 16th Street and North Ocean Boulevard (A1A)
Parking/Fees: limited metered parking
Hours: sunrise-sunset
Facilities: restrooms, picnic tables, and showers
Contact: Pompano Beach Parks and Recreation Department, 954/786-4111; taped beach report, 954/786-4005

3 POMPANO PUBLIC BEACH

Location: 10 North Pompano Beach Boulevard, at Atlantic Avenue in Pompano Beach
Parking/Fees: metered parking lot
Hours: sunrise-sunset
Facilities: concessions, lifeguards, restrooms, picnic tables, and showers
Contact: Pompano Beach Parks and Recreation Department, 954/786-4111; taped beach report, 954/786-4005

ACCOMMODATIONS

It is beyond us why anyone would come to Pompano Beach for a vacation or retirement. We just don't see it when far preferable beachfront communities like Delray Beach, Boca Raton, Fort Lauderdale, and Miami Beach are close by. A ride down A1A will reveal an oceanfront obscured by domino rows of 20-story condos with names like Ocean Monarch. At the opposite end of the scale you might see relics like the Budget Lodge and Food Mart, with Budweiser in neon on the door; the Sea Castle Resort Inn, which makes a mockery of the word "resort"; and a Ramada Inn with its sign blown out.

By the look of it, certain of the smaller motels and chain hotels won't survive the current transformation to an all-condo community. On the positive side, **Howard Johnson Plaza Resort** (9 North Pompano Beach Boulevard, 954/781-1300, $$) is right in the heart of the action by Pompano Municipal Beach, at Atlantic Avenue

THE GOLD COAST

and Pompano Beach Boulevard. There's also a **Holiday Inn** (1350 South Ocean Boulevard, 954/941-7300, $$$) with rooms on the Atlantic Ocean and the Spanish River. Scuba diving and snorkeling equipment can be rented, and there's a dock on the river.

The **Best Western Beachcomber** (1200 South Ocean Boulevard, 954/941-7830, $$) offers such amenities as a 300-foot private beach at affordable prices. Its neighbor is a **Sheraton Four Points Hotel** (1208 South Ocean Boulevard, 954/782-5300, $$$), which gives the south end of Pompano Beach a reassuring upscale franchise presence. At the low end, you can just about name your price at any the less stellar motels in Pompano Beach, of which there are many. Just drive the main thoroughfares and look for signs of desperation.

COASTAL CUISINE

Pompano Beach doesn't have much luster of its own, so it basks in the reflected glow of Fort Lauderdale and other better-tended communities in Broward County. Unsurprisingly, it isn't the bastion of haute cuisine that Fort Lauderdale can rightly claim to be. In Pompano Beach, you'll find places with names like **Chez Porky's** (105 SW 6th Street, 954/946-5590, $$) or novelty restaurants like the **Speed Cafe** (2401 NE 15th Street, 954/783-3488, $$), where you dine on wings and beef while seated inside custom cars. Other names drawn from Pompano Beach's plain-cloth dining scene: Red's Backwoods BBQ, Ronnie B's Taste of 50's, the Briny Irish Pub, Bru's Room Wing 'N' Ribs, and the East Coast Burrito Factory. Do you get the picture?

Having said that, there are first-class meals to be had in Pompano Beach at **Darrel & Oliver's Cafe Maxx** (2601 East Atlantic Boulevard, 954/782-0606, $$$$) and **Joe's Riverside Grill** (125 North Riverside Drive, 954/941-2499, $$$). And anyone visiting South Florida absolutely has to visit **Cap's Place Island Restaurant** (2765 NE 28th Court, 954/941-0418, $$$).

Cap's is one of the oldest restaurants in South Florida, having served Old Florida–style cuisine

before it became necessary to call it that. The restaurant has a tin roof, wood walls, and cozy, low-ceilinged rooms. It's been around since 1928 and has hosted presidents (JFK, FDR) and statesmen like Winston Churchill. Cap's is accessible only by a boat that shuttles diners from a dock in Lighthouse Point (at the aforementioned address) out to Cap's island locale. Dinner is served seven nights a week, starting at 5:30 P.M. Specialties include fresh hearts of palm salad, grouper chowder, and smoked mahimahi. Our hands-down entree recommendation is the sauteed seafood platter ($23.95).

Curiously, Cap's Place is the only restaurant in Florida that harvests and serves its own hearts of palm, which are taken from the Florida state tree, the sabal palm. They'll bring out a Saran-wrapped heart of palm for you to look at, and they'll tell the story of when and how they're harvested. (For every palm they take from their tract near Lake Okeechobee, they replant two.) Truth to tell, it's not exactly delicious, offering more texture than taste.

NIGHTLIFE

Duplicate bridge is very popular among those who live in Pompano's high-rise communities. We learned that in a local publication that serves the condominium communities of Fort Lauderdale and Pompano Beach. If you want something a little livelier than an evening of cards, hit the highway—Federal Highway (U.S. 1), that is. For a more detailed accounting of Pompano Beach after dark, we herewith refer you to the *Naked Came the Strangers* sidebar.

Lauderdale-by the-Sea

Lauderdale-by-the-Sea (pop. 6,300) has the funky look and feel of a Jersey Shore beach town. We intend that as praise. By comparison to the high-rise drudgery of Pompano Beach, Lauderdale-by-the-Sea's down-to-earth bustle is refreshing. Commonsensical height restrictions give the latter the look of an unretouched, old-fashioned beach town, with lots of low-to-the-ground motels and shops.

The heart of Lauderdale-by-the-Sea ("L-B-T-S," to locals) is the North Ocean Boulevard (A1A) at Commercial Boulevard. Single-story restaurants and shops proliferate in the vicinity. A real landmark is Anglin's Pier ($3 for anglers, $1 for strollers), the only privately owned pier on Florida's East Coast. Built by the federal government as a lookout for German U-boats during World War II, the pier was deeded to the landowner after the war. Snapper, snook, mackerel, cobia, and grouper are caught here. Someone landed a 1,040-pound hammerhead shark in 1965, and they've got the picture to prove it. Talk about catch of the day!

For more information, contact the Lauderdale-by-the-Sea Chamber of Commerce, 4201 North Ocean Drive, Lauderdale-by-the-Sea, FL 33308, 954/776-1000 or 800/699-6764, www.lbts.com.

BEACHES

Lauderdale-by-the-Sea Public Beach is steep and drops off quickly. A healthy stand of palms gives this mile-long strand a suitably beachy look. It attracts a real mix of people: families, bikers, locals, tourists. We kept flashing on some of the northern beaches we know, like Old Orchard Beach, Maine, and Seaside Heights, New Jersey. The proximity of stores and restaurants to the beach gives the area a feeling of liveliness and immediacy. A reef close to shore draws snorkelers and divers. They've even built an underwater "Shipwreck Snorkeling Trail," which begins seaward of Datura Street. The only thing that is missing from this picture-perfect beach is lifeguards.

4 LAUDERDALE-BY-THE-SEA PUBLIC BEACH

Location: Commercial Boulevard at A1A in Lauderdale-by-the-Sea

Parking/Fees: metered street parking
Hours: 24 hours
Facilities: concessions, picnic tables, and showers
Contact: Lauderdale-by-the-Sea Public Works Department, 954/776-0576

ACCOMMODATIONS

Lauderdale-by-the-Sea has some modest "resort motels" and "apartment motels" where rooms can be had for under $100 nightly in season and $25–35 out of season. Even the more upscale lodgings—**Clarion Lauderdale Beach Resort** (4660 North Ocean Drive, 954/776-5660, $$), **Costa del Sol Resort** (4220 El Mar Drive, 954/776-6900, $$), and **Villas by the Sea Resort and Beach Club** (4456 El Mar Drive, 954/772-3550, $$)—post bearable prices, by Gold Coast standards.

COASTAL CUISINE

The **Aruba Beach Cafe** (1 East Commercial Boulevard, 954/776-0001, $$) is the prime beachside perch in Lauderdale-by-the-Sea. It's larger than it looks from the street, with several on-premises bars and dining rooms. It's a great place for lunch, happy-hour drinks, and even dinner. Among the appetizers, try ahi sashimi, Bahamian conch fritters, or Caribbean lobster salad. For an entree, go for the blackened trio or fresh catches.

Adding to the non-franchised charm of this bustling beach town is the **Pier Coffee Shop** (Anglin's Pier, 2 Commercial Boulevard, 954/776-1690, $), which has been in business for nearly four decades. The grub is solid, basic stuff, and you can't beat the view and authentically funky ambience. Tourists generally ask for open-air booths, while locals sit inside. Regardless, you'll enjoy a long view of the Atlantic Ocean with your coffee and eggs.

While in the area, grab a glass of fresh-squeezed juice at **Mack's Groves** (4405 North Ocean Drive, 954/776-0910, $). It's the perfect rejuvenating tonic on a hot day at the beach.

THE GOLD COAST

THE GOLD COAST

NIGHTLIFE

Head to the Aruba Beach Cafe (see *Coastal Cuisine*) for a tropical drink or three. Go for the Mango Madness or Caribbean Iced Tea, which beats its Long Island cousin hands-down.

Fort Lauderdale

We believe in omens, and they were not good when we landed at Fort Lauderdale International Airport. Several things caught our attention en route to Fort Lauderdale's beach: First, a billboard announcing Paris Hilton's new fragrance (we weren't aware that vapidity had an aroma). Second, a sign for a local talk radio station, proudly exclaiming "Liberals Hate Us!" Third, we had arrived during Fleet Week, and lanes along the beach were closed in preparation for "McDonald's National Salute to American Heroes," a noisy air show trumpeting this country's military might at a time when the war in Iraq was going especially poorly. Fourth, Fort Lauderdale's beloved "Strip"—the commercial stretch along Atlantic Boulevard (A1A) between Sunrise

and Las Olas boulevards—was in the midst of a messy wholesale transformation from motels and hotels to soulless, imperious condos. The fifth and unkindest cut was a sign hooked to a chain-link fence at one of the scorched-earth construction sites. It read: "Progress Through Demolition." There's a philosophy to live by!

If you believe that demolition signals progress, than start cashing in your stock options for one of the seven-figure residential cells along Fort Lauderdale's ruined beach. We used to regard Lauderdale as paradise by the sea: clean, appealing, and accommodating to all. But that tolerant, welcoming attitude has been replaced by a cynical goose chase for the surplus loot of the wealthy. This transparently vulgar philosophy is shamelessly expressed in the choice of phrase used to market Fort Lauderdale: "Positively Posh." Such an attitude is, of course, positively rubbish. These days it saddens us to visit a city that was, at least for one of us, something of a second home and storehouse of treasured memories for nearly 40 years.

Yes, Fort Lauderdale's beach is being "supersized," to borrow a term from McDonald's deep-fat fryer. The city is demolishing its

Harbor Beach, Fort Lauderdale

© PARKE PUTERBAUGH

HURRICANE WILMA

South Florida had largely been spared the spate of hurricanes that hit in 2004 and 2005, but all things even out in the end and the region took a major hit from Hurricane Wilma in late October 2005. This was one serious storm system. Wilma registered the lowest barometric pressure (882 millibars) ever recorded in the Atlantic basin. Its maximum sustained winds were 175 mph. Officially, this made Wilma the most powerful hurricane on record in the Atlantic, surpassing Gilbert, Rita, Katrina, and the 1935 Labor Day storm. It was also the third Category 5 hurricane of 2005, itself a single-season record.

Hurricane Wilma made its first landfall at Cozumel, on the Mexican coast, and a second landfall at Cancun. Then it changed direction from southwest to northeast, drawing a bead on Florida as it crossed the Gulf of Mexico. The eye of the hurricane passed within 70 miles of Key West, marking the fourth time a hurricane had glanced off the Lower Keys in the 2005 season. Wilma was by far the worst, cutting electricity to the entire chain of Florida Keys and flooding the streets of Key West, whose man-made beaches – including popular Smathers and Rest beaches – were left severely depleted of sand.

Wilma made its third landfall at Cape Romano, on Florida's Southwest Coast, as a Category 3 storm packing 120 mph winds. Wilma crossed the state from west to east, bringing high winds and heavy rains from Marco Island to Fort Myers (on the West Coast) and from Miami up to north Palm Beach County (on the East Coast). Wilma was the worst hurricane to hit Fort Lauderdale and Broward County in half a century. Out in the open ocean, Wilma again intensified into a Category 3 hurricane, spinning off a wicked nor'easter that pummeled New England.

Across South Florida, six million people were left without power in Wilma's wake. Because the storm tore through the state's most populous region, property damage and loss of life were considerable. Nearly every home in Miami-Dade County lost power. Thirty-one people died and damage estimates reached $12 billion, making it the most destructive hurricane to hit Florida in 2005 (and nearly as damaging as Charley and Ivan in 2004). South Florida's schools stayed closed for a week, residents were ordered to boil water, and losses to the state's winter vegetable crop ran into hundreds of millions.

Try to picture the following scene, reported by the *Palm Beach Post*, in Wilma's aftermath: "The quantity of debris is daunting. Pieces of roofs, trees, signs, awnings, fences, billboards and pool screens are scattered across several counties." A week later, more than a million people still had no electricity.

The 2005 hurricane season stretched past the point of allotted letters (Q, X, Y, and Z aren't used), leaving meteorologists resorting to the Greek alphabet for naming storms. All totaled, there were 25 named storms in the Atlantic basin in 2005, including seven major hurricanes (Category 3 or larger) and three Category 5 monsters (Katrina, Rita, and Wilma).

The two-year onslaught of hurricanes and tropical storms has left many of us worried about Florida's future. How much more can one state take?

THE GOLD COAST

past in hopes of a future that looks like fool's gold to us. Perhaps they should rename it the Fool's Gold Coast. Certainly a lot of fools have bought into the dubious notion of an oceanfront condo, endlessly vulnerable to hurricanes and beach erosion, as a profitable investment.

Fort Lauderdale (pop. 163,000) has sunk billions in an effort to remake itself from a former Spring Break mecca and party town of great renown to an upscale vacation and convention destination. The latest phase is an all-too-eager capitulation to the easy money offered by permitting condo towers on the beach. The refurbishing is evident everywhere a tourist or traveler might go. If you can recall the way the beach used to look, then you may

THE DEATH OF FUN ON FORT LAUDERDALE'S STRIP

Spring Break and Fort Lauderdale are no longer on speaking terms, and the memories of those wild years have faded. It's very different today on Fort Lauderdale's Strip, the stretch of beach along Atlantic Boulevard (A1A) between Sunrise and Las Olas Boulevards. Those who have refashioned the town's image don't even like to hear it referred to as "the Strip" – too many echoes of the bad ol' days when Fort Lauderdale was out of control.

They have succeeded in dramatically transforming the beach's look and image. In fact, they have gone way too far in the other direction. Fort Lauderdale's Strip, whatever else you might say about it, at least had a discernible soul back in the day. With its funky bars, mom-and-pop motels, and T-shirt shops, the Strip had the down-to-earth feel of a beach accessible to all, regardless of means. Now it is genteel and affected, casting its neon rainbow upon people who think nothing of dropping $120 on dinner for two. They market the town as being "Positively Posh." That is a far cry from the days when Fort Lauderdale was known as "Party Town U.S.A."

The change came suddenly. Up through the mid-1980s, Fort Lauderdale actively courted Spring Break, which drew upward of 350,000 winter-weary collegiate revelers from such distant states as Maine and Michigan between February and April. The rites of spring had been practiced on the sands of Fort Lauderdale as far back as the 1930s. Yet only when *Time* magazine publicized the annual migration in 1959 – with an article in which a coed explained the allure by saying, "This is where the boys are" – did collegians descend en masse.

In 1960, the beach flick *Where the Boys Are* became a box-office hit, thanks in part to the sultry title tune by Connie Francis, the film's costar. In its wake, the Spring Break crowd doubled to an estimated 50,000. A street riot between bottle-throwing collegians and authorities erupted in 1961. Elvis Presley turned up in Fort Lauderdale in March 1964 to film scenes for *Girl Happy*, a cash-in film about the Spring Break phenomenon. Its soundtrack included such Elvis-sung lowlights as "Fort Lauderdale Chamber of Commerce" and "Do the Clam."

The political turmoil of the Vietnam era put a damper on Spring Break, or at least gave it a more urgent countercultural edge. One of us harbors still-potent memories of rock bands playing in the sand, braless hippie chicks, acres of bikinis, head shops, and the aroma of pot smoke and incense. After dying down in the mid-1970s due to war, gas crisis, and recession, the ritual rebounded spectacularly.

be shocked by all the changes wrought by the wrecking ball and crane. We certainly were.

Worse, there's no coherent aesthetic vision—just an ad hoc approach dictated by vague notions of what People with Money seem to want. The beach makeover began with a determined effort to send Spring Break packing in the late 1980s and the passage of a bed tax to fund redevelopment along the Central Beach. Some of the recent beachfront construction badly mimics the art deco theme that's made South Miami Beach such a success story. The rest of it doesn't even show that much imagination, consisting mainly of hypnotically dull and visually overwhelming condo towers.

Beach Place is the retail anchor along Atlantic Boulevard, and this is where Fort Lauderdale has become *Faux* Lauderdale. It is a 100,000-square-foot complex of shops and restaurants where you can drink and dine at a faux Irish pub, a faux piano bar, a faux Key West restaurant, a faux Cajun eatery, and so on. As phony as it may be, Beach Place has

In 1977, more than 100,000 revelers packed Fort Lauderdale Beach, spending in excess of $35 million. A sequel to *Where the Boys Are* was filmed in 1983 as Spring Break became a boisterous bacchanal that made *Animal House* seem like a tea party.

"There aren't any rules here," a security guard at the Holiday Inn Oceanside told the *Miami Herald*. "We don't care how many people they stick in the room or what they do as long as the door is closed." By this time, the Button – the Holiday Inn's neighbor and the most notorious bar on The Strip – boasted of dispensing 750,000 beers during Spring Break. Meanwhile, some residents and community leaders openly complained that the rites of spring ran counter to the city's best interests.

The watershed year for revelry was 1985. A record 350,000 collegians completely overwhelmed the streets of Fort Lauderdale. By now, Spring Break had degenerated to a Roman orgy. The *Miami Herald* described the scene at the Button: "The sweaty hordes, periodically hosed down by Button bartenders, watched or participated in contests that involved nudity, masturbation, beer enemas, drinking urine, and simulated oral sex onstage." One of the deejays was sentenced to 18 months in jail for promoting obscenity and actually served 90 days. The bar was fined $25,000 and ordered shut down for 60 days.

The town clamped down hard on Spring Break in 1986. The collegiate crowd, expecting to run wild in the streets, instead found a beefed-up police force ready to throw them in jail. More than 2,200 people were arrested that year, mostly on charges of disorderly conduct or violating a new ordinance against carrying open containers. A newly erected wall separated pedestrians from vehicles on Atlantic Boulevard, eliminating the possibility that a wandering drunk might pass out on your car hood. Capacity limits were enforced in hotels and bars.

The fun appeared to be setting in Fort Lauderdale. Some bar owners and shopkeepers griped about police-state tactics and their effect on the Spring Break economy, which sustained many businesses on the Strip.

Before you get too misty-eyed over the demise of erotic banana-eating contests, consider that seven collegians died in Florida during Spring Break in 1986. Most were drunken balcony-divers. Fort Lauderdale thereupon decided to send Spring Break packing, and Daytona Beach eagerly picked up the beat. By 1989 Spring Break had been effectively driven from Fort Lauderdale, as only 20,000 showed up that year.

"Fort Lauderdale is no longer the current Spring Break haven, and it will never be that Spring Break haven again," declared the executive director of the Broward County Tourist Development Council. The nail was officially pounded in the coffin when the Holiday Inn Oceanside and the Button were razed in the early 1990s to make way for a parking lot.

THE GOLD COAST

become a kind of sanctuary since the script for redevelopment along Atlantic Boulevard has descended into its final act of desecration with the erection of mausoleum-like condos. At least it's a clean, well-lit place where you can slurp an ice-cream cone, take a seat in the indoor courtyard, listen to a musician, and watch the milling crowd. It's not much, but it passes for community in a time of almost total artifice.

Away from the beach, Fort Lauderdale has grown like a goiter and, to our eyes, lost much of its appeal. Drivers honk their horns in a frustrated retort to the gridlock that engulfs every thoroughfare. Only moments after entering the downtown area on our latest visit our attention was drawn to the left lane, where we saw a wreck, an ambulance, and an unconscious victim receiving CPR. There are construction delays, too many vehicles, and too much unchecked growth here. It didn't used to be this way.

For a moment, we'll look on the bright side and rummage through Fort Lauderdale's more beguiling back pages. The city has historically been defined by the ocean and a network of inland canals that earned it the nickname "the Venice of America." There are 165 miles of canals in Fort Lauderdale and another 135 miles of them in the rest of Broward County. Frequent late-afternoon thunderstorms clear the air and cleanse the streets. This is a robustly wealthy municipality with chic malls and specialty shops; more restaurants per capita than any other American city; a mind-numbing 42,000 yachts lashed to docks in front of huge homes or berthed in the hundred area marinas; and impeccably manicured yards landscaped with citrus trees and colorful tropical flora.

Fort Lauderdale was built in 1838 as a fortification against the Seminole Indians and named for Major William Lauderdale. Fishermen and farmers settled here in the 1890s, and Fort Lauderdale incorporated in 1911. With the opening of South Florida to travel and tourism, Fort Lauderdale became a thriving resort whose permanent population grew steadily after World War II.

There's no great mystery to Fort Lauderdale's appeal. It can be summed up in one word: weather. The average year-round temperature is a near-perfect 75.4°F, and the mercury has never exceeded 100°F, thanks to the moderating effect of near-constant sea breezes. Here's a statistic to ponder on some cold, blustery day back home: The sun shines in Fort Lauderdale 3,000 hours per year. With ideal weather and a four-mile public beach as drawing cards, tourist visitation in 2004 surpassed 9.4 million and visitor expenditures totaled nearly $8 billion.

Somehow, back when wiser heads prevailed, Fort Lauderdale had the uncommon good sense to forbid construction on the seaward side of Atlantic Boulevard in the Central Beach area. Thus, drivers and pedestrians have always enjoyed an unobstructed view of the beach, and there's no better advertisement for a coastal community than that. Beyond the beach there are numerous other attractions in and around Fort Lauderdale. These include Riverwalk, a 1.5-mile linear park along the banks of the New River, and Las Olas Boulevard, an area of cafes and chichi boutiques about a mile off the beach. History and architecture buffs will want to check out **Stranahan House** (335 East Olas Boulevard, 954/524-4736), a riverside domicile that belonged to Fort Lauderdale's founder. Art aficionados will appreciate the sophisticated exhibits and collections at the **Fort Lauderdale Museum of Art** (1 East Las Olas Boulevard, 954/463-5184).

Kids will enjoy **Butterfly World** (3600 West Sample Road, Coconut Creek, 954/977-4400), which teems with myriad winged wonders in a rain-forest setting of flowers and gardens, and **Flamingo Gardens** (3750 Flamingo Road, Davie, 954/473-2955), which showcases the flightless pink wonders, as well as alligators, in a subtropical forest setting. If you have a swimmer among your brood, you might want to drop by the **International Swimming Hall of Fame** (1 Hall of Fame Drive, 954/462-6536), which lies right off the beach. Its mission: "Since 1965, ISHOF has promoted swimming, diving, water polo, synchronized swimming, open water swimming, water safety and aquatic art by honoring the great achievements and events in aquatic history." It foundered for years and was in danger of going under—many medals and memorabilia worth millions were pilfered by a crooked janitor—until a new director stepped in to set things right in 2005. Touring the wave-shaped museum costs $5 for adults and $10 for families.

Whatever else you do in this city, you simply have to ride the **Jungle Queen** (801 Seabreeze Boulevard, 954/462-5596). It cruises the city's canals and waterways, passing the spectacular winter domiciles of the wealthy. You're supposed to wave at them as they putter around their front yards: "There's Mr. Johnson now. Hi, Mr. Johnson!" The *Jungle Queen* stops at a Seminole Indian village, where you can buy snacks and trinkets. Such sights as a frightened, chattering spider monkey attached to a boy's head or a Seminole with missing fingers battling a gator won't soon be forgotten. Come and make

SO YOU WANT TO BE A GATOR WRESTLER?

Alligators are the signature species of Florida, at least from a tourist's perspective. Everywhere one turns, an Indian village features a floor show involving squirming, angry reptiles tussling with their Levis-wearing nemeses. That's right, gator wrasslin'.

And yet despite strong demand, those wrestling jobs have become harder to fill. The young Seminoles who used to wrassle gators are instead going to college or working at casinos, turning their backs on a proud heritage of snapping jaws and lost fingers. For the first time, job openings have been publicly advertised and are open to non-Indians of either sex. The pay is $12/hour and sensibly includes health benefits.

Basic job description:

* sneak up behind a 250-pound flesh-eating reptile that has 80 razor-sharp teeth
* grab tail of beast
* swing beast by tail in water to exhaust it
* climb atop beast's back and yank its head backwards
* pry open jaw to display 80 razor-sharp teeth to audience
* politely acknowledge applause
* collect tips

The next time you lose your shirt at one of Florida's Indian casinos, you might want to keep this career opportunity in mind. Your ticket home may be riding on your ability to wrassle. Our advice: Start practicing on the family dog.

THE GOLD COAST

your own memories! Fun for the whole family! Nightly dinner cruises are offered, too.

There are also gambling cruises, gondola tours, golf courses (upward of 90 of them along the Gold Coast), the Fort Lauderdale Historical Museum, and the Seminole Indian Casino and Bingo. There's no lack of things to do in Fort Lauderdale. We just wish we could recommend the city with the same unbridled enthusiasm we used to have for the place.

Let's return to the grievous catchphrase "Positively Posh," which positively smacks of nose-thumbing Palm Beach–style elitism. We grew up loving Fort Lauderdale not because of its snooty airs but for its natural beauty and openness to all. We have no affinity for the "international jet set" or pitches aimed at them, yet Fort Lauderdale is drunk in its hunt for big money these days. Catch a whiff of this fulsome marketing prose: "Cars are not the only indication that Greater Fort Lauderdale has come of age as a Positively Posh vacation destination. Hundreds of private

jets, costing as much as $30 million apiece, fly into three airports catering to private aircraft each day so owners can be whisked away to their 150-foot+ seagoing yachts tied up at their fabulous waterfront mansions or docked at the Bahia Mar Marina, home of the world's largest annual international boat show, or one of the many exclusive marinas in the area."

We urge Fort Lauderdale to dispense with its fixation on all things "posh" and return to a more egalitarian approach, promoting the city as a clean, civilized community with a splendid beachfront. But we fear we're wasting our breath, as the genie is out of the bottle.

For more information, contact the Greater Fort Lauderdale Chamber of Commerce, 512 NE 3rd Avenue, Fort Lauderdale, FL 33301, 954/462-6000, www.ftlchamber.com. Or contact the Greater Fort Lauderdale Convention and Visitors Bureau, 1850 Eller Drive, Suite 303, Fort Lauderdale, FL 33316, 954/765-4466 or 800/22SUNNY, www.sunny.com.

BEACHES

Fort Lauderdale City Beach runs for four miles along Atlantic Boulevard (A1A), from the southern border with Lauderdale-by-the-Sea down to Port Everglades. Angle-in beach parking is free for several miles along A1A, but spaces fill up quickly and the early birds get these highly desirable spots. There's also a large municipal parking lot near Las Olas Boulevard toward the south end of the beach, which costs $6 per day, and there are private lots located a block or two off the beach as well.

Though Fort Lauderdale City Beach has a history of renourishment, it's a pretty skimpy little strand at present. A pair of 2005 hurricanes—Katrina (yes, the same one that destroyed New Orleans) and Wilma (which did huge damage across South Florida)—accelerated the natural erosion process. Though Fort Lauderdale wisely prohibited construction on the seaward side of A1A, they did not preserve the dune system, leaving the beach unprotected and duneless from beach to sidewalk. The lack of any sort of buffer or speed bump in the form of vegetated dunes has left Atlantic Boulevard and all that new construction on its landward side—are you reading this, future condo owners of Fort Lauderdale?—vulnerable to wind and wave.

The federal government has gotten justifiably stingy about anteing up taxpayer money for the Sisyphean futility of beach renourishment. Nonetheless, a financing packaging involving the county, state, and feds was worked out, allowing Broward County to replace some of what's been stripped away by storms (particularly 2004's Hurricane Jeanne and 2005's Hurricanes Katrina and Wilma). This will benefit Fort Lauderdale's beach in the short term but do nothing to address problems over the long haul. Hurricanes and rising sea level will continue to bring untold grief and property damage to places like Fort Lauderdale, where towering condos and hotels built on the beach do not allow for retreat from an advancing ocean.

Short palms line the beach along A1A; many of the taller ones succumbed to blight back in the 1980s. We've taken many morning jogs along Fort Lauderdale's beach. We've hung out at its bars till the early morning hours, too. For many years we regarded it as one of the nation's premier municipal beaches, though its future is in doubt as unabated construction has overwhelmed it.

The heart of Fort Lauderdale City Beach—known as Central Beach—is along Atlantic Boulevard (A1A) between Sunrise and Las Olas Boulevards. Areas to the north and south—up by Oakland Park Boulevard (North Beach) and down toward Port Everglades (Harbor Beach), respectively—are less dense with beachgoers. The beach is widest and most deserted by the Port Everglades jetties. Parking and access are difficult unless you live in one of the harborside condos or are staying at the exclusive Lago Mar Resort and Club, so your best bet is to park at the Las Olas Boulevard lot and walk down to Harbor Beach—that is, if you wish to get away from the crowd. We like people-watching, and Fort Lauderdale can offer an eyeful when packed.

Along a portion of Atlantic Boulevard near Sunrise Boulevard, **Hugh Taylor Birch State Park** preserves a corner of Old Florida in the form of a coastal hammock. It's used by walkers, joggers, in-line skaters, bicyclists, and nature lovers who come to play and relax on an unspoiled tract right in the heart of the city. From here you can also cross Atlantic Boulevard to the beach via a pedestrian underpass. The park's 400-foot strip of beach is watched over by city lifeguards, so all the usual beach rules are in force. That means no surfing while lifeguards are on duty (9 A.M.–5 P.M.).

Just down from the state park is **Bonnet House** (900 North Birch Road, 954/563-5393), a 35-acre estate that belonged to a couple of Floridian artists. The grounds and mansion have been preserved and can be toured Tuesday–Sunday ($15 per person, free for kids under six). The stretch of beach in front of Bonnet House, known as Bonnet Beach, is a good place to escape the Central

Beach crowd while still being only steps from The Strip. Incidentally, $200,000 worth of damage was done to the grounds of Bonnet House by Hurricanes Katrina and Wilma, to give you some idea of those storms' devastation in this area.

The city of Fort Lauderdale has done a good job of providing public parking at or near the beach (particularly the Central Beach area). Three jumbo-sized lots—Oceanside (Atlantic at Las Olas), South Beach (on Seabreeze Boulevard), and Intracoastal (east side of Las Olas Bridge)—offer a combined 1,200 parking spaces. At South Beach, you pay $6 for all-day parking; the others are metered or computed hourly. In addition, there are metered spaces and small lots all along Atlantic Boulevard (A1A). Only Harbor Beach, at the south end, is a tough nut to crack for the public.

5 FORT LAUDERDALE CITY BEACH (NORTH BEACH)

Location: Oakland Park Boulevard south to NE 20th Street along North Atlantic Boulevard in Fort Lauderdale
Parking/Fees: metered street parking
Hours: 24 hours
Facilities: lifeguards and showers
Contact: Fort Lauderdale City Beach Lifeguard Office, 954/468-1595; beach report, 954/828-4597

6 HUGH TAYLOR BIRCH STATE PARK

Location: Sunrise Boulevard at Atlantic Boulevard (A1A) in Fort Lauderdale
Parking/Fees: $3.25 per vehicle entrance fee; $1 entrance fee per bicycle rider or walk-in visitor. Free street parking along A1A as well.
Hours: 8 A.M.-sunset (9 A.M.-5 P.M. on the beach)

Facilities: lifeguards, restrooms, picnic tables, showers, and a visitors center
Contact: Hugh Taylor Birch State Park, 954/564-4521

7 FORT LAUDERDALE CITY BEACH (CENTRAL BEACH)

BEST

Location: Sunrise Boulevard south to Las Olas Boulevard, along North Ocean Boulevard (A1A) in Fort Lauderdale
Parking/Fees: free street parking
Hours: 24 hours
Facilities: lifeguards and showers
Contact: Fort Lauderdale City Beach Lifeguard Office, 954/468-1595; beach report, 954/828-4597

8 FORT LAUDERDALE CITY BEACH (HARBOR BEACH)

Location: Las Olas Boulevard south to Port Everglades along South Ocean Boulevard (A1A) in Fort Lauderdale
Parking/Fees: $6 per day parking lot (Las Olas Boulevard at Ocean Boulevard) by the beach, plus metered street parking
Hours: 24 hours
Facilities: concessions, lifeguards, restrooms, picnic tables, and showers
Contact: Fort Lauderdale City Beach Lifeguard Office, 954/468-1595; taped beach report, 954/828-4597

RECREATION AND ATTRACTIONS

- **Bicycle Rentals:** Hot Scooter Rentals, 2908 East Sunrise Boulevard, Fort Lauderdale, 954/564-2155
- **Boat Cruise:** *Jungle Queen,* Bahia Mar Marina, 801 Seabreeze Boulevard, Fort Lauderdale, 954/462-5596

- **Dive Shop:** Lauderdale Diver, 1332 SE 17th Street, Fort Lauderdale, 954/467-2822

- **Ecotourism:** Anne Kolb Nature Center and West Lake Park, 751 Sheridan Street, Hollywood, 954/926-2480; Butterfly World, Tradewinds Park, Pompano Beach, 954/977-4400

- **Fishing Charters:** Extreme Fishing, 1005 Seabreeze Boulevard, Fort Lauderdale, 954/764-8723

- **Lighthouse:** Hillsboro Inlet Lighthouse, Hillsboro Inlet, Pompano Beach, 954/942-2102

- **Marina:** Bahia Mar Marina, 801 Seabreeze Boulevard, Fort Lauderdale, 954/764-2233

- **Pier:** Anglin's Pier, 2 Commercial Boulevard, Lauderdale-by-the-Sea, 954/776-1690

- **Rainy-Day Attraction:** Museum of Discovery and Science, 401 SW 2nd Street, Fort Lauderdale, 954/467-6637; Fort Lauderdale Museum of Art, 1 East Los Olas Boulevard, 954/525-5500

- **Shopping/Browsing:** Galleria at Fort Lauderdale, 2414 East Sunrise Boulevard, Fort Lauderdale, 954/564-1015

- **Surf Shop:** Obsession Watersports, 1804 East Sunrise Boulevard, Fort Lauderdale, 954/467-0057; Liquid Addiction, 929 Sunrise Land, Fort Lauderdale, 954/561-7675

- **Vacation Rentals:** Premier Vacation Rentals, 800/872-3043

ACCOMMODATIONS

Ocean-facing hotels and motels along Fort Lauderdale's Central Beach district can be found along a two-mile stretch of Atlantic Boulevard (A1A) between Sunrise and Las Olas Boulevards. A lot of less-fancy older motels are either gone or inevitably destined for oblivion in the name of "progress" (read: 20-story condos for the second-home wealthy). While they're not exactly to be mourned, what's replacing them is no cause for celebration.

The Sheraton chain has two venerable beachside sentinels: the **Yankee Trader** (321 North Atlantic Boulevard, 954/467-1111, $$$) and the **Yankee Clipper** (1140 Seabreeze Boulevard, 954/524-5551, $$$). These two hotels claim nearly 1,000 rooms between them. The Trader is at the beach's midsection, while the Clipper sits directly on the beach closer to Harbor Beach. How did the Yankee Clipper get away with its beachside placement, given the proscription against building on the beach? The answer is history. Predating the ordinance, Sheraton's Yankee Clipper has sat on this spot for nearly half a century. It was, in fact, the first oceanfront hotel in Lauderdale to be open year-round.

Despite its age, the Yankee Clipper has been periodically refurbished and modernized, and the rooms are first-rate. The hotel is really a miniature city, consisting of four towers and more than 500 rooms. There are pools all over the place. The main pool also has a bar right off the beach, and everything from cabanas and boogie boards to WaveRunners and Jet Skis can be rented here. They'll even set you up for a parasailing adventure.

Upscale hotel franchises are grouped together at the south end of the beach. These include the **Doubletree Oceanfront Hotel** (440 Seabreeze Boulevard, 954/524-8733, $$$), **Radisson Bahia Mar Beach Resort** (801 Seabreeze Boulevard, 954/764-2233, $$$), and **Marriott's Harbor Beach Resort** (3030 Holiday Drive, 954/525-4000, $$$$).

Middle-rank hotel franchises are further up toward the north end: **Howard Johnson Ocean Edge** (700 North Atlantic Boulevard, 954/563-2451, $$), **Ramada Sea Club Resort** (619 North Atlantic Boulevard, 954/564-3211, $$$), and **Holiday Inn Fort Lauderdale Beach Galleria** (999 North Atlantic Boulevard, 954/563-5961, $$$). For location—right at Sunrise and Atlantic Boulevards—the Holiday Inn can't be beat. Its proximity to the beach, Hugh Taylor Birch State Park, and Galleria Mall makes this Holiday Inn an ideal vacation base, and we've enjoyed many stays here over the years. Try to get an upper-floor room, as the beach view is incredible. The only downside is that some of the shops and bars directly behind it are a tad on the funky side. But it's got a nicely landscaped ground-level pool deck, and if you get an oceanfront room, you'll love the view and your stay. (Incidentally, the infamous Holiday Inn Oceanside—which long functioned as Spring Break headquarters and home of The Button, the notorious and ribald party palace—exists no longer.)

Affixed to Beach Place and rising behind it is **Marriott's Beach Place Towers** (21 South Atlantic Boulevard, 954/525-4440, $$$$). The words "luxury," "exclusive," and "premium" are invoked a lot in describing this property. Despite its proximity to the water, Marriott's Beach Place feels disconnected from the casual, let-it-hang-out experience of a real beach vacation, at least in the way such things used to be experienced along Fort Lauderdale's Strip. It is not strictly a hotel but one of those "vacation club" time-share resorts. As a partial "owner," you purchase a week or two in perpetuity for some fixed fee (e.g. $25,000), plus a yearly maintenance and membership charge. At the same time, non-owners can book a stay just like a regular hotel. In the winter high season, a one-bedroom villa starts at $254 and a two-bedroom villa goes for about twice that. Time was when that kind of money would buy you a whole week at some modest mom-and-pop on the Strip.

If you do want to pamper yourselves to the max, we'd unhesitatingly recommend **Lago Mar Resort & Club** (1700 South Ocean Lane, 954/523-6511, $$$$). For one thing, it really is on the beach—Harbor Beach, to be exact, at the quiet south end of Fort Lauderdale's urban beachfront. There's a broad fillet of sand here, not like the narrower, perpetually eroding strand along the Strip. Guests can lay out on the generally unpopulated beach behind Lago Mar or repose in hammocks strung between a small forest of palm trees. The resort has two impressively oversized pools on the property.

We especially enjoyed a dip in the balmy, undulating lagoon pool, which many of the rooms overlook. The rooms themselves are sumptuously decorated and, well, roomy.

What really sold Lago Mar to us was the air of quiet class that envelopes guests from the moment of arrival. Lago Mar looks and feels more like a residential apartment building than a hotel, and it's unobtrusively emplaced in a real neighborhood. For once, a luxury hotel doesn't sock it to you for parking (both valet and self-parking are complimentary). Room rates begin at $285 in season, and a one-bedroom poolside suite goes for $375–395. That's not inexpensive, but you really won't pay much less to stay at Marriott's Beach Place Towers or the other top-flight oceanfront resorts in town, and Lago Mar is a superior property in every conceivable respect. It even has an excellent on-site Northern Italian restaurant called Acquario. After a day spent hanging out on Harbor Beach, try the seared rare tuna in a tapanade of olives and sun-dried tomatoes and you'll go to bed happy. It worked for us.

Along the middle of the beach is a transitional melange of flyblown mom-and-pop motels, pricey new faux art deco hotels, and condos whose construction has brought dust, noise, and visual pollution to the beach. A couple of recent arrivals have all their South Beach wannabe moves down pat, practically screaming "art deco" in an area that, to our knowledge, has no such history.

If you wish to stay off the beach, we'd recommend the **Riverside Hotel** (620 East Las Olas Boulevard, 954/467-0671, $$$$), located on the New River near the shops of Las Olas. The rooms and grounds are understated and elegant, and the dining room is among our favorites in Fort Lauderdale. Moreover, the beach is just a short drive, walk, or jog east along Las Olas.

COASTAL CUISINE

Fort Lauderdale is a restaurant town. We could've written a book devoted just to dining out in Fort Lauderdale, and it would have to be updated often since the scene is so changeable. With all the evolution on the beachfront, the pace of change has accelerated even more furiously. There are now 3,500 restaurants in Broward County, most of them in the Fort Lauderdale metropolitan area. Suffice it to say that you cannot and will not go hungry in Fort Lauderdale—unless indecision drives you to starvation, that is. We have had no such problems, so grab your forks and get ready to dig in.

A longtime favorite, **15th Street Fisheries** (1900 SE 15th Street, 954/763-2777, $$$) overlooks the water from the 15th Street Marina. Inside, it is adorned with the accoutrements of a working fishery. It's a friendly, bustling place where you're made to feel welcome. The host greets you by saying "We're glad you're here," and buttons worn by the wait staff reiterate the message. Fresh seafood from Florida and elsewhere is served in creative ways. Selections are made from a large blackboard menu carted to your table by a server who explains the choices and answers questions. Favorite items are highlighted with stars.

From our perspective, the stars of the 15th Street Fisheries' menu include filet mignon of yellowfin tuna—a thick center cut marinated in a soy-ginger sauce and grilled (rare to medium-rare is best)—and snapper sauteed in white wine, ginger, garlic, and soy and topped with scallions. You can't go wrong with simple preparations of fresh catches like mahimahi, snapper, and tuna. The house specialty appetizer is flying fish—sweet, tasty little swimmers that are flash-fried tableside. Indeed, so much on the menu at 15th Street Fisheries is good that you'll want to return over and over to try it all.

Founded by football legend Don Shula—the Hall of Fame coach for the Baltimore Colts (1963–1969) and the Miami Dolphins (1970–1995)—**Shula's on the Beach** (321 North Atlantic Boulevard, 954/355-4000, $$$$) is attached to Sheraton's Yankee Trader Resort. Steaks are their mainstay; indeed, Shula's (which has several outlets around the country) is rated among the best steakhouses in America. If you're partial to gourmet training-table fare—you know, high-quality meat and potatoes—you won't be disappointed. We'd especially recommend the 22-ounce porterhouse—a thick, juicy slab of Black Angus that would sate the hungriest linebacker's appetite. This particular location also has an expanded menu and classy continental ambience. There are surf items—a changing list of fresh fish and such specialties as char-grilled Florida lobster—to complement the turf.

A few blocks up from Shula's is another class act near the beach, **Mark's Las Olas** (1032 East Las Olas Boulevard, 954/463-1000, $$$$). Chef Mark Militello owns three other restaurants in South Florida, including operations in Miami Beach (**Mark's South Beach,** at the Nash Hotel, 1120 Collins Avenue, 305/604-9050), Boca Raton (**Mark's at the Park,** in Mizner Park, 344 Plaza Real, 561/395-0770), and West Palm Beach (**Mark's City Place,** 700 South Rosemary Avenue, 561/514-0770). He's a culinary superstar, having won the James Beard Award for Best Regional Chef in the Southeast. At Mark's Las Olas, he does extraordinary things with seafood, such as grilled Florida lobster with jicama, yuca, and a vinaigrette of passion fruit and vanilla bean. Expect to pay about $150 for dinner for two, which may explain why some locals turn up their noses at what might superficially seem to be an overpriced tourist depot on their formerly unpretentious Strip. But Mark's does merit its gourmet stripes, so save up and splurge for a special night out.

Shooter's (3003 NE 32nd Avenue, 954/566-2855, $$) remains a popular spot to down drinks and watch boats cruise the Intracoastal. The huge, affordable menu ranges from pizza and burgers to pasta dishes and grilled grouper. Shooter's rocks and rolls like the wake from a speedboat, so don't be surprised if you have to wait for a table, even during midweek.

We've also enjoyed excellent seafood dinners at the **Sea Watch** (6002 North Ocean

Boulevard, 954/781-2200, $$$) and the **Old Florida Seafood House** (1414 NE 26th Street, 954/566-1044, $$$). The former is located on the ocean up at the north end of Lauderdale—technically, it's in Lauderdale-by-the-Sea—while the latter is situated in an old shopping center in an area known as Wilton Manors. Among the best seafood entrees we've ever had is stuffed Florida lobster, available at the Old Florida Seafood House and other restaurants around town at certain times of year. (The lobsters' numbers go up and down, and harvests are closely regulated.) The Florida lobster tastes nothing like its Maine cousin. This warm-water shellfish has no claws, and the tail is tender and almost flaky. In some ways we like it better than its more popular New England relative. There's nothing better than a Florida lobster, baked and stuffed with scallops, crabmeat, and light breading.

We're also bullish on **Catfish Dewey's** (4003 North Andrews Avenue, 954/566-5333, $$), a funky joint that serves Southern-style home cooking at down-home prices. Go for the all-you-can-eat specials, including fried catfish, if you're packing an appetite. With heaping helpings of catfish, hush puppies, cole slaw, and sweet tea placed on the table, Southerners like ourselves are in hog heaven at Catfish Dewey's, which also serves saltwater catches at reasonable prices. The abundant servings of local color—they attract some real characters, seemingly all of them in a boisterous good humor—come free of charge.

At the other extreme is **The Grill Room on Las Olas** (620 East Las Olas Boulevard, 954/467-0671, $$$$), inside the Riverside Hotel. The menu at this genteel hotel restaurant, housed in a room designed after the Singapore Officers Club, leans toward hearty surf-and-turf fare: a tasty New York strip steak, veal chop Oscar, grilled yellowfin with foie gras, all in the $20–40 range.

There's quite a scene at night—made up of equal parts dining, snacking, shopping, and people-watching—along Las Olas from SE 6th to SE 11th Avenue. Everything is fine

(as in upscale): "fine dining and shops," "fine art and design galleries," and "fine European clothiers." You'll find bridal salons, jewelers, and restaurants whose tables extend too far onto the sidewalk. The accent is French at **Cafe La Bonne Crepe** (815 East Las Olas Boulevard, 954/761-1515, $$) and **Le Cafe de Paris** (715 East Las Olas Boulevard, 954/467-2900, $$$), and Italian at **Timpano Italian Chophouse** (450 East Las Olas Boulevard, 954/462-9119, $$$$) and **Mancini's** (1017 East Las Olas Boulevard, 954/764-5510, $$$). "Bon appetit!" and/or "Al buon gusto!"

NIGHTLIFE

The club scene in Fort Lauderdale isn't exactly original, borrowing liberally from Southern California and South Miami Beach, but it can be lively and it does go late—as late as 4:30 A.M., if you're a raving insomniac. We're a bit distressed, however, to report that a few of the hottest nightspots from years past—namely, Baja Beach Club and Bermuda Triangle—exist no longer. Wha'ppen? The riotous Baja Beach Club is gone (but not forgotten), while the Bermuda Triangle has been replaced with a **Margarita Cafe** (219 South Atlantic Boulevard, 954/463-6872).

So…what to do in Fort Lauderdale? There are some tried-and-true nightspots where you can scare up some activity. If you're looking for something on the Intracoastal, try the ever-reliable **Shooter's** (3003 NE 32nd Avenue, 954/566-2855). The under-the-bridge area occupied by Shooter's and other close-by bars is particularly busy. Park on the street, feed the meter (charges are enforced 24 hours), and cruise from one joint to another. Our itinerant rambles have yielded everything from free hot dogs at a sports bar during Monday Night Football to a riotous New Year's Eve at Shooter's. Wildly lit boats parked four astride on the Intracoastal as wait staff gamely hopped from boat to boat with drink and food orders.

Squeeze (2 South New River Drive W, 954/522-2151) is an alternative-music club, and **The Poor House** (110 SW 3rd Avenue,

954/522-5145) doles out the blues. Back on the beach, places like the **Elbo Room** (241 North Atlantic Boulevard, 954/463-4615), **Quarterdeck** (1541 Cordova Road, 954/524-6163), and **Sloop John B** (239 South Atlantic Boulevard, 954/463-3633) rock loudly into the wee hours. You might hear a bar band playing "Mustang Sally" or a deejay spinning trance, techno, and hip-hop. Just case the joints (they're all within a few blocks of each other) till you hear what you like and wander in.

Finally, we should mention that Fort Lauderdale has been receiving a steady influx of gay people in recent years. Our theory is that after pioneering South Beach's revitalization, the gay community has begun trawling for greener, cleaner pastures since international *trendinistas* and the hardcore hip-hop crowd began descending on the place. They've certainly lessened South Beach's appeal in our eyes—and we can put up with just about anything.

John U. Lloyd Beach State Park

John U. Lloyd Beach State Park is a barrier-island beach with a lot of unlovely civilization lying over its shoulder. Condos loom to the north, planes streak in to nearby Fort Lauderdale International Airport, and industrial noise and traffic at Port Everglades intrude upon the calm. It makes for a weird clash of worlds, with New Florida superimposed upon Old Florida.

This state park looked like hell when we last visited, not just because of the urbanized environment bearing down on it but also due to erosion and damage wrought by recent hurricanes (particularly Hurricane Wilma, which roared across Broward County from the west) and the hazard of lying downdrift of the sand-trapping Port Everglades jetties. This explains why Fort Lauderdale's Harbor Beach has widened while the beach at Lloyd

is typically sand-starved. It was shocking to us, to say the least, to find virtually no beach sand here.

Signs warned of "severe beach erosion" and huge trees toppled into the surf or were listing precipitously in that direction. Spindly palm plantings were sparsely distributed among the sandy-soiled moonscape. Visitors tried to make the best of a bad situation. We saw Hispanic families gamely picnicking on the short, gullied bluffs above the beach, watching gargantuan tankers enter and exit Port Everglades as their blaring portable radios competed with the din of aircraft and industry.

The good news is that a big, wide Band-Aid has been applied to the vanished beach at Lloyd. A beach renourishment project, undertaken in late 2005, has at least temporarily restored the lost beaches of southern Broward County, from Lloyd south to the Dade County line (an area known as "Segment III" in Broward County). Sand pumped onto shore has created an artificial beach that's 100 feet wide. Moreover, the plan was to construct three "boulder mound erosion control structures" to "lock in" the sand. Will this be just another futile attempt to gerrymander nature with technology? We'll see, and of course we wish them good luck.

The 250-acre park at John U. Lloyd houses a concession stand (Loggerhead Cafe), where snacks can be had and canoes and kayaks rented. Behind Lloyd's 2.3-mile coastline lie a tidal creek, coastal hammock, and mangrove swamp. A nature trail loops around the island's densely forested interior. Though it is a lovely and instructional walk, the Barrier Island Trail tends to disappear underfoot in an obscuring carpet of Australian pine needles and sea grape leaves. Pay attention or you might lose your way!

Students of wetlands will be interested in the man-made red mangrove swamp on the west side of the park. It is a mitigation site for acreage destroyed during the expansion of Port Everglades in the late 1980s. Manatees live in the waterways, and sea turtles allegedly nest on the beaches—though there hasn't been much beach for them to nest on in recent times.

For more information, contact John U. Lloyd Beach State Park, 6503 North Ocean Drive, Dania Beach, FL 33004, 954/923-2833, www.floridastateparks.org.

BEACHES

9 JOHN U. LLOYD BEACH STATE PARK

Location: north end of North Ocean Boulevard, 0.25 mile north of Dania Beach Boulevard, in Dania
Parking/Fees: $5 entrance fee per vehicle
Hours: 8 A.M.–sunset
Facilities: concessions, lifeguards, restrooms, picnic tables, and showers
Contact: John U. Lloyd Beach State Park, 954/923-2833

Dania Beach

Dania Beach, Hollywood, and Hallandale Beach are clustered between (and overshadowed by) Fort Lauderdale and Miami Beach. We rather like Dania and, especially, Hollywood, although Hallandale Beach has gone to the dogs (and we don't mean greyhounds).

Dania Beach (pop. 28,500) was the first incorporated city in Broward County. In some respects, little has changed over the years but the name. Apparently desirous of the imprimatur conferred by the magical word "beach," Dania officially became Dania Beach in 1998. They promote it as "a dynamic waterfront community," but that's really a stretch. Largely a quiet community of older citizens, it is also the home of **Dania Jai-Alai** (301 East Dania Beach Boulevard, 954/920-1511). This pari-mutuel betting sport, touted as the world's fastest game, is kind of an extreme version of racquetball. It's played on a three-walled

© PARKE PUTERBAUGH

John U. Lloyd Beach State Park

court with scoop-shaped *cesta* (racquet) that flings the *pelota* (ball) at speeds up to 180 mph. Dania's Jai-Alai fronton is over 50 years old, and the sport itself may well date back 4,000 years.

Florida Atlantic University's Institute for Ocean and System Engineering (a.k.a. "Sea Tech") is located on the Intracoastal Waterway in Dania Beach. Dania Beach also has its own modest and likable city beach.

For more information, contact the Dania Beach Chamber of Commerce, 102 West Dania Beach Boulevard, Dania Beach, FL 33004, 954/926-2323, www.greaterdania.org.

BEACHES

Dania Beach Ocean Park,—also known as Frank C. "Tootie" Adler Park, which is a mouthful—is located at the end of Dania Beach Boulevard. It received a facelift in the 1990s, when the old wooden pier was replaced with a concrete pier. Fishing insomniacs love Dania Pier, which never closes. One early morning the only other person on the beach beside us was an obese homeless woman performing genital

THE GOLD COAST

ablutions in the surf. More typically, you'll see elderly people and anglers enjoying the day on this low-key beach.

Dania Beach has undergone a thorough makeover. A renourishment (the first since 1991) was completed in 2006. A new pier restaurant is under construction, as are chickee huts and bathrooms. Metered parking costs $1.25 per hour and is enforced 6 A.M.–11 P.M. Fortunately for Dania Beach, its renourishment was done *after* Hurricane Wilma passed through in 2005. As an enthusiastic lifeguard put it, "We haven't had this much sand in 15 years!" It's true—they'd lost a lot of dunes and beach width over the years. Hollywood Beach was not quite so lucky with the sandmen, as its renourishment *preceded* the hurricane. That's what you call bad timing.

10 DANIA BEACH OCEAN PARK (A.K.A. FRANK C. "TOOTIE" ADLER PARK)

Location: 100 North Beach Road at (A1A) in Dania
Parking/Fees: metered parking lot. Residents can purchase an annual parking sticker at Dania City Hall cashier's window. The cost is $37.10 (under 55) and $21.20 (55 and older).
Hours: sunrise–10 P.M.
Facilities: concessions, lifeguards, restrooms, picnic tables, and showers
Contact: Dania Beach Ocean Park, 954/924-3696

ACCOMMODATIONS

Small, nonfranchised motels along U.S. 1 are what you'll find in Dania Beach. Despite its unassuming charm, Dania Beach is not the first place that would enter our minds to book a Florida beach vacation. Places like the **Dania Beach Hotel** (180 East Dania Beach Boulevard, 954/923-5895, $), the **Blue Ocean Motel** (480 East Dania Beach Boulevard, 954/921-2775, $), and the yellow cinderblock

Ocean Terrace Motel (6040 North 4th Terrace, 954/922-4325, $) are unfancy, affordable, and the last of a dying breed in Florida: mom-and-pop motor courts by the beach.

COASTAL CUISINE

Our favorite place to chow down in Dania, the Fish Grill, has closed, but we have high hopes for the restaurant that's slated to open in late summer 2006 at Dania Beach Ocean Park. The Pier Restaurant will be the only pier in the country with an elevator leading up to it.

Hollywood

Though it pales in comparison its more famous neighbors, at least in terms of public perception, Hollywood (pop. 140,000) is a full-fledged city with five miles of sandy beach. The centerpiece of that beach is a paved 2.5-mile walkway called the Broadwalk (no, that's not a typo but an anagram). There are roughly 50 street-end public accesses onto the beach and Broadwalk. Since Miami Beach and Fort Lauderdale haven't learned how to say "no" to development, Hollywood has become an appealing alternative to both—especially at the beach, which can be fairly described as a well-kept secret.

The name "Hollywood" evokes fantasy and wealth, swimming pools, movie stars, and fast-talking hipsters who wear sunglasses after dark. Florida's Hollywood is a different scene altogether, though it does have a tangential tie to the Golden State. John W. Young, a California land speculator, initially planned Florida's Hollywood as a resort for the rich. To that end, he had the palm-lined Hollywood Boulevard run east to the Hollywood Beach Resort Hotel—the castle he built to house all the glittering Gatsbys he expected to descend on the place. After an initial burst of popularity, however, Hollywood fell from favor and has forever played second (or third) fiddle to its glitzy neighbors, Miami Beach and Fort Lauderdale.

THE GOLD COAST

Hollywood Beach Broadwalk

© PARKE PUTERBAUGH

In the later decades of the 20th century, Hollywood all but disappeared from the radar of American beachgoers. In fact, foreign visitors at times seemed to outnumber those from U.S., and a number of ethnic restaurants on and near the Broadwalk catered to their palettes. Canadians love Hollywood, highrailing it down from the Great White North to thaw out in winter or chill out in summer. During Florida's blistering summers, a sizable number of South Americans show up for a winter respite. We've seen German fräuleins and families from Ireland and England working on their sunburns. We've bantered with friendly, dreadlocked Jamaicans about the laid-back appeal and multi-ethnic makeup of Hollywood Beach.

American beachgoers should wise up, because in our view Hollywood is an understated, appealing city with low-density residences, lots of open space, and a neighborly feel to it. Attempts have been made to give Hollywood a makeover, but pro-development forces have generally met stiff resistance from those who want to maintain the status quo. Certain projects, such as the razing and rebuilding of the old Diplomat Hotel and the erection of the new Hollywood Beach Marriot—the latter being the end result of a contentious, controversial project long known as "Diamond at the Beach"—have finally come to fruition. The really good news is that the Broadwalk is getting an overdue $14 million makeover, which is being overseen by the farsighted Hollywood Beach Community Redevelopment Agency.

Hollywood was at one time a haven for oldsters, with nearly 60 percent of its population on the far side of 45. These days, only 35 percent of the population is over 45 and the median age is 39. We've noticed an increase in the city's vitality over the years, as if it's reversed the aging process. At one time we heard complaints like those of the Broadwalk shopkeeper who groused, "This city is run by an entrenched older establishment that is way behind the times. This beach hasn't changed in 30 years!" Well, it's changing now, but not so quickly that you can't recognize the place. In fact, Hollywood's evolution is proceeding at a seemingly reasonable pace. It almost looks like the 1980s to us there now.

There are beach towns on both coasts that

SANDY SOAP OPERA ON HOLLYWOOD BEACH

One beautiful spring afternoon we chanced upon a TV shoot on Hollywood Beach. It was quite a scene. As we sauntered up, the stars – lithesome, sexy Hispanic girls in revealing summer fashions – were standing around with hands on hips, waiting for the next take. They snapped into character and recited their lines when the director called for action. The plot apparently involved a catfight over a sinister macho man.

We asked a camera operator the name of the show. He smiled, shrugged his shoulders and said, "No comprende." Ah, yes, this was South Florida, the ultimate multiethnic melting pot. We recalled a Hispanic comedy album we'd seen entitled *You're in America Now, Speak Spanish!*

This much we understood: We were watching the filming of a Spanish-language soap opera. The love interest over which the two sexpots were quarreling was a portly, menacing *hombre* in a dark, three-piece wool suit. (In the simplistic code of TV and film, black clothes = bad guy.) He carried a fancy, silver-tipped cane, signifying he was a man of wealth and taste. Since we were sweating in T-shirts and cargo pants, we figured he must be dying in these stifling duds as the midday sun beat down. Between takes he wore a conspiratorial half-smile, as if to say he knew what a ridiculous figure he cut.

A table had been set up on the beach. In the scene's climax, he overturned it with a malevolent flourish, and the bickering young women fled his wrath. However, something didn't go right and the scene had been recut. Various assistants gathered up all of the stuff that flew off the table and rearranged it for take two. The actresses smoked cigarettes and chattered about their evening plans. They were an eye-catching sight. For all we knew, the tarts were superstars in their little corner of TV land.

We're hoping one day to stumble on this episode while channel surfing so that we can tell our children and grandchildren, "We were there!"

would happily turn back the clock to a time before developers did their damage. Hollywood, by contrast, has not given away the goose that laid the golden egg. Most motels on Hollywood Beach are still mom-and-pops, located right behind the dunes with easy access to an egalitarian beach. We couldn't have asked for more than what greeted us on a recent visit: a perfect cloudless afternoon; a wide, sparsely inhabited beach; and affordable eats, cheap thrills, and inexpensive novelty postcards.

For more information, contact the Greater Hollywood Chamber of Commerce, 330 North Federal Highway, Hollywood, FL 33020, 954/923-4000 or 800/231-5562, www.hollywoodchamber.org.

BEACHES

Hollywood Beach runs for 4.5 miles, from Balboa Street to the Hallandale border. They claim to have "over seven miles of beautiful white sand beaches," but this seems an exaggeration to us (though we don't dispute the beaches' beauty). Hollywood Beach is broken down into "north," "central," and "south" areas. The north end, where you'll find **North Beach Park,** is the most pristine and natural looking. **Central Beach** is the defined by the 2.5-mile Broadwalk, which runs from Sherman Street down to Georgia Street. With its shops, restaurants, and watering holes, this is the place to be in Hollywood and is among the best urban beaches on the Gold Coast. It's certainly near the top of our list. **South Beach,** on the other hand, is built up with hotels and condos and has suffered erosion problems. At this end of the beach, public access is gained only at Keating Park, a small public park.

If you're here to have fun, the Broadwalk is the place to be. This 27-foot-wide asphalt promenade has painted lines demarcating lanes for all the human traffic (walkers, bicyclists, in-line skaters, et al.). Lifeguards are stationed the length of the Broadwalk, which is easily accessible. Turn down any side street and you're bound to find a place to park near the Broadwalk. You pull into a spot and pay for a block of time ($1 per hour) at a nearby machine that will spit out a receipt to stick on the dashboard. Signs asking, "Have you paid the master meter?" are posted all over, and you'd better answer yes. There are also pay parking garages; the one on Johnson Street is closest to the heart of the action on the Broadwalk.

The Broadwalk is in the midst of a $14 million renovation that is bringing all sorts of improvements—crushed shell jogging path, tabby concrete bike path, colored pavers on the pedestrian path—that will separate the various forms of human traffic along its length. An 18-inch decorative wall will separate the Broadwalk from the beach. The only sour or sad note in all this is that Hollywood's beach renourishment occurred before Hurricane Wilma blew across from west to east, taking some of the sand back out to sea. The whole Broadwalk improvement project should be finished in early 2007 and parts are done now.

Restaurants and attractions such as miniature golf (play all day for $7!) line the Broadwalk. Shops dispense everything from groceries and electronics to T-shirts and henna tattoos. You can rent banana bikes, surreys, tandems, and more. Speed-demon kids whiz past on three-wheeled beach cruisers. Toward the north end of the Broadwalk, at Garfield Street, is Charnow Park. This city facility is outfitted with picnic tables, playground, and paddleball courts. It's a good place for families and those who want some respite from the Broadwalk bazaar.

The Hollywood Beach Theatre, an outdoor bandshell, is located on Johnson Street at the Broadwalk, and even if no one is performing, you can cool your heels on the seats. Live music is held 7:30 P.M.–9:30 P.M. on Monday, Tuesday, and Wednesday; it tends to lite jazz and easy listening (i.e. Vinnie Vincent, Cozy

Michaels, and the Swell Tones). The Broadwalk Friday Fest features "live music, specials and fun," every second and fourth Friday, and is a hipper, more youthful scene.

Surfing is permitted between Franklin and Meade Streets and between Georgia Street and Azalea Terrace, which are at the north and south ends of the Broadwalk, respectively. Boaters can launch nonmotorized craft here as well. Three reefs lie offshore at distances of a hundred yards, 0.5 mile, and 1.5 miles.

If you're coming for a full day, the best bet is to pay five bucks and park at North Beach Park, located at the north end of the Broadwalk. You can wander the beach or Broadwalk from here without worrying about the master meter. The beach belongs to the city of Hollywood, while the park grounds belong to the county. This 56-acre park has a picnic area with grills, a paved bike path, and the Turtle Cafe.

Hollywood's South Beach area is more built up and less accessible, though **Keating Park,** a small, shaded beachside park at Magnolia Terrace, provides an inviting break in the action.

Though it's not on the beach, **West Lake Park/Anne Kolb Nature Center** (751 Sheridan Street, 954/926-2480) is located along the east bank of the Intracoastal Waterway and is well worth the $1 it costs to get in. This 1,500-acre preserve is one of the largest urban parks we've ever seen. It has a 350-acre lake with a 2.5-mile shoreline, hiking trails, boat rentals, observation tower, and a vast expanse of lovely greenery that makes it easy to forget you're in a city. Environmental boat tours of the lake are offered daily. The Anne Kolb Nature Center has an exhibit hall (another $1 per person) devoted to the lake's mangrove ecosystem.

11 NORTH BEACH PARK

Location: 3601 North Ocean Drive (A1A), at the east end of Sheridan Street in Hollywood

THE GOLD COAST

THE GOLD COAST

Parking/Fees: $5 entrance fee per vehicle ($3 after 2 P.M.)
Hours: 8 A.M.-7:30 P.M. (to 6 P.M. during Eastern Standard Time)
Facilities: concessions, lifeguards, restrooms, picnic tables, and showers
Contact: North Beach Park, 954/926-2444

12 HOLLYWOOD BEACH (CENTRAL BEACH)

    BEST (

Location: Johnson Street at Broadwalk is the heart of Hollywood's central beach district, which extends along the Broadwalk from Sherman to Georgia Streets.
Parking/Fees: metered street parking and fee parking garages at Hollywood Boulevard and Johnson Street
Hours: 24 hours
Facilities: concessions, lifeguards, restrooms, picnic tables, and showers
Contact: Hollywood Beach Safety Department, 954/921-3423

13 HOLLYWOOD BEACH (SOUTH BEACH)

Location: along South Ocean Drive from Azalea Terrace to Magnolia Terrace in Hollywood.
Parking/Fees: metered parking lots
Hours: 8 A.M.-midnight
Facilities: none
Contact: Hollywood Beach Safety Department, 954/921-3423

14 KEATING PARK

Location: South Ocean Drive at Magnolia Terrace in Hollywood
Parking/Fees: metered parking lot
Hours: 8 A.M.-midnight

Facilities: restrooms
Contact: Hollywood Beach Safety Department, 954/921-3423

ACCOMMODATIONS

The Diplomat Hotel—for decades the "crown jewel of Hollywood Beach" before becoming a tarnished, time-worn bauble—closed its doors in 1991. The building sat idle for nearly a decade and was demolished with a spectacular implosion in 2000. Rising to new heights (32 stories!) on the very spot is the **Westin Diplomat Resort** (3555 South Ocean Drive, 954/602-6000, $$$$). It's a destination hotel, boasting fine-dining restaurants (Hollywood Prime and Satine), a bar/cafe (Nikita), and coffee and snack kiosk (Common Grounds) on the lobby level. The lobby is an impressively vaulted space with indoor palm trees, marble floors, and comfy chairs and sofas. There's an adjoining convention center and workout facility. The rooms are first-rate, with Westin's "Heavenly" beds, showerheads, and bath products.

The outdoor pools and decks are huge, warm and womblike, with the lower-level lagoon pool extending for a few hundred feet. It passes beneath the upper-deck, kid-friendly infinity pool. There is nothing not to like about the setup. They've even got a new beach as of mid-2005. Theirs had eroded away, through no fault of their own—the finger can be pointed at the sand-trapping Port Everglades, which has starved southern Broward County of beach-sustaining sediment—but has been widened to about 50 yards. Let's hope it stays put.

About a mile away from the Westin Diplomat is the **Diplomat Country Club** (501 Diplomat Parkway, Hallandale Beach, 954/457-2000, $$$$), a related operation that consists of more rooms, a golf course, and 30,000-square-foot spa. A shuttle runs between them, so guests can enjoy the facilities at both locations.

An old, hotly debated project called Diamond on the Beach, to be built on city-owned land, was intended to revitalize Hollywood Beach. Dragged out for years, it got mired in politics, controversy, and even criminality. Gus Boulis—a South Florida businessman who presided over a gambling (Sun Cruz gaming boats) and fast-food (Miami Subs) empire until he reportedly got whacked by the mob in 2001—was a principal in the Diamond on the Beach development company. The city of Hollywood terminated the lease agreement with Diamond on the Beach in 1999 and was ordered by the court to pay the developer $1 million in 2005. In place of Diamond by the Beach, the city signed a deal with Ocean Properties in September 2005 to build Marriott Ocean Village and Resorts. When completed, this colossus will stretch from Hollywood Beach to the Intracoastal Waterway at Johnson Street, the heart of Hollywood's Central Beach area. Perhaps we've given you too much detail, but the whole sordid saga is illustrative of the way business gets done in South Florida—which is to say it's like something out of a Martin Scorsese film about the mean streets of New York City.

We were impressed with the cheerful staff at the **Holiday Inn Sunspree Resort** (2711 South Ocean Drive, 954/923-8700, $$$). Room rates include access to a large swimming pool, health club, and beach.

You also have the option of stepping back into the Hollywood of yesteryear by staying at the **Ramada Inn Hollywood Beach Hotel** (101 North Ocean Drive, 954/921-0990, $$). It's a survivor from the city's first incarnation as a resort. Now it's a member of the Ramada chain. Built in 1925 and modeled along the Mediterranean lines of Addison Mizner's Palm Beach digs, the Hollywood Beach Hotel once served as a winter playground for wealthy northerners. Its fortunes have ebbed and flowed with the world economy (it's always been popular with an international clientele), and its reincarnation as a Ramada Inn basically tells you all you need to know about its stature these days.

Frankly, there's nothing wrong with the unpretentious, affordable hotels and motels that back right up to the Broadwalk. Don't expect turndown service or Mayfair toiletries, but such unfancy operations as **Motel Expo** (310 Grant Street, 954/923-0420, $) and the **Deane Motel** (300 Broadwalk, 954/927-9236, $) have been accommodating happy families for generations. They don't stand on ceremony here. When we went to the lobby of Motel Expo to ask prices, a hand-lettered note on the door read, "I am on the patio or in the laundry room."

COASTAL CUISINE

Because it has so many fixed-income, bargain-hungry natives and visitors, Hollywood is rife with mediocrity on the food front. It's no South Beach, but you can still scare up a memorable meal if you know where to look.

Top of the line is **Hollywood Prime** (3555 South Ocean Drive, 954/602-8393, $$$$), a classic New York–style steakhouse at the Westin Diplomat. It is a dining destination not just for guests and conventioneers but local businesspeople and residents who want to celebrate in style. The attentive wait staff will make you feel special. It's not a big place—just 22 tables and a few private rooms—but with its 25-foot ceilings, the room feels enormous. You come here to eat beef, pure and simple. The best choices on the menu are the dry-aged prime sirloin steaks, which are sized for two appetites: hungry (10-ounce, $29.95) and hungrier (16-ounce, $39.95). Each steak is served with a side of citrus-flavored sauce made from 22 ingredients, but the steak is pure perfection all by itself. So are the prime rib and, if you're not in the mood for beef, broiled tuna steak.

Everything comes à la carte, so bring your brightest gold card. A tasty Caesar salad, with lots of grated pecorino cheese, is a great starter, as are the chilled Malpeque oysters. Vegetable side dishes, which feed four, cost $9.95. We opted for the creamy, cheesy mashed potatoes and broccolini. Desserts are good, too, and we'd recommend the Grand Marnier crème brûlée or "ice cream creation"—five flavors,

SEMINOLE PARADISE: RESERVATIONS ABOUT THE RESERVATION

We made a road trip to the wilds of West Hollywood to check out the Hard Rock Hotel and Casino. It is sited on a parcel of land belonging to the Seminole Indian tribe. All we can say is that reservation life isn't what it used to be. While a massive infusion of greenbacks has lifted the quality of life for the cash-strapped Native Americans, their ancestors must be rolling over in their graves at the sight of all the debauchery – gambling, gluttony, boozing, and mindless shopaholic behavior – occurring on what we're constantly reminded is "sacred land."

The hotel and casino are just part of a complex of shops and clubs known as Seminole Paradise. (For the record, it's located right off S.R. 7/U.S. 441, just north of Stirling Road in Hollywood). The signage throughout this consumer wasteland depicts the midriff-bared torso of a svelte model. Surrounding her navel are snappy phrases trumpeting the "hot times" to be had here.

We came, we saw, we gambled – won $35 between us, in fact – but left with a hollow feeling inside. It seemed like just another chapter in the shameful exploitation of the Seminoles since Europeans first landed in Florida, except the Native Americans are helping to write this one themselves. And you can't really blame them. Who in their right mind turns down money in America?

We entered Seminole Paradise in the vicinity of Hooters, where waitresses in tight orange shorts and cleavage-baring T-shirts serve beer and cheesy chicken wings to a leering clientele. Next we came upon a series of clubs that provided fake evocations of a foreign country or musical genre. This is what culture has been reduced to in these plastic paradises: an overpriced mug of Harp beer at a faux Irish bar with neon cloverleaves called Murphy's Law or an earful of lite jazz in a purple-lit faux piano bar called Jazziz. At the latter, a shaven-headed oaf bellowed Billy Joel's "New York State of Mind" to a nearly empty room. We reminded ourselves that we were on an Indian reservation, and it seemed very weird indeed.

Of course, Seminole Paradise has a sports bar with numberless TV sets tuned to a multitude of games for the amusement of those for whom the season never ends. You can drink and play billiards at a phony upscale pool hall called Knight Time Trick Shot and Champagne Bar. The staged sights and sounds reach a crescendo at Legend's, a pricey concert attraction where imposters perform lifelike re-creations of such entertainment legends as Aretha Franklin, Marilyn Monroe, Elvis Presley, and the Blues Brothers.

They leave no arrowhead unturned at Seminole Paradise. To satisfy the prurient urges of horn dogs out for a night on the reservation, a strip club called Pas-

including raspberry sorbet and coconut. The signature dessert is a Valrhona chocolate cake. It takes half an hour to prepare, so place your order at the start of the meal. Also on the Westin Diplomat premises is **Satine** (3555 South Ocean Drive, 954/602-8930, $$$$), an Asian restaurant—complete with music and dance floor—that serves sushi and entrees such as steamed Florida snapper with bok choy, jasmine rice, ginger, and scallions.

At the other extreme, in terms of cost and atmosphere, is **Capone's Flicker Lite Pizza & Raw Bar** (1014 North Ocean Drive, 954/922-4232, $$). Flicker Lite is a combination pizza joint, restaurant, lounge, and liquor store set in a nondescript roadside strip along Ocean Drive in north Hollywood. The servers are characters, and the food is good, solid fare. The deck looks out on a pleasant scene: a waterway and view tower of the tree-filled West

sions – complete with a glaring, goateed bouncer at the door – has been situated on the backside of the complex.

Among the many shops where one can empty their purses or wallets, we were rendered speechless by a gimmick-driven clothier called Black Market and White House, which sells only black and white clothing. Niche marketing at its finest! By now, if you've worked up an appetite, you can drop $18-24 on a seafood entree at Bluepoint Ocean Grill.

All but hidden in a corner of the mall is the Seminole Okalee Indian Village & Museum, a grudging concession to Native American history drowned out by the surrounding mayhem. Now we'll pose the obvious question: What does any of this have to do with Seminole heritage and culture?

We'll leave you to ponder the answer, 'cause we're headed over to the casino. Upon entering, we briefly studied the musical memorabilia cases by the front door, which were heavy on the hard rock: Guns 'n' Roses, Motley Crue, Def Leppard. We saw Slash's top hat, Duff McKagen's vest, and Joe Elliott's ripped jeans. Thus edified, we peered over the rail into the "poker area," where people sat poker-faced as hands were dealt. An overweight woman with jiggling arm fat who was wearing a leopard-print top circulated among the gamblers, vending cigarettes from a tray. (Yes, you can light up here, and plenty of smoke signals are exhaled on the casino floor.)

"These people are dead and they just don't know it yet," we muttered to each other. "They're skeletons with skin on them."

Nonetheless, being chipper when-in-Rome types, we invested a miserly amount of our publisher's advance in the computerized slot machines. They have nickel slots, but you must wager a minimum of nine credits per play, so a five-cent slot machine is really a 45-cent slot machine. One of us scored two bars and a "Super 7" on the quarter slot, winning $27 on his very first press of the game button. The other won $16 on a Monopoly slot machine.

Mostly we absorbed the surreal ambience of a large, teeming casino in which every seat was taken. Affixed to posts throughout the casino are flat-screen TVs bombarding gamblers with sports events and rock videos. The slots all made burbling noises, and hundreds of them burbling simultaneously sounded like one of Philip Glass's minimalist compositions. It's vaguely soothing and must lull the public into a compliant mindset that causes them to play until they're depleted.

The patrons in the casino were enough to give us serious pause: gum-chomping losers, many of them grossly overweight; guys in cowboy hats who have never been near a horse; crab-faced old folks seriously afflicted with a gambling addiction. The universally stultified expressions worn by people who were none too alert to begin with told us it was time to leave. So we quit while we were ahead, exiting with serious reservations about Seminole Paradise.

THE GOLD COAST

Lake Park. We dined adjacent to a table full of postal clerks, while TV sets with bad color broadcast soap operas and CNN overhead. Very unpretentious.

Flicker Lite's "world famous" hand-tossed pizzas are made with a homemade sauce recipe. We opted for grouper and tuna sandwiches— thick, mouth-filling fillets accompanied by cole slaw, crispy fries, or pasta salad. Iced tea is served in huge plastic cups and was good enough that we caffeinated ourselves with several refills.

A few seafood restaurants along North Ocean Drive (A1A) overlook the Intracoastal Waterway. They cater simultaneously to the boating, dining, and party-cruising crowds. We snagged a decent seafood platter at **Martha's Tropical Grille** (6024 North Ocean Drive, 954/923-5444, $$), a second-floor dining room that's locally renowned

RENOURISHING SOUTH FLORIDA'S ERODED BEACHES

The largest beach restoration project in history was conducted along Miami Beach from 1977 to 1982 by the U.S. Army Corps of Engineers, which placed 14.5 million cubic yards of sand on 9.3 miles of shore – from Bal Harbour to South Beach – to create a new beach the width of a football field. The bill for the project was $60 million. Each year, roughly 200,000 cubic yards are required to maintain the beach at its desired width.

The euphemism for this procedure is "beach renourishment." Sand costs $2–10 per cubic yard, and 100,000 cubic yards are needed on average for each project. Even though such unprecedented investment might appear worth it from a cost-benefit perspective – the benefit being tourist-generated revenue – in reality the cost is quickly becoming prohibitive. Exhibit A is a "critically eroded" 38-mile stretch spanning either side of the Broward/Dade county line. Though 1.75 million cubic yards of sand were pumped onto these beaches in late 2005, some of it was lost immediately in places like Hollywood, where Hurricane Wilma blew across the state from west to east shortly after the new sand had been laid down.

Moreover, the sand supply itself for such projects is dwindling. Florida has come close to depleting its offshore sandbanks for purposes of beach renourishment. Already, Dade and Broward Counties have effectively consumed all the usable sand that can be dredged. They've been hungrily eyeing the Bahamas as an alternative source of sand, but Bahamian sand is way more expensive. One University of South Florida geologist compared the current crisis-driven response of beach renourishment to "taking aspirin for a brain tumor."

Though nature can do spectacular damage on occasion, it's usually of a kind that heals itself over time. The root causes of severe beach erosion along the East Coast of the U.S., especially in South Florida, are human-generated. The principal culprits are the flattening of dunes and dune vegetation for oceanfront developments; the erection of seawalls to protect homes and condos built too close to the water; and the construction of groins and jetties to hold inlets, harbors, and beaches in place. Blockage of the natural north-south flow of sand with the currents (a process known as "longshore transport") caused by these structures results in eroded beaches on the downdrift side. Being that it lies at the very bottom of the state, Miami Beach is downdrift of *everything:* all the inlets, jetties, groins, seawalls, and condos from Fernandina Beach south. That's 372 miles of arrested sand flow. No wonder Miami lost its beach. No wonder Hollywood, only 20 miles north, had no beach to speak of in 2004, remedied by extensive and expensive dredging soon thereafter.

Miami's renourished beach from the early 1980s has stuck around long enough to be judged a success. Before the infusion, waves were literally lapping at the lower floors of resort hotels. All the new sand was a consoling sight. Subsequently, dune plantings have helped stabilize the renourished beaches. A wooden boardwalk runs along and above the dunes, offering abundant public beach accesses The result is one of the more successful beach restorations in the world. Yet there have been setbacks, such as Hurricane Andrew (1992) and Hurricane Wilma (2005).

Meanwhile, the renourished Miami Beach strand remains a healthy width. Parts of Miami Beach are so wide that some visitors gripe about having to hike so far across the hot sand to get to the water. A decade from now, beachgoers who are able to complain of the same inconvenience should consider themselves lucky.

for its Floridian and Caribbean cuisine and Sunday brunches. The ground-level supper club has a different menu, and tourists can follow their broiled platter with dancing to the swingin' sounds of yesteryear.

Out on the Broadwalk, an unpretentious assortment of food stalls and restaurants with outdoor patios await hungry beachgoers. Some of them have an ethnic flair. **Istanbul** (707 North Broadwalk, 954/921-1263, $$) offers a taste of Turkey. **Nick's Bar & Grill** (1214 North Broadwalk, 954/920-2800, $$) makes a good stop for a casual meal of seafood, steak, or salad.

NIGHTLIFE

We were fascinated by the variety of ethnic pubs and restaurants along Hollywood Beach. **O'Malley's Ocean Pub** (101 North Ocean Drive, 954/920-4062), located on the ground floor of the Ramada Inn Hollywood Beach Hotel, is a cross between an Irish pub and surf bar. Wi-Fi Internet access, too! Certain street ends along the Broadwalk offer cozy saloons that cater to a particular clientele. For coffeehouse aficionados, two gathering places in close proximity are **Now Art Cafe** (1820 South Young Circle, 954/922-0506) and **Cafe Latte** (1840 South Young Circle, 954/926-6644). If you want to venture out a bit, the nightlife really pops at Seminole Paradise, the casino-shopping mall-restaurant-hotel complex in West Hollywood. (For more on this, see the *Seminole Paradise: Reservations About the Reservation* sidebar.)

Hallandale Beach

The last sand trap in Broward County is Hallandale Beach (pop. 36,000). This boomtown was formerly known as Hallandale, with the "Beach" having officially been appended in 2000. While Dania Beach has jai alai and Hollywood is Florida's greyhound racing capital, Hallandale Beach is home to **Gulfstream Park** (901 South Federal Highway, 954/456-

1515), Florida's premier horse-racing track. The Florida Derby and other races are held here mid-January–early May.

Hallandale has, to our jaded eyes, become "Hellendale." For years it has been an under-construction madhouse along the beach, where dust and noise are the rule as older buildings go down and condo towers go up. The most visually striking thing about Hallandale is its water tower, a rainbow-hued structure that resembles a teed-up golf ball. Since you can't miss this landmark, you won't miss Hallandale Beach's main beach, either, because its parking lot is located at the base of the colorful tower.

For more information, contact the Hallandale Beach Chamber of Commerce, 1117 East Hallandale Beach Boulevard, Hallandale Beach, FL 33009, 954/454-0541, www.ci.hallandale.fl.us.

BEACHES

Hallandale City Beach is a two-part affair. The north and south ends are each 300 feet long, with another football field's worth of private property separating them. North Beach is located where Hallandale Beach Boulevard meets Ocean Drive (A1A). It's shoehorned between condos, beneath a water tower, and behind a fire station. Most of the paved parking spots are for the fire department, but there's a dusty lot for beachgoers. You pay the $5 parking fee at the **Beachside Cafe** (2800 East Hallandale Beach Boulevard, 954/458-1055, $), a concrete hut serving everything from fast food to fish dinners (alcoholic beverages, too). Its sunbaked simplicity offers a fading snapshot of what fun used to be like in South Florida.

You won't have much fun on the beach proper, though, as it's a pitiful, eroded affair. It was pretty far gone before Hurricane Wilma walloped the area, and now it's almost beyond reclamation. How is a measly few feet of beach supposed to serve an entire community? Hallandale City Beach is hemmed in on both sides by condos and under relentless assault from the Atlantic Ocean, and it's too late to do much about it.

THE GOLD COAST

The south unit of Hallandale City Beach offers more of the same, the main difference being that the food concession—**Beachside South** (1800 South Ocean Drive, 954/458-5300, $)—is a bit more rudimentary, dispensing basic fare like burgers, chips, and sodas from a trailer. This part is landscaped with Australian pines, an exotic planting that other beach communities are working to eradicate.

15 HALLANDALE CITY BEACH (NORTH BEACH)

Location: Hallandale Beach Boulevard at A1A, in Hallandale Beach
Parking/Fees: $5 entrance fee per vehicle
Hours: 6 A.M.-10 P.M.
Facilities: concessions, lifeguards, restrooms, picnic tables, and showers
Contact: Hallandale Parks and Recreation Department, 954/457-1456

16 HALLANDALE CITY BEACH (SOUTH BEACH)

Location: just south of Hallandale Beach Boulevard, along A1A in Hallandale Beach
Parking/Fees: metered parking lot ($0.75 per hour)
Hours: 6 A.M.-10 P.M.
Facilities: concessions, lifeguards, restrooms, picnic tables, and showers
Contact: Hallandale Parks and Recreation Department, 954/457-1456

Golden Beach

The first barnacle on Dade County's oceanfront hull is Golden Beach, a wealthy residential municipality (pop. 900) within the Greater Miami sprawl, 11 miles north of Miami Beach, near the Broward County line. Golden Beach stretches from 194th Street down to Haulover Park. It's an off-putting place that really doesn't welcome visitors. One reason for Golden Beach's sour mood may be that the community was embroiled in and ultimately lost a protracted legal battle with neighboring Sunny Isles Beach and Miami Beach.

Actually, the town's real nemesis is the U.S. Army Corps of Engineers, and it had every right to be steamed when the corps dredged the ocean floor 1.5 miles offshore. Opponents were concerned that the process would damage and even destroy sensitive coral reefs. Golden Beach contended that the Corps ignored hired experts (a trademark of the Corps at the shore). The imbroglio was referred to as "South Florida's first big sand war." A three-year battle ended in late 1996 when a U.S. district court judge ruled that the corps could proceed. Golden Beach again filed for an injunction but was denied and the dredging began. A dredge the size of a football field worked round the clock for two months, pumping sand down to needy Sunny Isles Beach and Miami Beach. More than 700,000 cubic yards were removed.

While we side with grumpy Golden Beach on this one, we wonder if they were motivated by anything more than self-interest. What's needed is a sane approach to coastal development and beach renourishment so that communities are not pitted against one another, with reefs and offshore ecosystems being the ultimate losers. Golden Beach was tossed a bone in 2000 when an artificial reef was offered as compensation for all the sand that had been dredged and placed elsewhere.

Now Golden Beach itself is in dire need of sand. The entire stretch of coast from south Hollywood to Golden Beach has lost virtually all of its beach sand, an inevitable process accelerated by the hurricanes of 2004 and 2005. As expected, the Army Corps of Engineers is back, dredging like crazy to put another sandy Band-Aid in place. It's the myth of Sisyphus reenacted as an expensive, cautionary tale about the futility of messing with nature.

For more information, contact the Florida Gold Coast Chamber of Commerce, 1100 Kane Concourse, Suite 210, Bal Harbour, FL 33154, 305/866-6020, www.flgoldcc.org.

BEACHES

The unfriendly spirit of Golden Beach is expressed in signs that read: "Private Beach. Residents Only." With the open, accessible beaches of Hollywood and Miami Beach close by, Golden Beach has nothing to offer visitors but an unspoken directive to move along. In short, there is no public beach access in Golden Beach.

Well, perhaps in response to constant complaints, they've added four public parking spaces at Tweedle Park, near the south end of town ($1.25 per hour). Other than that niggardly gesture, there are no easements, no right-of-ways, no public accesses, nada. From end to end, the town is private property, mostly older hacienda-style homes that prohibit even a single glimpse of the ocean. You have to live here or be visiting someone who does to legally cross private property to get onto the beach (which is, by definition, public property seaward of the mean high-tide line). For this reason, we find some sort of karmic comeuppance in the fact that the state of Florida took Golden Beach's offshore sand to pump up the beaches elsewhere in Miami-Dade County. At least the public is welcomed on those renourished beaches.

Sunny Isles Beach

Sunny Isles Beach (pop. 17,000)—formerly just Sunny Isles and incorporated in 1997—is the most visitor-friendly of the pack of oceanfront communities in north Dade County. Its motto, emblazoned on pennants along Collins Avenue, is "We love our residents and visitors." They also love developers, as luxury high-rises are going up like gangbusters all along the oceanfront. We were not happy to witness the change, as Sunny Isles had always been a place

we looked forward to visiting, being safer and slower-paced than Miami Beach and more welcoming than Golden Beach and its ilk.

What Sunny Isles Beach mainly has to offer the touring public are hotels and motels, from single-story dinghies to towering dreadnoughts. The latter, unfortunately, have begun to elbow out many of the mom-and-pop motels and sun-baked apartments that defined this cheerful town in year's past. There are, in fact, a number of motels we'd love to recommend, but we realize it's only a matter of time before they, too, will sell out to developers.

Regardless of all the actual and impending changes, Sunny Isles Beach still draws visitors from all over the world. A local accommodations guide lists the languages spoken ("translation services available") at each hotel and motel. These include: Arabic, Bengali, Bulgarian, Cantonese, Catalan, Chinese, Creole, Czech, Dutch, Finnish, French, French-Canadian (yes, a separate listing), German, Greek, Hebrew, Hindi, Hungarian, Italian, Japanese, Korean, Mandarin, Polish, Portuguese, Russian, Serbo-Croatian, Spanish, Swedish, Tagalog, Ukrainian, Urdu, and Yiddish. Can you say, "Where's the beach?" in Tagalog? Oh, we almost forgot: English is spoken here, too. Often with a thick New York accent.

One lure to Sunny Isles Beach is its dive sites. In the offshore waters, divers can explore four artificial reefs—wrecks deposited between 1985 and 1991 to promote the formation of reef communities. For specifics on location and rules, call 305/375-DERM (350/375-3376).

For more information, contact the Sunny Isles Beach Resort Association, 17070 Collins Avenue, Sunny Isles Beach, FL 33160, 305/947-5826, www.sunnyislesfla.com.

BEACHES

Sunny Isles Beach is located near the intersection of Sunny Isles Causeway (S.R. 826) and A1A. It stretches for five miles, from 194th Street to Bayview Court. Some of it has been replenished from sand dredged offshore of neighboring Golden Beach. The town has provided 11 beach-access points along Collins Avenue. Metered parking can be found at each access; the meters run 24 hours a day, seven days a week, with a 12-hour limit. Newport Pier, located at the Newport Beachside Hotel & Resort, is the center of fishing and surfing activity. **Pier Park** has gotten hard to get to with all the construction going on. In fact, the parking lot is closed "until further notice" and one must park off-site and use a pedestrian walkway to get onto the beach. Not that we think it's worth the trouble these days. Really, about the only beach park in Sunny Isles that's worth a hoot is **Gilbert Samson Oceanfront Park,** a two-acre park at the town's midsection.

Haulover Beach is our preferred beach hereabouts, offering more than 1.25 miles of untrammeled nature in the middle of the heavily urbanized Gold Coast. It's a nice, well-tended beach, where the coarse brown sand is raked regularly for seaweed and litter. Located at the south end of Sunny Isles and extending down to Baker's Haulover Inlet (a man-made cut), Haulover has four large parking lots (where you'll pay a $5 entrance fee) and enough beach to accommodate all ages and lifestyle preferences.

You see, at least part of Haulover Beach is clothing-optional. It's one of the few nude beaches of any consequence in the state of Florida, and that fact has generated a bit of controversy. The benignly tolerant county of Miami-Dade had no objection to the revenue brought in by the fee-paying naturists. However, when their naked buns began overwhelming the beach, a hue and cry ensued.

The solution arrived at has been reasonable and fair. Up at the north end—out of view of families and others who might be offended—an 800-yard stretch of Haulover's 1.3-mile beach has been partitioned off for those who want to swim and sunbathe in the buff. The scene is self-sorted into gay and hetero sections (heavy on the former). Appropriately, a pink lifeguard stand is the line of demarcation for gay naturists. The scene is pretty mellow, with well-behaved sunbathers and little overt revelry. Certainly, it's less

"see and be seen" than South Beach. In fact, you really wouldn't want to see most of the gentle folk here without their clothing (trust us).

Issues of nudity aside, there's little not to like about Haulover Beach. It's a one-stop summer vacation, with a marina, restaurants, volleyball courts, picnic areas, children's playgrounds, tennis and golf centers—even a kite shop.

Down by the inlet at the south end of the beach is a jetty, which draws anglers and surfers. At Haulover Marine Center, you can charter a full or half day of drift and bottom fishing. Almost everything about the park is, uh, fishy. Haulover acquired its name from an early fisherman in the area, a man named Baker who would regularly haul his sponge boat from Biscayne Bay over the thickly wooded dunes to the ocean at this spot. The practice was adopted by succeeding generations of fishermen. "Baker's Haulover" appears on maps as early as 1823. Remnants of lush cypress groves and sea grape canopy can be admired as you walk to the beach from the lots at Haulover. Admiration mingles with sadness when you realize that all of south Florida's coastline looked like this not so long ago.

17 SUNNY ISLES BEACH

Location: 11 access points along Collins Avenue between 157th and 193rd Streets in Sunny Isles Beach
Parking/fees: metered street and lot parking
Hours: 24 hours
Facilities: none
Contact: Sunny Isles City Hall, 305/957-1311

18 GILBERT SAMSON OCEANFRONT PARK

Location: 17425 Collins Avenue, near foot of William Lehman Causeway in Sunny Isles Beach
Parking/fees: free parking lot
Hours: 24 hours

Facilities: restrooms, picnic tables, and showers
Contact: Sunny Isles City Hall, 305/957-1311

19 PIER PARK

Location: Sunny Isles Causeway (State Route 826) and Collins Avenue in Sunny Isles Beach
Parking/fees: metered parking lot
Hours: 24 hours
Facilities: lifeguards, restrooms, and showers
Contact: Sunny Isles City Hall, 305/957-1311

20 HAULOVER BEACH

BEST (

Location: 10800 Collins Avenue, in North Miami Beach
Parking/fees: $3.50 per vehicle entrance fee
Hours: sunrise-sunset
Facilities: concessions, lifeguards, restrooms, picnic tables, and showers
Contact: Haulover Beach Park, 305/947-3525

ACCOMMODATIONS

One used to be able to find enchanting oddball architectural touches outside some of the old motels and motor courts that once lined Sunny Isles Beach. In front of the old Sahara Beach Club Motel, for instance, were sculptured camels that dated from the building's construction in 1953. You won't see sights like these any longer, but we can remember not so many years ago when Sunny Isles Beach resembled a living museum of the kind of tourism that thrived when the area exploded as a vacation mecca in the middle of the 20th century.

Today you'll only find Taj Mahals of faded glory like the **Ramada Plaza Marco Polo Beach Resort** (19201 Collins Avenue, 305/932-2233, $$$). This old, historic 550-room leviathan has restaurants, a lounge, and shopping arcade. Not to be outdone, the tropically festooned **Newport Beachside Hotel & Resort** (16701 Collins Avenue, 305/949-1300, $$$)—formerly a Holiday Inn Crowne Plaza—has a deli, pub, club, and pier.

An omen of the misfortune awaiting Sunny Isles Beach is the imminent arrival of an unholy trinity of Trump Towers, soulless, 40-story

Haulover Beach

© PARKE PUTERBAUGH

THE GOLD COAST

luxury condos obliterating a half-mile of ocean-front in the 15800 block of Collins Avenue. Already in business is the **Trump International Sonesta Beach Resort** (18001 Collins Avenue, 305/692-5600, $$$$), a 22-story tower where rooms start at $329 in season. In his usual humble style, Donald claims to be "redefining" Sunny Isles. Donald describes his "vision" as "Trump Luxury Miami Style." That's right, way up here in Sunny Isles Beach, 10 miles above South Beach.

Surrounding the perimeter of the apocalyptic Trump Towers construction site is a fence adorned with a mural of "the Donald," with his Wookie-syle hair, flanked by a couple of business associates. It's hard to imagine anyone in this gaggle of pale-faced, desk-bound goons actually spending time on a beach. This makes it sadly ironic that they're "redefining" a beach that did not appear to need a drastic makeover. Goodbye, sweet old Sunny Isles. You're being Trumped into oblivion, whether you realize it or not.

COASTAL CUISINE

A sentimental favorite of longstanding is **Wolfie Cohen's Rascal House** (172nd Street at Collins Avenue, 305/947-4581, $$). For over 50 years, this hefty home of Manhattan-style delicatessen gourmandizing has occupied the heart of Sunny Isles' motel row, overwhelming diners with more than 400 menu items. These range from seafood to stuffed cabbage. Where else could you find salmon croquettes, stewed fruits, and chopped liver on a menu at the beach?

Wolfie's pièce de résistance is its famous corned beef sandwich, an "eating experience" piled higher than the proverbial condo. How popular is it? Well, one employee does nothing but carve corned beef all day long at his own station. If you can eat an entire corned-beef sandwich in a single sitting, you should immediately point your feet in the direction of the nearest gym to do some calorie-burning penance. We opted for the turkey sandwich (2.5 inches of roast turkey on rye) and

smoked salmon on a bagel with cream cheese. Wolfie's provides metal bowls full of accompaniments—pickles, slaw, and such. After overeating to our heart's content, we were further seduced by our chatty, touchy-feely waitress to split a slice of strawberry cheesecake for dessert.

The menu is vast and extensive, the company is colorful (*oy*, you've never heard such kvetching!), and the joint never closes. We never figured out where the "rascal" part comes in, but we did learn on our last visit that Andy Kaufman once worked at Wolfie's Deli in Los Angeles. That's endorsement enough for us.

NIGHTLIFE

Virtually all of the action that remains to be found in Sunny Isles is in the big hotels. The bar at the **Best Western Thunderbird Hotel** (18401 Collins Avenue, 305/931-7700)—a survivor from the mid-1950s and a reported hangout for the Rat Pack—is called **The Birdcage.** At the Newport Beachside Hotel & Resort (16701 Collins Avenue, 305/949-1300), you can still dance like it's 1999 at the **Seven Seas Lounge.** Parts of Sunny Isles Beach still resemble the Gold Coast back in the old days, but the past is fading fast if not altogether extinct.

Bal Harbour and Surfside

On the south side of Haulover Inlet are a pair of pleasant municipalities just above Miami Beach's frantic orbit. Bal Harbour (pop. 3,300) stretches from Haulover Inlet to 96th Street. It is the tonier of the two, with its "world famous" Bal Harbour Shops (located at Collins Avenue and 96th Street). If you get weak in the knees at the word "elegance," Bal Harbour is your kind of shopping mecca. Founded in 1965, this high-end mall—offering a half-million square feet of high-end shopping—is located one block off the ocean.

Its 90 stores include dozens of "the world's most elite shops," including Nieman Marcus, Prada, Cartier, Tiffany, Chanel, Dior, Versace, and Ralph Lauren.

Bal Harbour profited from Miami Beach's hard times, before its art deco renaissance. Now that glamorous shopping is again thriving in South Beach—on Lincoln Boulevard, to be exact—the Bal Harbour Shops have faced some formidable competition. Still, Bal Harbor Shops continues to distinguish itself as the nation's toniest, earning more per square foot than any other mall in America.

Surfside (pop. 5,000) occupies 10 blocks, running from 96th Street down to 87th Terrace. It's homey and residential—more like a suburb of Miami Beach than a resort destination.

For more information, contact the Florida Gold Coast Chamber of Commerce, 1100 Kane Concourse, Suite 210, Bal Harbour, FL 33154, 305/866-6020, www.village.bal-harbour.fl.us; or the Surfside Tourist Board, 9301 Collins Avenue, Surfside, FL 33154, 305/864-0722, www.town.surfside.fl.us.

BEACHES

The lapping blue-green waters off Bal Harbour and Surfside are safe and unthreatening, even to small children. **Bal Harbour** is all of 0.3 mile long, and it provides beach access at both ends: under the Haulover Bridge (102nd Street), where there's a metered lot, and at 96th Street, where there's a fee parking lot attached to the Sheraton. On good wave days, surfers fill the Haulover Bridge parking lot. The town has had to have its beach periodically renourished, which is par for the coast. A palm-shaded walking/jogging path extends from one end of Bal Harbour to another (all of six blocks!), and Surfside picks up the baton with its own beachside walkway.

Public access in similarly small-scaled **Surfside** extends down to 88th Street. Surfside provides access to a lifeguarded beach at 93rd Street and Collins Avenue, behind the community center. At 87th Terrace—Surf-

side's boundary with Miami Beach—the most remarkable bounty in Greater Miami greets you at North Shore Open Space Park (see *Miami Beach*).

21 BAL HARBOUR

Location: along Collins Avenue between 102nd and 96th Streets in Bal Harbour, with access points at both ends

Parking/fees: metered parking lot under the Haulover Bridge at 102nd Street and Collins Avenue. Fee parking at the Bal Harbour Shops and Sheraton Bal Harbour, at 96th Street and Collins Avenue.

Hours: 24 hours

Facilities: none

Contact: Bal Harbour Town Hall, 305/866-4633

22 SURFSIDE

Location: at street ends between 96th and 88th Streets in Surfside

Parking/Parking/fees: metered street parking

Hours: 24 hours

Facilities: lifeguards, restrooms, and showers

Contact: Surfside Town Hall, 305/861-4863

ACCOMMODATIONS

The **Sheraton Bal Harbour Beach Resort** (9701 Collins Avenue, 305/865-7511, $$$$) and **Sea View Hotel** (9909 Collins Avenue, 305/866-4441, $$$$) are pricey but well placed. The Sea View has been around for more than 50 years and is a European-style high-rise hostelry in the grand tradition. You'll pay $235–320 a night to stay here in season (mid-December–mid-April), and $165–245 the rest of the year. The Sheraton is a 16-story, 642-room contemporary monster breaching vertical space between the beach and the Bal Harbour Shops. It's got easy access to the beach and shopping, three restaurants, spa and health club, and a $12 million "fantasy

LITTLE HAVANA: THE CUBAN COMMUNITY IN MIAMI

Tony Wagner has been living in Little Havana since the early 1960s, when he was just a boy. He was born and raised in Cuba, where his father worked for the government until Fidel Castro's Communist revolution upended life in that island nation and sent families like the Wagners fleeing. Wagner, who gave us a guided tour of Little Havana, remembers the suddenness of their uprooting, and the hurt hasn't entirely gone away after four decades.

"The Cuban experience is a very particular and painful experience," he said with a rueful smile. Many of those who left rather than endure life under Castro landed in Miami. This community of exiled Cubans took root as "Little Havana" in what had been a poor neighborhood of elderly Jewish retirees.

Little Havana made national news in 1999 when "Little Elian Gonzalez" – which is how he was identified in the round-the-clock coverage on CNN and other networks – lived here with relatives. Gonzalez had been rescued at sea by a resident of Little Havana after the capsizing of a raft transporting him, his mother, her boyfriend, and others to the United States from Cuba. It was a miracle that he survived, but that was just the beginning of a long and torturous legal battle to keep his Cuban father from taking him home. The Cuban community in Miami wanted to stay in the U.S., while his biological father, the immigration service, attorney general Janet Reno, and Fidel Castro believed that the father's wishes should legally prevail. It was the biggest story out of Florida until the 2000 election fiasco.

The Elian Gonzalez story might have died down, but the passions it stirred in Little Havana didn't. In fact, there was a direct link between Gonzalez and the disputed 2000 election. The position of the Clinton administration, which sided with Reno, so enraged the Cuban community in Miami that they switched party allegiances and

poolscape." It's also got a price tag that starts at $305 a night in season.

On the more affordable side, **Baymar Ocean Resort** (9401 Collins Avenue, 305/866-5446, $$) is a three-story motel with a 300-foot beach, palm-fringed courtyard, and pool a few blocks south of Bal Harbour in Surfside. You'll pay $125 a night for an oceanfront room in season.

Miami Beach

To rephrase the late Richard Nixon, a frequent visitor to the Miami area during his troubled presidency, "Let us make one thing perfectly clear": Miami Beach (pop. 88,000) and Miami are two different places—technically, legally, and practically. The urban Frankenstein of Miami (population 375,000) is home to more than 60 cultural groups, the busiest cruise-ship harbor in the world, and one of the most heavily trafficked airports in North America.

How busy is Miami International Airport? It is claimed that of the nearly 10 million annual visitors to Greater Miami, 93 percent arrive by air and only 7 percent by car, boat, or train. Moreover, 55 percent of them are foreign visitors. No wonder Miami often feels as if it's not really a part of the United States. It is more of a stateless international community than your typical American city.

Miami is often referred to as the "city of the Americas." It is a fascinating polyglot of multi-ethnic neighborhoods like Coral Gables, Little Havana, Little Haiti, Hialeah, Biscayne Park, Bayside, and North Miami. This particular Miami is beyond the scope of this

voted for George Bush – this despite the fact that candidate (and vice-president) Al Gore said Elian should stay.

We saw pro-Bush signs (and none for Gore) staked around Little Havana in December 2000. The lingering association with Clinton ultimately hurt Gore in Little Havana, and those lost votes provided the slim-to-none margin that pushed Bush to apparent victory in Florida – and, therefore, the nation.

Little Havana (or "Calle Ocho") is presently undergoing a modest renaissance. The neighborhood informally runs from 37th to 8th Avenues and is solidly Cuban from 27th Avenue on down. As a matter of definition, the Little Havana Historic District runs from 17th to 8th Avenues. It is a lively bazaar. Maximo Gomez Park, a city park without so much as a square foot of greenery, provides tables and shelter where Cuban men play dominos and smoke cigars. You can hear the clicking of domino tiles and hearty laughter competing with street noise and the overhead sounds of jet traffic. (Little Havana is directly in the flight pattern for Miami International Airport.)

Moving along, we entered a cantina called Cafe Panza. In one room, Cuban men rolled dice while smoke curled from the ever-present cigars pressed between their lips. Over by the bar, curing hams hung overhead. In the back room, Cuban art – colorful, zesty, and surprisingly cubist in style, with a debt owed to Picasso – hung on the walls. Who would've thought you'd find Cuban cubism on the walls of a cantina in Little Havana?

It is these sorts of surprises that makes the area so delightful. Directly across the street is Bode & Moore, one of the most celebrated small cigar makers in the world. Shops like it abound in Little Havana, which teems with the sights and sounds of Cuban culture. We asked our host how many residents of Little Havana would return to Cuba if Castro were removed from power or died.

"What are we going to do, go back and start over?" Wagner retorted. "This is who we are now. We will stay here. This will be an extension of Cuba and vice versa. Rather than look at it negatively, like some people do in different parts of the country, I think it will make this nation a lot stronger. It is good for us as a people because we are more enculturated and have better diversity. We're Calle Ocho. We're international."

beach-themed book. After the Elian Gonzalez debacle, the Republican-plotted December 2000 "white riot" at the county courthouse (which cut short a legal recount of Bush-Gore presidential ballots), and the 2005 arrest in Miami of Luis Posada Carriles—a notorious Cuban terrorist and exile—that Miami is way beyond our comprehension, too. In 2006, the city of Miami was declared the road rage capital of America. We were not surprised.

Nonetheless, we mention Miami because visiting Miami Beach likely means having to pass through the city. This is especially true if you're an international traveler, since the airport is nestled in the thicket of Miami's westward sprawl, which stretches all the way to the Everglades.

By contrast, Miami Beach's evolution in the ensuing years has generally been positive. Back

in 1986, the rejuvenation of South Beach's Art Deco District was in its nascent stages. A goofy old photo shows one of us lifting the lid of a commode among a pile of them—colored in various art deco pastels—stacked on the porch of a property undergoing renovation. Presumably, those very toilet seats now accommodate the rear ends of wealthy tourists in any number of beautifully refurbished hotels. Bravo, we say. Miami Beach deserves commendation for its good works and good looks.

Latter-day Miami Beach—especially the lower third known as South Beach—is more spice than vice. South Beach is home to the Art Deco District, the most popular and accessible beaches in Greater Miami, and the hottest nightlife this side of New York City. One major reason for South Beach's resurgence has been its art deco–themed renaissance (see

THE GOLD COAST

© PARKE PUTERBAUGH

North Shore Open Space Park, North Miami Beach

the *Doing the Art Deco Dance in Miami Beach* sidebar). Within the Art Deco District, more than 1,000 buildings are now listed on the National Register of Historic Places. This made it the first historic district to pay homage to 20th century architecture. Its makeover has allowed South Beach to reconnect with its glory days of the early 20th century as a Tropical Deco resort paradise, and the architectural theme has been adapted all the way up to Fort Lauderdale.

Even if you're just mildly curious about the art deco brouhaha, you can spend some enjoyable hours strolling the district, admiring the architectural wonders and the civic spirit that helped rejuvenate them. The **Miami Design Preservation League** (1001 Ocean Drive, 305/672-2014) operates a beachfront welcome center, which is open 11 A.M.–6 P.M. daily. The Miami Beach Visitors Bureau has an information kiosk in the pedestrian mall at Lincoln Road and Washington Avenue. Both are good places to arm yourself with maps and literature before your stroll.

Miami Beach has also benefited from its broadminded acceptance of all people, regardless of race, creed, color, sexual prefer-

ence, and willingness to stay out till 4 A.M. in dance clubs. In this sense, it is a true melting pot—with the sun providing the heat—that's blended, assimilated, and color-blind. In fact, the whole of South Beach embodies the term "multiculturalism." Its human parade is as colorful as the exotic life forms that inhabit South Florida's tropical reefs. In short, South Beach is a functioning blueprint for a more fully integrated and mutually tolerant world. Not coincidentally, it knows how to throw a great party, too.

By way of orientation, Miami Beach runs from 87th Terrace down to the jetties at South Pointe Park. From Miami, three causeways cross Biscayne Bay to the barrier island occupied by Miami Beach. From north to south they are: I-195 (Julia Tuttle Causeway), which ends at 41st Street in Miami Beach; Venetian Causeway, a toll road that ends at 23rd Street; and I-395 (MacArthur Causeway), which ends at 5th Street.

The heart and soul of Miami Beach is South Beach ("SoBe" for short), which lies between 21st Street and South Pointe Park. The Venetian Causeway will bring you in at the north

DOING THE ART DECO DANCE IN MIAMI BEACH

As we were browsing the flamingo salt-and-pepper shakers at the Art Deco Welcome Center gift shop in Miami Beach, we struck up a conversation with the brassy woman behind the counter. "I'm a newcomer," she said, with a raspy chuckle. "I've only been here 68 years."

Without prompting, our cashier reminisced about the good old days in Miami back in the 1930s: "We used to go to the movies and walk. Everything was walking. Those were wonderful days." An old love song from the bygone big-band days played on the radio, and she hummed along. "I knew the lady who wrote that," she remarked. "Her husband was killed in the war. 'I'll Never Smile Again,' it was called."

Those days of war and upheaval are long gone, and life is good again in Miami Beach. In a way, it's a lot like it was in the pre-war days, as old things are now revered and even fashionable. Take the art deco architectural renaissance, which helped turn Miami from a morass of crime and poverty and into one of the liveliest and most fashionable communities in the world.

We were biding time in the gift shop as we waited to hook up with George Neery, who served as executive director of the Miami Art Deco Design Preservation League from 1990 to 1997. He led us on a brisk, informative walking tour of the Art Deco district, and we gained a richer appreciation of this style and the way it's defined and revived the area. He started out by noting that there's nothing original about Miami Beach. The palms are imported from Panama. The beach is artificial, having been created with imported sand. Even the natives aren't native. Everyone has come to Miami Beach from somewhere else.

As America's first vacation playground, the island of Miami Beach gave people something to do with two newly acquired things: disposable money and time. The first buildings, in fact, were constructed on the bayside, because oceanfront property had no value. People didn't know what to do on a beach, but they learned quickly.

The style known as art deco — an Anglicization of the French arts décoratifs — set the tenor for Miami Beach's construction from 1929 to 1942. Art deco caught on in the wake of the 1925 Paris Exhibition, whose formal name was the "1925 Exposition Internationale des Arts Décoratifs et Industriels Modernes." The modernist movement came together with Mediterranean Revival architecture — a Spanish influence that surfaced at the Pan American Exposition in San Diego — on these breezy shores.

Miami Beach was essentially created out of whole cloth to serve the leisure interests of suddenly prosperous Americans. Art deco provided a modern look that was whimsical and fun. They wanted to help people forget where they had come from (and would have to return to). Some of the design elements were inspired by the rounded corners and nautical details (such as portholes) of cruise ships, which were becoming streamlined and speedy — much like American culture itself. There were lots of ornamental elements, too: finials, faux window boxes, "eyebrows," friezes, ziggurats.

What began as whimsy has become an architectural tradition that defines the way Miami Beach looks and feels. Founded in 1976, the powerful Miami Art Deco Design Preservation League wants the 1,200 art deco buildings in Miami Beach to be regarded "like the pyramids," according to Neery. "We want people to come back in 100 years and see them here." League members have agitated, protested, and fought for individual buildings and their collective legacy.

Neery notes with pride that architects are more important than lawyers in Miami Beach. They may be more effective than lawyers, too, when it comes to preserving Miami Beach as an Art Deco enclave.

"We're like bees," says Neery. "You don't want to get the hive riled."

For more information, contact the Art Deco Welcome Center, 1001 Ocean Drive, Miami Beach, 305/531-3484; or the Miami Design Preservation League, 1001 Ocean Drive, Miami Beach, 305/672-2014, www.mdpl.org.

THE GOLD COAST

THE WOLFSONIAN

One of the most fascinating and unusual museums in the country, the Wolfsonian, can be found in the heart of South Beach's Art Deco District. While its location inside a restored Mediterranean-style building – formerly a storage company – nicely augments the museum's devotion to the decorative arts, the Wolfsonian is much more than a collection of pastel bathroom tiles and sculpted peacock feathers. The decorative arts are, in fact, only one facet of the 70,000-item collection. It is also a research and educational center, affiliated with Florida International University. It's committed to the history, restoration, and appreciation of the decorative arts, design, architecture, advertising, transportation, world fairs, and political propaganda from 1885 to 1945 in Europe and the Americas. Indeed, it's hard to say exactly what the Wolfsonian is, which is what makes it so endlessly fascinating and unusual.

Perhaps the unifying element of the place is that objects in the collection were typically very much ahead of their time. That is, they were created not as elitist objects to be hoarded, hidden, and envied by the rich and famous but mass-produced with the explicit intention of persuading or altering the perceptions of large numbers of people. Thus, the title of the museum-generated *Journal of Decorative and Propaganda Arts* is oddly accurate.

Still confused? Okay, here are some items on view at any given time in the changing exhibitions and semi-permanent installations: furniture, industrial design, glass, ceramics, metalwork, government-funded artwork, war recruitment posters, books, works on paper, paintings, sculpture, propaganda pamphlets, advertising graphics, and tourist brochures (yes!). On our most recent visit, we marveled over an exhibit on "modern seating" (i.e., chairs), which took up an entire floor of the museum. The Wolfsonian has a knack for making what would seem on paper to be a tedious theme and enlivening it in unexpected ways. We will never take our chairs for granted again.

The eclectic nature of this collection reflects the tastes of the institution's founder, Mitchell Wolfson, Jr. Upon opening the museum to the public in 1995, Wolfson announced, "This is a movement, a crusade, and a mission, and we're all zealots. ... Objects contain powerful information, and we have to learn to read them." By "propaganda," Wolfson means the 16th-century sense of the word, which is when the Catholic Church coined that Latinate term to denote the "propagation of the faith" (as Malcolm X would later say, "by any means necessary"). All of Wolfson's objects, in that sense, propagate the ideals of their times.

The Wolfsonian collection is, if nothing else, a rewarding visual delight not unlike the surrounding neighborhood of restored art deco and Mediterranean architecture. At the risk of sounding propagandistic, we'll end by saying a visit to Miami Beach is incomplete without a visit to the Wolfsonian. The museum is open weekdays (except Wednesday) 11 A.M.-6 P.M. (till 9 P.M. on Thursday). Sunday hours are noon-5 P.M. Admission is $5 for adults and $3.50 for seniors, students with ID, and children aged 6-12.

For more information, contact the Wolfsonian, 1001 Washington Avenue, Miami Beach, FL 33139, 305/531-1001, www.wolfsonian.org.

end, while the MacArthur Causeway will deposit you at the point where South Beach beats loudest and hottest. If you're not staying at one of the resorts or art deco hotels—and therefore have a legal parking space—you're best advised to park at one of municipal garages on 7th, 8th, 10th, 12th, 13th, and 17th Streets between Collins and Washington Avenues. You will otherwise drive in endless bumper-to-bumper traffic. Only lucky drivers snag a spot on the streets of South Beach, and the hungry meters require frequent feeding. We mention the traffic issue because South Beach can clog up as bad as midtown Manhattan at rush hour.

Bumper-to-bumper cars, exhaust fumes, frustrated drivers—they don't call Miami Beach "the sixth borough" for nothing.

Also, South Beach has lost some of its glamour as the hip-hop crowd has moved in. Over the years, the neighborhood has been descended on in waves: first, the gay and bohemian pioneers who redefined the aesthetic; then the moneyed international jet set; and, more recently, the rap and hip-hop crowd. Events like the Black Film Festival and the Hip-Hop Awards—set against the backdrop of SoBe's prolific club scene—have attracted growing numbers of African-Americans. During this decade some have even taken to referring to South Beach as *Soul* Beach. We know the hip-hop scene isn't for everyone, so if the prospect of a "Freak Week"-type celebration on the streets and clubs of Miami Beach doesn't sound like your cup of malt liquor, you may wish to check out what's happening here in advance of your visit.

For more information, contact the Greater Miami Convention and Visitors Bureau, 701 Brickell Avenue, Suite 2700, Miami, FL 33131, 305/539-3000 or 800/933-8448, www.gmcvb.com; or the Miami Beach Visitor Information Center, 1920 Meridian Avenue, Miami Beach, FL 33139, 305/672-1270, www.miamibeach-chamber.com.

BEACHES

Within Miami Beach's borders lifeguard stands are found at the ends of the following streets: 83rd, 81st, 79th, 74th, 72nd, 64th, 53rd, 46th, 35th, 29th, 21st, 17th, 14th, 13th, 12th, 10th, 8th, 6th, and 1st. The first three listed fall within the boundaries of **North Shore Open Space Park.** Running from 87th Terrace to 79th Street, this is one of the more delightful surprises in the Miami area. Originally set aside as an open space in 1972, its 40 acres have been batted like a volleyball between the state and the city of Miami Beach. At one time a state park, North Shore Open Space Park is currently leased to the city by the state. Who cares who runs it as long as they continue to maintain the attractive landscaping (lots of

shade and picnic areas) and dune walkovers? A bike/pedestrian path runs through the park. The entrance fee is only $1 per person. In the heart of high-rise heaven, it's a slice of the beach in its natural state.

Along Collins Avenue from 79th Street down to 21st Street, Miami Beach is one long strand used mainly by inhabitants of the barely believable wall of high-rise condos and hotels that line this route. Unless you're a lodger at one of these places, it's tough to find a spot to leave your car. Collins Avenue can be an adventure to navigate even without having to keep an eye out for parking opportunities. However, there are metered lots by the beach at **72nd, 64th, 53rd, 46th, 35th,** and **21st Streets.** Restrooms and showers can be found at all of them except 35th Street. There's also a municipal garage at 42nd Street. A boardwalk runs between 46th and 21st Streets—an area known as "mid-beach"—and parking lots can be found at either end. We ran the boardwalk one night around Happy Hour, and heard the happy chatter coming from ground-level courtyards and bar patios as we huffed and puffed. Miami Beach seems a very pleasant place indeed from the vantage point of this boardwalk.

South Beach is where 40 percent of Miami Beach's population resides, and it's a different story. SoBe says yes to parking and just about everything else, too. Anything goes (and comes off) along the stretch of South Beach from 17th to 5th Streets. Sights along the beach include completely nude sunbathing (though sunbathers are legally supposed to remove no more than tops), as well as thong bikinis that make a mockery of the word "swimsuit." We overheard one amazed and amused tourist say, "I've seen more cloth on a necktie!" The scene that greets you on South Beach can resemble an old *National Geographic* pictorial about Tahiti. Gorgeous lotion-lathered European and Hispanic women lounge unabashedly in the buff, while gay men sit cross-legged, conversing intently while staring into each other's eyes.

Within these boundaries falls **Lummus Park** (14th to 5th Streets), a breathtakingly wide stretch of sand backed by palm trees and "chickees" (thatch-roofed huts), colorful snack shacks, lifeguard stations, and a curvaceous walking, biking, and in-line skating trail. Chances are good you'll spot a model shoot out here on any given day. By the way, the ocean water is warm, relatively clear, and almost wavelessly calm. There's a slight drop-off about 10 feet from shore, at which point the bottom levels out and the water remains about chest-deep for several hundred feet. A recent swim took us further out to sea than we've ever been without getting in over our heads. A family's sense of ocean safety is furthered by the presence of 17 lifeguard stations between 79th Street and South Pointe Park. Play areas are set back from the water for the kiddies, though it's hard to imagine a child growing bored with the beach and ocean. Look sharp around 8th Street for the Asher sculptures next to a popular shaded pavilion (unofficially known as Asher Beach)—a donation to Miami Beach from the people of Israel.

South Pointe Park runs from 5th Street to a municipal fishing pier at the bottom of the barrier island, overlooking the shipping channel and Fisher Island. The park offers just about everything: lifeguards, showers, picnic shelters, concessions, playground, lighted pier, exercise course, and a restaurant. **Smith & Wollensky** (1 Washington Avenue, 673-2800, $$$$) specializes in steaks and chops ("a steakhouse to end all arguments"). It originated in New York City, and this relatively recent South Beach arrival is the only one outside the Big Apple. (Further evidence that Miami Beach is New York's "sixth borough.")

Because South Point Park lies outside the heart of the trendy SoBe bazaar, you will see fewer bulging thongs. The one bulge you will see is an ill-advised and much-despised construction called "the Towers." They are not just a visual blight, but an intrusion upon the nearshore regime that may impact beach and surf-zone dynamics at the south end. Since South Pointe has one of the finest breaks in South Florida, you can imagine how surfers and beach lovers feel about the Towers.

A final word about South Beach. A broad, flat apron of sand separates the sidewalk bazaar along Ocean Drive from the water's edge. It's a bit of a walk to the ocean's edge—so much so that referring to hotels and restaurants along Ocean Drive as "oceanfront" stretches credibility a bit. The beach isn't the principal preoccupation of many who flock to Miami Beach. They come for the social whirl, and often Ocean Drive is more crowded than the beach, even on the nicest days.

23 NORTH SHORE OPEN SPACE PARK

Location: Collins Avenue between 79th and 87th Streets in Miami Beach
Parking/fees: metered street parking, plus $1 entrance fee per person
Hours: 7 A.M.–8 P.M.
Facilities: lifeguards, restrooms, picnic tables, and showers
Contact: North Shore Open Space Park, 305/993-2032

24 72ND STREET BEACH

Location: 72nd Street at Collins Avenue in Miami Beach
Parking/fees: metered parking lot at 72nd and 73rd Streets between Collins and Washington Avenues in Miami Beach
Hours: 5 A.M.–midnight
Facilities: lifeguards, restrooms, and showers
Contact: Miami Beach Parks and Recreation Department, 305/673-7730, or Miami Beach Patrol, 305/673-7714

25 64TH STREET BEACH

Location: 64th Street at Collins Avenue in Miami Beach
Parking/fees: metered parking lot

Hours: 5 A.M.-midnight
Facilities: lifeguards, restrooms, and showers
Contact: Miami Beach Parks and Recreation Department, 305/673-7730, or Miami Beach Patrol, 305/673-7714

26 53RD STREET BEACH

Location: 53rd Street at Collins Avenue in Miami Beach
Parking/fees: metered parking lot
Hours: 5 A.M.-midnight
Facilities: lifeguards, restrooms, and showers
Contact: Miami Beach Parks and Recreation Department, 305/673-7730, or Miami Beach Patrol, 305/673-7714

27 46TH STREET BEACH

Location: 46th Street at Collins Avenue in Miami Beach
Parking/fees: metered parking lot
Hours: 5 A.M.-midnight
Facilities: lifeguards, restrooms, and showers
Contact: Miami Beach Parks and Recreation Department, 305/673-7730, or Miami Beach Patrol, 305/673-7714

28 35TH STREET BEACH

Location: 35th Street at Collins Avenue in Miami Beach
Parking/fees: metered parking lot
Hours: 5 A.M.-midnight
Facilities: lifeguards and showers
Contact: Miami Beach Parks and Recreation Department, 305/673-7730, or Miami Beach Patrol, 305/673-7714

29 21ST STREET BEACH/ SOUTH BEACH

Location: 21st Street at Collins Avenue in Miami Beach
Parking/fees: metered parking lot
Hours: 5 A.M.-midnight
Facilities: lifeguards, restrooms, and showers

Contact: Miami Beach Parks and Recreation Department, 305/673-7730, or Miami Beach Patrol, 305/673-7714

30 LUMMUS PARK/ SOUTH BEACH

BEST (

Location: Ocean Drive, between 5th and 15th Streets in Miami Beach
Parking/fees: fee parking lot and metered street parking
Hours: 5 A.M.-midnight
Facilities: concessions, lifeguards, restrooms, and showers
Contact: Miami Beach Parks and Recreation Department, 305/673-7730, or Miami Beach Patrol, 305/673-7714

31 SOUTH POINTE PARK/ SOUTH BEACH

Location: along Washington Avenue between 1st and 5th Streets, at the southern tip of Miami Beach
Parking/fees: metered parking lots
Hours: 5 A.M.-midnight
Facilities: concessions, lifeguards, restrooms, picnic tables, and showers
Contact: South Pointe Park, 305/673-7224

RECREATION AND ATTRACTIONS

- **Bike/Skate Rentals:** Bike & Roll, 760 Washington Avenue, Miami Beach, 305/538-2121; Fritz Skate Shop, 730 Lincoln Road, Miami Beach, 305/532-1954; Beach Scooter Rental, 1461 Collins Avenue, Miami Beach, 305/532-0977

- **Boat Cruise:** Miami Aqua Tours, Bayside Marketplace, Miami, 305/860-8654; Cruise Miami (clearinghouse for discount cruises), 800/338-4962, www.cruisemiami.com

THE GOLD COAST

- **Dive Shop:** South Beach Dive & Surf, 850 Washington Avenue, Miami Beach. 305/531-6110

- **Ecotourism:** Biscayne National Park, 9700 SW 328th Street, Homestead, 305/230-7275

- **Fishing Charters:** Another Reward Fishing Fleet, Miami Beach Marina, 300 Alton Road, Miami Beach, 305/372-9470

- **Lighthouse:** Key Biscayne Lighthouse, Bill Baggs Cape Florida State Park, Key Biscayne, 305/361-5811

- **Marina:** Miami Beach Marina, 300 Alton Road, Miami Beach, 305/673-6000

- **Pier:** South Pointe Park, 1 Washington Avenue, Miami Beach, 305/673-7224

- **Rainy-Day Attraction:** Miami Seaquarium, 4400 Rickenbacker Causeway, Key Biscayne, 305/361-5705

- **Shopping/Browsing:** Lincoln Road Mall (16th Street from Collins Avenue to Alton Road), Miami Beach; CocoWalk, 3015 Grand Avenue, Coconut Grove

- **Surf Shop:** X-Isle Surf Shop, 437 Washington Avenue, Miami Beach, 305/673-5900

- **Vacation Rentals:** Florida Sunbreak, 828 Washington Avenue, Miami Beach, 305/532-1516; Premier Vacation Rents, 4014 Chase Ave, Miami Beach, 818/766-6503

ACCOMMODATIONS

Do not stay in Miami, period. Cross the causeway bridge, pay the extra bucks, and stay somewhere along Miami Beach's 9.3 miles of oceanfront. Safe, affordable accommodations can be found in the mid-beach area of Miami Beach (near the famous, long-lived Fontainebleau, in the 4000 block of Collins Avenue) and in the less frenetic communities of Surfside and Sunny Isles Beach (see separate write-ups).

However, if you want to experience the deco dance of South Beach, you simply must book a room in the Art Deco District. In this roughly ten-by-four-block area, you will find more than 800 art deco buildings and 200 Mediterranean revival structures—including the late Gianni Versace's lavish 1930 mansion, at 1116 Ocean Drive—that have been restored since the preservation campaign began in the 1970s. The most desirable deco hotels line Ocean Drive between 5th and 14th Streets, but you must have a high tolerance for the endless party on the sidewalks below.

Before naming names, one small disclaimer. With the exception of the **Clay Hotel and Hostel International** (1438 Washington Avenue, 305/534-2988, $) and a few less trendy hotels outside the Art Deco District, it's not cheap to stay in South Beach. One of the most commendable non-trendies is the **Claremont Hotel** (1700 Collins Avenue, 305/538-4661, $). From the outside, it looks deco-esque, with a pink-and-beige pattern on a Bauhaus-style three-story building, but inside it's clean, comfortable, functional, and unaffected.

Among the more reliable of the more "pure" art deco lodges is the **Colony Hotel** (736 Ocean Drive, 305/673-0088, $$$). You can't miss its distinctive neon-rimmed, pastel blue entrance. Inside, it's all sleek marble and sharp angles, with a popular club and restaurant (Colony Bistro) on the premises and continental breakfast included with each of the 36 rooms. Two blocks off the ocean but fully embracing its spirit is **Hotel Astor** (956 Washington Avenue, 305/531-8081, $$$), which is as venerable as its name. Greeting all who enter is a stunning lobby paneled in an olive-green and black pattern that only a deco-phile could love. Built in 1936 and meticulously restored in recent years, the Astor has 41 rooms and a pricey, much-ballyhooed restaurant, the Astor Place Bar and Grill (305/672-7217, $$$$).

Combining luxury and beach access is the aptly named **Hotel Ocean** (1230 Ocean Drive, 305/672-2579, $$$). This Mediterranean-style complex overlooks the ocean at the north end of the Art Deco District, near the Versace mansion. Restored to 1930s splendor,

Hotel Ocean suggests the setting of a Somerset Maugham story. It's an airy, European-style place with low-key panache. Each room contains an interesting mix of art, furnishings, and personality. Our room was emblazoned "De Beaux Reues," which was painted on the wall and ceiling, and had an interesting mix of botanical and bird prints. Fittingly, a breezily casual French restaurant, **Les Deux Fontaines** (1230 Ocean Drive, 305/672-7278, $$$$), is on the premises.

Other delectable deco palaces are the Marlin, the Tides, and Essex House. The **Marlin** (1200 Collins Avenue, 305/604-5063, $$$$) is a fancy fish, a remodeled hostelry on the site of a former crack house. It might best be described as austere and techno. With its severe lines and liberal use of burnished metal, it is as utilitarian as a website. There's a recording studio in the basement and a sunken bar off the lobby. How expensive is it? Hey, they wouldn't even tell us the price! If money's no object, dive right in.

The **Tides** (1220 Ocean Drive, 604-5070, $$$$) is an example of a recent trend in South Beach architecture: monochromaticism, which is not to say monotonous. There's something appealing about the sandy color and pebbly texture of this 45-room, three-restaurant monolith, where a deluxe oceanfront room runs $350–475 per night. Classic and simple in architecture and decor, the Tides is the largest hotel on Ocean Drive.

Done up in mauves and browns, **Essex House** (1001 Collins Avenue, 305/534-2700, $$$) looks like a ship rising from the dry dock of Collins Avenue. Rooms are cleanly, sparely appointed, and rates reasonable, by South Beach Art Deco standards. Even if you don't stay at one of these places, by all means drop by for a drink. Each has its own look, history, character, and appeal. And they're all drop-dead fab, or try to be. Since perspectives on what's hot can change by the week, we'd advise checking out *South Beach Magazine*'s website (www.southbeach-usa.com) for a good, thorough orientation. Pay particular attention

to their "Fab Five List," and shine up your gold card.

If your main reason for coming to Miami Beach is to party, **The Clevelander** (1020 Ocean Dr., 305/531-3485, $$) is the place to dump your bags and let it all hang out. Its outdoor poolside bar is party central on the beach, but the rooms are actually quite nice and reasonably priced (for Miami Beach). As a friend told us, "The only disappointment was the fact that more expensive oceanfront rooms do not have balconies, so they are not a significant advantage over any other room in the place." So save yourself some money and avoid some noise in the bargain by booking a non-oceanfront room.

A word of warning about South Beach accommodations: You do not want to stay off the beach, if it can be avoided. On our last visit we were repulsed by the noisy, fumy, and litter-strewn streets in the vicinity of the Collins Avenue/Lincoln Road intersection. Why come to South Beach and pull up a block short of the ocean just to save some niggling amount on a room? If at all possible, stay on Ocean Drive or at those lodgings with Collins Avenue addresses that abut the beach. Otherwise you could wind up on a block that might as well be on the Lower East Side of Manhattan.

Since we brought up the name, we should give you the goods on the **Fontainebleau Hilton** (4441 Collins Avenue, 305/538-2000, $$$$), the monolithic resort dedicated to high rollers. Like its Vegas cousins, the Fontainebleau is lavishly tacky, with an ocean-sized swimming pool shaped like a tropical lagoon only a few hundred feet from the actual ocean. Be sure to wear your sunglasses inside to protect your eyes from the gleam of all the gold chains, polished Gucci loafers, and polar-white teeth.

Speaking of high-rises, South Beach is watching its stock and its skyline soar. The **Ritz-Carlton South Beach** (1 Lincoln Road, 786/276-4000, $$$$), and **Loews Miami Beach Hotel** (1601 Collins Avenue, 305/604-1601, $$$$) have opened in South Beach in recent years. Our favorite is Loews,

EAT AT JOE'S

Joe's Stone Crab restaurant (227 Biscayne Street, 305/673-0365, $$$) runs an ad in local papers that says more than a mouthful: "Before SoBe, Joe be." Established in 1913, Joe's has never looked back. This South Beach institution, located at the very southern tip of Miami Beach's barrier island, hasn't sacrificed an ounce of quality in its trend-resistant fare: fresh seafood that's simply prepared, with excellent service, no reservations needed or accepted. Needless to add, Joe's is extremely popular; an hour wait is not uncommon. The restaurant even published it's own cookbook – *Eat at Joes: The Joe's Stone Crab Restaurant Cookbook* – in 2000.

Joe's specializes in a native delicacy, the stone crab, which swims in the warm waters off Florida's Gulf Coast. They're like nothing you've ever eaten. For one thing, you eat only the claw. One claw per crab, in fact, is all the state allows commercial crabbers to harvest. The stone crab is protected under a law that prevents anything more than temporary capture during a brief season. The nets scoop them up, the crab is grabbed and the crusher claw twisted off, and the amputated crustacean is then tossed back overboard. The claws regenerate, like starfish arms.

In any given year, the kitchen staff at Joe's cracks about 400,000 pounds of Florida stone crabs. The claws are boiled and served cold, with drawn butter and spicy mustard sauce. Each claw is a natural work of art bearing the texture of fine china, colored ivory and rose with a black border. It provides an ample portion of delicate, tasty crabmeat. You can fill yourself on four stone crab claws. Seriously!

At Joe's the tuxedoed waiters (don't worry; diners can wear whatever they want) engage customers in solicitous patter. We lucked into Ozzie, an old surfer with a comically gruff demeanor, who has been at Joe's for 10 years. He offered, "Whatever I can do to make you happy, let me know." When we riposted, "A back rub might be nice," he responded, without missing a beat, "I'll give you a Miami back rub. Get up and face the wall over there, and I'll pat you down, then put on the handcuffs."

Many other fresh seafood items are offered, along with the wit. On one recent visit, we had an excellent grilled pompano and the cold seafood platter – a great deal including stone crabs, Florida lobster, and large shrimp. Side dishes are à la carte, but large enough to feed two diners.

One change has taken place at Joe's in the last decade. They've added a sleek, expensive back bar (thus shrinking the waiting area) and an annex where logoed merchandise and mail orders can be purchased. This unbridled commerce undercuts the old atmosphere, but it may just be a case of Joe trying to keep up with the Joneses. The surrounding area, once a dilapidated no-man's-land of ramshackle huts and dumps, is now home to a condo tower so obnoxiously tall, wide, mirrored, and against the grain that you understand why Joe's regulars complain. You wonder if the island won't eventually sink under the combined weight of the buildings and the egos of the men who build them.

In the meantime, you can still feast on stone crabs at Joe's, as well as the world's best coleslaw and hash brown potatoes. Although the menu is long and tempting, the trio of stone crabs, coleslaw, and hash browns is a can't-miss classic. If you order just as we've instructed, your old-time waiter will likely cock an eyebrow and smile as if to say, "Ah, a regular."

because they've used the historic neighboring St. Moritz (which they also own) as their architectural template. As a result—at least from the beach—the Loews doesn't overwhelm the neighborhood, despite its 18 stories. Loews, by the way, has a fabulous lobby bar and pool deck with a lively social scene.

To give the Ritz-Carlton its due, their 11-story beachfront hotel is a reconstruction of a 1950s art deco hotel (the DiLido). However, rack rates for the high winter season run $759–859 per night for "partial oceanview" rooms and more than that for their poolside "lanai" rooms. Two weeks here, and you could afford to build an in-ground pool at your own home! Besides, word-of-mouth on the hotel has not elicited the usual consistent Ritz raves. Frankly, it does seem a little out of place in casual, crazy-hip South Beach.

These lodgings probably will come to seem downright quaint as monolithic high-rise construction begins to dwarf anything and everything outside of the Art Deco district.

COASTAL CUISINE

The catch of the day in South Beach is **A Fish Called Avalon** (700 Ocean Drive, 305/532-1727, $$$), which has been serving some of the tastiest, most innovative seafood on the beach since 1989. It was opened by chef Gerry Quinn, an Irishman who had the chutzpah, before moving to Miami Beach, to launch an Irish restaurant in Paris. Specialties at A Fish Called Avalon include Bang Bang Shrimp: jumbo prawns cooked in a spicy, curry-based marinade and drizzled with a cooling mint sauce. It has won multiple "Taste of the Beach" awards. Popular entrees include Caribbean snapper, marinated in curry-based spices, served on black-bean salsa and topped with an orange sauce. Chilean sea bass is poetry on a plate: pan-seared quickly and served with a red and yellow pepper puree.

The superbly cooked food is just one of the many appeals of A Fish Called Avalon. Others include the cordial staff, live Latin-guitar accompaniment and, of course, the wonderful setting overlooking the passing parade on Ocean Drive. If you find it too humid or loud on the patio, head to the indoor dining room, whose art-filled decor makes for a memorable setting and meal. Top off your dinner experience with Guava Cheesecake, and then walk it off by entering the swarm along Ocean Avenue. Incidentally, A Fish Called Avalon is attached to a hotel called Avalon. Actually, it's the **Avalon Majestic** (700 Ocean Drive, 305/538-0133, $$$), comprising two separate and adjacent deco hotels. The smallish rooms are adequate but not exceptional; it's the location you'll be crowing about—and paying for.

Grillfish (1444 Collins Avenue, 305/538-9908, $$$) gets high marks for doing just that. They grill upward of 10 types of fish daily—it's all scrawled in chalk on a big blackboard over the doors to the kitchen—and they also saute seafood and serve it over pasta. All of it's good, and the restaurant's interior (especially the Middle Eastern–themed mural) and the picture-window view of bustling Collins Avenue add to the aesthetic experience. Even though we arrived exhausted from a long drive, the staff's sunnily hip attitude proved contagious. Our young waitress, a recently transplanted New Englander, was the perfect tonic for our harried mood. The chalkboard memo spotlights the freshest catches, but there are unchanging and ever-popular items at Grillfish, including a dynamite barroom seafood chowder (in tomato broth), shrimp scampi, and seafood fra diavolo. Finish it off with a slab of their key lime pie, which puts a unique, mango-accented twist on this local classic.

Miami Beach's cuisine often ignites national trends. Thai and Italian have been recent rages, but Cuban, Spanish, and Latin are the most authentically native. The restaurant scene in SoBe is highly competitive and therefore trendsetters and foodies have their hands full staying on top of it. These are among the most desirable and durable spots:

- **BANG** (1516 Washington Avenue, 305/531-2361, $$$$) has a hip New York cousin, BOOM.

- **Blue Door** (1695 Collins Avenue, 305/674-6400, $$$$) puts a French twist on American cuisine. Fancy surroundings, big wine list, lots of models, movers and shakers at your elbows, and fabulous sauces and accompaniments.

- **China Grill** (404 Washington Avenue, 305/534-2211, $$$$) is an influential purveyor of New World/fusion fare on the South Beach scene.

- **Emeril's Miami Beach** (1601 Collins Avenue, 305/695-4550, $$$) was inevitable, as this celebrity chef was bound to show up in South Beach sooner or later. Emeril does his N'awlins-style thing at Loews Miami Beach Hotel.

- **Larios on the Beach** (820 Ocean Drive, 305/532-9577, $$$) is a high-priced Cuban restaurant launched by salsa singer Gloria Estefan. It's gotten mixed reviews, as some find the salsa music better than the salsa.

- **Maiko** (1255 Washington Avenue, 305/531-6369, $$$) serves superlative sushi and sashimi.

- **Mark's South Beach** (1120 Collins Avenue, 305/604-9050, $$$$) has wowed SoBe with its Mediterranean menu and super chef, Mark Militello.

- **Nemo** (100 Collins Avenue, 305/532-4550, $$$$) serves New American cuisine in a chi-chi setting.

- **Starfish** (1427 West Avenue, 305/673-1717, $$$$) points the way with fresh, creative seafood.

- **Touch** (910 Lincoln Road, 305/532-8003) is a "modern influenced grill" that does everything to a turn; try the smoked, grilled margarita salmon. It's also an entertainment venue, with belly dancers, musicians, and deejays.

- **Wish** (801 Collins Avenue, 305/674-9474, $$$$) boasts a lush fountain court setting and gourmet seafood.

Also high on our (and everyone's) list is **Joe's Stone Crab.** Joe's is so much a beloved Miami Beach institution that we devoted an entire essay to the restaurant and its namesake specialty. (See the *Eat at Joe's* sidebar.)

Another enduring South Beach institution is the **News Cafe** (800 Ocean Drive, 305/531-0392, $$). Open 24 hours a day, it's best enjoyed over a morning platter of eggs and coffee, with a newspaper propped up in front of you. The food is just average but the atmosphere is unique, with a newsroom motif, stocked magazine rack, and view of the goings-on along the sidewalk and beach. If you just want a simple, decent sandwich sans hype, try **La Sandwicherie** (229 14th Street, 305/532-8934, $).

Though it's become a sizable national franchise, the **Crab House** (1551 79th Street Causeway, 305/868-7085, $$$) got its start on a small causeway island between Miami and Miami Beach. It has an appealingly informal atmosphere in the manner of a Chesapeake Bay crab house. Standard operating gear includes a wooden mallet, a nutcracker, and buckets for discards. Stone crabs and garlic crabs are house specialties. They also serve good seafood bisque and key lime pie. It's a good place if you want to escape the sometimes suffocatingly hip and overpriced South Beach scene.

NIGHTLIFE

On repeated visits to the area, we've noticed that the choices in South Beach fall to extremes: either hellish goth-rock dungeons or discotheques doling out deejayed hip-hop and electronic dance music. In South Beach, deco begat disco (or vice versa) and there's no escaping the racket, whether it's synth-driven, salsa-spiced, rave-minded, or trance-inducing. Miami's deejay-powered dance mix was originally marketed to a gay clientele at prison-fortress clubs with names like Hombre, but gays have faded into the background or fled to Fort Lauderdale.

South Miami nightspots, gay and straight alike, often go by one-word minimalist names. The roll call of SoBe clubs and bars—extant and defunct—includes Vivid, Touch, Opium, crobar, Felt, Drink, Level, Bash, Amnesia,

GET THEE BEHIND ME, MIAMI

At its southern end Miami dribbles on and on with seemingly no end in sight. If you're headed to the Keys and have decided that U.S. 1 is the straightest line between two points, you will become entrapped for what seems like forever inside a hamster wheel of redundant roadside commerce. By the time you've reached the relatively unblemished Overseas Highway and are cruising to the Keys, you will feel sullied and exhausted, as if you've run some sort of gauntlet. U.S. 1 out of Miami is a cow pie of capitalism so shoddy it's hard to imagine that Castro's brand of dictatorial communism could yield results any worse than this. And you will not want to gaze on another American flag anytime soon.

Some of the largest Stars and Stripes ever fabricated, joined by countless smaller ones, fly over car dealerships along this blighted stretch of highway. The size of their wind-whipped furls is matched only by the transparent gall of those who have hoisted Old Glory in these parts. There is an implied yet spurious relationship between the size of flags and the patriotism of the dealerships. The tautology goes like this: We fly more and bigger American flags, therefore we are a more trustworthy place to buy a Japanese car. A further irony rests in the fact that this parading of the red, white, and blue occurs deep in South Florida, a land swollen with illegal immigrants, drug runners, welfare cheats, pawnshop brokers trading in stolen goods, and people who can barely speak a word of English.

But flags are the least of the assorted horrors along this drive. You are dragged – as if in slow motion, thanks to all the stoplights and congestion – past mile after droning mile of seedy commerce that worsens as you plunge into the belly of the beast. It all starts at the end of I-95 in South Miami, where traffic is dumped onto U.S. 1. At this point, it is like any other bad case of suburban sprawl, thick with the sort of franchised mediocrity that makes every American city look more or less identical and almost negates the whole point of traveling anymore.

Still, we derived a measure of comfort from passing recognizable franchise names, even if they were of the Kentucky Fried Chicken and Miami Subs ilk. It did not last long as we proceeded farther south on U.S. 1, where the landscape deteriorates into a tawdry diorama of adult video shops, bail bondsmen, no-tell motels, off-brand gas stations, filthy fast-food stands, weed-choked lots, abandoned businesses, and the absurd specter of heavy machinery ravaging the countryside to erect more pointless enterprise on the very rim of the suffering Everglades.

Our advice is to avoid U.S. 1 out of Miami by taking Florida's Turnpike. This route, which swings west of the city, adds a few miles – as well as a few dollars in tolls – to the trip but saves considerable time and will spare you the sort of red-faced diatribes that were erupting in our car.

THE GOLD COAST

Kremlin, Liquid, and Twist. Often they have celebrity owners such as Prince, who opened Glam Slam in 1994 and partied there like it was 1999, though it only lasted until 1996. Glam Slam reopened under new ownership a year later and promptly closed again. So it goes in fickle, trend-hopping Miami Beach.

For dance-club aficionados, the scene in South Beach is as hot as it gets. God knows we tried to get into the groove, to bust a move on the trendiest nightspots South Beach has to offer. We dutifully made the rounds of Washington Street, between 5th and 15th Streets, stopping at every party palace to ponder the possibilities. Each was like a stage setting for a futurist play about the fascist takeover of the entertainment industry. Behind the obligatory velvet rope, a small committee of formally attired minions waited, one of whom invariably possessed the sort of physique and menacing smile that suggests severe corporeal punishment awaits should you get out of line.

You are slowly surveyed by this mute contingent—head to toe, toe back up to head—as you, in turn, survey the cryptic runes that pass for the club's name or logo, as well as the darkened windows, black curtains, and cat-house red and/or mausoleum black interior. Your inquisitiveness does not figure into the transaction. If you are deemed worthy, the velvet rope is briefly detached from one pole, and you are brusquely waved forward. You have earned the privilege of paying a cover charge of $20 to gain access to taped or turntable-spun music, overpriced drinks, and tragically hip attitudes for the rest of the evening.

After perusing several of these similar Washington Street scenes, we found that only **Club Madonna** (1527 Washington Street, 305/534-2000), a strip joint specializing in "European friction dances," held any appeal for us. This may have been because the three lithesome, spike-heeled, mini-skirted honeys waving us inside seemed glad we were alive. And they were democratic in their solicitations, inviting all comers to partake of their friction dances, no matter how ugly, shabby, or unhip. As long as you weren't penniless, you passed muster.

Yet, eschewing even the temptation of a friction dance, we continued down Washington Street to find a club desperate enough to wave us inappropriately attired yahoos (read: no tattoos, tuxes, or funereal goth attire) past its velvet rope. It was at this point that we understood a certain amount of mystique must be created out on the sidewalk, because no one in their right mind would set foot inside these tombs if they know how empty the charades truly are. The music runs to mind-numbingly loud hip-hop and dance remixes built around exhortations like "Put your hands in the air," "Get on your feet," and "Check yo' ass," which are repeated more times than Bill Withers sings "I know" in "Ain't No Sunshine."

If you must go to one of these clubs, the best is **Mansion** (1235 Washington Avenue, 305/532-1525). Formerly Mansion was the legendary Level, "the *Tyrannosaurus rex* of Washington Avenue." They were reliving the Studio 54 era on the night we visited, replete with guest appearances by disco divas, parade floats with characters dressed like Miss Liberty, transvestites in cowgirl outfits shaking their booties, and, of course, a line that stretched two blocks. Similarly packed, frenetic scenes are found at **crobar** (1445 Washington Street, 305/531-8225) and **State** (320 Lincoln Road, 305/531-2800). The latter was formerly known simply as 320; name changes and reincarnations are *de rigueur* with South Beach clubs, and it would take an Excel spreadsheet to keep track of it all.

These days, the hippest hip-hop haven is **Opium Garden/Prive** (136 Collins Avenue, 305/531-5535). We couldn't get in because P. Diddy had rented the club out for some sort of after-party bacchanal. Incidentally, your hotel might have cards or coupons that will help gain you access to certain SoBe clubs at a discount on particular nights. The hitch is that if these clubs have to hand out coupons to drum up business, they're not really in the hip vanguard.

You may find some lower-rung clubs on Washington Avenue that charge no cover at all. Avoid them at all costs, because they too are ripoffs. Draft beer costs $4 for Dixie Cup–sized mugs of domestic horse piss, and thimbles of club soda fetch nearly the same. You must shout to be heard, the bartenders can be as surly as the patrons, and the whole soulless scene made us want to toss a stool over the bar and hotfoot it back to the sanctuary of our high-priced hotel room.

In any event, hanging out with would-be glitterati in dance clubs is really not our cup of Tia Maria. Rather than wait for hours to catch glimpses of fashion robots, Bond-girl wannabes, dapper yuppie playboys, aging bon vivants, and gaudily attired Eurotrash, we prefer hanging out on Ocean Drive, where there's genuine amusement to be had at the open-air bars and on the egalitarian sidewalks. In fact, we advise all like-minded, disco-averse people to begin and end their nightlife on Ocean Drive. You really can't go wrong.

In our humble opinion, the best place to begin and end a night of carousing in SoBe is the **Clevelander** (1020 Ocean Dr., 305/531-3485). The party space is built around an outdoor pool that adds a splashy quality to proceedings at the five bars. Live music is provided by bands who mix disco, funk, R&B, and rock and roll. There's a large pool of musicians to draw from, as the music program at the University of Miami turns them out in profusion. We've noticed that people seem friendlier in open, unpretentious environments like the Clevelander than at the trendy Dracula's dens on Washington Street. We will note, with some dismay, that on our latest visit they were charging a $10 cover at the Clevelander and that some sort of runway-model event was happening. But this was a big-deal holiday weekend in SoBe and not the norm here. Thank God.

A few doors down from the Clevelander is the Latino-flavored **Mango's Tropical Cafe** (900 Ocean Drive, 305/673-4422). It's an indoor-outdoor club that gets as packed as any place we've ever seen. The operative exclamations are "Whoo-hoo!" and "Ariba!" Mango's is a hell of a lot of fun, regardless of what language you speak, and the festive Latin dance music will brighten your night. And don't just come here for drinking and dancing. Mango's menu, especially Caribbean mahimahi and tropical lobster tail, is a tropic-themed delight.

When you want to take a break from the South Beach blare, try the "coffee music bar" inside **Spec's** (501 Collins Avenue, 305/534-3667), a music megastore that retails CDs, tapes, and videos. The **News Cafe** (800 Ocean Drive) is also good for an evening-ending Irish coffee or eye-opening morning cup of java. The most original of all alternative hangouts is the **Laundry Bar** (721 North Lincoln Lane, 305/531-7700), a laundromat and lounge whose motto is "Get sloshed while your clothes get washed."

If you are headed out for an evening of booty-shaking see-and-be-seen fun, be aware that the bars on Ocean Drive fill up around 10 P.M. and the dance clubs on Washington Street don't really start hopping until midnight. Beyond the fact that club culture appeals to creatures of the night, part of the reason for the late hours is that it is often sticky, hot, and humid until well after 10 P.M. in South Beach. On a recent late-fall trip, we were mopping our brows on Ocean Drive as the temperature hung steady at 87°F while the humidity topped 95 percent—at 11 P.M.!

If you don't dig bars or clubs, you can still enjoy the nightlife of South Beach simply by watching the passing show on the sidewalk. Several evenings of South Beach voyeurism cost us nothing but the spare change we handed vagrants who ambled by, attached like remora fish to the belly of the sharks schooling along Ocean Drive. On a busy night you'll see sexy women in spiked heels, dolled-up guys with heavily oiled hair, Aristotle Onassis lookalikes and Jackie O clones, and the occasional homeless person. You might even see such incongruous sights as a sweater-clad iguana being led on a leash. Women hawk "Cuban" cigars. Many of the restaurants display plastic entree replicas on plates as street-level enticements. They're hard to miss, since the bistros along Ocean Drive have usurped the public's right-of-way as part of their dining area. Thus, you'll find yourself shuffling within inches of diners trying to enjoy their meals. For these and other reasons, we feel sometimes like strangers in a strange land in South Beach. But at least we're amused strangers, most of the time.

Just in case you were wondering whether any of the beautiful people ever connect with one another in a conjugal way, there's a column in a local coffee-table magazine for the rich and bored called "Sex on South Beach." Sample excerpt: "While discussing IPOs and the new Joop! Collection, I somehow remember working in the fact that I hate to be called Babie [sic] or Honey." As Joe South sang a long time ago, "These are not my people..."

WHO WILL UNLOCK VIRGINIA KEY'S POTENTIAL?

Miami officials have been issuing semi-regular proclamations about the "rebirth" of Virginia Key since we first laid eyes on it in the mid-1980s. It's all been talk, since little has been done and the 1,000-acre barrier island remains a squandered treasure. Then, in 2005, the city chose an architectural firm from Fort Lauderdale to create "the Virginia Key of tomorrow." A bloviating city commissioner said the project would make it "one of the most magnificent, one-of-a-kind regional parks in the country."

Right. And this edition of *Florida Beaches* will win the Nobel Prize for Literature.

Virginia Key deserves so much better than what she's been given. As Dade County's only beach for black people, it provided an alternative to the Jim Crow laws of the Deep South. Though the large black population in Miami had helped build and service the whites-only resorts of the 1920s and 1930s, they were not allowed on the sands of Key Biscayne and Miami Beach. As Pulitzer Prize–winning reporter Rick Bragg put it, "Think what it was like to live beside such cool beauty and not be able to stick a toe in it. For the people who did most of the heavy lifting in this utopia, it was a tropical paradise with a padlock."

However, partly in response to the service rendered to the nation by black soldiers in World War II, county leaders in 1945 designated this then-deserted barrier island as a public beach for black people. Until a bridge was built in 1947, blacks took a ferry over from the mouth of the Miami River. Small motels and cottages were built, and for two decades Virginia Key became a hotspot of African-American culture. Black families and church groups viewed it as a safe haven, and well-known entertainers and athletes made it a regular stop while in the area.

By the mid-1960s, the civil-rights movement opened other beaches in the area

Fisher Island

This private island off the southern tip of Miami Beach, across from Government Cut, has frontage on the Atlantic Ocean, so we are duty-bound to include it. Fisher Island (pop. 400) is beyond the means of most travelers and can only be reached via boat. Nonetheless, it is a beautiful 216-acre enclave of palm-caressed wealth dominated by the Mediterranean-style mansion of the late William K. Vanderbilt II, who obtained the island in 1925 from Carl Fisher (creator of Miami Beach) by trading him a 250-foot yacht. Surely it was the best deal any interloper has made since the purchase of Manhattan for a cache of beads and trinkets.

Fisher Island has 400 residents who have paid anywhere from $1 million to $7 million for their condo or villa—mostly part-timers from Brazil, Germany, Italy, France, and Russia. They preen and play on 18 tennis courts, a polo field, and an international spa. The island has a mile-long sand beach. The unusually white sand on Fisher Island was imported from the Bahamas. There are no public beach accesses and no lifeguards.

The karmic payback? Fisher Island is upwind from a sewage treatment plant on Virginia Key, and leaks are not uncommon.

For more information, contact the Inn at Fisher Island, 1 Fisher Island Drive, Fisher Island, FL 33109, 305/535-6020, www.fisherisland-florida.com.

ACCOMMODATIONS

The only way the public can recreate on the beach here is to stay at the posh, 60-room **Inn at Fisher Island** (1 Fisher Island Drive, Fisher Island, 305/535-6020, $$$$), which is part of the private Fisher Island Club. If you need to ask the price, you can't afford to stay here. We needed to ask, so we'll save you the humiliation: the average price of a room is $700 per night.

THE GOLD COAST

to African-Americans and a hurricane wiped out most of the structures on Virginia Key. Since then the key has gone to seed as the clueless and often corrupt Miami government has neglected one of the last remaining unspoiled beaches in South Florida – and the city of Miami's only beach holding, since Miami and Miami Beach are distinctly different municipal entities.

Not for long, though. The city has big plans for Virginia Key. Though civic groups have had some input, we have our doubts about what direction this "rebirth" will take. The mega-bucks developers, who always seem to get the final word, want to build condos, resorts, and "entertainment venues." In short, they want Virginia Key to echo the same mindless high-rise sprawl that runs in a nearly unbroken line down the Gold Coast.

The black community is understandably upset, as they want a civil-rights monument and park erected here. Environmental and outdoor-recreation proponents are also outraged at being ignored by city government. They want what has miraculously become a wildlife sanctuary – purely by default, not proactive policy – to stay that way. The endangered manatee has found Virginia Key to its liking, as has a diverse bird population.

The smart and honorable way to go would be to let nature take its course on Virginia Key, to celebrate this vital piece of African-American history, and to allow it to return to its shining incarnation as a symbol of accessibility and hope. One lawyer working with activists said, "This is a wonderful opportunity to redress the sins of the past." Ah, but another, wiser man once said, "Past is prelude," and this is, after all, Miami.

In other words, look for condos built with mysterious infusions of foreign cash, gated waterfront communities, and exorbitantly priced convention hotels. You can practically hear the jackals licking their chops in anticipation of another profitable plunder.

Key Biscayne and Virginia Key

These two keys in a pod, separated by a man-made cut, offer a less harried alternative to the shores of Miami Beach. There is neither the concentration of neon-scripted outdoor cafes and art deco hotels that one finds in South Miami Beach nor the density of high-rise condos that run like an unbroken wall in north Miami Beach. Instead, Key Biscayne (pop. 10,500) is upscale, low-key, and casually elegant, while Virginia Key is largely uninhabited.

The village of Key Biscayne's high-end real estate draws a mix of affluent buyers from here and abroad. Bounded by the Atlantic Ocean and Biscayne Bay on its sides and by 1,800 combined acres of parkland at its ends, Key Biscayne does make an idyllic hideaway. It's a watersports paradise, offering everything from exceptional windsurfing and sailing on Biscayne Bay (the U.S. Olympic sailing team trained here) to snorkeling and scuba diving among the reefs and wrecks offshore. Though the presence of money is as thick as the briny, humid air, Key Biscayne offers sizable swaths of undeveloped shoreline that are accessible to all.

For more information, contact the Key Biscayne Chamber of Commerce, 88 West McIntire, Suite 100, Key Biscayne, FL 33149, 305/361-5207, www.keybiscaynechamber.org.

BEACHES

Considering their size, Key Biscayne and Virginia Key are generously seeded with beach parks. Starting on Virginia Key—or actually just before it—is **Hobie Beach.** Lying on the north side of Rickenbacker Causeway, it is a terrific windsurfing spot. Picnic tables, sailboat rentals, and concessions can also be found at this unguarded bayside beach.

THE GOLD COAST

THE GOLD COAST

Virginia Key Beach has had a checkered history, having been closed periodically since the 1990s due to Miami's financial woes. To its eternal misfortune, Virginia Key Beach falls within the Miami city limits and is the city's only public beach. In order to save operating costs Miami elected to shut down its lovely beach park, which is one of the few things about the city that can be recommended without hesitation. After its closure, the park went from being a haven for families, windsurfers, and birdwatchers to a hangout for homeless derelicts and after-dark revelers who left behind broken bottles and garbage. Guess who got stuck with the cost of cleanup? The city of Miami!

Access to Virginia Key Beach, when and if it is open, costs $3 per car for Miami residents and $5 per car for nonresidents. The beach entrance sits across from the Miami Seaquarium and next to the city's yard-waste management facility. The Seaquarium suffered terrible losses of its marine life, including 20 sharks, as a result of Hurricane Wilma in 2005. For that matter, 98 percent of the population of Miami-Dade County was without power in the hurricane's aftermath—described by Florida Power & Light as the worst outage in its history—and low-lying Key Biscayne got hit particularly hard.

Out on Key Biscayne, **Crandon Park** and **Bill Baggs Cape Florida State Park** boast 2.3 and 1.5 miles of sandy shore, respectively. That's nearly four miles of public beach on one small key! Crandon is among the very finest beaches in South Florida and certainly tops in the Miami area. The lifeguarded beach is of a healthy width and gently slopes off as you enter the water, making it relatively safe for children. The sand is soft and free of shells, broken glass, and litter. We took an early-evening stroll along the beach at Crandon Park, and it occurred to us as the sun disappeared and the distant city skyline lit up that this was one of the few places in Miami where one could feel safe walking after dark. Incidentally,

the Biscayne Nature Center, an ecotourism enterprise based in Crandon Park, takes tour groups out on snorkeling trips; call 305/361-8097 for information and reservations.

Bill Baggs Cape Florida State Park occupies the north end of Key Biscayne. This used to be one of the loveliest and least spoiled coastal environments in Greater Miami until Hurricane Andrew blew through in 1992, clearing the park of vegetation. If the story ended there, it would be a sad testimony to nature's destructive might. Instead, this is a happier tale about nature's indomitable will to recover, especially with a human-assisted nudge. While it will take years for the trees to attain pre-hurricane heights, the tropical hammock thickets are dense and teeming with life again. In an odd sort of way, Andrew did the park a favor. By leveling the non-native Australian pines, it gave park naturalists a chance to start from scratch with native vegetation, and the park again looked like nature intended it. The park is geared toward nature-based recreation, including hiking, kayaking, and bicycling; bikes are rented inside the park. It is also home of Cape Florida Light, built in 1865; lighthouse tours are offered Thursday through Monday at 10 A.M. and 1 P.M.

The east-facing beaches of Key Biscayne and Virginia Key, incidentally, collect a lot of the ocean's debris. Seaweed accumulates in bale-sized mounds along the high-tide line. It's collected and hauled off in front of the Sonesta Beach Resorts but piles up along the natural beaches. This brown and beardlike harvest tends to attract insects, especially at dusk.

32 HOBIE BEACH

Location: along Rickenbacker Causeway between the mainland and Virginia Key
Parking/fees: free parking along the causeway
Hours: sunrise-sunset
Facilities: concessions, restrooms, picnic tables, and showers
Contact: Miami-Dade Parks, 305/755-7800

33 VIRGINIA KEY BEACH

Location: at Rickenbacker Causeway on Virginia Key, between Miami and Key Biscayne

Parking/fees: none

Hours: Virginia Key Beach is presently closed, though plans call for turning it into "a spectacular public park venue of national historical significance."

Facilities: none

Contact: Miami-Dade Parks, 305/755-7800

34 CRANDON PARK

Location: 4000 Crandon Boulevard, at the north end of Key Biscayne

Parking/fees: $5 per vehicle entrance fee

Hours: 8 A.M.–sunset

Facilities: concessions, lifeguards, restrooms, picnic tables, and showers

Contact: Crandon Park, 305/361-5421

35 BILL BAGGS CAPE FLORIDA STATE PARK

Location: 1200 South Crandon Park Boulevard, at southern tip of Key Biscayne

Parking/fees: $5 entrance fee per vehicle

Hours: 8 A.M.–sunset

Facilities: concessions, lifeguards, restrooms, picnic tables, and showers

Contact: Bill Baggs Cape Florida State Park, 305/361-5811

HURRICANE KATRINA

On the last days of August 2005, Hurricane Katrina destroyed the city of New Orleans, along with coastal communities in Mississippi and Louisiana. It is claimed to be the worst natural disaster in U.S. history. Half a million dwellings were wrecked in those two states. The bowl-shaped city of New Orleans got flooded to ruins when its levees were breached in the storm's aftermath.

However, the failure of New Orleans' man-made levees – whose repair and upkeep had been overlooked for years – shouldn't necessarily be blamed on Mother Nature. The real culprits, to our thinking, are the U.S. Army Corps of Engineers, for failures of oversight; the Bush Administration, which diverted sorely needed funding, equipment, and Louisiana National Guard personnel to Iraq; and the city of New Orleans, a crime-ridden cesspool with crumbling infrastructure that had for decades been referred to as "the city that care forgot."

Hurricane Katrina didn't just spread unimaginable death, misery, and damage across Louisiana and Mississippi. Florida took its lumps as well. South Florida strongly felt Katrina's impact, and even the Panhandle got brushed by the storm's outer fringes, adding insult to the injuries of Hurricanes Ivan and Dennis.

Katrina had barely strengthened into a Category 1 hurricane when it made landfall at Hallandale Beach, between Hollywood and Miami Beach, on Thursday, August 25. If you ever thought a Category 1 hurricane couldn't do much damage, ponder this: Hurricane Katrina dumped 15 inches of rain and blew down trees and telephone poles across South Florida. Severe flooding left two and a half feet of standing water across the area, and nearly 1.5 million customers were left without electricity. Moreover, 14 people died, directly or indirectly, due to Katrina. And the hot, humid days that followed only exacerbated residents' misery as they attempted to pick up the pieces.

Hurricane Katrina strengthened into a monster while crossing the Gulf of Mexico, where its top winds doubled from 80 mph to 160 mph. Of course, you know what happened next.

ACCOMMODATIONS

Aside from private condos, there are only a handful of places to stay on the beach in Key Biscayne, but they are top-flight luxury accommodations. One is the elegant **Sonesta Beach Resort** (350 Ocean Drive, 305/361-2021, $$$$). Warning: You will grow so comfortable here you might find it hard to leave. We certainly did, happily slouching in hammocks slung between palm trees on the beach. The Sonesta has a big, breezy beach that's swept clean of seaweed each morning. Cabanas, beach chairs, hammocks, palm trees, a big blue Olympic pool, a poolside tiki bar, and huge Jacuzzi—what more could you want from life than this?

The hotel itself is opulent, its walls adorned with paintings collected by the Sonesta family. These well-known patrons of the arts stock their Sonesta Hotels from a collection numbering 6,000 original artworks. The Sonesta Beach Resort survived 1992's Hurricane Andrew, although it required more than $20 million in restoration. The neighboring Sheraton, however, was destroyed by Andrew and never rebuilt.

For a long time, the Sonesta was the only game in town for upscale travelers (many of them well-to-do Latin Americans). Now there is competition: the **Ritz-Carlton Key Biscayne** (415 Grand Bay Drive, 305/365-9575, $$$$), which is one of the hottest properties in South Florida. A more affordable alternative to the Ritz and Sonesta is offered by the **Silver Sands Beach Resort** (301 Ocean Drive, 305/361-5441, $$$), whose flowering, plant-filled courtyard and 56 single-story units are a lot closer to the casual Old Florida look than its towering neighbors.

COASTAL CUISINE

The Sonesta Beach Resort has three on-premises restaurants. The **Purple Dolphin** (350 Ocean Drive, 305/361-2021, $$$$) specializes in fine dining and offers a Friday-night seafood buffet for $29. **Two Dragons** (350 Ocean Drive, 305/361-2021, $$$) serves Chinese and Thai items, as well as an extensive menu of sushi (try the Dragon Roll: eel, crab, avocado, and mango). At the more casual **Jasmine Cafe** (350 Ocean Drive, 305/361-2021, $), the menu includes soup, sandwiches, and lighter fare such as grilled shrimp quesadillas served with homemade guacamole and salsa. Try the conch chowder, a cumin-spiced concoction that takes a more Cuban approach to the soup than you'll typically find out on the Florida Keys.

Matheson Hammock County Park

South Miami-Dade County is beachless and mucky, but there are a couple of parks with swimming areas along Biscayne Bay. One of them is Matheson Hammock County Park, which lies south of Coconut Grove and east of Kendall. Constructed by the Civilian Conservation Corps in the 1930s, it is the oldest park in Miami-Dade County. Between the lushly vegetated grounds and the view of the Miami skyline and Key Biscayne across the bay, Matheson Hammock occupies a scenic corner of south Miami-Dade. As improbable as it sounds, there is even a sandy swimming beach here.

Though the sand has been trucked in, it's definitely more fun to recreate on than the grayish soil that lines the bay. The swimming area is a natural lagoon that has been enclosed to form a tidal-fed "atoll pool." Triathletes train here, finding the park a nice place to run and the atoll pool suitable for swimming laps.

Mainly, though, Mattheson Hammock is a family-oriented park with its picnic area and lifeguarded lagoon. There's even an alfresco restaurant, the **Redfish Grill** (open 5 P.M.–10 P.M. nightly). It's run by the owners of a fancy Coral Gables restaurant called Christy's. County parks don't get much nicer than this!

BEACHES

36 MATHESON HAMMOCK COUNTY PARK

Location: 9610 Old Cutler Road in South Coral Gables
Parking/fees: $3.50 entrance fee per vehicle
Hours: 6 A.M.-sunset
Facilities: concessions, lifeguards, restrooms, picnic tables, and showers
Contact: Matheson Hammock County Park, 305/666-6979

Homestead

Homestead (pop. 35,000) was nearly wiped off the map by Hurricane Andrew in 1992. It was the costliest natural disaster to that point in U.S. history—surpassed in 2005 by Hurricane Katrina—and Homestead took the most direct hit. Since then the city has rebuilt and is still rebounding. In Andrew's wake, President Bush (the first one) promised to rebuild Homestead Air Force Base, which was supposed to have been decommissioned. Today, Homestead Air Reserve Base is alive and well, serving as home for the Air Force's 482nd Fighter Wing. Plans to turn it into another major commercial airport for Miami were dropped in 2001 when environmentalists pointed out the harm that would come from wedging such a thing between two already sensitive and stressed National Parks (Biscayne and Everglades).

Seemingly trying to become South Florida's answer to Daytona, Homestead is home to a NASCAR motorsports complex—**Homestead-Miami Speedway** (1 Speedway Boulevard, 305/230-7223)—which can hold 60,000 people. That's almost twice the population of Homestead! If a car race in the heat and humidity of South Florida sounds appealing, then Homestead will be your kind of town. For most travelers, however, Homestead is bypassed en route to or from the Keys.

For more information, contact the Greater Homestead/Florida City Chamber of Commerce, 43 North Krome Avenue, Homestead, FL 33030, 305/247-2332, www.chamberinaction.com.

BEACHES

Homestead Bayfront Park, like Matheson Hammock County Park, features an atoll pool: an enclosed saltwater lagoon fed by tidal exchange, with a sandy shoreline. Located eight miles east of Homestead, this popular and well-equipped county park is adjacent to the visitors center for Biscayne National Park.

37 HOMESTEAD BAYFRONT PARK

Location: east end of Canal Drive (S.W. 328th Street) in Homestead
Parking/fees: $3.50 entrance fee per vehicle
Hours: 6 A.M.-sunset
Facilities: concessions, lifeguards, restrooms, picnic tables, and showers
Contact: Homestead Bayfront Park, 305/230-3034

Biscayne National Park

Biscayne National Park plays second fiddler crab to its better-known neighbor, Everglades National Park. One reason for this may be that 97 percent of its 181,500 acres are underwater. The park was created in 1968 yet remains something of a secret—at least by comparison to the Everglades and Pennekamp State Park on Key Largo. Mostly, it's visited by pleasure boaters, divers, snorkelers, and anglers. Within the park boundaries—which run from the south end of Miami to Key Largo—are 41 keys. There are also mangrove forests, living coral reefs, and 25 miles of mainland

THE GOLD COAST

THE GOLD COAST

shoreline. We took the snorkeling trip, which lasts all afternoon. Pray for a calm, wave-free day, otherwise all the rocking and rolling in the water might make you seasick. Heading out to whatever reef the guide decides to visit provides scenic sights on Biscayne Bay, and the snorkeling turns up colorful reef dwellers as long as the water hasn't been stirred up by waves and currents. You might ask about conditions before making the long trip out here and handing over your $35.

The point of entry for landlubbers is the Convoy Point Visitor Center, on Biscayne Bay. There is literature and exhibits at the center and picnicking on the grounds but not much else to do on the mainland. Daily trips include glass-bottomed boat tours at 10 A.M. ($24.45 for adults, $19.45 for seniors, and $16.45 for children under 12, plus $2.50 fuel surcharge) and a snorkeling excursion at 1:30 P.M. ($35 for adults, $29.95 for kids 12 and under, plus $2.50 fuel surcharge). Scuba-diving trips ($54 per person, plus $2.50 fuel surcharge) depart at 8:30 A.M. on weekends, as long as eight or more sign up. From November through May, round-trip boat drop-off and pickup and from Elliott and Boca Chita Keys ($35.95, plus $2.50 fuel surcharge) can be made through the park concessionaire, which also rents canoes ($12 per hour) and kayaks ($16 per hour) 9 A.M.–3 P.M. For information and reservations, call 305/230-1100.

Campgrounds are located on both Elliott Key and Boca Chita Key, which lie about eight and 10 miles offshore, respectively. Camping is $10 per night, and camping and docking your boat on either island costs $15 per night. Group sites (up to six tents and 25 people) go for $25 per night.

Elliott is 11 miles long and one mile wide.

There's a ranger station at the harbor, and a hiking trail runs along its coral spine. Boca Chita is small and round, a little puffball of a key by comparison. Both islands have restrooms, picnic areas and docks, and Elliott Key has showers and drinking water, as well. While there are no sand beaches, Elliott Key has a grassy one.

Boca Chita Key opened to the public in December 1996 after damage from Hurricane Andrew closed it for more than three years. Biscayne National Park was ground zero for the devastating Category 4 hurricane, which destroyed 90 percent of the mature red mangroves. However, the park's recovery has been impressive, and the park lucked out by avoiding significant damage during the 2005 blow-through of Hurricane Wilma. Come see the remarkable place for yourself!

For more information, contact Biscayne National Park, 9700 SW 328th Street, Homestead, FL 33033, 305/230-7275, www.nps.gov/bisc.

BEACHES

38 BISCAYNE NATIONAL PARK

BEST (

Location: Convoy Point Visitor Center at the east end of Canal Drive (S.W. 328th Street), nine miles east of Homestead
Parking/fees: free parking lots
Hours: 8:30 A.M.–5 P.M.
Facilities: concessions, restrooms, picnic tables, showers, and a visitors center
Contact: Biscayne National Park, 305/230-7275

KEY WEST AND THE SUNNY FLORIDA KEYS

To lovers of land's end, the Florida Keys make an endlessly fascinating set of ellipses for the East Coast. The more than 800 keys, not to mention the lion's share of Everglades National Park, fall inside massive Monroe County. Both are environmentally sensitive areas that have been subjected to extreme human-generated stresses. Theoretically they are protected, but both are, in fact, imperiled—particularly the beleaguered Everglades, whose hydraulic regime and biological makeup have been impacted by everything from sugar-cane operations to withdrawals of water for ballooning population centers.

At least you can still feel like you're getting away from it all, to some degree, down on the Keys or deep in the Everglades. The Keys extend for 108 miles in a southwesterly direction from the Florida mainland. You'll cross 42 bridges as you pass from the Upper Keys (Key Largo to Duck Key) to the Lower Keys (Grassy Key to Key West). When the road— good old U.S. 1, which originates 2,377 miles away in Fort Kent, Maine (on the Canadian border)—finally gives out toward the end of Whitehead Street in Key West, you're closer by far to the Cuban capital of Havana (90 miles) than to Miami (160 miles).

Out on the Keys people watch the sun set with a combination of Thoreauvian reverence and margarita-induced gaiety. Sunset-watching has been stylized into a touristy ritual in Key West, but even the commercialization takes a back seat to the actual spectacle, which is still jaw-dropping and awe-inspiring.

It's safe to say you won't come out to the Keys for the beaches. True sand beaches are few and far between on these coral-spined islands. A few notable exceptions are scattered between Marathon and Key West: Bahia Honda State Park (on Bahia Honda Key), Anne's Beach (on Lower Matecumbe Key), and

COURTESY OF ANDY NEWMAN/FLORIDA KEYS NEWS BUREAU/HO

THE SUNNY FLORIDA KEYS

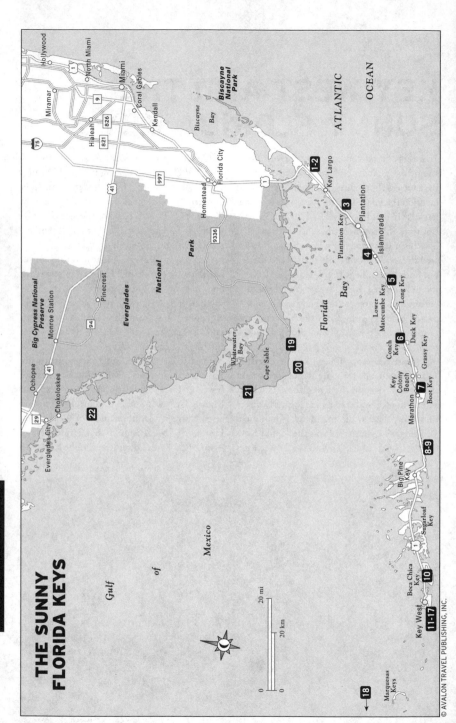

THE SUNNY FLORIDA KEYS

© AVALON TRAVEL PUBLISHING, INC.

BEST BEACHES

◖ **John Pennekamp Coral Reef State Park:** Best for Diving and Snorkeling (page 289)

◖ **Islamorada:** Best for Fishing (page 290)

◖ **Marathon:** Best for Fishing (page 298)

◖ **Bahia Honda State Park:** Top 25, Best for Camping (page 306)

◖ **Looe Key:** Best for Diving and Snorkeling (page 308)

◖ **Gulf Coast Keys:** Best for Canoeing and Kayaking, Best for Birdwatching and Wildlife-Viewing (page 329)

Sombrero Beach (in Marathon). The Keys have given birth to a laid-back way of life that finds its culmination in Key West, home base for the "Conch Republic" and as close to the tropics as America gets. Although alligators abound all over Florida, Monroe County is the only place in the state and nation where crocodiles can be found. We actually saw a sign on U.S. 1 that warned "Crocodile Crossing."

Even the deer are different down on the Keys. A unique species of dog-sized "key deer" make their home on a few islands in the Lower Keys. Between the crocs and the key deer, not to mention the crusty denizens of the Conch Republic, the Florida Keys provide a means of leaving the country without leaving the country, if you catch our drift.

Key Largo

Key Largo (pop. 13,000) is the largest of the Florida Keys. It's 33 miles in length from stem to stern. Yes, maritime metaphors are appropriate on Key Largo, because most vacation activities are done from a boat: fishing, diving, snorkeling, cruising the islands. Beaches are in short supply on Key Largo. Although your first inclination may be to make tracks down the Keys, enough points of historical and natural interest—and some genuine curiosities—can be found to justify a layover in Key Largo.

And if you come here to explore the wonders of John Pennekamp Coral Reef State Park, you might want to hole up here for a few days.

The most obvious curiosity about Key Largo is its fixation with Humphrey Bogart. This obsession originated with the 1948 movie *Key Largo,* which, obviously, derived its name from local geography. Beyond that, the Bogie connection is tenuous at best. With the exception of a few interior scenes filmed inside the Caribbean Club (MM 104.5), Key Largo was made on a soundstage in Hollywood, and Bogie himself never set foot on the Keys. Nonetheless, the largest town on this key, Rock Harbor, officially changed its name to Key Largo—presumably in hopes of translating Hollywood celebrity into tourist dollars. If you look closely, you will still find a sign for Rock Harbor on U.S. 1.

While this is harmless enough, it would be nice if Key Largo expended some of this same energy restoring other parts of town to a more nostalgic, if not idyllic, condition. For instance, the concept of zoning seems nonexistent, judging from the unending line of fast-food franchises and the scattershot development that finds an adult video shop next to a boat-propeller shop next to a fruit stand next to a church next to a T-shirt emporium next to a shell shop. A porno parlor, in fact, sits right across the street from John Pennekamp State Park. Incredibly enough, Key Largo remains

COURTESY OF STEPHEN FRINK/FLORIDA KEYS NEWS BUREAU/HO

A diver swims past a school of grunt while exploring the forward deck of the USS *Spiegel Grove*, off Key Largo, in the Florida Keys National Marine Sanctuary.

unincorporated, which explains the unregulated sprawl. Be especially wary of shell shops. They take whatever they legally can from the Keys and import coral and shells from other parts of the world where the environmental laws are lax, at best. Unsuspecting tourists buy this ecological plunder like saltwater taffy, contributing to one of the gravest of our many global eco-crises: the accelerated loss of our precious coral reefs.

While this may seem like carping, it does have some connection to Key Largo's most prominent drawing card, John Pennekamp Coral Reef State Park. The living reefs off Key Largo have been under assault from tanker wrecks, oil spills, agricultural runoff, coral poachers, prop dredge from small boats, and even the releases of uric acid from scuba divers. Swinish boaters even dump trash overboard, which sinks or washes ashore. Sadly, we have seen shameful masses of soggy detritus at the high-tide line on too many Keys beaches. Several divers have told us that underwater visibility has declined dramatically on the Keys. A management plan for the Florida Keys National Marine Sanctuary was implemented

in 1997. Though it was opposed by many Keys residents, who resent outside interference from a larger ruling authority, the plan has been widely hailed as a model for large-scale ecological undertakings. Still, it will take years to reverse the damage.

Key Largo gets a lot of mileage out of calling itself the "Dive Capital of the World." Established in 1960, John Pennekamp was the nation's first undersea preserve. The Key Largo National Marine Sanctuary was created in 1975. As part of the larger Florida Keys National Marine Sanctuary, Key Largo lays claim to six Sanctuary Preservation Areas, where fishing of all kinds—even with a hook and line—is prohibited. Other popular dive sites in the area include Molasses Reef and French Reef, with its underwater caves. Kayaking the waters of Florida Bay is an eco-friendly way to find some inspirational quietude.

Key Largo, like all of the Florida Keys, has increasingly become a destination resort—and, for retirees, destination of last resort—for the wealthy. This is unfortunate in that the lately arrived builders of trophy homes have been displacing those of more modest means who

HIGHWAY TO THE KEYS

U.S. 1 runs the 108-mile length of the Florida Keys, from Key Largo to Key West. Technically, however, it all begins in Florida City, below Homestead at the eastern boundary of Everglades National Park, where U.S. 1 officially becomes the Overseas Highway. The first mile marker (MM 126) is encountered here, and those numbers decrease as you make your way west down the Keys. The final mile marker (MM 0) is at the corner of Whitehead and Fleming Streets in Key West. On these narrow keys, mile markers function as addresses and directions. Often, the words "oceanside" or "bayside" will be included, as in "Harry Harris County Park, MM 92.5 oceanside."

These limestone spines are the remnants of coral reefs that died when sea level dropped during the last ice age. Most keys are so narrow you can see the Straits of Florida out of one eye and Florida Bay from the other. Although you travel west-southwest on the Overseas Highway, the Keys are frequently spoken of as being north or south of one another. We think "east" and "west" make more sense – look at a map to see why.

Ironically, Key West did not come by its name because it is the westernmost of the inhabited keys. It originally bore the Spanish name Cayo Hueso ("bone island"), which got misheard by English-speaking ears as Key West. Fortunately, that is an accurate name and, besides, "Key South" doesn't have quite the same ring.

Another bit of nomenclature: "Upper Keys" refers to the stretch from Key Largo to Islamorada. The "Lower Keys" extend from the western foot of the Seven Mile Bridge (Little Duck Key) to Stock Island. The "Middle Keys" include everything in between, with the town of Marathon as the hub. Key West stands alone at the end of the road, an entity unto itself.

Most people are familiar only with the bridged stretch of keys from Key Largo to Key West. However, more than 800 islands make up the entire 180-mile chain of Florida Keys, which extend from Biscayne Bay to the Dry Tortugas. The keys range in size from tiny mangrove islands to the sizable likes of Key Largo and Big Pine Key (the two largest). Forty-two bridges cross the Keys, ranging in length from 37 feet (Harris Gap, in the Lower Keys) to 35,716 feet (Seven Mile Bridge, which actually falls 1,244 feet shy of seven miles). The Keys average 2-6 feet above sea level, with the highest point found on Lignumvitae Key, which rises to 18 feet.

It was the unsinkable Henry Morrison Flagler who hatched the idea of linking the Keys by extending his Florida East Coast Railway from Homestead to Key West. Despite the project's cost, in terms of expense and human lives, the cross-Keys railroad was completed in seven years. Flagler rode triumphantly into Key West in 1912, shortly after his 82nd birthday. "Now I can die happy," he said. "My dream is fulfilled." (In fact, he died 16 months later.) His railroad survived until the raging, unnamed hurricane of September 2, 1935, destroyed 40 miles of track. The pilings survived, however, and the Overseas Highway (U.S. 1) was built on them.

By the way, sometime within the next decade you won't absolutely have to make the trip from Key Largo to Key West by car, if you so choose. The Florida Keys Overseas Heritage Trail – a joint undertaking between Monroe County and Florida's Departments of Environmental Protection, Transportation, and State Parks – will make it possible to bike or hike the 106 miles down the keys using abandoned railroad beds, former roads and newly constructed bikeways and walking trails. The trail will be part of Florida's ever-farsighted State Parks system.

PORT BOUGAINVILLE: ENTERING THE TWILIGHT ZONE

Come with us on a surreal side trip at the north end of Key Largo. This is a section of the Keys often missed by vacationers speeding on and off them via U.S. 1. Not so long ago, S.R. 905 was slated to become the main boulevard for a city known as Port Bougainville. All of the land had been purchased, lots platted, plans approved. In short, the deal was done. Port Bougainville would have been the largest development in the history of the Keys, with the building of 2,800 condos, two 300-room hotels, and yacht marinas. But environmentalists fought and banks foreclosed, and Port Bougainville was history.

The happy ending is that conservation groups, including the Friends of the Everglades, rescued this vital green buffer and estuary. Port Bougainville now belongs to the state, which purchased its 431 acres in 1988 for $22.8 million. The site is now a preserve being reclaimed by nature. If you're passing through, take the eye-opening drive along S.R. 905 north from its junction with U.S. 1 on Key Largo. At various intervals you can see where the streets of this phantom development had been laid out and where the vacation homes of the wealthy were going to be plopped among them. Some human habitations predating Port Bougainville still exist, but they occupy only the tip of Key Largo. S.R. 905, in fact, dead-ends at the gated tower of a private development, just past signs for the Ocean Reef Club and Key Largo Angler's Club.

Interestingly, the Key Largo wood rat – an endangered species driven to near-extinction by habitat loss, feral cats, and fire ants – is struggling to make a comeback at Port Bougainville. But don't cheer just yet – the wood rat's numbers are estimated to be 25-100 – approximately the size of the remaining population of Florida panthers. Which is to say, all but extinct.

have called the Keys home for much of their lives. In short, natives are being priced out of their own communities. We're not writing an editorial about social injustice but simply stating facts, which will likely not pertain if you're coming here to fish or relax.

Despite all the complications in the social matrix, the fact remains that there is nothing like the sight of mist rising off Florida Bay in the early morning in Key Largo. Rise with the sun to do something water-related, and you can't go wrong.

For more information, contact the Key Largo Chamber of Commerce, 106000 Overseas Highway, Key Largo, FL 33037, 305/451-4747 or 800/822-1088, www.keylargo.org.

BEACHES

It's a given that you're not really coming to the Keys for the beaches, because they are few and far between, and some of them aren't even "real," in that they've been created from trucked-in sand. Offshore coral reefs intercept the waves, so there's no physical mechanism for transporting sand shoreward to build up a beach. Having said that, you will find several beaches on Key Largo, but they're man-made. Two of them, **Cannon Beach** and **Far Beach,** are in John Pennekamp Coral Reef State Park. Cannon Beach is a small sliver of sand that features a replica of a 17th-century shipwreck, located 130 feet offshore, which attracts tropical fish and snorkelers. Swimming in the balmy waters is fine, but you really must pack snorkeling gear or you'll miss the best Cannon Beach has to offer. Far Beach, a short hop down Largo Sound, is a prettier site, lined with coconut palms that afford some shade.

Harry Harris County Park completes Key Largo's trio of faux sand beaches. It has a little something for everyone, from ballplayers (baseball fields, basketball courts) to boaters (two boat ramps, which are the best landings between Miami and Key West) to beachgoers (an enclosed tidal pool that's about as wide as a football field). Harry Harris apparently even appeals to evangelicals. One afternoon we watched a busload of people perform total immersion baptisms in the tidal pool, to much jubilation, weeping, and wailing on shore. There's also a large picnic area and children's playground. Wilkinson's Point is an interesting coral outcrop that extends about 100 yards into the water. On the north side, you can wander into the three-foot shallows of Florida Bay (wear shoes). It is a well-guarded fact that this is one of the best bonefishing areas around, and you don't even have to be in a boat to take advantage of it. County residents don't have to pay to use the park. Nonresidents must pay $5 on weekends and holidays but can enter for free at all other times.

1 CANNON BEACH

Location: John Pennekamp Coral Reef State Park, off U.S. 1 at MM 102.5 in Key Largo
Parking/Fees: $3.50 for one person; $6 for two people; and $0.50 each for all others. Camping fee is $26 per night.
Hours: 8 A.M.-sunset
Facilities: concessions, restrooms, picnic tables, showers, and a visitors center
Contact: John Pennekamp Coral Reef State Park, 305/451-1202

2 FAR BEACH

Location: John Pennekamp Coral Reef State Park, off U.S. 1 at MM 102.5 in Key Largo
Parking/Fees: $3.50 for one person; $6 for two people; and $0.50 each for all others. Camping fee is $26 per night.
Hours: 8 A.M.-sunset

Facilities: concessions, restrooms, picnic tables, showers, and a visitors center
Contact: John Pennekamp Coral Reef State Park, 305/451-1202

3 HARRY HARRIS COUNTY PARK

Location: east Beach Road at MM 92.5 in Tavenier, at the south end of Key Largo
Parking/Fees: free to county residents at all times. Nonresidents pay $5 per person on weekends and holidays, and nothing at other times. A $10 fee for use of the boat ramps is charged.
Hours: 7:30 A.M.-sunset
Facilities: concessions, restrooms, picnic tables, and showers
Contact: Monroe County Department of Parks and Beaches, 305/295-4385

RECREATION AND ATTRACTIONS (UPPER KEYS)

- **Bike/Skate Rentals:** Tavernier Bicycles and Hobbies, MM 91.9, Tavernier, 305/852-2859

- **Boat Cruise:** Key Largo Princess, Holiday Inn, MM 100, Key Largo, 305/451-4655

- **Dive Shop:** Capt. Slate's Atlantis Dive Center, 51 Garden Cove Drive, Key Largo, 305/451-3252

- **Ecotourism:** Florida Bay Outfitters, MM 104, Key Largo, 305/451-3018; Dolphin Cove Research and Education Center, MM 101.9, Key Largo, 305/451-4060

- **Fishing Charters:** Key Largo Fishing Guides Association, 305/451-9493

- **Marina:** Mangrove Marina, MM 91.7, Tavernier, 305/852-8380

- **Rainy-Day Attraction:** Florida Keys Wild Bird Center, MM 93.6, Tavernier, 305/852-4486

- **Shopping/Browsing:** Tavernier Towne Shopping Center, MM 91.2, Tavernier
- **Vacation Rentals:** Florida Keys Rental Store, MM 100, Key Largo, 305/451-3879 or 800/585-0584

ACCOMMODATIONS

Sheraton Beach Resort Key Largo (MM 97, 305/852-5553, $$$$) is as unobtrusive as a four-story hotel can possibly be. It is set among a 12-acre buttonwood grove that insinuates itself nicely into the visitor's consciousness. An on-premises restaurant/lounge called Treetops looks directly into the upper limbs of the native greenery. Located on Florida Bay, the resort—which was formerly part of the Westin chain—has benefited from the change of ownership, with a wholesale facelift and upgrading of facilities. There's a nice little bayside beach out back, with a waveless swimming area that's great for kids and a volleyball net set up in the water. Watersports adventures (parasailing, waterskiing, windsurfing, sailing, and more) can be arranged at the on-site marina. One of the best features is the pool area, where there's an ample-sized swimming pool for adults (no kids allowed) and another for families. A waterfall and beautiful murals divide the pools, the white noise generated by the former affording road-weary adults a respite from other folks' screaming kids. A nature trail through the buttonwood grove is a grace note to one of the more intelligently designed resorts we've encountered in our coastal wanderings.

Other interesting accommodations can be found in the area, none more intriguing than an underwater inn (you read correctly) named **Jules' Undersea Lodge** (MM 103.2, 51 Shoreland Drive, 305/451-2353, $$$$). Jules' carries scuba mania to new, er, lows—30 feet below sea level, to be exact. Originally an undersea research lab off the coast of Puerto Rico, the lodge was purchased by two seasoned divers who wanted to maintain an entrepreneurial attachment to their first love. A special "Luxury Aquanaut" package features a chef who swims into the cruise-ship-sized room (with TV, phone, etc.) to cook a meal on the premises. There's no question he earns whatever tips he gets.

Another original is **Amy Slate's Amoray Dive Resort** (104250 Overseas Highway, 305/451-3595, $$), which offers special packages that include an underwater wedding. (Imagine water bubbles rising from the happy couple's mouths as they burble, "I do.") Visitors can also book ecotours, courses in underwater photography, reef ecology, fish identification, and night diving at the Amoray. Rooms are adequate, and one- and two-bedroom apartments with fully equipped kitchens are also available.

One more local curiosity is the **Holiday Inn** (MM 100, 305/451-2121, $$$), notable for its unabashedly friendly service and the fact that the boat used in the 1952 film *The African Queen* is docked on the premises. The hotel's restaurant? Bogie's Cafe, natch! Here's looking at you, kid. The hotel has its own marina and will assist in booking watery expeditions. A casino boat and glass-bottom boat tours depart from the marina, and the hotel is only three miles from Pennekamp State Park.

COASTAL CUISINE

Key Largo's dining scene seems to be, at first glance, a bad stomach-acid trip of fast-food joints. The glowing familiarity of their signs apparently must entice enough unadventurous tourists to support the full smorgasbord of them represented here. Ah, but there are alternatives to being super-sized. For "Floribbean" cooking, check out **Gus' Grille,** located in the Marriott Key Largo Bay Beach Resort (MM 103.8, 305/453-0029, $$$). Off the beaten track and a bit more creative is **Flamingo Seafood Bar and Grill** (MM 106.5, 45 Garden Cove Drive, 305/451-8022, $$$).

Less pricey local hangouts are **Mrs. Mac's Kitchen** (MM 99.4, 305/451-3722, $$) and **Crack'd Conch** (MM 105, 305/451-0732, $$). Mrs. Mac's is a likeably ramshackle eatery that's gamely holding its own against the reef of franchises encroaching from all sides. Peeling wood paneling is covered with license plates, slogans, and snapshots of loyal customers, and the food is as homey as its interior. After all, the founder named Mrs. Mac's for his mom, whose homemade chili, conch chowder, and meat loaf are signature dishes. If it's available, you'll definitely want to check out the "Seafood Sensation," offered Thursday–Saturday nights: portions of delicious, simply prepared fish, fritters, crab, and shrimp. Crack'd Conch has been a landmark in the Upper Keys for years. It's a weather-beaten but rock-solid seafood house that serves reliable fare and large helpings.

Similar in its friendly atmosphere, attentive wait staff, and good reputation is the **Fish House Restaurant** (MM 102.4, 305/451-4665, $$). It has a fresh seafood market on the premises, where colorful fresh fillets glisten on beds of ice. Fresh catches usually include mahimahi, yellowtail, and snapper. In our opinion, the way to go from among several preparation options is pan-sauteed. They dip the fillets in egg wash, saute them in lemon and butter, and finish with a splash of sherry. Another good choice is "Matecumbe-style," in which fillets are baked with tomatoes, shallots, capers, basil, olive oil, and lemon juice. It sounds more like the Mediterranean than Matecumbe, but it's delicious all the same. The Fish House makes a really good key lime pie, to boot. Finally, the **Big Fish Grille** (MM99, 305/451-3734, $$) serves fresh local seafood and attracts locals who come for the live music, billiard tables, and dartboards. In other words, you can have your dinner and nightlife needs met under one roof.

A quick note: a couple of older favorites, such as Zappie's Bait Shop and Bar, have gone to that great dive bar in the sky. Indeed, friends of ours who used to love coming to the Keys have remarked that the unfancy old tiki-hut bars at which you could pull over, get a fruity drink, and prop up your bare feet are going the way of Nassau grouper and other endangered species. Perhaps they've become victims of their own (or Jimmy Buffett's) success, as up-scale types displace scruffy old-timers as this little corner of paradise (like everywhere else) get a moneyed makeover.

NIGHTLIFE

Key Largo is no Key West, but there's still a viable nightlife. **Coconuts** (528 Caribbean Drive, 305/453-9794), at the Marina del Mar Resort (near MM 100), is a triple-threat restaurant (with raw bar and menu full of fresh catches), outdoor bar, and indoor nightclub. On "Bluesday Tuesday," blues-rocking talent is brought in from all over. Wednesday through Saturday are variously given over to deejays, live bands, and solo acts. Live music and cool drinks are also on tap at the **Caribbean Club** (MM 104, 305/451-9970).

For an authentic Keys dive bar, find your way to the **Mandalay Marina and Tiki Bar** (80 East 2nd Street, 305/852-5450), which lies at the end of the road on the gulf side of Key Largo. It's unfancy as hell, full of local color, and has a clientele that looks like a Jimmy Buffett song come to life. We even heard a Jimmy Buffett song, "Cheeseburger in Paradise," performed—warbled badly, in actuality by a local duo. This is the place to come if you want to soak up native ambience in all its ragged glory. You'll see all kinds of cheeseburgers in paradise downing beers and swapping boat stories.

BEST❢ John Pennekamp Coral Reef State Park

This state park encompasses part of the only living coral reef in the lower 48 states. The reef, which extends three miles offshore, took thousands of years to form. The coral—a small, fleshy polyp—secretes a limestone home around itself, attaching to other coral dwellings. The result is a virtual underwater condominium that's home to 40 types of coral, 600 species of fish, and other marine life: Florida spiny lobsters, sea turtles, crabs, shrimp, and more. This undersea wonderland has been likened to a tropical rain forest.

Pennekamp's 150 square miles of protected ocean waters are home to a coral reef, mangrove swamps, and seagrass beds. The visual delights of the coral reef, not unlike a drugless LSD trip, can be appreciated several ways. The most popular—a 2.5-hour glass-bottomed boat tour—heads to Molasses Reef ($22 for adults, $15 for kids under 12; offered at 9:15 A.M., 12:15 P.M., and 3 P.M.). A 2.5-hour snorkeling tour speeds to the reef via motorboat, allowing 90 minutes of snorkeling ($28.95 for adults, $23.95 for kids under 12, plus $4 to rent masks, fins, and snorkels; offered at 9 A.M., noon, and 3 P.M.). A sailing and snorkeling tour makes the trip via catamaran, which is quieter and more relaxing but takes an additional 90 minutes for a total tour time of four hours ($34.95 for adults, $29.95 for kids under 18; offered at 9 A.M. and 1:30 P.M.). Reservations for all tours are strongly recommended.

Scuba tours originate at the dive shop ($45 per person; offered at 9:30 A.M. and 1:30 P.M.). Divers must be PADI-certified, and you can obtain that certification here. PADI open-water certification takes three or four days and costs $425—not a bad way to spend a vacation. For a brief taste of diving thrills, try the Day Resort Course ("Begin at 9 A.M. and be diving by 2 P.M."), which costs $150 and includes two reef dives. (Note that this is a non-certification course.) Other dive packages are offered; call 305/451-6322 for more information. You can also rent a powerboat at the marina and take off on your own adventure; call 305/451-6325 for boat rentals.

The main attraction at the visitors center is a 30,000-gallon saltwater aquarium. There are also exhibits and films on the reef ecosystem. A 47-site campground surrounds a pond behind the marina. Hiking paths explore the mangroves and uplands. A 2.5-mile mangrove wilderness trail follows a channel through mangrove forests. Canoes and kayaks can be rented at the marina, as can seacycles, Hobies, viewing rafts,

and bumper boats. Pennekamp even has a pair of man-made beaches, so bring swimsuits.

John Pennekamp Coral Reef State Park is open daily 8 A.M.–sunset, but the visitor center closes at 5 P.M. Park admission is $6 for every vehicle with two persons and $0.50 for each additional person.

For more information, contact John Pennekamp Coral Reef State Park, MM 102.5, Key Largo, FL 33037, 305/451-1202, www.pennekamppark.com. For tour information and reservations, call 305/451-6300

BEST (Islamorada

The town of Islamorada takes its name from two Spanish words, *islas moradas,* which translates as "purple islands." It was so christened by Spanish explorers for the violet sea snails that covered the shore once upon a time. A small town on a medium-sized key, Islamorada is a relaxing place to cast a fishing line and unwind. Fishing, in fact, is its main *raison d'être.*

Islamorada (pop. 6,800)—which occupies much of Upper Matecumbe Key—is our favorite of the more populous Keys between Miami and Key West. It embodies and preserves the laid-back Keys lifestyle, projecting the largely relaxed air of a fishing village (even though, truth to tell, there's little that's truly village-like about it in this day and age). For whatever reason, Islamorada's restaurants and resorts do a better job of grasping the essence of what the Keys are about than Key Largo, Marathon, and the boutique- and souvenir shop-lined streets of Key West. An excellent bike path runs for miles west of town, further proof of progressive minds hereabouts.

Islamorada was the first key to be colonized by European settlers: 50 Anglo-Bahamian conchs who established a community on Matecumbe Key. They built the first church and schoolhouse on the Keys at the turn of the century. All their hard work came to an untimely end when a hurricane destroyed the community on Labor Day 1935. A graveyard

© PARKE PUTERBAUGH

parasailing in Islamorada

world. The Atlantic Ocean meets the Gulf of Mexico here, with the Gulf Stream serving as an incubator.

For more information, contact the Islamorada Chamber of Commerce, P.O. Box 915, MM 82.5, Islamorada, FL 33036, 305/664-4503 or 800/322-5397, www.islamoradachamber.com.

BEACHES

Sand beaches are a precious and rare commodity out on the spiny Keys, and Islamorada is no exception. Private resorts, such as Cheeca Lodge, have man-made beaches and sandy lagoons, but Islamorada is otherwise devoid of them—with one quasi-exception on the bayside. **Upper Matecumbe County Park,** located behind the local library, isn't much more than a picnic and playground for the locals. People do swim in the bay, although it's not encouraged because tidal currents can be swift.

for these pioneers, many of whom were among the 423 who perished in the hurricane, can be found on the grounds of Cheeca Lodge, near the swimming pool. It is noted with a historical marker. A larger monument to hurricane victims sits on the Overseas Highway.

Islamorada justifiably markets itself as "the Sportfishing Capital of the World," boasting the largest charter fleet in the Keys (we counted 350 listings in the local Yellow Pages), as well as the world's greatest number of resident fishing vessels per square mile. Deep-sea and backcountry charters, as well as boat rentals, can be arranged at marinas in the vicinity, including **Bud 'n' Mary's** (MM 79.8, 305/664-2461) and **Papa Joe's** (MM 79.7, 305/664-5005), which lie opposite from each other on the ocean and bay, respectively. Also check out the action at Whale Harbor Bridge, which separates Upper Matecumbe Key from Windley Key. You'd have to be the world's unluckiest angler not to catch something in Islamorada, for the waters surrounding the Keys are the largest breeding and feeding grounds in the

4 UPPER MATECUMBE COUNTY PARK

Location: behind the Islamorada Public Library, at MM 81.5 on the bayside on Upper Matecumbe Key
Parking/Fees: free parking lot
Hours: 7:30 A.M.-sunset
Facilities: restrooms, picnic tables, and showers
Contact: Monroe County Department of Parks and Beaches, 305/295-4385

ACCOMMODATIONS

Cheeca Lodge (P.O. Box 527, MM 82, 305/664-4651, $$$$) is an "environmentally friendly" resort situated near the Hurricane Monument on the ocean side of Islamorada. We note the monument because the lodge's own sign is not much larger than a bumper sticker. That principle of understatement extends to the resort, where nature is allowed to play the starring role and side shows are held to

THE SUNNY FLORIDA KEYS

FISHING THE FLORIDA KEYS

In the Florida Keys, fishing is as automatic as breathing. Anglers head to the Keys in winter to cast for bonefish, tarpon, and other gamefish found in the mangrove-studded "backcountry" of Florida Bay. In the open waters of the Straits of Florida, sailfish, mackerel, kingfish, and more are taken November–March. Here is the lowdown on the fish species you're likely to cast for in the Keys:

- **Bonefish** – This fighting fish is pursued for sport only, since it is inedible. It is caught in the shallows from a poled boat or with waders, using crab or shrimp as bait.

- **Grouper** – Black grouper is unbeatable on the table, and the other types are delicious, too. Troll the bottom with cut or live bait. Unfortunately, they've been grossly overfished.

- **Mahimahi** (a.k.a. dolphinfish) – A superb eating fish, this iridescent, multicolored beauty is a surface dweller that schools beneath sea grass mats in summer.

- **Sailfish** – This leaping billfish has a raised dorsal fin that looks like a sail and a swordlike upper jaw. It's another desirable wall hanging best returned to the tropical waters it calls home.

- **Snapper** – Comes in many varieties: red (tasty but depleted), yellowtail, gray, mangrove, mutton, and more. They're hard to land but worth the effort.

- **Snook** – A gamefish found beneath bridges and around jetties, snook is a good, stealthy fighter, though its taking is strictly regulated in Florida; check the latest regulations.

- **Tarpon** – Its scales gleam like newly minted silver dollars. A leaping game fish that makes a coveted trophy, the tarpon is more often turned loose by anglers to leap some more.

Fishing tournaments are conducted throughout the year on the Keys. For information on places, dates, fees, rules, and awards, write Florida Keys Fishing Tournaments, P.O. Box 420358, Summerland Key, FL 33042. For an online calendar of fishing tournaments in the Florida Keys, go to www.flkinfo.com/tourney.htm.

For those who are fishing the Keys – or anywhere in Florida, for that matter – bear in mind that the following are overfished and in precipitous decline: bluefish, grouper, mackerel, marlin, snapper, swordfish, and tuna. In an article entitled "Maintaining Diversity in the Oceans," Dr. John Ogden – director of the Florida Institute of Oceanography – wrote the following:

"The unfortunate history of fishing is overfishing. The principal reasons are politics and greed. The United States spends approximately $500 million annually on fisheries research and management and has worked out the fisheries related aspects of the life histories of most commercially important species. Nevertheless, the United States does not effectively manage most of these fisheries."

a minimum. Okay, there is a par-3 golf course that might better have been left a tropical hammock. But much of the grounds remain in a natural state. Guests can wander a nature trail and gain an education along the way by reading about the plants and trees on the numbered trail guide. As a side note, part of the emerging environmental awareness in Florida is learning the difference between native and nonnative (a.k.a. exotic or invasive) species. Problematic exotics include the Australian pine, a tenacious grower that crowds out other species and blows over easily in a hurricane or big storm.

But back to Cheeca Lodge, where we're trying to decide whether to sit by the large, bathtub-warm pool, beside the saltwater lagoon, on the sand beach, or away from the action to the left of the pier. Chaise lounges line the property at all of these sites. Cheeca Lodge overlooks a blue million miles of ocean. The Tennessee Reef Lighthouse is visible off in the distance.

We got more relaxed here more quickly than at any other stop in our Florida travels. Even the beds seem unusually comfortable. The blue-and-white lodge reposes gracefully among swaying coconut palms and royal poincianas. They have an excellent kids program (Camp Cheeca) and two on-premises restaurants, so there's no reason to leave once you've checked in. Any excuse not to turn on the car while on vacation is welcome. Just chill out and let the laid-back aura of the Keys saturate your being.

At Cheeca Lodge, rooms go for $439–529 a night in season. If that is beyond your means, then be advised that Islamorada is chock full of places to stay at many different price points. These include other full-service resorts with private beaches such as the **Islander Resort** (P.O. Box 766, MM 82.1, 305/664-2031, $$$), **Chesapeake Resort** (P.O. Box 909, MM 83.5, 305/664-4662, $$$) and the **Plantation Yacht Harbor Resort** (87000 U.S. 1, MM 87, 305/852-2381, $$). Sprawling across 20 acres, the Islander has 114 suites and villas, a 0.25-mile-long coral-sand beach, and a lighted pier.

Hampton Inn (MM 80, 305/664-0073, $$$) is part of the hotel chain that made a big push in Florida in the 1990s. Located on the ocean, this Hampton has a pro dive shop, boat ramp, and daily scuba trips. There's also a glut of decidedly modest "resort" motels where rooms can be had for under $100 (half that out of season), if you're not particular about where you lay your head. And most anglers aren't.

COASTAL CUISINE

Atlantic's Edge (Cheeca Lodge, MM 82, 305/664-4651, $$$$) offers a stunning, glassed-in lookout over the ocean. It is the best interior view of open water in the Keys, being akin to standing on the bow of a ship. The outdoor **Ocean Terrace** (Cheeca Lodge, MM 82, 305/664-4651, $$$) is the lodge's more casual and affordable alternative. At both

restaurants, they will cook the catch of the day—either yours or theirs—in myriad ways. Ocean Terrace will fix 'em as follows: crusted with onions or plantains, jerk-grilled, braised, baked, or steamed. Atlantic's Edge will do all that and more: *a la nage,* meuniere, steamed, or blackened.

There are other good restaurants on Islamorada. If you want the freshest possible catch, priced reasonably and served in a casual setting among a crowd tilted toward locals, try **Islamorada Fish Company** (81532 Overseas Highway, 305/664-9271, $$). Be forewarned that pelicans will be eyeballing your meal from perches on the outdoor deck. They are envious for good reason. Seafood is served by the basket: tenderized deep-fried conch; catch of the day (mahimahi, snapper, cobia) served fried, grilled, Cajun-spiced, or teriyaki-marinated; and more. Preparations and presentation are uncomplicated, which is fitting since seafood this fresh doesn't need much more than a squeeze of lemon. Out of necessity, wooden clothespins are used to keep money and napkins from blowing off tables and into the water.

On our most recent visit, we turned down the driveway to **Island Grill** (85501 Overseas Highway, 305/664-8400, $$) and enjoyed another genuine Keys experience. By our elbows at the close-together tables were folks who arrived by boat and were enjoying the breeze and view of the blue-green water. One guy walked in and announced, "I drove two days to get here, and this is my first stop." He drained the first beer of his vacation in seconds flat, thanked the proprietor, and walked back out to his car. We enjoyed blackened tuna sandwiches, shrimp and grits, and cracked conch. The atmosphere was plenty satisfying, too.

You might also check out the two of the more down-home seafood eateries in the Keys, the **Green Turtle Inn** (MM 81.5, 305/664-9031, $$), which has been in business since 1947, and **Papa Joe's Landmark Restaurant** (MM 79.7, 305/664-8109), built in 1937 and ready to cook your catch for you. Right across

THE SUNNY FLORIDA KEYS

the highway is the equally venerable **Bud 'n' Mary's** (MM 79.8, 305/664-2461). **Uncle's Seafood Restaurant** (80900 Overseas Highway, 305/664-4402, $$$) is as close to traditional fine dining as one gets in the Upper Keys, specializing not only in seafood but Italian cuisine and wild game.

NIGHTLIFE

Woody's (MM 82, 305/664-4335) is the place to go in Islamorada if you're in the mood to rock out. In addition to being an Italian restaurant (some of the best pizza on the Keys), it's a low-slung joint that gets raucous to the sound of a house band that goes by the name (we kid you not) Big Dick and the Erections. Party hard, dude. On that note, one phenomenon that begs mentioning—though not thinking about too closely—is the preponderance of adult video venues in the Upper Keys. Perhaps the pickings are so slim at the local watering holes that XXX films serve as sexual surrogates. In any case, we don't want to know.

Lignumvitae Key Botanical State Park

The entirety of this 365-acre key—located one mile north of Lower Matecumbe Key in Florida Bay and accessible only by boat—is a botanical state park, and visitation is restricted to ranger-guided tours. Guided tours of Lignumvitae (pronounced *lig-num-VI-tee*) are given daily, except Tuesday and Wednesday, at 10 A.M. and 2 P.M. The official tour-boat concessionaire is **Robbie's Marina** (MM 77.5, Islamorada, 305/664-9814). Show up at Robbie's at least a half hour before tour time to catch the boat over to Lignumvitae Key, which costs $15 per person. Reservations are accepted but usually not necessary. The tour itself costs only $1 per person.

Lignumvitae Key is unique for its altitude (at 18 feet, it's the highest point in the Keys) and vegetation. It's basically the same stand of tropical species that once flourished all over the Upper Keys before man bridged them and reshaped the landscape. Thus, one of the last surviving stands of tropical virgin forest is preserved here. Lignumvitae ("tree of life") is the Latin name for a small, blue-flowered tree with wood so dense it doesn't float. This key is the last place in the western hemisphere it is known to grow. Other trees found in Lignumvitae's crazy tangle include gumbo-limbo, mastic, strangler fig, poison-wood, and pigeon plum. When you come out here, try to imagine what the rest of the Keys must have looked like when such forests covered them.

For more information, contact Lignumvitae Key Botanical State Park, P.O. Box 1052, Islamorada, FL 33036, 305/664-2540, www.floridastateparks.org.

Indian Key Historic State Park

This tiny, 11-acre key—located 0.75 mile southeast of Islamorada, and entirely preserved as a state park—is reachable by boat only. In recent years it has taken hits from hurricanes. In 1998 Hurricane Georges destroyed the dock and other facilities, limiting access to the island. The park remained closed for more than two years as repairs were made, reopening in early 2001. However, damage from the spate of hurricanes that blasted the Keys in 2005 again wrecked the dock, limiting access to canoes and kayaks only.

Indian Key was inhabited by Native Americans for thousands of years prior to the arrival of Spanish colonists in the 16th century. In the 18th century, the key became a haven for wreckers (who salvaged what they could from boats that ran aground on the reefs) and pirates (who plundered merchant vessels negotiating the Straits of Florida). Surprising as it may seem, Indian Key was at one time the most populous settlement between Jacksonville and Key West and served as the seat of Dade County. A hotel, general store, shops, wharves, and warehouses were built. Naturalist John James Audubon sketched birds here, and noted botanist Dr. Henry Perrine—who was especially curious about hemp(!)—conducted experiments with nonnative species. Perrine was killed here on August 7, 1840, during the second Seminole War.

Rich in history, Indian Key has preserved ruins, a restored boat dock, trails, and an observation tower. When guided tours resume, they will be offered every day but Tuesday and Wednesday at 9 A.M. and 1 P.M. The official tour-boat concessionaire is **Robbie's Marina** (MM 77.5, Islamorada, 305/664-9814). Show up at Robbie's at least a half hour before tour time to catch the boat over to Indian Key, which costs $15 per person. Reservations are accepted but usually not necessary. The tour itself costs only $1 per person. Call ahead for to check the status of park reconstruction and guided tours. At press time, Robbie's said they had "no clue" when trips to Indian Key might resume. "We're waiting on the government," he said. And we all know how long that can take.

For more information, contact Indian Key Historic State Park, P.O. Box 1052, Islamorada, FL 33036, 305/664-2540, www.floridastateparks.org.

Anne's Beach

Anne's Beach, located on Lower Matecumbe Key, is one of the real treasures of the Florida Keys. It was named for Anne Eaton. According to a plaque on a stone monument, Eaton "lived on this island for many years and dedicated herself to maintaining the beauty and serenity of these Keys. Anne helped bring this park to life." Would that there were more folks like her in this world.

To our thinking, Anne's Beach is the second-best beach in the Keys (numero uno being Bahia Honda State Park). Two entrance ramps

are situated about half a mile apart along the ocean side of U.S. 1. Follow the signs for Anne's Beach and park for free, barely a whisper off the road. The beach is nearly two miles long and made up of hard-packed sand. At its hardest, it has a claylike consistency. Walk in either direction and you will soon have a section of the beach to yourself.

If you don't want to traipse the wet sand, a wooden walkway runs above the tidal wetlands and dunes beneath a canopy of young trees. Several covered picnic areas have been built along the boardwalk, each with steps leading down to the water. The walkway parallels the beach for 0.25 mile, ending at the inlet that separates Upper and Lower Matecumbe Key. Across the inlet is a marina called Caloosa Cove.

For many years Anne's Beach was known to locals as Caloosa Beach. The beach is calm, waveless, and often thick with seaweed. Fly fishers wade out to try their luck in the turquoise waters. The most exciting activity is to shuffle along in knee-deep water and admire the critters at your feet and the birds wading contentedly just out of arm's reach. We had the unique experience of finding—among a thicket of litter we cleared from the mangrove roots—a message in a bottle. It was not from Sting. It was from a native of Melbourne, Florida, who wrote: "I am seven years old. I am now in Key West. If you find this, please write me. Signed, Toni Arjemi." Okay, Toni. We found your bottle. Let's do lunch.

BEACHES

5 ANNE'S BEACH

Location: eight miles west of Islamorada, at MM 73.5 on Lower Matecumbe Key
Parking/Fees: free parking lots
Hours: 7:30 A.M.-sunset
Facilities: restrooms and picnic tables
Contact: Village of Islamorada, 305/664-2345

Long Key

Long Key—located 10 miles west of Islamorada at MM 70—is the site of a state park and the town of Layton (pop. 200). Spaniards originally named this key Cayo Vivora ("Rattlesnake Key") for its serpent-like shape. Zane Grey, renowned author of Westerns, was one of Layton's most familiar faces. Henry Flagler built his Long Key Fishing Club here. The first of 42 bridges on Flagler's Key West Extension Railroad, in fact, was constructed at Long Key. Both Flagler's fishing club and cross-keys railway thrived 1912–1935. Then came the cataclysmic hurricane of 1935, which obliterated the railroad, whose supports later served as foundations for the Overseas Highway (U.S. 1).

Much of the south end of the island is occupied by **Long Key State Park.** Visitors can hike, canoe, and camp by the ocean in the 965-acre park. The most unique feature is the Long Key Canoe Trail, a mile-long paddle around a tidal lake rimmed with mangroves. Canoe rentals are cheap ($5 per hour, $10 per day) and the paddling is easy, especially if you time your trip so that you're on the water at high tide and the winds are calm. At low tide, the pool is only a few inches deep in some places, so you might wind up portaging over the shallows while birds stare incredulously, as happened to us. The basin is filled with bird life, including graceful egrets and long-beaked pelicans. The canoe trail is lined with numbered markers that correspond to items on a trail guide picked up at the kiosk where you sign in.

We followed our canoe adventure with a hike on the Golden Orb Trail, so named for a type of spider that is commonly seen in these parts. The female of the species is huge and slings massive icky-sticky webs straight out of science fiction in the trees overhead. The males, by contrast, are inconspicuous. The trail encompasses a variety of ecological zones in close proximity between ocean and bay, including a tropical hardwood hammock and an area where only scrubby, stunted trees grow. The Golden Orb Trail also crosses patches of tarry, anaerobic muck from which red and black mangroves rise via prop roots. Flaring off the trail, arrayed along a boardwalk that runs beside the ocean, are primitive campsites (highly recommended, if you don't mind lugging your gear a couple hundred feet). More developed sites lie along the park road beneath the shade of gumbo-limbo and other tropical trees, close to the water. You'll pay more for these, but look at it this way: At $31.49 per night, camping at Long Key costs about what you'd spend on taxes alone at an upscale resort. The park is currently restoring its shoreline in hopes of creating a natural sea turtle nesting area.

Long Key, by the way, has no beach. You can stroll the shore or wade in the shallows. But you will not find a sandy, swimmable beach. Just so you know.

For more information, contact Long Key State Park, MM 67.5, P.O. Box 776, Long Key, FL 33001, 305/664-4815 or 800/326-3521; www.floridastateparks.org.

Duck Key

Duck Key, located between Long and Grassy Keys at MM 61, quacked to life as a gleam in the eye of Bryan Newkirk, a mining baron and real estate agent who bought the key sight unseen in 1953. Wanting to turn it into a West Indian-style resort with a yacht basin and residential community, he built a private bridge to this small key, which lies to the side of the string of keys connected by the Overseas Highway. Though Newkirk's son (who directed the development) died of polio in 1955 and the resort changed hands several times thereafter, Hawk's Cay has managed to stay afloat over the decades. Now firmly established as a full-service resort, it is today much like the "complete island community" that Newkirk originally envisioned.

For more information, contact Hawk's

Cay Resort, MM 61, Duck Key, FL 33050, 305/743-7000 or 800/432-2242, www.hawkscay.com.

BEACHES

The beach at Hawk's Cay is typical of those you'll find on the grounds of resorts on the Upper Keys: to wit, a quarter inch of kitty litter sprinkled atop a hard coral spine and raked into neat furrows by groundskeepers early each morning. These are not the sort of beaches you'd write home about, but it's better than nothing.

ACCOMMODATIONS

Hawk's Cay (MM 61, 305/743-7000, $$$$) provides many things to do in an environmentally respectful setting, and therefore rates as one of the premier resorts in the Keys. Where to start? First, the rooms are large with high ceilings. As a reminder of the old days, bathroom doors are solid wood with crystal doorknobs. A library and game room are at ground level. In addition to burping videogames on which galaxies are conquered, there's a pingpong table at which one of us showed the other how the game is meant to be played.

Step outside and check out the pool—a large heated rectangle surrounded by comfortably padded chaise lounges. It is here that we saw an amusing animal blooper: a seagull skimming the surface of the pool, claws dragging water, in the hope that it might snare a fish. The outdoor courtyard also includes two Jacuzzis and a saltwater lagoon rimmed with chickees and more chaise lounges. The pool and lagoon look out on the Long Key Bridge, a 2.5-mile span that bridge-building visionary Henry Flagler pronounced his favorite.

Another lagoon serves as a staging area for Hawk's Cay's Dolphin Discovery Program. For $120, guests can learn about and swim among these marine mammals, which many scientists (and at least two beach writers) believe are as highly evolved as humans. The fun doesn't end at the porpoise pool. There's more: snorkeling, fishing, tennis, volleyball, a fitness trail, boating, parasailing, scuba diving, sunset cruises, ecology tours. Nightly room rates start at $279 in season (Christmas–late April) and run $229 and up the rest of the year.

COASTAL CUISINE

On-premises restaurants at Hawk's Cay range from the casual poolside **Indies Club** to **Waters Edge,** where a waterfront view is served gratis with your steak or seafood. At the **Palm Terrace,** a daily breakfast buffet is a good deal, with a heaping presentation of fruit, pastries, and hot items extending from one end of the room to the other.

Grassy Key

Located two miles east of Marathon, this key is home to the **Dolphin Research Center** (MM 59, 305/289-1121), formerly Flipper's Sea School (yes, that Flipper). Marine mammals are studied and cared for here, and interactive programs are open to the public, including Dolphin Encounter (a lecture and "playful, structured swim session" among the dolphins for $165). A less interactive and less costly program, DolphinSplash, will set you back $100. At the other extreme, you can make a day of it and participate in "Trainer for the Day" ($650) or "Researcher for a Day" ($500) programs. Although even Flipper might flip out at these prices, the programs are popular and fill up quickly. The Dolphin Research Center is open daily (except holidays) 9 A.M.–5 P.M. Call 305/289-0002 for information and reservations.

One of the Keys' favorite fishing resorts, **Rainbow Bend** (MM 58, 305/929-1505, $$$), is located on Grassy Key in a hurry-up-and-slow-down setting reminiscent of the way things used to be on the Keys.

For more information, contact the Greater Marathon Chamber of Commerce, 12222 Overseas Highway, MM 48.7, Marathon, FL 33050, 305/743-5417 or 800/262-7284, www.floridakeysmarathon.com.

Curry Hammock State Park

This relatively new arrival (it opened in 1999) is one of the most pleasant surprises in the Middle Keys. Accessible from Little Crawl Key, Curry Hammock State Park features a thick hammock of hardwood trees and the largest population of thatch palms in the country, not to mention mangrove swamps, seagrass beds, and wetlands.

The 970-acre park actually encompasses all of two keys (Little Crawl and Deer) and parts of two others (Fat Deer and Long Point). Curry Hammock has a shoreline that is wadeable, if not swimmable. A brand-new 28-site campground (open November 1–May 31) rivals the one at Long Key State Park, to which it bears a distinct resemblance.

For more information, contact Curry Hammock State Park, 56200 Overseas Highway, MM 56.7, Marathon, FL 33050, 305/289-2690, www.floridastateparks.org.

The clear waters of the Florida Keys provide snorkelers easy access to a wealth of living coral and marinelife.

COURTESY OF ANDY NEWMAN/TDC

BEACHES

6 CURRY HAMMOCK STATE PARK

Location: 11 miles west of Long Key, at MM 56.2
Parking/Fees: $3.50 for one person, $6 for two, and $0.50 for each additional person. Camping fee is $31.49 per night.
Hours: 8 A.M.–sundown
Facilities: restrooms, picnic tables, showers
Contact: Curry Hammock State Park, 305/289-2690

BEST Marathon and Key Colony Beach

The year-round population of Marathon is only 12,700, but that figure doubles in season, making it the second-largest city on the Keys. If Key West is the more populous Sodom at the end of the Overseas Highway, then Marathon is Gomorrah. In the bright light of day, it's as messy as can be. Beyond its obvious draw as a place to fish, dive, cruise the balmy waters, and escape the Great White North, Marathon functions as a vital commercial corridor for those residents scattered among the numerous keys between Islamorada and Big Pine Key. At night, Marathon morphs into a nonstop party, as sunbaked Jimmy Buffett look-alikes debate the relative merits of their boat engines over endless rounds of beer.

The city of Marathon stretches from Crawl Key (MM 57) to the foot of the majestic Seven Mile Bridge (MM 47). It came by its name as the result of Henry Flagler's quixotic endeavor to build "the railroad that went to sea." A base camp for hundreds of railroad workers was set up here in 1908. The grueling work of building the Seven Mile Bridge provoked one exhausted laborer to bemoan the "marathon effort" that lay ahead if they were going push

KEY LIME PIE

We make it a point to order key lime pie whenever we see it on a menu. We even ask for it when it's not listed, just in case there has been some tragic oversight at the menu printing plant. Why? Because we agree with food writer Craig Claiborne, who once said, "If I were asked to name the greatest of all regional American desserts, my answer might very well be key lime pie." Ours most certainly would be.

The basic ingredient of this pie is, of course, the key lime (*Citrus aurantifolia*), which takes its name from the Florida Keys, where key lime trees grow well in the chalky, rocky soil. This variety of lime differs greatly from the garden-variety lime most commonly found in grocery stores (*Citrus latifolia*). For one thing, key lime trees have thorns. The fruit is much smaller and rounder, the rinds are a splotchy brownish yellow, and the pulp is more acidic, which explains the widely admired and unmistakably tart taste.

Ah, but here's the rub. First of all, the key lime is not native to the Florida Keys, having been brought over from Asia in the early days of European exploration of the Caribbean. It's true that groves of these miniature limes were planted on the Keys in the 1800s, but they're no longer commercially grown there. Today, key limes are most often cultivated near Homestead and in Mexico and Guatemala.

Regardless of origin, the key lime makes a delectable pie. Though the fruit didn't originate in the Keys, the recipe for key lime pie certainly did, deriving from the introduction to the local population of Borden's canned condensed milk in 1856. Because there were no cows to produce fresh milk and no highways or railroads to ship it to them, the locals relied on condensed milk. It seemed only natural to combine the sour taste of key limes with the gooey sweetness of sweetened condensed milk.

The classic recipe for key lime pie is really quite simple: mix four egg yolks, a half-cup of key lime juice (about 10-12 key limes), and a can of sweetened condensed milk. Pour into a graham-cracker pie shell and bake for 15 minutes at 350°F. No green food coloring (real key lime juice is a dull yellow). No whipped cream. No gelatin. If you can't lay hands on key limes, regular limes can be substituted, but it won't be quite the same. Key lime juice is bottled and sold in grocery stores and gourmet shops, so there's really no excuse not to use the real thing.

If you must dress up the recipe, then make a meringue of the leftover egg whites. Beat the whites with a half-teaspoon of cream of tartar till foamy, then gradually add one-third cup confectioners' sugar and keep beating till stiff peaks form. Spread the meringue on top of the key lime mixture, then bake as previously instructed.

Ordering key lime pie comes as naturally to us as breathing, and restaurants all over the state insist their version is Florida's best. Therefore we've compiled a list of our favorites. We make no claims that this list is definitive, just that it reflects our myriad tastings and personal preferences. It should come as no surprise that our favorite slices of key lime pie are served in the Florida Keys in casual, unassuming environments.

1. Seven Mile Grill, Marathon

2. Manny and Isa's, Upper Matecumbe Key

3. Mangrove Mama's, Sugarloaf Key

4. Blond Giraffe, Key West

5. White Lion Cafe, Homestead

6. That Place on 98, Eastpoint

7. Grillfish, Miami Beach

8. Ophelia's By the Bay, Siesta Key

9. Crow's Nest, Venice

10. Joe's Stone Crab, Miami Beach

THE SUNNY FLORIDA KEYS

ahead to Key West before Flagler croaked. They succeeded; Flagler triumphantly rode into town on January 22, 1912, and the name Marathon stuck.

Prior to its incorporation in 2000, the fate of Marathon had largely been overseen by county commissioners involved in the real-estate trade. (This is a recurrent theme that plays throughout Florida's checkered history.) One member of this brainless trust had the nerve to pooh-pooh local environmentalists who were chagrined by a developer's razing of an ancient stand of gumbo-limbo trees. "You can refoliate things so fast in Florida," she offered, "it'll make your hair fall out." That is a fate we wish on her alone.

All of this makes Marathon's cluttered appearance inevitable. Every fast-food chain imaginable has an outlet along the Overseas Highway (U.S. 1) in Marathon. Like a series of blows to the head, their gaudy logos and touting billboards are particularly jarring in this otherwise magical setting. Why would anyone patronize these grease pits when fresh seafood is available at any number of affordable, locally owned outlets? (See *Coastal Cuisine* for alternatives to Wendy's and Papa John's.)

Despite it all, if you stick around long enough, you will grow entranced by Marathon and maybe even have your soul ensnared by the place. True, Marathon does not possess the blue, green, and red vistas of a postcard vision, but once the sun starts to fall upon your brow, the boats return to port, and the lights come on, the town and the key take on a certain tropical charm. From the perspective of a chaise lounge at a Marathon resort or a barstool at one of its many watering holes, the town begins to make a lot more sense than it does from the sweltering vantage point of the highway.

In Marathon, people find sanctuary from stormy or stale lives on the mainland. One bearded, permanently tanned barkeep ditched his businessman's life in Denver. "I got stupid and got respectable," he told us while drying glasses behind the bar. "I don't know what got into me." Now he dreamed only of living rent-free on a boat. "And in the evening, I can float to any bar on the island," he rhapsodized. Another Marathoner we met fled Detroit—where he'd worked for 18 years as a rivethead for General Motors—after a family tragedy. Now he toils in a restaurant kitchen. After several years scrubbing plates and pounding conch, his face glowed with the kind of ruddy contentment we saw all over the Keys. Another mainland expatriate retired as a schoolteacher in Kansas and came to the Marathon to write a book. After six years the book remains unwritten, but "there's still time, there's always more time," he philosophized.

To many who visit or live here, Marathon means fishing. Many seek respite from northern winters, renting or chartering boats to fish the waters of the Gulf Stream ("wider than a thousand Mississippi Rivers") or Florida Bay. The lure of big gamefish—marlin, sailfish, wahoo, tuna—is irresistible. Catches among the reefs close to shore include grouper and yellowtail snapper. From the bridges and shore, they stalk tarpon and snook. Divers comb the reefs of the Middle Keys, which are less crowded than those of Key Largo. Local dive shops offer certification and instruction.

If you're not enamored of angling or diving, you will likely keep on trucking out of town over the Seven Mile Bridge. That's unfortunate because Marathon has hidden charms and is worth poking around for at least a short while. Among the literature distributed by the local chamber is a helpful list entitled "50 Free Things to Do in the Marathon Area." One activity we would encourage all to try: "Walk, bike, skate, or jog on the old Seven Mile Bridge—breathe some really fresh air (1.9 miles each way)." While on your stroll, "Observe the fantastic array of sea life from the comfort of the bridge. See tarpon, sharks, stingrays, and more. The morning is the best time." Early evening works, too, and you will come away with an entirely different perspective on Marathon.

Also, by all means stop by the **Museum of Natural History of the Florida Keys** (MM 50, 305/743-9100), located at Crane

Point Hammock in Marathon. The museum encourages responsible appreciation and preservation of the ecosystems that make the keys special. They've also preserved artifacts of the pre-Columbian cultures that lived here. Naturally, they must touch on the mystique of pirates, smugglers, and wreckers, but this lore is intelligently presented. Other attractions on the 63.5-acre preserve include a coral reef, underwater cave, touch tanks, saltwater lagoon, tropical aquarium and terrarium, and one of the last stands of virgin tropical palm hammock in South Florida.

For more information, contact the Greater Marathon Chamber of Commerce, 12222 Overseas Highway, MM 48.7, Marathon, FL 33050, 305/743-5417 or 800/262-7284, www.floridakeysmarathon.com.

BEACHES

You won't come to Marathon for a beach vacation, but a couple of off-highway detours lead to bonafide beaches hereabouts. Just past MM 54 is a community called Key Colony Beach. To get there, turn south on Key Colony Beach Causeway. Without actually leaving land, you enter a filled-in mangrove swamp formerly known as Shelter Key. This is Key Colony Beach, an incorporated community of not quite 1,000.

The municipal oversight that comes with incorporation is undoubtedly one reason Key Colony Beach looks so enviably pleasant. The beach is an ocean-fronting, pearly white stretch of sand, all privately owned. In order to sample its charms, you must check into one of several motels that border it. The beach is dainty but clean, and the wave activity is a bit more brisk than on the beaches of the Upper Keys. An added enticement is the nine-hole, par-3 Key Colony Public Golf Course, which has been squeezed in among the houses.

Another off-highway detour leads to **Sombrero Beach.** To get here, turn east on Sombrero Beach Boulevard, just past an ancient Kmart at MM 50. You'll drive through a congested but well-tended residential area, and after two miles you'll come upon an arc

of bright white, hard-packed sand—natural sand, not pumped-in filler. Sombrero Beach continues around a bend, where it turns into a hardened reef and then picks up with a few more tiny pockets of sand (where we saw some solitary souls snoring contentedly at midday). The adjoining park includes a baseball field, playground, picnic shelters, and even a jug filled with a chemical that removes tar that might have gotten on your feet. (By the way, conch collecting is not allowed, no matter how tempting, and fines can reach $500.)

A third detour at MM 48 onto 20th Street (a.k.a. Boot Key Boulevard) is decidedly less pleasant. The street carries you over a drawbridge onto Boot Key. This mysterious key has a healthy chunk of ocean frontage, but you'll be too bummed out by the garbage dumped here and spooked by the unseen population of piratical boat-dwellers to stick around.

Incidentally, you may encounter printed references to a Chamber of Commerce Beach. It's supposedly on the bayside at the end of 33rd Street, next to the Marathon Yacht Club. The Marathon Chamber of Commerce used to occupy a small building by the turnoff, which is how it got its name. The name persists, but there's no beach to speak of and no reason to come looking.

Finally, at MM 54, on what is called Fat Deer Key, turn onto Coco Plum Drive to find a beach condo community possessing the upscale (for the Keys) look of Key Colony Beach but lacking public accommodations. The beach is long but private. We just wanted you to lay eyes on the most anomalous sight in the Keys—a 15-story condominium development called Bonefish Towers. Whoever permitted this boneheaded eyesore to be built out here should be filleted.

⑦ SOMBRERO BEACH

Location: Sombrero Beach Road in Marathon
Parking/Fees: free parking lots

THE SUNNY FLORIDA KEYS

Hours: 7:30 A.M.-sunset
Facilities: restrooms, picnic tables, and showers
Contact: City of Marathon, 305/743-0033

RECREATION AND ATTRACTIONS

- **Bike/skate Rentals:** Jerry's Watersports & Rentals, 4590 Overseas Highway, Marathon, 305/743-7298

- **Boat Cruise:** Florida Keys Sailing, Keys Fisheries & Marina, 35th Street Bayside (MM 49), Marathon, 305/289-9519

- **Dive Shop:** Abyss Dive Center, 13175 Overseas Highway, Marathon, 305/743-2126; Capt. Hook's Marina and Dive Center, 11833 Overseas Highway, Marathon, 305/743-2444

- **Ecotourism:** Marathon Kayak, 19 Sombrero Boulevard, Marathon, 305/743-0561

- **Fishing Charters:** Jerry's Charter Service, 585 82nd Street, Marathon, 305/289-7298

- **Marina:** Banana Bay Resort Marina, 4590 Overseas Highway, Marathon, 305/743-3648; Marathon Marina and Boatyard, 1021 11th Street, 305/743-6575, Marathon

- **Pier:** Old Seven Mile Bridge (world's longest fishing pier!), MM 47, Marathon

- **Rainy-Day Attraction:** Museum of Natural History of the Florida Keys, MM 50, Marathon, 305/743-9100

- **Shopping/Browsing:** Gulfside Village Shopping Center, MM 50, Marathon

- **Surf Shop:** Oasis Surf & Skate, 9575 Overseas Highway, Marathon, 305/743-5515

- **Vacation Rentals:** Land & Sea Vacations, 5701 Overseas Highway, Marathon, 305/743-6494

ACCOMMODATIONS

Key Colony Beach is a well-mannered, almost secret society of homes, condominiums, and beach resorts. Commendable motel choices out here include the **Key Colony Inn** (700 West Ocean Drive, 305/743-0100, $$) and the **Continental Inn** (MM 53.6, 305/289-0101, $$). They are affordable during the off-season and prices escalate during the choicer months (mid-December–mid-April). Both are clean and quiet.

Amenities at **CocoPlum Beach & Tennis Club** (109 Cocoplum Drive, MM 54.5, 305/743-0240, $$$$) include private beach, tennis courts, heated pool, sundeck, and Jacuzzi. The roomy villas range $1,500–2,500 a week in season. At the other end of the price scale is the **Hidden Harbor Motel** (2396 Overseas Highway, MM 48.5, 305/743-5376, $). Located on the bayside, it's clean and comfy, and every room has a boat slip at the private marina.

On Crawl Key, at the eastern end of Marathon, signs point to a sandy beach at the end of an unnamed road off the highway. It's called Valhalla Beach, and it's home to the **Valhalla Beach Motel** (MM 56, 305/289-0616, $), which rents totally unstylish but serviceable efficiencies by the night or week. The so-called sand beach is actually along a tidal creek, but in the Keys you take what beaches you can get and are grateful for them.

Of course, there are numerous places to stay along the Overseas Highway (U.S. 1), including the **Banana Bay Resort** (MM 49.5, 305/743-5500, $$), which has its own marina and watersports center, and **Hampton Inn & Suites** (1688 Overseas Highway, 305/743-9009, $$$), a sparkling gulfside property with its own dive center. We landed a room at the **Holiday Inn Marathon-Marina** (13201 Overseas Highway, 305/289-0222, $$) on a sweltering summer day and spent exactly seven hours in it. We dumped our bags, returned only to sleep and shower, and left with the dawn. We think that if you spend a lot of time in a motel room in the Keys, you're not doing something right.

There are dozens of other places to drop your bags in Marathon, many of them unfancy and cheap. The Greater Marathon Chamber of Commerce will happily help you book a room. Stop by their office at MM 53.

COASTAL CUISINE

If you're not into fishing, surely you're into eating fish. If so, Marathon is your meal ticket. It is home to two of our favorite waterfront eateries anywhere: Herbie's Raw Bar and the 7 Mile Grill. From the outside, **Herbie's Raw Bar** (MM 50.5, 305/743-6373, $$) is not much to look at, but looks are always deceiving in the Keys. Herbie's is a triple-threat wonder, with an outdoor restaurant, indoor bar, and screened-in dining and bar area. On our numerous visits here, we've feasted on ice cold raw oysters, piping-hot conch chowder, autumn salad (a house specialty), conch fritters, grouper fingers, cracked conch, crab and shrimp salad, and fresh catch of the day, prepared whatever way the wait staff suggests. The best bet for first-timers might be the blackened catch. Friendly interaction between tourists and locals is an off-menu specialty.

The **7 Mile Grill** (MM 47, 305/743-4481, $$) is a must visit, too. The formidable Seven Mile Bridge looms just beyond its outside dining area. You can't do much better than this low-key "grill" in the way of local color and cuisine. Again, order whatever is freshest. While waiting for your meal, scout the premises. It's a true Keys institution, with snapshots of local families and anglers, stuffed fish on the walls, beer cans along the ceiling, and novelty bumper stickers and placards that boast goofy slogans like "Sometimes I Wake Up Grumpy. Sometimes I Just Let Him Sleep." Other signs—"English for Florida" and "Give Me A Break, I Live Here"—tip you off to the local hot-button issues. Then there's the grub: wonderful seafood served with side dishes like rice and beans (which goes great with grouper). Finally, the key lime pie at the 7 Mile Grill is the best we've ever had. Everyone claims to make the best, of course, but the 7 Mile Grill backs up the boast with numerous awards and the evidence of your own taste buds. It's a sliver of tart, tangy perfection that makes us want to shout "Hallelujah!" and dance the Macarena when we're done. For some reason, the place

is closed on Wednesday and Thursday, so plan accordingly.

Just south of the 7 Mile Grill is **Porky's** (MM 47.5, 305/289-2065, $$), another local institution with much the same ambience but a different specialty: barbecue. Don't get us started singing the praises of Southern-style barbecue. That's a whole other book! Yet another favorite is the **Cracked Conch Cafe** (MM 50, 305/743-2233, $$). They raise their own conch on a farm and serve it every which way but bad. A shady mahogany tree makes an alfresco great setting for a quick cup of coffee, too.

Slightly more upscale dining can be had at **The Quay** (MM 54, 305/289-1810, $$$). Like Herbie's and the 7 Mile Grill, the Quay overlooks Florida Bay, making for great sunsets. It doesn't quite live up to its billing as "fine dining with the freshest seafood in the Keys"; with Maine lobster on the menu, this seems a dubious claim. The Quay's real selling point is its raw bar, housed in a wooden hut down by the water, where ice-cold raw oysters are served.

NIGHTLIFE

If the sun hasn't completely sapped your energy by day's end, you can run out the rest of your line at one of Marathon's many waterside lounges. Admittedly, Marathon will never be able to boast of the unbridled outrageousness of Key West, nor would its inhabitants wish to. The general tenor of nightlife in Marathon consists of sunset-watching happy hours, with local musicians playing "sunset music" as people chatter and sip Mexican beer or multicolored drinks.

Outrigger's Sports Bar and Brew Pub (MM 49.5, 305/743-5755) is about as wild as it gets in Marathon, with happy hours, deejays and/or live entertainment, bikini contests, wings specials, etc. For a quieter night out and earlier bedtime, angle over to **Angler's Lounge** (MM 48, 305/743-9018), located at the Faro Blanco Resort on the bayside. It has a happy hour, a dart board, and generally restrained music.

The Brass Monkey (MM 50, 305/743-4028), located by the Kmart Plaza, is the local rock and roll hangout of longstanding. We partied hardy here back in 1984, and live bands are still flogging classic rock till 3 A.M. nightly.

Boot Key

The Middle Keys put their worst foot forward on the mysterious Boot Key. It is, from all appearances, the favorite illegal trash dump for the Keys' government-flaunting residents. It is also another piece of evidence that they cannot properly care for these islands without outside oversight. Boot Key is a large, mostly uninhabited, and highly vegetated island that fronts the Atlantic Ocean for a long stretch. Instead of becoming the cleaned-up public treasure it ought to be, it has been reduced to a Hades of fast-food wrappers and abandoned appliances. Apparently, hundreds of live-aboard boaters—free spirits who dock at Boot Key Harbor, where they answer to no laws—have created all kinds of problems out here.

For the curious, turn onto 20th Street (MM 48) in Marathon and continue out to Boot Key. A modern drawbridge leads over an inlet to the key, which at first looks like a tree-covered refuge. Then the roadside flotsam hits your field of vision: rusted file cabinets, a pile of truck tires, bloated trash bags, and, finally, a heap of old kitchen appliances barricading the road. There's no development to speak of on Boot Key, but there is a beach—according to maps of the area, at least. Fascinated by the utter squalor, we pressed on, squeezing our car between a break in the appliances.

After fumbling among the litter-choked brush for a while, we gave up. Everywhere we roamed in the Keys, we came upon similar mounds of trash along the shore, where it gathers into obscenely large clumps. We turned the car around in a pock-marked driveway near the ocean. A scrawny black cat crossed our path, and beyond it we could make out several shacks, the flotsam from which covered the ground for yards in every direction.

Ironically, prior to trekking over to Boot Key, we'd just gotten an earful from some griping local outside the Chamber of Commerce, who was telling us that the government ought to "just get the hell on out of here and let us run the place the way we know how." With all due respect, we offer Boot Key as our case against self-governance.

On the way off Boot Key, we glanced into the bridge tender's hut at the center of the bridge. He was sound asleep, slumped on his stool. Could there be a more appropriate metaphor for Boot Key? More to the point, why don't they crack down on the human encroachment and illegal dumping? Why aren't the derelicts who've defiantly set up a militia-style boot camp on Boot Key sent packing?

In 2000 they couldn't even find money to pay the bridge tender. The newly incorporated city of Marathon squabbled with the county of Monroe over who should, um, foot the bill for the Boot Key bridge. They finally agreed to split the expense. Before working it out, a Monroe County commissioner actually offered to do the job himself. "I'm going to learn how to be a bridge tender!" he swore, sounding as gung-ho as Gomer Pyle. He couldn't have been any worse than the dozing gatekeeper we'd seen. But really, is this any way to run a city, a county, a key?

Greater Marathon Chamber of Commerce, 12222 Overseas Highway, MM 48.7, Marathon, FL 33050, 305/743-5417 or 800/262-7284, www.floridakeys marathon.com.

Pigeon Key

An afternoon spent on Pigeon Key will reward visitors in search of a more natural Keys environment and/or a slice of Keys history. This small key lies 2.2 miles west of Marathon. The original cross-Keys bridge (Seven Mile Bridge)

COURTESY OF ANDY NEWMAN/FLORIDA KEYS NEWS BUREAU/HO

the historic old Seven Mile Bridge in the Florida Keys near Marathon

passes through it, and that's how you'll get there now: by walking, jogging, biking, in-line skating, or break-dancing over the old bridge. Cars are not allowed, but a shuttle bus makes seven daily trips over from the Pigeon Key Visitors Center on Knight's Key (a small key at the foot of the Seven Mile Bridge), leaving hourly between 10 A.M.–4 P.M. The combined shuttle and visitor fee is $7 for adults and $4 for students.

Between 1908 and 1935, Pigeon Key served as a base camp for railroad workers, and historical buildings from those times survive. Since the days of railroad construction, Pigeon Key has been home to the U.S. Navy, a fishing camp, and the University of Miami's Institute of Marine Science. Today the Pigeon Key Foundation maintains the island as a research and education center; it's even affiliated with the Mote Marine Laboratory in Sarasota.

For more information, contact the Pigeon Key Foundation, MM 48, P.O. Box 500130, Marathon, FL 33050, 305/289-0025, www.pigeonkey.org.

Little Duck Key and Ohio Key

These two small, adjacent keys lie on the west side of the Seven Mile Bridge, with Little Duck Key at MM 40 and Ohio Key at MM 39. Having made the crossing, you are now officially in the Lower Keys. Little Duck Key is the site of the oceanside **Veterans Memorial Park** (formerly Duck Key County Park), where you'll find picnic tables, grills, and a concession stand, in addition to basic facilities and a bit of beach.

Ohio Key (a.k.a. Sunshine Key) is home to a 400-site camping resort spread out over 75 acres. Far from roughing it at the **Sunshine Key Camping Resort** (38801 Overseas Highway, MM 39, 305/872-2217, $), you are surrounded by stores, grills, game rooms, laundry facilities, tennis and shuffleboard courts, a marina, a fishing pier, and a beach.

For more information, contact the Lower Keys Chamber of Commerce, MM 31, P. O. Drawer 430511, Big Pine Key, FL 33043, 305/872-2411 or 800/872-3722, www.lowerkeyschamber.com.

BEACHES

8 VETERANS MEMORIAL PARK

Location: west end of Seven Mile Bridge, at MM 40 on Little Duck Key
Parking/Fees: free parking lot
Hours: 7:30 A.M.–sunset
Facilities: restrooms, picnic tables, and showers
Contact: Monroe County Department of Parks and Beaches, 305/295-4385

Bahia Honda State Park

The pearl of Keys beaches can be found at the popular Bahia Honda State Park, which takes up the entirety of Bahia Honda Key (at MM 36.5) and a small island at the southwest end of the park. It is the southernmost site in Florida's state park system, and one of the highlights of the Keys—especially since natural sand beaches are otherwise in short supply on these coral-spined islands. In addition, one of the largest remaining stands of the threatened silver palm tree can be found at Bahia Honda. Gumbo-limbo and yellow satinwood thrive here as well. These are not your typical mainland species, being native to subtropical islands.

A trek along the western end of the beach will bring you to the foot of the old Bahia Honda Bridge. This two-tiered structure—the last standing remnant of Henry Flagler's Overseas Railroad—spans Bahia Honda Channel. It is the deepest channel in the Keys and is also subjected to the strongest cross currents. It took extraordinarily large pylons to bridge what seemed to be Bahia Honda's bottomless depth. (*Bahia honda* means "deep bay" in Spanish.) This mile-long crossing proved more difficult to construct than the Seven Mile Bridge. Today, the abandoned bridge poses an eerie sight. Scuba divers explore the rich underwater life here, but one should only attempt this deep and treacherous dive with a seasoned pro.

Bahia Honda offers some of the finest camping we've ever seen on or near the beach. Nestled among a thick hammock, these sites make an inviting spot to drop anchor. There are two camping areas (Buttonwood and Sandspur) by the ocean and a smaller one on the bayside, totaling 80 sites. Hurricane Wilma really tore up the place when it roared through on October 24, 2005. In fact, the campgrounds' infrastructure had to be replaced and upgraded, and many downed trees removed. Buttonwood Campground didn't reopen until February 2006. A half dozen two-bedroom cabins that accommodate up to eight people can be rented nightly. (Reservations are accepted up to a year in advance and should be booked as early as possible.) A 19-slip marina and dive shop (305/872-3210) are at the south end of the park. Gear is rented and excursions—every-

thing from snorkeling to parasailing, kayaks to powerboats—are booked here all year long.

For more information, contact Bahia Honda State Park, 36850 Overseas Highway, Big Pine Key, FL 33043, 305/872-2353, www.floridastateparks.org.

BEACHES

Running for 2.5 miles, Bahia Honda is by far the longest natural sand beach on the Keys. Two named beaches are found inside **Bahia Honda State Park.** Loggerhead Beach, located by the concessions at the west end of the park, is small and protected. Sandspur Beach is long with shallow sandbars extending a good distance seaward. Wide it is not—10 yards at most—but the sand is pearly white and easy to walk on. Thick mats of seaweed accumulate at the high-tide line. This helps build up the dunes, and the park wisely lets nature take its course, opting not to clean it up.

On a low tide you can wade out as far as 100 yards from shore on the soft sand bottom. The crystal-clear blue-green water turns a darker brown where it meets the line of underwater aquatic vegetation at this point. We saw a fisherman about 1,000 feet offshore, and the water had yet to reach his waist. Kayaking is a popular pastime at Bahia Honda, as these buoyant vessels don't displace much water and therefore don't scrape bottom at low tide. Kayaks can be rented by the hour ($10 for a single, $18 for a double) or half-day ($30 for a single, $54 for a double).

⑨ BAHIA HONDA STATE PARK

BEST

Location: MM 36.5 on Bahia Honda Key
Parking/Fees: $5 per car entrance fee. Camping fees are $31.49 per night.
Hours: 8 A.M.-sunset
Facilities: concessions, restrooms, picnic tables, showers, and a visitors center
Contact: Bahia Honda State Park, 305/872-2353

West Summerland Key

Boy Scout and Girl Scout Camps, and little else, are located on this small key at MM 34 on the Overseas Highway (U.S. 1).

For more information, contact the Lower Keys Chamber of Commerce, MM 31, P. O. Drawer 430511, Big Pine Key, FL 33043, 305/872-2411 or 800/872-3722, www.lowerkeyschamber.com.

Big Pine Key

Big Pine Key is the unofficial hub and welcome center for the Lower Keys. Situated 25 miles north of Key West, at MM 29 on the Overseas Highway (U.S. 1), it is home to 5,000 human beings and 800 key deer. At eight miles long by two miles wide, Big Pine Key is the second largest of the Florida Keys in terms of land area. It is, unfortunately, fast becoming one of the most populous as well. That is because it is attracting a lot of the spillover from Key West, which is essentially built out.

That may be good news for Century 21, but it is terrible news for the endangered key deer, a stunted subspecies of the Virginia white-tailed deer that stands barely two feet tall at the shoulder. Two-thirds of the estimated population of key deer in the world live on Big Pine Key, and the rest are scattered on smaller keys. These little dears all too frequently become road kill, the victims of traffic zooming to and from Key West, even though the speed limit drops to 35 mph on Big Pine Key. As you well know, no one obeys the speed limit anymore and all too few give a hoot about nature. Fortunately, U.S. 1 is elevated over Big Pine Key, and culverts beneath it let the deer cross safely.

From the perspective of the key deer, Big Pine Key is a preserve of last stand. The island runs on a northwest axis and is much longer than the crossing via the Overseas Highway might suggest to the casual traveler. Despite the highway's ever-present danger, much of the island is a National Wildlife Refuge out of range of U.S. 1. All the same, your vigilant attention is requested when driving across Big Pine Key, particularly in the early morning

© PARKE PUTERBAUGH

Sandspur Beach, Bahia Honda Key

hours and at dusk. Within Key Deer National Wildlife Refuge is a spot called the Blue Hole: a borrow pit dug out in railroad days that now serves as home to alligators, turtles, and fish. An observation tower offers a safe place for humans to study the basking reptiles.

The ongoing carnage of the key deer makes the little white lie that opens the tourist brochure for Big Pine Key all the more specious. "These Lower Keys are by far the most unspoiled little islands in America," it reads. With a shopping center, Century 21 signs the size of mainsails, and residential areas that swell to the very borders of the Key Deer National Wildlife Refuge, this is a dubious claim. Big Pine Key's burgeoning growth was dealt a blow by a moratorium on new development imposed in 1995 (and rescinded in two years later). Tensions are ongoing between environmentalists and the builders and property owners on Big Pine Key. Some owners even complain that the key deer eat their flowers. Such an inconvenience! If it's so intolerable, go find another place to desecrate. After all, Big Pine Key is one of the last refuges for not only key deer but Caribbean pines, both of which are endangered. So slow down when you cross Big Pine Key and enjoy the scenery—perhaps even the sight of a scampering, dog-sized key deer.

Conservation efforts have allowed the key deer population on Big Pine Key and No-Name Key to stabilize at somewhere around 800. That's a far cry from the species low of 27 in 1957. Of course, that bit of good news has triggered calls to step up the building boom amid blather about "meeting the needs of both deer and people." There are already 5,000 residents crowded onto Big Pine Key. Enough is enough. Leave something for nature and build elsewhere.

For more information contact the Lower Keys Chamber of Commerce, MM 31, P.O. Drawer 430511, Big Pine Key, FL 33043, 305/872-2411 or 800/872-3722, www.lower-keyschamber.com.

ACCOMMODATIONS

If you happen to be staying on Big Pine Key, it's likely because you're fishing or taking a dive trip to Looe Key. Accommodations are limited and consist mainly of RV parks and rustic fishing camps. **Big Pine Key Fishing Lodge** (MM 33, 33000 Overseas Highway, 305/872-2351, $) rents efficiencies and campsites (tents and RVs). The evocatively named **Old Wooden Bridge Fishing Camp** (MM 31.5, 1791 Bogie Drive, 305/872-2241, $) has its own bait shop and private fishing bridge. There's also the modest **Big Pine Key Resort Motel** (MM 30.5, 30725 Overseas Highway, 305/872-9090, $).

COASTAL CUISINE

In general, the restaurants on Big Pine Key are as misconceived and out of place as the residential development that threatens the key deer. This isn't Miami, so what is something called the Baltimore Oyster House doing here? Ditto Bagel Island Cafe? Captain Anne's Sports Bar? Domino's Pizza, for god's sake? Closer to the spirit and locale of the Florida Keys is **Montego Bay Food & Spirits** (MM 30.2, 305/872-3009, $$), where you can at least order seafood.

NIGHTLIFE

The **No Name Pub** (Watson Boulevard, 305/872-9115) is the most popular hangout in the area, "a nice place if you can find it." Here's how to find this beer garden and pizza joint: From the stoplight at MM 31 on the Overseas Highway (U.S. 1), turn onto Key Deer Boulevard. Turn right at Watson Boulevard, then bear left at a fork in the road. Cross a bridge and you'll find the No Name Pub in a yellow house at the foot of the No Name Bridge. Its history dates back to 1936, making it refreshingly authentic and long-lived.

BEST(Looe Key

Looe Key lies in the Straits of Florida, seven miles southeast of Big Pine Key. It isn't really a key but a reef, named for a British frigate (HMS *Looe*) that sank here in 1744. Reachable by boat only, the appeal of Looe Key is the coral reef, which offers unsurpassed snorkeling and diving. Some claim it to be the most spectacular living reef in North America. The reef skirts the edge of the Gulf Stream, and the warm waters and varying depths help support a diversity of life forms. Diving and snorkeling trips can be arranged at outfitters all over the Lower Keys, such as **Strike Zone Charters** (MM 29.5, Big Pine Key, 305/872-9863) and the **Looe Key Reef Resort and Dive Center** (MM 27.5, Ramrod Key, 305/872-2215). Incidentally, Looe Key has been a National Marine Sanctuary since 1981.

For more information, contact the Lower Keys Chamber of Commerce, MM 31, P.O. Drawer 430511, Big Pine Key, FL 33043, 305/872-2411 or 800/872-3722, www.lowerkeyschamber.com.

Little Torch Key

Named for the torchwood tree, Little Torch Key can be found one mile south of Big Pine Key at MM 28 on the Overseas Highway (U.S. 1). It is home to three small resorts, including the **Dolphin Resort & Marina** (MM 28.5, 305/872-2685, $$), whose roll call of "beds, boats, bait, beer" sounds like just the ticket. A cut above your average Keys "resort"—which is, more often than not, a glorified motor court (and that's okay, too)—the Dolphin has some neat cottages and bungalows hidden among the greenery of this overlooked key.

For more information, contact the Lower Keys Chamber of Commerce, MM 31, P.O. Drawer 430511, Big Pine Key, FL 33043, 305/872-2411 or 800/872-3722, www.lowerkeyschamber.com.

Ramrod Key

Ramrod is the name of a ship that wrecked on a reef just offshore from Ramrod Key, which lies two miles west of Big Pine Key at MM 27. Here you'll find **Looe Key Reef Resort**

and Dive Center (MM 27.5, Ramrod Key, 305/872-2215, $$), a complete resort that has a motel, restaurant, dive shop, swimming pool, tiki bar, gas station, and convenience store. The room rates ($75–90 a night) are about as cheap as you'll find in the Keys. The motel is perfectly adequate, and the dive shop rules.

For more information, contact the Lower Keys Chamber of Commerce, MM 31, P.O. Drawer 430511, Big Pine Key, FL 33043, 305/872-2411 or 800/872-3722, www.lowerkeyschamber.com.

Summerland Key and Cudjoe Key

There's little reason to stop on these largely residential islands between Big Pine Key and Key West at MM 26 (Summerland Key) and MM 23 (Cudjoe Key), unless you're renting a home for a month or more. They go for around $2,500 a month, on average. (For a list of seasonal rentals, contact **Action Keys Realty,** 305/745-1323.) Summerland Key rates an airstrip and post office. Cudjoe Key earned a footnote from us in an earlier book for having pioneered a new low in real-estate mongering: the "condominium trailer park."

For more information, contact the Lower Keys Chamber of Commerce, MM 31, P.O. Drawer 430511, Big Pine Key, FL 33043, 305/872-2411 or 800/872-3722, www.lowerkeyschamber.com.

Sugarloaf Key

This ear-shaped island at MM 20 is receiving some of the developmental backwash from Key West. The island harbors a few communities and developments, including the town of Perky, renowned for its bat tower(!). Sugarloaf Key is followed by the Saddlebunch Keys, a grouping of small, uninhabited keys that are numbered one through five.

THE SUNNY FLORIDA KEYS

For more information, contact the Lower Keys Chamber of Commerce, MM 31, P.O. Drawer 430511, Big Pine Key, FL 33043, 305/872-2411 or 800/872-3722, www.lower-keyschamber.com.

ACCOMMODATIONS

Sugarloaf Lodge (MM 17, P.O. Box 440148, 305/745-3211, $$) is a "complete vacation resort" with 55 waterfront rooms, restaurant, tiki bar, pool, tennis courts, miniature golf, and shuffleboard. There's even a marina and an airstrip! Rooms for two run $140 in season (mid-December–April) and $100 the rest of the year. RV vagabonds who like to fish frequent a popular ocean-front KOA campground, the **Sugarloaf Key Resort** (MM 20, P.O. Box 420469, 305/745-3549, $).

Big Coppitt Key and Boca Chica Key

Boca Chica ("little mouth") has been the site of a U.S. naval air station since 1941. Big Coppitt is mostly inhabited by service families from the naval facility. That might suffice by way of description for this book's purposes, but there is a county beach out here. **Boca Chica Beach** is reachable by exiting the Overseas Highway (U.S. 1) at MM 10, where S.R. 941 (Old S.R. 4A) runs alongside the ocean. At its end is a county-maintained beach about a quarter-mile long where you'll find not much more than patches of sand and a few refuse containers. But it is a pet-friendly beach, so bring your canine for a romp on the beach (as many Key West residents do, since they don't have a comparably large and dog-tolerant beach).

THE SUNNY FLORIDA KEYS

HURRICANE RITA

Of the eight hurricanes that impacted Florida in 2004 and 2005 – well, *nine*, if you count 2005's Cindy, which was posthumously upgraded from tropical storm to hurricane – Rita and Cindy left the state the least scathed. Yet even those two left their marks.

Early in July 2005, Cindy came ashore at Alabama and swung northeast, briefly bringing wind and rain to Florida's Western Panhandle. A three-pack of named storms that came one after another – Arlene, Cindy and Dennis – had a cumulative effect upon the Panhandle, exacerbating all the damage that had been wrought by the "big one," Hurricane Ivan, in 2004.

On September 20, 2005, Rita passed within 50 miles of Key West – close enough to lash the vulnerable Lower Keys. Moving from the Straits of Florida into the Gulf of Mexico, Rita intensified into the season's second Category 5 hurricane, with 175 mph winds. It even surpassed Hurricane Katrina in strength, becoming the third-most powerful hurricane on record (behind 1988's Gilbert and the Labor Day storm of 1935, which decimated the Keys).

For a while, it looked like Rita might smack a Katrina-scarred Louisiana coast – they were holding their breath and saying prayers in New Orleans – but ultimately made landfall along the Texas coast, where it caused one of the most cataclysmic and deadly traffic jams in history. More than 100 people died in Texas while fleeing the storm, including 24 senior citizens whose bus caught fire. Making landfall on the Texas-Louisiana state line, Rita was directly blamed for $6 billion worth of damage in Texas.

Back on the Florida Keys, the damage caused by Hurricane Rita was mostly psychological. Rita was the third time the Keys had been under evacuation orders in 2005 – after Dennis and Katrina – and the ritual of boarding up and wondering what might be left when you returned had taken its toll. A month later, Hurricane Wilma pretty much sealed the deal, causing many to wave the white flag of surrender.

For more information, contact the Lower Keys Chamber of Commerce, MM 31, P.O. Drawer 430511, Big Pine Key, FL 33043, 305/872-2411 or 800/872-3722, www.lower-keyschamber.com.

BEACHES

🔟 BOCA CHICA BEACH

Location: from U.S. 1 at MM 10 on Big Coppitt Key, follow S.R. 941 (Old S.R. 4A) to the beach
Parking/Fees: free parking lot
Hours: 7:30 A.M.-sunset
Facilities: none
Contact: Monroe County Department of Parks and Beaches, 305/295-4385

Key West

The Overseas Highway (U.S. 1) comes to a stop on Whitehead Street in Key West, which is literally and figuratively the end of the road.

Key West (pop. 25,000) is the southernmost tip of the American land mass. It is well and truly isolated from the mainland by 42 bridges and 108 miles of narrow keys that barely poke above sea level. Most people who trek out here find Key West to be a worthwhile pot of gold at the end of the asphalt rainbow. Perhaps it is the tropical setting that makes Key West so appealing; though it falls shy of the tropics by 30 miles, that is just a technicality.

As it is in any far-flung province, especially in equatorial climes, the rules that apply in general society are more relaxed down here. In fact, they almost don't apply at all. People simply do not judge or ask questions in Key West. That is why it has historically attracted pirates, rumrunners, dope smugglers, offbeat literati, and every other kind of outlaw. Key West has also been for many decades a favored enclave of gays and lesbians.

Of course, all is not coconut milk and mangrove honey in Key West. With the steady influx of tourists and ongoing attempts at reshaping by developers has come a certain loss of intimacy. Although Ernest Hemingway was once quoted as saying, "I like Key West because

Duval Street is considered "the longest street in the United States."

COURTESY OF LEN KAUFMAN/TDC

THE CONCH REPUBLIC

You will frequently hear references in the Florida Keys to an entity called the Conch Republic. More an absurdist state of mind than an actual government, the Conch Republic is a legacy of the pirate mentality that has pervaded the Keys since the arrival of white men and the disappearance of the Calusa Indians. One of the most lucrative ways early whites and Bahamians (known as "Conchs") made their money in the early 1800s was by "wrecking": luring ships onto reefs with strategically placed lanterns and then waiting until the bounty (and drowned bodies) washed ashore.

Nowadays, the Conch Republic is largely a macho-buccaneer fantasy. The precipitating event that led to its formation was an April 1982 federal Border Patrol roadblock set up on U.S. 1 where the Keys meet the mainland. The intention was to check for drugs and illegal aliens. The result was widespread unrest among residents who grew sick of delays at the Soviet-style checkpoint.

The Lexington and Concord of the Conch Republic occurred at Mallory Square in Key West on April 23, 1982, when hundreds of protesters symbolically seceded from the United States and then quickly surrendered, requesting $1 billion in "foreign aid" from the state. This charade was followed by a weeklong party. What was genuinely amusing then is often obnoxious now, as the Conch Republic has become the *nom de guerre* of renegades who've tried to sabotage the work of the National Oceanographic and Atmospheric Administration, the Nature Conservancy, and a coalition of state and federal politicians.

Loosely affiliated with the right-wing "property rights" and "wise use" movements, the Conchs have succeeded in polluting the air with propaganda about how environmentalists and big government are taking over their corner of the world. The antigovernment strain runs deep in the psyche of the Conch Republic, which kids itself into thinking it's the last bastion of rugged individualism in America. Cluttered roadsides and littered shorelines argue silently but convincingly against self-governance. In short, not all Conchs take care of the Keys, yet they defiantly oppose state and federal efforts at protection and restoration of this national treasure.

In November 1996, Monroe County voters rejected Referendum No. 4 ("Shall we

people don't stare at me on the street," he'd undoubtedly find himself a harried celebrity today. A lot of changes have come to Key West in the last 20 years. Take the heart of Duval Street, between Truman and Front Streets, which is wall-to-wall with franchised stores and novelty bars that must depress the citizens of the Conch Republic. There's been a bloodless invasion of Key West by well-worn franchise names that have been branded into the American psyche. Worse, cruise ships now disgorge tourists at Mallory Square to prowl the downtown streets on souvenir-hunting junkets. As a result, Key West appears to be vying for the title of T-shirt capital of America, competing with the likes of Times Square, Venice Beach, Myrtle Beach, and Fisherman's Wharf. Everywhere in Key West

you see signs for cut-rate T-shirts ("4 for $10!") and rental scooters.

But that's not even the worst affront on Duval Street. Adult video stores and strip clubs exist, not in profusion but just enough to register an uncomfortable impression. Hired touts hector milling tourists, thrusting sheets of soon-to-be-litter into people's disinterested hands. In 1998, then-mayor Jimmy Weekley spearheaded an effort to make Key West "the cleanest little city in America." Considering Key West's renegade history, the town's got its work cut out for them. Our own view is that somewhere between irredeemable sleaze and antiseptic makeovers, there has to be a happy medium. Fortunately, the "Clean Key West" initiative has caught on and succeeded.

have a Florida Keys National Marine Sanctuary?") by a 55-45 margin. The following vignette is typical of what passes for democracy down here. A brave local woman spoke up at a public meeting to voice her opinion about sanctuary opponents. "The no vote is due to the pirate mentality in the Keys," she argued. "Don't expect those who are destroying the reef to vote for the sanctuary. The Keys belong to the nation, not just the residents of the county."

She was roundly booed by the Conchs, but we give her a belated standing ovation. Recognition is also due former U.S. Rep. Peter Deutsch, who put his job on the line by supporting the sanctuary. Despite the Conchs' saber-rattling theatrics, the 2,800-square-mile Florida Keys National Marine Sanctuary was established by an act of Congress in 1990. State approval came in January 1997, when a management plan for the sanctuary was approved by Governor Lawton Chiles and his cabinet. Its provisions include closing 19 small areas of the Keys to fishing and establishing rules to curb reckless boating. In addition, channel markings have been improved, seagrass beds have received enhanced protection, and scientific studies of dying reefs have been undertaken. It all sounds eminently reasonable to us.

So what's left of the Conch Republic? Well, they have a website (www.conchrepublic.com), an office (405 Patronia Street, Suite 2, Key West, FL 33030, 305/296-0213), and an online store where you can buy Conch Republic merch ("Official Gear of America's Tiny Islands Nation"). You can even apply for a bogus "citizen passport," designed by the Conch Republic's publicity-seeking "secretary general," Peter Anderson. Each April the Conchs celebrate "the independent and eccentric spirit of Key West" with 10 days of revelry: "drag" (pun intended) races involving female impersonators, mock sea battles, fiddling contests, and so forth. The Annual Conch Republic Independence Celebration turns 25 in 2007. For a taste of the more humorous side of the Conch Republic, here is their official manifesto:

"Dedicated to the fundamentally American spirit of a people unafraid to stand up to 'government gone mad with power' that embodied the founding of the Conch Republic in 1902. As the world's first Fifth World nation, a sovereign state of mind seeking only to bring more humor, warmth, and respect to a world in sore need of all three, the Conch Republic remains the country who seceded where others failed."

Key West has become occupied by upscale condominiums and hotels that block sunsets and water views in a town where these things were once available to one and all. The battle for Key West's soul is driven by the fact that tourism pumps more than a billion dollars a year into the economy of the Florida Keys. This bending in the direction of money is especially evident at Mallory Square, Key West's sacred spot of sunset-watching, which has become dressed up with new construction and brick courtyards in recent years. They now charge $15 to park at Mallory Square at sunset. (Alternatively, you can try to find a spot on nearby streets and feed the hungry meters.) The sunset-watching ritual has gotten very stylized, and even the geeks who perform for the crowd pre- and post-sunset crowd seem less like genuine characters and more like something from Hollywood casting.

We'll concede that Key West is choked with tourists, tacky souvenir shops, overpriced bars, and a roll call of franchises similar to that found in every other American city. But it's equally true that Key West retains something of its essential character despite the encroachments. There's still enough that's unique and individualistic about the place to make it worth visiting, albeit with a healthy skepticism and a wary eye.

Tourists, locals, snowbirds, and jet-setters converge uneasily and somewhat comically out here at land's end. Each clique comes with its own set of expectations and designs on the

THE SUNNY FLORIDA KEYS

place. Sometimes it's hard to tell hosts from parasites. Out at the intersection of South and Whitehead Streets, for instance, tourists line up to take pictures beside the painted buoy that identifies this spot as the southernmost point in the continental United States. It's a pilgrimage and photo op you simply must make, having come this far. Thus, Southernmost Point draws hordes of tourists and a handful of locals availing themselves of a chance to cadge tips. We watched one weather-beaten opportunist work the crowd, offering to snap pictures of the tourists with their own cameras. The beaming Middle American couple got to show the folks back home a snapshot of themselves beside the buoy, while the local—a character from a Jimmy Buffett song come to life—pocketed a buck or two. Only in Key West.

At the end of the road, people tend to get a little more surreal and devil-may-care. It can be something as incongruous as the distant sound of Bob Dylan's protest songs being performed by a Duval Street folksinger to tourists wearing flip-flops and Hawaiian shirts. Everything is topsy-turvy and carnivalesque. When Key West is alive, there is something in the blueness of the sky, the emerald of the water, the salt tang in the air, the crazy quilt of people, the endless singing, whistling, shouting, parading, and drinking that tells you this is it. This is land's end, and it's time to party.

BEACHES

Don't let anyone tell you Key West is not a beach town. They can be almost insistently paranoid on that point, particularly the hotel owners, who tell of having to endure tirades from disappointed families and couples who have come to Key West expecting a standard Florida beach vacation. Beleaguered concierges have had their heads chewed off by angry guests demanding, "Where's the beach?"

After combing the island's perimeter, we would like to counter the prevailing wisdom by asserting that Key West is indeed a beach town. You've just got to know where to look

for the beaches. For starters, don't stay downtown if being near the beach figures in to your vacation agenda. There are beaches along the south-facing side of Key West, running for about three miles from where South Roosevelt Boulevard (A1A) makes a 90-degree turn in the vicinity of Key West International Airport all the way down to Fort Zachary Taylor.

Smathers Beach is the longest stretch of beach, running along South Roosevelt for about three-fifths of a mile. It is a man-made beach that's widest around Atlantic Avenue. Ironically, despite being repeatedly washed away by hurricanes in 2005, Smathers Beach's sand has been recovered, sifted, and replaced—and is now wider and fluffier than ever. There's plenty of free parking on A1A and a bit of a seaside bazaar in progress, with people dealing their wares out of vans. You can rent Hobie Cats, sailboards, and snorkeling gear; buy ice cream, sandwiches, and cool drinks; purchase seashells (don't even think about it!); or snag a beach chair and umbrella for the day. The snorkeling off Smathers Beach is great, so dive in and enjoy the reefer madness, which is among the best off any beach in the United States.

The next two beaches are along Atlantic Avenue, which takes over from A1A in following the beachfront. **C.B. Harvey Rest Beach Park** (formerly just Rest Beach) and **Clarence S. Higgs Memorial Beach** are adjacent and indivisible. Rest Beach has picnic tables, a sunbathing dock and nothing more, but you can park across the road at McCoy Park, which has all the other necessary facilities. Higgs Beach is amply endowed with amenities, including a restaurant, showers, and tennis and volleyball courts. Both are festive beaches. Colorful sails, covered picnic tables, stands of shady palms, a paved bike path, and a beachside cafe make this a splendid spot for gathering rays, swimming, and snorkeling. Colorful characters cruise past on bikes and mopeds or streak by in a blur on in-line skates. A mixed crowd of gays, families, Europeans, oldsters, yuppies, and hippies congregate in an environment that embodies Key West at its relaxed, catholic, and tolerant best. If it's true that "it takes all kinds," then you'll find what it takes on these beaches.

A fence divides Higgs Beach from the private beach belonging to Wyndham Casa Marina Resort, a stretch of sand and beach chairs known as Kokomo Beach. Farther west, at the end of Vernon Avenue, is a very small beach known as **Dog Beach** that's popular with pet owners. Unless you're traveling with Fido, it's of no use or consequence to tourists. **South Beach** is a small swath of sand and hard-bottom beach a block away from the "Southernmost Point" marker. South Beach Restaurant (1405 Duval Street, 305/294-2727, $$) sits near this city beach—the southernmost public beach in the U.S.

Fort Taylor Beach, at the Zachary Taylor State Historic Site, is the final ocean-facing public beach in Key West's procession of them. It is a good beach, albeit difficult to maneuver around (necessitating a lot of careful scrambling over the rock reef until the water deepens), and a great sunset-watching spot—arguably even better than Mallory Square, though it lacks the entertaining diversion of crowds and street theater. As a final footnote, offered only out of a pathological need to be comprehensive, there is one public beach on the gulf side of Key West. Known as **Simonton Street Beach,** it is located downtown, a few blocks east of Mallory Square. You will find a boat ramp, public restroom, and so-called beach that is less than ideal for swimming.

To summarize, Key West is a beach town after all. Just realize that beaches aren't the primary focus of the Key West experience.

Now we must update an old story. In the mid-to-late 1990s, the beaches of Key West had become fouled by untreated sewage spewing from a treatment plant. (Prior to 1989, Key West didn't even treat its sewage—just let it run into the ocean.) Elevated levels of fecal coliform (bacteria found in human waste, and an indicator of other viruses and parasites) and enterroccus (an effluent-based bacteria that causes gastrointestinal problems) resulted in beach warnings and closures in Key West, which made national news in 1996. The crap even drifted out to the Dry Tortugas, where a health advisory had to be posted on the beach at Fort Jefferson.

But to give credit where credit is due, a state-of-the-art wastewater treatment plant is helping to remedy the situation. The plant even received an "Operations Excellence Reward" from the state Department of Environmental Protection in 2004. That's not to say Key West is home free. In fact, Higgs Beach was closed 124 days in 2004—fully a third of the year—due to bacterial contamination. And South Beach—well, you don't want to know.

During the worst bouts of bacterial infestation and beach closures in the 1990s, a Key West mayor actually said: "The fact is that people can still use the beaches. We just advise them not to go into the water." How's that for spin? It's hard to believe that a smallish key in open water has so thoroughly managed to foul itself. This black mark needs to be fixed. According to the National Resource Defense Council's latest "Testing the Waters" report, Monroe County (397) finished in a virtual dead heat with Okaloosa County (398) for total number of beach-closure days in 2004. Shame on both of you. (Note: These figures are computed by adding the number of days in a year that each beach in a given county had to be closed for health reasons.)

For the latest beach closures and health advisories, call 305/293-1653 from the Keys and 877/892-9585 outside them.

For general travel information about Key West, contact the Key West Chamber of Commerce, 402 Wall Street (Old Mallory Square), Key West, FL 33040, 305/294-2587 or 800/LAST-KEY, www.keywestchamber.org.

11 SMATHERS BEACH

Location: along South Roosevelt Boulevard (A1A) in Key West

Parking/Fees: metered street parking
Hours: 7 A.M.–11 P.M.
Facilities: concessions, restrooms, picnic tables, and showers
Contact: Key West Parks Department, 305/292-8190

12 C.B. HARVEY REST BEACH PARK

Location: along Atlantic Boulevard between Smathers Beach and Higgs Beach in Key West
Parking/Fees: free parking lot at Sunny McCoy Indigenous Park
Hours: 7:30 A.M.–11 P.M.
Facilities: picnic tables and restrooms
Contact: Key West Parks Department, 305/292-8190

13 CLARENCE S. HIGGS MEMORIAL BEACH

Location: west end of Atlantic Boulevard (A1A) in Key West
Parking/Fees: free street and lot parking
Hours: 7:30 A.M.–11 P.M.
Facilities: concessions, restrooms, picnic tables, and showers
Contact: Monroe County Department of Parks and Beaches, 305/295-4385

14 DOG BEACH

Location: south end of Vernon Avenue in Key West
Parking/Fees: Limited free street parking
Hours: 7:30 A.M.–11 P.M.
Facilities: none
Contact: Key West Parks Department, 305/292-8190

15 SOUTH BEACH

Location: south end of Duval Street in Key West
Parking/Fees: metered street parking
Hours: 7:30 A.M.–11 P.M.
Facilities: concessions, picnic tables, and restrooms
Contact: Key West Parks Department, 305/292-8190

16 FORT TAYLOR BEACH

Location: Fort Zachary Taylor Historic Site, south end of South Street in Key West
Parking/Fees: $5 per car entrance fee plus $0.50 per passenger. Pedestrian fee is $1.50 per person.
Hours: 8 A.M.–sunset
Facilities: restrooms, picnic tables, showers, and a visitors center
Contact: Fort Zachary Taylor State Historic Site, 305/292-6713

17 SIMONTON STREET BEACH

Location: north end of Simonton Street, on the bayside in downtown Key West
Parking/Fees: metered parking lot
Hours: 7:30 A.M.–11 P.M.
Facilities: restrooms
Contact: Key West Parks Department, 305/292-8190

RECREATION AND ATTRACTIONS

- **Bike/Skate Rentals:** Island Bicycles & Skateboards, 929 Truman Avenue, Key West, 305/292-9707; Key West Scooter and Bike Rental, 1313 Simonton Street, Key West, 305/296-1166

- **Boat Cruise:** Yankee Freedom Dry Tortugas Ferry, Lands End Marina (foot of Margaret Street), Key West, 305/294-7009;

THE SUNNY FLORIDA KEYS

Sunny Days Catamarans, Green and Elizabeth Streets, Key West, 305/294-7755

- **Dive Shop:** Subtropic Dive Center, 1605 North Roosevelt Boulevard, Key West, 305/296-9914
- **Ecotourism:** Eco-South Tours, A&B Marina, 700 Front Street, Key West, 305/292-1986; Blue Planet Kayak Tours and Rentals, 305/294-8087
- **Fishing Charters:** Key West Pro Guides, G-31 Miriam Street, Key West, 305/296-6602 or 866/259-4205; Key West Fishing, 9866/684-3474
- **Lighthouse:** Key West Lighthouse and Museum, 938 Whitehead Street, Key West, 305/294-0012
- **Marinas:** A&B Marina, 700 Front Street, Key West, 305/294-2535; Garrison Bight Marina, 711 Eisenhower Drive, Key West, 305/294-3093
- **Pier:** White Street Pier, C.B. Harvey Rest Beach Park, Key West
- **Rainy-Day Attraction:** Hemingway House, 907 Whitehead Street, Key West, 305/294-1575
- **Shopping/Browsing:** Mallory Square, 1 Whitehead Street, Key West, 305/296-4557
- **Vacation Rentals:** Rent Key West Vacations, 1107 Truman Avenue, 305/294-0990; Key West Vacation Rentals, 1075 Duval Street, Key West, 305/296-2561

ACCOMMODATIONS

The **Wyndham Casa Marina Resort** (1500 Reynolds Street, 305/296-3535, $$$$) is rife with history that dates back to its formal opening on New Year's Eve 1921. It was intended to be railroad and tourism magnate Henry Flagler's piece de resistance as a resort. He never lived to see its completion, but would no doubt be happy that the on-premises restaurant is named Henry's. Casa Marina thrived until World War II, when it was commandeered for Navy housing.

Marriott took it over in 1978, by which point the Spanish Renaissance–style resort had fallen into some disrepair, necessitating an expensive makeover. Wyndham acquired Casa Marina from Marriott in 2000. In fact, Wyndham combined two Marriott resorts—the Marriott Reach and Casa Marina—into a single 461-room mega-resort with the largest private beach in Key West. However, since the acquisition, there have been recurring complaints about the condition of the rooms and other matters. It is a given that keeping a hotel shipshape in the suffocating tropics entails a never-ending renovation, and Wyndham has apparently not been as vigilant as called for in that regard. At this point, the Wyndham Casa Marina Resort remains a popular convention hotel. But would you personally want to drop $330 a night to stay here? Neither would we. But we'll keep an eye on what they do with this historic property in the coming years.

Out on South Roosevelt Boulevard, across from Smathers Beach, there are three primary lodging choices. In order of ascending ritziness and cost, they are the **Key Wester Resort Motel** (3675 South Roosevelt Boulevard, 305/296-5671, $$), the **Best Western Key Ambassador Resort Motel** (3755 South Roosevelt Boulevard, 305/296-3500, $$$), and the **Sheraton Suites Key West** (2001 South Roosevelt Boulevard, 305/292-9800, $$$$). The Sheraton faces Smathers Beach at its prime south end. Sheraton offers the choicest digs if you want to stay on the beach in Key West.

In downtown Key West, near the intersection of Duval and Front Streets, lodgings include the **Hyatt Key West** (601 Front Street, 305/296-9900, $$$$), whose tropically landscaped acreage rambles down to the gulf's edge, and the **Crowne Plaza La Concha** (430 Duval Street, 305/296-2991, $$$), a restored property at the center of the Duval Street bazaar. Both are steps away from Mallory Square, the Conch Train tour's departure point, and the hottest bars and restaurants. Hyatt also owns a very interesting property at the west end of Key West, **Hyatt Sunset**

Harbour Resort (200 Sunset Lane, 305/292-3001, $$$$). It consists of 40 two-bedroom condos that come with kitchens, screened porches, and water views.

Okay. That is a sampling of the choices from among the flotilla of corporate giants that have streamed into Key West in our moneyed new age. At the other extreme are a host of funkier choices more in keeping with the let-it-all-hang-out spirit of the tropics and Key West's reputation as a haven for nonconformists. Many of these low-key motels and guesthouses are a bit frayed around the edges. It's the sun, the moisture, the tropics. It's okay. Unless you're hopelessly phobic with a fear of decay, there's no commandment saying you must hand over $300 a night for a perfectly sterile hotel room in Key West when you might find something for a third as much in a comfortably funky motel or "resort." An upstairs shutter may need a coat of paint and the air conditioner might groan like an ailing sea cow, but it's nothing to get freaked out about.

A lot of Key West's more modest but charismatic properties lie along Truman Avenue in the "Old Town" area. They include such old-timers as the 37-room **Key Lime Inn** (725 Truman Avenue, 305/294-5339, $$$). Painted a sun-faded greenish yellow, like the namesake key lime, and hidden among a forest of stunted trees, this one-acre "village" consists of cottages distributed randomly around the property. Buildings date from the mid-1800s to the mid-1900s, but all received a thorough renovation in 1999. The grounds are an enchantingly tropical tangle of key lime trees and dense, shady greenery. And you're just a few blocks from downtown.

Key West is also well suited to the guest house and bed-and-breakfast craze. It's got the old buildings, the distinctive architecture, the history, and the personality to be an "inn" kind of town. A classic high-end Key West bed-and-breakfast is the **Curry Mansion Inn** (511 Carolina Street, 305/294-5349, $$$), the circa-1855 Victorian home of Florida's first millionaire, William Curry. Another is **Eden House** (1015 Fleming Street, 305/296-6868, $$), a surprisingly affordable guesthouse. Built in 1924, it's got a bit of literary/bohemian history lurking in its past. Eden House remains an archetypal Key West hostelry, boasting clean and simple rooms with ceiling fans, plus a pool and garden cafe.

If you want assistance in booking a place to stay—be it hotel, motel, bed-and-breakfast, guest home, or whatever—call **Key West Reservations** (635 United Street, 305/293-9815), which offers free reservations for Key West and other keys.

COASTAL CUISINE

Duval Street is lined with restaurants that cater to the tourist trade. A closer look will ferret out smaller places that merit the locals' seal of approval. **Camille's** (703½ Duval Street, 305/296-4811, $$) is a perfect example. It looks something like a British tearoom crossed with a tropical diner. There are 10 tables and a counter with stools. A giant stuffed toucan sits in a perch by the window. The menu is creative and generally healthy, including garden veggie burgers and omelettes filled with shrimp, sun-dried tomatoes, and such. At lunch a grilled snapper sandwich is topped with pepper-jack cheese and shiitake mushroom salsa. Dinner usually includes two fish (mahimahi, snapper, or cobia), plus creative entrees by the French chef. Camille's is beloved by locals and those fortunate tourists who stumble onto it.

At the **Rooftop Cafe** (310 Front Street, 305/294-2042, $$$), you can either sit on a balcony overlooking the Mallory Square shopping district or inside beneath whirling fans. The food and ceremony are more elaborate than at Camille's, but it's worth it for the privilege of dining alfresco from a perch above the downtown bazaar. Three meals a day are served, with the top entrees being grilled mahimahi with macadamia nuts, brown butter, and fresh mango, and crab and shrimp cakes. The latter dish won the establishment a Florida "master chef" award. The key lime pie is among the best in Key West.

Close by is a Key West landmark, **Pier House** (1 Duval Street, 305/294-9541, $$$$), a casually classy gulfside resort with splendid guest rooms and suites, plus one of the best-known restaurants in town. At Pier House, get anything made with conch (sausage, fritters, chowder), expect a first-class array of fresh fish entrees, and finish it all off with a slab of key lime pie prepared frozen or chilled.

In late 2003, celebrity chef and Key West local Alice Weingarten moved a very popular restaurant she'd once had on Duval Street back into its original digs. A trip to Key West simply isn't complete without dinner at **Alice's Key West** (1114 Duval Street, 305/292-5753, $$$$). She takes a far-ranging and creative yet pleasingly accessible "fusion cuisine" approach to her menu, which ranges from Greek shrimp to Mediterranean chicken to Brazilian churrasco steak. We were most intrigued by the Cuban approach to ostrich, which was marinated in mojo (a delicious plate, served with plantains, black bean coulis, and a corn, avocado and tomato salsa). You can also get citrus-grilled mahimahi, seared yellowtail with black butter and capers, and shrimp crusted in a coconut and macadamia nut mixture. Save room for Alice's black-bottom key lime pie—yet another worthy variation on this regional classic.

They also do exquisite things with fish at **Nicola Seafood Restaurant** (601 Front Street, 305/296-9900, $$$$) in the Hyatt Key West Resort and Marina. Using native Florida and Bahamian ingredients, the chef prepares dishes with a continental flair. Barbados tuna is an enormous tuna steak marinated in orange-soy sauce, grilled medium rare, and placed atop of shredded vegetables and crispy grilled onions. Plantain-crusted black grouper is sauteed and surrounded with a pineapple-pepper salsa. Grated sweet potato coats a prime fillet of yellowtail snapper, which is sauteed till the exterior is crisp. Baked Florida lobster tail comes with a seafood stuffing that includes scallops and shrimp. Appetizers include a shrimp cocktail that's prepared like a mar-

garita, with the shrimp marinated in lime and served in a glass with a salted rim. Among the salads, the blackened Caribbean scallop Caesar is a winner. The conch chowder is delicious: the conch tender, the soup spicy.

One of the old reliables in Key West—it was old even when we first ate there and wrote about it in 1984—is **A&B Lobster House** (700 Front Street, 305/294-5880, $$$$). They serve both types of lobster known to well-traveled East Coasters: a Maine-style "lobster bake" (with corn and potatoes) and broiled Florida lobster tail (six or ten ounces). If you're not going for the latter, we'd recommend the very fresh fish offerings: black grouper piccata, pan-seared snapper, sesame-seared yellowfin, or seared Key West jumbo shrimp. The atmosphere is old-time elegance, and a meal here at A&B (founded in 1947) is like stepping into Key West's pre-hysterical past.

Looking for something cheap, quick, and good? We're fond of **Angelina's Pizzeria** (208 Duval Street, 305/296-3600, $), which claims to serve "the best slice in town." The pizza is fine any time of day but especially as a late-night pick-me-up during or after a bout of clubbing. Though the black-clad servers might look a little off-putting to tourists from Peoria, they are efficient and nice as pie, and Angelina's does indeed serve the best pizza we've had on the Keys—or anywhere, for that matter.

Affluent and upscale, latter-day Key West boasts a lot of high-end restaurants that are, if not exactly beyond our means, then certainly beyond our threshold of interest in a town that is, at its core, funky and low to the ground. If you want to drop a bundle, then that's your business, but in these laid-back environs we generally prefer pizza slices, grouper sandwiches, and cheeseburgers in paradise to rack of lamb. And they serve a mean cheeseburger at Sloppy Joe's, which is our next stop. Read on.

NIGHTLIFE

In Key West, the night starts young with the sunset-watching ritual at Mallory Square.

THE SUNNY FLORIDA KEYS

We'll briefly describe our latest experience one early summer evening. These days Mallory Square is bricked over and paved and bigger than ever. The entertainment, in the form of street performers doing bizarre things for tips, lately resembles some sort of stylized circus-cum-magic act you'd see in a Las Vegas lounge. For instance, a guy is bound in chains and hung from his feet. His Houdini-like trick is to extricate himself from the chains and safely return to earth. We wondered why anyone would attempt such a feat and who would want to observe it. Nonetheless, the sun has taken its bow and been applauded, so a big crowd has turned its attention to him. Before attempting the stunt he tells the crowd, "If I don't get a few good tips, I'm going back to my old job—jacking your car." And, he adds, "Remember that in Key West, it's hip to tip."

It's also okay to ignore this tomfoolery and walk away. And remember too that the setting sun, which is the best show of all, never asks for a tip. After sunset, one of us ponied up $8 for an "Ultimate Sunset Margarita," just to say he had such a thing in Key West. Served in a plastic cup, it was nothing special.

We make no secret of feeling ambivalent about the nightlife in Florida—and everywhere, for that matter—these days. That is to say, it seems to us that clubs and bars are no longer places where people have genuine experiences. Instead, they are served scripted evocations of formerly genuine experiences, from fake '50s retro to fake '60s coffeehouses to fake '70s discos. There are fake biker bars, fake British pubs, fake Caribbean-themed tiki bars, and plenty of places to serve the gold card–carrying yuppie. Key West has all these things, and big money has been leading it in the wrong direction, but it's still possible to overlook the fakery and ferret out a good time here.

So let's take a quick tour of Duval Street. Planning a night on the town in Key West is a simple matter. You walk up one side of Duval Street and then back down the other, keeping an ear cocked to the music spilling out of the bars. If it sounds good and the place is hopping, stop in for a drink or two. Then move on to the next place. Continue until wasted, and then walk, be driven or call a cab home. Repeat nightly until you have to leave town.

You'll find the likes of **Hard Rock Cafe** (313 Duval Street, 305/293-0230), **Planet Hollywood** (108 Duval Street, 305/295-0003) and **Hog's Breath Saloon** (400 Front Street, 305/292-2032) in Key West. This is notable because Key West used to be mercifully free of such franchised hot spots. On the premises of these glorified beer-and-burger joints are "merch shops." They sell logoed paraphernalia that informs the world you have drunk there. These days, even good old Sloppy Joe's has a merch shop. (*Sigh.*) There is no corner of the world immune to this sort of thing anymore—even a formerly feisty, independent-minded port o' call like Key West.

Despite all the crass merchandising, people manage to have a good time in Key West by force of will. We hit town hard on the heels of several nights in the Miami area, and it struck us just how much more friendly the debauchery is in Key West than in South Beach. Moreover, there are so many bars and clubs you are bound to find something that suits you. We heard "Wild Night" coming out of a bar, reminding us that every night has the potential to become a wild night here.

Casual hangouts like Hog's Breath attract swingin' yuppies and boat people. Old reliable saloons like the **Bull and Whistle** (224 Duval Street, 305/296-4545) and **Captain Tony's Saloon** (428 Greene Street, 305/294-1838) can be counted on to hire singers to belt blues, folk, and rock year after year. Tourists head to Jimmy Buffett's original **Margaritaville Cafe** (500 Duval Street, 305/292-1435), while locals gravitate to seriously fun and funky hideaways like the **Green Parrot** (601 Whitehead Street, 305/294-6133). There is no lack of gay clubs with darkened interiors and electronic dance beats streaming from the premises. Trendy restaurant/bars look down on the action from second-story decks along Duval.

FLORIDA KEYS TO HURRICANES:
NO MAS, POR FAVOR

Evacuating parts of Florida in advance of a hurricane has become an all-too-common exercise in frustration for those who live here. There is no mystery to this, as the low-lying peninsula sits like a welcome mat for the increasingly powerful tempests Mother Nature hurls its way.

Hurricanes operate on 30-year cycles in terms of intensity and number, and Florida grew like crazy during the most recent ebb in the cycle – roughly the quarter century from 1970 to 1995. Now that hurricanes are back to blasting Florida and the Gulf Coast with brutal force and numbing regularity, many who make their home in the Sunshine State are having second thoughts. A few winter snowstorms and cold snaps in the Rust Belt look like child's play compared to the destructive capability of a hurricane like Ivan, Charley, Katrina, Wilma, or the others that took extreme umbrage upon the state in 2004 and 2005.

That is why it was no surprise to us to read, in the wake of those record-breaking hurricane seasons, that some residents had begun throwing in the towel on the Keys and that home sales in South Florida had gone, well, south. Home sales in Broward County (Fort Lauderdale, Hollywood) dropped by 44 percent between October 2004 and October 2005. In Miami-Dade County, home sales declined by 48 percent during the same period. Though the real-estate and home-building industries tried to spin the situation as best they could, those statistics carry an obvious message: No one wants to live in the path of a hurricane.

The situation is especially dire on the Florida Keys, which have actually begun losing population. In a state whose population grew by an incredible 11 percent in just the first half of this decade, that is a shocking bit of news. But think about it rationally: As difficult as it is to face a hurricane on the mainland, it is exponentially more troublesome out on the Keys. Barely poking above sea level, they afford no protection. And exiting the Keys means traveling 100 miles down a two-lane highway over 42 bridges in the mother of all traffic jams.

In 2005, the Keys took a direct hit from four hurricanes: Dennis (July 8), Katrina (August 26), Rita (September 20), and Wilma (October 24). Each storm caused power outages, property damage, overflowing sewage, and evacuations that took as long as six hours. Perhaps the unkindest cut of all came when Hurricane Wilma delayed Key West's annual "Fantasy Fest" – a kind of decadent weeklong Halloween block party – by six weeks.

The Keys were estimated to have lost $50 million in tourist revenue from Wilma alone. And since tourism fuels the local economy, the hurricanes' impact extends beyond a wrecked boat, broken window, or flooded first floor.

"I'm sick of it all," Keys native Ron Kraig, who owned a boat-rental firm, told the *Miami Herald*. "This ain't paradise anymore. I want to cash in and move to the country."

We heard similar sentiments from waterlogged, battle-weary residents all over Florida. In a sense, it sounds like a multitude of factors – a more active hurricane cycle; hurricane strength further juiced by global warming; failing fisheries and eroding beaches; too many cars, roads, people, and buildings degrading the quality of life beyond tolerable limits – that are converging into the proverbial "perfect storm."

Toto, I don't think we're in Florida anymore.

For those about to rock (we salute you), there is **Sloppy Joe's** (201 Duval Street, 305/294-5717), open 9 A.M.–4 A.M. every blessed day. We always kick off our visits to Key West with a long evening here, just to make sure it's still alive and rocking. The idea of a world without Sloppy Joe's is unthinkable. It is the Plymouth Rock of watering holes on the East Coast.

However, our first pass through Sloppy Joe's on our latest trek to Key West was not encouraging. There was a guy onstage doing music and comedy, much like Steve Martin back in the early '70s. He had a puppet sidekick, and his humor was aimed at a dinner hour/early evening crowd of frumpy Midwestern tourists, many of whom were well on in years. They laughed heartily as this geographical joker lampooned their home states. He sang songs by Waylon and Willie and played "Stairway to Heaven" on the banjo. His routine included a fair share of "dumb Southerner" jokes and somewhat bluer fare. He asked, "Hey guys, do you remember your first blowjob?" And then: "How did it taste?"

His onerous shtick had nothing to do with the rocking side of Sloppy Joe's we have long depended on to help restore us to sanity after an entire coastline's worth of deejays, dance music, lounge pianists, dreadful comedians, hack cover bands and one-man acts doing glorified karaoke. So we decided to barhop some more and come back later, hoping for some sort of shift change at Sloppy Joe's in terms of performer and audience.

At **Dirty Harry's** (208 Duval Street, 305/294-3765) the question du jour was, "Who's getting fucked up tonight?" This query was shouted from the stage by the singer of a band called Slang. He wore a black T-shirt that read "Licensed Sex Therapist." The group played everything from Green Day to Guns 'n' Roses, with tips of the hat to Kid Rock and Bad Company. Slang was, in short, a good old-fashioned cover band. We were grateful to see a real band playing rock music on electric guitars. And although not all of their repertoire was to our liking, plenty of it fell

like high-decibel manna upon our rock-starved ears, which were ringing by the time we left.

Back at Sloppy Joe's, we struck up a conversation with a foxy lady (and Key West native) who told us that a group called Plunge was about to take the stage. "They're one of only two bands I'll go out to see," she told us. The other—we believe we heard this correctly—is the Masochists, who play at Hog's Breath. Under the influence of Plunge, which specializes in '80s New Wave covers, Sloppy Joe's began pulsing like the gloriously sloppy rock and roll club we've always known it to be. We hung out for a few sets and left feeling relieved at being able to report that live rock and roll still rules at Sloppy Joe's.

Moral of the story: Though Duval Street has largely sold its soul to the corporate franchise mentality, essential elements of Key West nightlife remain unchanged, if you know where to look. At its off-kilter best, Key West is still a wild kingdom on the edge of the tropics at the end of the civilized world.

Dry Tortugas National Park

The road may come to an end in Key West, but America dribbles on a bit longer. A clump of seven keys 70 miles west of Key West make up Dry Tortugas National Park (formerly Fort Jefferson National Monument). These islands were discovered in 1513 by Juan Ponce de Leon, who named them "Las Tortugas" for the proliferation of sea turtles. The name was amended to Dry Tortugas due to the lack of fresh water.

They've been an interesting part of American history. The Dry Tortugas have been the site of pirate activity and shipwrecks, lighthouses, a fortification (Fort Jefferson, on Garden Key), a naval fueling station, and a seaplane bases. These keys are also a haven for migratory birds and the remarkable diversity of life attracted to the submerged coral reefs and seagrass beds. Some pronounce the snorkeling here the best to be had in North America.

Franklin Roosevelt designated the Dry Tortugas and the surrounding underwater ecosystem a National Monument in 1935. It is now a 64,700-acre National Park, most of which (like Biscayne National Park, south of Miami) is underwater. The seven exposed coral reefs collectively amount to only 39 acres of dry land. Despite their remoteness, the Dry Tortugas are receiving increasing visitation—more than they can handle, some would argue. Visitation quadrupled between 1984 and 1998, when 72,000 people descended on the dry islands. Visitation peaked at 78,000 in 2002 and has since declined slightly. The human inundation has caused concern about reef preservation, fish populations, and the rare seabirds that pass through.

Primary activities are swimming, diving, snorkeling, fishing (a Florida saltwater fishing license is required), and birdwatching. Bush Key is a nesting area for sooty and noddy terns that's closed to the public April–September. Camping is allowed on Garden Key at a 10-site primitive campground overlooking a white-sand beach; there's also a group site for up to 40 people. On the grounds are picnic tables, grills, and toilets, but no sinks, showers, or phones. All supplies, including fresh water, must be brought over, and all refuse must be removed on departure.

The main point of arrival in the Dry Tortugas is Garden Key, 68 miles west of Key West, where Fort Jefferson is located and a park ranger is on duty. Other than by personal boat, there are two ways to get here from Key West: by ferry (roughly two hours each way) or seaplane (40 minutes). **Seaplanes of Key West** (3471 South Roosevelt Boulevard, Key West, 800/950-2359) provides half-day and full-day trips ($189 and $325, respectively, for adults). Boat services include the **Yankee Freedom Dry Tortugas Ferry** (Lands End Marina, 240 Margaret Street, Key West, 800/926-5332), which leaves at 8 A.M. and returns at 6:30 P.M. The cost is $129 for adults ($89 for

kids under 16) and includes breakfast, lunch, snorkel gear, and a 45-minute tour of Fort Jefferson. The high-speed catamaran **Fast Cat II** (Elizabeth and Green Streets, Key West, 305/292-6100 or 800/236-7937) makes the passage in two hours and allows visitors 4.5 hours to roam Garden Key. A round-trip ticket costs $110 for adults ($80 for kids under 16), leaving daily at 8 A.M. and returning by 6 P.M. If possible, make reservations at least a day ahead of time.

For more information, contact Dry Tortugas National Park, Box 6208, Key West, FL 33041, 305/242-7700, www.nps.gov/drto.

BEACHES

18 GARDEN KEY

Location: Dry Tortugas National Park
Parking/Fees: $5 entrance fee per person over 17. $3 per person, per night camping fee.
Hours: 8 A.M.-sunset
Facilities: concessions, restrooms, picnic tables, and a visitors center
Contact: Dry Tortugas National Park, 305/242-7700

Everglades National Park

Here is a national treasure that boggles the imagination: a 50-mile-wide stream creeping almost imperceptibly through a 1.5-million acre freshwater marsh (the world's largest) in a state that is home to more endangered species than any other except Hawaii. Among the endangered species that live primarily in the Everglades: Florida panther (down to an inbred population of 75), American crocodile (400), snail kite (1,500), Cape Sable seaside sparrow (4,000), Everglades mink, white ibis, and indigo snake. Above and beyond these

EVERGLADES NATIONAL PARK PHOTO

The endangered American Crocodile can be found in Everglades National Park.

threatened creatures, the Everglades is home to 1,000 plant and 120 tree species, 600 fish and reptile species, and 350 bird and 40 mammal species.

Established in 1947, Everglades National Park covers only 12 percent of the Everglades' watershed. It is essentially a slow-moving river whose headwater is Lake Okeechobee and mouth is Florida Bay. Water moves across a bed of porous limestone at depths ranging from a few inches to six feet. Mainly, the Everglades consists of vast fields of sawgrass dotted with islands of tropical hardwood hammocks. The Everglades are an ideal habitat for alligators and bird life. Until people took time to understand its hydrology and ecology, it was thought of as worthless swampland to be drained and plundered. Because of developmental pressure, pollution, and the withdrawal of water, the Everglades is now considered the most imperiled of the 336 properties in the National Park system. It has become an exploitable political issue, with even the environmentally unfriendly Bush administration attempting to tout its efforts at Everglades rehabilitation. So far, it's mostly been all talk and photo ops.

For our purposes, we'll use the death of the woman who wrote the book on the Everglades as our springboard into Everglades ecology. Her name was Marjory Stoneman Douglas. She died May 14, 1998, at age 108, in the Coconut Grove cottage where she'd lived for more than 70 years. Her book, *The Everglades: River of Grass* (1947), was the gauntlet hurled at the feet of nature's despoilers in South Florida. Much as the books of Rachel Carson did a decade later, *River of Grass* sounded a wake-up call. When *River of Grass* became an instant best-seller, it helped change the public perception of swamps in general and the Everglades in particular.

Some of the things Douglas warned about—draining, dredging, paving, development, channelization—are still going on. The Everglades' subtropical watershed has shrunk to less than one-sixth of its original 13,000 square miles. It has been strangled by 1,400 miles of levees and canals, polluted by runoff from 700,000 acres of sugarcane farms, and assaulted by development as suburbs expand on all sides. More than 70 percent of the flows into the Everglades have been diverted by agriculture and development. Populations of wading birds have plummeted by as much as 95 percent. The Everglades took 19 million years for nature to create and about 100 years for humans to very nearly destroy.

The prospect of losing America's most unique natural habitat finally motivated President Bill Clinton to protect what remains by buying 50,000 acres of surrounding farmland (sugar plantations that have been the beneficiary of federal tax subsidies), a deal finalized in 1997. Much of what's been lost in the Everglades is irreplaceable, and the job of restoration is formidable, if not impossible. To that end, the Clinton administration and the U.S. Army Corps of Engineers pushed a $7.8 billion plan for "replumbing" South Florida. Aiming at the restoration of the Everglades ecosystem, the plan consists of 68 projects over the next half-century. The park's gravest threat, according to some scientists, is the melaleuca, an introduced Australian tree that's spread like kudzu throughout the Everglades. Already it's turned half a million acres of open sawgrass prairie into a dense forest with practically zero biodiversity.

The main points of entry into the Everglades are Homestead in the east, and Everglades City in the west. Park headquarters and **Ernest F. Coe Visitor Center** lie 11 miles west of Homestead along S.R. 9336. The smaller **Royal Palm Visitor Center** is located four miles west of park headquarters. **Flamingo Visitor Center** is 38 miles southwest of headquarters, deep inside the park. The **Gulf Coast Visitor Center,** in Everglades City, is located on S.R. 29, four miles south of the Tamiami Trail (U.S. 41), which forms the northern park boundary. Another point of entry is **Shark Valley Visitor Center,** located on the Tamiami Trail (U.S. 41) about halfway between Miami and Everglades City. Coming from Miami, take Exit 25 off of Florida's Turnpike and proceed 25 miles west to Shark Valley Visitor Center.

Admission to the park is $10 per vehicle (good for seven days) or $5 per cyclist or pedestrian. Activities include canoeing, kayaking, hiking, airboat rides, and tram tours. There are campgrounds at **Long Pine Key** (108 sites, seven miles west of park headquarters on Route 9336) and **Flamingo** (234 sites, just west of the Flamingo Visitor Center). However, Flamingo was still shut down as this book went to press, due to damage from Hurricanes Katrina and Wilma, and a third campground—Chekika, located northwest of Homestead—had closed for good years earlier. The nightly camping fee is $14 per site ($28 for group sites); call 800/365-CAMP (800/365-2267) for reservations.

Flamingo Visitor Center and its facilities took a huge hit from the hurricanes of 2005. In fact, it was announced in December 2005 that Flamingo Lodge—which for 50 years had been the only place to stay in the park except for a tent or RV—would definitely never see the light of day again. Six feet of water and six inches of mud sealed the fate of the dilapidated, barracks-like lodge. There was talk about building a new lodge, but the National Park Service has no money for such bold initiatives at this cash-strapped juncture. As for the status of service and facilities elsewhere at Flamingo and other hard-hit areas in the park, call 305/242-7700.

So much for the Flamingo Lodge. When asked on her 100th birthday whether the Everglades themselves could survive, Douglas said, "I'm neither an optimist nor a pessimist. I say it's got to be done."

As previously noted, President Bill Clinton took a big step toward beginning the process by signing the Comprehensive Everglades Restoration Plan (CERP) on December 11, 2000—barely a month before he left office. For his own part, President George W. Bush pledged his support for the Everglades initiative at a photo op at Royal Palm Visitor Center in June 2001. He and brother Jeb Bush, governor of Florida, then signed an agreement in January 2002 guaranteeing that adequate water supplies are available to support the 30-year, $7.8

WAIST DEEP IN THE BIG MUDDY EVERGLADES

How much does Michael David Cushing like mucking about in the Everglades? Let's put it like this: He passed up tickets to a University of Miami vs. Florida State football game on a beautiful Saturday to lead a pair of beach bums through one of the watery "strands" along U.S. 41 in Everglades National Park. Instead of watching what turned out to be a huge upset victory for Miami (his alma mater), he took the plunge into sometimes chest-deep tannic water to show us the great natural beauty of the Everglades.

If being immersed in a swamp filled with alligators and water moccasins sounds like your worst nightmare, you may be surprised to learn that it's actually a pleasant traipse. Yes, there are gators, but they congregate in the deeper, fish-rich canals beside the highway. Moreover, they don't want to be around you any more than you want to be around them. If they are in the swamp, it won't be anywhere near a bunch of rustling, muck-about humans. Ditto with the snakes. Cushing claims in all his years of wandering never to have seen a snake or gator at close range. As for the spiders, you just have to walk around their formidable webs. Sometimes he'll reluctantly knock down a web in order to allow nervous humans to pass, commenting to the spider, "That will give you something to do this afternoon."

Cushing is the owner-operator of Dragonfly Expeditions, an outfitter that leads walking tours of the Everglades and longer ecotours to tropical destinations in the Caribbean and South America. He got interested in "mucking about" in the wild after being sent to Jamaica as part of a college project in adventure travel, cultural outreach, and personal growth. His knowledgeable, low-key disposition helps allay any fears one might have about swamp critters. Many think of swamps as forbidding, malodorous places that harbor dangerous animals, human criminals, and malevolent spirits. In reality, the swamp is a sweet-smelling arboretum of beautiful flowers, dappled sunlight, and clear, clean water. It is one of the coolest places to be on a hot day. While the rest of South Florida was broiling in humid 90°F heat, we were cool and comfortable in the swamp.

The water was waist-deep for much of our two-hour walk. After an initial plunge, we quickly adapted to slogging about like swamp foxes. Along the way, Cushing regaled us with facts about the Everglades and its current health (or lack thereof). Water flow into the 'glades is one-tenth of what it used to be, thanks to altered hydrology and human withdrawals in places like Miami (which was once part of the Everglades). Numerous varieties of snails hung from the trees, sedges, and grasses by the thousands, but they're mostly gone, many species sadly extinct. Alligators lying on the warm highway to thermoregulate themselves are often run over by speeding motorists. Their carcasses are laughingly referred to as "speed bumps." There's no question that the Everglades – an ecosystem unique in design, function, and scope – has been taken to the brink of ruin. A theoretically massive effort is underway to repair the 'glades. How successful it will be, given continuing population growth and Republican intransigence on environmental matters, remains to be seen.

Walking the Everglades with an expert like Cushing will introduce you to a hidden world of beauty amid towering bald cypress. Whatever you do, don't take an airboat tour. The boats are horribly loud and make a mess of the grasses as they pass over them. Moreover, you only get to see the "sawgrass prairie" areas of the Everglades and not the hidden depths of the tree-filled swamps. If you want to know the real Everglades, you really need to go mucking about.

For more information, contact Dragonfly Expeditions, 1825 Ponce de Leon Boulevard, Coral Gables, FL 33134, 305/774-9019 or 888/992-6337, www.dragonfly-expeditions.com.

billion Comprehensive Everglades Restoration Plan. Of course, some have questioned the president's sincerity.

"It appears to be a public-relations stunt aimed at whitewashing his extreme anti-environmental agenda," said Rodger Schlickeisen, president of Defenders of Wildlife. "Floridians aren't fooled by the president's photo opportunity. All he is saying, apparently, is that he won't fight against laws passed to protect the Florida Everglades."

Given that our nation is currently drowning in red ink, we sincerely hope that all the laws, initiatives, and good intentions on behalf of the Everglades do indeed reach fruition.

After all, it's got to be done.

For more information, contact the Everglades National Park Headquarters, Ernest F. Coe Visitor Center, 40001 S.R. 9336, Homestead, FL 33034, 305/242-7700, www.nps.gov/ever. Or contact Flamingo Visitor Center, Everglades National Park, Flamingo, FL 33034, 239/695-2945, www.nps.gov/ever; Gulf Coast Visitor Center, Everglades National Park, S.R. 29, P.O. Box 130, Everglades City, FL 33929, 239/695-3311, www.nps.gov/ever; Royal Palm Visitor Center, Everglades National Park (four miles west of park headquarters), 305/242-7700, www.nps.gov/ever; Shark Valley Visitor Center, Everglades National Park, 36000 SW 8th Street, Miami FL, 305/221-8776, www.nps.gov/ever.

BEACHES

Strange or incidental as it may seem, beaches exist on Cape Sable and numerous small keys facing the Gulf of Mexico along the western flank of Everglades National Park. One of the most interesting and out-of-the-way areas in the Everglades is the Flamingo Visitor Center, which lies at the end of S.R. 9336, nearly 40 miles southwest of the main visitors center and park headquarters. At Flamingo you'll find a restaurant, marina, picnic ground, and the 7.5-mile Coastal Prairie Trail, which leads to **Clubhouse Beach.** Unfortunately, it's a narrow mud beach that even a ranger describes as

"pretty nasty... not a very good place." Sometimes there's a bit of sand accumulation, but storm-driven waves regularly wash it away. In the stormy winter months, Clubhouse Beach can remain underwater much of the time. You can camp along the beach, but hordes of mosquitoes will likely make your life miserable. The skeeters are so bad that it's difficult to breathe during the day because of the bug cloud, and visitors are advised to wear long-sleeved shirts and head nets. And if you're thinking of going swimming, be aware that the shallow waters of Florida Bay are filled with stingrays and lemon sharks. It all sounds like a setting for an installment of *Survivor*.

This area of the park is much more hospitable to boaters than landlubbers. Because mosquitoes don't fly over open water, you can escape them pretty quickly on a boat. About 10 miles offshore is **Carl Ross Key,** where there's a primitive campground and a smallish beach. In 1960, Hurricane Donna split the key in two, causing neighboring Sandy Key to form. You're not allowed on Sandy Key, but you can watch roseate spoonbills and other birds attracted to it from Carl Ross Key.

The real jewel out here is **Cape Sable,** much of whose 15-mile length is shell beach. Camping is allowed at three beach areas (East, Middle, and Northwest Cape). Wilderness camping permits are obtainable at the Flamingo Visitor Center and cost $10 per stay for 1–6 people. To get to Cape Sable, which is accessible only by boat, exit the marina and head 10 miles due west along the shoreline. This is a scenic trip via canoe or kayak (which can be rented at the marina). Powerboats must swing away from the shoreline because of shallows; consult nautical charts and tide tables before setting out.

For more information about boat and tram tours; powerboat, kayak, and canoe rentals; and the restaurant and store at the Flamingo Visitor Center, contact the **Flamingo Lodge, Marina & Outpost Resort,** Flamingo, FL 33034; 239/695-3101. The Flamingo Marina has been reconstructed and day-use services have resumed, including back-country boat cruises, canoe and skiff rentals, and fuel servicing of boats (no overnight docking, though). The popular Florida Bay Boat Cruise will resume in November 2006. The Marina Store has reopened, and food and beverages can be purchased there. However, all restaurants are closed and there is no indication when or if they will reopen. The Flamingo Lodge is a goner. The heavily damaged lodge and cottages will be destroyed, and there is currently no timetable given for the reconstruction of overnight accommodations. Funding, obviously, is a big issue.

On the **Gulf Coast Keys** of Everglades National Park, boaters can explore any of 15 isolated keys with sandy, gulf-facing beaches on which to camp, fish, and sunbathe. People generally beach their boats, wade out, and cast lines into the Gulf of Mexico. Of these 15 campable keys, McLaughlin (a.k.a. Highland Beach), Pavilion, Rabbit, Picnic, and Tiger are the most noteworthy. Pavilion is the largest, with a mile-long beach. Highland has the biggest beach. Rabbit Key reveals a nice sand spit at medium-to-low tide. Camping on all the Gulf Coast Keys is primitive, but there are portable toilets at Rabbit, Pavilion, and Picnic Keys.

The number of campers at each key is restricted, and that limit is often reached between November and April. Canoeists and kayakers account for 80 percent of campers; the rest are anglers in powerboats. There's a boat ramp at the Gulf Coast Visitor Center in Everglades City, a small town whose economy is driven by tourism and recreational fishing. There are no facilities along the Gulf Coast between Everglades City and Flamingo, a distance of 100 miles. It is, in other words, a completely self-sustaining wilderness area that's yours for the enjoying.

The area offshore of Everglades City is evocatively known as the **Ten Thousand Islands.** From the Gulf Coast Visitor Center, a concessioner leads 90-minute boat tours ($26.50 for adults, $13 for children from 5 to 11) on the half-hour 9 A.M.–4:30 P.M.; call 239/695-2591 for information and reservations. Wildlife you're likely to spot on the offshore islands includes wading birds (herons, ibises, roseate spoonbills), manatees, bald eagles, and bottle-nosed dolphins.

19 CLUBHOUSE BEACH

Location: From the main park headquarters, 12 miles southwest of Homestead on S.R. 9336, proceed southwest along S.R. 9336 for 38 miles to Flamingo Visitor Center. From here, hike west for 7.5 miles to Clubhouse Beach along the Coastal Prairie Trail.

Parking/Fees: $10 entrance fee per vehicle; $5 entrance fee for pedestrians or bicyclists. A boat fee of $5 per powerboat and $3 per canoe or kayak is charged. A wilderness camping permit costs $10.

Hours: 24 hours (Everglades National Park) and 9:30 A.M.–4:30 P.M. (Flamingo Visitor Center). Visitors center hours are extended in season

Facilities: none

Contact: Flamingo Visitor Center, Everglades National Park, 239/695-2945

20 CARL ROSS KEY

Location: From the main park headquarters, 12 miles southwest of Homestead on S.R. 9336. Proceed southwest along S.R. 9336 for 38 miles to Flamingo Visitor Center. From here, Carl Ross Key is accessible only by boat. Departing the marina at the visitors center, proceed south for approximately 10 miles to Carl Ross Key. Bring nautical charts and tide tables.

Parking/Fees: $10 entrance fee per vehicle; $5 entrance fee for pedestrians or bicyclists. A boat fee of $5 per powerboat and $3 per canoe or kayak is charged. A wilderness camping permit costs $10.

Hours: 24 hours (Everglades National Park) and 9:30 A.M.–4:30 P.M. (Flamingo Visitor Center). Visitors center hours are extended in season.

21 CAPE SABLE

Location: From the main park headquarters, 12 miles southwest of Homestead on S.R. 9336, proceed southwest along S.R. 9336 for 38 miles to the Flamingo Visitor Center. From here, Cape Sable is accessible only by boat. Departing the marina at the visitors center, proceed due west along the shoreline for 10 miles to Cape Sable. Bring nautical charts and tide tables.

Parking/Fees: $10 entrance fee per vehicle; $5 entrance fee for pedestrians or bicyclists. A boat fee of $5 per powerboat and $3 per canoe or kayak is charged. A wilderness camping permit costs $10.

Hours: 24 hours (Everglades National Park) and 9:30 A.M.–4:30 P.M. (Flamingo Visitor Center). Visitors center hours are extended in season.

Facilities: none

22 GULF COAST KEYS

Location: From Naples, proceed east on U.S. 41 (Tamiami Trail) for 25 miles. Turn south on S.R. 29 and follow for three miles to the Gulf Coast Visitor Center, on the south side of Everglades City. There is a public boat ramp at the visitors center and many private ones in Everglades City. Consult nautical charts and tide tables before departing for offshore keys. The most popular and accessible of the Gulf Coast Keys are McLaughlin (a.k.a. Highland Beach), Pavilion, Rabbit, Picnic, and Tiger. Numerous smaller keys can be visited in this area, which is known as the Ten Thousand Islands.

Parking/Fees: $10 entrance fee per vehicle; $5 entrance fee for pedestrians or bicyclists. A boat fee of $5 per powerboat and $3 per canoe or kayak is charged. A wilderness camping permit costs $10.

Hours: 24 hours (Everglades National Park) and 9 A.M.–5 P.M. (Gulf Coast Visitor Center)

Facilities: restrooms (on Rabbit, Picnic, and Pavilion Keys)

Contact: Gulf Coast Visitor Center, Everglades National Park, 239/695-3311

THE SUNNY FLORIDA KEYS

NAPLES, SANIBEL-CAPTIVA, AND THE SOUTHWEST COAST

Florida's Southwest Coast is a far cry from the better-known area that lies on the same latitude about 100 miles east, separated by the Everglades and connected by Alligator Alley. There's no Miami, South Beach, Fort Lauderdale, or Hollywood in the southwest corner of the state. What you will find is Naples, a gleaming community on the gulf that recalls Fort Lauderdale back when it was a much more sylvan place. But there's nothing on the East Coast comparable to Marco Island or the islands of Sanibel and Captiva. The former is a once-paradisiacal isle that's now as overbuilt as it is out of the way. Sanibel and Captiva are sanctuaries that have been shown far more respect for the notion of building in concert with nature.

The Southwest Coast embraces three counties—Collier, Lee, and Charlotte—each of which has its own assets and peculiarities. Collier is the southernmost of the trio and

the second-largest county in Florida. More than 70 percent of Collier's land area is under preservation, but most of the preserves are inland and the coastline is overdeveloped at Marco Island and the unincorporated area north of Naples. Still, Naples is very nice, and Delnor-Wiggins Pass State Park is special.

Lee County's 52 miles of sandy beaches rank among the finest in the state from the standpoint of seclusion (Cayo Costa, the Captiva Islands, Lovers Key), perennial popularity (Fort Myers Beach), and a brilliantly planned combination of the two (Sanibel Island).

Only 17 miles long, Charlotte County has more than 120 miles of tidal coastline. Most of it is along Charlotte Harbor, a favorite spot for anglers. The county's rich history includes landfalls by Ponce de Leon and Hernando de Soto, and its name derives from King George III's wife, Charlotte So-

© PARKE PUTERBAUGH

phia. Despite the illustrious background, Charlotte County has done little to build on it, especially on its flyblown coast. There's just one county beach, at Englewood Beach, leaving it to the state of Florida to jimmy together some coastal holdings as part of its Barrier Islands GEOpark.

What all three counties on the Southwest Coast have in common is gulf beaches. That is to say, the beaches are flatter, with fewer dunes and smaller waves. Here on the gulf, you can watch the sun set over water, and as in Key West, sunset-watching is a daily ritual.

Cape Romano and Kice Island

If you've got a boat and a yen for adventure, then cross Caxambas Pass to Cape Romano and Kice Island. Located due south of Marco Island, they are actually a single entity since the pass between them closed. Morgan Beach, the gorgeous white strip of sand on the island's west side, is at least as long as Marco Island's strand—and there's not a single condo on it. Purportedly swimsuits can be removed with impunity here. Like, who's going to complain?

For more information, contact Rookery Bay National Estuarine Research Reserve, 300 Tower Road, Naples FL 34113, 239/417-6310, www.rookerybay.org.

BEACHES

1 MORGAN BEACH

Location: south of Marco Island, across Caxambas pass; accessible by boat only
Parking/Fees: none
Hours: sunrise to sunset
Facilities: none
Contact: Cape Romano/Ten Thousand Islands Aquatic Reserve, c/o Rookery Bay National Estuarine Research Reserve, 239/417-6310

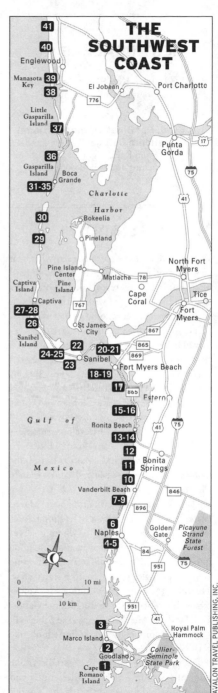

THE SOUTHWEST COAST

© AVALON TRAVEL PUBLISHING, INC.

BEST BEACHES

◖ **Lovers Key State Park:** Top 25, Best for Collecting Seashells (page 348)

◖ **J. N. "Ding" Darling National Wildlife Refuge:** Best for Canoeing and Kayaking, Best for Birdwatching and Wildlife-Viewing (page 355)

◖ **Bowman's Beach:** Top 25, Best for Collecting Seashells (page 360)

◖ **Captiva Beach:** Best for Collecting Seashells (page 365)

◖ **Cayo Costa Island State Park:** Best for Collecting Seashells (page 368)

Marco Island

There's an enormous gap between what you may hear or read about Marco Island and what your five senses reveal upon arrival. This chasm is the product of wishful thinking and outright misrepresentation. On paper, Marco Island appears to be heaven on earth. Far removed from urban sprawl, it is the southwesternmost developed island in Florida and the largest of the Ten Thousand Islands. But it's been developed into a nature-negating morass of condo towers, arrogant McMansions, golf courses, and total gatekept exclusivity.

Though we find such development inexcusable and un-American—using Emerson, Thoreau, Whitman, and Twain as our philosophical benchmarks—Marco Island is exactly what certain a certain class of rich, latter-day capitalists regard as their entitlement. Marco Island especially attracts a hefty population of affluent retired seniors, for whom it serves as a heavenly preview of what they imagine to be the afterlife: i.e., an eternal golf game and an upper-floor condo with a water view. They clog the roadways with their slow-moving, wide-bodied, gas-guzzling Monte Carlos, Cadillacs, and Mercedes-Benzes, and they will glower disapprovingly if you don't look like you "belong" here.

For us, Marco Island is a paradise gone tragically wrong—a three-mile-long island with a hundred-yard-wide beach that's about as hard to crash as a Mafia don's funeral. The thick, slick local media packet hails the "timeless beauty" and "unspoiled beaches" of "Florida's best-kept secret." They call Marco Island "secluded." They claim that it is "carefully planned" and "rich in diversity." And then they ask, "How can people living outdoors be so invisible?"

After searching in vain for anything secluded or carefully planned on Marco Island, we have prepared a different set of questions:

- The $64,000 question is, How could a place that didn't even exist 30 years ago be more overbuilt than the worst parts of north Miami Beach? How could such a beautiful and remote barrier island wind up covered by two unbroken miles of high-rise buildings?

- How could this have happened since the 1980s, by which time the lessons of coastal overdevelopment had become common knowledge?

- Why wasn't the Deltona Corporation, the prime mover behind Marco Island's development, more vigilantly regulated by state and county governments?

- How can the Marco Island Beach Association (MIBA), which oversees all aspects of beaches and "beautification," not object to the continued walling off of the beach, as with the Cape Marco project?

- Why should beach access be claimed by

© PARKE PUTERBAUGH

Tigertail Beach County Park on Marco Island

people who don't live here most or even part of the year and denied to year-round county residents?

• Using Marco Island as a case study, when will inviolable laws be passed to protect other coastal communities from foreign and out-of-state investors who seldom lay eyes on properties purchased for investment or tax-writeoff purposes?

There are various theories as to how Marco Island wound up becoming a poster child for development run amok. The most plausible is that Collier County decided to make Marco Island its golden goose. That is, they allowed the island to be purchased and privatized by the Deltona Corporation, which began snapping up property here in the 1960s. The trade-off for the county was a huge tax windfall from part-time residents who would, they presumed, not require much in the way of county services and infrastructure. Thus, the county's attitude was to surrender all principles of conscientious development out here in return for a sizable revenue stream benefiting the rest of the county.

When we first entered Marco Island in the mid-1990s, it was a shock to cross the hump-backed Judge Jolly Bridge and see an incongruous block of high-rises plopped on an island out in the middle of nowhere. Marco Island's skyline instantly put us more in mind of Manhattan Island than the "secluded" southwest coast of Florida.

In one sense, Marco Island does seem secluded. It's overwhelmed with buildings, but next to nobody's here. Much of the year you'll see condos, boats, and houses but few cars or people. Who really lives in this fantasy land? People might show up from time to time, but there is little sense of community. Marco Island mocks the very idea of community. It's more like an association of absentee owners and self-imprisoned paranoids.

If you can set aside the lingering image of Marco Island as a glut of condo and hotel towers arrayed like dominoes—and it takes a mighty effort, if you're disgusted by crass development—there are a few isolated spots where vestiges of the island's original charm survives. Foremost is Olde Marco Village. There is nothing old or historic about it. Olde Marco Village is simply the middle-class residential area that was here before Deltona went

CAPE MARCO: BIG CITY SKYLINE ON A SMALL FLORIDA ISLAND

If you're searching for an *Exxon Valdez*-like symbol for what is wrong with Marco Island, look no further than Cape Marco on the Gulf. Indeed, one can see no farther than this a monstrous development on the southern tip of Marco Island, because it completely blocks the gulf view. A complex of six skyscraping condominiums, ranging 12-26 stories, it is set on 30 acres and hogs 1,200 feet of beachfront. Cape Marco on the Gulf is so close to the water that it might as well be called Cape Marco *in* the Gulf. What is here is enough to give anyone who isn't making money off it a case of the heebie-jeebies.

Developer Jack Antaramian, an Aussie who's done big things — and we mean tall, not good — in South Florida, is responsible for Cape Marco. And, make no mistake, these condo towers are all about the bling. Units at Cozumel, a 24-story building completed in 1996, started at $990,000 for a two-bedroom-and-den configuration. Too steep? Hardly. It sold out!

In 1999 Marco Island's pliable city council approved a request to increase the height of a proposed building at Cape Marco although city staff recommended against it, claiming it would detract from the island's "small-town atmosphere." We applaud the sentiment, but Marco Island is about as small-town as The Bronx. Antaramian's lawyer made this argument for approval: "If you look up and down the beach, you have a kind of saw-tooth effect. That's part of the charm of Marco Island." This guy's good! He should be doing PR for Riker's Island.

The rest of the story played out as follows. In January 2000, with four sold-out condos already built and two more still on the drawing board at Cape Marco, Antaramian denied rumors he intended to sell his Marco Island holdings to Watermark Communities Inc. (WCI). Later in the year he did just that, and the fur really started flying. WCI's subsidiary, Bay Colony-Gateway Inc., built the Belize condominium 90 percent larger than even Antaramian had envisioned. Two condominium associations at Cape Marco sued the developer and the city of Marco Island, hoping to get it scaled back. Bay Colony-Gateway countersued, claiming they'd lost $10 million in sales at Belize due to "false information" spread by the condo groups.

How did all the fun 'n' games turn out? Well, Belize at Cape Marco was topped off at 25 stories in 2003. It became the largest luxury high-rise in Collier County, surpassing Cozumel at Cape Marco for that dubious honor. With units ranging 3,200-14,000 square feet, it was also the largest building ever developed by WCI. Both records will become history when Veracruz at Cape Marco, a frightful 26-story leviathan, is completed in late 2006.

Incidentally, Marco Island boosters do get one fact right in their description of the speculative fantasy world they inhabit. They boast that Marco Island was "once the home to conquistadors and pirates." Not much has changed. Pirates still plunder the island. They just happen to wear suits and ties.

on its rampage. A drive through here affords a glimpse at how cozy the island must have seemed to the original residents and retirees. Away from the high-rise Himalayas on the gulf, Marco Island has a sort of watery charm, with backstreet neighborhoods crossed by man-made canals.

However, the reality of Marco Island is that it serves as the ultimate bastion of good old-fashioned "I got mine"-ism. The local newspaper, the *Marco Eagle*, is a puff sheet for the business community, featuring upbeat stories on new construction. A running scorecard on the number of condominium units sold mimics the way some papers feature weather news on their cover. The chart is called "Marco Island Market Indicators," and it includes the dollar amount brought in by each real-estate transaction. What's confusing to us is that the place is already built out and yet it's under perpetual construction. When there's no more room to put anything how can they keep building? It makes no sense to us.

One interesting bit of archaeology on Marco was the discovery of a carved wooden figure of a half-man, half-panther. The Florida panther, an endangered species, used to roam freely hereabouts. The carved figure was claimed, in one local brochure, to "date back to A.D. 700–1450." (How's that for precise dating?) Naturally, the figure is long gone, allegedly to the Smithsonian, but gold replicas of the icon—cutely called "the Marco Cat"—are sold at local gift shops. The relic's disappearance and reincarnation as a souvenir trinket makes a fitting allegory for what has happened to this once quiet, lovely, and unspoiled island.

For more information, contact the Marco Island Chamber of Commerce, 1102 North Collier Boulevard, Marco Island, FL 34145, 239/394-7549, www.marcoislandflorida.com.

BEACHES

Just as it's hard for a rich man to enter the gates of heaven (per the Bible), it's hard for a poor one to get at the beaches of Marco Island. While public accesses are provided at South Marco Beach and Tigertail Beach, they are almost begrudgingly offered.

Take the **South Marco Beach Access.** This one public accessway along two unbroken miles of development is not much of anything. Collier County wrested a small walkway between high-rises for the public to gain passage onto the beach. You're required to park two blocks off the beach (at a cost of $3) and then scuttle along the side of a giant high-rise called The Apollo as though you're using the servant's entrance in the back. The beach is wide, flat, and expansive, but the proximity to these hideous buildings is oppressive. The beach itself ends a few hundred yards south at a development called Cape Marco, a towering architectural eyesore that blots out the very sky.

Tigertail Beach County Park, located at the north end of the island, is way more appealing. For the same $3 fee you get access to an undeveloped beach that runs for 0.5 mile. The drawback is that you're deposited beside a lagoon. If you walk along the lagoon, then you'll eventually curve around and come out on a spit. It's a round-trip hike that will take up to an hour. If you're not up for that, you can swim in the lagoon. Cabanas, kayaks, canoes, paddleboats, and windsurfing gear are rented. A nature trail flares off into beach hammock. There's a very modern playground for kids and a lunch spot with a deck (Todd's at Tigertail). The facilities at this 32-acre park are enormously impressive, but you should know that Tigertail Beach is not directly on the gulf. The fat cats of Marco Island have hogged all the gulfside beaches for themselves, you see.

❷ SOUTH MARCO BEACH ACCESS

Location: Park along Swallow Avenue, at the south end of Marco Island and walk two blocks to The Apollo condominium. A pathway beside it leads to the beach.

Parking/Fees: $3 entrance fee per vehicle; free for Collier County residents with beach parking permit from Naples City Hall

Hours: 8 A.M.–sunset

Facilities: none

Contact: Collier County Parks and Recreation Department, 239/353-0404

❸ TIGERTAIL BEACH COUNTY PARK

Location: Park entrance is at Fernando Drive at Spinnaker Drive, on the north end of Marco Island.

Parking/Fees: $3 entrance fee per vehicle; free for Collier County residents with beach parking permit from at Naples City Hall

Hours: 8 A.M.-sunset
Facilities: concessions, restrooms, picnic tables, and showers
Contact: Tigertail Beach County Park, 239/642-8414

ACCOMMODATIONS

The tone of Marco Island is set by the resort hotels on its beachfront. There's not a single mom-and-pop among them. Every building along the ocean adheres to a strict architectural dress code: tall, ramrod-stiff fortresses that are anything but welcoming.

Marco Island Marriott Resort, Golf Club and Spa (400 South Collier Boulevard, 239/394-2511, $$$$) is, to quote the late Frank Sinatra, "A Number One, top of the heap." That is to say, it's the largest (673 rooms) and most luxurious convention resort on the Gulf Coast. Here, you can indulge your inner CEO with an entire city's worth of amenities and an army of happy minions ready to cater to your every whim. Every minute of your stay at the Marriott can be choreographed by the staff, and you'll never have to leave the premises.

As far as we're concerned, all activities at this enormous complex are icing on the cake, with the pool area and beach being sufficiently entrancing to keep most folks happily occupied. Among the activities in a typical week: adult tennis clinics and tournaments, catamaran rides, "bead it" tutorials, tanning tips, a "ping-pong toss" competition, scuba diving, sailing seminars, scavenger hunts, shelling, body toning, "aqua-slimnastics," tropical drink-mixing classes, basketball shootarounds, bike tours, Skittles-counting contests, and the "Hermit Crabby 500." Each of these, of course, costs extra. For 18 holes of golf at Marriott's "Rookery at Marco" course guests will pay $149 if teeing off before noon; rates drop considerably after that. Of course, they do tons of convention business here. Families traveling without corporate pretext will pay $430–530 a night for a gulf-view room in the January–April high season. You'll pay $179–299 for the same room in late summer. Still way too much.

Other corporate sentinels—the **Hilton Beach Resort** (560 South Collier Boulevard, 239/394-5000, $$$$) and **Radisson Suites Beach Resort** (600 South Collier Boulevard, 239/394-4100, $$$$)—add to Marco Island's skyline. The only alternative to the high-rises is the **Paramount Suite and Hotel Beach Club** (901 South Collier Boulevard, 239/394-8860, $$$), across the street from the beach. While staying here requires a short walk to the beach access at South Marco, you don't have to pay the day-use charge at the public lot. The Paramount offers a low-key contrast (only 52 rooms and four stories) to Marco's condomania. A pool and racquetball courts are on-premises.

You can also go the condo-rental route. Here are a few local agencies specializing in vacation rentals: **Marco Beach Rentals** (1000 North Collier Boulevard, 239/642-5400) and **Marco Island Vacation Properties** (647 North Collier Boulevard, 239/393-2121).

COASTAL CUISINE

For all its high-class pretenses, Marco Island has a culinary reputation about one step up from convention food. This makes **Cafe De Marco** (244 Palm Street, 239/394-6262, $$$) an even more pleasant surprise than it would normally be. Located in "Olde Marco"—specifically, in the Port of Marco Shopping Village—Cafe De Marco is the finest restaurant on the island. Our dinner started with oysters Oscar (baked with crabmeat gratinee sauce and bread crumbs) and ended with peanut butter pie.

For entrees, one of us tried pasta *originale* (seafood, mushrooms, onions, and peppers, served with lobster sauce over linguine), and the other opted for grouper *fresca* (a hefty fillet simmered with garlic, butter, wine, shrimp, mushrooms, shallots, sun-dried tomatoes, carrots, and peppers). All fresh fish selections can be prepared "de Marco" (with mushrooms, shallots, garlic butter, and bread crumbs) or any other way you wish. Cafe De Marco is among our favorite restaurants in Southwest Florida. As for dessert—well, keep reading.

NIGHTLIFE

Whenever we asked about Marco Island's nightlife, we'd get an earful about lounge pianists and lite jazz. *Boring.* We also kept hearing about some guy who had been wowing the locals with dead-on impersonations of everyone "from Tony Bennett to Elvis." We fully intended to check him out, if only to indulge our appetite for irony. But, alas, a piece of peanut butter pie at Cafe De Marco got in the way.

This amazing concoction of peanut butter, chocolate chips, whipped cream, and chocolate sauce looked like a replica of a Marco Island high-rise. The more we picked at it, the larger it seems to grow. We guarantee that after devouring an anvil-like slab of peanut butter pie at Cafe De Marco, the only "getting down" you'll be doing tonight is a groan-filled belly flop onto your bed. It was more difficult to drive after eating a piece of this brain-fogging pie than if we'd knocked back several Manhattans on an empty stomach. It took a designated driver—the one in our party who had the sense to order key lime pie— to navigate the car back to the hotel.

Suffice it to say that we were sound asleep by 10 P.M. on a Saturday night, which caused us to miss both the nightclub impersonator and the jungle golf course we'd intended to play. The peanut butter pie is delicious beyond words, but unless you'll be sharing it with another person or two, please do as Nancy Reagan counseled would-be drug users and "just say no."

Naples

If Marco Island is the Miami Beach of Florida's southwest coast, then Naples is its Fort Lauderdale. Naples is neatly trimmed lawns, squeaky-clean streets, and upscale strip malls. Naples is golf courses and galleries and high-end clothiers and hundred-shop mall/marketplaces on or near the water. Naples is canals and yachts and carefree living on gulf and bay. There's even a touch of Palm Beach's upscale Worth Avenue along Naples' 5th Avenue and 3rd Street shopping districts. Naples also claims to be home to "the only true Teddy Bear Museum in the United States." (Oh, how we despise those faux teddy bear museums!)

All the comparisons with South Florida have an actual basis in fact, as Naples has become something of an escape route for those who cannot abide the high-stress, high-crime lifestyle that has overwhelmed Miami and Fort Lauderdale. Here's a statistic to ponder: the Relocation Crime Lab Index—a relative gauge of crime, based on statistics in 500 American cities, with a rating of 100 being exactly average—was 384 in Miami (no surprise there!), 199 in Fort Lauderdale, and 40 in Naples. The number of permanent residents gives no indication of how greatly Naples swells with the seasonal influx from wintering northerners. Peak season runs Christmas–April. According to *USA Today,* the Naples area claims the largest percentage of vacation property owners in the country, which means it's largely a land of second homes.

The city of Naples proper is long and narrow, bounded by the Gulf of Mexico on the west and the Tamiami Trail (U.S. 41) on the east. However, the city only technically ends there, as development continues and even accelerates beyond the city limits in unincorporated areas of Collier County, which are less restrictive of growth and development. The year-round population of Naples is only 22,000, but when you figure in all the adjoining unincorporated communities that press up against it, the metropolitan area is about 10 times that number.

Behind the facade of "luxury living," there are clashes in Naples between developers and environmentalists, as well as local citizens who want well enough left alone. Environmental interests are represented by The Conservancy, an enlightened group that does its best to preserve what remains of the area's subtropical ecosystems. This corner of the state has witnessed an extraordinary growth spurt in the

© PARKE PUTERBAUGH

Naples Beach

last two decades. Between 1980 and 1990, the Naples metropolitan area grew by 77 percent, giving it the dubious distinction of being the fastest growing in the U.S. Between 1990 and 2000, it grew by 64 percent.

They call Naples "the golf capital of the world," noting that Collier County has more golf courses per capita than almost anywhere else in the country. This is not something to whoop and holler about. The sudden impact of 70 golf courses and endless subdevelopments exacts a toll on the environment. The feisty Conservancy has taken on Deltona, at one time Florida's biggest developer, over Marco Island and neighboring Horr's Island. They've preserved nesting habitat for endangered loggerhead turtles, who lay 900–1,500 nests each year in Collier County. Yes, sea turtles do come ashore on the Gulf Coast, though not as many as on Florida's ocean-facing beaches.

Despite its rapid growth, the city of Naples has employed a modicum of urban planning— an anomaly in Florida—and the abundance of wealth means attractive homes and neighborhoods. Moreover, the town periodically imposes building moratoriums, and height limitations apply. This is why the really tall towers, such as the Ritz-Carlton Naples, fall outside Naples city limits in places like Vanderbilt Beach, which serve as a staging area for developmental sprawl.

The best news about Naples has to do with the way it's handled its beaches. Many east-west streets end at the Gulf of Mexico as public accesses, with metered parking and a walkway onto the beach. Add to this the romantic, strollable Naples Pier (on the gulf) and City Dock (on the Bay of Naples) and quiet neighborhoods with beautiful tree-lined streets, and there's much to like about Naples.

We said mostly. We already mentioned mounting population and environmental pressures. You should also know that they drive like maniacs in and around Naples. Tamiami Trail (U.S. 41) is a six-lane demolition derby whose contestants include reckless pickup truck renegades and terrified old folks with failing eyesight. To make matters worse, stoplights stay red for an awfully long time. In terms of traffic, U.S. 41 in Naples recalls the Miami/Fort Lauderdale corridor. In other respects, Naples is a privileged world apart.

CORKSCREW SWAMP SANCTUARY

Corkscrew Swamp Sanctuary, an Audubon Society preserve northeast of Naples, harbors the largest subtropical old-growth bald cypress forest in the world. It is an untouched oasis that makes one yearn for the lost days of 500-year-old primeval forests and hooting wildlife oblivious to humans. A highlight of the experience is a 2.25-mile boardwalk through marsh, prairie, pine upland, and cypress forest. There's also a Nature Store and rangers to answer questions.

To get to the preserve, take I-75 north to Exit 111 (Naples Park/C.R. 846) and exit east on Immokalee Road. Continue 15 miles and then turn left onto Sanctuary Road, which leads into the preserve. Corkscrew Swamp Sanctuary is open daily 7 A.M.–5:30 P.M. (to 7:30 P.M. mid-April–September). Admission is $10 for adults, $6 for college students with ID, $4 for those aged 6-18, and free for kids under six.

For more information, contact **Corkscrew Swamp Sanctuary,** 375 Sanctuary Road West, Naples, FL 34120, 239/348-9151.

For more information, contact the Naples Area Chamber of Commerce, 3620 Tamiami Trail North, Naples, FL 34103, 239/262-6376, www.napleschamber.org.

BEACHES

Within the heart of Naples, the beach is mostly quiet and residential, and nearly every east-west street that intersects Gulf Shore Boulevard ends at the beach with metered parking ($0.75 per hour) and public access. It's simple: you pull in a space, feed the meter, and step through a break in the shrubbery onto the beach. If you live here, the deal's even better: slap a beach parking sticker on your bumper (available at Naples City Hall), and you're entitled to park anywhere in town for free. Though there aren't any dunes on Naples Beach, they've at least seeded the back-beach area with dune grasses. The beach itself is of a decent width and flat as a pancake, bearing the usual imprint of tire marks from equipment used to clean it up each morning. When we last visited, dredges were pumping sand onto the beach to replace what Hurricanes Charley and Wilma stripped away.

Naples Beach encompasses the sandy whole of Naples, with public access at street ends from 33rd Avenue South up to the north end of town, just below Clam Pass County Park. Gulf Shore Boulevard parallels the gulf for most of the beach's 5.5-mile length. Down at the south end, below 21st Avenue South, Gordon Drive fronts the gulf. **Naples Municipal Beach and Pier** is located at by a palm-fringed, brick-tiled circle (at 12th Avenue South) in a neighborhood you don't have to fear walking around after dark. There is no charge to use Naples Pier; we've paid to walk or fish on many a pier that would give their pilings to look half this nice. The pier never closes, while the snack bar and bait shop are open till 5 P.M. daily.

In the midsection of Naples' municipal beach lies **Lowdermilk Park,** which is equipped with picnic tables, gazebos, play area, volleyball courts, and concessions. Lowdermilk is a few miles north of Naples Pier at the west end of Banyan Boulevard. Parking is metered.

Up at Naples' north end, the development gets more vertical and exclusive. Fear not; there are still ways to crash the beach. There's a 25-space access along **Gulf Shore Boulevard North,** near the west end of Seagate Drive. The real gem in north Naples is **Clam Pass County Park.** Heading there along Seagate Drive, you will come to a fork in the road. Bear left and you'll enter Clam Pass County Park, where you can spend a day at the beach for $3. Bear right and you'll come upon the rarefied Naples Grande Resort, where a day at the beach goes for around $300.

We took the $3 option and went to Clam

Pass, where we strolled the 0.75-mile wooden boardwalk that leads out to the beach. If you don't want to hike that distance, a tram will shuttle you there in six minutes. Kayaks, canoes, and sailboards are rented on-site. The 35-acre park includes a mangrove forest, a tidal bay humming with birds and wildlife, and a beach that runs for 0.6 mile. Best of all, it's never crowded.

4 NAPLES BEACH

Location: west ends of streets from 33rd Avenue South to Park Shore Drive in Naples
Parking/Fees: metered street parking; free for Collier County residents with a beach parking permit (obtainable at Naples City Hall)
Hours: 8 A.M.-11 P.M.
Facilities: none
Contact: Naples Community Services, 239/434-4687

5 NAPLES MUNICIPAL BEACH AND PIER

Location: 12th Avenue South at Gulf Shore Boulevard South in Naples
Parking/Fees: metered street and lot parking; free for Collier County residents with a beach parking permit (obtainable at Naples City Hall)
Hours: 24 hours
Facilities: concessions, restrooms, picnic tables, and showers
Contact: Naples Pier, 239/434-4696

6 LOWDERMILK PARK

Location: west end of Banyan Boulevard, at Gulf Shore Boulevard North in Naples
Parking/Fees: metered parking lot; free for Collier County residents with a beach parking permit (obtainable at Naples City Hall)
Hours: sunrise-sunset

Facilities: concessions, restrooms, picnic tables, and showers
Contact: Naples Community Services, 239/434-4687

7 GULF SHORE BOULEVARD NORTH ACCESS

Location: Gulf Shore Boulevard North near west end of Seagate Drive, in Naples
Parking/Fees: $3 entrance fee per vehicle; free for Collier County residents with a beach parking permit (obtainable at Naples City Hall)
Hours: sunrise-sunset
Facilities: none
Contact: Collier County Parks and Recreation Department, 239/353-0404

8 CLAM PASS COUNTY PARK

Location: From Tamiami Trail (U.S. 41), head west on Seagate Drive to intersection with Crayton Road; from here, follow signs to Clam Pass County Park
Parking/Fees: $3 entrance fee per vehicle; free for Collier County residents with a beach parking permit (obtainable at Naples City Hall)
Hours: sunrise-sunset
Facilities: concessions, restrooms, picnic tables, and showers
Contact: Collier County Parks and Recreation Department, 239/353-0404

RECREATION AND ATTRACTIONS

- **Bike/Skate Rentals:** Bike Route, 655 Tamiami Trail North (U.S. 41), Naples, 239/262-8373

- **Boat Cruise:** Naples Princess, 1001 10th Avenue South, Naples, 239/649-2275

- **Dive Shop:** Scubadventures, 971 Creech Road, Naples, 239/434-7477

- **Ecotourism:** Corkscrew Swamp Sanctuary, 375 Sanctuary Road, Naples, 239/348-9151

- **Fishing Charters:** A&B Charters, City Dock, 880 12th Avenue South, Naples, 239/263-8833
- **Marina:** Gulfshores Marina, 3470 Bayshore Drive, Naples, 239/774-0222
- **Pier:** Naples Municipal Beach and Fishing Pier, 25 12th Avenue South, Naples, 239/213-3062
- **Rainy-Day Attraction:** Conservancy Nature Center, 1450 Merrihue Drive, Naples, 239/262-0304
- **Shopping/Browsing:** 3rd Street South Association, 3rd Street between 14th Avenue South and Broad Avenue South, Naples, 239/649-6707
- **Surf Shop:** Board Room Surf Shop, 4910 Tamiami Trail North (U.S. 41), Naples, 239/649-4484
- **Vacation Rentals:** ResortQuest Naples/Marco Island,3761 North Tamiami Trail, Naples, 239/261-7577 or 888/239-5320

ACCOMMODATIONS

The **Naples Beach Hotel and Golf Club** (851 Gulf Shore Boulevard North, 239/261-2222, $$$) is a sprawling resort located near the center of town. Surprisingly, given that proximity, they occupy a significant expanse of land, on which is an 18-hole golf course (the oldest in Naples, dating to 1920), six Har-Tru tennis courts, and several buildings that offer different types of guest rooms. We stayed in the main building, a five-story salmon-colored beachside hotel.

The rooms are done in interesting color combinations. The walls in our room, for instance, were painted lavender. Instead of the typically banal pastel renderings of beach scenes on hotel walls, they'd hung stunning black-and-white photographs of nature scenes along the Gulf of Mexico by nationally renowned photographer Clyde Butcher (who lives in Fort Myers). A back door with a porthole opened onto a small balcony overlooking the gulf. The downstairs lobby is an enormous

hub for the bustling complex, where it's hard not to find something to do. Kids are especially well taken care of at the Naples Beach Hotel, which ranks among the top family resorts in the world. The resort offers creature comforts within friendly and human-scaled parameters.

The **Naples Grande Resort & Club** (475 Seagate Drive, 239/597-3232, $$$$) and the **Ritz-Carlton Naples** (280 Vanderbilt Beach Road, 239/598-3000, $$$$), by contrast, offer corporate plushing in a high-priced five-star environment. Room rates at the Ritz-Carlton start at $629 in winter at $209 in summer. The Naples Grande (formerly the Registry Resort & Club) is a relative bargain by comparison, with rates that begin at $429 in winter and $129 in summer.

To our jaded sensibilities, however, such grandiose erections miss the point of what it means to be at the beach. They inevitably represent (business)man's relationship to the natural world—which is to say distanced and arrogant—by brazenly overwhelming the landscape. We prefer downtown Naples or nearby Sanibel and Captiva Islands, where there's more of a willingness to blend in and harmonize.

If you're traveling on a budget, try the **Wellesley Inn** (1555 5th Avenue South, 239/793-4646, $$) or the **Best Western Naples Inn & Suites** (2329 9th Street North, 239/261-1148, $$). Both are modern, well kept, nicely landscaped, accessible to shopping areas, and half a mile or so from the beach. Moreover, you can take the money you save by staying here and eat like kings and queens in princely Naples.

COASTAL CUISINE

The **Dock at Crayton Cove** (842 12th Avenue South, 239/263-9940, $$$) overlooks the Bay of Naples from the historic City Dock. The relaxed air within starts with the two brothers who own and run the place. They amble around in faded Hawaiian shirts like two beach boys, but don't let their casual demeanor fool you. They are sticklers for quality, and they're constantly coming up with novel ways to fix favorite catches like grouper. There's sauteed banana-macadamia nut-crusted grouper and grouper fingers rolled in crushed pecans, lightly fried, and served with southern pepper jam and chile remoulade. There are also fresh catches prepared simply and served with key lime butter. Great grouper sandwiches at lunch, too!

The Dock at Crayton Cove has a sister operation, **Riverwalk at Tin City** (1200 5th Avenue South, 239/263-2734, $$$), housed in an converted processing plant at Old Marine Marketplace in Tin City, the former hub of Naples' fishing industry. The menu is more casually slanted, featuring items like grouper and chips and fried shrimp.

As one might expect in a moneyed community like Naples, there is a decided emphasis on fine dining. One of the more popular and long-lived spots serving high-end cuisine (and tab to match) is **St. George and the Dragon** (936 5th Avenue South, 239/262-6546, $$$$). It serves hearty surf-and-turf fare in a nautical-themed atmosphere (jackets required). And don't forget the fancy dining rooms at the Ritz-Carlton (the **Dining Room**, the **Grill**), Naples Grande Resort (**Brass Pelican, Lobby Restaurant,** and—coming in late 2006, the **Strip House**), and Naples Beach Hotel (**Broadwell's, HB's on the Gulf**).

If you're angling for fish in a more family- and pocketbook-friendly environment, **Kelly's Fish House Dining Room** (1302 5th Avenue South, 239/774-0494, $$$) has been serving seafood in its riverfront location since 1952. And for a good quick bite of a local specialty, head to **Gulf Coast Grouper and Chips** (338 Tamiami Trail North, 239/643-4577 and 11121 Health Park Boulevard, 239/594-0161, $).

NIGHTLIFE

If you want a good old-fashioned pub-crawl, Naples obliges with a passel of brew pubs. None of them is as rustic as they pretend to be, but the beer's cold and it beats the plastic revelry at dance clubs and hotel bars. The following serve lunch and dinner and have live music on weekends: **McCabe's Irish Pub & Grill** (699 5th Avenue South, 239/403-7170); **Old Naples Pub** (255 13th Avenue South, 239/649-8200); **Paddy Murphy's Irish Pub** (457 5th Avenue South, 239/649-5140); **Ridgeport Restaurant & Pub** (5425 Airport-Pulling Road, 239/591-1908); and **Village Pub** (4360 Gulf Shore Boulevard North, 239/262-2707).

Vanderbilt Beach

Vanderbilt Beach is in unincorporated north Collier County, an area that likes to link itself to Naples, obtaining cachet by proximity. Though the city of Naples ends just below Clam Pass County Park, the stretch of coastline from Vanderbilt Beach up to the Lee County line is referred to as "North Naples." Be forewarned that it is nothing like Naples. The roads are crowded; the place is a riot of construction; and gulf views are restricted to those who can get past the guard gates.

There is one similarity: With a population of 19,000, Vanderbilt Beach is almost as large as Naples. Lacking height restrictions, the buildings in Vanderbilt Beach are obscenely tall. The tallest resort hotels in the area, the Naples Grande and the Ritz-Carlton (see *Accommodations* in the *Naples* listing), actually lie *outside* Naples city limits. That doesn't prevent the latter from somewhat disingenuously referring to itself as the Ritz-Carlton Naples (shades of Florida's east coast, where the Ritz-Carlton Palm Beach is really in Manalapan).

For more information, contact the Naples Area Chamber of Commerce, 3620 Tamiami Trail North, Naples, FL 34103, 239/262-6376, www.napleschamber.org.

BEACHES

Great quantities of both money and sand have been pumped into Vanderbilt Beach, a locale where the erosion potential ranges from "high" to "extreme," according to coastal geologists. Beach access in the shadow of the Ritz-Carlton is about all you get at **Vanderbilt Beach County Park.** You'll get more beach and less development at nearby Delnor-Wiggins Pass State Park and Barefoot Beach Preserve.

VANDERBILT BEACH COUNTY PARK

Location: west end of Vanderbilt Beach Road (S.R. 862) in Vanderbilt Beach
Parking/Fees: $3 entrance fee per vehicle; free for Collier County residents with a beach parking permit from Naples City Hall
Hours: sunrise-sunset
Facilities: concessions, restrooms, picnic tables, and showers
Contact: Collier County Parks and Recreation Department, 239/353-0404

Delnor-Wiggins Pass State Park

One of Southwest Florida's most alluring beaches lies between Vanderbilt Beach and Wiggins Pass, where the Cocohatchee River empties into the Gulf of Mexico. This lushly vegetated park occupies the north end of a barrier island. Sea oats and cabbage palms line the open beach, while the island's backside is mangrove forest cross-cut by tidal creeks.

The fine-textured white-sand beach at Delnor-Wiggins Pass State Park can be accessed from five parking areas that run from the south entrance up to Wiggins Pass. Each lot has its own bathhouse. A boardwalk leads out to the pass, which is the only spot where fishing is permitted. There's also an observation tower from which one can survey all the natural splendor.

The park's only drawback has to do with the fact that swift currents at Wiggins Pass make

for hazardous swimming at that end. The fact that the park has the only lifeguard stand in Collier County is cause for both comfort and concern, so swim carefully.

For more information, contact Delnor-Wiggins Pass State Park, 1110 Gulf Shore Drive North, Naples, FL 34108, 239/597-6196, www.myflorida.com.

BEACHES

10 DELNOR-WIGGINS PASS STATE PARK

Location: north of Vanderbilt Beach at the west end of C.R. 846 (Bluebill Avenue/Immokalee Road)
Parking/Fees: $5 per car entrance fee
Hours: 8 A.M.-sunset
Facilities: lifeguards, restrooms, picnic tables, and showers
Contact: Delnor-Wiggins Pass State Park, 239/597-6196

Barefoot Beach County Park and Barefoot Beach Access

Barefoot Beach is a dual-entrance park consisting of a large preserve (south end) and a small access point (north end). Take it from us: **Barefoot Beach County Park** is where you want to be. To get there, you'll drive for a few miles through a stand of condos as thick as jungle bamboo, but it's worth putting up with speed bumps and signs warning you to stay on the main road. At the end of Lely Barefoot Road is the surprising payoff: 342 acres of dense tropical hammock, mangrove swamp, and open-sand beach.

Barefoot Beach County Park is the healthiest and most natural stretch of coast in mainland Collier County. The beach runs down to Wiggins Pass, a distance of 1.5 miles. A boardwalk meanders through the hammock and out to the beach. Facilities include a learning center, where naturalists lecture on such topics as shells, fossils, and artifacts. Exhibits on sea turtles and shorebirds underscore the need for habitat preservation. They also left us wondering how the gaping eyesore developments that we passed through to get here were allowed to happen. The protected gopher tortoise makes its home in the hammock.

Out on the beach, sea oats anchor low-lying dunes. Don't worry, they haven't been bulldozed away. The dunes are naturally smaller because wind and waves conditions don't favor dune formation on this part of the coast.

Barefoot Beach Access is little more than a parking lot and walkway to the beach at the end of Bonita Beach Road, on the Lee County line. Parking costs $3 at both the main park and its satellite access. The beach at the access is fine and the parking (100 spaces) is ample. However, your three sawbucks are better spent letting nature envelope you at Barefoot Beach County Park.

For more information, contact Barefoot Beach County Park, Lely Beach Boulevard, Naples, FL 33963, 239/353-0404, www.co.collier.fl.us/parks.

BEACHES

11 BAREFOOT BEACH COUNTY PARK

Location: From Bonita Beach Road, turn south on Lely Beach Boulevard and drive two miles into the park.
Parking/Fees: $3 entrance fee per vehicle; free for Collier County residents with a beach parking permit from Naples City Hall
Hours: 8 A.M.-sunset

Facilities: concessions, restrooms, picnic tables, showers, and visitors center
Contact: Collier County Parks and Recreation Department, 239/353-0404

12 BAREFOOT BEACH ACCESS

Location: From Bonita Beach Road, turn south on Lely Beach Boulevard and look for parking lot just inside the Collier County line.
Parking/Fees: $3 entrance fee per vehicle; free for Collier County residents with a beach parking permit from Naples City Hall
Hours: 8 A.M.-sunset
Facilities: none
Contact: Collier County Parks and Recreation Department, 239/353-0404

Bonita Beach

This coastal community is (pop. 13,500) is a microcosm of Fort Myers Beach, its accommodating neighbor to the north. For years Bonita Beach has been a sort of less harried and more out-of-the-way alternative, with its selling point being a more homey pace. However, the pace of growth and construction has accelerated markedly in this decade, and Bonita Beach is booming, for better or worse. It is close to, and closely allied with, the inland city of Bonita Springs (pop. 33,000). Bonita Beach and Bonita Springs have a combined population almost 50,000 residents. It is among the fastest-growing areas in the state, and looks to be the latest hot spot on the coast for the rich to plunder. Bonita Beach used to be a sweet nothing of a town. Now you see Tuscan-style villas and hacienda-type homes going up everywhere.

Still, Bonita Beach takes its tone from a county-wide ordinance we saw posted here: May 1–October 31 no one is allowed to shine lights on the beach, in deference to egg-laying sea turtles. They love their sea turtles. The *Fort Myers Beach Observer* runs a weekly

© PARKE PUTERBAUGH

Bonita Beach Park

"Turtle Count" (e.g., "21 nests, 13 hatched nests, 47 non-nesting emergencies"), compiled by community volunteers. One local women exclaimed that watching baby turtles emerging from nests "ranks up there next to my own kids being born." And it beats the heck out of watching other people's kids being born.

If you come to Bonita Beach, be aware that there are more than shelly gulf beaches to explore. The Audubon Society's Corkscrew Swamp Sanctuary lies due east (see the *Corkscrew Swamp Sanctuary* sidebar), and **Koreshan State Historic Site** (see the *Stranger Than Fiction: The Bizarre Tale of the Koreshans* sidebar) is worth a detour, too.

For more information, contact the Bonita Springs Area Chamber of Commerce, 25071 Chamber of Commerce Drive, Bonita Springs, FL 34135, 239/992-2943, www.bonitaspringschamber.com.

BEACHES

Lee County ranks among the most proactive in all of Florida in terms of providing public beach access to residents and visitors. We counted more than 10 "Lee County Beach Ac-

cess" signs along **Bonita Beach's** three-mile length. There are close to 50 of them throughout coastal Lee County, and that's in addition to the county's developed beach parks.

Accesses range from six-foot-wide easements between private properties to 50-foot walkways with parking spaces. They're identified by colorful pendants with coastal motifs, the semiotic equivalent of flagging you down and wishing you a nice day. Would that all counties were this generous and friendly! All of the accesses lead to the same wide, clean beach strand, of providing oases of seclusion in the middle of resort locales like Bonita Beach and Fort Myers Beach. Most accesses are close enough to motels, cafes, and condos to keep you from feeling like a shipwrecked South Sea adventurer, but far enough removed to at least let you daydream about the possibility.

From the south, the fun begins with **Bonita Beach Park,** at the west end of Bonita Beach Boulevard (just over the Collier County line, and almost touching that county's Barefoot Beach Access). The park has been upgraded with the addition of a picnic area, bathhouse, and volleyball courts. Parking is limited and costs $0.75 per hour. (Throughout Lee County, such parking fees are paid via a machine that's easier to use than an ATM; this looks to be the wave of the beach-parking future.) Doc's Beach House, right next door to Bonita Beach Park, is particularly inviting.

Two miles north of Bonita Beach Park is **Little Hickory Island Beach Park,** a small county park that shares the same long, semi-secluded beach.

13 BONITA BEACH PARK

Location: west end of Bonita Beach Boulevard

(C.R. 865) at 27950 Hickory Boulevard in Bonita Beach
Parking/Fees: metered parking lot (free if you display a beach sticker, obtainable for $35 at the Bonita Springs Recreation Center)
Hours: 8 A.M.-sunset
Facilities: concession, restrooms, picnic tables, and showers
Contact: Bonita Beach Park, 239/495-5811

14 BONITA BEACH PUBLIC ACCESSES

Location: 10 public accesses along Hickory Boulevard (C.R. 865) north of Bonita Beach Park

---

STRANGER THAN FICTION: THE BIZARRE TALE OF THE KORESHANS

From time to time, news erupts of a religious sect with a twisted world view and a charismatic leader who hoodwinks a bunch of lost souls into doing his bidding. Lest you think such scenarios are unique to our wayward modern age, you should pay a visit to the **Koreshan State Historic Site.** It is a spot of surpassingly strange historical interest on the Southwest Coast.

Here you'll find the reconstructed village of the Koreshans, who migrated here from Chicago in 1894. Led by one Dr. Cyrus Reed Teed, this sect believed that "the earth was a hollow sphere with the sun in the center and life existing on the inside surface of the sphere." They hoped to found a "new Jerusalem" that would eventually swell to eight million followers of "Koreshanity" (which rhymes with insanity). Ultimately, only 200 cultists showed up to practice Koreshanity at this swamp forest in remote Southwest Florida.

Teed believed all astronomical bodies were optical illusions. He rejected the scientific method, Copernican theory, atomic theory, and modern chemistry. Most of his followers were women whom he'd freed from the "desecration of maternity" in 1891 – a.k.a. the "Year of Koresh 52." Though the colony was purportedly celibate, rare were the times when Teed wasn't seen in public without a phalanx of lady friends.

He wrote that when he died, he'd rise to heaven and take his followers with him. Alas, when the prophecy didn't come to pass with his death in 1908, the county health officer ordered the sect to bury the putrefying corpse of their guru. Fittingly, Teed's grave was washed into the Gulf of Mexico during a 1921 hurricane. The last four surviving members of his sect deeded the land to the state in 1961.

Koreshan State Historic Site is located eight miles north of Bonita Springs, in the town of Estero. To get there, take I-75 to Exit 123 and proceed west on Corkscrew Road for two miles to the park entrance. Admission is $4 per car, and a guided tour of the Koreshan Settlement costs $2 for adults and $1 for children. There's a campground ($22 per night camping fee), and canoe rentals are available.

For more information, contact Koreshan State Historic Site, U.S. 41 at Corkscrew Road, Estero, FL 33928, 239/992-0311, www.floridastateparks.org.

Parking/Fees: free parking lots at several accesses; pedestrian easements only at others
Hours: 8 A.M.-sunset
Facilities: none
Contact: Lee County Department of Parks and Recreation, 239/461-7440

15 LITTLE HICKORY ISLAND BEACH PARK

Location: two miles north of Bonita Beach Boulevard on Hickory Boulevard (C.R. 865)
Parking/Fees: metered parking lot (no charge if you display a beach sticker; available for $35 at Bonita Springs Recreation Center)
Hours: 8 A.M.-sunset
Facilities: restrooms, picnic tables, and showers
Contact: Lee County Department of Parks and Recreation, 239/461-7440

ACCOMMODATIONS

Beach House Motel (26106 Hickory Boulevard, 239/992-2644, $) sits directly on the beach, just south of Little Hickory Island Beach Park. The units, from efficiencies and motel rooms to one- and two-bedroom apartments, are spread among eight detached two-story houses.

Across the road is the **Bonita Beach Resort Motel** (26395 Hickory Boulevard, 239/992-2137, $), a complex that stretches to the bay (actually, Hogue Channel). Bring your boat and tie up at the motel's dock. Neither place is fancy, but their very lack of pretension explains Bonita Beach's appeal—although the area is growing and changing, to our chagrin.

Will that appeal remain intact? We can't say for sure, but we suspect the worst. To rephrase Bob Dylan, something's happening in Bonita Beach, and neither we nor Mr. Jones know what it is. But here's a dead giveaway: Almost every other house along Hickory Boulevard (C.R. 865) has a "For Sale" sign staked out front.

Lovers Key State Park

Since Lovers Key, Inner Key, and Carl E. Johnson County Park were officially conjoined in

© PARKE PUTERBALGH

Lovers Key State Park

1998, Lovers Key State Park has swelled to 712 acres. It protects an ecosystem of beaches, estuaries, and wetlands that are recovering after invasion by nonnative species and disturbance by dredge-and-fill activities. You might see West Indian manatees, bottlenose dolphins, roseate spoonbills, marsh rabbits, and bald eagles at Lovers Key.

The entrance to Lovers Key is on Black Island, the barrier island just south of Estero Island (home of Fort Myers Beach). The $5 per vehicle entrance fee includes easy access via tram to the isolated beach at the park's south portion, on the far side of Oyster Bay, which is also an easy 10-minute hike from the parking lot. However you get there, it's a scenic, meditative trip ending at a wide beach with nature trails that wind back through the surrounding wetlands. Picnic pavilions large enough for family reunions are provided.

You can walk also out to the beach at the park's midsection. Two long wooden walkways cross mangrove-choked estuaries onto Inner Key and then Lovers Key, where you'll find a pearly-white, table-flat beach covered with shells and driftwood. Launches for motorized craft, canoes, and kayaks afford easy access to the Gulf of Mexico and Estero Bay. Anglers cast for trout and redfish and toss nets for mullet. The park's concession offers boat tours (sunset, dolphin-spotting, shelling) and fishing excursions. (For reservations, call 239/314-0110.) Canoes and kayaks are rented, too, so plan to take on the Great Caloosa Blue Wave Paddling Trail.

The beaches at Lovers Key are some of the wildest and most visually arresting on the Southwest Coast. We mentioned the locale while being interviewed for a Travel Channel special, *Florida's Best Beaches,* which we wound up narrating. No doubt influenced by the name "Lovers Key," the filmmakers declared it Florida's "most romantic beach." We tried to clear up the misconception, explaining it was a wilderness beach that probably got the name "Lovers Key" for the same grisly reason any number of Lovers Leaps were thus anointed.

We have no idea why it's called Lovers Key but can guarantee it's not because it's a popular or accommodating place to do the horizontal bop. Nevertheless, the filmmakers stacked the footage of Lovers Key with shapely bodies and groping couples. To us, this was the only dicey note in a TV special that has helped put this book on the map—not to mention reunite us with any number of lost acquaintances who called to say, "Hey, I just saw you guys on TV."

Even the overseers of Lovers Key State Park have been pleased with the outcome. On a recent visit, a clerk at the park's gift shop exclaimed, "A lot of people didn't even know we were here until that Travel Channel show. It's definitely brought people to the park."

The real appeal of Lovers Key is its seclusion. With its gray, skeletal driftwood formations and open horizon, the beaches here are superficially reminiscent of wilderness beaches in the Pacific Northwest. Bring your camera and prepare to spend at least half a day tramping the wild and secluded shoreline. It is, in short, a sanctuary for nature and for nature-loving humans, romantically inclined or not.

For more information, contact Lovers Key State Park, 8700 Estero Boulevard, Fort Myers Beach, FL 33931, 239/463-4588, www.myflorida.com.

BEACHES

16 LOVERS KEY STATE PARK

 BEST (

Location: entrance on Black Island, between Bonita Beach and Fort Myers Beach on C.R. 865

Parking/Fees: $5 entrance fee per vehicle with up to eight occupants; $3 for car and driver only; $1 per bicyclist or walker

Hours: 8 A.M.-sunset

Facilities: restrooms, picnic tables, and showers

Contact: Lovers Key State Park, 239/463-4588

Fort Myers Beach

Fort Myers Beach (pop. 7,000) is a rare specimen along the Southwest Coast: a beach town without affectations. The visual experience of arriving on Estero Island—the thin, seven-mile-long barrier island on which the town sits—recalls the best of the New Jersey shore, and we mean this as a compliment. That is to say, Fort Myers Beach is unpretentious and open to all, and this is part of its charm. From the south, you enter this long, beach-hugging community via Estero Boulevard. The more dramatic arrival is from the north, via San Carlos Boulevard and the dizzying Matanzas Skybridge, which air-drops you into a hustling, bustling epicenter of fun. Fort Myers Beach's assets include a long public pier, sun-baked mom-and-pop motels, condos painted various Life Savers-inspired hues, and low-key bungalows stretching for miles along Estero Boulevard (the main drag).

You will not find a wine-and-cheese crowd plotting their next golf game or shopping excursion. You will instead find jukeboxes blaring Southern rock and honky-tonk tunes, beer served in ice-cold pitchers, and sun-reddened revelers suddenly letting loose with rebel yells. These are the playful exclamations of folks "commonly referred to as having red body parts just below their heads," according to a local fact sheet. The editor of *Beach Bulletin,* a local publication, bragged that he'd written a song called "I Can't Love You 'Cause Your Dog Drank My Beer." Being Northern by birth but Southern by the grace of God (to quote a boast frequently plastered on pickup-truck bumpers), we felt right at home in Fort Myers Beach.

Like a happy-go-lucky nephew, Fort Myers Beach is seated at the gulfside banquet between the well-mannered great aunts of Naples and Sanibel-Captiva. Not that we don't revere those places, too, but sometimes we like to kick back and howl at the moon with the rest of the pack. You can do that at Fort Myers Beach, most of the time.

That's not to say life here is completely without contention. In 2006, battles rage about such issues as cars and the direction of development. Traffic seems to be the most pressing one. As a local official put it, "One two-lane

© PARKE PUTERBAUGH

Lynn Hall Memorial Park in Fort Myers

road is supposed to carry all our traffic off the island, and a four-lane road compressed into two lanes is supposed to bring all the traffic to our island." Happily, we can report that Fort Myers Beach hasn't lost any of its appeal even as this collective soul-searching continues and even in the wake of Hurricane Charley, which devastated the area in 2004.

Fort Myers Beach is nominally tethered to the much larger inland city of Fort Myers. With a population of 52,000, the latter city is nearly eight times as large. The beach community has traditionally championed what one local called "ticky-tackiness," while the big city to the east promotes itself as the "City of Palms." Fort Myers lines its streets with palms and its pockets with mounting revenue from suburban sprawl.

Fort Myers Beach, on the other hand, has styled itself as a combination family haven and redneck Riviera, happily going about its business of pleasing the occasionally uncouth yokels. Despite the airs put on by the City of Palms, the so-called yokels on the beach have shown way more foresight by instituting a height limit on buildings and making sure to keep the beaches of Estero Island, which are 75–100 yards wide at certain points, open and accessible.

Fort Myers Beach has spruced up Times Square, the popular grid of streets at the island's north end, where most of the big-time partying is done. Public access points have been shored up with attractive and clearly marked pennants, and the beaches are cleaned of seaweed and storm-generated scum, which can at times be an aesthetic problem. These are improvements worth making, and the town seems to improve without surrendering its soul.

The best news is that Fort Myers Beach remains an affordable place to which loyal vacationers return annually in droves. Admittedly, the traffic jams rank with the worst in any beach community, and the humid heat of summer could wilt the heartiest beachgoer. Indeed, some of the highest summertime temps anywhere in the country are posted here—check a weather page some time in July or August if you don't believe us. Nonetheless, there's much to like about Fort Myers Beach, and we hope they leave well enough alone.

For more information, contact the Fort Myers Beach Chamber of Commerce, 17200 San Carlos Boulevard, Fort Myers Beach, FL 33931, 239/454-7500 or 800/782-9283, www.fortmyersbeach.org.

BEACHES

The sandy beaches here are as wide open as the town's attitude toward visitors. Fort Myers Beach is the most popular vacation destination in Lee County, and it's easy to see why. Most of Estero Island's barrier beach is as spacious as it is inviting, enduring an occasional renourishment project to keep it that way. A series of **Fort Myers Beach Public Accesses,** extending from Flamingo Avenue north to Avenue A, are easy to find and use.

On our numerous drives along Estero Boulevard, we've counted 30 clearly marked signs and pennants over a five-mile span—a noble effort to provide public access. For the record, public beach accesses are provided at the ends of the following 30 streets, moving south to north: Flamingo, Gulf, Lanark, Aberdeen, Sterling, Dakota, Strandview, Gulfview, Bayview, Coconut, Hercules, Connecticut, Seaview, Pompano, Gulf Beach, Chapel, Mango, Delmar, Palm, Miramar, Avenue E, Alva, Avenue C, Avenue A, Canal, Belair Beach Club, Bay to Beach, Cane Palm, Casa Playa, and Vacation Villas. Some of the signs merely mark where an easement has been provided for pedestrians, while other signs sport a large "P," which designates free parking. Hurry, though, because spaces are limited.

Parking is by far the biggest hang-up in Fort Myers Beach, as traffic in peak season (Christmas–Easter) can become one long standstill on Estero Boulevard, the two-lane main drag. That's when the year-round population of 7,000 swells to over 40,000. Estero Island is liberally dotted with motels, and you're advised to park your car and walk or bike around town as much as possible. You can also catch a free ride with the LeeTrans shuttle service, whose buses sport eye-catching manatee logos on their sides. (Call 239/275-8726 for hours and routes.)

The beach is wide in most places, except for those older houses or lodgings with seawalls in front of them. Intended to hold the beach in place, these walls and groins actually create the opposite effect. In fact, the beaches on either side of the seawalls are wider. The sand is fine-textured and powdery near the dunes and hard-packed by the water. While the blinding white sand might seem inviting to anyone with a beach blanket, a cabana or lounge chair will make your hours on the beach far more comfortable. Bring your own or rent them on the beach.

At various unpredictable times of year, huge storms out in the gulf churn up seaweed and microscopic vegetation that accumulates on-shore in spongy red-brown masses, creating an olfactory stench. The rich bird life along Estero Island digs it, though, as it attracts bite-sized sea critters. We spent an entire morning enjoying the daredevil aerial show provided by gulls and pelicans, as well as the more dignified ballet of the herons and ibiscs, some of which are the size of wild turkeys. The former dive-bomb the water and disappear from view, only to resurface seconds later with some squirming varmint in their beaks. The latter stand still until they delicately duck their big bills into the water and pull out with a piece of gourmet sushi.

The beach along Estero Island invites strolling. Numerous benches along the way bear the message "Enjoy and Share." Though it's impossible to prove or refute, local boosters proclaim Fort Myers Beach to be "the world's safest beach." It is safe, with a very gradual drop-off and few waves.

While the beach is virtually unbroken along the entire length of Estero Island, various segments have names and boundaries. The area by the public pier is called **Lynn Hall Memorial Park.** It's a wonderful in-town beach park with a flat beach and minuscule waves. The park includes some nicely land-scaped grounds to the north, dotted with benches, picnic tables, and playground equipment. A block away are the rollicking shops and pubs of Times Square. The centerpiece, Fort Myers Beach Pier—informally known as Pelican Pier—is a pleasantly ramshackle affair that is indeed popular with pelicans. They stand around so stiffly on the ledges that you think they're wooden carvings. Signs provide step-by-step instructions on how to remove a fish hook from a pelican that's been accidentally snagged. If you come here, be aware that the parking meters are closely monitored by the gendarmes.

Just south of the pier is the most popular section of Fort Myers Beach. Along what's called Motel Row, the sociable beach is lined with volleyball nets, blaring radios, and the occasional surfer, with plenty of mingling between members of the opposite sex. People appear desirous and happy to make one another's acquaintance. Just for the record, it sometimes seems as if there's an unofficial contest in progress to see who can wear the smallest bikini in public.

At the northern tip of Estero Island, where Estero Boulevard dead-ends at a traffic circle, is **Bowditch Point Regional Park.** This inviting 17-acre park is inaccessible to cars, with only a few parking spaces provided for the handicapped. No problem, because you can walk up from the pier, ride a bike (bike racks are provided), or catch the free LeeTrans shuttle bus from Main Street Park in Fort Myers Beach. Picnic tables and grills are provided, and you'll also find a snack bar (Flip-Flops Café). A wide boardwalk fringed by palm trees leads out to the narrow beach, which becomes anorexically thin at its tip. From here you can see all the way over to Sanibel—an exciting vista unblemished by high-rises. Again, we'll mention the heat at Fort Myers Beach. The heat index hit 105°F when we last made our summertime traipse through the area, and we were told that had been about average.

17 FORT MYERS BEACH PUBLIC ACCESSES

Location: numerous beach access points along Estero Boulevard between Flamingo Avenue and Avenue A in Fort Myers Beach
Parking/Fees: metered or pay parking lots
Hours: 24 hours
Facilities: none
Contact: Lee County Department of Parks and Recreation, 239/461-7400

18 LYNN HALL MEMORIAL PARK

Location: 950 Estero Boulevard, beside Fort Myers Beach Pier
Parking/Fees: metered parking lot
Hours: 7 A.M.-10 P.M. (gates open 24 hours)
Facilities: concessions, restrooms, picnic tables, and showers
Contact: Lynn Hall Memorial Park, 239/463-1116

19 BOWDITCH POINT REGIONAL PARK

Location: 50 Estero Boulevard, at north end of Estero Island, above Fort Myers Beach
Parking/Fees: free parking lot at Main Street Park in Fort Myers Beach. Free trolley service from Main Street Park to Bowditch Point Regional Park.
Hours: 8:30 A.M.-sunset
Facilities: restrooms, picnic tables, and showers
Contact: Bowditch Regional Park, 239/463-1116

RECREATION AND ATTRACTIONS

- **Bike/Skate Rental:** Fun Rentals, 1901 Estero Boulevard, Fort Myers Beach, 239/463-8844

- **Boat Cruise:** Adventures in Paradise, Port Sanibel Marina, 14341 Port Comfort Road, Fort Myers, 239/472-8443
- **Dive Shop:** Seahorse Scuba, 15600 San Carlos Boulevard #19, Fort Myers Beach, 239/454-3111
- **Ecotourism:** Lovers Key State Park, 8700 Estero Boulevard, Fort Myers Beach, 239/463-4588
- **Fishing Charters:** Fort Myers Beach Fishing Charters, 414 Crescent Street, Fort Myers Beach, 239/463-6442
- **Marina:** Fort Myers Beach Marina, 703 Fisherman's Wharf, Fort Myers Beach, 239/463-9552
- **Pier:** Fort Myers Beach Pier (a.k.a. Pelican Pier), Estero Boulevard at San Carlos Boulevard, Fort Myers Beach, 239/765-9700
- **Rainy-Day Attraction:** Marine Science Center, Ostego Bay Foundation, 718 Fisherman's Wharf, Fort Myers Beach, 239/765-8101
- **Shopping/Browsing:** Times Square, Estero Boulevard at San Carlos Boulevard, Fort Myers Beach
- **Surf Shop:** West Coast Surf Shop, 1035 Estero Boulevard, Fort Myers Beach, 239/463-1989
- **Vacation Rentals:** Bluebill Vacation Properties, 2670 Estero Boulevard, Fort Myers Beach, 239/463-1141

ACCOMMODATIONS

A prolonged fight in the mid-1990s over a multistory convention center and hotel was called "the last straw" by a local activist. Well, the last straw was drawn, and the activists lost. The 12-story **DiamondHead Beach Resort** (2000 Estero Boulevard, 239/765-7654, $$$) is a vacation budget-buster in otherwise affordable Fort Myers Beach. Beachfront rooms here cost $200–330 a night, depending on time of year. (Christmas–Easter is the high season.) It's quite the tony resort, but the concept of "refined luxury," with prices to match, seems a little out of place here. It is rather exaggeratedly called "the anchor for the Main Street District."

For unpretentious seaside hideaways, you can do no better than the **Outrigger Beach Resort** (6200 Estero Boulevard, 239/463-3131, $$). The Outrigger charges family-friendly rates without cutting corners. This four-story, 144-unit motel complex reaches out toward the beach as if trying to embrace the sunset. For once the sign in front of a motel ("Look No Further. We Have the Best Beach!") doesn't lie. The beach just beyond the enormous sun deck is the widest on Estero Island, the sand powdery and white, and the water safe and warm. It is also far enough south of the pier to be considered off the beaten track.

The Outrigger has been serving unmatched hospitality since 1964. The staff is down-home friendly, the pace is relaxed, and many guests return for the same week (or weeks) each year. The tiki bar beside the pool is the best perch in town from which to watch sunset. Even locals come to the Outrigger at day's end to partake of the friendly patter. When the red disc makes its final plunge, someone bleats a long, sustained note on a conch shell, and the gathered throng applauds. The Thursday evening wine-and-cheese social is legendary among regular guests. Both a cafe and restaurant are on the premises, but if you want to cook your own meals, the homey rooms come with stocked kitchens and dinnerware for five.

Two excellent Best Westerns are located at the northern end of this island's ample beach. The **Best Western Beach Resort** (684 Estero Boulevard, 239/463-6000, $$$) is a five-story motel with a 450-foot beach. Every room is beachfront, with a balcony, kitchenette, and continental breakfast. Guests are within easy strolling distance of the pier and the bars and restaurants of Times Square. The **Best Western Pink Shell Beach Resort** (275 Estero Boulevard, 239/463-6181, $$$$) covers 12 palm-strewn acres and 1,500 feet of white-sand beach. It offers three pools, tennis, volleyball, shuffleboard, watersports, boat rentals, an on-site spa, and supervised children's activities. Plus, it offers easy access to the beach at Bowditch Point Regional Park.

COASTAL CUISINE

A longtime local resident claims the biggest problem with the Fort Myers Beach dining scene is consistency. One place we've heard nary a negative word about is **Charley Roadhouse Grill** (6241 Estero Boulevard, 239/765-4800, $$$). It looks like an old, nondescript steak house from the outside, but the interior is brightened by numerous saltwater aquariums, a garden atmosphere, and a seafood-heavy menu. Charley's has been in business for over 30 years, and the parking lot is always full at dinnertime.

Two waterfront restaurants—**Snug Harbor** (1131 1st Street, 239/463-4343, $$) and the **Gulfshore Grill** (1270 Estero Boulevard, 239/765-5440, $$—get thumbs-up for their fresh local seafood. The former, a popular spot for 35 years, has moved to a new location next to the Matanzas Skybridge. Both overlook the water, and you might even see dolphins playing outside the windows. Finally, **Smokin' Oyster Brewery** (340 Old San Carlos Boulevard, 239/463-3474, $$)— "S.O.B.," for short—has a popular raw bar with a big selection.

NIGHTLIFE

For those who dig draft beer, rowdy crowds, and loud jukeboxes, Times Square is the place to go. The most appealing places are **Pete's Time Out** (1005 Estero Boulevard, 239/463-5900) and **Top O' Mast Lounge** (1028 Estero Boulevard, 239/463-9424).

The **Tiki Bar** at the Outrigger Beach Resort (6200 Estero Boulevard, 239/463-3131) attracts a friendly crowd at sunset. Meanwhile, the **Junkanoo On the Beach** (3040 Estero Boulevard, 239/463-6139) kicks off its "party that never ends" with a happy hour that begins at 2 P.M.!

It did not escape our notice that a large contingent of Europeans have found Fort Myers Beach to their liking. This makes sense, as it's the most affordable place on the Southwest Coast. Germans flock to a unique nightspot called **Dusseldorf's on the Beach** (1113 Estero Boulevard, 239/463-5251). This cozy *Biergarten* stocks over 120 imported beers, including eight on tap. The place has a sense of humor, as its neon sign depicts a Bavarian holding a surfboard. Live polka music is offered Wednesday, Friday, and Saturdays. Roll out the barrel!

Bunch Beach

Few tourists find their way to this bay beach, but the road to it gets lined with locals' vehicles on weekends. Located between Estero and Sanibel Islands, there's nothing more to Bunch Beach than a boat launch and a few trash cans that collect beer bottles and picnic remains. Sociable locals bring their dogs, boats, boom boxes, fishing poles, and volleyball nets, then set up and have a good time. If you live in the area, it's a viable alternative to the parking

SINGING THE TOLL BRIDGE BLUES ON SANIBEL ISLAND

It now costs $6 to cross the bridge onto Sanibel Island. The exorbitant hike from $3 to $6 was implemented in 2004. That is a lot of money to pay, and if you go to and from the mainland twice a day during a week's vacation, you will hand over $84 to the toll collectors. Even the annual pass, offering unlimited access for a year, is no bargain at $600. Commuters into New York City pay less to enter Manhattan via its bridges and tunnels. So what gives?

The hike in rates was the end result of a contentious lawsuit between the City of Sanibel and Lee County. It has been a hot topic of conversation down here in recent years. The imbroglio began when inspectors discovered cracks in one of the bridges. It came down to repairing and rebuilding (Sanibel's wish) vs. building a whole new causeway (Lee County). The county won the suit and their new causeway will be open in stages in 2006 and 2007, an act that islanders called "paving paradise." Unmoved off-islanders derisively refer to Sanibel Island as "Sanctuary Island."

Also, you can blame the county, not the island, for the steep toll increase. All the bridge-toll money that had been collected over the years went into county coffers. The funds were supposed to be earmarked for bridge and causeway maintenance, but the county spent it on other things. When funds were needed to mend the bridge, none was available.

Sanibel sued, and the county won. The Lee County commissioners "punished" the island – in the words of Sanibel residents we spoke to – for its insubordination by doubling the toll. So far, the punishment has worked, albeit to no one's benefit. Visitor traffic is down since the toll was hiked – a fact bemoaned by local restaurant and shop owners – and it's hurt folks who work on Sanibel but live off-island. Crossings in March 2005 were down 37,000 from the previous year.

"You know politicians," sighed one resident. "They'll do whatever they think they can get away with." Meanwhile, the cost of the project continues to soar, reaching an estimated $134 million in December 2005.

Writing in the Fort Myers *News-Press*, guest editorialist Steve Brown put the imbroglio in perspective: "Lee County has dealt in bad faith with the city of Sanibel over the causeway, and innocent people are suffering the consequences. This is a call for everyone's help in convincing Lee County commissioners to lower unconscionable toll increases, take immediate action to ensure that the bridge is safe for travelers, and return the money rightfully owed to Sanibel."

problems in Fort Myers Beach and the pricey toll bridge to Sanibel Island.

BEACHES

20 BUNCH BEACH

Location: From Fort Myers Beach, proceed north on San Carlos Road (C.R. 865), then west on Summerlin Road (C.R. 869); turn south on John Morris Road and follow to beach.
Parking/Fees: free parking lot
Hours: 8 A.M.-sunset
Facilities: none
Contact: Lee County Department of Parks and Recreation, 239/461-7440

BEST Sanibel Island and J. N. "Ding" Darling National Wildlife Refuge

If American beaches were awarded the equivalent of Oscars, Sanibel Island's trophy case would be lined with gold statuettes in the following categories: Best Beach for Shelling, Most Sensibly Developed Beach, and Best Supporting Estuary. It would also be nominated for Best Special Effects (those sunsets!) and Best Soundtrack. In addition to enchanting bird and nature sounds, the latter would surely include Billy Joel's "I Love You Just the Way You Are," which could be Sanibel's theme song.

The reason for Sanibel Island's success is that the beach, island, and back bay are given starring roles. For the most part, humans respectfully maintain a low profile. Nature rules—or is at least treated as an equal—and restaurants, stores, and strip malls blend in with rather than obliterate the environment. There are no garish signs lunging for the consumer jugular. Development has been held in

check on Sanibel Island (pop. 6,064) through a series of ordinances and regulations that limit building heights to three stories and impose minimum setbacks from the water's edge. Building permits are decided on the merits, rather than simply rubber-stamped.

All of this oversight is still not enough, some of Sanibel's hard-liners will tell you. One of them put it like this: "If you saw what Sanibel Island looked like 20 years ago compared with the way it is today, you'd say it's gone to hell in a handbag. At the same time, when you look at the rest of Florida's coastline, it seems like a fairly idyllic place to be."

Indeed, it is. The island is entered via a series of causeways, leaving the bustling mainland world behind. It's built low to the ground, which gives trees a distinct height advantage. The island has 25 miles of bike trails—asphalt pathways for cyclists, skaters, joggers, and walkers that parallel the main roads. A free trolley system and cheap bike rentals mean you can put the car keys away, if you wish. This can be a real boon to those visiting during the high season, Christmas–Easter, when roads get choked to capacity.

Sanibel's first line of defense against traffic is its toll bridge. As motorists approach the island via the Sanibel Causeway, they must stop to pay a hefty toll—doubled to $6 in 2004—before crossing the first of three bridges. Even though the bridges were long paid for, the toll was kept in place to minimize the number of cars crowding onto the island. We've always though of it as a cover charge, but instead of getting into a South Beach dance club, you're allowed onto an island.

Sanibel's history dates back to around 500 B.C., when Caloosa Indians lived on the island. Spanish conquistadors came in the 1500s. Homesteaders farmed tomatoes, citrus, and coconuts in the 1800s. The Sanibel Lighthouse was built in 1884 to help provide safe passage to mainland ports. Ferries began shuttling the well-to-do over to the island enclave in the 1920s. One regular visitor was political cartoonist Jay "Ding" Darling, who displayed

SEASHELLOLOGY 101

Sanibel and its neighboring islands (Captiva, North Captiva, Cayo Costa) are recognized as the best shell-gathering spots in the United States. Shells wash ashore on these islands in incomprehensible mounds that accumulate on the beach, causing otherwise sane people to walk around for hours in a hunched-over position known as the "Sanibel stoop." The reason is that Sanibel extends westward into the Gulf of Mexico as a scoop to haul in a bounty of shells. In addition, the absence of inshore reefs allows shells to roll in with the tides.

Shells are deposited by waves and tide in parallel strips, each formed in the unending physical dialogue between land and water. There are bands for recent high and low tides. They're also at the mean high tide line, at lines marking spring tides (the highest high tides) and, at the very back of the beach. It's easier to walk between bands than on them, although these shell heaps make good benches for sunset watching.

Seashells are the calcified homes of soft-bodied mollusks, formed by secreting a liquid that hardens around them. Some 275 shell types wash ashore on Sanibel Island. Common finds include lightning whelks, the Florida horse conch (the state shell), cockles, coquinas, cones, pens, olives, augurs, tulip mussels, top shells, scallops, and sand dollars. Harder-to-find specimens are the Sanibel drillia, yellow Florida spiny jewel boxes, and a few kinds of tellins, one found in sand (great tellin), another on mudflats (rose petal tellin). The Holy Grail for Sanibel shell collectors is the lovely, speckled junonia, which is extremely rare. Whoever finds one gets his or her picture in the local paper.

Given Sanibel's seashell obsession, it's fitting that the only museum in the U.S. devoted exclusively to shells is on the island. Nearly a third of the 10,000 kinds of shells that have been identified worldwide are on display at the **Bailey-Matthews Shell Museum,** which opened in 1995.

If you do go shell-collecting on Sanibel or the adjacent islands, never take a live specimen. If a shell moves or appears to be occupied, leave it alone. Here is the official Sheller's Code. Repeat with one hand over your heart while the other holds a conch shell aloft:

"We realize that mollusks are part of our precious national wildlife resources, therefore

1. We will make every effort to protect and preserve them, not only for our own future enjoyment but for the benefit of generations to come;

2. We will leave every shelling spot as undisturbed as possible;

3. We will leave behind damaged and juvenile specimens so that they will live to multiply;

4. We will not collect live egg cases unless they are to be used for scientific study;

5. We will never 'clean out' a colony of shells;

6. We will practice and promote these conservation rules in every way possible."

The Bailey-Matthews Shell Museum is open 10 A.M.–4 P.M., Tuesday–Sunday. Admission is $7 for adults, $4 for children 5-16, and free for kids under five. For more information, contact Bailey-Matthews Shell Museum, 3075 Sanibel-Captiva Road, 239/395-2233.

an uncommon environmental awareness in his work for the time. Darling argued for the island's preservation, and the 5,000-acre National Wildlife Refuge on Sanibel's north side bears his name (more on this later).

The floodgates opened when the three-mile causeway linking Sanibel to the mainland opened in 1963. However, the island's slow-growth philosophy was already in place, and the worst environmental affronts have been held at bay, so to speak. About half the island's acreage is preserved. Showy hibiscus, feathery casuarinas, swaying coconut palms, and fragrant citrus blossoms are visible features of the Sanibel landscape, while businesses and shopping centers along Periwinkle Way are semi-hidden or at least modestly understated.

Environmental blight is less a concern on Sanibel Island than traffic tie-ups. If you can minimize your use of the automobile—getting around on foot or bicycle, riding trolleys, or just staying on property—your visit to Sanibel Island will be more enjoyable. The best piece of advice we can give is this: To maximize the Sanibel-Captiva experience, take it easy and let nature do all the heavy lifting.

Incidentally, Sanibel and Captiva Islands were joined years ago when Blind Pass closed up. Hurricane Charley breached Blind Pass temporarily (and also opened a new pass on North Captiva Island, which was split in two). You really can't speak of Sanibel without mentioning Captiva Island, and even North Captiva Island, in the same breath. All three are part of the Charlotte Barrier Chain, which has historically ranged between five and eight islands, depending on how many passes have opened or closed. The highest elevation on any of the islands is 14 feet. Even the low-lying Florida Keys have a higher point than that.

Here's what you'll find on Sanibel Island. Right after the causeway, there's a chamber of commerce stocked with the latest literature and helpful attendants. The causeway road soon meets Periwinkle Way, along which most of the island's restaurants and shopping centers are located. A left turn on Periwinkle will carry you out to the island's quiet east end, home to the Sanibel Lighthouse, Lighthouse Beach Park, and a T-shaped public pier. Turn right and you'll enter the commercial heart of Sanibel Island.

Continue in this direction, and Periwinkle Way will end at Tarpon Bay Road. A left turn on Tarpon Bay Road will lead to Gulf Drive, whose "East," "West," and "Middle" portions delineate the island's beach-facing south side, where most of the hotels, motels, resorts, and rental properties are located. Turn right on Tarpon Bay Road and you'll soon hook up with Sanibel-Captiva Road ("San-Cap," in local parlance), which runs along the bay side of the island. Tarpon Bay Road leads out to J.N. "Ding" Darling National Wildlife Refuge and over to Captiva Island.

J. N. "Ding" Darling National Wildlife Refuge (hereafter referred to as "Ding Darling") is the centerpiece of Sanibel Island with more than 6,000 wet and wild acres of open water, mangrove swamps, and brackish and freshwater marshes. The animal life seems positively giddy to have so much pristine habitat. They squawk and shout their approval all over the refuge till you think you've landed in nature's equivalent of a loony bin. But that's nature in the raw: howling, ecstatic, exclamatory. There's a lot of it on display at Ding Darling.

Ironically, the entire habitat was nearly destroyed by human recklessness during the 19th century and the first half of the 20th century. Restoration began with its establishment as a refuge in 1945. The refuge was nearly destroyed again when Hurricane Charley roared ashore on August 13, 2004. As much as 70 percent of the mangrove coverage was lost, and concerns were raised that the nesting of colonial birds might be impacted. Only time will tell just how extensive the impacts will be.

Facilities on the refuge include a visitors center, a boardwalk trail, two observation towers, alligator-viewing platforms, canoe trail, and five-mile wildlife drive. The latter can be driven, biked, hiked, or toured via tram.

We came on rented bikes, taking the dirt loop slowly to savor every sighting. Early morning and late afternoon are prime times for wildlife sightings, offering optimum lighting for photography, too. Inventories have logged 291 bird species on the refuge. We saw long-necked black anhingas and pink-feathered roseate spoonbills; graceful white egrets and ibises stalking the shallows on spindly legs; a red-shouldered hawk peering down pensively from a limb. We saw, and saw some more, and you should see, too.

We also paddled the refuge, taking the two-hour trail tour along a tidal creek. Along the way we learned about the estuarine ecosystem from an informed guide. We also had some wet, messy fun trying to master the technical points of maneuvering a two-person kayak. We bounced off mangrove prop roots, embankments, oyster reefs, and whatever other obstructions lay in our path. All part of the learning curve, and all in a day's play.

The refuge is open daily (except Friday) 7:30 A.M.–sunset. Admission is $5 per vehicle. A $12 site-specific pass provides a year's admission into the refuge. A $15 Duck Stamp is good for entry into any National Wildlife Refuge from July 1 through the following June 30.

The park concessioner for equipment rentals and guided tours is **Tarpon Bay Explorers** (900 Tarpon Bay Road, 239/472-8900). It's a one-stop outfitter of bikes, canoes, kayaks, and fishing equipment. You can rent a kayak or canoe ($20 for two hours) and explore the refuge on your own or take a guided tour. These include a daily 10:30 A.M. kayak trail tour ($30 for adults, $15 for kids) and a 4:30 P.M. sunset rookery paddle ($40 for adults, $25 for kids) on Monday, Wednesday, and Friday. Tram tours of the refuge depart daily (except Friday) at 10:30 A.M. and 2:00 P.M. and cost $10 for adults and $7 for kids.

For more information on Ding Darling, contact J. N. "Ding" Darling National Wildlife Refuge, 1 Wildlife Drive, Sanibel, FL 33957, 239/472-1100, www.fws.gov/dingdarling. Or, for more information on Sanibel

Island, contact the Sanibel-Captiva Islands Chamber of Commerce, 1159 Causeway Road, P.O. Box 166, Sanibel, FL 33957, 239/472-1080, www.sanibel-captiva.org.

BEACHES

The lovely beaches of Sanibel Island run for 14 miles along its southern face. Shelling is a big draw, with Sanibel having been deemed the best site for shell collecting in America and third best in the world (see the *Seashellology 101* sidebar). The preponderance of shelly material—from wholly preserved specimens to jagged shell fragments—makes walking barefoot on the beach uncomfortable. But if you wear shoes, you'll wind up crushing precious little shells with every step. The solution is to buy a pair of soft-soled, slipper-type "shelling shoes," which are carried by local retailers. Remember that you must leave all shells that still have living creatures inside.

Sunset on Sanibel Island is cause for celebration, though it's observed with less ritual than on Key West. People informally assemble on the beach. Some congregate up at Captiva Island's east end, just over the bridge from Sanibel. Shore birds turn out to observe the setting sun, too. Long lines of them assemble at the surf's edge, staring at the horizon as the sun slips into the gulf. Sundown colors the sky with fiery corals and electric blue-greens—a gorgeous solar spectacle unique to the skies of South Florida.

If you're booked at a hotel or resort along Gulf Drive, you will have instant beach access at your back door. If not, four public beaches are scattered along Sanibel Island's gulf side. They generally improve, in terms of beach quality and isolation, from east to west. At the eastern tip is **Lighthouse Beach Park,** home of Sanibel Lighthouse (a.k.a. Point Ybel Light), a refurbished concrete fishing pier, and Lighthouse Beach.

The city of Sanibel is currently negotiating with the U.S. Coast Guard to acquire the lighthouse, a unique rusted metal structure that looks more like the skeletal outline of a

© PARKE PUTERBAUGH

Sanibel Lighthouse at Lighthouse Beach Park, Sanibel Island

lighthouse. At Lighthouse Beach, there's also the historic Oil House (ca. 1899). A boardwalk crosses healthy dunes to the beach. Currents at this end of the island are strong, so it's not the best beach for swimming. The absence of lifeguards means you're best advised to swim elsewhere if you're got children in tow. Also, the $2 per hour parking fee is unusually steep.

The mid-island beach parks, **Gulfside City Park** and **Tarpon Bay Road Beach** are more conveniently situated. The latter is large, busy, and popular, and its size makes it the likeliest spot to nab a parking space.

Up at the west end is **Bowman's Beach,** the most remote of Sanibel's public beaches. It is also the best for shell collecting and sunset watching. Bowman's Beach is impressively wide along the accreting spit at Sanibel's west end. You're in for an altogether pleasant hike of about a quarter-mile from the parking lot to the gulf. En route, you'll pass through a succession of zones: beach grasses and shrubs, pines, wetlands, a canal, picnic tables shaded by sea grapes and pines, and finally the open beach. You'll see plenty of birds and subtropi-

cal fauna. The sand is soft and fine until you near the surf zone, where the sloping beach is full of whole shells and fragments.

Parking at these three gulf beaches is a more reasonable $0.75 an hour. Money is inserted in a machine that issues a sticker that must be displayed on the vehicle's dashboard. Make certain to "pay and display," because vigilant enforcement personnel will ticket you if time expires. Trust us on this point: we saw parking enforcement cops lying in wait for those who neglected to pay up. It's very much worth it, as Bowman's Beach is among the top beaches in Florida.

There's also a bayside beach on Sanibel's north shore. **Dixie Beach** lies at the end of Dixie Beach Road, off Periwinkle Way, in the middle of a subdivision. There's not much beach and little reason to come here. Also, beachside parks are found on the **Causeway Islands,** the two small islands crossed en route to Sanibel. Windsurfers and anglers flock to these palm-shaded islands.

21 CAUSEWAY ISLANDS

Location: along Sanibel Causeway (S.R. 867) between the mainland and Sanibel Island
Parking/Fees: free parking lots
Hours: sunrise-sunset
Facilities: restrooms, picnic tables, and showers
Contact: City of Sanibel Parks and Recreation Department, 239/472-9075

22 DIXIE BEACH

Location: On Sanibel Island, follow Periwinkle Way to Lindrin Road, turn right and continue for three miles to Dixie Beach Road. Turn right and follow for one mile to beach.
Parking/Fees: A (resident) or B (nonresident) parking permit required; these can be purchased at the Sanibel Police Department
Hours: sunrise-sunset
Facilities: picnic tables

Contact: City of Sanibel Parks and Recreation Department, 239/472-9075

23 LIGHTHOUSE BEACH PARK

Location: east end of Periwinkle Way at the tip of Sanibel Island
Parking/Fees: metered parking lot
Hours: sunrise–sunset
Facilities: concessions, restrooms, and picnic tables
Contact: City of Sanibel Parks and Recreation Department, 239/472-9075

24 GULFSIDE CITY PARK (A.K.A. ALGIERS BEACH)

Location: from Sanibel Island, take Periwinkle Way to Casa Ybel Road; follow to Algiers and turn south till it ends at Middle Gulf Drive
Parking/Fees: metered parking lot
Hours: sunrise–sunset
Facilities: restrooms and picnic tables
Contact: City of Sanibel Parks and Recreation Department, 239/472-9075

25 TARPON BAY ROAD BEACH

Location: Tarpon Bay Road at West Gulf Drive on Sanibel Island
Hours: sunrise–sunset
Parking/Fees: metered parking lot
Facilities: restrooms and picnic tables
Contact: City of Sanibel Parks and Recreation Department, 239/472-9075

26 BOWMAN'S BEACH

BEST (

Location: from Sanibel Island, proceed north on Sanibel-Captiva Road to Bowman's Beach Road, then turn south and follow to beach.

Parking/Fees: metered parking lot
Hours: sunrise–sunset
Facilities: restrooms, picnic tables, and showers
Contact: City of Sanibel Parks and Recreation Department, 239/472-9075

RECREATION AND ATTRACTIONS

- **Bike/Skate Rentals:** Finnimore's Cycle Shop, 2353 Periwinkle Way, Sanibel Island, 239/472-5577; Billy's Rentals, 1470 Periwinkle Way, Sanibel Island, 239/472-5248

- **Boat Cruise:** Captiva Cruises, McCarthy's Marina, 11401 Andy Rosse Lane, Captiva Island, 239/472-5300

- **Ecotourism:** Tarpon Bay Explorers, 900 Tarpon Bay Road, Sanibel Island, 239/472-8900

- **Fishing Charters:** Santiva Saltwater Fishing Team, 6211 Starling Way, Captiva Island, 239/472-1779

- **Lighthouse:** Sanibel Lighthouse, Lighthouse Beach Park, Periwinkle Way (east end), Sanibel Island, 239/472-6397

- **Marina:** Sanibel Marina, 634 North Yachtsman Drive, Sanibel Island, 239/472-2723; 'Tween Waters Marina, 15951 Captiva Drive, Captiva, 239/472-0249

- **Pier:** Sanibel Pier, Lighthouse Beach Park, Periwinkle Way (east end), Sanibel Island, 239/472-6397

- **Rainy-Day Attraction:** Bailey-Matthews Shell Museum, 3075 Sanibel-Captiva Road, Sanibel Island, 239/395-2233; Sanibel Historical Village & Museum, 950 Dunlop Road, Sanibel Island, 239/472-4648

- **Shopping/Browsing:** Periwinkle Place, 2075 Periwinkle Way, Sanibel Island, 239/472-2230

- **Surf Shop:** Sanibel Surf Shop, 1700 Periwinkle Way, Sanibel Island, 239/472-8185; Yolo Watersports/Jim's Rental's, 11534 Andy Rosse Lane, Captiva Island, 239/472-9656

- **Vacation Rentals:** Royal Shell Vacations, 1200 Periwinkle Way, Sanibel Island,

239/472-9111; Island Vacations of Sanibel and Captiva, 1101 Periwinkle Way, Sanibel Island, 239/472-7277

ACCOMMODATIONS

Hotels and resorts line Gulf Drive. The feeling is Old Florida personified, recalling a more placid era when people vacationed at low-key resorts, bungalows, and motor courts that sat beside (instead of towering over) the beach.

Choices along Gulf Drive range from brand-name dependables like **Best Western** (3287 West Gulf Drive, 239/472-1700, $$$$) and **Holiday Inn** (1231 Middle Gulf Drive, 239/472-4123, $$$$) to non-franchised charmers that tend to draw a loyal clientele of folks who return each year, often at exactly the same time. These include **Song of the Sea** (863 East Gulf Drive, 239/472-2200, $$$$), a European-style seaside inn, and the congenial, long-lived **Island Inn** (3111 West Gulf Drive, 239/472-1561, $$$$), which celebrated its centennial in 1995.

If money's no object, the **Casa Ybel Resort** (2255 West Gulf Drive, 239/472-3145, $$$$) beckons. Its signature is the faithfully recreated Thistle Lodge (ca. 1915), which now houses a pricey waterfront restaurant. (As you might imagine, paradise doesn't come cheaply at any of the island's venues, and rates at the above-mentioned resorts generally begin at $180 a night in season and drop by roughly a third out of season).

We're partial to the **West Wind Inn** (3345 West Gulf Drive, 239/472-1541, $$$$). It has a great location, being the westernmost beachside lodge on Sanibel Island. Up at this quiet, unhurried end of Sanibel, birds greatly outnumber beachcombers. The comfortable rooms at the West Wind have sliding-glass doors that face a heated pool in the center courtyard. The island trolley stops here, too.

If you're staying anywhere on Gulf Drive, the best perk of all is easy proximity to the beach. Remember that Sanibel Island is best approached as a place to kick back and relax. However much stress you've brought over, it

will begin exiting your pores as soon as you check in—especially if you minimize your use of the automobile.

COASTAL CUISINE

McT's Shrimp House (1523 Periwinkle Way, 239/472-3161, $$$) is a bit of a misnomer. Sure, they have shrimp, but the menu also includes artful preparations of grouper, snapper, and mahimahi. There's steamed and Cajun-style gulf shrimp (doused in a peppery sauce) or steamed rock shrimp (best dipped in melted butter). If you have a large appetite, order an all-you-can-eat platter of all three shrimp preparations. The seafood is on display for all to see behind the counter at the front of the restaurant. Even if it weren't, McT's does such a steady business that the constant turnover guarantees freshness.

Another popular seafood outlet is **Timbers Restaurant & Fish Market** (703 Tarpon Bay Rd., 239/472-3128, $$), a perennial winner in local "Best Seafood" polls ("Best Steak" polls, too). Canvas umbrellas, nautical artifacts, and murals make the large, ski lodge-style dining area seem more intimate. The house specialty is "crunchy grouper" and "crunchy shrimp," tasty preparations that involves rolling the seafood in crushed cereal crumbs. Fresh catch can be prepared to your specifications, too. (We prefer ours chargrilled or broiled with garlic butter.) The Timbers serves dinner only, but the on-premises fish market opens daily at noon.

Another Sanibel Island favorite is the **Lazy Flamingo II** (1036 Periwinkle Way, 239/472-6939, $$). It's an unfancy eatery popular with locals and tourists alike. They have a good raw bar that turns out ice-cold oysters on the half shell. They also smoke fish. An appetizer of smoked mahimahi, rolled in blackening spices and accompanied by cocktail sauce and crackers, is first-rate. They do good things with grouper, too.

We've also become fans of **Jacaranda** (1223 Periwinkle Way, 239/472-1771, $$$). Looks are deceptive at this Sanibel institution, which is much larger than it seems from the parking lot. You can dine in a relaxing, screened-in dining room that's open to the night air or opt for another section with air conditioning on really hot and humid nights. The ceiling fans and old wood beams create an authentic Old Florida atmosphere that enhances the enjoyment of the restaurant's specialty seafood and steak dishes. These include a sublime sesame-encrusted yellowfin tuna (available in appetizer or entrée portions), Florida snapper *en papillote* (baked in parchment), "SanCap Shrimp" (sauteed in Captain Morgan's Spiced Rum), and lump crabcakes. If you can't decide whether to go with surf or turf, try the combination steak and Florida lobster tail. Afterward, you can linger on the premises for drinks and live music in yet another area.

NIGHTLIFE

Whenever we're here, we dutifully but reluctantly look for nightlife. More often than not, we turn in early, reserving our energy for early morning kayaking adventures or bike hikes. Most visitors to Sanibel are on the same wavelength. Even on a Monday night at the height of the NFL season, only a handful of Sanibel stragglers bothered to take advantage of the "Monday night madness" that turns so many sports bars into raving palaces of beer foam, hot wings, and hollering, high-fiving maniacs.

A lot of Sanibel's restaurants and resorts have bars on the premises, including **Beaches Bar & Grill** (Sundial Resort, 1451 Middle Gulf Drive, 239/472-4151), **Delfini's Pool Bar** (Sanibel Inn, 937 East Gulf Drive,

---

SANIBEL-CAPTIVA CONSERVATION FOUNDATION

On Sanibel and the Captiva Islands, the mission to preserve land reflects the progressive bent of the locals. People are willing to pay the extra tariff it costs to come here precisely because the landscape has been kept natural and uncluttered, and because they're sick of all the other once-lovely beach communities that have been ruined by overdevelopment.

While it's not always true that economic and environmental needs can both be met, they converge as snugly as is possible on Sanibel and Captiva Island. Much of the credit for that goes to farsighted organizations like the Sanibel-Captiva Conservation Foundation. Since its incorporation in 1967, the foundation has secured over 1,800 acres.

The foundation doesn't just acquire land, either. They clear it of invasive and exotic plants, allowing native vegetation to fill the gaps. This new habitat provides food, shelter, and room to roam for native species of birds, mammals, insects, and marine life. The most crucial project undertaken by the foundation has been the securing of the Sanibel River, which is fed only by rain and allows the island to attract a more diverse assortment of wildlife than most barrier islands (including even the Captivas).

For a quick environmental education, drop by the foundation's nature center on Sanibel-Captiva Road. (Admission is $3 for adults and free for kids under 17.) On the premises are 4.5 miles of hiking trails, educational exhibits, a butterfly house, a nature shop, and a native plant nursery. Guided hikes (including beach walks), boat trips, programs, and activities are conducted. If you like what you see, become a member and donate some money to their land acquisition fund. That way you can return to the islands knowing that you've had some hand in their preservation.

For more information, contact the Sanibel-Captiva Conservation Foundation, 3333 Sanibel-Captiva Road, Sanibel, FL 33957, 239/472-2329, www.sccf.org.

239/472-3181), **Lazy Flamingo I** (6520 Pine Avenue, 239/472-5353) and **Lazy Flamingo II** (1036 Periwinkle Way, 239/472-6939), and **McT's Tavern** (1523 Periwinkle Way, 239/472-3161). The patio bar at the aforementioned **Jacaranda** (1223 Periwinkle Way, 239/472-1771) has a dance area and nightly live entertainment, with a 20-seat raw bar off to the side.

For a unique experience, hit **Ellington's Jazz Bar** (937 East Gulf Drive, 239/472-0494). Located in the Sanibel Inn, Ellington's features nightly jazz concerts with a string and brass band. Sanibel is also home to two theatrical venues. The Pirate Playhouse Company offers seasonal productions at the **J. Howard Wood Theatre** (2200 Periwinkle Way, 239/472-0006). The **Old Schoolhouse Theater** (1905 Periwinkle Way, 239/472-6862) stages musical theater and comedy, including a musical version of *Dracula*.

Captiva Island

The name "Captiva" is alleged to have derived from pirate Jose Gaspar, who would hold wealthy young women for ransom on then-undivided La Isla de Las Cautivas ("the island of captive women"). In this day and age, we believe there are few more desirable fates than to be held captive on Captiva Island or stranded on North Captiva Island.

The two Captivas lie perpendicular to Sanibel Island on a north-south axis. They are slender, sparsely populated, and densely wooded barrier islands. Captiva runs for six miles and North Captiva for 4.5 miles. Both have sand beaches along their west coasts.

Captiva Island (pop. 400) is connected to Sanibel Island via bridge, while North Captiva can only be reached by boat or small airplane. The two Captivas were carved from one when a 1926 hurricane split them. They were smashed head-on in 2004 by Hurricane Charley. There was much property damage on Captiva Island and much less on Sanibel, owing to their relative orientations and the hurricane's path. Blind Pass, which separated Captiva from Sanibel, completely filled with sand.

Sanibel bounced back, but it's taken Captiva longer to recover. For instance, every building at South Seas Resort, at Captiva's north end, was damaged, and the resort remained closed for a year and a half, reopening in March 2006.

Once you've crossed the bridge onto Captiva, you'll drive for a few miles before seeing any human habitations. Homes and rental villas are scattered among the sea grape, palm, and oak trees, but they are all but invisible from the road. You'll want to keep both hands on the wheel because Captiva Drive makes some gnarly hairpin turns on Captiva.

Captiva Island offers all kinds of outdoor activities for the family, biking being foremost among them. (Be careful, especially along Captiva's curves.) Beach bikes and more can be rented at **Jim's Rentals-Yolo Watersports** (11534 Andy Rosse Lane, Captiva, 239/472-9656). The teeming waters of Pine Island Sound Aquatic Preserve can be explored in kayak. Stop by **Wildside Adventures** (McCarthy's Marina, 11401 Andy Rosse Lane, 239/395-2925), which offers guided tours and kayak rentals for do-it-yourselfers.

For a mellower time, the **Captiva Memorial Library** (11560 Chapin Lane, 239/472-2133) is worth a visit. It stocks lots of books on shells, birds, wildlife, conservation, and Floridiana and is close to **Chapel by the Sea** (11580 Chapin Lane, 239/472-1646). This ancient landmark and its lovely cemetery are inspiring reminders of the early inhabitants of the island. Both lie at the end of Wiles Road.

Captiva Island is a pretty exclusive place, and—like Kiawah Island, South Carolina and Amelia Island, on Florida's East Coast—you will pay dearly to stay here. Steve Case, the founder and former CEO of America Online, reportedly bought up

the view from Andy Rosse Lane in Captiva Beach

© PARKE PUTERBAUGH

all the houses he could afford on Captiva as his pile of gold grew. That is the kind of company you will keep here, which is to say a rarefied and moneyed clientele. Many of these folks are normal in every way except for their net worth, but certain types do drag their one-dimensional, business-centric outlook with them everywhere they go—even on vacation.

For more information, contact the Sanibel-Captiva Islands Chamber of Commerce, P.O. Box 166, 1159 Causeway Road, Sanibel, FL 33957, 239/472-1080, www.sanibel-captiva.org.

BEACHES

A continuous beach runs the six-mile length of Captiva's west coast, with public access points dispersed along its length. Because the beach runs north-south, subtle differences in wave regime and seashell and sand distribution distinguish it from the beaches of Sanibel. For one thing, the surf is rougher and wavier on Captiva, and at the south end, near Blind Pass, swimming is discouraged because of undertow. The sand on Captiva is wide and slightly grayer than Sanibel's. The

dunes are largely intact, and small groves of trees grow right up to the sand. In either direction, Captiva Island begs to be combed for shells or the timeless experience of wandering a wild setting. There are no lifeguards, so it's best to swim within sight of companions.

The more vulnerable beach at Captiva has, alas, been worn down by strong currents and powerful hurricanes, and the local government has lately spent $3 million dumping sand on it. For much of 2005, a sand-pumping project kept the main beach off-limits, and much of the shore looked like a very long construction site. Where will they get the money or the sand to do such expensive cosmetic surgery next time?

To enjoy Captiva's beaches, come early because parking is limited. **Turner Beach** is located at Blind Pass, just over the bridge from Sanibel. A tiny dirt lot allows access to the beach and inlet. There's great surfcasting and sunset watching on the beach, but strong currents make for hazardous swimming.

At the north end of Captiva Road, to the left of the gate at South Seas Resort, is **Captiva**

Beach. This is the most popular access on the island—not that there's much competition—and the free lot has been enlarged. Still, it fills quickly, and unlucky day-trippers will find themselves heading back to Sanibel if they can't snag a spot here.

The 2.5 miles of beach at the north end of Captiva Island fall within the boundaries of the private South Seas Resort. However, anyone can legally roam the beach—below the mean high-tide line, that is—by walking up from public accesses south of here.

There are several other beach accesses in town, but these are right of ways only for pedestrians, and no parking is provided. For instance, at the end of Andy Rosse Lane, beside the popular Mucky Duck pub and restaurant, you can walk out to the beach, but don't try leaving your car here. Signs warn, "Cars Will Be Towed" and "Fine for Parking on Roadside."

Captiva Island is part of a barrier-island chain that also includes Sanibel, North Captiva, Cayo Costa, Cabbage Key, and Gasparilla Islands. If you want to explore the less-developed outer islands, you can rent a boat from a local marina or have them ferry you over and back. **Jensen's Twin Palms Marina** (15107 Captiva Drive, 239/472-5800) will take parties of up to six to North Captiva Island and back for $105. Call for reservations and to arrange drop-off and pickup times. Jensen's also services Cayo Costa Island, Cabbage Key, and Gasparilla Island. **Captiva Cruises** (McCarthy's Marina, 11401 Andy Rosse Lane, 239/472-5300) also offers regularly scheduled daily excursions to all the outer islands.

27 TURNER BEACH

Location: at Blind Pass, just over the bridge onto Captiva Island on gulf side
Parking/Fees: metered parking lot
Hours: sunrise-sunset
Facilities: restrooms

Contact: City of Sanibel Parks and Recreation Department, 239/472-9075

28 CAPTIVA BEACH

BEST (

Location: end of Captiva Drive on Captiva Island
Parking/Fees: free parking lot
Hours: 8 A.M.-sunset
Facilities: restrooms
Contact: Lee County Department of Parks and Recreation, 239/461-7400

ACCOMMODATIONS
South Seas Resort and Yacht Harbor (5400 Plantation Road, 239/472-5111, $$$$) claims the northern third of Captiva Island. This upper-crust establishment has a variety of accommodations—600 units in all, ranging from hotel rooms to two- and three-bedroom villas—on 330 acres and two miles of beach. It covers the complete range of wants for the leisure set: 21 tennis courts, 18 swimming pools, nine-hole golf course, three restaurants, watersports, boat rentals, planned activities and safe, gated security. In season you'll pay anywhere from $289 for a harborside room to $559 for a three-bedroom villa.

Though it's not in our nature to lavish fulsome praise on high-end venues, we found South Seas Resort to be as congenial as they come, with very few add-ons to the bills and an attentive staff. A biking trail and nature center are on the property, and the resort is commendably low-impact. For one thing, no building is taller than two stories. It is a possible to book cruises to North Captiva and Cayo Costa Islands from the marina here. Note that the resort has reopened after a complete makeover necessitated by Hurricane Charley.

As for less frilly lodgings, **'Tween Waters Inn** (P.O. Box 249, 239/472-5161 or 800/223-5865, $$$), located at Captiva's midsection, is a great jumping-off spot to wander the beach in either direction. It's outfitted with tennis courts, fitness center, day spa, and Old Captiva House, an award-winning continental restaurant. It also has the No-See-Um Lounge, named for the microscopic bugs that plague Southern climes. The 'Tween Waters Marina is also part of the complex, which truly earns its name by stretching from gulf to bay.

Beyond these two choices, cottage and villa rentals are the way to go on Captiva Island. Any number of companies handle rentals. Among them, **ResortQuest Reality** (1019 Periwinkle Way, 239/472-1511) covers Sanibel and Captiva Islands—even Fort Myers Beach—like a beach blanket.

COASTAL CUISINE

It's a rule of thumb that the farther one travels from the mainland, the higher the cost of eating out. On Captiva, the restaurant furthest away is **Chadwick's** (5400 Plantation Road, 239/472-5111, $$$$), at the entrance to South Seas Resort. Chadwick's offers a decent seafood buffet, along with a high tab and drowsy lounge entertainment.

Casual lunch and dinner options include the **Village Cafe** (14970 Captiva Drive, 239/472-1956, $$) and the **Green Flash** (15183 Captiva Drive, 239/472-3337, $$), so named for the last glinting rays of sunset, which cast an eerie green glow on the horizon.

For a novel dining experience head to the **Bubble Room** (15001 Captiva Drive, 239/472-5558, $$$), which must be seen to be believed. The servers are called "Bubble Scouts" and they sport Boy Scout uniforms and silly hats. The tables are museum display

HURRICANE CHARLEY

Two years of hurricane woes began with a bang when Hurricane Charley made landfall along Florida's West Coast on August 13, 2004. (Yes, it was Friday the 13th.) Just a day and a half earlier, Tropical Storm Bonnie had hit the Panhandle with high wind and heavy rain. The state was further spooked by Charley, which took a sudden eastward turn and slammed into the Sanibel-Captiva area, 100 miles south of where it had been expected to hit. By defying meteorologists' predictions, it caught Florida's Southwest Coast unprepared. It was too late to board up and evacuate, and so Lee and Charlotte Counties were utterly exposed when Charley roared ashore with 145 mph winds. A Category 4 hurricane, it was the most damaging since Hurricane Andrew in 1992.

"Our worst fears have come true," said a somber Governor Jeb Bush as he surveyed the devastation at Punta Gorda and Port Charlotte by helicopter. Two million people were without power after the storm. A week later 335,000 Floridians still had no electricity, and two weeks later 40 percent of Charlotte County residents remained in the dark.

Charley destroyed 12,000 buildings and left 19,000 others inhabitable. Florida's citrus industry suffered $150 million in losses. Beaches were heavily eroded and islands reconfigured. The state's Bureau of Beaches and Coastal Systems reported that North Captiva Island "completely disintegrated" along a 0.3-mile stretch where a new tidal pass had formed. Half of the island's 300 homes were substantially damaged. At the north end of Captiva Island, South Seas Resort closed for the better part of a year to rebuild. Charley also caused heavy damage in the Daytona Beach area as it exited the state.

Within Florida, Hurricane Charley was the deadliest of the 2004 and 2005 hurricanes, directly or indirectly causing 35 fatalities. (Hurricanes Dennis and Wilma claimed 32 and 31 lives, respectively.) Charley was just the beginning; Hurricane Frances crossed the peninsula from the other direction three weeks later, dealing a double blow to many interior locales that had just been hit by Charley.

cases filled with nostalgic gewgaws (Monopoly game money, old records, baseball cards, shoelaces, water pistols). The walls are covered with enough quirky memorabilia to keep necks craning throughout a meal. Oh yes, the food: ample portions of local seafood, baskets of "Bubble Bread" and sticky buns, and the best desserts on the island. There's a special menu and game room for kids, who dig this place. That's the double-edged sword here: If your inner kitty cat is not up to all the cuteness and kitsch, then you may want to consider less kooky cuisine.

For those who aren't up to the Bubble Room's gimmickry, **Redfish, Blufish** (14970 Captiva Drive, 239/472-1956, $$) is notable for its fresh seafood and inventive menu.

NIGHTLIFE

The Mucky Duck (11546 Andy Rosse Lane, 239/472-3434) is a pub-like place, with British maps and duck-motif decor. It's good for a quick lunch and for drinks and snacks at Happy Hour or later. The fare is pretty plain—fish 'n' chips and "super frankfurters" though we can recommend grouper or mahimahi sandwiches. The Mucky Duck features an assortment of sturdy draft beers (Bass, Harp, Guinness, John Courage, Pilsner Urquell) and a prime location (a dart's toss from the Gulf of Mexico). Alternatively, there's the **Crow's Nest Lounge** at the 'Tween Waters Inn (15951 Captiva Drive, 239/472-5800).

North Captiva Island

On North Captiva Island, habitation is limited to the north end, along Captiva Pass, the inlet separating it from Cabbage Key and Cayo Costa. The sheltered bay that sits in the crook of land to the east of the pass is called Safety Harbor, and passenger boats dock here. That is how most visitors arrive on North Captiva Island. If the logistics for spending a day here

can be ironed out, visitors have four miles of wonderfully secluded beaches to wander. The state of Florida owns a mid-island parcel of 350 acres that runs from beach to bay. There are no docks or facilities, and they don't encourage visitation.

Passenger service to North Captiva can be arranged through **Island Charters Water Transport** (Mattson Marine, Pineland Marina, 239/283-2008), on Pine Island. North Captiva can also be accessed via a 10-minute boat or water-taxi ride from Captiva Island; contact local marinas for boat rental and ferry fees.

Only 6,000 people a year set foot on North Captiva. There are no cars, hotels or grocery stores. However, many of the private homes on the island are part of a "rental pool" administered by the **North Captiva Island Club** (239/472-5836 or 800/576-7343). Hey, imagine renting a home on a semi-secluded island paradise. If you provision yourself well and can deal with the isolation—i.e., nowhere to go for cigarettes or Starbucks—you may well have the vacation of a lifetime.

For more information, contact the North Captiva Island Club, P.O. Box 1000, Pineland, FL 33945, 239/472-5836 or 800/576-7343, www.northcaptiva.com.

BEACHES

29 NORTH CAPTIVA ISLAND

Location: between Captiva Island and Cayo Costa Island; accessible via private boat or passenger ferry from Captiva Island, Pine Island, and Boca Grande
Parking/Fees: no parking or fees
Hours: 8 A.M.-sunset
Facilities: none
Contact: Cayo Costa Island State Park, 239/964-0375

Cayo Costa Island State Park

Just above North Captiva Island is an unblemished jewel known as Cayo Costa Island. Measuring seven miles long by one mile wide, Cayo Costa Island State Park is the least-visited park in the Florida State Park system. Owing to more than nine miles of blinding white and mostly deserted gulf beach, it has earned the nickname "Florida's Tahiti." While no naked women will swim out to greet your boat, the natural wonders of Cayo Costa more than compensate—although the island took a severe body blow from Hurricane Charley.

Among other things, the island was denuded of its canopy (especially the non-native Australian pines, whose riddance was actually welcome). What are remains are acres of recovering pine forest, oak-palm hammock, and mangrove swamps. Bird life is abundant, including bald eagles in spring. The island offers the best snorkeling and shelling on the Southwest Coast. You can hike the shoreline or a nature trail in the wooded area.

Twelve cabins are available for rent ($30 per night), and primitive tent camping is allowed ($18 per night) in a designated 30-site area at the north end. Reservations are accepted up to 11 months in advance, and they book quickly. If you're planning on coming between Thanksgiving and Easter, you'll likely need to book at least eight months ahead. Cabins sleep up to six. There's no electricity, and visitors must bring all necessary supplies, including food and drink, bug spray, and ice. Only restrooms, cold showers, and grills are provided. Caveat emptor: The experience of camping or renting a cabin may not be as sublime as in years past, at least until the island recovers from Charley's ravages. One camper came back complaining that Cayo Costa is "a hot, horrid little hell with barely working restrooms, non-functioning water fountains, and a wanting shower facility."

The lure for most visitors, especially during the winter months, is shelling, as over 400 species of shells have been found on the Cayo Costa beaches. The most varied shelling is at the northern tip of the island, along Johnson Shoals. Because shells are piled high and foot traffic is low, such hard-to-find species as murices, nautiluses, and spiny jewel boxes can be picked up in mint condition.

Cayo Costa is served by private ferry. The park concessionaire is *Tropic Star of Pine Island* (13921 Waterfront Drive, Pineland, 239/283-0015), which departs from the Pineland Marina. If you have a modest-sized party, an all-day boat rental may be cheaper than a group ferry ride and, if you know what you're doing, might be more exciting. Try **Port Sanibel Marina** (239/472-8443), on the Sanibel Causeway, or **Castaways Marina** (239/472-1112), on the west end of Sanibel Island. The latter also rents canoes and kayaks, which are especially good for exploring the nooks and crannies of the mangrove swamp on Cayo Costa's bayside. Conveniently, that is where the island's dock is located. For a $0.50 charge, a tractor-pulled open-air tram will spirit visitors across the island from bay to beach. It runs three times a day.

For more information, contact Cayo Costa Island State Park, c/o Barrier Islands GEOpark, P.O. Box 1150, Boca Grande, FL 33921, 239/964-0375, www.floridastateparks.org.

BEACHES

30 CAYO COSTA ISLAND STATE PARK

BEST (

Location: between North Captiva Island and Gasparilla Island; accessible via private boat or passenger ferry from Captiva Island and Boca Grande

Parking/Fees: $2 entrance fee per family, plus $0.50 per person fee for tram ride across island. Fees for overnight stay are $18 per campsite and $30 per cabin.

Hours: 8 A.M.-sunset

Facilities: restrooms, picnic tables, and showers
Contact: Cayo Costa Island State Park, 239/964-0375

Boca Grande

At 3:56 P.M. on Friday, Aug. 13, 2004—Friday the 13th, as fate would have it—the town of Boca Grande and the island of Gasparilla were changed forever. At that precise hour, Hurricane Charley—described as "a 10-mile-wide tornado"—landed on the southern tip of Gasparilla Island, bringing winds of up to 150 miles per hour. As it crossed the island, Charley paid a call to every home, cottage, and condo, tearing trees from their roots and flinging them onto cars and dwellings.

Fortunately, the state had declared a mandatory evacuation and most residents had fled to the mainland. It's a tribute to the resilience of the town and the island that nearly all businesses are up and running after months—and in some cases, up to a year—of being closed. Wiser and more wary residents pulled together to fill the gaps in state aid and insurance claims.

"We went from thinking one would never hit us to one would never miss us," one resident was quoted in the *Boca Beacon,* the island's weekly paper, which won an award for its hurricane coverage.

It's easy to understand why the diehards stayed behind. Boca Grande (pronounced "grand," with a silent "e") is like no other beach town in Florida. Boca Grande actually looks a bit like a New England fishing village. It is so casual, relaxed, and unpretentious that after a day spent walking its streets, lying out on its beaches, and talking to its natives, we felt as at ease here as we did in our hometowns.

It's rare in communities with prime coastal real estate that the tenor of life is set by townspeople and not big-money barons, but that's how it goes in Boca Grande. Back in the 1980s, the good folks of Boca Grande

banded together and built a bike path that extends the length of the island. The modest downtown area in this narrow, five-block-wide community preserves the often cited but rarely experienced Old Florida feel. Typical is the Temptation, a down-home restaurant and unofficial community center that's been doing business on this spot for more than half a century. For another glimpse at the town's back pages, check out two old but still-functioning marinas—Whidden's and Miller's—on the bay near 1st Street.

Oh, sure, there are condo developments at the north end, where a small chunk of Gasparilla Island extends into Charlotte County (a horse of an entirely different color). But Boca Grande manages to preserve the unhurried character that has been its calling card since the 1920s. The town occupies most of five-mile-long Gasparilla Island, which was named for pirate Jose Gaspar. The preferred mode of transportation is golf carts, because they're quiet and easy to get around in.

In the words of a woman who's lived here since the 1960s, Boca Grande is "a sleepy little island" that changes slowly and incrementally. Talking with us while watching waves break from her golf cart, she added that its 1,700 residents are "one big happy family."

Boca Grande has been a getaway for the wealthy, including familiar names like the DuPonts, Astors, and Eastmans. Often they'd stay at the Gasparilla Inn and become so charmed by the island that they'd build homes here. Fortunately, not everyone who lives here these days is rich and retired. It helps that Boca Grande is a bit out of the way for those movers and shakers who require easy access to airports and urban amenities.

The only thing we can complain about is the $4 per car bridge toll to enter the island. Built in 1958, the entrance bridges and the land at the north end were privately owned by the Gaspar family. The bridge is now maintained by the Gasparilla Island Bridge Authority. If you're making the trip with some frequency, you can buy discount passes for 30 or more trips at $2.25 per crossing.

In the spring, this sleepy little community wakes up for the annual tarpon run. In fact, Boca Grande proudly is the self-proclaimed tarpon-fishing capital of the world. Fishing for tarpon and golfing at the Gasparilla Inn are two reasons people with deep pockets come to Boca Grande. We'd suggest a third incentive, which doesn't require a lot of capital to experience: peace and quiet.

For more information, contact the Boca Grande Chamber of Commerce, 5800 Gasparilla Road, Suite A1, P.O. Box 704, Boca Grande, FL 33921, 239/964-0568, www.bocagrandechamber.com.

BEACHES

The sand on Gasparilla Island is powdery white, with linear mounds of coarse, shelly material. The beach is relatively narrow and diminishes to nothing at places where landowners (such as several "beach clubs") have built self-defeating seawalls. Although the town of Boca Grande has rebounded admirably from Hurricane Charley, the southern four miles of Gasparilla Island are described by the state as "critically eroded."

Almost all of Boca Grande's public beaches—certainly all the ones worth seeing—are at the south end of the island, where five discontinuous accesses are collectively referred to as **Gasparilla Island State Park.** There's parking at each of the accesses, which extend from the island's southern tip to the village's south end. From south to north, they are **Lighthouse Beach Park, Dunes Beach, Sea Wall Beach, Sea Grape Beach,** and **Sand Spur Beach.** Of the latter four, Sand Spur Beach offers the most in the way of parking and facilities: restrooms and picnic tables, plus the most swimmable of Gasparilla Island's beaches.

The most interesting vantage point is Lighthouse Beach Park, which looks across Boca Grande Pass to Cayo Costa Island. The pass is the main inlet into the bay, and tarpon use it as an expressway to blue crabs, upon which they feast and fatten themselves in the spring and summer. En route to their waiting smorgasbord in seafood-rich Charlotte Harbor, these glittering silver wonders are snatched from the waters of the pass by anglers looking to hook a trophy. The "world's richest" tarpon tournament is held each July. (Call the Boca Grande Chamber of Commerce for dates and entrance fees.)

Unfortunately, tarpon numbers are down precipitously. Even the Boca Grande Fishing Guides Association has been openly talking about "the devastating decline in health of our world famous tarpon fishery that has taken place during the past decade... Who would ever think that the very fishery that had made Boca Grande world famous would shrink in health to what we have witnessed during the past few years?"

It is another instance of killing the goose that laid the golden egg, which is essentially the story of the state of Florida.

Also at this southernmost beach are the 1890 Boca Grande Lighthouse, some huge oil-storage tanks, and a clump of old Coast Guard buildings that now serve as headquarters for the Barrier Islands GEOpark, a collection of island parks managed by the state, including Cayo Costa, Gasparilla Island, and Don Pedro Island State Parks. The oldest building on Gasparilla Island, the lighthouse still serves as a U.S. Coast Guard light and as a museum of local history (open Wednesday–Saturday 10 A.M.–4 P.M.). Surf-casting by the lighthouse is good, judging from the five-pound grouper we saw a screaming woman reel in seconds after casting her line. Swimming, though, is hazardous because of strong currents through the pass. We heard the unutterably sad story of children who drowned here when their parents weren't looking. As a general rule, inlets are not good or safe places for swimming.

In town, at the west end of 5th Street, a public parking lot sits beside a seawall. Boca Grande's seawalls have been around "as long as I've been coming here," according to a local with 30 years under her belt. The beach takes a beating, and with the seawall blocking its retreat, there is no beach—just rocks and the violent slapping of waves on concrete. Periodically, they renourish the beach, but it's all for naught, vanishing once again in a season or two. You can cast a line from the seawall, but forget about swimming or sunning on the beach, because there is none. **Boca Grande Public Beach Accesses** are found between 7th and 19th Streets, indicated by signs at the head of each street. Some of these street-end accesses offer half a dozen or so parking spots.

In early 2001, they were floating another renourishment scheme. Nearly three miles of beach would be extended 150 to 200 feet with sand from an offshore bar. The price tag was $11 million, with beachfront property owners picking up less than 10 percent of the tab (such a deal!). Valid concerns were raised by state officials about ecological ramifications and the impact and effectiveness of limestone boulder groins and an offshore breakwater to protect the artificial beach.

31 LIGHTHOUSE BEACH PARK (GASPARILLA ISLAND STATE PARK)

Location: south end of Gasparilla Island, at Boca Grande Lighthouse
Parking/Fees: $2 per vehicle parking fee
Hours: 8 A.M.-sunset
Facilities: restrooms, picnic tables, and a visitors center
Contact: Barrier Islands GEOpark, 239/964-0375

32 DUNES BEACH (GASPARILLA ISLAND STATE PARK)

Location: Gulf Boulevard at south end of Gasparilla Island
Parking/Fees: $2 per vehicle parking fee

Hours: 8 A.M.-sunset
Facilities: restrooms
Contact: Barrier Islands GEOpark, 239/964-0375

33 SEA WALL BEACH (GASPARILLA ISLAND STATE PARK)

Location: Gulf Boulevard at south end of Gasparilla Island
Parking/Fees: $2 per vehicle parking fee
Hours: 8 A.M.-sunset
Facilities: restrooms
Contact: Barrier Islands GEOpark, 239/964-0375

34 SEA GRAPE BEACH (GASPARILLA ISLAND STATE PARK)

Location: Gulf Boulevard at south end of Gasparilla Island
Parking/Fees: $2 per vehicle parking fee
Hours: 8 A.M.-sunset
Facilities: restrooms
Contact: Barrier Islands GEOpark, 239/964-0375

35 SAND SPUR BEACH (GASPARILLA ISLAND STATE PARK)

Location: Gulf Boulevard between Wheeler and 1st Streets in Boca Grande
Parking/Fees: $2 per vehicle parking fee
Hours: 8 A.M.-sunset
Facilities: picnic tables and restrooms
Contact: Barrier Islands GEOpark, 239/964-0375

36 BOCA GRANDE PUBLIC BEACH ACCESSES

Location: certain street ends between 7th and 19th Streets, identified with signs along Gulf Boulevard, in Boca Grande

Parking/Fees: free, limited street parking
Hours: sunrise-sunset
Facilities: none
Contact: Lee County Department of Parks and Recreation, 239/461-7440

RECREATION AND ATTRACTIONS

- **Bike/Skate Rentals:** Bike and Beach Rentals, 333 Park Avenue, Boca Grande, 239/964-0711

- **Boat Cruise:** Boca Boat Cruises and Charters, Uncle Henry's Marina Resort, 5800 Gasparilla Road, Boca Grande, 888/416-2628

- **Ecotourism:** Grande Tours, 12571 Placida Road, Placida, 239/697-8825.

- **Fishing Charters:** Boca Grande Fishing Guides Association, Boca Grande, www.bocagrandefishing.com (lists names and numbers of 51 fishing guides)

- **Lighthouse:** Boca Grande Lighthouse & Museum, Lighthouse Point Park, Boca Grande, 239/964-0060

- **Marina:** Miller's Marina, 220 Harbor Drive, 239/964-2232; Whidden's Marina, 190 East 1st Street, Boca Grande, 239/964-2878

- **Pier:** Gasparilla Pier (railroad trestle turned public pier at north end of Gasparilla Island), Boca Grande

- **Rainy-Day Attraction:** Old Theatre Mall, Boca Grande

- **Shopping/Browsing:** Railroad Depot and Railroad Plaza, 4th Street between Park Avenue and East Avenue, Boca Grande

- **Vacation Rentals:** Boca Grande Real Estate, 5700 Gulf Shores Boulevard, Boca Grande, 239/964-2211

ACCOMMODATIONS

Gasparilla Inn & Cottages (Palm Avenue and 5h Street, 239/964-2201, $$$$) is a magnet for those serious about getting away from it all. This yellow clapboard inn is so unpretentiously situated in its bayside neighborhood that we weren't positive we were entering a public inn at all. There's not even a sign out front. An air of casual exclusivity permeates its rooms and cottages. It's not on the beach, but it's not far from the public beaches. The 18-hole, par-72 golf course out back is the only one on the island. So entrenched is the code of tradition that President George Bush (not W but his daddy) was denied use of the golf course while staying on the island because it's strictly reserved for members and guests. Rates are based on the full American plan, with three meals included. They're highest during the "social season" (mid-December–mid-April), drop by a third during the "tarpon season" (mid-April–mid-June) and fall further still in summer and fall.

The **Anchor Inn** (450 East 4th Street, 239/964-2700, $$$) is a four-room B&B in a restored home whose courtyard is festooned with tropical plantings. Weekly room rates run $1,100–1,600 in winter and drop by almost half from mid-July–mid-December. Another option is the **Innlet on the Waterfront** (1150 East Railroad Avenue, 239/964-2294, $$), a 33-room hideaway favored by couples seeking weekend escapes.

COASTAL CUISINE

The Temptation (350 Park Avenue, 239/964-2610, $$$$) is an old reliable whose atmosphere is almost as palatable as the salads and fried seafood that make up the bulk of the menu. It's more than half a century old. "We wear it well, don't we?" bragged the woman who filled our water glasses. A mostly retired clientele gathers to dine on grilled shrimp salad, fried oysters, grouper fingers, and so forth. Lunch is a relative bargain, but nothing comes cheaply at dinner, where entrees run in the $19–27 range. Under the same roof is the **Caribbean Room,** a darkened bar festooned with ornaments and bric-a-brac. Island-oriented fare is served at more moderate prices.

Other seafood spots of longstanding are

PJ's Seagrille (321 Park Avenue, 239/964-0806, $$$$) and the **Pink Elephant** (491 Bayou Avenue, 239/964-0100, $$$). Neither is inexpensive, though the latter is a little ritzier (good wine list) and more ballyhooed.

Your stay is not complete without scoops of homemade ice cream at the **Loose Caboose** (4th Street and Park Avenue, 239/964-0440, $), which also dispenses soup, sandwiches, and more from the Railroad Depot.

NIGHTLIFE
If you're younger and friskier than Boca Grande's demographic median, head to **South Beach** (777 Gulf Boulevard, 239/964-0765), a bar and grill with lime-green decor and colorful fish on the wall. You can hoist a tall draft Guinness and order dinner from a menu that includes the usual bar-food staples (wings, steamed shrimp) as well as entrees like crispy grouper Gaspar and stuffed shrimp South Beach. From the indoor bar and dining room or alfresco patio, you can gaze across South Beach to the gulf. It's the best spot on Gasparilla Island to quaff a tall, cool one at sunset, and you may even want to stick around. Incidentally, South Beach was closed for repairs for two months after Hurricane Charley passed through.

Little Gasparilla Island, Don Pedro Island, Knight Island, and Palm Island

If, as Gertrude Stein suggested, a rose is a rose is a rose, then Little Gasparilla Island is a bouquet of hybrids. Not that long ago, this barrier island—stretching for seven miles, from Gasparilla Pass to Stump Pass—comprised four islands. Now, through natural sand movement and human intervention, the islands have been grafted together. Due mostly to the dredging of the Intracoastal Waterway, the narrow inlets

that once separated the islands—Little Gasparilla, Don Pedro, Knight, and Palm, with mangrove-covered Thornton Key sometimes included in the lineup—filled with sand. This created a long, thin sliver of an island that still retains its separate identities.

For instance, we heard that some folks on Little Gasparilla would be horrified to be associated with the upscale snowbirds on Palm Island. Being part of the same barrier system that created Sanibel, Captiva, North Captiva, Cayo Costa, and Gasparilla Islands, this island is blessed with a sublime combination of wide, hard-packed sand and uncrowded seclusion. Car traffic is virtually nonexistent because no bridge joins it to the mainland—just a barge ferry for residents on the south end. The primary modes of transportation are golf cart, moped, and bicycle. This limits the whims and priorities of the usual beach vacationer. We should all be so lucky. The utter carelessness afforded by carlessness can be a good thing.

So far, so good. But Little Gasparilla Island's rose has some thorns, too. The main one is that everything is ad hoc and nothing makes much sense. Perhaps this is to be expected when three government entities (county, state, federal) approach four conjoined yet separate islands with different agendas. For instance, Don Pedro Island State Park, near the south end of the barrier island, is a buried treasure that no visitor will quite know what to make of. Like Cayo Costa State Park, it can only be accessed by private boat, because there's no longer any ferry service. (Passengers used to be able to cross for $5, but the service was terminated.)

Moreover, you can't bike to Don Pedro from the north end of the island without illegally crossing the adjacent developments—Bocilla Bay and the Preserve at Don Pedro—of two developers who loathe each other. One built a fence and wall to force the other to hire private barges to bring his construction supplies. This might be funny if it weren't so juvenile.

Ideally, there would be no construction on such a fragile island. But we live in a compromised world, so we took Little Gasparilla

COWARDS OF THE COUNTY

Charlotte County seriously shortchanged its citizens and did a disservice to future generations. With a little courage, they could have acquired one of the nicest remaining tracts of unbuilt-upon barrier island beach in Florida. As it is, the county owns only an eroding little strip at Englewood Beach. By their actions, they lost a gorgeous 30-acre gulf-to-bay tract on Little Gasparilla Island that would have adjoined Don Pedro Island State Park. The story of how they let it slip through their fingers is a textbook example of local politics at its most myopic.

All of the circumnavigation required to get around on Little Gasparilla Island and the maze of private development that has marred its appeal could have been avoided had the Charlotte County Board of Commissioners cast a simple, logical vote in 1996. A plot of land, now developed as the Preserve at Don Pedro, could have been preserved in reality for a song. That song? Try "Bargain," by the Who.

The owner of the parcel, who really wanted to sell to the county, had significantly discounted his asking price. After the state kicked in grant money, Charlotte County's contribution toward the purchase of a tract appraised at $5 million would have been a mere $450,000. The Don Pedro tract was ranked second on a list of more than 40 such projects from all over Florida, and the state bent over backward to accommodate the hemming and hawing county commissioners.

However, "Bargain" was not the tune they chose to sing. Instead, the cowards of Charlotte County sang something more along the lines of "I Can't Explain." After dragging their feet for two years, they voted not to vote on the issue as a final deadline approached. The day after their vote-not-to-vote, land movers, cranes, and tractors were out at the preserve, knocking down trees and plotting out lots. Thanks to these stooges, Little Gasparilla Island will forever remain a confusing hodgepodge.

We don't mean to impugn all who sat on that commission. Two of them were staunchly in favor of the Don Pedro purchase. Moreover, there's a real hero in Charlotte County politics. The efforts of Joe Tringali, a three-term commissioner, led to the state's acquisition of the 133 acres now known as Don Pedro Island State Park. We suggest that the more reality-attuned residents of Charlotte County join together and sing "Won't Get Fooled Again," paying more attention to whom they put in office when election time rolls around.

We'll leave the last word to Jack Alexander, a local columnist who summed it up like this: "Politicians can be so dumb. And our County Commission could be in the *Guinness Book of Records* under 'Dumbest.'"

Island as we found it—and we found parts of it to our liking. Don Pedro Island State Park was wisely preserved. Palm Island has been developed with some sensitivity for the natural environment. And we enviously eyed the hidden homes on Knight Island, which are the sorts of hermitages where curmudgeons like us would love to spend our dotage.

For more information, contact the Englewood Area Chamber of Commerce, 601 South Indiana Avenue, Englewood, FL 34223, 239/474-5511 or 800/603-7198, www.englewoodchamber.com.

BEACHES

Of the seven miles of beach on Little Gasparilla Island, six are accessible only to owners or renters of private homes, or to guests at Palm Island Resort. The island's 1.3 miles of public beachfront fall inside **Don Pedro Island State Park,** at the south end.

Purchased by the state in 1989, Don Pedro stretches from bay to gulf. Its white-sand beach collects interesting deposits of shells and driftwood, as well as stunning, elevated sand dunes. The park is accessible only by boat, which you can tie up on the bayside dock for a $2 fee.

THE SOUTHWEST COAST

From here, a boardwalk leads out to the gulf beach. Facilities include restrooms and picnic pavilions, and there's an on-site ranger.

We felt like we'd stumbled onto a deserted Tahitian isle, until we bumped into a ranger. "What more could people want?" the beaming ranger asked, spreading his arms to indicate the bay-to-gulf splendor of this isolated gem. Well, maybe the 30 more acres that Charlotte County let get away (see the *Cowards of the County* sidebar).

37 DON PEDRO ISLAND STATE PARK

Location: south end of Little Gasparilla Island, accessible via private boat
Parking/Fees: $2 per boat docking fee
Hours: 8 A.M.–sunset
Facilities: restrooms and picnic tables
Contact: Barrier Islands GEOpark, 239/964-0375

ACCOMMODATIONS

The place to stay on Little Gasparilla Island is **Palm Island Resort** (7092 Placida Road, Cape Haze, 239/697-4800, $$$$). This vacation complex and real-estate venture fronts the Gulf of Mexico for two miles. Privately owned one- to three-bedroom villas are rented to vacationers. A two-bedroom gulf-front villa goes for $3,000–4,000 a week in the high winter season and drops to $2,000–2,730 July–mid-December.

Because of its relative inaccessibility and low-key nature, crowds are nonexistent even at the height of the season. Until 1998, cars were not allowed on Palm Island. Now your car, luggage, groceries, and whatever else you want to bring come over on the car barge from Placida. The car ferry is located at the end of Panama Boulevard, off C.R. 775 just north of Gulfwind Marina, and the resort's reception area is on Palm Island itself. Palm Island struck us as an appealingly secluded place with ample amenities and activities, including five swimming pools, 11 tennis courts, bike rentals, and a children's play area. The beach is inviting, if erosion-prone.

The tract that Palm Island occupies was purchased in 1980 by Garfield Beckstead, the man who rescued Useppa Island (east of Cayo Costa) in 1976. After studying the natural gifts of Palm Island—his new name for this chunk of Knight Island (justified, as there are plenty of palm trees)—he reportedly reduced the number of planned homesites by half. The island has 154 villas and 200 private homes.

For the time being, a balance between nature and human habitations has been struck. An early morning beach jog from Palm Island's villas to Stump Point—part of the 7,667-acre Cape Haze Aquatic Preserve—presented a living lab of marine ecology including live sea urchins, starfish, and sand dollars. Manatees are often spotted hereabouts. We saw fish leaping in the pass as we negotiated the driftwood-studded beach. For 10 minutes we stopped to watch an egret patiently surveying the gulf, cleaning its feathers while waiting for breakfast to appear in the teeming waters.

COASTAL CUISINE

All villas at Palm Island come with fully equipped kitchens, so you'll want to hit the Food Lion or Publix in Englewood before ferrying over. (Drop by the video store, while you're at it.) The resort's own eatery, **Rum Bay Restaurant** (Palm Island Resort, 239/697-0566, $$$), serves lunch and dinner. There's everything from bar food to the Cape Haze seafood platter (shrimp, scallops, and grouper broiled in lemon and butter). It's an appealing spot to hoist a drink at sunset or after dinner before taking a moonlit stroll back to the villa.

Manasota Key

Manasota Key is split between two counties, Charlotte and Sarasota, and the halves are visibly different. Charlotte County's portion of

Manasota Key falls within the town limits of Englewood (pop. 16,200). Most of Englewood, like neighboring Grove City and Lemon Pass, is an unplanned, unzoned mainland sprawl of homes, malls, and businesses. These towns serve as provisioning centers for the numerous gated private condo developments that dot the shoreline of Lemon Bay. If the signs staked in nearly every vacant lot along this corridor are any indication, more strip malls, drugstores, fast-food outlets, Wal-Marts, car dealerships, and mellifluously named developments are on the way.

It's business as usual in Charlotte County. It has the most elderly population in Florida, which explains a lot. The median age in Florida is 39.2 years. In Charlotte County, the median age is 53. To say that it's lacking in vision and vitality is an understatement.

To get to Englewood Beach from Englewood, turn west from C.R. 776 onto Beach Road, which leads over a drawbridge (below is Lemon Bay and the Gulf Intracoastal Waterway) and short causeway. Englewood Beach is a modest improvement over Englewood. The first thing you encounter on this thin barrier spit is Chadwick Park, home of Englewood Public Beach. Turn left and you'll be headed to a state-owned sliver of beach known as Stump Pass Beach (formerly Port Charlotte State Park). Turn right and you'll soon enter Sarasota County's portion of Manasota Key, with its more appealing temperament and better beach parks. Manasota Beach Road really is scenic up at this end, and passing beneath a canopy of tree limbs makes the drive a pleasant one.

For more information, contact the Englewood Area Chamber of Commerce, 601 South Indiana Avenue, Englewood, FL 34223, 239/474-5511 or 800/603-7198, www.englewoodchamber.com.

BEACHES

At its south end, the yin and yang of Manasota Key becomes evident. Manasota Key Road gives out at Stump Pass Beach, part of the state-owned Barrier Islands GEOpark. Step into the park's pine and mangrove canopy, and you'll be instantly calmed. From this natural habitat, the secluded beach stretches for a mile down to Stump Pass. The sand on **Stump**

Manasota Beach

© PARKE PUTERBAUGH

THE SOUTHWEST COAST

Pass Beach is gray-black and spongy—part of the Englewood Beach strand that has been renourished with dredge material. There's no entrance fee and no facilities beyond restrooms and a handful of parking spaces. One good way to visit is by bicycle, using the racks provided before hitting the beach.

The rest of Englewood Beach wears a generally downtrodden look. **Englewood Public Beach at Chadwick Park**—Charlotte County's only county-run gulf beach—has experienced severe erosion problems. A local journalist once likened the park to a "neglected old car," but it's received a modest cosmetic makeover in recent years. The picnic pavilions are decent, the visitors center has a new coat of paint and a fresh tin roof, and the parking lot has been paved. The park is within walking distance of a smattering of shops, restaurants, and bars.

Sarasota County claims north Manasota Key, which improves dramatically as you move north from Englewood Beach, exiting Charlotte County. (In this case, parting is not such sweet sorrow.) "Interval ownership" villas and mobile home parks are replaced by single-family homes and unadulterated nature. From here on out, it's clear sailing.

The first park in Sarasota County is **Blind Pass Beach** (a.k.a. Middle Beach), a 60-acre public preserve located along a curve a mile north of the Charlotte County line. The gulf-hugging road swerves dramatically and the barrier spit grows so thin that visitors park on the bayside and walk over to the beach. It's an exceptionally clean and modern facility, with a wild, healthy beach that stretches for over half a mile. Next to the parking lot is a nature trail dedicated to Frederick Duesberg (1910-1989). This winding, sawdust-covered trail offers a peek at the fragile bayside habitat, ending at a quiet lagoon. Fishing and kayaking are popular on the coves nestled along the bayshore. In the vicinity of Blind Pass the island is pretty fragile, and the road often has to be closed during nasty storms.

Another attractive, free Sarasota County facility, **Manasota Beach,** lies 1.5 miles above Blind Pass, at Manasota Key's north end. This 14-acre park fronts 1,400 feet of gulf beach, offering a boat ramp and dock on the bayside, too. They post year-round lifeguards here, among the first we'd seen on the Southwest Coast. The sand is coarse, fluffy, and shelly in spots.

Take note: Manasota Key is not an island, per se, because it connects with Venice to the north. But since the road doesn't extend to Venice, the key is island-like. In other words, you have to leave the key at Manasota Beach, via S.R. 776, to get to Venice.

38 STUMP PASS BEACH

Location: south end of Manasota Key Road, on Manasota Key
Parking/Fees: free parking lot
Hours: 8 A.M.-sunset
Facilities: restrooms
Contact: Barrier Islands GEOpark, 239/964-0375

39 ENGLEWOOD PUBLIC BEACH AT CHADWICK PARK

Location: Beach Road (C.R. 776) at Manasota Key Road, in Englewood
Parking/Fees: $1 parking fee per vehicle
Hours: 6 A.M.-11 P.M.
Facilities: concessions, restrooms, picnic tables, and showers
Contact: Chadwick Park, 239/473-1018

40 BLIND PASS BEACH

Location: one mile north of the Charlotte County line, at 6725 Manasota Key Road, on Manasota Key

Parking/Fees: free parking lot
Hours: 6 A.M.–11 P.M.
Facilities: restrooms, picnic tables, and showers
Contact: Sarasota County Parks and Recreation Department, 941/316-1172

41 MANASOTA BEACH

Location: north end of Manasota Key, at the west end of Manasota Beach Road
Parking/Fees: free parking lots
Hours: 6 A.M.–11 P.M.
Facilities: lifeguards, restrooms, picnic tables, and showers
Contact: Sarasota County Parks and Recreation Department, 941/316-1172

ACCOMMODATIONS

There are few motels worth recommending in Englewood Beach. The best bet on Manasota Key is a vacation home, condo, or villa rental. At the north end of the key, in Sarasota County, local regulations require a minimum one-month rental. Therefore, any short-term rentals on Manasota Key can only be had on the Charlotte County side of the line. Try **Surfside Realty** (1271 Beach Road, Englewood, 239/473-4050).

Toward the remote north end of Manasota Key is the **Seafarer Beach Resort** (8520 Manasota Key Road, 941/474-4388, $$), a small—eight rooms and four efficiency apartments—mom-and-pop motor court that possesses low-key charm. Most rates here are by the week, but daily rates are offered in the off-season.

SARASOTA, BRADENTON, AND THE CULTURAL COAST

In parts of Florida, "culture" is generally taken to mean gator wrasslin', dancing the Macarena, or drinking margaritas while wearing a stuffed parrot on your head. Refreshingly, real culture (with a capital C) can be found in Sarasota, which has a symphony, theater, museums, and bookshops that compare with those in cities many times its size. It's also where Ringling Brothers circus is headquartered, and Ringling money helped set Sarasota on its gilded path. We've dubbed this enlightened part of Florida—which includes the counties of Sarasota and Manatee—the "Cultural Coast." And whenever we're here, we try to linger because we feel right at home.

Just over the Ringling Causeway from Sarasota is tony St. Armands Circle, where you'll find exceptional shopping, restaurants and nightlife. Out on nearby Siesta Key, the residents are laid-back and well-read. South of here, the well-mannered city of Venice takes its architectural cues from its more famous counterpart in Italy. Between Venice and Sarasota are the Old Florida havens of Nokomis and Osprey, as well as lushly exclusive Casey Key. The only sour note in this coastal and cultural fantasia is Longboat Key, which exhibits all the snobbiness of a private country club.

Above Longboat Key is Anna Maria Island. This 7.5-mile island falls inside Manatee County, which is named for the beloved (and endangered) sea mammal. Spotting manatees is the Gulf Coast equivalent of whale-watching, and the county's parks department lists 15 manatee watch areas. Up here, people look after their beaches and manatees, and they've successfully held witless development at bay. Anna Maria Island is home to a conjoined trio of family-oriented beach communities: Bradenton Beach, Holmes Beach, and Anna Maria. Being the vacationer's equivalent of comfort food, they're impossible not to like

© PARKE PUTERBAUGH

if you've got any feeling for the beach life and Old Florida, not to mention white sands and golden sunsets.

Venice

In every possible way, Venice, Florida, is the polar opposite of Venice, California. Yet each of these popular, canal-filled beach towns—loosely based upon the grand Italian city of Venice—appeals to beach lovers in its own way. California's Venice is a fast-paced human parade that's equal parts freak show and *Baywatch* episode. If the human parade were moving any slower in Florida's Venice, it would be going backwards. When we last came to town, we actually saw a marquee announcing the "Johnny Mercer Birthday Show." Mercer was a bandleader from the swing era of the 1940s, but he's apparently still hot stuff in Venice. And there's nothing wrong with that.

The community of Venice is home to 20,000 well-rested folks, and the greater Venice area—which also includes the surrounding communities of South Venice, Nokomis, Laurel, and Osprey—accommodates a population of 90,000. This is the heart of AARP country, which means a lot of early-bird specials are served at local restaurants. It also means that the Venice area is comfortably non-trendy. Venice is the sum total of all the middle-American towns these retirees left behind in order to enjoy their golden years in the Florida sun. Since we're way closer to AARP membership than to the age at which one is first allowed to drink in bars, we'll just wish you many happy, sun-filled days, dear Venetians. You've earned your peace and quiet.

From its inception, Venice has been endowed with understated appeal. It fell within the borders of a 140,000-acre purchase of "wild Florida frontier land" by Mrs. Bertha Palmer, an heiress from Chicago who used her dead husband's fortune to build an elegant winter residence ("The Oaks") in nearby Osprey. She also used her influence to have

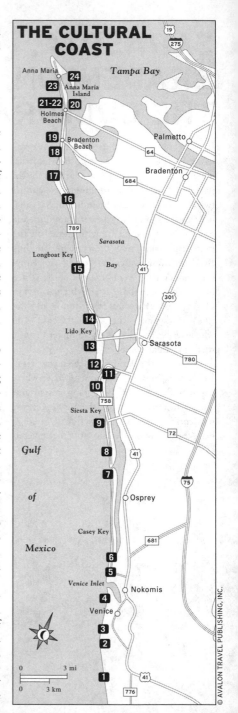

THE CULTURAL COAST

Anna Maria
Tampa Bay
Anna Maria Island
Holmes Beach
Palmetto
Bradenton Beach
Bradenton
Longboat Key
Sarasota Bay
Lido Key
Sarasota
Siesta Key
Gulf
of
Mexico
Osprey
Casey Key
Venice Inlet
Nokomis
Venice

0   3 mi
0   3 km

© AVALON TRAVEL PUBLISHING, INC.

BEST BEACHES

Casperson Park: Top 25 (page 383)

North Jetty Park: Best for Surfing (page 385)

Siesta Key Public Beach: Top 25, Best for People-Watching (page 389)

Coquina Beach: Top 25 (page 403)

Manatee Beach: Best for Families (page 404)

the railroad extended to Venice. A New York physician named Fred Albee chugged into the picture soon thereafter, promoting a new "master-planned community." Backed by railroad money, Albee set to work creating what he saw as a congenial mix of farming, industry, housing, commerce, and recreation, all the while establishing a Northern Italian architectural theme. Venice was incorporated in 1927. Throughout its history it has adhered, as best it could, to tasteful growth rather than slipshod sprawl, and the local preservation league is particularly effective.

Entering town these days, you drive down palm-lined streets past modest middle-class homes with roofs that need repairing or replacing. They don't make it easy for you to find the beach, maybe because they don't want you to. Venice really is less a vacation destination than a residential town. In Venice, you see open space in a way you don't in other towns. It doesn't look as if the developers have discovered what an unblemished jewel it is. (Don't you tell them, either!) One caveat: Car traffic often snarls in downtown Venice, due to a combination of too many timid drivers in barge-sized cars and too few bridges over the Intracoastal Waterway.

Naturally, this well-mannered and neatly manicured community is not in the market for party animals. As if to underscore that point, beachfront accommodations are at a minimum, bars are tame, and the primary recreational vehicles are golf carts and yachts. The latter bob in the town's harbor, from whose ends extend massive jetties that are popular with anglers and birdwatchers. Venice is also blessed with nearly five miles of beach, a sturdy fishing pier, and pleasant year-round weather.

For more information, contact the Venice Area Chamber of Commerce, 257 Tamiami Trail North, Venice, FL 34285, 941/488-2236, www.venicechamber.com.

BEACHES

The beaches of Venice are renowned for their deposits of sharks' teeth, which are a major part of the town's marketing campaign. Shark-adorned T-shirts proclaim Venice "The Shark Tooth Capital of the World." There's no need to freak out about shark attacks, though, because the teeth that wash up are the fossilized remnants of a massive shark burial ground located several miles offshore in a deep trench where they mysteriously go to die.

Of more concern than sharks, at least to the locals, is the fragility of the town's beaches. Venice's jetties are the cause of the erosion problems south of the harbor. In 1996, using sand dredged from an offshore bar, Venice undertook a massive, expensive renourishment of a 3.3-mile stretch of beach. This strand, from Casperson Park north to the harbor mouth, is a fine piece of work, and locals proudly extolled the virtues of "the new beach."

A decade later, the new beach is old news. In the summer of 2005, Venice Beach got a "new" new beach, adding as much as 150 feet of width to the same 3.3 miles that had been renourished before. (This job cost $12 million.) Coastal geologists refer to such actions as a "Band-Aid solution." Moreover, we've heard complaints that the renourished sand covers up the celebrated sharks' teeth. "Since the renourishment of Venice Beach, I have been unable to find teeth there," lamented a collector. But the beach is indeed wide and roomy, if artificially so, and three lifeguard stands provide year-round protection.

Starting from the south end of Venice, **Casperson Park** is an outstanding Sarasota County beach park with ample free parking and nearly two miles of beach. There are no lifeguards this far down, however. A well-marked nature trail runs through 177 acres of coastal hammock, tidal flats, and mangrove forests, affording peaceful diversion from the waves. Boardwalks run out to and along the beach besides a tangle of sea grape, jacarandas, and palm trees. Casperson is large enough to offer isolation—you can walk south for two miles to Manasota Key—in a gorgeous setting.

Moving north along Harbor Drive, we were impressed with the natural habitat left intact in Venice. Dunes exist on both sides of the road, with some of the errant sand spilling onto the asphalt. Up by Venice Fishing Pier is **Brohard Park,** a city-owned, county-maintained beach with a dirt lot, bait and gift shop (get your shark's-tooth T-shirts!), and a popular restaurant, Sharky's at the Pier. The beach beside the 740-foot pier is industrial-strength dredge fill, dark gray and sloping steeply to the surf zone. Brohard Park claims nearly a mile of shoreline. A sub-unit called **Service Club Park** has its own parking lot, picnic area, playground, and dune walkovers.

From the pier, Venice's beach stretches for two miles up to the jetties. **Venice Municipal Beach,** a 875-foot strand, is found at Harbor Drive and Venice Avenue, 1.4 miles north of

Casperson Park

the pier. Just offshore is a reef with large fossil deposits that are swarmed over by divers. The stretch from the pier to Venice Beach is combed by hopeful beachgoers looking for the allegedly commonplace shark teeth. For the record, we have never found a shark's tooth on Venice Beach. The T-shirts are easy to come by, though.

You can also get to the water's edge at South Jetty. There's no public beach here at the harbor, but the jetty area is used for strolling, fishing, and watching pelicans dive-bomb the water. You can also learn a lot about the role of jetties in beach erosion here. Currents transport sand from north to south, but the jetties interrupt that flow like a dam. Stand on the south jetty and look at North Jetty Park. Up there, the coast sticks out much further into the gulf, and the sand is powdery-white and natural. North Jetty has no need for the sort of renourishment required on the narrow, sand-starved beaches south of the harbor. You don't need a degree in coastal engineering to understand how extensively jetties have impacted Venice's beaches.

© PARKE PUTERBAUGH

THE CULTURAL COAST

1 CASPERSON PARK

 BEST (

Location: south of Venice Airport, on Harbor Drive in Venice
Parking/Fees: free parking lots
Hours: 6 A.M.–9 P.M.
Facilities: restrooms, picnic tables, and showers
Contact: Sarasota County Parks and Recreation Department, 941/316-1172

2 BROHARD PARK

Location: in Venice, near the Venice Fishing Pier
Parking/Fees: free parking lot
Hours: 6 A.M.–9 P.M.
Facilities: concessions, restrooms, picnic tables, and showers
Contact: Sarasota County Parks and Recreation Department, 941/316-1172

3 SERVICE CLUB PARK

Location: adjoining Brohard Beach at the north end, on Harbor Drive in Venice
Parking/Fees: free parking lot
Hours: 6 A.M.–9 P.M.
Facilities: restrooms, picnic tables, and showers
Contact: Sarasota County Parks and Recreation Department, 941/316-1172

4 VENICE MUNICIPAL BEACH

Location: west end of Venice Avenue, in Venice
Parking/Fees: free parking lot
Hours: 6 A.M.–9 P.M.
Facilities: concessions, lifeguards, restrooms, picnic tables, and showers

Contact: Sarasota County Parks and Recreation Department, 941/316-1172

RECREATION AND ATTRACTIONS

- **Bike/Skate rentals:** Beach Bikes & Trikes, 127 Tampa Avenue, Venice, 941/412-3821
- **Boat Cruise:** Bay Lady Cruises, 480 Blackburn Point Road, Venice, 941/485-6366
- **Dive Shop:** Scuba Quest, 2357 Tamiami Trail South, Venice, 941/497-5985
- **Fishing Charters:** Maverick Charters, Dona Bay Marina, 504 South Tamiami Trail, Nokomis, 941/966-1001
- **Pier:** Venice Fishing Pier, 1600 Harbor Drive South, Venice, 941/488-1456
- **Marina:** Crow's Nest Marina, 1968 Tarpon Center Drive, Venice, 941/484-7661
- **Rainy-Day Attraction:** Historic Spanish Point, 337 Tamiami Trail North, Osprey, 941/966-5214
- **Shopping/Browsing:** historic downtown Venice (along Venice, Tampa, and Miami Avenues)
- **Surf Shop:** V-Town Surf & Skate, 101 West Venice Avenue, Venice, 941/488-3896
- **Vacation Rentals:** Heritage Vacation Rentals, 908 Villas Drive, Venice, 941/488-2802

ACCOMMODATIONS

There are only two motels near the beach at Venice. They are the **Best Western Sandbar Beach Resort** (811 Esplanade North, 941/488-2251, $$$) and the **Inn at the Beach Resort** (101 The Esplanade, 941/484-8471, $$$). The former is directly on the beach and the latter a block away from it. Both are clean and above average but more pricey than one would expect to pay in modest Venice. At the Best Western, for instance, a two-bedroom gulf-view efficiency goes for $229 a night in season. The plethora of chain motels on U.S. 41, three miles west of the gulf,

THE CULTURAL COAST

are a budget-conscious alternative. But our rule of thumb is to avoid any motel with a Tamiami Trail (U.S. 41) address, as that congested corridor is nowhere near the beach.

COASTAL CUISINE

For our money, the best perch in Venice is topside at the **Crow's Nest Marina Restaurant and Tavern** (1968 Tarpon Center Drive, 941/484-9551, $$$). This airy two-story restaurant overlooks the yacht harbor from the south side. We've whiled away several evenings here, basking in the nautical decor and excellent food. Drinks are nursed downstairs, where lighter fare is available, while exquisitely prepared fresh seafood is served in the main dining room upstairs. Entrees are consistently interesting without going overboard. We started with an excellent seafood bisque that was tangy, robust, and liberally stocked with shrimp, crabmeat, and fish.

Suggested and affordable wines accompany the various entree descriptions. Grouper Key Largo is a worthy signature dish, accompanying a generous portion of grouper with succulent scallops, shrimp, and crabmeat. It is served over wild rice with a tureen of hollandaise sauce (tip that sucker over!). Another excellent choice is pan-seared pompano, served over delicious risotto, flavored with applewood bacon, and doused in a caper mushroom sauce. How about pan-seared medallions of monkfish, shrimp, and scallops with pesto garlic butter? If you've got any room for dessert, the Crow's Nest key lime pie compares favorably with that served in the Florida Keys.

NIGHTLIFE

We were given the lowdown by a lovely twentysomething waitress who was born and raised in Venice. "After midnight, Venice is done," was her summary statement. Venice's large retiree population and genteel, self-policing good manners allow for only so much rocking and rolling after sundown. What action there is can be found at **Sharky's at the Pier** (1600 Harbor Drive South, 941/488-1456).

Live music is offered Wednesday–Sunday, and it's a mix of rock, blues, and reggae, with a "calypso party" on Sunday evening. The outside patio is a great place to watch the sun go down and enjoy a frozen drink (a "deck delight"), but there's a limit: "For safety's sake," you are allowed only two frozen drinks on the patio.

The **Crow's Nest Tavern** (1968 Tarpon Center Drive, 941/484-9551) attracts whatever youngish Venetians are wont to party after the dinner plates have been cleared. Boogie nights bigger than these require a drive north to Sarasota, where the action is hotter and heavier.

Nokomis and Casey Key

Entering Casey Key at the town of Nokomis (pop. 400) via Albee Road (S.R. 789), you are embraced by vestiges of Old Florida. Nokomis is a casual little place that looks like the beach town that time forgot. Development tends toward low-key homes and small, sun-faded motor courts. Nokomis Beach is located where Albee Road meets the water, at Casey Key Road. Half a mile south, the key gives out at North Jetty Park, and Venice lies across the harbor.

Just about everything north of the jetty is residential, and the size of homes trends upward as you travel in that direction. Casey Key Road is a winding, bending, and at times breathtakingly thin and scenic thoroughfare. The homes here are lovely if ostentatious, not unlike Palm Beach. An area resident explained, "Casey Key is for people with money who want to show it off, but they're stuck with that road way out there."

Celebrities reportedly keep homes out here; it's certainly isolated enough to keep the prying eyes of the world at bay. The work of maintaining these estates keeps an army of laborers gainfully employed. Crews of painters, gardeners, repairmen, and landscapers can

© PARKE PUTERBAUGH

Nokomis Beach

THE CULTURAL COAST

be seen working on homesites at nearly every bend in the road.

For more information, contact the Venice Area Chamber of Commerce, 257 Tamiami Trail North, Venice, FL 34285, 941/488-2236, www.venicechamber.com.

BEACHES

The best beach in the Venice area is **North Jetty Park,** which lies across the harbor from Venice at the south end of Casey Key. The county park has much to offer: a wide, breezy beach, bay and gulf access, excellent jetty fishing, and viable surfing where the waves curl around the end of the jetty. Given the right conditions (e.g., a good south swell), North Jetty is one of the best surfing spots on the gulf. Lifeguards are on duty year-round, and volleyball nets, horseshoe courts, and concessions are on the premises.

Nokomis Beach is Sarasota County's oldest public beach, and the weathered benches, old wooden boardwalk, and flyblown showers affirm its age. The coarse, brown-sand beach at this 22-acre park runs for 0.3 mile. A popular family beach, Nokomis Beach has ample free

parking in large gravel lots, picnic pavilions, snack bar, lifeguards, and boat ramp on the Intracoastal Waterway. It is plain and unpretentious, and inviting for that very reason.

At the north end of Casey Key is **Palmer Point Beach.** Before local property owners closed Midnight Pass in 1983, Palmer Point was the northern tip of the barrier island. Now it's connected to Siesta Key, although no through road connects Casey and Siesta Keys. Regardless, the beach at Palmer Point is a secluded spot with 0.5-mile of gulf beach to wander, more often than not by yourself. You're also on your own in that there are no facilities or lifeguards.

For what it's worth, a heavily fortified $4 million estate at the north end of Casey Key was said to be owned by Joey Watts, a loan shark and associate of crime boss John Gotti.

5 NORTH JETTY PARK

Location: at the south end of Casey Key, at Venice Inlet

Parking/Fees: free parking lot
Hours: 6 A.M.–11 P.M.
Facilities: concessions, lifeguards, restrooms, picnic tables, and showers
Contact: Sarasota County Parks and Recreation Department, 941/316-1172

6 NOKOMIS BEACH

Location: Albee Road (S.R. 789) at Casey Key Road
Parking/Fees: free parking lot
Hours: 6 A.M.–11 P.M.
Facilities: lifeguards, restrooms, picnic tables, and showers
Contact: Sarasota County Parks and Recreation Department, 941/316-1172

7 PALMER POINT BEACH

Location: on Casey Key; walk south for 0.5 mile from Turtle Beach on Siesta Key
Parking/Fees: free parking lot at Turtle Beach
Hours: 6 A.M.–11 P.M.
Facilities: none
Contact: Sarasota County Parks and Recreation Department, 941/316-1172

ACCOMMODATIONS

Very little in the way of traditional beach accommodations can be found out this way, but beach-facing suites are available at the irresistibly named **Suntan Terrace Beach Resort** (117 Casey Key Road, Nokomis, 941/484-7110, $$) and **Gulf Sands Beach Apartments** (433 Casey Key Road, 941/488-7272, $$). A few miles up the road is **Gulf Surf Resort Motel** (3905 Casey Key Road, 941/966-2669, $$$), a trim and tidy motor court.

Siesta Key

Siesta Key (pop. 12,000) is split down the middle, literally and figuratively. The beaches are divided by an outcrop known as Point of Rocks. North of it, the constituent sand is powdery, white, and nearly 100 percent pure quartz in content. To the south, the sand is composed of shellier material. Likewise, the community is divided into two distinct halves, with the line of demarcation being Stickney Point Road. Turn right at the light, and there's a dense concentration of commercial activity. Turn left, and a quieter, laid-back, less harried stretch of shoreline unfolds. The community is further divided in its opinions on the reopening of Midnight Pass (see the *Open Midnight Pass!* sidebar), as well as other developmental and environmental issues.

Fortunately for all, however, the residents of Siesta Key are largely in agreement about the kind of place they want their island to be: an unpretentiously upscale escape from reality. It's just a great community, where construction workers will hold the door for you at the local 7-Eleven. The only serious drawback is traffic, which chokes the island at busier times of year.

On the plus side, Siesta Key claims one of the finest sand beaches in Florida, if not the world. Eight miles in length, the key extends from what used to be Midnight Pass north to Big Pass (which separates it from Lido Key). Siesta Key won the Great International White Sand Beach Challenge. Conducted by Woods Hole Oceanographic Institution, Siesta Key beat out 29 other entries due to its pure, floury white sand.

Beyond the professional commendations its sand has received, there's a discernible village character and way of life to be found on Siesta Key. We feel obliged to warn about one thing, however. On long, narrow keys like Siesta where only one main artery (Midnight Pass Road, in this case) runs its length, come prepared for heavy traffic. It's bumper to bumper in season and just plain bad the rest of the year. Incidentally, the whole concept of seasonality is dissolving as Siesta Key's fame spreads far and wide. We visited the island during what was reputed to be one of the slowest times of the year (the week after Halloween) and still hit more than a few traffic jams north of

THE CULTURAL COAST

OPEN MIDNIGHT PASS!

Siesta Key is split down the middle in all kinds of ways: the character of its north and south ends; the sand composition of its beaches; and public opinion surrounding Midnight Pass, a former inlet that separated Siesta Key from Casey Key. Why was it closed? As we understand it, some homeowners were worried about their swimming pools, which were subsiding in the saturated sands near the pass. Caving in to the argument of imminent risk to private property, the county brought in the bulldozers and the inlet was closed.

This was a shame, because it created a distance of 30 miles between inlets. Without Midnight Pass, the barrier island is unbroken from Stump Pass (south end of Manasota Key) to Big Pass (which separates Siesta and Lido Keys). A bay can get pretty polluted without the regular tidal flushing that inlets allow. Midnight Pass's closing has contributed to the decline in water quality of Little Sarasota Bay, which is studded with mangrove islands that serve as bird sanctuaries. The waters are also home to manatees, and some prize fish – including the odd tarpon – have been caught off bayside docks on Siesta Key.

A grassroots group has been agitating to get Midnight Pass reopened. It wouldn't take a lot to make it happen. A channel used by boaters nearly reaches the water now, stopping by the foot of the dunes at Palmer Point. Kayakers and small boaters carry their vessels over the dunes and launch in the ocean. A few well-placed sticks of dynamite, and Midnight Pass would be back in business. Oddly, some environmental groups oppose its reopening. They claim the ecological balance that's evolved since the inlet's closure in 1983 would be disrupted and the public beach at Palmer Point would be lost.

Midnight Pass has long been a hot-button issue in these parts and is symbolic of the types of decisions that lay ahead for coastal communities that must balance environmental well-being with economic growth. The fact that Midnight Pass was closed in the first place is a sad commentary on the sort of influence wielded by those with money and clout. In previous editions, we've stated up-front that we feel Midnight Pass should be opened.

Apparently, someone's been listening – if not to us, then to voices of reason in the community. Erickson Consulting Engineers was retained by the county in 2004 to open Midnight Pass. This is what we know about the project, which was posted on the Erickson website:

"Sarasota County is undertaking the work necessary to plan, design and permit a Project to Reopen Midnight Pass. This Project will restore tidal flows to Little Sarasota Bay, return the system to a marine environment, afford an access to the Gulf for boaters, provide sand for beach nourishment and stabilize the adjacent beaches. Present studies underway will provide the information needed to determine the environmental, economic (costs and benefits) and scientific merits of this Project."

We also know this much: As we went to press in 2006, two years after the permitting process was begun, Midnight Pass still wasn't open.

Stickney Point Road. Basically, snowbirds and Europeans come during the high season, while native Floridians make vacation getaways here the rest of the year. That's another way of saying it's always busy. With award-winning beaches, 50 miles of canals and waterways, and prime fishing opportunities—bridge fishing, surf casting, deep-sea trolling—it's no wonder Siesta Key is popular all year round.

There are two ways on and off the island: S.R. 72 (Stickney Point Road) at its midsection and S.R. 758 (Higel Avenue/Siesta Drive) at the northern "village" end of the island. Siesta and the other keys within easy reach of Sarasota—Casey, Lido, St. Armands, and Longboat—are celebrity-studded places. The rich and famous maintain part- and even full-time residences on these isles. Some of the names we heard bandied about on our last pass through Siesta Key include Michael Jordan (who played minor-league baseball in Sarasota), Tom Selleck, Jerry Wexler (famed producer for Atlantic Records), Brian Johnston (vocalist for hard rockers AC/DC), and Paul Reubens (Pee Wee Herman) and his parents. We even heard that Tom Cruise and Nicole Kidman roosted here in happier times. No doubt other celebs are ensconced behind tropical privacy hedges. Siesta Key is the kind of place that draws them like a magnet, because of its beautiful setting far from the stampeding paparazzi and nosy public. Besides, you won't find prettier sunsets over the water anywhere this side of Malibu.

For more information, contact the Siesta Key Chamber of Commerce, 5100-B Ocean Boulevard, Siesta Key, FL 34242, 941/349-3800 or 888/837-3969, www.siestakeychamber.com.

© PARKE PUTERBAUGH

Turtle Beach

BEACHES

Since Siesta Key falls inside Sarasota County, the public is well taken care of with beaches. The beaches on Siesta Key are markedly different. The main beach accesses—i.e., those with parking lots and facilities—are Turtle Beach and Siesta Key Public Beach. Between them is Crescent Beach. A string of street-end beach accesses lie north of Siesta Key Public Beach, off Beach Road and Ocean Boulevard. One last access can be found at Siesta Key's extreme north end, off Shell Road at Big Pass.

Starting from the south **Turtle Beach** is narrow and sloping. We found it to be alarmingly eroded on our latest visit. A spur road runs along the beach for about a quarter mile, offering public parking in dusty lots. The park itself has volleyball nets and a playground. Part of the paved road got washed out in 2005 by Hurricane Dennis. A nearly $8 million beach renourishment project at Siesta Key's south end has been delayed until late 2006. We actually saw an egret walking on the sidewalk down here, as if it had nowhere else to go.

The sand at Turtle Beach is coarse, brown, and shelly. That is precisely why turtles nest here—they can dig holes in the soft, mounded sand—and how the beach got its name. Writer Joy Williams has expounded on this beach, having owned land here that she's preserved through a conservation easement. "One Acre," her essay about Turtle Beach and Siesta Key, appeared in her book *Ill Nature*. It is a primer on Florida real estate that should be required reading. About the condos of Turtle Beach, she writes:

"The turtles still come to nest, and the volunteers who stake and guard the nests are grateful—they practically weep with gratitude—when the condo dwellers keep their lights out during the hatching weeks so as not to confuse the infant turtles in their late-night search for the softly luminous sea. But usually the condo dwellers don't keep their lights out. They might accommodate the request were they there, but they are seldom there. The lights are controlled by timers and burn bright and long. The condos are investments, mostly, not homes. Like the lands they've consumed, they're cold commodities."

Above an outcrop known as Point of Rocks,

the beach sand changes in composition from shell-based to quartz. At this point, the coastline describes a pronounced curve—hence the name **Crescent Beach**. Located at Siesta Key's midsection, this 2.5-mile beach can be accessed at two points: Point of Rocks, at the west end of Point of Rocks Road, and Stickney Point, at the west end of Stickney Point Road. Both are off Midnight Pass Road, which runs the length of the island. The only problem is parking, which is limited to a few spaces on the roadside. If you're staying at one of the B&B-style motels at Sara Sea Circle, Crescent Beach is just steps away from your room. With its nearshore reef formation, Crescent Beach offers the area's best scuba diving and snorkeling.

Siesta Key Public Beach is a 0.75-mile swath of sand on the north half of the island. Beach lovers should not miss an opportunity to spend time here. It is very nearly a perfect beach, consisting almost entirely of fine-grained white quartz crystals. Because it's so highly reflective, you won't singe your feet when walking across it on a hot day. It actually feels kind of cool, even in the scorching heat of high summer. There is a downside: because it so thoroughly reflects the sun's rays, it's easy to get burned, so slather on the suntan lotion. And because it is fine-grained, it is also hard-packed, so you might want to bring a beach chair or a chaise lounge for comfort's sake.

Siesta Key Public Beach draws a relatively attractive crowd. This beach park also has a full complement of facilities, including showers, a shaded picnic area, and a beachside cafe. A glorified grease pit, the cafe serves its purpose of assuaging hunger pangs while providing unintentional hilarity in the form of winged predators. It is the only restaurant we've ever been where the counter help hands over your food and then warns, "Watch out for the birds, sir." Hungry seabirds perch on the beams above diners' heads, waiting to pounce on untended fried shrimp or French fries. We saw them lurking and heard their shrieking. It was a scene straight out of Alfred Hitchcock's film *The Birds.*

In addition to all that's been mentioned, there is greenspace, benches, volleyball nets, and year-round lifeguards. The place has such a pleasant, beatific vibe that we almost joined a group of vegan belly dancers who were gyrating wildly around a bunch of dreadlocked conga drummers participating in a Ra-worshipping Sunday afternoon drum circle.

⓼ TURTLE BEACH

Location: south end of Siesta Key
Parking/Fees: free parking lots
Hours: 6 A.M.-11 P.M.
Facilities: restrooms, picnic tables, and showers
Contact: Sarasota County Parks and Recreation Department, 941/316-1172

⓽ CRESCENT BEACH

Location: Siesta Key
Parking/Fees: free limited parking at the west ends of Point of Rocks Road and Stickney Point Road
Hours: 6 A.M.-11 P.M.
Facilities: none
Contact: Sarasota County Parks and Recreation Department, 941/316-1172

⓾ SIESTA KEY PUBLIC BEACH

Location: south end of Beach Road, on Siesta Key
Parking/Fees: free parking lot
Hours: 6 A.M.-11 P.M.
Facilities: concessions, lifeguards, restrooms, picnic tables, and showers
Contact: Sarasota County Parks and Recreation Department, 941/316-1172

THE CULTURAL COAST

🔟 SIESTA KEY (NORTH ACCESSES)

Location: There are nine beach accesses at the north end of Siesta Key, off Beach Road and Ocean Boulevard: Avenida del Mare (No. 11), Calle del Invierno (No. 10), Plaza de las Palmas (Nos. 8 and 9), Calle de la Siesta (No. 7), Ocean Boulevard, (No. 5), Avenida Navarra (No. 4), Avenida Messina (No. 2) and Shell Road (No. 1).

Parking/Fees: limited free street parking

Hours: 6 A.M.–11 P.M.

Facilities: none

Contact: Sarasota County Parks and Recreation Department, 941/316-1172

RECREATION AND ATTRACTIONS

- **Bike/Skate Rentals:** Siesta Sports Rentals, 6551 Midnight Pass Road, South Bridge Mall, Siesta Key, 941/346-1797

- **Boat Cruise:** Sea Life Boat Tours, Mote Marine Aquarium, St. Armands Circle, Sarasota, 941/388-4200

- **Canoes/Kayaks:** Kayak Treks, 3667 Bahia Vista Street, Sarasota, 941/365-3892

- **Dive Shop:** Dolphin Dive Center, 6018 South Tamiami Trail, Sarasota, 941/924-2785

- **Ecotourism:** Mote Marine Laboratory & Aquarium, 1699 Ken Thompson Way, Sarasota, 941/388-2451; Myakka River State Park, 13207 S.R. 72, Sarasota, 941/361-6511

- **Fishing Charters:** CB's Saltwater Outfitters, 1249 Stickney Point Road, Siesta Key, 941/349-4400

- **Marina:** Siesta Key Marina, 1265 Old Stickney Point Road, Siesta Key, 941/349-8880

- **Rainy-Day Attraction:** John and Mable Ringling Museum of Art, 5401 Bay Shore Road, Sarasota, 941/359-5700

- **Shopping/Browsing:** St. Armands Circle, St. Armands Key, Sarasota, 941/388-1554

- **Surf Shop:** Underdog Skateboard and Surf Shop, 412 South Washington Boulevard, Sarasota, 941/331-1130

- **Vacation Rentals:** Siesta Key Realty, 5049 Ocean Boulevard, 941/349-8900

ACCOMMODATIONS

From the moment we set foot on **Sara Sea Circle,** we fell in love with it. Located at Siesta Key's midsection at Crescent Beach, Sara Sea Circle is a world within a world that's utterly unique, a kind of Shangri-La by the sea. The concept is this: nine B&B-style motels, banded together as "The Resorts of Sara Sea Circle," all of which hew to high aesthetic standards. Though each has its own courtyard and intricate landscaping, they're all informally linked with shared swimming pools and common greenspace.

They've done a great job of integrating adjacent resorts into a friendly whole. The landscaping is a truly amazing riot of bushes, trees, and flowering plants. Sara Sea Circle seems out of the way, but it isn't. It is an ideal spot for families or couples to vacation—the sort of place to which one would happily return year after year.

We stayed at the Captiva Beach Resort. Our room—actually, a suite with kitchenette—felt like home. The furniture was fine quality and the grounds impeccable. At the end of our stay, we found ourselves wondering why there aren't there more places like Sara Sea Circle. Maybe it just makes too much sense.

Here are all nine of the resorts of Sara Sea Circle: **Capri International** (6782 Sara Sea Circle, 941/349-2626, $$$), **Captiva Beach Resort** (6772 Sara Sea Circle, 941/349-4131, $$$), **Conclare—Sea Castle** (6738 Sara Sea Circle, 941/349-2322, $$$), **Sandy Toes Townhouses** (6810–6812 Midnight Pass Road, 941/922-9150, $$$), **Sara Sea Inn at the Beach** (6760 Sara Sea Circle, 941/349-3244, $$$), **Sea Club V Beach Resort** (6744 Sara Sea Circle, 941/349-1176 $$$), **Siesta Plaza Motel** (1120 Sun 'n' Sea Drive, 941/346-0579, $$$), **Tropical Shores Beach**

Resort (6717 Sara Sea Circle, 941/349-3330, $$$), and **Tropical Sun Resort** (6717 Sara Sea Circle, 941/349-3330, $$$).

At Siesta Key's less harried south end is a little masterpiece of an inn on the bayside. From the road you'd never imagine what lurks behind the modest facade of the **Turtle Beach Resort** (9049 Midnight Pass Road, 941/349-4554, $$$$). An enterprising couple, Gail and Dave Rubinfeld, have transformed an old fish camp into a unique and appealing getaway that's part older cottages and part newish inn. The 10 rooms at their Inn at Turtle Beach and 10 cottages strewn around the bayside property range from studios to one- and two-bedrooms. Each is individually decorated to reflect a different region or theme (e.g., "Country French," "Victorian," "Rainforest," "Montego Bay").

We stayed in "Key West," which evokes tropical surroundings with flowered rattan furnishings and airy, casual feel. Units each have kitchens and a private patio with hot tub. Also on premises are a pool, dock, and paddleboat. Next door is Ophelia's by the Bay, one of Florida's finest restaurants. Turtle Beach itself is right across the road. Turtle Beach Inn attracts everyone from honeymooners to vacationing families with pets. A seven-day minimum stay is imposed in the winter high season.

Most visitors to Siesta Key stay for a week or two, staying at the inn-like motels of Sara Sea Circle or renting a cottage or home. The high season on Siesta Key runs from mid-December through the end of April. Prices thereafter drop by a third. The only chain motel—**Best Western Siesta Beach Resort** (5311 Ocean Boulevard, 941/349-3211, $$$)—is actually closer to the beach-apartment standard in Siesta Key.

COASTAL CUISINE

Ophelia's by the Bay (9105 Midnight Pass Road, 941/349-2212, $$$$) has it all: setting (overlooking Sarasota Bay and its bird-filled mangrove islands), food (creative preparations using fresh ingredients), and atmosphere (casual, rarefied elegance). The dimly lit dining room, done in rich mauves and browns, is a romantic den, but we'd recommend the outdoor deck, mainly because the view is sublime and the breezes refreshing.

For an appetizer, try smoked trout with potato pancake or ask for a popular off-menu item, Szechuan tuna, which also comes in an entree portion. Generous hunks of pepper-coated, sushi-grade tuna are flash fried and served with noodles, soy-sherry sauce, and wasabi. Popular entrees include cedar-roasted salmon. Grilled on a plank, the fish develops a crisp, dark exterior and sweet, moist interior that picks up sublime accents from the wood.

The changeable menu might also include something like baked snapper crusted with dried, chopped black olives. You'll want to stick around for dessert, too. They make a killer key lime pie, and their crème brûlée is one of the richest served anywhere. It moved some fussy foreigners seated near us to exclamations usually reserved for the conclusion of operatic arias. You, too, will be singing the praises of Ophelia's and shouting "Encore!"

Of course, there's plenty of culinary action on an island as cosmopolitan as Siesta Key. **Summerhouse** (6101 Midnight Pass Road, 941/349-1100, $$$$) is the key's other great continental restaurant. For casual "Cali-Florida" waterfront dining, head to **Coasters** (1500 Stickney Point Road, 941/923-4848, $$$), at the east end of South Bridge. The **Siesta Fish Market** (221 Garden Lane, 941/349-2602, $$) is a rustic Old Florida–style seafood house. The **Wildflower Restaurant** (5218 Ocean Boulevard, 941/349-1758, $$) serves healthy vegetarian and seafood dishes. Two favorite breakfast spots are **Broken Egg** (210 Avenida Medera, 941/346-2750, $) and **Cafe Continental** (5221 Ocean Boulevard, 941/346-3171, $). We had cranberry scones and cappuccino at the latter, which is a French-style *patisserie*. While paying up, we overheard one guy proclaim the breakfast he'd just eaten to be the best he'd ever had, anywhere.

THE CULTURAL COAST

Virtually all motels, resorts, and rental properties on Siesta Key come with kitchens, so you can always toss a line from North Bridge (one of the best fishing spots on the Gulf Coast) and hook your own dinner.

NIGHTLIFE

From Siesta Key it's easy to head into Sarasota for an evening of jazz, opera, theater, or dance music. A popular subgenre of spliced, diced, and sampled hip-hop comes right out of Sarasota and can be experienced at **In Extremis** (204 Sarasota Quay, 941/954-2008). Any place advertising a deejay on its marquee will do for getting down.

Back on Siesta Key, the Siesta Village area has a few bar/restaurants with outdoor decks that come to life after dark. You might scare up some live music and a buzzing crowd at the **Beach Club** (5151 Ocean Boulevard, 941/349-6311), which is open every blessed night of the year. We parked our car in a free municipal lot and joined the swinging crowd at the **Daiquiri Deck** (5250 Ocean Boulevard, 941/349-8697). We were there for a Labor Day Weekend kickoff, and the crowd was loud, boisterous, and thirsty. They serve terrific grouper sandwiches and 40 kinds of frozen libations, including ones with grain alcohol in them. In other words, the Daiquiri Deck is like a post-collegiate frat party. There's a sister operation up at Madeira Beach, on Sand Key, if you're headed in that direction and want to keep the party going.

Sarasota

At the risk of sounding like nose-in-the-air snobs, which we're most definitely not—watching *Beverly Hillbillies* and *Sanford and Son* reruns is our idea of a good time—Sarasota (pop. 55,000) is something we never thought we'd see on the Gulf Coast of Florida: a genuine cultural capital. In fact, we strained our noggins to think of a city of comparable size in any state that offers so much in the way

of history, art, and contemplative wonders. Sarasota has museums, bookshops, colleges, and world-class opera houses, concert halls, and theaters. What's more, it's got inland parks, aquariums, and historic sites within easy reach. It also serves as a welcome mat for the superb beaches on the barrier islands of Siesta and Lido Keys.

Sarasota is a veritable three-ring circus of culture. The whole caravan got rolling in 1927, when John and Charles Ringling moved the Ringling Brothers and Barnum & Bailey Circus to Sarasota from Bridgeport, Connecticut. John and his wife Mable built their remarkable home and museums (see the *Step Right Up* sidebar). Numerous other worthy venues followed their lead. The **FSU Center for the Performing Arts** (5555 North Tamiami Trail, 941/351-8000) is home of the Sarasota Ballet and the award-winning Asolo Theatre Company, whose interior reconstructs a 1903 Scottish opera house. There's also the **Ringling Museum of Art** (5401 Bayshore Road, 941/351-1660), the **Sarasota Opera Association** (61 North Pineapple Avenue, 941/366-8450), and the **Florida West Coast Symphony** (Beatrice Friedman Symphony Center, 709 North Tamiami Trail, 941/943-4252). Sarasota's cultural centerpiece is the city-owned **Van Wezel Performing Arts Hall** (777 North Tamiami Trail, 941/953-3366), a stunning facility that was completely renovated in 2000.

In addition to these attractions, Sarasota is the springtime home of the Cincinnati Reds and the winter home—actually, the season runs December–June—of the Sarasota Kennel Club, which hosts greyhound racing. It is the jumping-off point to Florida's largest state park, Myakka River State Park, and home of Selby Botanical Garden. Finally, the Sarasota area is a mecca to anyone interested in archaeology. Three prehistoric sites of enduring interest lie close by: Spanish Point, Little Salt Springs, and Warm Mineral Springs.

The best way to get a handle on the area's many attractions is to obtain a copy of

STEP RIGHT UP: THE RINGLING MUSEUMS

Whereas much of Florida is a figurative zoo, Sarasota is more like a circus. Seriously. When John and Charles Ringling relocated their world-renowned Ringling Brothers and Barnum & Bailey Circus here in 1927, they inaugurated a tradition of circus mania that continues to this day. Currently, 15 circus companies are headquartered in Sarasota County. It is the largest concentration of big-top artists in the world. In celebration of that fact, the city of Sarasota planned to erect as many as 70 clown statues around town until a hue and cry from coulrophobes (those with a phobic fear of clowns) forced them to scale back the project.

To show its support, the community maintains the Sarasota Circus Hall of Fame, inducting new members each year. The names of these immortals are etched upon a gigantic bronze circus wheel in the middle of St. Armands Circle, at the end of Ringling Causeway on St. Armands Key.

This lush park was originally intended to be the entranceway to the Ringling Brothers' dream resort of Lido Beach. They never completed the resort, but the park is now a beautiful tribute to the marquee names of the circus world (Clyde Beatty, the Wallendas, Gunther Gebel-Williams, Lillian Leitzel, Emmett Kelly) and the lesser-known (the Nerveless Nocks, Loyal-Repensky Troupe, "Captain" Curtis, La Norma, Franz Unus). Gebel-Williams, hailed as "the greatest animal trainer of all time," died at home in Venice, Florida, on July 19, 2001.

Over on the mainland, the John and Mable Ringling Museum of Art and Circus Museum offers an earthly afterlife to circus artifacts. It is an impressive attraction – a fact that becomes obvious as you approach the ornate Italian Renaissance-style structure and catch your first gander of the 66-acre complex, replete with a world-class rose garden. An intriguingly eccentric and intelligent man, Ringling wasn't a miser like P. T. Barnum. (Barnum's last words: "How were the receipts at Madison Square Garden today?") Inspired by the East Coast manses of Henry Flagler and John D. Rockefeller – as well as that of Henry Plant in nearby Tampa – Ringling built a multifaceted paradise in Sarasota.

The Circus Museum is just one part of the tour. There's also Ringling's high-ceilinged, parquet-floored art museum, which houses an impressive collection of old Dutch masters, Madonnas, angels, Christ childs, and grim-visaged popes, plus a monumental series of works by Peter Paul Rubens. Just outside the art museum is a meditative sculpture garden, and beyond that the celebrated rose garden.

The Circus Museum is an exceptionally honest, understated, and eclectic tribute to what seems like a lost world. The working calliopes – disparagingly referred to as "the Devil's whistle" by fundamentalist fuddy-duddies in their day – make it easy to see how runaways might have been lured to the circus in the days before television, rock music, and Nintendo. It's all here: beautiful posters and prints, documentary photographs, equipment (including the human cannonball's cannon), circus wagons that look like prototypes for Ken Kesey's Merry Prankster buses, and Emmett Kelly's "Weary Willie" suit (a precursor of Johnny Rotten's wardrobe).

Then there's Ca d'Zan ("House of John"), the Ringlings' terra-cotta mansion. This 30-room bayfront palace was designed to suggest Mable's favorite pieces of architecture: the Doge's Palace in Venice and Old Madison Square Garden in New York.

Admission to the Ringling Museum of Art is $15 for adults, $5 for students, free for kids under five. This includes access to the art museum, courtyard, rose garden, circus museum, and Ca d'Zan. A cafe and gift shop are on-site, too. The complex is open daily 10 A.M.–5:30 P.M.

For more information, contact the John and Mable Ringling Museum of Art, 5401 Bay Shore Road, Sarasota, FL 34243, 941/359-5700, www.ringling.org.

THE CULTURAL COAST

"Sarasota Over My Shoulder," an informative brochure published by the Department of Historical Resources. The only downside to all this cultural capital is that you can get happily hung up on the mainland and neglect to cross the bridges to the beaches. Don't let this happen to you. In fact, make like a human cannonball and blast yourself toward the beach over the road named for the man himself, John Ringling Causeway (S.R. 789).

For more information, contact the Greater Sarasota Chamber of Commerce, 1819 Main Street, Suite 240, Sarasota, FL 34236, 941/955-8187, www.sarasotachamber.org or www.sarasota.com; or the Sarasota Convention and Visitors Bureau, 655 North Tamiami Trail, Sarasota, FL 34236, 941/957-1877 or 800/522-9799, www.sarasotafl.org.

Lido Key and St. Armands Key

Lido Beach is part of the city of Sarasota. It lies on Lido Key, a three-mile island located just above Siesta Key. Though only half as long as Siesta Key, Lido shares the same preponderance of soft, powdery white sand. Both keys' beaches are wide at the north end and thin dramatically to the south.

Ringling Causeway (S.R. 780) heads out to Lido Key from mainland Sarasota. En route, you'll cross three smaller keys: Bird, Coon, and St. Armands. The last of these is enfolded on three sides by Lido Key. The focal point of St. Armands Key is St. Armands Circle, an upscale shopping district that one local described to us as "our Rodeo Drive."

We've found St. Armands Circle to be nowhere near as off-putting and exclusive as the real Rodeo Drive or Worth Avenue in Palm Beach. Instead, it is a lively, accessible area that's something like CocoWalk, in the Miami suburb of Coconut Grove. Initially the centerpiece of John Ringling's dream resort community, St. Armands is a lushly landscaped traffic circle

from which side streets flare off like spokes. Many of its upscale boutiques and gift shops have daffy-sounding names like Soft as a Grape, To Die For!, Wet Noses, Tommy Bahama, and the Ted E. Bear Shop. While each no doubt appeals to a certain type of shopper, we were amused by the fact that our pressing quest for something practical—a roll of masking tape to seal a box of materials for mailing home—was unsuccessful at St. Armands' 120 or so shops. For that, we had to drive back to Sarasota.

For us, the most important side street off St. Armands Circle is the one that leads to Lido Beach. It's located halfway around the circle from Ringling Causeway and is, in fact, the continuation of Ringling Boulevard. Barely a quarter mile away is Lido Beach—a low-key, almost nondescript beach strip running the length of Ben Franklin Drive. Free parking is abundant, and there's little commercial buildup. If you hit Lido Beach at the right time, you'll have a wide, wonderful swath of sand all to yourself.

For more information, contact the Greater Sarasota Chamber of Commerce, 1819 Main Street, Suite 240, Sarasota, FL 34236, 941/955-8187, www.sarasotachamber.org or www.sarasota.com; or the Sarasota Convention and Visitors Bureau, 655 North Tamiami Trail, Sarasota, FL 34236, 941/957-1877 or 800/522-9799, www.sarasotafl.org.

BEACHES

Lido Key extends for 2.5 miles, from Big Sarasota Pass to New Pass. This long, unbroken strand is delightfully isolated in places. Given the large sums changing hands on St. Armands Circle, it's surprising that Lido Beach hasn't been overrun by condos and high-rises—except for an 11-story Ritz-Carlton and a 13-story Radisson Lido Key Beach Resort.

The good news is that Sarasota County owns 1.3 miles of gulf beach on Lido Key. A trio of county parks starts at Big Pass with **South Lido Beach.** This 100-acre nature preserve has a small (640 feet) gulf beach and a much lengthier shoreline along Big Pass (3,500 feet).

MOTE MARINE AQUARIUM AND LABORATORY

The Sarasota area tosses a lot of unique and tantalizing attractions at visitors. If you're staying awhile, many are worth checking out, including the Ringling Museum, Spanish Point, Selby Botanical Garden, Myakka River Excursions, and Jungle Gardens. There's one place that should be a required stop for any visit here: **Mote Marine Aquarium and Laboratory.**

Mote Lab is close to the beach, off the northeast corner of St. Armands Key on man-made City Island. It is a museum and a research lab that brings visitors as close to the coastal ecosystem as they can get without a wetsuit and snorkel. At the aquarium's entrance is a tiger-shark jaw; you're invited to run your finger over its four rows of razor-sharp teeth. Certain species are flirting with endangered-species status, so Mote has been tagging sharks in order to study their dwindling numbers and prevent their needless slaughter. They also have a 135,000-gallon shark tank.

At Mote, they're working to restock shark and other fish species-especially those impacted by disappearing wetlands habitat, which robs them of the first stage of their life cycle. All told, 200 live marine species are on display, including spiny lobsters, balloonfish, cowfish, urchins, sturgeons, barracudas, and octopuses. Kids can pick up specimens in touch tanks, ask questions of the helpful staff, and learn fascinating facts such as this:

Questions: How many hearts does an octopus have?

Answer: An octopus has three hearts.

Also open to the public is the Marine Mammal Visitor Center, which has tanks full of dolphins, manatees, and whales. This facility rehabilitates large injured sea animals, such as porpoises and sea turtles. We watched a pair of recuperating manatees bob around in their tank. These marine mammals are fed Romaine lettuce and other vegetarian fare. Their weekly grocery bill is $1,163. Mote is concerned with sturgeons, since much of the caviar that's sold comes from a criminal black market and is taken from these nearly extinct fish. (Just say no to caviar!) The center works to find aquaculture solutions to environmental disasters, too.

Sarasota Bay Explorers (941/388-4200) leads "sea life encounter" ecotourism trips that depart from Mote each weekday at 4 P.M. (also at 11 A.M. and 1 P.M. on weekends).This two-hour educational outing cruises Sarasota Bay and Robert Bay, exploring grass flats and mangrove islands. There are close encounters with dolphins, manatees, pelicans, herons, ibises, egrets, ospreys, eagles, and more. Binoculars are provided.

In the same generous, pro-nature spirit – and just down the block from Mote – is **Pelican Man's Bird Sanctuary** (1708 Ken Thompson Parkway, 941/388-4444). Pelican Man does for injured birds what Mote does for wounded ocean dwellers. This "open-air home and rehabilitation center" welcomes visitors, and admission is free.

General admission to Mote Marine Aquarium is $15 for adults, $10 for children 4-12, and free for kids under three. It is open every day of the year 10 A.M.-5 P.M. Admission includes access to the Aquarium, the Ann and Alfred Goldstein Marine Mammal Center, and Mote's new Immersion Cinema

For more information, contact Mote Marine Aquarium and Laboratory, 1600 Ken Thompson Parkway, Sarasota, FL 34236; 941/388-2451 or 800/691-MOTE, www.marinelab.sarasota.fl.us.

THE CULTURAL COAST

Huge dirt lots can take on all comers, and the picnic area on the bayside is very inviting.

There are two park entrances: a north one facing Sarasota Bay and a south one on Lido Beach. Within each section is a nature trail. The Northern Nature Trail explores a coastal ridge, mangrove swamp, and tidal swamp forest. The northern unit also has a canoe trail that winds along mangrove-lined waterways. The shorter Southern Nature Trail runs along a sandy-soiled coastal ridge. South Lido Park offers a lot to nature enthusiasts, so eat your Wheaties and get hiking or paddling. There is a posted boast that "We Are a Pesticide-Free Beach." If you're planning on swimming, then be advised that currents near the pass can be swift, so stick to marked areas only.

The main beach is **Lido Beach,** and it's located 0.5-mile southwest of St. Armands Circle on Ben Franklin Drive. The park claims 3,100 feet of beachfront and an enormous free parking lot. There's metered parking along Ben Franklin Drive to handle any spillover. Also at Lido Beach: a snack bar, gift shop, playground, beach rentals, and 25-meter heated pool with diving board. Lifeguards are on duty year-round. The beach itself is prone to erosion, which is dealt with by groins and periodic renourishment. However, Lido Beach looked pretty darned healthy when we came through in 2005. The crescent-shaped beach had to be 100 yards wide at its midsection.

A quarter-mile northwest of St. Armands Circle is **North Lido Beach,** a 77-acre preserve at the end of the road (but not the end of the key). There's another 3,000 feet of public beach at North Lido. It is more secluded up here than at Lido Beach, no doubt because parking is practically nil and there are no lifeguards or facilities. Basically, it's been kept in a wild state for the birds and the beachcombers who want to escape the crowds. Nude sunbathing was tolerated here well into the 1980s. Chances are that it still goes on, though disrobing is now technically illegal. Currents by the pass can be dangerous, so maybe nude sunbathing is the safest activity after all.

12 SOUTH LIDO BEACH

Location: South end of Ben Franklin Drive on Lido Key
Parking/Fees: free parking lot
Hours: 6 A.M.–sunset
Facilities: lifeguards (seasonal), restrooms, picnic tables, and showers
Contact: Sarasota County Parks and Recreation Department, 941/316-1172

13 LIDO BEACH

Location: 0.5 mile southwest of St. Armands Circle at Ben Franklin Drive on Lido Key
Parking/Fees: free parking lot
Hours: 6 A.M.–sunset
Facilities: concessions, lifeguards, restrooms, picnic tables, and showers
Contact: Sarasota County Parks and Recreation Department, 941/316-1172

14 NORTH LIDO BEACH

Location: north end of North Polk Drive on Lido Key
Parking/Fees: free parking lot
Hours: 6 A.M.–sunset
Facilities: none
Contact: Sarasota County Parks and Recreation Department, 941/316-1172

ACCOMMODATIONS

A row of hotels lies along Ben Franklin Drive southwest of St. Armands Circle. They offer resort-style amenities, with pools, lounges, and restaurants. The beach is wide, white, and breezy in front of them. In ascending order of cost and desirability, they are **Harley Sandcastle** (1540 Ben Franklin Drive, 941/388-2181, $$$), **Holiday Inn Lido Beach** (233 Ben Franklin Drive, 941/388-5555, $$$),

Radisson Lido Key Beach Resort (700 Ben Franklin Drive, 941/388-2161, $$$), and **Ritz-Carlton Sarasota** (1111 Ritz-Carlton Drive, 941/309-2000, $$$$).

COASTAL CUISINE

While the tone of St. Armands Circle is upscale, it is not dominated by huge flagship stores or faddish places like Planet Hollywood. Many one-of-a-kind shops and eateries can be found here, making for pleasurable shopping and strolling. With apologies to Jerry Lee Lewis, there's a whole lotta window shoppin' goin' on. A whole lotta eatin', too.

Morning strollers duck into **Morty's Bagel Cafe** (24 South Boulevard of Presidents, 941/388-3811, $) and **Barnie's Coffee & Tea Co.** (382 St. Armands Circle, 941/388-1195, $). The former turns out bagels as good as any in Brooklyn, while the latter serves eye-opening cups of java.

For dinner, we drifted to the **Columbia Restaurant** (411 St. Armands Circle, 941/388-3987, $$$), which is a must-stop on St. Armands Circle. Columbia originated in Tampa's Ybor City in 1905, and the St. Armands Circle location has been serving great Cuban food since 1959. The paella and *arroz con pollo* are to die for. We also heard commendations for **Chef Caldwell's** (20 Adams Drive South, 941/388-5400, $$$$), whose signature dishes are grilled venison, roasted duckling, and pecan-crusted snapper.

NIGHTLIFE

The outdoor patio at **Cha Cha Coconuts** (417 St. Armands Circle, 941/388-3300)—next door to the Columbia Restaurant on the northeast quadrant of St. Armands Circle—is about as wild as it gets on St. Armands Key. Even on weekends, the partying we witnessed was not enough to scare off the elderly couples contentedly strolling the sidewalks. Seldom is heard a discouraging word, and blaring rap and mindless dance beats are minimally encountered.

We headed into Sarasota and spent a pleasant evening browsing **Main Bookshop** (1962 Main Street, 941/366-7653), which is open until 11 P.M. seven days a week. This place is a monster, with the largest selection of remainders (out-of-print books sold at rock-bottom prices) outside of New York City. There are also hundreds of thousands of new books, posters, and prints, plus free coffee and reading areas.

Longboat Key

On Longboat Key (pop. 8,000), what you see is what you get: a sterile artificial paradise for those who can afford the real estate. At one time Longboat Key had a certain quaint charm based upon those who'd lived or visited for generations, but today it projects all the welcoming warmth of a bank lobby.

The tropical greenery is in place, as is typical of privatized hideaways on Florida's various coasts, but it's so obsessively tended and preternaturally lush that it exists in an almost disharmonious way with the landscape it means to decorate. Groundskeepers work overtime trimming hedges into perfectly shaped silos and meatballs. Dense thickets of greenery create an impenetrable wall around the premises of homes. There's nothing pleasing or artful about these horticultural presentations. To the contrary, they convey a demand for privacy that practically screams, "Stay off my property!" Oddly, given the enormous wealth, Longboat Key is just as undistinguished as it could be—boring, in fact. There's nothing much to see and little to remark on. Its prehistory is way more interesting than its present.

Longboat Key was a quiet fishing village for the first half of the 20th century. John Ringling tried to build a dream resort at the south end of the island in the 1930s, but the Depression forced him to abandon the golf course and hotel in midstream. Groundwork for serious development began when the Arvida corporation bought up land, including Ringling's holdings, in the late 1950s. Arvida is largely responsible for what has happened

THE CULTURAL COAST

THE WRONG PEOPLE HAVE ALL THE MONEY

We're lounging poolside at an upscale resort somewhere on the coast of Florida. There's no need to divulge the name or location, since the experience could happen anywhere. We've stuck this essay next to Longboat Key because this 12-mile island typifies the issue we are about to address – to wit, the way that wealth behaves and is courted at the beach.

The high-rise building behind the pool and Jacuzzi we're hanging out at has all the architectural charm of an armory. Everything about it encourages isolation, in the deepest existential sense of the word. There is no sense of community and few opportunities for interacting. The well-furnished cells in these condo towers go for stiff tariffs ($500 or more per night in season). The inhabitants while away the hours golfing or partaking or lying on the beach, both of which cost even more money. A cabana setup – basically, a chaise lounge and umbrella – can set you back $25 a day, plus tip to the attendant.

The resort tower in which these dark thoughts flood our heads blocks views and access to the beach to everyone who isn't staying here. Non-guests cannot cross the property to the beach without encountering an off-putting maze of guard gates, fences, checkpoints, and signs warning them off the property. Legally, the beach is public seaward of the mean high-tide line, and everybody has a right to be on it. The trick is crossing private property to get to the public beach. Hence, the need for public beach access, which is well served in some places and virtually nonexistent in others.

Several questions haunt us in our travels around the beaches of America: Who are the beaches for? Do those whose wealth purchases access to the most desirable locales really deserve the exclusivity? Shouldn't the best things about a democracy – including the grandest natural features of the very land itself – be accessible to all?

Back at the Jacuzzi, we're weighing the merits of mingling with strangers in this giant outdoor bathtub. With a sinking feeling, we realize that we have nothing in common with any of them. There are eight strangers in the Jacuzzi. Half are grossly overweight men with highballs in their hands. They have not set foot on the beach during their entire stay, and this is their first lungful of fresh air following eight hours of dull business conventioneering. The others are yuppie couples gossiping about a pending divorce: "Poor ol' Rob, he's gonna feel like he's been robbed when Julie's done with him – ha! ha! ha!"

on Longboat Key, bulldozing and scraping the key clean and then erecting private homes and condos for buyers with deep pockets.

There are marginal differences between opposing ends of the 11-mile island, which is almost evenly divided between Sarasota County and Manatee County. The south end is old-fogey land, where "I got mine"-ism is the reigning philosophy. Residents at the north end are younger and more attuned to history and nature, although there's not much left to preserve on either count. The north-enders refer to themselves as the "village idiots," because they're wild and crazy progressives

compared to the golf club–toting conservatives down south. The village area along Broadway Street does contain vestiges of a humbler past and is worth a look-see, just to catch a glimpse of how Longboat Key used to look.

Basically, the condo architecture is boring, the beaches hard to get at, and the general vibe unfriendly. That's not to say you can't have a good time if you come with family or friends. The beach is white and fine, the gulf inviting. A 10-mile bike path runs the length of the island, paralleling Gulf of Mexico Drive. But there's something distinctly generic about Longboat Key, as if nature's been factored out

At the poolside tiki bar, a well-heeled young couple stares wordlessly at each other. A pair of designer sunglasses dangles from a cord around his neck as he sips numbly on a frozen margarita. She's staring goofily into the middle distance, her lips – a marvel of the plastic surgeon's art – strained into a forced smile. A few old folks are tromping around, dripping wet in baggy swimsuits, muttering grumpily about dinner plans. The cabana clerk begins breaking down the setups on the beach. On the patio, a waitress prepares tables for the dinner hour. The sun is setting and the sky is beautiful, but the human landscape in the shadow of this gray building is depressing.

Some hours have passed, and we're dining in a restaurant to which we've been tipped off by some locals. A foursome walks in: two couples dripping money and self-importance. It quickly becomes apparent they've got more money than sense. Before the waiter can utter a word, one of the women blurts, "Ya got any salmon?" With all the available choices of native species plucked fresh from local waters, she wants salmon, flown in from the far side of the continent. Her jowly husband peers over his bifocals and scowls, "I ought to get broiled. Know it's better for you. But I don't like broiled. Always shrinks up to nothing."

Once the orders are placed and menus collected, the big-mouthed patriarch avails himself of a reserve of tasteless, unfunny, and tired jokes about the Clintons. When we leave, he's still at it, huffing and puffing, full of hot air and fried flounder.

No sooner have we returned to our high-priced room when there's a knock at the door. It's a maid bearing a rose and some chocolates. She offers "turndown service." What is this service? Typically, a chambermaid enters your room, often when you're out to dinner, to turn down the sheets, thereby making it infinitely easier for you to get into bed. A chocolate is placed atop the pillow, too. Our maid has brought a fresh flower as well. We're best friends but we don't exchange flowers. We politely decline the proffered turndown and the rose.

Our final thoughts have to do with soap – specifically, what a waste of soap there is in this place. Plastic-wrapped, scented, imported soaps made of the finest ingredients are stationed at every sink and tub (which number six in our two-bedroom condo). What happens to the 95 percent of the bar that isn't used? Isn't there a way – say, refillable tanks of liquid soap – to cut down on packaging and eliminate the discarding of countless bars of barely used soap?

The larger point that's dawned on us by day's end – after surveying all the wasteful extravagance – is that the wrong people have all the money. What makes them wrong, in our view, is the belief that the beach is "theirs."

of the equation, and you must bring your good times with you because they don't exist here.

We'll leave off by noting there are far better vacation spots worth touting in both counties that claim a share of Longboat Key. Who needs that sort of uptight elitism at the beach?

For more information, contact the Longboat Key Chamber of Commerce, 6854 Gulf of Mexico Drive, Longboat Key, FL 34228, 941/383-2466, www.longboatkeychamber.com.

BEACHES

The beaches of Longboat Key were severely eroded by hurricanes in 2004. Worse, some of the sand they paid $21 million to place on the thinning beaches in 2005 got washed away by Hurricane Dennis.

We don't feel too sorry for them, because it's hard to shake the feeling you're not really wanted on Longboat Key unless you're an owner or paying guest. The beach and ocean are hidden from view of the road along much of Longboat Key, with the exception of one beach-hugging stretch at its midsection. Surfers refer to the area as "Lookout," because it's the one place you can look out at the gulf from the road to gauge the surf. However, the view is spoiled by a plague of signs spiked into the sand that read "Private Property." So you must keep shuffling along, lest you threaten the security of their enclave. The good news is that getting off the island will make both you (the would-be visitor) and the cranky property owners of Longboat Key (the reluctant hosts) happy.

What bothers us most about Longboat Key is the lack of beach access and facilities for the public. The town of **Longboat Key** grudgingly offers four accesses between 3000 and 3500 Gulf of Mexico Drive. Each has a free wood-chip parking lot with 19–54 parking spaces and access to the island's white-sand beach. But there are no facilities—not a restroom, water fountain, or even a lousy garden hose to rinse off your feet—at any of them.

There's another clump of accesses with parking lots on the Manatee County side of Longboat Key. These accesses are located off Gulf of Mexico Drive near Atlas Street (50 spaces), Gulfside Road (50 spaces), and Broadway Street (50 spaces). Another leads to a hooked spit known as **Greer Island Beach**—and informally referred to as "Beer Can Island"—whose beach runs for 0.5 mile up to Longboat Pass. It is reachable from a parking lot at North Shore Road (26 spaces), just beyond the Longboat Key Bridge over to Anna Maria Island. There are no facilities—not so much as a stinking Portolet—at any of them, leaving us wondering what kind of day at the beach they want you to have on Longboat Key.

It should be noted there are a couple of city parks on the bay side of Longboat Key: Quick Point Nature Preserve, a tidal lagoon and mangrove wetland at the south end, and John M. Duarante Community Park, which preserves a sliver of coastal hammock at the opposite end of the island.

15 LONGBOAT KEY ACCESSES (SOUTH END)

Location: beach accesses with parking located at 3055 (near Neptune Avenue), 3174 (across from

Buttonwood Plaza), 3400 (near the Sea Horse Restaurant) and 3500 (near Long View Drive) Gulf of Mexico Drive on Longboat Key; in addition, there is a county-owned access at Triton Avenue
Parking/Fees: free parking lots
Hours: 5 A.M.-11 P.M.
Facilities: none
Contact: Longboat Key Public Works Department, 941/316-1966

16 LONGBOAT KEY ACCESSES (NORTH END)

Location: Beach accesses with parking are located on Gulf of Mexico Drive at Atlas Street, Gulfside Road, and Broadway Street on Longboat Key. In addition, there are beach-access easements (no parking) on Gulf of Mexico Drive at the Longboat Key Hilton, 6677 Gulf of Mexico Drive, Beachwalk, and Coral/Seabreeze Avenues
Parking/Fees: free parking lots
Hours: 5 A.M.-11 P.M.
Facilities: none
Contact: City of Longboat Key Public Works Department, 941/316-1966

17 GREER ISLAND BEACH (A.K.A. BEER CAN ISLAND)

Location: North Shore Road off Gulf of Mexico Drive on Longboat Key, just past Longboat Key Bridge
Parking/Fees: free parking lot
Hours: sunrise-sunset
Facilities: none
Contact: Manatee County Parks and Recreation Department, 941/742-5923

ACCOMMODATIONS

If you're not renting for a week or two, there are several resort hotels on the island. The best beachside locations belong to **Holiday Inn and Suites of Longboat Key** (4949 Gulf of Mexico Drive, 941/383-3771, $$$$) and **Longboat Key Hilton** (4711 Gulf of Mexico Drive, 941/383-2451, $$$$). We will give

Longboat Key this much credit: They've done a great job of minimizing signage with restrictive ordinances. No sign can be more than four feet tall, and neon is forbidden so that hotel, motel, restaurant, bar, and store signs do not assault the senses.

The island's best and best-known property is the **Longboat Key Club & Resort** (301 Gulf of Mexico Drive, 941/383-8821, $$$$). It is located at the south end, a mile from New Pass Bridge, on land formerly owned by John Ringling. He built a Ritz-Carlton on this spot in the 1930s, lavishly appointed with chandeliers and brass fixtures. Unfortunately, the Depression dashed his dream of a luxury beach resort, and the hotel was abandoned before completion. The "Ghost Hotel," as it was called by locals, stood for 30 years until its demolition in 1963. To this day, many older Sarasotans can spin yarns of adolescent misdeeds committed inside and on the grounds of the Ghost Hotel.

Today those grounds are occupied by six suite-filled towers, three restaurants, 36 tennis courts, and 45 holes of golf. If dad's a golf nut, mom likes tennis, and the kids just want to splash around a pool, the whole family will be happy at the Longboat Key Club. The buildings look a bit impersonal from the outside, but their well-appointed suites offer all the comforts of home: roomy rooms, balconies, and amenities like terrycloth robes, coffeemakers, and TVs everywhere you turn. Guest rooms run $335–435 in the high season (February–April) and drop by a third in summer. Two-bedroom suites run $820–1160 in the choicest months. That's a lot of jack for a room you'll inhabit for 24 hours or less.

The lately replenished beach at the Longboat Key Club is a wide, white ribbon. Nothing could be finer than gazing on the gulf from a cabana with a dog-eared book, a cool drink and the sun beaming overhead. Who needs golf when you've got gulf?

COASTAL CUISINE

For a glimpse at Longboat Key's back pages, turn onto Broadway from Gulf of Mexico Drive (S.R. 789) at a Chevron station at the north end. Back here low-slung bungalows and normal-looking yards impart a whiff of yesteryear. Three of the original "Whitney Beach cottages" still stand near the water in this small area, and two waterfront restaurants preserve the ambience of old Longboat Key.

Moore's Stone Crab (800 Broadway Street, 941/383-1748, $$$) is a gray, weathered structure that specializes in stone crab claws in season. When we last passed through, stone crab dinners were going for $22, while jumbos were fetching $40. The menu lists all sorts of seafood, but for a good sampling try "The One and Only Longboat Platter," which includes fried shrimp, oysters, scallops, fish fingers, and seafood chowder. You can dock your boat at Moore's. The glassed-in dining room overlooks the dock, upon which pelicans and seagulls perch. Moore's is the oldest seafood restaurant in Manatee County.

Euphemia Haye (5540 Gulf of Mexico Drive, 941/383-3633, $$$$) sets the standard for fine dining on Longboat Key. Its continental menu runs from fresh seafood to roast duckling.

We're partial to the **Mar Vista** (760 Broadway Street, 941/383-2391, $$$). It looks like an old bait shack, and that's exactly what it is. The ceilings are low and studded with grubstake. At lunch you can get a grilled grouper Rueben or a Caesar salad topped with fresh shrimp and crabmeat. At dinner, the chef whips up an array of made-from-scratch sauces for such dishes as triggerfish Kyoto (a sauteed fillet served with palm hearts, shiitake mushrooms, and soy-sherry butter). Sesame tuna is pan-seared and served with a pungent ginger wasabi soy sauce. If you've just got a yen for seafood simply prepared, go for Mar Vista's steamer pots.

NIGHTLIFE

Most of the night moves on Longboat Key are made by befuddled sea turtles looking to lay eggs on narrowing beaches that were for thousands of years their private property.

Anna Maria Island: Bradenton Beach, Holmes Beach, and Anna Maria

Anna Maria Island is the Cinderella who didn't get invited to the developers' black-tie ball on Longboat Key, and she hasn't regretted the snub one bit. In fact, Anna Maria looks prettier and more dignified than her sister key with each passing season. For starters, most of this 7.5-mile barrier island is accessible to the beach-going public, from Coquina Beach up to Holmes Beach. (The community of Anna Maria itself, at the north end, is a tougher nut to crack.)

No, this is not a nature sanctuary or National Seashore but a fully developed, family-friendly island. Growth here has been intelligently overseen, beginning with a concerted effort 30 years ago to enact and stick to a master plan. That plan includes a height limit of three stories and a respectful attitude toward Mother Nature. The coastline hasn't been dramatically tampered with or built on, and the result is a low-key sandy paradise that anyone would be proud to call home—or home away from home. If that's not reason enough to visit, consider that this stretch of Florida's West Coast once set a Guinness record for the most consecutive sunny days: 768 in a row. That's more than two years' worth!

Two bridges—Cortez (S.R. 684) and Palma Sola Causeway (S.R. 64)—connect Anna Maria Island to the mainland city of Bradenton. At the south end, Gulf Drive (S.R. 789) joins the island with Longboat Key. There are three relaxed and contiguous communities on the island: Bradenton Beach (pop. 1,700), Holmes Beach (pop. 5,000), and Anna Maria (pop. 1,800). The towns all exhibit a funky, sun-baked character (hand-painted murals, slapdash houses, screened-in porches, mom-and-pop businesses) and a genuine, lived-in authenticity. The island's inviting character has evolved naturally over generations as locals and loyal visitors have found a congenial common ground. These are the sort of unaffected beach towns we loved when we were kids. We strongly feel that people still want real communities and experiences like these when they go on vacation.

Anna Maria Island has tried to surmount the slippery slope of social class. Room and board are affordable, and much of the low-key, low-to-the-ground real estate is within easy walking distance of the beach. The three towns collectively impart philosophies of "Come one, come all" and "Don't worry, be happy." Anna Maria is the quietest and most residential, making it a great place to rent a vacation home or villa. Holmes Beach is the largest, with roughly 5,000 year-round residents and three miles of beach. Bradenton Beach has sunk the deepest taproot, centered around the renovated Bradenton City Pier (built in 1921). At this bayside complex, you can stroll and fish or sit on one of the many benches after polishing off a chili cheese dog basket.

For more information, contact the Anna Maria Island Chamber of Commerce, 5337 Gulf Drive North, Holmes Beach, FL 34217, 941/778-1541, www.annamariaislandchamber.org.

BEACHES

Because there are no gated gulf-front communities or horizon-obscuring high-rises on Anna Maria Island, the beach is part of every visitor's daily reality and a constant reminder of why people set aside two weeks from their stress-filled lives to come here. The beach is fairly consistent, with powdery white sand backed by anchoring vegetation and tree breaks. A beach-widening project on Anna Maria Island in summer 2005 was necessitated by all the sand lost during the previous hurricane season. The trouble is, quality sand is getting expensive, and the project itself necessitates beach closures—which interferes with the summer tourist season. Anna Maria Island lost a fair amount of vacation business in 2005 due to the renourishment projects, red tide, and the ever-present specter of hurricanes.

Public beach access is no problem on Anna Maria Island, except in the town of Anna Maria itself. Three county-run, gulf-facing beach parks (Coquina, Cortez, and Manatee) provide the facilities you'll need for an all-day visit if you're not staying directly on the beach. From south to north, here are the beaches of Anna Maria Island:

- **Coquina Beach**—This popular Manatee County park has both gulf beach and bayfront boating access. The mile-long coquina shell beach is white and hard-packed. A tree-lined beach lies on the west side of the road, and undeveloped natural habitat flourishes on the east. Picnic tables are set behind healthy sand dunes under a canopy of Australian pines. There's a playground and a lifeguarded safe swimming area. (Signs warn of a steep drop-off in the water.) Facilities include a cafe and concession kiosk at which beach chairs and umbrellas can be rented. The only negative at Coquina Beach is the line of cement groins on the beach.

- **Cortez Beach**—Another popular Manatee County park, Cortez Beach runs from the north end of Coquina Beach into the town of Bradenton Beach, from 5th to 13th Streets. Cortez is within walking distance of restaurants, shops, and bars. It's the site of a prime surf spot known as Three Piers—they're not really piers but erosion groins.

- **Palma Sola Causeway**—Beaches line the Palma Sola Causeway (Manatee Avenue/S.R. 64), the northernmost of two causeways linking Bradenton with Anna Maria Island. These sandy bay beaches have picnic tables and boat ramps.

- **Manatee Beach**—Located at the west end of Manatee Avenue in Holmes Beach, this is one of the most popular spots on Anna Maria Island. There's free parking in a sprawling dirt and shell lot, as well as lifeguards, volleyball nets, and one of the coolest beach cafes we've seen in a county park (see *Coastal Cuisine*). Holmes Beach Pier anchors the action here.

- **Holmes Beach**—Nearly three miles of beach can be accessed via various street ends in Holmes Beach off Gulf Drive between 28th Street (at the south end of town) and White Avenue (which divides Holmes Beach from Anna Maria). There are no facilities or lifeguards, just street parking and beach access.

- **Anna Maria Beach**—The gulf beach on the island's north end is accessible via dune walkovers at residential street ends, but there are neither facilities nor parking spaces. Your best bet is to park at the public lot by the post office at Spring Avenue and Gulf Drive, then walk west on Spring Avenue to the beach. A shore break at the south end of Anna Maria, in the vicinity of Beach and White Avenues, is another good surf spot on Anna Maria Island.

- **Anna Maria Bayfront Park**—Located on Bay Boulevard, this county park features 1,000 feet of beach on Tampa Bay. Anna Maria City Pier is located just south of the park, on Pine Avenue at Bay Boulevard.

Surfers, take note: the surf here on the south side of Tampa Bay is better than on the north, because the water's deeper and the waves pick up more juice. In fact, Anna Maria Island has been called "the surfing epicenter south of Tampa."

18 COQUINA BEACH

  BEST (

Location: south end of Anna Maria Island, off Gulf Drive (S.R. 789)

Parking/Fees: free parking lot

Hours: sunrise-sunset

Facilities: concessions, lifeguards, restrooms, picnic tables, and showers

Contact: Manatee County Parks and Recreation Department, 941/742-5923

19 CORTEZ BEACH

Location: between 5th and 13th Streets, off Gulf Drive in Bradenton Beach

Parking/Fees: free parking lot

THE CULTURAL COAST

Hours: sunrise-sunset
Facilities: lifeguards, restrooms, picnic tables, and showers
Contact: Manatee County Parks and Recreation Department, 941/742-5923

Hours: sunrise-sunset
Facilities: concessions, lifeguards, restrooms, picnic tables, and showers
Contact: Manatee County Parks and Recreation Department, 941/742-5923

20 PALMA SOLA CAUSEWAY

Location: along both sides and at both ends of the Palma Sola Causeway (Manatee Avenue/S.R. 64), which links Bradenton and Anna Maria Island, entering the latter at Holmes Beach
Parking/Fees: free parking lots
Hours: sunrise-sunset
Facilities: restrooms and picnic tables
Contact: Manatee County Parks and Recreation Department, 941/742-5923

22 HOLMES BEACH

Location: approximately 15 street ends between 28th Avenue and White Avenue off Gulf Drive in Holmes Beach
Parking/Fees: free street parking
Hours: sunrise-sunset
Facilities: none
Contact: Holmes Beach City Hall, 941/708-5800

21 MANATEE BEACH

  BEST

Location: 40th Street and Gulf Drive in Holmes Beach
Parking/Fees: free parking lot

23 ANNA MARIA BEACH

Location: west ends of streets from White Avenue north to Bean Point in Anna Maria
Parking/Fees: free parking lot at Spring Av-

Manatee Beach

© PARKE PUTERBAUGH

enue and Gulf Drive; no parking allowed on residential side streets that end at the beach
Hours: sunrise-sunset
Facilities: none
Contact: Anna Maria Public Works Department, 941/778-7092

24 ANNA MARIA BAYFRONT PARK

Location: off Bay Boulevard along Tampa Bay in Anna Maria
Parking/Fees: free parking lot
Hours: sunrise-sunset
Facilities: Restrooms and picnic tables
Contact: Manatee County Parks and Recreation Department, 941/742-5923

RECREATION AND ATTRACTIONS

- **Bike/Skate Rentals:** Ringling Bicycles, 3606 Manatee Avenue West, Bradenton, 941/749-1442; Iguana Have Fun, 13 Avenue of the Flowers, Longboat Key, 941/387-2100

- **Boat Cruise:** Lo-Seas II, 5501 Marina Drive, Holmes Beach, 941/778-1977

- **Dive Shop:** Sea Trek Divers, 105 7th Street North, Anna Maria, 941/779-1506

- **Ecotourism:** Ray's Canoe Hideaway, 1247 Hagle Park Road, Bradenton, 941/747-3909

- **Fishing Charters:** Findango Charters, 12507 44th Avenue West, Bradenton, 941/761-1715

- **Marina:** Bradenton Beach Marina, 402 Church Avenue, Bradenton Beach, 941/778-2288

- **Pier:** Bradenton Beach City Pier, Bridge Street at Sarasota Bay, Bradenton Beach, 941/779-1706; Holmes Beach Pier, Manatee Avenue at Gulf of Mexico, Holmes Beach; Anna Maria City Pier, 100 South Bay Boulevard, Anna Maria, 941/708-6130

- **Rainy-Day Attraction:** Anna Maria Island Historical Society, 402 Pine Avenue, Anna Maria, 941/778-0492

- **Shopping/Browsing:** Bridge Street, Bradenton Beach

- **Surf Shop:** West Coast Surf Shop, 3902 Gulf Drive, Holmes Beach, 941/778-1001

- **Vacation Rentals:** Island Real Estate, 6101 Marina Drive, Holmes Beach, 941/778-6066

ACCOMMODATIONS

You'll want to drop anchor on Anna Maria Island for a week or longer, so a house, villa, or apartment rental is the way to go. Weekly rates range from $500 for an efficiency to $2,000 for a nice gulfside house. If you write the Anna Maria Island Chamber of Commerce, your mailbox will sag under the weight of lodging-related brochures and catalogs.

A number of small motels and inns hang shingles on the island, mostly in Bradenton Beach. The 12-unit **Queen's Gate** (1101 Gulf Drive, Bradenton Beach, 941/778-7153, $$), is a cut above the island norm without being pretentious about it. The 36-unit **Catalina Beach Resort** (1325 Gulf Drive North, Bradenton Beach, 941/778-6611, $) is an "apartment motel" with rentals by the week, though some rooms can be had by the night. Often shuffleboard courts are attached to the various "beach clubs" and "resorts," which is a tip-off to the drowsy tenor of life on Anna Maria Island. For what it's worth, there are no brand-name motels or hotels on the island.

A touch of sophistication is available at **Harrington House** (5626 Gulf Drive, Holmes Beach, 941/778-5444, $$$), a beachside B&B. Built in 1925, this three-story coquina-block structure has been lavishly and lovingly preserved.

COASTAL CUISINE

You can stuff yourself silly on Anna Maria Island. At **Cafe on the Beach** (4000 Gulf Drive, Holmes Beach, 941/778-0784, $)—

THE CULTURAL COAST

located at the county-run Manatee Beach—we saw people the size of manatees taking advantage of a daily all-you-can-eat pancake breakfast special. The place also gets packed on Friday nights for the all-you-can-eat fish fry with live entertainment.

The best beachfront cuisine is at the **Beach Bistro** (6600 Gulf Drive, Holmes Beach, 941/778-6444, $$$$), a sit-down restaurant with linen tablecloths, rose-filled bud vases, and romantic sunset views. It has been decreed "one of Florida's top 20 restaurants" and is said to have the best food on the Gulf Coast. Consider a few of the seafood selections: Andrea's Floribbean grouper (crusted with coconut and cashews, pan-seared and oven-finished, drizzled with red pepper papaya jam) and their famous Bistro bouillabaisse (lobster, shrimp, shellfish, squid, and fish poached in a killer broth). Now for the tough part: the grouper is $28.95; the bouillabaisse, $34.95. **Bistro Land's End** (10101 Gulf Drive, Anna Maria, 941/779-2444, $$$) is less pricey and more casual.

The Sandbar (100 Spring Avenue, Anna Maria, 941/778-0444, $$) is a popular and affordable spot overlooking the gulf. The lunch menu features sandwiches, salads, and entrees. The seafood penne pasta and tuna tropic salads

hit the spot, and they came with a visual side dish of foaming waves slamming on the riprap just beyond the patio.

Another longtime favorite on the water is **Anna Maria Oyster Bar** (100 Bay Boulevard South, Anna Maria, 941/778-0475, $). Located at the end of 750-foot Anna Maria City Pier, just south of Anna Maria Bayfront Park, it offers a fresh grouper sandwich that will tickle your gills, plus the namesake oysters. The view of Passage Key, Egmont Key, and Sunshine Skyway off in the distance is a further enticement.

At **The Beach House** (200 Gulf Drive North, Bradenton Beach, 941/779-2222, $$), you'll swear you can hear the heartbeat of America. It's family dining in an airy wooden building with picture windows that frame the beautiful sunsets. Beachnut grouper is the signature dish for good reason: it's prepared with a nut crust, citrus-ginger sauce, and fruit salsa garnish. Scampi Anna Maria finishes a respectable second.

NIGHTLIFE

Head to the **D Coy Ducks Bar & Grill** (5410 Marina Drive, Holmes Beach, 941/778-5888) if you want to knock back a friendly drink in a pub setting. As for the rest of you, it's either shuffleboard or shuffle off to bed.

ST. PETERSBURG, CLEARWATER, AND THE BEACHES OF TAMPA BAY

Look at a map of Florida: the Tampa Bay area is like a giant whale that swallowed up a big chunk of the West Coast. The urban sprawl extends for miles, encircling the bay. Bridges that seem to go on for years cross enormous bodies of water en route to another blob in an endless spread-out metropolis that includes St. Petersburg, Tampa, and Clearwater, plus some cities you've likely never heard of that are nonetheless sizable (e.g. Largo, pop. 72,000). Tampa Bay is the closest Florida comes to Southern California, with its car-dependent cities that roll on with little evidence of planning.

One morning we were due to catch flights home from the Tampa airport. On the map, it didn't look to be that long a haul from our hotel room in St. Pete Beach. In reality, it took an eternity. The miles rolled on as we nervously watched the clock tick ever closer toward departure time. We drove the length of Sand Key, over Clearwater Pass Bridge, across blob-like Clearwater, and out toward the airport. We drove from streets onto causeways onto interstates onto off-ramps. Nervousness turned to panic as we screeched into the rental car lot, grabbed our bags and sprinted like mad to our respective gates. One of us broad-jumped onto the jetway just as the flight attendant began closing it. By a millisecond the flight was made. Moral of the story: We will never again underestimate the size of the Tampa Bay area, and neither should you.

Much of the Tampa Bay metropolitan area falls inside Pinellas County, which is the second-smallest (in terms of land area) and fourth-most populous county in the state of Florida. Putting these facts together yields another statistic: With more than 3,000 residents per square mile, Pinellas is Florida's most densely populated county. Its principal cities, St. Petersburg and Clearwater, merge with many smaller communities and booming Tampa,

© PARKE PUTERBAUGH

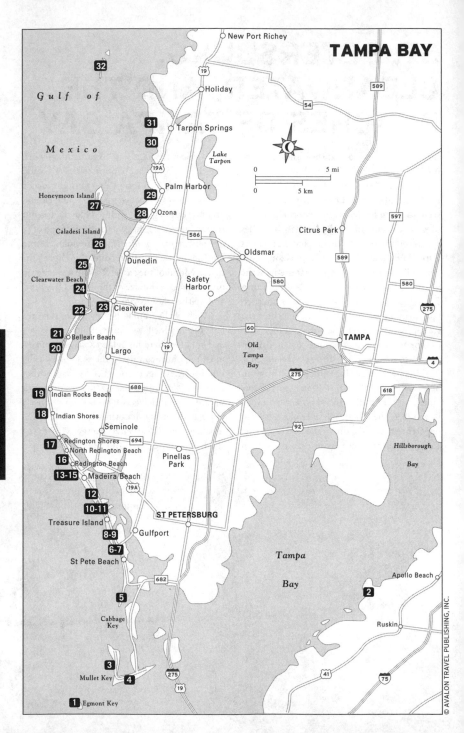

TAMPA BAY

BEST BEACHES

❰ Fort De Soto Park: Best for
Camping (page 411)

❰ North Beach: Top 25 (page 412)

❰ Treasure Island: Best for Fishing
(page 418)

❰ Treasure Island Beach Access:
Best for Families (page 420)

❰ Caladesi Island State Park:
Top 25 (page 440)

which is Florida's fourth-largest city. (For the record, Tampa falls in beachless Hillsborough County.) Collectively, they form a metropolitan area with a population of 2.4 million. That's a lot of gas stations and Taco Bells.

Fortunately, Pinellas County has 28 miles of beaches strung along a barrier-island chain that runs from Mullet Key (below St. Petersburg) to Anclote Key (above Tarpon Springs). In between, this beach-blessed county includes St. Pete Beach, Treasure Island, Sand Key, and Clearwater Beach. In addition, Caladesi Island and Honeymoon Island—two prize jewels in the state park system—lie west of the sound side city of Dunedin. If you can escape the asphalt sprawl east of the barrier islands, the beaches of Pinellas County will mellow your mood considerably.

Before continuing, we should remind you that this is a book about beaches, and therefore the bayside cities of Tampa and St. Petersburg are beyond our scope. If you want to learn more about these cities and other parts of the Tampa Bay metropolitan area that do not touch the Gulf of Mexico, contact the Tampa Bay Convention and Visitors Bureau, 400 North Tampa Street, Suite 2800, Tampa, FL 33602, 813/222-2753 or 800/448-2672, www.thcva.com.

Egmont Key

We'll start our Tampa Bay travels from the south, in Hillsborough County, where there's nothing in the way of sand beaches along the Gulf of Mexico. The sole exception is Egmont Key. Pull out a map and have a look. Manatee County runs to the tip of Anna Maria Island, while Pinellas County extends south of St. Petersburg. In between lies little Egmont Key, a straggler that somehow fell to Hillsborough County.

Egmont Key has a lot of history for a place that is so deserted today. Sitting at the mouth of Tampa Bay, it was the site of the first lighthouse (ca. 1848) on Florida's West Coast. During the third Seminole War, the key served as a holding camp for Seminole Indians pending their shipment to Oklahoma. Union forces captured Egmont Key during the Civil War. During the Spanish-American War of 1898, Fort Dade was built here to protect Tampa. The fort never saw much action, though it grew into a city of 300 residents and 70 buildings until being decommissioned in 1923. There's not much left of those days but ruins.

Today, Egmont Key is a combination state park, nature preserve, and historic site. The 380-acre key falls inside a narrow sliver of Hillsborough County. Egmont Key was delegated to Hillsborough County back in the 1920s to placate the Tampa Bay Pilots Association, who didn't want to enter different counties (and thus incur extra charges) when sailing up the bay and into port at Tampa.

Egmont Key lies two miles north of Anna Maria Island and two miles south of Fort De Soto Park. It was named while under British control for John Perceval, second Earl of

TAMPA BAY

TAMPA BAY

Egmont. It is the site of Egmont Key Lighthouse, which was erected in 1858. Until its automation in 1989, it was the only manned lighthouse in the United States. That same year, Egmont Key was made a state park. Today, the key's only full-time resident is a park ranger.

Egmont Key State Park has a 1.6-mile-long beach that's as pristine as any on Florida's West Coast. It's one of the best dive sites in the area, because submerged armament bunkers from its military past serve as fish-friendly reefs. Egmont Key is also notable for having the densest population of gopher tortoises in the world.

"They're almost a pain in the butt," jokes a ranger. "You can't take a step without having to move them out of the way." The fauna is typical of Gulf Coast barrier islands: sabal palms, red cedars, and more.

There's no charge to enter Egmont Key beyond what you'll pay to ferry over, if you're not piloting your own boat. There's no dockage, so you'll have to anchor off the beach. And there are no facilities of any kind.

The **Egmont Key Ferry** can be boarded at the ferry terminal in Fort De Soto Park. Ferries leave Fort De Soto at 10 A.M. and 11 A.M. daily and return from Egmont Key at 2 P.M. and 3 P.M. (Ferry service stops November–mid-February.) The cost is $15 per person and admission is first-come, first serve. Snorkeling gear costs $5 and a ride to the "Sunken Ruins" offshore of Egmont Key is an additional $10. For more information, call Hubbard's Sea Adventures at 352/867-6569.

For more information about Egmont Key, contact Egmont Key State Park, c/o Gulf Islands GEOpark, 1 Causeway Boulevard, Dunedin, FL, 727/469-5942, www.floridastateparks.org.

BEACHES

1 EGMONT KEY STATE PARK

Location: Located at the mouth of Tampa Bay, Egmont Key is accessible by boat only.

Parking/Fees: no entrance fee (and no docking, either)
Hours: 8 A.M.–sunset
Facilities: none
Contact: Egmont Key State Park, 727/893-2627

Apollo Beach

We're suckers for anything with "beach" in its name, so when we saw Apollo Beach on a map of the Tampa area, we decided to check it out. It's on the shore of Tampa Bay and not the Gulf of Mexico, so we should have passed since our beat is sandy beaches along the ocean or gulf. But then we noticed that there's a Surfside Avenue in Apollo Beach and decided to investigate.

We needn't have bothered. Apollo Beach (pop. 6,000) looks to be a floundering attempt at a retirement resort community. So we took a few pictures, looked around at the unsold lots, and went on our way.

We found cause for celebration a few miles south of Apollo Beach, at **E. G. Simmons Park.** This lovely, large, and shaded county park has a boat launch, fishing piers, a campground, picnic areas, and a public beach on its nearly 500 acres.

For more information, contact the Apollo Beach Chamber of Commerce, 6432 U.S. 41 North, Apollo Beach, FL 33572, 813/645-1366, www.apollobeachchamber.com.

BEACHES

2 E. G. SIMMONS PARK

Location: 19th Street NW, off U.S. 41 in south Hillsborough County
Parking/Fees: free parking lot
Hours: 8 A.M.–6 P.M.
Facilities: restrooms, picnic tables, and showers
Contact: E. G. Simmons Park, 813/671-7655

BRIDGE TO THE SKY: ST. PETERSBURG'S SUNSHINE SKYWAY

Driving across four-mile Sunshine Skyway Bridge (I-275) is like taking a dizzying amusement-park ride. At its highest point, it rises 19 stories above Tampa Bay. Connecting St. Petersburg to points south, it is the largest cable suspension bridge in the Western Hemisphere. One of the most memorable moments of our countless trips to Florida came in September 2005, when we raced across "the Skyway" at sunset while an FM classic-rock station blasted Steppenwolf's "Magic Carpet Ride." All that excitement for a $1 toll!

If you're into fishing, you're in for another kind of rush here. At either end, the Sunshine Skyway provides access to a pair of fishing piers. North Pier (on the St. Petersburg side) is a quarter-mile long. South Pier (on the Manatee County side, near Rubonia) is 1.5 miles long, making it the longest fishing pier in the world. These piers are remnants of the old Skyway Bridge, and you can drive out on them to park and fish. This is an absolute must-do if you're an angler.

BEST(Fort De Soto Park

South of St. Petersburg lies an island in the bay—actually a series of connected keys—entirely given over to a remarkable, expansive park. They call Fort De Soto a county park, but it is larger than some counties and feels more like a miniature Cape Cod or Outer Banks. The park occupies five keys, with V-shaped Mullet Key being the main stem and four smaller ones flaring off it.

The fort is named for Hernando De Soto, who sortied through here with his Spanish flotilla in the late 1530s, claiming the West Coast of Florida in the name of the mother country. This portended the extermination of the Tocobaga Indians, who had peacefully resided here until the gold-seeking conquistadors set about their slaughter. The fort named for De Soto is at the north end of the island, near the refreshment stand and souvenir shop (a nest of cheap trinkets not worth rummaging).

A 233-site campground occupies St. Christopher Key, off to the right from where the road enters the island. Campers enjoy a picture-perfect setting of tall, tropical plants and shrubs that offers cooling shade and a perfectly framed window on the water. Reservations can be made up to six months in advance (at www.pinellascounty.org/park). Bookings should be made as soon as you have dates in mind, as the campground is popular and fills up quickly. That said, they do not book 100 percent of the sites, leaving some available for walk-in campers. Camping costs $25 per night.

Massive picnic shelters at the **North Beach** and **East Beach** areas can be booked ahead of time. (Call 727/866-2484 for reservations.) Alternatively, you and your group can show up and take any table that hasn't previously been claimed. The tables and shelters seem endless in number. If you want to set a Guinness record for the world's largest picnic, Fort De Soto Park is the place to do it. Raccoons are hip to the picnickers' bounty, as we saw a number of large and aggressive ones rummaging around the trash bins on our last visit.

To get to Fort De Soto Park, take Pinellas Bayway (S.R. 682) to S.R. 679 and follow south for six miles to the park. En route, you will cross a populated island, Tierra Verde. For a paltry $0.85 in road tolls, the nature-filled, 1,136-acre wonderland at Fort De Soto Park is yours to enjoy.

For more information, contact Fort De Soto Park, 3500 Pinellas Bayway South, Tierra Verde, FL 33715, 727/582-2267, www.fortdesoto.com.

TAMPA BAY

Petersburg Skyway is visible from its shoreline, a breathtaking sight on a bright sunny day or as the setting sun colors the sky.

To be frank, beaches aren't really the calling card at Fort De Soto. It's the totality of nature and ample space to beat the crowd that make the trip worth the trouble. The park's ribbon-like miles of paved pathways are ideal for biking and in-line skating, and many visitors come equipped to do just that. They also tote their motorless boats and take advantage of the park's two-mile canoe trail. For motorboats, an 800-foot-long launch facility allows easy access to the bay and gulf. Those content to stay ashore can fish from the 500-foot Bay Pier and 1,000-foot Gulf Pier. Additionally, you can catch a ferry from Bay Pier to Egmont Key.

© PARKE PUTERBAUGH

North Beach, Fort De Soto Park

BEACHES

In 2005, Dr. Stephen Leatherman (a.k.a. "Dr. Beach") chose **North Beach** at Fort De Soto Park as the world's "#1 Beach" on his annual list. Indeed, the St. Pete Beach area hadn't fully recovered from the 2004 hurricane season when in September 2005 we found an impressive new sign at Fort De Soto Park hailing Leatherman's choice. Despite his accolades, advisories against swimming are posted on the gulf-facing North Beach ("No Swimming, Dangerous Currents"), and the stroll from the lot to the water is a lengthy one. People stroll and sun themselves on its endless deserted expanse. Rumors of nude sunbathing exist, and the beach is so enormous that proscriptions against disrobing would be difficult to enforce.

East Beach is Fort De Soto's designated swimming beach, and its still waters are inviting, if not conducive to the usual wave-filled fun one usually associates with a day at the beach. Facilities at East Beach are more compact than at North Beach, and it has a less dauntingly vast swath of sand. The St.

❸ NORTH BEACH

     BEST (

Location: From St. Petersburg, take the Pinellas Bayway (S.R. 682) to S.R. 679 and follow it south to the park for six miles. Turn right at park headquarters and follow to North Beach parking area.
Parking/Fees: $0.85 per vehicle in road tolls
Hours: sunrise–sunset
Facilities: concessions, restrooms, picnic tables, showers, and a visitors center
Contact: Fort De Soto Park, 727/582-2267

❹ EAST BEACH

Location: From St. Petersburg, take the Pinellas Bayway (S.R. 682) to S.R. 679 and follow it south to the park for six miles. Turn left at park headquarters and follow to East Beach parking area.
Parking/Fees: $0.85 per vehicle in road tolls
Hours: sunrise–sunset
Facilities: concessions, restrooms, picnic tables, showers, and a visitors center
Contact: Fort De Soto Park, 727/582-2267

TAMPA BAY

COASTAL CUISINE

On your way to Fort De Soto Park you'll cross the island of Tierra Verde, which has marinas and restaurants. Among them is the perennially popular **Fort De Soto Joe's Seafood Wharf** (200 Madonna Boulevard, 727/867-8710, $$). It's right on the water, and the glass walls and varnished wood make you feel as if you're aboard a boat. Early-bird dinners are generously offered noon–6 P.M. and priced fairly. Plates arrive amply filled. One afternoon we feasted on blackened mahimahi with sauteed vegetables, real mashed potatoes, and Caesar salad for only $7.95.

Pass-a-Grille

Pass-a-Grille (pop. 1,500) is a small community affixed to the southern end of St. Pete Beach like a barnacle on a ship's hull. Technically, it became a part of St. Petersburg Beach (now known as St. Pete Beach) in 1957, but it feels like a different place altogether. The name derives from an old ritual performed by Cuban fishermen (a.k.a. "Grillers") after a big catch. They preserved the fish by building fires on the beach and smoking the haul. One could see the fires when passing the island. Like the name, there's more than meets the eye in Pass-a-Grille. One of the best swaths of sand along the splendid stretch from St. Pete Beach to Clearwater Beach can be found in this unassuming area. There are no high-rises, and the whole of Pass-a-Grille—one of the oldest communities on Florida's Gulf Coast, with its history as a resort dating back to 1861—is a National Historic District.

The Don CeSar Resort divides the low-key neighborhoods of Pass-a-Grille from the commercial buildup of St. Pete Beach. The homes in Pass-a-Grille are attractive but not ostentatious, the yards well-landscaped but not overdone. The modestly idyllic layout at Pass-a-Grille ought to serve as a blueprint for other waterfront communities. (Alas, it's too late for most of them.) To top it off, the quaint

Gulf Beaches Historical Museum (115 10th Avenue, 727/552-1610) is located here. Its collection of island lore and artifacts can be perused on Thursday, Friday, and Saturday 10 A.M.–4 P.M. and Sunday 1 P.M.–4 P.M. (Note: It's closed on Thursday mid-May–mid-September.) Admission is free.

For more information, contact the Tampa Bay Beaches Chamber of Commerce, 6990 Gulf Boulevard, St. Pete Beach, FL 33706, 727/360-6957 or 800/944-1847, www.tampabaybeaches.com.

BEACHES

Pass-a-Grille Beach is a five-star winner. The sand is white and powdery, and the emerald gulf is warm and inviting. In fact, Pass-a-Grille is much wider than St. Pete Beach. Best of all, there's easy and ample access. Angle-in metered parking ($1 per hour) runs for 20 beach-hugging blocks, from 21st to 1st Avenues. All of it is mercifully uncongested by homes, hotels, or condos. So bring your quarters, beach blanket, suntan lotion, cooler, and paperback, and pass a day at Pass-a-Grille.

5 PASS-A-GRILLE BEACH

Location: along Gulf Way from 21st and 1st Avenues in Pass-a-Grille, just south of St. Pete Beach
Parking/Fees: metered street parking
Hours: sunrise-sunset
Facilities: concessions, restrooms, and showers
Contact: St. Pete Beach Parks Department, 727/367-2735

ACCOMMODATIONS

The affordable, well-situated **Island's End Resort** (1 Pass-a-Grille Way, 727/360-5023, $$) offers six rooms at the southern tip of Pass-a-Grille. It's as quiet and charming a place as you'll find at the beach. The comfortable, homey **Inn on the Beach** (1401 Gulf Way, 727/360-8844, $$) overlooks Pass-a-Grille Beach, offering airy rooms done up in brass, wicker, and ceramic tile. You might also like the **Keystone** (801 Gulf Way, 727/360-1313, $), a well-kept 30-unit motel that sits on the opposite corner from the Hurricane Restaurant and is, in fact, affiliated with that mammoth restaurant and entertainment complex. Read on.

COASTAL CUISINE

Pass-a-Grille boasts a number of bistros and cafe where you can get a bite on or near the water. For a relaxed, reasonably priced dining experience, **Sea Critters Cafe** (2007 Pass-a-Grille Way, 727/360-3706, $$) is the freshest catch in south St. Pete. The owner proudly dubs himself "a local beach bum born and raised on the beach." He's also enamored of all things Key Westerly, including odd artifacts, bric-a-brac, Jimmy Buffett's music, and "Duval Street key lime pie." He calls his restaurant's relaxing ambience "Key West attitude with no change in latitude." We raise our margaritas in salute to his well-executed fixation.

The smoked grouper dip is the perfect opener; all smoking is done on the premises. The smoked portobello mushroom and salmon appetizer also had us squawking like parrotheads at a Buffett concert. Signature dishes include Jambalaya, Florida-style crab cakes (with key lime aioli), cedar-planked salmon, and grouper. Without question, grouper is the way to go. You can order it grilled, blackened, jerked, pretzel-crusted, fried, and charcoal-grille. They even serve a grouper Reuben sandwich. A tradition at Sea Critters is the feeding of a thick, squirming school of sea catfish with buckets of bread. The owner has prepared a hilarious manual on "How to Properly Feed Catfish."

Another excellent choice is the **Hurricane Seafood Restaurant** (807 Gulf Way, 727/360-9558, $$$). The Hurricane is a dining and entertainment multiplex, with a downstairs cafe, outdoor deck, and Caribbean-themed upstairs operation called Stormy's. Grilled black grouper is what made the Hurricane famous, and they post other fresh catches

on the menu, too. Breakfast, lunch, and dinner are served daily. Try to catch a sunset here on a nice afternoon. (A bit of wisdom: they're almost always nice.) There's docking for those arriving by boat.

NIGHTLIFE

Hurricane's (807 Gulf Way, 727/360-9558) offers three places and ways to celebrate: **Stormy's,** an upstairs restaurant that becomes a dance club at 10 P.M.; the **Keys Club,** a piano bar where one sips single-malt Scotch or martinis while gazing at tropical fish suspended from the ceiling; and the **Hurricane Watch Rooftop Deck,** where you can drink in a 360° view along with a Hurricane Rum Runner or another frozen libation with a wacky name. Call for a prerecorded list of dinner and drink specials, as well as the best time to catch sunset that day.

St. Pete Beach

No, the proper name is not St. Petersburg Beach. Yes, St. Pete Beach is correct. Back in 1994, the name was officially changed to what people had informally been calling it for decades. St. Pete Beach (pop. 9,200) is the autonomous barrier-island community adjacent to the major city of St. Petersburg (pop. 250,000). The small city on the beach and the big city by the bay are joined by two causeways: Pinellas Bayway (at the south end) and Pasadena Avenue. Technically known as Long Key, though that name is rarely used, St. Pete Beach runs for seven miles from Pass-a-Grille to Blind Pass, which separates it from Treasure Island.

With the exception of cool, calm, and collected Pass-a-Grille, St. Pete Beach has been built up in herky-jerky fashion, lacking evidence of zoning and planning strategies, not to mention greenspace or adequate public beach access. It's not a bad place by any means, but a lot more could've been done with it. It's also somewhat snoozy and slow-

TAMPA BAY

going—more like Sunny Isles Beach than Miami Beach, to draw an East Coast parallel. This appraisal was confirmed by a fuzzy-faced kid named Nils, who was wielding the scoop at an ice-cream parlor we ducked into. He characterized St. Pete Beach as a place to "take a load off, man." In other words, you come here to chill.

Though affixed to the Tampa–St. Petersburg metroplex, St. Pete Beach doesn't feel like a big-city beach. It's well-stocked with hotels, motels, and restaurants (mostly franchised), and a newish glut of condos, plus the occasional sports bar and 7-Eleven, but it is not a wild and crazy strip of revving cars and jammed sidewalks. St. Pete Beach may lack personality but it's generally unthreatening.

The high season runs from Christmas through March. During this spell, you might see a smattering of Spring Breaking collegians, but you are more likely to spy families and foreign travelers. Traditionally, St. Pete Beach has been a favored spot for Midwesterners, but it's become a major destination for British tourists, too. They flock here in droves in the winter months. So pervasive are they that any number of British-style pubs serve British-style pub food. (They crossed the ocean to eat more of that gruel?) Newspaper and gift shops carry the dreadful British tabloids *The Sun* and *The Mirror*. A styling salon calls itself British Hairways.

In a sense, St. Pete Beach has become an American version of the Brits' "holiday camps," except that the gulf waters are generally balmy. In *Kingdom by the Sea*, Paul Theroux described the scene in Blackpool, a popular seaside resort: "Vacationers sitting under a dark sky with their shirts off, sleeping with their mouths open, emitting hog whimpers. They were waiting for the sun to shine, but the forecast was rain for the next five months." It's no wonder they love Florida.

Between international visitors—principally Britons, but also Germans and Canadians—and snowbirds from the North and Midwest, St. Pete Beach stays crowded from late December through early May. However, as has become the case all over Florida, the whole concept of seasonality is dissolving. The coastal communities have learned that when vacationers head home, that's the time to pull in convention business.

When we visited St. Pete Beach one November—which should be the least busy of all months—our resort was running at full occupancy. Hearing some strange calliope music, we opened a ballroom door and spied 500 elderly women wearing fezzes, clapping, hooting, and singing. And they say Spring Breakers go wild!

For more information, contact the St. Pete Beach Chamber of Commerce, 155 Corey Avenue, St. Pete Beach, FL 33706, 727/367-2735, www.stpetebeach.org; or the Tampa Bay Beaches Chamber of Commerce, 6990 Gulf Boulevard, St. Pete Beach, FL 33706, 727/360-6957 or 800/944-1847, www.tampabaybeaches.com.

BEACHES

The beach along St. Pete Beach is renourished (aren't they all?), wide, and long. If you're staying at one of the hotels, motels, or resorts on the beach side, you'll have instant access to the gulf, with its bejeweled waters, soft white sand, and inspiring sunsets. However, the Gulf Boulevard strip along St. Pete Beach is miserly with public access, given the size of the inland metropolitan area it's serving.

There's metered parking in two places: mid-island, off Gulf Boulevard between 44th and 50th Avenues, and toward the north end, off Beach Plaza between 66th and 70th Avenues. The former is known as **St. Pete Beach Access.** The latter—more favored by locals and surfers—is **Upham Beach.** Neither of them is as nice as the beach at Pass-a-Grille, which would be our first choice. However, if you're staying at a hotel, resort or condo on the beach, the point is moot, since beach access and parking come with the room.

6 ST. PETE BEACH ACCESS

Location: 4700 Gulf Boulevard in St. Pete Beach
Parking/Fees: metered parking lot
Hours: sunrise-sunset
Facilities: concessions, restrooms, picnic tables, and showers
Contact: St. Pete Parks Department, 727/582-2267

7 UPHAM BEACH

Location: between 66th and 70th Avenues, off Beach Plaza at the north end of St. Pete Beach
Parking/Fees: metered parking lot
Hours: sunrise-sunset
Facilities: restrooms and showers
Contact: St. Pete Beach Parks Department, 727/582-2267

RECREATION AND ATTRACTIONS

- **Bike/Skate Rentals:** Beach Cyclist Sports Center, 7517 Blind Pass Road, St. Pete Beach, 727/367-5001
- **Boat Cruise:** Captain Anderson Cruises, 3400 Pasadena Avenue South, St. Pete Beach, 727/367-7804
- **Dive Shop:** Treasure Island Divers, 146 107th Avenue, Treasure Island, 727/360-3483
- **Ecotourism:** Shell Island Cruises, Captain Mike's Watersports, Dolphin Beach Resort, 4900 Gulf Boulevard, St. Pete Beach, 727/360-1053
- **Fishing Charters:** Florida Deep Sea Fishing, 4737 Gulf Boulevard, St. Pete Beach, 727/360-2082
- **Lighthouse:** Egmont Key Lighthouse, Egmont Key, 727/893-2627
- **Marina:** Blind Pass Marina, 9555 Blind Pass Road, St. Pete Beach, 727/360-4281

- **Piers:** Merry Pier, 801 Pass-a-Grille Way, Pass-a-Grille, 727/360-6606; St. Petersburg Pier, 2nd Avenue East at Tampa Bay, St. Petersburg, 727/821-6164
- **Rainy-Day Attraction:** Salvador Dali Museum, 1000 3rd Street South, St. Petersburg, 727/823-3767
- **Shopping/Browsing:** Dolphin Village, 4600 Gulf Boulevard, St. Pete Beach
- **Surf Shop:** Suncoast Surf Shop, 9841 Gulf Boulevard, St. Pete Beach, 727/367-2483
- **Vacation Rentals:** Gulf Bay Realty, 9815 Gulf Boulevard, St. Pete Beach, 727/360-6969

ACCOMMODATIONS

The **Don CeSar Beach Resort** (3400 Gulf Boulevard, 727/360-1881, $$$$) rises at the south end of St. Pete Beach like a pink-stucco Taj Mahal. This neo-Mediterranean edifice—one of only eight hotels in Florida on the National Trust for Historic Preservation—houses one of Florida's premier resorts. Now owned by the Loews franchise, the Don CeSar is first-class all the way, with an unpretentious air that makes staying here a real treat. Particularly pleasurable is the outdoor pool deck, which has huge pools, hot tubs, and poolside bars where blenders work overtime mixing frozen drinks. A quick plunge in the gulf followed by a soak in the hot tub is especially refreshing in the cooler months. You could spend hours on the deck looking up at the architecture of the uniquely rouged Don CeSar (a.k.a. "the Pink Palace"). It's a splendid perch for watching the sun do its slow fade in late afternoon, too.

Everything you could want, including restaurants, fitness center, spa, and gift shops, is on-premises. We'd only quibble with the $10 per adult daily "resort charge" that is levied for local phone calls and use of the on-site spa. Those should rightly come with room fees that start at $339 (weekdays) and $394 (weekends) in the spring high season. The Don CeSar is far from alone in assessing a resort fee. It's become an all-to-common way to gouge guests, along with a daily charge for parking, without openly raising lodging rates (which are high to begin with).

St. Pete Beach's other tower of vacation power is the **Tradewinds Island Grand Beach Resort** (5500 Gulf Boulevard, 727/367-6461, $$$). It's like a small city—one with its own faux reggae theme song whose key line goes, "You got that Tradewinds feelin'!" Tradewinds is huge, occupying 18 acres of gulfside real estate. Its several towers contain 577 hotel rooms and suites. All feel like real living quarters, as they come with coffeemakers and refrigerators. If you get a room facing west—and it's worth the extra money—sunsets can be savored from the balcony.

Tradewinds is so oversized it's worth studying a map of the grounds before setting out from your room. There are many amenities and much to do. Just for starters: four heated swimming pools, a fitness club, body works salon, nine restaurants and bars, and a hefty slice of beach. A 0.25-mile waterway that loops through the property can be toured via paddleboat or gondola. Designed with families in mind, Tradewinds has a supervised children's program that will allow big kids to pursue their own playtime activities. They also own the **Tradewinds Sandpiper Hotel & Suites** (5500 Gulf Boulevard, 727/360-5551, $$$), an adjoining property. Staying there entitles you to use the facilities at the main resort.

Beyond these two St. Pete Beach sentinels, Gulf Boulevard is lined with motels and hotels of every description, condition, and price range. **Alden Beach Resort** (5900 Gulf Boulevard, 727/360-7081, $$$) is a well-maintained mid-rise alternative to the towers that have erupted on all sides. Occupying nine buildings, the Alden offers everything from a no-frills hotel room to a two-bedroom gulf-view apartment. The suites are comfortable, and you'll enjoy the swimming pools, shuffleboard courts, and wide beach out back.

COASTAL CUISINE

An old favorite on St. Pete Beach, Silas Dent's, burned down in the mid-1990s and got rebuilt as **Silas' Steakhouse** (5501 Gulf Boulevard, 727/360-6961, $$$). It continues to please old-timers and tourists by the galleon-load with its seafood, steaks, and award-winning prime rib. We especially like it because it was named for a grubby beachcombing folk hero who lived on nearby Tierra Verde.

A visit to this area would not be complete without a visit to Crabby Bill's. There are several locations, but the St. Pete Beach location of **Crabby Bill's** (5100 Gulf Boulevard, 727/360-8858, $$) is right on the beach and offers a gorgeous view to complement the extensive selection of seafood. They don't have strolling entertainers like the immortal Crabbo the Clown (who we encountered years back at the Indian Rocks Beach location). However, unintentional hilarity was provided the night we ate here by a slurring, boisterous drunk at the bar who loudly pontificated about the merits of high school football teams 40 years ago in northern Indiana.

If you're slumming for Southern-style comfort food, **Caldwell's Bar-B-Q & Grill** (7081 Gulf Boulevard, 727/363-6313, $$) has been serving ribs, chicken, beef brisket, pulled pork, and more since 1950. The food—barbecue platters, prime rib, barbecue ribs, and seafood combos—is hearty and inexpensive. Being Southern-bred chowhounds, we felt right at home.

This is a beach town whose culinary pulse tends toward chicken wings and grouper sandwiches. If you want something upscale, the **Maritana Grille** at the Don CeSar Resort (3400 Gulf Boulevard, 727/360-1882, $$$$) will oblige with creative and adventurous cuisine. The culinary approach is "Floribbean," but the menu might lead anywhere: from seared ahi tuna tartare to smoked salmon to wood-grilled beef tenderloin. We once had a warm lobster quesadilla served with a fruity dipping sauce stung with a hint of habanero. We were told more money is generated by Don CeSar's kitchens than its room charges. If you've ever eaten here, that claim is not hard to digest.

TAMPA BAY

At another extreme, the **Internet Outpost Cafe** (7400 Gulf Boulevard, 727/360-7806, $) is a way station for international travelers and a great place to start the day. They serve fresh blends of coffee and homemade muffins so moist they render you temporarily tongue-tied. Opened in 1997, it has caught on with visitors from Europe (where cyber cafes are as plentiful as sports bars are in the States). It's a civilized alternative to fast food or "family restaurant" spreads. Who knows? You might meet some budding Brigitte Bardot or Gerard Depardieu on whom you can try out your broken high-school French. There are eight terminals in a comfortable living room-style setting, and Internet access costs $2 per 15 minutes.

NIGHTLIFE

Follow the bouncing crowd to the sports bars of St. Pete Beach, where one can guzzle beer to the sight of bodies being blocked, checked, tagged, tackled, bloodied, and carried off. The theme of this sports-crazy area—home to pro football's Tampa Bay Buccaneers and pro baseball's Tampa Bay Devil Rays—is mined in popular clubs like **Undertow** (3850 Gulf Boulevard, 727/368-9000) and **Players** (6200 Gulf Boulevard, 727/367-1902).

Undertow started as a tiki hut and now has two full-service bars tended by bikini-clad babes. Volleyball is played on the beach and locals drive from Tampa to blow off steam. Players is a multi-room retreat in the Best Western Beach Front Resort with 32 TVs tuned in to sporting events and a modest menu of decent bar food. Their blackened-grouper sandwich helped make the sorry football game we watched here one night easier to swallow. Our alma mater, the University of North Carolina, got shellacked by Florida State, which at least made the bar crowd happy.

As an alternative to sports bars, hit the Corey Avenue Historic Shopping District. A renovated old movie house, the **Beach Theatre** (350 Corey Avenue, 727/360-6697), screens art-house films and independent productions you won't see at any 12-screen suburban multiplex.

BEST(Treasure Island and Sunset Beach

St. Pete Beach looks downright understated compared to Treasure Island (pop. 7,500), which takes the concept of family fun to il-logical extremes. It is a jammed-to-the-max

TED PETERS IS SMOKIN'!

One of our favorite places in the area requires an eastward bridge-hop over the St. Pete Beach Causeway (a.k.a. Pasadena Avenue) into South Pasadena. Here, you will find **Ted Peters Famous Smoked Fish** (1350 Pasadena Avenue South, 727/381-7931, $$), which has been serving the St. Petersburg area for half a century.

Fish are smoked 4-6 hours in wire mesh racks suspended over smoldering beds of Florida red oak coals. You sit at picnic tables or barstools on an outdoor patio and flag down one of the friendly waitresses. While some folks consider mullet worthwhile only as bait fish, we find it delicious and can highly recommend the smoked mullet at Ted Peters. Smoked Spanish mackerel and salmon are also mouthwatering. We prefer to order smoked platters, which includes the whole fish, to the smoked fish spread, which is more like tuna salad.

Two blocks east of Ted Peter's is **Florida Orange Groves and Winery** (1500 Pasadena Avenue South, 727/347-4025), which offers cold, fresh-squeezed orange juice. This is Florida's signature drink, so pull over and purchase a jug of liquid gold while you have the chance. Florida Orange Groves and Winery also dispenses some interesting libations you won't find mentioned in *Wine Spectator:* key lime wine, orange wine, watermelon wine, and grapefruit wine. Can you imagine the hangover?

vacationland of eccentrically named and oddly shaped motels, goofy golf courses, amusement parks, strip malls, beachwear emporiums, hotdog huts, ice-cream stands, souvenir shops, convenience stores, gas stations, restaurants, bars, and a few more convenience stores.

The island's resort destiny commenced in 1915 with the construction of The Coney Island, its first hotel. Beginning in the 1950s, the mangroves bordering the inland side of Treasure Island were filled in to create developments with names like Capri Isle and Isle of Palms. They really put the pedal to the metal in the 1970s. Treasure Island has been described by its boosters as a "mature, built-out city," though overbuilt is more like it.

The island derives its name from rumors that a Spanish galleon sank nearby in the early 1700s and still lies buried offshore. Treasure Island's swashbuckling motif is carried to absurd extremes by its motels, which include the Sea Chest, the Jolly Roger, the Buccaneer, the Swashbuckler, and the Treasure Chest. The real treasure on this 3.5-mile island is the beach, which you can't see from Gulf Boulevard for all the motels, hotels, and condos. Once you're laying out on it, however, you'll turn from a stressed-out road privateer to a contented landlubber.

At the island's less harried south end, reachable via West Gulf Boulevard, Sunset Beach is cloistered from the mayhem. Sunset Beach is to Treasure Island what Pass-a-Grille is to St. Pete Beach: i.e., a quiet stretch of residences and rental apartments that maintains its low-key island character by virtue of its isolation from the main drag. Like Pass-a-Grille, it once enjoyed small-town autonomy until 1955. The island communities of Sunset Beach, Boca Ciega, Treasure Island, and Sunshine Beach banded together that year to incorporate as the city of Treasure Island.

One of us has been visiting Treasure Island since the late 1970s, when a set of grandparents lived in nearby St. Petersburg. During that time, Treasure Island has changed very little, which is one of the reasons that we've enjoyed coming back. Sadly, during a recent visit we observed that the seeds of change are being planted in the form of the conversion of hotels and motels to condos. This is a phenomenon that's been sweeping much of Florida and the East Coast, and it's particularly sad to see it happen here.

During our latest trip to Treasure Island, we saw four new condos being constructed on the beach. An article in the *St. Petersburg Times* confirmed our fears and detailed the negative effects of condos on communities. During the past year, property values on Treasure Island had increased by 21.5 percent; the previous year, they had increased 13.5 percent. Much of the increase was due to the "flipping" of condominiums, which is when someone buys real estate not with the intention of living there but with the notion of reselling it for a quick profit. Another local publication decried the loss of traditional motels in the area.

We have been drawn back to Treasure Island year after year because of the intangibles: the "feel" of the island and the friendliness of nearly every bartender, waitress, and hotel staffer we've encountered. Something that also struck us was the longevity of those who work on the island. During the last four years, the same person has been taking our reservation at the Bilmar, the same maid has kept up our room during our stay, the same waitress at Foxy's has been serving our breakfast, and "Buddha Bob" has been serving us at the R Bar. These days, such consistency is very rare. We couldn't help but get an uneasy feeling that the conversion of hotels to condos, and the addition of new condos, will slowly—or quickly—change all that.

For more information, contact the Tampa Bay Beaches Chamber of Commerce, 6990 Gulf Boulevard, St. Pete Beach, FL 33706, 727/360-6957 or 800/944-1847, www.tampabaybeaches.com.

BEACHES

Like Miami Beach, Treasure Island has been artificially buttressed and is now so wide in places it's almost unfair to the rest of the world. The beach here is touted as "the largest white sand beach on the Gulf Coast" and "the widest beach on the Pinellas Suncoast." Isn't it cheating that its spectacular width is the result of not of natural processes but beach renourishment? It looks more like a glaring white desert than a beach.

At the island's southernmost tip, in the community of Sunset Beach, **Treasure Island Park** looks directly across Blind Pass at Upham Beach in St. Pete Beach. A public boardwalk extends for 0.6 mile over the dunes and along the pass. It's a great spot for sunset-watching. Free parking is available but there are no facilities. Treasure Island additionally boasts 45 dune walkovers at street ends from 77th to 127th Avenues. The access at **120th Avenue** is a little more substantial than the street-end walkovers found elsewhere on Treasure Island.

Pinellas County operates **Treasure Island Beach Access,** the island's main public beach, up around 100th Avenue. There are free parking facilities, showers, and drinking fountains, and benches line a cement jogging/biking path that runs for a mile or so, ending at the Holiday Inn. The city of St. Petersburg maintains **St. Petersburg Municipal Beach** on Treasure Island, directly across the street from the Howard Johnson, at 112th Avenue and Gulf Boulevard. A snack bar, 10 volleyball courts and other amenities are available. Metered parking costs only $0.50 per hour.

TREASURE ISLAND PARK

Location: south end of West Gulf Boulevard, in Sunset Beach on Treasure Island
Parking/Fees: free parking lot
Hours: 5 A.M.-1 A.M.
Facilities: none
Contact: Treasure Island Parks Department, 727/360-3278

TREASURE ISLAND BEACH ACCESS

Location: 100th Avenue and Gulf Boulevard, on Treasure Island
Parking/Fees: free parking lot
Hours: 5 A.M.-1 A.M.
Facilities: restrooms and showers
Contact: Pinellas County Parks Department, 727/464-3347

10 ST. PETERSBURG MUNICIPAL BEACH

Location: 112th Avenue at Gulf Boulevard, on Treasure Island
Parking/Fees: metered parking lot
Hours: 5 A.M.-1 A.M.
Facilities: concessions, restrooms, picnic tables, and showers
Contact: St. Petersburg Department of Leisure Services, 727/893-7335

11 120TH AVENUE ACCESS

Location: 120th Avenue at Gulf Boulevard, on Treasure Island
Parking/Fees: free parking lot
Hours: 5 A.M.-1 A.M.
Facilities: none
Contact: Treasure Island Parks Department, 727/360-3278

ACCOMMODATIONS

Top of the heap on Treasure Island is the **Bilmar Beach Resort** (10650 Gulf Boulevard, 727/360-5531, $$), a massive complex on 550 feet of beach. In keeping with the family-friendly tenor of Treasure Island, prices are reasonable and units come in a variety of shapes and sizes. Most have refrigerators and breakfast nooks.

We have stayed at the Bilmar for many years. It is an attractive and well-kept yet very reasonably priced hotel. The Bilmar is so well-liked by our families that one of our brothers spent part of his honeymoon there in 2001. But when we checked into the hotel in May 2005, there was the dreaded *c* word ("condominium"), with poster boards in the lobby cheerfully announcing that the Bilmar was converting to condos and directing those interested to the real-estate office on-site. Expressing our disappointment, we were reassured by the desk staff that "nothing is going to change, we are going to keep running this like a hotel..." Etc., etc.

When we opened the door to the room, we realized that a lot had changed already. The room had been completely remodeled, even though the hotel had been remodeled less than three years ago. Yes, the newly made-over room was extremely nice, and we liked the large flat-screen TV on the wall. The problem was that it didn't seem like we were staying in our own hotel room but in someone else's condo. Don't get us wrong; we still like the Bilmar. We're just not too thrilled about the condo conversion.

Next door to the Bilmar is the **Thunderbird Beach Resort** (10700 Gulf Boulevard, 727/367-1961, $$), which has the most spectacular neon sign in the area. You can't miss it. Of the accommodations bearing swashbuckling names, the **Buccaneer Beach Resort Motel** (10800 Gulf Boulevard, 727/367-1908, $) is the most presentable, and the rates are a bargain. Among the chain hotels, **Holiday Inn** (11908 Gulf Boulevard, 727/367-2761, $$$) and **Howard Johnson** (11125 Gulf Boulevard, 727/360-6971, $$) offer dependably clean and comfortable rooms.

COASTAL CUISINE

Portion size and low prices dictate the popularity of restaurants on Treasure Island, with pancake houses, hot-dog huts, and all-you-can-eat seafood buffets ruling the scene. **Gators on the Pass** (12754 Kingfish Drive, 727/367-8951, $$) is a colossal restaurant/nightclub complex (capacity 900) along Kingfish Wharf.

The menu is as large as the premises, ranging from ribs and chicken to grouper and mahimahi. The seafood chowder and gumbo are homemade from 60-year-old recipes, and the peel-and-eat shrimp can't be beat.

For all-you-can-eat snow-crab legs (on Tuesdays and Thursdays), go to the aforementioned **R Bar** (245 108th Avenue, 727/367-3400, $), a nondescript little restaurant on Treasure Island that serves a wide variety of seafood in an informal setting. The only entrees over $10 were snow crab, lobster, and filet mignon.

For the best view of the gulf go to **Caddy's** (see *Nightlife*) in Sunset Beach for breakfast, lunch, dinner, and/or to hang out after dinner.

NIGHTLIFE

Action central for nightlife at the south end of Treasure Island is **Caddy's** (9600 West Gulf Boulevard, 727/367-7427). It's an appealingly funky place with a rowdy but friendly clientele and decent menu (peel-and-eat shrimp, burgers, grouper sandwiches). Caddy's is elevated above the beach like an enormous lifeguard tower or tree fort. Don't be put off if there's a line of Harleys out front or the air is suddenly filled with the rumble of a hog revving its engine. This is as happy a mix as you'll find of people who wouldn't normally hang out together: yuppies, old-timers, beach nuts, sports fans, bikers, surfers, and rockers. Live music is provided by bands that have names like Naked People and Driving Blind, and classic FM rock blares the rest of the time. It's the sort of place you expect to find (but often don't) in every beach town.

Gators on the Pass (12754 Kingfish Drive, 727/367-8951) boasts "the world's largest waterfront bar." Tuesday is devoted to swing music; the rest of the time, they rock and roll all night (and party every day). In addition to live music, a menu of microbrews, and a nonsmoking bar, Gators works the sports-bar angle, with 28 televisions tuned into whatever games are on, especially anything Bucs-related. Here's a plan for an action-packed evening:

TAMPA BAY

start with a sunset dinner at Gators, then stroll the boardwalk to the gambling boats that depart from John's Pass and wager some of your hard-earned cash, and finally return to Gators for a rock and roll nightcap.

The aforementioned **R Bar** (245 108th Avenue, 727/367-3400) has live entertainment several nights a week featuring local musicians who are actually quite good and make the experience even more fun.

Lounges affixed to the larger resorts roll out the welcome mat for foreign visitors. One night, we popped into the bar at the Bilmar for a look-see. Between songs the burly singer asked, without irony, "Are there any Americans here?" We were the only ones. Each table of patrons called out their country of origin: "Deutschland! Wales! Scotland! England! Canada!"

Madeira Beach

At one time, Madeira Beach (pop. 4,500) was a fun and funky beach town. While Treasure Island was adopted by teeming teen hordes from St. Petersburg, Madeira Beach became the favorite haunt of the young and restless from Tampa, who lovingly dubbed it "Mad Beach." Then the condo brigade grabbed a chunk of the community chest and since then, to paraphrase Paul Revere and the Raiders, kicks just keep getting harder to find. As the cost of living has risen, the marginal group-house tribes were elbowed out and the town opened itself to tourists. As a result, more visitors to Mad Beach come from Europe and Canada than from Tampa these days.

Even with all the changes, Mad Beach is still a fun though slightly less funky beach town. Bits and pieces of the old spirit still exist, rearing its head in subtle, unexpected ways. For example, we fell into conversation with a friendly, long-haired clerk at a convenience store. Half an hour later, we were still discussing the recordings of Lou Reed ("Lou changed my life," he offered), John Cale, Nico, and the New York Dolls.

Those who aren't retired make their living servicing tourists in commercial fishing. Ma-

---

SAND KEY: A SLIVER OF OLD FLORIDA

Sand Key encompasses eight communities extending for "14 miles of heaven," from John's Pass to Clearwater Pass. The towns along this barrier-island charm bracelet are collectively marketed as the Gulf Beaches on Sand Key. From south to north, they are Madeira Beach, Redington Beach, North Redington Beach, Redington Shores, Indian Shores, Indian Rocks Beach, Belleair Shore, and Belleair Beach. They are a varied lot, ranging in character from tourist-friendly beach towns to quieter residential communities.

There's something for everybody on Sand Key: hotels and motels for tourists, beach parks for mainland day-trippers, condos and single-family homes for those who have sunk roots into the sand. If you look closely, parts of Sand Key appear unchanged from the 1950s. You'll spy little L-shaped cottage courts and mom-and-pop motels — worlds within worlds right off the main road. The fact that you can pull into a place like the Wit's End Motel, Sea Fever Motel, or dozens of other hidden charmers like them is encouraging to those of us who fret that development has completely blanked out the past. If the way things used to be is the way you like things to be, check out Sand Key.

For more information, contact Gulf Beaches on Sand Key Chamber of Commerce, 501 150th Avenue, Madeira Beach, FL 33708, 727/391-7373 or 800/944-1847, www.usa-chamber.com/gulf-beaches.

deira's mayor, a hepcat named Charlie Parker, boasts, "More grouper is brought into John's Pass than any other place in the state." Seafood is celebrated every October with a three-day festival at John's Pass Village—the commercial hub of Madeira Beach—that draws over 100,000 people.

For more information, contact the Gulf Beaches on Sand Key Chamber of Commerce, 501 150th Avenue, Madeira Beach, FL 33708, 727/391-7373 or 800/944-1847, www.usachamber.com/gulf-beaches.

BEACHES

Beginning at John's Pass (south end of Sand Key) and stretching for 2.5 miles, the beach at Madeira is a dazzling white strand. It's not quite as wide as Treasure Island's, but it's impressive nonetheless. The fishing is unsurpassed at **John's Pass Beach and Park**—a judgment confirmed by a capped jetty filled with anglers. Dune walkovers lead to 500 feet of beach (no lifeguards). Heading north along Gulf Boulevard, beach access is provided at numerous street ends. Parking is catch-as-catch-can. From south to north, access points are located at 129th through 137th Avenues, plus 141st, 142nd, and 148th Avenues, and at the end of Bayshore Drive. At 144rd Avenue and Gulf Drive is **Kitty Stewart Park**. This small beach turnout has eight parking spaces and a lone picnic shelter.

Pinellas County's Park Department oversees **Madeira Beach Access,** which is not the best of their parks. A sign warns "No Loitering on Beach." This made us wonder, who isn't loitering on a beach? Isn't that the point? Metered parking ($1 per hour) is available. The beach is thinning in places, with remnants of wooden piers and groins in the water. Beach rentals are reasonably priced: $2 an hour or $7 all day for a double chaise lounge. Again, no lifeguards.

At the north end of Madeira Beach is **Archibald Memorial Beach,** a larger city-run park with concessions and facilities.

12 JOHN'S PASS BEACH AND PARK

Location: On Gulf Boulevard at 129th Avenue in Madeira Beach
Parking/Fees: metered parking lot
Hours: sunrise-midnight
Facilities: restrooms, picnic tables, and showers
Contact: Madeira Beach Public Works Department, 727/391-1611

13 KITTY STEWART PARK

Location: Gulf Boulevard at 143rd Avenue in Madeira Beach
Parking/Fees: metered parking lot
Hours: sunrise-midnight
Facilities: picnic table and a shower
Contact: Madeira Beach Public Works Department, 727/391-1611

14 MADEIRA BEACH ACCESS

Location: Gulf Boulevard at 144th Avenue in Madeira Beach
Parking/Fees: metered parking lot
Hours: 7 A.M.-sunset
Facilities: concessions, restrooms, and showers
Contact: Pinellas County Parks Department, 727/464-3347

15 ARCHIBALD MEMORIAL BEACH

Location: Gulf Boulevard and Municipal Drive at 153rd Avenue in Madeira Beach
Parking/Fees: metered parking lot
Hours: sunrise-midnight
Facilities: concessions, restrooms, picnic tables, and shower
Contact: Madeira Beach Public Works Department, 727/391-1611

TAMPA BAY

TAMPA BAY

RECREATION AND ATTRACTIONS

- **Boat Cruise:** Europa Sea Kruz, 150 153rd Avenue #202, Madeira Beach, 727/393-2885

- **Ecotourism:** Hubbard's Sea Adventures, 150 John's Pass Boardwalk, Madeira Beach, 727/393-1947

- **Fishing Charters:** Snug Harbor Charter Service, 13625 Gulf Boulevard, Madeira Beach, 727/398-7470

- **Marina:** Hubbard's Marina, 150 John's Pass Boardwalk, Madeira Beach, 727/393-1947

- **Rainy-Day Attractions:** Books to the Ceiling, 15126 Municipal Drive, Madeira Beach, 727/392-3070

- **Shopping/Browsing:** John's Pass Village and Boardwalk, 150 128th Avenue, Madeira Beach, 727/397-1571

- **Surf Shop:** Overhead Surf Shop, 12991 Village Boulevard, Madeira Beach, 727/397-3249

- **Vacation Rentals:** Era Total Realty Services, 13030 Gulf Boulevard, 727/393-2534

ACCOMMODATIONS

The **Shoreline Island Resort Motel** (14200 Gulf Boulevard, 727/397-6641, $$) is an "exclusively all-adult" motel, with all guests and visitors required to be over the age of 21. For the prurient-minded, "adult" does not mean what you're thinking. La-Z-Boy recliners, not heart-shaped tubs, are provided with each room, and the emphasis is on peace and quiet. Shoreline is a clean and polite five-building complex with hands-on service from the same family who has owned and operated it for the past 30 years. Four of the buildings are directly on the gulf, opening onto 400 feet of beach.

In Mad Beach, you'd expect to find a place called the **Wits End Motel** (13600 Gulf Boulevard, 727/391-6739, $). Name aside, this motel's beachfront location, heated pool, fully equipped efficiency apartments, and reasonable rates will actually help restore your sanity.

Situated on 600 feet of beach, the 149-room **Holiday Inn** (15208 Gulf Boulevard, 727/392-2275, $$) has tennis and volleyball courts, a restaurant, sports bar, and heated pool. We spent a memorable evening on barstools at the poolside tiki bar listening to some honeymooning Aussies get progressively louder with each can of brew. As the sun went down the sky took on a rosy hue, matching the ruddy faces of the happy couple.

COASTAL CUISINE

For a great grouper sandwich head to **Dockside Dave's** (119 Boardwalk Place, 727/392-9399, $$), just over the bridge from Treasure Island. This unpretentious little spot has a simple menu including seafood and some of the best onion rings around. Dave's prepares each order individually, so take time to relax and celebrate the fact that you have no deadlines to meet or place to go.

Up at John's Pass Village, the **Friendly Fisherman** (150 128th Avenue, 727/391-6025, $$) serves terrific waterfront views along with breakfast, lunch, and dinner. It's a family-friendly place where food is served at wooden tables, many of which overlook the marina. For broiled, fried, or char-grilled grouper brought in fresh from the adjacent docks, the Friendly Fisherman will do just fine.

Johnny Leverock's Seafood House (565 150th Avenue, 727/393-0459, $$) is a gulf-side chain with a firm foothold in these parts. There's also one down in St. Pete Beach and one up in Clearwater Beach. Just be sure to order fresh fish prepared as simply as possible (char-grilled or blackened). Otherwise you'll be ordering off a menu that isn't much different from that of any inland Red Lobster franchise.

NIGHTLIFE

Some of our best night moves on Sand Key were made on miniature golf courses. There are several in the area, each more ludicrously landscaped than the last. Our favorite was

Smugglers Cove Adventure Golf (15395 Gulf Boulevard, 727/398-7008), a clean, well-lit course of 18 interesting holes that reward skill as often as dumb luck. Obviously, the pirate motif is a recurring theme. One hole takes place on a shipwrecked galleon's deck, and another runs alongside a lagoon filled with live alligators. During one memorable round in our beach bum vs. beach bum competition, the score was tied as we went to the last hole. It was a tricky spiraling sucker that forced us to confront the age-old question: Play it safe or go for broke? One of us played it safe and won. The other went for broke and lost the game. Lost poorly, in fact. Words were exchanged.

Redington Beach, North Redington Beach, and Redington Shores

Between them, the three towns of Redington Beach (pop. 1,500), North Redington Beach (pop. 1,500), and Redington Shores (pop. 2,500) hold sway over four miles of beachfront. "Hold sway" is a fairly accurate description, as these are mostly single-family bedroom communities whose beaches are utilized primarily by residents. That is especially true in Redington Beach, which is as uptight as they come.

The grip loosens the farther north you go, with Redington Shores being the most visitor-friendly of the three. In fact, it attracts an esoteric mix of vacationers, especially in summer when travelers from Canada, England, France, Germany, Italy, and Denmark beat a path here. No, our eyes weren't deceiving us when we spied a Danish-American restaurant along Gulf Boulevard. "Danish lobster tails," anyone?

For more information, contact the Gulf Beaches on Sand Key Chamber of Commerce, 501 150th Avenue, Madeira Beach, FL 33708, 727/391-7373 or 800/944-1847, www.usa-chamber.com/gulf-beaches.

BEACHES

The beach is within walking distance of most homes in these three communities, which is great if you live here. Otherwise, you can just forget about it, especially in Redington Beach, which has absolutely no public beach access. **North Redington Beach** has public access with spotty parking at various street ends. Among them, 171st and 173rd Avenues have lots.

Redington Shores also has street-end accesses, beginning at 175th Avenue and continuing up to 184th Avenue. **Redington Shores Beach Access,** at 182nd Street, offers ample free parking and an extremely wide beach, but watch out for exposed rocks in the water.

16 NORTH REDINGTON BEACH/REDINGTON SHORES ACCESSES

Location: various street-end accesses in North Redington Beach and Redington Shores
Parking/Fees: limited free street parking
Hours: sunrise-sunset
Facilities: none
Contact: Redington Shores Town Hall, 727/397-5538

17 REDINGTON SHORES BEACH ACCESS

Location: Gulf Boulevard at 182nd Avenue in Redington Shores
Parking/Fees: free parking lot
Hours: 7 A.M.-sunset
Facilities: restrooms and showers
Contact: Pinellas County Parks Department, 727/464-3347

ACCOMMODATIONS

Each of the 125 rooms at the **Doubletree Beach Resort** (17120 Gulf Boulevard, 727/391-4000, $$$$) has a balcony overlooking the gulf and

TAMPA BAY

there's a dining room and lounge on the premises. This repackaged former Hilton resort is one of the nicer corporate lodges on Sand Key. You'll pay dearly for the privilege ($290 and up a night in high season), however.

Some of the smaller gulf-front properties, such as the three-story **Sandalwood Beach Resort** (17100 Gulf Boulevard, 727/397-5541, $$), offer a considerable break on price in homier surroundings. If you're looking to rent a condo, contact **Suncoast Resort Rentals** (16401 Gulf Boulevard, 727/393-3425).

COASTAL CUISINE

Shells Seafood Restaurant (17855 Gulf Boulevard, 727/393-8990, $$) is a Florida chain that rises above the pedestrian franchised norm. Shells has won top honors among locals for a decade for "casual seafood" and big helpings. While some of the menu is given over to the obligatory fried platters—hey, this is a family restaurant—Shells also has some excellent seafood pasta dishes and an array of fresh fish, which they'll char-grill or blacken. They're open for lunch and dinner. St. Pete Beach also has a **Shells** (6300 Gulf Boulevard, 727/360-0889, $$).

A popular new entry on the seafood scene is **Ballyhoo Grill** (16699 Gulf Boulevard, 727/320-0536, $$$). It, too, is part of a regional chain, like Shells and Johnny Leverock's.

North Redington Beach boasts an anomaly for this stretch of the Gulf Coast: a continental restaurant, the **Wine Cellar** (17307 Gulf Boulevard, 727/393-3491, $$$). Catering to both locals and European visitors, the Wine Cellar serves seafood platters (called King Neptune's Quartet) as well as frog legs *provencale.* The place is huge, with room for dancing nightly after the plates are cleared.

NIGHTLIFE

The **Friendly Tavern** (18121 Gulf Boulevard, 727/393-4470) in Redington Shores has been around for half a century, and the name of the place pretty much tells you why. A broad selection of foreign beers adds to the brew-ha-ha.

They sell food, too, including shrimp steamed in beer. Finally, they boast of being "the original Gulf Coast home of laser karaoke."

Indian Shores and Indian Rocks Beach

The most congenial of the Sand Key communities, Indian Shores and Indian Rocks Beach are populated with a mix of year-round residents, regular seasonal visitors, and vacationers from all over the map. Indian Shores (pop. 1,700) is justifiably proud of its five-story height limit on buildings and wide-open beaches, which host a popular "Taste of the Beaches" fair each May.

Likewise, Indian Rocks Beach (pop. 5,100) has three miles of beaches whose welcoming spirit is as warm as the gulf waters. To add to the communities' appeal, creative local entrepreneurs cater to the needs of one and all. The conspicuous absence of fast-food franchises and corporate logos offers a lesson from which many beach towns could take a cue.

© PARKE PUTERBAUGH

Indian Rocks Beach

SUNCOAST SEABIRD SANCTUARY

The largest wild bird hospital in the United States is **Suncoast Seabird Sanctuary,** located in Indian Shores. At full capacity, this rescue, rehabilitation, and re-release facility is haven for more than 500 birds, with an average of 25-30 wild birds arriving each day. Almost all the birds have been injured – either directly or indirectly – by humans. The main sources of injury are fish hooks and monofilament fishing lines, which can cause so much damage to birds that, even when recovered from their wounds, some cannot be re-released into the wild. Other injuries are caused by flying into power lines and windows or ingesting pesticides and other pollutants.

However they fall, the birds are diagnosed, treated, and put through an extensive recuperative process. The ultimate goal is to re-acclimate each bird to the outdoors in an aviary with others of its species. The public is encouraged to view the aviary, treatment rooms, and facilities, where the staff have pioneered new techniques in avian medicine. These include safe anesthesia, prosthetic feet, artificial bills, and successful captive breeding of Eastern brown pelicans. Happily, 80 percent of the birds that survive the first 24 hours are eventually re-released into the wild.

It all started on December 3, 1971, when zoologist Ralph Heath, Jr. came upon a wounded cormorant walking in a daze alongside Gulf Boulevard. He took in the bird, named him Maynard, and fixed his wing. The feathers really started flying as word of Maynard's rescue made the rounds. Wounded birds started showing up at Heath's doorstep, and he couldn't turn them away. He opened the sanctuary soon thereafter and runs it to this day. Money is raised completely by donations, and much of the work is done by volunteers.

Do yourself and your kids a favor and make Suncoast Seabird Sanctuary part of your vacation itinerary. It's enough to make anyone's spirit take wing.

For more information, contact Suncoast Seabird Sanctuary, 18328 Gulf Boulevard, Indian Shores, FL 34635, 727/391-6211, www.seabirdsanctuary.org.

TAMPA BAY

For more information, contact the Gulf Beaches on Sand Key Chamber of Commerce, 501 150th Avenue, Madeira Beach, FL 33708, 727/391-7373 or 800/944-1847, www.usa-chamber.com/gulf-beaches.

BEACHES

As you might expect in towns that roll out the welcome mat so unhesitatingly, public access to the five miles of shoreline in Indian Shores and Indian Rocks Beach is quite generous. There are accesses with limited free parking at the west ends of 20 out of 27 avenues in **Indian Rocks Beach.** Most also have outdoor showers but little else.

Pinellas County oversees two excellent beach parks here, too. One is **Tiki Gardens-Indian Shores,** which has public parking on the east side of Gulf Boulevard ($0.50 per hour), meaning you must cross this busy thoroughfare to

get to the beach. Luckily, the button on the pedestrian signal at the crosswalk has a hair trigger, so you don't have to wait long to cross. The beach is a renourished strip of white sand backed by modest dunes.

Parking is free at **Indian Rocks Beach Access,** but the sand is thinner, grayer, and shellier than at Indian Shores. There are basic facilities (showers, restrooms) at both county parks but no lifeguards.

18 INDIAN ROCKS BEACH ACCESSES (SOUTH)

Location: west ends of avenues in Indian Rocks Beach
Parking/Fees: free limited street parking
Hours: 6 A.M.-11 P.M.

Facilities: picnic tables and showers
Contact: Indian Rocks Beach Public Works Department, 727/595-6889

19 TIKI GARDENS–INDIAN SHORES

Location: 19601 Gulf Boulevard in Indian Shores
Parking/Fees: metered parking lot
Hours: 7 A.M.-sunset
Facilities: restrooms and showers
Contact: Tiki Gardens-Indian Shores, 727/549-6165

20 INDIAN ROCKS BEACH ACCESS

Location: 1700 Gulf Boulevard in Indian Rocks Beach
Parking/Fees: free parking lot
Hours: 7 A.M.-sunset
Facilities: restrooms and showers
Contact: Indian Rocks Beach access, 727/588-4852

RECREATION AND ATTRACTIONS

- **Dive Shop:** Indian Rocks Tackle & Dive Center, 1301 North Gulf Boulevard, Indian Rocks Beach, 727/595-3196

- **Ecotourism:** Suncoast Seabird Sanctuary, 18328 Gulf Boulevard, Indian Shores, 727/391-6211

- **Fishing Charters:** Jaws Too Fishing Charter, 401 2nd Street, Slip #1, Indian Rocks Beach, 727/595-3276

- **Marina:** Redington Shores Marina, 17811 Gulf Boulevard, Redington Shores, 727/391-1954

- **Pier:** Redington Long Pier, 17490 Gulf Boulevard, Redington Shores, 727/391-9398

- **Rainy-Day Attraction:** Indian Rocks Area Historical Museum, 1507 Bay Palm Boulevard, Indian Rocks Beach, 727/593-3861

- **Vacation Rentals:** Suncoast Vacation Rentals, 19823-C Gulf Boulevard, Indian Shores, 727/596-4067

ACCOMMODATIONS

The lodgings here are geared for vacation-length rentals of one and two weeks and even a month. Typical of the Old Florida–style offerings is **Tommy's On the Beach** (2302 Beach Trail, Indian Rocks Beach, 727/463-1976, $$), a three-unit beach house built well behind the dunes yet within an easy stroll of the gulf. It's popular for family reunions and honeymoons, delivering a unique lodging experience.

A nice but unglamorous "apartment motel" right on the gulf, the **Anchor Court Apartments & Motel** (940 Gulf Boulevard, Indian Rocks Beach, 727/595-4449, $$) has a heated pool, shuffleboard, and tennis. The **Holiday Inn Harbourside** (401 Second Street, Indian Rocks Beach, 727/595-9484, $$$) is a Key West–style all-suites resort on 15 acres alongside the Intracoastal Waterway. It's appointed with two heated pools, tennis and volleyball courts, and a marina from which fishing charters and dolphin-watching excursions can be taken.

COASTAL CUISINE

"Don't Worry, Be Crabby!" is the motto of **Crabby Bill's Seafood** (401 Gulf Boulevard, 727/595-4825, $$), a wild and wacky family seafood restaurant in Indian Rocks Beach. The fun starts when you walk in the door. We were greeted by a woman in a crab headdress, and a few steps behind her skulked Crabbo the Clown. Upon entering, you're shown to seats at one of the long picnic tables, where you'll quickly make friends with total strangers. Crabbo the Clown led the packed house in foot-stomping, hand-clapping sing-alongs. If you're not ready for noisy family fun, you might wish to eat elsewhere. Of course, since this is the best seafood place for miles, you

TAMPA BAY

must eat here and you *will* enjoy it! If two crabs like us can leave happy, then you will, too.

Crabby Bill's fondly recalled memories of communal Maine clambakes and Pacific Northwest smokehouse dinners. You order from the menu on a paper placemat or off handwritten signs listing "today's specials" that cover the walls. The prices are reasonable, the seafood is fresh, and the portions are huge and hearty. Crabs are obviously the specialty here. But how could we resist a pound of grilled yellowfin tuna for $17?

The dining experience is not unlike a giant family reunion, with people chatting, guffawing, staring enviously at other diners' plates, and offering ordering suggestions of their own. One friendly man proffered a piece of fish from his own plate to convince us how good it was. Forget Woodstock, we'll take Crabby Bill's! There are four other Crabby Bill's in the area, and they're all good, but this is the original. In fact, the Indian Rocks Beach location is still run by Bill himself.

Guppy's (1701 Gulf Boulevard, Indian Rocks Beach, 727/593-2032, $$) is a stylish but unpretentious restaurant serving lunch and dinner across from Indian Rocks Beach Access. The menu offers interesting variations on old standards, like a smoked salmon sandwich on pita that was so delicious it was sad to see it disappear. The same could be said for the Jamaican jerk grouper with pineapple salsa. We vowed to try the grouper fajitas the next time. You can sit on a patio that overlooks the boulevard and beach or stay inside, away from car noise.

One of the more expensive restaurants on Sand Key, the **Salt Rock Grill** (19325 Gulf Boulevard, Indian Shores, 727/593-7625, $$$$), merits its tariffs with an upscale, art-filled interior and a menu of surf-and-turf preparations pit-grilled over citrus and oak embers. If you're looking to splurge, Salt Rock Grill is the place to do it.

NIGHTLIFE

Along the stretch of coast between St. Pete Beach and Sand Key, the preponderance of pubs can sometimes make you feel as if you've been dropped by cosmic transporter into Merrie Olde England. Actually, it's the other way around, as many Britons make the trip to Florida's West Coast for sun 'n' fun of a sort they rarely get back home. You could design a pub crawl that began down in St. Pete Beach and ended in Indian Rocks Beach at the **Red Lion Pub** (1407 Gulf Boulevard, 727/596-5411) or the draft house simply known as **The Pub** (20025 Gulf Boulevard, 727/595-3172). Two other popular pubs are **Mahuffer's** (19201 Gulf Boulevard, Indian Shores, 727/596-0226), which is also known as Sloppy John's, and **J.D.'s** (125 Gulf Boulevard North, Indian Rocks Beach, 727/595-1320). Cheers, mate!

Belleair Shore and Belleair Beach

The two Belleairs are almost all residential, and their tone is one of strident privacy. We encountered this astonishing boast about Belleair Shore in a local publication: "No commercial activity is sanctioned within the town." We also encountered this telling statement: "Beaches in the community are public [note: this is a matter of state law, not community largesse], but access is private." In short, these are year-round bedroom communities for executives who commute to the neighboring cities of Tampa, St. Petersburg, and Clearwater. They got theirs, and they want you and yours nowhere near them.

In the fall of 2000, the mayor of Belleair Beach (pop. 1,751) resigned from office. He had been involved in a money-laundering scheme, and his criminal trial was deadlocked. Rather than face another trial, he confessed to stealing $250,000. His fellow citizens raced to his defense as a "man of honor" in hopes of averting prison time for their mayor of 12 years. We can't help but marvel at the great gulf when it comes to white-collar and blue-collar crime. The mayor of Belleair Beach makes off with a quarter mil and his punishment is being forced

CLEARWATER VS. THE CHURCH OF SCIENTOLOGY

Clearwater is "the spiritual headquarters of the Scientology religion," according to the church's website. It is Scientology's Mecca or Jerusalem, if you will, a holy city, a place of pilgrimage. It is home to the largest single church of Scientology on the planet (and, presumably, in the solar system), as well as dozens of buildings in the downtown area, which serve as offices for its staff of 1,200 and lodgings for the 2,000 adherents who they say come here daily. The church paints a rosy picture of how this strange metro-marriage came to be, but the facts and the surveys and news stories tell an altogether different tale. The truth is that Scientologists, given cold shoulders wherever they'd previously put down roots, hit Clearwater in 1975, armed with a plan to "take control of the city," according to a *New York Times* article based on records seized in an FBI raid. Their efforts to take over Clearwater were deceptive, at best, and diabolical, at worst: "Government and community organizations were infiltrated by Scientology members. Plans were undertaken to discredit and silence critics. A fake hit-and-run accident was staged in 1976 to try to ruin the political career of the mayor. A Scientologist infiltrated the local newspaper."

The church furtively purchased the historic Fort Harrison Hotel in downtown Clearwater, hiding behind the name of a dummy corporation. The impressive structure now serves as its world headquarters. The church boasts that its presence has helped to reduce the city's crime rate and pumps much needed revenue into the local economy (and yet, having attained IRS status as a religion after a contentious decades-long battle, it pays no taxes). Oddly, even though they're a major presence in Clearwater – and guide the footsteps of such celebrities as Tom Cruise and Michael Jackson – we could find no references to Scientology in the voluminous literature generated by the Greater Clearwater Chamber of Commerce. Conversely, locals blame the church for the decline of downtown, and have not exactly thrown their arms around their alleged benefactors. Indeed, the church's own surveys – taken prior to a major wrongful death trial brought against Scientology by the family of a member who died in their custody – show that four out of five Clearwater residents have "negative" feelings toward Scientology, regardless of whatever boost in the local economy may accrue from its presence. Both the Scientologists and the city that serves as their unwilling host remain wary of one another. It's the oddest metropolitan standoff we've encountered in our travels.

One caveat: It's not our purpose here to debunk or deconstruct Scientology. (Just Google "Scientology" and "cult" and draw your own conclusions.) Our perspective is that of beach bums who've been visiting here since about the time Scientology arrived, in 1975. In downtown Clearwater, uniformed members of the Church of Scientology now walk the streets. The secrecy and authoritarian tactics of this religious sect has added a palpable and an undeniable level of the bizarre to Clearwater's social aura.

to resign. Some homeboy robs a 7-Eleven of $200 and is tossed in the slammer for 25 years and branded society's scourge.

For more information, contact the Gulf Beaches on Sand Key Chamber of Commerce, 501 150th Avenue, Madeira Beach, FL 33708, 727/391-7373 or 800/944-1847, www.usa-chamber.com/gulf-beaches.

BEACHES

Beach accesses exist at the ends of 7th, 13th, 19th, and Morgan Streets in **Belleair Beach.** There is limited parking near the accesses, "as required by Florida state law," which was pointed out to us by a seemingly reluctant city administrator. In other words, the Belleair communities provide the public with no more than they legally must.

21 BELLEAIR BEACH ACCESSES

Location: 7th, 13th, 19th, and Morgan Streets in Belleair Beach
Parking/Fees: free limited street parking
Hours: 7 A.M.-sunset
Facilities: none
Contact: Belleair Beach Public Works Department, 727/595-4646

ACCOMMODATIONS

Belleair Beach Resort (2040 Gulf Boulevard, 800/780-1696, $$$) offers apartments, efficiencies, and a few rooms at weekly and monthly rates (even nightly, when available). A heated pool and barbecue grills are on the premises. There are no other resorts or motels in either community, and what few condo rentals exist are generally let out on a seasonal basis only.

Sand Key County Park

The entire 14 miles of barrier island between John's Pass and Clearwater Pass is known as Sand Key, but something weird happens north of Indian Rocks Beach. The transition is as surreal as anything at the Salvador Dali Museum in St. Petersburg. You leave a calm, relaxed environment that's welcoming to all and enter something comparable to Baghdad's Green Zone or Pyongyang. This is a land of security gates, horizon-obstructing monoliths, steamrollers, speed bumps, cranes, fences, and barricades. What has occurred to engender such rampant paranoia and reckless overdevelopment at the north end of Sand Key? The towering condos at the north end of the island, a sliver that technically belongs to the city of Clearwater, are the architectural equivalent of extended middle fingers.

Fortunately, Sand Key is crowned at its tip by Sand Key County Park, one of the finest beach parks on the Gulf Coast. Sand Key

boasts an extraordinarily white, shelly sand beach that is among the widest we've ever laid our beach towels on. It runs for a mile on the south side of Clearwater Pass. Parking is metered ($1 per hour) and abundant (nearly 800 spaces). Lifeguards, which are rarer than gulls' teeth on the Gulf Coast, are on duty year-round 9:30 A.M.–4:30 P.M. The park offers cabana rentals, a playground, and even a dog park, which opened in 2003. The park occupies 90 wonderful acres, 25 of which have been added due to natural accretion since the original purchase of 65 acres back in the mid-1970s. Nine wooden boardwalks take you over the dunes and on to the beach. The park's dunes and native vegetation evoke what the whole of Sand Key must have looked like at one time in the not-so-distant past.

For more information, contact Sand Key County Park, 1060 Gulf Boulevard, Clearwater Beach, FL 34630, 727/588-4852, www. pinellascounty.org/park/sand_key_park.

BEACHES

22 SAND KEY COUNTY PARK

Location: north end of Gulf Boulevard on Sand Key, at Clearwater Pass
Parking/Fees: metered parking lots
Hours: 7 A.M.-sunset
Facilities: concessions, lifeguards, restrooms, picnic tables, and showers
Contact: Sand Key County Park, 727/588-4852

Clearwater Beach

By comparison to the more colorful and down-to-earth communities strewn along Sand Key, Clearwater Beach (pop. 110,000) is overbuilt and commercialized. Hotel and condo towers dominate much of the gulfside skyline along Clearwater Beach (not to mention that part of

TAMPA BAY

PINELLAS COUNTY RECREATION TRAIL

The Pinellas County Recreation Trail is a 33.7-mile wonder that runs from St. Petersburg to Tarpon Springs, passing through the communities of Seminole, Largo, Clearwater, and Dunedin. Walkers, joggers, in-line skaters, and bicyclists use the trail. Created in a rails-to-trails conversion, it occupies the site of an old railroad line. We first crossed its path, so to speak, in Dunedin, where it passes through the center of town. The trail makes a spectacular overpass of U.S. 19A north of Dunedin, near the causeway to Honeymoon Island. The section of the trail from here to Crystal Beach swings closest to the gulf.

We salute the county for funding such an ambitious project, which is a far better use of tax dollars than yet another road-construction project. Other counties around Florida would do well to emulate the Pinellas County Parks Department, which seeded the county with splendid beach parks and this magnificent recreation trail.

A free "Guidebook to the Pinellas Trail" comes with detailed maps and en route listings of parks, restaurants, pay phones, bike shops, convenience stores, and places of interest — including osprey-nesting platforms!

For more information, contact the Pinellas County Planning Department, 14 South Fort Harrison Avenue, Clearwater, FL 34616, 727/464-4751.

Sand Key onto which Clearwater spills over). Meanwhile, older motels and efficiencies cut from plainer cloth cower in the shadows, set back like bleacher seats far from the home plate of the Gulf of Mexico. Lacking any sort of middle ground, the combination of exclusive beachside resorts and humbler hostelries relegated to the shadows creates its own forms of class-warfare pathology, and all hell breaks loose when cruisers, boozers, and losers hit town to blow off steam.

Clearwater was a very different place many centuries ago. The Native Americans who lived in the area called it Pocatopaug ("clear water") for the freshwater springs that bubbled up along shore. Conquering Spaniards forced the Indians to move inland, and the area languished until the construction of Fort Harrison in 1841 on the bluffs overlooking Clearwater Harbor. In 1880, Clearwater became a resort community with the construction of the Orange Bluff Hotel, followed by the Seaview and Belleview Hotels. The Belleview still does business as the **Belleview Mido Resort Hotel** (25 Belleview Boulevard, 727/442-6171, $$$), a golf resort on the Intracoastal Waterway that claims to be the largest occupied wooden structure in the world.

In the present, Clearwater Beach bustles without exhibiting much personality, although we will give them credit for trying. On one recent visit, we were stopped on the pier by a well-dressed fellow with a clipboard. He was soliciting visitors' opinions of the beach for an independent survey. We suggested reining in development, and he admitted the town was concerned about traffic and overdevelopment. Are they concerned enough to do something about it? Possibly so, but can you undo what's already been done?

For more information, contact the Clearwater Beach Chamber of Commerce, 100 Coronado Drive, Clearwater, FL 33767, 727/447-7600 or 888/799-3199, www.beachchamber.com.

BEACHES

We'll be the first to admit that appearances can be deceiving and that on some levels **Clearwater Beach** merits a second look. In our first edition, we had little good to say about it. Subsequent visits have led us to revise our opinion, at least of the beach. This much is true: At the south end, Clearwater Beach is dominated by high-rise hotels, and the streets are choked by traffic and construction.

A pleasant change takes place north of the Radisson Resort (formerly Adams Mark), where Clearwater Beach has provided one of the nicer municipal beaches on Florida's West Coast. The table-flat, powder-soft sands of Clearwater Beach runs for about a mile. There's plenty of sand to go around, and they've been generous with parking, too. Metered lots ($1 an hour) and a gated pay lot ($1.50 per hour) run beside the gulf along Mandalay Avenue. It's lifeguarded year-round, which is rare on the West Coast.

The centerpiece of Clearwater Beach is a concrete pier, known as Pier 60, at Causeway and Gulf Boulevards. There's plenty of activity— fishing, shops, restaurants, beach concessions—on and around Pier 60. At its foot are well-maintained picnic shelters and a shaded playground. Inspired by Key West's sunset-watching ritual, Clearwater Beach initiated a late-afternoon rite of its own in 1995. "Sunsets at Pier 60" features a similar cast of characters (clowns, jugglers, tightrope and stilt walkers, singers, and musicians) vying for spare change as the sun pulls its daily vanishing act. The gathering lasts two hours before and after sunset. For more information on this "nightly festival of fun for the whole family," call 727/449-1036.

You see all kinds of people on Clearwater Beach: oldsters reposing in the shade of the pier with mass-market paperbacks; families taking a break from their Mickey Mouse vacation in Orlando; teenage kids seeing how little they can get away with wearing in public; and oodles of Aussies and Brits enjoying a sunny seaside holiday.

Evidence of the British presence is everywhere, especially at the numerous British-themed "pubs" that make U.K. travelers feel right at home (as if you should feel right at home when you're traveling). In Clearwater Beach, you can knock back a pint, trade quips, and toss darts. The European influx occurs mostly in the winter months, while American tourists and locals crowd beaches in the summer, when school is out and the water is warm.

A cautionary note: though the north end of Clearwater Beach is indisputably nice, developmental mayhem is amiss even here. A letter to the editor of the *Clearwater Times* put it perfectly: "Enough is enough! I have had it with the hypocrisy demonstrated by the Clearwater mayor and city commission, chastising everyone who disagrees with them while courting developers as if they were the second coming." It is time to put on the brakes in Clearwater Beach.

North Clearwater Beach (a.k.a. North Beach) runs along Mandalay Avenue north of Acacia Street. Up at this quieter, more residential part of town, beach access can be gained from numerous street ends, but parking is nearly impossible.

Finally, a word about popular **Ben T. Davis Beach,** a long, narrow beach along Courtney Campbell Causeway, which links Tampa and Clearwater. If you don't mind the lack of waves, it's a great place to catch some sun, bring your dog, play volleyball, or tear around the water on a Jet Ski. Needless to say, it's mainly frequented by locals, as no one in their right mind would travel to the Tampa-Clearwater area to recreate on a causeway beach.

23 BEN T. DAVIS BEACH

Location: Along Courtney Campbell Causeway, between Tampa and Clearwater
Parking/Fees: free roadside parking
Hours: 24 hours
Facilities: none
Contact: City of Tampa Recreation Office, 813/282-2909

24 CLEARWATER BEACH

Location: on Somerset Street, 1.3 miles north of Clearwater Pass
Parking/Fees: fee parking lots ($1 per hour)
Hours: 24 hours
Facilities: concessions, lifeguards, picnic tables, restrooms, and showers

TAMPA BAY

A DAY IN THE LIFE OF CLEARWATER BEACH

Here are four views of Clearwater Beach made at different times on the same weekend day in late August. Look at it as a kind of beach diary.

MORNING: The gray half-light of dawn brings out walkers, runners, scavengers with metal detectors, and other early birds. At 7 A.M., more than a few people are already bobbing in the water. No doubt they're here to beat the heat of high noon, which can make the tepid gulf waters feel more like a Jacuzzi than a refreshing plunge. The water is so warm that numerous dead fish have washed ashore. On the beach, John Deere tractors pulling sand rakes clean the beach, arranging the sand in neat furrows for another day of trampling by happy human feet. A couple of city workers with drills sink two-foot-long bits into the sand at various intervals. Why? We have no earthly idea. Maybe we'll make a call *manana*. Maybe not.

Since we no longer hang out at bars till the wee hours and the thought of enduring deejayed dance music in clubs fills us with dread, we are able to rise and shine at an early hour, seeing another side of beach life that seldom figured into earlier editions of this book. Thus we embark on a seven-mile dawn run along Clearwater Beach, passing the aforementioned swimmers, beach tractors, and fellow joggers. If you want to find your own private stretch of sand isolated from Clearwater Beach's central bustle, walk or jog north. Two miles north of the city beach, the crowds thin out, the cottages and condos end, and the island narrows. This tip is actually part of Caladesi Island State Park. If you make it up to the north end, at the pass separating Clearwater from Caladesi, your reward will be a park bench shaded by a palmetto tree that bears the legend: "I Love This Beauty All Around Us."

NOON: The day has gotten firecracker hot. We wade into the gulf. It is like walking into warm soup. The water temperature is in the upper 80s. People aren't swimming but bobbing like dumplings in chicken stock. Rental chair-and-umbrella setups run the length of the beach. We hear every language and accent imaginable. Kids scamper about. Teenage girls lay on their stomachs, chatting on cell phones. Bearish-looking

---

Contact: Clearwater Beach Lifeguard Station, 727/462-6963

25 NORTH CLEARWATER BEACH (A.K.A. NORTH BEACH)

Location: along Mandalay Avenue, from Acacia Street north to the end of Clearwater Beach Island
Parking/Fees: free limited street parking
Hours: 24 hours
Facilities: none
Contact: Clearwater Beach Lifeguard Station, 727/462-6963

RECREATION AND ATTRACTIONS

- **Boat Cruise:** Dolphin Encounter, Clearwater Beach Marina, Clearwater Beach, 727/442-7433

- **Dive Shop:** Scuba Quest, 25712 U.S. 19 North, Clearwater, 727/726-7779

- **Ecotourism:** Osprey Bay Kayaks, 17910 U.S. 19 North, Clearwater, 727/524-9670

- **Fishing Charters:** Dixie Queen Charters, Clearwater Marina, Clearwater Beach, 727/446-7666

- **Marina:** Clearwater Municipal Marina, 25 Causeway Boulevard, Clearwater Beach, 727/462-6954

- **Pier:** Pier 60, Causeway Boulevard and

dads with brawny physiques cradle their kids while playing pirates with them in the water. Middle-aged dudes with radios tuned in to the Gators game look distressed with each turnover and elated with each TD. Without getting in over our heads, we wade out to a sandbar, going from neck-deep to knee-deep water. A little further out, boats and Jet Skis tear around the gulf, making wake and noise. It is "hot hot hot," just like the calypso song. Many beachgoers lay on the sand, bronzing their hides beneath the unforgiving sun. You can smell tanning lotion in the air.

SUNSET: Folks line the beach, chatting quietly or peering meditatively at the sun as it turns from a fiery orange to a deep red and slowly slips behind the horizon. Vendors hawk their wares on Pier 60 – mostly homemade jewelry and other crafts, like picture frames lined with seashells. A young rock band, slightly punky and surprisingly good, plays at a makeshift amphitheater just off the sand. Our hats are off to any band of teens that covers "Love Me Two Times," by the Doors. There are street performers – clowns, jugglers, and whatnot – but the scene doesn't have the manic intensity of Key West's Mallory Square sunset ritual. For one thing, sunset at Clearwater can be viewed from a beach, and a big one at that, and people are spread out all along its length. They appear to have reconnected with some ancient sun-worshiping animal instinct, because even the rowdiest teens pause to gaze silently upon the solar spectacle.

NIGHT: The strip along Clearwater Beach draws teens in great numbers, and they cruise and dawdle in clumps along its length. We're having dinner on an outdoor deck overlooking the brawl. Rap music streams in Doppler-effect fashion as vans full of would-be reprobates cruise past. Every now and then someone really winds out the gears on their motorbike, filling the air with the sound of rebellion. People look for the party, but the party is always just out of sight, moving ahead of them or behind them, elusive and frustrating. Up at the Shephards' resort/restaurant/party complex, The Wave nightclub and tiki bar draw party animals dressed to undress later, if you catch our drift. And the cars cruise till the wee hours, up and down the drag, looking for the party.

TAMPA BAY

Gulfview Boulevard, Clearwater Beach, 727/462-6466

- **Rainy-Day Attraction:** Clearwater Marine Aquarium, 249 Windward Passage, Clearwater, 727/767-2244

- **Shopping/Browsing:** Pier 60, Causeway Boulevard and Gulfview Boulevard, Clearwater Beach, 727/462-6466

- **Surf Shop:** Mandalay Surf Company, 499 Mandalay Avenue, Clearwater Beach, 727/443-3884

- **Vacation Rentals:** Florida Beach Rentals, 612 Mandalay Avenue, Clearwater Beach, 727/447-3529

ACCOMMODATIONS

The presence of so many towering buildings on the beach bears testimony to the fact that Clearwater Beach just can't say no to development. Such considerations as aesthetic appeal, quality of life, and a community's right to beach access and open space are apparently secondary to the rubber-stamping of grossly oversized constructions that are justified in the holy name of "economic development."

We say this not because we categorically despise high-rises at the beach but because Clearwater Beach is so thoroughly saturated with them. They exist in profusion both on the north side of Clearwater Pass and the northern sliver of Sand Key onto which Clearwater's developmental tentacles extend like an aggressive form of cancer.

There is a pecking order on Clearwater Beach in terms of beach proximity. The more prestigious likes of **Hilton Clearwater Beach Resort** (400 Mandalay Avenue, 727/461-3222, $$$$), **Radisson Resort on Clearwater Beach** (430 South Gulfview Boulevard, 727/443-5714, $$$$), and **Holiday Inn Sunspree Resort** (715 South Gulfview Boulevard, 727/447-9566, $$$) claim the beachfront. They're all roughly the same height, price, and appearance (to wit: tall, high, and upscale). The Radisson, which was for many years the Adam's Mark Hotel, has received a total refurbishing and has the advantage of sitting adjacent to the wide, sandy city beach.

Across the street are such mid-level chains as **Howard Johnson** (325 South Gulfview Boulevard, 727/442-6606, $$$$), as well as some of the more palatable mom-and-pops. A block behind it, on Coronado Drive, are the everyday small hotels and motor courts which look to have been here since the 1950s. If you're really light in the wallet, cruise these non-franchised motels. They are not very fancy and some are frankly uninviting, but many have an unpretentious charm and are at least clean and affordable.

The problem with Clearwater Beach is how completely the high-priced corporate sentinels dominate the beach. For instance, the 425-room Hilton offers "10 acres of sandy white beach," and the Holiday Inn claims "1,000 feet of private white sandy beach." How'd they acquire so much of the shoreline? Shouldn't Clearwater worry about how it will provide its growing population with sufficient beach access? The irony is that erosion is severe in front of these hotels, some of which literally have no beach—just a seawall separating the gulf from the hotel. You have to walk up to the municipal beach to swim and lay out.

COASTAL CUISINE

At **Frenchy's South Beach Grill,** one of us got the mixed grill platter: mahimahi, grouper, and shrimp scampi, served with healthy green salad and rice, fresh and fairly priced at $14.95. The other had wasabi-crusted tuna with garlic chive butter and was equally pleased. They *really* tout the grouper sandwich at Frenchy's, which is the place to go in the Clearwater area for this Florida staple menu item. Frenchy's is a two-story, restaurant/bar complex that faces the traffic and nighttime bustle of Mandalay Avenue. Our waitress sighed heavily as a couple of scooters roared past.

Done up in orange and coral tones, **Frenchy's Rockaway Grill** (7 Rockaway Street, 727/446-4844, $$) is a great place for a full dinner, light bite, or a cool drink at sunset. This beachside bistro is a friendly, bustling place with occasional live entertainment. We heard an acoustic guitarist tackling everything from Van Morrison to Jimi Hendrix. (Morrison got tackled behind the line of scrimmage, while Hendrix shook off several defenders and dove for a first down.) There are fish on the walls—ceramic, ocean-themed murals—and fish on the plates. The house specialty is crabmeat-stuffed grouper with hollandaise sauce. They also prepare chicken, pork, and seafood in a sweet, piquant jerk sauce. Frenchy's lies at one end of a metered public parking lot. (The meters are enforced daily till 1 A.M., so feed them accordingly.) The original **Frenchy's Cafe** (41 Baymont Street, 727/446-3607, $$) is close by, on the bay side. They're best known for award-winning grouper sandwiches.

Seafood and Sunsets at Julie's (351 South Gulfview Boulevard, 727/441-2548, $$) is an anomaly: a modest, fairly priced non-franchised eatery on Clearwater Beach. Regular menu items include grilled mahimahi, and posted specials—such as grilled red snapper atop black beans and rice—will complicate your decision. The decor is yellowish, the ambience marginally New Agey, the food hearty and wholesome, and the tab absurdly reasonable. One caveat: Desserts come from a bakery and are just okay.

Leverock's Seafood House (551 Gulf Boulevard, 727/446-5884, $$) has the best location: by the foot of the bridge over Clearwater Pass, where the setting and view are splendid. Leverock's has a number of indoor dining rooms and an outdoor dining area. However, the food is pretty ordinary, or at least our meals have been, with the selection comparable to Red Lobster. Yet it's so popular that people happily wait for tables. To our jaded palettes, Leverock's doesn't take enough advantage of fresh Florida catches and ingredients. But at least the view and drinks are worthwhile, and the crowds seem sated.

The seafood buffet at **Shephard's Restaurant and Lounge** (619 South Gulfview Boulevard, 727/441-6875, $$$) groans with peel 'n' eat shrimp, crawfish, crab legs, baked grouper, stuffed flounder, and more. The buffet costs $22.95 per person, and if a mountainous display of fresh seafood served seven nights a week sounds like a winner, hustle yourself over here. You might wind up doing the hustle afterward, as Shepherd's transforms into a club geared toward live Top 40 dance music after the plates are cleared. Incidentally, Shepherd's also operates a 40-unit gulfside resort, complete with huge heated pool and waterfront tiki bar. I like the restaurant, **Shephard's Beach Resort** (601 South Gulfview Boulevard, 727/442-5107, $$) boasts reasonable rates and a great location.

Britt's Laguna Grill (309 South Gulfview Boulevard, 727/445-1755, $$$) is set in a big yellow house and has an extensive menu that ranges from wraps to wood-fired pizzas. On the seafood front, there are lots of oyster appetizers, and we're partial to the "Cajun Trio" (grouper, salmon, shrimp) entree.

The best deal we found on breakfast was at the **Waterfront Restaurant** (490 Mandalay Avenue, 727/442-3684, $$), where we scored a hearty platter of eggs, pancakes and bacon for just $2.99.

NIGHTLIFE

Our first experiences of Clearwater Beach after dark sent us retiring to the safety of our hotel room. On subsequent visits we discovered the **Beach Bar & Grill** (454 Mandalay Avenue,

727/446-8866), a down-to-earth hangout with live bands, a boisterous crowd and a bountiful beer selection. That is much closer to our idea of a good time.

Dunedin

This picture-perfect small town along the West Coast of Florida boasts neighborhoods full of tidy homes, an attractive harbor, and a Main Street so spotlessly clean and quiet it could be set in Kansas. Its shaded Main Street is lined with distinctive restaurants and gift and antique shops that dispense knickknacks like a carving of a weeping sailor.

But things are not quite as they seem in placid Dunedin (pop. 37,500), which lies four miles north of Clearwater. Despite the high-end exterior, we were surprised by what we heard and saw on our first visit here some years back.

First, a store owner stood in the sidewalk and, with cigarette in hand, complained bitterly about business and announced his intention to "get the hell out." Next, while walking to Dunedin's tiny **Historical Society Museum** (349 Main Street, 727/736-1176), we ran into a teen gang who were signifying a little too loudly. More curious still was the poster in the front window of a local gay nightclub. Tonight was "Undie Monday," with revelers encouraged to "screw your nut into someone else's bolt." By our reckoning, Dunedin exists somewhere between divinity and depravity.

The town boasts Scottish immigrants among its founders (hence the name "Dunedin," derived from the city of Edinburgh). It was, at one time, a major seaport with the largest fleet of sailing vessels in Florida. It is the oldest town south of Cedar Key. Each spring, Dunedin's roots spring to life with the Highland Games, a celebration of all things Scottish. You're greeted at the edge of town by a rendering of a bag-playing Scotsman in a kilt. The local paper is called the *Dunedin Highlander*.

Little changes in Dunedin, which is surprising since it's just three miles north of booming Clearwater. Dunedin lies along U.S. 19A, facing St. Joseph Sound. It is blocked from direct gulf frontage by Caladesi and Honeymoon Islands and has no beaches. We've included Dunedin because it serves as a jumping-off point, via Dunedin Causeway, to Honeymoon Island and Caladesi Islands. A lot of its appeal derives from its calm-water harborage. A small, pretty harborside park is located where the road makes a series of perpendicular turns. People fish off the T-shaped dock and snap pictures at sunset photo ops. A few steps from the water, a brick facade announces the entrance to Main Street.

For more information, contact the Dunedin Chamber of Commerce, 301 Main Street, Dunedin, FL 34698, 727/733-3197, www.dunedin-fl.com.

BEACHES

Two pristine west coast barrier islands—one completely uninhabited (Caladesi) and one nearly so (Honeymoon)—are just a bridge away from Dunedin. See *Caladesi Island State Park and Honeymoon Island State Park.*

ACCOMMODATIONS

The four-story **Inn on the Bay** (1420 Bayshore Boulevard, 727/734-7689, $$) directly overlooks the bay. Waterfront rooms have balconies from which one can watch incomparable Gulf Coast sunsets. Rooms are spacious and comfortably outfitted with kitchenettes. Just off the fourth-floor lobby is a restaurant, the **Dolphin's Smile,** and at ground level, a poolside tiki bar. You can't get closer to the water than this, and you're only a hop, skip, and jump from the causeway to Honeymoon and Caladesi Islands.

A couple of lately arrived franchise motels are **Holiday Inn Express** (975 Broadway, 727/450-1300, $$), on U.S. 19A, and **Best Western Yacht Harbor Inn** (150 Marina Plaza, 727/733-4121, $$), near the water.

COASTAL CUISINE

There's something of a "restaurant row" on the south side of Main Street in Dunedin. A handful of eateries have registered on the broader metropolitan area's culinary radar. The **Black Pearl** (315 Main Street, 727/734-3463, $$$$) is a fine-dining spot that serves duckling, lamb, scampi, cedar-planked salmon, and veal *paillards* in an elegant setting. They also have a superlative dessert menu that includes homemade licorice ice cream.

A few doors down, **Kelly's Chic-a-Boom Room** (319 Main Street, 727/736-0266, $$) does double duty as a restaurant (serving breakfast, lunch, and dinner) and music club. The atmosphere is playfully retro, like a kind of hip speakeasy, and crowds queue up for the food and fun. A couple of bands playing at Kelly's when we last passed through bore names like the Black Honkeys and the Vodkanauts. It's our kind of joint.

Also on Main Street is **Casa Tina** (369 Main Street, 727/734-9226, $), which takes a refreshingly healthy approach to Mexican food.

Sea Sea Riders (221 Main Street, 727/734-1445, $$) takes its name from an old soul song, "C.C. Rider," recorded by Wayne Cochran, Mitch Ryder, and Elvis Presley. It's sited along U.S. 19A at Dunedin's harborfront park. Occupying an Old Florida home dating from 1916, this is the place to come for fresh seafood in the Dunedin area.

NIGHTLIFE

Returning from an evening in Clearwater Beach some years back, we thought we'd drive past **1470 West** (325 Main Street, 727/736-5483) to see how "Undie Monday" was progressing. From the open front door came shrieking disco-diva music. The place was as loud as it was empty (well, it was Monday). These days, 1470 West is still hanging on, still booking female impersonators. Dunedin must be a tolerant community, as 1470 has held fast to its spot on Main Street for many years.

A block up Main Street, the corner bar,

Skip's Place (371 Main Street, 727/734-9151), gets packed with locals in a less hysterical setting.

Lest we forget, Dunedin is the springtime home of the Toronto Blue Jays. They play at **Dunedin Stadium** (311 Douglas Avenue, 727/733-0429). In fact, they signed a deal that will keep them here till 2017.

Caladesi Island State Park and Honeymoon Island State Park

A graceful, arching span leads over the Gulf Intracoastal Waterway to Honeymoon Island. First, the bad news: at the island's east end is an unsightly block of condos. However, these quickly yield to unblemished nature. Pay the $5 per car entrance fee and you've got the run of this lobster-shaped island. Your choices of destinations and activities at Honeymoon Island State Park:

- A two-mile sand spit along a roadless, gulf-facing beach, along which you can hike your way to splendid isolation.

- A sociable beach by the public parking lots, where most folks drop their blankets and chairs to minimize the hassle of beachgoing on a hot day. People-watching can be good on a busy weekend. Signs warn that in-shore waters are stingray habitat, so shuffle your feet to avoid a sting.

- Hiking trails on an arm of the island shielded by the spit. You can bird-watch and study the abundant plant life, including the dominant Florida slash pine, the regal-looking sabal palm (the Florida state tree), the low-to-the-ground saw palmetto, and 200 other species.

- Well-landscaped picnic grounds on the gulf and sound sides of the island. They've provided volleyball nets in the picnic and play areas, so you can bump, set, and spike in as nice a setting as one could ask for.

- **Cafe Honeymoon,** which offers a lot more than the average park concession stand. They have a decent menu (burgers, dogs, fish sandwiches), ice cream and snacks, and a beer selection that includes locally brewed

© PARKE PUTERBAUGH

Honeymoon Island State Park

Dunedin Piper Ale. They also carry beach supplies, attire, and games, postcards, and bait. The umbrellas and chairs that have been set up on the beach can be rented—for $5 an hour or $15 per day—at the cafe. Cafe Honeymoon closes at 4 P.M. daily.

Caladesi Island State Park offers all that and less. This uninhabited island is reachable by private boat or passenger ferry from Honeymoon Island ($9 round-trip for adults, $5.50 for children 4–12, and free for kids under four). There's a bayside marina with 108 slips, if you're piloting your own craft. At the ferry landing is a concession stand, wooden bathhouses, shaded picnic areas, playground and boardwalk nature trails. Boardwalks cross the island from the marina to the gulf, where the sand is as white, fluffy and fine as flour. With 3.5 miles of beach, it's possible to escape the crowd and spend a perfect day on Caladesi Island. We took a long walk to the end of the island and back with only shorebirds for company.

For ferry information, call the **Caladesi Connection** at 727/734-5263. For reservations (accepted but not required) and schedules, which vary by time of year, call 727/734-1501. Ferries run seven days a week, weather permitting, generally 10 A.M.–5 P.M. In order to regulate crowds, they'll tell you the maximum stay on the island is four hours. This is hardly an enforceable rule, so follow your conscience. Overnight boat camping is permitted—on a first-come, first-served basis, but boaters must register before sundown. Tent camping is prohibited on the island.

Out on the beach, you can pay for a set-up of two chaise lounges and an umbrella, plunked in the sand where the boardwalk meets the beach, for $5 an hour or $15 for a four-hour "day." The more appealing alternative is to create some distance from your fellow beachgoers by walking down the beach. Solitude is easily gained out here.

The scene along causeway is worth noting, too. Those who don't want to pay the state-park entrance fee simply set up camp beside the causeway. Folks sit in beach chairs with their feet in the water, reading the *St. Petersburg Times*. They bike, jog, and rollerblade along a concrete path. They launch small boats or fish from the shallows. It's a bonafide scene in and of itself.

For more information, contact Caladesi Island and Honeymoon Island State Parks, 1 Causeway Boulevard, Dunedin, FL 34698, 727/469-5918, www.floridastateparks.org.

BEACHES

26 CALADESI ISLAND STATE PARK

 BEST (

Location: south of Honeymoon Island; reachable by passenger ferry or private boat only
Parking/Fees: $5 per vehicle entrance fee on Honeymoon Island, plus a $7 per person round-trip ferry charge ($3.50 for children 4–12, free for kids 3 and under) to Caladesi Island. A $3.25 docking fee is charged per private boats on Caladesi Island. An additional $8 fee is charged if you're docking overnight.
Hours: 8 A.M.-sunset
Facilities: concessions, restrooms, picnic tables, and showers
Contact: Caladesi Island State Park, 727/469-5918

27 HONEYMOON ISLAND STATE PARK

Location: from U.S. 19A on the north end of Dunedin, turn west onto Dunedin Causeway (S.R. 586/Curlew Road) and follow onto island
Parking/Fees: $5 per vehicle entrance fee
Hours: 8 A.M.-sunset
Facilities: concessions, restrooms, picnic tables, and showers
Contact: Honeymoon Island State Park, 727/469-5918

TAMPA BAY

Ozona, Palm Harbor, and Crystal Beach

Between Dunedin and Tarpon Springs, three retirement communities—Ozona, Palm Harbor, and Crystal Beach—are arrayed along U.S. 19A. The beaches around here are pretty small potatoes, so the recreational focus is on fishing piers and boat ramps. Away from congested U.S. 19A, there's not much more to Crystal Beach (pop. 1,000) than a church, youth center, town hall, post office, and a couple small businesses, and the homes of those who quietly live here.

Ozona (pop. 2,000) is a bit larger. This bayside community has no beaches but it does have a boat ramp on Bay Street. What really caught our attention was the sight of Spanish moss hanging in live oak trees—which is about as far south as we've seen such a thing.

Palm Harbor (pop. 80,000) is a hell of a lot larger. In fact, for a still-unincorporated community, Palm Harbor is soaking up population like a sponge. In that respect it reminded us of Port St. Lucie (on Florida's East Coast), and that is not a compliment. One thing we did like is **Wall Spring Park,** a new county park that's been opening in phases. It is built around a natural spring that pumps 4.2 million gallons of water a day. There's not much more out here now than a few picnic tables, but in the offing are boardwalks, nature trails, a canoe/kayak launch, and an observation pier.

For more information, contact the Greater Palm Harbor Area Chamber Of Commerce, 32845 U.S.19 North, Suite 210, Palm Harbor, FL 34684, 727/784-4287, www.palmharborcc.org.

BEACHES

On the gulf in Palm Harbour is **H.L. "Pop" Stansell Park.** This pleasantly wooded park's five acres include a pier, boat ramp, and three picnic shelters. The Pinellas County Recreation Trail passes within a block of it. The beach is just a short strip with more mud than sand.

Ozona doesn't have a beach, but it does have the **Ozona Beach Grill** (315 Orange Street, 727/781-5100, $), which will do if you want to duck in for a bite after having searched in vain for beaches.

Though its enticing name suggests white sand and clear water, the beach at **Crystal Beach** is only 150 feet long. It sits behind Crystal Beach Community Church, at the west end of Crystal Beach Avenue. Though the beach affords a perfect setting for the church's sunset services, the rest of us are better off heading to Caladesi Island or Honeymoon Island. Still, the beach is easily accessible from the Pinellas County Recreation Trail and is adjacent to Live Oak City Park, a community park. Park benches beneath palm trees afford peaceful spots to relax beside the water. We watched a bikini-clad girl with a sailboat tattooed on her lower back launch a kayak into the water and paddle out toward the offshore keys. There's a small wooden fishing pier if you're inclined to drop a line. Though it's only a mile or so off U.S. 19, you're light years removed from its maniacal bustle.

28 H.L. "POP" STANSELL PARK

Location: from U.S. 19A in Palm Harbor, turn west on Florida Avenue and proceed to park.
Parking/Fees: free parking lot
Hours: sunrise-sunset
Facilities: restrooms and picnic tables
Contact: Palm Harbor Recreation and Parks Department, 727/785-9862

29 CRYSTAL BEACH

Location: Crystal Beach Avenue at South Gulf Road in Crystal Beach

TAMPA BAY

Parking/Fees: free parking lot
Hours: sunrise-sunset
Facilities: none
Contact: Crystal Beach Community Church,
727/784-8222

ACCOMMODATIONS

A resort that's the size of an entire town can be found in Palm Harbor. The **Westin Innisbrook Resort** (36750 U.S. 19 North, Palm Harbor, 727/942-2000, $$$$) is one of Florida's premier sports resorts, placing a major emphasis on golf. There are four courses here, including the celebrated Copperhead course, home to the annual Tampa Bay Classic (a PGA Tour event). In addition to 72 holes of championship golf, the 1,000-acre resort has 11 tennis courts, six swimming pools (including the Loch Ness Monster pool), and a wildlife preserve. There are 700 guest suites in 28 lodges along the golf courses. Six restaurants, including a world-class steakhouse, are arrayed about the grounds. The Gulf of Mexico is close by, but this leafy resort in the rolling hills of north Pinellas County is really more about golf than gulf.

Tarpon Springs

Tarpon Springs (pop. 22,500) is not a beach town, but it has a storied relationship with the Gulf of Mexico and its estuaries. Water is the defining element of this small city. Tarpon Springs is dissected by the Anclote River and several bayous, bays, and lakes, and it is bordered by the Gulf of Mexico. There are 50 miles of waterfront, lending credence to the boast that it is the "Venice of the South." However, the town's name is a misnomer. There are no springs in Tarpon Springs, whose name came from a chance remark made by a landowner's daughter in the late 1800s. She saw fish jumping in the bayous and said, "Look at those tarpon spring!" Manatees have been showing up in the waters of beautiful Spring Bayou in recent years. Maybe they should change the name to "Manatee Springs."

The town center is two miles from the coast, where Tarpon Avenue (S.R. 582) meets Pinellas Avenue (U.S. 19A). The historic district—a reminder of those years the area served as a winter haven for wealthy Northerners—is a pleasant place to stroll and shop. The top at-

Fred H. Howard Park and Beach

© PARKE PUTERBAUGH

TAMPA BAY

traction is the Sponge Docks, on Dodecanese Boulevard and the south bank of the Anclote River. Here, a community of Greek sponge divers still plies their trade.

At one time sponging was the largest industry in Florida. A sponge-collecting industry took root in 1905, earning Tarpon Springs the title "Sponge Capital of the World." Greek immigrants are skilled at this trade, a throwback to the time when the original Greek Olympic Games featured a competition for "excellence in skin diving to gather sponges." They don heavy diving suits, lead-weighted belts, and metal diving bells straight out of a Jules Verne novel. Then they descend to pry live sponges from the gulf's bottom with small rakes. Pollution, overharvesting, and a sponge blight killed the trade in the 1940s, and the town declined with it.

Today, Tarpon Springs survives with a more modest sponge fishing industry and a shrimping fleet. The industry's rehabilitation is the direct result of environmental standards put into place in the 1960s and enforced to this day. Today there are roughly 20 active spongers working out of Tarpon Springs. They've had to resort to importing them from the Greek islands, since so few locals take up the occupation. It's a rough way to make a living. You work against currents at depths of 30–60 feet for 2–3 hours at a time. You might be gone for several weeks and venture as far as 100 miles offshore. Out of 5,000 species of sponges, only five have commercial value. Sponge harvests remain low because of pollution in the gulf and shrimp boats, which destroy sponges by raking the bottom.

"It's real, it's a way of life," says George Billiris, a sponge merchant and former diver. "It's not something cooked up to entertain tourists." We asked this garrulous old Greek if he still dives. "No, but next summer I'm going to get all the old divers together," he said. "There's six of us. Wait—no, five. The count changes every year. Anyway, we're going out on a dive for two weeks. The last hurrah."

Tarpon Springs, like many other spots in Florida, has grown rapidly in recent years, and there's new construction all along the water. Still, the largely Greek community has maintained its character and certainly nothing much has changed down by the historic sponge docks, where you can learn all about sponge diving on a 40-minute exhibition trip ($7 for adults, $3 for kids 6–13). You will be told that a sponge diver wears 172 pounds worth of gear and must walk at a 45° angle against the current. A diver actually demonstrates his livelihood, dropping over the side and reappearing moments later with a sponge. You can have you're picture taken with him, and he'll autograph it for you. Of course, we did this.

Back on the docks, you can purchase sponges in all shapes, sizes, and varieties at the onshore sponge and souvenir shops. Whether you're looking for an artist's stippling sponge, a loofa, or a simple yellow sponge, they're piled high in well-organized bins and sell for $4 and up. A natural wool sponge will set you back $10. Once you've tried it, you will never want to clean yourself with anything else. You can also buy gimcracks like a coconut-shell bird feeder. It's touristy in a tolerable way. Bouzouki music plays over speakers and a voice occasionally cuts in: "Come join us for an exciting cruise! Look for dolphins! See the lighthouse and bird sanctuary! Our boat has onboard restrooms and a full-service bar!"

For more information, contact the Greater Tarpon Springs Chamber of Commerce, 11 East Orange Street, Tarpon Springs, FL 34689, 727/937-6109, www.tarponsprings.com.

BEACHES

The word "beach" doesn't often come up in connection with Tarpon Springs. However, the town is home to the northernmost of Pinellas County's beach parks, Fred H. Howard Park and Beach. The park is a bit hard to find but worth the quest. A byzantine set of turns is required from U.S. 19A. Start by heading west on Klosterman Road (S.R. 880) and then follow the signs. You'll eventually pass beneath Spanish moss–draped oaks along

TAMPA BAY

Sunset Drive and enter Fred H. Howard Park. The mainland part of the park has nine sizable picnic shelters, as well as a kayak trail and new playground. It's a nice spot for a shaded picnic, but you're still not at the beach.

Lo and behold, a causeway appears, leading out to a small, palm-lined island that materializes like some kind of mirage. **Fred H. Howard Park and Beach** is a real revelation: a thriving, energetic beach scene that looks like a scaled-down version of Miami's South Beach. We know this sounds crazy, but our eyes did not deceive us on a late-summer weekend in 2005. The place was popping and hopping. The mile-long causeway leading out to it has plenty of angle-in parking on the left side, and people park, fish, swim, and party along its length. Windsurfers sail the breezy waters between the island and mainland. The island is ringed with palms, and people swim along all sides of it. No lie: we saw more bikinis at Howard Park than on any other beach between Clearwater and Pensacola.

It's claimed that nearly two million people a year visit Fred H. Howard Park and Beach, which is one of Florida's great county parks. We struck up a conversation with a friendly group of high-schoolers soaking up rays and vibes. A kid with braces was unreservedly enthusiastic about his hometown hangout: "Isn't this beach just the greatest?" he exclaimed. We had to agree.

Just south of Howard Park, at the west end of Gulf Road, is the town-run **Sunset Beach.** A favorite with locals, it's more popular as a picnic area (with 15 shelters) and boat launch than a beach, though it does have a small swimming area.

SUNSET BEACH

Location: west end of Gulf Road in Tarpon Springs
Parking/Fees: free parking lot
Hours: sunrise–10 P.M.

Facilities: restrooms and picnic tables
Contact: Tarpon Springs Parks Department, 727/942-5610

31 FRED H. HOWARD PARK AND BEACH

Location: From U.S. 19A in Tarpon Springs, turn west on Klosterman Road (S.R. 880) and follow signs to the park
Parking/Fees: free parking lots
Hours: 7 A.M.–sunset
Facilities: restrooms, picnic tables, and showers
Contact: Fred H. Howard Park and Beach, 727/937-4938

RECREATION AND ATTRACTIONS

- **Bike/Skate Rentals:** Outdoor Gear, 212 East Tarpon Avenue, Tarpon Springs, 727/943-0937
- **Boat Cruise:** St. Nicholas Boat Line, 693 Dodecanese Boulevard, Tarpon Springs, 727/942-6425
- **Ecotourism:** Island Wind Tours, Tarpon Springs Sponge Docks, 600 Dodecanese Boulevard, Tarpon Springs, 727/934-0606
- **Fishing Charters:** Dolphin Deep Sea Fishing, 810 Dodecanese Boulevard, Tarpon Springs, 727/937-8257
- **Lighthouse:** Anclote Lighthouse, Anclote Key State Park, Anclote Key, 727/469-5942
- **Marina:** Tarpon Springs City Marina, Tarpon Springs, 727/937-9165
- **Pier:** Sunset Beach, Gulf Road, Tarpon Springs, 727/942-5610
- **Rainy-Day Attraction:** Coral Sea Aquarium, 850 Dodecanese Boulevard, Tarpon Springs, 727/938-5378
- **Shopping/Browsing:** Sponge Exchange, 735 Dodecanese Boulevard, Tarpon Springs, 727/934-9262

ACCOMMODATIONS

Most of the motels in Tarpon Springs are located on U.S. 19A. Trust us; you do not want to stay on U.S. 19A. Located in the historic district is **Spring Bayou Inn Bed & Breakfast** (32 West Tarpon Avenue, 727/938-9333, $$), a turn-of-the-century home with five rooms. It overlooks Spring Bayou, and a prettier spot you could not wish to see.

COASTAL CUISINE

You should definitely sponge a meal in Tarpon Springs. How often do you find authentic Greek food? Excellent restaurants can be found in the blocks near the sponge docks. Our favorite is **Mykonos Mayerion** (628 Dodecanese Boulevard, 727/934-4306, $$), which is as authentically Greek as any restaurant in the island nation. The paper placemats at Mykonos bear a map of Greece and its cultural highlights. Greek writing lines the walls. You hear Greek spoken in the restaurant.

And the food! Mykonos serves amazing appetizers you can make a meal out of: dolma (grape leaves stuffed with rice and topped with lemony sauce); cold marinated octopus, spreads for the homemade bread that are flavored with garlic or caviar; and pan-fried kefalotyri cheese. A big, pizza-shaped block is served on an iron platter, covered with oil and set aflame. "You're not scared, are you?" asked our smiling waitress as a nearby table recoiled from the plume of flame that rose when she touched a match to the oil. This sizzling, must-try appetizer really starts making noise when they squeeze lemon on it just prior to placing the platter in front of you.

There's more: tangy, healthful Greek salads, topped with big squares of feta cheese and swimming in oil and vinegar. Entrees such as Greek shrimp (cooked in olive oil, lemon, garlic, oregano, and feta cheese) and lightly sauteed, tender-sweet calamari. Pan-fried fish such as smelt, sand perch and grouper. Homemade yogurt and baklava for desert. And Greek coffee to top it all off, so thick and black you practically need to consume it with

a spoon. The food at Mykonos is as good as it is inexpensive. You cannot order wrong and will not leave hungry.

The largest restaurant in Tarpon Springs—indeed, one of the largest in all of Florida—is **Louis Pappas' Riverside Restaurant** (10 West Dodecanese Boulevard, 727/937-5101, $$). They seat around 1,000 and serve seafood "fresh from the docks," including Grouper 3rd Generation (dipped in a sauce of lemon, garlic, and mustard, then floured and fried), Greek-style octopus (broiled in lemon and olive oil), and *kalamarakia* (fried baby squid). The prices are right, with entrees running in the $8.95–11.95 range. For a lighter bite, our favorite bakery in town is **Parthenon Pastry Shop** (751 Dodecanese Boulevard, 727/938-7709, $).

Anclote Key Preserve State Park

Anclote Key lies three miles off the coast of Tarpon Springs. It is the northernmost in a string of barrier islands that includes Honeymoon and Caladesi Islands. There is no road or state-run ferry to Anclote Key, so this four-mile island gets mentioned far less frequently than they do. Yet the entirety of its western shoreline is one long, secluded beach, backed by healthy dunes held in place by sea oats.

"If you like a completely natural beach, this is the place," a ranger at Caladesi exclaimed, and he wasn't just whistling Dixie. There's even an old lighthouse at the southern end of the island. This decommissioned Coast Guard beacon (ca. 1886) has lately been restored by a local organization.

Excursion boats head out to Anclote Key. (Try **Island Wind Tours,** 600 Dodecanese Boulevard, 727/934-0606.) Private boats can be rented in Tarpon Springs if you want to make the trip yourself. There are no facilities, running water, or rangers on duty. The state built picnic tables and a boardwalk over the dunes, but vandals destroyed them and used the pieces for firewood.

"We're too short of manpower to keep an eye on everything," said the Caladesi ranger, "so there's no more boardwalk or picnic tables." Primitive camping is allowed. Most campers drop their gear on the beach, which is the best place to escape the mosquitoes.

For more information, contact Anclote Key Preserve State Park, 1 Causeway Boulevard, Dunedin, FL 34698, 727/469-5942, www.floridastateparks.org.

BEACHES

32 ANCLOTE KEY PRESERVE STATE PARK

Location: three miles west of Tarpon Springs, in the Gulf of Mexico
Parking/Fees: none
Hours: 8 A.M.-sunset
Facilities: none
Contact: Anclote Key Preserve Sate Park, 727/469-5918

TAMPA BAY

THE NATURE COAST

The Nature Coast spans eight of Florida's least-traveled coastal counties (Pasco, Hernando, Citrus, Levy, Dixie, Taylor, Jefferson, and Wakulla), which perhaps explains why so much nature still survives here. Collectively known as the Big Bend, these counties honestly have little to offer in the way of beaches. For reasons having to do with wave regime and sediment supply, beaches simply don't form along the Big Bend.

What these counties do have to offer is unique in the United States: hundreds of thousands of preserved, pristine acres of wetlands, forests, and spring-fed rivers. There are countless species of flora and fauna, including some of the world's few remaining Florida panthers and manatees. Glimpses of the similarly endangered Old Florida can be spotted all over, as well. The Nature Coast is a haven for such exotic Native American–derived place names as Weeki-Wachee,

Withlacoochee, Chassahowitzka, Sopchoppy, Ochlockonee, and Suwannee.

The quieter, more subtle charms of the Nature Coast are lost upon those speeding south toward Tampa Bay on U.S. 19. But those who pause and look around will find a hidden wonderland conducive to camping, canoeing, kayaking, fishing, hiking, photography, and other uplifting, restorative activities.

Holiday, New Port Richey, and Port Richey

You've heard of "the real Florida," which is the motto of the state park system in its preservation efforts. U.S. 19 through Pasco and Hernando counties might be described as "the surreal Florida." It stands alone among all our

© PARKE PUTERBAUGH

THE NATURE COAST

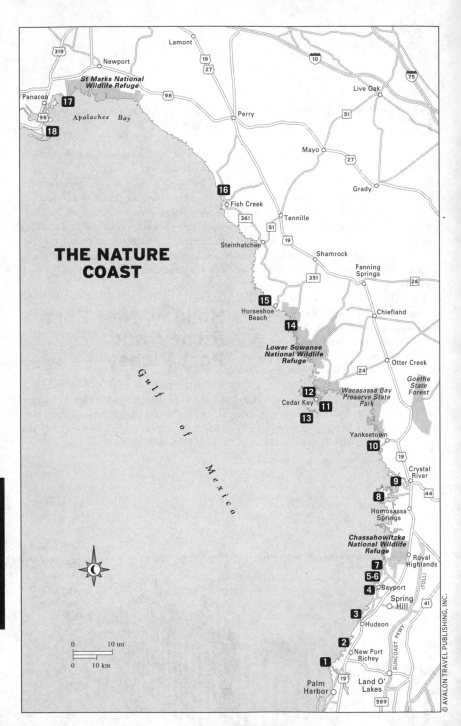

THE NATURE COAST

BEST BEACHES

◖ **Chassahowitzka National Wildlife Refuge:** Best for Canoeing and Kayaking (page 456)

◖ **Kings Bay (Crystal River National Wildlife Refuge):** Best for Diving and Snorkeling (page 456)

◖ **Homosassa Springs State Wildlife Park (Homosassa Springs):** Best for Birdwatching and Wildlife-Viewing (page 457)

◖ **Cedar Keys National Wildlife Refuge:** Best for Canoeing and Kayaking (page 468)

◖ **St. Marks National Wildlife Refuge:** Best for Birdwatching and Wildlife-Viewing (page 476)

coastal travels as the most unremittingly over-built thoroughfare of franchised commerce in existence. Pasco County is the ugliest coastal county in the state of Florida because of it. For at least 25 miles the strip-mall sprawl and man-made devastation of the landscape are daunting to navigate and depressing to behold. Moreover, It obscures any differences that might otherwise distinguish hideous Holiday (pop. 32,000) from Port Richey (pop. 3,200) or New Port Richey (pop. 16,500). Port Richey wishfully bills itself as "the Little City on the River," but from the vantage point of U.S. 19, it's all one big, ugly anaconda of stores, service stations, and strip malls.

U.S. 19 in this vicinity is a 20-mile strip mall, a numbing procession of Chinese buffets, mortgage lenders, printers, makers of signs and banners, dentists, storage facilities, muffler shops, tanning salons, hardware stores, and so on. A supper club sits directly across the highway from a strip club. You pass the same franchises so repeatedly that you might actually believe you're driving in circles. Of course, there are plenty of insurance companies and auto-body shops to deal with the collisions that are routine and inevitable along this four-lane blacktop. Heaven help the fool who doesn't keep up with speeding traffic, and beware of lane-changing cretins screeching around

you to shave a few seconds off their mindless sprint from stoplight to stoplight. Between NASCAR-driver wannabes and slow-moving retirees, you are in for a white-knuckle ride on this trip to hell or Home Depot, which are more or less the same thing.

We wish we could offer an alternate route for combating Pasco County, but U.S. 19 is the only way through this mess. How could such a monstrous defiling of what was once an appealingly isolated corner of the state been allowed to happen? It makes a mockery of the term "Nature Coast," as nature has been obliterated to make way for more retail sprawl, housing subdivisions, and golf courses than you can shake a five-iron at. They euphemistically refer to the permissive mindset that enabled this vile morass as "a progressive business climate." The end result is that nature—the only real asset they can claim—has taken a beating. In place of unmolested acreage upon which black bears and Florida panthers should be roaming you'll find an endless, redundant procession of Eckerd's, Wal-Mart, McDonald's, Taco Bell—in short, all of the usual suspects in the franchised dimming of the American mind.

So take a sedative or antidepressant, insert a soothing CD in your car stereo, and motor through this blight as best you can. No pulling

THE NATURE COAST

THE EIGHT COUNTIES OF THE NATURE COAST

North of Tarpon Springs, the Florida coast undergoes a dramatic transformation. The human population thins and the beaches all but disappear along a 200-mile stretch known as the Nature Coast. It lies along the interior elbow along that separates the north-south Florida Peninsula from the east-west Florida Panhandle. For this reason, the area is also referred to as the Big Bend. The backdrop of sandy beaches ends at Honeymoon Island (in Pinellas County) and doesn't reappear until St. George Island (in Franklin County). That's not to say there are no sand beaches along the Nature Coast, just that they're rare and small in size. And even if there's a fringe of sand beach along the shore, the bottom of the gulf is muddy and mucky, not sandy.

The Nature Coast/Big Bend area consists of eight gulf-fronting counties. From the south, they are Pasco, Hernando, Citrus, Levy, Dixie, Taylor, Jefferson, and Wakulla. Slogan makers have branded the Nature Coast/Big Bend "a land that time forgot," and parts of it are also referred to as the Forgotten Coast. There are exceptions: Pasco and Hernando Counties have been all too well remembered along the U.S. 19 corridor, which is as blighted by retail development as any big-city beltway. But by and large, the Nature Coast/Big Bend/Forgotten Coast is a condo-less sanctuary where nature reigns supreme.

All totaled, 980,000 acres of land in these eight counties have been set aside for conservation or recreation, and they are home to at least 19 endangered or threatened animal species. It is impossible to mention all of the natural sights, parklands, and preserves within this vast region, but here is a county-by-county look at some highlights.

- **Pasco County** has 15 miles of gulf coastline, including several small beaches off the beaten track in Holiday, Hudson, and Port Richey. However, it is bisected by the grossly overbuilt U.S. 19 corridor, making Pasco one county you'll want to pass through. Having negotiated this hazardous four-lane blacktop too many times, we decided AC/DC must have had U.S. 19 in mind when they wrote "Highway to Hell."

- **Hernando County** claims to be "the heart of the Nature Coast," but it is growing too fast – the population having shot up by 62 percent in 10 years – and U.S. 19 is an overbuilt, traffic-choked horror show. Relief can be found in an expansive state forest and the swamps along its meandering rivers, the Withlacoochee and the Weeki Wachee. On the coast, you'll find glimpses of Old Florida at Bayport and Pine Island. The rest of Hernando County's 15 miles of coastline is swamp forest that falls inside Chassahowitzka National Wildlife Refuge.

- **Citrus County** declares itself "Mother Nature's Theme Park." With one-third of the county's land area under preservation, this is a fair boast. Citrus County has seven

over for triple-bacon cheeseburgers. Restroom breaks only. You'll thank us later.

For more information, contact the Pasco County Tourism Development Council, 7530 Little Road, New Port Richey, FL 34654, 727/847-8129 or 800/842-1873, www.visitpasco.com.

BEACHES

A quieter bit of yin to U.S. 19's obnoxious yang is offered at a trio of county parks in southwest Pasco County. First up is **Anclote River Park,** on the mouth of the Anclote River at the west end of Bailey's Bluff Road in Holiday. Boaters and fishers will have a good time out here, but the real surprise is the sandy strip of beach that is lifeguarded all summer long.

Neighboring **Anclote Gulf Park** lacks a beach but is worth mentioning because it has a fishing pier that's often swamped with happy anglers. Both parks have a picnic area and

pristine rivers, numerous lakes, a state forest, and Chassahowitzka National Wildlife Refuge. People come to Citrus County to fish and to commune with nature – especially the manatees drawn to its pure, spring-fed rivers. The springs from Crystal River north to the Suwannee River make for world-class snorkeling.

* **Levy County** is right at the bend in the Big Bend. To the south, the unassuming community of Yankeetown nestles beside the bucolic Withlacoochee River. At the center is Cedar Key, an island hideaway surrounded by extensive nature preserves that include Waccasassa Bay Preserve State Park, Cedar Key Scrub State Reserve, Cedar Keys National Wildlife Refuge, and Lower Suwannee National Wildlife Refuge. Many of the lovely offshore islands, especially Atsena Otie and Seahorse Key, are ringed with sandy beaches begging to be visited by boat or kayak.

* **Dixie County** is bounded by the Suwannee and Steinhatchee Rivers and the Gulf of Mexico. It is great in size (704 square miles) but small in population. It is peaceful and serene on the gulf at places like Shired Island and Horseshoe Beach. Excellent fishing, an appealing natural setting, and the splendid isolation that comes from being in the proverbial middle of nowhere are Dixie County's calling cards.

* **Taylor County** has the longest coastline – 60 miles! – of any Florida county but only one accessible sand beach: Hodges Park, in Keaton Beach. A lack of beaches shouldn't discourage anyone from visiting this sparsely populated county, which calls itself the "Forest Capital" of Florida. Ninety percent of Taylor County is covered by trees, and the Forest Capital State Museum in Perry celebrates this fact. The county's many rivers – including the Steinhatchee, Econfina, and Aucilla – attract canoeists and kayakers. Winter runs of trout and redfish draw anglers, and fishing the grass flats keeps them occupied in spring and fall. Scalloping and crabbing are popular, too.

* **Jefferson County** is the only county in Florida that touches the state of Georgia and the Gulf of Mexico. Its brief, six-mile coastline lies at the head of Apalachee Bay. All 9,000 acres between U.S. 98 and the gulf in Jefferson County belongs to St. Marks National Wildlife Refuge. Most of the county is forest and marshland. At 235 feet, the county seat of Monticello is one of the highest points in Florida.

* **Wakulla County** is given over to vast tracts of Apalachicola National Forest, St. Marks National Wildlife Refuge, and Wakulla Springs State Park. Four rivers – the St. Marks, Sopchoppy, Ochlockonee, and Wakulla – run through the county. There's plenty of great canoeing and hiking in Wakulla County. The 16-mile Tallahassee-St. Marks Historical Railroad State Trail runs from the state capital to the St. Marks River, and the Florida National Scenic Trail – a 1,300-mile work in progress – also crosses the county. Beach lovers have but a few sandy slivers, but anglers who love flats fishing are right at home here.

playground. Close by is **Key Vista Natural Attractions Park,** which has a boardwalk, trail, and fishing. All three of these watery-recreation-based parks in Holiday are on Bailey's Bluff Road.

Port Richey—as opposed to "New" Port Richey, the fast-growing community that lies inland—claims **Robert K. Rees Memorial Park.** It, too, has a small but natural strip of sandy beach, boardwalk, and seasonal life-

guards, plus canoe access to the gulf. Lifeguards are rare along the lower reaches of Florida's West Coast, where there are broad, sandy beaches and real waves to worry about. It's odd indeed that Pasco County should have not one but three lifeguarded county beach parks.

Port Richey Waterfront Park has a picnic table, fishing pier, playground, but no beach. Sited on one of the last undeveloped waterfront parcels in Pasco County, it was slated to become a huge commercial arena, but the Trust for Public Land purchased it in 1997 and then deeded it to the city of Port Richey. On the developmental front, some stories still do have happy endings.

1 ANCLOTE RIVER PARK

Location: west end of Bailey's Bluff Road in Holiday
Parking/Fees: free parking
Hours: sunrise-sunset
Facilities: concessions, lifeguards (seasonal), restrooms, picnic tables, and showers
Contact: Anclote River Park, 727/938-2598

2 ROBERT K. REES MEMORIAL PARK

Location: west end of Green Key Road in Port Richey
Parking/Fees: free parking lot
Hours: sunrise-sunset

Facilities: concessions, lifeguards (seasonal), restrooms, and picnic tables
Contact:, Robert K. Rees Memorial Park, 727/834-3252

Hudson and Aripeka

A brief but welcome respite from U.S. 19's mindless sprawl is offered in northwest Pasco County, where a smaller state road forks off toward the coast while U.S. 19 swings a bit inland. Old Dixie Highway (S.R. 595) detours into an older Florida shaped by cracker houses, coastal scenery, and pristine wetlands.

Five miles north, on Old Dixie Highway, lies Aripeka (pop. 1,000), an unincorporated town that shares the same zip code as Hudson. We spotted some shirtless, red-skinned men fishing from a bridge, which just about said it all. Aripeka is a jumble of small homes, a church, and very little else. It has a sandy coastline, fish camp, and rundown marina. Signs that urged us to "Beware of Dog" were willingly heeded.

For more information, contact the Pasco

Robert J. Strickland Memorial Park, Hudson

© PARKE PUTERBAUGH

THE NATURE COAST

County Tourism Development Council, 7530 Little Road, New Port Richey, FL 34654, 727/847-8129 or 800/842-1873, www.visit-pasco.com.

BEACHES

One mile west of U.S. 19 via Clark Street in Hudson (pop. 40,000) is **Robert J. Strickland Memorial Park** (a.k.a. Hudson Beach). This side of Hudson has a resort atmosphere and fronts a highly appealing sand beach. It is a pleasant surprise to find such a clean and inviting beach in so cankerous a county. The beach is small but the sand is pearly white and fairly wide, leading to slippery-bottomed, waveless water. Watch out for oyster shells and rocks.

A full complement of facilities, including picnic shelters and summer lifeguards, can be found here. Parking is free and abundant. The beach is bounded by a boardwalk, and you can get a good view of the surrounding area from the pavilion. This popular park gets especially crowded on warm days. The neighborhood itself has a homey atmosphere and looks to have been around a lot longer than the retail clutter out on U.S. 19.

❸ ROBERT J. STRICKLAND MEMORIAL PARK (A.K.A. HUDSON BEACH PARK)

Location: at the west end of Clark Street in Hudson

Parking/Fees: free parking lots

Hours: sunrise-sunset

Facilities: concessions, lifeguards (seasonal), restrooms, picnic tables, and showers

Contact: Hudson Beach Park, 727/861-3010

ACCOMMODATIONS

A more than adequate beachfront motel and perfectly pleasant seaside restaurant sit side by side along the gulf in Hudson. The former is the **Inn on the Gulf** (6330 Clark Street, 727/868-5623, $$) and the latter is Sam's (see *Coastal Cuisine*). On an offbeat note,

Gulf Coast Resort (13220 Houston Avenue, 727/868-1061, $) is an "RV nudist park on 40 wooded acres." Just imagine the human manatees on display.

COASTAL CUISINE

Sam's Hudson Beach Restaurant (6325 Clark Street, 727/868-1971, $) has an unfancy setting—you eat at picnic tables under an open-air pavilion—but the menu is surprisingly extensive and tilted toward seafood items. Sam's specialties: shrimp, oysters, and clams.

Hernando Beach

Proceeding north on Old Dixie Highway (C.R. 595) from Pasco County, you will cross the Hernando County line. While C.R. 595 loops back out to U.S. 19, another blue highway, Shoal Line Boulevard (C.R. 597), runs along the gulf to Hernando Beach (pop. 2,000). This waterfront community consists of a sizable spread of homes built along an extensive series of canals, docks, marinas, seawalls, an extensive juncus marsh, and a muddy, shelly, and rocky shoreline. It's suburbia with boat slips instead of two-car garages. (Memorable street name: Campanero Entra.) There's not much out here for travelers beyond a clump of seafood restaurants, such as **BJ Gator's** (4054 Shoal Line Boulevard, 352/596-7160, $$). Hernando Beach reminds us of a bonsai version of Fort Lauderdale in its earliest days, when it was aiming to become the Venice of America.

For more information, contact the Greater Hernando County Chamber of Commerce, East Fort Dade Avenue, Brooksville, FL 34601, 352/796-0697, www.hernandochamber.com; or the Hernando County Tourist Development, 16110 Aviation Loop Drive, Brooksville, FL 34609, 352/754-4405 or 800/601-4580, www.co.hernando.fl.us/tourdev.

BEACHES

There are no sand beaches in Hernando Beach, but the county operates four small parks in the area, three of which do have beaches. Running from south to north, the first is **Hernando Beach Park.** Despite the name, it's at least a mile from the Gulf of Mexico. Nonetheless, it's a very attractive and large (135 acres) park filled with trees and native vegetation. Hernando Beach Park is ideal for younger kids, as it has an extensive playground, sturdy observation tower, and safe swimming area at a man-made beach along Jenkins Creek. Across the road is **Jenkins Creek Park,** a small parcel with a fishing pier and boat launch for canoes and small powerboats.

About a mile north of here is **Rogers Park,** which has a boat launch into a manatee-frequented area of the Weeki Wachee River. It also has a picnic area, artificial beach, and the friendliest group of ducks we've encountered. One even tried to get in our car. A $2 admission fee is charged in summer only.

ACCOMMODATIONS

Aside from chain motels on U.S. 19 and I-75, there's the **Hernando Beach Motel** (4291 Shoal Line Boulevard, 352/596-2527, $). It's nothing fancy, but if you're in the area to fish or get away from it all, it will fit the bill just fine. The motel's 14 units range from one-bedroom efficiencies with full kitchen and bath to two-bedroom, two-bath condos.

COASTAL CUISINE

Just across the river from Rogers Park, in Weeki Wachee, is an inviting seafood, steak, and rib house called **Otters** (5386 Darlene Street, 352/597-9551, $$). It's set inside a rambling brown wooden house. On our visit, the belting of Frank Sinatra provided an interesting contrast to the quacking of ducks across the Frances Carlisle Bridge. (We prefer the quacking.)

◨ HERNANDO BEACH PARK

Location: 6400 Shoal Line Road (C.R. 597), a mile west of Hernando Beach on Jenkins Creek
Parking/Fees: free parking lot
Hours: sunrise-sunset
Facilities: restrooms, picnic tables, and showers
Contact: Hernando County Parks and Recreation Department at 352/754-4031

◨ ROGERS PARK

Location: 7244 Shoal Line Boulevard (C.R. 597), on the Weeki Wachee River, five miles west of Weeki Wachee
Parking/Fees: $2 per vehicle entrance fee
Hours: sunrise-sunset
Facilities: concessions, lifeguards (seasonal), restrooms, picnic tables, and showers
Contact: Hernando County Parks and Recreation Department, 352/754-4031

Bayport and Pine Island

The historic town of Bayport (pop. 250) is located at the mouth of the Weeki Wachee River. Because of this prime location, it served as Hernando County's major port before the Gulf Coast railroads went into service in 1885. Some of the old vernacular architecture is still intact, and some is collapsing along the side of Cortez Boulevard (C.R. 550). This road links Bayport and neighboring Pine Island (pop. 400) with U.S. 19, which lies seven miles east.

The drive through this area is an unbridled delight. Spanish moss drapes down from the limbs of gnarled oak trees, and salt-marsh wetlands spread in all directions. Think of it as Florida's Mont-Saint-Michel, because during winter storms parts of the roadway are inundated at high tide, while on the lowest tides you can walk out almost a mile from shore. The infamous "No Name Storm" of 1993 badly tore up the area, and many residents had to be rescued by helicopter and boat.

For more information, contact the Greater

© PARKE PUTERBAUGH

Alfred A. McKethan Pine Island Park

Hernando County Chamber of Commerce, East Fort Dade Avenue, Brooksville, FL 34601, 352/796-0697, www.hernandochamber.com; or Hernando County Tourist Development, 16110 Aviation Loop Drive, Brooksville, FL 34609, 352/754-4405 or 800/601-4580, www.co.hernando.fl.us/tourdev.

BEACHES

Cortez Boulevard ends in Bayport at **Bayport Park,** a small gulfside park with two boat ramps, a fishing pier, and picnic pavilion (but no beach to speak of). From Bayport Park, backtrack down Cortez Boulevard (C.R. 550) and turn onto serpentine C.R. 495. (There's a roadhouse called the Bayport Inn, with an address of 4835 Cortez Boulevard, at the intersection.) You will scarcely believe what you'll encounter at the end of the road after three miles of salt marsh and mudflats: a palm-fringed island. This sandy oasis is called **Alfred A. McKethan Pine Island Park,** and it occupies a three-acre point of land in the middle of nowhere.

Pine Island is home to a surprisingly festive beach scene. The tiny island is rimmed by a beach created from sand that's been trucked in and spread inside a seawall. There's a large, sandy playground with a volleyball court and things for kids to climb on and slide down. A nearly waveless beach and staffed lifeguard stand make Pine Island as safe as milk. The park's cafe is another surprise, going way beyond burgers and dogs all the way to cappuccino and key lime pie. Entry is $2 per car, the park is open till 9 P.M., and parking is abundant. Pine Island draws all shapes, sizes, ages, and accents, but we especially heard a lot of Spanish voices amid the happy din. It's as pleasant and unexpected a surprise as one will find on the Nature Coast.

6 BAYPORT PARK

Location: west end of Cortez Boulevard (C.R. 550), in Bayport
Parking/Fees: free parking lot
Hours: sunrise-sunset
Facilities: restrooms and picnic tables
Contact: Hernando County Parks and Recreation Department, 352/54-4031

7 ALFRED A. MCKETHAN PINE ISLAND PARK

Location: on Pine Island Drive, at the west end of C.R. 495, eight miles northwest of Weeki Wachee
Parking/Fees: $2 per vehicle entrance fee
Hours: 8 A.M.-9 P.M.
Facilities: concessions, lifeguards (seasonal), restrooms, picnic tables, and showers
Contact: Hernando County Parks and Recreation Department, 352/754-4031

BEST Chassahowitzka National Wildlife Refuge and Crystal River National Wildlife Refuge

The Nature Coast earns its name partly through the extraordinary confluence of six National Wildlife Refuges (Chassahowitzka, Crystal River, Lower Suwannee, Pinellas, Cedar Keys, and St. Marks). As most ecotourists know, National Wildlife Refuges are federally owned conservation lands managed by the U.S. Fish and Wildlife Service. They have been set aside to protect habitat and to ensure that future generations will have wildlife and wilderness to enjoy—and 40 million Americans a year do just that.

There are currently 632 National Wildlife Refuges in the United States, encompassing 96 million acres and providing haven for 200 endangered or threatened species. The state of Florida claims 28 refuges, most of which are vital wintering grounds for waterfowl and other migratory birds. They also set unbreachable boundaries for the never-ending development that otherwise threatens to turn Florida into a giant strip mall and subdevelopment.

Chassahowitzka National Wildlife Refuge is located southwest of Homosassa, sprawling across southern Citrus County and northern Hernando County. The refuge covers 30,500 acres of bays, creeks, estuaries, brackish marshes, fringing hardwood swamps, and mangrove islands. It stretches along a mostly inaccessible coastline, from the Homosassa River down to Raccoon Point, below the mouth of the Chassahowitzka River. Refuge headquarters can be found on U.S. 19, a mile north of the Citrus County line. The refuge itself is accessible by boat only, and the idea is to keep it that way in order to preserve the unspoiled estuarine habitat.

However, the Citrus County Parks and Recreation Department, through a lease arrangement, maintains the 40-acre **Chassahowitzka River Campground and Recreation Area** within the refuge. Day-use facilities include a boat ramp, canoe and kayak rentals, and there's a natural spring to marvel at. Chassahowitzka lies 1.7 miles west of U.S. 19 at the end of Miss Maggie Drive (C.R. 480). A modest fee of $2 per vehicle is charged. The stellar campground at Chassahowitzka River has 92 sites, both primitive ($15 per night) and with hookups ($20 per night).

Because most of the land surface in the refuge is mudflats and salt marsh, there are no hiking trails. About 250 species of birds, 50 species of reptiles and amphibians, and 25 species of mammals can be found here. Fishing is allowed in the pure, spring-fed creeks that sluice through the wetlands.

By comparison, Crystal River National Wildlife Refuge is a shrimp, encompassing a mere 46 acres of islands in **Kings Bay.** But it's an important habitat for manatees. This area's many natural springs pump 600 million gallons of water a day, making Kings Bay the most significant warm-water refugium for the beleaguered mammal. (Odd as it may seem, outputs of warmed water from power plants along the Florida coast also serve as manatee refuges.) Approximately 25 percent of the nation's manatees congregate in Kings Bay, which is why its refuge islands are so critical.

Commercial marinas and dive shops can be found at the end of Kings Bay Drive and Paradise Road in Crystal River. Diving, snorkeling, and swimming are the activities of choice, while fishing is prohibited on the refuge. Peak time for manatee viewing is December–March. To learn more about the manatee, visit the Manatee Education Center at Homosassa Springs State Wildlife Park, seven miles south of Crystal River on U.S. 19.

For more information, contact Chassahowitzka and Crystal River National Wildlife Refuges, 1502 Southeast Kings Bay Drive, Crystal River, FL 34429, 352/563-2088, www.chassahowitzka.fws.gov, www.crystalriver.fws.gov;or Chassahowitzka River Campground and Recreation Area, 8600 West Miss Maggie Drive, Homosassa, FL 34446, 352/382-2200, www.bocc.citrus.fl.us/parks/chass_camp/campground.htm.

BEST(Homosassa Springs and Homosassa

Fully one-third of Citrus County's 682 square miles have been set aside as federal, state, or county conservation land and, as a result, it is a vital home to 12 endangered species, including the Florida black bear, manatee, scrub jay, peregrine falcon, and Southern bald eagle. There are uniquely fascinating destinations along Citrus County's coastal backroads. This self-proclaimed "soul of the Nature Coast" and "Mother Nature's theme park" is home to Native American archaeological sites dating back 10,000 years; historic remnants of Spanish and pioneer settlements; and truly remarkable natural springs where manatees can be closely observed.

A few towns are worth visiting, too. Homosassa, Homosassa Springs, and Crystal River are closely tied to the coast. You can fish for tarpon in the gulf, dive and snorkel in spring-fed rivers, and bird-watch in the coastal wetlands. There's even a legitimate sand beach. Many come here to snorkel and dive among the spring-fed rivers and caves carved into the underlying limestone. Boat tours and rentals are available in Homosassa and Crystal River. In eastern Citrus County, the 57-mile Withlacoochee State Trail is a rails-to-trails conversion that follows the course of the Withlacoochee River from Trilby (in northern Pasco County) to Citrus Springs (in northern Citrus County).

Homosassa Springs (at U.S. 19/98 and C.R. 490) and Homosassa (three miles west, near the gulf) in particular have enticing points of interest. In Homosassa (pop. 2,100), six acres at **Yulee Sugar Mill Ruins State Historic Site** (352/795-3817) are all that remain of a 7,000-acre sugar plantation run by David Levy Yulee, who became Florida's first U.S. senator. The mill has been partially restored, and can be self-toured. The park is off Yulee Drive in Homosassa, three miles west of U.S. 19.

In Homosassa Springs (pop. 6,300), the attraction is **Homosassa Springs State Wildlife Park.** This lovely 180-acre nature park was initially preserved by the good citizens of Citrus County. They bought the land and deeded it to the state, which set about its restoration and refurbishment into a wildlife park.

The park is along the lines of a high-class alligator farm. Visitors walk a 1.1-mile loop trail and gaze at caged critters—flamingos, hawks, bald eagles, alligators, and more—some of which are recovering from injuries in the wild. You will never get closer to a bald eagle or a crested caracara than at Homosassa Springs. The biggest thrills are the cages harboring a Florida black bear, a bobcat, and the endangered Florida panther. The remaining population of Florida panthers in the wild is estimated at 50, and these last survivors are not genetically healthy.

The majestic panther needs room to roam, but there's very little room left in Florida, where developmental sprawl has invaded nearly every corner. The caged Florida panther seemed sulky and withdrawn, and who

THE NATURE COAST

can blame him? In the wild, these stealthy creatures are rarely seen by human eyes. Here, it's on display to any tourist with a point-and-shoot. We couldn't resist studying the majestic creature ourselves, just as he couldn't resist hungrily eyeing the flamingos across the trail. One thing's for sure: If the Florida panther goes extinct, we'll all share in the blame, the shame, and the reckoning.

The park is one of the few places where manatees may be observed at close range. From an underwater observatory, visitors can watch them swim about the warm natural springs in which they feed and live. Up close, they look like gray, fleshy submarines.

Homosassa Springs State Wildlife Park also has a museum, children's education center, and numerous exhibits and activities. Your visit begins with a narrated trip by pontoon boat up a shallow creek to the west visitors center, where the loop trail and animal exhibits are located. You can also drive up to this west entrance, but it's more fun to park at the east entrance (on U.S. 19) and ride the boat. En route, you pass beneath a canopy of sweetgum, red maple, bayberry, sweet bay, longleaf pine, and magnolia, plus those remaining bald cypress that weren't cut down for the pencil factory that used to operate nearby. Overhanging boughs provide cooling shade during the ride. Up in the canopy you'll spy an occasional golden orb spider, a giant whose enormous webs are a wonder of nature. Dragonflies buzz beside the boat. The whole adventure is a glimpse at Florida's natural heritage, as it was (and still ought to be).

The park's east entrance and visitors center are located on U.S. 19 in Homosassa Springs, beside a Ramada Inn. Homosassa Springs State Wildlife Park is open daily 9 A.M.–5:30 P.M. The last ticket is sold at 4:30 P.M., but it's recommended you get here by 1 P.M. in order to fully enjoy all the park has to offer. Admission is $7.95 per adult and $4.95 for kids 3–12.

For more information, contact Homosassa Springs State Wildlife Park, 4150 South Suncoast Boulevard, Homosassa, FL 34446, 352/628-5343. www.floridastateparks.org. Or, for more information about Homosassa Springs and Homosassa, contact the Citrus County Visitors and Convention Bureau, 9225 West Fishbowl Drive, Homosassa, FL 34448, 352/628-0305 or 800/587-6667, www.visitcitrus.com.

COASTAL CUISINE

The most popular dining spot in Citrus County is **KC Crump Restaurant and Ramshackle Cafe on the River** (11210 West Halls River Road, 352/628-1500, $$). This converted 1870s fishing lodge overlooks the Homosassa River.

We wove our way via backroads to Old Homosassa after soliciting recommendations for seafood in the area. Everyone sent us to **Charlie Brown's Crab House** (5297 South Cherokee Way, 352/621-5080, $$), which specializes in Florida hard-shell blue crabs served Chesapeake Bay style—which is to say spiced and steamed. The house specialty is garlic crabs, which are wok-fried in whole garlic, spices, and oil. Moved by the backwater bayou ambience, we also tried the blackened catfish. *Everything* here is good, be it grouper fingers or gator tail. Bargain-priced lunch specials are served 11 A.M.–4 P.M. If you're famished at the dinner hour, try Charlie's seafood combo: a mound of fish, shrimp, scallops, and oysters for $15.95. While dining, you can gaze out the windows onto Monkey Island—an actual island prowled by playful squirrel and spider monkeys.

Ozello

Out in the middle of a sliced-and-diced watery nowhere of mangrove islands and teeming marshlands is Ozello (pop. 200). C.R. 494 (Ozello Trail) winds its way out to Ozello from U.S. 19. Out by the Gulf of Mexico is **Ozello Community Park,** which has a boat ramp, fishing pier, and picnic tables, but no real beach.

For more information, contact the Citrus County Visitors and Convention Bureau, 9225 West Fishbowl Drive, Homosassa, FL 34448, 352/628-0305 or 800/587-6667, www.visitcitrus.com.

BEACHES

8 OZELLO COMMUNITY PARK

Location: west end of C.R. 494 (Ozello Trail), in Ozello
Parking/Fees: free parking lot
Hours: sunrise-sunset
Facilities: restrooms and picnic tables
Contact: Citrus County Parks and Recreation Department, 352/795-2202

COASTAL CUISINE

If you're seeking local ambience and victuals, be sure to stop at **Peck's Old Port Cove** (139 North Ozello Trail, 352/795-2806, $$). The locally harvested crab and fish are highly recommended.

Crystal River

Crystal River (pop. 4,000) is the second largest incorporated town in Citrus County (after Inverness, the county seat) and the largest on the coast. The town bills itself as "Where Man and Manatee Play," which is, perhaps, an unintentional koan. If man is playing with manatee, that is not good. If man and manatee are playing separately, that is probably good. If man is playing too close to manatee, it is potentially tragic. We've heard and witnessed too many tales about bone-headed human behavior around this endangered species to swallow the idea that man and manatee can somehow exist in harmony. For instance, we saw one unsupervised lad of seven who would not be satisfied until he had actually ridden on the back of a manatee. But that pales in comparison to reckless boaters who routinely inflict injury and even death upon these gentle sea mammals, which now number a mere 3,200 in the United States. For the most part, two things kill manatees: red tides and reckless boaters. Recent years have been particularly hard ones for the beleaguered

© PARKE PUTERBAUGH

Fort Island Gulf Beach, Crystal River

THE NATURE COAST

manatee population: 276 died in Florida in 2004 and 366 died in 2005—the worst year since a 1996 red tide bloom drove the number of manatee deaths to 400. In the midst of all this, it's come to light that the state of Florida is actually considering *downgrading* manatee's endangered status based on a new criteria. Do you see why we think they've lost their minds down here?

Crystal River attracts manatees because of its warm springs. Manatees cannot tolerate water temperatures below 68°F, and the millions of gallons issuing daily from thermal springs in coastal Citrus County are a constant 72°F. The town lies east of Kings Bay, which is fed by Florida's second largest springhead and connected (via the Crystal River) to the Gulf of Mexico. With its steady, comfy water temperature and glassine pure water, Kings Bay is the most popular nesting area in the state for the West Indian manatee.

The land along the north bank of the Crystal River once teemed so vibrantly with life that the original pre-Columbian inhabitants constructed religious temples, shrines, and mounds in homage. The area was first inhabited around 200 B.C. by Native Americans of the Deptford culture, followed by the Weedon Island culture (A.D. 300–900), and then the Safety Harbor culture. The Safety Harbor posse was chillin' here in 1539 when Hernando de Soto showed up looking for what the rappers call "shine" (gold).

All of this can be explored in depth at the **Crystal River State Archaeological Site** (3400 North Museum Point, 352/795-3817). The visitors center here contains artifacts of all three cultures, and park personnel can answer any questions after you've taken a self-guided tour of the grounds. The park is two miles north of Crystal River on U.S. 19.

One curious note about the local citrus crop: Originally, this area was dominated by David Yulee's sugar plantation, but a major freeze in 1894 sent the citrus industry farther south, where it remains today. One of Florida's old-est citrus varietals, the "Homosassa orange," is still grown hereabouts, but don't expect to find roadside stands selling fresh-squeezed OJ, as on Florida's East Coast. We learned it's too much trouble for local farmers to produce this gold elixir. A few highway stands still sell citrus by the bag, however.

For more information, contact the Citrus County Visitors and Convention Bureau, 9225 West Fishbowl Drive, Homosassa, FL 34448, 352/628-0305 or 800/587-6667, www.visitcitrus.com.

BEACHES

Believe it or not, there's a real sand beach in Crystal River, and it's called **Fort Island Gulf Beach.** From U.S. 19, head west on Fort Island Turnpike for 10 miles. Five miles out you'll see a turnoff to Fort Island Trails Park, which offers boat launches and picnic tables in a sylvan setting. We watched a big black vulture in a dead tree, and it watched us back, no doubt wishing we were road kill. The remainder of the drive to the beach is well out of sight of human habitations, passing miles of big sky and salt marsh that are especially beautiful in the golden glow of late afternoon. Nearing the park you will also see, disturbingly, the twin stacks of a power plant off to the right.

The beach at Fort Island is a 0.25-mile crescent of soft brown sand—the last sand beach of any size you'll see for maybe 100 miles, until you round the Big Bend in the vicinity of St. George Island. It's safe, snug, and protected by lifeguards who are on duty in the summer months. Parking, picnic tables, showers, and a boat launch are provided, but Fort Island Gulf Beach is otherwise a pretty bare-bones setup.

'Tis a curious spot, this little beach at the end of the road. On our last visit we saw a few sights that gave us pause. One was a group of young revelers partying around a pickup truck with a large Confederate flag hoisted from the rear. Further up the beach, a mother forcefully struck her two-year-old son for lobbing a handful of sand at his sister. And so our bliss at being on a beach at the end of so long a road was tempered by the people we encountered on it.

9 FORT ISLAND GULF BEACH

Location: nine miles west of U.S. 19 via Fort Island Turnpike, in Crystal River
Parking/Fees: free parking lot
Hours: sunrise-sunset
Facilities: lifeguard (seasonal), restrooms, picnic tables, and showers
Contact: Citrus County Parks and Recreation Department, 352/795-2202

RECREATION AND ATTRACTIONS

- **Bike/Skate Rentals:** Lenco Bicycles, 800 North Suncoast Boulevard, Crystal River, 352/795-8688
- **Boat Cruise:** Crystal River Manatee Dive & Tour, 267 Northwest 3rd Street, Crystal River, 352/795-1333
- **Dive Shop:** American Pro Diving Center, 821 Southeast U.S. 19, Crystal River, 352/563-0041
- **Ecotourism:** Homosassa Springs State Wildlife Park, 4150 South Suncoast Boulevard, Homosassa, 352/628-5343
- **Fishing Charters:** Apollo Deep Sea Fishing, 1340 Northwest 20th Avenue, Crystal River, 352/795-3757
- **Marina:** Twin Rivers Marina, 2880 North Seabreeze Point, Crystal River, 352/795-3552
- **Rainy-Day Attraction:** Crystal River State Archaeological Site and Museum, 3400 North Museum Point, Crystal River, 352/795-3817
- **Shopping/Browsing:** Heritage Village, North Citrus Avenue, Crystal River
- **Vacation Rentals:** Greenbriar Rentals, 2432 North Essex Avenue, Hernando, FL 34442, 352/746-5921 or 888/446-5921

ACCOMMODATIONS

As this area gets hip to ecotourism, more motels and marinas around Kings Bay and along Crystal River offer guided manatee-viewing tours, diving and fishing treks, and canoe/kayak rentals. One of the best places to lay over is **Best Western Crystal River Resort** (614 Northwest U.S. 19, 352/795-3171, $$), which sits right on Kings Bay. Its 114 rooms blend nicely with the natural landscape, and the nearby waters are easily accessed via the on-site dive shop and marina, where boats of all kinds can be rented. For landlubbers, the bay can be vicariously enjoyed from the tiki bar.

COASTAL CUISINE

Adjacent to the Best Western in Crystal River (see *Accommodations*) is **Crackers Bar & Grill** (502 Northwest 6th Street, 352/795-3999, $$), a beef-and-seafood place with a full bar.

Yankeetown

In the South, the old historical saw "George Washington Slept Here" has been amended to "Elvis Presley Played Here." In Yankeetown (pop. 600), that rebel yell is for real. The King took up temporary residence here in the summer of 1961 to film *Follow That Dream*, one of his many forgettable movies. To commemorate its ties to the King, the road from Inglis (a dot on the map along U.S. 19/98) to Yankeetown was renamed Follow That Dream Parkway (C.R. 40). The 6.8-mile drive passes hundreds of acres of unspoiled tidal flats and wetlands, with islands in the distance. You can follow your dream to some excellent fishing and boating, or (in our case) an unforgettable sunset.

Yankeetown got its name from the Northerners who began coming here in the 1920s. Today, the community is a scattering of modest dwellings in a woodsy, watery setting. The Withlacoochee River empties into the Gulf of Mexico, and vast stands of grasses extend into the gulf. The town landmark is the Izaak Walton Lodge, named for the 17th-century author of *The Compleat Angler*. A Briton who never set foot in Florida, Walton offered fishing's "serenity" as an alternative to hunting's "savagery." The lodge offers lodging, food, and fishing expeditions.

Yankeetown is a slowed-down vision of the way Florida used to be. We've heard locals have been buying up property so they can preserve its dreamy isolation. More power to 'em, because we love the place. Now back to that aforementioned sunset. We arrived at Yankeetown Landing, at the end of the road, as the setting sun disappeared behind a bank of clouds, only to reappear on the horizon for one last golden glinting before vanishing for good. This late-August afternoon had been extremely hot (92°F) and so humid that we felt like pieces of damp laundry. But a cooling onshore breeze sprang up as the sun dimmed. We sat on a wooden pier, drinking it in and surveying the open canopy of sky above vast expanses of marshland, open water and small offshore islands. A couple of locals were casting their lines in the water, and one complained that he'd only had one nibble all evening, "a hard-hitting catfish." The grayish-orange hues of the dimming day settled on the land and water, and the breeze picked up, rustling the palmetto trees' dry, browning boughs.

We really didn't want to leave. Moments such as these are too precious to be abandoned. Don't forget to savor them when you find yourself in a piece of paradise off the beaten track such as Yankeetown.

For more information, contact the Withlacoochee-Gulf Area Chamber of Commerce, 167 C.R. 40, P.O. Box 427, Inglis, FL 34449, 352/447-3383.

BEACHES

Near the end of Follow That Dream Parkway is **Yankeetown Park** (a.k.a. Vassey Creek Park), which offers teeming bird and marine life, pleasant isolation, ripples for waves, and a narrow, crescent-shaped swath of sand. Just around the corner, at the very end of C.R. 40, is Levy County Boat Ramp, a launch site with access to grass flats where the fishing is reputedly excellent.

10 YANKEETOWN PARK (A.K.A. VASSEY CREEK PARK)

Location: west end of C.R. 40 in Yankeetown
Parking/Fees: free parking lot
Hours: sunrise–sunset
Facilities: restrooms and picnic tables
Contact: Levy County Mosquito Control Department, 352/486-5127

ACCOMMODATIONS

The **Izaak Walton Lodge** (6301 Riverside Drive, 352/447-2311, $) is an 80-year-old lodge that rents out guest rooms, suites, and villas. It was built by a member of the Izaak Walton League of America, who dedicated it to "the spirit of conservation." Rooms are inexpensive, but the building (a two-story wood lodge with a gigantic limestone fireplace) is priceless. The area can be explored via bike and canoe, which are available at the lodge, but many come for the fishing. Boat rentals and guided trips are available.

COASTAL CUISINE

The gourmet dining room at the Izaak Walton Lodge is called **The Compleat Angler** (6301 Riverside Drive, 352/447-2311, $$$), after the classic text on fishing by the lodge's namesake. The food is prepared with more flair than one might expect in a place as far removed as Yankeetown. Specialties include red snapper topped with crabmeat and bernaise sauce, Cajun oysters and scallops, and steak au poivre. The changeable breakfast menu might include seafood omelettes or eggs Benedict. It's almost too good to be believed.

Cedar Key

Cedar Key calls itself the "gem of the Nature Coast," and this is a not-unfair self-appraisal.

© PARKE PUTERBAUGH

Cedar Key

It is several things in one: a working fishing community, an artists colony, a historic village (settled in the 1840s), an archaeological site, a grouping of islands, and a state of mind somewhere between coastal Maine and Greenwich Village. One of the more articulate waitresses we met in town went so far as to liken Cedar Key, with its tight-knit population of 1,000 and genial eccentricities, to the Big Sur community of the 1960s. That's overstating the case, but it is easy to see how such happy thoughts might arise.

Good vibes begin as you approach Cedar Key on S.R. 24 from U.S. 19 at Otter Creek. It's a 20-mile trip that cuts through Cedar Key Scrub State Reserve, an unbroken natural habitat free of rusted trailers, burnt-out junkyards, and trash heaps. A different visual diversion is offered via C.R. 345, accessed from U.S. 19 in Chiefland. This route runs through cattle and horse-ranch country before hooking up with S.R. 24 nine miles from Cedar Key.

The highway ends in the town of Cedar Key, which unfolds around a small circular knob of land. (We were struck by the resemblance of Cedar Key to Stonington, Maine.) The fishing docks of Cedar Key are built around a cul-de-sac, with the grid of the village behind them. The streets of village are numbered and lettered. As one local pundit put it, "Cedar Key is very laid-back, quiet, no tall buildings, one grocery store, one gas station, one policeman on duty, and no crime." If anything, there appeared to be *fewer* places out here than there were when we last passed through. Downtown Cedar Key is little more than a tiny grocery store, a few gift and craft shops, and a boarded-up lounge (the L&M) that appeared to be slated for some sort of transformation.

Cedar Key is more than the town that bears its name. It is also a group of more than 100 keys that range in size from one acre to 165 acres. There is, in fact, no Cedar Key, per se. The town itself occupies Way Key, the largest of the 100 islands. The first settlement was actually on Atsena Otie Key (the Creek Indian name for "Cedar Island"), which lies directly offshore and can be seen from the village docks. Thirteen of the islands make up Cedar Keys National Wildlife Refuge, set aside by President Herbert Hoover in 1929. The outermost, Seahorse Key, was added to

THE NATURE COAST

the refuge by President Roosevelt in 1936. It is a world-renowned bird sanctuary and the highest point of land on the Gulf Coast, with a sand ridge that rises 52 feet. Seahorse Key is also the site of a pre–Civil War lighthouse that's now used by the University of Florida.

All this talk of cedar refers to the red cedar forests that once blanketed the islands. The wood was cherished by the Native Americans for many purposes, but white settlers, beginning in 1855, used it mainly in the thriving pencil trade. Eberhard Faber bought land and built a factory to take advantage of the timber boom, which went bust by 1900 when all the trees were gone. Two notable enterprises came to a better end here. The first was the trans-Florida railroad, which linked Cedar Key to Fernandina Beach in 1861. The second was naturalist John Muir's marathon trek from Wisconsin, chronicled in *A Thousand-Mile Walk to the Gulf* (1867). Upon his arrival in Cedar Key, Muir wrote: "Today I reached the sea and many gems of tiny islets called keys."

Another railroad enterprise involving Cedar Key was nipped in the bud. Railroad baron Henry Plant plotted to extend his Gulf Coast Railway through here, but Cedar Key refused to become a station stop on his line and wouldn't even let his supply boats dock in the harbor. Two local museums cover the area's fascinating history, dating back to pre-Columbian times. They are the **Cedar Key State Museum** (170 Museum Drive, 352/543-5350), which is open Thursday–Monday, and the **Cedar Key Historical Society** (2nd Street, 352/543-5549), which is open daily.

Despite some inevitable encroachment — e.g., a few condos on stilts—Cedar Key stubbornly retains its independent edge. Fishing is the one thing that touches everyone's life, including visitors who reap the bounty at local restaurants. The quirky local paper, the *Cedar Key Beacon,* is filled with tide tables, fishing reports, and tips. Fishing fanatics, naturalists, birdwatchers, painters, photographers, and those who love the mystique of land's end have been smitten with Cedar Key. Cedar Key is also a popular weekend getaway for city-dwellers from Tallahassee and Gainesville.

Regardless of what draws you to Cedar Key, it resembles coastal Maine in one other essential respect: the bestowing of "local" status. "You are a local if your grandparents were born here," said one longtime resident. Local or not, you will likely come to feel right at home on Cedar Key.

For more information, contact the Cedar Key Chamber of Commerce, 480 2nd Street, P.O. Box 610, Cedar Key, FL 32625, 352/543-5600, www.cedarkey.org.

BEACHES

There's a small manmade beach at **Cedar Key City Park,** located at 2nd and Dock Streets. Frankly, this little patch of hard-packed sand is the least of Cedar Key's charms and the last reason to come here. On the west side of town, at G and 1st Streets, a small natural sand beach called **Sand Spit Park** is where locals sometimes go to watch sunset or collect sand dollars. There's also a public pier at the west end of Dock Street.

The real beaches are found on keys like Atsena Otie and Seahorse, which are part of Cedar Keys National Wildlife Refuge (see separate write-up). At Atsena Otie, a secluded key 0.5-mile offshore, a hard-packed sand beach faces the gulf. If you don't have a boat, you can get there is via **Island Hopper Boat Tours and Rentals** (City Marina, 352/543-5904). This rental, cruise, and ferry service operates at the main dock in Cedar Key, next to the Seabreeze Restaurant. They will take you to Atsena Otie and pick you up later in the day. They also conduct several daily cruises to the many offshore keys.

11 CEDAR KEY CITY PARK

Location: 2nd and Dock Streets, in Cedar Key
Parking/Fees: free parking lot
Hours: sunrise–10 P.M.
Facilities: restrooms, picnic tables, and a shower
Contact: Cedar Key City Hall, 352/543-5132

12 SAND SPIT PARK

Location: 1st and G Streets in Cedar Key
Parking/Fees: free street parking
Hours: 24 hours
Facilities: none
Contact: Cedar Key City Hall, 352/543-5132

RECREATION AND ATTRACTIONS

* **Boat Cruise:** Cedar Key Island Hopper, City Marina, Cedar Key, 352/543-5904

* **Dive Shop:** Aztec Dive Center, 1005 Northwest 19th Avenue, Chiefland, 352/493-9656

* **Ecotourism:** Atsena Otie Key, Cedar Keys National Wildlife Refuge, Chiefland, 352/493-0238

* **Fishing Charters:** Barhopper Charters, Cedar Key, 352/543-0118

* **Kayak Rentals:** Kayak Cedar Keys, 3rd Street Dock, Cedar Key, 352/543-9447

* **Marina:** Cedar Key Marina, Cedar Key, 352/543-6148

* **Pier:** Cedar Key Public Fishing Pier, Dock Street (west end), Cedar Key

* **Rainy-Day Attraction:** Cedar Key Historical Museum, S.R. 24 and 2nd Street, Cedar Key, 352/543-5549

* **Shopping/Browsing:** Cedar Key Historic District, Cedar Key

* **Vacation Rentals:** Island Place, 1st and C Streets, P.O. Box 687, Cedar Key, 352/543-5307

ACCOMMODATIONS

For such a secluded place, Cedar Key has a variety of accommodations, ranging from the motel-like **Faraway Inn** (3rd and G Streets, 352/543-5330, $) to the historic **Island Hotel** (2nd and B Streets, 352/543-5111, $$). Listed on the National Register of Historic Places, the Island Hotel dates back to 1861. It's one of the few structures that survived the hurricane of 1896, which otherwise wiped out Cedar Key. Nowadays the Island Inn is run by a couple who wanted to move back to the States after 10 years of running a fishing business in the Bahamas. The decent-sized rooms have ceiling fans, heavy furniture, and broad plank walls. The place exudes personality. There are no phones or TVs at the inn, but it's reputedly well-stocked with ghosts—13 of 'em, according to a psychic.

Cedar Key Bed & Breakfast (3rd and F Streets, 352/543-9000, $$) is a meticulously restored, oak-shaded Victorian home (circa 1880). By contrast, **Island Place** (1st and C Streets, 352/543-5307, $$) consists of three-story villa-style condos that are available by the night or longer. A swimming pool and hot tub are on-premises, and the town docks are just down the street.

The contemporary and tidy **Cedar Cove Beach and Yacht Club** (192 2nd Street, 352/543-5332, $$) is the closest thing to a beachfront motel on Cedar Key. Options include efficiencies, studios, and townhouses. Cedar Cove sits beside Cedar Key City Park and has a pool, hot tub, sauna, fitness room, and an excellent restaurant (see *Coastal Cuisine*). The "yacht club" is an oddly amusing affectation.

There are also townhouses, cottages, and campgrounds on Cedar Key. Contact the Cedar Key Chamber of Commerce (352/543-5600) for an illustrated booklet of places to stay.

COASTAL CUISINE

Fishing is king in the pristine offshore waters, and every day brings in a royal catch of grouper, yellowtail, redfish, flounder, mackerel, croaker, and mullet. Much of the bounty is catchable by surfcasting or dangling a line right off the village docks. The shallow near-shore waters are also ideal for oysters and clams. Farm-raised Cedar Key cherrystone clams are as tender and tasty as their Long Island cousins. Other local favorites include heart of palm salad, smoked mullet, stone crab claws, blue crabs, and soft-shell crabs.

THE NATURE COAST

From its upstairs dining room, overlooking the water, we were pleasantly surprised by the mullet and cherrystone clam dinners served at **Seabreeze on the Dock** (520 Dock Street, 352/543-5738, $$). Served with drawn butter, the clams were small, tasty, and fresh. Mullet are those giddy fish you see leaping above the surface of the water. They are netted, not hooked, and used mostly for bait, but they also make good eating. Some consider the lowly baitfish unworthy of human consumption, but not us. A bit more gamy and rich than most fish, mullet are also small and bony, so appoint one of your party to be the designated Heimlich maneuver provider. Seabreeze serves its mullet dredged in meal, fried, and accompanied by cole slaw and baked potato. By meal's end you'll be leaping giddily, too.

The dining room at the **Island Hotel** (2nd and B Streets, 352/543-5111, $$$) has long been hailed as the gourmet seafood restaurant of choice and is the original source for much of what is considered local cuisine on Cedar Key. Nowadays it has some serious competition—and competition is a good thing—from The **Island Room Restaurant at Cedar Cove** (192 2nd Street, 352/543-6520, $$$). We enjoyed a dinner here as fine as any we've had in Florida. Chef Peter Stefani's crab cakes alone make dining here worth the trip. They contain more Cedar Key blue crab than breading and are delicately held together by "secret" ingredients, sauteed, and served with lemon beurre blanc. The Stefanis farm-raise their own clams, making one of their clam appetizers a must. They're available steamed (with white wine, olive oil, garlic, and herbs) and baked three ways (casino, Rockefeller, or diablo). Clams also figure in *linguine alla vongole*, a delicious pasta entree. The Stefanis make their pasta fresh daily and they grow their own herbs, as well. A tireless couple!

Fettucini crab carbonara (with smoked bacon, onion, and a touch of cream) is heavenly, and grouper Savannah (a pecan-crusted fillet served with sherry beurre blanc) is among the Island Room's most popular entrees. The wine list is dotted with interesting, unusual selections, and desserts are made fresh. Dinner is served daily, and they offer a Sunday brunch, too. Why not book a room at the Cedar Cove motel so you can be first in line when the doors open at 5 P.M.?

NIGHTLIFE

After your peanut-butter pie plate has been cleared upstairs at the **Seabreeze on the Dock** (see *Coastal Cuisine*), mosey downstairs to the lounge and pass some time. On the night we visited, a bewhiskered country gentleman was singing along with music uploaded to the house P.A. via his laptop computer, which sat conspicuously on a chair beside him. The irony struck us hard. We could not have been in a more out-of-the-way place, and yet we were being entertained by cyber-country karaoke. One moment he was importuning, "Take the ribbons from your hair," and the next he was crooning, "All my exes live in Texas." Truly bizarre.

One of the best things the **Island Hotel** has going for it—besides its rich history—is the wonderful Neptune Room, a mega-friendly watering hole dominated by a painting that has hung behind the bar for as long as the hotel has been here. Just the thought that John Muir may have laid eyes on this painting filled us with amazement as we sat back at Friday happy hour here. Others who come here are more impressed by the signed picture of Jimmy Buffett.

The place was packed and the relaxed crowd mellowed out by the sounds of a live pianist tinkling in the back room. We overheard some classic chatter: "You know, I have a low opinion of money" and "I parked my car last Wednesday and haven't moved it since. I'll take a ride when I run out of beer." A mountain-sized man strode barefoot into the bar and began making howling noises when he spotted his friends. No one batted an eye. In fact, the bartender already had the guy's regular potion ready when he sidled up to the bar. Our kind of place.

Waccasassa Bay Preserve State Park and Cedar Key Scrub State Reserve

Nearly all of the coast between Yankeetown and Cedar Key falls within the confines of the 30,788-acre Waccasassa Bay Preserve State Park, which is home to the northernmost mangrove forest in the United States. Two-thirds of the acreage is salt marsh or mud-bottomed, serpentine tidal creeks (over 100 of the latter!), which are the liver and kidneys of the natural world. Large as it is, this preserve is but a sliver of the gulf hammock that used to cover the state in pre-development times.

While access to Waccasassa Bay is limited, the rewards are unsurpassed for anglers, photographers, birdwatchers, and campers. Nature's sublimity is quite enough, but the occasional sighting of bald eagles, manatees, and black bears makes the experience positively magical. Primitive campsites on the Waccasassa River are accessible by canoe or kayak. Canoes can be launched where S.R. 326 crosses the Waccasassa River in Gulf Hammock and on C.R. 40A at Covass Creek, near Yankeetown. The preserve can also be entered from Cedar Key. Certain activities are seasonally restricted. Call in advance for details.

Adjacent to Waccasassa Bay Preserve State Park is Cedar Key Scrub State Reserve. Its 4,000 acres of pine flatwoods and sand pine scrub is fringed by salt marsh. Because it is a state *reserve* (and not a *preserve*), limited hunting is permitted from September through mid-November. There's also fishing, hiking, and canoeing, but no camping.

For more information, contact Waccasassa Bay Preserve State Park and Cedar Key Scrub State Reserve, P.O. Box 187, Cedar Key, FL 32625, 352/543-5567, www.floridastateparks.org.

Cedar Keys National Wildlife Refuge and Lower Suwannee National Wildlife Refuge

Cedar Keys National Wildlife Refuge comprises 13 islands offshore from the town of Cedar Key. These islands in the gulf have sand beaches and no habitations on them, save for an inoperative lighthouse on Seahorse Key. (These days, that lighthouse is used by the University of Florida as a marine research and environmental education center.) The islands can be visited by private boat or commercial operator, such as Island Hopper Boat Tours in Cedar Key. The public is allowed on the beaches but cannot visit the island interiors. In the case of Seahorse Key, the entire island is off limits during bird-nesting season, which runs March 1–June 30. Seahorse Key is basically a gigantic sand dune with a central ridge that's 52 feet tall, making it the highest elevation on Florida's Gulf Coast.

The one exception to the rules regarding visitation is the latest acquisition, Atsena Otie Key. This formerly inhabited (the last homes were removed a century ago) and now marvelously isolated key came perilously close to being developed as recently as 1996. The state, in the form of the Suwannee River Water Management District, came to the rescue in 1997, purchasing the island for $3 million. Now it is owned by the state and managed as part of Cedar Keys National Wildlife Refuge. The island has a short nature trail, educational kiosks, and a dock.

Atsena Otie lies 0.5-mile offshore from Cedar Key. Visitors can walk among the ruins of two cedar mills, both of which were destroyed in a devastating 1896 hurricane. Drawbacks to visitation are snakes (especially cottonmouths) and mosquitoes, which can be

THE NATURE COAST

hellish in the warmer months. The best time to visit Atsena Otie Key is during the cooler winter months.

The Lower Suwannee National Wildlife Refuge protects 52,000 acres in the watershed of the lower Suwannee River. It is home to such endangered and threatened species as the bald eagle, the eastern indigo snake, the manatee, and the gulf sturgeon, plus three species of sea turtles. In addition, 250 bird species have been identified as residents or visitors. A boardwalked trail leads out to the Suwannee River. Thirty miles of refuge roads are open to vehicles, and many more miles of old logging roads can be explored on foot or by bike.

For more information, contact Cedar Keys and Lower Suwannee National Wildlife Refuges, 16450 Northwest 31st Place, Chiefland, FL 32626, 352/493-0238, www.cedarkeys.fws.gov (Cedar Keys) or www.lowersuwannee.fws.gov (Lower Suwannee).

BEACHES

CEDAR KEYS NATIONAL WILDLIFE REFUGE

 BEST (

Location: The refuge consists of 13 islands in the Gulf of Mexico offshore of Cedar Key, including Atsena Otie, Seahorse, Snake, and North keys.

Parking/Fees: free day use; accessible by boat only

Hours: Beaches on the Cedar Keys are open sunrise-sunset. The islands' interiors are closed to the public at all times. Seahorse Key is entirely closed to the public March 1-June 30.

Facilities: restroom (Atsena Otie Key) and a visitors center (10 miles west of Chiefland, on C.R. 347)

Contact: Cedar Keys National Wildlife Refuge, 352/493-0238

MANATEE SPRINGS STATE PARK

This state park is not on the coast, but it's not far from it (23 miles, to be exact). At Manatee Springs State Park, an underground spring pumps 117 million gallons of water to the surface daily. That's 81,250 gallons a minute! The water from this limestone aquifer is a constant 72°F. In winter, the run from the spring to the Suwannee River attracts manatees, who come to warm themselves. A long, winding boardwalk, bordered by a cypress-gum swamp, follows the spring run out to the Suwannee River. One cool November morning we saw three of them – two adults and a juvenile – swimming around Manatee Springs. They surfaced frequently, noisily exhaling and then inhaling, and then they dove and swam some more.

Most visitors discreetly and respectfully observed the manatees' comings and goings, but an older couple – one in a kayak, the other loudly flapping around in diving gear – chased them all over the place. Does nature never know a moment's peace from the reckless intrusions of human beings? The boardwalk is really as close as one needs to get to the endangered manatees. Think about it: Would you want hordes of nosy manatees chasing you around a heated pool?

A $4 per vehicle entrance fee is charged at Manatee Springs State Park. Facilities include 86 campsites, canoe rentals, picnic area, and nine miles of hiking trails. To get here, take U.S. 19/98 north through the town of Chiefland, then turn west on C.R. 320 and continue for six miles to the park.

For more information, contact Manatee Springs State Park, 11650 Northwest 115th Street, Chiefland, FL 32626, 352/493-6072www.myflorida.com.

Suwannee

You've surely heard "Old Folks at Home," the classic Stephen Foster song that begins with the line "Way down upon the Suwannee River"? Well, you can't get any farther down the Suwannee River than Suwannee (pop. 300), a fishing village at the mouth of this wide, wild, and wonderful waterway. If you're a disciple of blue highways, you'll love the 23-mile scenic drive down C.R. 349 from U.S. 19/27/98 in Old Town to Suwannee.

The Suwannee is a slow-moving blackwater river that defines the laid-back pace of life in the Deep South and embodies what remains of its mystery as well. The river gets its start in the Okefenokee Swamp, curling 260 nautical miles through remote parts of north-central Florida before emptying into the Gulf of Mexico in two places, designated East Pass and West Pass. The village of Suwannee lies on West Pass. The village is a fisherman's haven, offering freshwater fishing in the river and saltwater fishing in the gulf.

For more information, contact the Suwannee River Chamber of Commerce, P.O. Box 373, Old Town, FL 32692, 352/542-7349, www.suwanneeriverchamber.com.

ACCOMMODATIONS

Those with a yen to cast a line may want to drop anchor at **Bill's Motel and Fish Camp** (C.R. 349, 352/542-7086, $), which offers bait and tackle, saltwater and freshwater guides, and kitchenettes where you can feast on your catch. There are also several RV parks in the area, such as **Munden Camp** (Munden Road, 352/542-7480, $). Established in 1863—that is not a typo—this is "the *original* Suwannee campground." You'd better believe it!

COASTAL CUISINE

You can break bread on Suwannee's waterfront at **Salt Creek Shellfish Company** (C.R. 349, 352/542-7072, $$) and the **Suwannee Cafe** (Corbin Street, 352/542-0500, $).

Shired Island County Park

Shired Island County Park adjoins the Shired Island unit of Lower Suwannee National Wildlife Refuge, west of the Suwannee River on the Gulf of Mexico. To get here, take C.R. 351 out of Cross City. The turnoff from U.S. 19/27/98 isn't well marked, but there's an Ace Hardware store at the northwest corner of the intersection. Follow C.R. 351 for eight miles, than take a left fork onto C.R. 357 another 12 miles to Shired Island, which is properly pronounced "shared." En route you will pass flyblown trailers and dead critters in the road. We noticed the charred, flattened remnants of a small boat in a canal. (Some rural folks make a trash heap of their beloved "country.") The pavement gives out and the road ends with no warning, but if you turn right just before the dead end, you will find yourself at Shired Island County Park. Your cue will be a pair of beat-up dumpsters. When we visited, one of the dumpsters bore the charming graffiti "Horseshoe Boys Make Better Lovers." Apparently, the lads of Shired Island and nearby Horseshoe Island have some issues.

For more information, contact the Dixie County Chamber of Commerce, Evans Square, U.S. 19, P.O. Box 547, Cross City, FL 32628, 352/498-5454, www.dixiecounty.org.

BEACHES

The word "park" is used rather loosely at **Shired Island,** as it more closely resembles a gypsy encampment. Modest RVs are scattered about the property. We're told there's a 14-day limit on camping, but some of the RVs looked as though they'd been here since the Reconstruction. The smoke streaming from wood fires filled our nostrils. We saw no humans stirring but felt like we were being watched. It was a tad eerie, if truth be told.

There is a real sand beach with a small stand of cabbage palms along the shore. We snapped a picture, dipped our toes in the water, and

THE NATURE COAST

were happy to leave, just as those who were silently studying us from their trailers were no doubt happy to have us leave. Again, fishing is what's done along this stretch of coast. There's a boat ramp on the federal side of Shired Island, and bank fishing is popular among anglers.

14 SHIRED ISLAND COUNTY PARK

Location: at the end of C.R. 357, 20 miles south of Cross City
Parking/Fees: free parking lot. Camping fees are $14 per night for RVs and $8 per night for tents
Hours: 24 hours
Facilities: restrooms, picnic tables, and showers
Contact: Dixie County Coordinator, 352/498-1240

Horseshoe Beach

Don't come looking for a beach in Horseshoe Beach (pop. 300). This town at the end of the road looks like a development aborted well shy of build-out. Some nice-looking weathered-wood houses perch atop cinderblock stilts. There's even an unusual home that looks like a big boat hoisted onto dry land. The road into Horseshoe Beach gives out at an asphalt circle. We turned off our car and listened to the gulf lap against the rocks. On this gray day, we stared into a monochromatic tableau of water and sky. Out in the water are a string of small, forested keys. No doubt they'd be fun to explore, if you had a boat. Horseshoe Beach was utterly isolated, despite the presence of a marina, dry dock facility, canals, and homes.

For more information, contact the Dixie County Chamber of Commerce, P.O. Box 547, Evans Square, Highway 19, Cross City, FL 32628, 352/498-5454.

BEACHES

Horseshoe Beach has only the merest sliver of sand at **Butler and Douglas County Park.** You can park your RV or plop your tent here, and there are picnic pavilions, a boat ramp, and indoor showers. Fishing is the reason to come out here, as Horseshoe Beach is surrounded by water on three sides: two canals and a bay (named Horseshoe Cove). Folks also take scallops from the water in season.

15 BUTLER AND DOUGLAS COUNTY PARK

Location: at the end of 4th Avenue West in Horseshoe Beach
Parking/Fees: free parking lot. Camping fees are $14 per night for RVs and $8 per night for tents
Hours: 24 hours
Facilities: restrooms, picnic tables, and showers
Contact: Dixie County Coordinator, 352/498-1240

COASTAL CUISINE

If you should ever find yourself in Horseshoe Beach at dinnertime (hey, stranger things have happened), duck into the **Crimson Crest Restaurant** (Main Street, 352/498-0005, $). This humble house of home cooking serves a seafood buffet 5–9 P.M. on weekends. Beyond that, you're on your own out here.

Steinhatchee

If you're traveling north up the coast, advance notice of this fishing community at the mouth of the Steinhatchee River is served in the nearby town of Jena, just over the Dixie County line. The turnoff along C.R. 361 to Steinhatchee (steen-HATCH-ee) is announced by 30 or so small signs for local businesses that have been staked into the earth. The town

THE NATURE COAST

gull-covered pilings in the Gulf of Mexico at Steinhatchee

© PARKE PUTERBAUGH

itself (pop. 800) is more pleasant than this initial assault. It is oriented toward boating and fishing, with a modest clump of commercial enterprises aimed at the angler, like the full-service **River Haven Marina** (S.R. 51, 352/498-0709).

Steinhatchee is a self-described fishing village (although commercial fishing in Dead Man's Bay has been severely restricted by a state-mandated "net ban"). Fish camps are everywhere, so come armed with rod and reel and RV. There are no beaches, but people head here in summer to go scalloping in Dead Man's Bay, and all year-round to catch speckled trout, Spanish mackerel, redfish, and flounder in the saltwater flats. The old bridge to Jena now serves as a fishing pier and gets packed when redfish run up the Steinhatchee River. The river is a beautiful sight, with an attractive overview offered from the C.R. 361 bridge. It looks like the sort of place Charles Kuralt would have ferreted out for his Sunday-morning *Eye on America,* with the sounds of lapping water and laughing gulls audible as the camera holds steady on the peaceful river and forested fringe.

For more information, contact the Perry-Taylor County Chamber of Commerce, 428 North Jefferson Street, Perry, FL 32347, 850/584-5366, www.taylorcountychamber.com.

ACCOMMODATIONS

Steinhatchee Landing (S.R. 51, 352/498-3513, $$) consists of 20 cottages (wood frames, tin roofs, open porches) strewn about an attractive property on the river. **Steinhatchee River Inn** (S.R. 51, 352/498-4049, $)—an all-suites motel 0.5-mile downriver—is run by the same owner. These properties are the nicest accommodations in Steinhatchee, but there are acceptable, inexpensive alternatives geared toward unfussy anglers, such as the **Ideal Fish Camp and Motel** (114 Riverside Drive SE, 352/498-3877, $).

COASTAL CUISINE

If you didn't manage to net your own dinner, drop by **Roy's** (S.R. 51 at C.R. 361, 352/498-5000, $$), whose glassed-in dining room looks out on the river and its grassy wetlands. The fare and service are unexceptional, and prices are on the stiff side. Still, we netted

THE NATURE COAST

good grouper sandwiches (the menu's only bargain), and the salad bar is a belly-buster. Roy's has been a local favorite since 1969. Check out the roof of the place for your best recommendation: 500 hungry seagulls.

Big Bend Wildlife Management Area

Feeling adventurous, we followed a sign to **Dallus Creek Landing,** part of the Tide Swamp Unit of the Big Bend Wildlife Management Area. Sandy roads along C.R. 361, between Steinhatchee and Keaton Beach, lead into this state of Florida gameland. We rumbled our rental car along four miles of backroads before reaching a dead end at a picnic area and boat landing overlooking a breathtaking marsh. Along the way, we noticed the variety of tree species—oaks, maple, ash, gum, and palms. If you ever wanted to see overlapping ecotones, this is it. Spanish moss drapes the limbs of live oaks, and towering coconut palms jut high above the forest canopy.

Another area worth visiting on the same reserve is **Hagen's Cove.** Like Dallus Creek Landing, it's a good crabbing and scalloping area with a boat ramp, picnic area, and wildlife observation tower. Camping is available by permit at both Dallus Creek Landing and Hagen's Cove January 16–October 31.

One of the great attractions of Big Bend Wildlife Management Area is the 105-mile **Big Bend Saltwater Paddling Trail.** There are six primitive campsites along the route. If you're making the trip in its entirety (as opposed to a day paddle along one of its sections), the Big Bend Trail must be paddled from north to south. It runs from the Aucilla River (which divides Jefferson and Taylor Counties) down to Salt Creek Landing, in the town of Suwanee. Through paddlers must have a permit from the Florida Fish and Wildlife Conservation Commission to use the campsites. For permits and/or to purchase a 40-page paddling guide (which costs $15), call 850/488-5520.

For more information, contact the Big Bend Wildlife Management Area, 663 Plantation Road, Perry, FL 32347, 850/838-1306, www.myfwc.com/recreation/big_bend.

Keaton Beach

Keaton Beach (pop. 500) is one of those places that appeals to those who wish to be as far from crowds as possible. It is typical of the small villages along Florida's rural Big Bend, where the beachless gulf is lined with houses of weathered wood perched on cinderblock stilts and often beside canals.

Keaton Beach was forever changed in 1993, when a ferocious storm blew Keaton Beach and neighboring Dekle Beach right off the map. Referred to as the "No Name Storm," it was a bonafide hurricane that formed quickly and was missed by meteorologists. Packing winds of 110 mph, the No Name Storm slammed Taylor County's unsuspecting coastal towns with a 25-foot storm surge. It hit with the force of a tidal wave, inundating low-lying areas as far as a mile inland.

Eleven people were killed in Keaton Beach and Dekle Beach, and survivors tell of clinging with their babies to roof-mounted TV antennas to keep from being washed away. The proprietor of the Keaton Beach Marina recalled, "My dad looked out the window and said to my mom, 'We'd better leave.' Then he looked out again and saw the van wash away. We weren't going anywhere."

There's a plaque commemorating the dead in Keaton Beach. The No Name Storm set back the pace of development by decades. There used to be three or four good restaurants and motels in Keaton Beach. Now, there's just one of each (although a row of anomalous "luxury townhomes" has sprouted in recent years). And so nature has seen to it, in its indifferent and inevitable way, that the Nature Coast remains as nature intended it.

For more information, contact the Perry-Taylor County Chamber of Commerce, 428 North

Jefferson Street, Perry, FL 32347, 850/584-5366, www.taylorcountychamber.com.

BEACHES

There is a sand beach in Keaton Beach. At the end of the road that winds through sleepy Keaton Beach lies **Hodges Park,** which has two picnic shelters, a new fishing pier and gazebo, and a sand beach that runs for a couple hundred yards. It's bounded at one end by a rock jetty at the mouth of Blue Creek. The water is generally so calm that the Gulf of Mexico looks like a gigantic saltwater lake. We walked the beach several times in amazement and appreciation—not just for the beach but the abundant bird life along it.

16 HODGES PARK

Location: end of Keaton Beach Drive, in Keaton Beach
Parking/Fees: free parking lot
Hours: sunrise-sunset
Facilities: restrooms and picnic tables

Contact: Taylor County Public Works Department, 352/838-3528

ACCOMMODATIONS

Since the No Name Storm laid waste to Keaton Beach, the pickin's out here have been mighty slim but are ever so slowly rebounding. The obvious choice is **Keaton Beach Marina, Motel, and Cottages** (Keaton Beach Road, 850/578-2897, $). **Louise Henrichs Beach Rentals** (850/578-2039) handles vacation properties by the weekend, week, or month. Otherwise, camping is king along this isolated stretch of coast.

NIGHTLIFE

Just outside Keaton Beach a sign at Joe's Video announced an unbeatable deal: rent two videos, get one free. Unfortunately, Joe's had closed years ago and the deserted building's windows were broken. A sign on the same road pointed to something called the "Haunted Hayride." We followed it to a driveway where a funky-looking truck with "Haunted Hayride" spray-painted on its side was parked. But Halloween had been three weeks earlier, so the

Hodges Park, Keaton Beach

© PARKE PUTERBAUGH

THE NATURE COAST

Haunted Hayride was history. Again, we'd missed the boat (or the hayride). So much for nightlife in Keaton Beach. As the nice marina lady put it, "If you're looking for quiet, this is the place. Even cell phones don't work here."

Dekle Beach

Dekle Beach (pronounced "DEE-kle") is an eerily quiet outcropping of homes three miles north of Keaton Beach. It doesn't show up on maps, but a road sign along C.R. 361 points to it. We followed the arrow to a smattering of homes, two blocks deep, facing the gulf. Dekle Beach was another casualty of 1993's No Name Storm, which devastated the town. (See *Keaton Beach* for a fuller account.)

Some of the surviving or rebuilt homes out here are nice vacation dwellings of weathered wood, hoisted high on cinderblock leggings, while others are dumpy-looking ground-level boxes. Eagles Nest, a five-house resort, has a fishing pier that extends 0.25 mile into the gulf. Some neighboring dwellings are fronted only by pilings—all that remains of docks that collapsed in the storm. Near the asphalt circle where Dekle Beach comes to an end, we found a postage stamp-sized patch of sand that we'd hesitate to call a beach.

For more information, contact the Perry-Taylor County Chamber of Commerce, 428 North Jefferson Street, Perry, FL 32347, 850/584-5366, www.taylorcountychamber.com.

ACCOMMODATIONS
The **Eagles Nest** (Route 2, Box 18, 850/584-7666, $$) consists of five houses arrayed around the gulf and a canal. The homes are rented by the day, week, or month. At $500 or so per week for a two-bedroom, two-bathroom home, it's a steal—especially if you're into isolation, fishing, and sunsets. (What rational person wouldn't be?) **Louise Henrich's Beach Rentals** (850/578-2003) handles other rental properties in and around Dekle Beach.

Adams Beach

Being devotees of blue highways and out-of-the-way places, we set out in search of an intriguing dot on the map labeled Adams Beach. Unlike Keaton Beach and Dekle Beach—intriguing dots on the map that exist in reality—we could find hide nor hair of Adams Beach. Perhaps it was a figment of some mapmaker's imagination. Maybe it's a fictional, Stephen King–style conjuring that comes to life only at Halloween, when it's visited by the horror merchants behind the Haunted Hayride (see *Nightlife* in *Keaton Beach*). Confounding the mystery is the cryptic notation—written in an old brochure about Florida's "hidden coast"—that "cows often wade here."

The truth of the matter is that a small settlement did once exist but was wiped out half a century ago by a hurricane. Any attempted rebuilding since 1993's devastating No Name Storm has been thwarted by stringent new setback and septic regulations. Nowadays Adams Beach is just a bunch of dwellings at the ends of dirt roads named for those who live on them (e.g., Dennis Howell Road, J.L. Gibson Road). We saw this message posted in front of a church in the area: "To belittle is to be little." Amen.

We did find Adams Beach Road, a short spur at a 90° bend along C.R. 361 that leads to a physical barrier by the Gulf of Mexico. Beyond the barrier lies broken beer bottles and other signs of late-night misbehavior.

For more information, contact the Perry-Taylor County Chamber of Commerce, 428 North Jefferson Street, Perry, FL 32347, 850/584-5366, www.taylorcountychamber.com.

Econfina River State Park and Aucilla River State Canoe Trail

The Econfina (eco-FEEN-a) and Aucilla (aw-SILL-la) are two canoeable rivers in northwest

Taylor County. Econfina River State Park encompasses 3,377 acres of forest, salt marsh, pine flatlands, and oak and palm forests. Nine miles of hiking, mountain-biking, and horseback trails run through the park. For a map and information about put-ins, contact Econfina River State Park (address below) and request a brochure entitled "Historic Big Bend Saltwater Paddling Trail."

To get to the Econfina, take U.S. 98 west from Perry for 20 miles, then turn south on S.R. 14 and follow it to the river. To get to the Aucilla, continue west on U.S. 98 (past S.R. 14), take the first left after Cabbage Grove Road onto an unmarked road, and follow signs to the boat ramp and river. The Aucilla divides Jefferson County and Taylor County, with the boat ramp falling on the Taylor side. The dark, tannic Aucilla and the clear, spring-fed Wacissa River meet at Nutall Rise in Jefferson County, much of whose southern end falls inside St. Marks National Wildlife Refuge.

For more information, contact Econfina River State Park, 1022 DeSoto Park Drive, Tallahassee, FL 32301, 850/922-6007, www.floridastateparks.org.

ACCOMMODATIONS

There are campsites, motel rooms, condo rentals, and a swimming pool at **Econfina on the Gulf** (Route 1, Box 255, Perry, 850/584-2135, $), which also has a seafood restaurant that's open weekends and some weekdays.

Newport

The tiny community of Newport (pop. 30) is 20 miles south of Tallahassee on U.S. 98 at the St. Marks River. You're near the end of Florida's Big Bend are on the Panhandle. Newport was once the fifth-largest city in Florida (with a population of 1,500). Now it's not much larger than a crawdad mound, serving mostly as the gateway to St. Marks National Wildlife Refuge. Newport is the home of a popular oyster bar. If you're into local color, Ouzts'

is typical of the sort of funky eateries strewn along U.S. from Newport to Pensacola.

For more information, contact the Wakulla County Chamber of Commerce, 23 High Drive, P.O. Box 598, Crawfordville, FL 32326, 850/926-1848, www.wakullacounty.org/chamber.

COASTAL CUISINE

If you like cold beer and oysters, **Ouzts' Too** (7996 U.S. 98, 850/925-6448, $) is the real deal. It's also something of a phoenix. Built in 1969, Ouzts' Oyster Bar burned to the ground in 2000 and came back as Ouzts' Too. Already the grubstake of Ouzts' regulars covers the rebuilt restaurant's walls. It just goes to prove you can't keep a good honky-tonk oyster bar down.

Though it's just a large cinderblock hut on the west bank of the St. Marks River, Ouzts' is a colorful place. It also proves that the Cajun influence in cooking, drinking, and music is not confined to the bayous of Louisiana. That influence can be found all across Florida's Panhandle.

At Ouzts' they'll shuck you a dozen cold, fresh Apalachee Bay oysters. They're known for smoked mullet, bacon-wrapped shrimp, and shrimp pie, too. Breakfast, lunch, and dinner are served daily. Ouzts' also rents canoes, which can be paddled to Natural Bridge (seven miles upriver) or the community of St. Marks (three miles downriver).

The regulars at Ouzts' are a cigarette-smoking, beer-guzzling, hell-yessing bunch. This roadhouse can get pretty wild after dark. They have a regular Thursday night jam (mostly bluegrass), if you're up to braving the scurvy characters. At lunch a few years back we sat near an enormous good ol' boy who made longneck beers disappear like magic while unleashing an incoherent monologue punctuated with fits of snuffling laughter. A mustachioed river rat started ragging on rich northerners: "Heck, we could take these oysters up to New York City and git four times what we git for a dozen down here." A bushy-bearded fellow swiveled on his stool and fixed us with an unnerving stare. We minded our own business and enjoyed the bivalves and brew. You should, too.

BEST⟨ St. Marks National Wildlife Refuge

Wakulla County gets high marks for land preservation. Much of its land—68,000 wild acres of marsh, open water, diked impoundments, and slash pine and palmetto forest, plus 31,000 acres of open water in Apalachee Bay—belongs to St. Marks National Wildlife Refuge. Forty miles of the Florida National Scenic Trail pass through here, and another 36 miles of trails cross the refuge.

Located at the head of Apalachee Bay, the refuge takes its name from the St. Marks River, which empties into the Gulf of Mexico on refuge land. The visitors center and most accessible refuge lands lie 20 miles south of Tallahassee, along C.R. 59.

The refuge has four units, so make the visitors center your first stop in order to orient yourself, ask questions, and collect maps and trail guides. Walk the short Plum Orchard Pond Trail, directly behind the visitors center. The path and boardwalk skirt a pond and swamp. You'll spy a variety of tree species—pines, palms, and hardwoods—and some scintillating natural sights. Nearly 300 bird species have been identified on the refuge.

At the end of C.R. 59 (11 miles from the U.S. 98 turnoff in Newport) is St. Marks Lighthouse. The present structure dates from 1866, when the 1842 original was rebuilt after being blown up during the Civil War. The tower's red top houses an electric lamp that's visible for 15 miles. The 80-foot lighthouse is a mandatory photo opportunity. Next to it is a wildlife-viewing stand. Close by is an impoundment surrounded by a levee and filled with native and migratory birds. We saw wood

ducks, cormorants, egrets, herons, and ibises. Alligators sun themselves on the banks.

You can camp on the refuge only if you're a through-hiker on the Florida National Scenic Trail. Other opportunities for outdoor recreation include hiking, picnicking, bird- and wildlife watching, boating, fishing, and crabbing.

The entrance fee at St. Marks National Wildlife Refuge is $4 per car. A $2 fee is charged to use the Aucilla River Boat Ramp.

For more information, contact St. Marks National Wildlife Refuge, 1255 Lighthouse Road, P.O. Box 68, St. Marks, FL 32355, 850/925-6121, www.fws.gov/saintmarks.

BEACHES

We spread out a giant map of Wakulla County and looked for any road that might lead to a beach. Most of the coast is saltwater marsh, so we weren't hopeful. Still, Wakulla Beach Road looked promising, so we turned off U.S. 98 and proceeded four miles down a sandy, mildly rutted road through St. Marks National Wildlife Refuge. We passed pickup trucks and hunters carrying bows and arrows, tracking hapless critters through the woods. Soon we were at the muddy end of the road, face to face with a flock of scurrying fiddler crabs. We won't stretch credibility by calling it a beach, but there is a 24-hour boat launch here, and it is yet another open window onto the wide, wonderful gulf.

Edward Ball Wakulla Springs State Park

Wakulla Springs State Park is located 14 miles south of Tallahassee and seven miles northwest of Newport. The natural feature the park is named for is one of the deepest and largest freshwater springs in the world. Water flows up the limestone aquifer and out of the ground at the rate of 600,000 gallons per minute. There's a swimming beach at the spring's headwaters, as well as a dive tower from which one can jump into the lake's pure, limpid 70°F waters. We found the dive-tower rules unusual enough to warrant inclusion:

* No jumping while boats are near tower.
* Only two persons may jump at a time.
* No swimming over the spring.
* No jumping from the rails.
* No gainers, inwards, or handstands.

Park admission is $4 per vehicle. Tours via glass-bottom and pontoon boats depart hourly and cost $6 per adult ($4 for kids under 12). A network of trails crisscrosses the 3,000-acre forest in and around the park.

For more information, contact Wakulla Springs State Park, 550 Wakulla Park Drive, Wakulla Springs, FL 32327, 850/224-5950, www.floridastateparks.org.

ACCOMMODATIONS

Overlooking the spring-fed lake is the state park's man-made centerpiece, **Wakulla Springs Lodge** (550 Wakulla Park Drive, 850/224-5950, $$). This venerable old lodge was constructed in 1937 by railroad magnate Edward Ball. Its 27 rooms have marble floors and antique furnishings. Rooms run $85–105 a night. If you are laying over in Wakulla County, Wakulla Springs Lodge is the best and practically the only place to stay (save for The Inn at Wildwood on U.S. 98). The lodge and park are listed on the National Register of Historic Places and designated a Natural National Landmark. You can also dine here at the **Ball Room Restaurant,** which serves breakfast, lunch, and dinner.

In the lodge's lobby is an enormous Plexiglas case in which a giant 12-foot alligator known as Old Joe is interred. Old Joe was known in these parts as "the most photographed wild alligator in existence" until some morons killed him in 1966. A $5,000 reward was offered, but the perpetrators were never caught. A sign above the case says it all: "This is Old Joe's one and only cage."

Shell Point

Shell Point (pop. 300) occupies a knob of land extending into the gulf at the Wakulla County's coastal midsection. Most of the county is taken up by St. Marks National Wildlife Refuge and Apalachicola National Forest. However, out on this tip—which includes the small communities of Shell Point, Live Point, and Oyster Bay—private homes line the gulf and Shell Point Resort is at the end of the road. It's not the bustling, upscale place the word "resort" might invoke, but it's an interesting hideaway on what is sometimes called "the Forgotten Coast."

For more information, contact the Wakulla County Chamber of Commerce, 23 High Drive, P.O. Box 598, Crawfordville, FL 32326, 850/926-1848, www.wakullacounty. org/chamber.

BEACHES

Shell Point Beach is a sandy and muddy tidal flat at the head of Apalachee Bay. Along the beach, a concrete seawall protects the modest homes scattered along its length. It proved useless in 1998, when a four-foot wall of water from Hurricane Georges damaged a lot of homes. The county maintains a small beach park on this narrow, sandy shore—one of only two sand beaches in Wakulla County.

17 SHELL POINT BEACH

Location: From U.S. 98 east of Medart, turn south on Spring Creek Highway (C.R. 365) and follow for 1.5 miles to a fork in the road. Take the left fork (Shell Point Road/ C.R. 367) and follow to its end at Shell Point Beach.
Parking/Fees: free parking lot
Hours: sunrise-sunset
Facilities: restrooms, picnic tables, and showers
Contact: Wakulla County Parks and Recreation Department, 850/926-7227

ACCOMMODATIONS

Shell Point Resort used to consist of a marina, motel, and restaurant. The marina's still there, but the modest cinderblock Shell Point Motel was torn down in 2005. (The Shell Point Restaurant is gone, too.) Dry your eyes, however, because a much nicer place, **The Inn at Wildwood** (3896 Coastal Highway, 850/926-4455, $$) opened up in fall 2005. This "nature-based lodge" is located on U.S. 98, and it is huge by Wakulla County standards, with 71 rooms.

Panacea

The town of Panacea (pop. 1,200) isn't quite the curative for body and spirit that its name promises. Still, it's a haven for retirees and home for working fishermen. It also symbolized home for one of the many lost souls in the books of Frederick Exley, one of our writerly inspirations. (See Exley's *Pages from a Cold Island*.)

You will find a handful of seafood eateries by the side of the road and one noteworthy attraction: the **Gulf Specimen Marine Laboratory** (222 Clark Drive, 850/984-5297). The lab's specimen tanks present an array of bizarre and beautiful underwater life forms found in the Gulf of Mexico, from jellyfish and hermit crabs to sharks and stingrays. Touch tanks with starfish, sea pansies, clams, and sand dollars will give the kiddies some icky thrills.

Admission is $4.50 for adults and $2 for children under 12, and the museum is open seven days a week.

For more information, contact the Wakulla County Chamber of Commerce, Old Wakulla County Courthouse, 23 High Drive, Crawfordville, FL 32326, 850/926-1848, www.wakullacounty.org.

BEACHES

Mash Island Park is located southwest of Panacea on Ochlockonee Bay. There used to be a beach here until hurricanes severely eroded it, wrecking the beach, pier, and restrooms. Mash Island Park was still closed as we went to press in 2006, and a county parks administrator told us they were "hopeful" that it might reopen sometime before the end of the year. This park was in bad shape as we put the last edition of this book to bed in 2000. Half a decade later, after being walloped by Hurricanes Ivan and Dennis, it's in even worse shape.

18 MASH ISLAND PARK

Location: from Panacea, take U.S. 98 south for three miles, then turn west on Mashes Sands Road (C.R. 372) and follow two miles to the park
Parking/Fees: free parking lot
Hours: Park is temporarily closed and may reopen sometime in 2006.
Facilities: restrooms and picnic tables
Contact: Wakulla County Parks and Recreation Department, 850/926-7227

COASTAL CUISINE

They likes to eat in this part of the state, and what they likes to eat is seafood. The **Harbor House** (107 Mississippi Avenue, 850/984-2758, $$) has a good broiled seafood platter and quiet, civilized atmosphere. **Angelo's Seafood Restaurant** (U.S. 98, 850/984-5168, $$) features raw oysters, heads-on shrimp, and seafood Creole.

APALACHICOLA, ST. GEORGE ISLAND, AND THE FORGOTTEN COAST

The counties at the east end of Florida's Panhandle have the best of both worlds: great, sandy Panhandle beaches and the appealing isolation of the Nature Coast/Big Bend area. Franklin County is large in size (545 square miles) but small in population (under 11,000). They call it "Florida's Final Frontier" and the "Forgotten Coast."

Franklin County claims 60 miles of coastline on its four barrier islands: Dog, St. George, Little St. George, and St. Vincent. Only St. George Island is conventionally developed, and much of its east end is a state park. On the mainland, the appealingly laid-back town of Apalachicola has long been famous for its oysters and lately been gaining attention for its inns and restaurants.

Neighboring Gulf County (pop. 14,000) puts its best foot forward at Cape San Blas and St. Joseph Peninsula. Their hilly dunes and sugar-sand beaches are world-class. The smaller peninsula at Indian Pass is an undiscovered gem, too. And ongoing efforts to monitor the unique ecosystem of St. Joseph Bay Aquatic Preserve—an all-volunteer effort done in conjunction with the University of Florida's Lake Watch Program—gets two enthusiastic crab claws up from us.

Alligator Point

At the east end of Franklin County, a peninsular knob juts into Apalachee Bay. On the map, Alligator Point looks like a barrier island that has been welded to the mainland at one end, with the thinnest sliver of sand extending westward into the bay. The turnoff to Alligator Point (pop. 100) from U.S. 98 lies just south of a bridge over the Ochlockonee River.

So what's out here? For one thing, a lot of private homes have been plopped on this

© PARKE PUTERBAUGH

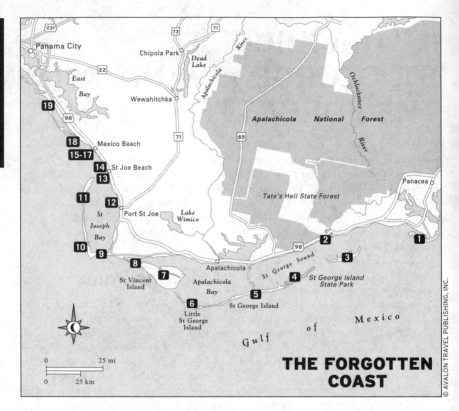

THE FORGOTTEN COAST

© AVALON TRAVEL PUBLISHING, INC.

eroding peninsular sliver. At one point along its midsection, the stilt-like pilings on which homes have been built are practically standing in water. There are no houses along one stretch, where hurricanes look to have razed the place. On the backside, road signs warn of flooding, and it's obvious that storm overwash is a not-infrequent hazard.

For more information, contact the Carrabelle Area Chamber of Commerce, U.S. 98 (Carrabelle Mini Mall), P.O. Drawer DD, Carrabelle, FL 32322, 850/697-2585, www.carrabelle.org.

BEACHES

1 ALLIGATOR POINT

Location: scattered accesses along C.R. 370 at Alligator Point

Parking/Fees: free street parking
Hours: sunrise-sunset
Facilities: none
Contact: Franklin County Parks and Services Department, 850/927-2111

ACCOMMODATIONS

Most of the construction at Alligator Point is ill-advisedly located along the narrow peninsular spit on the island's west side. If you want to rent a house at Alligator Point, contact **Coastal Shores Realty** (53 Coastal Highway, Crawfordville, FL 32327, 850/984-5800). Many come out here to camp at **Alligator Point KOA** (C.R. 370, 850/349-2525) or use the facilities at **Alligator Point Marina** (3461 C.R. 370, 850/349-2511), a full-service marina, bait shop, restaurant, and lounge.

BEST BEACHES

(St. George Island: Best for Fishing (page 484)

(St. George Island State Park: Top 25 (page 486)

(St. Joseph Peninsula State Park: Top 25, Best for Camping (page 496)

Lanark Village

Lanark Village (pop. 1,000) used to be the site of Camp Gordon Johnson, an army base where personnel were trained for amphibious assaults. Some of those who passed through Camp Gordon landed on the beaches of France during the D-Day invasion. They practiced by staging landings on nearby Dog Island. Since 1996, there's been an annual three-day reunion of veterans who served at Camp Gordon. **Camp Gordon Johnson Museum** is located in a small house on 4th Street. It's open on Saturdays only from 1000 hours till 1400 hours (that's 10 A.M.–2 P.M. to you civilians).

The camp existed for three years, then a developer came in and replaced the tar-paper barracks with rows of concrete ground-floor condos. Lanark Village was advertised in big-city newspapers across the Midwest back in the 1950s, so most of its residents are retirees from Chicago, Wisconsin, Pennsylvania, and so forth. For someone desiring a quiet, convivial place to retire, Lanark (LAN-ark) Village practically sells itself. A lot of folks come down to visit a friend or relative and wind up liking it so much they stay.

This quiet gulfside community has its own post office, fire department, boat club, and six-hole golf course. Lanark residents also have a community center where they meet to swap stories, and gossip over coffee. Some apartments are available for rental and occasionally come up for sale. There are no beaches in serene Lanark, and seemingly no one under retirement age, either.

"That's what we need, younger people to get involved," the septuagenarian president of the Lanark Village Association told us. We think it's fine just the way it is.

For more information, contact the Carrabelle Area Chamber of Commerce, U.S. 98 (Carrabelle Mini Mall), P.O. Drawer DD, Carrabelle, FL 32322, 850/697-2585, www. carrabelle.org.

Carrabelle and Carrabelle Beach

Carrabelle (pop. 2,000) calls itself "the pearl of the Panhandle," and with its watery setting, that is no idle boast. Its south side faces St. George Sound, on the Gulf of Mexico. On the west side, it is bounded by the Carrabelle River, formed by the confluence of the Crooked and New Rivers. Carrabelle is a small town that hasn't changed much in the last half century. According to a resident who's been around that long, it hasn't changed at all. (No wonder they call it the Forgotten Coast!)

Carrabelle is the sort of town that doesn't miss an opportunity to trumpet its novelty tourist attraction: "The World's Smallest Police Station," which is located inside a phone booth. Mostly, Carrabelle is populated by those who work the water—fishers, shrimpers, oystermen—and those who have come to retire on its quiet shores. There are a good number of docks and marinas from which one can charter a fishing boat. It is the logical place to

THE FORGOTTEN COAST

Carrabelle Beach

begin or end a trip down the Gulf Coast. The real appeal of Carrabelle is its location on the water, the absence of high-powered tourism, and the air of honest community it projects as a result.

For more information, contact the Carrabelle Area Chamber of Commerce, U.S. 98 (Carrabelle Mini Mall), P.O. Drawer DD, Carrabelle, FL 32322, 850/697-2585, www.carrabelle.org.

BEACHES

Just west of town is **Carrabelle Beach,** a lengthy strand that gets a little larger each time another storm chews away more trees and highway roadbed to uncover the underlying sand. Thanks to a couple of hurricanes in the 1990s (Earl and Opal), Carrabelle Beach has already doubled in length to about 3.5 miles. At this rate, it won't be long before the 13-mile stretch from Carrabelle to Eastpoint is all beach. Of course, this will necessitate relocating U.S. 98.

Carrabelle Beach provides free parking and concrete picnic tables. A boardwalk leads to the beach. There's not much action on this laid-back beach. Just bring your chair, towel, and book, and prepare to spend a good, old-fashioned day at the beach.

② CARRABELLE BEACH

Location: one mile west of Carrabelle on U.S. 98
Parking/Fees: free parking lot
Hours: sunrise–sunset
Facilities: restrooms and picnic tables
Contact: Florida Department of Transportation (District 3), 850/697-3838

ACCOMMODATIONS

Island View Inn (1714 U.S. 98 East, 850/697-2050, $) benefits from its location on the gulf, where it looks out on St. George and Dog Islands. There are cottages (with or without full kitchens), free boat slips for guests, boat rentals, an RV park, and two fishing piers. The atmosphere is friendly and the attitude down-home. In their own words, "We love fishin' and bluegrass pickin'."

A modest step up the lodgings ladder is

© PARKE PUTERBAUGH

The Moorings (1000 U.S. 98, 850/697-2800, $), which is still plenty cheap. It's also a marina-motel combo, offering excursions to Dog Island and as docking services for those with their own boats. Directly across from Carrabelle Beach is a 48-site campground called **Sting Ray Station RV Park** (U.S. 98, P.O. Box 929, 850/697-2638, $). You couldn't ask for a better location.

COASTAL CUISINE

A beloved old seafood restaurant, Julia Mae's, closed down since the last edition of *Florida Beaches*. The owner sold off the gulfside property for a tidy profit, and that was that. And that leaves such local favorites as **The Shrimp House** (201 West 11th Street, 850/697-2098, $$) and **Harry's Georgian Restaurant** (113 St. James Avenue NW, 850/697-3400, $$).

NIGHTLIFE

You might notice (as we have) the number of bars and lounges, some open and others out of business, in Carrabelle. **Harry's Bar and Lounge** (306 Marine Street, 850/697-9982) is one of them. Hey, if you worked on the water, wrestling with shrimp nets, crab traps, and oyster bars, you'd want to knock back a tall cool one as you hit dry land, too.

Dog Island

Long, narrow, and sandy barrier islands begin reappearing on the Panhandle side of the Big Bend around Franklin County. The first east-west barrier of any size is Dog Island (pop. 12), which lies 3.5 miles offshore. There are no bridges to the seven-mile island, which has insured that it's remained relatively undeveloped. Eleven hundred acres have been set aside as the Jeff Lewis Wilderness Preserve, with the Nature Conservancy and the Barrier Island Trust involved in their acquisition and management.

Around 100 small homes dot the island.

There is one small inn and no stores on Dog Island, necessitating provisioning trips to the mainland via private boat or ferry. (For a ferry schedule or private run over, call Captain Raymond Williams at 850/657-3434.) The soothing sounds of the surf, the seasonal comings and goings of 270 bird species, and an isolated beach make Dog Island a special place.

For more information, contact the Carrabelle Area Chamber of Commerce, U.S. 98 (Carrabelle Mini Mall), P.O. Drawer DD, Carrabelle, FL 32322, 850/697-2585, www.carrabelle.org.

BEACHES

Six miles of white-sand beach run along **Dog Island's** south side. An area of sand dunes rising as high as 50 feet is referred to as "the mountains." Inland are freshwater marshes and stands of live oak and slash pine. Hiking trails crisscross the preserve. Anyone who would say there is not much to do out here really means "there is no place to shop or watch TV." In other words, they don't get it.

3 DOG ISLAND

Location: 3.5 miles south of Carrabelle in the Gulf of Mexico
Parking/Fees: no parking; free day use of beach
Hours: sunrise-sunset
Facilities: none
Contact: Nature Conservancy, Northwest Florida Chapter, 850/643-2756

ACCOMMODATIONS

The **Pelican Inn** (Dog Island, 850/697-4728, $$) was built in the 1960s and is the only commercial structure on Dog Island. The inn has eight efficiency apartments with sliding glass doors that open onto the gulf. It's what's *not* available that's most appealing. The Pelican Inn has no TVs and just one cell phone in case of emergency. (The mailing address is Pelican Inn, P.O. Box 123, Apalachicola, FL 32329.)

THE FORGOTTEN COAST

BEST⟨ St. George Island

St. George Island (pop. 1,000) was the first serious stretch of sand reachable by road and bridge we'd laid eyes on since leaving the Clearwater area on Florida's West Coast. The "road and bridge" provision, of course, excludes Dog Island (see separate entry), which lies just east of St. George Island and is reachable by boat only. The mainland approach to St. George Island is the town of Eastpoint, which is basically one long seafood-offloading dock. The four-mile ride out to St. George Island along S.R. 300 is a real dipsy-doodle: part roller-coaster bridge, part causeway crossing man-made keys nearly at sea level. On the east side of the bridge lies St. George Sound; on the west side, Apalachicola Bay. Wonderfully plump oysters, tasty small calico scallops, and serious eating fish like grouper, redfish, mackerel, and flounder are plucked from these teeming gulf and bay waters.

St. George Island is long and narrow, oriented northeast to southwest. The island is

St. George Island Public Beach

roughly 20 miles in length, with nine miles at the eastern end preserved as St. George Island State Park. From the point where the causeway meets the island at its midsection, it is four miles to the state park guard station. Four miles of paved road continue into the park, and four miles of dirt road lie beyond that. The state park is the natural treasure and saving grace of St. George Island, which is otherwise succumbing to willy-nilly development.

It is a lovely island, many of whose natural features remain intact, but it is in the process of a transition that can only portend more of the sorts of things that make havens like this one less appealing: more houses, more traffic, more people (which is to say, more people who can afford it). Ultimately, there will be fewer uncrowded beaches and less of the backside habitat that made the island attractive in the first place. One piece of tourist literature had the audacity to claim, "Strict building codes and low-density zoning regulations have preserved the beauty of St. George." Yeah, and voting in Florida is as smooth as a pair of silk drawers. Those who are plotting St. George's future would do well to study the story of the goose that laid the golden egg.

We were struck by several ironies during our time on the island. First of all, signs warn of penalties as high as $1,000 for disturbing sea oats or $500 for riding vehicles on the dunes. Yet it is perfectly legal for earth-moving equipment to raze the dunes, vegetation and all, in order to put up another vacation home. On an otherwise peaceful Saturday, we saw lots being flattened and heard the whirring of band saws as home construction proceeded apace. Another irony: while looking for a place to mail postcards, we were told there was not a post office or even a street-corner mailbox on the island. "Put your mail in the private mailbox outside one of the real-estate offices and raise the flag," we were told by a convenience-store clerk. "That's what everyone else does." Let us get this straight: developers more or less get to do anything they want on St. George, yet the island lacks a mailbox so

© PARKE PUTERBAUGH

WE DREAM OF JEANNI

Jeanni McMillan is the genial genie behind Journeys of St. George Island (formerly Jeanni's Journeys) This ecotourism outfit specializes in boat trips to the surrounding barrier islands and waterways. Jeanni leads her journeys March 5-December 31. Destinations include Little St. George Island, St. Vincent Island, and Dog Island. She also leads trips up the Apalachicola River and to Owl Creek, in Apalachicola National Forest.

She'll take you fishing, crabbing, oystering, or shelling. You can travel by motorized boat or paddle a kayak or canoe. Jeanni is kid-friendly, too. She'll teach kids how to make sand sculptures, and she leads "kids-only" trips. Prices are reasonable, given the time, equipment, and expertise. A three-hour guided trip (e.g., "oyster adventure," "shelling and swimming") for up to six costs $250. Four- to six-hour excursions run $300, and you can choose from a variety of outings and locales. All-day trips to Dog Island or St. Vincent Island are $450. Kayak and canoe paddles of four to five hours can be arranged for $60 per person. Jeanni's knowledge of the area is vast and her enthusiasm genuine.

For more information, contact Journeys of St. George Island, 240 East 3rd Street, St. George Island, FL 32328, 850/927-3259, www.sgislandjourneys.com.

that some fiction about its isolation from the ways of the mainland world can be preserved. Where is the sense in any of this?

The best evidence of folly at work on St. George greets the eye upon one's arrival on the island. Directly on the beach sits a stunningly ugly row of narrow, vertical shotgun cottages. Pressed as close together as New York City brownstones, painted in loud colors, they act as a wall to obstruct views of the beach. One other note: at the west end of the island, the road gives out at a private development, St. George Plantation, with a guard gate. The real affront here is that boaters cannot launch from the west end of St. George Island and cross the man-made channel to Little St. George Island. Fording this brief cut is the simplest way to get there, but boaters must instead take a different approach. Lot by lot, gate by gate, and dollar by dollar, St. George Island is under siege. Since it is being developed rather late in the game, you might think they would have learned from mistakes made during the big-bucks building boom that brought many island environments to their knees.

Okay, enough bashing of St. George Island. We're only pointing all this out because there's still much that's good about the island and much left to preserve. At present, the island's year-round residents number 1,000, but that is growing every year. Many visitors come from Tallahassee and Atlanta. Typically, they vacation here and like it so much they build a second home, which they then rent out through a local realtor in the summer months. During quieter times of year, they live here themselves, subsidizing their mortgage with summer rental income. Thus, in the summer you see lots of families on the island. Many of the rental homes have four or five bedrooms and sleep 8–10 people, so families share a rental for a one- or two-week vacation. Here are a few sample home names and weekly prices, for your information (and amusement): Loafer's Glory ($1,225 summer, $695 winter), Stairway to Heaven ($1,175 summer, $655 winter), Beachy Keen ($1,095 summer, $595 winter). In general, weekly beach-house rentals run about $1,110–1,200 in summer and $600–700 in winter. This is the reverse of the scenario in South Florida, where winter is the high season.

You'd be hard pressed to find a nicer place to kick back and relax than St. George Island.

We just hope that prudent reins are applied to growth and development so that it remains that way.

For more information, contact the Apalachicola Bay Chamber of Commerce, 99 Market Street, Apalachicola, FL 32320, 850/653-9419, www.baynavigator.com/chamber.

BEACHES

First, a fact: the tallest spot in Franklin County is a 55-foot sand dune on St. George Island. Ride along St. George Island via bicycle, as we did for its entire paved length, and you'll appreciate the ground-level view of the dunes. They are more substantial, for obvious reasons, in St. George Island State Park than on the inhabited parts of the island. Not to beat a dead horse, but just compare the high, hump-backed dunes in the state park with the modest mounds along Gorrie Drive.

The beaches of St. George Island are wide and fine, brownish-white, and gently sloping across a broad berm. A ridge of small, mostly whole shells identifies the high-tide line. The water temperature out here on the Panhandle explains why late fall and winter is a down time, compared to peninsular South Florida. The gulf cools precipitously after September, bottoming out at around 60°F December–February. It warms up quickly in March and hits a peak around 80°F for much of the summer. This is a great beach for hiking, and these are great beach roads for biking. (For cheap bike rentals, drop by Island Adventures, on East Gulf Drive.)

St. George Island State Park is the island's natural highlight. A couple of miles past the entrance station is a large parking lot and a wooden pavilion with showers and picnic tables that faces the beach. The same complement of facilities is repeated a few miles farther down. A campground on the Apalachicola Bay side of the island comes with full hookups. Alternatively, backpackers can hike a 2.5-mile trail through pine flatwoods from the developed campground out to Gap Point, where primitive camping is permitted.

St. George Island Public Beach is located where the causeway meets the island. There's a free parking lot but no visitor facilities even though they've been long promised and are long overdue. Mother Nature has done her part, providing an ample strand that stretches for miles in either direction.

The beach has coarse brown shelly sand, small dunes, and some seaweed on the shore. On our latest visit, it was late summer and the water was bathwater-warm. Big puffy clouds filled the sky. Ghost crabs scuttled into jumbo crab holes. By contrast to the white sand and emerald water of the mid-Panhandle, St. George Island has a different look and feel that puts us in mind of North Carolina's Outer Banks. We were charmed by the older houses along the beach road, especially a modest single-story pink cinderblock one called "Sandy Beaches" that had a ceramic alligator out front. It seemed emblematic of the unhurried, unpretentious beach life in decades past.

We wandered the wave-washed beach at sunset, walking till our footsteps became a mantra. It was a peaceful and rejuvenating way to end what had been a long day. We can only imagine what an entire week or two out here on this slow-moving island would do for body and soul.

4 ST. GEORGE ISLAND STATE PARK

🏕️ 🥾 **BEST** (

Location: From the south end of Bryant Patton Causeway (S.R. 300) on St. George Island, turn east on Gulf Drive and follow the road four miles to the park entrance.

Parking/Fees: $4 per vehicle entrance fee. Camping fees are $10 per night with full hookups and $8 without

Hours: 8 A.M.-sunset

Facilities: restrooms, picnic tables, and showers

Contact: St. George Island State Park, 850/927-2111

THE FORGOTTEN COAST

5 ST. GEORGE ISLAND PUBLIC BEACH

Location: on St. George Island at Bryant Patton Causeway (S.R. 300) and West Gorrie Drive

Parking/Fees: free parking lot

Hours: 24 hours

Facilities: restrooms and picnic tables

Contact: Franklin County Planning Department, 850/653-9783

RECREATION AND ATTRACTIONS

- **Bike/Skate Rentals:** Island Adventures, 115 East Gulf Drive, St. George Island, 850/927-3655

- **Boat Cruise:** Governor Stone, 268 Water Street, Apalachicola, 850/653-8700

- **Dive Shop:** Captain Black's Dive Center, U.S. 98, Port St. Joe, 850/229-6332

- **Ecotourism:** Journeys of St. George Island, 240 East 3rd Street, 850/927-3259

- **Fishing Charters:** Rockfish Charters, 923 East Gulf Drive, St. George Island, 850/927-3839

- **Lighthouse:** Cape St. George Lighthouse, Little St. George Island

- **Marina:** Rainbow Marina, 123 Water Street, Apalachicola, 850/653-8139

- **Pier:** "Think of St. George Island as a massive fishing pier jutting five miles out into the Gulf of Mexico across one of the most productive estuaries in the world."—John B. Spohrer, Jr., *Fish St. George Island.*

- **Rainy-Day Attraction:** Apalachicola National Estuarine Research Reserve, 261 7th Street, Apalachicola, 850/653-8063.

- **Shopping/Browsing:** Avenue D and Commerce Street, Apalachicola

- **Vacation Rentals:** Collins Vacation Rentals, 60 East Gulf Beach Drive, St. George Island, 850/927-2900 or 800/423-7418; and Prudential Resort Realty, 123 West Gulf Drive, St. George Island, 850/927-2666 or 800/332-5196

ACCOMMODATIONS

St. George Island is geared to the rental of vacation homes for stays of one or more weeks. During the high summer season, you will pay $600–2,000 a week for a vacation rental, depending on size, amenities, and location, location, location. They all have evocative names like Sea Spell, Serendipity, Island Dream, and A Bit of Paradise. Would you be surprised to learn that one of the largest, most lavishly appointed and expensive is called Doctor's Orders? A broad selection of rental properties is handled by Collins and Prudential.

There's only one motel (The Buccaneer), one B&B (St. George Inn), and one other overnight property (Resort Island Inn). The last of these is a new construction without a shred of personality inside the guard-gated "Plantation," a development that takes up much of the west end of St. George Island.

The Buccaneer (160 West Gorrie Drive, 850/927-2585, $$) is a plain-looking yellow cinderblock motel with a pirate painted on the front. It looks like it could've drifted up from Treasure Island on Florida's West Coast. It's smack-dab on the beach at the end of the causeway. We were pleasantly surprised by the clean, quiet rooms and condition of the furniture. There's a heated pool in the interior courtyard and a wooden walkover to the beach. The Buccaneer is a more than acceptable old-school beachfront motel.

The **St. George Inn** (135 Franklin Boulevard, 850/927-2903, $$$) is homier than a motel and less expensive than a house rental. (We were quoted a rate of $134 a night in summer.) Located a block from the beach, it is a white Victorian three-story, trimmed in blue with wraparound porches. It feels more like a rambling hotel than a bed-and-breakfast, and the rooms are homey and well appointed. The TV is ingeniously stashed in a built-in cabinet over the closet, with doors that shut to hide the idiot box.

COASTAL CUISINE

Set sail for the **Oyster Cove** (201 East Pine Street, 850/927-2600, $$$), located on the sound side of St. George Island. Ascend the stairs, be seated, and start your culinary adventure with a bowl of Louisiana seafood gumbo, a thickened stew made from homemade roux. For the Oysters St. George appetizer, local oysters are topped with herbs, garlic, and parmesan cheese. Of all the cheeses, parmesan has the best taste and texture when paired with baked oysters.

Chef Nathan Montgomery's namesake dish, A.J. Montgomery, consists of amberjack with tomatoes and artichoke hearts in a light wine sauce thickened with caraway and served atop angel-hair pasta. Also highly recommended is the Chef's Combo: baby gulf shrimp, sweet calico scallops, and chunks of grouper sauteed in "sauce divine" (mushrooms, green onions, garlic, parmesan, butter, and white wine). Stone crab claws and Florida lobster turn up on the menu in season. We snagged a platter with a broiled half-lobster, tender stone crab claws, and a portobello mushroom stuffed with minced mahimahi and three cheeses. We topped it all off with a very good key lime pie.

Another commendable island eatery is **Finni's Grill & Bar** (40 West Gorrie Drive, 850/927-3340, $$$), which has a beach-facing outdoor deck and an indoor dining room. The emphasis is on seafood, such as the signature dish grouper jalamango: a spicy grilled fillet served with a chutney-style tropical fruit accompaniment. If you want a change from seafood, try the chicken St. George, which is grilled and served with roasted bananas, black beans, and rice.

The **Blue Parrot Oceanside Cafe** (68 West Gorrie Drive, 850/927-2987, $$$) is very popular but somewhat overpriced. You sit in white plastic chairs at white plastic tables and order dishes that run from $16.95 (crabcakes) to $21.95 (seafood platter). Ten bucks seems too much to pay for a grouper sandwich, though they make a very good one. And $7.50 is a lot to pay for a frozen mango daiquiri, though that, too, is very tasty. Tiki torches welcome you and

the deck bustles with hungry families and hanger-outers. One guy we talked to had fled Florida for Hawaii and just returned "to get divorced and get joint custody of my five-year-old boy." He talked about the many places he'd lived, and his harrowing experiences in Atlanta, where he was shot, run over by a truck, and hit so hard with a baseball bat that his jaw was broken in five places. What can you say to that? We ordered another frozen mango daiquiri and silently counted our blessings.

Just off the island, in Eastpoint, is a first-rate seafood restaurant, **That Place on 98** (500 U.S. 98, 850/670-9899, $$). Facing St. George Bay, they serve chilled oysters on the half shell, fried oysters with mustard-horseradish sauce, oysters Rockefeller, and "Oysters 98" (bacon, parmesan, mozzarella, garlic, onions, Worcestershire sauce). There are great fish sandwiches at lunch and seafood platters at dinner. And their key lime pie, balancing sweetness and tartness, is among the best this side of the Keys. By the way, try to sit on the weathered-wood deck. The tangy gulf breezes will complement your meal perfectly.

NIGHTLIFE

Being a family island that doesn't even have mailboxes, St. George isn't oriented to wild and woolly goings-on. It is generally quiet out here. Most of the island's modest commercial buildup is located within a few blocks of the causeway. However, if you want to knock one back at happy hour, sunset, or after dark, try **Finni's Grill & Bar** (40 West Gorrie Drive, 850/927-3340). Then there's **Harry A's Porch Club and Oyster Bar** (10 West Bayshore Drive, 850/927-9810), the island's oldest tavern and a popular spot to down oysters, sandwiches, and suds.

At the aforementioned **Blue Parrot** (68 West Gorrie Drive, 850/927-2987), they've got great drinks that are best enjoyed on the outdoor deck. Groovy grouper sandwiches, too.

Little St. George Island (Cape St. George State Reserve)

St. George Island used to be 29 miles long until the Army Corps of Engineers cut a channel west of center in 1954 to allow boats to enter the Gulf of Mexico more quickly. So St. George Island (20 miles long) has a son, Little St. George Island (nine miles long). Separating the two islands is man-made pass Bob Sikes Cut. Unfortunately, you cannot cross the pass from St. George Island unless you're a property owner or guest at St. George Plantation. This pretentious development at the west end of the island is a private, gated community.

Little St. George Island is part of the Apalachicola National Estuarine Research Reserve. The completely undeveloped island is managed by the National Oceanographic and Atmospheric Administration and the Florida Department of Environmental Protection. Little St. George Island is open to the boating public for swimming, fishing, bird-watching, and hiking. Primitive camping is permitted at either end, provided you call with the date(s) and number of people and let them explain a few rules. Foremost is that fires must be built on the beach and only dead wood taken. There's a public dock on the island, but the recent spate of hurricanes severed it from the shore. "It wasn't connected to the land the last time we checked," according to a reserve spokesperson. You might have to anchor offshore, but if you're camping at either end of the island, this will be the best alternative anyway.

The midsection of the boomerang-shaped island juts out at Cape St. George. Three lighthouses have occupied the island since in 1833. Hurricanes subjected the latest lighthouse (erected in 1852) to severe erosion and made it non-operational. It actually listed off-center by 10°. The leaning lighthouse was moved back to perpendicular by the Cape St. George Lighthouse Society, which raised $250,000 to do it.

For more information, contact the Apalachicola National Estuarine Research Reserve, 261 7th Street, Apalachicola, FL 32320, 850/653-8063, www.ocrm.nos.noaa.gov/nerr/reserves/nerrapalachicola.

BEACHES

The Beaches Are Moving is a controversial but well-researched book by coastal geologist Orrin Pilkey. His proposition—that barrier islands are unstable landforms that shouldn't be built upon—is unpopular with developers and other profiteers. But proof of Pilkey's premise can be seen at **Little St. George Island,** which has moved 400 yards north—at the rate of about 10 feet a year—in little more than a century.

The beach runs for nine lovely miles. It's marred only by residual damage done to the island's dune ridges in the 1960s. Believe it or not, they were flattened during military training exercises carried out on Little St. George Island. Thanks, Uncle Sam!

6 LITTLE ST. GEORGE ISLAND

Location: due west of St. George Island
Parking/Fees: no parking or fees; public docking available at Government Dock
Hours: 24 hours
Facilities: none
Contact: Apalachicola Estuarine National Research Reserve, 850/653-8063

Apalachicola

We fell in love with this scenic and unassuming small town, nestled 75 miles west of Tallahassee and 65 miles east of Panama City on U.S. 98. Apalachicola (pop. 2,400) lies on the west bank of the Apalachicola River, where it empties into Apalachicola Bay. We

REFRIGERATOR MAGNATE: THE JOHN GORRIE STORY

A little-known fact: The scientific basis for modern refrigeration and air conditioning was largely pioneered in Apalachicola. The inventor was John Gorrie (1803-1855), a South Carolina-born and New York-trained physician who'd been looking for a way to cool down yellow fever and malaria patients. Using a system of pumps, coils, and tanks, he devised an apparatus that produced bricks of ice. He called his invention the "ice machine." In 1851 he was granted the first U.S. patent for mechanical refrigeration. His research eventually led to the invention of the air conditioner by Willis Haviland Carrier, for which Carrier was granted a patent in 1906.

Gorrie's ice machine, which made life in the sultry South more bearable, is celebrated at John Gorrie Museum State Park in Apalachicola. Gorrie never profited from his invention, whose widespread promulgation was opposed by (of all things) the ice lobby: i.e., those who cut, sold, stored, and shipped block ice from the wintry north to other parts of the country. The museum is open 9 A.M.-5 P.M., Thursday-Monday. This is one place where the overused exclamation "cool" really applies.

For more information, contact John Gorrie Museum State Park, 6th Street and Avenue D, Apalachicola, FL 32320, 850/653-9347, wwww.floridastateparks.org.

love the low-key working waterfront along Water Street and by the historic downtown. Apalachicola hosts the annual Florida Seafood Festival the first weekend of November, and for good reason: there is no fresher seafood than that plucked from the waters surrounding Apalachicola. In fact, 90 percent of the bivalves harvested commercially in Florida come from the Apalachicola Bay.

There is only one stoplight in Franklin County: a blinking red in downtown Apalachicola. There are few fast-food franchises and plenty of wonderful hometown restaurants. Just don't come to Apalachicola looking for sand beaches. Those are found on close-by islands: Dog, St. George, Little St. George, and St. Vincent. Apalachicola does make a good jumping-off point for fishing trips or island exploration. Spend a night at one of the restored bed-and-breakfasts and enjoy some seafood meals. While you're here, tune in 100.5 FM ("Oyster Radio"), an eclectic and entertaining radio station. You might just be tempted to stick around town for good.

Local history can be explored on foot with a map of landmarks (available at inns, restaurants, and the chamber of commerce). At various times, lumber, cotton, and shipping have contributed to Apalachicola's fortunes. Today, it's seafood that drives the economy, and they're generating revenue from tourism, too. Deservedly so, in our opinion.

For more information, contact the Apalachicola Bay Chamber of Commerce, 99 Market Street, Apalachicola, FL 32320, 850/653-9419, www.baynavigator.com/chamber.

ACCOMMODATIONS

Apalachicola is ideally suited to inns. Its old homes are sprawling and architecturally distinguished, and the natural setting is conducive to whiling away the afternoon on a verandah. The pale yellow **Coombs House** (80 6th Street, 850/653-9199, $$)—a classic example of steamboat gothic architecture—has been meticulously restored. Its dark-toned hardwoods (black cedar, tiger oak) reflect the muted opulence of a bygone area. Each room has been furnished by owner Lynn Wilson, an antiques collector and interior designer. Everything about the inn is lavish, but the rates are reasonable.

Another hostelry worth touting is the **Gibson Inn** (57 Market Street, 850/653-

2191, $). This tin-roofed, three-story Victorian dates from 1907. Entering the lobby is like stepping into the past. Hang out on the wraparound porch and you'll swear time is standing still. Once you've adapted to the slower ways, you'll appreciate the wisdom of a local who explained, "Sitting on the porch of the Gibson in a rocker, watching the world go by. ... That is what Apalachicola is all about." In addition to 31 rooms and bargain rates ($85–175 per night), the Gibson Inn has a first-rate dining room that offers surf (oyster, shrimp, and Cajun grouper) and turf (oven-roasted prime rib).

The **Apalachicola River Inn** (123 Water Street, 850/653-8139, $) is part of a complex that also includes a marina and restaurant. The color scheme is pink and the modest motel-style rooms all face the river. Best of all, it adjoins Boss Oyster, one of our absolute favorite Florida restaurants.

COASTAL CUISINE

The oysters in Apalachicola are plucked from the waters of the bay using old harvesting techniques. They're plumper, thicker shelled, and tastier than those found elsewhere. The Surgeon General's warnings aside, we love raw oysters, and Apalachicola's are the best. **Boss Oyster** (123 Water Street, 850/633-9364, $$) is the be-all and end-all of oyster bars, and it rules the waterfront in Apalachicola. You can sit on the breezy deck and watch the fishing boats come and go while digging into a tasty plate of bivalves.

They prepare oysters in so many ways it takes an eight-page stapled menu to describe them all. How do they prepare oysters? Let us count the ways: raw, with cocktail sauce, or steamed, with melted butter, or baked and served with a multitude of accompaniments. There's Oysters Max (parmesan cheese, capers, garlic, herbs), Oysters Captain Jack (bacon, jalapenos, Colby cheese, hot sauce), Oysters Bienville (shrimp, mushrooms, garlic, cheddar), Oysters Monterray [sic] (blue crab, sherry, Monterey jack), Oysters Diana (olives,

feta, garlic, herbs). The list goes on and on. If you're undecided, try a Boss Oyster Combo: a dozen oysters served three different ways (your choice). They encourage you to submit your own ideas for toppings: "See your name on the menu. ... Become famous!" We came up with one called Barbequed Bliss: baked oysters topped with crumbled bacon, barbeque sauce, chives and melted cheddar cheese.

They offer other seafood delicacies, too: steamed blue crabs, double-battered Boss Buffalo shrimp, po' boys, smoked fish dip, and a belly-busting Golden Fried Seafood Platter that serves two. Their oyster Caesar salad places hot, fried Buffalo oysters atop romaine with Caesar dressing. Order a smoked mullet and you'll get a plateful with crackers and hot sauce. They serve iced tea in glasses as large as rain barrels. They also make a wicked Snickers cheesecake and an authentic key lime pie. On your way out, grab a T-shirt, which features renderings of a bivalve and Boss Oyster's motto: "Shut Up and Shuck!"

Higher up the culinary totem pole, in terms of atmosphere and sophistication, is **Chef Eddie's Magnolia Grill** (133 U.S. 98, 850/653-8000, $$$$), where the menu tends toward rich and hearty sauces (béarnaise, bordelaise, lobster) adorning lamb, quail, filet mignon, and whatever's fresh at the fish market. Chef Eddie Cass' best-known dish is the Ponchartrain: sauteed mahimahi topped with shrimp, artichokes, almonds, and cream scampi sauce.

Tamara's Floridita Cafe (17 Avenue East, 850/653-4111, $$$) is owned by a Venezuelan woman who's come to Apalachicola with some extraordinary recipes. Pecan-crusted grouper with jalapeno cream sauce and margarita chicken with honey tequila glaze are two of her most memorable preparations. Her dense key lime pie is a worthy departure from the traditional. Paintings of musicians (James Brown, Alberta Hunter) line the walls, and the restaurant is located downtown, within easy walking distance of the inns of Apalachicola.

The Hut (U.S. 98, 850/653-9410, $$) is

an unfancy hole-in-the-wall that does seafood and steaks at nice prices. The Friday lunch special (a spread of fried seafood) is legendary. Another longtime local favorite, dating from 1903, is the **Apalachicola Seafood Grill** (100 Market Street, 850/653-9510, $$). It claims to serve "the world's largest fried fish sandwich." They also have a huge selection of fresh seafood. It's on the corner of Market Street and Avenue E, near the only traffic light in Franklin County.

The bottom line is that you really can't go wrong eating seafood anywhere in the vicinity of Apalachicola Bay.

NIGHTLIFE

Nothing ever changes in Apalachicola. The closest thing to a change is that the old **Dixie Theatre** (21 Avenue F, 850/653-3200) has begun showing movies for the first time in 34 years. One of the first movies shown was *Fahrenheit 911,* which suggests there's a progressive element in this community.

St. Vincent Island National Wildlife Refuge

At 12,358 acres, St. Vincent Island is huge. For comparison's sake, it is five times as large as Little St. George Island. It appears to be shaped like a conch shell: wide on its east and south faces, the island tapers to a point at its northwest end. The shape and size of St. Vincent are explained by the fact it lies at the western end of a barrier-island chain. Because it's at the end of a westward-moving "sand cell," a series of parallel dune ridges have formed over the millennia, some reaching heights of 35 feet (which is tall in these parts).

The island has varied inland habitats, including freshwater lakes, oak hammocks, and upland pine forests. For much of the last century it was a private game preserve, stocked with exotic fauna ranging from sambar deer

to zebras. In 1968, the Nature Conservancy purchased the island, which it then sold it to the federal government. Because of the diverse habitats and the endangered and threatened species it attracts—sea turtles, indigo snakes, wood storks, peregrine falcons, bald eagles— St. Vincent Island National Wildlife Refuge is one of Florida's most precious coastal locales. In the 1990s, endangered red wolves were introduced to the island.

St. Vincent is open for visitation during daylight hours. It is closed only during public hunts (for white-tailed deer, sambar deer, wild pigs, and raccoon), held during four-day periods from November through January. Camping is prohibited, but 80 miles of sand roads serve as hiking trails. We paddled to the island via kayak and had a wonderful time poking around with our guide from **Broke-a-Toe's Outdoor Supplies and Services** (Indian Pass, Cape San Blas, 850/229-9283). On the bay side we visited a site where pottery shards dating back 4,000 years often turn up. He also showed us "the spaces"—watery chutes on the bayside into which Native Americans chased fish and then blocked their exit.

Private operators ferry visitors over and back from the mainland for a nominal fee. **St. Vincent Island Shuttle Services** (850/229-1065) charges $10 for adults and $7 for children under 10 for drop-off and pickup. They also rent bikes to adults only for exploring the island ($25 per bike and ferry trip). They operate during daylight hours and ask that you call before coming. The shuttle departs from Indian Pass Boat Launch, at the end of Indian Pass Road (C.R. 30-B). FYI, there are no public docking facilities on St. Vincent Island.

For more information, contact St. Vincent National Wildlife Refuge, P.O. Box 447, Apalachicola, FL 32329, 850/653-8808, southeast.fws.gov/stvincent.

BEACHES

Strange as it sounds, given its 14 miles of isolated beaches, swimming is among the least

THE FORGOTTEN COAST

popular activities on **St. Vincent Island National Wildlife Refuge.** The gulf water off its beach isn't as pure and appealing as it is on St. George Island because it doesn't get the twice-daily tidal flushing that occurs through the passes flanking St. George. Moreover, hurricane-engendered erosion has narrowed St. Vincent's beaches, which in places have retreated to the point where tree stumps sit the surf zone. So while the island as a whole rates highly, its beaches aren't its primary asset.

7 ST. VINCENT ISLAND NATIONAL WILDLIFE REFUGE

Location: six miles offshore from the mouth of the Apalachicola River
Parking/Fees: no parking or fees; no public docking
Hours: sunrise-sunset
Facilities: none
Contact: St. Vincent National Wildlife Refuge, 850/653-8808

Indian Pass

Indian Pass (pop. 850) is one of the best-kept secrets along the Forgotten Coast. It's the name of both a pass and a small community in southeast Gulf County. It's tucked along a scenic loop road that leaves U.S. 98/C.R. 30 near Apalachicola and rejoins it at Port St. Joe. Whereas most folks head out to Cape San Blas and St. Joseph Peninsula, this road less traveled runs east along Indian Peninsula, inside of which is Indian Lagoon. The tip of Indian Peninsula practically touches the west side of St. Vincent Island; between them is Indian Pass. Some of the better-quality oysters in an area that's renowned for them come from the bay around here.

Indian Pass is more secluded than Cape San Blas, which is to say there are fewer vacation homes and less than 1,000 year-round residents. There are also a few campgrounds and boat launches. The biggest news to come out of Indian Pass lately was the sighting of a giant, iguana-like creature by a reliable ecotourism guide and a couple of nervous customers.

The guide told us the story: "It was an eight-foot black reptile. It rose out of the

© PARKE PUTERBAUGH

Indian Pass, looking over at St. Vincent Island

water, undulating and red-eyed, with a serpent's head, and it looked mean. The tail came out of the water, and it was pointed. We all thought we saw teeth, and they were not cow teeth—they were shredding teeth."

It turned out to be a marine iguana that had been imported from South America and kept as a "pet" until it escaped. The story goes that it was eventually caught and sold to a zoo.

For more information, contact the Gulf County Chamber of Commerce, 104 Fourth Street West, Port St. Joe, FL 32456, 850/227-1223, www.gulfcountybusiness.com.

BEACHES

Curiously, the controversial practice of beach driving—which is hell on the beach—is permitted along Indian Peninsula and part of Cape San Blas. There are two designated beach entrance/exit points at **Indian Pass** and three on Cape San Blas. A permit is needed to drive on the beach. It can be obtained at the office of the Gulf County Tax Collector for a fee of $15 per year for area property holders and $150 for everyone else. Wisely, driving on the beach is forbidden at dusk during turtle-nesting season.

The beach along Indian Peninsula is more for anglers and amblers than swimmers. The bay bottom is silty and the water is more occluded than that found off St. George Island and St. Joseph Peninsula. It's not polluted, however, and once you're a few hundred yards offshore, it becomes clear as a bell.

8 INDIAN PASS

Location: From U.S. 98/C.R. 30, turn east on C.R. 30-B and follow for two miles to Indian Pass

Parking/Fees: Free parking lot. Beach driving requires a permit, available for $15 per year for county property holders and $150 for non-property holders. Call the Gulf County Tax Collector, 850/229-6116.

Hours: sunrise–sunset

Facilities: none

Contact: Gulf County Planning and Building Department, 850/229-8944

ACCOMMODATIONS

As you approach the Gulf of Mexico on Indian Pass Road, a large, lovely two-story structure rises on stilts above the cabbage palms off to the right. This is **Turtle Beach Inn and Cottages** (140 Painted Pony Road, 850/229-9366, $$$), a four-room B&B with two "tower" cottages for larger groups. A path on the property leads to a secluded beach. The perfect getaway!

Indian Pass Road dead-ends at Indian Pass, where you'll find the only other accommodations: the clean, well tended **Indian Pass Campground** (Indian Pass Road, 850/227-7703, $). In addition to camping, you can rent kayaks and canoes for paddling over to St. Vincent Island. If you'd rather not sweat the crossing yourself, **St. Vincent Island Shuttle** (Indian Pass Road, 850/229-1065) will take you over and pick you up at a prearranged time. While swimmers might think St. Vincent looks temptingly close, the current through the pass can be treacherous. And there are no lifeguards within 50 miles.

COASTAL CUISINE

We found a joint worth crowing about out in the middle of nowhere. **Indian Pass Raw Bar** (8391 S.R. C-30, 850/227-1670, $) is the place to go for some of the freshest and best-tasting oysters on the Panhandle, which is to say in the entire United States. Funky and weather-beaten with barely decipherable lettering, it looks like a country store from the outside. Indeed it was a gas station and convenience store many years ago. Inside, in an unfancy room with a bar and some tables, they serve raw oysters ($4.50/dozen), baked oysters, shrimp, and crabs, plus beer, wine, and soft drinks to wash it all down.

Cape San Blas

Viewed on a map, Cape San Blas and the peninsula that shoots up from it look like an arm that's been bent at the elbow. The undulating shoreline at the southern end of St. Joseph Bay is the bulging biceps. Cape San Blas is the crooked elbow protruding into the Gulf of Mexico. The long forearm, bent slightly inward at its wrist-like tip, is St. Joseph Peninsula. The peninsula extends for about 20 miles, enclosing St. Joseph Bay and protecting the mainland town of Port St. Joe. Severe beach erosion is evident just inside the elbow of the cape, necessitating repeated shoring up from road crews.

Does the gulf want to open an inlet and make a barrier island of St. Joseph Peninsula? Only the next major hurricane knows for sure, but we'll offer this word to the wise: where the peninsula flares off from Cape San Blas is the most highly erodable section of coastline in the state of Florida. An amazing 1,600 feet of width has been lost in the last 80 years, and erosion occurs at the rate of 36 feet per year. In other words, build out here at your peril.

Vacation homes and condos are sited all along the skinny peninsula, though stores and restaurants are few and far between. Formidable dunes are found inside St. Joseph Peninsula State Park, at the western end of the peninsula. Cape San Blas, with its treacherous offshore shoals, has been the site of five lighthouses; three were destroyed by storms and the encroaching gulf. The latest one (constructed in 1885) was made to be moved. That is good because shifting sands necessitated its relocation in 1918. In the lighthouse's history, one can discern the wisdom of the biblical warning against building one's house on sand.

For more information, contact the Gulf County Chamber of Commerce, 104 Fourth Street West, Port St. Joe, FL 32456, 850/227-1223, www.gulfcountybusiness.com.

BEACHES

The white ribbon of sandy beach along the gulf looks almost like it's been dusted with frost. The healthiest beach is at **St. Joseph Peninsula State Park** (see next write-up). Beyond that, the county has provided two beach parks, one near Cape San Blas (Salinas Park) and one between the cape and the state-park entrance (Cape Palms Park).

Salinas Park is a wide, accreting, south-facing beach. Boardwalks lead over the dunes to a usually uncrowded beach. A gazebo perches atop the tallest dune. Facilities at Salinas include picnic tables and a playground, with the only sour note being that they've been the frequent target of vandals.

Cape Palms Park offers a parking area and boardwalk to the beach along the peninsula's midsection. The park has a covered pavilion and picnic tables, playground, grills, showers, and good landscaping.

9 SALINAS PARK

Location: on C.R. 30-E (Cape San Blas Road), 0.25 mile west of its intersection with C.R. 30, on Cape San Blas
Parking/Fees: free parking lot
Hours: sunrise–sunset
Facilities: restrooms, showers, and picnic tables
Contact: Gulf County Planning and Building Department, 850/229-8944

10 CAPE PALMS PARK

Location: five miles northwest of Cape San Blas on St. Joseph Peninsula, via C.R. 30-E (Cape San Blas Road)
Parking/Fees: free parking lot
Hours: sunrise–sunset
Facilities: restrooms, picnic tables, and showers
Contact: Gulf County Planning and Building Department, 850/229-8944

St. Joseph Peninsula State Park

St. Joseph Peninsula State Park occupies the upper portion of a lengthy spit, protruding northwesterly from Cape San Blas. This undefiled park is far from major population centers (Tallahassee is 75 miles distant) and truly merits its claim of isolation. There are nine miles of gulf beach, 10 miles of bayshore, and 2,516 acres of parkland, much of it hardy sand-pine scrub and pine flatwoods. A roadless area at the north end is a wilderness preserve. From the end of the road to the tip of the peninsula is 7.5 hikeable miles.

You can easily find a remote spot on the beach and fish, swim, and sunbathe. Kayaking and scalloping are popular on the bayside. Birdwatchers know St. Joseph Peninsula as a prime location for sighting hawks—especially the sharp-shinned hawk—during their fall migration. A total of 209 bird species have been catalogued on the peninsula. Monarch butterflies pass through en route to Mexican wintering sites. Mammals include deer, foxes, skunks, and bobcats.

Incidentally, T. H. Stone, to whom the park was dedicated in 1967, built the first bathhouse here in the early 20th century.

For more information, contact St. Joseph Peninsula State Park, 8899 Cape San Blas Road, Port St. Joe, FL 32456, 850/227-1327, www.floridastateparks.org.

BEACHES

Four boardwalks and an access path from the cabin area lead onto the white-sand beaches of **St. Joseph Peninsula State Park.** The dunes were still recovering from damage inflicted by Hurricane Opal (1995) and Hurricane Earl (1998) when Hurricane Ivan (2004) and Hurricane Dennis (2005) meted out more punishment. On average, they've lost three feet of elevation and up to 40 percent of their size. Many of the stabilizing sea oats were taken out by the storms. Even though the beach and dunes have been adversely impacted by this spate of hurricanes—a sad reality all over the Panhandle—they are still lovely to look at and play on.

11 ST. JOSEPH PENINSULA STATE PARK

▲ ⌇ 🧍 🎿   **BEST (**

Location: west end of St. Joseph Peninsula, via C.R. 30-E (Cape San Blas Road)
Parking/Fees: $4 per vehicle entrance fee. The camping fee is $20 per night. Primitive camping in the wilderness area is $3 per night for adults and $1 for kids under 16. Cabins rentals are $80 per night
Hours: 8 A.M.-sunset
Facilities: concessions, lifeguards, picnic tables, restrooms, and showers
Contact: St. Joseph Peninsula State Park, 850/227-1327

ACCOMMODATIONS

Eight furnished cabins on the bayside bear cute names like "Starfish," "Trout," "Conch," and "Snapper." They are available for rental ($80 per night, depending on time of year), and 119 campsites with hookups are located in two areas on the gulf. Primitive hike-in camping can be done on the wilderness preserve. The cabins blend in with the landscape, and they're a cut above the typically dilapidated state-park lodgings. Cabin and camping reservations are accepted up to 11 months in advance.

Port St. Joe

We've included Port St. Joe (pop. 4,500) more as a biohazard warning than for any relevance as a coastal destination. Port St. Joe lies along the inner shoreline of St. Joseph Bay, serving as a gateway to Cape San Blas and St. Joseph Peninsula. It's the only town of any size along Gulf County's coast, but it is better passed through than lingered over. You've heard of such public-relations handles as the "Nature

Coast" and the "Forgotten Coast"? We call the area between Port St. Joe and Panama City the "Chemical Coast."

Arizona Chemical has mammoth industrial operations on the waterfront in Port St. Joe. The smokestack emissions will have you holding your nose while crossing the bridge in or out of town. The smell is like Vienna sausages boiled in vinegar. Rundown shacks list within sight of the dark, satanic mills. It's another all-American eyesore, with the worst aspects of industry and franchising sucking the life out of what surely once was an appealing stretch of the Gulf Coast. At least there's a legitimate bit of state history here. Port St. Joe is known as the "Constitution City" for having been the site of Florida's first constitutional convention in 1838.

You may need to patronize some of the businesses in Port St. Joe since there are precious few of them on Cape San Blas, but you're best advised to make your time here as brief as possible. There is one bright spot: a large, recently built marina with 120 wet slips and charter boats has improved the town's lot.

Fore more information contact the Gulf County Chamber of Commerce, 104 West 4th Street, Port St. Joe, FL 32457, 850/227-1223, www.hometown.com/gulfco.

BEACHES

Frank Pate Park, at the end of 5th Street on St. Joseph Bay, has a boat ramp and fishing pier, plus tennis courts, picnic area, and playground. There's even a bit of sand on the shore, but you really don't want to swim here.

12 FRANK PATE PARK

Location: south end of 5th Street in Port St. Joe
Parking/Fees: free parking lot
Hours: 24 hours
Facilities: restrooms and picnic tables
Contact: Port St. Joe City Hall, 850/229-8261

RECREATION AND ATTRACTIONS

- **Dive Shop:** Captain Black's Dive Center, 301 Monument Avenue (U.S. 98), Port St. Joe, 850/229-6330

- **Ecotourism:** Broke-a-Toe's Outdoor Services and Supplies, 7155 Leeward Street, Cape San Blas, 850/229-9283

- **Fishing Charters:** Premier Sportfishing, 340 Marina Drive, Port St. Joe, 850/227-9720

- **Lighthouse:** Cape San Blas Lighthouse, Cape San Blas

- **Marina:** Port St. Joe Marina, 340 West 1st Street, Port St. Joe, 850/227-9393

- **Pier:** Frank Pate Park, 5th Street at Monument Avenue (U.S. 98), Port St. Joe

- **Rainy-Day Attraction:** Constitution Convention State Museum, 200 Allen Memorial Way, Port St. Joe, 850/229-8029

- **Vacation Rentals:** Cape San Blas Vacation Rentals, 4320 Cape San Blas Road, Port St. Joe, 850/229-6916

St. Joe Beach and Beacon Hill

The line demarcating Eastern and Central time zones falls between Beacon Hill and Mexico Beach, in Bay County. Election-night controversy was engendered in November 2000 when TV networks, vying to be the first to call the state of Florida for Bush or Gore, did so before the polls had closed on the Central time zone side of the line. In so doing, they essentially disenfranchised Panhandle-dwelling voters.

A sandy shore reappears on the mainland as the protective influence of the outlying St. Joseph Peninsula disappears. Most of St. Joe Beach consists of boxlike two-story houses that block the view of the gulf from the road and sit precariously close to the water. Some of the homes in Beacon Hill look like they've been around forever. Others appear to have popped up overnight, such as a plague of connected units, painted in garish colors, that lines the gulf side of U.S. 98 on the east end of town.

For more information, contact the Gulf County Chamber of Commerce, 104 Fourth Street West, Port St. Joe, FL 32456, 850/227-1223, www.gulfcountybusiness.com.

BEACHES

Access is catch-as-catch-can in **St. Joe Beach,** where any lot that doesn't have a home on it serves as an impromptu easement onto the beach. Pull onto the shoulder and follow the sandy trails to the beach, like everyone else does. **Beacon Hill Community Park** is a handsome facility located on the inland side of U.S. 98. It sits on a dune ridge near the Beacon Hill Lighthouse, whose beacon aids navigation into St. Joseph Bay. The park is oriented toward ballgames and picnicking, but it does have a boardwalk leading out to the gulf.

⓭ ST. JOE BEACH

Location: various trails lead to the beach from pulloffs along U.S. 98 in St. Joe Beach.
Parking/Fees: free roadside parking
Hours: sunrise-sunset
Facilities: none
Contact: Gulf County Planning and Building Department, 850/229-8944

⓮ BEACON HILL COMMUNITY PARK

Location: on U.S. 98 in Beacon Hill, by the Beacon Hill Lighthouse
Parking/Fees: free parking lot
Hours: sunrise-sunset
Facilities: restrooms and picnic tables
Contact: Gulf County Planning and Building Department, 850/229-8944

COASTAL CUISINE

There are a couple of inviting beachfront venues in Beacon Hill: **Regan's Pub & Oyster Bar** (8066 West U.S. 98, 850/647-2800, $) and **The Wonder Bar** (8141 West U.S. 98, 850/647/9920).

Mexico Beach

As we entered Mexico Beach, we realized that we were nearing the end of the Forgotten Coast. Mexico Beach (pop. 1,300) isn't exactly forgotten, nor is it very memorable. It's a linear, no-frills beach town that likes to refer to itself as "the quiet alternative." The majority of homes in Mexico Beach are sun-faded, candy-colored box-like structures. Some have faded too much, however, and are in need of fixing up.

In 1995, Hurricane Opal devastated Mexico Beach on the gulf side of U.S. 98. Proving the old adage that those who forget history are condemned to repeat it, the majority of the post-hurricane construction has been on the gulf side of the road. Why not just paint a target on the back door? Glancing blows from Hurricanes Ivan and Dennis have not helped the beach profile in this vulnerable community. The east end of town is more appealing, because the development is on the inland side of the highway, where it hasn't obstructed the view of the splendid white-sand beaches and sparkling Gulf of Mexico.

Even though it's technically just inside Bay County, Mexico Beach is more closely aligned with the adjoining Gulf County communities of Beacon Hill and St. Joe Beach. In fact, it's appears to have been informally adopted by Gulf County, even though it resides in a different county and time zone.

For more information, contact the Mexico Beach Community Development Council, P.O. Box 13382, Mexico Beach, FL 32410, 850/648-8196 or 888/723-2546, www.mexicobeach.com/cdc.

BEACHES

Mexico Beach has done a commendable job of providing public access to its 3.5 miles of beaches. A couple of small beach parks, **Wayside Park** (at 7th Street) and **Sunset Park** (at 19th Street), are sited at the east and middle parts of town, respectively. Sunset Park is next to El Governor Motel (and was once known as El Governor Park). At the west end of town is **Canal Park,** which includes the Mexico Beach Pier, at the foot of 37th Street.

There are also four dune walkovers strewn at various intervals along U.S. 98. Parking is free at all of the parks and accessways. Mexico Beach is a kid-friendly beach, as the west end of St. Joseph Peninsula blocks and tames the waves, leaving Mexico Beach's shoreline calm and undertow-free.

15 WAYSIDE PARK

Location: 7th Street and U.S. 98 in Mexico beach
Parking/Fees: free parking lot
Hours: sunrise-sunset
Facilities: restrooms and showers
Contact: Mexico Beach Town Hall, 850/648-5700

16 SUNSET PARK (A.K.A. EL GOVERNOR PARK)

Location: 19th Street and U.S. 98 in Mexico Beach
Parking/Fees: free parking lot
Hours: sunrise-sunset
Facilities: concessions, restrooms, picnic tables, and showers
Contact: Mexico Beach Town Hall, 850/648-5700

17 CANAL PARK

Location: 37th Street at U.S. 98 in Mexico Beach
Parking/Fees: free parking lot
Hours: sunrise-sunset
Facilities: concessions, restrooms, picnic tables, and showers
Contact: Mexico Beach Town Hall, 850/648-5700

ACCOMMODATIONS

The most arresting structure in Mexico Beach is **El Governor Motel** (U.S. 98, P.O. Box 13325, 850/648-5757, $), a five-story motel that looms like the Empire State Building in this otherwise low-to-the-ground community. Cut from plain cloth and boasting an outdoor pool and bar, El Governor sits so close to the gulf that it looks like it could topple forward into it during the next big blow. As a matter of fact, its seawall was heavily damaged by Hurricane Ivan in 2004.

A more mannerly place to lay over in Mexico Beach is the **Driftwood Inn** (U.S. 98, 850/648-5126, $$), a two-story Victorian B&B that's also on the beach side. Beyond that, vacation rentals are available through **Mexico Beach Harmon Realty** (1432 U.S. 98, 850/239-4959), and there are three RV parks in the area.

COASTAL CUISINE

The **Toucan Restaurant and Oyster Bar** (812 U.S. 98, 850/648-3010, $$) has two outdoor decks and an indoor dining room. The cuisine is finer than you'd have any right to expect in Mexico Beach, including such entree offerings as tequila lime chicken, salmon in a bag, and local oysters.

Tyndall Air Force Base

Twenty-five miles of Panhandle real estate between Mexico Beach and Panama City is claimed by massive Tyndall Air Force Base. It's a city in its own right, with 21,000 personnel supporting the stated mission of "air superiority

THE FORGOTTEN COAST

for F-15 Eagle pilots" (i.e., top guns). As you pass through Tyndall AFB on U.S. 98, signs beside the road read: "Global Power. Global Reach. For America."

Tyndall's military mission does not completely exclude the public from enjoying the land it occupies. On a 12-mile peninsula that stretches to the west, bounded by East Bay and St. Andrews Bay, roads and boardwalks can be used by hikers and mountain bikers. The beach along Crooked Island, which juts into the Gulf of Mexico, is open to the public most of the time, provided you've obtained the necessary passes. For a map and a recreational permit to hike, bike, or hit the beach, you must register at the Natural Resources Office. We've detailed the necessary bureaucratic hurdles below.

For more information, contact Tyndall Air Force Base, Panama City, FL 32403, 850/283-1113, www.tyndall.af.mil.

BEACHES

Crooked Island—10 miles of deserted barrier island that adjoins Shell Island to the west—is accessible to the public, albeit with restrictions. You must obtain a recreational pass at the Natural Resources Office, and to do so you must first get a gate pass from the visitors center. Here's the drill:

Tyndall Air Force Base is located between Mexico Beach and Panama City on U.S. 98. Gate passes are obtained at the visitors center, by the entrance gate at Sabre Drive. Vehicle registration is required for a gate pass, which must be shown any time you enter a gated area. Now proceed to the Natural Resources Office. Pass through the Sabre Drive gate, take the first left (Dejarnette Road) and park at the only building on the right. The Natural Resources Office will issue a recreational pass, which is good for the entire year. You must provide a picture ID, vehicle registration, and proof of car insurance.

With your recreational pass, you can now make an amphibious assault on the beach. There are two access points: **Crooked Island East** at the east end, and **Tyndall Beach** (a.k.a.

Crooked Island West) at the west end. The unmarked access road to Crooked Island East is at the eastern border of the base, near the city limits of Mexico Beach. Carry your recreational pass or military police will ticket you. Don't bring your dog or litter the beach. (Believe it or not, litter is a problem out here.) What kind of oaf would litter the beaches of an Air Force base that was kind enough to let them play out here?

Tyndall Beach is accessible from the west side of the base, near Panama City. Turn south onto the base from the main gate (Florida Avenue), located at the first stoplight east of Panama City on U.S. 98, over the Dupont Bridge. Once inside, take the first left and the next right, then turn right at the third stop sign and proceed to the beach. You'll find a boardwalk and pavilion with a restroom and shower. The pass between Crooked Island and Shell Island has closed, creating one long island where there had been two. Hurricane Opal initiated the closure in 1995, and Hurricane Earl sealed the deal in 1998.

A final note: Public access is granted under normal conditions. When we're at war and the military is in a state of high alert, recreational passes may not be granted. The status of public access is stated on marquees at the base entrance, and you should call before visiting. For detailed information on public access and recreation at Tyndall Air Force Base, call the Natural Resources Office at 850/283-2641.

18 CROOKED ISLAND EAST

Location: From U.S. 98, turn south onto the easternmost access road within the boundaries of Tyndall Air Force Base, just west of Mexico Beach.

Parking/Fees: free parking lot

Hours: sunrise-sunset (Note: This area is sometimes off-limits to the public. Check the marquees as you enter Tyndall AFB or call the Natural Resources Office for current status.)

Facilities: restrooms, picnic tables, and showers

Contact: Natural Resources Office at Tyndall Air Force Base, 850/283-2641

19 TYNDALL BEACH (A.K.A. CROOKED ISLAND WEST)

Location: Enter the main gate (Florida Avenue) at Tyndall Air Force Base. Take the first left and the next right, then turn right at the third stop sign and proceed to the beach.

Parking/Fees: free parking lot

Hours: sunrise-sunset (Note: This area is sometimes off-limits to the public. Check the marquees as you enter Tyndall AFB or call the Natural Resources Office for current status.)

Facilities: restrooms and showers

Contact: Natural Resources Office at Tyndall Air Force Base, 850/283-2641

PANAMA CITY BEACH: THE PANHANDLE'S PLAYGROUND

Panama City Beach's bleached-white sand and emerald water are a sight for sore eyes. For many decades this lengthy anaconda of a beach town has served as a family-oriented warm-weather vacation mecca. Since the 1990s it has also drawn collegiate Spring Breakers from all over the country in the winter months. "PCB" dominates the coast of Bay County along the Panhandle's midsection. The town stretches for 26 miles across a sandy peninsula. To the east is the busy port and military town of Panama City, which is the antithesis of—and not to be confused with—Panama City Beach.

Panama City Beach exhibits different personalities depending on the time of year. From February through Easter, PCB attracts collegiate Spring Breakers—as many as a half-million back in the roaring Nineties but a fraction of that in recent years. Just before Spring Break 2005, Panama City Beach mayor Lee Sullivan told *USA Today*, "It's the last dance. I believe this will be the last big Spring Break." The inevitable selloff of Club La Vela for "redevelopment" (read: condos) will signal the death knell. And even though Club La Vela says it plans to reopen elsewhere, it won't be the same. From Easter through Labor Day, PCB has always plied the summer tourist trade, although all the newly built and under-construction condos have made it tough for vacationing families to find affordable places to stay. From Labor Day through February, PCB goes into a virtual state of hibernation.

St. Andrews State Park

It's no mystery why St. Andrews State Park is the most popular and highly rated beach in

© PARKE PUTERBAUGH

BEST BEACHES

◖ St. Andrews State Park: Best for Camping, Best for Diving and Snorkeling (page 504)

Bay County. Not only is the beach here and on adjoining **Shell Island** beautiful, but the spacious park (1,260 acres) includes a lake, marshlands, two hiking trails, and full facilities for camping (176 sites), swimming, fishing (including gulf and bay piers, rock jetties, and a boat ramp), picnicking, snorkeling, canoeing, kayaking, and diving.

Upon entering the park, the road to the right leads to Shell Island Shuttle and the road to the left heads to the campground. There's a place called Button Marsh Overlook. It's a low swale between dune ridges that's a freshwater marsh most of the year and a full-fledged lake during the rainy season. Herons, turtles and alligators populate the area. If you're up for a short walk, be sure to visit Gator Lake Overlook and Nature Trail.

For more information, contact St. Andrews State Park, 4607 State Park Lane, Panama City Beach, FL 32408, 850/233-5140, www.floridastateparks.org.

BEACHES

Stephen Leatherman, the ubiquitous "Dr. Beach" (see *Enter Sandman: Dr. Beach and the Ratings Game* sidebar), rated **St. Andrews State Park** the best beach in the United States in 1995. Thought it's since taken big hits from hurricanes, St. Andrews remains a lovely place, with mesa-like sand cliffs backing a wide beach that runs for 2.5 miles. Along the water's edge are a wealth of life forms, including starfish, urchins, and an endless field of shells.

The east end is called Jetty Beach (for obvious reasons). The inlet separating St. Andrews from Shell Island is a deep-water shipping channel watched closely by the Coast Guard.

It's fun to walk out along the jetty and watch the boaters and surfers. At certain times of year, we were told, it is among the best surfing spots in Florida. Just don't let the Coast Guard catch you blocking the inlet.

Shell Island is also a park holding, offering more of the same exquisite beach and a less crowded spot from which to snorkel off the jetties. The Shell Island Shuttle takes passengers over and back every half hour 9 A.M.–5 P.M. in spring and summer. (Round-trip fare is $11.50 for adults and $5.50 for kids.) The shuttle service also offers snorkel packages ($18.95 for adults and $12.95 for kids 12 and under). For information on shuttles and boat rentals at St. Andrews, call the **Pier Concession Store** (850/233-4004). Also on the property is the **Jetty Dive Store** (850/233-0197).

◱ SHELL ISLAND

🔱 🏃 🏊 ⛱

Location: due east of Panama City Beach, in St. Andrews Bay

Parking/Fees: Shell Island is accessible by boat only. Private operators in the Panama City Beach area run shuttles to and from the island. Shell Island Shuttle, a concession operating within St. Andrews State Park, charges $11.50 per round trip for adults and $5.50 for children. Call the Pier Concession Store at 850/235-4004 for times of operation, which vary seasonally.

Hours: 8 A.M.-sunset

Facilities: none

Contact: St. Andrews State Park, 850/233-5140

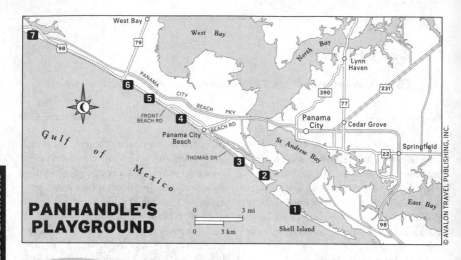

PANHANDLE'S
PLAYGROUND

© AVALON TRAVEL PUBLISHING, INC.

2 ST. ANDREWS STATE PARK

   **BEST ◖**

Location: Three miles east of Panama City
Beach at east end of Thomas Drive (S.R. 392)
Parking/Fees: $5 entrance fee per vehicle.
The camping fee is $24 per night.
Hours: 8 A.M.-sunset
Facilities: concessions, restrooms, picnic
tables, showers, and visitors center
Contact: St. Andrews State Park,
850/233-5140

Panama City Beach

It pains us to say this, but we can no longer
recommend Panama City Beach as a vacation
destination and are extremely disappointed
with what has been allowed to happen here in
a veritable blink of an eye.

What's happened is simple: Panama City
Beach has been destroyed in a matter of a few
years by the most egregious building boom
we've ever witnessed in an American beach
town. The destruction could not have been
more thorough had Hurricane Katrina made
landfall at PCB and parked itself here for a
week. The impact of this transformation has
been immediate and far-reaching. An esti-

mated 6,000 rooms have been lost as hotels
and motels get sold, razed and replaced with
armory-like high-rise condominium towers.

As a manager at Club La Vela ruefully put
it to us, "With an average of four people per
motel room, that's 24,000 fewer people per
week that Panama City Beach is able to accommodate during Spring Break. Our numbers
were way down this year." Beyond killing off
Spring Break, the condo-building boom has
kept vacationers away in droves.

What has happened is shocking and sicken-
ing. We used to love PCB's older motor courts
and unfancy, family-friendly ways. The area
known as Miracle Strip once bustled with activity. Now it is a fenced-off construction zone
that's unrecognizable, shadowy and dead, with
hardly an open hotel or motel to be found.
Cranes are everywhere, as legions of hardhats
erect beachside mausoleums for the investor
class. There's something horribly wrong with
this picture.

Real estate has become the place to make a
killing since the stock market began sputtering
and stalling. As a result condos have been rising on Panama City Beach faster than bamboo
in a rainforest. The scam goes something like
this: Units in a proposed beachfront condominium for which ground has not even been
broken are auctioned via lottery and sell out

© PARKE PUTERBAUGH

St. Andrews State Park

in a matter of hours. The lottery winners, who need only put down a $5,000 deposit, turn around and resell the unbuilt units they've just purchased to another speculator, who in turns does the same in a process known as "flipping." During this fool's gold rush, real-estate values in Panama City Beach have been doubling every six months.

This insane pyramid scheme will fall apart when buyers find themselves unable to sell their units for a profit and can't even recoup their investment. Then there will be a panic followed by a spectacular collapse of the real-estate market. Suddenly thousands of unwanted condo units in these drab, hurricane-vulnerable buildings will be available at fire-sale prices. Meantime, the sadder but wiser community of Panama City Beach will survey the ugly concrete towers that permanently transformed their beach while chasing off the tourists who'd long sustained their economy, and they'll wonder, "What the hell happened?"

Meanwhile, area businesses that depend on a regular stream of visitors have felt the pinch from the community's transformation. It's impacted restaurants, bars, amusement parks, convenience stores, drugstores—you name it, and it's closed or imperiled in PCB. Some of the oldest businesses on the beach have shut their doors for good. We heard the same refrain—"Business is down all over"—from one end of town to another. Club La Vela might eventually have to change its motto from "Party With Thousands" to "Party With Hundreds." Or dozens. A restaurateur confided to us that Club La Vela might be the next big landmark to go on the auction block.

And yet if you were to look at this evolution as a simple matter of economics, you might be tempted to conclude that PCB is booming. Rows of skyscraping condos stretch for miles. When we last passed through we heard that 38 more had been permitted and were awaiting groundbreaking. Each new project sells out as soon as the developers can obtain the necessary permits. Why is this happening in Panama City Beach? Because it is a bargain relative to all the other conquered corners of the Florida coast. Condos in PCB fetch $400 per square foot, versus $1,000 in Miami Beach. One 200-unit condo that existed only on paper

ENTER SANDMAN:
DR. BEACH AND THE RATINGS GAME

Panama City Beach has made extensive and prominent use of a number-one ranking that one of its beaches received from Dr. Stephen Leatherman, world-renowned architect of an annual beach-ratings list. The beach he rated so highly in 1995 for *Conde Nast Traveler* was St. Andrews State Park. As anyone who's been there knows, Panama City Beach is very different from St. Andrews in that there are no Wal-Marts, pancake houses, or Matterhorn-sized condominium projects at the latter. Moreover, St. Andrews has a back-beach area with sculpted dune formations that give some inkling of what the whole of Panama City Beach must have looked like at one time. You cannot blame PCB for capitalizing on its proximity to St. Andrews, though there is something misleading about acting like they are one and the same.

The man who pronounced St. Andrews the best beach in the world is widely known as "Dr. Beach," a handle that plays off his PhD in coastal geology. He is professor of Environmental Studies at Florida International University and director of their coastal research lab. Since 1991, Leatherman has annually rated the beaches for Conde Nast. Unfortunately, no sooner had he ranked St. Andrews number one than Hurricane Opal plowed through, ravaging the sparkling white sand, narrowing the beach, and flattening the dunes. Recent hurricanes have further damaged the beach, and when we were last there in September 2005, the air was toxic with red tide and large, dead fish lined the shore. Still, Panama City Beach touts St. Andrews' Number One ranking in 1995 as if it was announced yesterday.

Leatherman's lists, which change a lot from year to year, are received as gospel, and they are admittedly fun to read and to compare with years past. We do have to wonder a bit about the methodology, though. Take, for example, Leatherman's assertion that he examines 650 beaches around the country, subjecting each destination to a very rigid rating scale. (We have an image of a guy in a white lab coat stalking the beaches, pausing to hold a stethoscope to the sand.) His scientific scale involves

sold out within two and a half hours of going up for auction.

In record time, Panama City Beach has become as overbuilt and blighted as any locale on the East Coast, including North Miami Beach. Condos line the beach side of the road while there's retail decrepitude on the landward side. Yet as bad as PCB looks now, it will only get worse. And who are the beneficiaries? Certainly not long-time residents, who have watched their town get sold off to the highest bidders: out-of-town speculators who have no sense of the community and likely have never ever laid eyes on the condo units they hope to "flip." Someone's getting rich while an entire community is getting reamed.

"I don't like it," said a clerk at a convenience store with whom we spoke about the archi-

tectural carnage. "They're tearing everything down and putting up condos. Soon there won't be anything to do." She shrugged at what was basically a done deal. Most folks on the lower rungs of the socioeconomic ladder silently accept these blows against their community. What can they do? They're essentially powerless spectators watching the demise of their community while others with no ties to it profit obscenely. That's how it goes.

How quickly everything has changed. In previous decades, parts of Panama City Beach were actually known by separate names and had discernible personalities. Nowadays few residents have memories long enough to use the older names. For example, what used to get called "Biltmore Beach" is today referred to as East Panama City Beach. The one sectional

50 criteria, such as sand softness, water and air temperature, number of sunny days, currents, smell, pests, litter, access, crowds, and crime rate.

We don't mean to impugn Dr. Leatherman's unimpeachable credentials. His *Barrier Island Guidebook* – a brief, non-technical overview of processes that shape coastal barriers – is one of our bibles. Yet simple math shows that if this assertion is to be believed, he must "very rigidly" measure and assess 32,500 criteria (50 multiplied by 650) per year in order to calculate his final ratings. That works out to about 89 criteria assessed on a daily basis. Only on-site inspections will do, given such subjective measures of beach worthiness as "softness" and "smell." This necessitates constant travel to the coastal margins. Moreover, what about the wrenches that an atypical day at the beach might throw into the works? How is time of year accounted for? What if you visited Panama City Beach in December and Malibu in June? Would you be seeing each place at its best or worst, and is that a fair measure of overall merit? What about beaches that have been artificially renourished? Are they docked for not being natural or given added points for their people-pleasing width?

No, we're not envious of Dr. Beach, who's got too much ground to cover and too many criteria to track. Meanwhile, his annual Top Ten list has made him the Casey Kasem of coastal scientists. He is widely cited by other Florida beach towns that have shown up on his lists. We recall a newspaper story out of Siesta Key, which felt that it had undeservedly been left off the good professor's Top Ten. They bade him visit, he was duly impressed, and Siesta Key turned up on his 1992 list.

We are somewhat amused by his celebrity, since academics rarely get to cash in at the pop-culture trough. At the same time, we've got to hand it to him for coming up with such a marketable idea. The one thing that makes it a bit of a gimmick (albeit an entertaining one) is that the beaches don't change from year to year as dramatically as his lists do.

In the introductory portion of this book, we've come up with a list of what we consider to be Florida's best beaches. Please don't think we're jumping on anyone's bandwagon. Just so you know, we've been drawing up such lists since we began working on our first beach book in 1984 – well before either Leatherman or Letterman got into the Top Ten list-making game.

identification that's still in regular (though declining) usage is Miracle Strip. This seven-mile stretch along Front Beach Road between Thomas Drive and Panama Beach City Pier is also known as Middle Panama City Beach. And West Panama City Beach refers to a string of small communities—Laguna Beach, Santa Monica, Sunnyside, Hollywood Beach, and Inlet Beach—between S.R. 79 and Phillips Inlet. Since Panama City Beach's incorporation as a massive linear municipality in 1969, those other names have gone into gradual disuse. Technically and practically, it's all Panama City Beach now. Just for the record, Phillips Inlet—the western boundary of PCB—is not an actual inlet but a coastal dune lake.

Panama City Beach lies well north of the warm subtropical meccas way down on the Florida Peninsula. If you should find yourself in Panama City Beach some winter day, you may wind up with the shivers. We spent one of the coldest days of our lives in PCB during a blustery December. The mercury dropped well below freezing after nightfall, and the wind was stiff and penetrating. In Florida? Yes, in Florida. This experience drove home the point that PCB must make hay when the sun shines—which explains why it adopted Spring Break after Fort Lauderdale and Daytona Beach had sent it packing.

Of course, these days they're looking for more bigger bucks than a bunch of half-naked, beer-swilling Spring Breakers can deliver. Panama City Beach has willingly made a deal with the devil, and it looks like hell as a result.

For more information, contact the Panama

LOOK OUT JOE, HERE COMES ARVIDA

Outside of its coastal strip, a huge portion of Bay County is owned by a single corpo-ration. The Jacksonville-based St. Joe Company is far and away the largest private landowner in the state of Florida, with 1.2 million acres. Most of it is Panhandle tim-berland, though they also own 39 miles of coastline. Its holdings in Florida amount to an area the size of the state of Delaware.

St. Joe is an old industrial company (founded in 1936) involved in timber and paper. Lately, it decided to become a modern real-estate company. To that end, St. Joe lured Peter Rummell, the former head of the Disney empire's "Imagineering Group," to become its CEO in 1996. A year later, St. Joe acquired a controlling interest in Arvida, the mammoth, Boca Raton–based developer. The idea was to pair St. Joe's huge land-holdings with Arvida's expertise at developing large-scale residential projects.

East of Destin, the Panhandle hasn't quite been ruined by bamboo-thick develop-ment like the rest of Florida. Therefore investors and developers have pounced on this last frontier like birds of prey on road kill. Already, St. Joe/Arvida has con-structed massive residential developments on its Panhandle acreage. How's this for hubris? In 2002, St. Joe actually proposed renaming the Panhandle "Florida's Great Northwest." They thought "panhandle" sounded too declassé.

Here's a typical news nugget from Walton County, reported without an eye being batted: "Walton County has approved WaterSound North – another St. Joe-Arvida project on the east end of the county north of Highway 98, along the Intracoastal Waterway. The first phase consists of 478 homes on 560 acres. The development will eventually cover over 1,400 acres and have 1,000 homes. Plans have already been approved for a 150-acre commerce park nearby."

As for Bay County, check this out item from 2004: "The state has issued a blanket wetlands permit to allow St. Joe to develop 18,000 acres in Bay County north of the East Bay and Panama City Beach. This area is west of S.R. 79, near the planned international airport."

Oh, yeah, the airport. Panama City Beach already has an airport that's only 10 years old and hardly overtaxed by air traffic. But St. Joe wanted a new one, so it twisted arms in Tallahassee, Florida, and Washington, DC – which is to say the Bush brothers, U.S. president, and Florida governor, respectively. And so the Panama City-Bay County International Airport is on the drawing board, with 80 percent of its projected $200 million cost to be borne by taxpayers. Such a sweet deal! Okay, some pesky environmental permits are holding things up, but you know how the Bush administration works – i.e., these things can be handled.

As *Miami Herald* columnist and novelist Carl Hiaasen wrote: "If St. Joe pulls this off, even its critics would have to marvel. What a feat for a private company to get a big-city airport built purely to advance its own agenda. Of course, it helps that the attorney overseeing the St. Joe's Bay County projects was co-chairman of the Bush presidential campaign in the Panhandle."

Some of the locals are none too pleased with the big plans drawn up by St. Joe/Ar-vida and their county commissioners. What chance do ordinary people have when the deck's stacked so blatantly in favor of those with money and power?

"People in rural Bay County have been fighting the illegal annexation of their community for years with no help from the Bay County Commission," complained a letter-writer to the *Panama City News-Herald*.

Isn't that always the way it seems to go?

City Beach Convention and Visitors Bureau, P.O. Box 9473, Panama City Beach, FL 32417, 850/233-5070 or 800/PC-BEACH, www.thebeachloversbeach.com; or the Greater Panama City Beaches Chamber of Commerce, 415 Beckrich Road, Suite 200, Panama City Beach, FL 32407, 850/235-1159, www.pcbeach.org.

BEACHES

Swimming in PCB can be tough if you're an adult. The water is so shallow for so great a distance that unless you're willing to walk out more than 100 feet and swim through a floating mass of seaweed, you will find total immersion to be nearly impossible. We had to lay in the water, as if in a bathtub, to get our heads wet. It barely came up to our knees. That makes it a really safe beach for young kids but little fun for people who really want to swim or ride waves. Why is this so? We're guessing these inshore shallows have something to do with the sand renourishment that's been necessary to restore eroded beaches after a decade's worth of serial hurricanes. Perhaps the sand added to the system has been reworked by wind and waves, forming a huge sandbar. In any case, it doesn't make for great swimming.

Between St. Andrews State Park to Phillips Inlet, Panama City Beach encompasses 26 miles of sandy gulf shoreline. The water changes colors at different times of day, from emerald to azure to coral, and the white, nearly pure quartz sand provides a striking contrast. Any randomly chosen part of this shoreline, if viewed from dune line to water—sans the motels and high-rises—is what the word "beach" conjures in most people's desert-island fantasies.

All that said, for a city in desperate need of—no, entirely dependent upon—the public swarm from March through September, PCB has not done very well at providing public beach access. West of St. Andrews State Park, a few street endings lead to dune walkovers, but parking is minimal (and more often nonexistent), and the public beaches along the

Miracle Strip are scarce. Granted, most who come here are staying at oceanfront hotels or condos and don't need public beach access. But what about the visitors whose motels don't abut the ocean? And what about city and county residents? As former President Bill Clinton once said, "We can do better." (He, of all people, should know.)

The best public accesses in PCB are **Bay County Pier and Park** (a.k.a. M. B. Miller Park), at the center of the Miracle Strip, and **Panama Beach City Pier** (a.k.a. Dan Russell Municipal Pier). Both provide free parking and facilities. The Panama City Beach Convention and Visitors Bureau maintains an information center a stone's throw from County Pier, which has a half-mile of beach and free parking. City Pier (which lies west of County Pier) is home to B's Pier Cafe an impressively broad beach. The pier and beach are open all night.

Two smaller beach parks in PCB are **Thomas Drive Park,** in East Panama City Beach, and **Bid-o-Wee Beach,** between the county and city piers. Thomas Drive Park lies just east of Club La Vela and Spinnaker (see *Nightlife*). It's got 80 or so parking spaces, basic facilities, and a boardwalk to the beach. Bid-o-Wee Beach isn't really a formalized access but one of the few remaining undeveloped beachfront parcels in PCB. The county and city parks departments couldn't offer us any information on it, and neither claimed responsibility for its ownership or upkeep. It lies between the Fiesta and Fontainebleau Hotels on Front Beach Road. Just park by the side of the road and walk the crossovers to the beach, noting the natural look of the dunes. It is, as one local put it to us, "the beach the way it used to be." Up in **West Panama City Beach,** a number of marked accesses (at least a dozen, by our rough count) lead onto the beach.

PCB has an interesting (read: not very effective) system for patrolling its beaches: they hoist colored flags. Recently they've upgraded their flag system to five: blue flag (dangerous marine life), green flag (low hazard: calm conditions), yellow flag (medium hazard: moderate surf and/or currents), red flag (high hazard: high surf and/or strong currents), two red flags (water closed to public). While lifeguards are stationed at the two piers, the rest of PCB's 26 miles is watched by the Panama City Beach Patrol, which scoots up and down the beach on big-wheeled carts.

The big problem at Panama City Beach is rip currents. The United States Lifesaving Association, has spoken critically of Panama City Beach's surf-rescue system. In their defense, 26 miles is a lot of beach to keep tabs on and adequate funding for such a big job is an issue.

3 THOMAS DRIVE PARK

Location: 7,000 block of Thomas Drive in Panama City Beach
Parking/Fees: free parking lot
Hours: sunrise-sunset
Facilities: restrooms and showers
Contact: Bay County Parks Division, 850/784-4066

4 BAY COUNTY PIER AND PARK (A.K.A. M.B. MILLER PARK)

Location: between 13,623 and 14,401 Front Drive Road in Panama City Beach
Parking/Fees: free parking lot
Hours: sunrise-sunset
Facilities: lifeguards (seasonal), restrooms, picnic tables, showers, and visitors center
Contact: Bay County Parks Division, 850/784-4066

5 BID-O-WEE BEACH

Location: between the 13,000 and 14,000 blocks of Front Beach Road in Panama City Beach
Parking/Fees: free roadside parking

Hours: 24 hours
Facilities: none
Contact: Panama City Parks and Recreation Department, 850/233-5040

6 PANAMA BEACH CITY PIER (A.K.A. DAN RUSSELL MUNICIPAL PIER)

Location: 16,000 block of Front Beach Road in Panama City Beach
Parking/Fees: free parking lot
Hours: 24 hours
Facilities: concessions, lifeguards (seasonal), restrooms, and showers
Contact: Panama Beach City Pier, 850/233-5080

7 WEST PANAMA CITY BEACH ACCESSES

Location: numerous marked accesses along Front Beach Road between City Pier and Phillips Inlet in West Panama City Beach
Parking/Fees: free roadside parking
Hours: sunrise-sunset
Facilities: none
Contact: Bay County Parks Division, 850/784-4066

RECREATION AND ATTRACTIONS

- **Boat Cruise:** Captain Davis Queen Fleet, 5550 North Lagoon Drive, Panama City Beach, 850/234-3435
- **Dive Shop:** Panama City Dive Center, 4823 Thomas Drive, Panama City Beach, 850/235-3390
- **Ecotourism:** Shell Island Shuttle, Pier Concession Store, St. Andrews State Park, 4607 State Park Lane, Panama City Beach, 850/235-4004
- **Fishing Charters:** Captain Anderson's Marina, 5550 North Lagoon Drive, Panama City Beach, 850/234-3435

- **Marina:** Captain Anderson's Marina, 5550 North Lagoon Drive, Panama City Beach, 850/234-3435
- **Piers:** Panama Beach City Pier (a.k.a. Dan Russell Pier), 16101 Front Beach Road, Panama City Beach, 850/233-5080; County Pier (a.k.a. M. B. Miller Park), 12213 Front Beach Road, Panama City Beach
- **Rainy-Day Attraction:** Gulf World Marine Park, 15412 Front Beach Road, Panama City Beach, 850/234-5271
- **Shopping/Browsing:** Alvin's Island, 12010 Front Beach Road, Panama City Beach, 850/234-3048
- **Surf Shop:** Liquid Dreams Surf Shop, 545 Beckrich Road, Panama City Beach, 8850/230-0572
- **Vacation Rentals:** Beachfront Condominiums, 2317 Magnolia Drive, Panama City Beach, 850/234-3935 or 800/242-6636

ACCOMMODATIONS

There's a lot of beach in Panama City Beach, and there are sure a lot of condos along it. The town is like the world's longest run-on sentence. What you won't find enough of, however, is overnight accommodations. The old one- and two-story beachfront motels have become an endangered species, displaced by predatory condos. What has happened in PCB is tantamount to putting a shark in a koi pond.

You can find a few old motels of longstanding still doing business: the **Fiesta Motel** (13623 Front Beach Road, 850/235-1000, $$), **Bikini Beach Resort** (11001 Front Beach Road, 850/234-3392, $$), and the **Majestic Motel** (10901 Front Beach Road, 850/230-1400, $$). However, many more have been torn down. When we last passed through, for instance, The Trade Winds Motel was a mound of rubble, although its sign still stood, bearing the self-evident message "Motel Closed" as well as the words "Condo Sales on Site."

Most of PCB's remaining accommodations can be found along the Miracle Strip, a dense-ly developed seven-mile stretch along Front Beach Road. The **Holiday Inn Sunspree Resort** (11127 Front Beach Road, 850/234-1111, $$$) and the **Edgewater Resort** (11212 Front Beach Road, 850/235-4044, $$$$) anchor the strip at the pricier end. The Holiday Inn offers clean, well-kept rooms and balconies overlooking the gulf, plus upscale amenities like a fitness center, beachside tiki bar, swan boats, cabanas, and chaise lounges. One of the city's few lifeguard stands is directly behind the Holiday Inn.

The Edgewater is a golf and tennis resort spread out among 15 buildings on the beach and across the highway. Units in the five high-rise buildings on the beach offer eye-popping views of the emerald water and white sand from their balconies. The villas on the inland side offer homey comforts and conveniences. The Edgewater, with a total of 540 units, is a city-within-a-city.

A recent arrival on the beachfront is **Legacy by the Sea** (15325 Front Beach Road, 850/249-8601, $$$). It's as tall as the condo towers further down the beach but operates like a hotel. The idea of a luxury hotel in Panama City Beach is a bit of a wishful anomaly, and we wonder exactly how a brand-new building figures it can lay claim to any sort of "legacy." Still, we're grateful that it isn't a condominium.

At one time not so long ago, four hotels in close proximity were collectively known as the Boardwalk Beach Resort. Of those four, none of the originals remains. However, the **Boardwalk Beach Resort** (9400 South Thomas Drive, 850/234-3483, $$$$) lives on as a condominium, convention center, and hotel. A tall sucker, too.

Just for the record, the ugliest condo we've ever seen is right on the beach at PCB. It's called **The Summit** (8743 Thomas Drive). Admittedly it's an odd name for a building that is, in fact, an architectural nadir. This 15-story, 30-unit-wide structure looks like the sort of institution from which one would try to escape. Sling some barbed wire around the property and it could pass for a prison. Unfortunately, Panama City Beach has been overtaken by such constructions.

COASTAL CUISINE

If, as doctors often advise, breakfast is the most important meal of the day, you're in luck in Panama City Beach. With a Pancakes Plus, Blue Top Waffle Shoppe, Thomas Drive Waffle & Omelet House, three Waffle Shoppes, and five Waffle Houses—not to mention five McMuffin-vending McDonald's—we deduced that breakfast may be the only meal served with any regularity to visitors (especially Spring Breakers), who nurse their hangovers with pancakes and bottomless mugs of coffee. We stumbled onto a deal at the **All-American Diner** (10590 Front Beach Road, 850/235-2443, and 15406 Front Beach Road, 850/233-6007, $), where we snagged an all-you-can-eat breakfast for about six bucks.

Lunch and dinner are different propositions. The choices are as staggering as the appetites brought to them by an army of people who have been playing on the beach all day. Many a beachfront eatery proclaims itself a "grille" or "pub." The advantage of hitting such places—such as **Hammerhead Fred's Grill & Bar** (8752 Thomas Drive, 850/233-3907, $$), to name one of the more popular ones—is that you can eat, drink, and party on the same premises. **Shuckums Oyster Pub & Seafood Grill** (15618 Front Beach Road, 850/234-3214, $$), another friendly indoor/outdoor saloon, is located at the west end of the Strip. Local oysters are their forte and each order is shucked in front of you.

The best-known seafood restaurant in town is unquestionably **Capt. Anderson's** (5551 North Lagoon Drive, 850/234-2225, $$$), which was voted the best seafood restaurant in Florida by readers of *Southern Living* magazine three years in a row. Capt. Anderson's is an oasis of stability in maddeningly volatile PCB. The seafood dishes are reliably good. The service is prompt, efficient, and friendly. The restaurant is extremely well-run by the Patro-

nis brothers, Yonnie and Theo. It is so beloved an operation that even the employees stick around. Two of its workers have been there more 50 years, and 30 have worked here for a quarter-century or longer. That's loyalty.

We too feel loyal to Capt. Anderson's, making sure to dine there every time we come to PCB. On our most recent visit, we had their signature appetizer, broiled shrimp in a plate of spicy oil, for starters, and then moved on to grouper imperial (broiled fillet topped with crabmeat) and one of their fisherman's platters. The World's Finest Seafood Platter (drum roll, please) is heaped with crab, shrimp, scallops, and fish, served fried ($20.95) or broiled ($22.95). We'd recommend getting it broiled and—although it'll hike the price by $9—adding a half stuffed Florida lobster. This underwater crustacean, which we prefer to its better-known New England counterpart, is available seasonally from August to March.

Capt. Anderson's most popular menu items are shrimp (cooked five different ways) and grouper. If it's listed, you should by all means order scamp. No, not "scampi." Scamp is a member of the grouper family and tastes so good that fishermen tend to keep what little they catch for themselves.

You really can't go wrong with any seafood item at Capt. Anderson's. As Yonnie Patronis told us, with no false modesty, "The seafood in this market is as good as you'll find anywhere in the world." Capt. Anderson's does a huge business, serving up to 2,000 meals a night at the height of the season, but they are equipped to do so professionally and efficiently.

The fishing fleet unloads its daily catch outside the picture windows, and you can watch the show from the patio bar, a popular watering hole for locals and a great place to start a memorable dining experience. The decor showcases nautical artifacts around mahogany walls, slate floors, coral-tree chandeliers, and even a fireplace (in Florida?!). Crab traps filled with whelk shells hang from the ceilings. There are several large dining rooms, and you'd better memorize the route if you hope to find your way back from the restroom.

Capt. Anderson's is open for dinner six nights a week; they also have an oyster bar and cocktail lounge on the sizable (capacity 660) premises. They do an out-the-door-popular business from Spring Break through summer's end, and then shut down from mid-November to early February. "Once school opens up, it's like turning off a spigot," owner Jimmy Patronis says.

Nearby, on Grand Lagoon, is **Hamilton's** (5711 North Lagoon Drive, 850/234-1255, $$$), another popular seafood house that specializes in cooking fresh catches over mesquite hardwood and charcoal. An interesting assortment of Greek and Cajun-tinged salads and entrees are on the menu, including snapper etoufee, snapper Lafont (stuffed with shrimp, crab, and cheese), snapper St. Charles (sauteed in olive oil), and shrimp Christo (baked in olive oil with Greek seasonings).

While we seldom mention any restaurant that is not on or near the water, **Canopies** (4423 U.S. 98, 850/872-8444, $$$) is a rare treat, offering casual fine dining. Canopies is located two miles east of Hathaway Bridge in Panama City. Their grilled grouper with crispy crawfish tails and Cajun hollandaise sauce is irresistibly fine. Ditto the trio of grouper, salmon, and tuna with citrus beurre blanc.

NIGHTLIFE

Two clubs in Panama City Beach have dominated the nightlife for many years: **Club La Vela** (8813 Thomas Drive, 850/234-3866) and **Spinnaker** (8795 Thomas Drive, 850/234-7882). Both are the size of airplane hangers, and they are adjacent to each other, along Thomas Drive at the east end of PCB. Club La Vela is the more lascivious of the two, especially since Spinnaker began repositioning itself as a more family-friendly kind of place.

Club La Vela boasts of being the "largest nightclub in the USA," with 48 bar stations, 13 dance floors, five bandstands, and a capacity of 7,000. Regular features include wet T-shirt and bikini contests and male and female

revues. The statistics at Spinnaker are only slightly less staggering: 34 bar stations and three stages for live music. At the height of Spring Break, admission to Club La Vela runs $25 (ouch!) and $15 at Spinnaker. Both are open 10 A.M.–4 A.M.

Sharky's Beach Club (15201 Front Beach Road, 850/235-2420) made headlines back in 1998 when it was the site of a series of Tuesday contests entitled "Sex on the Beach." Participants "gathered in a circle and simulated sex acts," according to a newspaper account. Some of the simulations went too far for the local constables, who arrested three women. Spring Break fun at Sharky's these days is less libidinous than that, but it's still a fun place to party. The other popular hangout is **Hammerhead Fred's Island Grill & Bar** (8752 Thomas Drive, 850/233-3907). The party tent at Hammerhead Fred's is always a hot spot over Spring Break.

Beyond these titans of the nightlife, after-dinner activities in PCB range from the virtuous to the venial. That is to say, there's praying and sinning. Praying can be done at **Noah's Ark Recreation Center** (12902 Front Beach Road, 850/234-6062), which is housed inside a large wooden boat. It offers family entertainment to keep the young'uns from ending up at the sorts of places whose doors we darkened, where the only praying done is for the speedy delivery of one's next beer and all eyes are glued to nearly naked angels.

The best known and least shocking of these establishments is **Hooters** (12709 Front Beach Road, 850/230-9464). The Hooters concept normally seems desperately lame—waitresses with orange gym shorts and tight T-shirts accentuating their hooters—but in PCB it seems to work because they're basically dressed no differently than the beach bunnies strolling the sand. The location in PCB is only the Hooters franchise that's located directly on the beach. The food is stunningly mediocre (cheesy, sodium-doused wings are a specialty), but the grouper sandwich is passable and the beach view is a winner.

Along these same lines, but less coy about their motives, is a harem's worth of exotic dance clubs in Panama City (the military town across the bay) and Panama City Beach. One day we found ourselves stuck in traffic behind a van with this come-on affixed to its rear: "Topless Dancers—Follow Me." And so we did. We were particularly impressed with the talent at **Show N Tail** (5518 Thomas Drive, 850/233-1717). If you think we're overdoing it, keep in mind that this is the Florida Panhandle, where you're never far from a military base or a rowdy beach (or both), and topless clubs are part of the landscape.

One forlorn night not long after Labor Day, we angled into a place called the Big Easy, on Front Beach Road. The choice was pretty much made for us, since nothing else was open. It was big and friendly, with draft beer served in plastic pitchers, plenty of classic rock on the CD jukebox, and pool tables and dartboards to pass the time. We watched waves of restaurant workers come in for a nightcap after their shifts, and had us a fine time in the sort of bar we love to frequent. Alas, the Big Easy is no more, as it got "bought off" and who knows or cares what's there now. However, **The Big Easy 2** (17190 West U.S. 98, 850/234-6770), located out on the highway, is still serving a thirsty crowd (no pool tables, though). So is **Foghorn's** (8011 Thomas Drive, 850/235-1243), which does have pool tables and such.

One of the longest-running beach bars in Panama City Beach was Salty's but it got closed and razed, and a condominium is going up in its place. There are rumors that the owners are taking a year off and will open will reopen a new Salty's on Thomas Drive. What's left? Well, you can still go to **Schooners, the Last Local Beach Club** (5121 Gulf Drive, 850/235-3555). They serve lunch and dinner (fried oysters, grilled grouper), have live entertainment (bands with names like Sticks & Stones and Latitude), and have an extremely loyal clientele who will probably riot if it ever closes down.

But back to Salty's, which held its "last dance" on September 25, 2004. The symbolism seemed appropriate. In a very real sense, the curtain is descending on Panama City Beach as it was known and loved for generations.

SEASIDE AND THE STYLISH COMMUNITIES OF SOUTH WALTON COUNTY

Seaside and its surrounding communities in Walton County collectively compose the most stylish corner of the Florida coast. Imagine a string of tony, tasteful, and exclusive communities like Key Biscayne (on Florida's East Coast) arrayed in a row, and that is the surprising lay of the land up here on the Panhandle. Walton County's 26 miles of beaches are renowned for their blindingly white, powdery quartz sand, mountainous sand dunes (though hurricanes have pared back their height), and glistening, turquoise gulf waters. Add the remaining pockets of tasteful, low-key architecture, numerous gourmet restaurants, and miles of lovely white quartz-grained sand beaches, and you've got a county to which savvy vacationers gravitate.

Walton is best known for the designer beach town of Seaside. It is also home to Grayton Beach and Topsail Hill Preserve State Parks, which have breathtaking, windswept beaches. In addition, there are the older beach towns of Seagrove and Grayton Beach; the low-rise, high-end residential communities of Dune-Allen Beach and Blue Mountain Beach; and the tony stylings of Sandestin, a mammoth condo and golf resort.

Having praised Walton County to the skies in past editions, we feel must come down to earth in this one, because things have been changing at an alarming rate. As Joni Mitchell sang, they've paved paradise and put up a parking lot—not to mention more residential developments than a county as kissed by nature as Walton should have to endure. Walton County's natural assets are being sorely tested by this reckless and sudden assault, much of which has been triggered by the relentless plundering of the St. Joe/Arvida corporation. All we ever seem to see on the roads in south Walton County these days is cement trucks churning batches of concrete for the next gulf- or sound hogging development that's been green-lighted by the

© PARKE PUTERBAUGH

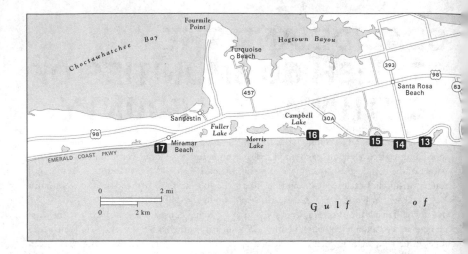

pliable county commission. In other words, south Walton County is falling all over itself to become the next South Florida. Therefore, you should take with a grain of salt any puff pieces you might read in *Southern Living,* the Sunday newspaper's travel section, or an airline magazine when they exclaim over the quaint, unspoiled beaches of south Walton County.

Inlet Beach and Carillon Beach

Traveling from east to west, the first links in the chain of beach communities in south Walton County are Inlet Beach and Carillon Beach. As still-embryonic communities, they don't make much of an impression beyond the signs announcing their existence, such as "Downtown Carillon: "Shop - Eat - Jazz - Fun." Voila! Instant community. Or so they'd have you believe.

We recall a roadside produce stand hereabouts where oranges grown on the other side of Florida and grapes picked in California were being sold. To us it seemed a kind of symbol for south Walton County, where everything is ever so slightly faux. At the same time we bear in mind that faux with good taste is preferable to wretched with bad taste.

For more information, contact the South Walton Tourist Development Council, C.R. 331 and U.S. 98, P.O. Box 1248, Santa Rosa Beach, FL 32459, 850/267-1216 or 800/822-6877, www.beachesofsouthwalton.com.

BEACHES

Camp Helen State Park, occupying 183 acres at Inlet Beach, became part of the Florida state parks system in 1997, and not a moment too soon. The acreage is covered with old live oak trees, Spanish moss hanging from their gnarled limbs. One of the oaks that has collapsed is propped up with a concrete pillar like an old man leaning on a cane. The park's centerpiece is Inlet Beach Pier, located at Phillips Inlet (which is actually an outflow for Lake Powell, a coastal dune lake). Camp Helen has picnic pavilions and a gleaming new visitor center with exhibits.

The state of Florida purchased the land for $13.5 million. It was spared the fate of becoming another exclusive beach community when Gulf Coast Community College drew up a management plan for the tract. The 183-acre state park is home to two dozen species of endangered or threatened plants and animals, including snowy and ploving pipers and loggerhead sea turtles. It is also the site of an old log lodge that dates back to the 1930s. Until its acquisition, the property belonged to a

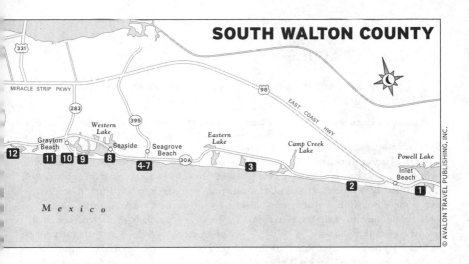

© AVALON TRAVEL PUBLISHING, INC.

SOUTH WALTON COUNTY

textile manufacturer in DeFuniak Springs that used it as a summer camp for its employees from 1932 until 1989. Those were the days when companies actually gave a hoot about their loyal workers. Some of the old buildings survive on the grounds.

Various groups are working to acquire more land surrounding Lake Powell—one of the largest coastal dune lakes in Florida, located on the Bay-Walton County line. We wish them well, because preserved land is sorely needed on the Panhandle, where everything's being developed faster than you can say "bulldozer."

■ CAMP HELEN STATE PARK

Location: off Scenic C.R. 30-A at Phillips Inlet, in Inlet Beach
Parking/Fees: $2 per vehicle entrance fee
Hours: 8 A.M.-sunset
Facilities: restrooms, picnic tables and a visitor center
Contact: Camp Helen State Park, 850/233-5059

ACCOMMODATIONS

Don't look for resorts or restaurants at this end of the county, but for vacation rentals in Inlet Beach, try **Panhandle Realty** (850/234-6823).

Rosemary Beach

Twenty-eight miles east of Destin, at the far end of "Scenic 30-A," Rosemary Beach is a work in perpetual progress. It was initially inspired by Seaside's "neotraditional" example. Indeed, Andres Duany, who co-created Seaside's town plan, also worked on the plan for Rosemary Beach, and some of the same architects have designed these handsome luxury residences and businesses. Where Seaside was done up in pastels, Rosemary Beach is executed in earth tones—"rosemary green" being one of them—and is described as "old Caribbean" with "singular homes, open spaces, and intimate courtyards, woven together by lanes, sand paths and boardwalks."

Blah, blah, blah. Don't believe a word of it. The "cottages" and "carriage houses" are packed so close together that Rosemary Beach looks more like the New York City borough of Queens.

Nowhere in south Walton County has the "new urbanism" concept overshot its mark wider than at Rosemary Beach. Duany, who coauthored *Suburban Nation: The Rise of Sprawl and the Decline of the American Dream*, must wonder what he hath wrought. Here, in this instant city of absentee homeowners, part-time residents, and real-estate speculators,

---

BEST BEACHES

◖ Grayton Beach State Park: Top 25 (page 529)

◖ Topsail Hill Preserve State Park: Top 25 (page 535)

---

one finds more construction workers than vacationers. They generate a ceaseless cacophony of hammering, sawing, and buzzing. Foremen in hard hats bark orders into cell phones as they trudge through faux village streets barely wide enough for two of the ubiquitous SUVs to pass one another.

The fulsome prose in a Rosemary Beach tourist brochure puts it like this: "On a perfect beach, a new town is taking shape…" But it has been taking shape at a nonstop, breakneck pace for 10 years, exploding like an aggravated form of cancer. In 2001, it drove one guy off the deep end. Claiming he'd had all he could take of the runaway construction and associated noise, he anonymously threatened to blow up something in Rosemary Beach, necessitating evacuation. Aside from that brief respite, the pace of construction and its attendant annoyances have continued unabated since. At least there's now a "Solace Day Spa" in town if the clamor drives you batty.

Behind all the barriers, tractors, cranes, tubes, wires, pipes, bricks, cement trucks, and asphalt rollers, one can see that Rosemary Beach superficially offers all the same features as Seaside: a town center with two town greens (which are the size of postage stamps), a town hall, neighborhood pools, paths, and boardwalk. However, the sense of community is completely contrived because Rosemary Beach is utterly exclusive, wealth-dependent, off-putting, and imitative. The accolades it bestows upon itself must make the shills who write it cringe at night before drifting off to sleep. Take these well-spun lines, obviously intended to reassure those who came for peace and quiet and not the ceaseless din of a construction zone: "Our town will have a different look every time you visit… but the Rosemary Beach Tradition will remain the same." Only in America can a city that didn't exist in 1995 refer, without irony, to its "tradition."

One of the most annoying things about Rosemary Beach is that even though it is oppressively upscale, it projects the pretense of being just another funky, down-to-earth beach village. You see such faux downscale affectations as Shabby Slips—a high-priced shoppe that, best as we can figure, sells stuff to toss over designer furniture to make it look old—and Carpenter's Market, a faux ramshackle roadside shack that offers such downhome Old Florida victuals as guacamole, pate, and gourmet crackers.

Oh, it's nice in Rosemary Beach, to be sure, suffocatingly so. Every square inch has been meticulously groomed, sculpted, and retrofitted to give you as authentic a sense of historical legacy as one of the European villages at Busch Gardens. It looks real, in other words, but it has no soul. And it's now as built out and hemmed in as North Miami Beach. Had the developers stopped about halfway through what's here now and let the "community" really grow in a natural way, they might have succeeded in creating something along the lines of Seaside—which, by comparison, seems like the anomalous miracle it probably is. There is no guiding vision to Rosemary Beach. It is a concept without an endpoint, just "more, more, more," as Billy Idol shouted in "Rebel Yell." We started shouting ourselves on the latest pass through town as we were forced to detour around all the construction and an army of workers. Signs read: "Pardon Our Construction! Shops Are Open." And what is that hideous three-story colossus that extends from the highway to the so-called green?

SOUTH WALTON COUNTY

Nineteen strung-together communities make up "the beaches of south Walton County." It's a different world once you cross Phillips Inlet and leave Panama City Beach behind. Whereas the architectural parameters that define Panama City Beach tend to be honky-tonk and high-rise, Walton County riffs mostly on a Florida vernacular theme, pioneered by Seaside's experiment in New Urbanism. If Panama City Beach epitomizes the 7-Eleven mentality, Walton County's mind-set is more along the lines of Starbucks. Panama City Beach is overbuilt, and Walton County seemed to, at least in the past, proceed with caution lest it become like its neighbor.

At the same time, the heavily Republican south end of the county (where the beaches are) has talked of secession, chafing at the restrictions and wanting to put the pedal to the metal in terms of development. It would be a shame if Walton County went the way of so many others in Florida. We do not need more Destins and Marco Islands, with shady outside investors subverting the local public's will in order to erect godawful condominium blocks for absentee owners. Please, heed a pair of beach bums who have seen it all: Leave well enough alone!

Between Inlet Beach and Dune-Allen Beach runs the 18-mile Scenic County Road 30-A Bike Path. About half its length is off-road, and the rest parallels Scenic County Road 30-A, the great gulf-hugging highway that spans the length of the county. We can imagine nothing nicer than working up a good sweat and/or appetite by spending the day cruising scenic south Walton on a two-wheeler.

Just for the record, none of south Walton's 19 "coastal communities" is incorporated. Not even Seaside.

Paradoxically, Rosemary Beach's impact and example might wind up being even more pervasive than Seaside's. The desire to create a community was never the highest priority here. It's really been driven by speculative marketing—in a word, greed. As more of these "communities" along Scenic C.R. 30-A pile on the development, property values for every piece of land on or near the coast has risen beyond the wildest fantasies of longtime landowners. As a consequence, state and local governments will be unable to afford a single sliver more than what they already own. Thus, there will be no new beach parks or open spaces than what already exists. From here on out, it's all "in-fill."

The construction frenzy that has overtaken Rosemary Beach, Seacrest Beach, Seagrove, WaterColor, Grayton Beach, Santa Rosa Beach, Dune-Allen Beach, Blue Mountain Beach, and Miramar Beach will eventually spread across the entire Panhandle. It will even engulf those counties east of here that like to refer to themselves as the "Forgotten Coast." This is not some cynical dystopian prediction. It is happening as you read these words.

As a ranger at Grayton Beach State Recreation Area ruefully told us, "We've just got to hold on to what little we got left."

For more information, contact Rosemary Beach, P.O. Box 611070, Rosemary Beach, FL 32461, 850/231-2900 or 888/855-1551, www.rosemarybeach.com.

ACCOMMODATIONS

When the construction dust finally settles, the **Pensione in Rosemary Beach** (Town Center, 888/855-1551, $$$) may emerge as one of the smarter things created here. An overnight lodge anywhere along Scenic C.R. 30-A is welcome, and the Pensione is classy but not overly ostentatious: eight rooms on three floors within a brief stroll of the Gulf of Mexico. Breakfast comes with the room. It's served at **Onano** (850/231-2436), the "neighborhood cafe" on the ground floor. Onano also features "Northern Italian" cuisine at night, as well as fresh local seafood.

Fully one-third of the homes in Rosemary Beach are available for vacation rental. Carriage houses range in size 400–1,000 square feet and rent for roughly $1,200–2,100 per week. Cottages have anywhere from two to six bedrooms ($1,540–8,000 per week). Eight thousand dollars a week?! It's your money. You can browse units online at www.rosemarybeach.com.

Seacrest Beach

Seacrest Beach lies 26 miles east of Destin, along Scenic C.R. 30-A. It is the first in a consecutive trio of "sea"-named communities, the others being Seagrove Beach and Seaside. Seacrest is another recently introduced development of cottages reposing between the dunes that have been modeled after the tasteful and stringently controlled example of Seaside, the mother of all "new traditionalist" coastal communities. Really, though, it's a singularly unappealing burlesque of Seaside. A riot of non-native stubby palms have been planted, accentuating the designer fakery. Just west of Seacrest, a beach access point named **Gulf Lake Beach** has appeared at Camp Creek Coastal Lake.

For more information, contact South Walton Tourist Development Council, C.R. 331 and U.S. 98, P.O. Box 1248, Santa Rosa Beach, FL 32459, 850/267-1216 or 800/822-6877, www.beachesofsouthwalton.com.

BEACHES

2 GULF LAKE BEACH

Location: at Camp Creek coastal lake on Scenic C.R. 30-A, just west of Seacrest
Parking/Fees: free small parking lot
Hours: 24 hours
Facilities: none

Contact: Beach Services Department, South Walton Tourist Development Council, 850/267-1216

Seagrove Beach

Seagrove Beach predated its neighbor to the west, Seaside, by many years. Having been founded in 1949, it is the second-oldest community (behind Grayton Beach) in south Walton County. People speak of "old" Seagrove and the slower, quieter life along this part of the Panhandle before it was discovered. But while Seagrove has longevity, Seaside has a master plan, which is another way of saying that the former community occupies a much longer stretch of Scenic C.R. 30-A but leaves a less distinct impression. One thing that does stand out is an enormous high-rise condominium that shoots from the ground to a height of 21 stories. Known as One Seagrove Place and dating back to the 1970s, it is an absurd non sequitur along Scenic C.R. 30-A. But in all fairness, while it sticks out like a sore thumb, it was constructed before building regulations were put in place. We were told no more high-rises of its kind will be built along Scenic C.R. 30-A, as four stories is the maximum permissible height.

We'll see how long that holds. We've learned that a business-driven entity called the South Walton Community Council is tired of permitting delays, building restrictions, scenic corridors, and all the other things that once made this stretch of coast such a delightful departure from the numbingly overbuilt Florida norm.

Seagrove Beach took its name from the groves of live oak that grow right down to the "sea" (or, more accurately, gulf). One of the most ecologically interesting aspects of the area is the mixed forest of hardwoods (oaks, magnolias, hickories, and hollies) and sand pines found among the rolling dune fields. While Seagrove is a mishmash of old

© PARKE PUTERBAUGH

Deer Lake State Park

Florida bungalows, new traditional cottages, and the aforementioned condo colossus, one can find some nice places to rent and have a decent meal.

For more information, contact the South Walton Tourist Development Council, C.R. 331 and U.S. 98, P.O. Box 1248, Santa Rosa Beach, FL 32459, 850/267-1216 or 800/822-6877, www.beachesofsouthwalton.com.

BEACHES

The beaches of south Walton County are beautiful (although hurricanes have claimed some of their former width). Their appeal is all the more pronounced because they are so relatively unspoiled. Happily, public beach access is readily available in Seagrove Beach, starting east of town at Deer Lake. Surrounding one of Walton County's unique coastal dune lakes is **Deer Lake State Park.** As with Topsail Hill Preserve State Park (to the west), it is more of a preserve than a park. The lack of facilities beyond Portolets makes the experience all the more rewarding for those who like nature in the raw. The park encom-

passes 172 acres around the lake and beach and 10 times that area on the inland side of Scenic C.R. 30-A, for a total of 1,920 acres. A one-third mile boardwalk provides access to the beach, though in the wake of 2005's hurricane season, the stairs at the beach were washed away. Temporarily (we hope), a sign reads, "Danger! Beach Closed Until Further Notice." The boardwalk crosses the extensive back-dune area, through the pine flatlands, over the dunes, and out to the beach. It is an absolutely wonderful walk.

In Seagrove Beach proper, there are 18 neighborhood accesses—that is, pedestrian easements, via dune walkovers at the ends of 18 streets, onto the beach. They usually abut condos and subdivisions and are mainly used by their residents. Several that provide public parking as a legal easement onto the beach are the **Seagrove Beach** (adjacent to One Seagrove Place), **Pelayo Beach,** and **San Juan Beach** accesses. **Santa Clara Park** has parking for 49 vehicles. **Walton Dunes** is a three-acre parcel next to the condo of the same name.

EDEN GARDENS STATE PARK

If you're looking for a short jaunt off the beach, take C.R. 395 north from Seagrove for a few miles. You'll wind up at Point Washington, a dot on the south shore of Choctawhatchee Bay, facing Tucker Bayou. There's not much here but state forestland, a fishing dock, a ferry landing, and Eden Gardens State Park. Delightful picnic grounds look out over the bayou near Wesley Mansion, a two-story, antique-filled Greek Revival mansion dating from 1897 that serves as the centerpiece of this quiet, idyllic spot. The house and grounds belonged to William Henry Wesley, a lumber baron, and his descendents, and was deeded to the state in 1968.

The house is open for hourly guided tours 9 A.M.–4 P.M. Thursday–Monday. In addition to a nominal $1.50 per adult ($0.50 for kids) for the tour, it costs $2 per vehicle to enter the 115-acre park. (The state added 100 acres in 2000.) The grounds, reflecting pool, and four gardens – camellia, rose, azalea, and butterfly – are particularly attractive when in flower, with March being the peak month for color.

For more information, contact Eden Gardens State Park, 422 Harvest Road, Point Washington, FL 32454, 850/231-4214, www.floridastateparks.org.

3 DEER LAKE STATE PARK

Location: between Seacrest Beach and Seagrove Beach on Scenic C.R. 30-A
Parking/Fees: free parking lot
Hours: 8 A.M.–sunset
Facilities: restroom and picnic tables
Contact: Deer Lake State Park, 850/231-0037

4 SEAGROVE BEACH

Location: east side of One Seagrove Place (condo tower), on Scenic C.R. 30-A in Seagrove Beach
Parking/Fees: limited free street parking
Hours: 24 hours
Facilities: shower
Contact: Beach Services Department, South Walton Tourist Development Council, 850/267-1216

5 PELAYO BEACH

Location: beside the Pelayo development on Scenic C.R. 30-A in Seagrove Beach
Parking/Fees: free small parking lot
Hours: 24 hours

Facilities: shower
Contact: Beach Services Department, South Walton Tourist Development Council, 850/267-1216

6 SANTA CLARA PARK

Location: between Pelayo and San Juan accesses on Scenic C.R. 30-A in Seagrove Beach
Parking/Fees: free parking lot
Hours: 24 hours
Facilities: restrooms, picnic tables, and showers
Contact: Beach Services Department, South Walton Tourist Development Council, 850/267-1216

7 SAN JUAN BEACH

Location: across from the south end of San Juan Street, on Scenic C.R. 30-A in Seagrove Beach
Parking/Fees: free small parking lot
Hours: 24 hours
Facilities: shower
Contact: Beach Services Department, South Walton Tourist Development Council, 850/267-1216

ACCOMMODATIONS

Seagrove Villas and Motel (Scenic C.R. 30-A, 850/231-1947, $$$) is a rarity along condo-crazed "Scenic 30-A": an actual beach-front motel, just like beach towns are supposed to have. It has a small pool, too. Nightly room rates run $82–180 (suites $120–280), depending on the season. We learned that this "villa motel" is actually owned by the giant Resort-Quest (formerly Abbott Resorts), a vacation house and condo-rental firm, making it seem not so quaint as on first glance.

There are no other motels or hotels in Seagrove Beach, but many properties—ranging from one-bedroom apartments to six-bedroom homes—can be rented through such firms as **Garrett Realty Services** (3723 East Scenic C.R. 30-A, 850/231-1544).

COASTAL CUISINE

Seagrove lays claim to an excellent restaurant: **Cafe Thirty-A** (Scenic C.R. 30-A, 850/231-2166, $$$$). It serves a broad menu whose primary emphasis is seafood, while also whipping up beef, lamb, poultry, and vegetarian dishes with a creative, contemporary flair. Sophisticated and pricey, it's a great place to spend a long, leisurely evening. At the other extreme, **Seagrove Village Market** (3004 South C.R. 395, 850/231-5736, $) has some of the best and most reasonably priced burgers and grilled fish on the beach.

Seaside

Driving along Scenic C.R. 30-A between Panama City and Destin, you can be forgiven for doing a double take when you pass through Seaside (pop. 1,027). It certainly brought expressions of disbelief to our faces when we first visited in the early 1990s. After we gained some familiarity with the area and its brief history, disbelief turned to admiration and, finally, the desire to return and perhaps buy homes here with the nest egg accumulated from sales of this book. (Talk about a pipe dream!) Seaside is exactly what it appears to be when you first lay eyes on it: a fairy tale come to life.

The components of Seaside's fairy tale would have to include such literary citations as *Gulliver's Travels* (its small-scale charm brings to mind the make-believe village of Lilliput) and *Lost Horizon* (the novel that propounded Shangri-La, an idyllic valley where one can lead a life of endless contemplation). If you've never seen it before, it's pleasantly shocking to stumble on a village as outwardly clean and wholesome as Seaside. It looks like *Leave It to Beaver* land, although it takes a lot of wealthy Ward Cleavers to afford Seaside's mortgages.

Victorian-style dwellings encircle an unpretentious town center that includes a teeny-tiny post office, upscale small shops, a village green with bandstand, a cozy bed-and-breakfast (Josephine's), one of the best restaurants in Florida (Bud & Alley's), and bicycle- and pedestrian-friendly brick streets. Each cottage must have a white picket fence and porch. Lawns are forbidden. Only native vegetation can be grown on homeowners' lots. It's all laid out, chapter and verse, in the Seaside Urban Code and Construction Regulations. While it may all smack of "father knows best" paternalism, at least father is an enlightened despot and not an irrational or tasteless tyrant.

Even the dune crossovers at the street-end beach accesses break the mold. Inventive wood pavilions (designed by different craftsmen) lead over the dunes and onto the beach. Each is architecturally distinguished, providing zigzagging ramps to the sand. Of course, nothing this special happens by accident. Seaside was painstakingly plotted by developer Robert Davis and husband-and-wife architects Andres Duany and Elizabeth Plater-Zyberk (who head the Miami firm Arquitectonica). Their idea was to interpret the local vernacular architecture of the Florida Panhandle in a "new traditional" community. Fortunately, they had a blank slate, as there was very little along Scenic C.R. 30-A. They designed Seaside to be on the cutting edge of the New Urbanism, which

© PARKE PUTERBAUGH

dune walkover in Seaside

actually employs classic older approaches to designing neighborhoods. The idea is to create opportunities for residents to interact with one another as they did in the "old days." At least that's the theory.

Groundbreaking in Seaside dates to the early 1980s. Very little had to be razed before Seaside rose. Though seemingly every other square inch of Florida's coastline had been plundered, this prime stretch escaped notice (though it is being plundered now, Seaside excepted).

Our incredulity extends to the local bookstore, **Sundog Books** (Four Corners, 850/231-5481), which dutifully carries bestsellers alongside tasteful collections of new and classic literature, as well as serious works of science, nature, and philosophy. Books are stacked with studied haphazardness in the manner of an absent-minded professor's library, further rewarding browsing.

One local proudly and accurately referred to Seaside as the "Nantucket of the South." It does have something of the timeless look of a New England fishing village. From the road, Seaside struck us as having the slightly surreal look of a Hollywood back lot or some sort of slick

"Biosphere 2000" experiment whose concept of the future has much to do with revisiting the past. It was envisioned in much the same way by film director Peter Weir, who made Seaside the surreally normal centerpiece of *The Truman Show,* a film starring Jim Carrey.

Initially, Seaside's contrived normalcy had us wondering whether there was substance behind the whitewashed facade. The answer is a provisional yes. They have designed a town that aims to reestablish connections, jump-starting the lost notion of community. All of Seaside's merited architectural and environmental accolades aside, what most appeals to us is its stability as a community and far-ranging influence as a template for other "new urbanism" developments, from luxury resorts to inner-city reclamation projects.

This aspect was recognized when Seaside and its founders won the Urban Land Institute's Award for Excellence in 2003. Architectural historian Vincent Scully has written extensively and fondly about Seaside, though he has wondered out loud whether Seaside can "survive" its success.

"There's never been a real-estate success

like this in the history of mankind," Scully told the *Seaside Times* in 2004. "It's changed the whole coast. It really is that the town is a work of art that counts here. ... You really feel the grandeur of nature and brotherhood of mankind."

Seaside's stability as a community is obvious if you stick around awhile. Everywhere you turn, little things point that out: volunteers working to clean up the coastline and protect sea turtle nests; annual 10K races to benefit the Clean Beaches Council; an annual wine festival (aptly named Seeing Red); health fairs; a two-day "Back to Nature Festival"; repertory theatre productions; enriching and challenging lyceum programs; live concerts on the grassy green at Town Center; an informal bocce ball league; outreach events to surrounding Walton County communities; and plans for a community performing arts center (in partnership with the University of West Florida). There's even a graveyard now.

In other words, people have invested more than money into the Seaside concept; they live and die in Seaside now, and want to be buried here. This brilliant idea, conceived 25 years ago, has become an ongoing act of vision. Arguments even erupt over which part of town is "the real Seaside." We prefer the Old Florida homes of Savannah and Tupelo Streets on Seaside's "east side."

We're not deluding ourselves into thinking Seaside is an alternative available to everyone. It is decidedly upscale, attracting moneyed aesthetes who appreciate quality. Nevertheless, Seaside doesn't project the exclusionary paranoia of gated communities that have popped up all over Florida. What's more, it's surrounded on three sides by state parks and conservancy lands, and on the fourth by one of the prettiest beaches anywhere. Those who come here appreciate the harmonious interplay of natural and man-made elements. In this sense, unless its example is perverted and burlesqued—as it has been in Rosemary Beach and other faux "communities" in Walton County—Seaside might well be the coastal community of the future. It deserves to become a blueprint for positive change.

For more information, contact the Seaside Visitors Center, 121 Central Square, P.O. Box 4730, Seaside, FL 32459, 850/231-4224 or 800/277-8696, www.seasidefl.com.

BEACHES

The beaches in the Seagrove, Seaside, and Grayton Beach area are nearly perfect. We don't make this claim lightly. They rate highly on every index one can possibly apply to beaches. The sand is the texture of light brown sugar, clean and cool, singing and squeaking beneath your feet. The water is emerald inshore and azure offshore. It is a slice of Tahiti on the gulf where the water is swimmable nine months a year. Only from November through February, when water temps hover in the 60–65°F range, can one not slip in comfortably.

The beaches in and around **Seaside** are backed by dunes that were battered mercilessly by hurricanes in the last decade. They're not the mighty dunes of yesteryear, rising to heights of 30 feet or more, but they're slowly coming back. The pace of recovery has been aided by dune-restoration projects.

Seaside's beachfront has weathered some severe storms in the past two decades—most notably, Hurricane Opal in 1995. Owing to its design, Hurricanes Charley, Frances, Ivan, and Dennis (in 2004 and 2005) had relatively little lasting impact on Seaside, where other Panhandle beach communities suffered far greater losses. This has nothing to do with lucky charms and everything to do with the fact that the dunes were never bulldozed to make way for homes. Moreover, the existing dunes have been protected and restored with native vegetation. Consequently, the beach itself has remained in place. Seaside's efforts to keep its beach clean and healthy have been contagious. In fact, Walton County is the only county in the nation in which all of the beaches have earned Blue Wave certification from the Clean Beaches Council.

While in Seaside, check out the pavilions at the ends of Tupelo, Savannah, East Ruskin,

West Ruskin, Pensacola, Odessa, and Natchez Streets. Each is unique, offering some kind of commentary on the environment that is graceful and/or playful. Our favorite is the Natchez Street Pavilion, which rises to a peak and then falls again—like a wave!—with what looks like a beach umbrella as its crowning touch. The hurricanes of 2005 didn't completely bypass the area, though they temporarily knocked out one pavilion.

🞼 SEASIDE

Location: various street ends along Scenic C.R. 30-A in Seaside
Parking/Fees: no public parking; accesses are for use of Seaside property owners, renters, and their guests
Hours: sunrise-sunset
Facilities: none
Contact: Seaside Visitors Center, 850/231-4224

RECREATION AND ATTRACTIONS

- **Bike Rentals:** Seaside Swim & Tennis Club, Seaside Avenue at Forest Street, Seaside, 850/231-2279
- **Boat Cruise:** Choctawhatchee River Boat Tours, Point Washington, 850/231-4420
- **Fishing Charters:** Angry Fish Charter Company, Grayton Beach, 850/622-0611
- **Dive Shop:** Sea Cobra, U.S. 98, Sandestin, 850/837-1933
- **Ecotourism:** Point Washington Wildlife Management Area, C.R. 395, Point Washington, 850/265-3676
- **Rainy-Day Attraction:** Sundog Books, Seaside, 850/231-5481
- **Shopping/Browsing:** Silver Sands Factory Stores, U.S. 98, Miramar Beach, 850/864-9780
- **Vacation Rentals:** Seaside Cottage Rental Agency, 2311 Scenic C.R. 30-A, P.O. Box 4730, Seaside, 850/231-4224 or 800/277-8696

ACCOMMODATIONS

There are about 260 properties for rental in Seaside and 350 cottages in all. There will be no more than that due to prohibitions on new construction. The only real-estate activity is in resales. Cottage rentals of a week or longer are an alluring option in Seaside, not only for their proximity to the superlative beach but also because the buildings themselves are so airy and architecturally distinguished. For cottage rentals in Seaside, call **Seaside Cottage Rental Agency** (2311 Scenic C.R. 30-A, 850/231-4224). Two-bedroom cottages run $1,800–2,400 for a weekly rental in summer. Rates drop 12 percent in spring and fall, and 20 percent in winter.

For briefer stays, try **Josephine's Bed & Breakfast** (101 Seaside Avenue, P.O. Box 4767, 850/231-1940, $$$$), a French country inn that combines first-class elegance with the casual setting of life at the beach. The rooms are done in various color schemes and have different personalities. "Josephine" (#4) has dark green carpeting and silver fern walls, while "Napoleon" (#6) has burgundy carpeting and complementary tones throughout. Both are upstairs rooms that share a verandah from which the gulf is visible. All seven rooms and two suites at Josephine's have private baths, TVs, microwaves, coffeemakers, and working fireplaces.

Guests are served a full breakfast at 9 A.M. in the dining room. At night, Josephine's becomes one of the premier fine-dining restaurants in the area. Incidentally, there are a lot of great dining options hereabouts—at least as many in the small towns of Seaside and Grayton Beach as in the larger Panhandle cities of Panama City Beach and Destin.

COASTAL CUISINE

Bud & Alley's (Cinderella Circle, P.O. Box 4760, 850/231-5900, $$$$) is one of Florida's finest restaurants. The name refers not to the owners but to a pair of beloved pets. "Bud" was a dachshund belonging to Robert Davis—the driving force behind Seaside, who also had an early hand in the restaurant—and "Alley" was a cat belonging to co-owner Scott Witcoski. None of this has much to do with anything, but the playful name reflects the likable bent of the restaurant, which occupies six areas (indoors and outdoors) and harmonizes with the beautiful beach it overlooks.

The culinary orientation is toward healthful dishes prepared with local ingredients. An herb garden out back is used extensively by the kitchen. How about an appetizer of shrimp steamed in court bouillon and served with cocktail sauce? Or sauteed soft-shell blue crab, served with remoulade atop fresh tomato slices? On the entree front, we've sampled a hearty mixed grill that included homemade sausage, buttertender filet mignon, and grilled triggerfish. A popular dish flash-sears sushi-grade yellowfin tuna coated with sesame seeds and serves it over balsamic-marinated greens with wasabi and soy. Every desert is good, but Kahlua crème brûlée and tiramisu stand out. The latter deserves a berth in the dessert hall of fame.

In the town center is **Shades** (83 Central Square, 850/231-1950, $$), which has a casual feel that, like everything in Seaside, has been meticulously cultivated. They make terrific iced tea, an essential in the South. The menu runs from peel 'n' eat shrimp, hot wings, and tasty salads to citrus crab cakes, tuna, and mahimahi. It's a good lunch stop. The **Hurricane Oyster Bar** (850/534-0376, $$) is a nice new arrival, with a dozen raw ones going for $7.

NIGHTLIFE

You may never make it off the roof of **Bud & Alley's.** We've found ourselves at the restaurant's **Tarpon Deck Roof Club Bar** for many a late-day sunset. The breeze, conversation, setting, and libations are so stimulating that we've stayed well past the daily ringing of the bell for sunset. They have a contest to see who can guess the exact time the sun will set; whoever comes closest gets free drinks. The Tarpon Deck is Seaside's sole late-night scene. On some nights, bands play in the courtyard below, but even without it the taped music

(reggae and rock) is the perfect backdrop for frozen margaritas, Corona and lime, or a bracing iced coffee. From the rooftop deck one can study the amazing array of colors in the sky before and after sunset, ever changing in an intoxicating visual feast.

For livelier nightlife, head to the legendary Red Bar in Grayton Beach. If you're really desperate, Panama City Beach and Destin are only a half hour east and west, respectively. Another nightlife option closer to Seaside is **Cash's Discount Liquors** (16199 U.S. 331 South, Freeport, 850/835-4321), located 10 miles north in Freeport. Cash is a chain of package stores and attached lounges. This Cash's—the chain's home base—can get particularly wild. Incidentally, we counted ten Cash's Discount Liquors franchises on the Florida Panhandle. Another place we've admittedly only heard about is The Matador. Allegedly it's in Niceville. ("But nobody really knows where it is," we were told.) Locals get down so profoundly that the place has its own unique odor, a fusion of alcohol and hard partying.

We'd advise letting those at The Matador gore themselves and just stay put in Seaside, where the quiet is almost remarkably *loud*. Seaside was designed in the manner of a classic American small town and the sidewalks roll up early. After hanging out at Bud & Alley's, you can always buy a bottle of wine at Modica Market to take back to wherever you're staying. Why would you want to leave a place as relaxing and quiet as Seaside?

WaterColor

WaterColor is the "neotraditional" planned community that picks up at Seaside's western flank. A pale imitation of Seaside, the color scheme is designer pastels and, as best we can make out, the style—created by Boston architect Graham Gund—is faux New Orleans. The entire 499-acre development is owned by St. Joe/Arvida, the largest private landowner and developer in Florida.

Needless to say, WaterColor is upscale (the average unit costs $1.22 million) and tasteful in the quaint, anal-retentive way of instant cities. For example, it has crushed-shell pathways and a posted speed limit of 17 mph. In the window of WaterColor Market hangs a sign: "Fresh Daily Necessities and Niceties." It's all just a bit too cute.

Right now, WaterColor is about the size of a landscape painting, though soon it will be larger than a Thomas Hart Benton mural. At buildout it will have 1,140 homes, beach and tennis clubs, a boathouse, and 100,000 square feet of commercial space. As a result, you are never far from the din of construction noise here. We paddled to the far reaches of Western Lake, which WaterColor borders, and could hardly hear ourselves think over the sound of hammers and band saws.

For more information, contact WaterColor, 34 Goldenrod Circle, Santa Rosa Beach, FL 32459, 850/534-5001 or 866/426-2656, www.watercolorvacations.com.

BEACHES
Between Seaside and WaterColor is **Van Ness Butler Jr. Regional Beach Access.** Right now, there's little more than a parking lot and a path to the water from which you can enjoy for free what people in WaterColor have paid more than $1 million each to access.

🔟 VAN NESS BUTLER JR. REGIONAL BEACH ACCESS

Location: Along Scenic C.R. 30-A in WaterColor
Parking/Fees: free parking lot
Hours: sunrise-sunset
Facilities: none
Contact: Beach Services Department, South Walton Tourist Development Council, 850/267-1216

ACCOMMODATIONS
Two things are worth noting for travelers at WaterColor. For overnight stays, there's the lovely, luxurious **WaterColor Inn** (34 Goldenrod Circle, Seagrove Beach, FL 32459, 850/534-5050 or 866/426-2656, $$$$), with prices so high ($270–530 per night) it will make your nose bleed. Housed therein is an innovative seafood restaurant, **Fish Out of Water** (850/534-5050, $$$), that serves Gulf favorites with "an Asian accent" and WaterColor Market.

Grayton Beach State Park

Grayton Beach State Park preserves a world-class beach and coastal environment. A visit to Grayton Beach makes one appreciate the vastness of Florida's dune fields in their natural state. Barrier dunes of pure quartz sand roll back from the beach for some distance, giving way to salt marsh, slash pine flatlands, and scrub-hickory hammock. It is this varied landscape, incorporating not only the beach but the environments behind it, that makes Grayton Beach an exceptional experience.

The dunes are in a cycle of recovery from hurricanes in 1995, 1998, 2004, and 2005. Hurricane Opal sheered off about half of the frontal dunes' 30-foot height in places, but sand fencing and replanting programs accelerated their restoration. However, recent hurricanes claimed some of their bases, and their profiles have steepened as a result. On our last visit the walkover to the beach was in splinters and a path through the sand had been forged with two-by-fours and yellow police tape. We expect it will be repaired by the time you read this. In any case, Grayton's mile-long beach runs contiguously with those of Seaside and Grayton Beach, the communities that flank it, providing opportunities for lengthy beach hikes.

The 2,200-acre park is dotted with lily ponds and marshes and is also home to West-

© PARKE PUTERBAUGH

Western Lake in Grayton Beach State Park

ern Lake, one of the most formidable of Walton County's brackish coastal dune lakes. Unique to this area, they breach their boundary with the gulf several times a year. The park offers 37 campsites and 15 two-bedroom cabins. Camping at Grayton Beach is particularly pleasurable after the worst of summer's heat and bugs have died down. The clear, aquamarine water remains swimmable through October and sometimes beyond. There are hiking trails here as well, with the Dune Trail and Pinewoods Loops each taking about half an hour. It's well worth the slog to see what lays in the extensive back-beach area.

Canoes are available for rent ($10.75 per half-day). We spent a glorious morning paddling around beautiful Western Lake. Its waters were teeming with redfish, mullet, and bass, as well as alligators. We were never far from reminders of civilization, however, with the ceaseless din of sawing and swearing emanating from new homes and condos being built at WaterColor; the whir of cars and trucks speeding along Scenic 30-A; and the buzz of planes and military helicopters. To all this, the birds, crickets, frogs and jump-ing fish provided a lovely counter-chorus. So get out on one of Walton County's coastal dune lakes and discover what the fuss is really all about.

For more information, contact Grayton Beach State Park, 357 Main Park Road, Santa Rosa Beach, FL 32549, 850/231-4210, www.myflorida.com.

BEACHES

10 GRAYTON BEACH STATE PARK

                                BEST (

Location: between Seaside and Grayton Beach on Scenic C.R. 30-A

Parking/Fees: $5 per vehicle entrance fee. The camping fee is $19 per night, and cabin rentals are $110 nightly.

Hours: 8 A.M.-sunset

Facilities: restrooms, picnic tables, and showers

Contact: Grayton Beach State Park, 850/231-4210

Grayton Beach

If Seaside is a neoclassical sculpture, then Grayton Beach (pop. 300) is a piece of folk art: ramshackle, unpretentious, unschooled. To put it another way, Seaside takes a studied, academic approach to Florida vernacular architecture, while Grayton Beach is a mishmash of styles—including authentic tin-roofed bungalows that look one hard rain shy of collapsing—and late-model vacation homes. Seaside is an instant community, while Grayton Beach has deep roots. Seaside is upscale and exacting, Grayton Beach is laid back and down to earth. Get the picture?

The town of Grayton Beach is separated from Seaside by Grayton Beach State Park. Their proximity belies the fact that the two communities are light years apart. Grayton Beach offers a truer glimpse of Old Florida, with some glancing blows from the "new traditional" imperatives that are threatening to alter the area's longtime appeal. Grayton Beach is by far the oldest community in coastal Walton County, having been developed in the 1920s. It was the first beach town to pop up between the Panhandle bookends of Apalachicola and Pensacola. Grayton Beach looks comfortably aged and unchanged, with its sandy, tree-lined streets and old homes built of weathered cypress. Its antiquarian ways have not only kept old-timers happy but attracted an artsy, offbeat element.

Most notably, from an outsider's perspective, Grayton Beach claims several excellent restaurants; a bar that exudes more personality than every club in Panama City Beach put together; and a re-creation of impressionist Claude Monet's garden in Giverny, France, dubbed **Monet Monet** (100 East Scenic C.R. 30-A, 850/231-5117).

For more information, contact the South Walton Tourist Development Council, C.R. 331 and U.S. 98, P.O. Box 1248, Santa Rosa Beach, FL 32459, 850/267-1216 or 800/822-6877, www.beachesofsouthwalton.com.

BEACHES

On the east side of Grayton Beach is Grayton Beach State Park (see previous entry). **Grayton Beach** proper has public accesses at the ends of Garfield and Pine Streets. Significant on-street parking, right before the boardwalk entrance to the beach, makes the former particularly appealing if you're just passing through town. The hurricanes of 2005 left one of the dune walkovers in splinters, necessitating a makeshift path delineated by yellow police tape.

11 GRAYTON BEACH

Location: at the end of Garfield Street in Grayton Beach

Parking/Fees: free street parking

Hours: 24 hours

Facilities: none

Contact: Beach Services Department, South Walton Tourist Development Council, 850/267-1216

ACCOMMODATIONS

With the demise of Patrone's Hideaway—a funky conglomeration of rental units that was home to an art gallery and zoo that featured a 1,000-pound pig—Grayton Beach has no overnight lodgings per se. This former haven, which was as unique as the town's Red Bar, was torn down to make way for seven single-family homes. We were amused by the spin the developer put on it. As if skimming a tidy profit played no part in the deal, he said: "We're reverting the property back to the 1890 plat, so the lots there will be just like the other lots in Grayton Beach."

Now your only choice, besides cabins or campsites in Grayton Beach State Park, is to contact a real-estate agency about a vacation rental. **Rivard Real Estate** (15 Pine Street, Santa Rosa Beach, 850/231-5999) appears to have the market cornered hereabouts.

COASTAL CUISINE

Criolla's (170 East Scenic C.R. 30-A, 850/267-1267, $$$$) puts a Caribbean and Creole twist on its culinary offerings, which include pan-seared salmon served with fried, skewered soft-shelled crawfish. (Yes, crawfish go through a molting stage just like their blue crab relations.) Prices are on the high side but worth the splurge.

Picolo (70 Hotz Avenue, 850/231-1008, $$) is the restaurant part of an operation that also includes the vaunted Red Bar (see *Nightlife*). Entrees include half a dozen nightly preparations that go for reasonable prices. And you can always linger to hear the house jazz band, a blues band, surf group, or whatever's on the CD player at the Red Bar.

NIGHTLIFE

We fell in love with—and felt at home in—the **Red Bar** (70 Hotz Avenue, 850/231-1008) from the moment we set foot in the place. The room is indeed painted as red as Rudolph's nose, with European film posters and other bric-a-brac on the walls and red Christmas lights strung throughout. In this red-light district, you can catch live jazz or listen to CDs from an extensive collection behind the bar. We heard *The Best of Van Morrison* in its entirety one night—the perfect accompani-

ment to an after-dinner drink and some casual eavesdropping. Van Morrison is one of our musical heroes, and on this night at the Red Bar he never sounded better. The crowd is eclectic, making the people-watching as good as you'd find in any big-city hangout. The casual cosmopolitan ambience is not surprising, considering it's owned by Belgian brothers named Ollie and Philippe. Be aware that in summer, the Red Bar and its restaurant, Picolo, can get out-the-door popular.

Blue Mountain Beach, Santa Rosa Beach, and Dune-Allen Beach

Here are three more communities in the string of pearls along the gulf in south Walton County. You'll mostly find residential cottages along this stretch of Gulf Coast. They're tasteful to a fault, being reflexively imitative of the style of Seaside without the aesthetic organizing principles that

© PARKE PUTERBAUGH

Fort Panic Park, Dune-Allen Beach

SOUTH WALTON COUNTY

BED TAXES FOR BETTER BEACHES

Walton County has beautiful beaches and a smart way of preserving them for future generations. They subsidize land acquisition, facilities, and maintenance via a bed tax. Two-thirds of the 3 percent bed tax levied on lodging in south Walton County goes to the beaches. It is estimated that the tax generates $2 million annually for land acquisition and beach renourishment. No public funds or ad valorem taxes have been laid out for beach projects in Walton County, where it's all been done with the bed tax. The program is relatively recent, with the first tax-subsidized beach access built in 1988.

The county classifies its accesses in two ways. "Neighborhood accesses" are public easements that give residents and renters who are not directly on the beach a means of getting there without trespassing. There's virtually no parking or facilities at a neighborhood access, though some have an outdoor shower ("freshwater washdown," in engineering parlance). "Regional accesses" are public beach accesses that offer parking and more in the way of facilities, such as restrooms and picnic tables. All accesses have crossovers to protect the dunes. In Walton County, the boardwalks, crossovers, gazebos, and so forth are built not with wood but a wood polymer that holds up against the elements by resisting weathering, splintering, and cracking.

That is just another way that Walton County is a leading light on the issue of beach access. They're also bullish on land acquisition, developing regional accesses out of parcels in Seagrove Beach and west of Seaside. This is all very impressive for a relatively sparsely populated county. In neighboring Okaloosa County, by contrast – especially along Destin's privatized shoreline – they look enviously at Walton County's generous bounty of public beaches.

"We're very serious about public beach access in Walton County," says Malcolm Patterson, executive director of the South Walton Tourist Development Council, "and we spend a lot of money on it. People in Destin fuss all the time because they can't get to their beaches." No such problem exists in Walton County.

There's a lesson here for planning boards, county commissioners, and enlightened developers who are willing to listen: You can't lose by making beaches accessible to the public. Besides, it's simply the right thing to do.

---

bind it all together. These houses, painted in various lollipop-inspired hues, are almost too cute (especially the orange-foam ones). Since these communities are imitating Seaside, which itself is imitating an idealized past, there's a lot of faux flying around.

Still, better to use Seaside as a model than to have no models at all—or bad ones. Nonetheless, the communities are in danger of losing their appeal due to rapid overdevelopment. A development called the Sanctuary at Redfish was being built during our last trip through. All the new condos, villas, and mini-manses are shoving out the old cinderblock vacation huts of yesteryear. No doubt tensions between old and new are simmering beneath the sunny surface.

Blue Mountain Beach derives its name from its dunes. They rise as high as 70 feet, making this the highest point along the Gulf of Mexico in the United States. It's real rolling terrain, which is unusual for Florida. Blue Mountain Beach is one of the nicest towns in Walton County, with lovely coastal dune lakes hereabouts. We'd noticed that the hurricanes of 2004 and 2005 helped push the shoreline further in and flushed the county's coastal dunes lakes, which have never seemed so full or so beautiful.

Santa Rosa Beach lies between Blue Mountain Beach and Dune-Allen Beach. Oyster Lake, one of the county's more impressive coastal dune lakes, is the primary natural feature in Dune-Allen Beach, which is otherwise distinguished by more cutesy cottages and the doubtful promise of "Caribbean-style coastal living."

For more information, contact the South Walton Tourist Development Council, C.R. 331 and U.S. 98, P.O. Box 1248, Santa Rosa Beach, FL 32459, 850/267-1216 or 800/822-6877, www.beachesofsouthwalton.com.

BEACHES

Blue Mountain Beach has a bona fide public beach, with parking for a dozen or so cars, at the south end of C.R. 83. From here, you can walk onto the beach via an arty wooden gazebo reminiscent of those up in Seaside. At the south end of C.R. 393 is **Ed Walline Park,** a slightly more developed beach park along this slightly less developed coastline. There are picnic tables, a decent-sized parking lot, and a boardwalk to the beach. The beach here was nearly wiped out by recent hurricanes and tropical storms. The boardwalk was impassable in late 2005, while bulldozers were mounding sound in an attempt to save what little beach is left here. Right across from Ed Walline Park, curiously enough, is Miss Lucille's Gossip Parlor. Wonder what they're talking about these days—the loss of beaches, the endless construction, the high-priced fake shoppes, the phony Seasides springing up everywhere. That's what we'd be discussing.

Santa Rosa Beach harbors a treasure known as **Gulf View Heights.** Hidden behind Goatfeathers Raw Bar and Restaurant are picnic shelters, restrooms, and parking for up to 25 cars. Finally, an access at the end of Spooky Lane provides the local condo inhabitants an easement onto the beach. A new arrival on the beach at Dune-Allen is **Fort Panic Park,** with ample off-street parking, showers, and walkways.

12 BLUE MOUNTAIN BEACH

Location: south end of C.R. 83 in Blue Mountain Beach

Parking/Fees: free parking lot
Hours: 24 hours
Facilities: picnic tables and showers
Contact: Beach Services Department, South Walton Tourist Development Council, 850/267-1216

13 GULF VIEW HEIGHTS

Location: next to Goatfeathers Restaurant on Scenic C.R. 30-A in Santa Rosa Beach
Parking/Fees: free parking lot
Hours: 24 hours
Facilities: restrooms, picnic tables, and showers
Contact: Beach Services Department, South Walton Tourist Development Council, 850/267-1216

14 ED WALLINE PARK

Location: south end of C.R. 393 in Santa Rosa Beach
Parking/Fees: free parking lot
Hours: 24 hours
Facilities: restrooms, picnic tables, and showers
Contact: Beach Services Department, South Walton Tourist Development Council, 850/267-1216

15 FORT PANIC PARK

Location: west of Dune-Allen Realty on Scenic C.R. 30-A in Dune-Allen Beach
Parking/Fees: free parking lot
Hours: 24 hours
Facilities: picnic tables and showers
Contact: Beach Services Department, South Walton Tourist Development Council, 850/267-1216

ACCOMMODATIONS

Contact **Dune-Allen Realty** (5200 Scenic C.R. 30-A, 850/267-2121 or 888/267-2121) for a listing of gulfside condo and cottage rentals.

COASTAL CUISINE

We lucked into a lunch special to beat them all: soft-shell crab and amberjack platters for $4.95 each at **Goatfeathers** (3865 West Scenic C.R. 30-A, 850/267-3342, $$). It is an appealing, reliable seafood restaurant and market that takes its name from a quote that owners Pat and Eleanor Miller saw on the wall of a restaurant in (of all places) Austria. The quote is attributed to Ellis P. Butler, an obscure American humorist. The name stuck when the Millers bought the restaurant, then called Over the Market, in 1988. It fits this friendly, unpretentious place.

The equally friendly and busy **Snapperheads** (3711 West Scenic C.R. 30-A, 850/622-5615, $$) offers similar lunch specials and dinner menus. You can't go wrong at either place.

A culinary landmark in Blue Mountain Beach, **Basmati** (3295 West Scenic C.R. 30-A, 850/267-3028, $$$$) is a gourmet restaurant in a striking two-story wooden home. They specialize in Asian fare and sushi.

Just down the road is **Donut Hole II** (6745 U.S. 98, 850/267-3239, $). Though the name suggests a Dunkin' Donuts–style hole in the wall, this is a modestly upscale bakery-diner with an excellent selection of baked goods, including key lime–glazed donuts and tarts. They serve a killer breakfast, as well as lunch and dinner from their diner-themed menu. We hit the Donut Hole on the way to Topsail Hill Preserve State Park, and it provided us with the caloric input to hike the tall dunes. The key lime–glazed items had us both smacking our lips like sated housecats. Incidentally, the original Donut Hole is in Destin.

Oddly, we were passing through the area just days after Hurricane Katrina. A sign on the door was offering half-price to Louisiana and Mississippi evacuees. These civic-minded souls were also collecting money for the Red Cross and matching the first $2,500. We've always liked the Donut Hole, but we like it even more now.

Topsail Hill Preserve State Park

This recently established and therefore largely undiscovered state park has been called the most pristine coastal property in the state of Florida. Without hesitation we'd place Topsail Hill Preserve State Park near the top of our list of favorite Florida beaches. We must, however, attach the necessary disclaimers. As stated, Topsail is difficult to get to, though access has improved. When we first fumbled our way onto the preserve, the sandy access roads were rutted with gaping holes, and the mile-long drive to a clearing behind mountainous sand dunes was extremely bumpy.

By 2000, the main access road had been graded, and at its end was a parking lot, portable toilet, and boardwalk to the beach. Topsail has increased its holdings from 350 acres to 1,643 acres. Today, its beach extends for 3.5 miles. A network of trails has been cut, including a 2.5-mile nature trail around the south side of Morris Lake.

Topsail Hill largely remains an undeveloped state park, meaning that facilities are minimal. Spanish moss hangs from the trees and spongy deer moss covers the ground in this scrub forest environment. The preserve affords nesting sites for herons and egrets. Taking the road less traveled on our initial visit, we sloshed barefoot through muck and marsh that serve as a watery border between two lily ponds and a coastal dune lake. Working our way around Campbell Lake, we marveled at water as clear and calm as glass. Coastal dune lakes like this one are substantial bodies of water, occupying upward of a hundred acres. Next, we scaled a 50-foot sand cliff whose summit presented a glorious sight: a quarter-mile of dune ridges and swales between us and the Gulf of Mexico. We delicately plotted a seaward path through them, making sure not to disturb the vegetation.

Mainly, we followed other sets of footprints, using the markings to find our way back out. ("Did we turn left or right at this pile of driftwood?" was our befuddled query when we briefly lost our way.) We couldn't help but notice the number of pawprints left by animals... large animals, by the look of them. Finally, we found a break between dunes that had been sensuously sculpted by the wind. There, dead ahead, lay the aqua-blue gulf and one of the most stunningly secluded white-sand beaches we've ever seen.

In 2002, a shared-use trail to the beach was added, along with a free tram that shuttles visitors between the beach and day-use parking lot.

For more information, contact Topsail Hill Preserve State Park, 7525 West Scenic C.R. 30-A, Santa Rosa Beach, FL 32459, 850/267-0299, www.floridastateparks.org.

BEACHES

16 TOPSAIL HILL PRESERVE STATE PARK

 BEST (

Location: between Dune-Allen Beach and Sandestin, turn south on Topsail Road at U.S. 98, the beach is a 300 yard walk from the parking lot

Parking/Fees: free parking lot

Hours: 8 A.M.-sunset

Facilities: restroom

Contact: Topsail Hill Preserve State Park, 850/267-1868

ACCOMMODATIONS

In 1998, the state acquired a commercial RV park on U.S. 98, which has been renamed **Gregory E. Moore RV Resort** (7525 West Scenic C.R. 30-A, Santa Rosa Beach, 850/267-0299 or 877/BEACH-RV) and is officially part of park operations. There are 156 campsites, which cost $38 per night. Fifteen cabins are also available for weekly ($575) or monthly ($1,100) rentals.

Sandestin

Sandestin did not exist until 1971, when an Atlanta real estate consortium purchased a

2,400-acre parcel of land eight miles east of Destin on U.S. 98, stretching from Choctawhatchee Bay to the Gulf of Mexico. The acreage was filled with scrub pine, oak, marshes, and clear coastal dune lakes. It had previously survived Indian wars and pirate attacks, not to mention bomb detonations and rocket tests by our own armed forces. It also dodged several less appetizing attempts at development, including one by Walt Disney, who briefly considered building Disney World here. Another came from the folks who brought us the Indianapolis Speedway; they had plans to cover this exquisite area with asphalt until one of the local landowners backed out at the last minute.

After extensive planning to ensure quality development, groundbreaking took place in 1973, and the area was christened Sandestin, combining the names of neighboring towns Santa Rosa Beach and Destin. The master plan calls for 40 percent of the property to remain in a natural state at buildout. This is misleading, however, since much of that natural land will consist of golf courses, which is a wholly unnatural use of land. However, in Sandestin's favor, its Burnt Pine golf course was constructed without disturbing wetlands—and, in fact, wetland plantings were added to aid in erosion control. At least environmental issues have been factored into the developmental equation at Sandestin.

The largest self-contained resort on the Gulf Coast, Sandestin owns 7.5 miles of beachfront and bayshore property. In 1998, the Vancouver-based Club Intrawest—which mainly owns ski resorts—acquired Sandestin. These days at Sandestin you'll find four golf courses, nine pools, tennis courts, 26 miles of biking and hiking trails, a 98-slip marina (from which fishing, sailing, and cruising charters can be arranged), a health club, four residential "villages," a gaggle of gulf-front condominiums, an excellent waterfront restaurant and lounge, and a beachside complex with a beautiful heated pool and boardwalk access ramp to the Gulf of Mexico. On the way is the village at Baytowne Wharf, a pedestrian-oriented community inspired by Charleston and New Orleans. For more information, contact Sandestin Golf and Beach Resort, 9300 U.S. 98 West, Destin, FL 32550, 850/267-8150 or 800/622-1922, www.sandestin.com.

BEACHES

The wedge-shaped Sandestin runs beside the gulf for a few miles. The dunes have been left relatively undisturbed, though if nothing at all were here the dune fields would roll inland for a good distance like they do at nearby Topsail Hill Preserve State Park. Regardless, the beach at Sandestin and neighboring Tops'l Beach & Racquet Resort is exceptionally wide, white, and powdery soft, with the turquoise waters of the gulf providing eye-popping vistas. Not surprisingly, you can't access the beach at Sandestin unless you are a resort guest or property owner.

ACCOMMODATIONS

Sandestin Golf and Beach Resort (9300 U.S. 98 West, 850/267-8150, $$$$) offers a full line of rentals, including rooms at a 175-unit bay-front inn and 600 units in the resort's beachfront condos and bayside golf villas. A real deal can be had in the off-season (November–mid-March), when rooms rates drop precipitously and privileges include free use of the world-class fitness center. We've stayed in both a golf villa and a beachfront condo, preferring the latter's views and easy access to the beach. (But we don't golf.)

The Southwinds condo where we bunked down had a gulf-facing balcony and was plushly appointed; there was absolutely nothing not to like. Also on the beachfront at Sandestin is the **Sandestin Hilton Resort** (4000 Sandestin Boulevard South, 850/267-9500, $$$$). Hilton leases the land from Sandestin and provides ample outdoor activities (golf, tennis) and stellar beach access.

COASTAL CUISINE

Sandestin's Elephant Walk, their stately beachfront restaurant, has gone extinct. We had a wonderful meal there some years back, capped by their signature dish, Grouper Elizabeth. It was named for Elizabeth Taylor, who starred in the B movie from which the restaurant took its name. Perhaps the motif was a tad esoteric, come to think of it, but we sure miss the place.

What was Elephant Walk is now **Finz Loft** (Sandestin, 850/267-4800, $$$$). It specializes in Gulf seafood "with a Southern influence." Finz also has a more casual family dining setting downstairs. From either area, you can view the lulling gulf beach and waters.

Acme Oyster House (140 Fisherman's Cove, 850/622-0200, $$$) is a recent arrival to the Baytowne Merchants mall at Sandestin. It's an offshoot of the famous original in New Orleans' French Quarter, which has been around since 1910. You come here for fresh oysters, po' boys, jambalaya, and ice-cold Dixie Beer.

Miramar Beach

Miramar Beach is the most westward of south Walton County's gulf-hugging communities. For years, the community was a mixed bag that displayed elements of Walton County's low-key approach to beach development alongside Okaloosa County's rubber-stamping permissiveness. Because it sits on what is called "Old Highway 98," a loop road off the four-lane franchise heaven of U.S. 98, we held out hope that it would retain some of its Old Florida charm. In the last edition of this book, we wrote, "Ultimately, we fear whatever funky character Miramar Beach still possesses is Destin-ed to be snuffed out."

Our fears were borne out. In the process, an old adage was also verified: when you try to appeal to everyone, you end up appealing to no one. Miramar had previously shown potential to learn from the well-documented mistakes of Destin to the west and to emulate more sensibly planned communities to the east, like Grayton Beach, Seaside, and Seagrove.

Miramar Beach tried to play it both ways and ended up with a mish-mash that disappoints more than it delights. Thus you see high-rise condos going up in one section and chunks of coast left untouched in another (at least for now). Tony luxury projects like Mediterranean have beautifully landscaped grounds, but behind it rises a KFC billboard. Condo units have been constructed where sand dunes used to be. These are not grandfathered lean-tos that predate coastal environmentalism. These are handsome new homes costing nearly seven figures, and many are yet to be occupied. What fool would plunk down a million bucks for an abode with one foot in Davy Jones' locker and the other on a banana peel?

Incredibly, homes have been built shotgun-style on eroding bluffs overlooking a perilously narrow beach. They're goners, it's safe to say. But they're sure painted pretty. The operative philosophy around here seems to be that if you paint a home in some kind of designer color—forest green, frivolous peach—that

© PARKE PUTERBAUGH

Miramar Beach

you have instantly become like Seaside. The charade is doubly obnoxious because they're all but in the surf zone and have adopted none of the New Urbanism design practices that's made Seaside so truly unique, allowing it to weather storms on the coast better than neighboring communities.

One afternoon we sat in our car in disbelief, watching a bunch of bulldozers trying to shore up dunes across the street from a couple of badly placed condos. They've stripped away all of the dunes in these parts and, by our reckoning, "Majestic Sun Condo," "Surfside Condo," and the rest are all doomed.

What was Walton County—which almost too loudly trumpets its progressive coastal philosophy—thinking to allow this retro stupidity to take place? More to the point, no homeowner would live here without insurance, and most private insurance premiums for such risky settings are prohibitively expensive, if even available any longer, so the only recourse is for the federal government to underwrite the flood insurance on these. As a result, all taxpayers (including you, dear reader) will foot the bill to rebuild these vacation homes for the rich when the inevitable storm blows them away.

The shame of it is that Miramar Beach still has some lingering appeal. Ah, but what they could have accomplished with a little foresight and conviction!

For more information, contact the South Walton Tourist Development Council, C.R. 331 and U.S. 98, P.O. Box 1248, Santa Rosa Beach, FL 32459, 850/267-1216 or 800/822-6877, www.beachesofsouthwalton.com.

BEACHES

The prime public-access point onto **Miramar Beach** is located on Old U.S. 98 between Newman Drive and Avalon Estates. From the ample free parking lot, five wooden dune walkovers lead to a typical Panhandle beach, which is to say one that's nearly perfect in sand texture, coloration, size, and water temperature. The beach is backed by rounded mounds

SOUTH WALTON COUNTY

of protected dunes. Miramar Beach access is a joint venture between the South Walton Tourist Development Council, which maintains the facilities and walkovers, and a restaurant called Pompano Joe's (see *Coastal Cuisine*). There's also a pedestrian access onto the beach at Gulf Street, on the west side of the Mainsail Resort, for those in the neighborhood.

17 MIRAMAR BEACH

Location: on Old U.S. 98, between Newman Drive and Avalon Estates in Miramar Beach
Parking/Fees: free parking lot
Hours: 24 hours
Facilities: concessions, restrooms, and showers
Contact: Beach Services Department, South Walton Tourist Development Council, 850/267-1216

ACCOMMODATIONS

East of Miramar's public beach, the beachfront assumes the names of the high-rise condominiums that have effectively usurped access to the beaches for anyone but the occasional inhabitants of these ghastly buildings. One of them, Hidden Dunes, is particularly well-named, as it blocks any view of the dunes from the highway. **Mainsail** (114 Mainsail Drive, 850/837-4853, $$$) is the most inviting of the "gulfside family resorts," offering affordable off-season rates. Next to it, however, is Edgewater, a sloping structure that looks about as inviting as a stealth bomber.

West of the public beach, the beachfront is likewise named after resort developments—in this case, **Surfside** and **Seascape.** Each of these gargantuan monoliths is claimed to be one of south Walton County's 19 beach communities, though this stretches the word *community* beyond credibility. We'd describe only five of the posited 19—Seagrove Beach, Seaside, Grayton Beach, Santa Rosa Beach, and Miramar Beach—as actual communities in the sense that we understand the term. That is to say, a place with roots, stability, a little history, a permanent population, and some meaningful interaction among them.

COASTAL CUISINE

Pompano Joe's (2237 Old U.S. 98 East, 850/837-2224, $$) is a reasonably priced seafood house with a relaxed nautical ambience and a great location overlooking Miramar Beach. Come in at lunchtime for some inexpensive specials, which include a dynamite amberjack sandwich and salad. Fried and grilled seafood entrees include mahimahi, amberjack, and grouper, the gulf-plucked favorites you'll see on most every Panhandle menu. Our suggestion: char-grilled grouper with jalapeno pineapple salsa.

   The Whale's Tail (1373 Scenic Gulf Drive, 850/650-4377, $$) is located right on the beach at Seascape Resort. Though it looks like a ramshackle beach bar, it's a locally popular spot for breakfast, lunch, and dinner, as well as late-night imbibing.

DESTIN, FORT WALTON BEACH, AND THE EMERALD COAST

The "Emerald Coast" is the marketing handle for a single Panhandle county, Okaloosa, much of whose 24-mile coastline falls inside Eglin Air Force Base. The two beach towns here are Destin and Fort Walton Beach. Destin's principal asset is a harbor with a huge fleet of charter-fishing boats. It is the self-styled "World's Luckiest Fishing Village." Despite its name, Fort Walton Beach doesn't have gulf beaches, strictly speaking. Those are on Okaloosa Island, a built-up area sandwiched between Eglin parcels. Okaloosa Island has beachside hotels and motels, Destin is home to fishing boats and good restaurants, while Eglin has deserted beaches. And what beautiful beaches they are.

BEST(DestIn

Destin is a city out of control. It is overrun by traffic and condo construction that never seems to end. This town, the centerpiece of Okaloosa County's "Emerald Coast," is given to some misconceived and reckless development. (However, Panama City Beach has lately been giving it a run for the money.) The traffic on U.S. 98 is so constant and thick that the inevitable wrecks keep a fleet of criminal lawyers and personal-injury attorneys busy.

The modus operandi is one we've seen often while combing the coastline. It goes down something like this: Build quickly and recklessly with speculators' cash. Never ask whose money it was, how they got it, why the big hurry, or what the wishes of the community might be. Build as close to the water as possible, heedless of beach erosion and now-common hurricane scenarios. Block views of the gulf with condo towers and prohibit public access to the beach with guard gates, walls, and fences. Sell them to the second-home wealthy, usually out-of-

© PARKE PUTERBAUGH

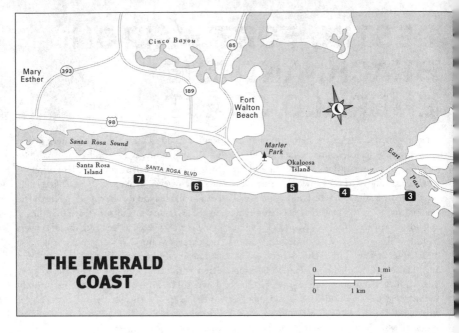

THE EMERALD COAST

THE EMERALD COAST

staters and foreigners. Name the condos for the very natural features they have destroyed or obscured (e.g. "Sea Dunes," "The Sandpiper"). Finally, watch as the units go eerily and wastefully unoccupied much of the year. That is what happens when absentee landowners hold title to real estate purchased for tax or investment purposes.

That is Destin, in a coconut shell. The first sight you behold upon entering the city from the east is a fortress called Destiny-by-the-Sea. The beach is blighted by rows of 10-story beige condos. Like most boomtowns, Destin has no sense of proportion or discernible identity. It's cash rich but sense poor. Every vacant plot of land along U.S. 98 is slated for development, though the growth here is already maxed out and overwhelming.

Bounded by Choctawhatchee Bay and the Gulf of Mexico, Destin's real destiny is to double in size and population in the next decade. The current population is said to be 12,162, though it seems much larger. One of us lives in a small town of 25,000 that seems positively rural compared to Destin.

How can this be? The operative term is "full-time residents." Units in Destin's glut of condo towers are basically a second-home write-off only occasionally occupied by their absentee owners.

"The problem, if you grew up here, is that we've lost a lot more than we've gained," we were told by a Panhandle old-timer. "I don't know what's going on here. Well, greed is what's going on here, to put it simply. They can't put up condos fast enough. It's a sad thing."

It did not need to turn out like this. Destin has some beautiful beaches that would otherwise receive our highest commendations. To its credit, Destin does have an intriguing harbor, a dining scene that ranks with the best on the Panhandle, and a bit of beachy redemption in the form of Henderson Beach State Park. We love Destin Harbor (see *The World's Luckiest Fishing Village* sidebar) and head down there to remind ourselves that it's not all bad in Destin. Walking along the harbor docks, you'll pass shirtless charter-boat mates with permanent tans and cigarettes dangling from their lips. They're often cutting

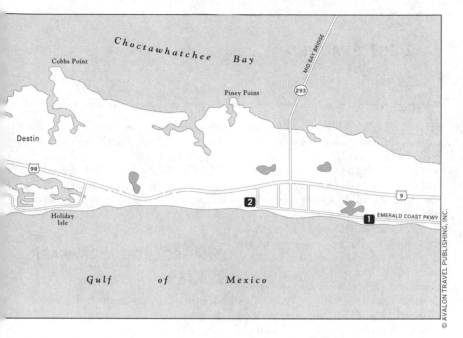

Choctawhatchee Bay

Cobbs Point

MID BAY BRIDGE

Piney Point

293

Destin

98

Holiday
Isle

2

9

EMERALD COAST PKWY

1

Gulf   of   Mexico

© AVALON TRAVEL PUBLISHING, INC.

fish, hosing down their boats, and generally going about the business of keeping the craft they work on shipshape.

Still, we found ourselves far preferring towns to the east (e.g., Seaside and Grayton Beach) and west (Pensacola Beach). Why? Because these beachfront communities have been through many of the same battles as Destin but have emerged with decent public beaches and a better handle on development. Destin just doesn't get it and therefore doesn't deserve the business of beachcombers—not when better options lay close by.

For more information, contact the Destin Area Chamber of Commerce, 4484 Legendary Drive, Destin, FL 32541, 850/837-6241, www.destinchamber.com; or the Emerald Coast Convention and Visitors Bureau, 1540 Miracle Strip Parkway (U.S. 98), Fort Walton Beach, FL 32548, 850/651-7131 or 800/322-3319, www.destin-fwb.com.

BEACHES

After ranting about Destin, it may seem odd to rave about a great public beach here. But that is because it's a state park that did not come to fruition because of any community largesse. **Henderson Beach State Park** takes its name from the landowners who sold it to the state in 1983, making it the first purchase in the Save Our Coast program. At the time, Destin was still unincorporated and seemingly incapable of doing anything in the way of public beach access on its own. Thanks to the Hendersons, who wanted to see the unique natural features of the area preserved, the public has access to 6,000 feet of unblighted beachfront along the Gulf of Mexico.

Naturally, it didn't come without a fight. "Those of us who want to preserve something of our beachfront are grateful they did it," a longtime local told us. "But the developers, the money people, were loathe to see a square inch of real estate given up for anything other than their own enrichment."

The 250-acre park, located two miles west of the Walton County line and just east of Destin, is a habitat for sand pine, scrub oak, Southern magnolia, dune rosemary, and wildflowers. Henderson Beach State Park

THE EMERALD COAST

BEST BEACHES

(Destin: Best for Fishing (page 539)

has a boardwalk, bathhouses with outdoor showers, six dune walkovers, picnic pavilions, and grills. A 60-site campground east of the public beach, with full facilities and a boardwalk to the gulf, is spread around four loops. The sites are shaded, offering more protection than you might expect at the beach. A three-quarter-mile nature trail winds its way through steep dunes and a sculpted maritime forest at the park's interior. When we hiked it, there were big puffy cumulus clouds rising behind it in a deep blue sky—a beautiful sight.

Another fine beach park, **James Lee County Park,** lies on Old U.S. 98 near the county line. Lee has the same public-private arrangement as Miramar's county beach access. A decent and affordable restaurant called the Crab Trap is attached to the property, overlooking the Gulf of Mexico. Parking is free, and six dune walkovers, picnic pavilions, restrooms, and showers are provided. It is popular with families because the water is shallow and clear. Surfing and volleyball round out the action at this fun spot.

A small access point at 7th Street abuts the west end of Henderson Beach. Other accesses are supposedly located south of the harbor via Gulf Shore Drive, off of U.S. 98. This jut of land is called Holiday Isle, and its condo crush rivals the upper reaches of Miami Beach. Both of the "public beach accesses" we came across were no more than niggling easements between high-rises.

We did, however, stumble on an excellent parcel of state-owned land at the very end of Gulf Shore Drive. It's an unnamed but lovely dune-covered sand spit that has formed off Holiday Isle at East Pass. Park on the side of the road and have a look and a stroll. Un-

less you're a condo owner or resort guest, it's about all you'll see of Destin's beachfront at this end.

Incidentally, the east end of Destin is one gigantic shopping mall of overpowering size, including the fabled upscale Silver Sands Shopping Mall and others that aren't quite so upscale.

1 JAMES LEE COUNTY PARK

Location: along Old U.S. 98 near the Walton County line
Parking/Fees: free parking lot
Hours: 6 A.M.–8:30 P.M.
Facilities: concessions, restrooms, picnic tables, and showers
Contact: Emerald Coast Convention and Visitors Bureau, 850/651-7131

2 HENDERSON BEACH STATE PARK

Location: 17000 Emerald Coast Parkway (U.S. 98) in Destin
Parking/Fees: $4 entrance fee per vehicle. The camping fee is $21 per night.
Hours: 8 A.M.–sunset
Facilities: restrooms, picnic tables, and showers
Contact: Henderson Beach State Park, 850/837-7550

RECREATION AND ATTRACTIONS

- **Bike/Skate Rentals:** Island Sports Shop, 1688 Old U.S. 98, Destin, 850/650-9126

Destin Harbor

- **Boat Cruise:** Southern Star Dolphin Cruises, 78 Harbor Boulevard, Destin, 850/837-7741

- **Dive Shop:** Emerald Coast Scuba, 110 Melvin Street, Destin, 850/837-0955

- **Ecotourism:** Fred Gannon Rocky Bayou State Park, 4281 S.R. 20, Niceville, 850/833-9144

- **Fishing Charters:** Destin Fishing Fleet Marina Charter Service, 201 U.S. 98 East, Destin, 850/837-1995

- **Marina:** Harborwalk Marina, 66 U.S. 98 East, Destin, 850/650-2400

- **Rainy-Day Attraction:** Destin History and Fishing Museum, 108 Stahlman Avenue, Destin, 850/837-6611

- **Shopping/Browsing:** Silver Sands Factory Stores, 10562 U.S. 98 East, Destin, 850/654-9771

- **Surf Shop:** Innerlight Surf and Skate, 852 Harbor Boulevard, Destin, 850/650-5509

- **Vacation Rentals:** Emerald Coast Vacation Rentals, Holiday Plaza, 12773 Emerald Coast Parkway, Suite 110, Destin, 850/637-6100;

ACCOMMODATIONS

This may shock and amaze you (it did us), but the beach vacation mecca of Destin has few beachfront hotels and motels worth recommending. That is because it has few beachfront hotels and motels, period. An exception is the **Sea Oats Motel** (3420 U.S. 98 East, 850/837-6655, $$), an attractive, contemporary property directly on the white-sand gulf beach. Also, the **Holiday Inn Destin** (1020 U.S. 98 East, 850/837-6181, $$$) sits beckoningly at the edge of the gulf and boasts of having "Destin's largest outdoor pool." This circular tower offers a rare chance to stay directly on the beach in walled-off Destin. Try to get a beach-view room, as all rooms have balconies but views from some angles aren't so scenic. Holiday Inn Destin is one of the more upscale, well-tended hotels we've stayed at in this chain. Right across from Henderson Beach State Park is **Comfort Inn Destin** (19001 U.S. 98, 850/654-8611, $$).

By and large, however, the most viable lodging option in Destin is a vacation rental in a beachfront high-rise. The average weekly rental in summer is $1,500. If that's beyond your means, you can always camp at **Henderson**

THE EMERALD COAST

© PARKE PUTERBAUGH

THE WORLD'S LUCKIEST FISHING VILLAGE

With its glut of condos and paucity of public beach accesses, Destin's crowded gulf-front real estate sounds a bum note. However, a sweeter chord is struck down by Destin Harbor, where a sizable fishing fleet gives visitors a chance to find out why Destin is referred to as the "World's Luckiest Fishing Village."

In one sense, the deep-sea fishing bonanza doesn't have as much to do with luck as with submarine geology. What is referred to as the "100-fathom curve" – the point offshore at which the water reaches a depth of 100 fathoms (600 feet) – draws closer to the mainland at Destin than any other spot on the Florida coast. What this means is that when you sail out of Destin, you'll reach deep water more quickly than from any other point in the state. You can be fishing in a 100 feet of water within a few miles of shore.

The Destin Marina Fishing Fleet Charter Service represents 40 fishing boats. The scene down along the harbor bustles in summer and is slower in winter. On a gray, foggy day, you can almost convince yourself that you've stumbled into a New England fishing village. Boats of all sizes take parties of all sizes into the gulf for fishing trips, setting off as early as 6 A.M. Deep-sea fishing is extremely popular in Destin, particularly on summer weekends. (You're advised to book reservations months in advance.) Weekdays in season are more flexible. Out of season, it's easier still to arrange a guided fishing trip on short notice. You can walk up and do it.

Here are the bottom-line basics: Parties of up to six can expect to pay between $380 for four-hour (half-day) trips, $570 for six-hour trips, and $750 for eight-hour (full-day) trips into the Gulf of Mexico. Each additional angler will pay about 10 percent of the base cost. The most common catches are grouper, amberjack, triggerfish, king mackerel, wahoo, and dolphin. If you're after billfish – blue marlin, white marlin, and sailfish – you'll travel 50–60 miles offshore. At that point you're looking at a 12-hour round trip costing around $1,075. Even if you're not dropping a grand to tussle with a marlin, it's fun to stroll the docks and checking out the catches as they're hauled off and cleaned.

Destin's charter-boat captains and crew genuinely like what they're doing. We went out with **Capt. George Eller** (Destin Harbor, 850/650-1534) on his 42-foot sportfisher, the *Bounty Hunter*. He obviously loves what he's doing. "It's not a job, it's a lifestyle," he says. "You have to want to do it. If you wake up and say, 'Damn, I have to go to work,' you won't make it. I get up and wander down to the harbor. If a trip comes along, peachy keen, but if not, 'Let's go get breakfast.'"

It's a nice life. "Another day in paradise," says Eller. "We believe that. Not many places can compare with this. The lifestyle here is pretty laid back. There are no smokestack industries for a hundred miles."

He makes the experience appealing to his passengers, too, with his enthusiasm for sportfishing. "Until you've experienced the thrill of catching a 25-pound king mackerel on a 20-pound line," he says, "you haven't lived."

For more information, contact the Destin Marina Fishing Fleet Charter Service, 201 U.S. 98 East, Destin, FL 32540, 850/837-1995. www.charterdestin.com.

Beach State Park (17000 U.S. 98, 850/837-7550, $) for $21 a night.

COASTAL CUISINE

Destin's cuisine is its strongest suit, but here is yet another Pyrrhic victory. Quite simply, the prices at many seafood restaurants lining U.S. 98 are exorbitant. This is not to say the seafood isn't fresh or the preparations worthy. (After all, Destin is the self-billed "World's Luckiest Fishing Village"). But, come on—fried seafood platters for over $20? Certain places serve sushi, but at inflated prices that rival a big-city raw-fish palace like Hatsuhana.

Still there are so many restaurants in Destin (300, by one count) that you can't help but score a satisfying meal if you know where to go. A lot of them are grouped together along Harbor Boulevard.

Start by following us to the **Boathouse Oyster Bar** (288 U.S. 98 East, 850/837-3645, $), a shack that sits beside a dock on the harbor. It is refreshingly lacking in pretension, lacking a phone or even a restroom (you use the marina's next door). We copped a dozen cold, tasty raw oysters, devoured while admiring the coral reef of colorful graffiti and grubstake affixed to the walls and ceiling. The Boathouse has live music seven nights a week, too.

Another perennially popular spot, right on the harbor where the charter fishing fleet does its business, is **AJ's Seafood and Oyster Bar** (168 U.S. 98 East, 850/837-1913, $$). The atmosphere is casual but polished, with ceiling fans, varnished picnic tables, and a chipper wait staff. Our waitress was a French-accented stunner. When we walked into AJ's on our latest visit, can you guess what was playing? "Margaritaville"! What are the chances of that happening in Florida? (About 50/50, to be quite honest.) At least it was the less frequently heard live version.

But AJ's is not so upscale that it doesn't welcome—hell, it downright encourages—a biker clientele, right down to the parking area reserved "for Harleys only." Raw oysters and smoked yellowfin tuna dip are essential appetizers. AJ's serves seafood with a New Orleans accent. Their grouper sandwich ($11) is broiled in butter and served with remoulade. The belly-busting "Run of the Kitchen" fisherman's platter is $26. Not cheap but you won't complain over the quality or quantity. By the way, if you want to party, head to AJ's Club Bimini after dark.

In the same affordable vein, we dug the **Crab Trap** at James Lee County Park (3500 Old U.S. 98 East, 850/654-2722, $$) and the **Back Porch** (1740 Old U.S. 98 East, 850/837-2022, $$), where char-grilling fish is the name of the game.

A great view of the water can be had at the **Lucky Snapper** (76 U.S. 98 East, 850/654-0900, $$$). Luckily, snapper is our favorite Florida fish, and they also do grouper all kinds of ways here. After consulting with our waiter—bronzed snapper? Caribbean-style tuna? sauteed triggerfish?—we opted for blackened grouper with fried crawfish and pineapple corn relish, served atop brown rice, and were not disappointed. Don't pass up the heads-on steamed shrimp, either.

We also lucked out by chumming U.S. 98 for early-bird offerings and posted dinner specials at the more expensive joints, hooking a nicely prepared mullet dinner at **Harbor Docks Seafood & Brew Pub** (538 U.S. 98 East, 850/837-2506, $$$) for under $10. And then we stuck around and spent much more than that on excellent sushi.

The finest preparations in town can be found at the popular **Marina Cafe** (404 U.S. 98 East, 850/837-7960, $$$$), which moved to a larger new location a few years back. The environment is relaxing as you look out over Destin Harbor and rows of condos on the beachfront from its picturesque windows. Brown-toned faux-painted walls that are refreshingly free of artwork create a meditative setting. A sushi bar in one corner serves such creations as dragon rolls (stuffed with fried soft-shelled crab and topped with eel). Brace yourself for sticker shock, as menu items average around $25. But if you come 5–6 P.M.

FISH OUT OF WATER:
A CALIFORNIAN CLEANS UP DESTIN HARBOR

At first, we paid him little mind. He was the first mate aboard a fishing boat we took out of Destin Harbor. Our group's deep-sea fishing excursion into the Gulf of Mexico got waylaid by winds and choppy seas. (Just our luck: Destin's charter boats get grounded by wind and wave only once every 45 days or so.) Instead of hauling in king mackerel we cruised the protected harbor and enjoyed an otherwise nice day – sunny and warm, like it usually is in Destin.

The first mate – a blond-haired, bronze-skinned sea salt who looked to be in his 30s – didn't say much at first. He paced the deck, obscured behind opaque shades and a sun visor. Though he kept to himself, idly tossing lines in the water to pass the time, he wore an amiable smile and seemed to want to join the conversation. It didn't take much to draw him out.

His name was Mark Walker. He's a transplanted Californian who loves working on the water. A good guy, he headed east when his son moved to Destin so that he could be a responsible dad. Walker brought with him a sorely needed environmental ethic that has benefited the Destin area more than the oily opportunists who have overbuilt the beachfront and fouled the harbor would ever realize or concede. He deserves some kind of award for all the volunteer work he has done cleaning up Destin Harbor. For six months he did nothing but harbor cleanup, donating $70,000 of his own money and time, by his account.

"Nobody else was going to do it," he says. With a shrug he adds, "The money's gone. The harbor lives."

He has taken a proprietary interest in Destin Harbor's health and well being. "Nobody messes with my pond," says Walker. He's served as the official Community Service Officer for the harbor. Among other things, he enlisted smokers for his harbor-area "butt pickup patrol," forcing them to confront the litter that they and their ilk generate. "That puts them off discarding cigarette butts pretty quickly," he says, chuckling. In particular, he enjoys raising environmental awareness by speaking at local schools. "They're good little warriors," he notes.

The more he talks, the more animated he gets and the livelier are his casts from the deck. Each toss causes the unspooling monofilament line to sing in a high-pitched tone, and then there's a small splash as the rig hits the water.

"I'm trolling my favorite spots in the harbor for a trout," he explains. "I figured I might hit a 10-pounder, but I probably won't 'cause all I got's a little spoon."

Walker has mapped the harbor floor, which required countless hours diving down where God knows what toxic muck has been buried and entrained in the sediment. Learning of this, the U.S. Environmental Protection Agency called to ask, "Why are you not dead?" Walker has protected himself from the harbor's chemical horrors by coating his skin in Vaseline and treating his eyes with boric acid and ears with isopropyl alcohol. These trade secrets came east with him from California. He told his EPA inquisitors, "Man, I'm from Los Angeles. I grew up in a sewer."

He's also worked as a lifeguard and divemaster. He likes body surfing, but his real avocation is environmental activism. Even so, he knows what buttons not to push in Destin. "If I came on like Greenpeace and started telling on people, I'd be dead by now," he says. "The word 'environmentalist' scares people to death." So Walker works within the system, leading by example and making friends and recruits. Water quality at Destin Harbor has improved, but ask if he'd eat anything he caught here and the answer is "No. Nevah." All the same, between cleanup efforts and a boost from nature, things are looking up. Hurricane Opal, which left the harbor looking like a war zone of wrecked boats, brought a new sand floor to Destin, and 17 marine species have returned.

daily, they have a buy-one-entree-and-get-one-free deal that's an absolute steal.

Any seafood item at the Marina Cafe is bound to be good but we'd especially commend those using fresh local catches: grouper, tuna, mahimahi. We tried flash-seared pepper-crusted tuna (served atop artichoke hearts and green beans) and grilled mahimahi (in a citrus thyme beurre blanc). The meal begins with a basket full of hot, fresh bread, and your waiter upends a wine bottle full of herbed olive oil for dipping. The menu is very a la carte—entrees come with minimal veggie accompaniment, side dishes such as garlic braised spinach run around $5, and appetizers (designated "small plates" in the new parlance) run in the $8–12 range. We split a heaping platter of buttermilk-marinated fried calamari served with a spicy caper pomodoro dipping sauce. The crab cake, scallop, and shrimp appetizers are also pure heaven! If you make it to dessert, try one of their fortified coffees. Black Gold adds five liqueurs—including frangelico, amaretto, and cinnamon schnapps—to the steaming brew.

Another favorite spot is **Cafe Grazie** (1771 Old 98 East, 850/837-7240, $$$), a bustling Italian restaurant that does everything right, from warm bread served with an olive oil, roasted garlic, and red pepper dip prepared at your table to entrees like the house specialty grouper parmesan. You'll enjoy this festive place and its cuisine immensely.

Lest we forget, a good place for breakfast or a mid-day pastry is the **Donut Hole** (635 U.S. 98 East, 850/837-8824, $). We love its kindred operation over in Walton County, and this is the original.

NIGHTLIFE
Nightown (140 Palmetto Street, 850/837-7625), a multi-tiered dance club/disco, is still king of Destin's nightlife. If deejayed dance music is your thing, this self-billed "ultimate dance club" is the place to go. We're too old and cynical to affect dance-floor moves without irony or embarrassment, and the music is egregious to our ears. That is why we're more

likely to head over to Destin Harbor and hanging out with the Parrotheads at **AJ's Club Bimini** (168 U.S. 98 East, 850/837-1913) or amble over to the **Boathouse Oyster Bar** (288 U.S. 98 East, 850/837-3645), which is the most down-to-earth joint in town.

Eglin Air Force Base

Spreading its wings to embrace 724 square miles of land plus 97,963 square miles of test and training area in the Gulf of Mexico, Eglin Air Force Base is the largest in the free world. The 33rd Fighter Wing, heroes of the 1990 Persian Gulf incursion, is based at Eglin. The sight of parachuting pilots and the sounds of low-flying jets are not uncommon around here.

Eglin owns 3.5 miles of beach at the east end of Santa Rosa Island and about 15 miles at the island's midsection. Sandwiched between these parcels is Okaloosa Island—the name that locals have given the unincorporated commercial area south of Fort Walton Beach. Eglin's holdings are, in the words of one lifelong local, "jewels of emptiness." Indeed, they are beautiful to behold from U.S. 98, with white sand mounded so high that it almost resembles a snowy winter landscape. The beaches of Eglin are not entirely off-limits to the public. At least the eastern parcel of **Eglin Beach,** near Destin Bridge, is accessible. For the military community, there's Eglin Community Beach Center, a seasonal beach club with a big deck, food concession, and gorgeous strip of beach. The beach is open to all, with a few rules (e.g., no walking on dunes, as a beach-restoration project is in progress). Beach access is free, except for down by the jetties, which requires a $7 recreation permit obtainable at Eglin Air Force Base's Natural Resources Branch on S.R. 85 in Niceville; call 850/882-4164.

North of Santa Rosa Island, much of Eglin is open to outdoor recreation. Strewn among the base's vast acreage are 15 tent camping areas, 20 fishing holes, and 52 miles of boat and canoe routes that run through eight bayous and rivers. There are no proven trails but many miles of sandy roads. To obtain a recreation permit, drop by the Natural Resources Branch or write in advance of your visit. The permitting and fee structure is somewhat complicated but basically boils down to the following:

For a $7 recreational permit, you can hike, bike, or ride horses on Eglin's 264,000 acres. A permit to camp costs $5 and is good for up to five consecutive days in designated primitive campsites only. A fishing permit costs $12; a hunting permit, $40; and a combined permit, $50. They are good for a fiscal year.

Public tours of Eglin Air Force Base were canceled in the mid-1990s due to budget cutbacks. However, the **Air Force Armament Museum** (100 Museum Drive, Eglin AFB, 850/882-4062)—which sits right outside the gates at the intersection of S.R. 85 and S.R. 189—is open daily 9:30 A.M.–4:30 P.M. There is no admission charge.

For more information, contact Eglin Air Force Base, Natural Resources Branch, 107 S.R. 85 North, Eglin Air Force Base, FL 32542, 850/882-4164, www.eglin.af.mil.

BEACHES

▣ EGLIN AIR FORCE BASE

Location: west side of Destin bridge, off U.S. 98 on Okaloosa Island
Parking/Fees: free parking lot
Hours: sunrise–sunset
Facilities: none
Contact: Public Affairs office at Eglin Air Force Base, 850/882-2878, ext. 333

Fort Walton Beach and Okaloosa Island

Fort Walton Beach is home of Eglin Air Force Base. Yet even before Fort Walton Beach became home to the largest air force base in the free world, the area held strategic value.

The first settlers arrived 10,000 years ago. They were a nomadic people whose wanderings came to a halt along this coast, where they set up a sophisticated civilization with skilled artisans, intricate religious ceremonies, and a political structure. One of their temple mounds, completed around A.D. 1400, still exists right in the center of town, along with one of the largest collections of native pottery in the Southeast. They can be found at the **Indian Temple Mound Museum** (139 Miracle Strip Parkway, 850/243-6521), which offers a remarkable glimpse at pre-Columbian culture unlike any other on the Florida Panhandle. Interestingly, Temple Mound was the first municipally owned museum in Florida.

It was near this Indian temple mound that George Walton—for whom the town was named—set up camp during the Civil War to guard the coast against Union invasion. After the war, veterans of "Camp Walton" returned to the area to homestead. One of them, John Thomas Brooks, established Brooks Landing on Santa Rosa Sound, near the Indian temple mound. The town that grew from this settlement was named Fort Walton in 1932. "Beach" was added in 1953 to attract vacationers. And why not? The beaches of Fort Walton, with their blanket of nearly pure white quartz sand, are among the nicest in the state of Florida.

Today, the city of Fort Walton Beach has a population of over 22,000, and the Greater Fort Walton area a whopping 90,000. Most of the residents live on the mainland. Okaloosa Island, where the beaches are located, is technically unincorporated, although businesses out there use Fort Walton Beach as a mailing address. Thus Fort Walton Beach technically has no gulf beaches (though it does have beaches on Choctawhatchee Bay). If you want beaches, then Okaloosa Island is where you need to be.

As military towns are wont to be, Fort Walton Beach—connected to the beaches by a bridge on U.S. 98—can get a little rough

John Beasley Wayside Park, Fort Walton Beach

© PARKE PUTERBAUGH

around the edges. It has the obligatory complement of pawn shops, tattoo and piercing parlors, and other businesses that serve the military community. At the same time, there's a cute, low-to-the-ground bunch of shops along the Miracle Strip in "downtown" Fort Walton Beach. One of them advertises "hippie things." Unfortunately, we also saw a sign of the times that read: "Now Selling: The Historic Gulfview Hotel District—A Primary Home Condominium Community."

Please, Fort Walton Beach, don't become another Destin.

For more information, contact the Greater Fort Walton Beach Chamber of Commerce, 34 Miracle Strip Parkway Southeast (U.S. 98), Fort Walton Beach, FL 32549, 850/244-8191, www.fwbchamber.org; or the Emerald Coast Convention and Visitors Bureau, 1540 Miracle Strip Parkway (U.S. 98), Fort Walton Beach, FL 32548, 850/651-7131 or 800/322-3319, www.destin-fwb.com.

BEACHES

Destin, Fort Walton Beach, and Okaloosa Island are marketed together as the Emerald Coast, a reference to the blue-green hue of the gulf. The words "Emerald Coast" and an accompanying logo adorn Fort Walton's Beach's water tower. While Destin attracts its share of upscale vacationers, Okaloosa Island has a far more appealing and accessible beach.

Starting from the east, the island thins to almost nothing on the narrow strip of land between Destin and Fort Walton Beach. The gulf looks to be encroaching upon the road. For a couple miles the beach has been flattened by recent hurricanes. Along this stretch, people pull over and walk to the beach carrying surfboards under their arms.

The fun begins after you cross over a bridge onto a barrier island. Its proper name is Santa Rosa Island, but the three-mile commercial corridor that falls between Eglin-owned parcels is called Okaloosa Island. Whatever you call it, the island stretches west to the tip of Fort Pickens at Pensacola Pass, 40 miles away.

According to a local geologist, the sands that make up Santa Rosa Island "are among the whitest and most homogenous throughout the entire world." The source of this pure quartz sand is the Appalachian Mountains,

THE EMERALD COAST

and the conduit is the Apalachicola River, 130 miles east of Fort Walton Beach. As world temperatures rose at the end of the last ice age, continental ice sheets began melting and the runoff surged down rivers to the sea.

One such river was the Apalachicola, which transported chemically weathered and eroded bits of Appalachian quartz to the Gulf of Mexico. The fine-ground, polished white sand grains began arriving 5,000 years ago. Reworked by waves and currents, these deposits formed a barrier island that grew west from Destin, a process that continues today.

Needless to add, the beaches on Okaloosa Island are superfine in more ways than one. Starting from the east, the first public beach is **John Beasley Wayside Park.** This free county park is located on U.S. 98, a few hundred feet east of the Visitors Welcome Center. Open 8 A.M.–5 P.M. daily, the center is full of local literature and is staffed by helpful folks.

A quarter mile west is **Brackin Wayside Park and Boardwalk,** which has a huge pier as its centerpiece. There's free parking, a gulfside restaurant (Harpoon Hanna's), several shops, volleyball nets on the beach, and lifeguards on duty in-season.

Just around the corner, where Santa Rosa Boulevard picks up along the beachfront after U.S. 98 cuts inland, are seven numbered beach accesses. The first three have seasonal lifeguards, picnic pavilions, and facilities. The only problem here is that there's public parking but not nearly enough of it. **Access #1** is next to Pandora's Lounge and also bears the name Blue Dolphin Beach Walk. The smaller, unnamed **Access #2,** adjoining the Breakers, has a dirt lot. **Access #3** bears the name Seashore Beach Walk. Like #1, it has some cute gazebos, a paved lot, and a boardwalk out to the beach. **Accesses #4, #5, and #6** are unimproved, with small gravel lots and portable toilets. The fourth adjoins the Carousel Beach Resort, the fifth is next to Island Echoes Resort, and the sixth is marked with a wooden sign. A seventh access is located just before the gate to Eglin Air Force Base. The distance between accesses #1

and #7 is all of two miles, so if one lot is filled just move down to the next.

An interesting footnote: The easternmost unit of the tri-state Gulf Islands National Seashore is on Okaloosa Island. The Okaloosa Area is a bayside facility, with free parking on, and access to, Choctawhatchee Bay. The bay's calm water is ideal for sailboarding and sailing, and its shallow depths mean safe, wave-free swimming for kiddies. A concessioner rents sailboards, sailboats, paddleboats, and beach equipment, and also sells snacks and drinks.

4 JOHN BEASLEY WAYSIDE PARK

Location: along U.S. 98 on Okaloosa Island, 1.25 miles east of Fort Walton Beach
Parking/Fees: free parking lot
Hours: 6 A.M.–8:30 P.M.
Facilities: lifeguards (seasonal), restrooms, picnic tables, showers, and a visitor center
Contact: Emerald Coast Convention and Visitors Bureau, 850/651-7131

5 BRACKIN WAYSIDE PARK AND BOARDWALK

Location: along U.S. 98 on Okaloosa Island, one mile east of Fort Walton Beach
Parking/Fees: free parking lot
Hours: sunrise-sunset
Facilities: concessions, lifeguards (seasonal), restrooms, picnic tables, and showers
Contact: Emerald Coast Convention and Visitors Bureau, 850/651-7131

6 OKALOOSA ISLAND ACCESSES (#1-3)

Location: marked and numbered accesses

along Santa Rosa Boulevard, on Okaloosa Island
Parking/Fees: free parking lots
Hours: 6 A.M.-8:30 P.M.
Facilities: lifeguards, restrooms, picnic tables, and showers
Contact: Emerald Coast Convention and Visitors Bureau, 850/651-7131

7 OKALOOSA ISLAND ACCESSES (#4-7)

Location: marked and numbered accesses along Santa Rosa Boulevard, on Okaloosa Island
Parking/Fees: free parking lots
Hours: 6 A.M.-8:30 P.M.
Facilities: restrooms (seasonal)
Contact: Emerald Coast Convention and Visitors Bureau, 850/651-7131

RECREATION AND ATTRACTIONS

- **Bike/Skate Rentals:** Plus Skateshop, 186 Miracle Strip Parkway, Fort Walton Beach, 850/244-6525
- **Ecotourism:** Adventures Unlimited Outdoor Center, 8974 Tomahawk Landing Road, Milton, 850/623-6197
- **Fishing Charters:** Destin Fishing Fleet Marina Charter Service, 201 U.S. 98 East, Destin, 850/837-1995
- **Marina:** Fort Walton Beach Yacht Basin, 104 Miracle Strip Parkway South, Fort Walton Beach, 850/244-5725
- **Pier:** Public Fishing and Observation Pier, Brackin Wayside Park and Boardwalk, 1400 U.S. 98 East, Okaloosa Island
- **Rainy-Day Attraction:** Indian Temple Mound Museum, 139 Southeast Miracle Strip Parkway, Fort Walton Beach, 850/833-9595
- **Shopping/Browsing:** Fort Walton Beach Main Street, Miracle Strip Parkway, Fort Walton Beach, 850/664-6246

- **Surf Shop:** Islander's Surf Shop, 191 Miracle Strip Parkway SE, 850/244-0451.
- **Vacation Rentals:** Southern Resorts, 656-C Santa Rosa Boulevard, Okaloosa Island, 850/243-0339

ACCOMMODATIONS

Several spiffy new motels and hotels have opened up on Okaloosa Island over the past decade. Flanking the pier and boardwalk at Brackin Wayside Park is the **Ramada Plaza Beach Resort** (1500 Miracle Strip Parkway, 850/243-9161, $$). Down a bit from that is **Holiday Inn Sunspree Resort** (573 Santa Rosa Boulevard, 850/244-8686, $$$), which was formerly Days Inn & Suites. Both offer the comforts of restaurants, lounges, and poolside bars, nicely landscaped grounds, and more than adequate beach access.

All that and more is available at the **Sheraton Four Points Hotel** (1325 Miracle Strip Parkway, 850/243-8116, $$$), which is a veritable oasis of greenery and creature comforts set a comfortable distance back from the generic drabness of the Miracle Strip. The hotel tower faces the beach, and a landscaped courtyard with spa and heated pool feels well removed from the churning world beyond. To put it all in perspective, the beach in back of the hotels and motels of Okaloosa Island has powdery white sand that will help make you forget whatever it costs to stay here.

A few budget motels are located on Okaloosa Island as well. We tried staying at one of them years back, lured by the $30 room rate. As they say, "You get what you pay for." We wound up sharing a wing—not to mention a whole mess of wings, judging from the remains of a chicken dinner left on the sidewalk—with some kerchief-headed dudes who were grilling and drinking outside their motel room a few doors down from us.

COASTAL CUISINE

Shoney's, Krystal Burgers, Morrison's Cafeteria, and Olive Garden are among the restaurants recommended by the Fort Walton Beach

THE EMERALD COAST

Chamber of Commerce, so you know the dining scene is nothing to write home about. But with a little rooting around, Fort Walton Beach and Okaloosa Island are capable of a few surprises.

Right on the beach is the **Crab Trap** (1450 Miracle Strip Parkway South, 850/243-5500, $$). It's the centerpiece of a complex of shops and restaurants on the rebuilt boardwalk at Brackin Wayside Park. The Crab Trap ("where the cool crabs hang out") has a seafood-heavy menu and a great view of the water. Another "view" restaurant, **Angler's Beachside Grill** (1030 Miracle Strip Parkway South, 850/796-0260, $$), is located at Fort Walton Pier. In addition to a seafood-heavy menu, they have a Sunday afternoon crawfish boil.

One of Florida's oldest seafood restaurants, **Staff's** (24 Miracle Strip Parkway South, 850/243-3482, $$) has been serving seafood and steaks in a family atmosphere for nearly a century, having opened in 1913. The restaurant has a very ordinary interior but a good menu of local catches like scamp, red snapper, and triggerfish. If you can't make up your mind, get the fried seafood platter, which costs $20.95 and includes free dessert. The seafood is fried crispy and served in huge portions. Afterward, we were pleasantly surprised by Staff's key lime pie.

Another popular choice is **High Tide Restaurant & Oyster Bar** (1203 Miracle Strip Parkway South, 850/244-2624, $$), located where Santa Rosa Boulevard meets Miracle Strip and then peels off to Okaloosa Island. If you're in a non-seafood mood, hit **Brooks**

Bridge Bar-B-Que and Cafe (240 Miracle Strip Parkway SE, 850/244-3003, $).

NIGHTLIFE

While in the Fort Walton Beach area, we opted to do as the locals do, which is to say pursue the seven deadly sins. The two most popular nightspots are a raucous nightclub and a raunchy strip club. **Cash's Cabanas** (106 Santa Rosa Boulevard, 850/244-2274), including Cash's Road Kill Cafe and Cash's Faux Pas, has for 30 years offered live entertainment to servicemen, working stiffs, and party animals.

Sammy's (1224 Santa Rosa Boulevard, 850/243-0693), an exotic dance club, is home to a bevy of "Sammy's Angels" willing to take it all off for slavering construction workers, lonely old men, and our boys in blue. As Sammy's parking lot was packed to the gills, we felt obliged to investigate. A sign inside the establishment lays out the protocol: "This is no time to be shy, If you'd like an Angel at your table, just ask, 'Can I buy you a drink?'" Further pointers are offered in an essay entitled "The Naked Truth About Table Dances," which includes such irrefutable brilliance as, "Most guys offer about $20 per dance. That's about 50 cents per thrill." Finally, this disclaimer: "Sammy's is not responsible for lost or broken hearts." Or squandered paychecks.

From here, the nightlife get progressively seedier. For further descents into Dante's Inferno, feel free to scout around town, where tattoos, palm readings, strippers, masseurs, and (no doubt) knuckle sandwiches are readily available.

PENSACOLA BEACH, PERDIDO KEY, AND THE WESTERN PANHANDLE

Welcome to the western frontier of Florida's Panhandle. In years' past, Santa Rosa and Escambia counties did indeed seem like an uncharted, and a welcoming, frontier. Between them, they're home to nearly 50 miles of fine-grained, Grade A white quartz sand.

Santa Rosa County's coast is little more than unincorporated Navarre Beach, which is technically leased from Escambia County, but Escambia is home to some of our perennial favorite beach sites—Pensacola Beach, the Gulf Islands National Seashore, and Perdido Key State Park. Though the "frontier" flavor out here began to go sour in the 1990s with the hideous high-rises on Perdido Key, the overridingly sweet spirit of the area was always available at the great cultural institution, the Flora-Bama Lounge. This palatial playhouse for party animals, with its seven different indoor/outdoor bar areas right on the beach, straddled two state lines at the Panhandle's end; it never failed to provide us a good time.

But the Flora-Bama Lounge is gone, wiped out by Hurricane Ivan, and the big blows of the last two years have, literally, reshaped the entire character of the western Panhandle and beyond, ripping up the Alabama, Mississippi and, of course, Louisiana coastlines as well. Bridges from the mainland to the barrier islands of Santa Rosa Island and Perdido Key have also been washed out, coast roads rendered impassable and anything smaller than a high-rise condo pretty much sent to the four winds. Navarre Beach itself lost much of its formerly prize-winning beach and no beach in the area escaped punishment. This is a tragedy, because these were some of the best on the Gulf Coast. Slowly the area is springing back to life—and a version of the Flora-Bama is even in the planning stages—but it's safe to say that it will be a good while before the frontier is as welcoming as it once was.

© PARKE PUTERBAUGH

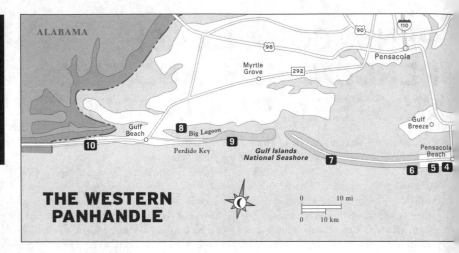

ALABAMA

Myrtle Grove

Pensacola

Gulf Breeze

Gulf Beach

Big Lagoon

Perdido Key

Gulf Islands National Seashore

Pensacola Beach

THE WESTERN PANHANDLE

0   10 mi

0   10 km

Navarre Beach

Except for a portion of Eglin Air Force Base's inaccessible coastal holdings, Santa Rosa County's only claim to gulfside real estate is Navarre Beach (pop. 3,000). This town, if you can call it that, lies between Eglin Air Force Base and the Santa Rosa Area of Gulf Islands National Seashore, with the latter falling inside Escambia County. Navarre Beach is a four-mile sliver of attempted development along a forlorn, windswept stretch of Santa Rosa Island, south of the mainland town of Navarre, also unincorporated but much larger. Every time they make headway building condos and selling property, nature sends a hurricane Navarre Beach's way. Dunes get flattened, sheets of sand obliterate the highway, and buildings take a beating. Opal and Georges were the main offenders in the 1990s, and Ivan, Dennis, and Katrina have belted the beaches in the past few years. Check the *Pensacola News Journal*'s photo archives for some stomach-churning aerial shots of Navarre Beach houses knocked over like dominoes and others squashed like giant bugs by July 2005's Dennis, whose eye made landfall here.

Even before the latest hurricanes, Navarre Beach possessed a ghost-town aura. Though seemingly too isolated to catch fire as a vaca-

tion or retirement destination, that hasn't stopped a boom in the construction of 15-story condos and mini-manses-on-stilts, which are going up everywhere. Still they insist on calling Navarre Beach an "undiscovered paradise." The irony is that with the arrival of such constructions—and the damage to them in recent years to hurricanes—it is no longer either undiscovered or paradisiacal.

The gravest man-made (as opposed to meteorological) affront to the serenity of this barrier island is the Portofino, which, though it uses a Pensacola Beach address, is actually in Navarre Beach. "An exclusive island vacation rental resort and spa," the Portofino's numerous high-rise towers have been, against all common-sense planning and zoning tradition, wedged along the bay-front and cater to people who want body-fat analysis, skin-fold testing, body wraps, and waxing as part of their vacation regimen. At least after all the hurricanes, with the main road heading west to Pensacola Beach (SR399) buried by sand, the Portofino could truly be marketed as "isolated."

For more information, contact the Navarre Beach Chamber of Commerce, 1917 Navarre School Road, P.O. Drawer 5430, Navarre, FL 32566, 850/939-3267 or 800/480-7263, www.navarrefl.com/nbacoc.

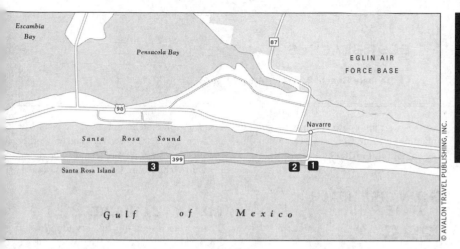

THE WESTERN PANHANDLE

© AVALON TRAVEL PUBLISHING, INC.

BEACHES

About a mile's worth of Navarre Beach is undeveloped, county-owned public beach. That part of **Navarre Beach** extends from the point at which the Navarre toll bridge deposits traffic on the island to the gate at Eglin Air Force Base. There are 12 separate county-owned, sequentially numbered beach accesses distributed through Navarre Beach. At each, there are a few free parking spots and a boardwalk over the dunes to the gulf. For those who are so inclined, nude sunbathers frequent the east end of Navarre Beach. No lifeguards are on duty.

We were amazed to find ourselves, post-Ivan but pre-Dennis, with virtually the whole of the beach to ourselves one fine day, sharing it only with some paratroopers on maneuvers off in the distance at Eglin. We marveled at the expanse of beach, the fineness of the sand, and the penetrating air-force blue of the water.

The best new addition to Navarre Beach—and to this whole end of the Panhandle—was **Navarre Beach State Park.** The state park opened in March 2004 on what was formerly U.S. Navy land. It embraces 130 acres from the gulf to the Santa Rosa Sound, and contains 10 campsites with full hookups. Campsites can be reserved up to 11 months in advance (call 800/326-3531 for reservations). Vacan-

cies are rare, so plan ahead. The day-use area has access to 4,000 feet of beach on the gulf and Santa Rosa Sound. The park has bathhouses, picnic pavilions, and a boardwalk that winds through the salt-marsh ecosystem. The **Navarre Beach Fishing Pier** (8579 Gulf Boulevard, 850/936-6188) is also run by the state, though it has been here several years. Open daily 8 A.M.–sunset, the 1,200-foot pier is a good place to catch cobia, mackerel, flounder, bonito, kingfish, pompano, and redfish. Nearby, you can get anything in the way of beach equipment at the Eco-Beach Store (8460 Gulf Boulevard, 850/936-7263), including bikes, kayaks, canoes, baby strollers, fishing charters and snorkel gear.

Note: We leave the above description intact, despite the fact that this wonderful park was damaged by Hurricane Ivan in September 2004 and completely shut down by Hurricane Dennis in July 2005. As this book was going to press, the park was still closed but we have the utmost faith in the Florida State Parks system to get this place up and running as soon as humanly possible. In the meantime, if you're a do-gooder, they need volunteers to help clear up the mess.

Another piece of good news for Navarre Beach is that a toll is no longer charged to cross the Garcon Point Bridge (S.R. 399) over

BEST BEACHES

(**Navarre Beach:** Best Nude Beach (page 556)

Santa Rosa Sound onto Navarre Beach. The tollbooths were, in fact, being torn down during our last visit in 2005.

1 NAVARRE BEACH STATE PARK

Location: 8660 Gulf Boulevard (U.S. 98), at west end of Navarre Beach on Santa Rosa Island
Parking/Fees: $4 per vehicle entrance fee, and $28 per night camping fee
Hours: 9 A.M.–sunset
Facilities: restrooms, picnic tables, and showers
Contact: Navarre Beach State Park, 850/936-6055 (Note: Temporarily closed in 2006 due to hurricane damage).

2 NAVARRE BEACH

　　　　　BEST (

Location: Gulf Boulevard (U.S. 98), at west end of Navarre Beach on Santa Rosa Island
Parking/Fees: free parking lot
Hours: 24 hours
Facilities: lifeguards (seasonal), restrooms, picnic tables, and showers
Contact: Santa Rosa County Engineering Department, 850/939-2387

ACCOMMODATIONS

The only hotel on the island, a two-story 253-room **Holiday Inn,** was so badly damaged by Hurricane Ivan that it was razed in early 2006 (as was another Holiday Inn in Pensacola Beach). Plans have been made to build a replacement at Navarre Beach, but no opening date has been set. The only other option, then, is a vacation rental. For those, try **Gulf Properties** (8460 Gulf Boulevard, 850/939-4748).

COASTAL CUISINE

There were restaurants aplenty along Gulf Boulevard and Navarre Parkway, and we were partial to one with good food, brew, beachside ambience, and local color: **Barracuda's Bar and Grill** (8469 Gulf Boulevard, 850/939-0093, $). You guessed it. Ivan wiped it out, though the owners have plans to rebuild it on the same spot. Miraculously, another local favorite located just down the road, **Crocodile's** (8649 Gulf Boulevard, 8650/939-8777, $$) survived; it puts a Louisiana spin on local seafood catches. Things are indeed catch as catch can these days at Navarre Beach.

Gulf Breeze

Gulf Breeze (pop. 6,189) is six miles south of Pensacola on U.S. 98, at the western end of a spit that juts into Pensacola Bay between Santa Rosa Island and the mainland. The Santa Rosa County line extends out with the spit. Thus, even though Pensacola, Gulf Breeze, and Pensacola Beach all line up on a north-south axis, Gulf Breeze belongs to a different county. This can be problematic if you're heading out to Pensacola Beach from Pensacola (or vice versa), because Santa Rosa is a largely dry county where nothing stronger than beer can be sold. (The latest effort to change that state of affairs was voted down in November 1998.) A word to the wise: they

NAVARRE BEACH BLUES

The good news for Navarre Beach was the March 2004 opening of Navarre Beach State Park. The bad news was the September 2004 arrival of Hurricane Ivan and then, nine months later, the arrival of Dennis, the eye of which made landfall right here on July 10, 2005. A storm tide of up to 12 feet caused flooding and "overwash" across the island as severe as that caused by Ivan and 1995's dreaded Opal. The most severe type of beach and dune erosion (condition IV) also occurred. As the official report on the storm put it, "Few dunes, natural or man-made, survived the impact of Dennis."

The beach is now very narrow throughout Navarre Beach and all but gone in some places. The extensive flooding and overwash severely damaged the roads and utilities. Beach access walkways have been destroyed throughout the community. The Navarre Fishing Pier sustained complete destruction to two sections. And the recently completed Navarre Beach State Park was severely impacted having all its dunes, roads, paved parking areas, boardwalks, beach access walkways, and one large bathhouse/concession building destroyed. Navarre Beach, once hailed by "Dr. Beach" as among the finest in the country and used by Steven Spielberg as the backdrop for *Jaws 2*, had, even prior to this, been suffering in recent years from severe erosion.

They're still working on rebuilding the dunes, as each whopper of a hurricane has made it a task comparable to Sisyphus's attempt to roll a boulder up a hill. The latest dune and beach restoration project, costing Santa Rosa County and FEMA (meaning all U.S. taxpayers) $13.6 million, was scheduled for completion by July 2006. The project is expected to add two million cubic yards of sand to a 4.1-mile stretch that includes Navarre Beach State Park; the new beach will be widened 150 feet and be backed by 14-foot dunes. We will see.

lie in wait in Gulf Breeze for those who have been drinking and driving. The behavior is inarguably illegal and reprehensible, and you stand a good chance of getting caught in Gulf Breeze.

Gulf Breeze serves as headquarters for the Florida district of **Gulf Islands National Seashore** (1801 Gulf Breeze Parkway, 850/934-2600). You can obtain maps and literature on the six areas that make up Gulf Islands National Seashore in Florida. Three are directly on the coast: Santa Rosa (between Navarre Beach and Pensacola Beach), Fort Pickens (west end of Santa Rosa Island, near Pensacola Beach), and Perdido Key. Fort Barrancas is southwest of Pensacola, near Pensacola Naval Air Station. Okaloosa is on Choctawhatchee Bay, near Fort Walton Beach.

The remaining area is Naval Live Oaks, which surrounds the headquarters and visitor center in Gulf Breeze. It is worth the short detour to drop by and orient yourself to the National Seashore's extensive holdings in the western Panhandle, and also to walk the trails and view the exhibits at Naval Live Oaks. This area is a Native American archaeological site and former federal tree farm where live oaks were grown to provide a supply of timber to build ships for the U.S. Navy from 1830 to 1860. Now it is a quiet haven for nature study where visitors can walk among salt marsh, live oak hammock, and sand pine-scrub communities.

A public fishing pier in Gulf Breeze juts out into Pensacola Bay (at 1 Gulf Breeze Parkway, 850/934-5147). It never closes and costs only $2 per person.

For more information, contact the Gulf Breeze Area Chamber of Commerce, 1170 Gulf Breeze Parkway, Gulf Breeze, FL 32561, 850/932-7888, www.gulfbreezechamber.com.

Santa Rosa Area (Gulf Islands National Seashore)

The Santa Rosa Area of Gulf Islands National Seashore runs for seven miles between the west end of Navarre Beach and the east end of Pensacola Beach. Three parking lots (without facilities) are strewn along its length, as are seven dune walkovers, offering instant access to the snow-white gulf beach. A spot along this area's midsection has been named **Opal Beach** (after the destructive 1995 hurricane), and it includes newly constructed parking lots and picnic clusters, including shelters, restrooms, showers, and dune crossovers. Sadly, they may have to open another memorial section, called Dennis Beach, because that devastating July 2005 hurricane so severely damaged the road and seashore it had to close until spring 2006.

When the seashore is up and running again, Opal Beach will remain the park's fee-collection area, with the National Seashore's standard $8 per vehicle charge applying. Your receipt is good for seven days at Opal Beach and all other fee-applicable areas of Gulf Islands National Seashore, including Fort Pickens and Perdido Key. The road through the

HURRICANE DENNIS

Another hurricane season from hell roared to life in 2005, picking up where it had left off in 2004. Arlene, the year's first tropical depression, formed very early in the season, on June 8. Three days later, Tropical Storm Arlene made landfall on the Western Panhandle. It brought light flooding but little damage, and relieved residents – still coping with the catastrophic losses from 2004's Hurricane Ivan – felt they'd dodged a bullet. But then came Hurricane Dennis, which had the Panhandle's name on it.

Dennis was the fourth named storm of 2005 – the first time in recorded history there'd been that many named Atlantic storms so early in the season. Dennis was a menace, growing into the most powerful July hurricane in a century and a half. It made landfall at snake-bit Pensacola Beach on Sunday, July 10, as a Category 3 storm with 120 mph winds. Compact and fast-moving, Dennis caused relatively small property losses compared to 2004's Ivan. Still, the beleaguered Panhandle could barely stand another round of flooding, and the natural environment took a beating.

The storm's impact was most heavily felt on its east side. Dennis caused more damage along the Eastern Panhandle and Big Bend than any hurricane since 1995's Opal. The oyster beds of Apalachicola Bay were left in shambles, and across the Panhandle as much as eight linear feet of beach was lost to erosion. The combination of 2004's Ivan and 2005's Dennis left many areas virtually beachless and much beachfront construction vulnerable to the next big blow. Beach and dunes from Navarre Beach east to St. George Island suffered erosion categorized as "major," according to Florida's Bureau of Beaches and Coastal Systems.

At hard-hit Navarre Beach, "Few dunes, natural or man-made, survived the impact of Dennis," according to the bureau's report. "Scour of the beach and upland contours significantly lowered elevations by three to six feet. The beach is now very narrow."

The road on Santa Rosa Island was left impassable in places, and several units of Gulf Islands National Seashore (Live Oak, Santa Rosa, Fort Pickens, Perdido Key) were knocked out of commission for many months, their geological and biological features having been severely altered. Nature is surely resilient, but if you revisit certain Western Panhandle locales – even now – they may be unrecognizable to your eyes.

Santa Rosa Area and the three undeveloped roadside parking lots will remain free. Incidentally, the Florida National Scenic Trail passes through the Santa Rosa Area, with the beach itself being the trail. If you're going to be in the area for a week, you should invest in a $25 annual pass, which will quickly pay for itself (and then some).

For more information, contact Gulf Islands National Seashore, 1801 Gulf Breeze Parkway, Gulf Breeze, FL 32563, 850/934-2600, www. nps.gov/guis.

BEACHES

🖪 SANTA ROSA AREA (GULF ISLANDS NATIONAL SEASHORE)

🚶 🏄

Location: between Navarre Beach and Pensacola Beach, along S.R. 399 (Gulf Boulevard) on Santa Rosa Island
Parking/fees: There are three free parking lots along S.R. 399 and an $8 per vehicle entrance fee at Opal Beach day-use picnic area. The entrance fee is good for seven days at all units of Gulf Islands National Seashore.
Hours: 8 A.M.-sunset
Facilities: none
Contact: Gulf Islands National Seashore, 850/934-2600

Pensacola Beach

Pensacola Beach (pop. 2,738) is a gulfside community—located two bridges, 8.5 miles, and 15 minutes from downtown Pensacola, at the western end of Santa Rosa Island—which has managed to maintain a relatively low-key aura reminiscent of what beach towns all over the country used to be like. In Pensacola Beach, the town overseers kept growth in check, not prohibiting it but just slowing it down to a manageable level. The result was, as

of 2004, a community that had its fair share of condos and hotel towers (with the emphasis on "fair"), along with vast stretches of older beach homes and one that looked relatively unblemished compared to the reckless development that has scarred neighboring Perdido Key and big-money sellouts like Destin.

All that changed in September 2004, when Hurricane Ivan brought wind and storm surges so severe that they knocked out a seemingly indestructible bridge leading from the mainland city of Pensacola to the barrier island (an image that made the national news). Needless to add, winds and flooding that severe caused major beach and dune erosion at Pensacola Beach, with some estimates as high as 50 yards of beachfront lopped off just like that. Structural damage was extensive, too, with hundreds of homes and businesses destroyed, and the sounds of hammers, saws, pumps, and dredges will be heard for years to come. Nine months later, the eye of Hurricane Dennis made landfall only a few miles east of Pensacola Beach, though miraculously not doing nearly the damage that Ivan did, perhaps because much of Ivan's damage had yet to be rebuilt.

We have always loved Pensacola Beach and we hope and pray that when all the dust and sand is cleared, the locals continue to retain some control over the low-key flavor of this peerless community, which has been a beacon of stability on the beach. All the same, some locals complain that Pensacola Beach is heading in that direction, with the governing Santa Rosa Island Authority giving realtors and developers whatever they ask for.

Right now, though, Pensacola Beach is all torn up, and so are we about this state of affairs. We'd be remiss to insist the town has recovered from these devastating storms. There are huge piles of rusty, twisted metal scrap along the road, wood and sawdust mounded in pyres, hillocks of rubble that was once part of a home or a condo, broken or dented furniture and appliances left at curbs. We found ourselves muttering, "How much more can one town take?" Even the beachside pay phone we tried to use didn't work because the sand had been so blasted by the wind into the metal casing that the buttons wouldn't move.

In Pensacola Beach, at the best of times, the beach life rules, and one day soon those good times will return. When they do, you can walk along the sand in either direction until your feet blister. Eventually, we hope, you'll be able to jog, bike, or stroll along the asphalt recreation trail that ran along the bay side of Via de Luna Drive (S.R. 399) for eight miles, extending from residential Pensacola Beach out to the gate at Fort Pickens. You can take your longboard out to the point at Fort Pickens and surf with the old-school crowd. You can eat, drink, and be merry without having to wander too far.

Most of the retail/commercial build-up is located compactly in the area between the foot of Bob Sikes Toll Bridge and the public beach parking lot. Here, you'll find a water tower painted like a beach ball. Three miles west, also on S.R. 399, is Pensacola Beach's other colorful water tower. These towers serve as bookends for the community, which is bordered by units of Gulf Islands National Seashore: Santa Rosa, to the east, and Fort Pickens, at the west end of the island.

Pensacola Beach is family friendly, tourist friendly, surfer friendly—just plain friendly. There's always been a little something for everybody out here without the interests of any one group—come-lately condo owners, longtime homeowners, transient vacationers, day-trippers from Pensacola and environs—dominating Pensacola Beach's relaxed way of life. Traditionally, crowds peak in summer, when as many as 250,000 people might be enjoying the island's beaches. Those numbers, of course, are down now because there are fewer rooms to stay at in Pensacola Beach after the hurricanes. Pensacola Beach even attracts a civilized Spring Break crowd, which tends to consist of families trying to escape college kids and college kids trying to escape each other.

Do bear in mind that this is not South Florida. Pensacola's climate is not subtropical, and there is no Gulf Stream warming the waters. While you'll swim comfortably from late April through September, Pensacola Beach is not a year-round playground. They do have a touch of winter here, with traces of snow from time to time. That said, the beaches of the Panhandle, especially along Santa Rosa Island, are some of the prettiest in Florida. They are also, unfortunately, disappearing. Read on.

For more information, contact the Pensacola Area Convention and Visitor Information Center, 1401 East Gregory Street, Pensacola, FL 32501, 850/434-1234 or 800/874-1234, www.visitpensacola.com; or the Pensacola Beach Visitor Information Center, 735 Pensacola Beach Boulevard, P.O. Box 1208, Pensacola Beach, FL 32562, 850/932-1500 or 800/635-4803, www.visitpensacolabeach.com.

BEACHES

Santa Rosa Island is 48 miles long from stem to stern. That's a lot of beach, and Escambia County claims a fair length along its west end.

© PARKE PUTERBAUGH

Pensacola Beach

The nearly pure quartz sand glistens like a bed of granulated sugar. However, there's trouble in paradise. The beaches of Santa Rosa Island have taken a beating from an onslaught of hurricanes: 1995's ferocious Hurricanes Erin and Opal, 1997's Hurricane Danny, 1998's one-two punch of Hurricanes Earl and Georges, and of course, Ivan, Dennis, and (to a lesser degree) Katrina. On the Fort Pickens side of the island, it's sad to see all the ghostly stalks of trees that have died from saltwater intrusion when the hurricane overwashed the island. Meanwhile, the beach itself has been disappearing at an alarming rate all along Santa Rosa Island. From 1999 to 2001, they lost 74 feet of beach width. Gone with the waves. There was only one volleyball net's width of beach by the Pensacola Beach pier. They lost 65 acres of sand, their greatest asset, along the 7.5 miles of Pensacola Beach.

This was sending area officials, resort owners and merchants into a tailspin. What do you do about an economy built on tourism when the very thing that draws people is disappearing grain by grain? You go shopping for two million cubic yards of sand and the money to pay for it. That is what happened in Pensacola Beach, where they tried to figure out how to raise the $10–20 million necessary for a beach renourishment project. They succeeded, but much of it washed away again in the cataclysm of hurricanes that repeatedly assaulted Pensacola Beach in 2004 and 2005.

Meanwhile, an elderly Pensacola Beach activist, 75-year-old Ann Sonborn, made national headlines for her efforts to ensure that the sugar-white beaches of Pensacola remain that way. She and other watchdogs patrolled the beaches to make sure the Santa Rosa Island Authority didn't cheat by using red clay, rocks, dirt, and brown sand. "I like white sand," she told the Wall Street Journal. Don't we all? Despite her best efforts, the sand at Pensacola Beach was renourished in 2003 by pumping offshore sand onto the beach. The result is not as bad as we've seen elsewhere, though small, shelly shards and off-white sand grains can be seen. To compare Pensacola Beach at present with the way it used to look, head out to the Fort Pickens end of Gulf Islands National Seashore, where sand was not pumped onto the beach. Predictably, much of the new sand on Pensacola Beach has already moved offshore again, creating a popular sand bar. Something tells us this was not part of the original plan. All thing's considered, however, it's still a wonderful beach.

The heart of Pensacola Beach is the enormous free public parking lot located where the bay bridge deposits traffic onto the island. Just look for the colorful water tower, painted to resemble a beach ball. At this point you can turn left toward Navarre Beach, right toward Fort Pickens, or straight into the public parking lot at Pensacola Beach. This area has long been known as **Casino Beach,** because a casino for social activities like teas and dances (not gambling) used to be out here. A concrete boardwalk runs along the beach, and the beachside Bikini Bar offers refuge from the sun. The old pier was destroyed by Hurricane Opal in 1995; a sturdy concrete replacement opened in the spring of 2001.

Like the parking, the facilities here are free and ample. The pier is 1,471 feet in length, making it the longest on the Gulf of Mexico. It sustained hurricane damage but, as this book was going to press, was being repaired and restored. A volleyball tournament was in progress on a recent visit, as enviably tanned and fit people played with professional intensity. The scene around the pier and the bandshell was lively, with groups of shaggy-haired, shirtless guys in various stages of feeling fine banging on congas and strumming guitars, trying their best to revive the spirit of Woodstock. One strummed a guitar (badly) while another beat on a cloth-covered African drum. They took stabs at "Evil Ways" and "All Along the Watchtower." Another fellow danced to their music. When "Evil Ways" fell apart due to the duo's uncertain rhythm and faulty strumming, the

THE WESTERN PANHANDLE

bongo-beater exclaimed, "Keep it goin', man, I was just gettin' a groove goin'."

Everyone is friendly here. Even the 17-year-old Lolitas say hi and smile at you when they walk past, as do the bikers and rapper wannabes. The most interesting phenomenon we encountered was the number of young women arriving solo, cell phones clamped between their teeth or held in their hands as they tiptoe from the asphalt lot onto the hot sand.

The beach and parking lot at Casino Beach are so oversized that they seem uncrowded even when there are significant numbers of people packing the beach. We've been to Pensacola Beach at different times of year—in early summer, at the height of Spring Break (which is but a tremor compared to Panama City Beach's annual beachquake), as well as in fall and winter (the deadest times of year)—and never failed to find a parking space. Across the way, facing Santa Rosa Sound, is Quietwater Beach Boardwalk. It's an area of shops and restaurants with a "quiet water" beach on the bayside.

In addition to all the parking by Casino Beach, smaller lots and roadside accesses are strung along the western end of **Pensacola Beach,** extending all the way to the entrance gate at Fort Pickens. Only one of these free accesses, which is called **Fort Pickens Gate,** has a full complement of facilities: picnic pavilions, dune walkovers, restrooms, and showers (but no lifeguards). This is the same beach you'd pay $8 to enter via the gate at Fort Pickens. One other access, by the San de Luna condominium complex, has only a paved parking lot. Numerous "Beach Access" signs are staked in the sand at periodic intervals to allow renters and homeowners on the bay side of the road access to the beach via dune crossovers. You can also park beside the road and use the crossovers.

Also, from Memorial Day to the end of September, Pensacola Beach operates a free "Tiki Trolley" that will whisk you to and from all points along the beach.

4 CASINO BEACH (PENSACOLA BEACH)

Location: south end of Pensacola Beach Road, in Pensacola Beach
Parking/fees: free parking lot
Hours: 24 hours
Facilities: concessions, lifeguards (seasonal), restrooms, picnic tables, and showers
Contact: Santa Rosa Island Authority at 850/932-2257

5 PENSACOLA BEACH (WEST ACCESSES)

Location: 10 beach-access points (one with a parking lot) between Casino Beach and Fort Pickens, along S.R. 399 in Pensacola Beach
Parking/fees: free roadside parking at dune crossovers and a free parking lot by San De Luna condominium complex
Hours: 24 hours
Facilities: none
Contact: Santa Rosa Island Authority, 850/932-2257

6 FORT PICKENS GATE

Location: 0.25 mile east of the entrance gate to Fort Pickens (Gulf Islands National Seashore), on S.R. 399 in Pensacola Beach
Parking/fees: free parking lot
Hours: 24 hours
Facilities: restrooms, picnic tables, and showers
Contact: Santa Rosa Island Authority, 850/932-2257

RECREATION AND ATTRACTIONS

- **Ecotourism:** Naval Live Oaks, Gulf Islands National Seashore, 1801 Gulf Breeze Parkway, Gulf Breeze, 850/934-2600

- **Fishing Charters:** Moorings Charter Fleet, 655 Pensacola Beach Boulevard, Pensacola Beach, 850/932-0304

- **Marina:** The Moorings, 655 Pensacola Beach Boulevard, Pensacola Beach, 850/432-9620

- **Pier:** Pensacola Beach Pier, Pensacola Beach; Fort Pickens Pier, Gulf Islands National Seashore, 850/934-2600

- **Rainy-Day Attraction:** National Museum of Naval Aviation, Pensacola Naval Air Station, 1750 Radford Boulevard, #B9, Pensacola, 850/453-6289

- **Shopping/Browsing:** Quietwater Beach Boardwalk, Quietwater Beach Road (bayside), Pensacola Beach

- **Surf Shop:** Innerlight, 203 Gulf Breeze Parkway, Gulf Breeze, 850/932-5134 and 1020 North 9th Avenue, Pensacola, 850/434-6743

- **Vacation Rentals:** JME Management, 27 Via de Luna Drive, Pensacola Beach, 850/932-0775.

ACCOMMODATIONS

Of the 1,200 hotel rooms that existed before Ivan, only 780 were available for visitors by the beginning of 2006. Of the 12 major hotels at the beach, only five were opened. Of the ones we've liked in years past, the best spot, in terms of location and condition, is the **Hampton Inn** (2 Via de Luna Drive, 850/932-6800, $$$). This four-story tower—unlike the typically serviceable but unfancy Hampton Inns that line interstates across the country—has been designed as a resort with vacationers in mind. Two enormous heated pools on a beach-facing deck pose an inviting detour either en route to or from the gulf. Gulfside rooms have private balconies. Rooms are spacious and airy, and the rate (averaging

$135–175 per night, in season) includes a formidable continental breakfast, plus drinks and snacks at night. The inn was so damaged by Ivan and Dennis that it was closed down, completely renovated, and reopened, better than ever, in spring 2006.

Other comparably priced gulfside lodges that we liked were the Clarion Inn and Resort and a popular eight-story Holiday Inn, located at the west end of Santa Rosa Island. Both were damaged so badly they've been torn down; only the Holiday Inn, as of March 2006, is planned to be rebuilt. The newest resort hotel on the beach is **Hilton Gardens Inn** (12 Via de Luna, 850/916-2999, $$$). It not only survived the hurricanes, but is building a 92-room tower addition, a further sign that Pensacola Beach is slowly moving up the ranks of Florida beaches in terms of recognition and desirability. Our biggest fear in this regard is that, because construction costs have doubled since late 2004, only the priciest of hotels and residential development will replace all the mom-and-pops and beach bungalows that were destroyed by the storms. For now, it's wait and see.

For a slight drop in room rates but not room quality, the **Comfort Inn Pensacola Beach** (40 Fort Pickens Road, 850/934-5400, $$$) is directly opposite the public parking lot at Casino Beach. If you don't mind being across the beach and not directly on it, you will save a few bucks per night (and it's probably why the inn was saved from Ivan). Besides, you're literally next door to the Sandshaker, home of the almighty Bushwhacker (see *Nightlife*). As regards the increase in room rates here, a bit of a rise is expected, given that it's a seller's market. However, a sign outside the visitors center on our last pass through reminded folks that "Price Gouging Is Against the Law."

COASTAL CUISINE

We are happy to report that nearly all of our favorite dining and drinking establishments survived Ivan and Dennis. Though some had to close for renovations, they are back up and running in 2006. The complex of shops at Quietwater Beach Boardwalk, on the bay side of the island near the foot of the toll bridge, houses several good restaurants. First, there's **Jubilee Topside** and **Jubilee Bushwhackers** (400 Quietwater Beach Road, 850/934-3108, $$$), sister operations that face the bayside beach known as Quietwater Beach. The house-specialty barbecued oysters are brushed with a tangy barbecue butter and topped with cheese, then broiled and served with a dipping sauce. Amberjack and grouper sandwiches, a heaping fried seafood platter, and plenty of non-seafood entrees fill the menus as well. The enclosed outdoor bar in the back often jumps to the sounds of reggae bands.

Speaking of which, they serve jammin' Jamaican jerk chicken and shrimp at **Sun Ray Restaurant & Cantina** (400 Quietwater Beach Road, 850/932-0118, $$$), a Caribbean/Mexican restaurant in the same complex. Sun Ray has the feel of a good old Baja surfer's bar. In fact, we heard a gaggle of old surfers, including one vintage board bum with wavy hair and ruddy complexion, waxing fondly about the surf out at "the Point" that day as they laid waste to mounds of fajitas. That seems to be the way to go here, as one sizzling pan of fajitas after another—filled with Cajun shrimp, jerk chicken, and steak—exited the kitchen. Also intriguing are the Caribbean seafood dishes: Montego Bay shrimp, red snapper, shrimp ceviche, and a saffron-saturated paella. Wash it all down with a Corona or one of their tall, cool drinks like the Key Lime Pie—a liquid version of the popular dessert, spiked with coconut liqueur—and you'll have found a great way to beat the heat.

As we were finishing dinner on a Saturday night over Spring Break, our waiter—a wiry-haired old hippie in a tie-dyed Sun Ray T-shirt—advised us to stick around for the Latin dancing. We demurred but will certainly return to Sun Ray's to further delve into their Mex-Carib menu.

A convenience store away from the Jubilee complex is the popular **Flounder's Chowder and Ale House** (800 Quietwater Beach Road, 850/932-2003, $$$). Much like Jubilee, there are indoor and outdoor dining areas, live music on occasion, and a festive beachside atmosphere that extends to the menu. "Eat, drink, and flounder" is their motto, and we happily obeyed, anteing up for Fred Flounder's Old Fashioned Florida Seafood Platter (consisting of grilled fish, shrimp scampi, fried oysters, scallops, and stuffed blue crab, all for $19.95) and a blackened sampler (chunks of grouper, tuna, and chicken). They also char-grill various fresh fish (snapper, mahimahi, grouper, yellowfin tuna), and baked stuffed flounder is a house specialty.

Flounder's shares ownership with **McGuire's** (600 East Gregory Street, 850/433-6789, $$$), a popular Irish pub in downtown Pensacola that serves steaks, burgers, ribs, and seafood in a convivial pub atmosphere, complete with an on-premises brewery and lots of dim-lit, dark-wood nooks and crannies. McGuire's ("over 20 years of feasting, imbibery, and debauchery") occupies the site of Pensacola's old firehouse. In addition to the pure, additive-free beer they turn out—we recommend a sampler of six homemade brews, lined up in a row of short glasses, with special kudos to the #2 "Irish Red"—they have a 7,500-bottle wine cellar. While touring the cellar, one of us got to handle a bottle of vino valued at $5,000. No time for slippery fingers!

Peg Leg Pete's (1010 Fort Pickens Road, 850/932-4139, $$) is a prized hangout for locals and those visitors lucky enough to stumble upon it. It's out toward Fort Pickens; turn right when you arrive on the island and head west for about a mile. There's an upstairs bar/restaurant with an outside deck, a downstairs hangout (the Underwhere Bar), and a sand volleyball court bedecked with sponsors' beer logos. Peg Leg's is a great place to come for beer and drinks, raw oysters and steamed shrimp, and ample servings of local color. And their key lime pie—which is pale yellow and not too tart, melding perfectly with its graham-cracker crust—rates high on our statewide tasting of this delicacy.

A popular day-starting spot on Pensacola Beach is **Bagelheads** (5 Via de Luna, 850/916-3287, $). It is a friendly place run efficiently by a small army of youthful helpers. We could overlook the Starbucks-style affectations (white chocolate scones, parmesan bagels) if they weren't so skimpy with the cream cheese. Good coffee and tasty pastries, though.

NIGHTLIFE

Begin your evening in Pensacola Beach with a Bushwhacker, a local specialty that originated at a beachside bar called **The Sandshaker** (731 Pensacola Beach Boulevard, 850/932-2211). This rummy, slushy concoction migrated up from the islands with a local bartender. It's the perfect way to launch an evening in Pensacola Beach. A well-made Bushwhacker tastes like a Caribbean milkshake and gives the imbiber both an alcohol buzz and a sugar rush. Several liqueurs are involved, crème de cacao prominent among them. Although it tastes like dessert, it packs a disarmingly potent punch. Locals come to the Sandshaker in late afternoon and early evening for drinks, gabbing, and sunset-watching on the deck, where a troubadour can often be found strumming a tune. One we'd like to hear: "Wasting away again in Bushwhackerville..."

The Sandshaker shook the entire community of Pensacola for reasons other than their potent drink in 2003. In December 2003 the bar was raided by local police and federal drug agents, capping a three-year cocaine-trafficking probe. Several employees were arrested and the lounge closed for a while. It gets stranger. The *Pensacola News Journal* reported that, in addition to Sandshaker staff, others arrested included prominent Pensacolans like a former Texaco executive who sat on the Board of Governors at Pensacola Junior College; a popular soccer coach at Gulf Breeze High School; a state probation officer and vice president of the Florida Council on Crime and Delinquency; and a mental health counselor. After such disillusioning news, we may need mental health counseling ourselves. Or maybe just another Bushwhacker. Remarkably, the bar survived its legal troubles and the

hurricanes and is still serving the frozen libation for which it's best known.

The nightlife rises to a comfortable simmer but never really boils over in Pensacola Beach. Typically, you'll see gaggles of buzz-cut military guys, baseball-capped frat boys, and dudes who pour cement and nail boards together standing around telling their latest "drunk as hell" stories while deciding where to make their next move.

A little Pensacola Beach trivia: the oldest bar on the island is **The Islander** (43 Via de Luna Drive, 850/932-3741). They've added an upstairs area, the Cypress Bar, for live music on the weekends (no cover). Ivan literally blew off the Islander's roof, but it's intact and in good spirits, and we have now adopted its motto for all future nightlife: "Never leave a place where you're having a good time to go somewhere else where you only think you'll have a better time." There's also a **Hooters** (400 Quietwater Beach Road, 850/934-9464), but don't get your hopes or anything else up, as the girls wear white T-shirts and shorts instead of the revealing getups into which they're squeezed like sausages at other Hooters. As we regard wholesome pulchritude more appealing than sleazy attire anyway, we actually found this Hooters to be more appealing than its sister acts.

Pensacola proper is a rocking little city, especially in the historic district around Palafox Place, called Seville Quarter. You'll find all kinds of bars and hangouts on Palafox and its warehouse-lined side streets. We gravitated to an alternative club called **Sluggo's** (130 Palafox Place, 850/435-0543), where we caught the bands Sugarsmack and Squatweiler, both from back home in North Carolina. The music was loud and bracing, and we hung out till the wee hours. The good time we had in the company of Pensacola's friendly alternative community was worth the next morning's ringing in our ears.

Finally, a word to the wise: the town of Gulf Breeze, which must be crossed when going from Pensacola Beach to Pensacola (and vice versa), lies in a different county (Santa Rosa).

The police force in Gulf Breeze vigilantly nabs drunk drivers en route, so don't drink and drive. We'd hate for you to party your way into a jail cell, lawyer's fees, fines, tripled insurance rates, loss of license, and other messy bringdowns that follow a DWI arrest. It's not worth the hassles, nor is it fair to put others at risk. But you already know that. Just don't forget it.

Fort Pickens Area (Gulf Islands National Seashore)

Note: We are leaving intact our descriptions of this exceptionally beautiful beach destination, even though Fort Pickens Road, Fort Pickens Campground, and the lands on the Fort Pickens Area of Gulf Islands National Seashore were heavily damaged by storms in 2004 and 2005. Eventually, this area will be seen and enjoyed again by the public. Indeed, Fort Pickens was within days of reopening after Ivan in June 2005 when Tropical Storm Arlene damaged the newly constructed roadway. It was followed by Tropical Storm Cindy, Hurricane Dennis, and Hurricane Katrina—an almost unfathomable onslaught. And now, at last, for a piece of good news: The National Park Service reopened Fort Pickens to hikers, bikers, and boaters by April 2006, and they hope to have the reconstructed park road and campground open to the public sometime in early 2007.

The west end of Santa Rosa Island is the site of an old army fort whose batteries and emplacements are open to visitors. The history is rich and the remains of the fort and its batteries, which saw active service 1834–1940, are impressively large. Fort Pickens itself took 21.5 million bricks to build. It's worth taking a self-guided tour of the fort, its cannons, and emplacements. A brochure can be picked up at the visitors center. There's also a museum detailing the natural history of the area. History aside, the real marvel at Fort Pickens is seven

unspoiled miles of gulf beaches. In addition, there are picnic areas, a bayside fishing pier, a bayside campground, a bike path, a camp store, and more. It's a nature lover's bonanza, and history buffs don't make out too shabbily, either.

The island thins precipitously for the first couple of miles past the entrance gate. This is due to Hurricane Opal, which nearly breached Santa Rosa Island at this spot. Actually, the island—and indeed the whole Panhandle—suffered major meteorological blows in 1995. Hurricane Erin's high winds toppled trees in August and Hurricane Opal's storm surge overwashed the island in October. Today, the park service road veers close to the lapping waves, and tendrils of sand blow across the asphalt. There was, in fact, a heated debate about relocating the road farther west, but arguments in favor of providing visitors with an ocean view won out. The trees at Fort Pickens suffered terribly from wind and waves. If the trunks didn't snap or split, the roots died from saltwater intrusion. Dunes were overtopped and flattened. The narrowed beach at Fort Pickens is still quite visibly reeling from the hurricanes of the past 12 years, and it's unclear whether the future holds recovery or regression. Yet for now this end of the island remains a great place to ditch the crowd and find your own hidden sliver of beach.

For more information, contact Gulf Islands National Seashore, 1801 Gulf Breeze Parkway, Gulf Breeze, FL 32561, 850/934-2600, www. nps.gov/guis.

BEACHES

Driving west from the entrance station, you hit a pair of gulfside parking lots identified only as "Public Beach." There are about 30 spaces at each and no facilities. **Langdon Beach** is the official named beach at Fort Perkins, with a large lot, picnic pavilions, dune walkovers, and seasonal lifeguards. Across the road is Langdon picnic area, a bike path, and the remains of an old battery. A short distance up the road, across from Campground Loop A, is Dune

Nature Trail, a boardwalk with informative nature signage that leads a quarter mile out to the beach. A small parking lot is located near the camp store, and there is another beach boardwalk across the street. At this point, the road loops around the island's tip, where the remnants of Fort Pickens, a visitors center, and a museum are located.

You can park beside the cement wall that rims the perimeter and stroll through the fort, tour the small museum, or fish from the bayside pier. You don't need a saltwater fishing license to toss a line at Fort Pickens; it's all included in the $8 entrance fee. Continuing around the loop, you'll encounter Battery 234 and Battery Cooper. A sand trail leads to the beach from each. There's great wilderness beach strolling out at this end. As a note to surfers, the tip of the island known as "the Point" is a favorite with longboarders. People also come from all over the southeast to snorkel and dive around the jetties at Fort Pickens.

Incidentally, Fort Pickens made national headlines in July 2001 when an eight-year-old boy was attacked by a 250-pound bull shark while playing in knee-deep water. His uncle wrestled the seven-foot shark to shore, a park ranger shot it, a volunteer firefighter removed the boy's severed arm from the shark's mouth, and his aunt administered CPR to the bleeding boy on the beach. A month later, Jessie Arbogast was still recovering in the hospital, having lost most of his blood. It was a miracle he survived at all.

Just for the record: in the year 2000, there were 51 reported shark attacks in the United States, 34 of them in Florida—and only one fatal.

7 LANGDON BEACH

Location: three miles west of Pensacola Beach, on Fort Pickens Drive at the west end of Santa Rosa Island
Parking/fees: The road into the park will be

closed to cars and campers until early 2007. $8 entrance fee per vehicle. The entrance fee is good for seven days at all units of Gulf Islands National Seashore. Camping fee is $20 per night. For camping reservations, call 800/365-2267.
Hours: 7 A.M.-midnight (CDT) and 7 A.M.-10 P.M. (CST)
Facilities: concessions, lifeguards (seasonal), restrooms, picnic tables, showers, and a visitor center
Contact: Gulf Islands National Seashore, 850/934-2600

ACCOMMODATIONS

The shaded, 200-site campground at Fort Pickens affords quick and easy walking access to gulf and bay beaches. It is, moreover, the only designated campground on Santa Rosa Island. You can camp for a week at Fort Pickens ($20 per night) for the cost of one night's hotel lodging in Pensacola Beach. For reservations, call 800/365-2267 and mention the designation code GUL. The campground will reopen in early 2007, barring further calamities.

Big Lagoon State Park

Big Lagoon State Park is exactly that: a big lagoon between Perdido Key and Pensacola, along a section of the Gulf Intracoastal Waterway. Its 700 acres include sandpine scrub, salt marshes, inland swamps, and sandy beaches. There's nearly a mile worth of beaches, broken into "East" and "West" designations. They're safe for children since they don't face the gulf's waves.

The park is a bonanza for nature lovers, with trails, boardwalks, an observation tower (at East Beach), abundant bird life in the lagoons and uplands, fishing in the grass beds, and a variety of habitats in a relatively small area. Tall pines shade a 75-site campground. A boat ramp provides ready access to the

Intracoastal Waterway. If you find yourself in the area, Big Lagoon should be an obligatory stop. And if you are feeling romantic, the park can be used for weddings (for an $80 fee). Needless to add, the park is undergoing lengthy restorations following the hurricanes and tropical storms of recent years. Check the state parks website for the latest information on the status of all facilities.

For more information contact Big Lagoon State Park, 12301 Gulf Beach Highway, Pensacola, FL 32507, 850/492-1595, www.floridastateparks.org.

BEACHES

⑧ BIG LAGOON STATE PARK
🏕️ 🚶

Location: 10 miles southwest of Pensacola on C.R. 292A
Parking/fees: $4 per vehicle entrance fee. Receipt is also good for admittance to Perdido Key State Park. The camping fee is $17.84 per night.
Hours: 8 A.M.-sunset
Facilities: restrooms, picnic tables, showers, and a visitor center
Contact: Big Lagoon State Park, 850/492-1595

Perdido Key Area (Gulf Islands National Seashore)

Note: We are leaving the descriptions of this exceptionally beautiful beach intact, even though the road and many of the park facilities were destroyed by Hurricane Ivan and Hurricane Dennis in 2004 and 2005, respectively. Happily, park officials have completely rebuilt the road through the Perdido Key Area; they are rebuilding the wrecked infrastructure as well. Outdoor showers and restrooms are available, as are new picnic pavilions. The nature trail boardwalk is being rebuilt, as well.

The westernmost unit of Gulf Islands National Seashore in Florida occupies six glorious miles on Perdido Key. Indeed, it is by far the best thing about Perdido Key. For one thing, the road only extends three miles into the park, but the beach extends 4.5 roadless miles farther. It is possible to find solitude by walking east along the beach. You can even saddle up the backpack for a wilderness beach campout. Primitive camping is permitted and costs no more than the $8 admission to the National Seashore, although they do ask that you obtain a free permit from the park ranger if you intend to park your car overnight. This formality is not required if you arrive by boat (which most campers do). The other stipulation is that campers must walk at least a half-mile east of the paved road before setting up. Call 850/934-2623 for more camping information.

For more general information contact Gulf Islands National Seashore, 1801 Gulf Breeze Parkway, Gulf Breeze, FL 32561, 850/934-2600, www.nps.gov/guis.

BEACHES

The developed beach out here is named for Rosamond Johnson, the first black serviceman from Escambia County to die in the Korean War. Before desegregation, this was the only beach in the area open to African-Americans. At **Johnson Beach,** there are covered picnic pavilions on the beach side of the road and a nature trail on the lagoon. A concession stand and lifeguards are present from Memorial Day to Labor Day. As has been noted, you can elect to ditch the crowds—not that they're ever huge, by urban-beach standards—by proceeding east to the end of the park road and then hiking along the beach to your own sandy sanctuary. At the far eastern tip of Perdido Key is the west jetty that holds open the mouth of Pensacola Bay.

🎧 JOHNSON BEACH

Location: 15 miles southwest of Pensacola, via S.R. 292, at the east end of Perdido Key

Parking/fees: $8 entrance fee per vehicle. The entrance fee is good for seven days at all units of Gulf Islands National Seashore. There is no charge for primitive camping on the beach, but you are asked to register at the ranger station and to avoid the dunes and vegetated areas.

Hours: 8 A.M.–sunset

Facilities: concessions, lifeguards (seasonal), restrooms, picnic tables, and showers

Contact: Gulf Islands National Seashore, 850/934-2600

Perdido Key

The state of Florida's amazing shoreline and this guidebook both deserve a happier ending than the one provided by Perdido Key. The key runs for 16 miles, all but the last mile of which lie inside Florida. Between the Perdido Key unit of Gulf Islands National Seashore and Perdido Key State Park, a generous allotment of nearly 10 miles of beach have been set aside for preservation and recreation. The problem here is not the key itself but the community of Perdido Key, which is actually an unincorporated part of Escambia County (read: subject to minimal building and zoning regulations). It is glutted with high-rise condos on the gulf side of the road, and more are on the way, if developers continue to have it their way. Even after visits from Hurricanes Ivan, Dennis, and Katrina, the development continues apace.

How bad is it? Bad enough that a two-year moratorium on construction had to be imposed. In 1998, however, the moratorium was lifted, and the earthmovers have been at it again. The cap on living units is 4,116, but some feel that this has been ignored and that, when approved but not-yet-built developments are factored in, the construction may in fact have surpassed the cap by as many as 2,000

units. Keeping tabs on the developmental mayhem afoot on Perdido Key is bit like trying to plug a leaky dike. In 2000, a lawyer from Destin, another ruined community, filed a $15 million lawsuit against Escambia County to force the construction of a 19-story beachfront condo called Windemere. "This project is going to get built," he stated. "We're going to get to develop it one way or the other. They're going to get their condos."

Then, in September of that same year, a Texas developer pitched a $390 million Marriott resort and convention center that would overwhelm 213 acres of Perdido Key. It would sit next to the Lost Key Plantation golf club and involve construction of a 300-room gulf-side hotel, another 120-unit hotel on the bay side, as many as 500 time-share units and 1,455 condo units, plus a 132,000-square-foot convention center. The "project coordinator" claimed with a straight face that it would not overload the island. He's unintentionally on the money in the sense that the island is already overloaded, so what difference would a few thousand more units make? Too much is never enough! Bring it on!

To put this in perspective, the year-round population on Perdido Key is 1,600 and the number of units is nearly triple that, which means that a lot of high-rise housing sits idle much of the time. Why were these monstrosities not built on the north side of the road, a location no less proximate to the gulf that would have provided a buffer from hurricanes and beach erosion while allowing the public to see and use the beaches? And how could any of this have happened in a place that is a designated coastal high-hazard area—that is, an evacuation area in the event of a Category 1 hurricane?

At "buildout"—a developer's euphemism for maximum planned or permitted construction—Perdido Key will be top-heavy with 8,000 units, and the state route that runs through it will be widened to four lanes. At least some of the locals are up in arms over all this unchecked growth. The Perdido Key As-

HURRICANE IVAN

The third major hurricane to hit Florida in one month was also the first of the 2004 season to reach Category 5 (winds of 155 mph or more) status. Before barreling down on Florida, Ivan killed 68 people in the Caribbean. In particular, it damaged or destroyed nearly 90 percent of the buildings on Grenada and left half the residents homeless. Bearing down on Florida, Ivan triggered evacuations on the Keys, the West Coast, and the Panhandle.

Ultimately, the slow-moving storm zeroed in on the western Panhandle, making landfall as a Category 3 hurricane along the Florida-Alabama line in the early morning hours of September 16. Even before coming ashore, its outer fringes had spawned killer tornadoes in Panama City Beach. But Pensacola and Perdido Key bore the brunt of Ivan's wrath. Century-old oak trees that had weathered numerous hurricanes were toppled, and the hurricane wiped out a section of the I-10 bridge linking Pensacola with Gulf Breeze and Pensacola Beach. Over a million people were without electricity, and a power-company spokesman said the utility's 80-year-old infrastructure had been "basically destroyed in eight hours."

Hurricane Ivan was bigger than Charley, more powerful than Frances, and caused three to four more times damage than either of them. It was the worst hurricane to hit the Panhandle since Opal in 1995, killing 19 people in Florida and causing $13 billion in property damage. Ivan's 30-foot storm surge and 130 mph winds wrought geological havoc upon beaches and bays. Moreover, as the *Palm Beach Post* reported, the hurricane "eviscerated dozens of homes down to their foundations and left others as bare skeletons, ready to crumble in the next stiff breeze."

We have never seen beaches as badly wracked by a hurricane as those of Santa Rosa Island (including Navarre Beach and Pensacola Beach) and Perdido Key in the aftermath of Ivan. Even a full year later, the area looked as if it had been hit by a bomb. Recovery seems a long ways off – and another assault, by Hurricane Dennis in 2005, only set the process further back. We really wonder if it will ever be the same out here.

Ivan will long be remembered as the storm that wouldn't go away. After causing severe flooding in the southeast, Ivan exited the mainland at North Carolina's Outer Banks. Over the open ocean it split into several storm systems, one of which turned south, circled around, and came back to torment Florida some more – East Coast, West Coast, and (yes) the Panhandle.

sociation and the Escambia County Citizens Coalition are fighting the county commission and the developers as best they can with pockets that don't go nearly as deep as their adversaries'. In so doing, they run the risk of "slap suits": lawsuits filed by developers to intimidate residents who challenge their projects.

What bothers us is that in the race for dollars, a lot of facts about beach preservation get overlooked or distorted. Consider a press release whose warm and fuzzy message misrepresented an alarming situation. One

mid-August evening in 1998, a gaggle of 80 sea turtle hatchlings emerged from a nest out behind the misnamed Eden Condominium. Instinct would lead them to follow the light of the moon to the Gulf of Mexico, but they were confused by artificial lighting from the condo and headed for the pool instead. Here was the condo manager's take on what turned out to be a narrowly averted tragedy: "This was a great opportunity to see a spectacular event of nature. The [condo] visitors pitched right in and helped in the rescue effort. They just loved it!"

We took a different sort of sounding from the natural world. As we drove through this tall forest of condos, we could hear frogs in the swamps. Their loud collective croaking sounded like didgeridoos in those brief vacant stretches between human constructions. We figured they were saying something like, "We want our ecosystem back!" We also heard other critters making noises that sounded like "creepy... creepy... creepy." We couldn't agree more.

With four heavily developed miles of condos reaching as high as 18 stories, plus bayside developments and golf courses, it is disingenuous to open a piece of visitor-information literature with the heading, "PERDIDO KEY. SHHHH!!! OUR SECRET!" Perdido Key is no secret—just ask the sea turtles—and this "building-frenzied key," as the *Pensacola News-Journal* accurately described it, is home to some of the tallest and ugliest constructions anywhere in Florida. What can you say about a community that sites golf courses atop wetlands, a shopping center atop an Indian burial ground, and condo towers atop a narrowing beach? Nothing more than they've got it all wrong on Perdido Key.

A final anecdote. The first edition of this book didn't go nearly so far in its criticism of development on Perdido Key, and yet one of us received a phone call at home from an outraged woman who identified herself as a member of the Perdido Key Chamber of Commerce and the manager of a condominium property. After ranting and raving for 20 minutes, she delivered her coup de grace: "You don't know *nuthin'* 'bout Perdido Key!"

Unfortunately, we know way too much about Perdido Key.

For more information, contact the Perdido Key Area Chamber of Commerce, 15500 Perdido Key Drive, Perdido Key, FL 32507, 850/492-4660, www.perdidochamber.com.

BEACHES

In the middle of the developed stretch of Perdido Key is a 2.5-mile, 247-acre respite known as **Perdido Key State Park.** The beach here has lost a good deal of its width as the cumulative result of numerous hurricanes since 1995. There are two bathhouses at Perdido Key and a long beach to lie on. The price is right, too: $2 per vehicle or nothing at all if you can produce a receipt from Big Lagoon State Park. The state park system honored its pledge: "Perdido Key State Park will reopen as soon as possible. Thank you for your patience and understanding." The park reopened in the spring of 2006.

10 PERDIDO KEY STATE PARK

Location: 17 miles southwest of Pensacola, along S.R. 292 on Perdido Key
Parking/fees: $2 per vehicle entrance fee (free with a receipt from Big Lagoon State Park)
Hours: 8 A.M.-sunset
Facilities: restrooms, picnic tables, and showers
Contact: Perdido Key State Park c/o Big Lagoon State Park, 850/492-1595

ACCOMMODATIONS

They call Perdido Key a family-oriented beach, but there is not a single motel or hotel room to be found on the beach. The closest you can get is **Best Western Perdido Key** (13585 Perdido Key Drive, 850/492-2775, $$), which is hundreds of yards from the beach. However, any number of high-rises like the aforementioned **Eden** (16281 Perdido Key Drive, 850/492-3336, $$$$) will rent by the week in summer and by the day the rest of the year. Rental rates at Eden run about $1,000–1,400 per week for a one- or two- bedroom condo in season and drop by as much as 40 percent out of season. Condo rental rates on Perdido Key vary from one concrete housing project to another, so shop around. By the way, you can't miss Eden: It's the gargantuan sloping condo that dominates the horizon like a breaching whale. It looks like anything but the biblical Eden.

THE FALL AND RISE OF THE FLORA-BAMA LOUNGE

Having reached the end of the road, we are somewhat saddened at having to be the bearers of sad news. The legendary **Flora-Bama Lounge, Package & Oyster Bar** (17401 Perdido Key Drive, 850/492-0611) was razed in April 2005, after sustaining irreparable damage the previous September. The Flora-Bama has since reopened as an open-air deck bar with an indoor tent.

Flora-Bama Lounge had in recent years been engulfed by a fortress of high-rise condos that, literally, loomed right up to its back door like Japanese sci-fi monsters. What seemed a laid-back roadhouse complex in the best flyblown Florida beach tradition came to look lost by comparison amidst this condo blight. Nonetheless, it never failed to amuse and entertain us, and a trip to this end of the Panhandle was incomplete without a visit to the Flora-Bama, the most happening place within 50 miles of Perdido. The roadhouse had 11 bars, 500 feet of beach, and, live music nightly. The bands who were playing during our last visit, just prior to Hurricane Ivan, included the Beat Daddys, Knee Deep, and Phat Taxi. We walked into the middle of a Miss Summer Bikini Contest, held on Sunday afternoons. The whole ramshackle operation resembled a folk-art sculpture made out of weathered wood, canvas, and beer cans. The crowd could be as rough hewn as the architecture. Nothing dangerous, you understand, just a bunch of good ol' boys and gals blowing off steam, y'know?

The Flora-Bama Lounge hosts a number of annual events, the most notable being the Interstate Mullet Toss (yes, a fish-throwing contest, held in late April) and the Frank Brown International Songwriters Festival. Frank was a Flora-Bama employee who lived to the ripe old age of 95. The music festival named for him is an 11-day showcase in early- to mid-November that draws some of the best players in the Southeast. The idea behind the festival is to promote the belief that "music makes the world a better place."

A little history lesson for perspective: The Flora-Bama was built by Greek-Americans from Pensacola, Ted Tampary and Constantine and Anthony Theodore. Though it was due to open on July 4, 1964, it was burned down by the owner of a rival establishment. Rebuilt in half the time, it was at first a drive-in liquor store. The most recent owners are Joe Gilchrist and Pat McClellon. "Do it with us on the line" is their motto, and we have done it with them on many occasions. One Sunday afternoon, around the time church was letting out in most places, we wandered into the Flora-Bama Lounge to find a pair of dudes with hair down to their belt loops entertaining a packed house with a song with the refrain, "I can't wait till I get sober so I can get drunk again." The crowd, which included many women, was smiling, hoisting mugs, and singing along.

They still don't have a proper building, per se – that will happen "sometime, we hope," we were told – but at least the Flora-Bama lives on. You can't keep a good bar down.

COASTAL CUISINE

Locals love **Triggers** (12700 Gulf Beach Highway, 850/492-1897, $$), whose specialty and namesake is triggerfish, a delicate-tasting deepwater catch that's serve fried, blackened, broiled, grilled, sauteed, char-grilled, stuffed, Cajun-style, in a salad, in a bisque, or as part of a combination plate. Give us a combination plate with triggerfish and mullet, and we're happy as clams.

The Reef (14110 Perdido Key Boulevard, 850/492-9020, $$) has undergone a nice transformation in the past five years to become a staple of Perdido Key's dining and nightlife scenes. When the former ramshackle biker bar was sold, the new owners added an upstairs restaurant (breakfast, lunch, dinner) but retained the live-music and pool-hall venue downstairs. The menu is small and unfancy but sufficient enough for hungry beach bums. The signature item is barbequed shrimp, which is a treat in the Paul Prudhomme style: melted butter, cayenne pepper, rosemary, served with buttered loaf you dip and allow to melt in your mouth. It's mouth-watering, sinus-clearing, and spirit reviving. The blackened grouper salad is an $8 bargain, with crisp lettuce, cheese, carrots and healthy chunks of fresh fish.

A card displayed on the table boasted "Good Ole American Wine" and a sign on the door said "NASCAR Headquarters." The **Shrimp Basket** (14600 Perdido Key Drive, 850/492-1970, $) offers all-you-can-eat specials and an appealingly funky atmosphere where customers wear flip-flops. More upscale is **Orleans Restaurant** (14110 Perdido Key Drive, 850/492-4004, $$), a restaurant that doubles as a jazz venue. Hey, you're closer to what's left of New Orleans than you may realize, and a time zone earlier than the rest of Florida.

NIGHTLIFE

Our favorite Panhandle establishment, the Flora-Bama Lounge, has made a phoenix-like recovery from hurricane devastation. See *The Fall and Rise of the Flora-Bama Lounge* sidebar for more about this bit of good news. Yee-haw!

We asked our friendly barkeep at **The Reef** (14110 Perdido Key Boulevard, 850/492-9020) where all the bikers went when the ownership changed, and she said, "They still come here…

we got a Biker Night on Thursdays!" Darned if they don't. Actually, it was a Locals Night *and* Biker Night (one and the same?), with a free buffet, "free money," and "lots of prizes." It remained a mystery how they determine who is a biker and/or local, but free food and cash are indeed nice ways to thank their most loyal clientele.

Live music, with no cover charge, is featured nightly Wednesdays–Sundays, and we lucked into a band called the Landsharks playing on a Saturday night for a drinking crowd during the high summer season. They were more accomplished than their surroundings, performing an eclectic mix of songs by Ides of March ("Vehicle"), John Mayer ("Your Body Is a Wonderland"), and Neil Diamond ("You Are the Sun, I Am the Moon"). The shaven-headed guitarist looked like a Joe Satriani wannabe, and the paternal bassist, who played an eight-string bass guitar (in a bar band?!), actually yawned.

Being a bar band, they were forced to play "Happy Birthday" for a barfly named Cliff. They insisted he dance "the hucklebuck" while they performed an uptempo "Happy Birthday." ("Put your drink down, Cliff, you can hucklebuck better thataway!"). They assured him he'd get laid that night, which didn't seem to make him particularly happy. And the human parade came and went all around us: girls with cigarettes in their mouths, their boyfriends studying us to see if we or their girls smiled a little too familiarly at one another. Just another Saturday night on the Redneck Riviera in the friendliest biker bar we've ever been in.

RESOURCES

Travel Resources

FAST FACTS ABOUT FLORIDA

- **Average hours of sunshine each year:** 3,000
- **Capital:** Tallahassee
- **Distance from the southern tip of Florida to the Equator:** 1,700 miles
- **Florida sales tax:** 6 percent
- **Greatest distance from any point in Florida to the nearest beach:** 60 miles
- **Land area:** 58,560 square miles
- **Land area rank:** 22nd
- **Leading industries:** tourism, citrus growing, commercial fishing
- **Number of acres of state parks:** 723,000
- **Number of annual out-of-state visitors:** 74 million
- **Number of known springs:** 320
- **Number of lakes of one acre or larger:** 7,800
- **Number of miles of sandy beaches:** 1,100
- **Number of linear miles of shoreline:** 1,800
- **Number of miles of tidal shoreline:** 8,462
- **Number of rivers:** 166
- **Number of saltwater marine species:** 1,200
- **Number of state parks:** 162
- **Population rank of U.S. states:** 4th
- **Population:** 17,400,000 (most recent U.S. Census estimate, 2004)
- **State animal:** Florida panther
- **State beverage:** orange juice
- **State bird:** mockingbird
- **State flower:** orange blossom

© PARKE PUTERBAUGH

FLORIDA'S PRO SPORTS TEAMS

There are nine professional sports teams in the state of Florida, listed below with contact information.

MAJOR LEAGUE BASEBALL

- **Florida Marlins**
Dolphins Stadium, 2267 Dan Marino Boulevard, Miami, FL 33056, 305/623-6100, www.marlins.mlb.com

- **Tampa Bay Devil Rays**
Tropicana Field, One Tropicana Drive, St. Petersburg, FL 33705, 888/326-7297, www.devilrays.com
    One of us has a soft spot for the Devil Rays because they annually keep his beloved Baltimore Orioles out of last place.

NBA

- **Miami Heat**
American Airlines Arena, 601 Biscayne Boulevard, Miami, FL 33132, 786/777-4328, www.nba.com/heat
    Team leader Shaquille O'Neal has earned a sheriff's badge, adding law enforcement outside the arena to all the enforcing he does in the lane.

- **Orlando Magic**
Waterhouse Centre, 8701 Maitland Summit Boulevard, Orlando, FL 32810, 407/916-2400, www.nba.com/magic

NFL

- **Miami Dolphins**
Dolphins Stadium, 2267 Dan Marino Blvd., Miami, FL 33056, 305/623-6100, www.miamidolphins.com

- **Jacksonville Jaguars**
Alltel Stadium, 1 Alltel Stadium Place, Jacksonville, FL 32202, 904/633-2000, www.jaguars.com
    The Jags are perennial playoff contenders.

- **Tampa Bay Buccaneers**
Raymond James Stadium, One Buccaneer Place, Tampa, FL 33607, 813/879-2827, www.buccaneers.com

NATIONAL HOCKEY LEAGUE

- **Florida Panthers**
Bank Atlantic Center, One Panther Parkway, Sunrise, FL 33323, 954/835-7000, www.floridapanthers.com

- **Tampa Bay Lightning**
St. Pete Times Forum, 401 Channelside Drive, Tampa, FL 33602, 813/301-6500, www.tampabaylightning.com
    One of the premier teams in pro hockey, the Lightning were surprising winners of the 2004 Stanley Cup.

- **State freshwater fish:** Florida large-mouth bass
- **State nickname:** "The Sunshine State"
- **State reptile:** alligator
- **State saltwater fish:** sailfish
- **State saltwater mammal:** manatee
- **State shell:** horse conch
- **State song:** "Old Folks at Home" (a.k.a. "Suwannee River"), by Stephen Foster
- **State stone:** agatized coral
- **State tree:** sabal palm
- **Time zones:** Eastern (east of Apalachicola River), Central (west of Apalachicola River)
- **Who Named Florida:** Ponce de Leon, who called it "Pascua Florida" ("flowery Easter") on Easter 1513
- **Year granted statehood:** 1845

TIPS FOR SAVVY TRAVELERS

First, an observation gleaned from decades on the road. In general, the more you pay for a hotel room, the less you'll receive in the way of services and amenities. Exorbitant room charges are only part of the billing at large, upscale hotels (especially in Florida). Separate charges may be levied for parking a car, using an on-premises fitness center, and getting a beach cabana or lounge chair. Nothing is given away. (For more on this, see *The Great Hotel Surcharge Scam* section below)

Moreover, every unasked-for service provided—from the hijacking of your car by valets to the delivery of luggage to your room by bellhops—requires tipping. Our advice is to avoid inflated rates and surcharges by staying at a good midlevel hotel chain like Hampton Inn, Fairfield Inn by Marriott, or Holiday Inn Express (our favorites), where rooms are dependably clean and comfortable, parking spaces are free, and a complimentary continental breakfast is served each morning. Ask yourself how much time you spend in a room while on a beach vacation anyway. If you're hibernating in a hotel room, you might as well stay at home, where you can watch TV for free.

Here are some travel tips we've compiled in our many years of coastal wanderings:

- If you're flying, the best rates come with a minimum 21-day advance purchase. You can sometimes catch some last-minute deals, too. We've had success with Travelocity (www.travelocity.com) and their "Fare Watcher" service. But trust us on this one: book at least three weeks in advance, if at all possible.

- Carry your AAA and/or AARP card and always ask for an discount—not just at hotels but also at theme parks and attractions. By all means join a hotel chain's frequent guest club, which allow members to accrue points toward free future stays and include useful benefits like guaranteed late checkout. We're partial to Holiday Inn's Priority Club and Hilton's HHonors.

- Coupon booklets offering discount hotel rates can be useful if you're traveling without reservations or if there's still time to cancel an existing one. These "Roomsaver" booklets are found at highway rest areas and some gas stations and restaurants near interstate exits. You can also access and print them out at www.roomsaver.com.

- Try to stay at places that include a free continental breakfast or breakfast bar as part of the room rate. At the very least, siphon a cup of coffee from the lobby coffeemaker before checking out.

- Check in for at least two nights whenever possible. If hotel policy means you can't check in before 4 P.M. and must check out by 11 A.M., a one-night stay will have you in and out in a hurry, with only 19 hours of access to a room. A two-day stay will allow you to enjoy a full day and parts of two others. And you'll only have to unpack and pack once.

- When making hotel reservations, specify as precisely as possible the type of room you want so there will be no unpleasant surprises at check-in. If you want two beds, nonsmoking, ground level and ocean view, then spell it out to the reservation clerk or make the correct choices online. Always get a confirmation number and also print out your reservation, if you've made it online.

- Don't be shy about asking for an early check-in or late checkout. All they can do is say no. Bear in mind they want to court and keep loyal customers, not make you mad.

- Avoid inflated in-room phone charges and surcharges by using calling cards and cell phones. Never dial a long-distance call from a hotel phone. You might as well throw money out the window.

- Avoid hotel valets by asking for the self-parking option, if possible. Otherwise you will be forced to turn your car over to a youthful stranger and pay dearly for this larceny.

- Politely refuse bellhop service if you'd rather carry luggage to your room. Don't even make eye contact with anyone on the premises wearing a funny uniform.

- Place the "Privacy, Please" or "Do Not Disturb" sign on the door handle as you're leaving to avoid an intrusive evening "turn-down service" while you're out to dinner. You really don't need a chocolate placed on a fluffed-up pillow.

- Placing the privacy sign on your door will also spare you and yours a rude awakening by maids wanting to clean the room at an unconscionably early hour.

- If you'd rather not watch TV in the hotel fitness center, unplug the set and hide the remote control under a stack of towels. You can now buy a universal remote that will turn off TVs in airports, lobbies, and anywhere else you'd rather not be bothered by the boob tube. Gadget of the year, in our opinion.

- When patronizing a breakfast buffet (free or otherwise), wear a jacket and fill each pocket with fruit and snacks for the road. Who says there's no such thing as a free lunch?

- As much as possible, plan your vacation to minimize driving once you've reached your destination. It's not really a vacation if you're having to do a lot of driving. You do enough of that at home, don't you?

The Great American Surcharge Scam

It felt like heaven sleeping on the "Heavenly Beds" at the Westin Diplomat in Hollywood, but upon awakening we felt like entered some sort of nightmarish Kafka-esque reality when we studied the bill that had been slipped under the door. From over 20 years on the road we've come to learn that the more expensive the hotel, the less you get with your room, and the surcharges can mount quickly.

For instance, we had to pay $26 for two days' parking at the Diplomat in Hollywood. The business center at the hotel wanted to assess us $6 for the "service" of handing a package we'd prepared to a FedEx employee at the end of the day. The unkindest cut was a $2.50 per-call charge for dialing toll-free numbers from our room. Adding to the absurdity was the levying of a "state telecom tax" ($0.23) and a "county telecom tax" ($0.13), bringing the grand total to $2.86 per toll-free call. Our bill for toll-free phone calls alone came to $29—about what it would cost to stay for a night at a typical Motel 6.

And have you ever ordered room service? In addition to the already inflated prices on these menus, they'll tack on a $2 "room delivery fee" plus an 18 percent gratuity. We once calculated that a bagel with cream cheese delivered to our room would cost $11—roughly the cost of 50 bagels purchased in a grocery store. At one upscale resort, we calculated that a bowl of "mixed berries" would have set us back about $20, after all the surcharges were added to the listed fee of $10 for the miserly bowl of fruit. A cabana beside a pool at the same resort was going for a daily fee of $75–150. Also, use of the fitness rooms was complimentary, but a $25 daily fee for use of the locker room was applied. Can you realistically enjoy the former without the latter? Surely, even the wealthiest individual is going to notice the absurdity of being touched at every turn.

You can see where we're headed with this. The nickel-and-diming of the traveler—especially the business traveler, who doesn't notice and could care less about these add-ons, because his or her company is footing the bill—is mounting to a point where the basic room charge is just the starting point for a slew of extra charges. As capitalism must press ever onward with its prerogative for profit, these pesky additional fees are where the lodging industry has turned to swell the customer's bill.

TOLL-FREE PHONE NUMBERS

Airlines

Miami Airport is serviced by nearly 100 airlines and is the ninth-busiest airport in the world. Here is a selective list of some of the larger airlines that fly to Florida:

- Aeromexico, 800/237-6639
- Aeroperu, 800/777-7717
- Air Canada, 888/247-2262
- Air France, 800/237-2747
- Air Jamaica, 800/523-5585
- Alitalia, 800/223-5730
- American Airlines, 800/433-7300
- America West, 800/235-9292
- Bahamas Air, 800/222-4262
- British Airways, 800/247-9297
- Canadian Airlines, 800/426-7000
- Continental Airlines, 800/523-3273
- Delta Airlines, 800/221-1212
- Finnair, 800/950-5000
- Lufthansa, 800/645-3880
- Mexicana, 800/531-7921
- Northwest Airlines, 800/225-2525
- Pan Am, 800/359-7262
- Qantas Airways, 800/227-4585
- Southwest Airlines, 800/435-9792
- Swiss Air, 800/359-7947
- Transbrasil, 800/872-3153
- United Airlines, 800/241-6522
- USAirways, 800/428-4322

- Varig Brazilian Airlines, 800/468-2744
- Virgin Atlantic Airways, 800/862-8621
- ValuJet, 800/825-8536

Car-Rental Companies

Here is a list of the major car rental companies operating in Florida:

- Alamo Rent-A-Car, 800/327-9633
- Avis Rent-A-Car, 800/331-1212
- Budget Rent-A-Car, 800/527-0700
- Dollar Rent-A-Car, 800/800-3665
- Enterprise Rent-A-Car, 800/261-7331
- Hertz Rent-A-Car, 800/654-3131
- National Car Rental, 800/227-7368
- Thrifty Car Rental, 800/367-2277.

Hotels and Motels

For your convenience, here is a list of major hotel chains operating in Florida:

- Best Western, 800/780-7234
- Candlewood Suites, 800/226-3539
- Clarion Hotels, 877/423-6423
- Club Med, 888/932-2582
- Comfort Inn & Suites, 877/424-6423
- Courtyard by Marriott, 800/321-2211
- Crowne Plaza, 800/227-6963
- Days Inn, 800/329-7466
- Doubletree Inn, 800/222-8733
- Econo Lodge, 877/423-6423
- Embassy Suites, 800/362-2779
- Fairfield Inn, 800/228-2800
- Four Seasons, 800/819-5053
- Hampton Inns, 800/426-7866
- Hilton Hotels, 800/445-8667
- Holiday Inn, 800/465-4329
- Howard Johnson, 800/446-4656
- Hyatt Hotels, 888/591-1234
- Inter-Continental, 800/424-6835
- La Quinta Inns, 866/725-1661
- Marriott Hotels, 888/236-2427
- Motel 6, 800/466-8356
- Omni Hotels, 888/444-6664

- Quality Inn, 877/423-6423
- Radisson Hotels, 800/333-3333
- Ramada Inn, 800/272-6232
- Red Roof Inn, 800/733-7663
- Renaissance Hotels, 800/468-3571
- Residence Inn, 800/331-3131
- Ritz-Carlton, 800/241-3333
- Rodeway Inn, 877/424-6423
- Sheraton Hotels, 888/625-5144
- Shoney's Inn, 800/552-4667
- Sleep Inn, 877/423-6423
- Staybridge Suites, 800/238-8000
- Super 8 Motels, 800/800-8000
- Travelodge, 800/578-7878
- W Hotels, 888/625-5144
- Westin Hotels, 888/625-5144

General Information

For all kinds of information about Florida, contact Visit Florida, 661 East Jefferson Street, Tallahassee, FL 32301, 850/488-5607 (not a toll-free number), www.visitflorida.org. Visit Florida is a public/private partnership that acts as the official tourism marketing corporation for the State of Florida.

SUGGESTED READING

The books listed below have informed or entertained us and may deserve a look from you, too.

Amory, Cleveland. The Last Resorts. New York: Grosset & Dunlap, 1952.

Beatley, Timothy, et al. An Introduction to Coastal Zone Management. Washington, D.C.: Island Press, 1994.

Carr, Archie. A Naturalist in Florida. New Haven: Yale University Press, 1996.

De Hart, Allen. Adventuring in Florida: A Sierra Club Guide. Revised edition. San Francisco: Sierra Club Books, 1995.

Exley, Frederick. Pages from a Cold Island. New York: Random House, 1974.

Grow, Gerald. Florida Parks: A Guide to Camping and Nature (7th ed.). Tallahassee: Longleaf Publications, 2001.

Hiaasen, Carl. Sick Puppy. New York: Warner Books, 2001.

Hiaasen, Carl. Stormy Weather. New York: Warner Books, 1996.

Hiaasen, Carl. Tourist Season. New York: Warner Books, 1987.

Myers, Ronald L. and John J. Ewel. Ecosystems of Florida. Orlando: University of Central Florida Press, 1990.

Nelson, Gil. Exploring Wild Northwest Florida. Sarasota: Pineapple Press, 1995.

Pilkey, Orrin, et al. Living with the East Florida Shore. Durham, NC: Duke University Press, 1984.

Roberts, Diane. Dream State: Eight Generations of Swamp Lawyers, Conquistadors, Confederate Daughters, Banana Republicans, and Other Florida Wildlife. New York: Free Press, 2004.

Rymer, Russ. American Beach: A Saga of Race, Wealth, and Memory. New York: HarperCollins, 1998.

Vansant, Amy. The Surfer's Guide to Florida. Sarasota: Pineapple Press, 1995.

Whitney, Ellie, D. Bruce Means, and Anne Rudloe. Priceless Florida: Natural Ecosystems and Native Species. Sarasota: Pineapple Press, 2004.

Williams, Joy. The Florida Keys: A History & Guide (10th ed.). New York: Random House, 2003.

Beach Activities

SWIMMING

Parts of Florida are swimmable all year-round. For years, one of us took an annual New Year's Day dip in the Atlantic Ocean at Fort Lauderdale, and it was easy as pie, with water temps in the comfortable mid-70s. Roughly from

Palm Beach south, the Atlantic Ocean receives a thermal boost from the Gulf Stream, which passes closest to land hereabouts.

We've found parts of Florida's West Coast to be swimmable in late fall and early winter, too. One November afternoon, we took a swim off Siesta Key. The water temperature in the Gulf of Mexico hovered around 76°F. It felt balmy to us, especially as we basked in the knowledge that folks back home were wearing overcoats and raking leaves.

Some of the locals, however, looked at us as if we'd lost our minds. They claimed the water was just too cold for them this time of year.

"We're used to the summertime, when the gulf is in the high 80s, low 90s," said a ranger at a coastal park. "When it gets below 80, it's too cold for us."

We've heard this refrain over and over. A smile, a shake of the head: too chilly for us blood-thinned natives.

One day on Treasure Island we were treated like freaks for entering the water. A strolling couple stopped to ask, "You're not going swimming, are you?"

Was there a problem—Sting rays? Red tide? Shark attacks?

"You're a better man than I," said the husband. "Yesterday, I waded up to my waist, and it was so cold my bowels haven't been the same since."

Oh, come on. We're hardly polar bears when it comes to braving frigid waters. At 72°F, the gulf felt eminently swimmable on this warm, sun-dappled afternoon.

We described it as "refreshing." They described it as "too damn cold."

Now, we will admit you'll likely get nowhere near the water on the northern Florida coast November–March. Winter can extend its frosty tentacles as far down as Jacksonville, on the East Coast, and all along the Panhandle. We have been in the deep freeze in Panama City Beach and Seaside, exclaiming at the unexpected frigidity.

The concept of seasonality is much more pronounced in northern Florida than it is on the subtropical southern end of the Florida peninsula. As a result, South Florida has its high season (in terms of tourism) in the winter months, while summer is the peak time on the Panhandle.

How cold is too cold to swim? Your water-temperature tolerance has a lot to do with where you live and what you're used to, but the following scale will hold true for most people.

85°F and above: uncomfortably hot

80–85°F: bathwater warm

75–80°F: perfect temperature

70–75°F: refreshingly cool

65–70°F: uncomfortably cool

60–65°F: intolerably cold

59°F and below: hypothermia (wetsuits only!)

FISHING

Florida's recreational fishing industry brings in $3 billion a year in revenues. We're poor fisherman at best, and no serious angler would ever consult us for advice on the finer points of casting a line. We'd be laughed right out of the water, if not cut up for bait. However, there is one piece of advice we can unabashedly offer anglers of any level of competence who are considering a fishing trip to Florida. That is, get hold of the excellent magazine *Florida Fishing and Boating*, published by the nonprofit **Florida Sports Foundation** (2930 Kerry Forest Parkway, Tallahassee, FL 32309, 904/488-8347, www.flasports.com). This detailed, lavishly illustrated journal spells out all you need to know about Florida rules and regulations, license requirements, size and bag limits, best fishing spots for every species from amberjack to tarpon, best times of year to catch various species, names and numbers of reputable fishing charters, tournament information, and more. How popular is fishing? Well, there are 3.4 million registered anglers in the state of Florida.

To get you started, here are some general rules regarding fishing in Florida's waters—which include not just the Atlantic Ocean, Gulf of Mexico, and Straits of Florida but also 1,711 streams and rivers and 7,800 freshwater lakes. First, everyone ages 16–64 needs a fishing license, whether you are fishing in freshwater or saltwater. Fees vary according to residency and length of license. Non-resident freshwater and saltwater licenses are $16.50 for seven days and $31.50 for one year. For Florida residents—meaning that the state has been a person's primary residence for at least six months prior to license application—a combination freshwater/saltwater license is $25.50.

Call 888/347-3456 to obtain a license (for which service $3.25 plus a 2.5 percent surcharge will be added to your license fee or fees). You will be issued a license number and can start fishing the same day. (Your permanent license will be mailed out within 48 hours.) Fishing licenses can now also be obtained online at www1.wildlifelicense.com/fl with a slightly smaller service charge ($2.25 plus 2.5 percent) appended to the transaction. The money from fishing fees is used by the Florida Fish and Wildlife Conservation Commission to improve and restore marine habitat and to fund fisheries research and public education.

There are also established and strictly enforced saltwater limits on oysters, crawfish, queen conch, stone crab claws, blue crab, and Florida spiny lobster. Serious consequences await anyone injuring or killing sea turtles, manatees, porpoises, manta rays, coral, sea fans, and pelicans and other seabirds.

Specific fishing regulations, including the latest regulation changes—as well as a wealth of fishing facts, tips, and forecasts—are online at www.floridafisheries.com.

NUDE BEACHES

Let's be candid: For many, nude beaches offer the titillating hope of copping a peek at hot bods and the voyeuristic guilt of actually doing so. Honest-to-god naturists, however, just want to be left alone. The best way to do so is to find a secluded spot and act discreetly. This is not always possible in Florida, where condos overlook and tourists overrun nearly every sandy spot and where the terrain (unlike California) doesn't provide rocky, cliff-backed coves where privacy and seclusion can be easily gained.

In Florida, it seems, no nudes is good nudes. It is difficult to get naked without getting in trouble. As one naturist put it, "If you want to go nude, you have to be plain-out choosy and careful. Though a number of beaches around the state have earned a reputation as skinny-dipping beaches, one by one, they have been, shall we say, redressed by local law."

However, a subculture of beach nudity does exist in Florida. The "clothing optional" epicenter is, oddly enough, in the most populous corridor: the northernmost part of North Miami Beach. At the north end of Haulover Beach, one can skinny-dip or expose naked flesh to the sun's rays legally and without fear or disfavor. During National Nude Week each July, festivities are held at Haulover. In March, an annual Tropical Pig Roast is held here, too. Another celebrated hot spot for nude sunbathing is South Beach, where the people-watching is much better than Haulover Beach. And don't forget Playalinda Beach, up at Canaveral National Seashore, where naturism has persisted despite resistance from authorities and old fogeys.

Other beaches in Florida where nudity is practiced and tolerated:

- Guana River (between Ponte Vedra Beach and St. Augustine)
- Blind Creek Beach (near Jensen Beach)
- Boca Chica Beach (near Key West)
- St. George Island (easternmost end, inside St. George Island State Park)
- St. Vincent National Wildlife Refuge (an island offshore from Apalachicola)
- Navarre Beach (on land belonging to Eglin Air Force Base, along the western Panhandle)
- Santa Rosa Beach (a unit of Gulf Islands National Seashore, between Pensacola Beach and Navarre Beach)

- Fort Pickens (a unit of Gulf Islands National Seashore, west of Pensacola Beach)
- Perdido Key (a unit of Gulf Islands National Seashore)

For more information, contact South Florida Free Beaches/Florida Naturist Association, P.O. Box 530306, Miami Shores, FL 33153, www.sffb.com.

Health and Safety

AVOIDING SUNBURN

In the old days, before the ozone layer was depleted—before anyone knew there was an ozone layer—the beach was one big tanning salon. People who hadn't been outdoors all year suddenly spent two weeks in the sun on a beach towel. Slathering themselves with suntan lotion from forehead to feet, they submitted exposed flesh to eight hours of slow ultraviolet roasting. Everyone wanted, and many still want, a deep, dark tan.

We don't want to spoil your day at the beach, but here are the latest facts about what's really going on under the sun. You won't get this information from the manufacturers of sunscreens and other expensive lotions designed to make you feel safe while sunbathing beneath the thinning ozone layer. Many of the products on the market misleadingly offer "all-day protection," lulling sun-worshippers into a false sense of security.

According to researchers at the Memorial Sloan-Kettering Cancer Center, no sunscreen on the market offers protection from malignant melanoma, which is the most severe form of skin cancer (albeit the rarest). Writing in *Mother Jones,* Michael Castleman called the sunscreen industry the "sunscam industry," claiming it willfully endangers the lives and health of beachgoers. His greatest animus is aimed at the Skin Cancer Foundation (SCF), which annually warns consumers that "sunscreen should continue to be an integral part of a comprehensive program." What the SCF neglects to mention is that it is heavily funded by the sunscreen industry. Castleman argues that sunscreens might even contribute to skin cancers. By prolonging the amount of time people spend in the sun, they prevent sunburn, which is human skin's "only natural melanoma warning system." Statistics show that melanoma rates are growing 6 percent a year and that people are 12 times as likely to contract melanoma today than in 1950. Meanwhile, sunscreen sales continue to rise.

The real risk to human skin is UVA radiation, a longer-wave form of sunlight than the UVB radiation that causes sunburn. While UVB radiation does damage the skin's outer layer, UVA penetrates the its elastic fibers and collagen, causing you to "leather" while you weather. More insidiously, UVA penetrates the cloud cover, putting people at risk on days when they'd never suppose a hazard existed. Of course, beachgoers will continue to bask in the sun. And why shouldn't they? It's their vacation, for crying out loud. Well, to keep you from crying out loud from severe sunburn, here are some tips for safer sunbathing.

- The key to sitting safely in the sun is covering up. Buy or rent a beach umbrella. Wear a hat, ideally with a wide brim to deflect sun from the eyes. Sunlight is a contributing factor in cataract formation.

- Keep susceptible or overexposed parts of your body covered with clothing or towels. If you're sunbathing, turn over frequently and take a break in the shade every hour or so.

- As much as possible, stay out of the sun 11 A.M.–3 P.M., when its rays are most intense.

- Wear protective clothing. Try out new lines of beachwear made from fabrics alleged to block UVA and UVB rays.

- Use a sunscreen that blocks both UVA and UVB radiation. Read the label and look for ingredients like Parsol 1789 (avobenzone), titanium dioxide, and zinc oxide (that white stuff you see on lifeguards' noses).

- Liberally apply sunscreen to cool, dry skin a

half-hour before hitting the beach. This will allow it to penetrate the skin's fibers. Reapply sunscreen throughout the day, because sweat and water weakens and removes it. Don't believe products claiming to be "waterproof."

- Newer sun lotions contain antioxidant vitamins and enzymes that are said to suppress growth of cancerous cells during sunbathing. They are indeed more effective than old sunscreens, but as one dermatologist stated, "It's not possible to have pigment darkening without sun damage. It's too good to be true." The most effective antioxidant is L-ascorbic acid (a form of Vitamin C). Still, long-term suppression of skin cancers has not been verified and you are, in effect, lab rats for the antioxidant industry. So even if you use the latest generation of antioxidant-fortified sunscreens, cover up and use common sense.

- Those at greatest risk for melanoma due to sun exposure are fair-skinned Caucasians, people with naturally red or blond hair, and those with freckles on their upper back. Melanomas are also on the rise among Chinese, Japanese, Hawaiians, and Filipinos—populations once thought immune. A family history of melanoma is also, obviously, a contributing factor.

- If you feel flush after sun exposure, use "after sun" lotions that contain sun-protective nutrients. Some natural substances, including aloe vera, chamomile, and marigold, also provide relief and trigger healing.

- Finally, you aren't going to die because you didn't know all this until now. Even the sunscreens and suntan lotions you used in the past provided some measure of protection from UV radiation. Just play it smart and take added precautions from now on. That way, we'll catch you at the beach when we're all in our nineties.

RIP CURRENTS

A day at the beach is not entirely without hazard. You risk the pain of sunburn and stings from jellyfish, man o' war, and sea lice. Less common risks include respiratory infection from red tide and the remote possibility of shark attacks. By far, the biggest hazard facing ocean swimmers is getting caught in a rip current (a.k.a. rip tide and run-out). Unlike shark bites, rip currents happen all too often.

Statistics bear out their danger. In a recent 10-year period, Miami-Dade County led the state with 30 rip-current fatalities, while Volusia County (home of Daytona Beach) placed a close second with 29. Rip currents occur in the Gulf of Mexico, too. Bay County (home of Panama City Beach) placed third on the list with 24 deaths.

Rip currents form as part of a cell-like circulation when longshore currents moving in different directions converge near the beach and then turn away from shore. Sand and sediment are moved seaward by rip currents, and their deposition results in the formation of offshore bars. These currents can reach 100 feet in width and extend 1,000 feet into the ocean.

The strong pull of a rip current and a panicked swimmer's reflexive instinct to paddle against it can result in tragedy. However, the current's narrowness can work to a cool-headed swimmer's advantage. If you swim parallel to shore instead of toward it, you will soon exit the rip current and can then return safely.

To avoid trouble, don't swim alone. Stay within sight of lifeguards and pay heed to posted warnings on lifeguard stands or towers. If you get caught in a rip current, keep calm. (Admittedly, this is easier said than done.) Call for help by waving your arms in the air, and then swim parallel to shore to release yourself from the current's grip. If you have kids, inform them of this life-saving strategy before they enter the water. Have the young ones wear water wings or life vests, and always keep an eye on them. Move away from inlets, where currents can be especially hazardous and not always visible.

Having heard too many tragic tales of lives lost, we cannot stress this enough: If you're caught in a rip current, stay calm and swim parallel to shore. Make sure kids wear flotation devices, and never let them out of your sight.

SEA LICE

Sea lice rank low on the list of swimming hazards, but they can be troubling enough to impact business at the beach if there's an outbreak. That is because these microscopic nuisances are a real pain in the butt—and anywhere else they happen to bite an unsuspecting swimmer. Think of them as mosquitoes of the sea.

Sea lice are actually the juvenile form of the thimble jellyfish. Their bite is bothersome and, at worst, can leave susceptible victims feeling poorly for days with mild nausea, fever, sleeplessness, and discomfort. This dermatitic scourge—which also goes by the name "seabather's eruption"—can drive people off the beach if word gets around. In an outbreak area, one in every four swimmers will contract it. The area affected is usually that part covered by a swimsuit, because that is where they get trapped. In a scientific paper published in 1995, Mary T. Russell wrote, "The suspected organism, barely visible except under excellent lighting, appears like a speck of finely ground pepper. Its size is approximately that of a pinhead floating on the surface layers of the water."

Sea-lice outbreaks occur along a 250-mile stretch of Florida's East Coast but especially in Palm Beach County, where the Gulf Stream current comes closest to shore. Peak season for sea lice runs April–July. Their numbers wax and wane on an unpredictable long-term cycle.

If you encounter sea lice, treatment of the ensuing dermatitis includes taking an antihistamine for the itching and applying hydrocortisone cream to the rash. The only way to protect yourself from sea lice when there's an outbreak is to avoid the water or, ahem, wear a smaller bathing suit. Doing the latter might make beachgoing an even more enticing proposition!

Flora and Fauna

ALLIGATORS AND CROCODILES

Both alligators and crocodiles are found in Florida, though gators are far more prevalent. Here are some facts about these aquatic predators, many of them gleaned from our visit to the excellent St. Augustine Alligator Farm.

- There are 14 species of crocodiles and two species of alligators. The American alligator *(Alligator mississippiensis)* is the species native to Florida. The rare Chinese alligator *(Alligator sinensis)* is endangered and perhaps extinct.
- The range for alligators and crocodiles overlaps only at the southern tip of Florida.
- An alligator has 80 teeth, all of them sharp, and its jaws can exert a biting force of 4,000 pounds per square inch (psi). By contrast, a human's biting force is only 200 psi.
- Both male and female alligators hiss, and males also roar loudly across long distances.
- The adult alligator's diet consists of fish, small mammals, birds, and sometimes even deer and cattle. Crocodiles eat fish, mammals, waterfowl, and human beings.
- Alligators can reach a top speed of 25 mph in water and 11 mph on land. To put it another way, they can run a 5:45 mile. Can you?
- Estimated number of human beings killed by crocodiles each year: 2,000
- Number of human beings in Florida attacked by alligators 1973–1990: 127
- Number of human deaths in Florida attributable to alligators 1973–1990: 5
- The maximum sentence and fine for feeding a wild alligator in Florida: 60 days and $500
- An adult alligator eats only 25 percent of its body weight yearly. That is a *slow* metabolism.
- How can you distinguish an alligator from a crocodile? If you can get close enough, the fourth tooth on either side of a crocodile's lower jaw visibly projects outside the snout when its mouth is closed.

- Average length of an alligator: 6–12 feet. Maximum length: 19 feet.
- Alligators were trapped to near-extinction in this country, necessitating their placement on the endangered species list in 1967. After a remarkable recovery, they were removed from the list in 1987.

SEA TURTLES

Here's a statistic that might surprise you: 90 percent of all sea turtle nesting in the United States occurs in Florida. Most of it is done on Florida's East Coast, with a smaller run on the Gulf Coast. Two endangered species (the green turtle and the leatherback) and one threatened species (the loggerhead) make Florida their nesting area. The densest concentration of nesting occurs between Volusia County and Palm Beach County—and especially in south Brevard County and Indian River County. During egg-laying season (May–August) as many as 20,000 turtle nests, each containing 100 eggs, are laid here.

While we're doing the math, let's factor in some sad subtractions. For every 1,000 eggs that will hatch 50–60 days later, only one juvenile will survive to adulthood. The silver lining: For every hatchling that makes it to adulthood, life expectancy is as high as 80 years. Average adult weights run around 400 pounds for loggerheads, greens, and Kemp's ridleys, and 1,000 pounds (half a ton!) for leatherbacks.

Looking more closely at one productive area, Hutchinson Island—which straddles St. Lucie and Martin Counties—has landed as many as 7,000 sea turtle nests in one season, though the number dwindled to a low of 3,522 in 1997. Partly due to greater public sensitivity, the number of nests jumped to nearly 6,000 in 2000, before tapering off again in 2004.

In 2004, Hurricanes Frances and Jeanne destroyed 3,670 loggerhead nests and 840 green turtle nests in the Archie Carr National Wildlife Refuge alone. Yet it could've been worse. The year 2004 saw an unusually low number of nests laid. Some in the scientific community speculate the turtles instinctively backed off from egg-laying, sensing the coming cataclysms. Laugh if you will, but 2005 conversely turned out to be a record year for green turtles along Florida's central East Coast (10,000 nests in Brevard County alone!). It also reversed a five-year trend of declining numbers for loggerhead turtle nests and set a record for the endangered Kemp's Ridley (57 nests in Brevard County).

The turtles' nesting rituals have been going on for 175 million years, since the first pregnant sea turtle waddled ashore on some isolated coastline to carefully dig a deep hole with her front legs, squat above it, and deposit a pile of eggs the size and shape of Ping-Pong balls. After securing the nest by covering it with sand, the mama turtle waddles back to the ocean, never to see her brood. Only a few hours of a sea turtle's life are spent on land.

Turtle walks are intended to show respectful human beings this miraculous visitation. As such, they must be carefully regulated. Turtle walks are limited to groups of 50 and led by state-licensed marine biologists. On Hutchinson Island, they are overseen by Florida Power & Light's Environmental Education Department. Sightings are not guaranteed, although they generally occur all but one or two nights a season. The epic struggle of sea turtles has had the positive effect of generating near-unanimous sympathy among humans, aiding efforts to curb behavior that interferes with egg laying and hatching. However, it has also made turtles a loved-to-death tourist attraction, like puffins in Maine, otters in Monterey, and whales in Massachusetts.

Flashes from cameras, headlights from cars, and even handheld flashlights can startle a skittish mama sea turtle or distract hatchlings from making their seaward march. If a sea turtle is prevented from laying her eggs, she'll simply turn around, return to the ocean, and drop her load there—a needless tragedy. As for the babies, disorienting lights can lead them astray from the moonlight they instinctively follow to the ocean. Many communities urge hotel, cottage and condo owners to keep lights off at night during nesting season. Adding to the hatchlings' woes, raccoons and feral pigs raid sea-turtle nests, and shorebirds and seabirds snatch them from land and water.

The goal of a turtle walk is to find a sea turtle about to lay eggs. If a bucket-sized hole has been dug and the turtle is squatting over it, laying is imminent. Biologists use infrared telescopes and binoculars to tell when such a moment is at hand. They patrol beaches to rid them of human intruders, count nests laid by each species, and spot candidates for a turtle walk. When one is found, the news is radioed to the guide, who quietly leads the group onto the beach. There they form a semicircle at the turtle's head. Most are hushed into reverent awe by this extraordinary spectacle, the most moving aspect of which is the mother turtle's tears. As she drops her eggs, tears flow unabated. She is not weeping with joy or sadness, however. Her tear ducts simply keep her eyes moist and clear them of sand and other irritants. Nevertheless, her tears further make this age-old ritual a humbling experience. You'll want to run home and hug your own mother.

Turtle walks are held on Friday and Saturday nights in June and July. Beginning in late April, call FP&L's Environmental Information Line (800/334-5483) for reservations and information.

MANATEES

One of the more visible species teetering on the brink of extinction in Florida is the West Indian manatee. This gentle giant inhabits waters along the Florida coast, including estuaries, bays, canals, and rivers. The average adult manatee is 10 feet long and weighs 1,000 pounds, although they can grow as large as 13 feet and weigh as much as 3,000 pounds. These submarine-shaped herbivores forage for plant material in shallow waters. Being mammals, they break the surface to breathe air every three to five minutes.

It takes manatees a long time to reproduce. Males reach sexual maturity at nine years and females at five, and their gestation period is 13 months. Manatees can live to 60 years or more, though they rarely reach such an age in Florida. That is because they are massacred by boat propellers, drowned in canal locks and flood-control structures, strangled in crab trap lines, and choked by fish hooks and monofilament line. Sometimes they're deliberately harassed, injured, and even killed by sadistic humans.

Manatees are tracked by marine biologists who identify individuals by unique patterns of boat-prop scars. The current population of manatees in the U.S. is estimated to be around 3,000. Their cause is not aided by recurrent red tides along the Gulf of Mexico, which are likely triggered by human pollution. During one such outbreak, 83 manatees died in a three-week period along the short stretch of coast from Venice to Naples.

Manatees are legally protected by the Marine Mammal Protection Act of 1972, the Endangered Species Act of 1973, and the Florida Manatee Sanctuary Act of 1978. The Save the Manatee Club, an advocacy organization cofounded by Jimmy Buffett, raises money and awareness. Beyond that, it's up to each individual to act responsibly so that the manatee population can be stabilized.

Here are some rules governing human interactions with manatees. Be sure to follow them!

- Do not enter designated manatee sanctuaries for any reason.
- Do not pursue, corner, or follow a manatee while swimming or diving.
- Do not disturb a resting manatee.
- Do not attempt to feed or give water to manatees.
- Do not ride, poke, prod, grab, or otherwise disturb a manatee at any time.
- Do not separate a manatee calf from its mother or any single manatee from a group.

- *Do* observe idle, slow-speed, caution, no-entry, and safe-operation zones when boating.
- *Do* use snorkeling gear and not scuba gear when observing manatees.
- *Do* stay out of seagrass beds, which are prime habitat for manatees.
- For more information, contact the Save the Manatee Club, 500 North Maitland Avenue, Maitland, FL 32751, 407/539-0990, www.savethemanatee.org.

Environmental Concerns

HURRICANES AND FLOODS

The Saffir-Simpson Hurricane Scale

Hurricanes are grouped into five categories, based on maximum sustained wind speed. Within each of the categories, certain degrees of flooding and property damage can be expected to occur. The following list is adapted from materials from the National Oceanographic and Atmospheric Administration (NOAA). By now, everyone in Florida just about knows them by heart. In 2005, three hurricanes reached Category 5 strength. Although none of them made landfall at Category 5, Hurricane Katrina hit Louisiana at Category 4 strength and Rita and Wilma came ashore as powerful Category 3 hurricanes.

Tropical Storm: winds 39–73 mph

Category 1 Hurricane: winds 74–95 mph No real damage to buildings. Damage to unanchored mobile homes. Some damage to poorly constructed signs. Also, some coastal flooding and minor pier damage. (examples: Irene 1999 and Allison 1995)

Category 2 Hurricane: winds 96–110 mph Some damage to building roofs, doors, and windows. Considerable damage to mobile homes. Flooding damages piers and small craft in unprotected moorings may break their moorings. Some trees blown down. (examples: Bonnie 1998, Georges 1998, and Gloria 1985)

Category 3 Hurricane: winds 111–130 mph Some structural damage to small residences and utility buildings. Large trees blown down. Mobile homes and poorly built signs destroyed. Flooding near the coast destroys smaller structures with larger structures damaged by floating debris. Terrain may be flooded well inland. (examples: Keith 2000, Fran 1996, Opal 1995, Alicia 198,3 and Betsy 1965)

Category 4 Hurricane: winds 131–155 mph More extensive curtainwall failures with some complete roof structure failure on small residences. Major erosion of beach areas. Terrain may be flooded well inland. (examples: Hugo 1989 and Donna 1960)

Category 5 Hurricane: winds 156 mph and up

Complete roof failure on many residences and industrial buildings. Some complete building failures with small utility buildings blown over or away. Flooding causes major damage to lower floors of all structures near the shoreline. Massive evacuation of residential areas may be required. (examples: Andrew 1992, Camille 1969, and Labor Day 1935)

FEMA and Federal Flood Insurance

Federal flood insurance is available through the National Flood Insurance Program (NFIP) and is administered by the Federal Emergency Management Agency (FEMA). The agency was created in 1968 to aid victims of natural disasters like hurricanes and floods. In reality, it has become the single greatest factor driving coastal overdevelopment in the last 30 years. Essentially the government has underwritten the risk of construction in Special Flood

TOP 10 REASONS HURRICANE SEASON IS LIKE CHRISTMAS

10. Decorating your home's exterior (okay, boarding up windows)

9. Dragging out boxes that haven't been used since last season

8. Last-minute shopping excursions in crowded stores

7. Regular TV shows pre-empted by "specials"

6. Family members coming to stay with you

5. Lots of calls from out-of-state friends and family

4. Buying foods you wouldn't normally shop for... and in large quantities

3. Getting time off from work

2. The warm glow of candles

1. At some point you will have a tree in your house!

We don't know who to credit for the above list, since it came to us via not one but several Internet contacts. (You know how these things circulate.) But it seemed too funny not to include in this book. We edited it somewhat for our own purposes.

Hazard Areas (SFHA) by offering relatively low-cost flood insurance. Nearly the entire Gulf Coast, from Florida to Texas, falls inside an SFHA.

What began as a benevolent idea was exploited by speculators and is now little more than welfare for the wealthy and a windfall for the real-estate industry. Virtually no one would purchase beachfront property if federal flood insurance weren't available. Flood-insurance premiums from private companies are prohibitively expensive, if coverage is available at all. After Katrina, some insurers stopped offering it at any price to Gulf Coast residents.

Nationwide, the country's fourth-largest insurer, went one step further than that. In August 2005 the company announced it would no longer write new homeowner's policies in Florida. That decision applied to single-family houses, condominiums, mobile homes, and boats, and was made even after Nationwide was given approval to raise its rates by as much as 25 percent. Nationwide became the seventh insurance company to

announce it was bailing out on Florida after the 2004 hurricane season.

Perversely, we've noticed that the condo-building frenzy in Florida has, if anything, accelerated. It doesn't help that local developers and zoning boards flout federal government guidelines. The feds prescribe minimum setbacks—a suggested distance from the high-tide line on which to build safely. Although these guidelines are routinely ignored, homeowners are still granted cheap, federally subsidized flood insurance. In Florida, county officials claim to lack the manpower to enforce guidelines. Why should a developer, homeowner, or local government be concerned, as long as taxpayers will pick up the tab when it's time to rebuild?

Though we've been railing about NFIP since the mid-1980s, few Americans were even aware of its existence until 2005. After Katrina, no one can claim ignorance of FEMA or NFIP. Who can forget the total lack of preparedness by an agency so stocked with unqualified political cronies that it couldn't function with even minimal competence?

The National Flood Insurance Program was designed to be self-funding through premiums, but it has not worked out that way. As the *Washington Post* reported, "[NFIP] has no reserves, heavily subsidizes some of its riskiest customers, and relies on the Treasury to bail it out when losses exceed income."

Nearly half of all money paid out by NFIP since 1978 has gone to communities on the Gulf Coast. In 2004, NFIP paid $2 billion to property owners flooded by Hurricane Ivan and three others—double the historical average. Losses in 2005 from Katrina and Rita alone topped $10 billion, forcing the program to borrow billions from taxpayers with no guarantee of repayment.

To pay off these losses, Congress increased NFIP's borrowing cap to $3.5 billion. It's estimated the loans won't be paid back for a decade—and then only if no comparable catastrophes occur on the Gulf Coast. (Ha!) Even before Katrina broke the bank, forecasters predicted that property damage from hurricanes on the Atlantic and Gulf coasts would annually top $50 billion by 2030. Even FEMA estimates that 30,000 single-family homes and condos within 500 feet of the ocean or gulf will be underwater in 25 years, based on conservative projections that sea-level rise will swamp two linear feet of beach per year.

In Florida, the rising tide is expected to consume way more than that—as much as 1,000 linear feet of coast in some regions. Given the stark realities, it's obvious that "business as usual" by FEMA has got to stop. It is time for common sense to prevail: to wit, no more federal underwriting of flood insurance in high-hazard coastal areas. Period.

RED TIDE

Red tide is the name given to a toxic outbreak that sometimes occurs along the Gulf of Mexico in warmer months. A red tide can blanket the beaches with dead fish. The toxin that kills them also becomes airborne in sea spray and wind. Exposure to this malevolent mist can cause watery eyes, sore throats, headaches, and respiratory distress. Moreover, no one wants to swim in infected waters, making red tide another economy-killer in Florida. Even more damaging is the effect red tide has on fishing and aquaculture, necessitating bans on harvesting oysters, clams, mussels, and scallops.

Red-tide outbreaks are caused by single-celled dinoflagellates *(Gymnodinium breve)* that are propelled by whiplike tails. (We observed their movements through a microscope at Sarasota's Mote Marine Aquarium.) When these microorganisms enter their toxic stage, they produce a reddish-brown pigment. At that point their cells burst, releasing a poison that's carried landward by wind and tide. The initial burst occurs 10–40 miles offshore. Smaller sea animals are most susceptible to the poison.

Though marine biologists understand the mechanism by which the toxin is released, they still don't know precisely what initiates the process. Educated guesses point to the usual culprit: human-generated pollution. Sewage runoff, boat spew, and other pollutants upset the chemical balance in the waters through which the microorganisms tumble, and red tide is their defense mechanism. They've become so commonplace that red-tide hotlines have been set up in Manatee County (941/745-3779) and Sarasota County (941/346-0079). Call for the latest conditions if you're headed this way.

We encountered a relatively mild red tide one November—much later in the year than usual—in Venice. The smell was bad enough to floor Hulk Hogan, and our respiratory systems were irritated, too. The sight of dead fish and small creatures decomposing in stinking mats of seaweed kept people off the beach.

We also crossed paths with a more devastating red tide in 2005. Warm, polluted gulf waters stirred up from the rancid depths by Hurricane Katrina triggered a particularly virulent outbreak that affected both the West Coast and Panhandle.

When we visited St. Andrews State Park,

SUMMARY OF HURRICANES AND TROPICAL STORMS IMPACTING FLORIDA, 2004

Name	Date and Time of Landfall	Category # (Maximum Wind Speed)	Location of Landfall	Coastal Area Impacted	Property Losses	Deaths (in FL)	Interesting Fact
Tropical Storm Bonnie	Thursday, August 12 (2 P.M.)	Tropical Storm (65 mph)	St. George Island	Eastern Panhandle	minor	0	Bonnie and Charley made landfall within a day of each other – a first for Florida.
Hurricane Charley	Friday, August 13 (3:45 A.M.)	Category 4 (145 mph)	Cayo Costa	Southwest Coast: Lee County barrier islands (including Sanibel & Captiva)	$14 billion	35	Costliest storm since Hurricane Andrew (1992). Damaged Florida's citrus crop.
Hurricane Frances	Saturday, September 4 (1 A.M.)	Category 2 (105 mph)	Sewall's Point, Hutchinson Island	East Coast: Palm Beach to St. Augustine Beach West Coast: Pinellas County	$8 billion	23	Spawned 106 tornadoes, second in history only to Hurricane Beulah (1967).
Tropical Storm Frances	Monday, September 6 (2 P.M.)	Tropical Storm (65 mph)	St. Marks	Big Bend: Cedar Key to Alligator Point	minor	0	Frances impacted the East Coast, West Coast, and Panhandle of Florida.
Hurricane Ivan	Thursday, September 16 (2 A.M.)	Category 3 (130 mph)	Gulf Shores, Alabama	Panhandle: Perdido Key to St. Joseph Peninsula	$13 billion	19	Most destructive Panhandle hurricane since Opal (1995).
Hurricane Jeanne	Saturday, September 25 (midnight)	Category 3 (120 mph)	Gilbert's Bar, Hutchinson Island	East Coast: Hutchinson Island to St. Augustine Beach West Coast: Pinellas County	$6 billion	6	Jeanne was Florida's fourth hurricane in a year – the first time a state had been hit by four hurricanes since 1886.

SUMMARY OF HURRICANES AND TROPICAL STORMS IMPACTING FLORIDA, 2005

Name	Date and Time of Landfall	Category # (Maximum Wind Speed)	Location of Landfall	Coastal Area Impacted	Property Losses	Deaths (in FL)	Interesting Fact
Tropical Storm Arlene	Saturday, June 11 (1 P.M.)	Tropical Storm (70 mph)	Perdido Key	Western Panhandle	minor	1	First named storm of record 2005 season.
Hurricane Dennis	Sunday, July 10 (2:25 P.M.)	Category 1 (80 mph)	Pensacola Beach & Navarre Beach	Panhandle: Pensacola Beach to Shell Point	$2 billion	32	Greatest damage on eastern Panhandle since Hurricane Kate (1985).
Hurricane Katrina (first landfall)	Thursday, August 25 (6:30 P.M.)	Category 2 (105 mph)	Bal Harbour & North Miami Beach	South Florida: Hollywood to Key West	$2 billion	14	Strengthened as it crossed Everglades and Gulf of Mexico.
Hurricane Katrina (second landfall)	Monday, August 29 (6:10 A.M.)	Category 4 (145 mph)	Grand Isle, Mississippi	Panhandle: minor impacts from Pensacola Beach to Panama City Beach	$60 billion (in LA and MS)	0	Costliest natural disaster in U.S. history. Destroyed 500,000 homes in three states.
Hurricane Ophelia	Thursday, September 8th	Category 1 (75 mph)	passed offshore near Flagler Beach	Northeast Florida: Flagler Beach to Fernandina Beach	minor	1	Never made landfall in Florida, but did great damage along North Carolina coast.
Hurricane Rita	Saturday, September 24 (2:30 A.M.)	Category 3 (120 mph)	Sabine Pass, Louisiana	Florida Keys	$8 billion (in TX)	0	Rita passed within 50 miles of Key West; was also the second Category 5 hurricane in the Gulf of Mexico in less than a month.
Tropical Storm Tammy	Wednesday, October 5 (7 P.M.)	Tropical Storm (50 mph)	Mayport	Northeast Florida: Flagler Beach to Fernandina Beach	minor	0	Caused heavy rainfall in the Southeast and New Hampshire's worst flooding in 25 years.
Hurricane Wilma	Monday, October 24 (6:30 A.M.)	Category 3 (120 mph)	Cape Romano	Southwest Florida: Marco Island to Naples South Florida: Key West to Cape Canaveral	$12 billion	31	Most intense Atlantic hurricane on record. Biggest storm to hit Broward County since Hurricane King (1950).

near Panama City Beach, the toxic stench literally took our breath away. Piles of dead fish—big ones, not juveniles—lay rotting along the shoreline. The air was palpably nasty, hitting our lungs like we'd been sucker-punched. Coughing and wheezing, we retreated after giving the beach a cursory once-over.

A few days later, down at Nokomis Beach, we overheard a woman ask, "Excuse me, is it dangerous to swim here?" The lifeguard replied, "No, just red tide and dead fish." Just what everyone wants to see on vacation, right? Earlier that morning we'd tried swimming at Crescent Beach, on Siesta Key. The water was urine yellow, the beach stank, and we went in only up to our knees for fear of contracting infection. Finally, we gave up and headed to the motel pool.

It's sad to be driven to a pool by red tide and pollution. It's like having to drink bottled water instead of what comes out of the tap. Who would've thought we'd wind up paying for water? Likewise, who would've thought we'd wind up swimming in pools instead of the gulf or ocean? Has it really come to this?

FLORIDA'S AILING FISHERIES

The bestseller *The Perfect Storm* sketched a poignant portrait of the hard lives of commercial fishermen in a world of dwindling fish populations. In early 2000, the National Academy of Sciences brought together leading marine biologists to study the global fish crisis. Their unanimous conclusion: Overfishing, not global warming or pollution, is the "single greatest threat to the diversity of life in the world's oceans."

In April 2006, a special edition of *Mother Jones* magazine charted the full extent of the problem. It ain't pretty. "The world's oceans—including U.S. waters—have been overfished for decades, causing long-term disruption to marine ecosystems," reports *Mother Jones*. "Many commercially important fish stocks, like the legendary Atlantic cod, are seriously depleted despite many years of federal and state regulation. According to the latest numbers from the Department of Commerce, at least 28 percent of the fish stocks are officially 'overfished' and another 19 percent are 'subject to overfishing.'"

It would be easy to point a finger at the United States, third-largest exporter of seafood in the world (behind Thailand and Norway), but there's blame enough to circle the globe several times. Florida claims some of the most disingenuous politically motivated "experts" making policy on fisheries issues. James Fensom, a two-term member (and chairman for two years) of the federal Gulf of Mexico Fishery Management Council, resigned in disgust in 2005. He wrote a blistering letter to Governor Jeb Bush, who'd originally appointed him, citing corporate corruption among the board members. He wrote, that his successor "should not be in a leadership position in any fishing organization, should not be a commercial or recreational fisherman who generates income by harvesting fish, should not be an immediate family member of a scientist who receives grants from the National Marine Fisheries Service, and should not be a family member of an employee of the National Marine Fisheries Service."

Fensom added that during his two terms, "There has never been a member who has declared a conflict of interest on an issue and declined to vote," and some members with a financial stake in the outcome of a vote "strain all logic and applicable science in an effort to maintain current fishing limits."

The bottom line is that commercial fishing—the business that fills fisherman's platters and all-you-can-eat buffet troughs from Maine to Florida—is a phenomenally inefficient industry. Around the world, $124 billion is spent annually to produce $70 billion worth of fish. The $54 billion shortfall is covered by government subsidies. The world's fishing fleets use large nets to drag the sea floor, destroying coral and hauling in everything within reach. Twenty-seven million tons of fish are killed in the hauling process and then tossed overboard. And we're rapidly running out of fish to catch. Of the world's major fishing grounds, 44 percent are being fished to capacity, 31 percent are exploited, 16 percent are overfished, 6 percent are depleted (nothing left), and only 3 percent have been left alone to recover from overfishing.

In order to protect the spawning grounds of the gag grouper, the U.S. National Marine Fisheries Service proposes a fishing ban in two 100-square-mile blocks of the Gulf of Mexico. They're also considering an extensive reserve around the Dry Tortugas to protect a variety of reef fish.

But no one knows what to do about a "dead zone" the size of New Jersey that extends into the gulf from the mouth of the Mississippi River. The culprit is fertilizer and pesticide runoff from factory farms, which enters the gulf via the Mississippi and its tributaries. This chemical soup triggers algal blooms and hypoxia (low oxygen levels), leaving a huge area virtually devoid of life three months a year. The Midwestern agribusiness lobby has thus far stymied federal action on the matter. One has to wonder how a political system that allows this to happen can be said to serve our best interests. By 2006, the dead zone had grown even larger. Nothing has been done by the federal government to stem it in the past five years.

Given government inertia, it falls to "we the people" to do the right thing. Despite all the bad news, there are still ways to enjoy seafood and support local fishing fleets while allowing endangered and threatened species to regenerate. The best way is to follow the guidelines listed below, gleaned from *Mother Jones* and Seafood Watch. As you can see, you won't go hungry by choosing good alternatives to overfished and endangered species. Contact elected officials, too, and urge them to supported legislation that will meaningfully address the fisheries crisis.

Endangered – Avoid
- Atlantic cod
- Atlantic flounder
- Atlantic haddock
- Atlantic halibut
- Blue crab
- Blue marlin
- Bluefin tuna
- Chilean sea bass (a.k.a., Patagonian toothfish, Antarctic cod, and icefish)
- Conch, queen
- Eastern oyster
- Orange roughy
- Pompano
- Shark
- Shrimp or prawns
- Red or yellowtail snapper
- Sturgeon
- Swordfish
- Tropical grouper
- White abalone

Sustainable – Good Choices
- Alaskan salmon
- Albacore tuna
- Calamari
- Catfish
- Crab (except Chesapeake blue crab)
- Crayfish
- Lobster
- Mackerel
- Mahimahi (a.k.a. dolphinfish, dorado)
- Mullet
- Mussels
- New Zealand cod
- Pacific halibut
- Sardines/herring
- Sole
- Scallops
- Snapper (gray, lane, mutton, yellowtail)
- Squid
- Striped bass
- Tilapia
- Trout
- Tuna (albacore, bigeye, yellowfin)

BEACHES AND BUTTHEADS: THE LITTER PROBLEM

While littering is obnoxious, it is more than just an aesthetic problem. This is especially true at the beach, where litter often ends up in the ocean. More than two million seabirds and 100,000 sea animals die each year along U.S. shores from discarded plastic. They die from ingestion, strangulation, and drowning after getting caught in our useless discards. Although plastic takes up to 450 years to decompose, 20 million tons of it are produced annually in the U.S. alone. Every hour Americans throw away 2.5 million plastic bottles.

The problem isn't just limited to plastic. Americans create four pounds of garbage per person every day. With only 5 percent of the world's population, we produce—if that's the right word—half the world's waste: plastic, paper, glass, aluminum, rubber, motor oil. You name it, we throw it away.

At the beach, the temptation to litter is greater than elsewhere. People are on vacation, subsisting on fast food and convenience-store fare, with all its disposable packaging. They're not focused on reducing waste and rarely given the opportunity to recycle. Although beach municipalities need to do much more, so do thoughtless consumers. In our view, litter is an attitude problem. When someone tosses a cigarette butt or fast-food wrapper out the window or on the beach, they're not just breaking the law but extending a middle finger to the world. In effect they are saying, "With this totally stupid and irresponsible act, I hereby leave the world through which I pass an uglier place."

The following list of "Florida's Dirty Dozen" tallies the flotsam deposited on Florida beaches. The information—types of garbage, total pieces, and percentage relative to all debris collected—comes from Florida's Center for Marine Conservation, based on beach clean-ups.

1. Cigarette butts: 111,422 (17.6 percent)
2. Plastic pieces: 34,087 (5.4 percent)
3. Glass beverage bottles: 32,497 (5.1 percent)
4. Plastic food bags/wrappers: 32,211 (5.1 percent)
5. Plastic caps/lids: 30,669 (4.8 percent)
6. Plastic straws: 29,619 (4.7 percent)
7. Foamed plastic pieces: 29,552 (4.7 percent)
8. Metal beverage cans: 27,688 (4.4 percent)
9. Paper pieces: 22,573 (3.6 percent)
10. Plastic beverage bottles: 21,461 (3.4 percent)
11. Foamed plastic cups: 17,641 (2.8 percent)
12. Glass pieces: 13,328 (2.1 percent)

Total: 402,748 (63.6 percent)

Here's how long it takes various types of litter to decompose in the ocean, according to the Florida Sea Grant. A beautiful poster with this information is available online for $1 at www.reefrelief.org.

1. Glass bottles and jars: maybe forever
2. Monofilament fishing lines: 600 years
3. Disposable diapers: 450 years
4. Plastic bottles: 450 years
5. Plastic six-pack rings: 400 years
6. Aluminum cans: 200 years
7. Styrofoam cups: 50 years
8. Biodegradable diapers: one year
9. Waxed milk cartons: three months
10. Cardboard boxes, apple cores: two months
11. Paper towels, newspapers: 2–6 weeks

Index

A

accommodations: 578–579; *see also specific place*
Adams Beach: 474
Air Force Armament Museum: 548
airlines: 578
Alex's Beach: 166, 167
Alfred A. McKethan Pine Island Park: 455, 456
Algiers Beach: *see* Gulfside City Park
Alligator Point: 479–480
alligators: 233, 326, 584–585
Amber Sands Beach: 145
Amelia Island: Amelia Island Plantation 39–41; Fernandina Beach 30–36; geology 35; south end 41–42
Amelia Island Museum of History: 30–31
Amelia Island Plantation: 39–41
Amelia Island State Park: 41–42
American Beach: 36, 38
Anastasia State Park: 68–69
Anclote Gulf Park: 450
Anclote Key Preserve State Park: 445–446
Anclote River Park: 450, 452
animals: 584–587
Anna Maria: 402–406
Anna Maria Bayfront Park: 403, 405
Anna Maria Beach: 403, 404–405
Anna Maria Island: 402–406
Anne Kolb Nature Center: 245
Anne's Beach: 295
Apalachicola: 489–492
Apollo Beach (Canaveral National Seashore): 112, 113

Apollo Beach (town): 410
aquariums: 395
archaeological sites: 460, 548
Archibald Memorial Beach: 423
Aripeka: 452–453
Art Deco District: 259–260, 261
Atlantic Beach: 47–49
Atlantic Dunes Park: 210
Atsena Otie Key: 463, 467–468
Aucilla River State Canoe Trail: 474–475
Avalon Beach: 155, 156

B

Bahia Honda State Park: 305–306
Bailey-Matthews Shell Museum: 356
Bal Harbour: 256–258
Barefoot Beach Access: 344
Barefoot Beach County Park: 343–344
baseball: 93, 149, 180–181, 392, 575
basketball teams: 575
Bathtub Reef Beach Park: 172, 173
Bay County Pier and Park: 509, 510
Bayport: 454–455
Bayport Park: 455
beach access: *see specific place*
beaches: driving rules 100–101; litter 594; rating lists 506–507; renourishment 32, 165–166, 234, 250; suggested activities 579–582
Beachwalk/Pasley Park: 166
Beacon Hill: 497–498
Beacon Hill Community Park: 498
bed taxes: 532

Beer Can Island: 400
Belleair Beach: 429–431
Belleair Shore: 429–431
Ben T. Davis Beach: 433
Bethune, Mary McLeod: 93
Betsch, MaVynee: 37
Beverly Beach: 79–80
Bicentennial Park: 85, 86
Bid-o-Wee Beach: 509, 510
Big Bend: 447–478
Big Bend Wildlife Management Area: 472
Big Coppitt Key: 310–311
Big House Problem: 195
Big Lagoon State Park: 567–568
Big Pine Key: 307–308
Big Talbot Island State Park: 43, 44
biking: 363, 474–475
Bill Baggs Cape Florida State Park: 276, 277
birds/birdwatching: Cedar Keys National Wildlife Refuge 467–468; Homosassa Springs State Wildlife Park 457–458; J. N. "Ding" Darling National Wildlife Refuge 357–358; Long Key State Park 296; Lower Suwannee National Wildlife Refuge 467–468; Merritt Island National Wildlife Refuge 115–116; Pelican Man's Bird Sanctuary 395; St. Marks National Wildlife Refuge 476; Suncoast Seabird Sanctuary 427; Ten Thousand Islands 328; Waccasassa Bay Preserve State Park 467
Biscayne National Park: 279–280
Blind Creek Beach: 162, 163–164
Blind Pass Beach: 377–378

Blowing Rocks Preserve: 177
Blue Mountain Beach:
531–534
boat tours: 174
Bob Graham Beach: 166
Boca Chica Beach: 310–311
Boca Chica Key: 310–311
Boca Chita Key: 280
Boca Grande: 369–373
Boca Grande Public Beach
Accesses: 371–372
Boca Raton: 212–217
Bonita Beach: 344–347
Bonita Beach Park: 345–346
Bonita Beach Public Ac-
cesses: 346–347
Bonnet House: 234–235
Bonsteel Park: 140
bookstores: 524
Boot Key: 304
Bowditch Point Regional
Park: 351, 352
Bowman's Beach: 359, 360
Boynton Beach: 206–208
Boynton Beach Oceanfront
Park: 207, 208
Brackin Wayside Park and
Boardwalk: 550
Bradenton Beach: 402–406
Briny Breezes: 207
Broadwalk: 244–245
Brohard Park: 382, 383
Bryn Mawr Access: 155, 156
Bryn Mawr Beach Access:
166, 167
Bulow Creek State Park: 87
Bunch Beach: 354–355
Burney Beach Front Park: 38
Burt Reynolds and Friends
Museum: 183
Burt Reynolds Institute For
Theatre Training: 183
Burt Reynolds Jupiter The-
atre: 183
Burt Reynolds Park: 183
Bush, George W.: 202
Butler and Douglas County
Park: 470
butterfly ballots: 202
Butterfly World: 232

C
Ca d'Zan: 393
Caladesi Island State Park:
439–440
Caloosa Beach: see Anne's
Beach
Camp Godon Johnson Mu-
seum: 481
Camp Helen State Park:
516–517
camping/campgrounds: 306,
323, 328, 411, 456
Canal Park: 499
Canaveral National Sea-
shore: 111–114
Cannon Beach: 286, 287
canoeing: Aucilla River State
Canoe Trail 474–475;
Chassahowitzka River
Campground and Recre-
ation Area 456; Grayton
Beach State Park 529;
Gulf Coast Keys 328; J. N.
"Ding" Darling National
Wildlife Refuge 357–358;
Jonathan Dickinson State
Park 174; Waccasassa Bay
Preserve State Park 467
Canova Beach: 133–134
Canova Beach Park: 133
Cape Canaveral: 116–119
Cape Marco: 334
Cape Palms Park: 495
Cape Romano: 331
Cape Sable: 327, 329
Cape San Blas: 495
Cape St. George State Re-
serve: 489
Captiva Beach: 364–365
Captiva Island: 357, 362,
363–367
Captiva Memorial Library:
363
Carillon Beach: 516–517
Carlin Park: 182, 184
Carl Ross Key: 327, 328–329
Carrabelle: 481–483
Carrabelle Beach: 481–483
car rentals: 578
Casey Key: 384–386

Casino Beach: 561–562
Casperson Park: 382, 383
Castillo de San Marcos Na-
tional Monument: 64
Causeway Islands: 359
Cayo Costa Island State
Park: 368–369
C.B. Harvey Rest Beach
Park: 314, 316
Cedar Key: 462–466
Cedar Key City Park: 464
Cedar Key Historical Soci-
ety: 464
Cedar Key Scrub State
Reserve: 467
Cedar Keys National Wild-
life Refuge: 467–468
Cedar Key State Museum:
464
Central Beach: 244
Chapel by the Sea: 363
Charlotte County: 374
charters: see specific place
Chassahowitzka National
Wildlife Refuge: 456–457
Chassahowitzka River
Campground and Recre-
ation Area: 456
Chastain Access: 172, 173
Cherie Down Park: 118
Church of Scientology: 430
Circus Museum: 393
Citrus County: 450–451
citrus fruit: 147, 418
Clam Pass County Park:
339–340
Clarence S. Higgs Memorial
Beach: 314–315, 316
Clearwater: 430
Clearwater Beach: 431–437
clothing-optional beaches:
112, 114–115
Clubhouse Beach: 327, 328
coastal cuisine: see specific
place
Coastal Hammock Trail:
213
Coastal Science Center: 170
Cocoa Beach: 119, 122–129
Coconut Drive Park: 158

Coconut Point Park: 138, 139
Conch Republic: 312–313
Conn Beach: 150, 151
Coquina Beach: 403
Coral Cove Park: 179–180
Corkscrew Swamp Sanctuary: 339
Cortez Beach: 403–404
Crandon Park: 276, 277
Crescent Beach Park: 73
Crescent Beach (Siesta Key): 389
Crescent Beach (town): 72–74
crocodiles: 584–585
Crooked Island: 500–501
Crystal Beach: 441–442
Crystal River: 459–461
Crystal River National Wildlife Refuge: 456–457
Crystal River State Archaeological Site: 460
Cudjoe Key: 309
Cultural Coast: 379–406
Curry Hammock State Park: 298
Cushing, Michael David: 326

D

Dallus Creek Landing: 472
Dania Beach: 241–242
Dania Beach Ocean Park: 241–242
Dania Jai-Alai: 241
Dan Russell Municipal Pier: 509, 510
Darling National Wildlife Refuge: 357–358
Davis Beach: 433
day in the life of Clearwater Beach: 434–435
Daytona Beach/Daytona Beach Shores: 89–102
Daytona International Speedway: 91
Daytona USA: 90–91
Deerfield Beach: 219–223
Deerfield Public Beach: 220–221

Deer Lake State Park: 521, 522
Dekle Beach: 474
Delnor-Wiggins Pass State Park: 343
Delray Beach: 208–212
Delray Beach Public Beach: 210
Destin: 539–547
Destin Harbor: 544, 546
development issues: 374, 387
Diamond Coast: 178–217
Disney World: 120–121
dive shops: *see specific place*
Dixie Beach: 359
Dixie County: 451
Dodgers: 149
Dog Beach: 315, 316
Dog Island: 483
Dollman Park: 163, 164
Dolphin Research Center: 297
Don Pedro Island: 373–375
Don Pedro Island State Park: 374–375
Dr. Flea's: 198
Dry Tortugas National Park: 322–323
DuBois Park: 181, 183
DuBois Pioneer Museum: 181
Duck Key: 296–297
Dune-Allen Beach: 531–534
Dunedin: 437–439
dunes: 106, 528–529, 534–535, 554–555
Dunes Beach: 370, 371

E

East Beach: 411, 412
Econfina River State Park: 474–475
ecotourism: 32, 52, 395, 485; *see also specific place*
Eden Gardens State Park: 522
Edgeton Bicentennial Park: 132–133
Ed Walline Park: 533

Edward Ball Wakulla Springs State Park: 476–477
Eglin Air Force Base: 547–548
Eglin Beach: 547
Egmont Key: 409–410
Egmont Key State Park: 410
E. G. Simmons Park: 410
El Governor Park: 499
Elliott Key: 280
Elliott Museum: 170
Emerald Coast: 539–552
endangered fish: 593
Englewood Public Beach at Chadwick Park: 377
environmental issues: 387, 546, 587–594
Everglades National Park: 323–329
Exchange Park: 158

F

facts about Florida: 574, 576
Far Beach: 286, 287
fauna: 584–587
Federal Emergency Management Agency (FEMA): 587–589
Fernandina Beach: 30–36
ferry service: 410, 440
53rd Street Beach: 263, 265
Fisher Island: 274
fish/fishing: general discussion 580–581; Destin Harbor 544; Islamorada 290–292; Marathon 300; Navarre Beach Fishing Pier 555; overfishing 592–593; Pompano Beach 223, 225; Steinhatchee 470–471
fishing charters: *see specific place*
Flagler Beach: 80–82
Flagler, Henry Morrison: 63, 285
Flagler Museum: 196
Flagler Park: 106–107
Flamingo: 325
Flamingo Gardens: 232

flea markets: 198
Fletcher Beach: 171, 172
flood insurance: 587–589
Flora-Bama Lounge, Package
  & Oyster Bar: 572
Florida Keys: 281–329
Florida Keys Overseas Heri-
  tage Trail: 285
Floridana Beach: 140
Florida Orange Groves and
  Winery: 418
Florida panthers: 457–458
Florida West Coast Sym-
  phony: 392
food: *see specific place*
football teams: 575
Forgotten Coast: 479–501;
  see also Nature Coast
Fort Clinch State Park:
  28–30
Fort De Soto Park: 411–413
Fort George Island: 44–45
Fort Island Gulf Beach:
  460–461
Fort Lauderdale: 228–240
Fort Lauderdale City Beach:
  234, 235
Fort Lauderdale Museum of
  Art: 232
Fort Lauderdale's Strip:
  230–231
Fort Matanzas National
  Monument: 74–75
Fort Myers Beach: 349–354
Fort Myers Beach Public
  Accesses: 350, 352
Fort Panic Park: 533
Fort Pickens Area, Gulf
  Islands National Seashore:
  566–567
Fort Pickens Gate: 562
Fort Pierce: 157–159
Fort Pierce Inlet State Park:
  156–157
Fort Taylor Beach: 315, 316
Fort Walton Beach:
  548–552
46th Street Beach: 263, 265
Fountain of Youth: 65
Frank Butler Park, East: 70

Frank C. "Tootie" Adler
  Park: *see* Dania Beach
  Ocean Park
Frank Pate Park: 497
Frank Rendon Park: 95, 96
Frederick Douglass Memo-
  rial Beach: 162, 163
Fred H. Howard Park and
  Beach: 443–444
Frieda Zamba Aquatic Com-
  plex: 81
FSU Center for the Perform-
  ing Arts: 392
Futch Memorial Park: 135

G

Gamble Rogers Memo-
  rial State Recreation Area:
  82–83
Garden Key: 323
gardens: 209, 232, 294
Gasparilla Island: 369–373
Gasparilla Island State Park:
  370–371
gated communities: 57
Gate Station Beach: 59, 60
gator wrestling: 233
Gilbert Samson Oceanfront
  Park: 254
Gilbert's Bar House of Ref-
  uge Museum: 170
Glasscock Beach: 165, 166
Gold Coast: 218–280
Golden Beach: 252–253
Golden Orb Trail: 296
Golden Sands Beach Park:
  145
golf: 54–55, 193
Gonzalez, Elian: 258
Gorrie, John: 490
Grassy Key: 297
Grayton Beach: 530–531
Grayton Beach State Park:
  528–529
Green Turtle Beach: 162,
  163
Greer Island Beach: 400
Guana River: 58–59
Gulf Beaches Historical
  Museum: 413

Gulf Breeze: 556–557
Gulf Coast Keys: 328, 329
Gulf Islands National
  Seashore: Fort Pickens
  Area 566–567; Gulf Breeze
  557; Perdido Key Area
  568–569; Santa Rosa Area
  558–559
Gulf Lake Beach: 520
Gulf Shore Boulevard North
  Access: 339, 340
Gulfside City Park: 359, 360
Gulf Specimen Marine
  Laboratory: 478
Gulfstream: 207
Gulfstream County Park:
  207, 208
Gulfstream Park: 251
Gulf View Heights: 533
Gumbo Limbo Nature
  Center: 213

H

Hagen's Cove: 472
Hale Groves: 147
Hallandale Beach: 251–252
Hallandale City Beach: 251,
  252
Hammock: 77–79
hanging chads: 202
Harry Harris County Park:
  286–287
Haulover Beach: 254, 255
Hawk's Cay: 296–297
Hawley Education Center:
  177
health tips: 582–584
Henderson Beach State Park:
  541–542
Herman's Bay Access: 163,
  164
Hernando Beach: 453–454
Hernando Beach Park: 454
Hernando County: 450
Higgs Beach: 314–315, 316
Highland Beach: 212
Hightower Beach Park: 131
hiking: Econfina River State
  Park 474–475; Honey-
  moon Island State Park

439; John D. MacArthur
Beach State Park 188;
Jonathan Dickinson State
Park 174; Pinellas County
Recreation Trail 432;
Topsail Hill Preserve State
Park 534
Hillsboro Beach: 223
Historical Society Museum:
437
Historic First Coast: 27–71
H. L. "Pop" Stansell Park:
441
Hobe Mountain Trail: 174
Hobe Sound: 176–177
Hobe Sound Beach: 176–177
Hobe Sound National Wild-
life Refuge: 175–176
Hobe Sound Nature Center:
176
Hobie Beach: 275, 276
hockey teams: 575
Hodges Park: 473
Holiday: 447, 449–452
Hollywood: 242–251
Hollywood Beach: 244–246
Holmes Beach: 403, 404
Homestead: 279
Homestead Bayfront Park: 279
Homestead-Miami Speed-
way: 279
Homosassa: 457–458
Homosassa Springs: 457–458
Homosassa Springs State
Wildlife Park: 457–458
Honeymoon Island State
Park: 439–440
horseback riding: 42
Horseshoe Beach: 470
hotels: 578–579
House of Refuge Beach:
171, 173
Howard E. Futch Memorial
Park at Paradise Beach: 135
Howard Park and Beach:
443–444
Hudson: 452–453
Hudson Beach Park: 453
Hugh Taylor Birch State
Park: 234, 235

Huguenot Memorial Park:
44–45
Humiston Park: 150, 151
hurricanes: general discus-
sion 19–21; environmental
issues 587–589; Florida
Keys 321; humor 588;
Hurricane Charley 19, 366,
590; Hurricane Dennis
557, 558, 591; Hurricane
Frances 19, 169, 590; Hur-
ricane Ivan 21, 557, 570,
590; Hurricane Jeanne
19, 171, 590; Hurricane
Katrina 20, 277, 591;
Hurricane Ophelia 591;
Hurricane Rita 310, 591;
Hurricane Wilma 229, 591;
Saffir-Simpson Hurricane
Scale 587; statistical data
590–591
Hutchinson Island: 159–164

I

Indialantic: 134–136
Indian Harbour Beach:
132, 133
Indian Key Historic State
Park: 294–295
Indian Pass: 493–494
Indian River citrus fruit: 147
Indian River Heritage and
Citrus Museum: 147
Indian River Shores: 148
Indian Rocks Beach: 426–429
Indian Rocks Beach Access:
427–428
Indian Shores: 426–429
Indian Temple Mound
Museum: 548
Inlet Beach: 516–517
International Swimming
Hall of Fame: 232
Irene H. Canova Park: 133
Islamorada: 290–294

J

Jacksonville: 45–46
Jacksonville Beach: 50–56

jai-alai: 241
James H. Nance Park: 135
James Lee County Park: 542
Jaycee Beach Park: 150, 151
Jefferson County: 451
Jenkins Creek Park: 454
Jensen Beach: 164–168
Jensen Beach/Sea Turtle
Beach: 165–166
Jetty Beach: 503
Jetty Park: 118
J. N. "Ding" Darling
National Wildlife Refuge:
357–358
Joe's Stone Crab Restaurant:
268
John and Mabel Ringling
Museum of Art and Circus
Museum: 393
John Beasley Wayside Park:
550
John Brooks Park: 162, 163
John D. MacArthur Beach
State Park: 187–189
John Gorrie Museum State
Park: 490
John Pennekamp Coral Reef
State Park: 289–290
Johnson Beach: 568–569
John's Pass Beach and Park:
423
John U. Lloyd Beach State
Park: 240–241
Jonathan Dickinson State
Park: 174
Juan Ponce de Leon Land-
ing: 138, 139
Jungle Hut Road Park: 78,
79
Jungle Queen: 232
Juno Beach: 185–187
Juno Beach Park: 186–187
Jupiter: 180–185
Jupiter Beach Park: 181–184
Jupiter Inlet Lighthouse: 180
Jupiter Island: 173–176

K

Kathryn Abby Hanna Park:
46

kayaking: 188, 328, 357–358, 456
Keating Park: 245, 246
Keaton Beach: 472–474
Kelly Seahorse Ranch: 42
Kennedy Space Center: 116–117
Key Biscayne: 275–278
Key Colony Beach: 298, 300–304
Key Deer National Wildlife Refuge: 307–308
Key Largo: 283–289
key lime pie: 299
Key Vista Natural Attractions Park: 451
Key West: 311–322
Kice Island: 331
Kimberly Bergalis Memorial Park: 157–158
Kings Bay: 456–457
Kitching Creek Trail: 174
Kitty Stewart Park: 423
Klondike Beach: 113
Knight Island: 373–375
Koreshan State Historic Site: 345, 346

L

Lake Worth: 203–205
Lake Worth Municipal Beach: 204
Lanark Village: 481
Langdon Beach: 566–567
Lantana: 205
Lantana Municipal Beach: 205
Lauderdale-by-the-Sea: 226–228
Lauderdale-by-the-Sea Public Beach: 227
Leatherman, Stephen: 506–507
LePore, Theresa: 202
Levy County: 451
Lido Beach: 396
Lido Key: 394, 396–397
Lighthouse Beach Park (Boca Grande): 370, 371
Lighthouse Beach Park

(Sanibel Island): 358–359, 360
Lighthouse Point Park and Recreation Area: 104–105
lighthouses: *see specific place*
Lightner Museum: 64
Lignumvitae Key Botanical State Park: 294
litter: 594
Little Duck Key: 305
Little Gasparilla Island: 373–375
Little Havana: 258–259
Little Hickory Island Beach Park: 346, 347
Little St. George Island: 489
Little Talbot Island State Park: 43–44
Little Torch Key: 309
Lloyd Beach State Park: 240–241
lodging surcharges: 577–578
Loggerhead Park: 186, 187
Longboat Key: 397–401
Long Key: 296
Long Key Canoe Trail: 296
Long Key State Park: 296
Long Pine Key: 325
Looe Key: 308–309
Lori Wilson Park: 124
Los Angeles Dodgers: 149
Lovers Key State Park: 347–348
Lowdermilk Park: 339, 340
Lower Suwannee National Wildlife Refuge: 467–468
Lummus Park: 263–264, 265
Lynn Hall Memorial Park: 351, 352

M

MacArthur Beach State Park: 187–189
Madeira Beach: 422–425
Madeira Beach Access: 423
Main Beach: 31–32, 33
Main Street Pier and Beach: 94, 95
Malacompra Beach Park: 78–79

Manalapan: 205
Manasota Beach: 377, 378
Manasota Key: 375–378
Manatee Beach: 403, 404
manatees: 456–457, 459–460, 468, 586–587
Manatee Springs State Park: 468
mansions: 195
maps: Cultural Coast 380; Diamond Coast 179; Emerald Coast 540–541; Florida Keys 282; Forgotten Coast 480; Gold Coast 219; Historic First Coast 28; Nature Coast 448; Panhandle's Playground 504; Quiet Coast 73; South Walton County 516–517; Southwest Coast 331; Space Coast 111; Sports Coast 85; Tampa Bay 408; Treasure Coast 142; Western Panhandle 554–555
Marathon: 298, 300–304
Marco Island: 332–337
marinas: *see specific place*
Marineland: 75–76
Marine Science Center: 103
Mary McLeod Bethune Beach Park: 107
Mash Island Park: 478
Matanzas Beach: 74
Matheson Hammock County Park: 278–279
Mayport: 46–47
M. B. Miller Park: 509, 510
McLarty Treasure Museum: 143
McMillan, Jeanni: 485
Melbourne Beach/Melbourne Shores: 136–140
Mel Fisher's Treasure Museum: 143
Merritt Island National Wildlife Refuge: 115–116
Mexico Beach: 498–499
Miami Beach: 250, 258–273
Miami Design Preservation League: 260

Mickler's Landing: 56–57
Middle Cove Beach Access: 162, 163
Midnight Pass: 387
Midtown Beach: 199
Miramar Beach: 536–538
Mission of Nombre de Dios: 64
Morgan Beach: 331
Morikami Museum and Japanese Gardens: 209
Mosquito Lagoon: 112
motels: 578–579
Mote Marine Aquarium and Laboratory: 395
mountain biking: see biking
Murkshe Memorial Park: 124, 125
Museum of Arts and Sciences: 93
Museum of Natural History of the Florida Keys: 300–301
Museum of Weapons and Early American History: 65
museums: Apalachicola 490; Cedar Key 464; Daytona Beach 93; Delray Beach 209; Dunedin 437; Eglin Air Force Base 548; Fort Lauderdale 232; Fort Walton Beach 548; Jacksonville 45; Lanark Village 481; Marathon 300–301; Miami Beach 262; North Hutchinson Island 155–156; North Indian River County 147; Palm Beach 196; Pass-a-Grille 413; Sanibel Island 356; Sarasota 392–393; Sebastian Inlet State Park 143; St. Augustine 64–65; Stuart 170; Vero Beach 150

N

Nance Park: 135
Naples: 337–342
Naples Beach: 339, 340
Naples Municipal Beach and Pier: 339, 340
National Flood Insurance Program (NFIP): 587–589
Nature Coast: 447–478
Navarre Beach: 554–556
Navarre Beach Fishing Pier: 555
Navarre Beach State Park: 555, 556, 557
Navy Seal Museum: 155–156
Neptune Beach: 49–50
Newport: 475–476
New Port Richey: 447, 449–452
New Smyrna Beach: 105–109
nightlife: see specific place
Nokomis: 384–386
Nokomis Beach: 385, 386
Normandy Beach Access: 163, 164
North Beach (Clearwater Beach): 433, 434
North Beach (Fort De Soto Park): 411, 412
North Beach Park (Hollywood): 244, 245–246
North Beach Park (Vilano Beach): 61
North Captiva Island: 367
North Clearwater Beach: 433, 434
North Hutchinson Island: 155–156
North Indian River County: 144–148
North Jetty Park: 385–386
North Lido Beach: 396
North Ocean Park: 225
North Peninsula State Park: 85, 86
North Redington Beach: 425–426
North Shore Open Space Park: 263, 264
nude beaches: 112, 114–115, 254, 396, 555, 581–582

O

Ocean Cay Park: 182–183, 184
Ocean Inlet Park: 207
Ocean Park: 137, 138
Ocean Reef Park: 190, 191–192
Ocean Ridge: 206–208
Ocean Ridge Hammock Park: 207–208
Ohio Key: 305
Okaloosa Island: 548–552
Okaloosa Island Accesses: 550–551
Oldest Wooden Schoolhouse: 65
Old Salt Road Park: 78, 79
120th Avenue Access: 420
Opal Beach: 558–559
Ormond Beach: 86–89
Ormond-by-the-Sea: 84–86
overfishing: 592–593
Overseas Highway: 271, 285
Ozello: 458–459
Ozello Community Park: 458–459
Ozona: 441

P

Pablo Historical Park: 51
Painters Hill: 79
Palma Sola Causeway: 403, 404
Palm Beach: 194–203
Palm Beach Shores: 189–194
Palm Beach Shores Park: 191, 192
Palm Coast: 77–79
Palmer Point Beach: 385, 386
Palm Harbor: 441–442
Palm Island: 373–375
Panacea: 478
Panama Beach City Pier: 509, 510
Panama City Beach: 504–514
Panhandle: 502–514
panthers: 457–458
Paradise Beach Park: 135
Pasco County: 450
Pasley Park: 166
Pass-a-Grille: 413–414

Pass-a-Grille Beach: 413
Patrick Air Force Base: 129–130
Peanut Island: 190
Pelayo Beach: 521, 522
Pelican Beach Park: 130–132
Pelican Man's Bird Sanctuary: 395
Pensacola Beach: 559–566
Pepper Park: 155, 156
Perdido Key: 569–573
Perdido Key Area, Gulf Islands National Seashore: 568–569
Perdido Key State Park: 571
Peter's Point Beach Front Park: 32–33
Phil Foster Park: 190
Phipps Ocean Park: 199
Pier Park: 254, 255
piers: *see specific place*
Pigeon Key: 304–305
Pine Island: 454–456
Pinellas County Recreation Trail: 432
Playalinda Beach: 112–113, 114–115
Pompano Beach: 223–226
Pompano Public Beach: 225
Ponce Inlet: 102–105
Ponte Vedra Beach: 56–58
Port Bougainville: 286
Port Richey: 447, 449–452
Port Richey Waterfront Park: 451–452
Port Salerno: 173–174
Port St. Joe: 496–497
Port St. Lucie: 160–161
professional sports: 93, 149, 392, 575

QR

Quiet Coast: 72–83
rainy-day attractions: *see specific place*
Ramrod Key: 309
reading suggestions: 579
recreational activities: see *specific place*
Redington Beach: 425–426

Redington Shores: 425–426
Redington Shores Beach Access: 425
Red Reef Park: 214–215
red tide: 589, 592
Rees Memorial Park: 451
renourishment: 32, 165–166, 234, 250
rental cars: 578
resources: 574–594
restaurants: *see specific place*
Rest Beach: *see* C.B. Harvey Rest Beach Park
Reynolds, Burt: 182–183
Richard G. Edgeton Bicentennial Park: 132–133
Richard G. Kreusler Park: 199, 200
Ringling Museum of Art: 392, 393
Riomar Beach: 150–151
rip currents: 583–584
Ripley's Believe It or Not!: 65
River to Sea Preserve: 76
Riviera Beach: 189–194
Riviera Beach Municipal Beach: 190–191, 192
Robert J. Strickland Memorial Park: 453
Robert K. Rees Memorial Park: 451
Robert P. Murkshe Memorial Park: 124, 125
Robinson, Jackie: 93
Rocks, The: *see* Chastain Access
Rogers Park: 454
Ron Jon Surf Shop: 123
room surcharges: 577–578
Rosemary Beach: 517–520
Round Island Park: 154–155

S

safety tips: 582–584
Saffir-Simpson Hurricane Scale: 587
Sailfish Marina: 190
Salinas Park: 495

sand dunes: 106, 528–529, 534–535, 554–555
Sandestin: 535–536
Sand Key: 422
Sand Key County Park: 431
Sand Spit Park: 464, 465
Sand Spur Beach: 370, 371
Sanibel-Captiva Conservation Foundation: 362
Sanibel Island: 354, 355–363
San Juan Beach: 521, 522
Santa Clara Park: 521, 522
Santa Lucea Beach: 171, 172
Santa Rosa Area, Gulf Islands National Seashore: 558–559
Santa Rosa Beach: 531–534
Sarasota: 392–394
Sarasota Bay Explorers: 395
Sarasota Circus Hall of Fame: 393
Sarasota Opera Association: 392
Satellite Beach: 130–132
scuba diving: 279–280, 289–290, 308–309, 456–457
Seabranch Preserve State Park: 173–174
Seacrest Beach: 520
Sea Grape Beach: 370, 371
Sea Grape Beach Access: 145, 146
Seagrove Beach: 520–523
Seagull Park: 130
Seahorse Key: 463–464, 467
sea lice: 584
seashells: 356
Seaside: 523–527
Seaside Park: 32, 33
Sea Turtle Beach: 165–166
Sea Turtle Preservation Society, The: 137
sea turtles: 585–586
Sea Wall Beach: 370, 371
Sebastian Fishing Museum: 143
Sebastian Inlet State Park: 141–144
Seminole Paradise: 248–249

Service Club Park: 382, 383

72nd Street Beach: 263, 264

Sexton Plaza: 150, 151

Shell Island: 503

Shell Point: 477–478

Shell Point Beach: 477

Sheppard Park: 123, 124

Shired Island County Park: 469–470

shopping: *see specific place*

Sidney Fischer Park: 123, 124

Siesta Key: 386–392

Siesta Key Public Beach: 389

Simmons Park: 410

Simonton Street Beach: 315, 316

Singer Island: 189–194

64th Street Beach: 263, 264–265

Smathers Beach: 314, 315–316

Smyrna Dunes Park: 106, 107

snorkeling: 177, 279–280, 289–290, 308–309, 456–457

soap operas: 244

Sombrero Beach: 301–302

South Beach Access: 41, 42

South Beach Boardwalk: 157, 158

South Beach (Hollywood): 244

South Beach (Key West): 315, 316

South Beach (Miami Beach): 260, 262–265

South Beach Park (Boca Raton): 214–215

South Beach Park (Vero Beach): 151

South Cocoa/North Patrick Beach: 124, 125

Southeast Museum of Photography: 93

South Inlet Park: 215

South Jetty Park: 157, 158

South Lido Beach: 394, 396

South Marco Beach Access: 335

South Palm Beach: 205–206

South Patrick Residents Association Park: 130

South Patrick Shores: 129–130

South Pointe Park: 264, 265

South Ponte Vedra Beach: 59–60

South Ponte Vedra Beach Recreation Area: 59, 60

South Walton County: 515–538

Southwest Coast: 330–378

Space Coast: 110–140

Spanish River Park: 214–215

spectator sports: *see* professional sports

Spesser Holland North Beach Park: 137–138

Spesser Holland South Beach Park: 138–139

sponge fishing industry: 443

Spooky Lane Access: 533

Sports Coast: 84–109

Spring Break: 230–231

spring training: 149, 180–181, 392

Spyglass Beach: 73, 74

St. Andrews State Park: 502–504

Stansell Park: 441

St. Armands Key: 394

St. Augustine: 62–68

St. Augustine Alligator Farm: 65

St. Augustine Beach: 69–71

St. Augustine Lighthouse and Museum: 65

Steinhatchee: 470–472

St. George Island: 484–488

St. George Island Public Beach: 486, 487

St. George Island State Park: 486

St. Joe/Arvida Company: 508

St. Joe Beach: 497–498

St. Joseph Peninsula State Park: 495, 496

St. Lucie County: 160–161

St. Lucie Inlet Preserve State Park: 174–175

St. Marks National Wildlife Refuge: 476

Stokes Beach: 166, 167

St. Pete Beach: 414–418

St. Pete Beach Access: 415, 416

St. Petersburg Municipal Beach: 420

Stranahan House: 232

Strickland Memorial Park: 453

strip clubs: 224

Stuart: 168–173

Stuart Beach: 170, 172

Stump Pass Beach: 376–377

St. Vincent Island National Wildlife Refuge: 492–493

Sugarloaf Key: 309–310

Summer Beach: 36

Summer Haven: 75

Summerland Key: 309

sunburn: 582–583

Suncoast Seabird Sanctuary: 427

Sunny Isles Beach: 253–256

Sunnyland Beach: 140

Sunset Beach (Tarpon Springs): 444

Sunset Beach (town): 418–422

Sunset Park: 499

Sunshine Skyway Bridge: 411

Sun Splash Park: 94, 95

surfing: 124, 142–143, 181–182, 385–386

surf shops: *see specific place*

Surfside: 61, 257

Surfside Park: 157–158

Suwannee: 469

swamp tours: 326

Swap Shop Circus: 198

swimming: 579–580

T

Tampa Bay area: 407–446

Tarpon Bay Road Beach: 359, 360

Tarpon Springs: 442–445
Taylor County: 451
Ted Peters Famous Smoked Fish: 418
Teed, Cyrus Reed: 346
Ten Thousand Islands: 328
Tequesta: 179–180
theme parks: Daytona USA 90–91; Disney World 120–121; Marineland 76
35th Street Beach: 263, 265
Thomas Drive Park: 509, 510
Thurman, Howard: 93
Tiger Shores Access: 166, 167
Tigertail Beach County Park: 335–336
Tiki Gardens-Indian Shores: 427, 428
toll bridges: 354
toll-free telephone numbers: 578–579
Tomoka State Park: 87
Tom Renich Park: 85, 86
Topsail Hill Preserve State Park: 534–535
tours: St. Augustine 66; swamp tours 326; wildlife 358
Tracking Station Beach: 148
travel resources: 574, 576–579
travel tips: 576–578
Treasure Coast: 141–177
Treasure Island: 418–422
Treasure Island Beach Access: 420
Treasure Island Park: 420
Treasure Shores Beach Park: 145
Tropical Storm Arlene: 591
Tropical Storm Bonnie: 590
Tropical Storm Frances: 590
Tropical Storm Tammy: 591
Turner Beach: 364, 365
Turtle Beach: 388, 389

Turtle Beach Nature Trail: 162, 164
turtles: 585–586
Turtle Trail Beach Access: 145, 146
21st Street Beach: 263, 265
27th Avenue Park: 107
Tyndall Air Force Base: 499–501
Tyndall Beach: 500, 501

UV
Upham Beach: 415, 416
Upper Matecumbe County Park: 291
U.S. 1: 271, 285
Usina Beach: 59, 60
vacation rentals: *see specific place*
Vanderbilt Beach: 342–343
Vanderbilt Beach County Park: 343
Van Ness Butler Jr. Regional Beach Access: 528
Van Wezel Performing Arts Hall: 392
Varn Beach Park: 79
Vassey Creek Park: 462
Venice: 380–384
Venice Municipal Beach: 382, 383
Vero Beach: 148, 150–154
Vero Beach Museum of Art: 150
Veterans Memorial Park: 305
Vilano Beach: 60–62
Virginia Forest Access: 166, 167
Virginia Key: 274–275
Virginia Key Beach: 276, 277

WXYZ
Wabasso Beach Park: 145, 146

Waccasassa Bay Preserve State Park: 467
Wagner, Tony: 258
Wakulla County: 451
Wakulla Springs State Park: 476–477
Walker, Mark: 546
Walline Park: 533
Wall Spring Park: 441
Walton County: 515–516, 532
Walton Dunes: 521
Walton Rocks Beach: 162–163, 164
Washington Oaks Gardens State Park: 77
WaterColor: 527–528
Waveland Beach: 163, 164
Way Key: 463
Wayside Park: 499
wealthy behavior issues: 398–399
Western Panhandle: 553–573
West Lake Park: 245
West Palm Beach: 197, 198
West Panama City Beach: 509, 510
West Summerland Key: 307
Wilbur-by-the-Sea: 102
wildlife: 584–587
Wilson Creek Trail: 174
wineries: 418
Winterhaven Park: 104
Wolfsonian: 262
World Golf Hall of Fame: 54–55
World's Luckiest Fishing Village: 544
Worth Avenue: 196–197
Yankeetown: 461–462
Yankeetown Park: 462
Yulee Sugar Mill Ruins State Historic Site: 457
Zorayda Castle: 65

Acknowledgments

During our research for three editions of *Florida Beaches* and one older, out-of-print East Coast beach guide—a period that spans nearly a quarter-century—we have repeatedly combed every corner of Florida's coast. Along the way, we have made friends with many helpful natives. It would take a whole other book to mention them all by name, but several are worth singling out for going that extra mile for and with us. They are Susan McLain (Daytona Beach), Jayna Leach (Panama City Beach), and Stacie Mae Brady (Seaside). We'd also like to thank several past and present employees of Visit Florida, the official state tourism agency, who have always been extremely helpful. They are Doug Luciani, Kelly Grass, Brandy Henley, and Lisa Sloan. Special thanks also to John and Leigh Forrester, old friends in Ponte Vedra Beach who have often put us up (and put up with us).

This book was originally published by a fine independent publisher called Foghorn Press. From the days of the "old" Foghorn, we'd like to remember and thank Vicki Morgan, David Morgan, Kyle Morgan, Holly Haddorff, Jean-Vi Lenthe, Donna Leverenz, and Dawn Lish. After Foghorn was acquired by Avalon Travel Publishing, we worked on the second edition of *Florida Beaches* with Marisa Solís. Now this totally revised third edition is being published by Avalon's Moon imprint. We're thrilled to be with Moon, whose books we've read and regarded highly. For all of our good fortune with our several beach books, we are indebted to our agent and longtime friend, Anne Zeman.

We feel privileged to work with a super-competent and friendly group of people, starting at the top with Avalon publisher Bill Newlin and associate publisher Donna Galassi. Our in-house editors—Ellie Behrstock, Kay Elliott, and Cinnamon Hearst—have been a steady source of helpful ideas and encouragement, and are a pleasure to work with. We appreciate their patience, too, as we turned in this book a full year later than intended. (We had a good excuse: eight hurricanes.) We're also indebted to production coordinator Darren Alessi, graphics coordinator Tabitha Lahr, cartography editor Kevin Anglin, and indexer Judy Hunt, all of whose contributions have made this a better book.

On the home front, we'd like to recognize our wonderful moms, Helen Puterbaugh and Penny Bisbort, and siblings: Mark Puterbaugh, Anne Sherrill, Patty Stevens, and Mary Nell Stone. A special shout-out to Mark for helping with Treasure Island and Sand Key. Many of the insights in those entries are his. Our wives—Carol Hill Puterbaugh and Tracey O'Shaughnessy Bisbort—have tolerated our long absences with good cheer and more understanding than we'd likely muster if the shoe (or flip-flop) were on the other foot. We'd also like to salute our own little sand-castle builders, Hayley Anne Puterbaugh and Paul James Bisbort, who have already shown great promise as beach bums.

Finally, a salute to the endless cast of home-grown Florida characters with whom we've crossed paths, from Stanley the Mad Innkeeper to Crabbo the Clown, who have kept us chuckling at life's rich pageant.

www.moon.com

For helpful advice on planning a trip, visit www.moon.com for the **TRAVEL PLANNER** and get access to useful travel strategies and valuable information about great places to visit. When you travel with Moon, expect an experience that is uncommon and truly unique.

 HANDBOOKS | METRO | OUTDOORS | LIVING ABROAD

OUTDOORS

"A smart new look provides just one more reason to travel with Moon Outdoors. Well-written, thoroughly researched, and packed full of useful information and advice, these guides really do get you into the outdoors."

—GORP.COM

ALSO AVAILABLE AS FOGHORN OUTDOORS ACTIVITY GUIDES:

101 Great Hikes of the
  San Francisco Bay Area
250 Great Hikes in
  California's National Parks
Baja Camping
Bay Area Biking
California Beaches
California Camping
California Fishing
California Golf
California Hiking
California Recreational
  Lakes & Rivers
California Waterfalls
California Wildlife
Camper's Companion
Easy Biking in Northern
  California

Easy Hiking in Northern
  California
Easy Hiking in Southern
  California
Florida Beaches
Florida Camping
Georgia & Alabama Camping
Great Lakes Camping
Maine Hiking
Massachusetts Hiking
Montana, Wyoming & Idaho
  Camping
New England Biking
New England Cabins
  & Cottages
New England Camping
New England Hiking
New Hampshire Hiking

Northern California Biking
Oregon Hiking
Pacific Northwest Hiking
Southern California
  Cabins & Cottages
Tom Stienstra's Bay Area
  Recreation
Utah Camping
Utah Hiking
Vermont Hiking
Washington Boating
  & Water Sports
Washington Fishing
Washington Hiking
West Coast RV Camping

MOON FLORIDA BEACHES

Avalon Travel Publishing
An Imprint of
Avalon Publishing Group, Inc.

AVALON
publishing group incorporated

1400 65th Street, Suite 250
Emeryville, CA 94608, USA
www.moon.com

Editor: Cinnamon Hearst
Acquisitions Manager: Rebecca K. Browning
Copy Editor: Ellie Behrstock
Graphics Coordinator: Tabitha Lahr
Production Coordinator and
    Interior Designer: Darren Alessi
Cover Designer: Gerilyn Attebery
Map Editor: Kevin Anglin
Cartographers: Suzanne Service, Kat Smith
Cartography Director: Mike Morgenfeld
Indexer: Judy Hunt

ISBN-10: 1-56691-496-5
ISBN-13: 978-1-56691-496-3
ISSN: 1522-6425

Printing History
1st Edition – 1998
3rd Edition – October 2006
5 4 3 2 1

Text © 2006 by Parke Puterbaugh
    and Alan Bisbort.
Maps © 2006 by Avalon Travel Publishing, Inc.
All rights reserved.

Some photos and illustrations are used by permission and are the property of the original copyright owners.

Front cover photo: Beach at Marathon Key
© James Randklev
Title page photo: John D. MacArthur State Park
© Parke Puterbaugh
Chapter opener photos: page 17, Lake Worth Municipal Beach; page 27, Mickler's Landing, Ponte Vedra Beach; page 72, Flagler Beach; page 84, Daytona Beach; page 110, Cocoa Beach; page 141, Hummiston Park, Vero Beach; page 178, Red Reef Beach, Boca Raton; page 218, Hollywood Beach Broadwalk; page 281, Pigeon Key; page 330, Andy Rosse Lane, Captiva; page 379, Siesta Beach, Siesta Key; page 407, North Beach, Fort De Soto Park; page 447, Cedar Key; page 479, Mexcio Beach; page 502, Rick Seltzer Park, Panama City Beach; page 515, Camp Helen State Park; page 539, Destin Harbor; page 553, Pensacola Beach; page 574, Manatee Beach

Printed in the United States by Malloy, Inc.

Moon Handbooks and the Moon logo are the property of Avalon Travel Publishing, an imprint of Avalon Publishing Group, Inc. All other marks and logos depicted are the property of the original owners. All rights reserved. No part of this book may be translated or reproduced in any form, except brief extracts by a reviewer for the purpose of a review, without written permission of the copyright owner.

Although every effort was made to ensure that the information was correct at the time of going to press, the author and publisher do not assume and hereby disclaim any liability to any party for any loss or damage caused by errors, omissions, or any potential travel disruption due to labor or financial difficulty, whether such errors or omissions result from negligence, accident, or any other cause.

KEEPING CURRENT

We are committed to making this book the most accurate and enjoyable guide to Florida's beaches. You can rest assured that every beach in this book has been carefully reviewed in an effort to keep this book as up-to-date as possible. However, by the time you read this book, some of the fees listed herein may have changed and certain businesses or locales may have changed unexpectedly.

If you have a favorite gem you'd like to see included in the next edition, or see anything that needs updating, clarification, or correction, please drop us a line. Send your comments via email to feedback@moon.com, or use the address above.